REAL ESTATE LAW DIGEST

THIRD EDITION

JAMES A. DOUGLAS
Member of the New York Bar

PATRICK J. HAMILL
Member of the New Jersey Bar

EILEEN R. POLLOCK
Member of the New York Bar

WARREN, GORHAM & LAMONT
Boston • New York

WARREN, GORHAM & LAMONT, INC.
210 SOUTH STREET
BOSTON, MASSACHUSETTS 02111

ISBN 0-7913-0749-2

Library of Congress Catalog Card No. 90-083524

PRINTED IN THE UNITED STATES OF AMERICA

HOW TO USE THIS BOOK

This Third Edition of Real Estate Law Digest has been completely revised and updated, incorporating both the latest developments in real estate law and the significant case law from the recent past. The relevant decisions of federal and state courts have been carefully reviewed, selected, and edited to present a comprehensive yet accessible overview of the law as it exists today. Because real estate law is constantly evolving, the reader should check the continued validity of a point of law in any given case.

Case digests summarize the decisive facts, issues, holdings, and rationales offered by the courts. The digests are organized in sections and arranged topically. The Table of Contents lists each topic heading and its page number in the text. In addition, each chapter starts with a synopsis listing the sections contained in that chapter. The Table of Cases and the Index, keyed to section numbers, offer alternative research aids.

SUMMARY OF CONTENTS

TABLE OF CONTENTS

PART A

FORMS OF OWNERSHIP

PART B

ESTATES AND OTHER INTERESTS IN PROPERTY

PART C
LANDLORD AND TENANT

PART D
CONDOMINIUMS AND COOPERATIVES

PART E
RECORD AND NOTICE OF OWNERSHIP

PART F
GOVERNMENTAL USE RESTRICTIONS

PART G

PRIVATE USE RESTRICTIONS

PART H

CONSTITUTIONAL RIGHTS ON PRIVATE PROPERTY

PART I

ADJOINING LANDOWNERS

PART J

TRESPASS AND NUISANCE

PART K

WATER AND WATERCOURSES

PART L

ROADS, HIGHWAYS, AND STREETS

PART M
SALES CONTRACTS

PART N
OPTIONS TO PURCHASE

PART O
PURCHASER'S REMEDIES FOR PROPERTY DEFECTS

PART P
BROKERS AND BROKERAGE AGREEMENTS

PART Q
TRANSFER BY DEED

PART R
EMINENT DOMAIN

PART S

OTHER METHODS OF TRANSFER AND RESTRAINTS ON ALIENATION

PART T

LIENS AND ENCUMBRANCES

PART U

MORTGAGES AND DEEDS OF TRUST

PART V
GOVERNMENTAL REGULATION OF TRANSACTIONS

PART A
FORMS OF OWNERSHIP

1.00
PARTNERSHIPS AND JOINT VENTURES

1.05
Partnerships

Georgia Parties entered into a partnership to build and sell a house. Division of profits from the venture was specified, but there was no provision for sharing losses. Defendant purchased a lot, taking title to the property in her own name, obtained financing, and the house was erected. Eventually, the house was sold at a loss, defendant receiving $18,000 over the existing indebtedness. Plaintiff sued, claiming to hold a contractor's lien for $18,000. *Held:* An individual cannot hold a lien on his own property; a lien is a claim that one has on the property of another. A partner does not have the right to a common-law materialman's or contractor's lien on partnership property. Because the parties agreed that the house was partnership property, plaintiff could not claim his share of the assets by enforcing a lien against defendant. *Stephens v. Clark*, 268 SE2d 361 (1980).

Minnesota Beach and Anderson entered into an oral partnership to own and operate an amusement park. After Beach filed for dissolution of the partnership, the partners resolved the suit by entering into an oral stipulation agreement before a court reporter that gave Beach possession of the amusement park, for which he was to pay Anderson $85,000. Anderson refused to abide by the settlement, claiming it was invalid under the Statute of Frauds. *Held:* The stipulation did not fall within the Statute of Frauds and was thus binding on Anderson. The agreement, although oral, did not involve the transfer of real property. Under state law, a partnership interest is considered personal property, so the stipulation involved the transfer of personalty, not realty. Realty acquired by a partnership with partnership funds becomes personal property, and its transfer along with a partnership interest is considered merely ancillary to the partnership transfer. *Beach v. Anderson*, 417 NW2d 409 (1988).

Missouri Partners were in the business of raising hogs on land that was owned by defendant and upon which improvements had been made using partnership profits. No rent for use of the land or the improvements was ever paid by the partnership, and there was no agreement regarding disposition of fixed assets in the event of dissolution. In an action for an accounting and dissolution of the partnership, the lower court awarded all fixed assets of the partnership to defendant. Plaintiff appealed, arguing that since the improvements were made with partnership assets and used by the partnership, he should be entitled to half their value. *Held:* Reversed for plaintiff. Since the improvements were made with partnership assets for purposes of the partnership business, they were personal property of the partnership, and the nonlandowning partner was entitled to his proportionate share of their value. *Gauldin v. Corn*, 595 SW2d 329 (Ct. App. 1980).

New York In 1964, plaintiff and defendant executed a partnership agreement to practice medicine. In 1971, they formed a professional corporation. The doctors practiced out of an office they and their spouses owned as tenants in common. Upon dissolution, plaintiff sought partition of the premises; however, defendant claimed that a provision of the partnership agreement barred partition. *Held:* For plaintiff. Once the doctors formed a professional corporation, the partnership agreement became a nullity. Partition of the premises was fair and reasonable. *Notar-Francesco v. Furci*, 539 NYS2d 801 (App. Div. 1989).

North Carolina Simmons and Wood formed a partnership into which each contributed personally owned real estate. The partnership then leased the parcel to the defendant under a 10-year lease with two 5-year renewal options. Some time later, the partners decided to dissolve the partnership, and Wood transferred his interest to Simmons and his wife. The defendant then exercised the first of its two renewal options. Later that year, Simmons and his wife, plaintiff, separated and the parcel was conveyed to plaintiff. Plaintiff recorded her deed before defendant recorded its original lease or renewal options. She then brought an action to eject defendant on the theory that title passed to her unencumbered by the lease. Defendant argued that title had been in the partnership and it was never conveyed. *Held:* Plaintiff was a bona fide purchaser of the parcel and her interest was not encumbered by the lease. Wood conveyed a fee simple interest to Simmons and plaintiff, and Simmons conveyed a fee simple interest to plaintiff. *Simmons v. Quick-Stop Food Mart, Inc.*, 296 SE2d 275 (1982).

North Dakota Mortgagor, a property development partnership, defaulted on loans secured by mortgages on partnership real estate. Mortgagee commenced a foreclosure action against the real estate and a separate contract action against the individual partners who each signed separate guaranties. The actions resulted in two judgments for the full amount of the debt plus interest. In effect, the partners would be personally liable to the extent that the price realized at foreclosure fell short of the balance due on the debt. The partners brought suit to set aside the judgment against them. *Held:* The deficiency judgment was upheld. Recovery by mortgagee on the partner's guaranties was not precluded by the antideficiency statute any more than would be so in the case of a guaranty executed by a guarantor unrelated to the primary obligor. Merely because partners are always personally liable to partnership creditors does not mean that the guaranties added nothing to the partner's primary obligation under the partnership debt. *Mandan Sec. Bank v. Heinsohn*, 320 NW2d 494 (1982).

1.10 Limited Partnerships

7th Circuit Group of investors became limited partners in a real estate development scheme pursuant to an agreement that provided that the limited partners could be asked to increase their total capital contributions. Two capital calls were made within the next two years. When the enterprise began to fail, the limited partners sued for violation of Rule 10b-5 of the Securities Exchange Act of 1934. They claimed that the two capital calls each represented a separate "purchaser" of a security and thus were actionable under Rule 10b-5. They argued that each decision as to whether or not to comply with the call was an investment decision in the same sense as the original commitment, and therefore a distinct "purchase" of a security. The general partners contended that the only "purchase" had occurred when the original agreement was signed. *Held:* A limited partner's investment in response to a capital call constitutes a purchase of a security. The court said that the crucial fact is "whether an investment decision remains to be made by the party from whom disclosure is withheld, and not upon when the agreement to purchase or sell was executed." *Goodman v. Epstein*, 582 F2d 388 (1978).

New York Plaintiff, an attorney and limited partner of defendant, a limited partnership, provided defendant with 12,500 hours of legal services during a 20-year period. Plaintiff sued to recover fees to which he said he was entitled. The trial court held that he was not entitled to fees, and he appealed. *Held:* Affirmed for defendant. The appellate court was swayed by the fact that there had been no express agreement to pay plaintiff for his long-term legal services. It recognized the existence of several letters between plaintiff and defendant regarding payment for legal services, but found them unpersuasive. Those letters, according to the court, did not overcome the fact that plaintiff knew that he had no express agreement to be compensated and that he continued to perform services in the face of warnings that the partners were not willing to be billed for services rendered. *Swan v. Dolphin Lane Assocs.*, 459 NYS2d 801 (App. Div. 1983).

Texas Limited partnership was formed between builder, who was general partner, and limited partners, who agreed to advance money to builder for construction of multiple dwelling units and then buy them from him when completed. After the buildings were completed, general partner issued a financial report showing the buildings to be making a profit; however, several months later, he admitted the information was inaccurate and the buildings were losing money. The partnership was dissolved, and the limited partners brought suit against the general partner to recover their capital investment on the ground that his mismanagement had constituted a breach of fiduciary duty to them. The general partner contended there was insufficient evidence to show that limited partners suffered any damage proximately caused by his conduct. *Held:* Limited partners were entitled to recovery. Where a fiduciary relationship has been breached, limited partners may recover for restitution of their contributions, not merely proximate damages. *Watson v. Limited Partners of WCKT, Ltd.*, 570 SW2d 179 (Civ. App. 1978).

1.15 Joint Ventures

Georgia A joint venturer sued to clear title to property on which bank, a creditor of the other joint venturer, had a lien. The parties had formed, by self-styled agreement, a joint venture to acquire and develop property. They never registered the trade name of their business and acquired the property not in the name of the joint venture but in their own names as tenants in common. Joint venturer argued the land was partnership property and, under state law, not subject to levy. *Held:* No valid joint venture existed. For a partnership to protect its real property from judgment creditors of individual partners, title must be taken in partnership name. Therefore, the judgment lien attached to the property where title was held by joint venturers as tenants in common. *Morgan Guar. Trust Co. v. Alexander Equities, Inc.*, 268 SE2d 660 (1980).

Kansas Builders formed a corporation to construct houses, and received free office space, secretarial services, and other benefits from a licensed real estate broker. The builders agreed with buyers to construct a house for them, and the broker agreed to sell their existing house at a guaranteed price. When the builders failed to complete the house, the broker agreed to finish it, but numerous lien holders foreclosed on the property. When the buyers finally purchased the house at a sheriff's sale, they sued both the corporation and the broker for damages. The broker argued that it was not engaged in a joint venture with the builders and therefore was not liable for damages. *Held:* The broker was liable. A number of factors, including the sharing of office space and secretaries, the financial ties, and the broker's agreement to complete the house, indicated the existence of a joint venture. The broker was therefore jointly liable with the builders for the buyers' damages. *Modern Air Conditioning, Inc. v. Cinderella Homes, Inc.*, 596 P2d 816 (1979).

New Jersey Plaintiff and defendant owned real estate in joint ventures. Defendant managed the properties, receiving a management fee of 5 percent. Defendant was also a licensed insurance broker and obtained insurance for the property, retaining the normal commissions for his personal use. When plaintiff discovered this, he insisted that defendant reimburse the joint venture for the amount of the commissions. Defendant refused, claiming that plaintiff must have realized what was happening, since defendant kept the commissions on life insurance that he obtained for plaintiff and his family. Defendant conceded, however, that he never expressly told plaintiff about keeping the property insurance commissions. *Held:* The managing party could compensate himself only in ways known to the other. Since plaintiff had no duty to audit or inspect the venture's books, he was entitled to assume that defendant had made full disclosure of any personal benefits. Accordingly, the court ordered a new trial to determine whether plaintiff had actual knowledge of the retained commissions. If plaintiff had such actual knowledge, then defendant did not breach any fiduciary duty. Otherwise, defendant would have to reimburse the joint venture. *Silverstein v. Last*, 383 A2d 718 (1978).

Oregon A licensed real estate agent committed $20,000 toward the acquisition of real property worth $125,000. The agent was in jeopardy of forfeiting his investment if he could not secure another substantial investor. The agent then entered into a joint venture with defendant. Defendant supplied $80,000 and the balance was secured by a joint promissory note. The agent was to refinance the property and pay defendant $100,000 within 60 days, plus $27,000 as guaranteed profit. The agent was to make all installment payments and to improve the property, but the agent breached these obligations and defendant had to assume them. After the project showed an accounting profit, the agent did not receive a return of capital or profit. He sued, demanding reimbursement. *Held:* Defendant was to receive both his guaranteed profit and investment capital before the agent would receive anything. Oregon law requires a joint venturer to receive his share of the assets even if he failed to perform all required duties. Defendant could, however, set off any damages proved against proceeds to which plaintiff was entitled. *Zdroy v. Dickenson*, 654 P2d 1127 (Ct. App. 1982).

Washington Four couples owned property containing a lake and a dam. The dam gave way, flooding downstream property. Downstream property owners sued owners of the lake for damages. They settled with two of the couples, the defendants, for $5,000 each. Subsequently, the court granted a motion of summary judgment against all owners of the lake on the issue of liability. The other two couples, plaintiffs, settled for $750,000. Plaintiffs sued defendants for contribution, alleging the property was purchased as a joint venture. *Held:* The parties were merly co-owners without an agreement, express or implied, for contribution or indemnity. They did not contract to engage in an enterprise in which they had a common objective and community of interest, and made independent decisions with regard to purchasing, managing, and selling the property. *Goeres v. Ortiquist*, 658 P2d 1277 (Ct. App. 1983).

2.00 TRUSTS

2.05 In General

1st Circuit Taxpayer, a business trust with transferable shares, was owned by two brothers who also had controlling interest in a corporation that leased commercial property from the trust. Based on IRC § 543(a)(2) the government assessed taxes on the theory that the trust's earnings constituted personal holding company income and should be taxed at higher rates. Taxpayer argued that the rental income did not represent "personal holding company income" as defined in Section 543(a). *Held:* For taxpayer. The trust's property was leased to the corporation, not to the trust shareholders as individuals. As corporate shareholders, the brothers were not entitled to personal use of corporate property; therefore, neither were the trust's lease revenues within Section 543(a) nor were the shareholders "individuals entitled to the use of the property." *Silverman & Sons Realty Trust v. Comm'r*, 620 F2d 314 (1980).

2.10 Fiduciary Duties of Trustee

Illinois Plaintiffs appointed defendant trustee of a land trust. The property was subject to a mortgage held by a savings and loan association. Defendants lent plaintiffs $15,000, secured by a junior lien on the trust property. Subsequently, plaintiffs defaulted on the mortgage. The savings and loan foreclosed and purchased the property at the foreclosure sale, wiping out defendant's junior lien. Defendant purchased the property from the savings and loan without notifying plaintiffs. Plaintiffs sued for breach of fiduciary duty, and defendant sought to recover the funds it had lent plaintiffs. *Held:* Defendant's purchase of trust property was a conflict of interest and a breach of its fiduciary duty to plaintiffs. As trustee, defendant had access to inside information concerning the property. A conflict of interest was also created when defendant acquired a junior lien on the trust property. Defendant was not entitled to repayment unless it could prove the loan was made fairly, with full disclosure and with plaintiffs' informed consent. *Home Fed. Sav. & Loan Ass'n v. Zarkin*, 432 NE2d 841 (1982).

New Mexico Prior to his death, decedent deeded half of his land to his spouse and the other half to his son. The wife deeded her half to the son and conveyed an interest in the house to her daughter. When the son gave an oil and gas lease to a third party, the daughter asserted rights in the royalty payments. The trial court held that the father had conveyed the land to his son subject to an express trust in favor of the daughter. *Held:* Reversed. The evidence in the trial court did not support the findings of fact since there was no direct evidence showing that an express trust existed or that the father had intended to create one. Mere evidence that the father treated his children equally was not sufficient. *Thomas v. Reid*, 608 P2d 1123 (1980).

Texas Beneficiaries of an express trust brought an action for an accounting and recovery of trust monies allegedly mishandled by the trustee in his dealings with rental property. *Held:* A trustee cannot avoid liability for acts of his agent in respect to trust property and, unless the trust instrument expressly provides for the use of agents, the trustee is without power to delegate his fiduciary duty. Where a trust instrument vested management of property within the sole discretion of the trustee, the trustee is obligated to perform all acts himself. *Corpus Christi Bank & Trust v. Roberts*, 587 SW2d 173 (Ct. Appl. 1979).

2.15 Constructive Trust

Florida Plaintiff and his mother owned the mother's home as joint tenants. The mother persuaded her son to quitclaim his interest to her to facilitate the sale of the house because she planned to move. The mother died before the property could be sold. Unknown to her son, after the property had been conveyed to her, the mother executed a will giving one half of the property to a religious organization. The son sued to have the quitclaim deed set aside and a constructive trust or a resulting trust declared. *Held:* A constructive trust existed, entitling the son to have his original title as joint tenant restored. When one person having legal and equitable title to property transfers it to another with whom the person has a confidential relationship to hold for a particular purpose, a constructive trust arises in favor of the transferor and may be enforced when the transferee acts to harm the transferor's interest. Fraudulent intent it not necessary for imposition of a constructive trust. *Mayer v. Cianciolo*, 463 So. 2d 1219 (Dist. Ct. App. 1985).

New York Plaintiff and grantee each contributed one half of the down payment on vacation property. Although the deed was listed in grantee's name only and grantee alone obtained a mortgage for the balance of the purchase price, plaintiff and grantee shared the cost of meeting monthly expenses on the property equally. The arrangement was apparently intended to prevent plaintiff's wife, from whom plaintiff was seeking a divorce, from making claims on the property. When plaintiff and grantee ended their relationship, a dispute arose over the property's disposition. *Held:* Plaintiff was not barred from recovery by the doctrine of unclean hands, because if any fraud had been committed, it had been directed at plaintiff's wife and not at grantee. Any oral agreement by plaintiff to relinquish his claiims to the property was unenforceable because plaintiff could surrender his interest in the property only by conveying it in writing. Plaintiff was due an undivided one-half interest in the property, not a lesser amount representing his actual expenses in purchasing and maintaining the property, because that was the parties' intention. *Higgins v. Normile*, 515 NYS2d 148 (App. Div. 1987).

3.00 JOINT TENANCIES

3.05 Creation

Alabama Plaintiff conveyed two plots of land jointly to herself and to her nephew, defendant, via a deed providing for receipt of a fee simple interest by the survivor. Before the sale, plaintiff filed a motion alleging she had previously conveyed her interest in the land to third parties. Defendant alleged that plaintiff's deed to third parties was void because it destroyed defendant's survivorship interest. *Held:* The court first determined the deed conveyed a joint tenancy, not a tenancy in common. Thus, the nature of the survivor's interest depended upon case law. The court concluded that the conveyance was governed by the case of *Bernhard v. Bernhard*, 278 Ala. 240, 177 So. 2d 565 (1965), which required that survivorship interests like that of defendant be held indestructible. Plaintiff contended that subsequent case law overruling *Bernhard* should have governed. The court disagreed, holding that the case law came into being after plaintiff's conveyance to herself and defendant and was not retroactive in effect. The case was remanded for consideration of whether the deed was effective to convey a life estate pur autre vie, i.e., for grantor joint tenant's life. *Johnson v. Keener*, 425 So. 2d 1108 (1983).

Alabama Land was conveyed to plaintiff and his deceased wife by a deed granting them the land "as tenants in common and with equal rights and interest . . . and unto the survivor of the said Grantees, at the death of the other. . . ." Plaintiff's deceased wife sought to convey her interest in the property to her son, defendant, subject to her life estate. Plaintiff argued the property was his under the survivorship provision of the deed. *Held:* For plaintiff. The deed to plaintiff and his wife contained "tenancy in common" language, creating a tenancy in common for life with a contingent remainder in favor of the survivor. The right of survivorship in one tenant in common is not destructible by an act of the other. Therefore, a person taking property by deed from such cotenant had no interest in the property after the grantor's death. *Durant v. Hamrick*, 409 So. 2d 731 (1981).

Georgia The will of a 1970 decedent devised land to her son and daughter as joint tenants and not as tenants in common and to the survivor of them in fee simple. The son died, and his widow sued the daughter for his interest in the property. *Held:* The daughter was entitled to the entire property. Although before 1976, Georgia had abolished joint tenancy as it existed in common law, a right of survivorship created by contract or will was recognized. Thus, the son and daughter had held vested life estates with cross-contingent remainders. *Williams v. Studstill*, 306 SE2d 633 (1983).

Iowa Decedent and his business partner acquired land for their cattle business and conveyed an undivided one-half interest to decedent and his wife as joint tenants with survivorship rights. The land was sold shortly before decedent's death, and the contract contained a provision continuing any joint tenancy of the vendors. Decedent's mother and sister contended that the land was a partnership asset and that decedent's interest should have been included in the estate to pass by intestacy. *Held:* Title to the property indicated that decedent intended the property to be owned by him and his wife jointly, not as a partnership asset. *In re Estate of Allen*, 239 NW2d 163 (1976).

Texas Two brothers each had an undivided one-half interest in property. They both executed deeds purported to convey to the other all of the property upon the death of the grantor. One brother died and his will, without mentioning the property in question, named a third party as his devisee. *Held:* The devisee had no interest in the land. The deeds were valid. They were not ineffective wills. It was necessary to consider the two deeds as one transaction and to give effect to the intent of the grantor. Upon the death of one brother, the surviving brother became the owner of the land in fee simple. *Terrell v. Graham*, 576 SW2d 610 (1979).

Washington A father deeded property to his sons as joint tenants at a time when a community property agreement was in force between one of the sons and his wife. When that son died, the surviving son brought an action to quiet title to the property in himself. *Held:* The widow retained an undivided one-half interest in the property. The joint tenancy originally created was between the one son and the community of the other son and his wife. The widow's half share in the community interest in the joint tenancy was not extinguished by her husband's death; instead the community property agreement, which stated that all community property was to vest in the survivor, controlled, entitling her to her late husband's share as well. *Lyon v. Lyon*, 670 P2d 272 (1983).

Wisconsin Deceased was owed money on a land contract resulting from the sale of a motel. His widow, who had joined in the contract, petitioned to have herself declared a joint tenant in her deceased husband's interest in the contract. The trial court found that the widow was not a joint tenant, and she appealed from that ruling. *Held:* Where the deceased was entirely responsible for the construction and business operations of the motel, there was no evidence that the deceased and widow intended to share the proceeds of the contract, or that widow expressed any interest in the proceeds. Thus, there was no evidence of any promise or intent on the part of the deceased to create a joint tenancy. Absent such evidence, widow could not claim status of joint tenant. *In re Estate of Weger*, 238 NW2d 522 (1976).

3.10 Termination

8th Circuit Husband and wife were joint tenants with right of survivorship. In 1976, the property was conveyed to a third party by a quitclaim deed purportedly signed by husband and wife. Wife's signature was a forgery, however. Subsequently, the property changed hands several times. Upon husband's death, wife brought a diversity action in federal court to quiet title. *Held:* The 1976 quitclaim deed from the husband to the third party effectively transferred the husband's interest in the joint tenancy. One joint tenant is free to convey his interest in the joint tenancy to a third party at any time, without the knowledge or consent of the other joint tenant. Such a conveyance severs the joint tenancy, leaving the third party and other joint tenant as tenants in common. Husband's attempt to transfer wife's interest by a forged signature was ineffective, however. *Hockett v. Larsen*, 742 F2d 1123 (1984).

California To prevent foreclosure while her husband was out of town, a wife deeded the couple's house to a lender under what was, in effect, a refinancing agreement at very high interest. With the lender's knowledge, but without consulting her husband, the wife forged her husband's signature on the deed. When the wife defaulted on the new financing arrangement, the house was sold. The husband sued to quiet title to the property and cancel the forged deed. *Held:* The deed was a valid and effective conveyance of the wife's interest only. It had the effect of severing the joint tenancy and making the grantee and his assigns tenants in common with the husband, with a one-half interest in the property. *Handy v. Shiells*, 235 Cal. Rptr. 543 (Ct. App. 1987).

Illinois Decedent, who held real estate as joint tenant with his brother, had executed a mortgage on the jointly held property to secure payment of a friend's note. When the surviving brother sued to quiet title to the entire property, decedent's heir (the friend mentioned above) counterclaimed that he had inherited an interest in the property as tenant in common. *Held:* Under Illinois law, a conveyance severs a joint tenancy, while a judgment lien does not. The surviving brother was sole owner of the property. Disavowing its dicta in earlier cases, the court held that the mortgage was a lien and therefore did not sever the joint tenancy. The decedent's interest in the property ceased to exist on his death, as did the mortgage lien. *Harms v. Sprague*, 473 NE2d 930 (1984).

Illinois A joint tenant who held property jointly with her surviving sister conveyed the property from herself as joint tenant to herself as tenant in common, expressly to dissolve any rights of survivorship between herself and her sister. When the sister predeceased the joint tenant, representatives of the sister's estate sought a declaratory judgment giving effect to the joint tenant's conveyance. *Held:* Basing its decision on a statute that dispensed with the "straw man" requirement in the creation of joint tenancies, the court held that the joint tenant's deed was effective in converting the joint tenancy into a tenancy in common. *Minonk State Bank v. Grassman*, 432 NE2d 386 (App. Ct. 1982), aff'd, 447 NE2d 386 (1983).

Oklahoma Plaintiffs acquired real property from individual joint tenants. In 1973, state tax authorities filed a warrant against the joint tenants for back taxes. One of the joint tenants died in 1975, and her interest in the property terminated. At that time, the state had not issued an execution against the property. When plaintiffs acquired the property, they brought an action to remove the lien. *Held:* For plaintiffs. The state's unexecuted tax lien on the property terminated upon the death of the joint tenant. The court applied the common-law rule that a lien on a party's interest in joint tenancy property is extinguished on the joint tenant's death, since the joint tenancy itself is thereby severed. *Ladd v. State*, 688 P2d 59 (1984).

Pennsylvania Brother and sister were deeded certain property as joint tenants with a right of survivorship. Subsequently, they listed the property for sale and an agreement for sale was executed by the brother with the written consent of the sister. The brother died and the sale was consummated by the sister. The brother's estate alleged that the decedent was entitled to one-half the proceeds of the sale. *Held:* The agreement for sale, executed prior to the death of the brother, terminated the joint tenant's right of survivorship because equitable interest in the property had already passed to the purchaser. The estate was entitled to one-half the proceeds of the sale. *Yannopoulos v. Sophos*, 365 A2d 1312 (1976).

3.15 Partition

Kansas Two brothers (plaintiffs) and their sister (defendant) owned as joint tenants with the right of survivorship some realty upon which there was a single-family dwelling. Defendant, who occupied the residence, refused to agree to the sale or leasing of the property by plaintiffs. As a result, plaintiffs commenced an action for partition of the property. The trial court granted plaintiffs' motion for a summary judgment, and defendant appealed, asserting that property held in joint tenancy could not be the subject of involuntary partition. *Held:* Affirmed for plaintiff. The court's affirmation was supported by case law of 18 states (and no current authorities to the contrary) holding that property held in joint tenancy can be partitioned. It also noted that, under the circumstances, partition was the only equitable solution because it gave plaintiffs the choice of not sharing the property with defendant and prevented defendant from continuing to enjoy the property to the practical exclusion of plaintiffs. *Hall v. Hamilton*, 667 P2d 350 (1983).

Maine Defendant appealed the Commissioner's report partitioning a parcel on which were located a barn, a farmhouse, a garage house, and a cottage. Defendant argued that the report dividing the property into a lot of 49,000 square feet with three buildings on it, and a lot of 54,000 feet with the cottage on it, failed to adequately state the comparative values of the shares. *Held:* The report partitioned the property on the basis of values including financial, utilitarian, or sentimental advantages and stated that both the quality and quantity of the property were considered. Defendant failed to prove that the division resulted in an inequality so substantial as to constitute gross error and the report was therefore sustained. *Easton v. Hackett*, 352 A2d 748 (1976).

Michigan Plaintiff and her husband, defendant, conveyed two parcels of land to themselves and their three sons by deeds stating that the conveyances were made to defendant and his wife and the sons, all single men, as joint tenants with rights of survivorship. Plaintiff and defendant divorced. Plaintiff sought judicial partition of the two parcels, but her request was denied on the grounds that the deeds conveyed by the spouses created in them a joint tenancy with rights of survivorship that could not be partitioned. Plaintiff contended that the deed created a survivorship in the sons, but the interest created in the spouses was a tenancy by the entirety, which, upon divorce, became a mere tenancy in common. *Held:* For plaintiff. An estate between spouses will be presumed to create a tenancy by the entirety absent a showing of intent to create a different estate. The mere use of the term "joint tenants" does not by itself indicate that a joint tenancy has been conveyed. The deed's designation of a plaintiff as defendant's wife and of the sons as single men supported a creation of a tenancy by the entirety. Therefore, the divorce converted the tenancy to a tenancy in common, which is entitled to partition. *Butler v. Butler*, 332 NW2d 488 (1983).

Virginia Judgment creditor filed a complaint to compel partition of land held in a joint tenancy with right of survivorship. *Held:* Partition should be granted. A joint tenant can both convey his interest to a stranger, thus defeating the right of the survivor, and also force partition of the property. The law should therefore be able to compel partition on behalf of a judgment creditor where the debt is first incurred and then left unpaid while property exists of value sufficient to pay that debt. *Jones v. Conwell*, 314 SE2d 61 (1984).

West Virginia Husband and wife, who were separated, held the wife's home as joint tenants with right of survivorship. The husband's creditors sought to foreclose to enforce liens against the property. *Held:* "Creditors of one joint tenant may reach that joint tenant's interest and force partition either in kind or by sale, but only if 'the interest of the other person or persons so entitled will not be prejudiced thereby.' *W. Va. Code*, 37-4-3." Although there should be a fairly strong presumption that business property may be reached in a creditor's suit, "when creditors seek to subject a jointly owned family house to the satisfaction of outstanding judgments, the court must look carefully to the issue of prejudice of the non-debtor spouse." The court, noting a widespread reluctance in the United States to allow creditors of one spouse to sell the family house to satisfy debts, made it clear that in such cases the statutory element of prejudice should be treated expansively, citing the loss of an unassignable low-interest mortgage as one example of possible prejudice. *Harris v. Crowder*, 322 SE2d 854 (1984).

3.20 Contribution

Oregon A mother and son purchased real property together as joint tenants with a right of survivorship. At the time of the mother's death, the two, as co-obligors, owed $40,000 secured by trust deeds on the purchase price. The son, as personal representative, took the position that her estate was liable for one-half the balance due on the purchase price. The other heirs filed objections to the son's position on contribution. *Held:* For the objecting heirs. At the time of the mother's death, the entire property vested solely in her son. If the law were to require contribution from the mother's estate for half of the debt, the estate would receive no benefit. Contribution is an equitable remedy used to prevent unjust enrichment. If it were used in these circumstances, it would result in unjust enrichment rather than prevent it. *Bonner v. Arnold*, 676 P2d 290 (1984).

4.00 TENANCIES BY THE ENTIRETY

4.05 Creation

Florida Plaintiffs' parents acquired the subject property as an estate by the entirety. After plaintiffs' mother died, their father remarried and conveyed the property to himself and his second wife as an estate by the entirety. The second wife, however, did not join in the conveyance. After plaintiffs' father died, both plaintiffs and the second wife claimed interests in the homestead property. *Held:* Plaintiffs were entitled to a remainder interest in the homestead property. The applicable law was the "homestead" provision of the Florida Constitution of 1885, under which the gratuitous conveyance of homestead property from husband to wife, where there were children, was void unless there was joinder by the wife. Defendant's reliance on case law construing the amended version of the "homestead" provision to waive the joinder requirement was unjustified because the amendment did not take effect until after the attempted conveyance as an estate by the entirety and after the father's death. *Robbins v. Robbins*, 411 So. 2d 1024 (Dist. Ct. App. 1982).

Indiana A mortgage was executed on a family farm owned in tenancy by the entirety. On default and suit to foreclose, the wife testified that she never signed the mortgage or authorized her husband to do so. *Held:* The mortgage was valid since the husband signed for his wife as her agent. An implied agency will be inferred based upon the circumstances and the parties' actions. There was a long history of the husband conducting the family business with the wife's tacit approval. Additionally, she failed to revoke his implied authority by objecting to his signing her name on an earlier note and mortgage. *Moehlenkamp v. Schatz*, 396 NE2d 433 (1979).

4.10 Rights and Duties of Cotenants

Massachusetts A husband had owned a residence with his wife in a tenancy by the entirety since 1954, along with several properties he owned by himself. Defendant bank levied on these properties to satisfy a debt owed by defendant. Between 1954 and the time of the sheriff's sale of the properties, the Massachusetts Equal Rights Amendment (ERA) had gone into effect. The wife sued to enjoin the sheriff's sale, asserting that the ERA invalidated the Massachusetts rule for tenancies by the entirety. *Held:* Although the Massachusetts rule conflicted with the provisions of the ERA, the tenancy would stand because it was created before the state adopted the ERA. *West v. First Agricultural Bank*, 419 NE2d 262 (1981).

North Carolina Plaintiff and her husband owned real estate as tenants by the entirety. The house located on the property and its contents were insured by defendant for $30,000. Subsequently, plaintiff's husband intentionally set fire to the house, completely destroying it. At the time of the fire, plaintiff and her husband were indebted for $20,000, which was secured by deeds of trust on the house. An insurance policy contained a loss-payable clause favorable to the bank. Shortly after the fire, defendant paid the balance due on the trust note. Plaintiff sued defendant for the remaining $10,000, claiming she was entitled to the money because the property was owned by the entirety. *Held:* An estate by the entirety in personal property is not recognized in North Carolina. The insurance proceeds were incapable of entirety ownership and had to be considered divisible property. It was ordered that half of the $10,000 balance be paid to plaintiff, while the other half would be forfeited by the husband. *Lovell v. Rowan Mut. Fire ins. Co.*, 274 SE2d 170 (1981).

4.15 —Right of Survivorship

Florida Two brothers each owned an undivided one-half interest in property. Each executed a deed creating a tenancy by the entirety between himself and his wife in an undivided one-half interest in the property. During probate of the second brother's will, it was contended that an undivided one half of an undivided one-half interest passed to decedent's wife by the deed and that the remaining one-fourth interest passed by his will into his estate. *Held:* The deed created a tenancy by the entirety, so that upon the death of either spouse, husband's entire interest would vest a full title in surviving spouse. *Baumgardner v. Kennedy*, 343 So. 2d 1323 (Dist. Ct. App. 1977).

Florida Purchase-money mortgage was granted to a husband and wife for the sale of their residence in New York. The couple moved to Florida. After the husband's death, his widow claimed sole ownership of the mortgage, although the husband's will devised the mortgage to his sons. *Held:* The trial court ruling that an undivided one-half interest was owned by the widow and the remainder passed to the husband's estate was reversed and remanded. A major issue was whether New York or Florida law should apply. The court held that since the mortgage was a "movable," ownership of it would pass under Florida law, which recognizes estates by the entirety in personal property. *In re Estate of Siegel*, 350 So. 2d 89 (Dist. Ct. App. 1977).

New Jersey Shortly after a New Jersey married couple entered into a contract to sell their home and before the closing was held, the husband died. The state Inheritance Tax Bureau then claimed that one half of the proceeds from the sale of the property was includable in the husband's estate, stating that a recent addition to the state administrative code permitted application of the equitable conversion doctrine for tax purposes. *Held:* The application of the doctrine of equitable conversion in these circumstances was rejected. Since the property had not been sold, there was no cash traceable to the deceased husband during his lifetime. The court, in reversing the decision by the tax bureau, concluded that the inherent right of survivorship provided by a tenancy by the entirety could not be destroyed by the signing of a contract. *In re Estate of Houghton*, 371 A2d 735 (1977), aff'd, 383 A2d 713 (1978).

4.20
Termination

Florida A husband who owned property in his own name conveyed the property to his wife and himself as tenants by the entirety. The wife did not join in the conveyance. Their son attempted to have the conveyance declared void after the husband's death. *Held:* The conveyance was valid, even without the joinder of the wife. While Article X, Section 4(c) of the Florida constitution requires joinder of the wife where there is an attempt to alienate the homestead property, joinder is not necessary in order to transfer sole title from the husband alone to husband and wife as tenants by the entirety. *Jameson v. Jameson*, 387 So. 2d 351 (1980).

New York Husband sued for divorce and wife counterclaimed for a separation decree. The husband's complaint was dismissed and the wife withdrew her counterclaim for the decree. The court nonetheless awarded the wife sole and exclusive possession of the marital home as well as support payments. On appeal, the appellate divison ordered that the marital home be sold and the proceeds be divided according to the parties' respective equities in the property. The wife appealed. *Held:* The court of appeals reversed, since the appellate division was without authority to order the sale of the marital home. The parties owned the property as tenants by the entirety, and that tenancy could not be destroyed unless one of the parties died or the marriage relationship was altered by some judicial decree (divorce, separation, or annulment). Since no divorce or separation decree had been granted, the court could not order the sale of the home. *Kahn v. Kahn*, 401 NYS2d 47 (1977).

4.25
Effect of Divorce

Florida Ex-wife brought an action for partition of property now owned by herself and her ex-husband as tenants in common. The lower court ruled that ex-husband's claim of homestead was not applicable and ordered partition and sale of the property. Ex-husband appealed. *Held:* The Florida constitution, Article 10, Section 4, mandates that homestead interests should be protected from forced sale wherever possible, but not at the expense of others owning interests in the property. In this case, both parties agreed that the property was indivisible and that forced sale was the only method through which the ex-wife could obtain beneficial enjoyment of her one-half undivided interest in the property. In addition, the trial court had not granted to the ex-husband exclusive possession of the family home as alimony or child support. Under these circumstances, partition and forced sale were permissible. *Tullis v. Tullis*, 360 So. 2d 375 (1978).

Michigan After her former husband's remarriage and death, wife filed a quiet title action in an attempt to gain sole possession of property that she had purchased with husband as tenants by the entireties when they had been married but that had not been sold at the time of their divorce decree. *Held:* Wife could not gain sole title and control of the property. After the divorce decree became final, husband and wife held the property as tenants in common. Therefore, wife must share the property as a tenant in common with husband's heirs. *Brown v. Prisel*, 293 NW2d 729 (1980).

New Jersey In a divorce proceeding, the wife contended that certain real property was acquired by the husband during marriage and therefore was an asset subject to equitable distribution. The realty was acquired by the husband and his mother, as joint tenants with right of survivorship, prior to the marriage, and the mother died before the filing of the divorce complaint. *Held:* Although the survivorship right was created when the joint tenancy was established, it did not become effective until the mother's death, at which time the husband acquired an undivided fee ownership in the entire tract of land. Therefore, upon the death of his mother, which was during his marriage, the husband acquired a substantive interest in the premises within the contemplation of the equitable distribution statute. *Gauger v. Gauger*, 376 A2d 523 (1977).

New York Defendant mortgaged a property owned by himself and his wife as tenants by the entirety, but forged his wife's signature on the documents. The couple later divorced, the loan went into default, and a foreclosure action was brought. *Held:* The divorce extinguished the right of survivorship the foreclosure purchaser would otherwise have had. Despite the general rule that the rights of the mortgagee are fixed at execution, the inchoate rights of the mortgagee follow those of its mortgagor. *VRW, Inc. v. Klein*, 503 NE2d 496 (1986).

4.30
Effect of Separation

New York When husband and wife separated, they agreed that the family home, which they held as tenants by the entirety, would be sold and the proceeds shared equally. Before the sale could occur, the wife died. The administrators of her estate sought half the proceeds of the sale, contending that the separation agreement terminated the tenancy by the entirety, converting it to a tenancy in common. *Held:* The husband was entitled to all the proceeds. Conversion of a tenancy by the entirety into a tenancy in common required certain definitive acts, such as a judicial decree of separation, a conveyance of the property in which spouses join, or execution of a written instrument clearly expressing agreement by husband and wife to divide the property. None of these requirements was met by the separation agreement, which the court held constituted, at most, an executory contract to divide the proceeds when a sale occurred. *In re Estate of Violi*, 482 NE2d 29 (1985).

4.35
Effect of Death

Maryland Calvin and Cecelia held a farm as tenants by the entirety. Carlton paid $100 for a written option to purchase the farm, which was extended without additional consideration. Calvin died, and Carlton wrote Cecelia accepting the offer to sell. Cecelia refused to convey the property and Carlton sued. *Held:* Under the Maryland Statute of Frauds, the written extension of the option was insufficient because of absence of consideration. Therefore, the issue became whether there was an offer to sell the property, which Carlton accepted by his letter. The general rule is that the death of an offeror revokes the offer or causes it to lapse. The continued vitality of the offer depended on the continued assent of both Calvin and Cecelia. Since upon Calvin's death, his assent was no longer possible, the offer lapsed. Therefore, no outstanding offer existed, and Carlton's letter was a mere offer to buy, which Cecelia refused. *Beall v. Beall*, 434 A2d 1015 (1981).

5.00
TENANCIES IN COMMON

5.05
Creation

Missouri Unmarried man and woman were deeded a farm as man and wife.

There was no testimony to show the contribution of either party to the purchase price of the farm. The woman sued the man to quiet title and to partition. *Held:* Reversed in part. Even though the parties were tenants in common, the trial court should have taken into account the contribution of each grantee toward acquisition of the property before making a decision regarding the interest of each party upon partition. While there was no substantial evidence to support the trial court's decision to order the sale, rather than partition, of the farm, the sale pursuant to the order of the trial court to a third party purchaser could not be set aside. *Brooks v. Kunz*, 597 SW2d 183 (1980).

Oregon An unmarried couple purchased a house in 1972. Of the $2,000 down payment, the man paid $500 and the woman $1,500. The man made monthly mortgage payments, and the woman paid household expenses. In 1974, the couple split up, with the man continuing to live in the house and paying the mortgage. *Held:* Since the couple intended to pool their resources for their common benefit during the period they lived together, they should be viewed as equal cotenants in common, subject to the following: The man had to pay the woman $500, representing the difference in the down payment. He also had to pay her one-half the fair rental value of the house for as long as he lived there. The woman had to pay one-half the monthly mortgage from 1974, when the couple stopped living together. *Beal v. Beal*, 557 P2d 507 (1978).

5.10 Rights and Duties of Cotenants

1st Circuit Three parties claimed ownership of land subject to condemnation. Two of them entered into a stipulation to divide the condemnation proceeds, and rested their claim on a clear chain of title that was held by one of those parties and that went back to the son of an owner of the property who had died intestate. The third party rested its claim on the interest held by the late owner's daughter. The latter claim, however, was based only on a missing deed. *Held:* The condemnation proceeds would have to be divided between the parties claiming title from the son and the party claiming title from the daughter. Although the case law may require an award of full compensation to the party with the strongest title, those claiming title from the son could have acquired no more than the undivided half-interest he had inherited from his father. The only, and therefore the best, evidence relating to the half-interest derived from the daughter was presented by the third party. *United States v. 79.31 Acres of Land*, 717 F2d 646 (1983).

Arkansas Lessor leased premises in its shopping center to several tenants. Each lease contained a mutual release of liability arising from any damage covered by insurance. After a fire in defendant tenant's premises, plaintiffs cotenants sued, claiming defendant's negligence caused the fire. The parties each had fire insurance that covered their losses. Defendant moved for summary judgment. *Held:* For plaintiffs. Plaintiffs were not claiming under or through the lease. The lease released lessee and lessor but did not waive a cause of action in negligence against a cotenant. In addition, plaintiffs' insurance policies were not purchased for the mutual protection of all cotenants, so neither this cause of action nor subrogation would be barred by the existence of insurance. *Gift Box v. Scott*, 613 SW2d 395 (1981).

Florida A man and woman lived as husband and wife in a house to which they had taken title in both their names as husband and wife. When the man died, his legal wife sued the woman, seeking to recover possession of and title to the entire house or, in the alternative, partition. *Held:* The man and woman had an estate in common in the house, with no right of survivorship, making the woman and the estate cotenants after the man's death. A cotenant in exclusive possession that uses the property for her own benefit and from which she receives no rent is not accountable to cotenants out of possession unless the cotenant in possession holds adversely or as a result of an ouster. The suit brought by the wife placed the woman on notice that the cotenant out of possession claimed adversely to her. Therefore, the woman was liable for half the reasonable rent from the date the complaint was served. *Diedricks v. Reinhardt*, 466 So. 2d 375 (Dist. Ct. App. 1985).

Michigan Plaintiff's decedent was killed in an incident that occurred during a dragstrip race on property owned by defendants, who were mother and son, as tenants in common. The son operated the dragstrip, without any participation by the mother. Plaintiff was awarded damages against both parties. *Held:* Judgment against the other reversed. Recovery of these damages is based upon the failure to use reasonable care in the operation of the dragstrtip, and not upon mere ownership of the property. Such personal liability cannot attach to the mother without evidence that she was involved in the dragstrip business. *Merritt v. Nickelson*, 287 NW2d 178 (1980).

Michigan Property owners, as tenants in common, brought a trespass action against neighboring landowners, alleging that the neighbors' employees had removed earth from plaintiffs' property to use as landfill on defendants' land. Only one plaintiff tenant testified that he did not give his consent for the earth to be taken. The court of appeals held that plaintiffs had not satisfied their statutory burden of proof that the earth was taken without their consent, since each cotenant did not submit evidence of his or her lack of consent. *Held:* The testimony of one tenant that he did not grant consent, together with the circumstantial evidence of the others' nonconsent, was sufficient to satisfy plaintiffs' burden of proof. *Weisswasser v. Chernick*, 252 NW2d 766 (1977).

Montana Co-owners acquired an inn and entered into an agreement setting forth their rights and obligations concerning the property. After experiencing financial difficulties, a majority of co-owners decided to sell the inn to purchasers. One co-owner objected to the sale. Purchasers initiated a quiet title action against objecting co-owner, alleging that his claimed ownership interest placed a cloud on their title. He counterclaimed, asserting that co-owners had no authority to transfer his ownership interest. *Held:* Co-owners' majority vote was sufficient to validate sale. Their original agreement stated that all decisions were to be made by majority vote, unless otherwise specified. The agreement did not specify a majority vote for the sale of the property. The agreement controlled, even though co-owners held their interests as tenants in common. *Felska v. Goulding*, 776 P2d 530 (1989).

Nebraska Farmer, as lessee, planted crops on property owned by tenants in common. A dispute arose among the tenants, and a judicial sale followed. The farmer sought compensation for his unharvested crop, which was sold with the land. Two of the tenants in common argued that they owed nothing because they had terminated their interest in the lease prior to planting. *Held:* Under the equitable principle of unjust enrichment, the two tenants are liable to the farmer to the extent that the crops increased the judicial sale price. In reaching this result, however, the majority held that, in spite of case law precedent, a tenant in common may effectively terminate his leasehold interest to avoid liability arising directly therefrom. *Ahrens v. Dye*, 302 NW2d 682 (1981).

Ohio Widow took the statutory share in her husband's estate in lieu of an undivided one-sixth interest in the family residence. The rest of the interest in the house was held by other family members. Executrix for the husband's estate sued to evict the widow and for back rent. *Held:* The widow was not subject to eviction, but she was liable for reasonable rent. Any co-owner has a right to possess the property, and the widow acquired a possessory interest in the house through her statutory share of the estate. *Collins v. Jackson*, 517 NE2d 269 (1986).

Utah Defendant and her spouse owned land as joint tenants. To finance the repayment of $8,400 to a finance company, they executed a deed of trust. Subsequently, the husband was held liable for a money judgment unrelated to the land. The creditor levied upon the husband's interest in the land, and at a sheriff's sale, plaintiffs acquired that interest. As a result, a tenancy in common was created between the defendant and the plaintiffs. The interests of all were subject to the deed of trust to the finance company. When that obligation fell into default, a trustee's sale was held. Defendant outbid plaintiffs and took a deed to the entire interest. Plaintiffs sued to recover their half interest or the purchase amount. *Held:* Plaintiffs were restored their half interest. It was wrong for defendant to use her money to purchase at the foreclosure rather than to prevent the default. However, defendant's payment was held to be a payment of her personal liability to the finance company and not an advance for the benefit of cotenants. *Jolley v. Correy*, 671 P2d 139 (1983).

Vermont Property had been leased by tenants to the state of Vermont. Subsequently, a judgment creditor obtained a judgment against the property. Tenants, however, granted the state an option to purchase the property between the granting of the judgment and its recording. Tenant agreed to convey title by a warranty deed free and clear of all liens and encumbrances, if the state elected to exercise the option. The state filed a cross-claim against the judgment debtor and his cotenant, alleging breach of warranty. *Held:* For the state. When they signed the option agreement and the warranty deed, the cotenants jointly obligated themselves to convey free and clear title to all property. They held a common purpose in jointly granting the property. Therefore, cotenant was liable to the state, even though the lien did not attach to his interest in the property. *Northeast Petroleum Corp. v. Agency of Transp.*, 446 A2d 1164 (1983).

5.15
Ouster of One Cotenant by Another

Ohio Widow took the statutory share in her husband's estate in lieu of an undivided one-sixth interest in the family residence. The rest of the interest in the house was held by other family members. Executrix for the husband's estate sued to evict the widow and for back rent. *Held:* The widow was not subject to eviction, but she was liable for reasonable rent. Any co-owner has a right to possess the property, and the widow acquired a possessory interest in the house through her statutory share of the estate. *Collins v. Jackson*, 517 NE2d 269 (1986).

South Carolina Decedent left property to his five children. After decedent's death and until 1935, three of the children lived on the property in separate homes. In 1935, York, one of decedent's children, began to occupy and cultivate the entire tract of land. York and his descendants remained on the land through 1969, when his widow and descendants conveyed part of the property to a church. In 1975 a surviving nephew sued to partition the land among the tenants in common. York's descendants argued they had held the land adversely for over 20 years so as to oust the other cotenants. *Held:* York's descendants had not acquired title by ouster. No circumstances between 1935 and 1969 had overcome the strong presumption that a tenant in common holds possession in recognition of the cotenancy. York's activities of farming and collecting rent were insufficient to overcome the presumption. Further, the conveyance in 1969 to the church could not be the basis of an acquisition of title by ouster because it occurred within ten years of the action in 1975. *Felder v. Fleming*, 295 SE2d 640 (1982).

Utah Plaintiff sought damages for her cousin's exclusive use of grazing land that she and the cousin held in common. Plaintiff had asked the cousin to utilize the land only in proportion to his ownership, but he continued to graze to maximum capacity. *Held:* When a cotenant out of possession makes a clear, unequivocal demand to use land that is in the exclusive possession of another cotenant and that cotenant refuses to accommodate the other tenant's right to use the land, the tenant out of possession has a claim for relief. Damages were based on an estimated amount of feed grazed by his livestock. Although a cotenant is generally not entitled to contribution for improvements made without his cotenant's consent, the cousin was allowed to deduct from damages the cost of certain repairs. *Gillmor v. Gillmor*, 694 P2d 1037 (1984).

5.20 Partition

Alabama Husband and wife owned property subject to a mortgage as tenants in common, with a one-quarter interest owned by the husband and three quarters by the wife. When they defaulted on the mortgage, mortgagee purchased the property at the foreclosure sale. The property was redeemed and reconveyed by deed to husband and wife. The wife's heirs sued the husband's heirs, seeking partition and sale of the property. The trial court decreed the sale and allocated three quarters of the proceeds to the wife's heirs and one quarter to the husband's heirs. The husband's heirs appealed, arguing that the foreclosure ended the original tenancy and the redemption created a new one. *Held:* Affirmed. Under Alabama law, the exercise of a redemption right within the statutory period following foreclosure restores legal title to the mortgagors as if there had been no sale. *Foster v. Hudson*, 437 So. 2d 5298 (1983).

Nebraska After a son and a daughter inherited land intestate from their father, they divided it by use. The daughter and her family occupied and improved the area classified as pasturage, while the son and his family occupied and improved the part classified as cropland. Subsequently, the son's family sought partition. *Held:* The land would have to be partitioned by sale, rather than by partition in kind, despite the presumption in favor of partition in kind in Nebraska. Partition in kind would result in a complex settlement granting the parties rights that they did not want or could not use. *Nordhausen v. Christner*, 338 NW2d 754 (1983).

New Mexico Two couples purchased adjacent lots and agreed to combine the lots into a common tenancy, with each party owning an undivided one-fourth interest. Twenty years later, seller sold his interest in Lot *A* to buyer under a warranty deed, which did not specifically limit the grant to seller's interest. Subsequently, second cotenant sued seller to quiet title, claiming that the unilateral sale by one cotenant, without the consent of other cotenants, served to partition the estate and terminate the cotenancy agreement. *Held:* Conveyance of seller's interest did not effect a partition, regardless of the extent of the interest conveyed. A cotenant may convey his interest in the common estate to a stranger without the knowledge or approval of other cotenants. Generally, a cotenant cannot convey an individual or undivided interest in a specific parcel of a commonly held tract; however, the conveyance is permitted if it does not substantially prejudice the partition rights of cotenants. State law recognizes that under certain circumstances a conveyance that purports to grant complete ownership of a specific tract within the common estate may actually transfer only the vendor's undivided interest in the estate. In this case, the conveyance of an interest in Lot *A* did not disturb the existing cotenancy relationship between the parties in Lot *B*. *Landskroner v. McClure*, 765 P2d 189 (1988).

New York In 1964, plaintiff and defendant executed a partnership agreement to practice medicine. In 1971, they formed a professional corporation. The doctors practiced out of an office they and their spouses owned as tenants in common. Upon dissolution, plaintiff sought partition of the premises; however, defendant claimed that a provision of the partnership agreement barred partition. *Held:* For plaintiff. Once the doctors formed a professional corporation, the partnership agreement became a nullity. Partition of the premises was fair and reasonable. *Notar-Francesco v. Furci*, 539 NYS2d 801 (App. Div. 1989).

PART B

ESTATES AND OTHER INTERESTS IN PROPERTY

6.00
FEE SIMPLE ESTATES

6.05
Fee Simple Absolute

Alabama Daughter of decedent, who died intestate, appealed the trial court's decision granting an undivided one-half interest in decedent's property to the widow and to the daughter under the homestead laws. Because the homestead was valued at more than $6,000, the daughter contended that her mother was only entitled to a life estate in the property under state law (Ala. Code, tit. 7, §661). *Held:* The trial court was correct in granting an absolute fee simple interest in the widow irrespective of the value of the property. Revisions in Sections 661 and 663 of Title 7 were intended to allow widows to obtain title to the homestead of their deceased husbands, and not merely to occupy the estate. *Mordecai v. Scott*, 320 So. 2d 642 (1975).

Mississippi Grantor had conveyed by deed a life estate in land to his son and daughter-in-law, with the remainder fee interest to their issue after their death. Grantor executed another deed four years later for the purpose of making absolute to his son and daughter-in-law title to the land. The son died childless, leaving his wife his sole heir at law. Heirs of the grantor sued to determine whether the grantor had conveyed a contingent remainder interest in the land to the two grantees or whether he had retained a contingent remainder interest that could pass to his heirs. *Held:* Fee simple title to the property was vested in the widow. Under the doctrine of worthier title, since the son and daughter-in-law had no issue at the time of execution of the second deed, the grantor had with a contingent reversionary interest that was alienable by him in his lifetime, and he conveyed that interest to his son and daughter-in-law by the subsequent warranty deed, vesting them with fee simple absolute title. *All Persons v. Buie*, 386 So. 2d 1109 (1980).

New Jersey Landowner deeded parcel to the United States for use as a life-saving station. The United States deeded its interest in the parcel to the state. Grantor's successors brought an action for possession, alleging that the original deed to the United States conveyed an estate in fee simple determinable, which terminated when the grantee stopped using the parcel as a life-saving station. *Held:* The original deed conveyed a fee simple absolute. Under state law, a fee simple determinable is a fee estate that automatically expires upon the occurrence of a stated event. Language creating a determinable fee is strictly construed to avoid forfeiture. While the deed described the use for which the property was acquired, it did not contain words of limitation or refer to a reverter. There was no evidence in the deed, the price paid, or the circumstances of an intent to return the property to the landowner if the contemplated use of the property ended. *United States Trust Co.*

v. State, 543 A2d 457 (Super. Ct. App. Div. 1988).

West Virginia Husband and wife executed a joint will that, by its terms, was irrevocable. The will left all realty and personalty, including the family farm, to the surviving spouse. On the death of that spouse, all that property "which shall not have been disposed of" went to six named children of each spouse from different marriages. The husband died first, and the widow wrote a holographic will leaving the farm to her son. On her death, the son submitted the holographic will to probate. *Held:* The devise of the farm to the son was valid, because the wife had acquired a fee simple interest in all the property covered by the joint will. The court applied a state statute specifying that a fee simple is created by a deed or will unless a contrary intention appears therein. Far from indicating that the wife was to receive a mere life estate in the property, the gift to the offspring in the joint will was simply a provision for the disposition of a possible residuum. *Seifert v. Sanders*, 358 SE2d 775 (1987).

6.10 Fee Simple Determinable

Kentucky In 1869, decedent conveyed land to railroad for use as a depot. The deed contained a possibility of reverter upon cessation of use. The railroad ceased to use the property for depot purposes in the late 1940s, and conveyed the property to defendant in 1969. Decedent's heir claimed a reversion of title and brought an action to quiet title. Defendant claimed that a state statute provided that every possibility of reverter and right of reentry created before July 1, 1960, ceased to be enforceable 30 years after creation, unless a declaration to preserve it had been recorded before July 1, 1965. This procedure had not been followed. *Held:* The statute was inapplicable in this case. The property automatically reverted to decedent's heirs in the late 1940s, upon cessation of use, and the 1960 statute had no effect on reversions that had already occurred. The railroad's quitclaim deed in 1969 conveyed nothing to defendant. *Caldwell v. Brown*, 553 SW2d 692 (1977).

Nebraska Plaintiffs' predecessors had given land to a school district in 1891. The deed stated that it was "to become null and void as soon as the land ceased to be used as school property." *Held:* This indicated an intent to give a fee simple determinable estate and although the land was later sold to the defendants, the plaintiffs had already lost their right of reversion, since by statute the possibility of reversion ended 30 years after the estate was given to the school district. *Heedleston v. Nebraska Jewish Educ. Soc'y*, 186 NW2d 904 (1971).

Wyoming Husband and wife conveyed land to the county. The deed specified that the conveyance was for "the purpose of constructing and maintaining thereon a County Hospital in memorial to the gallant men of the Armed Forces." The county later sold the land and hospital to a private company, which moved the hospital and put the land up for sale. The grantors sought recovery of the land, alleging that the deed created either a fee simple determinable or a fee simple subject to a condition subsequent with a right of reversion to the grantors if the land ceased to be used for a hospital. *Held:* The intent of the grantors was to pass all the estate. The deed did not clearly state that the estate would automatically expire if the land was not used for the stated purpose and did not show the grantors' intent to convey a fee simple determinable. The use of language stating that the conveyance was made in "memorial" was insufficient to create a fee simple determinable because no time limit for preserving the memory was stated. *Wood v. Board of County Comm'rs*, 759 P2d 1250 (1988).

6.15 Fee Tail

Missouri Plaintiff brought a quiet title action to construe a deed that created an estate tail. The first taker under the deed took a life estate and plaintiff, his only child, took a contingent remainder in the fee. Plaintiff was subsequently adopted from his natural father, who subsequently died. Under Missouri law, where a remainder is limited to the heirs of the body of a person to whom a life estate is given, after termination of the life estate, the heirs of the body of such life tenant shall be entitled to take as purchasers in fee simple. Another Missouri statute provides that when a child is adopted, all legal relationships between such child and his natural parents cease. Defendants argued that plaintiff had no valid interest in the land. *Held:* Under Missouri law, the heir of the body takes not by descent but as a substituted purchaser from the original donor. The plaintiff therefore takes as a purchaser under the deed and not by inheritance from his natural father so that his interest in the land was not extinguished by the adoption statute. *Morris v. Ullbright*, 558 SW2d 660 (1977).

6.20 Fee Simple Subject to Condition Subsequent

7th Circuit Texas railroad company purchased a right-of-way from trustee of bankrupt railway under a deed without warranty of any kind. The bankruptcy railway had acquired the right-of-way subject to a reversionary clause that provided that the property would revert to the grantors or their successors if the property ceased to be used for railroad purposes. Sale of the right-of-way was approved by the court; however, purchaser's access to the right-of-way was subsequently barred. The purchaser sued, stating seller violated the purchaser's rights under the court orders approving the sale. *Held:* Bankrupt railway possessed no interest capable of being conveyed to purchaser. Evidence in the case demonstrates that the bankrupt seller was not using the property for any railroad purpose since it never repaired destroyed rail tracks and failed to maintain the tracks. Since the original grantor envisioned actual use and maintenance of tracks constructed on the right-of-way, the mere holding or property for future disposition was not a railroad purpose contemplated by the parties. Under Texas law, a reasonable reading of the reversion clause requires the property to revert when the original grantee ceased using the property for railroad purposes; therefore, the continued use of the track by a third party rail operator does not prevent the reversion clause from being triggered. *In re Chicago, Rock Island & Pac. RR*, 865 F2d 807 (1988).

Pennsylvania Land was granted to a railroad, subject to a reverter clause. The clause permitted the grantor or his successors in interest to repossess the land a year after giving written notice, should the land cease to be used for railroad purposes. When the land ceased to be used for railroad purposes in 1976, the grantor's successors began to farm it. The successors did not give written notice until three years later, when the township to which the railroad had released its interest sued to quiet title. *Held:* The grant to the railroad subject to the reverter clause had given the railroad a fee simple interest subject to a subsequent condition. Since the condition in question, nonuse or abandonment, had occurred, and the successors had given the written notice more than a year before the time of this proceeding, the successors now held the land in fee simple absolute. The successors' repossession of the land before giving written notice may have been wrongful, but it did not diminish their reversion rights. *Emrick v. Bethlehem Township*, 485 A2d 736 (1984).

Tennessee Testator bequeathed property to his wife under a general power of disposition subject to a condition subsequent that the property should pass to his children in the event his wife should ever remarry. Years after testator's death, the wife, who had not remarried, sold the property. A daughter-in-law and several grandchildren refused to join in the deed, and suit was brought by the wife and prospective purchasers for a judicial determination. The lower court ruled that by virtue of the general power of disposition, the wife owned a fee simple absolute. *Held:* Reversed. The applicable state statute, which raises a presumption that every conveyance passes the entire estate of the grantor, applies only to life estates and leaseholds, and not to a fee simple subject to a conditional limitation. Accordingly, the condition subsequent continues in the property whether held by the wife or subsequent purchasers. *Hall v. Hall*, 604 SW2d 851 (1980).

Texas In 1949, plaintiff conveyed a surface estate in a five-acre tract to defendant's grantor. The conveyance specified that a cotton gin was to be constructed on the tract, and that the use of the tract was to be restricted to the operation of a cotton gin. In the event the land was ever used for any other purpose, title was to revert to the grantor. After defendant acquired title to the tract in 1967, he constructed a grain elevator on the property. In 1973, plaintiff sued to exercise her right of reverter and contended that the language of the original conveyance constituted a conditional limitation. *Held:* A conditional limitation exists when the estate is limited by the happening of an event which, when it happens, gives the grantor the right to terminate the estate by reentry. As the language of the 1949 conveyance was an expression of a condition subsequent, plaintiff was required to have exercised her right of reentry before the expiration of the three-year statute of limitations for the recovery of land. Where plaintiff had not done so, defendant retained title to the tract. *Field v. Shaw*, 535 SW2d 3 (Civ. App. 1976).

7.00 LIFE ESTATES

7.05 Creation

North Dakota A husband deeded property in which only he held an interest to his daughter, reserving a life estate to himself and his wife. After his death, the daughter sued to quiet title in her own favor, arguing that her surviving mother's life estate was invalid under the common-law rule that a reservation in a deed or conveyance cannot convey an interest to a third party who is a stranger to the title. *Held:* The common-law rule is rejected. Even if the deed should have conveyed the interest to the wife rather than reserved it to her, it would be putting form over substance to deny the obvious intent of the grantor for that reason. *Malloy v. Boettcher*, 334 NW2d 8 (1983).

Texas A premarital agreement provided that "the property presently owned by each of the parties shall be and remain the separate property of that respective party" and gave each party the right to "control, manage and dispose of" his property. It made, however, no reference to homestead rights. Although the husband and wife each owned a house, they resided in the wife's house during their marriage, allowing the husband's son to occupy his father's house. When the wife died, the husband remained in the wife's house, claiming that the homestead laws entitled him to live there for the rest of his life. *Held:* The husband had a life estate in the house. Texas statute provides that homestead rights are the same whether the property involved is separate or community property. The wife's son's argument that the premarital agreement constituted a waiver was not valid since the agreement did not state that the right to dispose of the separate properties was "free from any claim" arising out of the marriage. *Hunter v. Clark*, 687 SW2d 811 (Ct. App. 1985).

Wyoming A father had conveyed a half interest in land to his son and his son's wife, retaining a life estate for himself, in consideration of an agreement by the son and wife to take care of him. *Held:* The father was not entitled to have the deed set aside on the ground that taking care of him was a condition subsequent which the son and his wife had breached. The deeds contained no reference to such an agreement; and even if such care were a condition subsequent, the fact that the father had left the premises and refused to accept such care made performance of the agreement impossible. *Zullig v. Zullig*, 502 P2d 198 (1972).

7.10 Powers of Life Tenant

Florida Eighty-three-year-old married woman sued to enforce a contract under which she claimed a right to reside in a house formerly owned by a 79-year-old widower. The widower had deeded the house to her, but retained a life estate in the house. The two also signed a contract, which stated that neither party would have the right to dispossess the other from the premises. Thereafter, when the relationship became strained, the widower changed the locks. *Held:* The contract was unenforceable because there was no consideration. Since a life tenant cannot be evicted, the woman had not given up any rights when she agreed not to evict the widower. *Maszewski v. Piskadlo*, 318 So. 2d 226 (Dist. Ct. App. 1975).

Illinois One part of decedent's will provided that his wife would have the right to live in his home until she died, remarried, or vacated the premises to establish a new residence. Another part of his will provided that if his wife ceased to live in the house for any reason, or died, the proceeds would go to a trust fund set up for his daughter. The wife became ill and had to be taken to a nursing home, and the daughter contended that the house should be sold for the benefit of her trust. *Held:* The term "for any reason" may be read in the context of the whole agreement. The wife was entitled to a part of the proceeds of the sale equal to the value of her life estate interest in order to pay her medical bills. *First Nat'l Bank v. Baker*, 342 NE2d 337 (App. Ct. 1976).

Nebraska Plaintiff acquired a life estate in farmland, with the remainder to his children. Subsequently, he sued to partition the land. The guardian ad litem for the children (still minors) objected. *Held:* A life tenant may not partition land with minor remaindermen unless the court determines that the partition is in the minors' best interest. That was not the case here. If partition were permitted, the minors would be deprived of the anticipated appreciation of the land, and given instead more risky interests in trusts and insurance policies. *Williams v. Nebraska Wesleyan Univ.*, 332 NW2d 694 (1983).

7.15 Rights of Remaindermen

Alabama A woman's property subject to a remainder interest in her children was redeemed at a foreclosure sale. There was no evidence that any money was actually paid to effect the redemption. Title later passed to the defendant, whom the children sued to quiet title to their mother's life estate and their own remainder interests. *Held:* A redemption also redeems for the benefit of remaindermen, and subsequent conveyances of title are taken subject to the remaindermen's interest. It did not affect the children's interest that they had contributed nothing toward the redemption. *Scotch v. Hurst*, 437 So. 2d 497 (1983).

Iowa Grantor signed a quitclaim deed, which granted her farm to the first remainderman, with a reserved life estate, only if the remainderman survived grantor. If the first remainderman did not survive grantor, then the farm would be conveyed to a second remainderman. Both remaindermen died before grantor. Executors and administrators of the estates of the three parties sought to quiet title in their parties' heirs. *Held:* Title is quieted in heirs of the second remainderman subject to the life estate. The Iowa Contingent Remainder Act abolished the common-law rule of the destructibility of contingent remainders; therefore, the rule that a contingent remainder fails if the contingent remainderman does not live until the condition precedent occurs does not apply to instruments executed on or after July 1, 1925. Instead, a deed is construed to effectuate the intent of the grantor and passes all interests of the grantor in the property, unless a contrary intent can be reasonably inferred. In this case, since the deed placed a contingency only on the first remainderman, the grantor intended survivorship to be a prerequisite only for the first remainderman to acquire an interest. *Davies v. Radford*, 433 NW2d 704 (1988).

Michigan Plaintiff conveyed a warranty deed to defendants, reserving a life estate. Defendants entered into a lease with an oil company, collecting delay rentals and a bonus payment. Plaintiff sued, contending that as life tenant he was entitled to these payments. *Held:* For plaintiff. A life tenant of an estate is entitled to income from the property, and a remainderman is entitled to the principal. In this case the delay rentals represented a reservation of the right to drill and thus were ordinary rentals payable to the life tenant. The lease granted a "profit a prendre," a right to carry on mining operations, which does not transfer any present interest in the minerals in place. The bonus payment was for the right to use the surface of the land and not payment for oil and gas in place and was therefore allocable to the holder of the present possessory interest, the life tenant. *VanAlstine v. Swanson*, 417 NW2d 516 (1987).

Virginia Property owner conveyed a life estate to his daughter with the remainder to her children. Both the daughter and the granddaughter sold portions of the property. The granddaughter predeceased the great granddaughter. When the great granddaughter died, her husband sued to eject the purchasers of the portions of the property that had been sold. *Held:* Ejectment was denied because the sales were valid. The remainder vested at the birth of the remainderman and not, as the great granddaughter's husband would have it, at the death of the life tenant. *Mullins v. Simmons*, 365 SE2d 771 (1988).

8.00
DOWER AND CURTESY

8.05
Relinquishment and Termination

4th Circuit Widow brought action in 1983 to recover her dower in real property owned by her husband during their marriage. The husband conveyed the property in 1971. Although he died in 1974, the widow first learned of the conveyance in 1983. *Held:* The action was timely. Va. Code Ann. §64.1-37 permits a widow to bring an action of ejectment to recover dower. Laches had no application because the 15-year statute of limitations applicable to actions of ejectment would apply. *Devers v. Chateau Corp.*, 748 F2d 902 (1984).

Arkansas Owner of land that held oil-producing wells died intestate and was survived by his widow and eight children. Under state intestacy laws, the children received the estate subject to the widow's dower and homestead rights. The widow and the children signed an agreement, which provided that "[widow] shall receive thereunder a one-ninth interest" in lieu of sums she would have received under an oil and gas lease. The widow subsequently conveyed her mineral interests in the royalty deeds to a third party. Suit was brought to determine ownership of the royalty interest in oil plaintiff was purchasing. *Held:* The agreement was intended to define only what widow would receive in lieu of her dower and homestead and was not to be considered as a conveyance of an absolute estate to one-ninth interest in mineral rights. To convey legal title, it is necessary that there be words expressing the fact of a sale or transfer of title. Since no words of conveyance are used in the agreement, it lacks the language necessary to convey a fee simple interest. Evidence presented in the case shows that the parties' intent was to settle what the widow would receive from any proceeds of oil and gas leases so that they could lease the lands without delay. *Davis v. Griffin*, 770 SW2d 137 (1989).

Kentucky In a divorce settlement, decedent and his first wife contracted to convey his land to their children, and the contract was incorporated in the divorce judgment. Plaintiff, decedent's second wife and widow, brought suit alleging her entitlement to dower in decedent's land. After the trial court ruled in favor of plaintiff, the children of decedent's first wife appealed. *Held:* Plaintiff was not entitled to dower. Under Kentucky law, a widow does not have dower in property sold but not conveyed by her husband before their marriage, as in this instance. The contract and divorce judgment subjected the land to a constructive trust from the time of execution of the contract. As a result, plaintiff's claim of a dower right in the land failed. *North v. North*, 638 SW2d 711 (Ct. App. 1982).

9.00 COMMUNITY PROPERTY

9.05 Interests of Spouses

California Married couple purchased a house as joint tenants through a joint mortgage, using the wife's premarital property as a down payment. Later payments were to be made from community property funds. When the marriage was dissolved, the wife objected to apportioning a half interest in the house to each spouse. She argued that she had intended not to make a gift to her husband but to retain a separate interest in the house. *Held:* The presumption that each joint tenant had a half interest in the house would stand, for lack of sufficient evidence to rebut it. There was no evidence of an understanding between the spouses that the wife was acquiring the house for herself, and the fact that she did not intend to make a gift was not sufficient to overcome the presumption. *In re Marriage of Lucas*, 614 P2d 285 (1980).

Washington Plaintiff and his brother acquired property by a deed expressly providing that they take it as joint tenants. At the time, a community property agreement between the brother and his wife was also in force. After his brother died, plaintiff brought suit to quiet title to the property. *Held:* Plaintiff and the widow held the property as tenants in common, each holding an undivided half-interest in the property. The community property agreement did not sever the joint tenancy, but created a joint tenancy between plaintiff and the community of his brother and widow. Because the law favors community property agreements over joint tenancies, the agreement controlled and the brother's half-share of the community interest in the joint tenancy went to the widow. *Lyon v. Lyon*, 670 P2d 272 (1983).

Washington Husband and wife maintained and improved their residence, which the wife had acquired before the marriage. The wife, without the husband's knowledge, conveyed the house to a daughter by a prior marriage. After the wife's death, the husband sued the daughter for the increase in the value of the house during the marriage. *Held:* It is presumed that the increased value of the property is community property if community funds were used to effectuate value-enhancing improvements. However, the community has no right to increases in value from other causes, such as inflation. *McCoy v. Ware*, 608 P2d 1268 (1980).

9.10
Release and Termination

Texas Prior to divorce, wife conveyed all of her interest in community property to her husband. The disclaimer deed contained no reference to consideration and expressly stated the conveyance was intended by her as a relinquishment of all interest. *Held:* A disclaimer of rights in community property will not be given effect if there is no consideration and if the instrument expressly negates an intent to make a gift. *Campbell v. Campbell*, 587 SW2d 513 (Ct. App. 1979).

Washington Husband and wife separated in 1943 but were never divorced; their subsequent conduct was found to establish that they had renounced their marriage. Prior to his death in 1972, husband made a gift of one half of property acquired by the couple before their final separation. Husband had solely controlled the property for almost thirty years after the separation. The trial court held that, since the marriage was a nullity after the final separation, the husband had obtained sole title to the community property by adverse possession and his gift of one-half of the property was valid. *Held:* Affirmed. While possession of community property by a spouse can never be hostile to the interests of the other spouse, the termination of the marriage relieves the managing spouse of his or her duty to act for the benefit of the lapsed community. The separation in 1943 removed any legal barrier to husband's claiming adversely to wife in the property. *Peters v. Skalman*, 617 P2d 448 (1980).

10.00
AIR RIGHTS

10.05
Nature and Incidents

New York Plaintiff was a tenant on a lot the air rights to which were sold to defendant, along with the lot owner's consent to a zoning lot merger. Plaintiff objected, claiming that he was a party in interest whose consent should have been obtained. *Held:* Plaintiff's consent was not needed. Although he may have had an interest in the structures on the lot, he did not have an interest in "a tract of land," as the term is used in the statute. Nor did plaintiff have an interest in the lot's air rights. *MacMillan, Inc. v. CF Lex Assocs.*, 437 NE2d 1134 (1981).

11.00 MINERAL (SUBSURFACE) RIGHTS

11.05 Nature and Incidents

U.S. Supreme Court Plaintiffs, the owners of lapsed mineral interests, challenged the constitutionality of an Indiana statute that provided that mineral leases not used for 20 years automatically lapsed unless the mineral owner filed a statement of claim in the county recorder's office. "Use" of mineral interest was defined in the statute to include actual or attempted production of minerals, payment of rents or royalties, and payment of taxes. *Held:* The statute was constitutional. First, the legitimate state goal of encouraging mineral interest holders to develop their interests and generate taxable income was furthered by the statute. Second, the statute did not extinguish property rights without adequate notice. Plaintiffs had no constitutional right to notice that the 20-year period was about to expire. The two-year grace period provided for in the statute was sufficient time for plaintiffs to become familiar with its terms. *Texaco, Inc. v. Short*, 454 US 516 (1981).

U.S. Supreme Court Respondent discovered water on a mining claim, Claim 22, that it had purchased from the federal government, and used the water to prepare for commercial sale sand and gravel removed from the claims. The district court held respondent was entitled to access to Claim 22's water, and the court of appeals affirmed. *Held:* Reversed. Water was not a "valuable mineral deposit" under 30 USC 22 so as to entitle respondent to exploration. Although "water" may be a mineral in the broadest definition, respondent could not "mine" it because it was not the type of valuable mineral that Congress intended to make the basis of a valid claim. *Andrus v. Charlestone Stone Prods. Co.*, 436 US 604 (1978).

5th Circuit In 1968, after a mother donated land to her son and daughter, they sold the "usufruct," defined as the right to possess property and receive its fruits, back to her mother for $10. In 1972, the daughter conveyed her interest in the property to the son, reserving a mineral servitude. Several years later, the mother died and the son and daughter inherited the property. The daughter died and in 1978, the son and daughter's heirs leased the property for mineral exploitation. The son claimed that the heir's mineral servitude was created in 1968 and extinguished after 10 years of nonuse. *Held:* The transaction in which the mother donated property to her children and immediately rebought it for nominal consideration was void as a disguised reservation of usufruct in violation of state law. Therefore, the son and daughter acquired ownership of the property only upon their mother's death. The mineral servitude was created in 1975, when the daughter inherited an interest in the property, not in 1968, when the mother donated it. Because mineral operations began in 1978, the servitude was not extinguished by 10 years of nonuse. *Lyons v. Fisher*, 847 F2d 1158 (1988).

6th Circuit Petitioner operated a coal tipple that crushed and prepared coal for transport. Federal mine inspectors determined that the operation violated the Surface Mining Control and Reclamation Act (the Surface Mining Act) by causing imminent environmental danger, and ordered an immediate halt to the tippling operations. Petitioner sued in U.S. District Court to enjoin the secretary of the interior from enforcing the cessation orders. The secretary argued that the district court lacked jurisdiction over the dispute because petitioner failed to exhaust all administrative remedies provided by Section 525 of the Surface Mining Act. *Held:* For the secretary. Petitioner could not seek judicial review of the cessation order until it underwent administrative review. Once the administrative process had been completed, the secretary's final order would then be reviewable "on the record." The administrative relief provisions of the Surface Mining Act would be rendered superfluous if petitioner were allowed judicial review before attempting to obtain relief from the secretary. *Shawnee Coal Co. v. Andrus*, 661 F2d 1083 (1981).

U.S. District Court, Colorado Defendant constructed a portion of his house on national forest land. The United States claimed that defendant's action constituted a trespass and sought to compel him to vacate the land. Defendant argued that he should be allowed to remain and pay damages. *Held:* Defendant, who failed to procure a deed or pay taxes on the land, was a trespasser. The fact that the house was constructed on once-valid mining claims did not give him any rights to the land, because he did not conduct mining operations. Defendant's argument that it had taken the United States 15 years to take action after the park boundary was established did not succeed, because no right of prescription may be obtained against the U.S. government. *United States v. Osterlund*, 505 F. Supp. 165 (1981), aff'd, 671 F2d 1267 (10th Cir. 1982).

California In a land grant, the state, as grantor, reserved to itself all mineral rights in the subject property. The grantee thereafter laid claim to natural steam deposits, arguing that such a resource is a water right, not a mineral right. *Held:* For the state. Geothermal resources are considered in a class with mineral interests generally, inasmuch as natural steam is an energy source and not a conventional water resource. *Pariani v. State*, 164 Cal. Rptr. 683 (1980).

Georgia A corporate landowner held title to land under a deed that specifically exempted mineral rights. Because the grantor had neither attempted to work the mineral rights nor paid taxes on the rights for seven years, the landowner filed a petition with the county clerk seeking title by adverse possession under a Georgia statute. *Held:* The landowner's claim was defeated by its failure to release its petition for forwarding until after grantor paid the taxes. As a matter of law, the petition was not filed until the clerk was instructed to file it, despite its having been stamped "filed" on an earlier date. *ITT Rayonier, Inc. v. Hack*, 328 SE2d 542 (1985).

Kansas Plaintiffs' predecessors in interest granted an oil and gas lease on land they owned, and conveyed to defendants' predecessors in interest a one-half royalty interest. The royalty contract covered royalties payable to landowners under future, as well as existing, oil and gas leases. The contract had no termination date and was binding upon the heirs and assigns of landowner. Plaintiffs, who then owned the land, sued defendants to have the royalty interest declared void as a violation of the rule against perpetuities. *Held:* For plaintiffs. The interest conveyed under the royalty contract was contingent because there was no guarantee of any production. The interest was void under the rule against perpetuities as it might not have vested within 21 years plus a life in being. *Cosgrove v. Young*, 642 P2d 75 (1982).

North Dakota Cooper owned a mineral interest in certain property that was seized and transferred by sheriff's deed. Prior to issuance of the deed, Cooper conveyed the mineral interest to defendant, who previously had received and recorded an option to acquire royalty rights. In the subsequent action to quiet title, defendant claimed priority over the sheriff's deed because the conveyed mineral interest related back to the recording of the earlier royalty option. *Held:* A purchase does not relate back to an option unless the interest purchased is identical to the interest reserved in the option. A royalty interest is fundamentally distinguishable from a mineral interest, and under the facts of the present case, the recorded option was not sufficient to give notice of the mineral interest that defendant acquired. *Texard Oil Co. v. Mosser*, 299 NW2d 191 (1980).

Ohio Plaintiff lessor of property brought suit against her lessee, arguing inter alia that the lease was terminated by operation of a clause continuing the lease as long as "paying quantities" of oil or gas were found on the premises. *Held:* "Paying" quantities of oil or gas produced under a royalty agreement exist where the value of either exceeds the actual costs of producing it. Amortization of the initial expenses or the value of a lessee's labor in the project is not to be included as an item of "actual" cost. Additionally, where lessor must share royalties, he may be required to make a division order before the royalties are paid even though the lease does not require it. *Blausey v. Stein*, 400 NE2d 408 (1980).

Oklahoma Owners of mineral interests brought an action to terminate defendant's oil and gas lease on the grounds that the property was not yielding "paying quantities" of oil and gas. *Held:* In determining whether paying quantities are being produced, depreciation deductions shall be treated as a proper item of expense. *Stewart v. Amerada Hess Corp.*, 604 P2d 854 (1979).

Pennsylvania Decedent acquired title to a tract of land from mining corporation, which reserved in the deed all mineral rights. The county condemned the land "in fee simple" for an airport and issued decedent a condemnation award. Mining corporation was not notified of the proceedings and no portion of the award was earmarked for mineral rights. Subsequently, mining corporation conveyed its mineral rights in the property to decedent. Fourteen years later, when decedent's estate learned that a contractor hired by the county had excavated and removed coal, it sued for trespass. *Held:* Absent evidence that the court knew of the existence of a separate mineral estate, the condemnation in fee simple must be held to have intended to condemn all estates in the land. The case was remanded to determine if notice requirements to the mining corporation were satisfied and if the statute of limitations had expired. *Captline v. County of Allegheny*, 459 A2d 1298 (Commw. Ct. 1983), cert. denied, 466 US 904 (1984).

Texas When plaintiffs' predecessor and defendants conveyed the surface estates of their tracts, the deeds of exchange reserved to each party the mineral rights in the acreage otherwise deeded over. The reservation covered "all of the oil, gas, and other minerals of every kind and character, in, on, under and that may be produced from said tract of land," together with easements necessary for exploration and extraction. Uranium was discovered on a tract conveyed to plaintiffs' predecessor. Plaintiffs as surface owners sued defendants to establish ownership of the uranium. *Held:* Uranium is a mineral within the ordinary and natural meaning of the word and, as part of the mineral rights, was retained in the defendants' conveyance of their tract to plaintiffs. In order to eliminate title uncertainty for others in the future, uranium henceforth would be deemed part of the mineral estate unless specified otherwise by the parties. The effect of the extraction of the mineral was significant, in that if all reasonable methods of extracting the mineral would destroy the surface, the mineral would be held to form part of the surface estate. *Moser v. US Steel Corp.*, 676 SW2d 99 (1984).

Texas A conveyance of land reserved an interest in oil, gas, and other minerals. The grantee's successor in interest brought an action against the grantors for a declaratory judgment as to the ownership of lignite (coal) deposits on the land. At one point, the lignite outcropped on the surface and there were other lignite veins that ran just below the surface. *Held:* The lignite deposits were included in the conveyance and not included in the mineral reservation. Generally, if a mineral lies "at the surface," the surface owner has title to the mineral. The term "surface" refers not only to the surface top, but also to a depth shallow enough that it must have been contemplated that the mineral's removal would be by a method that would destroy or deplete the property's surface. *Reed v. Wylie*, 597 SW2d 743 (1980).

Utah Surface owner's predecessor entered into an agreement with owner of mineral estate, granting it surface rights for oil and gas production, in exchange for 2.5 percent of the value of the oil and gas produced. Surface owner purchased the surface interest and a half-interest in royalties from ranch company. Previously, company had granted a half-interest in the royalties to another purchaser. Surface owner argued that it was entitled to the entire 2.5 percent. *Held:* Surface owner was entitled to the entire payment because it was a covenant that ran with the land: (1) the covenant touched and concerned the land, (2) the original parties intended that it run with the land, (3) predecessor's grant of surface easements in exchange for the payment established mutuality of estate, and (4) the covenant was in writing. The payment was not a royalty and so was not freely assignable. A royalty payment is a share of production; the agreement described the 2.5 percent payment in terms of a money payment, not in terms of creating a share of production. *Flying Diamond Oil Corp. v. Newton Sheep Co.*, 776 P2d 618 (1989).

11.10 Leasing

U.S. Supreme Court Just before lessee Gulf Oil Corporation's 50-year lease to produce and market oil and gas expired, lessor arranged to sell the remaining gas to an intrastate purchaser. Petitioner was an interstate pipeline that had contracted with Gulf to buy gas from the leased property and in behalf of which Gulf had obtained a certificate of public convenience and necessity from the Federal Power Commission (FPC) authorizing service of unlimited duration. Petitioner moved for a determination by the FPC that the remaining gas reserves could not be diverted to the intrastate market without abandonment authorization pursuant to Section 76 of the Natural Gas Act. The FPC granted the motion. *Held:* The FPC acted within its statutory powers in requiring lessor to obtain permission to abandon interstate service. The issuance of the certificate of unlimited duration created a federal obligation to serve the interstate market until abandonment authorization had been obtained. The FPC reasonably concluded that under the act the obligation to continue service attached to the gas, not as a matter of contract but as a matter of law, and bound lessors. The service obligation imposed by the FPC therefore survived expiration of the private contract that gave rise to the FPC's jurisdiction. *California v. Southland Royalty Co.*, 436 US 519 (1978).

5th Circuit The parties entered into a mineral lease, which provided that the owner would be paid a one-eighth royalty on all oil and gas production from the leased land. A letter agreement was executed simultaneously with the lease, and provided for an additional royalty of 7.5 percent of the total minerals produced and sold. It was unclear whether a proportionate reduction clause in the lease applied to the royalty interest described in the letter agreement. *Held:* The ambiguity in the lease and letter agreement should be resolved in favor of nonproportionality as it was the lessee who drafted the agreement and subsequently assigned the royalty interest described therein. *Richland Plantation Co. v. Justiss-Mears Oil Co.*, 671 F2d 154 (1982).

9th Circuit The U.S. Department of the Interior's proposed sale of oil and gas leases on the outer continental shelf off the California coast was challenged on the ground that it would violate the Coastal Zone Management Act. The act requires that federal activities "directly affecting" the coastal zone be consistent with state coastal zone management plans. *Held:* The lease sale "directly affected" the California coast. The sale was the first link in a chain of events that could lead to changes in the coastal zone resulting from the development and production of oil and gas. A narrower definition of "directly affecting" proposed by the department of the interior would diminish state influence and defeat the major purpose of the act. *California v. Watt*, 712 F2d 584 (1982).

9th Circuit Plaintiffs sued to compel the issuance of oil and gas leases pursuant to the Mineral Lands Leasing Act. Plaintiffs' original offer was rejected on the ground that the application contained a defective signature. After the defect in the application was aired, the lands were withdrawn from those leased under the act. *Held:* The act grants the secretary discretion as to whether or not a lease for oil and gas entry should be issued. Plaintiffs' offer to lease did not vest in them any right to the lease. *Burglin v. Morton*, 527 F2d 486 (1976).

10th Circuit Plaintiff Indian tribe brought an action against the secretary of the interior and certain oil and gas lessees claiming that notices of the sale of leases on the reservation were inadequate under 25 CFR §171.3. Plaintiff also alleged failure to comply with the National Environmental Protection Act (NEPA). *Held:* The notice regulation was not complied with, so plaintiff was entitled to damages for the loss of higher bids that proper notice would have attracted. But the court denied plaintiff equitable relief (i.e., lease cancellation) because the damage award was deemed sufficient. The NEPA claim for injunctive relief was barred by the doctrines of laches and unclean hands. The court also held that plaintiff was entitled to rentals on the leases while the action was pending because, although cancellation was denied, plaintiff could prove the secretary violated the notice regulation. *Jicarilla Apache Tribe v. Andrus*, 687 F2d 1324 (1982).

10th Circuit Plaintiff, an oil and gas company, obtained oil and gas leases on federally owned land in Oklahoma. The Mineral Lands Leasing Act and the leases themselves provided that the leases could remain in effect beyond their initial 10-year terms only so long as they produced oil and gas in paying quantities. One year after the initial terms had expired, the

United States terminated the leases for inadequate oil and gas production. Plaintiff, in an action for a declaration that its leases remained in effect, contended that it had produced oil and gas on nearby nonfederal property, and claimed that production from the nonfederal property constituted production from federal property under the terms of an Oklahoma drilling and spacing order. The Oklahoma order placed federal and neighboring nonfederal property in a single unit. *Held:* The secretary of the interior had never approved the Oklahoma communitization order and was therefore not bound by it and had the right to terminate the leases. *Kirkpatrick Oil & Gas Co. v. United States*, 675 F2d 1122 (1982).

Alabama A lease of five acres contained a "catch-all" or "Mother Hubbard" clause extending its coverage to all contiguous or adjacent land owned by the lessor. Lessor claimed by adverse possession a one-acre strip adjoining the five acres described in the lease. When lessor sought to lease the strip to a third party, lessee sued claiming that the land was included in his lease under the Mother Hubbard clause. Lessor argued that the lease was ambiguous because it specifically described five acres of land. *Held:* A Mother Hubbard clause applicable to excess acreage or a small strip of land adjoining an interest conveyed is enforceable. Moreover, there was no ambiguity in the instant conveyance because the reference to five acres was merely a system for calculating payments. The lease clearly provided that the land would be deemed to contain five acres for the purpose of paying any bonus regardless of whether it contained more or less. *Whitehead v. Johnston*, 467 So. 2d 240 (1985).

Kansas Lessees under an oil and gas lease violated the lease by dumping salt water on the land, failing to maintain fences, and leaving open pits on the premises, resulting in damages to lessors' land and cattle. Lessors locked out lessees and refused their tender of delay rental payment, contending that the lease was void. The lease made no provision for cancellation or forfeiture as a remedy for its breach. *Held:* Because of the flagrant nature of lessees' breach of the covenant restricting their use of the surface, cancellation was an appropriate remedy. Given the continuing nature of the breach, damages were impracticable; but lessees were not required to tender rental payments while lessors were attacking lessees' title. *Thurner v. Kaufman*, 699 P2d 435 (1984).

Ohio Coal and clay lease provided that lessee, in return for the right to mine lessor's land, was to pay a minimal rent as royalty, and that lessee's failure to perform any of the covenants would result in forfeiture. Although lessee paid its rent on a timely bais, it did not mine the land. Lessor sued seeking forfeiture, claiming that lessee had an implied duty to mine. *Held:* Since a mineral lease includes an implied covenant to develop the land, lessee had a duty to make reasonable efforts to mine it where there was no express disclaimer. It was clear from the language of the lease that timely payments of rent did not relieve lessee of this duty. *Ionno v. Glen-Gery Corp.*, 443 NE2d 504 (1983).

Nebraska Plaintiff, oil and gas lessee, had a lease that provided for a primary term of six months and as long thereafter as oil or gas was produced. After the lease's primary term, plaintiff, for financial reasons, was compelled to remove his equipment from the leased premises. Landowners then gave defendant another oil and gas lease on the property. By this time, the price of oil had risen from $3 to $40 per barrel. Plaintiff brought an action to quiet title and to enjoin defendant from operating the well. *Held:* Defendant had title to the leasehold at the time the price of oil had risen to $40 per barrel. The lease expressly provided that its term would end when oil and gas production ended. Therefore, plaintiff's leasehold interest ended when the well stopped producing oil and plaintiff left the premises. *Kirby v. Holland*, 316 NW2d 746 (1982).

Oklahoma Landowners leased oil and gas rights to defendant. The lease permitted assignment only with the written consent of lessors. When defendant assigned a portion of the lease to a third party without permission, the owners sued, seeking cancellation and forfeiture. *Held:* The clause restricting alienation was invalid as an unlawful restraint on alienation. The right to give or withhold consent to an assignment by the lessee inured only to the lessors personally and not to their successors, grantees, heirs, or assignees. Lessors could convey their estate to others and they would still have the power to consent to the alienation of property that they did not even own. Restraints upon alienation where there are no provisions for forfeiture or reversion are "disabling restraints" and void. *Shields v. Moffit*, 683 P2d 530 (1984).

Oklahoma Lessee purchased an oil and gas lease from the state in 1956. The oil and gas lease was held in full force and effect beyond the five-year primary term. When production from the well ceased in January 1975, lessee drilled a new well, which began to produce in June 1975. State brought an action to quiet title to the oil and gas lease, arguing that the lease ended once the original well ceased production, and that construction of a new well did not reactivate the lease. It argued that under Oklahoma law, an oil and gas lease lasts only as long as production is in paying quantities. *Held:* Under Oklahoma law, a lease lasts as long as it has ability to produce, even when it is not producing, if a reasonable and prudent operator makes a diligent effort to restore production. A temporary production stoppage by itself does not terminate an oil and gas lease if it is for a reasonable time and was caused by mechanical problems. On these facts, lessee exercised due diligence in commencing the restoration of production by drilling a second well. *State ex rel. Comm'rs of the Land Office v. Amoco Prod. Co.*, 645 P2d 468 (1982).

Washington by the terms of a strip-mining lease, lessee was obligated to pay a basic minimum rental whether or not there was any production. Complaints of environmentalists led to extended litigation, and lessee terminated the lease without commencing operations. The lessor sued for the minimum rentals. *Held:* The Washington Supreme Court reversed the court of appeals and excused lessee from paying rent under the doctrine of commercial frustration. Because neither lessor nor lessee did or could reasonably have foreseen the public outcry in opposition to the strip mining project, lessee was commercially frustrated in its purpose under the lease. The purpose of the lease clause, which provided for a minimum annual rental "irrespective of whether lessee produces any minerals from the leasehold," was not to allocate to lessee the entire risk of unforeseeable events, but to discourage idleness and procrastination when mining is permissible. *Weyerhaeuser Real Estate Co. v. Stoneway Concrete, Inc.*, 637 P2d 647 (1981).

West Virginia By the terms of an 1890 mineral lease, lessee was given the right to use the surface of the property for the erection and maintenance of buildings, machinery, telephone and telegraphic lines, "and other improvements necessary" to the mining operations. Successor lessors objected to lessee's planned construction of electric power lines to service mine shafts, arguing that such use was inconsistent with the lease. *Held:* The proposed use was within lessee's rights under the lease. A mineral severance deed, coupled with specific surface uses, gave lessee broad rights to surface utilization necessary to the mining activities. *Buffalo Mining Co. v. Martin*, 267 SE2d 721 (1980).

Wyoming Plaintiff lessors had a 5 percent royalty interest in an oil and gas lease. Defendant lessee's predecessors had paid plaintiffs' ad valorem and severance taxes. After defendant became lessee, it unintentionally paid these taxes for three years. When it discovered this, defendant deducted the taxes it had paid from plaintiffs' production payments. Plaintiffs sued for recovery of the taxes. *Held:* There was no contract between the parties for the payment of ad valorem and severance taxes. Evidence of past conduct of defendant in paying the taxes for the first three years of its lease could not be relied on to establish a contract because, under Wyoming law, such evidence was admissible only to interpret ambiguous contract provisions. The rule in Wyoming requiring royalty interest owners to pay ad valorem and severance taxes on their interests in the absence of an agreement to the contrary applied. *Ashland Oil Co. v. Jaeger*, 650 P2d 265 (1982).

11.15 Profit à Prendre

Idaho For 25 years, a mining firm mined quartzite rock from property it mistakenly believed was located on unpatented, government land. When it learned that the land was privately owned, the mining firm sued to quiet title to the property. *Held:* The private owner retained title. The mining firm had not established right to mine the rock on a profit à prendre theory through prescription. To acquire a prescriptive right, one must use the privilege without actual possession of the land. The doctrine of adverse possession rather than prescription applies when a claimant exercises a substantial possessory interest in the land, as in this case, where the mining firm conducted large-scale operations. *Oakley Valley Stone, Inc. v. Alastra*, 715 P2d 935 (1985).

Michigan Plaintiff conveyed a warranty deed to defendants, reserving a life estate in the property. Plaintiff then sued to recover payments collected by defendants from an oil and gas lease on the property. *Held:* Payments from oil and gas lease were for the right to drill and to invade the present possessory interest in the land, and since the life tenant was entitled to income from the property and had the right to use the surface of the land, such payments were allocable to plaintiff as life tenant. The court said that the lease granted a profit à prendre, i.e., a right to mine the land, not a present interest in the minerals in place. *VanAlstine v. Swanson*, 417 NW2d 516 (1987).

12.00 FIXTURES

12.05 Definition

Alaska Husband appealed a lower court decision that a small building on a certain property was not a trade fixture and was therefore subject to a supplemental property division. *Held:* The building was not carried as an asset on the financial statements or books of the purported owner, and was not listed in the depreciation schedules in its tax returns. The company canceled its insurance on the building after the real property was transferred to the wife as part of a property settlement. The trial court's determination that the building was not a trade fixture was proper. *Penney v. Penney*, 541 P2d 359 (1975).

Colorado Lease for a restaurant allowed tenant to make improvements, which could be removed upon termination, provided there would be no damage to the premises. The tenant made unremovable improvements, which were not completed until after the lease terminated. On the date of completion, several mechanic's and materialman's liens had been filed against the landlord. The landlord sought to have mechanic's liens that arose in connection with the installation of the fixtures discharged, arguing that it lacked a property interest in the improvements by virtue of the lease. *Held:* The lease did not change the character of the property as far as the rights of the lien claimants were concerned. The owner, not the short-term tenant, benefited from the unremovable improvements. Therefore, the liens were valid against the owner. *A-1 Plumbing & Heating Co. v. Thirteenth St. Corp.*, 616 P2d 141 (Ct. App. 1980).

Idaho Farm tenant who removed the underground cables of an irrigation system when he vacated the premises was accused by the landlord of committing waste on the ground that the system was a fixture. *Held:* The irrigation system was a fixture, and the tenant had committed waste by removing it. The system met the three tests for a fixture: (1) The system was annexed to the land, in that it was attached to cement slabs and buried in the ground; (2) it was adapted to the use made of the land, because irrigation was necessary to farming; and (3) it was intended to be a permanent part of the land, since the previous gravity system was destroyed when the irrigation system was installed. *Rayl v. Shull Enters., Inc.*, 700 P2d 567 (1984).

Iowa Owner of a mobile home moved it to a plot of land, removed the hitches and wheels, and set it on a cement foundation. Owner then sold plaintiff the land on which the home was situated, pursuant to a contract stating that the land was sold "together with . . . all attached fixtures." A judgment creditor of owner attempted to enforce execution against the home. Plaintiff sued for an injunction, claiming that the home was sold to him under the land contract. *Held:* Creditor could not enforce execution against the mobile home. The home was a fixture included under the terms of the contract because (1) its removal would be as expensive and damaging as the removal of a permanent home; (2) the home was used as a homestead, the use for which the land had been appropriated; and (3) the home was intended to be permanently attached to the land. *Ford v. Venard*, 340 NW2d 270 (1983).

Montana Lessor leased a portion of its right-of-way, authorizing the lessee to construct a warehouse on the property. The lease provided that prior to the end of the term the lessee would remove all structures not belonging to the lessor and would restore the premises to their former state. A judgment creditor of the lessee subsequently obtained a lien against the lessee's real property and sought a declaratory judgment that the warehouse was real property. *Held:* The warehouse was personal property. The provision in the lease for removal of all structures at the end of the term indicated a clear intent of the parties that the warehouse was to be personal property. *Pacific Metal Co. v. Northwestern Bank*, 667 P2d 958 (1983).

Ohio Appellee had constructed a basic oxygen furnace designed for and devoted to steel production. The furnace was taxed as real property on the assumption that it was a fixture. Appellee sought to have the assessment nullified. *Held:* The primary test for the difference between a fixture and a chattel is whether the property is devoted to the business conducted on the premises or is devoted primarily to the use of the land on which the business is conducted. The furnace was, therefore, not a fixture. *Wheeling-Pittsburgh Steel Corp. v. Jefferson County Bd. of Revision*, 271 NE2d 861 (1971).

12.10 Annexation to Realty

California Plaintiff leased a boat from the city, and the county taxed it as real property. Plaintiff filed for a refund, contending that the vessel was personal property, not a fixture, because it floated and was not affixed to any land, and that lessee's possessory interest in the vessel was not subject to taxation. *Held:* The vessel met the tests of a fixture, and thus was taxable as real property. The city intended it to be a permanent addition to the realty. Although the vessel floated, it was securely fastened to the wharf and movement was minimal. *Specialty Restaurants v. Los Angeles County*, 136 Cal. Rptr. 904 (Ct. App. 1977).

Michigan City officials, as part of a tax assessment, based their valuation of plaintiff's banking facilities on both the realty itself and on certain fixtures such as night depository equipment, vault doors, and "drive-in" teller installations. The bank, lessee of the premises, argued that the equipment was exempt by operation of the general property tax laws since it was installed as trade fixtures and not intended to be permanent accession to the property. *Held:* The tax valuation was not improper. The equipment had been physically annexed to the realty and fully integrated into the building. Although, as between landlord and tenant they were treated as removable fixtures, for other purposes they may be treated as realty. *Michigan Nat'l Bank v. City of Lansing*, 293 NW2d 626 (Ct. App. 1980), aff'd, 322 NW2d 173 (1983).

Oklahoma Premier purchased a mobile home in which C.I.T. took a security interest by assignment of an installment sales contract that stated that Premier was not to make the mobile home a part of any real estate. C.I.T. failed to perfect its security interest. Premier affixed the mobile home to a concrete foundation on land it owned, then sold the land and mobile home to buyers, who mortgaged the mobile home to the bank. The bank properly recorded its mortgage. When the buyers filed for bankruptcy, the property was awarded to the bank, and C.I.T. sued in replevin. *Held:* The bank was entitled to the mobile home in satisfaction of its mortgage, because a mobile home affixed to a permanent foundation was real property; and a subsequent mortgage holder had priority over an unperfected holder of a purchase money security interest. In light of the three factors that determined whether property was a fixture—annexation to realty, appropriateness of structure to use of realty, and intent to make structure permanent—the mobile home was a fixture to the real estate. However, the provision of the original unperfected sales contract that the mobile home would not become part of real estate was not binding on a subsequent mortgagee without notice. *CIT Fin. Servs. v. Premier Corp.*, 747 P2d 934 (1987).

12.15 Tenant's Right to Remove

Arkansas During his lease, the tenant installed lighting fixtures, carpeting, heating, air conditioning, and display cases. Upon termination, the tenant removed these installations, and the landlords sought compensation for such removal based on a lease provision that the tenant was to keep the lease premises in good condition, order, and repair. *Held:* The installations were trade fixtures, which could be removed by the tenant upon termination of the lease. *Sparkman v. Etter*, 458 SW2d 129 (1970).

New York Restauranteurs built a prefabricated diner on leased property. The lease provided that the diner was restauranteurs' personal property and could be removed even if removal resulted in injury to the freehold. Restauranteurs sold the diner to buyers, retaining a security interest. Buyers later defaulted and abandoned the property, and the county obtained a tax deed. When the restauranteurs attempted to foreclose, they learned of the tax deed, and sued the county. *Held:* The diner was a trade fixture and could be removed only if there would be no damage to the underlying property. The county was not bound by the terms of the prior lease, which allowed removal of the diner regardless of damage. It was a question for the jury whether restauranteurs could remove the diner without causing damage to the freehold. *JKSP Restaurant, Inc. v. County of Nassau*, 513 NYS2d 716 (App. Div. 1987).

Oregon Prior to the institution of condemnation proceedings, lessor instituted a forcible-entry and detainer action against lessee for failure to pay rent. When the condemnation proceedings commenced, the parties stipulated that the issue of whether the lease was terminated would be determined in the award proceedings. The lessee asserted a right to compensation for the taking of his trade fixtures, which he had not removed. *Held:* As a general rule, a lessee may remove his trade fixtures, prior to surrendering possession or eviction. However, where the lessee is a party to a pending action disputing the lessee's possession, and the property is taken while such action is still pending, the lessee has a reasonable time thereafter to remove his trade fixtures. Since the taking here prevented the lessee from removing his trade fixtures, he was entitled to compensation. *State Highway Comm'n v. Demarest*, 503 P2d 682 (1972).

Texas Lease agreement between defendant and a shopping center tenant gave the latter the right to remove any "improvements, fixtures, furnishings, kiosks" at the end of the lease term, "provided that all amounts payable to the Landlord under the terms of the lease . . . have been paid." The tenant constructed a kiosk, which was not attached to the shopping mall. When the tenant defaulted in the rent payments, either defendant landlord or the builder took possession of the structure. Plaintiff, a trustee of the tenant's bankrupt estate, claimed the kiosk was a permanent, immovable fixture and sought to recover its value from defendant. Defendant instead offered to give the structure to plaintiff. Plaintiff sued and lost. He then appealed. *Held:* The trial judge had cause to believe that the intention of the parties was that the right of removal be subject to a condition precedent (i.e., payment of rent). When the right to removal is not exercised within a reasonable time, the right is forfeited. Equity itself would not allow recovery in favor of plaintiff based upon the facts of the case. *Fenlon v. Jaffee*, 553 SW2d 422 (1977).

13.00 EASEMENTS

13.05 Creation

10th Circuit In 1903, a city instituted condemnation proceedings to acquire an easement over lands owned in fee by an Indian tribe subject to trust responsibility of the United States. The easement was to erect a waterworks system over the land and create a watershed and basin. The United States sued to quiet title in the lands to which the city claimed the easement, alleging that the easement was invalid since the government was not named in the 1903 proceedings. The government also claimed that various activities conducted on the land and allowed by the city were invalid. *Held:* The validity of the easement was not affected by the failure to name an indispensable party to the proceedings. Under Oklahoma law, the rights obtained by the grant of easement are only those necessary to the reasonable and proper enjoyment of the easement. *United States v. City of McAlester*, 604 F2d 42 (1979).

Maine A newly enacted statute gave the public unlimited right to use intertidal land for "recreation." Oceanfront property owners sought an injunction limiting public use of the beach. *Held:* The act was unconstitutional and an injunction was granted. Established rules of property law in Maine held that oceanfront owners owned their land subject to an easement permitting public use only for fishing, fowling, and navigation. A general recreational easement was not encompassed in or reasonably related to these permitted public uses. Additionally, defendants failed to prove that a public easement by local custom had been established. The courts and legislature cannot alter long-established property rights to accommodate new recreational needs because of the constitutional protection against taking property without compensation. *Bell v. Town of Wells*, 557 A2d 168 (1989).

Maryland Plaintiffs, owners of property abutting a lake, sued local authorities to prevent destruction of their lake bed by the accumulation of silt caused by drainage of runoff waters. County officials had obtained easements from another property owner in order to install pipes and route surface waters into the lake from a nearby construction project. *Held:* The easements granted to the county were invalid. The chain of title of the grantors contained a restriction that forbade conveyance of easements to parties who are not heirs of the owners. In addition, the grantors held an easement appurtenant over property of their estate and therefore cannot separate such easement from their title. Moreover, its injection of vast quantities of silt into the lake amounted to an excessive use tantamount to destruction of the underlying fee. *Anne Arundel County v. Litz*, 412 A2d 1256 (Ct. Spec. App. 1980).

New York Deceased was the president and sole stockholder of corporation-defendant. He conveyed, by an unacknowledged and unattested letter, what the trial court found to be an easement, despite absence of such words as "grant," "easement," or "right-of-way," over a certain parcel. He subsequently conveyed the servient tenement to corporation-defendant. *Held:* The conveyance of the easement, though unacknowledged and unattested, was enforceable against the grantor and all those taking the servient tenement with notice of it; and the deceased's knowledge could be imparted to the corporation-defendant. *Yager Pontiac, Inc. v. Fred A. Danker & Sons, Inc.*, 343 NYS2d 209 (App. Div. 1973), aff'd, 356 NYS2d 860 (1974).

Oregon Landowners sued to enforce a nonexclusive easement for the use of an access road across defendant's land. Defendant claimed that his contract of sale for the land was made free and clear of any encumbrances and that since plaintiffs had purchased the property subsequent to defendant's purchase, they could not claim the right to an easement. *Held:* The contract of sale that passed the interest to defendant specifically included the right of other owners to use the road. Thus, plaintiffs' right to the easement was vested to defendant's contract of sale. *Chaffee v. Fine*, 540 P2d 371 (1975).

Virginia Purchaser bought a lot in a waterfront subdivision and blocked the use of the landing from other landowners. The landowners sued, claiming that they had easement rights in the landing. *Held:* The landowners had no easement rights. Although there were references in the conveyance to a recorded plot showing an area marked "landing," the second did not show an estoppel beyond the plot against the landowner. In addition, the word "landing" is ambivalent, and whether an easement in a landing is necessary to the enjoyment and value of properties depends on the circumstances of the particular case. *Jones v. Beavers*, 269 SE2d 775 (1980).

13.10
—Express Grant

New York Plaintiff and defendant owned adjacent property that was previously owned by grantor, who conveyed the parcels to different parties. When grantor had conveyed defendant's property to defendant's predecessor in interest he "excepted and reserved" to himself and to plaintiff's predecessor in interest a right-of-way across defendant's parcel. Defendant sought to bar plaintiff's use of her property, and plaintiff claimed title to an easement over defendant's parcel. *Held:* Plaintiff was not entitled to an express easement over defendant's property. No express easement was created by grantor's "reservation" of an easement for the benefit of plaintiff's predecessor in interest. The rule in New York was that a deed with a reservation or exception by grantor in favor of a third party did not create a valid interest in favor of that party. *Estate of Thomson v. Wade*, 509 NE2d 309 (1987).

New York Factory's fire exit led to road by way of a driveway located on an adjacent parcel. The adjacent landowner sought to block use of the driveway by the factory. The factory owner petitioned for declaration of an easement across the adjacent parcel, relying on the fact that the previous owner of the adjacent parcel had joined in the application for a certificate of occupancy for the factory that included plans for the fire exit. At the time the certificate of occupancy was applied for, the previous owner of the adjacent parcel leased the factory parcel through a company he owned. *Held:* No express easement was created by the owner of the adjacent parcel's joining in the request for a certificate of occupancy for the factory. An express easement requires a writing that establishes unequivocally the grantor's intent to impose a permanent restriction on the servient estate. The jointly sought certificate of occupancy benefited the former owner's own corporation; there was no evidence the former owner intended to grant an easement to future tenants of the factory. *Willow Tex, Inc. v. Dimacopoulos*, 503 NE2d 99 (1986).

Texas On January 1, 1963, plaintiff granted defendant an easement to complete construction of an abandoned oil well on his property. The grant was for five years or until the well was plugged and abandoned, and would expire after 30 years in any event. The agreement further provided that if it was still in effect 10 years later, plaintiff was to be paid $1,000. On January 5, 1973, defendant mailed check for $1,000 that reached plaintiff's bank on January 8, 1973. Plaintiff directed the bank to return the check, since the payment was not timely. When plaintiff blocked any access to the well, defendent obtained an injunction to prohibit interference with its easement. Plaintiff contended that the injunction was invalid because defendant failed to make timely rental payment. *Held:* The law does not favor a forfeiture, and, unless compelled to do so by language that will admit no other construction, forfeiture will not be decreed. Therefore, since there was no provision for forfeiture in the agreement, and since the only applicable limiting term of the agreement related to the well being plugged and abandoned, the injunction had been validly issued. *Gheen v. Diamond Shamrock Corp.*, 529 SW2d 289 (Civ. App. 1975).

Virginia Purchasers of real property sued the owners of adjacent property, alleging they had an easement to the pool located on defendant's property. Defendants had sold the house and property to plaintiffs' predecessor in title by a contract that gave the right to use the pool "to the purchaser and his family." There was no mention of pool privileges in the deed conveying the property. Plaintiffs contended that their predecessors assured them that the pool privilege was an easement that ran with the land, even though it was not included in plaintiffs' deed. *Held:* The use of the pool by the original purchasers was a license, not an easement. The language in the sales contract was not sufficient to establish an express easement. The absence of any provision for its use plus the oral testimony of defendant indicated the use was intended to be limited to plaintiffs' grantor. *Bunn v. Offutt*, 222 SE2d 522 (1976).

West Virginia Property owner conveyed a permanent easement for a right-of-way to defendant. The deed, which was recorded, was not signed by the owner's wife, who was named as a grantor in the deed but whose sole interest in the real estate was an inchoate dower interest. The property owner thereafter conveyed all of his property to plaintiff, who sought to have the deed conveying the easement to defendant declared void because of the wife's failure to sign the deed. *Held:* The conveyance was upheld. Since the husband intended to convey the easement and there was no condition precedent that the wife should sign before delivery became effective, the validity of the deed was not affected by the absence of the wife's signature. The deed became effective with regard to the husband, who fulfilled a prior executory contract to grant the easement. *Parish v. Pancake*, 215 SE2d 659 (1975).

13.15
—Express Reservation

Missouri Original owner of a subdivision, by her acknowledgment on the plat, reserved to herself an easement for the use of all roadways in the plat without otherwise making reference to the roadways or their use. Plaintiffs came to own part of the subdivision, which was frequently flooded and valuable only for the topsoil that could be removed from it. All but two of the remaining lots in the subdivision were residential in character. Defendants, owners of some of these lots, blocked a subdivision road to prevent plaintiffs' dump trucks from gaining access to it, alleging that the trucks were damaging the subdivision roadways. Plaintiffs sought to enjoin defendants. *Held:* The original owner's reservation granted plaintiffs' predecessor an easement that ran with the land, giving access to plaintiffs. As the original owner did not limit the right to use the roadways, plaintiffs were entitled to drive their trucks throughout the subdivision. *Goad v. Bennett*, 480 SW2d 77 (Ct. App. 1972).

Oregon Plaintiffs, purchasers of subdivision lots, held deeds granting them an easement for use of a road in the subdivision and reserving the same easement to the other subdivision owners. Defendant did not own any of the subdivided tracts, but he had been granted an easement over one of them by the subdividers for access to the roadway easement to service his property, which was adjacent to the subdivision. The plaintiffs brought suit against the subdividers to construe the reservation in the deed. *Held:* In the absence of evidence that the subdividers owned other land, or evidence indicating that they desired the reservation for assignment to nonsubdivision landowners, the reciprocal agreements did not reserve to the subdividers an interest in the roadway easement that they could convey to owners of land not in the subdivision. *Ambrosek v. Barker*, 504 P2d 740 (1972).

13.20
—Implied Grant

Florida Owners of a parcel bordered on the north by a creek sought an easement acrosss neighbor's parcel on the west. The neighbor's parcel had a remote grantor in common with the owners'. The neighbor argued that the owners had acquired land north of the creek, which had access to a road. *Held:* For the owners. The relevant Florida statute provided that an implied easement exists where there is no practicable means of egress, with "practicable" meaning without the use of a bridge. The creek could be crossed by four-wheel drive vehicles during the dry season, but the water level at the "ford" reached three feet during an engineer's inspection in July. Therefore, the court found an easement was necessary. *Lykes Bros. v. Clements*, 501 So. 2d 1302 (Dist. Ct. App. 1986).

Massachusetts Lot A was sold at a tax sale. The trustees for adjacent lots sought to prevent the buyer from using sewer and water lines that ran under their lots. The buyer argued that the adjacent lots were burdened by an easement for the water and sewer lines in favor of Lot A. *Held:* For the buyer. Easements by implication have been recognized when land was formerly in common ownership, when use of one part of the land was made for the benefit of another part until severance of ownership, and when the use of one part is reasonably necessary for the enjoyment of the other part. The court found that intent of the grantor and grantee could be presumed where title to Lot A passed involuntarily as a result of a tax sale. *Flax v. Smith*, 479 NE2d 183 (App. Ct. 1985).

Minnesota The original titleholder built an apartment building with a parking lot on one portion of his property; on the other, he built a house with a garage, but without a driveway. The original purchasers of the house painted and finished it before their purchase, forming a well-traveled dirt road from their garage to the parking lot of the apartment building. The original titleholders allowed the purchasers to continue to drive across the parking lot. This arrangement continued for 14 years, when new owners barricaded the entrance to the garage, forcing the new purchasers to park on the street. The new purchasers sued for an implied easement. *Held:* For the new purchasers. The original purchaser's use of the easement during the painting and finishing of the house was long-continued and apparent enough to demonstrate that the original titleholder intended the easement to be permanent. Moreover, the easement was necessary to beneficial enjoyment of the land. *Rosendahl v. Nelson*, 408 NW2d 609 (Ct. App. 1987).

Oregon Plaintiffs sold part of their land to defendants, including a roadway permitting access to the remaining portion of plaintiff's property. Plaintiffs claimed an easement by implied reservation. *Held:* For plaintiffs. The circumstances permitted an inference that, had plaintiffs put their minds to the matter, they would have intended to create a roadway easement by implied reservation across defendants' property. The same result would follow when considered from the standpoint of the reasonable expectations of a person receiving conveyance of the land. *Cheney v. Mueller*, 485 P2d 1218 (1971).

Pennsylvania Plaintiffs and defendants were granted land by a common owner. Their parcels were separated by a road, the title of which was retained by the common owner. Both deeds referred to the road, and a map showing it was recorded. The road, however, was not a highway and was not dedicated to public use. When plaintiffs began developing their land for commercial use, defendants purchased the land on which the road was located and obstructed it. Plaintiffs sought a decree granting an easement by implication. *Held:* Where descriptions in a deed refer to a road that is neither a highway, nor dedicated to public use, as a boundary, grantee acquires an easement by implication. *McAndrews v. Spencer*, 290 A2d 258 (1972).

13.25
—Grant by Necessity

9th Circuit Person who acquired a homestead on lands in the public domain sued to enjoin the construction of a road across his homestead by an individual who applied for a homestead for adjoining property. Plaintiff argued that the road was a continued trespass and the government contended that it was an easement of necessity. *Held:* The homesteader was vested with all the incidents of fee simple ownership although legal title remained in the government. There was no easement of necessity since the government retained access to its property across land that the government still held. *United States v. Clarke*, 529 F2d 984 (1976).

Arizona A landowner brought an action for access over a developer's property to an airport. The trial court denied the easement, and the landowner appealed, arguing that an easement by necessity should be implied. *Held:* Affirmed. A property owner is not entitled to an easement of necessity unless he proves that the property cannot be effectively used without the easement. *Chandler Flyers v. Stelear Dev. Corp.*, 592 P2d 387 (1979).

Arkansas Owner of landlocked property petitioned to condemn a right-of-way across an adjoining tract. The county court appointed viewers, as required by Ark. Stat. Ann. § 76-110, who then laid out the right-of-way, which was affirmed by the circuit court. Owners of adjoining tract appealed, arguing that owner already had access to the property through its frontage on a navigable watercourse. *Held:* Affirmed. The court found that the petitioner must demonstrate a reasonable necessity for a road, not an absolute necessity. Although Section 76-110 referred to access to a public road or navigable watercourse, it was adopted over a century ago, in 1871. Because travel today is usually by motor vehicle, even for short distances, it was unreasonable to require owner and her visitors to travel by boat. *Attaway v. Davis*, 707 SW2d 302 (1986).

Colorado Plaintiff held oil and gas leaseholds that lacked access to a public road. Plaintiff filed a condemnation petition seeking an easement of necessity across defendant's property. *Held:* Plaintiff did not have a cause of action, because the Colorado constitutional and statutory condemnation provisions allowed only owners of a fee interest to seek condemnation. The provisions were construed against lessees to protect the owners of adjacent servient estates from repeated condemnation litigation each time an estate changed hands. In contrast, a taking by a fee owner was permanent. Even if lessees were permitted to seek condemnation, plaintiff could not do so, because a property owner could not create the necessity for an easement across the property of a third party by subdividing its land into "landlocked" leaseholds. *Coquina Oil Corp. v. Harry Kourlis Ranch*, 643 P2d 519 (1982).

Florida Plaintiff owned landlocked property. He sued neighboring landowners, a private owner and a public water management district, claiming an easement of necessity under Fla. Stat. § 704.01. The water district argued it was not a "person" as defined in the statute, and it had not waived sovereign immunity. *Held:* A review of the statutory definition of "person" indicated that the legislature intended to include agencies such as the water district. The court noted the strong public policy in Florida to provide access to hemmed-in lands. If no cause of action against the state existed under the statute, public policy would be frustrated where private property was surrounded by state land. *South Fla. Water Management Dist. v. Layton*, 402 So. 2d 597 (Dist. Ct. App. 1981).

Massachusetts When the common grantor originally divided a tract, both parcels held access to public roads. Subsequently, the respondents' access was severed by eminent domain proceedings. Respondents asserted that they should be entitled to an implied easement (easement by necessity) across plaintiff's land. Plaintiff sought to register the land free of any such encumbrance. *Held:* Implied easements arise from the circumstances surrounding the execution of instruments, including the physical condition of the premises. When circumstances change subsequent to the execution of instruments, that fact cannot retroactively change the intention of the grantor. Where an eminent domain proceeding severed access to the premises, the proper remedy was in damages in the condemnation award. *Darman v. Dunderdale*, 289 NE2d 847 (1972).

Texas Defendant purchased Lots 14 and 3A. Access to Lot 3A was blocked by a lake and two other properties. Subsequently, defendant constructed a road down the boundary line of the two other properties and used it to gain access from Lot 14 to a boat deck on Lot 3A. The owners of adjoining properties sued to enjoin the use of the road, while defendant claimed an express easement, or an easement by necessity or estoppel. *Held:* For the owners of the adjoining properties. There was no showing that the previous owner of defendant's properties ever possessed a right of access to Lot 3A. Since the previous owners did not have a right of access, they could not subsequently create one by an express easement, and the court could not create it through an easement by necessity. *Jordan v. Rush*, 745 SW2d 549 (Ct. App. 1988).

Virginia When houses were being built on Lots 19 and 20 of a subdivision, construction vehicles used a driveway belonging to Lot 20 to gain access to Lot 19. Subsequently, plaintiffs purchased Lot 19, and defendants purchased Lot 20. Rather than build a new driveway, defendants, who had ample frontage on a road, continued to use plaintiffs' driveway to gain access to the property. When defendants obstructed plaintiffs' access to the driveway, plaintiffs sought to enjoin the obstruction, claiming an easement by necessity. Plaintiffs argued that a new driveway would be costly, that it would be difficult to reach their garage, and that their property value would be diminished. *Held:* If another means of access exists, though less convenient or more expensive to develop, no way of necessity arises. The factors cited by plaintiffs fell short of constituting a necessity. *Fones v. Fagan*, 196 SE2d 916 (1973).

Washington The county conditioned approval of plaintiffs' application to subdivide their landlocked property into residential lots upon plaintiffs providing a connecting road. The county would not condemn a right-of-way, but agreed to help construct a road if plaintiffs obtained a right-of-way and transferred it to the county. Plaintiffs brought a private condemnation action pursuant to Washington law, which permits condemnation of private land by private parties. *Held:* Plaintiffs could not condemn a right-of-way for use as a public connecting road. Public policy behind allowing a private condemnation cause of action is to prevent landlocked property from becoming useless. Plaintiffs could condemn a right-of-way for a use compatible with the uses to which the land was being put by its owners. However, the power to condemn private property did not extend to creating a public access road for a subdivision development, so plaintiffs could not transfer a right-of-way to the county. *Brown v. McAnally*, 664 P2d 1153 (1982).

13.30 —Grant by Prescription

3d Circuit For more than 50 years, plaintiff and its predecessors in title used the sidewalk in front of a bank building and the air space above the same for the maintenance and changing of a theater marquee. The bank owned the sidewalk subject to a public easement of passage. When the city then vacated the sidewalk giving the bank fee simple title, free of all encumbrances, to the former sidewalk, the bank decided to construct a new building which would block the sidewalk. Plaintiff claimed an easement by prescription to maintain its marquee. *Held:* An easement can be acquired by prescription in and above a sidewalk, title to which is in private hands subject to an easement in favor of the public, by regular use of such sidewalk in a way not used by the public. *RKO–Stanley Warner Theatres, Inc. v. Mellon Nat'l Bank & Trust Co.*, 436 F2d 1297 (1970).

9th Circuit For 31 years, Indians had used a road across settlers' property to reach their tribal lands. When the settlers padlocked a gate across the road, the Indians responded by shooting off the locks. The United States intervened as trustee for Indian tribes and claimed an easement by prescription. One issue was whether the Indians' use of the road was continuous. *Held:* "Continuous use" to right-of-way by prescription does not mean constant use; rather, if the claimant had used the right-of-way whenever he desired, without interference by the owner of the servient estate, the use was continuous and uninterrupted. *Confederated Salish & Kootenai Tribes v. Vulles*, 437 F2d 177 (1971); accord *Gleason v. Phillips*, 470 P2d 46 (1970).

Arkansas Stahl's property was bisected by a public road. Thompson owned a house north of Stahl's property. Two dirt roads were created by constant use, leading from the public road on Stahl's property to the Thompson house. Stahl's property north of the public road was wild and unimproved. Stahl claimed the roads were used by permission; Thompson claimed a prescriptive easement over the roads.

Held: A prescriptive easement was acquired. The use of wild, unimproved land is presumed to be permissive until those using the land demonstrate their claim by open and notorious conduct. Here, witnesses testified that the roads had existed for 30 years. Stahl's predecessor in title testified that the use of the land was without permission. Under the circumstances, open, hostile, and adverse use was established. *Stahl v. Thompson*, 641 SW2d 721 (1982).

California Defendants habitually crossed to their land over a portion of a neighboring plot that they mistakenly believed to be their own. However, they never paid taxes on the plot. When plaintiff sued to quiet title, defendants counterclaimed for adverse possession and a prescriptive easement. *Held:* Possession by defendants was hostile and adverse for purposes of title by adverse possession or establishing a prescriptive easement. However, defendants' failure to pay taxes on the plot precluded a claim of adverse possession, but it did not bar a claim of easement by prescription. *Gilardi v. Hallam*, 636 P2d 588 (1981).

Florida An action was brought for a declaratory judgment and injunctive relief to prevent defendant from erecting a public observation tower on its beach property on the theory that the public had obtained a prescriptive easement over the property. *Held:* The public's use of the beach was not adverse to defendant's use, and, therefore, no prescriptive easement had been created. Even if such an easement were presumed to exist, defendant's tower would not be a use inconsistent with the public's continued use of the beach. *City of Daytona Beach v. Tona-Rama, Inc.*, 294 So. 2d 73 (1974).

Georgia In 1962, plaintiff purchased a home and began using a driveway to access his residence. In 1986, defendant purchased the adjoining lot and proposed to move plaintiff's driveway to prepare for commercial development. Both parties acknowledged plaintiff's right to a prescriptive easement covering the driveway; however, defendant offered to create an express easement over a new driveway in exchange for the old one. After the negotiations stalled, plaintiff sought to enjoin defendant from blocking the driveway or altering the path of the original easement. *Held:* Plaintiff had acquired a prescriptive easement that may not be altered by the owner of the servient tenement. Since an owner may not acquire a prescriptive easement if he shifts the easement's path during the period of prescription, it follows that once the easement is acquired, the owner of the servient tenement may not alter the easement's path. *Thomason v. Kern & Co.*, 376 SE2d 872 (1989).

Georgia Plaintiff owned property through which it had opened some roads. Defendant owned several nearby, noncontiguous tracts that he wished to develop into a residential subdivision. Subsequently, defendant began to widen and gravel the roads on plaintiff's property, claiming he had established prescriptive title to the roads for over 20 years. Evidence showed the road was used from 1916 to the mid-1960s, and it had since become overgrown. Plaintiff sued to enjoin the alleged trespass. *Held:* For plaintiff. Case law held that a showing of repairs is required during the prescriptive period, in order to give notice to the owner of one's intention to claim the road as private. There was no evidence that defendant had made repairs during the prescriptive period. *Chota, Inc. v. Woodley*, 309 SE2d 132 (1983).

Idaho Landowners sued when a county attempted to abandon a road that crossed private property, claiming that the road was public. This claim was based partly on the fact that the road was maintained by the forest service, which had an easement over the private property. *Held:* The expenditure of funds by the forest service to maintain a road abandoned by the county did not occur at public expense and, therefore, did not make the road public. The court determined that the federal government had a private easement as an abutting owner that survived an abandonment of the public road. The forest service's expenditures were to maintain its private easement. *French v. Sorensen*, 751 P2d 98 (1988).

Illinois Plaintiffs sued to establish that a roadway owned by defendant had become a public highway because of prescriptive use in excess of the requisite 15-year period. They sought to enjoin defendant from barricading the roadway, which was used as a shortcut to and from the local airport. Defendant claimed (1) he had no notice the roadway was claimed as a public highway, (2) the use was not hostile, as he granted permission to some of the users, (3) the public use was not confined to a definite and specific right-of-way, and (4) the use was not continuous and uninterrupted, as he blocked the road at least one day a year. *Held:* Prescriptive use was established and the injunction was granted. There is a presumption that the public use was prescriptive. (1) Defendant's testimony showed that he was aware of the public's use of the roadway. (2) Permission was only granted to a small number of users. Defendant failed to show that the use was under some license inconsistent with the public's claim of right. (3) The roadway was established where the use was over substantially the same strip. (4) Defendant's obstruction was not an interruption, since it was not submitted to for such duration as to raise a fair presumption of abandonment. *King v. Corsini*, 335 NE2d 561 (App. Ct. 1975).

Maryland Plaintiff brought a trespass suit against defendants involving the use of a road through plaintiff's farm. Defendants claimed an easement by prescription. When the use of the road began, there was a family relationship between the then owners of the dominant and servient estates, and the trial court held that the evidence of the family relationship proved that the use of the road was merely permissive. *Held:* The family relationship, without more evidence, was insufficient to support the finding that use of the road was necessarily permissive. *Zehner v. Fink*, 311 A2d 477 (Ct. App. 1973).

Massachusetts For more than 20 years, a door on the third floor of plaintiff's building opened onto a balcony that connected it to a fire escape attached to defendant's building. In June 1983, defendant acquired the building and performed renovations, in the course of which it demolished the fire escape. Plaintiff, meanwhile, had also performed renovations, with the intention of renting the third floor separately, a move that required the continued existence of the fire escape to meet building code regulations. Plaintiff sued. *Held:* Plaintiff had an easement by prescription in the fire escape. Although plaintiff had not made continuous physical use of the fire escape, the nature of the fire escape did not require continuous physical use. *Brooks, Gill & Co. v. Landmark Properties*, 503 NE2d 983 (App. Ct. 1987).

Massachusetts The owners of a parking lot adjacent to defendant's property sought to enjoin defendant from using their lot. Defendant claimed it had a prescriptive easement, based on its use of the land in a manner that was open, notorious, adverse to the owner, and continuous for a period of at least 20 years. During 12 of the 20 years, the lot was shared by defendant's predecessor and the tenants of the previous owners of the lot. The lease permitted tenants to sublet the leased property without the owners' consent. *Held:* Defendant had not acquired a prescriptive easement, because defendant's predecessor's use of the parking lot was not "notorious." There was no evidence the owners knew of and assented to use of the lot by defendant's predecessor, nor was there anything to put them on notice that defendant was using the lot, since defendant's predecessor's cars were indistinguishable from those of tenant's employees. *Boston Seaman's Friend Soc'y v. Rifkin Management*, 473 NE2d 702 (App. Ct. 1985).

Michigan Plaintiff sued to permanently enjoin a continuing trespass by defendant on his property. Defendant had a gravel driveway that crossed a portion of plaintiff's lot, which defendant had used from the time that plaintiff's predecessor in title owned the property. *Held:* The circumstances were such that plaintiff should have been aware of the use of its property. The nature of the use was such that it was made under a claim of right. Defendant was not required to make expressions of adverse intent to indicate hostile use. Defendant acquired a prescriptive easement, and the date of the commencement of the statutory period was when the driveway was built and not when plaintiff purchased. *Mumrow v. Riddle*, 242 NW2d 489 (Ct. App. 1976).

Minnesota Landowner blocked an access road located on his property that led to a beach in order to prevent use of the beach by the public. These efforts were not entirely successful in stopping pedestrians, who would walk around the obstructions. Plaintiff sued to obtain a declaration that the public had acquired a prescriptive easement across the property. *Held:* The former landowner had sufficiently asserted his ownership and intention to prevent public usage of the access way. Even though the public circumvented his barriers, his actions broke the continuity of the adverse use, and so the requisite period of 15 years was never completed. *Rice v. Mieler*, 238 NW2d 609 (1976).

Montana A survey conducted incident to the purchase of land revealed that its southern portion had long been used by a neighbor for agriculture and other purposes, though the neighbor had not paid taxes on that portion. Plaintiff purchaser brought an action to quiet title, and defendant neighbor counterclaimed for a prescriptive easement or adverse possession. *Held:* Defendant could not be granted an easement by prescription, because he was in possession of the property during the statutory period; and "easement" is by definition a nonpossessory interest. He could not be awarded adverse possession, because he had not paid the taxes throughout the statutory period. *Burlingame v. Marjerrison*, 665 P2d 1136 (1983).

New York Plaintiffs brought an action for a declaratory judgment that they had acquired an easement by prescription over a gravel road on defendants' land. They also sought to enjoin defendants from interfering with their use. The trial court enjoined plaintiffs from asserting a claim to a prescriptive easement, and they appealed. *Held:* Affirmed. The neighborly relationship between plaintiffs and defendants' predecessors in interest created an implication that the use of the disputed roadway was permissive. Where permission can be implied from the beginning, an adverse use will not arise until there is an assertion of a hostile right that is made known to the property owner. Plaintiffs had not shown that they had asserted such a right. Instead, it was shown that the use of the roadway arose from a cordial and cooperative relationship. *Hassinger v. Kline*, 457 NYS2d 847 (App. Div. 1983).

Oregon In 1951, plaintiffs gave neighbors permission to use their driveway to access a public road. The neighbors sold their property in 1964, and the assignees mistakenly believed they had easement rights in the driveway. Plaintiffs and assignees used the driveway and shared maintenance expenses but never discussed its use or ownership. In 1978, assignees sold the property to defendants, who also mistakenly believed they had an easement to use the driveway. Plaintiffs sued to enjoin defendants' use; defendants claimed an easement by prescription. *Held:* For defendants. Plaintiffs had granted neighbors a nonassignable license to use the driveway, which was revoked when the neighbors sold the property in 1964. The use of the driveway by defendants and their assignees was adverse in that it was open, notorious, and continuous for over 10 years. The fact that defendants' and assignees' use of the driveway was based on a mistaken belief was sufficient to prove the element of hostile intent. *Hanscam v. Sousa*, 641 P2d 86 (1982).

Utah Plaintiffs drove their cattle once a year across defendant's land to a federal grazing area. This practice continued for over 20 years. At one point, defendant built a gate at the boundary of the land, sometimes giving plaintiffs the key, and sometimes not, in which case plaintiffs cut the fence. Plaintiffs sued to establish an easement by prescription. *Held:* Plaintiffs had an easement by prescription in gross, since the easement was not appurtenant to any dominant estate. Plaintiffs' use of the land was open, notorious, adverse, and continuous for 20 years, so as to establish a prescriptive easement. *Crane v. Crane*, 683 P2d 1062 (1984).

Washington Plaintiff sued to establish a prescriptive easement on the property of an adjacent landowner. In 1966, plaintiff had constructed a residence accessible by a road that plaintiff believed to be a public right-of-way but that was on private property, as he learned in 1972. He continued to use the road on a daily basis to reach his house. Defendant argued that there was insufficient evidence to conclude plaintiff's use of the road was adverse, because he had thought that the road was public. *Held:* A declaration of adverse intent is not necessary to establish a prescriptive easement, for whether the use had been adverse is one of fact. Plaintiff used the right-of-way as an owner, not in recognition of the title of the true owner, and a prescriptive easement was thus established. *Dunbar v. Heinrich*, 605 P2d 1272 (1979).

West Virginia Airport authority sued to enjoin the county board of education from building a school 3,000 feet from an airport and from seeking alterations in flight patterns over the proposed school. The airport argued that it had acquired a navigation easement over the site by virtue of frequent aircraft overflights. *Held:* A navigation easement in airspace used by aircraft over lands adjacent to an airport cannot be acquired by prescription. First, the available decisions have consistently held that easements may not be acquired by prescription against the state. Second, practical problems arise in defining "navigation easements," such as whether changes in the type or number of overflying aircraft could modify or cancel the easement, whether multiple flight patterns would result in multiple navigation easements, and by what manner an easement could be established if multiple tracts of land were involved. *Sticklen v. Kittle*, 287 SE2d 148 (1981).

Wyoming Defendants discovered that a town road crossed their property, and were sued by the town when they tried to block the road. *Held:* The town had a prescriptive easement over the property for the road. The presumption that the town's use was permissive was rebutted by the use and maintenance of the road for over 30 years. *Koontz v. Town of Superior*, 746 P2d 1264 (1987).

13.35
—Grant by Eminent Domain

Georgia Transit authority built a subway tunnel under plaintiffs' condominium complex. Testing of the trains caused the buildings to vibrate. Attempts at refinement failed to solve the problem, and a costly alternative was rejected by the authority. The authority sought condemnation of a noise and vibration easement covering the affected areas. *Held:* The authority must either condemn the fee or continue construction and take all necessary steps to alleviate the problem. The law contemplates the taking of an actual property interest, but not merely purchase of the right to damage. The question of whether a condemning authority may acquire by eminent domain a noise and vibration easement without taking the further step of condemning the fee itself was noted by the court as one of first impression anywhere. *Metropolitan Atlanta Rapid Transit Auth. v. Trussell*, 273 SE2d 859 (1981).

Nebraska When an easement to construct drainage facilities was obtained on plaintiff's land by eminent domain, plaintiff challenged the reduction of his property taxes by only 50 percent, claiming that the value of the land should have been reassessed to nothing. *Held:* The reassessment stood. The taking of the easement did not diminish plaintiff's title to the land, simply the land's value. Plaintiff's theory that the value of the land to which the easement applied should have been considered separately from the rest of the property was rejected. *Voltmer Family Farms v. Richardson County*, 343 NW2d 755 (1983).

13.40
—Creation by Estoppel

Texas The Haskinses owned two contiguous parcels of land at the end of a roadway that led across Gouge's land to a state highway. Gouge sold a portion of his land at the point of intersection of the roadway with the highway to Winters. Before the conveyance, Winters observed a member of the Haskins family using the roadway and was told by Gouge that they had a right to use it. After Winters purchased the property, he put up a gate across the roadway at the point of egress to the highway, and offered Haskins a key to the lock on the gate. Winters stated that he did not want an easement across the land, but had no objection to the Haskinses using the roadway to gain access to their land. The Haskinses sued for an easement by estoppel. *Held:* For Winters. Use of the roadway by the Haskinses did not estop Winters from denying the existence of an easement, because such use, as well as Winters's knowledge of the Haskinses' use of the roadway, was as consistent with a permissive use of the roadway as an easement. *Haskins v. Winters*, 641 SW2d 603 (Ct. App. 1982).

Texas Property owner purchased a tract in 1949 that was separated from a public highway by a strip of land owned by a corporation. The public highway could be reached only through the use of a public road on the corporation's property. The property owner obtained an easement and used the road without interference until 1972, when he conveyed the property. After the conveyance, the corporation constructed a gate on its road, preventing access to the highway. The grantee sued for an easement by estoppel. *Held:* For the grantee. One who attempts to create an easement by estoppel must show that he relied to his detriment upon some representation by the owner of the servient state. In view of the grantee's knowledge of his grantor's unchallenged use of the road, it was reasonable for him to conclude that his access to the property would be similarly unrestricted, and to take title to the property in reliance on that conclusion. *Exxon Corp. v. Schutzmaier*, 537 SW2d 282 (Civ. App. 1976).

13.45 Scope

5th Circuit One group of cotenants granted defendant the right to construct a single pipeline across the subject land. The remaining cotenants granted defendant the right to lay pipelines across the subject land. Defendant built one pipe and then another, and plaintiff, the successor in title to all the cotenants, sought title to the subject land. *Held:* Defendant was indeed limited to construct just one pipeline; however, plaintiff was entitled only to damages for construction of the second line and not to sole possession of the subject land. *Texas Mort. Co. v. Phillips Petroleum Co.*, 470 F2d 497 (1972), cert. denied, 411 US 948 (1973).

10th Circuit The United States owned a power line right-of-way. It permitted eight homes and a service station to be erected beneath its wires between 1950 and 1966. When construction of a ninth home was proposed, the United States objected, claiming that the house would be an unreasonable interference with its easement since it would increase the cost and difficulty of inspecting and repairing the wires. *Held:* The United States could not object. For over 16 years, it and those who owned the land beneath the power lines had acted as though the landowners were privileged to build homes on the right-of-way despite the additional trouble caused the United States. That conduct defined the scope of the easement. *United States v. Cross*, 477 F2d 317 (1973).

Alabama The owner of an easement across a stretch of beach sought to build a pier appurtenant to the easement. The owner of the beach objected. At trial, testimony by the grantor regarding his intent for the extent of the easement was admitted, since the language of the easement was ambiguous. *Held:* The owner of the easement could not build a pier, since the easement was granted with the intent that it be used solely for pedestrian access. *Fouts v. Beall*, 518 So. 2d 1236 (1987).

Alabama A manufacturer granted a sewer line easement to a sewer board to connect its property with a waste treatment plant and to avoid dumping waste in the river. The easement was granted for $5, and evidence indicated it would have cost the manufacturer $50,000 to privately treat the waste. The easement conveyed to the sewer board was for an underground pipeline, but the sewer board built an above ground line. Although the line took one year to construct and was plainly visible, the manufacturer did not object to the above ground placement until a year and a half after construction, when it sued to remove or change the location of the line. *Held:* For defendant. The sewage easement was vital to the public welfare. In addition, relocation of the line would cost at least $250,000, and it would be against the public interest to compensate the present owner of the property who had already benefited by purchasing the property at a reduced rate. *Consolidated Foods Corp. v. Water Works & Sanitary Sewer Bd.*, 319 So. 2d 261 (1975).

Arizona Developer was constructing a shopping mall on two parcels of land, one of which was accessible only through an easement granted by Neffson to developer's predecessor in interest. Neffson filed for an injunction against use of the easement by shopping mall customers from the second piece of land. *Held:* For Neffson. An easement appurtenant to a dominant parcel may not be used to benefit a nonappurtenant parcel. The fact that the two parcels were adjacent and commonly owned was irrelevant. *DND Neffson Co. v. Galleria Partners*, 745 P2d 206 (1987).

Connecticut Defendant's predecessor in interest granted plaintiff an easement on her property for the purpose of transmitting electricity. The deed reserved in grantor, her heirs and assigns, the right to use the land in any way that would not interfere with plaintiff's generation of electricity. Defendant, a factory, purchased the property and built a parking lot and used it as a loading site. It also constructed a building that encroached on the easement. Four or five years later, plaintiff sued to enjoin defendant from interfering with its easement. *Held:* For defendant. For four or five years, plaintiff acted in acquiescence of defendant's activities and allowed it to make substantial investments in paving part of the easement and providing loading facilities. Equitable relief was denied plaintiff as the balance of equities favored defendant. *Connecticut Light & Power Co. v. Holson Co.*, 440 A2d 935 (1981).

Michigan A cable television franchise requested permission to use the poles of the light company, which were located on property designated a "public utility" easement on a subdivision plot, in order to gain access to subscribers in the subdivision. For purposes of the subdivision control act, which regulates plotting, "public utility" includes gas, electricity, water, steam, telephone, sewer, or other services of a similar nature. A property owner, over whose property the easement extended, challenged the right of the franchise to use the easement. *Held:* The cable television franchise was permitted to use the utility poles. Despite the absence of two-way communication, cable TV is analogous to the telephone in providing communication service and transmission of intelligence. *White v. Detroit Edison Co.*, 281 NW2d 283 (1979).

13.50
—Enlargement

Louisiana When a lessee, contrary to its lease with defendant, expanded into the parking area of a shopping area, the holder of a nonexclusive easement over the entire parking area sued for injunctive relief. *Held:* Although plaintiff's lease entitled it to seek injunctive relief without having to prove inadequacy of legal remedies or irreparable harm, the court refused to enforce this otherwise enforceable clause in view of the exceptional circumstances of the case. The harm to defendant, the other tenants of the shopping center, and the community served by the shopping center from the destruction of a $4 million building would outweigh any harm caused to plaintiff. Plaintiff could have been adequately compensated in damages. *J. Weingarten, Inc. v. Northgate Mall, Inc.*, 404 So. 2d 896 (1981).

New York The owner of the dominant estate had an easement giving him access to a public highway via a right-of-way through defendant's development. When owner acquired additional parcels adjacent to his dominant estate, he sought to extend the use of the right-of-way to these parcels, although the additional parcels had independent access to a public street. *Held:* A right-of-way created to serve a specific tract of land may not be used to serve another. *Zeh v. Karker*, 351 NYS2d 478 (App. Div. 1974).

Washington The predecessors in title to Parcel A granted to the predecessor owners of Parcel B a private road easement across Parcel A for "ingress to and egress from" Parcel B. The new Parcel B owners, the Browns, purchased Parcel C and sought to combine the two parcels by moving the single-family house on Parcel

B to a location that straddled the boundaries of Parcels B and C. The new Parcel A owners, the Vosses, put up obstacles to bar the easement, and the Browns sued to enjoin them from interfering with their use of the easement. The Vosses countersued to enjoin the Browns from using the easement other than for Parcel B. *Held:* If an easement is appurtenant to a particular parcel of land, any extension thereof to other parcels is a misuse of the easement. However, although the easement was being misused, at least in a technical sense, the trial court had properly refused to grant the injunction against continued misuse given the fact that the Browns had spent $11,000 on their new house. *Brown v. Voss*, 715 P2d 514 (1986) (en banc).

13.55
—Overburdening

Maine Fifteen or more individuals shared a common, identical easement allowing them to use a 400-foot beach for recreational activities. One of the parties was a campground owner, who expanded the campground to 170 sites. When this resulted in severe crowding during the summer, other easement holders brought suit. *Held:* Plaintiffs were entitled to injunctive relief. The campground owner had overburdened the easement. His practice of allowing his business invitees to use the beach impaired the reasonable enjoyment of the common facilities by all easement holders. *Poire v. Manchester*, 506 A2d 1160 (1986).

13.60
Easement of Access

9th Circuit A timber company sought to build access roads across national forest land to land in Montana owned by the company. This land was wholly surrounded by national forest land, and environmentalists brought suit to stop the company. *Held:* The national forest service was required to provide the company with reasonable access to the company's land by virtue of a provision of the Alaska National Interest Lands Act of 1980, 16 USC § 3210(a). The company may also have been entitled to an easement by necessity or to other statutory rights of access. *Montana Wilderness Ass'n v. United States Forest Service*, 655 F2d 951 (1981), cert. denied, 455 US 989 (1982).

Alabama Landowner sold two parcels to a telephone paging company and one parcel to his son. A survey after the sale found that paging company's buildings encroached on the son's parcel. The son gave the paging company an easement over a portion of his parcel for guy wires and existing buildings. Later, the paging company put shells over a portion of the parcel it claimed previously was a dirt driveway. The son claimed the easement did not permit that use. The paging company sued. *Held:* The paging company was entitled to a permanent injunction as owner of the dominant estate to permit them to use the driveway to access a building that encroached on the son's property. An easement is construed to allow the owner of the dominant estate to use a driveway across the servient estate. In addition, testimony established that the paging company's use of the easement was consistent with the use of the property prior to its sale. *Sprinkle v. American Mobilephone Paging*, 525 So. 2d 1353 (1988).

Arkansas Plaintiff had an easement for invitees to his land to cross over defendant's land. When plaintiff tried to sell his land, defendant allegedly interfered with the sale by ordering plaintiff's invitees off defendant's land when they were unaccompanied by plaintiff. Plaintiff sought injunctive and monetary relief. *Held:* Plaintiff's unaccompanied invitees could not, as defendant requested, be required to present defendant with written evidence of their status in order to cross his land. However, plaintiff was not entitled to compensation for the failure of the prospective sale of his house, because there was no evidence of damages. *Bean v. Johnson*, 649 SW2d 171 (1983).

Arizona A landowner brought an action for access over a developer's property to an airport. The trial court denied the easement and the landowner appealed, arguing that an easement by necessity should be implied. *Held:* Affirmed. A property owner is not entitled to aircraft access, absent evidence that the property could not be effectively used without such access. *Chandler Flyers v. Stelear Dev. Corp.*, 592 P2d 387 (1979).

Maine Owners of lake shore property sued for a declaratory judgment to permit them to use a road across adjacent property as the only means of access to the lake. The trial court granted judgment, declaring that they had a right of access; the adjacent property owners appealed. *Held:* Affirmed. At the time of the conveyance, when the dominant and servient estates were severed, the grantor reserved the right-of-way across the adjacent property by implication. *LeMay v. Anderson*, 397 A2d 984 (1979).

Missouri The process of building sewer lines obstructed a road that linked a landlocked property to a highway. The owner of the landlocked property sued the sewer company, claiming it had interfered with his easement of access. *Held:* The landlocked owner was entitled to damages for interference with his easement because the sewer company's actions constituted a nuisance. However, since the interference was temporary in nature, the proper measure of damages was the reduction in value of the landlocked property during the period of interference, not the difference in fair market value of the property before and after construction of the sewer. *Mondelli v. Saline Sewer Co.*, 628 SW2d 697 (Ct. App. 1982).

Nebraska Developer conveyed a portion of its tract, which contained a department store, to plaintiff and conveyed the rest to a builder for further development as a shopping center. Plaintiff sued to enjoin the builder from interfering with plaintiff's use of storm and sanitary sewer lines and an access road for which it alleged there was easement on defendant's tract. The developer alleged that the conveyance to plaintiff contained an implied grant for utility lines and the conveyance to the builder impliedly reserved the easements. *Held:* Where the parties contemplated that there would be joint use of the utility lines, parking facilities, and access roads, and these facilities were constructed with the knowledge of the builder and could be removed only at great cost, the injunction was granted. The builder was barred by failing to act until the disputed facilities were constructed. *Cape Co. v. Wiebe*, 241 NW2d 830 (1976).

13.65
Right-Of-Way Easement

Georgia Property owner in a platted subdivision began an addition to his building. A neighboring landowner brought an action to enjoin the addition, contending that it would encroach on the subdivision's right-of-way. *Held:* The original owner recorded a subdivision plat showing a street. He, as a matter of law, created easements in favor of the property owners. No presumption of abandonment arose because 20 years did not run. The case was remanded for the jury to determine whether defendants encroached on the easements. *Smith v. Clay*, 236 SE2d 346 (1977).

Idaho Defendants had purchased an easement that granted them a right-of-way "exclusively for their use" along a route that effectively bisected their neighbor's land. They paved a roadway along the right-of-way at their own expense. Some years later, plaintiff acquired the neighbor's parcels on either side of the roadway and sought permission to use defendants' roadway. Defendants asked in return that plaintiff reimburse them for their construction costs and contribute to ongoing maintenance. Plaintiff filed an action to quiet title, claiming that he was entitled to use the road over his land without outlay on his part. The trial court held that the exclusivity of defendants' easement precluded use of the road by plaintiff. *Held:* Reversed and remanded. The phase "exclusively for their use" was ambiguous. Further evidence was needed to determine whether the parties to the deed intended (1) fee simple ownership conveyed to the defendants; (2) an easement right-of-way excluding all others, including the servient owners; or (3) an easement right-of-way excluding all but the servient owners. It was extremely unlikely that the neighbor would have agreed to an easement that left one half of her tract inaccessible to the other half. *Latham v. Garner*, 673 P2d 1048 (1983).

Maryland Appellants' deed referred to a plat of the land previously conveyed to plaintiffs that depicted an abutting roadway passing between plaintiffs' and their neighbors' land. After the original landowner's efforts to dedicate this roadway to public use failed, plaintiffs sought a judgment declaring them fee simple owners of the roadway and barring appellants from using it. *Held:* Although plaintiffs had fee simple title to part of the roadway, appellants had an easement by plat reference to use the roadway. *Boucher v. Boyer*, 484 A2d 630 (1984).

Texas Property owner brought an action for declaratory judgment that she had a right to use an alley betwen her property and an adjacent piece of property. After a nonjury trial, judgment was granted for the property owner. On appeal to an intermediate appellate court, the judgment was reversed. The property owner then appealed. *Held:* Property owner was entitled to declaratory judgment. When the trial court rendered judgment, there was an implied finding of fact. Since the question of public dedication of the alley was a question of fact, the trial court's decision must stand. *Viscardi v. Pajestka*, 576 SW2d 16 (1978).

Utah Owner of property abutting an undedicated public thoroughfare sued to prevent the installation of power lines within the highway easement. *Held:* In a case of first impression, the construction as approved by municipal authorities did not constitute an additional servitude which would entitle plaintiff to injunctive relief or damages. Transmission of power is consistent with the permissible uses of a public right-of-way. *Pickett v. California Pac. Util.*, 619 P2d 325 (1980).

Utah Plaintiffs brought an action to establish a right-of-way by prescription over defendant's land. Plaintiffs and their predecessors had crossed the land for 40 years, using it for timber, picnics, camping, and grazing of sheep. The lower court dismissed the complaint. *Held:* Plaintiff's activity created an easement by prescription, even though the land was used sporadically. *Richards v. Pine Ranch, Inc.*, 559 P2d 948 (1977).

Vermont Grantor of lakeshore lots had reserved rights-of-way across the lots for the benefit of those who might build to the rear of them. The grantor subsequently attempted to establish boating and docking rights-of-way by granting such rights in deeds to property to the rear of the lakeshore lots. *Held:* It may be inferred that the original reservation did not include the right to build a dock or maintain a boat landing. *Edwards v. Fugere*, 287 A2d 582 (1972).

13.70 Maintenance and Repairs

Connecticut Plaintiff sued to recover the cost of repairs it incurred in restoring a protective dike damaged by the city when it laid sewer lines. The owner granted the city an easement for the construction of the pipelines, but the easement was silent as to expenses for repairs to the dike. *Held:* Where there was no showing that the action of plaintiff in rebuilding the dike interfered with the city's pipeline or that preserving the breach was necessary for the city's use of the easement, the award of damages was proper. The owner of an easement has a duty to make such repairs as are necessary for the owner of the land to have reasonable use of his estate. Plaintiff was not required to allow the land to remain exposed to risk of harm from flooding. *Center Drive-in Theatre, Inc. v. City of Derby*, 352 A2d 304 (1974).

Idaho Landowners sued a reservoir district that owned an easement over their property for an irrigation canal and maintenance roads on either side. While driving on the road, the landowner's truck fell into the canal when the road's edge gave way. *Held:* It is an easement owner's duty to maintain and repair the easement so as not to create an additional burden on the servient estate. The reservoir district must be held to the general standard to use ordinary care in the management of the easement. The case was remanded to determine whether the failure to maintain the road was a breach of its duty. *Rehwalt v. American Falls Reservoir Dist.*, 550 P2d 137 (1976).

Illinois A lakeside owner's association sued the city to compel it to repair erosion damage along two lakes located within their development. The association claimed that the lakes were part of an easement granted to the city allowing it to conduct and store storm water. However, the easement provision contained a declaration of covenants and restrictions, which stated that the association was responsible for all common areas of the development. The city refused all repair requests made by the association, claiming that the declaration released it from all repair obligations. *Held:* The easement imposing liability on the city was superseded by the declaration of covenants. The instrument conveying the easement incorporated the declaration and thereby held the association responsible for maintenance. Generally, the owner of an easement has the duty to keep an easement in repair. However, no duty to repair exists if there is an agreement to the contrary. *Briarcliffe Lakeside Townhouse Owners Ass'n v. City of Wheaton*, 524 NE2d 230 (App. Ct. 1988).

Missouri Pipeline operator had an easement for the construction and operation of its pipeline across land whose owner otherwise had full rights of use and development. The pipeline operator sued the owner when construction on the land by the owner forced the operator to relocate its pipeline. *Held:* The operator was entitled to damages, despite the fact that the terms of the easement had not forbidden the owner to build on the land. The grant allowed the easement holder certain rights that landowner had substantially interfered with. *Mississippi River Transmission Corp. v. Wachter Constr., Inc.*, 731 SW2d 445 (Ct. App. 1987).

Texas Corporation purchased a pipeline easement that provided that the pipe was to be at sufficient depth to permit cultivation of farmland above it. Because of soil erosion, the pipe, which had originally been laid 48 inches deep, was severed by a plow 22 inches below the surface. When the corporation sued to recover for damages to the pipe, it contended that it had no duty to maintain the easement and that its sole obligation was to construct the pipe at the proper depth. The landowner answered that the corporation had previously reburied the pipe when it was exposed by erosion and therefore had understood its obligations to include pipeline maintenance. *Held:* The corporation had a duty to maintain its easement, since it was clearly the intent of the parties that cultivation would continue throughout the year. *Mapco, Inc. v. Ratliff*, 528 SW2d 622 (Civ. App. 1975).

13.75 Succession and Transferability

U.S. District Court, Pennsylvania Government sued to enjoin the operation of a commercial campground and the construction of a toilet on property over which it possessed a flowage easement. The terms of the easement restricted the use of the land and prohibited the construction and maintenance of habitable structures. *Held:* Where the owners of property in fee purchased the land subject to the government's easement, which prohibited the construction of structures upon the land, the camping structures, whether or not motorized, were within the meaning of the easement, and maintenance of the campground and construction of the toilet was enjoined. *United States v. Zorger*, 407 F. Supp. 25 (WD), aff'd, 546 F2d 421 (1976).

Arizona Agreement between the state and original landowners made at the time the state acquired a right-of-way provided that the state was to put in crossovers so that the landowners would have direct access to both the northbound and southbound lanes of the highway. In condemnation proceedings one issue was whether the agreement created a right as to subsequent owners and lessees. *Held:* The agreement created an easement appurtenant to the land, which ran with the land and gave any subsequent owners and lessees rights incident to the easement and damages for its loss. *State ex rel. Herman v. Schaffer*, 515 P2d 593 (1973).

Mississippi Landowner sued to enjoin defendant from interfering with his easement to use a private road on defendant's land. Defendant answered that since the easement was acquired by adverse possession, it was personal and did not run with the land for the benefit of plaintiff. *Held:* An easement is an interest in land distinguishable from a license, which merely confers a personal privilege. An easement acquired by prescription is equivalent to the conveyance of such right by deed. The easement runs with the land. *Logan v. McGee*, 320 So. 2d 792 (1975).

Texas Grantor owned a life interest in the surface of a tract of land that included Lots 1 and 2. During his lifetime, the grantor conveyed Lot 1 to Individual *A*, and Lot 2 to Individual *B*. After grantor's death, *A* contended that he had an easement appurtenant over Lot 2, since it had been necessary to cross Lot 2 to reach Lot 1 when grantor owned both lots. *Held:* An easement appurtenant attaches to the land and passes with it. However, a life tenant cannot alienate any greater interest in property than an interest that ceases with his life. Moreover, there must be unity of title between the alleged dominant and servient estates, and a life interest in a servient estate is not sufficient to establish the unity of title necessary to support the grant of an easement appurtenant beyond the duration of a life estate. Therefore, since the grantor could not have expressly granted an easement across Lot 2 that extended beyond her life estate in the property, *A* could not have acquired an easement appurtenant over the lot. *First Nat'l Bank v. Amarillo Nat'l Bank*, 531 SW2d 905 (Civ. App. 1975).

13.80
Easements in Gross

Connecticut Plaintiff owning landlocked plot claimed an easement across defendant's plot to the sea, based on the recognition of such an easement in prior deeds to defendant's lot. However, one of the previous owners of plaintiff's lot had conveyed all his interest in what became defendant's plot to defendant's predecessor, reserving the easement only to himself and not his heirs and assigns. *Held:* The easement across defendant's plot was appurtenant, and so did not lapse at the death of plaintiff's predecessor, as it would have had it been in gross. According to the court, an easement should be deemed appurtenant when it would be of value to anyone who owned the land. *Kelly v. Ivler*, 450 A2d 817 (1982).

Maine Defendant held title to property containing an obsolete mill and attached dam. Defendant was granted a license by the town to demolish the mill. Subsequently, however, the town objected to the demolition, arguing that it had an easement in the dam, which once was used to collect water for the town's fire protection system. Defendant cited a 1969 agreement between the town and landowners relieving them of any obligation to support the now-obsolete water system. The town cited language in the agreement that it should continue to have the same rights in the dam as it "presently possesses." *Held:* For defendant. The rights held by the town amounted to an easement in gross over the dam and not an easement appurtenant to land, because the town owned no such land. An easement in gross in a structure can be terminated by voluntary destruction of the structure. Without an interest in the land, the town had no enforceable rights to prevent demolition of the dam. *Inhabitants of Sabattus v. Bilodeau*, 391 A2d 357 (1978).

13.85
Extinguishment

6th Circuit Easement granted for $995 by plaintiffs' predecessors provided that if a pipeline for the transportation of coal slurry "shall cease to be used for the purpose set forth herein for the period of one year," the easement would be terminated. The granting clause twice employed the word "purposes" to refer to rights of "constructing, maintaining, operating, altering, repairing, replacing, and removing one pipeline for the transportation of coal slurry." When the pipeline was not used for over one year to transport coal slurry, although it was maintained in readiness to do so, plaintiffs sought a declaration of rights as to the easement. *Held:* In light of the meager price paid for the easement, the easement was terminated despite language to the contrary in the granting clause. *Golden v. Henderson*, 456 F2d 376 (1972), cert. denied, 409 US 861 (1973).

Connecticut Plaintiffs and defendant were owners of adjoining property. Plaintiffs accessed their home by two routes: a main entrance and a right-of-way created by an easement bisecting defendant's property. The easement contained a clause that terminated the easement if any new building was erected or if any existing building was enlarged. Plaintiffs, easement owners, informed defendant of their plans to construct an addition to their home. Defendant initially failed to respond; however, defendant declared the easement terminated upon initiation of construction. Plaintiffs sought an injunction to restrain defendant from interfering with their use and enjoyment of the easement. *Held:* According to the express terms of the deed, the easement terminated when plaintiffs enlarged their home. An easement that is conditioned on the nonoccurrence of a particular event is automatically terminated when that event occurs. *Eis v. Meyer*, 555 A2d 994 (App. Ct. 1989).

Georgia A landowner conveyed two parks to the county. The parks were never used, and the county later reconveyed the parks to the landholder's successor in exchange for park land elsewhere. The former parks were divided further, and 30 years later, the owner of two of the original lots sued, arguing that he and his predecessors in title had acquired a recreational easement to the parks. *Held:* For the developer. The lot owner was estopped from asserting his rights under the easement. An easement may be extinguished by estoppel if the owner of the servient tenement acts inconsistently with the continued existence of the easement and in so doing relies on the conduct of the dominant owner evidencing an intent not to make use of the servient tenement in the future. The lot owner sat idly by while the park land was sold and developed. To restore the recreational easement would place an unreasonable hardship on purchasers of the lots. *Rolleston v. Sea Island Properties, Inc.*, 327 SE2d 489, cert. denied, 474 US 824 (1985).

Indiana Plaintiffs acquired at a tax sale a tract of land subject to pipeline easements. In a suit against the holders of the easements, plaintiffs argued that the easements were extinguished, since a tax deed passes title that is free and clear of liens and encumbrances. Although a question of first impression in Indiana, the rule in other jurisdictions is that a "prior easement of record survived a tax sale if it was separately assessed and separately taxed." Plaintiffs contended that the taxes paid by defendants on the pipeline were personal property taxes on the pipe itself. *Held:* Since an easement is an estate or interest in real property, the tax paid by defendants was a tax on real property separately assessed. While one tract of land can be taxed to several different owners, the legislature could not have intended that two or more interests in the property should pass by a tax deed where only one owner is delinquent in his tax payments. The tax sale therefore, did not pass the easement to plaintiffs. *Budnick v. Indiana Nat'l Bank*, 333 NE2d 131 (Ct. App. 1975).

Louisiana Plaintiff sought construction of a servitude agreement whereby the use of a deep water well was shared by the owners of three adjoining lots for irrigation purposes. The servitude was created in 1941 as part of a partition agreement. In 1951, the well dried up because of a lowered water table. Soon thereafter, one of the lot owners employed a contractor to redig the well and change the casing. This lot owner now claimed the right to charge the other lot owners for use of the well. *Held:* Redrilling on the same right did not create a new well, but amounted to a continuation of the old servitude, which plaintiff was entitled to use freely, provided he payed the pro rata share of the cost of the well's maintenance. *Vincent v. Meaux*, 325 So. 2d 346 (Ct. App. 1975).

Massachusetts The U.S. government acquired a pipeline easement over plaintiff's land to connect a fuel depot to a fuel oil pier. When the fuel depot land was later sold to a private company, and the oil pier was sold to the Massachusetts Port Authority along with the easement, plaintiff sued to quiet title to his property, arguing that the easement had been extinguished under state law. *Held:* Federal law applies. The federal government's easement was unconditional and perpetual. It did not depend upon the continued use of the pipeline and could be sold by the government. The proposed use recited in the declaration of taking was not a limitation, but a demonstration of the existence of a public use. *Boorstein v. Massachusetts Port Auth.*, 345 NE2d 668 (1976).

New York The board of education commenced action to establish the right of its employees and students to use an abandoned railroad bridge that spanned its property and defendant's. Plaintiffs alleged that for over 20 years its employees and students continuously used the railroad bridge as a means of access. Following negotiations, each party released its rights to the property outside the boundary line without any mention of the bridge. Soon after, defendant blocked its side of the bridge, impeding access to plaintiffs' property. After many unsuccessful attempts to have the obstructions removed, plaintiffs declared that they acquired title by adverse possession or, alternatively, that they had a prescriptive easement across the property. *Held:* The boundary line agreement, by its terms, released any right of plaintiffs to defendant's land. Assuming a valid easement existed, it would have lawfully been terminated by its release to the servient owner. *Board of Educ. v. Ryewood Farms, Ltd.*, 533 NYS2d 988 (1988).

Vermont In a property dispute over spring rights, the owners of the servient estate contended that the dominant estate had no right to use the spring since they did not participate in the cost of the original construction or repairs. *Held:* The dominant estate's right to use the spring was not lost by their failure to share in the expense of construction. The case was remanded for a determination of the contribution which would be required from each party to defray the cost. *Thomas v. Clark*, 346 A2d 189 (1975).

13.90
—Abandonment

Arizona Three companies agreed to establish a joint parking lot across their adjoining parcels. When the owner of Tract C leased his property to a company, which tore up a portion of the parking lot, the owner of Tract B sued for an injunction. The owner of Tract B had put up a sign on its portion of the parking lot limiting parking to its customers. Defendant installed billboards and a minipark on the lot. *Held:* The agreement granted the owner of Tract B a parking easement for the nonexclusive use of its customers, business patrons, and visitors. However, where the only benefit to the owner of Tract B would be to permit the use of the area for auction purposes every nine months, and defendant would be required to remove its billboard and minipark, injunctive relief was denied. The owner of Tract B abandoned its rights and failed to object to defendant's use of the property. *Bayless Inv. & Trading Co. v. Berkins Moving & Storage Co.*, 547 P2d 1065 (Ct. App. 1976).

Maryland County held an easement on part of landowner's property for use as a street, while the landowner retained fee simple title to the bed of the street. When the county sought to condemn part of the land for use as a park, it claimed that the property should be valued subject to the easement. The landowner argued that use of the land as a park was not included in the scope of the easement and that closure of the street established an intent to abandon the easement as a matter of law. The lower court granted the county's motion for summary judgment and the property owner appealed. *Held:* Summary judgment reversed. The question of abandonment is an issue of fact, not law, and therefore is for the trier of fact to decide. *Peck v. Baltimore County*, 410 A2d 7 (1979).

Oregon Defendants granted plaintiffs an easement over their land to a county road. When plaintiffs found another way to reach the road, they rarely used the route over defendants' land. This situation continued for 23 years, and the easement route became impassable. Plaintiffs then announced their intention to repair the route, and brought suit to enforce the easement. *Held:* For plaintiffs. There was no language in the deed of easement evidencing an intent to end the easement once grantees used an alternative means of access, and nonuse alone does not suffice to extinguish an easement. Also, there was no evidence that defendants' use of the easement route was continuous and adverse so as to establish a claim of adverse possession. *Abbott v. Thompson*, 641 P2d 652 (1982).

Pennsylvania Plaintiffs sued to enjoin defendant from maintaining an easement of ingress and egress over their land, contending that the easement had been abandoned. *Held:* While the owners of the dominant tenement erected a gate and a fence between the tracts and defendant made infrequent use of the right-of-way, the easement was not abandoned. Abandonment requires proof of intention to abandon, coupled with either (1) adverse possession by the servient tenement, (2) affirmative acts by the owner rendering the use impossible, or (3) obstruction by the dominant tenement in a manner inconsistent with further use. The easement was therefore not lost through abandonment, nonuse, or adverse possession. *Piper v. Mowris*, 351 A2d 635 (1976).

Pennsylvania Deed to defendants' property contained an easement permitting them to operate a millrace on plaintiff's property in connection with a gristmill that existed on their land until 1948. When defendants sought to reopen the millrace, which had not been used since 1930, plaintiff claimed that the easement had been abandoned. *Held:* The nonuse of the millrace, coupled with the tearing down of the gristmill in 1948, constituted an abandonment of the easement. *Ruffalo v. Walters*, 348 A2d 740 (1975).

13.95
Conveyance to Bona Fide Purchaser Without Notice

U.S. District Court, North Dakota Owners of land subject to a lease granted the United States an easement for waterfowl production purposes. When the lease expired, the lessees purchased the property, with notice of the easement, but then began claiming the land in violation of the easement. The United States sought an injunction, and the purchasers answered that since they had been lessees under a lease executed prior to the granting of the easement, they had prior rights. *Held:* Any prior rights enjoyed by the lessees were extinguished on the expiration of the lease, since the lessees did not purchase the premises under an option to purchase, which, had the lease contained one, would have preserved the lessees' priority. *United States v. Albrecht*, 364 F. Supp. 1349 (1973), aff'd, 496 F2d 906 (8th Cir. 1974).

Massachusetts Attorney for the purchaser of property had seen a registered plan disclosing the existence of an easement and had allowed his client to accept a deed referring to the easement. On appeal, the respondent argued that he was a purchaser in good faith. *Held:* The knowledge of the attorney was properly imputed to the purchaser. Since the purchaser had knowledge of the easement's existence, he was not a purchaser in good faith. *Quinn v. Hintlian*, 346 NE2d 374 (App. Ct. 1976).

Ohio Defendant's predecessor in interest granted an easement to plaintiff's predecessor in interest, but the easement was not recorded. Though both properties changed hands several times, the easement was not recited in any of the deeds. When plaintiff sought to enforce the easement, its purported location was in a ditch, and plaintiff had an alternate route around defendant's land. *Held:* Plaintiff could not enforce the easement, because it was unrecorded. Also, an easement by necessity could not be claimed, since another route existed, and the claimed easement was not even passable. *Tiller v. Hinton,* 482 NE2d 946 (1985).

13.100 Public Trust Easement

U.S. Supreme Court Plaintiff's title to California tidal land was based on a nineteenth century patent issued by the federal government, which confirmed a land grant made by the Mexican government before the acquisition of California. Defendant municipality wished to make extensive use of the land for water engineering projects and claimed it had a public trust easement in the land, based on the state's claim to have acquired a public trust easement in all tidal land when it entered the Union. *Held:* Defendant municipality had no easement. The easement claimed by the municipality would so far derogate plaintiff's fee interest that it could not survive the patent proceedings. It had to have been presented to the federal patent commission in the last century or be barred. *Summa Corp. v. California ex rel. State Lands Comm'n*, 466 US 198 (1984).

Massachusetts Plaintiff granted the state a conservation easement in her land restricting its development but reserved the right to the use of a single-family residence on the property. She contested the tax assessment of her land at full value. *Held:* The easement did not reduce the value of the land, because it was unenforceable. Plaintiff's exception for the use of a single-family residence failed to state what part of the land could be used for this purpose. Grantors of conservation easements must identify a parcel of land, separate from the house, that is subject to development restrictions. *Parkinson v. Board of Assessors*, 481 NE2d 491 (1985).

14.00 LICENSES

14.05 Nature and Incidents

Georgia Landowner sued to enjoin defendants from using a road across her property that she contended had been constructed by defendants without her knowledge or consent. Defendants stated that they enjoyed a parol license to use the road and had expanded and improved the road in reliance on the license. *Held:* The evidence supported the lower court's finding that there was an express grant of a license to defendant. Furthermore, under state law (Ga. Code § 85-1404), an executed parol license may support an equitable estoppel where expense has been incurred. *Jordan v. Coalson*, 219 SE2d 439 (1975).

Minnesota Village ordinance prohibited persons from dwelling in trailers for periods longer than three days unless they applied for and obtained a permit. A permit issued to a mobile home owner limited the location of the mobile home on the property to a period not to exceed five years. On expiration of the five-year period, village council refused to renew the permit and failed to specify the reasons for its decision. The homeowner sued to obtain a permit. *Held:* A permit, specifying time limitation, is in the nature of a contract and automatically terminates at the expiration of the contract period. There exists no property right to an extension, and it is not necessary for the council to give its reasons for its decision of nonrenewal. *Paal v. Village of Wells*, 232 NW2d 808 (1975).

Vermont Landowner was granted a license permitting the construction of wires over an adjacent landowner's property. In 1969, the parties executed a lease, which provided that for consideration of one dollar, the wires would remain on the property. The rent was never paid, and the adjacent landowner advised the lessee that unless the amount due was paid, the wires would be removed. The lessee sued to obtain an injunction to prohibit the lessor from interfering with the wires. *Held:* The lessee had no right to an injunction on the basis of the license, because the license was terminated by the lease. The lease was not invalid for lack of consideration, since the lessee failed to pay the consideration required. *Carbonneau v. Lague, Inc.*, 352 A2d 694 (1976).

14.10 Termination

District of Columbia A gift shop operated a shop in a hotel lobby under an agreement, labeled a "license" agreement. When the ownership of the hotel changed, the agreement with the gift shop was terminated. The gift shop sued to maintain possession. *Held:* The gift shop was not entitled to continued possession. The agreement was a license rather than a lease. It did not grant the shop an estate in property, nor did it provide for specific space in the hotel. Therefore, the agreement was revocable. *Union Travel Ass'n v. International Assocs.*, 401 A2d 105 (1979).

Maryland Construction company was licensed by a landowner to remove sand and gravel. The license agreement contained no remedy provisions in the event of a default. When the licensee defaulted on payments due under the agreement, the landowner sought injunctive relief, which would, in essence, have forfeited the agreement. *Held:* The payments due under the license were technically royalties. In the absence of an express provision empowering a lessor or royalty owner to declare a forfeiture, a court will not enforce a forfeiture for the nonpayment of royalties. *Ammendale Normal Inst., Inc. v. Schrom Constr. Co.*, 288 A2d 140 (1972).

Ohio Grocery store demanded that customer leave its premises after he was observed making written notations of prices for certain goods. *Held:* A customer is a licensee whose license may be revoked at will. When such a license is revoked, the customer becomes a trespasser and the owner of property may thereafter cause him to leave the premises. *Mosher v. Cook United, Inc.*, 405 NE2d 720 (1980).

South Dakota A railroad granted property to plaintiff via a quitclaim deed in which railroad retained for itself the right to license its rights with respect to electric transmission lines across the property. Defendant subsequently purchased the electric transmission lines from the party who was then the licensee. At this time, railroad terminated the license it had issued to the licensee and issued a new license agreement to defendant. Plaintiff then sent defendant a notice of revocation of license and demanded that the electric transmission lines be removed from the property. When defendant refused to remove the lines, plaintiff brought suit for injunctive relief and damages. *Held:* The effect of the reservation clause in the quitclaim deed to plaintiff was to retain in railroad its right to license its rights in the electric transmission lines. Termination of the license after defendant purchased the lines vested no new rights in landowner, and defendant was properly granted a license by railroad. *Ellwein v. City of Watertown*, 315 NW2d 693 (1982).

PART C
LANDLORD AND TENANT

15.00
TENANCY BY LEASE

15.05
Creation

Georgia In 1980, an oil company "leased" a tract of land from landowner for 10 years. Under the lease agreement, landowner was to retain possession, use, and responsibility for maintenance of the property, which included a service station and a grocery store. In return, the lease agreement required landowner to purchase gasoline exclusively from the oil company. Landowner sold the property in 1981. When purchaser began obtaining gasoline from an independent distributor, the oil company brought action seeking damages for breach of the lease agreement. The trial court awarded damages to the oil company, and purchaser appealed. *Held:* Reversed in favor of purchaser. The court of appeals found that despite its denomination as a lease, the agreement between landowner and oil company constituted neither a lease nor a covenant running with the land; therefore, it was not binding upon purchaser. *Halley v. Harden Oil Co.*, 357 SE2d 138 (1987).

Massachusetts Lessor and lessee held discussions regarding possible modifications to a long term lease. These discussions resulted in a letter of intent. When lessor subsequently sued to recover possession, the lessor used the rights it would acquire under the terms of the letter as a defense. *Held:* The letter of intent was not an operative document, but merely a memorandum contemplating the execution of other documents, such as a lease. Because the letter was written in the future tense, the court determined the parties had intended the letter to serve as an outline for future action rather than a binding agreement. *Mendel Keen, Inc. v. Workshop, Inc.*, 508 NE2d 853 (1987).

New Hampshire After title passed, seller of house remained on the property despite buyer's demand to vacate. When seller was away, buyer entered the house without permission, removed seller's property, and changed the locks. Seller brought an action for trespass and for violation of a statute restricting a landlord's rights against a tenant of residential property in the absence of consent or judicial authorization (N.H. Rev. Stat. Ann. § 540-A:3). Buyer claimed the statute did not apply in the case of a tenancy at sufferance. *Held:* The statute was applicable. The provision of the purchase and sale agreement allowing seller to occupy the premises for two days after the closing and title passage was a provision for a two-day lease. The statute was applicable only to tenancies of leased premises and would not have applied in the case of a seller holding over after conveyance and without agreement. Although at common law no action for trespass to land or goods would lie against the landlord who entered and removed the goods of a tenant whose prior tenancy had been converted to a tenancy at sufferance, the statute at issue expressly provided procedures for terminating such tenancies. *Hill v. Dobrowolski*, 484 A2d 1123 (1984).

New Jersey In an action for breach of lease, the tenant alleged that the purported lease did not contain all the essential terms of a lease and therefore was not binding. *Held:* The document purported to be the lease set forth, in substantial detail, the essential elements of a commercial lease as applicable to the premises and the intended use by the tenant. It incorporated the names of the parties, the length of the term, the annual rent, warranties by the landlord, and provisions regarding rent abatement. Despite its lack of provisions for maintenance and insurance, it was clear that the agreement was intended to be a binding lease. *Berg Agency v. Sleepworld-Willingboro, Inc.*, 346 A2d 419 (Super. Ct. App. Div. 1975).

Utah Lessor appealed from an action it had commenced to have a lease declared invalid. The trial judge declared the lease to be voidable and allowed the lessee to stay on as a tenant from year to year. Lessor maintained that the lease was void, and therefore the lessee was a trespasser. *Held:* Where party goes into possession and pays rent under a voidable lease, a landlord-tenant relationship is created, not on terms of the lease, but on terms implied at law. The term that the law necessarily implies is one that will be fair to both parties. Here a tenancy from year to year was suitable. *Thomas J. Peck, Inc. v. Lee Rock Prods., Inc.*, 515 P2d 446 (1973).

15.10 Validity of Leases

Georgia Plantiff leased property from defendant under the mistaken belief that defendant was the owner thereof. In fact, defendant was a lessee whose term was set to expire three years before the plaintiff's "lease" ended. *Held:* In plaintiff's suit for breach of contract, sublessee could readily have ascertained when the rights of the sublessor were to expire, and is therefore charged with notice by implication. So much of the sublease as extended beyond the primary lease was without consideration; therefore, no recovery can be made. *Gulden v. Newberry Wrecker Serv.*, 267 SE2d 763 (1980).

Hawaii Lessor sued for breach of a so-called contract to lease based on failure of the lessees to make payments and execute the lease. *Held:* Where the contract to lease named the parties to the agreement, described the property, specified the rent and terms of payments, set forth the duration of the lease, and provided that the lessor would subordinate her fee interest upon certain specified terms and conditions, there was a lease that was sufficiently definite and capable of enforcement. The subordination clause was not so indefinite and uncertain as to render the lease unenforceable. The evidence sustained a finding that the lessor was ready, willing, and able to perform her end of the agreement. *Malani v. Clapp*, 542 P2d 1265 (1975).

Illinois A new owner refused to renew tenant's lease, and the tenant moved to have his correspondence with the previous owner declared a lease. The tenant had sent the previous owner a check for two months' rent and one month's security with a letter stating that acceptance of the check would guarantee the owner's issuing a three-year lease on the premises commencing immediately at a stated rent. The tenant's letter also contained terms for renewal options and a purchase option. The previous owner acknowledged receipt of the check and replied that tenant's terms were accepted with the consideration of tenant's first check and subsequent monthly payments, and that an executed lease would be forthcoming. *Held:* The correspondence was a lease. It contained the essential elements: a definite agreement as to the extent of the property, a definite term, price of rental, time and manner of payment, and intention of the parties that it constitute a lease. *Feeley v. Michigan Ave. Nat'l Bank*, 490 NE2d 15 (App. Ct. 1986).

Indiana Tenants who had signed a lease for an apartment decided, prior to moving in, not to take possession and to sublet the premises. Tenants then noticed several defects and requested a city inspection. The inspector found that the landlord was in violation of the municipal code for maintaining a rental unit without an occupancy permit. Believing they could not legally find a sublessee and that their lease was void, tenants informed landlord they would no longer assume responsibility for subleasing the apartment. Landlord sued tenants for rent and damages. *Held:* For tenants; the lease was unenforceable because it violated the municipal code. A contract made in violation of a statute is void. Landlord should not be permitted to continue to rent substandard housing with another individual as subtenant. *Noble v. Alis*, 474 NE2d 109 (Ct. App. 1985).

Mississippi Taxpayers sued the county board of supervisors to set aside a lease of sixteenth section school lands at an allegedly grossly inadequate rate. The taxpayers had reported the matter to the attorney general, the district attorney, and the county attorney, but no action had been taken. The board alleged that the taxpayers lacked standing to bring the suit. *Held:* Sixteenth section school lands were held in trust by the state for school purposes administered by the county supervisors as a public trust. Since the state refused to take official action, taxpayers had standing to sue. *Keys v. Carter*, 318 So. 2d 862 (1975).

New York A property owner conducted extensive negotiations for the leasing of its property as a parking lot. After an agreement was reached, the owner drafted and signed an instrument, but did not deliver it to the prospective lessee. When the owner leased to a third party, the prospective lessee sued for specific performance or, alternatively, for money damages for the alleged breach. *Held:* The prospective lessee was not entitled to recovery. Delivery of the lease was required to make it effective; the drafting and signing of an agreement did not validate it. *219 Broadway Corp. v. Alexander's, Inc.*, 387 NE2d 1205 (1979).

New York An owner of a service station leased the premises to himself. The subtenant occupied the premises and paid rent to the landlord-tenant, who deposited the payments into his personal bank account. Upon expiration of the lease with himself, the owner attempted to recover possession of the service station from the subtenant. *Held:* For the subtenant. The court ruled that one person cannot be both landlord and tenant, that is, an individual cannot contract with himself or lease space to himself. If there is a merger of tenant and landlord, the tenancy is "extinguished" by the interest of the owner. Thus, the lease that the owner supposedly drew up with himself was invalid. In addition, there was a clear intention on the part of both the owner-landlord and the subtenant to lease the space to the latter, and the subtenant did in fact occupy the premises and pay rent to the alleged "tenant." *Schmaeling v. Schmaeling*, 487 NYS2d 494 (Dist. Ct. 1985).

Texas Defendant executed a "Lease and Operating Agreement" that provided that defendant would install a self-service gasoline operation on the premises of a convenience store owned by "lessors." In return, lessors would exclusively sell defendant's gas in exchnge for a percentage of sales and a fixed monthly "rent." Plaintiff bought the store from lessors and sought to enter into an agreement with another gas distributor. When defendant objected, plaintiff sought a declaratory judgment stating that the original agreement was a personal contract binding only upon its signatories, and not a lease. *Held:* The contract was not a lease. It contained no granting clause that would indicate that the oil company intended to transfer interest in, and possession of, property. A lease is created only if there is language indicating that one party intends to dispossess himself of the premises and the other party to occupy them. *Vallejo v. Pioneer Oil Co.*, 744 SW2d 12 (1988).

16.00 EXISTENCE OF LANDLORD–TENANT RELATIONSHIP

16.05 In General

Iowa Farm employee was injured in a gas explosion in the house on the farm where he lived incident to his employment. He sued the farm owner, relying in part on Iowa's landlord-tenant act. *Held:* Plaintiff's claim under the landlord-tenant act was rejected because plaintiff had no rental agreement with farm owner; his agreement was with the partnership that employed him. *Poyzer v. McGraw*, 360 NW2d 748 (1985).

Oregon Pursuant to use agreements with the port, individuals used storage units in a building owned by the port to store boats. The county sought to tax these storage units, relying on a statutory provision that deemed port property held under a lease to be taxable, unless used for berthing ships. The port contended that the use agreements gave merely a nonpossessory license, not a leasehold, citing restrictions in the agreements prohibiting commercial use and giving the port free access to the units for inspection. *Held:* The use agreements were taxable as leases. The agreements contained the three elements of a lease: description of property, duration of term, and consideration. They also provided that either party must give 30 days' notice of termination. A license, unlike a lease, was generally terminable at will without notice. Since the agreements granted sufficient control over the premises to fulfill the requirement of possession, the restrictions cited by the port were insufficient to reduce users' interests in the storage units to a nonpossessory license. *Port of Coos Bay v. Department of Revenue*, 691 P2d 100 (1984) (en banc).

16.10 Promise to Lease

5th Circuit Agent for a company seeking office space orally agreed with landlord to rent space, and landlord promised to hold the space until a lease could be signed. After some months, agent's new superior decided against renting the property, and landlord could not rent the space in a changed market. Landlord sued. *Held:* Landlord did not have an enforceable contract, but he succeeded under claims of detrimental reliance and respondeat superior. Though the agent clearly did not have the authority to bind his company himself, the company's preparations to move in made it reasonable to believe it would sign the lease. *Breaux v. Schlumberger Offshore Servs.*, 817 F2d 1226 (1987).

Massachusetts A prospective tenant signed a lease with an agent to rent office space in a building owned by the landlord. At that time, the agent told the tenant that a deal would be made when the tenant signed the lease, and that the lease would then be forwarded to the landlord for a countersignature. One month before the proposed commencement of the lease period, the agent informed the tenant that the deal would not be completed. The potential tenant sued the landlord for damages. *Held:* For the tenant. The agent's assurance to the prospective tenant that the necessary countersignature would be provided constituted a guaranty that the transaction would be authorized by the landlord. The landlord and his agent gave the tenant reasonable assurance that a deal would be made; therefore, the landlord was liable for compensatory and punitive damages suffered by the tenant as a result of the breach. *Greenstein v. Flatley*, 474 NE2d 1130 (App. Ct. 1985).

Missouri Owner of land along highway signed a lease with a billboard company that was not enforceable unless the company signed an acceptance. On February 10, the company erected a sign before it had signed the acceptance. Landowner informed the company it needed an immediate decision, but the company said it would decide by February 15. The company signed the acceptance on February 13. That same day, landowner entered into a lease with a competitor, and sent the company written revocation. The company did not inform landowner of its acceptance until February 14. The company sued to enforce the lease. *Held:* For landowner. The company failed to exercise reasonable diligence to notify landowner of its acceptance of the contract before the revocation. Landowner was not estopped from revoking its offer because the company erected a sign in reliance on landowner's agreement to hold the offer open, as the company alleged. Landowner did not induce the company's performance by any such promise. *National Advertising Co. v. Herold*, 735 SW2d 74 (Ct. App. 1987).

17.00 STATUTE OF FRAUDS

17.05 Requirements

Georgia Tenant occupied the landlord's premises, allegedly under an oral five-year lease. The tenant submitted a written draft to the landlord, who disagreed with every material term and demanded revisions, but no lease was ever executed. After five months, the tenant gave notice and moved out. The landlord brought suit for specific performance or damages, and the tenant raised the Statute of Frauds as a defense. The landlord contended that the tenant's occupancy and payment of rent was sufficient past performance to take the lease out of the Statute of Frauds. *Held:* A prerequisite to invoking the past performance exception to the Statute of Frauds is an oral contract sufficiently definite and certain in all essential particulars to render it enforceable. Here the parties did not agree on any terms. *Smith v. Top Dollar Stores, Inc.*, 198 SE2d 690 (1973).

Missouri Tenants brought an action against a landlord for return of a security deposit. The tenants contended that the landlord had orally released them from the last month of their 12-month lease. The landlord maintained the alleged oral termination was ineffective, and therefore he was entitled to apply the deposit to the last month's rent. Although the lease ran for one year, it was executed two weeks before the commencement of the term. *Held:* The court found the lease to be for more than a year and subject to the Statute of Frauds. Although the traditional rule is that a lease subject to the Statute of Frauds could not be modified orally, the court adopted the "modern trend," holding that an executory oral agreement of recission is sufficient to terminate an agreement within the Statute of Frauds so long as the unexpired term of the lease is less than that required by the statute to be in writing. *Gee v. Neiberg*, 501 SW2d 542 (1973).

New York Plaintiff claimed that he and defendant orally agreed that defendant would lease plaintiff's building after plaintiff renovated it. Defendant, however, never signed a lease and never occupied the building. Meanwhile, plaintiff spent $400,000 in improvements in reliance on the oral agreement. Plaintiff sued to recover the value of the work under a theory of quantum meruit. *Held:* The cause of action was not barred by the Statute of Frauds, because it was not an attempt to enforce an oral lease or an oral agreement to enter into a lease. Instead, it was an acknowledgement that no actual contract existed and a request to enforce a contract implied in law to compensate plaintiff for expenditures made in reliance on defendant's representations. *Farash v. Sykes Datatronics, Inc.*, 452 NE2d 1245 (1983).

17.10
Admissibility of Parol Evidence

Minnesota Plaintiffs signed a lease for shop space in which they promised to keep "said premises" in compliance with applicable codes. They sued the landlord when code violations made the building unusable, claiming that the landlord had promised to bring the building into compliance. *Held:* The term "said premises" in the lease was ambiguous, and so parol evidence would be admissible to determine the intentions of the parties with respect to responsibility for repair. *Nord v. Herreid*, 305 NW2d 337 (1981).

18.00
TENANCY FOR YEARS

18.05
Creation

North Carolina The city was a tenant under a 10-year lease containing an option to purchase premises used for metered parking. At the end of the term, the city decided not to exercise the option and instead negotiated for a lower price. While the negotiations continued after the term expired, the city "bagged" the meters and exercised no control over the property, although it continued to pay rent until the negotiations collapsed and the meters were removed, seven months after the expiration of the term. The property owners then brought suit for five more months rent, contending that by its holding over, the city had created a tenancy from year to year. *Held:* When a tenant holds over after the expiration of the term of an estate for years, a presumption of a tenancy from year to year arises. However, that presumption is rebuttable by a contrary showing of the intent of the parties. Here the evidence supported a finding that the city did not intend to create a tenancy from year to year. *Gurtis v. City of Sanford*, 197 SE2d 584 (1973).

18.10
Termination

New York Defendants who, subject to a lease, purchased property that had been severely damaged by fire, gave notice to lessee, who had vacated the premises owing to the damage, that his lease was terminated pursuant to the terms of the lease because the premises had been found untenantable because of destruction by fire. Tenant commenced an action for a declaration, inter alia, that he had a valid and existing lease. *Held:* Upon the sale of the building, the terms of the lease inured to the benefit of the purchasers, who became landlords. Nothing in the language of the lease indicated that the right of termination incorporated therein was intended to be limited. *Jim, Jack & Joe Realty Corp. v. Rothenburg*, 432 NYS2d 110 (1980).

Wisconsin Lease provided that the lessee could terminate "at any time after the first nine months of the term, by giving lessor not less than two (2) months notice." At the end of seven months, the lessee gave two months notice. The lessor asserted that this was an improper termination, as the lease required the lessee to wait nine months before attempting termination. *Held:* "After . . . nine months" is definitive of the word "term," not "notice." The clause vests an absolute right in the lessee to limit the term to nine months. *International Trading Co. v. JC Penney Co.*, 173 NW2d 680 (1970).

18.15
—Under Reserved Power

Delaware An oil company, as tenant, reserved the right to terminate a lease, contingent on either its failure to obtain acceptable licenses or permits within a reasonable time, or the taking of appeals against the granting of such licenses or permits. However, when the oil company had obtained all necessary licenses and permits and notified the landlord of its desire to proceed with the lease, the landlord refused. The oil company sought specific performance, to which the landlord answered that the promises of the oil company under an executory lease were illusory due to the termination clause and, therefore, the agreement was unenforceable for lack of mutuality. *Held:* Regardless of whether the promises of the oil company were illusory under the executory agreement (which the court held they were not), the oil company had obtained the permits without appeals against it, so the contingencies under which the lease could be terminated could no longer arise, and the conditional promise became absolute. *Mobil Oil Co. v. Wroten*, 303 A2d 698 (Ch. 1973), aff'd, 315 A2d 728 (1974).

18.20
—By Rescission

9th Circuit Landlords and tenant signed a commercial lease in 1969 containing two 5-year options to renew, with the rent during the option periods tied to property taxes. At the time the lease was entered into, property taxes were based on fair market value, which had been increasing. However, the passage of Proposition 13 in 1978 limited tax increases on real property, so that property taxes did rise with the value of the leased premises, as landlords had expected. When tenant notified landlords it was exercising its first option to renew, landlords decided to rescind the lease, claiming that Proposition 13 frustrated the contract and excused their performance. *Held:* Landlords' performance was not excused under the doctrine of frustration. Application of the doctrine in California was limited to cases of extreme hardship. Although landlords would receive less profit than anticipated, the difference was not so great as to render performance of the lease extremely impracticable. *Waegemann v. Montgomery Ward & Co.*, 713 F2d 452 (1983).

18.25
—By Abandonment

Texas Landlord filed suit against tenant, a dentist, alleging abandonment of the leasehold and nonpayment of rent, and seeking recovery of past and future rents due under the lease. Tenant cross-claimed for loss of business revenues, and argued that the premises were not habitable. *Held:* Since landlord had sent a notice to quit the property and had filed an eviction action, the lease had been terminated by the landlord, and no claim for future rents could be maintained under an abandonment theory. *Fidelity Management Co. v. Herod*, 600 SW2d 380 (Civ. App. 1980).

19.00 PERIODIC TENANCY

19.05 Creation

North Carolina Tenant, satisfied with the terms of an oral lease offered by landlord, took possession of the property. When landlord presented tenant with a written lease that varied from the oral agreement, tenant refused to sign it. However, tenant continued to occupy the premises and pay rent, which was accepted by the landlord. The pollution from landlord's nearby plant caused tenant to abandon the premises. Tenant then sued landlord for damages arising from constructive eviction and nuisance. Landlord argued that because oral leases were void in North Carolina, tenant was merely a tenant at will subject to eviction at any time. *Held:* Tenant had a cause of action in nuisance and constructive eviction because he was more than a tenant at will. When a tenant takes possession under an invalid lease and pays rent that the landlord accepts, he becomes a periodic tenant. The periodic tenancy in this case was held to be a month-to-month tenancy. *Kent v. Humphries*, 281 SE2d 43 (1981).

20.00 TENANCY AT WILL

20.05 Creation

Connecticut Plaintiff occupied a room in defendant's hotel for three months and never signed a lease. After defendant changed the locks to the room, plaintiff sued for forcible entry and detainer. *Held:* For defendant. Plaintiff was a transient occupant of a hotel; he was to be treated no differently from other registered guests. The short duration of his occupancy and the rudimentary nature of the accommodations furnished were further indications that only a temporary living arrangement was intended. *Bourque v. Morris*, 460 A2d 1251 (1983).

New York The lease between a homeowner and his tenant provided the tenant with the privilege of termination of the lease agreement at "a date of his own choice." On the homeowner's death, his estate moved to evict the tenant. *Held:* For the tenant. Homeowner's estate could not evict the tenant at will. The lease created a life tenancy terminable at the will of the tenant by expressly and unambiguously granting him the right to terminate at the date of his choice, without reserving a similar right to landlord. *Garner v. Gerrish*, 473 NE2d 223 (1984).

Texas Landlord leased tenant a tract of land for a 20-year term. The lease also provided for a term "so long thereafter" as the lessee, his heirs, successors or assigns used the land to operate equipment for processing natural gas and petroleum. Tenant and his son complied with the terms of the lease. Several years after the 20-year term expired, landlord sued to terminate the lease on the ground that the "so long thereafter" provision made the lease indefinite and created a tenancy at will terminable by either party at any time. *Held:* The lease did not create a tenancy at will; the parties intended to create a perpetual right to lease the land. Despite the lack of a termination date, the lease would end on the date tenant ceased to use the land as specified. *Philpot v. Fields*, 633 SW2d 546 (Ct. App. 1982).

West Virginia Landlord sued to void a 15-year lease for a two-car garage on the ground that a termination provision by tenant on 30 days' notice annulled the lease and created a tenancy at will. *Held:* The lease's provisions were proper and were not the subject of objection. An option of tenant to terminate the lease upon 30 days' notice to landlord alone does not invalidate the lease or convert it to a tenancy at will. The general rule is that, where a lease is for a definite term of years and complies with the formal requisites of such terms, it creates a tenancy for years and not a mere tenancy at will. *Thomas v. Goodwin*, 226 SE2d 792 (1980).

21.00 TENANCY AT SUFFERANCE

21.05 Nature and Incidents

Georgia A lease provided for no automatic renewal or extension provisions, but instead stipulated that should the landlord acquiesce in the tenant's remaining on the property after the expiration of the term, the tenant would be a tenant at will. When the lease expired, the landlord leased to another and gave notice of this new lease to the tenant, requesting that he leave. When the tenant refused, the landlord brought a summary dispossess action. The tenant maintained that the action was not brought because he was not given notice as required for tenants at will. *Held:* The tenant would be a tenant at will only if landlord acquiesced in his continued occupancy. Since the landlord did not acquiesce, but insisted he remove himself, the tenant was merely a tenant at sufferance and not entitled to notice. *Wilson v. Lee*, 200 SE2d 480 (1973).

Massachusetts Plaintiff purchased an apartment building occupied by defendants as tenants at will of the former owner. Plaintiff notified defendants that they could remain at a higher rental or vacate. None of defendants agreed to the higher rental, and plaintiff initiated action for possession. Defendants contended that the notice was insufficient to terminate their tenancies. *Held:* When the reversion was sold, all tenants at will became tenants at sufferance of the new owner. By common law, such a tenant was entitled to no notice at all. By statute (Mass. Gen. L. ch. 186, § 13), however, when, as here, a tenancy at will is terminated by operation of law, a new owner may not recover possession "until after the expiration of a period, equal to the interval between the days on which the rent reserved is payable, from the time when the tenant receives notice in writing of such termination." The letter to the tenants informing them of the new landlord was sufficient notice of termination of the tenancy at will by operation of law and, since the statutory period had elapsed when this action was filed, no other notice was required. *Rubin v. Prescott*, 289 NE2d 902 (1972).

22.00 PUBLIC HOUSING

22.05 In General

1st Circuit The Department of Housing and Urban Development (HUD) became mortgagee in possession of an apartment building after the owner defaulted on the HUD-insured mortgage. The building was in poor repair and in violation of the local building code. HUD made some repairs, but did not take care of all the problems. One of the tenants, who had left the property, sued HUD for damages or restitution of rental payments, alleging that HUD failed to maintain her apartment in habitable condition. *Held:* The tenant could obtain restitution of rent paid during the period that HUD breached its obligation to maintain her apartment in habitable condition. The National Housing Act, which governed public housing issues, required HUD to take reasonable steps to maintain housing projects. *Conille v. Secretary of Hous. & Urban Dev.*, 840 F2d 105 (1988).

22.10 Entitlement

U.S. Supreme Court The Brooke Amendment to the Housing Act of 1937 provided that a low income family living in a federal housing project shall pay as rent a specified percentage of its income. HUD included as rent a reasonable amount for utilities, and issued regulations to that effect. Tenants brought a civil rights suit under 42 USC § 1983 against the local housing authority, alleging failure to comply with these regulations. They claimed the authority overcharged them for utilities, and violated the rent ceiling imposed by the Brooke Amendment. *Held:* For tenants. The legislative history of the Brooke Amendment indicated that private causes of action were permitted. Further, the provision calling for a "reasonable" allowance for utilities was not too vague to confer on tenants an enforceable right under 42 USC § 1983. *Wright v. City of Roanoke Redevelopment & Hous. Auth.*, 479 US 418 (1987).

6th Circuit Although a tenant had left a public housing unit owing rent, the housing commission granted her application for a certificate of family participation, which allowed her to obtain Section 8 benefits. The tenant later received a notice to quit for reasons other than nonpayment of rent. When the tenant again applied for a certificate to enable her to seek Section 8 housing elsewhere, the housing commission refused, citing the back rent she owed from the public housing tenancy. *Held:* For the tenant. Under 24 CFR § 882.209(e)(1), a public housing authority is required to issue a new certificate to a family already receiving Section 8 assistance unless the family owes rent under the lease to its current owner. The court distinguished its earlier ruling in *Baker v. Cincinnati Metropolitan Housing Auth.*, 675 F2d 836 (6th Cir. 1982), allowing a public housing authority to deny certificates to new applicants who owe back rent for previous non-Section 8 tenancies in public housing. The cited regulation did not apply to new applicants and currently assisted Section 8 families. *Bakos v. Flint Hous. Comm'n*, 746 F2d 1179 (1984).

7th Circuit Applicants seeking federally subsidized housing under the Section 8 program were denied housing based on unfavorable reports from previous landlords. Applicants sued, claiming that the lack of admission standards, procedural rights, and opportunity for a hearing in the Section 8 program violated their due process rights. *Held:* Applicants did not have a protected property interest in receiving Section 8 benefits. Section 8 is not an entitlement program, but involves the allocation of limited and valuable benefits among a large pool of eligible applicants. An applicant becomes entitled, as opposed to eligible, to Section 8 only after a private owner accepts its application. Further, the class of eligible applicants would not benefit from a costly and elaborate hearing procedure. *Eidson v. Pierce*, 745 F2d 453 (1984).

23.00 TENANT'S DUTY TO PAY RENT

23.05 In General

6th Circuit Plaintiff landlord leased industrial property to a manufacturing corporation on a long-term lease. After one year, the lessee was merged into another corporation, a wholly owned subsidiary of defendant. Defendant later dissolved its subsidiary and sold all assets, including the leasehold, to another corporation, which subsequently defaulted on the rentals. Landlord sued defendant, arguing that as parent and sole shareholder of the dissolved subsidiary, it was secondarily liable for the rent. *Held:* For plaintiff. Where a lease is treated as an asset of a dissolved corporation (as opposed to a case in which the lease is merely abandoned) and where it is assigned to a third party in liquidation, the shareholders of the dissolved corporation remain liable under the lease. In addition, the court found that equity was best served by "piercing the corporate veil" in cases involving several successively controlled entities, even though the parent corporation was never in actual possession. *Middendorf v. Fuqua Indus., Inc.*, 623 F2d 13 (1980).

Florida Tenant and landlord entered a five-year lease for a restaurant. For four years, portions of the restaurant were flooded after heavy rains because of leaks. During the fourth year, the tenant withheld rent payments, and then abandoned the premises early in the fifth year. The landlord then sued for the unpaid rent. *Held:* The landlord was entitled to the unpaid rent. The tenant's failure to abandon the premises for four years vitiated any privilege he may have had to abandon the premises as uninhabitable. *Bass v. Wollitz*, 384 So. 2d 704 (1980).

Georgia During a disagreement between a landlord and tenant over the expiration date of a commercial lease, the tenant mailed a check for the current month's rent bearing the notation "payment in full." The landlord informed the tenant that the payment was unacceptable. Three months later, he obliterated the notation and negotiated the check. In a suit for recovery of rent due, the court found an accord and satisfaction, entering judgment for the tenant. The landlord appealed. *Held:* The court was correct in finding an accord and satisfaction had been reached. In such circumstances, the landlord must either accept the condition or reject the check outright. He cannot accept the proceeds under protest and argue that the check was only partial payment. Nor may he modify the effect of his acceptance by striking out "payment in full" before indorsing the check. In this case, negotiating the check was tantamount to acceptance of the tenant's "payment in full" condition. *Alston v. Insured Credit Serv., Inc.*, 237 SE2d 680 (1977).

Hawaii The tenant leased two parcels of land from the landlord with rent to be agreed upon at 10-year intervals. However, in the event they could not agree, the lease provided that the annual rent would be based on a formula derived from the market value of the land as determined by appraisers selected by the parties. After a failure to agree on rent, appraisers were chosen and determined a rent based on the "highest and best use" of the land. Then tenant objected, arguing that the market value should be based on the actual use of the land rather than the highest and best use. When the tenant refused to pay the rent, the landlord sued for eviction. *Held:* The landlord is entitled to collect the rent determined by the appraisers. When the parties agreed to submit any dispute to the appraisers, they were bound to the result unless fraud or plain error could be shown. *Loyalty Dev. Co. v. Wholesale Motors, Inc.*, 605 P2d 925 (1980).

Maryland At tenant's request, landlord performed work on rented commercial property and submitted a bill for $2,983. When tenant failed to pay the bill, the landlord moved to evict for failure to pay "additional rent." Tenant claimed the charge was not rent and thus he was not subject to eviction. *Held:* For the landlord. In reaching its conclusion, the court examined a provision in the lease entitling the landlord to "additional rent" for "all other sums of money or charges required to be paid by Tenant under the lease, whether or not the same be designated 'additional rent.'" Another provision required tenant to pay landlord within 20 days for "all other work" that landlord might do on the premises. *University Plaza Shopping Center, Inc. v. Garcia*, 367 A2d 957 (1977).

Minnesota A commercial lease called for lessee to pay a pro rata share of real estate taxes above the 1976 base level, based on lessee's share of building space. The terms of the lease specifically referred to real estate taxes "levied against the property" and provided that the payments due from lessee because of additional real estate taxes would be divided by 12 and paid monthly along with regular rents. The lease also called for a retroactive adjustment if taxes were not assessed by January 1. A dispute arose as to taxes levied in 1981, but not payable until 1982. The lease had terminated in February of 1982. *Held:* When a tenant agrees to pay taxes *levied* during a lease, the tenant is obligated to pay those taxes imposed during the term of the lease, even though the taxes are not due and payable until expiration of the lease term. *Columbia Assocs. v. Propper Oil Co.*, 402 NW2d 223 (Ct. App. 1987).

Ohio Landlord and tenant entered into a one-year written lease ending March 31, 1986. In January 1986, landlord gave tenant three days' notice to vacate premises for nonpayment of rent. Tenant moved from the premises at the end of January without paying that month's rent or the rent on the remaining two months of the lease. The landlord rented the apartment in March, and sued to recover rent for January and February. *Held:* A landlord's election to evict a tenant for nonpayment of rent did not relieve the tenant of future obligations to pay rent under the lease, or until a new tenant was found, whichever came first. *Briggs v. MacSwain*, 508 NE2d 1028 (1986).

South Carolina A commercial tenant leased a parcel described in the lease as a "theater lot" and built a movie theater there. The lease obligated landlord to make a parking area available to tenant without further charge, with tenant responsible for its paving and maintenance. Tenant was also required to pay taxes "upon the leased premises and improvements thereon." Landlord maintained that tenant had to pay taxes on the parking lot. *Held:* For tenant. The parking lot was not part of the leased premises. Tenant paid rent under the lease for the theater lot only; access to the parking area was at no extra charge. The fact that tenant made improvements and was responsible for repairs did not convert the parking area into leased premises. The provision of the lease governing payment of taxes did not include appurtenances such as the parking area. *Litchfield Co. v. Kiriakides*, 349 SE2d 344 (Ct. App. 1986).

South Dakota A lessee attempted to make an "in kind" payment to the lessor of 11 cows in lieu of cash. The lessor refused to accept this type of payment, and the lessee brought suit. *Held:* For the lessor. The Supreme Court of South Dakota ruled that the 11 cows did not constitute a cash payment as required by the terms of the lease, but were merely a promissory note to serve as collateral until a proper payment was made. In addition, the Court held that the lessee's failure to tender cash constituted a breach of the lease, and was grounds for him to lose occupancy of the premises. *Dale v. Pelton*, 365 NW2d 1 (1985).

Texas Decedent left her house equally to two sons. Plaintiff sued his brother for rent for the time he lived in the house after their mother's death. *Held:* For plaintiff. Defendant had contended the debts were barred by the statute of limitations. However, the evidence showed that defendant orally agreed to repay the debts. If a promise to repay is made before an action on the debt is barred by the statute of limitations, a valid contract is created that will support the creditor after the original limitations period has expired. Defendant admitted he had agreed to pay half the fair market rental value of the home, but claimed that he did so merely to keep his brother from badgering him, and had no intention of actually paying. Nonetheless, the meaning reasonably conveyed by the parties, rather than their uncommunicated subjective intention, controlled whether a contract has been formed. Defendant's words, rather than his intentions, were controlling. In addition, defendant's argument that the agreement lacked consideration because the brothers were tenants in common was found without merit, because defendant's occupancy was exclusive, rather than shared. *Fuqua v. Fuqua*, 750 SW2d 238 (Ct. App. 1988).

23.10
—Rent Increases

U.S. District Court, Maryland Tenants in a federally assisted, private housing project sued their landlords for increasing their rent without giving them notice and an opportunity to be heard. The tenants alleged that their constitutional rights to due process and equal protection were violated. *Held:* Tenants in federally assisted projects have no property rights in, or entitlement to, occupancy of their premises at a fixed rent. They therefore have no right to notice and a hearing before their rents are increased or the terms of their leases changed. *Fenner v. Bruce Manor, Inc.*, 409 F. Supp. 1332 (1976).

U.S. District Court, New York Lessor sued his lessee, the U.S. Postal Service, to adjust the rental to reflect monetary inflation. The lease agreement was for a 10-year term and gave the tenant the option to renew four times for five-year periods at moderate rental increases. The lessor claimed that the lessee, the federal government, had caused the inflation. *Held:* Reformation of a contract is available only when the express language fails to reflect the agreement. Since the lessor did not claim that the expressed contract did not reflect their agreement, and since inflation was not a ground for escape from the contract terms, the lessor was not entitled to relief, even if the lessee's policies caused the inflation. *Brubrad Co. v. United States Postal Serv.*, 404 F. Supp.

691 (ED 1975), aff'd, 538 F2d 308 (2d Cir. 1976).

Alabama A 51-year ground lease provided for rent from the twenty-first year through the twenty-fifth year at a fixed rate or equal to "30 percent of the value of the leased premises as determined by an appraisal." An appraisal was made that did not take into account the existence of the lease. Tenants sued for a declaratory judgment, seeking to have the lease taken into account in valuing the property. *Held:* The lease should not be considered in valuing the premises. Since the lease was ambiguous and there was no parol evidence as to the parties' intent, the court turned to case law, finding that cases from other jurisdictions supported the contention that the lease should not be considered. In addition, the parties originally bargained with respect to unimproved land and reasonably expected the appraisal 20 years later to be based on the same. *First Nat'l Bank v. Duckworth*, 502 So. 2d 709 (1987).

Hawaii Landlord and tenants were unable to agree on a renewal rent for a long-term lease. An arbitration panel selected in accordance with the lease determined a rental valuation of $720,000. The dissatisfied tenants disrupted the arbitration proceedings, and landlord obtained a court order compelling new arbitration. A redetermination reached the same amount. The court confirmed the valuation, but would not award attorney fees to landlord. Landlord and tenants appealed. *Held:* Affirmed in part, reversed in part. Tenants' disruption of the arbitration proceedings denied the landlord a speedy resolution of the rental determination in breach of the lease. Such a breach triggered a lease provision requiring tenants to pay landlord's legal fees. *Gadd v. Kelley*, 667 P2d 251 (1983).

Louisiana Lessor and lessee agreed that lessee should pay only taxes above the amount paid in 1981. The parties were unaware that a statute had eliminated property taxes in 1971 and reinstated them in 1982, so lessor had paid no taxes in 1981. When lessor received a tax bill in 1983 of $86,000, it sued lessee, seeking reimbursement of the entire amount. *Held:* For lessee. The lease provision requiring lessee to pay increases over the base year amount showed the parties believed that lessor was paying some tax. Since there was a good faith agreement to share the tax burden, equity did not permit the lessor to gain an unfair advantage based on the admitted mutual error. *Falstaff Brewing Corp. v. Consolidated Fibres*, 487 So. 2d 138 (Ct. App. 1986).

Massachusetts Tenant refused to sign a lease that contained a provision that she assume all costs of removing lead paint. Subsequently, landlord sought to increase the rent by $100. Tenant refused to pay; landlord sent her a notice to quit, and commenced a summary process action. Tenant counterclaimed for damages under Mass. Gen. L. ch. 186, § 18 (1986). Section 18 imposes liability on a landlord who takes reprisals against a residential tenant who has sought relief or complained in writing to a landlord concerning a violation of his rights. *Held:* The landlord's act of reprisal after tenant's oral refusal to sign the lease did not justify an award of damages under the statute. The legislature expressly required that a complaint to a landlord be in writing for the landlord's reprisal to be found actionable. *Manzaro v. McCann*, 519 NE2d 1337 (1988).

New Jersey Under tenant's original lease, tenant paid landlord the rent after she received her public assistance check on the third of each month. A new landlord purchased the building, terminated the original lease and offered tenant a new lease with a rent increase. Rent was due on the first of each month, with a $25 penalty if not paid by the fifth of the month. Tenant never executed a new written lease, but remained in possession and paid the increased rent. However, she failed to pay late charges for the months her rent was late. Landlord sought possession for nonpayment of the late charge. *Held:* Tenant could not be evicted. In a dispossess action for nonpayment or late payment of rent, a tenant may raise the defense that the failure to abide by the tenancy's rent payment requirements stemmed from an unreasonable change in the renewal lease. By accepting some of the lease changes imposed by the landlord, tenant did not impliedly accept all changes. Her refusal to pay the late fee constituted a valid refusal to accept the lease change. New Jersey's Anti-Eviction Act limits the eviction of tenants to "reasonable grounds." Landlord's lease change to include a late fee was unreasonable when tenant always made her payment after receiving her assistance check. *447 Assocs. v. Miranda*, 559 A2d 1362 (1989).

Washington Tenants resided in landlord's retirement community under "lifetime leases," which provided that rent increases were to be linked to the cost-of-living index. After rents rose faster than those in local housing markets, tenants threatened to move out. Subsequently, landlord limited increases to a proportion of the annual escalations in the community's operating costs. Within seven years, inflationary pressures caused landlord to reinstate the original formula. He sought to raise rents, via a surcharge, to the level they would have reached had the cost-of-living formula been used for the past seven years. Tenants claimed landlord had waived the right to use the formula and that therefore the surcharge was not authorized under the lease. *Held:* The surcharge was invalid. Landlord had waived both the right to apply the original formula for rents due during the seven-year period and the right to use the rent that might have been charged in one year as the basis for an adjustment in any succeeding year. *Panorama Residential Protective Ass'n v. Panorama Corp.*, 640 P2d 1057 (1982).

23.15
—Holdover Tenants

7th Circuit Tenant spent $2.5 million to build a grain elevator on land it leased. When landlord went bankrupt, the trustee raised the rent from $100 to $6,000 per month, based on the value of the improved property. Tenant refused to pay, but remained on the property and purchased it two months later. Tenant was found liable for the $6,000 rent during the holdover period. Tenant appealed. *Held:* For tenant. Under Iowa law, if the lease authorizes tenant to construct and remove improvements, tenant retains title even to seemingly permanent improvements. Tenant's title to the elevator continued during the holdover period, because the terms of a holdover tenancy are presumed to be the same as under the lease. In various contexts in which tenants have constructed improvements, courts have assessed rent based on the unimproved value of the property. Therefore the holdover rent should have been determined on the basis of the unimproved value of the property. *In re Chicago, Rock Island & Pac. RR*, 753 F2d 56 (1985).

D.C. Circuit Landlord informed tenant, a restaurant, that it intended to terminate its lease under a provision allowing early termination. Tenant, after unsuccessfully seeking a declaratory judgment, vacated the premises. The landlord sued for liquidated damages of triple rent and attorney fees for the tenant's holdover. *Held:* For landlord. The lease specified that valid notice of termination was the only legal predicate necessary for recovery of liquidated damages and costs, and that in the event of a holdover, tenant would be liable for triple rent and legal fees. It was immaterial that tenant believed in good faith that its holdover was valid. The lease did not require a finding of bad faith before liquidated damages could be imposed. *Horn & Hardart Co. v. National Rail Passenger Corp.*, 843 F2d 546 (1988).

Colorado Before the term of the lease was to expire, landlords notified tenants in writing that the monthly rent would be increased from $3,000 to $6,000. Tenants continued to occupy the building without a written lease and paid landlords only $3,000 per month. Landlords sued, claiming that the lease had been renewed with a modified rental. *Held:* For tenants. The lease included a holdover clause limiting the amount of rent in the event of a holdover. The lease also required that all amendments and modifications be in writing. The judgment of the lower court finding the lease had been renewed with an increased rental could not stand unless the provision requiring modifications to be in writing had been waived. *Williams v. Colorado Springs College of Business*, 736 P2d 419 (Ct. App. 1987).

Connecticut Lessor and a commercial tenant signed a lease providing for a five-year term with a perpetual renewal provision. When the tenant refused to vacate after the expiration of the initial term, the landlord sued to recover possession and for damages. The tenant continued to make payments of $175 per month after the expiration of the original term, which was the rental during the term. *Held:* Where the tenant continued in possession wrongfully, it became a tenant at sufferance, whose obligation was to pay the reasonable rental value of the property occupied without the lessor's consent. Damages representing the difference between the fair market rental of the property and the $175 per month were properly awarded. *Lonergan v. Connecticut Food Store, Inc.*, 357 A2d 910 (1975).

Texas Husband and wife leased an apartment. Wife separated from husband and moved out of the apartment without informing landlords. Husband remained in possession of the apartment and held over after the lease expired. Subsequently, wife divorced husband. Landlords brought suit against ex-wife and husband for failing to pay rent during the holdover period and for failing to maintain the premises. Ex-wife argued that she was not obligated to the landlords. *Held:* Ex-wife was liable for unpaid rent accrued during husband's holdover period and damages for failing to maintain the premises. By not notifying landlords that she ceased to hold under the lease, ex-wife failed to rebut the presumption that a holding by husband was also a holding by ex-wife. Landlords' knowledge that she was not occupying the premises during the period of husband's holding over did not overcome the presumption of a joint holding over. Ex-wife's liability was based on her signing the lease, not on her marital status. *Marynick v. Bockelmann*, 773 SW2d 665 (Ct. App. 1989).

23.20 Rent Control and Rent Stabilization

U.S. Supreme Court A landlord group challenged a rent control ordinance enacted by the city that allowed a hearing officer to consider tenant hardship when determining whether to approve a proposed rent increase. The landlords argued that the ordinance was unconstitutional price control, and the objective of alleviating individual tenant hardship was an improper policy for the legislature to adopt in a rent control ordinance. *Held:* For the city. The Court said it would be premature to consider the constitutionality of the tenant hardship clause on the record because there was no evidence the provision had in fact ever been relied upon by a hearing officer to reduce a rent. The ordinance did not require a hearing officer to reduce a proposed rent increase on grounds of tenant hardship. The Court recognized that the protection of consumer welfare, including protection of tenants, was a legitimate and rational goal of price regulation. Within this scheme, the hardship provision was a rational attempt to accommodate the conflicting interests of protecting tenants from rent increases while insuring landlords a fair return on their investments. In light of the Court's conclusion that the ordinance's hardship tenant provisions served a legitimate purpose of protecting tenants, the ordinance did not violate the equal protection clause for treating landlords differently on the basis of whether or not they have hardship tenants. *Pennell v. City of San Jose*, 485 US 1 (1988), aff'g 721 P2d 1111 (1986).

U.S. Supreme Court A landlord group challenged a rent control ordinance, claiming that its rent-setting formula, which was based on a fair return to landlords on their investments rather than on the value of their properties, resulted in an unconstitutional taking, since it failed to account for inflation. The landlord group also argued that the ordinance violated federal antitrust law. The California Supreme Court held that the ordinance was facially constitutional under federal and state due process clauses and did not violate antitrust law. A rent control ordinance was valid if it guaranteed the landlord a fair return on investment; it need not guarantee a fair return on the value of the property. The U.S. Supreme Court agreed to hear an appeal on the antitrust issue. *Held:* The ordinance did not violate federal antitrust law. The rent ceilings were imposed upon landlords by the city. Section 1 of the Sherman Act applies only to unreasonable restraints of trade effected by a "contract, combination . . . or conspiracy" between separate entities. A restraint imposed unilaterally by government is not concerted action. *Fisher v. City of Berkeley*, 475 US 292 (1986), aff'g 693 P2d 261 (Cal. 1984).

D.C. Circuit These two cases were decided in favor of tenants in low-rent public housing who had been overcharged for rent. In determining the amount of equitable relief due to each of the overcharged tenants, the U.S. district court refused to order reprocessing of past rents in either case. The court had also retained an improperly computed rent schedule in one of the cases. The tenants appealed the court's measurement of damages. *Held:* It was within the court's discretion not to order reprocessing of rents to measure damages. However, the record did not support the decision to leave the improperly computed schedule in effect indefinitely. *Thompson v. Washington; Marshall v. Harris*, 551 F2d 1316 (1977).

U.S. District Court, Illinois Plaintiff, an applicant for low-income public housing, challenged the validity and constitutionality of a public housing authority's policy of denying applicants Section 8 housing if they are indebted to the authority for rent arrearages from a prior tenancy. Plaintiff contended that the policy amounted to an unauthorized collection practice and that income level was the exclusive criterion for determining eligibility for Section 8 housing. *Held:* The court found that the authority's arrearage policy did not violate federal housing regulations nor the applicant's constitutional right of equal protection. *Kohl v. Housing Auth.*, 9 Hous. & Dev. Rep. 1055 (1982).

California City's rent control ordinance provided for administrative adjudication of excess rent claims and imposition of treble damages. Rent control board awarded tenant restitution of excess rent, treble damages, and authorized immediate rent withholding by tenant. Landlord asserted that the administrative adjudication provision violated the judicial powers clause of the California constitution. *Held:* The administrative adjudication of rent control claims did not violate the judicial powers clause. Such administrative action was reasonably necessary to accomplish the agency's legitimate regulatory purpose. However, imposition of treble damages and the order authorizing immediate rent withholding was beyond the board's authority. The power to award treble damages poses the risk of arbitrary, disproportionate results. Allowing tenants to immediately withhold rents would give the board's order immediate practical effect; the landlord would have no opportunity to first apply for judicial review. *McHugh v. Santa Monica Rent Control Bd.*, 777 P2d 91 (1989).

California An association of mobile home park owners challenged the constitutionality of a mobile home park ordinance. The ordinance empowered a local review board to approve rent increases based on twelve nonexclusive factors. A hearing was to be held within 90 days after application for an increase was received, and a decision was to be rendered within 15 days after the hearing. *Held:* The ordinance, by stating its purpose as counteracting rent increases and setting forth 12 nonexclusive considerations, provided adequate legislative guidance to the board for its determinations on rent increases. The lack of a specific formula for calculating rent increases did not render the ordinance unconstitutional. The court also found that the 105-day period before a decision was rendered on an application was not excessive. *Carson Mobilehome Park Owners v. Carson*, 197 Cal. Rptr. 284 (1983).

California The passage of Proposition 13 in 1978 caused a substantial reduction in property taxes to plaintiff, a commercial landlord. The city passed an ordinance requiring 1979 rents to be reduced by an amount equal to 80 percent of a landlord's Proposition 13 savings. Plaintiff challenged the constitutionality of the ordinance as an impairment of plaintiff's contractual obligations. *Held:* The ordinance was constitutional because it did not substantially impair the obligations of plaintiff's leases. Plaintiff was not deprived of any gains reasonably to be expected under the leases, and plaintiff retained 20 percent of its unexpected windfall. Moreover, the ordinance was of only one year's duration; thereafter plaintiff would receive all the savings of Proposition 13. *Rue-Ell Enters. v. City of Berkeley*, 194 Cal. Rptr. 919 (Ct. App. 1983).

District of Columbia Tenant challenged a judgment, awarding unpaid rent, which did not allow a rollback of the rent on the basis of legislatively mandated rent control. The trial court ruled that the application of a rollback would be unconstitutional as applied to the landlord because it would deprive the property of economic value. Tenant appealed. *Held:* It was error for the trial court to declare the legislation unconstitutional as applied to the landlord. The court made no general finding of constitutional infirmity, but instead projected as to what would happen if rent control were to be imposed on such landlord and announced its displeasure with the projected results. Accordingly, the case was reversed and remanded. *Cobb v. Bynum*, 387 A2d 1095 (1978).

Massachusetts Two adjacent row houses, containing three dwelling units each, had long been owned and operated as a single economic unit. However, in 1983, one of the row houses was sold to defendants, who promptly moved into the unit. Because owner-occupied two- and three-family houses are exempt from rent control, defendants requested and obtained a certificate of exemption based on their occupancy of the row house. One of the tenants objected, petitioning for judicial review, because the exemption does not apply to any "building" that contained four or more rental units prior to August of 1982. *Held:* For defendant landlords. The rent control board's finding was supported by substantial evidence, since the properties were situated on separate lots and were separated by a 12-inch brick party wall. The board's decision to interpret the reference to a "building" in terms of the physical characteristics of the structure and not the economic reality was not inappropriate. *Entis v. Rent Control Bd.*, 503 NE2d 640 (1987).

Massachusetts Landlords challenged the imposition by the rent control board of charges for filing petitions for individual rent adjustments. The landlords contended that the charges were taxes, rather than fees as purported, and that they were unrelated to the costs of the services occasioned by the petitions. *Held:* The charges were validly imposed. Fees were imposed only on those utilizing a particular government service; and the fees covered the board's reasonably anticipated costs of providing the services. *Southview Coop. Hous. v. Rent Control Bd.*, 486 NE2d 700 (1985).

Massachusetts Plaintiff purchased an apartment building, which he intended to convert to a condominium. When he applied to the rent control board for a 10 percent rent increase in the 26 units that remained as rental apartments, the board granted him only a 6.8 percent increase. The appeals court said that although the 6.8 percent rate was confiscatory and unconstitutional, plaintiff did not have a constitutional right to a 10 percent raise, and remanded the case to find a reasonable minimum rate of return. The supreme judicial court reversed. *Held:* The 6.8 percent rate of return was not confiscatory. Plaintiff chose to finance 100 percent of the cost of the building, incurring a large 9 percent interest rate. The rent control board was not bound to consider the landlord's financing arrangements in setting rates, and the landlord's choice of financing did not justify imposing higher rents. *Zussman v. Rent Control Bd.*, 359 NE2d 29 (1976).

Massachusetts Tenant lived in an apartment under the jurisdiction of the rent equity board. A new owner purchased the building and demanded a rent increase that would take effect less than 12 months from a previous increase imposed by the former owner. Tenant filed a grievance with the rent equity board. *Held:* The rent increase by the new owner was prohibited. The purpose of the city's rent control ordinance, which prohibited a landlord's receiving more than one rent increase in a 12-month period, was to prevent rent gouging by successive landlords. The successor landlord's notice to the tenant of the rent increase was insufficient to terminate a tenancy at will. *Maguire v. Boston Rent Equity Bd.*, 518 NE2d 882 (App. Ct. 1988).

New Jersey Town council voted to repeal a vacancy decontrol ordinance in March 1982. However, it was discovered that the ordinance had never been legally passed as required by a majority of council members, and in October 1982 the council again passed an ordinance repealing vacancy decontrol retroactive to March 12, 1982. The owner of a residential complex that had relied on the invalidity of the March ordinance to relet vacated apartments at higher rents moved to annul the retroactive provisions of the October ordinance. *Held:* The retroactive portion of the ordinance was unanimously overturned. Retroactive application of a rent control ordinance and the impairment of existing contract rights must have a strong, rational public purpose to be sustained. Here there was no housing emergency or a pattern of exorbitant rent increases; rather, the ordinance was to correct a claimed procedural defect. *South Hamilton Assocs. v. Mayor of Morristown*, 493 A2d 523 (1985).

New Jersey Owners of one or two condominium units, which they rented to tenants, sued the township rent board seeking relief from enforcement of a rent control ordinance. Owners claimed that an exemption from the ordinance of housing of two units or less applied to owners of two or fewer condominiums in one building. *Held:* Plaintiffs' units were exempt from rent control. The court saw no reason why the drafters of the ordinance would have intended to treat condominium owners differently from owners of other single-dwelling units. The reasons for the exemption were the same: landlords of one or two units were seen as more caring of tenants' needs, more equal in bargaining power, and less able to comply with burdensome rent control provisions than larger landlords. Further, the state's condominium law prohibited discrimination against condominium units by enactment of zoning ordinances that were not applicable to all buildings of similar type. *AMN, Inc. v. South Brunswick Township Rent Leveling Bd.*, 461 A2d 1138 (1983).

New Jersey Apartment owners sued to challenge a rent control ordinance, on the ground that since greater rent increases were not permitted at the end of multiyear leases than at the end of single-year leases, the ordinance denied it equal protection. *Held:* To overturn a classification on equal protection grounds, the owner must establish that there was no rational basis for the classification. Where the apartment owner did not submit such proof, it was presumed that the municipal governing body had a rational basis for concluding that the base rents of apartments subject to multiyear leases should be subject to the same standards as single-year leases. *Troy Hills Village v. Township Council*, 350 A2d 34 (1975).

New York Tenant of a rent stabilized apartment objected to a term in her renewal lease requiring the rental of a garage, arguing that it violated Section 60 of the Rent Stabilization Code, which required landlords to offer lease renewals on the same conditions as the expiring lease. Tenant argued that before signing the original lease, she had the choice whether or not to rent the space and that she should have been given the same opportunity before signing the renewal lease. *Held:* The fact that the tenant originally had the option to rent the garage space was irrelevant, for it was not a provision of the lease, but part of the initial negotiations. *David v. New York City Conciliation & Appeals Bd.*, 450 NE2d 229 (1983).

New York Tenants whose apartments were subject to rent control challenged the legality of a rent control agency's use of the average experience of a small fraction of the buildings involved to arrive at a standardized increase factor to determine the percentage increase of maximum base rents. The law required that the computation be based on a building-by-building basis. *Held:* The agency had a limited operational budget and it would take years to make the adjustments building by building. In order to preserve the existing rent-controlled units and enable landlords to maintain their buildings, the substitution of a statistical average was proper. The method used must be sound, fair, accurate, and representative. *Tenants' Union, Inc. v. Beame*, 351 NE2d 731 (1976).

New York Defendants were landlords of an apartment building occupied by plaintiffs, who used their apartments in their professional practice. Landlords served two of plaintiffs a notice declaring that their respective leases would be terminated, despite renewal options. Plaintiffs sought protection under the rent stabilization laws, which would allow them to renew their leases. *Held:* Premises used primarily for professional purposes are not entitled to the protection of rent stabilization laws. *Gallin v. Mendelson*, 541 NYS2d 811 (App. Div. 1989).

New York Defendant municipality adopted a resolution declaring a housing emergency with respect to buildings with 16 or more units, pursuant to a statute that empowered municipalities to declare such emergencies where the vacancy rate was less than 5 percent. Landlord sued to have the resolution declared void. *Held:* For the landlord. The board improperly based its decision on a vacancy report prepared by consultants that showed a 3.2 percent vacancy rate as to rental housing in general. The report did not reflect the vacancy rate of buildings with a minimum of 16 units. In the absence of proof of the report's accuracy, the board lacked legal grounds to declare an emergency. *Colonial Arms Apartments v. Mount Kisco*, 480 NYS2d 895 (App. Div. 1984).

New York Tenant entered into a three-year lease that gave a rent concession for the first two months of the lease. Tenant's renewal leases did not contain a similar provision. Section 60 of the Rent Stabilization Code provided that renewal leases must be offered on the same terms and conditions as the expiring lease. Tenant filed a complaint with the rent board that he was overcharged by the amount of the two-month concession during each of the renewal leases. The owner maintained that the two-month rent concession was intended as a one-time only inducement to rent the apartment. *Held:* Section 60 of the Rent Stabilization Code required the owner to include a two-month rent concession in each of the renewal leases. Tenant's failure to question the rent at the time of previous renewals did not amount to a waiver because the protections of the Rent Stabilization Code could not be waived. *Century Operating Corp. v. Popolizio*, 455 NYS2d 789 (App. Div. 1982).

New York A landlord alleged that he was automatically entitled to a rent increase for improvements to a tenant's apartment, without first obtaining approval of the Division of Housing and Community Renewal (DHCR). The tenant maintained that the Tenant Protection Act and Rent Stabilization Code exclusively granted the DHCR the power to issue rent increases. *Held:* Under the Rent Stabilization Code, before a rent increase may be issued for apartment improvements, the landlord is required to first obtain approval from the DHCR. Approval is necessary even when the tenant has given written consent to the rent increase. *Aron Assocs. v. De La Cruz*, 535 NYS2d 512 (Civ. Ct. 1988).

23.25 Percentage Rental Agreements

9th Circuit Oil companies leasing state-owned lands over which their pipelines passed challenged the constitutionality of a regulation that based rentals on the volume of oil and gas passing over the leased land. The state argued that it was acting in a proprietary capacity as a landlord rather than as a sovereign imposing a tax, thus excluding it from constitutional challenge. *Held:* For the oil companies. The state's conduct was vulnerable to constitutional attack because its charge placed a burden on interstate and foreign commerce that could not be justified under the facts of this case. A rent based on the volume of interstate and foreign commerce passing through the state's land was invalid. *Western Oil & Gas Ass'n v. Cory*, 726 F2d 1340 (1984), aff'd, 471 US 81 (1985) (per curiam).

U.S. District Court, Missouri Retailer leased a store in a shopping center. The agreement called for a fixed minimum rental plus a percentage and required the tenant to keep the premises open during business hours for the full 25-year term of the lease. During the next five years, the retailer incurred operating losses in excess of $1 million, but the shopping center landlord refused to permit the store to be closed. The tenant then sued to have the "keep open" clause deemed unconscionable and inequitable. *Held:* The clause was not unconscionable. An unconscionable agreement is one that no man in his right senses would make and that no fair and honest man would accept. The court pointed out that the "keep open" clause was not unusual in this type of percentage rental commercial lease. Furthermore, the lease had been negotiated at arm's-length and in good faith. *JJ Newberry Co. v. Mixon*, 440 F. Supp. 20 (ED 1977).

California Lessee leased property from an investment company for a term of 52 years. The lease required that the property be improved and operated as a mobile home park. Rent was set at $15,000 per year, or 7 percent of the current market value of the property, and was to be recalculated in 1985 and adjusted accordingly. During the initial lease period, regulations were enacted that severely limited the use of the property. In 1985, the parties were unable to agree upon the fair market value of the property for purposes of recalculating the rent. The lessee claimed that the value should be determined based on all facts, including zoning restrictions; the investment company demanded that the value be determined by an arbitrator according to the highest and best use the vacant and unimproved premises could offer, without regard to any current or hypothetical use of the property. *Held:* For the lessee. In appraising the fair market value of the property, the appraiser must consider the impact of zoning restrictions and ordinances that affect the possible different uses of the property and the ability of the owner to put the property to a more valuable use. The appraisal must be made in accordance with the highest and best use of the land without regard to the present lease. However, the appraiser must consider, if appropriate, the impact any legal impediment to a change of use has on the value. *Humphries Inv. Inc. v. Walsh*, 248 Cal. Rptr. 800 (Ct. App. 1988).

Colorado The lessor rented a gasoline station to the lessee for a rental based on the gallonage of gasoline sold, with a monthly minimum of $250. For 17 years, the lessee operated the gas station with monthly rentals averaging $750 per month. When the lessee closed the station, but continued to pay the $250 per month minimum, the lessor brought an unlawful detainer action. The lessee argued that it was under no obligation to operate a gas station on the premises. *Held:* The lessor is entitled to terminate the lease. It was the intent of the parties that there would be a continuous operation of the service station on the premises, and the minimum rental amount was simply to set a floor to the gallonage payments and was not intended to provide an alternative basis of computing the rent. *Continental Oil Co. v. Bradley*, 602 P2d 1 (1979).

Illinois The lease agreement for a 24-hour truckstop restaurant provided that lessee would pay 5 percent of all gross sales over $35,000 to the lessor as additional rental. Lessor interpreted gross sales to include the full amount of receipts for the sale of lottery tickets in the Illinois state lottery and brought a complaint for accounting of gross sales. *Held:* The money received from the sale of lottery tickets was not intended by the parties to be included in gross sales. Only the commissions and bonuses belonged to lessee and only those amounts increased lessee's sales. The remainder of the lottery receipts, although temporarily in lessee's possession, were not lessee's property. Only amounts that are income to a lessee are received by the lessee within the meaning of gross sales. *Anest v. Bellino*, 503 NE2d 576 (App. Ct. 1987).

New York Landlord brought suit to enforce a lease provision that landlord would obtain a percentage rent between the time tenant exercised the option to purchase and when title to the property was conveyed. *Held:* Landlord was entitled to the percentage rent due under the lease where there was no evidentiary proof that the closing was unreasonably delayed by landlord, and where there was no showing of extrinsic evidence to resolve any ambiguity with respect to tenants' obligation to pay rent after exercising the option to purchase. Landlord was also entitled to attorney fees under the lease. *WA Olson Enters. v. Agway, Inc.*, 431 NE2d 289 (1981).

New York A lease provided for a term of 50 years with a fixed rental for the first 25 years. The rental for the next 25 years, if the parties could not agree, would be 5 percent of the value of the land as determined by an appraisal. The two appraisers appointed by the parties could not agree on a value, and a third appraiser was appointed. The third appraiser and defendant's appraiser agreed on a figure substantially higher than that of plaintiff's appraiser. Plaintiff sued for summary judgment to set aside the appraisal for use of an improper valuation method. *Held:* Summary judgment for defendant. The appraisers were not limited to the market value technique as argued by plaintiff. Fixing the value of the land free of encumbrances and without considering the long-term lease was not an error. *Olympia & York 2 Broadway Co. v. Produce Exch. Realty*, 462 NYS2d 456 (App. Div. 1983).

North Carolina Commercial tenant's lease called for a fixed monthly rent, plus a percentage of "all" sales. The tenant moved to a new location, and although he had the right to assign or sublet, he could not find a new tenant, so he broke his lease. The landlord sued, claiming as damages the balance of fixed rent during the lease term but also the percentage rental based upon the tenant's sales at his new location. *Held:* Rental based on "all sales" applied only to sales conducted at the rented premises. Since the tenant had the right to sublet or assign, the landlord could not have expected that the tenant would conduct business on the premises during the entire lease term. Since the lease provided that the premises could be used for any lawful purpose, the assignee or subtenant might not have carried on a retail business giving rise to a percentage rent obligation. *Loew's of Shelby, Inc. v. Hunt*, 226 SE2d 232 (1976).

Pennsylvania Lessor and lessee entered into a percentage lease for a parking garage. The lease provided for a minimum annual rental plus 50 percent of gross receipts from lessee's operations in excess of $220,000, exclusive of sales, excise, or similar taxes. After an excise tax was imposed on the use or occupancy of commercial or industrial property, lessee deducted the tax from its gross receipts and remitted 50 percent of the balance to lessor, thus in effect making lessor pay one half of the tax. *Held:* The lease defined "gross receipts" as those *received* by lessee exclusive of any sales, excise, or other taxes. Thus, only those taxes that were first included in lessees's gross receipts could be excluded in computing the rent. Since the excise tax was not collected from customers, it was not deductible from gross sales. *Arel Realty Corp. v. Meyers Bros. Parking Corp.*, 393 A2d 669 (1978).

Tennessee Lessee operated a business on

property under an assigned lease from the owners. A clause in the original lease provided for payment, as additional rent, of a sum equal to 2 percent of the gross sales of the business in excess of $200,000. At the time of the assignment, lessees operated a convenience market, but later placed pinball machines in the market. The owners claimed that income from the machines should be included in the term "gross sales." *Held:* Income from the pinball machines should not be included as part of the "gross sales." Under Tenn. Code Ann. § 47-2-106(a), pinball machines constitute an "activity" and not a "sale," since no title passes from seller to buyer. Furthermore, the original lease did not contemplate inclusion of revenue from pinball machines, and the use of the word "sales" in the lease tended to limit the kind of income to be used in calculating the additional rental. *Borchert Enters. v. Webb*, 584 SW2d 208 (Ct. App. 1978).

Texas Lessor of a motel sued lessee claiming, inter alia, that the term "total gross room revenues," which was used as the basis for calculating rent due, included both the basic room charge as well as income from television rentals. *Held:* As used in the contract, the term "total gross room revenues" included all income derived from room rentals, including the television earnings. *Cocke v. Pacific Gulf Dev. Corp.*, 594 SW2d 545 (Civ. App. 1980).

23.30 Acceleration of Rent

Louisiana Landlord leased property to tenant for the operation of a fast-food fish and chips restaurant. One provision of the lease required tenant to procure and maintain specific types and amounts of insurance on the property. Another provision gave landlord the option of accelerating rent payments if tenant breached any other provision of the lease (including the insurance provision) and landlord gave written notice to tenant of such breach. After tenant repeatedly violated the rent provision and received repeated notice of such violations, landlord accelerated all future rents due under the lease. Tenant contended that the acceleration would be unlawful as an award of punitive damages, which were generally not allowable in the state of Louisiana. *Held:* Acceleration clauses in leases are lawful and binding on the parties. Therefore, an award of accelerated rents would not be an award of punitive damages. *Bray v. Arthur Treacher's Fish & Chips*, 409 So. 2d 1274 (Ct. App. 1982).

Mississippi A lease provided that in case of default, the lessor could declare the lease forfeited, and lessee would be liable for "all rents remaining unpaid" under the lease. When lessee defaulted on the rent, lessor sued lessee and its guarantors to collect rent for the remainder of the lease term. Defendants claimed that no rent was owed except for the amount past due at the time the suit was filed. *Held:* For defendants. Lessee's obligation under the lease to pay "all rents remaining unpaid" was unclear. The court interpreted the clause to refer to all payments past due, and not as an acceleration clause. A contract to accelerate the maturity of a debt gives a harsh remedy and will not be deemed effective unless it is clear and unequivocal. Preference should be given to the construction that will prevent the acceleration of maturity. *Frey v. Abdo*, 441 So. 2d 1383 (1983).

23.35 What Constitutes Nonpayment

New Jersey Landlord brought an action for dispossess of tenants who had withheld rent because of the failure of their building's central air-conditioning system during a heat wave. The lease obligated the landlord to supply air conditioning. The tenants contended that the landlord breached an implied covenant of habitability. *Held:* The landlord breached implied covenant of habitability. A covenant to pay rent and a covenant of habitability are mutually dependent and the tenants could abate rent. *Park Hill Terrace Assocs. v. Glennon*, 369 A2d 938 (1977).

South Carolina A commercial lease required tenant to pay the rent on or before the fifteenth of the month and stated that time was of the essence. If the rent was not paid on time, landlord had a choice of remedies, including the right to evict tenant and terminate the lease. Tenant's bookkeeper mailed the June rent on the eighth of the month, but misaddressed the envelope, so that the payment never reached its destination. By June 19, landlord's agent had not received the June rent; subsequently, landlord sued for ejectment. *Held:* Landlord was entitled to possession. The lease terms were unequivocal and had been bargained for between the parties. They allowed no exceptions for "good faith inadvertence." A creditor assumes the risk of nondelivery of mailed payments only if he authorizes remittance by mail and the payment is duly mailed and addressed. *Hairston v. Carolina Wholesale Furniture Co.*, 353 SE2d 701 (Ct. App. 1987).

23.40 Landlord's Remedies for Nonpayment

U.S. Supreme Court A tenant stopped paying rent because the leased premises had severely deteriorated owing to the landlord's failure to repair. When the landlord threatened to oust the tenant under the forcible entry and wrongful detainer (FED) statute unless the rent was paid, the tenant argued that the statute violated due process. He claimed it improperly limited the triable issues to the tenant's default and precluded defenses based on the lessor's breach of duty to maintain the premises. *Held:* The treatment by the state of the undertakings of a tenant and those of a landlord as independent rather than dependent covenants did not violate the due process clause. The purpose of the FED statute is to provide landlords with a simple proceeding for speedy recovery of possession of leased premises when a tenant stops paying rent. A tenant may sue the landlord in a separate action after the tenant has been dispossessed, but the tenant may not raise the landlord's breach of duty as a defense to the FED action. *Lindsey v. Normet*, 405 US 56 (1972).

3d Circuit Landlord posted a notice of distraint on the premises when a subtenant fell behind in rent payments. Subtenant sued, claiming the distraint procedure violated due process. Landlord argued no state action was involved. Subtenant claimed the state was present by virtue of the Pennsylvania statute that offered distraint as a remedy for nonpayment of rent. *Held:* For the landlord. When a private individual utilizes a self-help remedy recognized by the state, his actions are not attributable to the state. Statutory approval of an action is deemed state action only when the statute delegates a state power to a private individual. Settlement of debtor-creditor disputes was never a traditional state function. *Luria Bros. v. Allen*, 672 F2d 347 (1982).

8th Circuit When tenants breached a lease by abandoning the premises, the landlord sued for rent due and other items such as utility charges. The tenants claimed that landlord failed to fulfill his duty to mitigate damages. *Held:* The landlord, by retaking possession of a leased premises which had been abandoned by tenants, had a duty to use reasonable efforts to mitigate the damages caused by the tenant's breach of the lease. The trial court's finding that landlord had used reasonable efforts to mitigate damages would not be disturbed absent a finding that the lower court's conclusion was clearly erroneous. *Condor Corp. v. Arlen Realty & Dev. Corp.*, 529 F2d 87 (1976).

Arkansas Landlord sued tenant for overdue rent, and the court clerk issued a writ of attachment based on landlord's affidavit that tenant was about to remove her property from the state. Tenant filed a counterclaim alleging that attachment of her property without notice and a hearing under the state prejudgment attachment provisions violated due process. *Held:* The provisions were unconstitutional. The court overruled its decision in *Springdale Farms, Inc. v. McIllroy Bank & Trust*, 663 SW2d 936 (1984) for failure to apply the "balancing of interests" test of the U.S. Supreme Court for use in due process cases. The test requires the court to consider (1) the private interest affected by official action; (2) the risk of erroneous deprivation of such interest and the value of additional safeguards; and (3) the government's interest, including fiscal and administrative burdens additional requirements would entail. The court concluded that the risk of erroneous deprivation of a debtor's property and the benefit of additional safeguards substantially outweighed any burden the government would incur. *McCrory v. Johnson*, 755 SW2d 566 (1988).

Georgia When tenant failed to pay rent for one month, landlord demanded possession of the apartment. Tenant refused to leave the premises and was issued a dispossessory warrant. *Held:* The dispossessory warrant was valid although the landlord had failed to terminate the lease before demanding possession. Although the Georgia "terminate lease then demand possession" rule was initially applied only to holdover tenants, its application was subsequently extended to nonpayment of rent. However, while a tenant cannot become a holdover until the lease is terminated, a tenant's default in rent permits the landlord to demand possession without the formality of terminating the lease. *Metro Management Co. v. Parker*, 278 SE2d 643 (1981).

Georgia Tenant who had moved from landlord's home but left her personal belongings, sued the landlord for damage to her property. Landlord counterclaimed for unpaid rent and moved for a directed verdict. *Held:* Motion denied. Landlord did not have a common-law lien allowing her to retain tenant's household goods as security for unpaid rent. A landlord's right to distrain for rent was to be exercised through the use of legal process. *Messmore v. Roth*, 366 SE2d 318 (Ct. App. 1988).

Kentucky Public housing tenant found guilty of forcible detainer for lease violations was unable to meet the requirement of Ky. Rev. Stat. Ann. § 383.255 that she deposit rental monies with the court and her appeal was dismissed. At issue was the constitutionality of the statute requiring an indigent tenant to deposit rent with the court in order to perfect an appeal. *Held:* An indigent person has no constitutional right to supersede a judgment without posting security, but he does have the right under the Kentucky Constitution to one appeal without doing so. The deposit provision of the statute should be disregarded when an appellant is unable to deposit rent because of poverty. However, if tenant appellant fails to make the deposit, the provision of the statute that stays enforcement of the district court's judgment is not triggered, permitting the landlord to obtain possession of the premises before an appeal is disposed of. *Fickey v. Cross Creek Apartments, Ltd.*, 700 SW2d 807 (Ct. App. 1985).

New Jersey Upon a default in rent, landlord notified tenant that it was terminating the lease. Four months later, landlord relet the property at a higher rental and sued tenant for the rent due during the interim four months. The tenant argued that landlord's excess rent from its new tenant for the remaining term should be applied to reduce the damages owed for the period the property was vacant. The lease provided that damages were the difference between rent reserved and rent collected during the remainder of the unexpired term; and damages would "become due and payable in monthly payments, during the remainder of the unexpired term. . . ." *Held:* The excess rent from the new lease should not be applied to reduce the rent due for the months the property was vacant. Courts had construed similar lease provisions as providing that after a lease is terminated, a separate cause of action for damages accrued each month for rent due until the end of the lease. *NJ Indus. Properties v. YC & VL, Inc.*, 495 A2d 1320 (1985).

New Jersey Landlord directed a municipal constable to distrain tenant's goods for nonpayment of rent. Under the New Jersey distraint statute, no notice or hearing was required. Tenant asserted the distraint constituted "state action" in violation of the due process clause. *Held:* The distraint was state action. It was conducted pursuant to a state statute and was expressly authorized by the state. The landlord, having been assisted by a constable who was a state official, was a state actor. The court then held that the statute was unconstitutional because it permitted landlords to deprive tenants of their property without making an evidentiary showing of their right to do so. *Callen v. Sherman's, Inc.*, 455 A2d 1102 (1983).

New York Tenant signed a 20-year lease for commercial property, which lease contained a clause providing that landlord could accelerate all future rent if tenant defaulted in making any monthly payments. The clause required neither formal notice of default nor a grace period to pay arrears. Tenant failed to pay one month when rental check was misaddressed. Landlord met with tenant to discuss the situation, but tenant refused to pay arrears or to pay the next month's rent. Landlord sued to collect remaining rent on 20-year lease, and tenant objected, saying enforcement of acceleration clause would constitute "penal forfeiture" of its interests under the lease. *Held:* Landlord had the right to enforce the acceleration clause. While acceleration clauses will not be upheld where the default is trivial or unintentional and is promptly cured, here tenant did not want to act to cure its default, despite the fact that landlord arranged a meeting to resolve the problem. *Fifty States Management Corp. v. Pioneer Auto Parker, Inc.*, 415 NYS2d 800 (1979).

Oregon Tenant rented office space from landlord under a month-to-month tenancy, with rent to be paid in advance on the first of each month. Tenant gave landlord notice that he was terminating his tenancy effective the next month, but failed to pay rent due for that period. The landlord notified the tenant about the delinquent rental payment, but the tenant refused to settle. Less than 20 days after the rent was due, the landlord locked the doors and posted a notice declaring repossession and a possessory lien, and proceeded to remove the tenant's property. The tenant sued, claiming conversion and improper lien execution. *Held:* The landlord's violation of the 20-day statutory notice requirement prior to executing a lien did not result in conversion. Since the landlord preserved the chattels and permitted repossession after receiving payment, his actions did not rise to the level of conversion. *Jordan v. Wilhelm*, 770 P2d 74 (Ct. App. 1989).

Pennsylvania A commercial lease was made contingent upon approval of lessee's beer distributor's license. Lessee did not take possession immediately because it had not received its license and it failed to pay rent for the first three months of the term. Lessor then exercised its option to terminate for nonpayment of rent, and entered into a new lease with another lessee. The first lessee, alleging it had an exclusive lease, sought to enjoin execution of the new lease. *Held:* The lease clearly provided for rent to be paid commencing February 1, 1976, and for the lessor to terminate the lease for failure to pay rent. The clause making the agreement contingent upon approval of a beer license was a condition subsequent: If the license were disapproved, lessee's obligation to pay rent would be discharged. Until this event, lessee was protected from entrance of another beer distributor in the shopping center. Lessee's failure to pay rent constituted a breach of the lease, and lessor could therefore contract with a new lessee. *Village Beer & Beverage, Inc. v. Vernon D. Cox & Co.*, 475 A2d 117 (Super. Ct. 1984).

23.45
—Right to Legal Expenses

Florida Lease for commercial space included a clause in which lessee agreed to pay "reasonable attorney's fees" in any suit for collection of rental. When lessee defaulted on rent and lessor sued, lessor retained an attorney for a contingent fee of 25 percent of full recovery. When the parties reached a settlement of more than $418,000 in rental arrears, a hearing was held in a lower court on the lessee's liability for attorney fees, and the court held that the lessee should pay $52,000. *Held:* The amount of attorney fees was excessive, and the case was sent back to the lower court to reduce the amount. Although a contingent fee arrangement was perfectly valid, the fee should be "a fair measure of the value of the services actually performed by the attorney." The court award had constituted a rate of $340 per hour, rather than a more reasonable rate of $60 to $100 per hour. *Kaufman & Broad Home Systems, Inc. v. Sebring Airport Auth.*, 366 So. 2d 1230 (Dist. Ct. App. 1979).

New York A dispute between landlord and tenant as to the basis for calculating escalation charges in a commercial lease culminated in a declaratory judgment for the landlord. The landlord demanded that tenant pay litigation costs, relying on a lease provision that permitted the landlord to recover attorney fees in connection with performing an obligation on account of tenant. *Held:* Tenant was not required to pay landlord's fees incurred in a declaratory judgment action. Landlord could recover attorney fees only if the litigation arose from an obligation tenant owed to a third party. *Frank B. Hall & Co. v. Orient Overseas Assocs.*, 446 NYS2d 59, aff'd, 453 NYS2d 680 (1982).

23.50
Waiver of Tenant's Default

Georgia Tenant signed a 10-year lease. After six years, tenant defaulted on rent payments, and the landlord sued, seeking repossession as well as past due rent. While the action was pending, both sides settled the dispute for an agreed-upon sum. The amount was tendered by the tenant with the understanding that the dispossessory proceeding would be dismissed; and the tenant resumed making rental payments. However, 12 months later, the tenant received notice that the dispossessory action had been placed on a trial calendar. He then filed a motion to require compliance with the agreement, requesting dismissal of the action. *Held:* Delivery of the agreed-upon sum with the express intention of settling the dispossessory action, together with the acceptance of monthly rental payments, amounted to acceptance of the settlement and required dismissal of the action. *Mutual Ins. Co. v. Dublin Pub, Inc.*, 378 SE2d 497 (Ct. App. 1989).

New York A landlord and tenant entered a lease agreement that provided that the rent would be paid monthly and would be due on the first day of the month. For several years, the tenant made many late payments, but the landlord made no objection and accepted all the late checks. However, when a new landlord purchased the premises, and the tenant did not pay on the first of the month, the new landlord sued to evict the tenant. *Held:* The landlord is entitled to evict the tenant. The waiver of strict compliance of the lease provisions does not apply to the new landlord since he had no notice of the waiver and had no way of knowing about it when he took possession. *Tehan v. Thos. C. Peters Printing Co.*, 421 NYS2d 465 (App. Div. 1979).

Washington Tenant who leased commercial space in landlord's shopping center was served notice that back rent was due. The notice also alleged breach of maintenance covenants. Tenant sent landlord a check for four fifths of the rent. Landlord notified tenant it was terminating the lease and then cashed the check. In a suit by landlord for unlawful detainer, tenant claimed that landlord's acceptance of the check waived any default as to prior unpaid rent. Landlord argued that it accepted the check not as rent but as partial damages for breach of maintenance covenants. *Held:* For tenant. There was no basis for an unlawful detainer action, because landlord never advised tenant that it considered the check damages. Tenant was justified in assuming that the check was collected as rent and that landlord waived any default as to prior unpaid rent. *First Union Management v. Slack*, 679 P2d 936 (Ct. App. 1984).

23.55 Destruction of Premises

5th Circuit Lessee abandoned the premises, alleging constructive eviction. Lessor's assignee filed suit for unpaid rent. Lessee brought a third-party action against lessor, and lessor counterclaimed for anticipatory breach. Subsequently, the premises were destroyed by a tornado. The lease provided that destruction of the prmises terminated the lease. Lessor's assignee amended its complaint to incorporate the anticipatory breach theory. The lessee answered that, by suing for unpaid rent, lessor's assignee had chosen to treat the lease as valid, and could not now assert an anticipatory breach by the lessee. Therefore, lessee argued, the lease continued in effect until terminated by the tornado. *Held:* Lessor's counterclaim for anticipatory breach prior to the tornado acted as an acceptance of the repudiation. The lessor's assignment to the assignee was a limited one that did not deprive lessor of its powers under the lease. Therefore, the acceptance of the repudiation justified a claim based on anticipatory breach for rent due on the remainder of the lease. *Farmers & Bankers Life Ins. Co. v. St. Regis Paper Co.*, 456 F2d 347 (1972).

Illinois Defendant, a store owner, leased adjacent premises from plaintiff, another landlord, in order to expand its store. Before the expansion could take place, the main store was completely destroyed by fire. Although the new premises were undamaged, defendant had no use for them alone. Defendant declared the lease terminated because of the doctrine of commercial frustration. The landlord sued for beach of the agreement, which called for cancellation in the event of destruction of the leased premises, but was silent as to damage to the original store. *Held:* A commercial tenant may cancel a lease without penalty when both landlord and tenant know that the value of the lease to the tenant depends upon some particular condition or state of events and when the event that frustrated the purpose of the lease for the tenant was not reasonably foreseeable. In this case, the value of the new premises depended upon the continued operation of the original store, and the fire in the main store was not reasonably foreseeable. The court noted that continued operation of defendant's store in plaintiff's premises would require a complete change in the overall nature of the business. *Smith v. Roberts*, 370 NE2d 271 (App. Ct. 1977).

Texas The lease descrption of premises, on which lessee operated a retail clothing business, included the land as well as the building, and failed to specify the use of the premises. A fire gutted the building, leaving it unfit for commercial purposes and lessee suspended rent payments. Six months later lessor advised that, the building having been restored, the premises were ready for reoccupancy. Lessee did not resume occupancy and did not pay rent for the remainder of the term. Lessor sued for the unpaid rent, and the trial court ruled that lessee was required to pay the amount. *Held:* Affirmed. The general rule in Texas is that the lessee of land (as opposed to the lessee of improvements alone) upon which improvements are destroyed by fire subsequent to the execution of the lease contract, cannot be relieved of the express covenant to pay rent unless it is so stipulated in the lease. The lease in question failed to so stipulate. *Gonzalez v. Cavazos*, 601 SW2d 202 (Civ. App. 1980).

23.60
Late Charges

Georgia In the course of an action to regain possession of its apartment, landlord demanded past due rent from tenant, including a late charge of $50 that landlord claimed it was entitled to under the lease. Tenant refused to pay the late charge. The trial court held the late charge was usurious. Landlord appealed. *Held:* Reversed. A lease providing for a late charge is not a loan and does not have to comply with usury laws. The appellate court defined the real issue as whether the late charge was enforceable as liquidated damages or was an unlawful penalty. The court upheld the late charge because the lease stated the late charge "is due for services required of the agent/owner," indicating the parties intended to provide for damages. *Krupp Realty Co. v. Joel*, 309 SE2d 641 (Ct. App. 1983).

New Jersey Under tenant's original lease, tenant paid landlord the rent after she received her public-assistance check on the third of each month. A new landlord purchased the building, terminated the original lease and offered tenant a new lease with a rent increase. Rent was due on the first of each month, with a $25 penalty if not paid by the fifth of the month. Tenant never executed a new written lease, but remained in possession and paid the increased rent. However, she failed to pay late charges for the months her rent was late. Landlord sought possession for nonpayment of the late charge. *Held:* Tenant could not be evicted. In a dispossess action for nonpayment or late payment of rent, a tenant may raise the defense that the failure to abide by the tenancy's rent payment requirements stemmed from an unreasonable change in the renewal lease. By accepting some of the lease changes imposed by the landlord, tenant did not impliedly accept all changes. Her refusal to pay the late fee constituted a valid refusal to accept the lease change. New Jersey's Anti-Eviction Act limits the eviction of tenants to "reasonable grounds." Landlord's lease change to include a late fee was unreasonable when tenant always made her payment after receiving her assistance check. *447 Assocs. v. Miranda*, 559 A2d 1362 (1989).

New York Landlord brought a summary proceeding to evict tenant for refusing to pay a $50 late fee when she was over 10 days late on her monthly rent of $405. Tenant claimed the fee was unconscionably high. *Held:* The $50 late fee was excessive and amounted to an unconscionable penalty. If tenant had to pay this fee every month it would amount to an annual interest rate of 450 percent. In addition, the late fee was invalid because the premises were subject to the Emergency Tenant Protection Act, under which landlords could charge only a regulated rent. Any additional consideration received by landlords had to be approved by the Division of Housing and Community Renewal. The $50 late fee had not been approved. *Spring Valley Gardens Assocs. v. Earle*, 447 NYS2d 629 (Rockland Co. Ct. 1982).

23.65 Security Deposits

Massachusetts Residential tenants notified landlord they were terminating their tenancy and vacated the premises. After an inspection, the landlord retained the full security deposit for damages it claimed were in excess of ordinary wear and tear. Tenant sought treble damages pursuant to Mass. Gen. L. ch. 186, § 15B(7) for wrongful conversion of their security deposit. The trial court found that damage to the premises amounted to $311.44 and awarded three times the remainder of the security deposit plus costs and interests. Landlord appealed, asking the award be reduced to actual damages in the absence of bad faith on her part. *Held:* Tenants were entitled to treble damages. The language of the statute was unambiguous, and the legislative history indiated that the legislature did not intend to include a bad faith requirement. *Mellor v. Berman*, 454 NE2d 907 (1983).

Ohio Tenants sued landlord for withholding their security deposit, claiming double damages and attorney fees. *Held:* For tenants. Ohio's landlord-tenant statute provides for double damages for wrongful withholding of a security deposit. A miscalculation was wrongful for purposes of applying the penalty provisions. *Smith v. Padgett*, 513 NE2d 737 (1987).

Ohio Tenants sued landlord for withholding their security deposit and failing to supply an itemized accounting of the withholding, as required by the Ohio Landlord-Tenant Act. The statute permitted a tenant to recover the deposit, plus damages equal to the amount wrongfully withheld. *Held:* For the landlord. The damages provision of the statute applied only to the amount of the security deposit that remained after legitimate damages were deducted. Since tenants in this case owed more for rent and expenses than the security deposit would cover, they were not entitled to damages. *Vardeman v. Llewellyn*, 476 NE2d 1038 (1985).

Pennsylvania The attorney general sued, claiming that landlord had unlawfully withheld money for unnecessary cleaning services from the security deposits of former tenants in violation of the Landlord and Tenant Act. The action sought to impose civil penalties and to enjoin landlord from further illegal acts. Landlord objected, claiming the attorney general failed to state a cause of action. *Held:* For the attorney general. The allegations, if proved, violated Section 2 of the Unfair Trade Practices and Consumer Protection Law, which provided that "[f]ailing to comply with the terms of any written guarantee or warranty given to the buyer at, prior to, or after a contract for the purchase of goods or services is made" is a deceptive practice. *Commonwealth v. National Apartment Leasing Co.*, 529 A2d 1157 (Commw. Ct. 1987).

Washington Tenant leased premises from landlord for a health spa and deposited $5,900 "as partial consideration" for the execution of the lease. The lease further provided for return of the deposit if the tenant fully complied with all of the terms of the lease. When the tenant defaulted on the lease, the landlord sued and recovered damages without tenant being given any credit for the $5,900 deposit. On appeal, the tenant argued that the full judgment without credit for the deposit is actually a double recovery. *Held:* The landlord is entitled to a judgment without credit for the deposit. The deposit is additional rent that the tenant agreed to pay subject to its right to earn a rebate in the amount of the additional rent by faithful performance of the lease. By defaulting, the tenant lost its earn-back privilege. *Block v. Olympic Health Spa, Inc.*, 604 P2d 1317 (Ct. App. 1979).

Wisconsin Tenant sued to recover her security deposit from landlord. Relief was granted and was affirmed on appeal. Tenant then filed a motion for costs and appellate attorney fees. She was represented throughout by a legal services organization. *Held:* For tenant. The purpose of the statute under which relief was granted at the trial level was to encourage attorneys to pursue tenants' claims where the anticipated monetary recovery would not justify the expense of legal action. If attorney fees were not recoverable on appeal, landlords could defeat the statutory purpose by the simple expedient of an appeal. An award of attorney fees was proper even if the tenant was represented at no charge by a legal services organization. *Shands v. Castrovinci*, 340 NW2d 506 (1983).

23.70 Liability of Guarantor

Colorado A retail corporation leased commercial premises. The corporation president signed the lease and a manufacturer of the corporation was guarantor. The guarantee contained a broad consent-for-modifications clause, under which the guarantor expressly consented to any modifications made in the terms of the lease. Several years later, the corporation president sold his interest in the corporation. The new owners moved the store to larger premises in the same shopping center, and executed an amendment to the lease providing for higher rent. The new owners defaulted, and the lessor sued the manufacturer-guarantor, although the manufacturer was not a party to the amendment. *Held:* For the guarantor. The removal of the corporation president as lessee, which meant the guarantor could no longer rely on his performance, together with the change in premises and significantly increased rent combined to make the "amendment" in fact a new lease. Where no part of the original premises is covered by a new agreement, that agreement goes beyond a mere modification of the original, and falls outside even a broad consent-for-modifications clause. *Green Shoe Mfg. Co. v. Farber*, 712 P2d 1014 (1986).

23.75 Sharecrop Leases

Idaho Landowner and farmer entered into an oral lease entitling the landowner to one third of the farmer's crop. The landowner later confirmed the oral agreement in a letter, but failed to file a security interest in the crop. The farmer, who was responsible for expenses under the lease, obtained fertilizer and seed on credit from a supplier. Much of the crop was subsequently delivered to the supplier and applied to the debt. The landowner sued to compel delivery of his third of the crop. *Held:* For the landowner. A tenant farmer could not transfer title to a landowner's share of a crop or to convert that share into a mere security interest. *NBC Leas-*

ing Co. v. B & T Farms, Inc., 733 P2d 721 (1987).

23.80
Tenant's Right to Withhold Rent

U.S. District Court, Massachusetts The U.S. Postal Service, lessee, informed its landlord of the need to repair a deteriorating roof on the property. The landlord made inadequate repairs and the postal service was forced to replace the roof at its own expense. The postal service withheld rent to recover its costs. The landlord sued to evict, asserting that the postal service's sole remedy for failure to repair was cancellation of the lease. *Held:* The postal service had the right to make necessary repairs and offset the costs by withholding rent, provided it could prove the repairs were necessary and reasonable. The Massachusetts high court recognized the developing trend treating certain lease covenants as interdependent, especially regarding a tenant's duty to pay rent and landlord's duty to maintain the premises, particularly in light of a statement in the lease that the landlord agreed to maintain the premises "in consideration of the aforesaid rental." *Reed v. United States Postal Serv.*, 660 F. Supp. 178 (1987).

24.00
OTHER DUTIES OF TENANT

24.05
Relinquishing Possession

9th Circuit Farmers leasing land from an Indian tribe were informed by the Bureau of Indian Affairs (BIA) that their tenancy would be terminated unless they complied with lease conditions. The tenants did not comply, but continued to plant crops on the land. The BIA moved for ejectment; the farmers continued to plant and deposited the proceeds with the court. The court ultimately ruled tenants were in trespass. The parties then sought a determination of their rights in the crop proceeds. *Held:* For the BIA. Although Arizona limited the liability of a tenant in good faith possession to rent arrears, the farmers were not holding over in good faith since they failed to appeal the BIA's determination that they were in default. The court applied the common-law rule of waygoing crops, which provides that a tenant who plants a crop knowing the lease term will expire before the crop can be harvested loses the entire crop upon termination of the lease, less costs. *Andersen v. Bureau of Indian Affairs*, 764 F2d 1344 (1985).

Arkansas A tenant who remained in her apartment for 10 days after receiving a three-day notice to vacate was charged and convicted of criminal trespass. She appealed. *Held:* The conviction was reversed, on the ground that a general law, such as the trespass statute, does not usually apply in situations where there is a statute specifically addressing the question. While the language of the trespass statute might seem to cover defendant's situation, there were specific remedies in other statutes for holdover and unlawful detainer by tenants. In addition, the criminal trespass statute had not been applied historically in landlord-tenant cases. *Williams v. City of Pine Bluff*, 683 SW2d 923 (1985).

Georgia When tenant failed to pay rent for one month, landlord demanded possession of the apartment. Tenant refused to leave the premises and was issued a dispossessory warrant. *Held:* The dispossessory warrant was valid although the landlord had failed to terminate the lease before demanding possession. Although the Georgia "terminate lease then demand possession" rule was initially applied only to holdover tenants, its application was subsequently extended to nonpayment of rent. However, while a tenant cannot become a holdover until the lease is terminated, a tenant's default in rent permits the landlord to demand possession without the formality of terminating the lease. *Metro Management Co. v. Parker*, 278 SE2d 643 (1981).

Idaho After the landlord-gas company gave proper notice of termination of a distribution and consignment agreement with an operator of one of its bulk plants, the operator failed to vacate the premises. The gas company filed an unlawful detainer action, and the operator counterclaimed for damages alleging that the gas company's actions interfered with his right to sell his business. *Held:* Counterclaims are improper in unlawful detainer actions. The consignment and distributor agreements provided either party the right to terminate by giving five days' notice. The gas company was therefore entitled to possession. *Texaco, Inc. v. Johnson*, 539 P2d 288 (1975).

New York Railroad leased a pier from the city for 70 years under leases and permits that required the railroad to maintain the pier in good condition. The railroad remained in possession and continued to pay rent for 11 years after its last permit expired. The city's successful action for breach of the covenant to keep the pier in good condition was reversed by the appellate division, which held that the covenant was not in force because, after the permit expired, the relationship was that of licensor-licensee. *Held:* By remaining in possession, the railroad became a holdover tenant, and there was an implied continuation of all the terms of the previous agreement, including the covenant to maintain the premises. *City of New York v. Pennsylvania RR*, 333 NE2d 361 (1975).

24.10 Repairs

11th Circuit After being notified by landlord that the lease was terminated due to deteriorating conditions, tenant sought a declaratory judgment clarifying the landlord's obligations for repair, maintenance, and replacement. The landlord counterclaimed for damages and termination of the lease. *Held:* The landlord's counterclaim was barred by res judicata, since the same complaint had been raised unsuccessfully by landlord a year earlier in state court. The tenant was not required to remedy any defect on the premises that existed before the state action was filed. The tenant, however, was required to comply with the conditions of the lease from that date forward. *Capitol Funds, Inc. v. Arlen Realty, Inc.*, 755 F2d 1544 (1985).

Arkansas Texaco leased a service station under a lease requiring lessor to make major repairs. Texaco subleased the station to plaintiff. Texaco later subleased the station to a third party who orally subleased the station back to plaintiff, who remained as proprietor. During plaintiff's term as proprietor, a section of the stone wall collapsed, injuring plaintiff. Texaco's subleases with plaintiff and the sublessor provided that Texaco would maintain the premises in good repair. *Held:* Summary judgment against plaintiff; sublessee had the duty to repair. Arkansas follows the common-law rule that the lessor owes no duty of repair to the lessee. The lease agreements between lessor and Texaco and between Texaco and the third party were not applicable to the oral agreement between the third party and plaintiff because of lack of privity. *Hurst v. Feild*, 661 SW2d 393 (1983).

Illinois Commercial tenants asked landlord to fix a brick wall that appeared to be in danger of imminent collapse. Landlord refused, arguing that the lease made tenants responsible for repairs to the premises. *Held:* The maintenance clause of the lease did not obligate lessees to make structural repairs such as those required here. Despite the lease clause making lessee generally responsible for repairs, a lessee was not obligated to make structural alterations necessitated by extraordinary and unforeseen events, unless the lease explicitly provided otherwise. Since the lease did not use the term "structure," lessee's repair obligation did not include repairs involving structural changes. *Expert Corp. v. LaSalle Nat'l Bank*, 496 NE2d 3 (Ct. App. 1986).

New York Landlord complied with Environmental Protection Agency directive to dump sewage into city sewage system rather than nearby bodies of water and sued tenant for the cost of compliance. The lease required the tenant to remove conditions that constituted a violation of law, or of a regulation, if the violation resulted from tenant's "manner and use" of the premises. *Held:* The violation did not result from the character of tenant's use of the premises; occupancy by any tenant would have necessitated installation of a new sewer system. This case is different from those in which tenants must comply with local laws or regulations because of the property. *Bush Terminal Assocs. v. Federated Dep't Stores, Inc.*, 424 NYS2d 28 (App. Div. 1980).

Wyoming Lease obligated the tenant to make all necessary repairs and return the property in good condition at the conclusion of the lease term. During the course of the lease term, the property was inspected by governmental authorities and substantial repairs were required to comply with the building and safety codes. Both the tenant and the landlord refused to make the required major repairs and the tenant moved out when governmental action was imminent. The landlord brought an action for a declaratory judgment. *Held:* The landlord is responsible for repairs that are substantial and structural in nature and that will survive the term of the lease, if the repairs were not the result of actions by the tenant. *Scott v. Prazma*, 555 P2d 571 (1976).

24.15 Liability for Damage to Premises

10th Circuit Tenant's employee, believing that a fire had been extinguished in the store, turned off the sprinkler system. The fire was not out and caused considerable damage before it was brought under control a second time. Landlord sued tenant, claiming that his store was damaged because of the conduct of tenant's employee. Tenant denied the allegations of misconduct and affirmatively alleged that under the express terms of the lease the tenant was not liable for any loss or damage resulting from fire "irrespective of the cause thereof." *Held:* The unambiguous exculpation clause excused tenant from liability for damage resulting from any negligence of its employees. *Schechter v. SS Kresge Co.*, 579 F2d 1231 (1978).

Alaska Commercial tenant negligently caused a fire that destroyed the premises. The landlord, which was required under the lease to furnish fire insurance, subrogated its claim to the insurer, who thereupon filed suit against the tenant. The insurer argued that although the lease obligated landlord to furnish fire insurance for the benefit of tenant, the tenant was liable under a separate lease clause indemnifying landlord for losses due to negligence. *Held:* Subrogation claim dismissed. Where the landlord has contracted to provide fire insurance and where the lease does not specify tenant's liability for fire damage, the tenant is an implied co-insured for subrogation purposes. *Alaska Ins. Co. v. RCA Alaska Community, Inc.*, 623 P2d 1216 (1981).

Iowa Tenant sued landlord for withholding part of its security deposit. Landlord counterclaimed for additional damages not included in the original deduction. Tenant contended that Iowa Code § 562A.12, which provides that a landlord has 30 days to return a security deposit, prevented a landlord from making a claim for damages once the 30-day period for return of the deposit had passed. *Held:* The court rejected tenant's statutory interpretation. The statute referred only to the return of the security deposit and could not be read as imposing a statute of limitations on the landlord's claim for damages. The landlord was free to pursue an action for damages after returning tenant's deposit. *Whitehorn v. Lovik*, 398 NW2d 851 (1987).

Kansas A sublessee negligently caused a fire that damaged the building. Landlord sued lessee in tort for negligence and requested lessee summary judgment, because a third party had caused the fire. The trial court granted summary judgment and defendant lessee appealed. *Held:* Defendant lessee was liable to the landlord for the negligence of its sublessee. The lessee has an implied obligation to use reasonable diligence in protecting the property and to return it to landlord in the condition in which it was received. Where the general duty is violated, even though it arises out of the terms of a contract and is caused by a third party, the breach of duty constitutes a tort actionable on the theory of negligence. *Marcellus v. KOV, Inc.*, 615 P2d 170 (1980).

Louisiana Plaintiff, owner of a five-story building, sued a former lessee for failure to properly maintain the building and timely vacate the premises at expiration of the lease. Prior to expiration of the lease, plaintiff inspected the building and found extensive structural damage. Defendant argued that during his 18 years' tenancy, any requests for repairs by plaintiff had been made at defendant's expense, and that plaintiff acquiesced in any deficiencies in maintenance by knowledge of the defects and by renewing and extending the lease. *Held:* For plaintiff. Plaintiff's alleged knowledge of damage to its property did not waive defendant's duty under the original lease and renewal leases to return the property in good order at the expiration of the lease. Plaintiff did not acquiesce in any violation of a prior lease, and defendant was required to maintain and surrender the building in good order. *Bernard Co. v. Factory Outlet Shoes, Inc.*, 503 So. 2d 647 (Ct. App. 1987).

Michigan Landlord and his insurer sued tenant for negligence when her three-year-old daughter set fire to the apartment, rendering it uninhabitable. The lease did not address tenant's liability for fire damage resulting from her negligence, but it required tenant to keep the premises in good repair and return them in the same condition, reasonable wear and tear excepted. *Held:* For tenant. Absent an express and unequivocal agreement by a tenant to be liable to lessor or lessor's insurer in tort for negligently caused fire damages to the premises, a tenant has no duty to the lessor or insurer that would support a negligence claim. However, tenant was liable for rent during the period the premises were uninhabitable. *New Hampshire Ins. Group v. Labombard*, 339 NW2d 527 (Ct. App. 1986).

Wisconsin Delco purchased a commercial building but did not assume the mortgage. Subsequently, mortgagee foreclosed against the property. The building sold for $250,000 less than the mortgage, and mortgagee sued Delco for the deficiency, claiming that by failing to pay property taxes, allowing the roof to deteriorate, and causing severe water damage, Delco had committed waste upon the property. Delco claimed as a successor owner that did not assume the mortgage, it was not liable to the mortgagee for waste. *Held:* For mortgagee. A mortgagee's lien interest is sufficient to entitle the mortgagee to bring an action for waste, and a nonassuming grantee's status is not so unique as to insulate it from a waste action and prevent the mortgagee from preserving its security interest. *Prudential Ins. Co. of Am. v. Spencer's Kenosha Bowl, Inc.*, 404 NW2d 109 (Ct. App. 1987).

24.20
Taxes and Assessments

Kansas Landlord and tenant concluded in 1961 a 10-year lease whereby the tenant would operate a bowling alley and would pay the increases in taxes on the property, starting with the year 1967, over and above the taxes for 1962. The lease was renewed for a second 10-year term in 1971. However, from 1967 to 1974, the tenant did not pay the tax increases over and above the 1962 taxes, and the landlord sued for the tax payments for that period. *Held:* The landlord was not entitled to tax payments from 1967 to 1974. At no time, until 1974, did the landlord request payment of the tax increases, including at the time of the renewal of the lease in 1971. Therefore, the landlord had waived all right to the past tax increase payments, but was entitled to collect these payments in the future. *Crestview Bowl, Inc. v. Womer Constr. Co.*, 592 P2d 74 (1979).

New York Under a commercial lease, tenant was liable for paying any increases in taxes during the term of the lease. Tenant refused to pay the increase imposed as of July 1, 1985, for the 1985–1986 tax year. Seeking a declaration that it was not obliged to pay any of the increase, tenant argued that landlord imposed the increase primarily because two stories had been added to the property for landlord's own benefit. *Held:* It is not ordinarily the aim of a tax escalation clause to hold tenant responsible for increases in real estate taxes that result from improvements on the property redounding solely to the benefit of the landlord. Thus, tenant was not responsible for the part of the increase resulting from the improvements. However, tenant was responsible for its proportionate share of tax installments falling due after its lease expired, since the tax obligation was imposed and accrued on July 1, regardless of when installments were due. *Credit Exch., Inc. v. 461 Eighth Ave. Assocs.*, 511 NE2d 47 (1987).

West Virginia Lessor sued the lessee for failing to pay the full amount due under the lease. The lease, begun in November 1967, provided that the lessee would pay the amount of taxes in excess of the "full first year's assessment." The lessor argued that, under the clause, the lessee was to pay the excess in taxes over the 1968 taxes for each succeeding year of the lease. Defendant argued that the first full calendar year was 1968, and that therefore the lessee had to pay the excess over 1969 taxes. *Held:* Since the clause was ambiguous on its face, it was interpreted in view of the entire lease and in favor of the lessor. *Moore v. Johnson Serv. Co.*, 219 SE2d 315 (1975).

24.25
Maintenance of Business Hours

U.S. District Court, Missouri Under the terms of its 25-year lease, plaintiff was "to keep the entire demised premises open during business hours" for the duration of the lease. After having sustained operational losses over an extended period, plaintiff wanted to discontinue the business and petitioned for a declaratory judgment, asking the court to find that its contractual obligation was limited to the payment of the annual rental and to declare the keep-open clause unconscionable. Defendant moved for dismissal for failure to state a claim upon which relief could be granted. *Held:* Motion to dismiss the petition granted. There is no support for plaintiff's position in Missouri law. Its characterization of the questioned clause as unconscionable was inappropriate. There was no disparity in the parties' bargaining position or capacity. The court will not set aside an otherwise valid lease simply because one party no longer finds the arrangement as profitable as it first anticipated. *JJ Newberry Co. v. Mixon*, 440 F. Supp. 20 (ED 1977).

Texas Lease for a drive-in grocery business allowed the lessees to cease operating if they determined that it was no longer economically feasible to do so, but they would continue to be liable for the guaranteed annual rent. The lease also permitted the lessor to establish a gas-pumping facility on the premises at his own expense. The lessor installed and operated such a facility. The lessees closed the store, and the lessor brought suit for damages, contending that the closing of the store locked up the equipment to operate the gas station. *Held:* The lease did not require the lessees to keep the store open for the lessor to operate his station, but on the contrary, specifically allowed them to close it. They were therefore not in breach of their contract. *Daniels v. Shop Rite Foods, Inc.*, 502 SW2d 894 (1973).

24.30
Restrictions on Use of Premises

California Tenant in a mobile home park obtained a license to serve as a foster parent and housed children in her mobile home. Park owners claimed that her operation of the foster home violated a park rule that the park be used only for residential purposes and prohibiting business or commercial activity. Tenant sued to enjoin the park owners' unlawful detainer action. *Held:* For the park owners. Tenant's operation of a foster home violated the rule against operating a business on the leased site. Although tenant claimed she made no profit, she was held to be operating a business because she had no other employment and was reimbursed for her services. *Morris v. Green River Village Mobilehome Community*, 232 Cal. Rptr. 581 (Ct. App. 1986).

New Hampshire A long-term lease specified that the premises were to be used to operate a restaurant for the sale and consumption of food and nonalcoholic beverages. The tenant, who wished to operate a full-service restaurant, sought a declaration that the lease permitted the sale of alcoholic beverages. *Held:* The lease did not permit the sale of alcoholic beverages. When the lease specified only that lessee could sell nonalcoholic beverages, lessor manifested his desire to limit the sale and consumption of beverages on the premises to that variety of beverages only. In this context, the lease was intended to prohibit what it did not explicitly permit. *Elca of NH, Inc. v. McIntyre*, 523 A2d 90 (1987).

25.00
DUTIES OF SHOPPING CENTER TENANT AND LANDLORD

25.05
Duties of Tenant

Arizona Lessor, a shopping center developer, brought a forcible detainer action to recover possession of a supermarket. Lessee had ceased operations and vacated the premises. Eight months later, ignoring lessor's termination of the lease, lessee reopened part of the premises as a liquor store and sublet the remainder.

Lessor contended that lessee had violated an implied covenant of continuous operation contained in the lease. *Held:* For lessor. The lease provided for percentage rent, lessor was required to build to suit as a supermarket, and competition was restricted, suggesting that lessee's continuous operation was clearly within the contemplation of the parties. The court also found that the base rent was inadequate, and this, together with the provision for percentage rent, implied a covenant of continuous operation. *First Am. Bank & Trust Co. v. Safeway Stores, Inc.*, 729 P2d 938 (Ct. App. 1986).

New Mexico Lessor sued to enjoin lessee, a shopping center tenant, from establishing a competing business within a two-mile radius of the shopping center in violation of its lease. Lessee argued at trial that the radius clause was an unlawful restraint of trade. *Held:* The radius clause was enforceable, because it was ancillary to a lawful lease. The court noted that the clause was a reasonable corollary to another clause providing for percentage rent above a certain minimum. Although lessee had pointed out that its gross income had not been high enough to trigger the percentage rent clause, the court said that there was no evidence to show that percentage rent would not be paid during the remaining lease period if the radius clause were enforced. The court also noted that no harm to the public had been intended, and that, while there was some restriction on competition, the restriction was limited in time and place and was subsidiary to the main purpose of the lease. *Winrock Enters., Inc. v. House of Fabrics, Inc.*, 579 P2d 787 (1978).

New York Jury found both the landlord and tenant negligent and jointly liable for plaintiff's injuries sustained when she fell over a snow-covered planter box located about 20 feet from the entrance to the tenant's store. However, the trial judge ruled that an indemnity clause of the lease agreement obligated the tenant to pay the landlord's share of the judgment. The tenant appealed, arguing that the accident had not occurred "in and about" its premises as specified in the agreement. The appellate division found in the tenant's favor, and the landlord appealed. *Held:* The agreement in question clearly supported the landlord's right to indemnification. The phrase "in or about" is frequently used to mean "around" or "on the outside of." Consequently, in this case, "in or about" must be held to include the sidewalk area where the accident occurred. Courts do not generally look unfavorably upon agreements that, by requiring the parties to carry insurance, afford protection to the public. *Hogeland v. Sibley, Lindsay & Curr Co.*, 366 NE2d 263 (1977).

Oklahoma A shopping center owner sought to terminate the lease of "anchor" tenant on grounds of failure of consideration, alleging that tenant breached an implied covenant to operate its business in such a manner as to generate percentage rentals and to attract customers to the shopping center. *Held:* The lease expressly excluded any warranty by tenant as to the volume of sales it would generate and provided for a substantial and adequate minimum rental. Had the minimal rental been only nominal, the court might have found an implied covenant. *Mercury Inv. Co. v. FW Woolworth Co.*, 706 P2d 523 (1985).

Pennsylvania Defendant, a commercial tenant in plaintiffs' shopping center, withheld rents after plaintiffs violated a non-competition clause by leasing space to a competing jewelry and gift concern. Plaintiffs commenced an action for unpaid rent and obtained a confession of judgment award as provided for in the lease. *Held:* Judgment for plaintiffs vacated. The obligation to pay rent is not independent of the landlords' duty to abide by a commercially indispensable lease covenant; therefore, defendant was justified in refusing to pay rents. *Teodori v. Werner*, 415 A2d 31 (1980).

Tennessee A supermarket's shopping mall lease specified that the lessor would not lease to a grocery in the same complex, and that tenant could not use the premises for a drug store without the lessor's permission or for an illegal purpose. Nothing was said about tenant's right to sublet or assign. Subsequently, the tenant subleased to a clothing and general merchandise store. The lessor claimed the sublease was inconsistent with the original lease, and constituted a breach of the implied warranty of continuous occupancy. *Held:* The sublease was valid. The lessor's agreement not to lease to a grocery did not suggest that the tenant had to use the premises for a similar business. The interdependent nature of the shops in the mall did not warrant such an implication. *Kroger Co. v. Chemical Secs. Co.*, 526 SW2d 468 (1975).

25.10 Duties of Landlord

3d Circuit The lease for a shopping center snack bar contained a restrictive covenant. The lease also set out the items that could be sold at the snack bar. Later, the shopping center leased space to a restaurant. The snack bar lessee sued for damages and an injunction. *Held:* No injunction was issued, because the overlap between the snack bar's sales and the restaurant's sales was less than 50 percent. In any event, restrictive covenants are to be narrowly construed in favor of competition. *Carousel Snack Bars v. Crown Constr. Co.*, 439 F2d 288 (1971).

Connecticut Defendants leased space from plaintiff for the operation of a miniature golf course in a glass-enclosed shopping mall. The mall attracted large numbers of young loiterers who, although not playing golf, would stand and watch the golfers through windows surrounding the course. Although a security guard would attempt to disperse the trespassers, one of defendants' employees was assaulted and their cash box was burglarized. Defendants' business was drastically reduced, causing them to quit the premises. Consequently, defendants did not tender any further rent payments, although the lease term had not yet expired, so plaintiff sued to recover lost rent. Defendants alleged that plaintiff violated the covenant of quiet enjoyment in the lease. *Held:* A covenant of quiet enjoyment pertains to actions by landlord or others claiming title to the property and not to trespassers. Plaintiff had no knowledge or control over the trespassers and therefore cannot be held liable for a breach of covenant of quiet enjoyment. Large crowds and trespassers could have been foreseen by defendant when leasing property in a large shopping mall, therefore defendants were liable for the rent. *Net Realty Holding Trust v. Nelson*, 358 A2d 365 (Super. Ct. 1976).

Michigan Plaintiff was shot during an armed robbery in a drug store in a high crime area. Plaintiff sued the drug store, alleging that the store breached its duty to exercise reasonable care for the safety of its patrons by not providing armed and visible security guards. *Held:* The store did not have the duty to protect patrons from the unforeseeable acts of third parties. A merchant's duty of reasonable care does not include the duty to provide an armed security guard to deter criminal acts of third parties. The common law imposes no duty upon a person to aid or protect another. The landlord owes only a duty to exercise reasonable care to protect an invitee. *Williams v. Cunningham Drug Stores, Inc.*, 418 NW2d 381 (1988).

New Jersey Plaintiff, owner of a small shopping center, sought a declaration that a restrictive covenant in the original lease with a former tenant did not prevent him from leasing another store to a new supermarket. The current tenant, a chain drugstore, who had a sublease agreement with former tenant, counterclaimed to enforce the restrictive covenant. *Held:* For plaintiff. Although the agreement between former tenant and the drugstore was actually an assignment and not a sublease, entitling the drugstore, as tenant assignee, to the rights of tenant-assignor, the restrictive covenant was applicable only "so long as lessee handles food or food products at retail." Therefore the drugstore, which sold food in 7 to 10 percent of its space, could not enforce the restrictive covenant. Nor was plaintiff precluded by laches from challenging the validity of the restrictive covenant, because no prospective supermarket tenant had previously appeared, and there was no evidence the drugstore's business would be harmed by leasing to a supermarket. *Berkeley Dev. Co. v. Great Atl. & Pac. Tea Co.*, 518 A2d 790 (Super. Ct. Law Div. 1986).

New York Shopper fell and hurt herself in the driveway of a supermarket's parking lot, owing to a hole in the driveway. Both the supermarket-lessee and the owner-lessor were sued. *Held:* Where the landlord has breached a covenant to repair, he is liable both to the tenant and to those on the land with the tenant's permission. This was true even though the supermarket retained control of the driveway under the lease and was therefore also liable. *Putnam v. Stout*, 345 NE2d 319 (1976).

New York A tenant's store in a shopping center occupied an ideal location for which the tenant paid a premium rent. Many, if not all, of the shoppers who entered the center passed the tenant's store. This changed, however, when the owner of the center erected a huge department store. The flow of traffic by the tenant's store diminished drastically; moreover, the corridor was no longer pleasing to the eye because it became a dingy, artificially lighted hallway. The tenant sued for damages. The lease contained this provision: "Landlord reserves the right to make changes, additions, alterations, or improvements in or to such common areas (defined as the parking lot, corridor, sidewalks, and mall); provided, however, that there shall thereby be caused no unreasonable obstruction of tenant's right of access to the demised premises or any unreasonable interference with tenant's use of the demised premises." *Held:* The tenant still had access to and the use of his store, notwithstanding the changes the owner had made. While the tenant may not enjoy the same volume of business as before, he would be able to carry on. Hence, the owner had acted reasonably and done no more than the tenant had agreed he might do. *MNS Brandell, Inc. v. Roosevelt Nassau Operating Co.*, 345 NYS2d 608 (App. Div. 1973).

South Carolina Plaintiff lessee of shopping center premises sued for an injunction to prevent lessor from erecting a building in violation of the lease. *Held:* Although the proposed building would violate the terms of the lease, the lessee on several occasions expressed its acquiescence in the lessor's plans and, therefore, could not enjoin the breach. *Genesco, Inc. v. Palmetto Plaza Shopping Center, Inc.*, 265 SE2d 34 (1980).

Utah A shopping center was developed on adjoining properties owned separately by two individuals. The two owners agreed to set aside parcels for use as parking facilities. A successor in interest of one of the owners made a lease that encumbered a portion of the parking area owned by it. The lessor agreed to indemnify the lessee if the agreement limiting the area to parking was enforced. The adjoining owner sued to enforce the restrictive covenant. *Held:* The agreement created a covenant running with the land. The court ordered removal of the structures placed thereon. The court declined to balance the equities and compensate the injured party by monetary damages without requiring removal of the structures. The court stated that balancing the equities was inappropriate where the violation was deliberate and willful. With full knowledge of the covenant, the parties took a calculated risk it would not be enforced. Having taken the risk, they must bear the consequences. *Papanikolas Bros. v. Sugarhouse Shopping Center*, 535 P2d 1256 (1975).

26.00 LANDLORD'S DUTY TO REPAIR

26.05 In General

D.C. Circuit Owners of a building failed to make needed repairs, with the result that the local government ordered the building vacated. The tenant's business, a restaurant, was closed, and the tenant did not reopen in another location. The tenant brought suit for damages. The trial court charged the jury that the tenant was entitled to compensation as measured by the fair market value of a going business. *Held:* Since the business could have been relocated, the tenant was entitled to (1) loss of net profits, (2) fixed expenses, and (3) value of prepaid items for which tenant would not receive benefit, but only for the period of time reasonably required to relocate such a business, and in no event beyond the date at which the tenant could have been required to vacate the premises. *Arnold's Hofbrau, Inc. v. George Hyman Constr. Co.*, 480 F2d 1145 (1973).

Indiana Landlord who was not in the business of renting property, leased a single-family residence to tenants. Tenant fell and was injured on steps landlord had promised to repair but never had. Tenants sued on theories of negligence, breach of covenant to repair, breach of implied warranty of habitability, and negligence per se based on tenants' belief that the condition of the steps violated a rule of the administrative building council. *Held:* For landlord. Landlord had not expressly covenanted to repair the property at the inception of the lease. There was no implied warranty of habitability in Indiana with respect to the rental of single-family used homes by nonmerchants, because they do not have better knowledge than consumers and are not in a better position to absorb loss. Finally, under Indiana law, violation of an administrative rule is not negligence per se. *Zimmerman v. Moore*, 441 NE2d 690 (Ct. App. 1982).

New York A commercial tenant's employee was severely burned while attempting to relight a pizza oven on the lessor's premises. The tenant and employee sued lessor for injuries sustained. *Held:* The lessor is entitled to summary judgment dismissing the claim against him. An out-of-possesion lessor is not liable for injuries that occur on the leased premises unless the lessor has retained a contractual responsibility to keep the premises in repair. In the present case, the tenant assumed the burden of maintaining the premises and equipment, thereby eliminating lessor's liability. *Tanoury v. Cancilla*, 540 NYS2d 91 (1989).

26.10
Tort Liability for Failure to Repair

9th Circuit Plaintiff was seriously injured from a fall on property leased from the federal government and used as a recreational center. Plaintiff sued, claiming the government had breached its duty of care, either to correct the dangerous condition or to warn of the possible danger. The government was granted summary judgment based on Cal. Civ. Code § 846, which restricted the liability of landowners who open their land to public recreational use. *Held:* Reversed. The statute provided an exception for individuals who paid a fee for use of the center. Therefore the limitation of liability of the statute did not apply. The Ninth Circuit remanded the case to the district court on the issue of the government's duty of care. *Graves v. United States Coast Guard*, 692 F2d 71 (1982).

Alabama Two women consented to share an apartment in landlord's building. Shortly after moving in, however, a fire caused extensive damage to their personal belongings. Evidence presented at trial showed that the fire was probably caused by a staple driven through an electric wire located in the wall space of the damaged apartment. There was also proof that landlord had made periodic inspections while the apartment was being built. A jury ruled that landlord was liable, and landlord appealed. *Held:* Reversed. Landlord had breached no duty or obligation to the two tenants. A landlord is under no duty to inspect his premises for latent defects. Nor is he liable for the work of the independent contractors who installed the electrical wiring, since there was no evidence that he directed their work. Landlord could be held responsible only if he knew of the defect and concealed this fact. There was no evidence that landlord was aware of the staple in the wire. *Osborn v. Brown*, 361 So. 2d 82 (1978).

Colorado Commercial landlord hired a contractor to remove pipes from his building. The contractor, with the landlord's knowledge, began using an electric torch on walls made of wood and cork. Shortly thereafter, a fire broke out that caused considerable damage and ultimately resulted in condemnation of the entire building. A tenant, owner of a box company located in the building, sued both the landlord and the contractor. He argued that the landlord had been negligent in selecting the contractor, had failed to supervise the work adequately, and had breached a covenant of quiet enjoyment. *Held:* Generally speaking, a building owner is not liable for the negligence of an independent contractor. However, a landlord will be responsible for an independent contractor's acts if the contractor is engaging in an "inherently dangerous" activity. The court remanded the case to the lower court for a jury to decide whether the use of an electric torch was the sort of activity for which the landlord should be liable. *Western Stock Center, Inc. v. Sevit, Inc.*, 578 P2d 1095 (1978).

Florida Tenant sued apartment owners to recover for injuries sustained when tenant ignited gas fumes while trying to turn on the gas stove and hot water heater. The accident occurred shortly after tenant moved in. The trial court entered summary judgment in favor of the landlord. The district court of appeals affirmed, referring to the rule of *caveat lessee*, which means that once possession passes to the tenant, the landlord is not liable for injuries caused by the condition of the leased premises. *Held:* Reversed. The owner of a residential dwelling unit leased to a tenant for residential purposes has a duty reasonably to inspect the premises before allowing tenant to take possession, and to make repairs necessary to transfer a reasonably safe dwelling unit to the tenant. This applies unless defects are waived by the tenant or the duty is modified by agreement between the parties. *Mansur v. Eubank*, 401 So. 2d 1328 (1981).

Illinois Subtenant's employee was injured when she fell in her employer's parking lot. The employee sued the sublessor for failure to maintain the premises. The sublessor had covenanted with the prime lessor to keep the premises in repair. However, the sublease made plaintiff's employer responsible for repairs. *Held:* For the sublessor. Generally, it is the tenant in possession, in this case plaintiff's employer, who is liable for injuries sustained by third persons because of a failure to keep the property in repair. Since the sublessor never promised the subtenant it would repair, the general rule of lessor immunity applied and the sublessor owed no tort duty to third persons. *Wright v. Mr. Quick, Inc.*, 486 NE2d 908 (1985).

Illinois Tenant was injured by a defective oven while in a neighboring tenant's apartment. Tenant sued landlord, alleging landlord breached its duty to maintain appliances in safe condition, a covenant in the neighbor's lease as well as in tenant's. Landlord moved to dismiss, contending that (1) the lease imposed no duty of repair, which would give rise to a tort action, and (2) tenant lacked standing to sue because she did not allege breach of a lease she had entered into. *Held:* Tenant had a cause of action in tort. Restatement (Second) of Torts § 357 imposes tort liability upon a landlord who breaches a covenant to repair the premises. The court rejected landlord's argument that liability should apply only to common areas. The landlord's duty of repair was not merely a contractual duty, but a tort duty extending to persons on the premises with lessee's consent. *Dial v. Mihalic*, 438 NE2d 546 (1982).

Maryland Pursuant to the Rent Escrow Act, tenant notified landlord of serious defects in the dwelling, but no action was taken to repair them. Tenant then brought a rent escrow action. After $1,000 had accumulated in escrow, the court awarded the funds returned to tenant. Landlord appealed, claiming the court did not have jurisdiction to order payment if the tenant had failed to request a hearing. *Held:* For tenant. The purpose of the act was to provide tenants with a mechanism for encouraging the repair of serious and dangerous defects within the dwelling unit. To conclude that the court lacked jurisdiction because tenant had not requested a hearing would be to frustrate legislative goals. *Neal v. Fisher*, 541 A2d 1314 (1988).

Massachusetts When landlord began eviction proceedings against tenant for nonpayment of rent, tenant counterclaimed that landlord had breached its implied warranty of habitability and covenant of quiet enjoyment. Tenant also sought consequential damages for emotional distress, which landlord allegedly caused her both negligently and intentionally. She claimed that landlord was unable and unwilling to remedy the recurrent floodings in her apartment, causing her to suffer great emotional anguish. *Held:* Landlord knew or should have known that all flooding could have been stopped by cementing over a porous wall. Landlord also knew or should have known that his inaction and indifference would be likely to cause emotional harm; therefore, his conduct was outrageous. In addition, since there was evidence that tenant's emotional distress was severe, all of the elements necessary for recovery of damages for the infliction of emotional distress were present. *Simon v. Solomon*, 431 NE2d 556 (1982).

Massachusetts Tenants who withheld rent because of rat-infested conditions were sued by landlord for nonpayment. Tenants counterclaimed for damages for, inter alia, emotional distress. *Held:* Tenants were not entitled to damages for emotional distress. The evidence showed that the landlord did not knowingly or recklessly cause tenants emotional distress and had attempted to alleviate the rat infestation. Moreover, the statute on which tenants based their claims for damages provided a remedy only for economic loss. *Wolfberg v. Hunter*, 432 NE2d 467 (1982).

Massachusetts Lease provided that the landlord could, 10 days after giving notice of nonpayment, enter and repossess the premises if the tenant defaulted on its monthly payment. The landlord entered the premises for the purpose of repossessing, but without giving notice. While padlocking and boarding up the front and rear doors of the store, he inadvertently activated the burglar alarm, which he silenced by disconnecting it. Six days later, the store was burglarized. The tenant brought suit for the losses sustained due to the burglary. The trial court held for the tenant, and the landlord appealed. *Held:* By failing to comply with the notice requirement, the landlord entered wrongfully. The rule of damages applicable to such a situation is liability for loss naturally and proximately resulting from the act of the tortfeasor. The court found that theft was a foreseeable result of the landlord's failure to reset the burglar alarm; consequently, the landlord was liable for the losses sustained from the burglary. *Gidwani v. Wasserman*, 365 NE2d 827 (1977).

Montana Tenant's spouse was killed by an electric shock in apartment after repeatedly asking landlord to repair the electrical system. Testimony established that the electrical system was not properly grounded. Tenant sued for wrongful death and survival. *Held:* Prior to this case, the Montana Supreme Court had held there was no implied warranty of habitability in residential leases, and that "repair and deduct" was tenant's exclusive remedy. But noting that the Residential Landlord and Tenant Act of 1977 had adopted the doctrine of implied warranty of habitability which allowed tenants to recover for injuries from latent dangerous defects, the court held that the wrongful death and survival action could be maintained. The case was remanded to determine whether landlord breached its duty of ordinary care. *Corrigan v. Janney*, 626 P2d 838 (1981).

Ohio Pursuant to a statutory duty requiring landlords to keep premises in habitable condition, landlord hired an independent contractor to make plumbing repairs. The contractor allegedly negligently caused a fire resulting in damage to tenants' apartment. Tenants sued the contractor and landlord alleging the contractor's negligence. Landlord contended he was not liable for the negligence of an independent contractor. *Held:* For tenants. Whether the duty is assumed by the landlord or is nondelegable and imposed by statute, the landlord may not insulate himself from liability for negligent performance of his duty by hiring an independent contractor. *Strayer v. Lindeman*, 427 NE2d 781 (1981).

26.15 Assumption of Risk by Tenant

Louisiana Tenant fell on a wobbly stairway. On a previous occasion, the tenant had fallen on the same stairway, receiving a gash requiring 21 stitches. No suit was filed at that time, but the landlord was requested to repair the stairway. The tenant instituted suit for damages based upon this second fall, and landlord raised contributory negligence as a defense. *Held:* The general rule is that where a tenant has knowledge of a defect in the premises, continued use does not constitute contributory negligence, unless it would appear to a reasonable man that use of that portion of the premises is apparently and imminently dangerous. The fact that a prior accident occurred did not ipso facto render the tenant's use of the premises unreasonable under the circumstances. Since the jury did not find that the tenant acted unreasonably, its verdict would not be disturbed. *Wilson v. Virgadeno*, 258 So. 2d 572 (Ct. App. 1972).

Kansas Tenant had used the sidewalk during the year preceding her injury, although she knew it was corroded. The landlord argued she had either assumed the risk that she would trip or had been negligent, thereby relieving him of any liability. *Held:* Tenant had no choice except to use the sidewalk, since it was the only practical way to get into the leased premises. To hold that she had thereby relieved the landlord of responsibility for her personal safety would make meaningless the rule that a tenant can recover for personal injuries resulting from a defect the landlord has agreed to repair. *Richardson v. Weckwork*, 509 P2d 1113 (1973).

Washington Tenant slipped and fell descending a stairway equipped with insufficient handrails. A local building ordinance required handrails extending the full length of the stairway, and tenant fell on the bottom step, which had no handrail. Tenant sued on a theory of negligence per se, to which landlord raised assumption of risk as an affirmative defense. *Held:* Assumption of risk was not an appropriate defense to negligence per se based on violation of a public safety statute. Unlike assumption of risk in cases of contractual duties, duties imposed by statutes designed to enhance public safety cannot be waived by private agreement or understanding. *Cramer v. Van Parys*, 500 P2d 1255 (Ct. App. 1972).

26.20
Covenant to Repair

7th Circuit Landlord appealed court's award to tenant for breach of landlord's obligation to repair the stores it operated. Landlord claimed the only remedies available to tenant under the lease were abatement of rent for unusable portions of the buildings or making repairs itself and charging them to the landlord. Tenant cross-appealed, contending that expert testimony it attempted to introduce on how the state of disrepair of the stores diminished their leasehold value was improperly excluded by the lower court on the ground that tenant had subleased only part of the property. *Held:* Tenant had the right to sue landlord for damages. Although the lease did not provide for such right, it could not limit any remedies available to tenant under state law unless tenant waived them. Since there was no waiver, the remedy of damages was available to tenant. However, the trial court erred in excluding the expert testimony because it had a reasonable basis in fact. A tenant was not required to sublease its property in order to establish damages for breach of a landlord's covenant to repair. *American Nat'l Bank & Trust Co. v. K-Mart Corp.*, 717 F2d 394 (1983).

Colorado Lessor brought an unlawful detainer action to recover possession of a penthouse apartment. The lease provided that the lessor would paint every three years. When the lessor did not paint the premises as per the lease provision, the lessees contracted to have it done and withheld rent as a setoff for the painting expenses. *Held:* The lessees are entitled to a setoff of the costs incurred as a result of the lessor's failure to perform her express covenant to repaint. *Shanahan v. Collins*, 539 P2d 1261 (1975).

Connecticut Lease provided that the landlord was responsible for building maintenance. The tenant began to hear "sizzling" sounds emanating from the bathroom walls, but the landlord ignored repeated requests to inspect the problem until finally the landlord's agent listened, but never entered the bathroom. Subsequently, a pipe fitting burst, and the tenant was scalded by hot water. The tenant brought suit, and the landlord, though conceding that it had "control" of the plumbing, argued that it could not have had actual or constructive knowledge of the defect, a prerequisite for its liability for breach of its duty to keep that portion of the demised premises over which it retained control in reasonably safe condition. *Held:* The existence of the "sizzling" noise, which suggested steam escaping from a leaking pipe, was sufficient evidence for a jury to conclude that the landlord had constructive notice of the defect. That is, a reasonable inspection would have disclosed the defect. *Pollack v. Gampel*, 313 A2d 73 (1972).

Illinois Landlord sought to evict tenants for nonpayment of rent. The tenants admitted that they were in arrears, but argued that the landlord could not evict them because they were relieved of the obligation to pay the full rent so long as their apartments were defective and unfit for human habitation. The tenants said the landlord had expressly promised to make repairs needed to render their apartments fit to live in, but he had failed to do so. The trial court held that even if this was true, the tenants were obliged to pay the rent and could be evicted if they did not. *Held:* The landlord's performance of his promise to put premises in good repair is a condition precedent to the tenant's duty to pay rent, at least where the repairs are needed to make the premises habitable. Consequently, a landlord may not evict a tenant who withholds rent for untenantable premises while the landlord himself is shirking his contractual obligation to repair them. *Jack Spring, Inc. v. Little*, 280 NE2d 208 (1972).

Massachusetts Commercial tenant sought indemnification from landlord for damages paid to a customer who was injured as the result of water leakage from a defective roof. Under the lease, landlord was obligated to make repairs, but he failed to do so after receiving notice from tenant. *Held:* An express covenant to make needed repairs is equivalent to an indemnity agreement; therefore, tenant may recover damages upon landlord's negligent failure to repair. *Great Atl. & Pac. Tea Co. v. Yanofsky*, 403 NE2d 370 (1980).

Michigan When an oil company sued a gas station operator, the gas station operator counterclaimed that the company failed to make repairs to the roof as required by the lease, and that his personal injury was caused by the disrepair. The oil company's motion for summary judgment on the counterclaim was granted by the court of appeals. The court cited the principle that an action in tort by a tenant cannot be based upon breach by the landlord of a covenant to make repairs. The state supreme court overruled this principle and reversed the case. *Held:* Landlord could be held liable for personal injuries resulting from landlord's failure to perform under a covenant to make repairs. The gas station operator had stated a claim upon which relief could be granted. *Mobil Oil Corp. v. Thorn*, 258 NW2d 30 (1977).

New York Shopper fell and hurt herself in the driveway of a supermarket's parking lot, due to a hole in the driveway. Both the supermarket-lessee and the owner-lessor were sued. *Held:* Where the landlord has breached a covenant to repair, he is liable both to the tenant and to those on the land with the tenant's permission. This was true even though the supermarket retained control of the driveway under the lease and was therefore also liable. *Putnam v. Stout*, 345 NE2d 319 (1976).

New York Tenant did not have to repair defects, its covenant notwithstanding, unless the landlord completed the repairs it had covenanted to make. A pier owned by the city had been badly damaged by an explosion. The city leased the pier to lessee, covenanting to rebuild the pier before the term began. Lessee covenanted to keep the premises in good repair during the term and, when the term was up, to surrender them "well and sufficently repaired, painted and in good order and condition." The city made extensive repairs, enough that lessee took possession when its term began. However, the city then refused to do any more work and left the pier in disrepair. Lessee deferred maintenance of the pier until the city finished rebuilding it. This impasse continued until the end of the term, causing lessee to surrender the premises without making any of the repairs required by its covenant. The city sued lessee for damages. *Held:* There was no breach by lessee of its covenant; lessee's duty to repair defects arising during the term was dependent on performances by the city of its covenant to rebuild, a covenant it had never fully performed. *Farrell Lines, Inc. v. City of New York*, 330 NYS2d 358 (1972).

26.25 Code Violations

7th Circuit Landlord violated local ordinance requiring that residential rental property be heated at stated minimum temperatures. Consequently, tenant was forced to keep a kettle of boiling water on the stove in order to heat her kitchen. The kettle overturned, scalding her children, and she commenced suit in tort against the landlord. *Held:* The cause of action can be maintained, and no summary judgment will lie for the landlord on the issue of proximate cause. The injuries could be shown to have been the direct and foreseeable consequence of landlord's negligence per se. *Enis v. Ba-Call Bldg. Corp.*, 639 F2d 359 (1980).

Connecticut A city ordinance made issuance of a certificate of occupancy a prerequisite to renting units in a building and prohibited recovery of rent on any unit for which a certificate had not been obtained. Landlords' application for certificates of occupancy was denied, but they continued to rent to tenants. Tenants sued, alleging landlords' collection of rent on uncertified units violated the state Unfair Trade Practices Act. Evidence established that landlords' buildings were in violation of housing and health codes. *Held:* For tenants. Although landlords had not specifically violated the prohibition on *recovery* of rent without certificates of occupancy, having only *received* rent, landlords had offended public policy by failing to ensure minimum standards of habitability. Their conduct was unfair and deceptive within the meaning of the Unfair Trade Practices Act. The case was remanded to permit tenants to present evidence on the issue of damages. *Conaway v. Prestia*, 464 A2d 847 (1983).

Connecticut Hot-water pipe in an apartment building burst, scalding a tenant. The local housing code provided that the plumbing system was to be pressure tested to disclose leaks. The plumbing in this building, which was of recent construction, had not been so tested. Tenant brought suit for damages, citing as one specification of negligence defendants' failure to have the test carried out. Defendants contended that, since the code section in question was in a chapter entitled "Drainage and toilet systems," it did not cover hot water pipes. *Held:* Regardless of the title, the section clearly and unambiguously referred to plumbing systems generally, and other sections under the same title referred to hot water tanks, etc. Therefore, the section was fully applicable. *Pollack v. Gampel*, 313 A2d 73 (1972).

Maryland Under the terms of a lease the landlord was to build a warehouse protected by a sprinkler system that would comply with the Maryland fire rating bureau requirements and U.S. government standards for buildings used to store government material. When the building was certified as completed, tenant took possession. However, the sprinkler system did not comply with the requisite standards until two months later, and tenant refused to pay the first two months' rent. When the landlord brought suit to recover the rent, tenant counterclaimed for damages owing to lost profits as a result of noncompliance with standards. *Held:* Where a lease required compliance with fire rating bureau requirements, but the landlord tendered as ready for occupancy a building which did not do so, tenant was entitled to go to the jury on its claim for damages. *S&S Bldg. Corp. v. Fidelity Storage Corp.*, 310 A2d 778 (1973).

Massachusetts Plaintiff, a tenant at sufferance in an apartment in defendant's building, sought an order compelling defendant to make repairs in compliance with the state building code and the state sanitary code. The parties stipulated that there were continuing violations of both codes. Defendant contended that plaintiff, as a tenant at sufferance and already under a court order to vacate the premises, was not entitled to the relief sought. The lower court issued a preliminary injunction to correct violation of the building code and sanitary code. *Held:* Affirmed. The relevant sanitary code statute states that any tenant who rents space in a building for residential purposes may file a petition to obtain relief under that code; the building code section that plaintiff sought to enforce describes a tenant who rents space as one entitled to sue; this section was not concerned with tenant-owner relationships, but rather rehabilitation and preservation of the state's housing stock. *Brown v. Guerrier*, 457 NE2d 630 (1983).

Massachusetts Plaintiff was injured when she slipped down an exterior flight of stairs, which had no landing at the top, leading from her leased apartment directly to the ground. She claimed there was snow and ice on the steps that caused her to slip. She objected to the exclusion at the trial of a building code provision requiring landings on such staircases. *Held:* Plaintiff was granted a remand because of the exclusion of evidence of the building code provision, which was clearly intended to eliminate or minimize the risk of falls, with resulting injuries, in passing through a doorway which opens directly to the top step of a set of stairs. It could contribute to the jury's decision as to the landlord's negligence. *Perry v. Madeiros*, 343 NE2d 859 (1976).

Ohio Tenant, just prior to moving from premises, notified landlord of two broken steps on stairway. A month later, tenant was injured when a third step collapsed. *Held:* Violation of the landlord's statutory duty to repair constituted negligence per se, leaving only the question of proximate cause to be resolved. Ohio statutory warranty of habitability did not expressly establish a cause of action in tort against a landlord for failure to make statutorily required repairs and also required proof of notice of the defect or attempted notice by tenant. *Shroades v. Rental Homes, Inc.*, 427 NE2d 774 (1981).

Oregon Tenant fell down a stairway within the demised premises. The stairway had no handrail, a violation of Portland's building code. The landlord argued that, under common-law rules, a landlord is not liable to his tenant for injuries caused by a dangerous condition existing at the time that the lessee took possession unless the condition is known to the landlord but unknown to the lessee, who would not be expected to discover the condition. The tenant contended that the violation of the building code was negligence per se, despite the fact that she was aware of the lack of a handrailing. *Held:* Since the court has adopted the rule that violation of an ordinance is negligence per se, it would be unreasonable to modify that concept with the notion that the ordinance only imposed a duty on the landlord when the violation of the building code was latent. This would effectively nullify any protection that such ordinances provided the tenant. *Lapp v. Rogers*, 510 P2d 551 (1973).

26.30
Exculpation From Liability for Failure to Repair

D.C. Circuit A construction contract provided that the contractor would "adequately protect adjacent property. . . ." The owners of the building under construction also owned the building on the adjacent property. When the lessee of that building discovered that part of the floor area was sinking, the owners promised to repair the floor, and undertook to do so. However, the repairs were negligently done, and the city ordered the premises closed. The lessee brought an action for damages to its business. The owners contended that they were insulated from liability by the provision of the construction contract. *Held:* The provision concerning protecting adjacent property did not clearly set forth an intent on the part of the contractor to exculpate the owners from their own negligence. Such an exculpatory clause must be clearly set forth before it will be given effect. *Arnold's Hofbrau, Inc. v. George Hyman Constr. Co.*, 480 F2d 1145 (1973).

Alabama Plaintiff lessee sued landlord for damages caused by a fire in his apartment, alleging the cause to be landlord's negligence in failing to repair the ceiling lighting of the common breezeway from which all tenants entered their apartments. The lease exculpated landlord in case of injury to person or property of lessee. Specifically, the exculpatory clause waived damages caused by the failure to repair fixtures or appurtenances located in the building. The trial court found for landlord and plaintiff appealed. *Held:* Affirmed. Exculpatory clauses are valid in Alabama. They have been recognized as a specific exception to the general rule that a party may not contract against the consequences of his own negligence. However, if damages resulted from landlord's active negligence stemming from some willful or wanton misconduct, the landlord could be sued for personal injuries. *Matthews v. Mountain Lodge Apartments, Inc.*, 388 So. 2d 935 (1980).

California Tenant tripped over a rock on a stairway in the landlord's building and was injured. A jury awarded the tenant $3,500 in damages. On appeal, the landlord argued that he should not be held liable, because the lease contained a clause disclaiming the landlord's liability for any injuries suffered on the premises. *Held:* The exculpatory clause was void as against public policy. In affirming the judgment for the tenant, the court pointed to six relevant factors: (1) Leases are increasingly subject to government regulation; (2) the landlord was providing an essential service; (3) the apartment building was open to the general public; (4) the lease was the product of unequal bargaining strength; (5) the lease was a standard form contract of adhesion; and (6) the tenant was being made to assume the risk of someone else's carelessness. *Henrioulle v. Marin Ventures, Inc.*, 143 Cal. Rptr. 247 (1978).

Mississippi Tenant slipped and injured herself on a stairway leading to her apartment. Her lease contained an exculpatory clause stating that landlord would not be liable for any personal injury or property damage caused by his negligence. When tenant sued landlord, the latter raised the exculpatory clause as a defense. *Held:* The landlord was liable for tenant's injuries. Although the court noted the general rule of caveat emptor for conveyances under leases, it also noted the exception for common areas of premises leased to multiple tenants. With respect to those areas, landlord has a duty of reasonable care. The court, noting that only a minority of states had declared exculpatory clauses void as against public policy, decided that Mississippi should join the minority. The majority rule was characterized by the court as a relic from the days when residential leasing was rare, and whose application in modern times would be unfair to tenants lacking bargaining power equal to that of landlords. *Cappaert v. Junker*, 413 So. 2d 378 (1982).

Mississippi The tenant leased space for a store from the landlord. The lease agreement provided that the landlord was to maintain the roof, foundation, and exterior walls of the building, while the tenant would maintain the rest of the premises. The agreement also contained an exculpatory clause that held the landlord harmless from any damages to persons or property on the premises and held the tenant liable for such damages. When the roof began to leak, the tenant notified the landlord but nothing was done, and the tenant made no repairs herself. When she suffered almost $17,000 in damages, she sued the landlord. *Held:* The tenant was not entitled to damages. The exculpatory clause was enforceable, since it was fully understandable division of risk and did not reflect fraud, over-reaching or unequal bargaining power. Under the exculpatory clause, damages would not be awarded even though the landlord was specifically required by the lease to keep the roof in good repair. *Smith v. Smith*, 375 So. 2d 1041 (1979).

New York Landlord, operator of a large shopping center, and the major tenant in the center were both sued by a customer who was injured in a fall in front of the tenant's store. After a trial, the jury allocated liability as 60 percent the owner's and 40 percent the tenant's. The landlord countersued the tenant, claiming that the tenant was responsible for all damages pursuant to an indemnification clause in the lease. Under this provision, the tenant agreed to maintain insurance on the premises for injuries to customers and to hold the landlord harmless for any losses, and to obtain policies in which the insurers would indemnify the landlord against losses. *Held:* Since this was a commercial agreement bargained at arm's length, the tenant was liable for all the damages. This was not a situation in which the landlord was exempting himself from liability for his own negligence but, rather, one in which the parties were allocating the risk of liability to third parties between themselves, through the use of insurance. *Hogeland v. Sibley, Lindsay & Curr Co.*, 366 NE2d 263 (1977).

Texas Plaintiff lessee sued defendant lessor for injuries incurred when he fell through a plate glass door. Plaintiff alleged the door was dangerous for use and defendant failed to exercise ordinary care in warning plaintiff. Defendant filed a motion for summary judgment, based on an exculpatory clause in the lease stating that landlord had no liability for injury caused by structural defects in the premises. *Held:* For defendant. Exculpatory clauses between landlord and tenant are generally upheld as to future liability for negligence unless there is gross disparity in bargaining power between the parties. *Porter v. Lumbermen's Inv. Corp.*, 606 SW2d 715 (Civ. App. 1980).

Virginia Plaintiff landlord sued defendant tenant for fire damages caused by tenant's negligence. Defendant pointed to a provision in the lease that relieved lessee of liability resulting from an "accidental fire." *Held:* For defendant tenant. The court concluded that the term "accidental fire" would include an act of negligence; it would not include an intentional act. Further, noting the trend in the law, the fact that landlord was to carry fire insurance is another factor in the court's construction of the accidental fire exculpatory provision, relieving the lessee from liability for his negligence. *Monterey Corp. v. Hart*, 224 SE2d 142 (1976).

26.35 Responsibility for Fire Damage

Florida A complaint filed on behalf of two children who were killed in a trailer fire alleged that (1) the electrical wiring in the trailer was so defective and dangerous that the electric authority had terminated service to the trailer; (2) the lessor of the trailer had a duty to make repairs before allowing the tenant to take possession; (3) the lessor knew of the defects; and (4) as a result of the termination of electric service and the lessor's failure to make repairs, the tenants were compelled to use candles at night. The complaint further alleged that the use of candles was reasonably foreseeable and known by the lessor to be unreasonably hazardous to small children. The trial court dismissed the petition for damages. *Held:* Reversed. The complaint against the lessor was sufficient to create a jury issue on causation. *Southeast Bank v. JAMA Mobile Home Parks*, 490 So. 2d 1057 (Dist. Ct. App. 1986).

Illinois Tenants rented a decaying building and made improvements. Seeking to secure the building from vandalism, tenants leased an adjacent larger building from the same landlords. Tenants were unable to improve the larger building and let the second lease lapse. Landlords were subsequently cited for numerous code violations on the larger building and failed to respond. The building caught fire, apparently as a result of arson, and the fire spread to and destroyed tenants' improved building. Tenants sued landlords for negligence, alleging that landlords breached their duty to maintain and secure the larger building. *Held:* The evidence was sufficient to uphold a jury verdict for tenants on grounds of negligence. Landlords had notice of building code violations and that vagrants had access to the larger building, but failed to maintain and secure the building as required by city ordinance. Landlords could not delegate their duty to maintain the property to tenants, although tenants had retained access to the building, since tenants had no contractual or common-law duty to maintain the building. *Chem-Pac, Inc. v. Simborg*, 495 NE2d 1124 (App. Ct. 1986).

New York Premises were partially destroyed by fire while the lessees were in possession. Lessors restored the premises to their original condition at the commencement of the lease pursuant to the lease covenant to repair, but did not restore lessees' improvements to the leasehold. Lessees then defaulted on the lease, and lessors sued to recover unpaid rent. *Held:* Lessors were not obligated under the lease to restore the leasehold improvements and were therefore entitled to the rent for the remaining term pursuant to a valid acceleration clause. *Silver v. Moe's Pizza, Inc.*, 503 NYS2d 86 (App. Div. 1986).

North Dakota A fire started in a tenant's apartment. The fire chief ascribed the fire to a cigarette dropped negligently into the cushions of the couch and left to smolder. During the time the cigarette could have been dropped, the tenant was not the only smoker in the apartment: Her daughter and a co-worker who had spent the night on the couch were also present. None of them admitted to having left a cigarette to smolder. The landlord sued the tenant for negligence, alleging that the fire was caused by the couch or the apartment, both of which were in her exclusive control at the time of the blaze. *Held:* The tenant could not be presumed responsible for negligence based on her control of the apartment. According to the fire chief's testimony, it was the cigarette, not the couch or apartment, that caused the fire. Since there was no evidence to prove that it was the tenant herself who dropped the cigarette, a jury instruction on res ipsa loquitur was reversible error. *Victory Park Apartments, Inc. v. Axelson*, 367 NW2d 155 (1985).

Washington A commercial lease contained a waiver of subrogation clause, which provided that lessor and lessee waived their rights of recovery for any losses resulting from fire covered by insurance. After a fire damaged the leased premises, as well as other parts of the same building owned by lessor, lessor sued the lessee. *Held:* The waiver clause applied only to insured losses on the leased premises. The lessor was entitled to seek recovery from the lessee for loss of property not covered by the lease and for any uninsured loss of property covered by the lease. Where a lease that relates to specified premises does not refer to any other property, a waiver in the lease cannot be extended to relieve lessee from liability for damage to property not subject to the lease. *Millican of Wash. v. Wienker Carpet Serv.*, 722 P2d 861 (Ct. App. 1986).

Wisconsin Tenant injured in a fire set deliberately by the grandson of another tenant sued the landlord for negligence and was awarded actual and punitive damages. Evidence established that the landlord was aware of serious security problems at the low-income housing complex, including previous suspicious fires, lack of security nights and weekends, broken locks, and an inoperable fire alarm system. Witnesses testified that a reasonable owner would have corrected these problems to reduce the risk of fire. The landlord contended he could not afford to make any improvements. *Held:* The award of punitive damages was justified. The landlord's failure to act to reduce the risk of fire constituted reckless disregard of the tenant's safety and evidence of "outrageous" conduct justifying an award of punitive damages, given the landlord's knowledge of problems at the complex and the history of suspicious fires. *Brown v. Maxey*, 369 NW2d 677 (1985).

27.00 OTHER DUTIES OF LANDLORD

27.05 Maintenance of Common Areas

Kansas The grandmother of a university student sued for personal injuries suffered in a fall in an unlighted stairwell while visiting her granddaughter's dormitory. The granddaughter rented a room under a written agreement with the university. The lower court granted defendant summary judgment on the basis that no landlord-tenant relationship existed. *Held:* Reversed and remanded. Although the agreement was not a true lease, the university owed a landlord's duty to exercise reasonable care in keeping common areas of the residence hall in safe condition for residents and invited guests. The lessor-lessee relationship is liberally construed to include a lease of a portion of university property to students. *Burch v. University of Kansas*, 756 P2d 431 (1988).

Maryland Tenant sued the landlord after tenant's son was seriously injured when he fell through the lower half of a glass exit door after running down a corridor. The tenant claimed the landlord was negligent in not having used a heavier glass at the time the building had been constructed some years before. From a verdict for the tenant, the landlord appealed. *Held:* The test is whether the landlord conformed to established custom in the particular instance, provided that customary construction and maintenance is not inherently dangerous or obviously improper. The evidence established that the landlord complied with custom in choosing the plate glass. There was no evidence of any inherent danger in the use of such glass. A landlord cannot be found negligent because the glass in doors might not withstand a blow from a running child. The mere fact that stronger materials could have been used in construction or were available for replacement was insufficient to support a finding of negligence. *Bernstein v. Reforzo*, 379 A2d 181 (1977).

Nebraska A tenant on the second floor of a two-story building sued her landlord after she slipped on dog excrement and fell down a flight of stairs. She claimed that the stairway constituted a common area under the landlord's control and that the landlord was negligent in not supervising the maintenance of animals belonging to other tenants. After a jury verdict in favor of the tenant, the landlord's motion for a new trial was sustained. *Held:* Reversed and remanded. The Nebraska Supreme Court ruled that the landlord was not liable for the tenant's injuries because the stairway, which constituted a separate entrance exclusively to tenant's apartment, was not a common area under the landlord's control. In addition, the landlord had no responsibility to supervise maintenance of tenants' animals. *Hiatt v. Tallmage*, 365 NW2d 448 (1985).

Ohio Tenant was injured by a fall on ice that had accumulated at the entrance of her apartment building following a snowstorm. She sued the landlord for negligence, citing Ohio Rev. Code Ann. § 5321.04(A)(3), which required landlords to "[k]eep all common areas of the premises in a safe and sanitary condition." *Held:* Landlord was entitled to summary judgment. The common law of Ohio did not recognize a duty of landlords to clear ice and snow from common areas absent an express provision in the lease. Had the statute cited by tenant been intended to abrogate the common-law rule, it would have provided so expressly. It was tenant's duty to protect herself from the obvious and apparent dangers of accumulated ice and snow. *LaCourse v. Fleitz*, 503 NE2d 159 (1986).

Ohio Plaintiff rented an apartment from defendant. On January 24, 1982, she slipped on snow and ice on the walkway from her apartment to the sidewalk and fractured her ankle. She sued the landlord, and his motion for summary judgment was granted. *Held:* Affirmed. The walkway was not a "common walkway" for which the landlord had a legal duty to keep clear of snow and ice. Tenants of the three other apartments had their own walkways, and the mere fact that another tenant infrequently used the same walkway would not make it a "common approach." Here the tenant had possession and control over the area, and her son had regularly removed snow and ice in 1978 and 1979. Since the landlord retained no control or possession, he was under no legal duty to keep the area clear. *Porter v. Miller*, 468 NE2d 134 (Ct. App. 1984).

Texas Plaintiff, patron of defendant retail grocer, fell on icy sidewalk in front of the store. The premises were leased under terms that obligated landlord to maintain common areas, including the removal of ice and snow. Plaintiff argued that defendant lessee breached its duty to keep the premises in safe condition and to prevent injury to business invitees. *Held:* Summary judgment for lessee affirmed. As set forth in controlling decisions, an occupier of premises must keep such premises in a reasonably safe condition and warn invitees of dangerous conditions. The "occupier of premises" means the party in control thereof. Since the landlord by the terms of the lease retained control of exterior sidewalks and undertook responsibility for removal of ice and snow, defendant grocery was not an "occupier of premises" and had no duty to maintain common areas. *Howe v. Kroger Co.*, 598 SW2d 929 (Civ. App. 1980).

27.10 Maintenance of Parking Facilities

Maine Lessee was to become the exclusive tenant of a building and an adjacent parking lot upon the expiration of the lease of another tenant with which the lessee shared the building. However, when the other tenant's lease expired, the lessee had lost interest in the exclusive use of the building and lot, and instead negotiated an amendment to its original lease, giving up any rights to the other half of the building and any ultimate leasehold rights in one half of the parking area. The lessor attempted to build a drive-up teller facility on part of the parking area, to which the lessee objected. At issue was the question of whether the lessee retained any rights to the other half of the parking area. *Held:* Under the instruments lessor and lessee were tenants in common as to the use of the parking area, and neither had the right to appropriate any particular portion of the lot for a use which excluded the other from that portion without consent. *Bank of Maine v. Giguere*, 309 A2d 114 (1973).

Wisconsin Landlord covenanted to supply its tenant with not less than 18 parking spaces, and, in the event that less than 18 were available, the tenant would receive credit against its rent. The landlord constructed a new building next to the demised premises and assigned the parking spaces to other tenants. The tenant brought suit for an injunction, contending that it was still entitled to the spaces, as they were still available. The landlord argued that available meant "not needed by the landlord." *Held:* As a matter of law, available means physically usable. Since these spaces existed, they were available. *American Mut. Liab. Ins. Co. v. Fisher*, 206 NW2d 152 (1973).

27.15 Limitation on Competition by Other Tenants

Georgia Tenant, a travel firm, sued lessor for violating a restrictive covenant in its lease, which provided that lessor would not lease to any other businesses competitive to tenant's in the same complex. Tenant sought damages for lost profits under both its breach of contract claim and its allegation of fraud. *Held:* Tenant was entitled to lost profits under the fraud claim, but could not seek them under the breach of contract claim. The measure of damages recoverable for a lessor's breach of covenant not to rent other stipulated premises for a competing business is the difference in value between plaintiff's leasehold with the covenant against competition unbroken and the same leasehold with the covenant broken. However, allegations and evidence of loss of profits are material to show damages sustained. *Gilmore Int'l Travel, Inc. v. Equitable Life Assurance Soc'y of the United States*, 358 SE2d 279 (Ct. App. 1987).

Montana Lessees operated a restaurant under a lease from a hotel that provided that the hotel would not permit a competing full restaurant service to be maintained in the hotel without lessees' consent. When the hotel sublet a portion of the hotel for a Mexican restaurant that would operate only when lessees' restaurant was closed, lessees filed for a declaratory judgment barring the other restaurant. *Held:* The second restaurant is barred by the lease agreement. The lease satisfied the requirements of an enforceable restrictive covenant: (1) it must be restricted in respect to time or place, (2) it must be for good consideration, and (3) that it must be reasonable and in the public interest. *O'Neill v. Ferraro*, 596 P2d 197 (1979).

Texas A commercial lease forbade the landlord to lease to potential competitors of the tenant within a specified area. However, the landlord was a partnership (all of whose members had signed the lease), and one of the partners did lease to a competitor within the designated area. This partner argued that this type of anticompetition covenant is void as to a partner, such as himself, with no connection to the restrained property. *Held:* The anticompetition covenant was valid. Contracts otherwise in restraint of trade will be enforced where each party is legally tied to the subject property. Being a partner and participating in the partnership's affairs were sufficient connections. *City Prod. Corp. v. Berman*, 610 SW2d 446 (1980).

27.20 Duty to Deliver Possession

Connecticut In a summary process action to recover possession of premises, a landlord appealed a decision in favor of the tenant within 14 days, as provided by the general statute relating to appeals. Tenant claimed the appeal was untimely, since the summary process statute provided that appeals must be taken within five days. *Held:* The purpose of summary process statutes is to secure prompt hearings and final determinations, and, therefore, the five-day statute applies to all appeals by either the landlord or the tenant. *Henry Knox Sherrill Corp. v. Randall*, 358 A2d 159 (1976).

Hawaii The tenants were involved in a dispute with their landlord, who "found the situation intolerable." The tenants were served an eviction notice, with which they did not comply. The tenants subsequently reached an agreement with the landlord to retain possession of the premises, but the landlord later changed his mind. The landlord then padlocked the door of the apartment. The tenants brought suit, charging that they were locked out without cause or court order. *Held:* For the tenants. The Residential Landlord-Tenant Code, Hawaii Rev. Stat. § 521-63(c), states that "[i]f the landlord removes or excludes the tenant from the premises overnight without cause or court order so authorizing, the tenant may recover possession or terminate the rental agreement and, in either case, recover an amount equal to two months rent or free occupancy for two months, and the cost of suit, including reasonable attorney's fees." The court ruled there was no reason to depart from a strict interpretation of the legislation and awarded two months' rent and attorney fees to the tenants. *Kaiama v. Aguilar*, 696 P2d 839 (1985).

New York Lease drafted by the landlord stated that tenant could take possession if and when previous tenant left. In addition, the lease provided that if the premises were not vacated by a certain date, either party could cancel the lease on 60 days' notice, and the lease would expire at the end of that period. When the previous tenant did not vacate by the specified date, the prospective tenant sought to cancel the lease by giving notice. The landlord claimed that the lease was still in effect because the premises were ready for the tenant's occupancy before the end of the 60 days. *Held:* The termination was valid because the lease did not indicate that a salvage period after the specified date was intended. The lease is to be construed against the lessor as drafter, and no new liability not explicitly clear in the lease will be imposed upon a tenant by interpretation of an ambiguous clause. *67 Wall St. Co. v. Franklin Nat'l Bank*, 333 NE2d 184 (1975).

27.25 Gas and Electricity

California In an attempt to harass his tenants into leaving their homes, landlord terminated gas service for 60 days, preventing heating and cooking. Tenants sued under a state statute that imposes a $100 per diem penalty in cases of willful landlord termination of utility services. *Held:* The trial court's imposition of $26,000 in damages, both actual and punitive, was neither excessive nor unjust. The landlord's unreasonable and "atrocious" conduct distinguishes the court's holding from that in *Hale v. Morgan*, 584 P2d 512 (1978). *Kinney v. Vaccari*, 612 P2d 877 (1980).

27.30 Quiet Enjoyment

7th Circuit Tenant leased a building from landlord exclusively for the operation of a radio broadcast station. The landlord anounced that it planned to build a taller building next to the tenant's building. Tenant sued, claiming that construction of the taller building next door would distort and destroy its radio transmission and that the action constituted a breach of the implied covenant of quiet enjoyment. *Held:* For defendant. In order to find a breach of lessee's right to quiet enjoyment, it is necessary to first find that lessee has a right to the use of the airwaves extending across the space where the new building is to be constructed. Illinois law does not imply an easement for light or air in a lease, nor by analogy will it imply an easement for radio frequencies. Neither party could reasonably have expected the property surrounding the tenant's building to remain undeveloped; therefore, the parties did not intend to imply a right of passage for tenant's radio signals. Tenant had the duty to bargain for any unique provisions affecting the transmission of radio waves; an easement for unobstructed radio waves cannot be read into the lease. *Infinity Broadcasting v. Prudential Ins. Co.*, 869 F2d 1073 (1989).

District of Columbia Tenant's theater lease provided for the right of tenant to be reimbursed for defaulted obligations of landlord. Under the lease, landlord was obligated to provide adequate construction and insulation to prevent noise or odors that emanated from a restaurant from penetrating to the theater. After unsuccessfully attempting construction, theater sued restaurant to enjoin loud entertainment. Landlord appealed award of attorney fees to reimburse theater, and restaurant appealed award to reimburse landlord. *Held:* The legal action taken by theater was reasonable and appropriate in light of landlord's failure to perform its soundproofing obligations. Attorney fees were therefore reimbursable. In addition, because the restaurant breached its lease by providing loud entertainment the damages assessed against it were proper. *Sundown, Inc. v. Canal Square Assocs.*, 390 A2d 421 (1978).

Florida Tenant in the business of selling patio furniture signed a lease with a shopping center landlord. Landlord later leased adjacent space to an exercise studio. Loud music, screams and yells were heard from the exercise studio, causing walls to vibrate and a painting to fall off the wall in the furniture store. The store lost customers and employees because of the noise. Landlord promised to insulate the walls, but failed to do so. The furniture store owner moved out. Landlord sued for breach of the lease, and the store owner pleaded constructive eviction. *Held:* Tenant was constructively evicted. Landlord's explicit covenant with tenant of peaceable enjoyment of the premises had been breached. Landlord had the means of securing tenant's quiet enjoyment, but failed to take action until tenant moved out, when it insulated the store. *Barton v. Mitchell Co.*, 507 So. 2d 148 (Dist. Ct. App. 1987).

Maryland Tenant who was subjected to "unbearable" noise from the apartment above vacated his apartment after repeated complaints to landlord without effect. Landlord sued tenant for breach of lease, and tenant counterclaimed, alleging nuisance, a breach of covenant of quiet enjoyment and constructive eviction. *Held:* For tenant. The court took the less traditional view that a landlord who has the authority under the lease to restrict excessive noise or other offensive conduct has an obligation to protect the right of tenants to quiet enjoyment, and should evict an offending tenant. The traditional view that breach of quiet enjoyment and constructive eviction cannot be based upon disturbances by another tenant was rejected because it was predicated on past treatment of tenants as parties over whose conduct the landlord had no control. Tenant also had a cause of action for nuisance. *Bocchini v. Gorn Management Co.*, 515 A2d 1179 (Ct. Spec. App. 1986).

Massachusetts When plaintiff attempted to organize tenants to resist a rent increase, the landlord demanded rent for an empty conference room that he had previously allowed plaintiff to use free of charge for weight training and locked plaintiff out of the room. Plaintiff sought damages against the landlord under Mass. Gen. L. ch. 186, §§ 14, 18 for interference with the quiet enjoyment of residential premises and for taking reprisals against a tenant for organizing a tenant's union. *Held:* Tenant was entitled to awards of three months' rent under Section 14 and one months' rent under Section 18. The landlord's single act of locking plaintiff out of the conference room violated both sections and constituted two separate injuries. *Ianello v. Court Management Corp.*, 509 NE2d 1 (1987).

Mississippi A landlord rented a property to a commercial tenant without informing him of zoning restrictions that made the property unsuitable for the tenant's business. The tenant invested over $5,000 in repairs to the premises before learning of the zoning. The tenant never inquired about zoning, and the landlord, although he knew of the zoning restrictions, claimed not to have thought about it when negotiating the lease. The tenant sued the landlord for breach of the covenant of quiet enjoyment and for fraud, and was awarded actual as well as punitive damages. The landlord contested the punitive damages on appeal. *Held:* For the landlord. Punitive damages are assessed only in extreme cases, requiring not only fraud, but willful and intentional wrong or gross negligence and reckless conduct. The landlord appeared to have represented the property as suitable only on the basis of vague parol evidence, and the zoning ordinance had not been effectively enforced by the city in the past. *Gardner v. Jones*, 464 So. 2d 1144 (1985).

Texas A gynecologist executed a lease contract for the rental of an office for his practice. The doctor and lessor agreed to an expressed covenant of quiet enjoyment conditioned upon the payment of rent. Months later, anti-abortion protesters began picketing the building. After several complaints from the doctor, the landlord failed to take action. The doctor then abandoned the premises and refused to pay additional rent, claiming that the landlord breached the covenant. *Held:* The landlord's failure to act amounted to a constructive eviction and breach of the covenant. The failure to act interfered with the doctor's use and enjoyment of the leased premises, allowing him to abandon the premises within a reasonable time after the incident. *Fidelity Mut. Life Ins. Co. v. Kaminsky*, 768 SW2d 818 (Ct. App. 1989).

Washington Lessee sued to recover damages and injunctive relief against a lessor, which allegedly had breached its duty to repair a wall that was structurally unsound. *Held:* Although the lease contained no express covenant of quiet enjoyment, such a covenant arises by implication in every lease. The lessor's acts and omissions, however, result in liability only when there is a breach of an underlying duty; but where lessor breached the lease and evidenced a motive or intention to destroy an interest of the lessee, tort damages may lie. *Cherberg v. Peoples Nat'l Bank*, 564 P2d 1137 (1976).

27.35
Mitigation of Damages Caused by Tenant's Breach

Colorado Lessees were in default of their lease. Lessor entered into a new lease with another company, which paid lessor a $130,000 "entry premium" for the right to the lease. Lessor sued the lessees and guarantors for breach of the lease, and they argued that the premium should have been applied as a setoff to mitigate lessor's damages from their abandonment of the lease. *Held:* The premium could be set off. The fact that the monetary benefit to the lessor is in the form of an "entry premium," rather than increased rent should have no legal significance to the proper measure of damages as long as the premium is paid prior to the expiration date of the defaulting tenant's lease. Prohibiting the offset of an "entry premium" would place the lessor in a financially more advantageous position than if the lessees had fully performed their obligations and would impermissibly allow the lessor to reap a windfall from the default. *La Casa Nino, Inc. v. Plaza Esteban*, 762 P2d 669 (1988).

New Jersey After tenant broke his lease, the landlord waited 15 months before re-renting the apartment, even though other tenants were interested in the vacant apartment, and sued the defaulting tenant for nearly $5,000. *Held:* Where another "suitable tenant can be found, landlords should not be allowed to recover unpaid rent." The court did state that landlords could collect reasonable expenses incurred in reletting the premises, but only when such expenses could be proved. Finally, the court made it clear that its decision applied only to *residential* leases, and left open "the question of whether a similar rule should be adopted in commercial settings." *Sommer v. Kridel*, 378 A2d 767 (1977).

North Dakota Tenant entered into a five-year lease for premises to be used as a grocery store. When the business failed, the tenant leased the building to a subtenant, who was later adjudicated a bankrupt. The landlord then listed the premises with a broker, but at an annual rent of $33,600, which was $12,600 greater than the rent provided in the original lease with the tenant. The landlord was unable to relet the premises at the higher rental and sued the original tenant for accrued rent. *Held:* A landlord has a duty to mitigate damages that arise out of a tenant's default. Since the new rental figure exceeded the old one by more than 50 percent, the landlord's listing of the premises with a broker did not constitute a good faith effort to mitigate damages. *MARSON, Inc. v. Terwaho Enters.*, 259 NW2d 289 (1977).

Oregon Landlord rented office space for a five-year term to a tenant who defaulted after two years. After six months, the landlord found a new tenant at a higher rent and for a longer term than the original lease, but subsequently this tenant also defaulted. After a year, the landlord relet the premises to a third tenant, who occupied the premises through the expiration of the original term. The landlord then sued the original tenant for the difference between the total rent left unpaid over the unexpired term, less the total rent paid by the two subsequent tenants during that term. *Held:* The landlord's efforts to relet the premises for a higher rent and an extended term were reasonable and entitled him to damages from the original tenant. The marketability of the premises could be inhibited by limiting the term, and the higher rent was consistent with fair market value. The landlord had therefore properly acted to mitigate damages. *United States Nat'l Bank v. Homeland, Inc.*, 631 P2d 761 (1981).

27.40 Protection of Tenants From Crime

4th Circuit A female tenant was attacked outside her apartment building. The Supreme Court of Virginia had decided in 1974 that a landlord had no duty to protect tenants from criminal acts of third parties. However, tenant maintained that the subsequent enactment of the Landlord and Tenant Act, requiring landlords to "keep all common areas . . . of the premises in a clean and *safe* condition," superceded the 1974 precedent. *Held:* Tenant was not entitled to protection against criminal acts under the statute. The word "safe" in this context meant from of structural hazards, not secure against criminal activity. The court, noting the need to balance tenant protection against the cost of such protection, deemed this a policy issue to be resolved by the legislature. *Deem v. Charles E. Smith Management, Inc.*, 799 F2d 944 (1986).

D.C. Circuit Tenant was criminally assaulted in the hallway of an apartment house. *Held:* Landlord had both actual and constructive notice that crimes were being committed against tenants in the common areas of the building. Consequently, the landlord was under a duty to protect the tenants. The standard that the landlord was obliged to maintain was that which he was in fact following at the time the tenant became a resident, and which standard was not thereafter maintained. The general rule of law that a person is not under a duty to protect another from criminal attacks does not apply to "modern day urban apartment living. . . ." The landlord has an implied contractual duty to provide reasonable protective measures. *Kline v. 1500 Mass. Ave. Apartment Corp.*, 439 F2d 477 (1970).

U.S. District Court, Kansas When tenant moved into landlord's apartment complex, a security guard was on duty at night. Over the course of tenant's lease, the guard took on additional work, and the landlord did not provide additional guards. One night tenant was raped by burglars in her apartment. She sued the landlord, alleging a breach of express and implied warranties to maintain security. *Held:* An award of $390,000 to tenant was justified, because landlord had failed to maintain the level of security existing at the beginning of the lease, which failure was in breach of the implied warranty to maintain conditions. Such finding was supported by evidence of advertisements and conversations with tenant regarding security. The damage award was not excessive in light of testimony that tenant suffered psychological damage as a result of the attack and required continuing psychiatric care. *Flood v. Wisconsin Real Estate Inv. Trust.* 503 F. Supp. 1157 (1980).

California Plaintiff, a former tenant in defendant's building, was raped and assaulted in the dimly lit lobby. The common areas of the building were unsafe, and the lock on the front door was broken. Defendant had actual and constructive notice that the lobby was in dangerous condition, that the building was in a high-crime area, and that tenants were fearful for their safety. Plaintiff sued for personal injuries. *Held:* Defendant, who had notice of dangerous conditions, failed to exercise reasonable care by securing the building. Although landlords traditionally had no duty to protect tenants from the criminal acts of others, recent case law has created a duty on the part of a landlord to take reasonable steps to protect tenants from crime. *Kwaitkowski v. Superior Trading Co.,* 176 Cal. Rptr. 494 (1981).

California A resident of a large apartment building was shot and killed as he walked past a neighbor's apartment. The assailant had a history of psychotic behavior and was rumored to possess a gun. Tenants frequently complained to the building manager of the tenant's threatening actions; however, the landlord failed to respond to the complaints or to investigate the assailant's background. The parents of the deceased asserted that the landlord had a duty to monitor or control the behavior of the assailing tenant. *Held:* The landlord had no legal duty to monitor tenant's conduct. While tenant's conduct may have been a nuisance, the landlord could not have foreseen that tenant would fatally shoot the victim. The landlord's failure to evict the nuisance tenant was not the proximate cause of the shooting. Plaintiffs failed to establish what action the landlord could have taken with respect to tenant's deteriorating mental condition, or that tenant was not legally entitled to keep a handgun in her apartment. *Davis v. Gomez,* 255 Cal. Rptr. 743 (Ct. App. 1989).

District of Columbia Landlord appealed a trial judge's jury charge that a landlord owes a duty of reasonable protection against criminal acts of third parties to his tenants and guests in an urban multiple-unit apartment house. Tenants had complained about the security of the front door on several occasions prior to the shooting and robbing of plaintiff tenant in the common hallway of the apartment house. *Held:* The landlord owes the duty to tenants and guests. The trial judge was correct in his charge and in letting the case go to the jury. There was evidence of criminal incidents in the hallways and of the continuing ineffectiveness of the front door in excluding unauthorized persons from entry. Action had been taken by neighboring buildings to improve their security and tenants' concern had been expressed to landlord, giving him notice of the inadequacy of security in his building. *Spar v. Obwoya,* 369 A2d 173 (1977).

Hawaii Condominium owners lent their unit to guests while they were away on their honeymoon. Late one night, two assailants passed through common areas of the development and entered the guests' apartment. The assailants shot one guest and raped another after robbing the apartment. The condominium project was in a high-crime area, and there had been previously unsolved cases of rape, robbery, and break-ins in the complex. There also were rumors that an extra master key was floating around. The victims sued the condominium association for negligence. *Held:* For the victims. When a condominium association performs all the traditional duties of a landlord, it also assumes the landlord's duty of care to protect resident condominium owners and their guests from foreseeable criminal acts of third parties. *Moody v. Cawdrey & Assocs., Inc.*, 721 P2d 707 (1986) (per curiam).

Illinois Plaintiff, who was raped by an intruder, sued landlord, alleging the assault resulted from landlord's failure to repair a burglar alarm in her apartment in violation of a lease provision requiring landlord to repair defects. Landlord contended that under Illinois law a landlord does not owe a tenant a duty of protection against criminal acts. *Held:* For landlord. Landlord installed the burglar alarm voluntarily and had at most a contractual obligation to keep it operable. He did not promise plaintiff she would be protected from criminal harm by third parties. His liability was limited to damages reasonably foreseeable by breach of his duty to repair the alarm, i.e., the cost of repair. In addition, plaintiff failed to establish that the inoperable alarm was the proximate cause of the rape. It would be speculative to assume that a working alarm would have prevented the crime. *Carrigan v. New World Enters., Ltd.*, 446 NE2d 265 (1983).

Louisiana Plaintiff's five-year-old son was murdered in a development owned and managed by defendant. The mother alleged that the development had control of the surrounding premises where the murder occurred, and that the development was aware of hazardous conditions but failed to correct them. She sued the development, alleging the proximate cause of her son's death was defendant's failure to correct the unsafe conditions. The development moved for summary judgment. *Held:* Motion granted. Absent a special relationship between the landlord and tenant, or breach of an implied or express obligation by the landlord to provide security, the landlord has no duty to protect tenants from harm sustained as a result of a third party's actions. *Cornelius v. Housing Auth.*, 539 So. 2d 1250 (Ct. App. 1989).

Maryland Tenant's father was shot and killed in the underground parking garage of an apartment house. There were no known prior incidents of crime in the building. The landlord was installing additional security measures at the time of the incident owing to an increasing crime rate in the neighborhood. The tenant contended that the landlord had a duty to protect tenants from criminal assaults. *Held:* The landlord does not have a special duty to protect tenants unless malfeasance or negligence can be shown. Here, the landlord had no prior knowledge of any criminal activities on the premises. *Scott v. Watson,* 359 A2d 548 (1976).

Missouri A window latch of tenant's third-floor apartment was broken, so that an intruder could gain entry from the fire escape. Landlord knew a burglar had previously entered the apartment through balcony doors. Tenant repeatedly reported the broken latch, and, subsequently, tenant was raped by an intruder who entered through the unsecured window. She sued, alleging the landlord was negligent in failing to take precautions to prevent an intruder from gaining access to the fire escape and the window of her apartment. *Held:* Tenant's complaint stated a cause of action against the landlord for negligence in maintaining the fire escape. A landlord has a duty of due care to secure the common premises safe against foreseeable risks. Tenant alleged landlord knew of the dangerous condition of the window. There was no logical reason, the court wrote, why a dangerous condition of common premises, proximately causing injury on private premises, could not occasion liability. *Aaron v. Havens,* 758 SW2d 446 (1988) (en banc).

Nebraska A female tenant in an apartment building had her front door kicked in and, although she made daily requests to have the lock repaired, no action was taken for a week. At the end of the week, she was sexually assaulted in her apartment by a male tenant who had in the past made frequent lewd displays. The tenant's lawsuit resulted in summary judgment for the landlord and an appeal by the tenant to the Supreme Court of Nebraska. *Held:* Reversal and a new trial were granted by the court on a straight *Kline*-style analysis. References were made to the foreseeability of the criminal act, the reasonableness of precautionary measures, and the proximate causation of injury by the absence of such measures. *KSR v. Novak & Sons, Inc.,* 406 NW2d 636 (1987).

New Jersey A downstairs tenant sued her landlord for negligence and breach of the implied warranties of habitability and quiet enjoyment for failing to evict a disruptive upstairs tenant. The downstairs tenant claimed that upstairs tenant had violent fights with his wife and allowed continual drug traffic through his apartment. When the downstairs tenant told the landlord's agent about a motorcycle gang fight upstairs, the agent promised to evict the upstairs tenant. A year and a half later, the upstairs tenant discharged a shotgun through the downstairs ceiling, blowing the downstairs tenant across the room and causing her injuries that required surgery. The upstairs tenant was eventually evicted after yet another incident. *Held:* The downstairs tenant was not entitled to damages beyond a small rent abatement. Before the gang fight, landlord was not on notice as to the upstairs tenant's destructive tendencies. The shotgun incident was not foreseeable, because none of the preceding incidents would have led a reasonable person to expect a criminal assault on another tenant. Finally, damages for injuries attributable to a breach of the implied warranty of habitability are recoverable only when the breach is based on a failure to provide adequate security in the common areas; tenant was injured in her own apartment. *Williams v. Gorman,* 520 A2d 761 (Super. Ct. App. Div. 1986), cert. denied, 526 A2d 182 (1987).

New York The tenant, a rape victim, lived in an apartment. Early one morning, a stranger followed her to the building's main entrance and through the building's unlocked front door. Tenant unlocked the inner door, but could not escape before the door could self-lock. Tenant sued the landlord for negligence in leaving the outer door in disrepair. *Held:* The landlord could not be held liable for failure to install a self-locking outer door. Municipal law requires a landlord to lock the outer door of a building when the outer door opens directly to a lobby where some apartments are located. Since the victim admits that the rapist entered the building by following her through the self-locking inner door, she failed to produce any evidence that the landlord breached a duty owed to her. *Robinson v. New York City House. Auth.,* 540 NYS2d 811 (App. Div. 1989).

New York Burglars broke into the apartment of a senior citizen and stole her savings and jewelry, breaking both locks. Tenant asked the superintendent to replace the landlord's lock, but was told it would take two or three days. Tenant hired a locksmith the next day, paid $120, and withheld $120 from the rent. Landlord sued for $120, arguing tenant was not authorized to make repairs. *Held:* Tenant gave landlord adequate notice of 18 hours before arranging to have repairs made. Landlord was given sufficient opportunity to repair a condition materially affecting tenant's safety and the apartment's habitability. Therefore, landlord was obligated as a matter of law to reimburse tenant for reasonable expenses incurred in making repairs herself. *Jangla Realty Co. v. Gravagna,* 447 NYS2d 338 (Civ. Ct. 1981).

Oklahoma Tenant, who was assaulted and raped in her rented condominium apartment, sued the condominium owners for negligence in failing to repair a broken lock on glass doors when they knew the lock was broken and were aware of other rapes in the complex. *Held:* A split court found that tenant had a cause of action. A landlord has a duty to maintain security in the common areas of leased premises, as well as a duty to make repairs upon notification that the premises are inadequately secured owing to defective materials. Finally, a landlord may be liable for failure to exercise reasonable care in carrying out its undertaking to provide services to protect person or property. *Lay v. Dworman,* 732 P2d 455 (1986).

Pennsylvania Tenants sued landlord for compensatory and punitive damages for physical and emotional injuries they sustained when they were robbed at gunpoint in the garage of landlord's apartment complex and then abducted. At the time of the attack, the complex provided security services for the grounds and entrances but not for the garages. In the five-year period preceding the attack, the crime rate in the area had risen substantially. Twenty-one reported incidents had occurred in the complex. Numerous requests were made by occupants for increased security at the garages but were not answered by landlord. Tenants argued that landlord breached its duty to provide adequate protection from foreseeable criminal actions of third persons. *Held:* A landlord has no general duty to protect tenants against criminal attacks. However, a landlord may incur a duty, if he provides a program of security by, for example, hiring guards. When a landlord offers a program to protect the premises, he must use reasonable care in performing the task. The duty, however, is not one of an insurer, and landlord is not liable unless his failure is the proximate cause of the harm. *Feld v. Merriam,* 485 A2d 742 (1984).

27.45
Liability for Dangerous Conditions

5th Circuit An escalator in a building leased by the Hyatt Corporation had been turned off and used as a stationary stairway connecting the hotel and the lobby. The formerly stationary escalator began moving rapidly, hurling plaintiffs to the lobby floor, and resulting in injuries of varying degrees. Plaintiffs alleged that Hyatt was strictly liable for their injuries. *Held:* Hyatt was liable for injuries sustained. According to the terms of its lease, Hyatt assumed custody of the escalator. Since the escalator created an unreasonable risk, Hyatt, as guardian, was strictly liable for damages caused by the defective escalator. *Blansit v. Hyatt Corp.,* 874 F2d 1015 (1989).

Alabama Tenants' son was injured by a dilapidated shed on landlords' property. He sued landlords for damages, arguing that they had negligently failed to warn him of a known hidden danger. *Held:* Landlords were not liable for the son's injuries. Although landlords failed to disclose the unreasonable risk of physical harm presented by the hidden, deteriorating shed, tenant father also knew of the danger, which knowledge shifted the burden to warn from landlords to him. The shed was not an attractive nuisance because it did not attract the son; prior to the time of his injury, he did not even know the shed existed and discovered it only after chasing his puppy. *Julian v. Linden,* 545 So. 2d 23 (1989).

California Tenant, who was injured when he slipped in the shower and broke the glass shower door, sued the landlord on grounds of strict liability and negligence. The landlord claimed that as purchaser of the apartment complex from a previous owner, it was unaware of the fact that the shower doors were made of untempered glass, a hazardous condition. *Held:* Landlord should be tried on ground of strict liability as well as negligence. Landlords engaged in the business of leasing dwellings are strictly liable in tort for injuries resulting from latent defects existing when the premises were let. California courts had previously applied the doctrine of strict liability only to those in the chain of commerce. Although landlord had purchased the building and had no relationship with the builder, it made implicit representations of habitability that warranted a strict liability standard. The landlord could be held liable for negligence owing to its failure to exercise ordinary care to inspect the premises for safety when it purchased the property. *Becker v. IRM Corp.,* 698 P2d 116 (1985).

Georgia A local ordinance required "every dwelling" to have a smoke detector. Tenant of a mobile home, whose wife died in a fire, sued landlord for negligence in failing to provide smoke detectors as required under this ordinance. *Held:* The ordinance applied to mobile homes. Its wording was ambiguous, since it was not clear whether mobile homes were included in the term "every dwelling" or were excluded by not being specifically enumerated. The court therefore interpreted the ordinance broadly to fulfill the legislative purpose of promoting public safety. *Kirk v. Lithonia Mobile Homes, Inc.,* 352 SE2d 788 (Ct. App. 1987).

Illinois Plaintiff slipped and fell in the vestibule of a multi-unit apartment building owned by defendants. The outer door of the vestibule could not be kept shut and repeatedly blew open. As a result, water, ice, and snow accumulated on the floor. The accumulation caused plaintiff to slip and fall, fracturing a bone. Plaintiff sued to recover for personal injuries sustained owing to defendant's negligence. *Held:* Defendants were responsible for negligent maintenance. The broken door caused an unnatural accumulation to be formed, which was not caused by water, ice, or snow being tracked in by residents. The problem had been longstanding, and building personnel failed to correct the condition. Since defendants had control of the premises and notice of the hazard, they had the duty to prevent or remove the dangerous condition. *Turner v. Cosmopolitan Nat'l Bank,* 536 NE2d 806 (App. Ct. 1989).

Missouri Plaintiff sued owner of apartment complex for injuries in a collision with a bicycle in an adjoining parking lot. The driveway had a downhill grade and an expert witness testified that a safety bump should have been installed to prevent a bicycle from speeding. The jury awarded plaintiff $850,000 on her claim that landlord was negligent in failing to install a speed bump, but the trial court set the verdict aside. *Held:* Reversed with instructions to enter judgment on the verdict. A landlord owes a duty to make common areas of leased premises reasonably safe, which duty extends to driveways and parking lots. There was evidence the resident manager had received complaints about bicycles being driven at excessive speeds. Based on the evidence, the jury could have found that a speed bump would have greatly reduced the risk of accident. *Jackson v. Ray Kruse Constr. Co.*, 708 SW2d 664 (1986) (en banc).

Ohio A four-year-old, who had been playing with friends without adult supervision, walked from the apartment building property where he lived to an adjacent railroad right-of-way and attempted to board a moving train. His right leg had to be amputated below the knee. The child's parents sued landlord, alleging that it breached a common-law duty to the tenants to keep its outside common areas in a safe condition by fencing off or otherwise blocking the paths leading to the railroad tracks. *Held:* For landlord. Generally, a landlord is not required to protect against conditions existing beyond the territorial limits of its property. Courts have uniformly held that a landlord is not required to fence property simply because it abuts railroad tracks. The danger of a moving train is an open, obvious one, comparable to the dangers posed by street traffic. A landlord has no duty to place a fence between its property and a railroad right-of-way. *McKinney v. Hartz & Restle Realtors, Inc.*, 510 NE2d 386 (1987).

Utah A low window in tenant's third floor apartment was set in a slanting wall so that it protruded into the room. Tenant fell through the window and broke her back. She sued the landlord for breach of the duty of reasonable care in not securing the window. *Held:* For tenant. The landlord had a duty to exercise reasonable care toward his tenants. If a reasonably prudent person should have known that the window design was dangerous, the landlord could be held liable for not taking safety precautions. Although the window was constructed in compliance with the building code and by a licensed architect, a finding of a design defect was not precluded. *Williams v. Melby*, 699 P2d 723 (1985).

Virginia Landlady had hired a carpenter to install a door. Tenant tripped and fell over a piece of wood, four inches high, that the carpenter had left nailed across the apartment threshold. Tenant sued landlady. *Held*: For landlady. Landlady could not be held liable for every defect or risk resulting from repairs. Tenant did not contend that landlady was negligent in selecting a contractor or that she knew of the dangerous condition. Generally, a landlord is not vicariously liable to a tenant for an independent contractor's negligence in making repairs. Exceptions may apply if the contractor's torts arise out of his use of a dangerous instrumentality or if the work is inherently dangerous. *Kesler v. Allen*, 353 SE2d 777 (1987).

28.00 LANDLORD'S WARRANTIES

28.05 Implied Warranty of Habitability

California Tenant argued that landlord had breached the warranty of habitability by failing to provide security guards despite an express warranty to do so. Tenant cited a handbook he received when he moved in stating that 24-hour security guards would be provided and a letter stating that the handbook was made part of the lease by reference. *Held:* The trial court should have considered the handbook and letter as evidence to determine whether there was an express warranty to furnish security guards. A landlord's duty to provide adequate building security is part of the warranty of habitability, although this does not mean a landlord must furnish security guards unless he has expressly warranted to do so. *Secretary of Hous. & Urban Dev. v. Layfield,* 152 Cal. Reptr. 342 (Ct. App. 1978).

Illinois Tenants responded to a suit for rent by claiming that the landlord had breached an implied warranty of habitability, citing problems with heat, sewage, toilets, collapsed ceilings, and infestation. There was no local building code. *Held:* The implied warranty of habitability applies to all leases of residential real estate regardless of the existence of building codes. To constitute a breach of warranty, a defect must be substantial, rendering the premises unsafe or unsanitary, and thus unfit for occupancy. Damages are the difference between the fair rental value of the premises if they were as warranted and the fair rental value in the defective condition. *Glasoe v. Trinkle,* 479 NE2d 915 (1985).

Illinois Plaintiff, tenant of a single-unit dwelling, sustained injuries when the back steps collapsed underneath her feet. She sued the landlord for damages under an implied warranty of habitability theory. *Held:* Recovery was denied and the court refused to apply the warranty to a single-unit dwelling. In a multiple-dwelling situation, no one tenant has exclusive possession of the building, so it is more expedient for the landlord to carry the burden of protecting the tenants. However, in a single-unit, tenant-occupied dwelling, no such rule of expediency need apply; the tenant can care for the building as easily as the landlord. *Dapkunas v. Cagle,* 356 NE2d 575 (1976).

Massachusetts Tenant, who was without heat for a portion of the preceding month, withheld a portion of her rent. Landlord brought an action for summary process and tenant counterclaimed for damages. The trial court awarded damages to tenant, and landlord appealed. *Held:* Affirmed. Tenant's obligation to pay rent abated when she notified landlord of his breach of the warranty of habitability. *Berman & Sons, Inc. v. Jefferson,* 396 NE2d 981 (1979).

New Jersey Tenants, upon moving into their apartment, informed the landlord that a front-door lock was defective. Despite promises of action, the landlord failed to repair the lock. Eight days after the initial complaint, tenants' apartment was burglarized and $6,100 of their personal property was stolen. *Held:* While the mere relationship between landlord and tenant does not impose upon the former a duty to protect the latter from crime committed by third persons, landlord's failure to fix the lock increased the foreseeable risk of theft. Therefore, tenants' loss was a foreseeable consequence of landlord's negligence, landlord's conduct was a proximate cause of the loss, and landlord was liable. *Braitman v. Overlook Terrace Corp.,* 346 A2d 76 (1975).

New York Tenants of seven high-rise apartment buildings sued their landlord when trash accumulated in front of their buildings and maintenance came to a halt because of a strike of the maintenance and janitorial staff. Tenants sued for an abatement of rent for these conditions, arguing that the landlord was in violation of various state and local health requirements, and had thereby breached the implied warranty of habitability. *Held:* Landlord had breached the implied warranty of habitability. There had been extensive and lengthy violations of the health code that affected the tenants and entitled them to a 10 percent abatement in rent for the period of the strike. *Park West Management Corp. v. Mitchell,* 391 NE2d 1288 (1979).

New York The administrator of city-owned property attempted to recover an apartment from a tenant on grounds of nonpayment of rent. Tenant claimed breach of the warranty of habitability because the bathroom ceiling had fallen into the bathtub, rendering the apartment uninhabitable. *Held:* For the tenant. Damages can be assessed against an administrator for breach of warranty of habitability. The clear language of Section 235-b of the Real Property Law, providing for an implied warranty of habitability, applies to all landlords and tenants, including New York City and its tenants. *Department of Preservation & Dev. v. Sartor,* 487 NYS2d 1 (App. Div. 1985).

South Carolina Two teenage girls who were staying with a tenant were killed by a fire resulting from defective wiring in the furnace control box. The estates sued the landlords, who had also built the building. *Held:* For landlords. A landlord has no duty to maintain leased premises in a safe condition, nor is a landlord liable for any defect in the premises, absent some special agreement. Even where there is such an agreement, liability lies in contract, not tort. There is no implied warranty of fitness or habitability in leases. In addition, the wiring was performed by an independent subcontractor, and the landlords were not responsible for the negligence of subcontractors. *Young v. Morrisey,* 329 SE2d 426 (1985).

Vermont Landlords appealed a judgment awarding tenant reimbursement of all rent paid and additional compensatory damages for breach of the implied warranty of habitability. Landlords failed to repair the substantial problems, including no keys, a broken toilet, leaking water pipes, and sewage odor. Tenant proceeded to make repairs herself. *Held:* The rent award and compensatory damages were proper; an implied warranty exists that the landlord will deliver and maintain premises that are safe, clean, and fit for human habitation. Substantial violations of the applicable housing code are prima facie evidence of a warranty breach, with damages measured by the difference between the warranted value of the dwelling and its actual value in the defective condition. *Hilder v. St. Peter,* 478 A2d 202 (1984).

28.10
Implied Warranty of Fitness for Intended Use

Arkansas Lessee, the owner of a retail boat business, entered into a verbal commercial lease with lessor. A month-to-month lease was used since lessee did not want to assume responsibility for repairs to the building. No agreement was made as to who would assume responsibility for wiring and other repairs. Five years after the lease was entered into, the building was damaged by fire. While evidence showed that the fire had originated in the building's circuit box, its cause could not be determined. Lessee sued for damages on the basis of express and implied warranties of habitability. *Held:* Time has dissolved any warranty of the fitness existing in premises that are over 20 years old. An implied warranty of fitness has been previously recognized in the sale of a new building and extends to sales involving parties not in privity with the original vendor builder. However, the implied warranty expires after a reasonable time, and this case involves a building over 20 years old. *Sanders v. Walker,* 767 SW2d 526 (1989).

Minnesota Less than a year after opening a jewelry store, tenant discovered that his premises had been burglarized. Entry into the vault area of the store was made through the ceiling, which consisted only of the thin floor of an equipment room directly above the store. The construction of the building, therefore, allowed easy access into the vault from above, and this had never been called to tenant's attention. Tenant sued landlord. *Held:* Landlord was liable on the ground that it breached its duty to inform tenant of sufficient facts to enable tenant to determine whether the premises were suitable for a jewelry store. An exculpation clause in the lease, in which the tenant specifically agreed to assume responsibility for all damages arising from his use of the building, did not bar recovery. The clause did not bar claims against the landlord for failure to disclose conditions existing prior to the signing of the lease. *Vermes v. American Dist. Tel. Co.,* 251 NW2d 101 (1977).

North Carolina Plaintiff's friend agreed to rent a second floor duplex for one week. When plaintiff and two other men leaned against the wooden railing surrounding the second floor deck, it gave way, causing plaintiff injuries. The deck railing was well maintained and its only purpose was to prevent people from walking off the deck. Plaintiff sued lessor for breach of an implied warranty of fitness. *Held:* The court, applying the law of South Carolina, the site of the injury, held that a landlord, absent express warranty, owes no duty of care to a tenant to keep the premises in repair. Even when breach of an express agreement to repair is established, neither tenant nor a third party would be entitled to damages for personal injury caused by a defective condition of leased premises. *Williams v. Riley,* 289 SE2d 102 (1982).

28.15
Implied Warranty of Suitability in Commercial Leases

Texas Tenant who rented medical office space experienced numerous problems of a serious nature with the building and services the landlord was required to provide. Tenant vacated the premises and discontinued rent payments. *Held:* The court extended residential property warranties to commercial property tenants to find an implied warranty of suitability in commercial leases. This warranty states that the premises are suited for their intended commercial purpose. Landlord's breach of the implied warranty of suitability justified tenant's abandonment of the premises and discontinuance of rental payments. *Davidow v. Inwood N. Professional Group,* 747 SW2d 373 (1988).

29.00
LANDLORD'S DUTIES TO THIRD PERSONS

29.05
In General

New York Employee of tenant supermarket fell and injured herself descending a stairway built by the supermarket. The lease required the supermarket to maintain the premises and make all repairs, but landlord reserved a right to make repairs at the supermarket's expense. Although landlord had not examined the staircase, the employee sued both supermarket and landlord, alleging that the staircase was inadequately lit and had a handrail too close to the wall. *Held:* Because landlord reserved the right to inspect and make repairs at the supermarket's expense, it could be held responsible for the accident, even though it had no actual notice of the defects and was not in possession of the premises. Under city ordinance, it owed a duty directly to the employee to remedy the defect, a remedy the lease permitted it to perform. *Guzman v. Haven Plaza Hous. Dev. Fund Co.,* 509 NE2d 51 (1987).

New York Plaintiff was accosted at knifepoint on a public sidewalk and forced to accompany the assailant to a nearby building belonging to a city housing project. The assailant gained access to the building via an unlocked door and once inside, he robbed plaintiff and sexually assaulted her. During the two-year period prior to this assault, the building's locks had been broken, and it had been the scene of at least five criminal acts against tenants involving unauthorized entry. Plaintiff sued the city housing authority, alleging negligence for failing to adequately secure the property. *Held:* The housing authority owed no duty to plaintiff, who was neither a tenant nor a guest, to protect her from the intentional actions of the assailant. Because the housing authority had no relationship to the unidentified wrongdoer and because the injured plaintiff had no connection to the premises independent of the crime itself, the housing authority's duty to maintain the building did not extend to her. Nor was plaintiff within the zone of foreseeable harm. *Waters v. New York City Hous. Auth.,* 513 NYS2d 356 (1986).

New York Parents of an injured child sought to recover damages for injuries sustained by the child when she fell from steps leading to a mobile home. Defendant, owner of the trailer park, denied any statutory duty to maintain the stairs even though he provided electric, water, and sewer connections. Defendant asserted that no stairway was present when the lease was issued, and that he neither participated in its design nor provided materials for its construction. Defendant also contended that after leasing the lot he surrendered all dominion and control. *Held:* A landlord is not liable in negligence for conditions that exist upon the land after the transfer of possession and control. Landlord had no statutory duty to maintain stairs on the leased premises in a safe condition since he did not participate in their design or construction. *Hildenbrand v. Porto,* 534 NYS2d 461 (App. Div. 1988).

29.10 Invitees

Delaware The employee of a shopping mall tenant was abducted from the mall lot after closing and raped. The landlords were aware that minor crimes has been committed in the lot, but they provided only one after-hours guard, despite recommendations that more were necessary. The landlords were sued. *Held:* The landlords were liable for compensatory damages but not for punitive damages. By extending security over the mall common areas, the landlords had created an expectation of safety by business invitees. The landlords had been negligent in performing their duty to provide security, but their conduct had not been outrageous. Therefore, they did not merit punitive damages. *Jardel Co., Inc. v. Hughes,* 523 A2d 518 (1987).

Idaho Employees of a gift shop that leased space from Holiday Inns were injured when attempting to move security gates owned by the gift shop. The gates were known to be unstable. The employees sued Holiday Inns. *Held:* For employees. The rule that an owner is not required to protect invitees from open and obvious dangers is not absolute. Where an employee is required by an employer to perform dangerous work on landowner's premises, the landowner can be found liable. Since the employer is shielded from liability by workmen's compensation laws, these cases will necessarily involve the employee-invitee and the landowner, with the landowner required to show reasonable care for the protection of the employee-invitee, even though the dangerous condition is known to the employee-invitee. The question of whether employees assumed the risk of injury is one for a jury. *Keller v. Holiday Inns, Inc.,* 691 P2d 1208 (1984).

Kansas The grandmother of a university

student sued for personal injuries suffered in a fall in an unlighted stairwell while visiting her granddaughter's dormitory. The granddaughter rented a room under a written agreement with the university. The lower court granted defendant summary judgment on the basis that no landlord-tenant relationship existed. *Held:* Reversed and remanded. Although the agreement was not a true lease, the university owed a landlord's duty to exercise reasonable care in keeping common areas of the residence hall in safe condition for residents and invited guests. The lessor-lessee relationship is liberally construed to include a lease of a portion of university property to students. *Burch v. University of Kansas,* 756 P2d 431 (1988).

Mississippi A grocery store patron injured her back when her shopping cart hit a pothole in the parking lot and started to overturn. The store's operator leased the building from a shopping center owner under a lease providing that the operator had the free use of the parking lot, which was maintained by the owner. The patron sued the operator. *Held:* A lessee-occupant owes a duty of reasonable care to its invitees, notwithstanding a maintenance agreement with the landlord. A jury could conclude that the operator controlled the premises and had a duty to repair or warn. *Wilson v. Allday,* 487 So. 2d 793 (1986).

Missouri Plaintiff was accidentally shot during a drug raid while visiting an apartment rented by the assailant from defendant landlord. Plaintiff asserted that prior to the date he was shot, another drug raid and shooting had occurred in the apartment building. Plaintiff sued, alleging negligence in failing to screen tenants and in protecting against dangerous activities. *Held:* Plaintiff failed to state a cause of action against the landlord for breach of a duty to protect an invitee from dangerous activities. The petition lacked any allegation that a dangerous condition of the common premises caused injury in the private premises. Absent this allegation, the landlord had no liability for the invitee's injuries. *Conroy v. Solon Gershman Inc.,* 767 SW2d 381 (Ct. App. 1989).

New Jersey Plaintiff, leaving defendant's supermarket, was knocked to the ground in the parking lot and her purse was snatched. She was injured and sued the supermarket, claiming it had been negligent in failing to warn her of prior muggings on its premises and failing to provide a safe place to shop and park. *Held:* A landholder has a duty of reasonable care to safeguard business invitees from criminal acts of third persons. It was reasonable for the jury to find that, absent warnings, hiring one guard primarily to remain inside the store was an insufficient response in light of the history of attacks on the premises. The landholder–business invitor is in the best position to provide either warnings or adequate protection for its patrons where they are in risk of injury. *Butler v. Acme Mkts., Inc.,* 445 A2d 1141 (1982).

New York Plaintiff, a boy of fourteen, was bitten by a German shepherd dog owned by a tenant of a house owned by landlady. Plaintiff sued the landlady. There was evidence that the landlady was aware of the vicious tendencies of the dog. Landlady moved for summary judgment. *Held:* Dismissal of motion for summary judgment affirmed. The general rule is that landlord is not liable for attacks by tenant's animals where landlord has no knowledge of the animal's nature. However, here evidence indicated that the landlady, knowing of the dog's vicious nature, nevertheless rented to tenant, allowed him to keep the dog on the premises, and took no protective measures. The court distinguished this situation from one where tenant obtains an animal after entering into the lease. In this situation, landlord, by leasing the premises to a dog owner, had affirmatively created a reasonably foreseeable risk, as to which landlady had a public policy duty to protect third persons. *Strunk v. Zoltanski,* 468 NE2d 13 (1984).

New York When a supermarket customer sued an executor of the lessor's estate for injuries sustained when her shoe caught in a hole and she fell in a driveway adjoining the supermarket and lot, the executor argued that the mere existence of a covenant by the lessor to repair did not render him liable. *Held:* A landlord may be liable for injuries to persons coming onto his land with the consent of the lessee solely on the basis of his contract or covenant to keep the premises in repair. *Putnam v. Stout,* 345 NE2d 319 (1976).

Oregon A customer was injured by robbers in the parking lot of a shopping mall. She sued the owners of the mall, arguing that they had a duty to take precautions against negligent or criminal conduct on the part of third persons and to provide a sufficient level of security to afford reasonable protection. She also questioned the lack of warnings alerting customers to the risk of criminal activity. *Held:* The jury could have found from the evidence that mall owners were negligent. They knew of and had acted on reports of criminal incidents, so they should have been on notice that more security was needed. *Brown v. JC Penney Co.,* 688 P2d 811 (1984).

Pennsylvania Plaintiff, a general maintenance worker, was employed by defendant municipal agency to inspect city-owned property scheduled for demolition. While descending a staircase to determine whether utility appliances had been removed, he sustained injuries caused by a faulty set of interior stairs. *Held:* Judgment for defendant. A landlord's liability does not depend solely on the status of the injured party, whether licensee or invitee, but on other variables as well. These include the purpose of the invitation, the likelihood that the invitee will realize the danger and take steps to protect himself, the nature of the land, and the purpose for which it is used. In this case, the facts compel the conclusion that defendant owed no duty to this particular invitee. Plaintiff knew the house was to be demolished and that as a rule no repairs are made to such properties. Consequently, to find liability under such circumstances would be "patently unjust." *Atkins v Urban Redevelopment Auth.,* 414 A2d 100 (1980).

Tennessee Shopping center patron was assaulted in the parking lot and sued the shopping center association on the ground that the center had breached its duty to protect invitees from violence in that there were no security guards. The patron further alleged that since there had been previous assaults in the lot, the center had notice that precautionary measures were required. *Held:* There is no duty on the owners or operators of a shopping center to protect patrons from acts of violence unless they know or have reason to know that criminal acts about to occur pose imminent probability of harm to an invitee. Since the shopping center association could never prevent the presence of a criminal in its lot, there was no liability. *Compropst v. Sloan,* 528 SW2d 188 (1975).

29.15 Licensees

Massachusetts Tenant's visitor fell down a dark stairway of a building. The visitor brought an action against the building owner, alleging nuisance and negligence in failing to maintain a light bulb on the second floor. *Held:* The landowner owed the visitor a duty to use reasonable care in the maintenance of the premises. The amount of light cast on the stairway in question was relevant to the issue of negligence; also, violation of a safety statute was evidence of negligence. However, plaintiff could not recover damages for nuisance. *Lindsey v. Massios,* 360 NE2d 631 (1977).

Minnesota A reception guest slipped and broke a leg on freshly spilled soda pop on premises that had been rented to the hostess for the reception. The guest brought suit against the lessors of the premises, contending that they had a duty to guard against hazardous situations caused by guests. *Held:* Since the premises had been turned over to the hostess for the reception, the lessors had no control over the premises. A landowner who retains no control is not liable for the tenants' negligence in maintaining the premises. *Filipczak v. International Bhd. of Elec. Workers Local 110,* 195 NW2d 433 (1972).

North Carolina While visiting a tenant, a young man drowned in a pool located in the apartment building. There was a sign posted at the entrance to the swimming pool stating, "No lifeguard on duty—swim at your own risk." Decedent's estate sued the landlord on the ground that the pool had been constructed improperly and a lifeguard should have been provided. *Held:* Decedent was a licensee because he had entered the premises solely and exclusively in pursuit of his own pleasure. Thus, the landlord's only duties to the decedent were to refrain from injuring him willfully or through wanton negligence, and from doing any act that increased the hazard to decedent while he was on the premises. Since he had posted a warning sign and since state regulations do not require the presence of a lifeguard, the landlord was not negligent. Nor was there sufficient evidence that the pool had been negligently constructed. *Andrews v. Taylor,* 239 SE2d 630 (Ct. App. 1977).

29.20 Notice of Hazardous Conditions

Colorado Plaintiff brought this action against defendant landlord under the rule of negligence per se for a code violation. Plaintiff had been injured when he fell over a stairwell that had handrails below the height requirements of the town's building code. Defendant had not built the building and the certificate of occupancy had been issued when it was built, indicating that the building had passed inspection. *Held:* Since defendant had no notice of the condition, she was not liable. Although it had been held that failure to obey an ordinance is negligence per se, this is not an inflexible rule. Here, defendant was not the builder and the property had been approved for occupancy, indicating compliance with the applicable ordinances. In light of these circumstances, there is no reasonable basis for applying negligence per se. *Singleton v. Collins,* 574 P2d 882 (Ct. App. 1978).

Massachusetts In a suit by a guest of tenant for injuries caused by a defective porch railing, defendant landlord argued that the porch was part of the demised premises and that no duty of reasonable care was owned. *Held:* Judgment for plaintiff guest. Landlord knew of the defect and had a reasonable opportunity to make needed repairs. In such a case, the landlord's negligent failure to make repairs is actionable by third parties. *Young v. Garwacki,* 402 NE2d 1045 (1980).

New York While in the backyard of defendant's premises, an infant was bitten by a dog owned by defendant's lessee. Lessee had an oral lease with lessor that prohibited dogs. Defendant's parents allowed the dog, since it was represented as a "good dog" and was observed by the parents on several occasions as having a gentle character. Plaintiff sued defendant landlord for injuries sustained. *Held:* The child could not maintain an action against the landlord since, at the time the lease was adopted, the landlord had no knowledge of the dog's vicious tendencies. New York law requires a landlord who knows of the vicious tendencies of a tenant's dog to take reasonable measures to protect individuals from dog attacks. The fact that the dog was an Afghan hound, usually aloof and gentle to strangers, prevented the court from implying knowledge of vicious propensities based on the breed. *Plue v. Lent,* 537 NYS2d 90 (App. Div. 1989).

Wisconsin Tenants, who were moving out of the top floor of landlord's two family house, enlisted the help of a neighbor in moving heavy items. During the move, the neighbor fell from the second-story porch when a wooden railing gave way because of dry rot. When the neighbor sued, the landlord denied any knowledge of the defective railing, despite the testimony of the tenant who said that the landlord had been warned about it several times. *Held:* The landlord is liable. The landlord's general cloak of immunity at common law is abrogated. Landlords must use "ordinary care" to discover defective conditions. *Pagelsdorf v. Safeco Ins. Co. of America,* 284 NW2d 55 (1979).

29.25 Latent Defects

Georgia Defendant leased a building to a tenant. After the lease expired, tenant continued as a tenant at will. Tenant never gave defendant notice of any defect in the property nor did tenant request that defendant inspect the premises. Plaintiff, who was working for the tenant to make repairs on the building, was injured when an overhead door fell on him. He sued the landlord. *Held:* After fully parting with possession and the right of possession, a landlord has liability to a third party for a latent defect only if the landlord is aware of it and of the need to repair it. The landlord has no duty to inspect the premises to disclose the existence of any latent defects. Plaintiff argued that the lack of a system to catch the door if the chains broke was a latent defect. Even if that were so, there was no guarantee that defendant would have discerned the defect in the exercise of ordinary care. *Davis v. Smith,* 314 SE2d 471 (1984).

30.00 EVICTION

30.05 Notice of Eviction

Alaska Tenant in a low-income housing complex improperly disposed of garbage, walked around nude, hit a car in the parking lot, and allowed odors to waft from his apartment. The landlord gave tenant only 10 days under the notice to terminate instead of the 20 days allowed by Alaska law. Tenant argued that he could not be evicted, because of insufficient notice. *Held:* For landlord. The statute gave tenant 10 days from receipt of the notice in which to correct the breach giving rise to the termination effort and another 10 days to move out. The statute permitted tenant to save his lease only if the breach was remediable by repairs or the payment of damages or otherwise. Tenant's breaches were irremediable, so the 10-day provision was pointless in this case, and landlord did not have to comply strictly with the 20-day notice provision. *Taylor v. Gill St. Invs.,* 743 P2d 345 (1987).

Arkansas After she failed to pay rent, landlord served tenant a notice to vacate in 10 days. She failed to vacate and, consequently, was convicted of a misdemeanor, fined, and sentenced to a 30-day prison term under an Arkansas statute prohibiting unauthorized tenant holdovers after eviction notices. She appealed her conviction, arguing that the statute was unconstitutional. *Held:* Tenant's conviction was valid. The statute (1) did not deny her procedural due process because it required ten days' notice to vacate and a hearing to determine if a tenant's refusal to vacate was justified; (2) did not circumvent the civil statute, put a "chilling" effect on a tenant's right to assert defenses, or mandate criminal conviction or a fine as a result of what the tenant might have considered to be a justified refusal to pay rent; and (3) was a valid exercise of state's police power. However, tenant was improperly sentenced to a jail term and her fine was reduced. *Duhon v. State,* 774 SW2d 830 (1989).

District of Columbia Landlord sued to evict a tenant at sufferance and argued that the rent control regulation requiring him to state the reasons for the eviction in the notice to quit created a new tenancy and deprived him of property without due process. *Held:* Eviction controls in an emergency rent control program are constitutional, and the regulations in question were not unreasonable or oppressive. *Jack Spicer Real Estate Inc. v. Gasseway,* 353 A2d 288 (1976).

Massachusetts At-will residential tenant was served a letter by the owner terminating the tenancy for several acts of voluntary waste allegedly caused by tenant. The letter gave tenant two days to quit the premises before owners would begin eviction proceedings. Tenant failed to vacate the premises, and owners sued for summary process eviction. *Held:* A statutory notice to quit was required to terminate a residential tenancy at will prior to a summary process action, even where the action is predicated upon voluntary waste committed by the tenant. State statute dictates that a tenant at will should receive the longer of the rental period or 30 days' notice to quit. As a matter of law, voluntary waste does not terminate a tenancy for the purpose of allowing a landlord to commence eviction proceedings against a tenant. Since a significant amount of time elapses between the filing of a summary complaint and a judgment of eviction, the elimination of the notice period would not eliminate any ongoing damage to the premises. *Bech v. Cuevas,* 534 NE2d 1163 (1989).

New York Landlord commenced a summary proceeding to recover possession of commercial leasehold premises. The commercial tenant ignored notices of default and termination of lease because they were signed by an attorney with whom the tenant had never previously dealt and not by the owner or attorney named in the lease. The district court dismissed the proceeding. *Held:* Affirmed. The default provision refered only to "the landlord serving a written five (5) days' notice upon the Tenant" to be followed by "a written three (3) days' notice of cancellation." The printed provision of the lease also contained a rider that referred to a named attorney as escrowee, but did not specify that notice of default or of termination of the lease could be given by the landlord's agent or by another attorney. Therefore, the notices were insufficient and the tenant was entitled to ignore them as not in compliance with the lease provisions concerning notice. *Siegel v. Kentucky Fried Chicken,* 492 NE2d 390 (1986).

Texas Tenants challenged the constitutionality of eviction procedures that allowed private moving and storage companies to remove tenants' belongings from landlords' premises pursuant to a writ of restitution. The belongings could be reclaimed only after a payment of moving expenses and storage fees. If the property was not claimed within 30 days, it was advertised for sale and auctioned. *Held:* The procedures of the writ of restitution did not violate tenant's procedural due process rights. The procedure for executing the writs of restitution adequately accommodated competing interests. Tenants were given a full judicial hearing and posted notice on the premises prior to the execution of the writ. Tenants' substantive due process rights were not violated by the county or its constables because there was no causal connection between the constable's acts in executing the writ of restitution and the subsequent deprivation of constitutional rights caused by warehousemen who charged unreasonable storage charges. Removal and storage of the property was a reasonable alternative to placing the property at risk in a public area. *Merritt v. Harris County,* 775 SW2d 17 (1989).

30.10 Tenant's Defenses

U.S. Supreme Court Landlord brought an action to evict tenant for nonpayment of rent. *Held:* Since the right to recover possession of real property was protected at common law, the Seventh Amendment entitles either party to demand a jury trial in a proceeding by a landlord to recover possession of premises for nonpayment of rent or other default. In the average landlord-tenant dispute, where the failure to pay rent is established and no substantial defenses exist, it is unlikely that the defendant tenant would request a jury trial. The trial court's power to grant summary judgment where no genuine issues of fact are in dispute offers a bulwark against the use of a demand for a jury trial as a means of delay. *Dave Pernell v. Southall Realty,* 416 US 363 (1974).

4th Circuit Plaintiffs entered into a one-year lease with a landlord participating in the Section 8 program. When the landlord refused to renew the lease and attempted to evict them, plaintiffs argued that the eviction action was in retaliation for their use of legal aid attorneys to persuade the landlord to drop an earlier eviction action because of lack of notice. Plaintiffs claimed they were entitled to a hearing before the housing authority before they could be evicted. *Held:* Although Section 8 requires the housing authority to make a finding of "good cause" before approving eviction, it does not necessarily require a full-fledged hearing. Due process in this case would have been adequately provided by an eviction proceeding in state court. *Swann v. Gastonia Hous. Auth.,* 675 F2d 1342 (1982).

11th Circuit Defendant, a private landlord, initiated eviction proceedings against plaintiffs before their leases had expired. Plaintiffs, who were tenants participating in the Section 8 Existing Housing Assistance Payments Program, argued that they could not be evicted until the end of the lease term. Defendant relied upon a lease provision permitting termination at will by either party on 30-day written notice. *Held:* Despite the lease provision for termination at will, the Section 8 plaintiffs had a constitutionally protected interest in the continued occupancy of their apartments until their leases expired. Defendant could evict plaintiffs during the lease term only for "good cause," as determined by the state housing authority. The statute creating the Section 8 program provides the Department of Housing and Urban Development (HUD) with the sole authority to issue notices to vacate, and the landlord with the right to make representations to HUD for termination of tenancy. These provisions would be meaningless if defendant were permitted to evict Section 8 tenants mid-term without a determination of "good cause" or HUD review. *Jeffries v. Georgia Residential Fin. Auth.*, 678 F2d 919, cert. denied, 459 US 971 (1982).

D.C. Circuit Tenant withheld rent to protest unsafe conditions and housing code violations. Landlord brought a summary proceeding to evict tenant for nonpayment of rent. *Held:* A tenant has the right to remain in possession of premises without paying rent when the landlord allows them to become unsafe and unsanitary in violation of the housing code. Any attempt by the landlord to evict the tenant will not be sustained on the ground of failure to pay rent, for the tenant is exercising his legal rights. *Robinson v. Diamond Hous. Corp.*, 463 F2d 853 (1972).

Louisiana Lessee appealed his eviction for violating a provision of his lease forbidding alterations of the premises without lessor's written consent. Lessee had made allegedly minor repairs in the air-conditioning system, which involved cutting holes in the roof to provide for new pipes. No written permission was requested or given; however, lessor watched as the work was being done and did not protest to lessee or attempt to stop the work. *Held:* Reversed. The requirement for written consent was vitiated by lessor's implied consent to the work. *Ford v. Independent Bakers Supply, Inc.*, 385 So. 2d 580 (1980).

New Jersey Under tenant's original lease, tenant paid landlord the rent after she received her public-assistance check on the third of each month. A new landlord purchased the building, terminated the original lease and offered tenant a new lease with a rent increase. Rent was due on the first of each month, with a $25 penalty if not paid by the fifth of the month. Tenant never executed a new written lease, but remained in possession and paid the increased rent. However, she failed to pay late charges for the months her rent was late. Landlord sought possession for nonpayment of the late charge. *Held:* Tenant could not be evicted. In a dispossess action for nonpayment or late payment of rent, a tenant may raise the defense that the failure to abide by the tenancy's rent payment requirements stemmed from an unreasonable change in the renewal lease. By accepting some of the lease changes imposed by the landlord, tenant did not impliedly accept all changes. Her refusal to pay the late fee constituted a valid refusal to accept the lease change. New Jersey's Anti-Eviction Act limits the eviction of tenants to "reasonable grounds." Landlord's lease change to include a late fee was unreasonable when tenant always made her payment after receiving her assistance check. *447 Assocs. v. Miranda,* 559 A2d 1362 (1989).

New Jersey Plaintiff bank granted a $30,000 loan for the purchase of an apartment building. When the owner defaulted on mortgage payments, plaintiff commenced foreclosure proceedings and demanded possession of the premises. The tenants argued that plaintiff had no right to possession absent compliance with New Jersey's Anti-Eviction Act. The statute prevents landlords from summarily removing tenants without good cause and without prior demand and notice. *Held:* Mortgagees are not "landlords," and are therefore not subject to Anti-Eviction Act requirements, which apply only in true landlord-tenant relationships. The court held that the legislature and not the judiciary has the power to subject foreclosing mortgagees to the statute. *Guttenberg Sav. & Loan Ass'n v. Rivera,* 428 A2d 1289 (1981).

Wisconsin When a local oil company purchased the assets of a national oil company, it gave the operator of a service station leased on a month-to-month basis notice of termination of the tenancy. The operator counterclaimed that the oil company was estopped, since it had promised him a new lease if he would stay on, and sought damages. *Held:* Where the evidence regarding the alleged promise was lacking in detail, the record precluded enforcing the contract on the basis of estoppel. The court properly refused to consider the damage remedy as a counterclaim where it arose from collateral agreements, but not from the lease itself. Counterclaims in eviction actions may include any claim related to the property arising out of the transaction or occurrence that is the subject of the claim but not transactions that are collateral to the lease. *Rossen Oil Co. v. Heiman,* 242 NW2d 176 (1976).

30.15 Retaliatory Eviction

3d Circuit Landlord owned virtually all residential property in the borough. Tenants, members of the borough governing body, sued landlord for civil rights violations, alleging landlord retaliated against tenants for adopting a budget and tax structure at odds with landlord's proposals by refusing to renew leases. *Held:* Landlord and corporation did not engage in state action for purpose of the federal civil rights statute. The fact that the state incorporated the borough was a ministerial act that did not transform landlord into a state actor. The court also rejected tenants' argument that the corporation owned by landlord was actually a "company town" performing all the functions of government. Landlord's control over municipal services does not mean his actions are governmental. In a company town situation, only actions connected with the exercise of governmental functions may be regarded as state action. In his role as landlord, he was a private party, not an instrument of the state. *Robison v. Canterbury Village, Inc.,* 848 F2d 424 (1988).

California Seven days after tenant had reported landlord to the police for sexually molesting tenant's daughter, landlord sent a notice to tenant to "pay rent or quit." The notice announced an immediate rent increase from $200 to $650 per month. When landlord sent tenant a 30-day notice of termination and tenant refused to move, landlord commenced an unlawful detainer action. Tenant raised retaliatory eviction as a defense. *Held:* Retaliatory eviction may be raised as an affirmative defense in an unlawful detainer action. The strong public policy interest in protecting those who report violations of the law from intimidation would not significantly impair the public policy of preserving the summary nature of unlawful detainer proceedings. *Barela v. Superior Court,* 636 P2d 582 (1981).

California Tenant alleged that landlord terminated its lease in retaliation against tenant's employees who had refused to testify falsely in landlord's favor in lawsuits brought against landlord by other tenants. The trial court refused to hear tenant's defense of retaliatory eviction, holding the defense was available only for residential tenants. *Held:* A valid defense of retaliatory eviction is available to commercial tenants if, on balance, the public policies furthered by protecting a tenant from eviction outweigh the state's interest in ensuring that unlawful detainer proceedings are truly summary. The public policy furthered by allowing the retaliatory eviction defense where a landlord was alleged to have punished witnesses for refusing to perjure themselves outweighed any resulting delay. *Custom Parking, Inc. v. Superior Court,* 187 Cal. Rptr. 674 (Ct. App. 1982).

Maine Tenant at will and landlord had a dispute as to the amount of rent, with landlord claiming tenant owed what amounted to 13-weeks' rent payments. Tenant subsequently filed a complaint with the city building code enforcement body concerning substandard conditions. Upon inspection, violations were found and landlord was contacted. Landlord then tried to regain possession of the premises. Tenant charged retaliatory eviction. *Held:* Landlord was entitled to a writ of possession of the apartment. Although tenant had filed the complaint about code violations within six months prior to the dispossess action, which by statute is presumed to be retaliatory, the landlord had successfully rebutted the presumption of retaliation by establishing a nonretaliatory motive for the eviction, that is, the back rent alleged to be due. *Perreault v. Parker,* 490 A2d 203 (1985).

Minnesota Landlord orally agreed to make certain repairs for tenants who leased a house on a month-to-month basis. When landlord failed to make repairs demanded by tenants, tenants withheld rent. Landlord served them with a 30-day notice to quit and brought an unlawful detainer action when they did not. *Held:* By statute, a landlord who serves a notice to quit within 90 days of a demand for repairs has the burden of proving that the eviction was not retaliatory. A nonretaliatory eviction is one wholly unrelated to and unmotivated by any good faith activity on the part of the tenant protected by the statute. Where there was a clear relationship between the notice to quit and the tenant's protected activities, the landlord failed to meet his burden. *Parkin v. Fitzgerald,* 240 NW2d 828 (1976).

Ohio Major repairs were made on tenant's apartment as a result of tenant's complaints. At a hearing requested by tenant, her rent was reduced and was to be deposited in an escrow account until the repairs were finished. A week later, landlord served tenant with notice of termination. When tenant refused to vacate, landlord filed a forcible entry and detainer action, asserting the apartment could not continue to be rented, because of the repairs. *Held:* Tenant met its burden of proving landlord's eviction was retaliatory and in response to tenant's complaints about the apartment. The court considered the temporal proximity of the parties' actions, as well as evidence they were causally linked. Landlord failed to prove she had a valid justification for the attempted eviction. She did not establish actual intent to make repairs or that repairs would have effectively deprived tenant of the use of the apartment. *Karas v. Floyd,* 440 NE2d 563 (Ct. App. 1981).

30.20
Partial Eviction

California Landlord leased-back a portion of rented premises from tenant and thereafter enlarged and sublet the property to a third party. Tenant stopped paying rent and sued for damages, claiming constructive eviction. Landlord sued for eviction on the basis of nonpayment of rent. *Held:* A partial actual eviction relieves a tenant from the obligation to pay rent only if such "eviction" is from a substantial portion of the premises. The extent of interference is a question of fact for the trial court, which here ruled against tenant. *Dussin Inv. Co. v. Bloxham,* 157 Cal. Rptr. 646 (1979).

New York Major tenant in a shopping plaza possessed the right under its lease to use the existing plaza parking area in common with the other tenants. The plaza owners leased two thirds of the parking area to a fast-food franchise, which proceeded to demolish the parking lot and construct a restaurant on the site. Tenant sued for partial eviction. The trial court held that tenant was not actually partially evicted, since the encroachment of the restaurant did not result in a loss of ingress or egress, and tenant appealed. *Held:* Reversed. Tenant had acquired an easement for the use of the parking area appurtenant to its leasehold. Lessors were liable for knowingly breaching tenant's lease, interfering with tenant's easement, and partially evicting tenant from its leasehold. Although tenant failed to show a loss of business resulting from the demolition of the parking lot, adequate parking was important to tenant's business, and tenant was thus deprived of the full use of the leased premises. As to damages, tenant, having elected to pay the rent as it became due, was entitled to claim damages, but was estopped from demanding a full refund of the rent already paid. *487 Elmwood, Inc. v. Hassett,* 486 NYS2d 113 (App. Div. 1985).

New York Landlord of commercial property painted over the doors of tenant's store entrance with opaque paint. Tenant withheld rent, claiming actual partial eviction. *Held:* In the absence of physical expulsion from demised premises, there can be no actual eviction such as to justify withholding of rent. However, the landlord's actions are compensable in damages by a suit at law. *Broadway Copy Serv., Inc. v. Broad-Wall Co.,* 431 NYS2d 13 (App. Div. 1980).

30.25 Constructive Eviction

4th Circuit Tenant leased a store in a shopping center. From the beginning of its occupancy, tenant complained to landlord that the roof leaked. Despite attempts at repair, the situation continued unabated. Defendant closed the store for business reasons having nothing to do with the leaking roof and attempted, without success, to sublease the property. Landlord sought the balance of the rent due. *Held:* The condition of the roof prevented tenant from using or subleasing the premises. Therefore, constructive eviction barred landlord's action for damages. *Jaffe-Spindler Co. v. Genesco,* 747 F2d 253 (1984).

Florida Tenant of commercial property under a five-year lease abandoned premises four years after initial complaint of leaking roof. In landlord's suit for a money judgment, tenant asserted constructive eviction. *Held:* Notwithstanding the waiver rule in the 1979 Landlord and Tenant Act, tenant's failure to abandon for such a considerable time negated his claim of constructive eviction. Waiver of privilege to abandon cannot be inferred from the passage of time alone. However, under the totality of circumstances presented, tenant's actions were unjustified. *Bass v. Waollitz,* 384 So. 2d 704 (Ct. App. 1980).

Illinois Tenant's one-year lease was to begin November 1. The apartment was filthy and the manager promised to clean it by October 29, at which time he said she could move in early. Tenant did so, but the apartment was still uninhabitable, and she moved out that night. The landlord, unable to rent the apartment for three months, refused to return tenant's security deposit. Tenant sued for constructive eviction and asked for attorney fees, costs, and for twice the amount of the security deposit, based on a state statute holding a landlord liable for twice the amount of a security deposit wrongfully withheld. *Held:* Plaintiff was constructively evicted, because landlord's failure to fix the apartment permanently deprived tenant of enjoyment of the premises. However, the statute awarding double the security deposit did not apply. Landlord was not withholding the deposit for property damages, but as a setoff against damages it believed in good faith it was due for breach of the lease. *Applegate v. In-*

land Real Estate Corp., 441 NE2d 379 (App. Ct. 1982).

Illinois Tenants leased space in a building that was subsequently condemned. They defaulted on three months' rent, then vacated the premises, and landlord terminated the lease. Tenants sought part of the condemnation award based on their improvement of the property and landlord's failure to maintain the premises. *Held:* Tenants' failure to pay rent terminated their leasehold interest and extinguished their interest in the condemnation award. A tenant's obligation to pay rent could be discharged upon a constructive eviction, but there could be no constructive eviction unless the premises were vacated. If tenants remained on the premises, they were obligated to pay rent. Because they failed to do so for three months, landlord was justified in terminating the lease. Tenants therefore had no leasehold interest on the date of the condemnation award and had no interest therein. *City of Chicago v. American Nat'l Bank,* 408 NE2d 379 (App. Ct. 1980).

Maryland Tenants sued landlord, complaining of poor janitorial service, lack of heat and hot water, and other deficiencies. They sought a declaratory judgment that landlord had substantially breached the lease, and tenants were constructively evicted. They also sought damages, including those caused by loss of a five-year renewal option provided for in their lease. The trial court granted landlord summary judgment, holding that tenants' failure to vacate the premises prior to the end of the original term waived their claim of constructive eviction and right to renewal. *Held:* Summary judgment vacated and case remanded. Tenants' claim that landlord provided inadequate services could support a claim of constructive eviction if the deficiencies were found to be sufficiently serious. Since tenants did not abandon the premises until the original term expired, they could not seek relief for the original rental term, but were not precluded from asserting constructive eviction regarding their option to renew. *Stevan v. Brown,* 458 A2d 466 (Ct. Spec. App. 1983).

Nevada The county health district ordered a drive-in theater closed because its water quality failed to meet the state's standards. The lessee filed a constructive eviction complaint against the lessor, who counterclaimed for breach of the lease agreement. *Held:* Failure of the landlord to perform the government-ordered alterations constituted constructive eviction. Any alteration or repair ordered by a public authority is ordinarily outside the tenant's common-law duty to repair, and the expenses of compliance are more properly regarded either as capital expenditures or as necessary carrying charges to be paid out of rent. Correction of the water problem was costly and necessary for the continued operation of the theater. Because the lease was for five years and only nineteen months remained when the theater closed, the benefit of the expenditure reverted to the lessor. *Portal Enters. v. Cahoon,* 715 P2d 1324 (1986).

Nevada Tenant sued for damages for breach of lease, claiming he was constructively evicted. Tenant was unable to operate his business since he was denied a certificate of occupancy because landlord refused to comply with a municipal ordinance requiring construction of a fire wall. Tenant offered to build the wall and deduct the expense from his rent, but landlord refused. Landlord then changed the locks on the premises and took possession of the property. *Held:* Tenant was actually and constructively evicted, and could recover damages for breach of the lease, including lost profits. Structural repairs requiring a substantial alteration of the premises must be made by the lessor. The landlord was therefore under a duty to construct a fire wall, and his failure to do so amounted to constructive eviction. Moreover, changing the locks amounted to actual eviction. *Polk v. Armstrong,* 540 P2d 96 (1975).

New Mexico A commercial tenant of a building that was purchased by a new owner was paying a below market value rent. Tenant's lease contained an option to renew for two additional terms at the same rent. On three occasions, the new owner notified tenant of a substantial increase in rent, stating that defendant's previous managerial services, which were the reason for the low rent, were no longer needed. The owner sued to rescind the lease, and tenant counterclaimed, alleging breach of the covenant of quiet enjoyment. *Held:* The landlord's actions did not evidence malice or bad faith. Repeated demand letters are not in themselves acts of malice and do not constructively evict tenants. Tenant's delay in vacating the premises was not justified by landlord's actions. *El Paso Natural Gas Co. v. Kysar Ins. Agency,* 645 P2d 442 (1982).

New York Lessees defaulted on their lease when lessors failed to restore damaged leasehold improvements following a fire. Lessors sued to recover the upaid rent, and lessees argued that lessors' failure to obtain a new certificate of occupancy constituted constructive eviction because this rendered occupation of the premises illegal. *Held:* The absence of a certificate of occupancy did not relieve lessees of their obligation to pay rent. Lessors had made no covenant to obtain a certificate of occupancy, which could be obtained only by restoring the leasehold improvements. Therefore, lessees did not deprive defendants of a benefit to which they were entitled. In addition, lessees were not deprived of the right of possession, a necessary element of constructive eviction. *Silver v. Moe's Pizza, Inc,* 503 NYS2d 86 (App. Div. 1986).

Texas Landlord refused to replace a heating and air conditioning system despite a provision in the lease that landlord would pay for such repairs and despite repeated requests from tenant. Almost a year later, tenant abandoned the premises and demanded payment for its losses. When tenant did not renew its property insurance when it became due, as required under the lease, landlord sued for breach of lease. *Held:* Landlord's failure to repair was a constructive eviction entitling tenant to damages. Tenant's delay in abandoning the premises was for a reasonable period. The constructive eviction relieved tenant of the obligation to pay rent; therefore, tenant was also relieved of the duty to pay for insurance. *Downtown Realty v. 509 Tremont Bldg.,* 748 SW2d 309 (Ct. App. 1988).

30.30 Wrongful Eviction

D.C. Circuit Landlord evicted tenant, who had not paid rent, by packing and removing all her possessions, which forced her to pay for a motel until she found other lodgings. Tenant sued for actual and punitive damages. Landlord argued that he was entitled to exercise his common-law right to self-help. *Held:* Tenant is entitled to judgment for actual, but not punitive, damages. Landlord's common-law right to self-help had been abrogated by statute, so tenant had a right not to have her possessions interfered with except by legal process. *Mendes v. Johnson,* 389 A2d 781 (1978).

Maine Tenants, recipients of public welfare, sought to enjoin their landlord and others from evicting them in violation of the state human rights act. *Held:* A violation of the statute can be shown only where a landlord seeks an eviction "solely" because the tenant receives welfare, and not merely because such status is a contributing or even the predominant reason. If tenant complaints, late rental payments, or other matters caused the landlord to seek eviction, the existence of such factors prevents application of the statute. *Vance v. Speakman,* 409 A2d 1307 (1980).

New York Landlord entered plaintiff's parents' rent-controlled apartment after their deaths, removed the contents and discarded or destroyed them. Plaintiff sued defendant landlord for conversion, seeking $100,000 in damages, and moved for summary judgment. *Held:* For plaintiff. A landlord has no right under state law to retain or destroy personal property of a tenant, even where the tenant is legally displaced. Since defendant knew plaintiff was involved with his parents' tenancy and failed to contact him, defendant was liable for conversion as a matter of law. *Glass v. Weiner,* 480 NYS2d 760 (App. Div. 1984).

Washington When a tenant was evicted by her landlord, she sued to recover damages for wrongful eviction, including storage expenses connected with her moving. *Held:* The damage award by the trial court was adequate. The tenant recovered all the expenses that reasonably flowed from the landlord's wrongful act, including moving expenses. An honest attempt to mitigate damages was required, such as removal of her things from storage within a reasonable time. Damages could not be recovered for loss of use since they resulted from the unreasonably long storage period. *Sverson v. Marine Bancorp,* 546 P2d 454 (1976).

30.35
—Resort to Self-Help

Arkansas Tenants, who were delinquent in rent, were asked by landlord to vacate the premises. While tenants were away from home, landlord entered the house and removed all their personal property. Landlord relied on a provision in the lease permitting the landlord to take immediate possession of the premises should tenant fail to pay rent and on another provision that gave him the right to take possession and to remove tenants' property if they left the premises unoccupied while rent was due and unpaid. Tenants sued for wrongful and constructive eviction and conversion. *Held:* For tenants. Landlord's resort to self-help to evict a holdover tenant violated Arkansas forcible entry and detainer statutes. The protections of these statutes could not be waived, invalidating the lease provisions that purported to authorize landlord's conduct. *Gorman v. Ratliff,* 712 SW2d 888 (1986).

Nebraska A fire made commercial premises unfit for the continued operation of tenants' business and tenants stopped paying rent, as permitted by the lease, although they did not abandon the premises. Landlord changed the locks on all the doors to the premises and refused to give tenants keys to the new locks. Landlord did not deny tenants access during daylight hours. Tenants did not try to remove their property, even after landlord sent written notice that their property would be removed and placed in storage. The property was placed in storage after an action for conversion had been commenced, but before trial. *Held:* The partial lockout was a breach of the covenant of quiet enjoyment, but landlord did not convert tenants' property. Landlord was not asserting any claim to the property and did not prohibit tenants from removing it. Moreover, by their own admission, tenants made no request for its possession. *Polley v. Shoemaker,* 266 NW2d 222 (1978).

Utah A dispossessed tenant sued the

manager and the unknown owners of the apartment in which she had lived, alleging forcible eviction, conversion of her property, and intentional infliction of emotional distress. The manager moved for summary judgment of the complaints on the ground that he was acting only as agent for the owner of the property and within the scope of his agency. *Held:* The manager was not entitled to summary judgment. If an agent commits a tort while acting on behalf of his principal, the fact that he is an agent does not insulate him from liability to the injured party. The manager freely admitted that he retained the tenant's property without aid of judicial process. Seizing a tenant's property by self-help is a civil wrong and is actionable as a tort. Therefore, the manager could be held liable for conversion. *Pentecost v. Harward,* 699 P2d 696 (1985).

30.40 Tenant's Right to Relocation Benefits

9th Circuit Tenants living in a YWCA residence were evicted in a plan to convert the building to federally subsidized low-income housing. The project received Department of Housing and Urban Development financing and Section 8 rent subsidies. Tenants sued for federal relocation assistance, claiming they were displaced persons entitled to benefits under the Uniform Relocation Assistance (URA) program. The government argued that relocation assistance was not available for a privately owned project. *Held:* The district court properly granted the government's motion to dismiss. The legislative history and statutory framework of URA demonstrated that the program applied only where displacement was caused by a government agency. Despite the degree of federal involvement in the YWCA project, the conversion was private and not covered by URA. *Isham v. Pierce,* 694 F2d 1196 (1982).

30.45 Protected Tenancies

Georgia Public housing authorities sought to dispossess a tenant who was found by the police with marijuana in his apartment. The 10-day notice of eviction contended tenant had conducted himself unlawfully and disturbed neighbors' peaceful enjoyment of their accommodations. Tenant contended his conduct did not endanger other tenants or property and that he was entitled to 30 days' notice. *Held:* For tenant. Under the lease, management could give notice for good cause, including serious interference with the rights of other tenants, damage to premises, or creation of physical hazards. There was no evidence of complaints by neighbors, interference with rights of other residents, or damage to premises. Although tenant technically violated the terms of the lease by his illegal conduct, this violation was not sufficiently severe to warrant 10-day's notice. *Housing Auth. v. Brown,* 349 SE2d 501 (Ct. App. 1986).

New Jersey Plaintiff owned a three-story building that housed commercial enterprises and two private rental apartments. Defendant occupied an apartment as a month-to-month tenant. Plaintiff notified defendant that his tenancy would terminate at the end of the year and stated that he intended to personally occupy the apartment. Defendant failed to vacate the apartment, and plaintiff filed an action for possession. *Held:* The owner of a mixed-use building has recourse to provisions of the state Anti-Eviction Act. The act prohibits removal of certain residential tenants without "good cause." Good cause for removal includes a showing that the owner of a building of three residential units or fewer would personally occupy the unit. The presence of commercial uses does not affect the rights of residential tenants or owners under the act and has no relevance in determining whether owner would be deprived of the right to personally occupy a building. Accordingly, *Cabrera v. Mordan,* 220 NJ Super. 373, 532 A2d 272 (Law Div. 1987), is overruled to the extent it holds otherwise. *Durruthy v. Brunert,* 549 A2d 456 (Super. Ct. App. Div. 1988).

New Jersey A longtime resident in an 18-unit apartment building accepted part-time janitorial duties in return for a rent reduction. After a few years, the building was sold and the new landlord terminated resident's duties and sought possession of the apartment. N.J. Stat. Ann. § 2A: 18-61.1(1)(3) limits a landlord's right to evict a tenant in order to retain possession for himself to those premises with three or fewer residential units. However, N.J. Stat. Ann § 2A: 18-61.1(m) permits the removal of a janitor whose job is terminated and whose tenancy is conditioned on that employment. *Held:* The court held for the tenant, reasoning that the purpose of Subsection (m) was to permit a landlord to promptly provide living space for a new building-related employee, where employment calls for that person's presence in the building. Here, there was no proof indicating such a need. Furthermore, the court was satisfied that the requirement of the subsection that tenancy be conditioned on employment, required that such employment and the provision of living space be simultaneous. *Cruz v. Reatique,* 514 A2d 549 (Super. Ct. Law. Div. 1986).

New York Granddaughter moved into her grandmother's rent-controlled apartment in Manhattan. She still maintained an apartment in Queens, which she sublet to a friend. She paid $100 toward the grandmother's rent, and after the grandmother was hospitalized and died in September, she paid the September and October rent. When granddaughter told landlord of the grandmother's death, he served notice of termination of lease and notice to quit. Section 56(d) of the New York City Rent and Eviction Regulations exempted from eviction a member of the deceased tenant's family who was living with tenant. *Held:* For landlord. Section 56(d) protects only members of a deceased statutory tenant's family. The "living with" requirement connotes permanence. The granddaughter never put her name on the grandmother's mailbox, she left her furniture in the Queens apartment, had her telephone there, and her bank accounts were in Queens. These facts indicated only temporary residency. *829 Seventh Ave. Co. v. Reider,* 493 NE2d 939 (1986).

New York Tenants occupying loft space sued to challenge a regulation of the New York City Loft Board, permitting the landlord of an interim multiple dwelling to evict a residential occupant who has no lease on the ground that the unit is not the primary residence of the occupant. Tenants argued that the Multiple Dwelling Law, which protects residential tenants of illegally converted loft buildings from eviction, does not make "primary residence" a qualification for protection. Thus the regulation imposed an additional requirement not found in the statute. *Held:* The regulation was properly based on the legislative purpose of the Multiple Dwelling Law. The law was addressed to the problems of residential tenants, not to tenants' nonresidential use of premises. Tenants' reading of the law did not comport with the law's purpose of alleviating the housing shortage. *Lower Manhattan v. New York City Loft Bd.,* 487 NE2d 889 (1985).

New York Tenant signed a renewal lease in her name alone, although her sister was living with her. Soon after, the tenant moved out of the apartment. The sister remained and began paying the rent with her own checks. When the term of the lease expired, the landlord contested the sister's right to a renewal lease under the city's Rent Stabilization Law. *Held:* For the landlord. The rent stabilization law did not define the term "tenant." The court refused to apply the broad definition of "tenant" contained in the Rent Control Law, because rent stabilization was intended as a less stringent regulation than rent control. The court further ruled that in accepting the sister's rent checks, the landlord did not waive its right to contest the sister's continued occupancy. *Sullivan v. Brevard Assocs.*, 488 NE2d 1208 (1985).

New York Plaintiffs, who owned a cooperative apartment, rented two rooms from the cooperative for their maids. The cooperative board decided to put the maids' rooms to more profitable use, and served a 30-day termination notice for the rooms. Plaintiffs sued, claiming a landlord-tenant relationship existed between themselves and the board, bringing the rooms within the rent control law. *Held:* Any landlord-tenant relationship between the parties was incidental to plaintiffs' status as shareholders in the cooperative corporation. The rent control statute excluded dwellings owned as a cooperative, and was enacted to protect tenants from overreaching landlords, not for situations where a party was both a tenant and a shareholder in the landlord corporation. *Cohen v. Brown, Harris, Stevens, Inc.*, 485 NYS2d 745 (1984).

New York In 1983, tenant was sentenced to 15 years imprisonment, although he was eligible for parole after four years. He continued to pay rent, and his roommate continued to live there. The Omnibus Housing Act excluded from the protections of the rent control laws housing not occupied by the tenant as his primary residence. Landlord brought a holdover proceeding against the incarcerated tenant. *Held:* For landlord. Tenant had not resided in the apartment since 1983 and would not be returning in the foreseeable future. Even if tenant and his roommate had lived together at one time, the roommate was not entitled to occupy the apartment under N.Y. Real Prop. Law § 235-f which protected unrelated persons *sharing* a dwelling, and contemplated that the occupant live in the apartment together with the tenant. *Chris-Mac Co. v. Johnpoll,* 513 NYS2d 582 (App. Div. 1987).

Vermont In return for his work for employers, employee received wages and the right to occupy a house on employers' farm. When employee was fired, he and his family were permitted to remain in the house. They claimed that the employers told them they could stay if employee worked half days. Two weeks later, the employers forcibly evicted employee and his family from the house, claiming they had given the family a week or two to move out when employee was fired. They argued the family was not entitled to the protection afforded to tenants, since their occupancy was incidental to employee's employment. *Held:* The family's occupancy was not incidental to employee's employment. After employee was fired, he and his family remained as tenants, not employees, with the rent paid in the form of employee's work for half days. *Tatro v. Lehouiller,* 513 A2d 610 (1986).

30.50 Forcible Entry and Detainer

6th Circuit Tenants were served with notice by posting by their landlord, the housing authority, in forcible entry and detainer actions to repossess their apartments. The tenants sued for a declaratory judgment invalidating the posting method of service allowed by the Kentucky statute as depriving them of proper notice. Testimony showed that many tenants never saw the postings. *Held:* Service by posting violated due process. The standard for notice in forcible entry and detainer actions should be the same as in any in personam suit, "notice reasonably calculated, under all the circumstances, to apprise interested parties of the pendency of the action and afford them an opportunity to present their objections." Kentucky was required to give notice by mail instead of by posting. *Lindsey v. Greene*, 649 F2d 425 (1981), aff'd, 456 US 444 (1982).

Alaska Landlord filed an action for forcible entry and detainer against tenant united with a cause of action for rent arrearages. When default judgment was entered on the second cause of action, the tenant argued that the default judgment was void because of a lack of jurisdiction. *Held:* Since the court had no statutory jurisdiction over actions for forcible entry and detainer at the time the action was brought, the court also lacked jurisdiction over the secondary claim for rent under the special form of summons used in forcible entry and detainer actions. *McDowell v. Lenarduzzi*, 546 P2d 1315 (1976).

Arizona A commerical lease provided that in the event one party to the lease sued the other, the prevailing party would recover attorney fees. Landlord brought a forcible entry and detainer action against tenant for nonpayment of rent. Tenant won, and applied for attorney fees. The court denied the application on the ground that Arizona's forcible entry and detainer statute did not provide for attorney fees. Tenant appealed. *Held:* Affirmed. The purpose of a forcible entry and detainer action is to provide a summary and speedy means of obtaining possession of the property, and allowing the interjection of the issue of attorney fees into the proceeding would detract from the summary nature of the action. In Arizona, forcible entry and detainer is strictly a creature of statute and cannot be expanded by a lease provision. *DVM Co. v. Stag Tobacconist, Ltd.*, 671 P2d 907 (1983).

California Seven days after tenant had reported landlord to the police for sexually molesting tenant's daughter, landlord sent a notice to tenant to "pay rent or quit." The notice announced an immediate rent increase from $200 to $650 per month. When landlord sent tenant a 30-day notice of termination and tenant refused to move, landlord commenced an unlawful detainer action. Tenant raised retaliatory eviction as a defense. *Held:* Retaliatory eviction may be raised as an affirmative defense in an unlawful detainer action. The strong public policy interest in protecting those who report violations of the law from intimidation would not significantly impair the public policy of preserving the summary nature of unlawful detainer proceedings. *Barela v. Superior Court*, 636 P2d 582 (1981).

Connecticut Plaintiff, who was locked out of a hotel room he had occupied for three months, brought a forcible entry and detainer action pursuant to Conn. Gen. Stat. § 47a-43. Defendant moved to dismiss on grounds that (1) plaintiff was dispossessed by changing the lock and not by physical force and (2) plaintiff was a transient occupant and exempt from the forcible entry and detainer statute. The trial court granted defendant's motion on both grounds. *Held:* Affirmed, but only on the second ground. The use of physical force was not a requirement of Section 47a-43, which required only a finding that possession could not be regained without damage to the premises. Changing the lock was within that definition. However, plaintiff was not protected under the statute, because, despite his desire to make the room his permanent home, he knew he was a transient occupant of the hotel. *Bourque v. Morris*, 460 A2d 1251 (1983).

Iowa Landlady and month-to-month tenants entered into a sham warranty deed transaction so that landlady could circumvent city upgrading requirements. When tenants defaulted on their rent, landlady began a forcible entry and detainer action in equity. Tenants argued that (1) landlady could not pursue her remedy in a court of equity because, having engaged in the sham warranty deed transaction, she lacked clean hands and (2) the action was barred by Iowa Code § 648.18 because it was not commenced within 30 days of the first missed rental payment. *Held:* Landlady was entitled to possession. First, tenants could not complain of landlady's lack of standing because they, too, were participants in the transaction and lacked clean hands. Second, since this was a monthly tenancy, each missed rental payment was a separate cause of action on which landlady had 30 days to act. At least one missed rental payment was due within 30 days before commencement of the action. *Garrison v. Fetters,* 383 NW2d 550 (1986).

Ohio Mobile home park tenants violated park regulations by owning a dog. Landlord gave tenants a written notice asking them to remove the dog, and when they did not, he sent another notice advising them their lease would be terminated by a specified date. When tenants did not leave the premises, landlord brought a forcible entry and detainer action against them for holdover. *Held:* Landlord improperly relied on the notice provisions of Ohio Rev. Code Ann. § 5321, the landlord-tenant law applicable to apartment tenants. The statute pertaining to the termination of mobile home park tenancies was Ohio Rev. Code Ann. § 3733.13. Forcible entry and detainer proceedings against mobile home park tenants are governed by Ohio Rev. Code Ann. § 1923.02(A)(10), which applies only where tenants have defaulted in payment of rent or breached the terms of a rental agreement. Landlord's complaint was also defective in not having cited the violation of park regulations or any other breach of the rental agreement. *Schwartz v. McAtee,* 488 NE2d 479 (1986).

Ohio Plaintiff filed an eviction action (forcible entry and detainer) in municipal court at a time when defendant had a case pending against plaintiff in common pleas court involving a challenge to title of the same property. The municipal court stayed the action pending resolution of the title suit. *Held:* Judgment reversed. An action for forcible entry and detainer relates solely to the issue of the right of possession, and, therefore, questions involving conflicting claims to title are irrelevant and beyond the jurisdiction of the municipal court. A quiet title suit is of no relevance in determining whether the plaintiff has a present legal right to possession. *State ex rel. Carpenter,* 400 NE2d 391 (1980).

Oregon Plaintiff sold a mobile home to defendant and orally rented her a site for the mobile home for $100 monthly rent. Subsequently, when defendant asked for a written lease, plaintiff wrote a lease providing for $200 rent. Defendant refused to sign and attempted to continue paying $100 per month, but plaintiff refused to accept it, and brought a forcible entry and detainer action. Defendant counterclaimed for statutory damages for plaintiff's failure to furnish a written lease and deposited the rental into court. *Held:* For defendant. Under the Uniform Residential Landlord and Tenant Act, a tenant who counterclaims and tenders to court any outstanding rent may retain possession of the premises if the award plus tendered rent equals or exceeds the amount of rent adjudged to be owed. However, the withholding remedy is not available to a tenant who brings an original action instead of a counterclaim. *Napolski v. Champney,* 667 P2d 1013 (1983).

Oregon Landlord brought a forcible entry and detainer action to recover possession of an apartment and attorney fees. The trial court awarded possession but denied attorney fees. *Held:* Attorney fees should have been awarded to the landlord. The forcible entry and detainer statutes and the Residential Landlord and Tenant Act are not unrelated statutes. The latter statute provides for an award of attorney fees in any action on a rental agreement. *Executive Management Corp. v. Juckett*, 547 P2d 603 (1976).

31.00 ASSIGNMENTS

31.05 Right to Assign

Maryland Tenant-bank had a lease that contained a strict prohibition against assignment without consent of the landlord, which included assignment by operation of law. Assignment was a default under the lease. When tenant-bank merged with a second bank, tenant-bank's leasehold rights were transferred to the second bank by operation of law. Landlord did not consent to the transfer and notified both banks of its intent to terminate the lease. Suit followed. The second bank argued that the nonassignment clause should not preclude assignments by corporate merger. *Held:* The court of appeals refused to allow a corporate merger exception to a nonassignment clause in a commercial setting. To do so would vitiate the "operation of law" language and would negate the intention of the parties. A more liberal provision should have been negotiated ab initio. *Citizens Bank & Trust v. Barlow*, 456 A2d 1283 (1983).

Nebraska Corporation held identical leases with various landlords on grocery store buildings. Because of labor difficulties, the corporation closed the stores, which reopened under new management. The agreements between corporation and new management were originally structured as lease assignments. However, the landlords refused to consent to the assignments and informed the corporation that they would consider it in default if it assigned the leases. To avoid this, the assignments were replaced by subleases, which were permitted under the leases. The landlords argued that the original assignments were still in effect and sued for possession. *Held:* The leases had not been violated, because no prohibited assignments had been made that remained in effect beyond the period in the leases for curing default. It was not necessary for the parties to formally rescind the assignment or to reassign the leases before they could enter into valid subleases. The landlords' claim that the subleases were actually assignments was rejected. The corporation's right of reentry was a reversionary interest sufficient to qualify the transfer as a sublease rather than an assignment. In any case, the corporation retained a reversionary interest because the subleases expired before the basic lease. *American Community Stores Corp. v. Newman*, 441 NW2d 154 (1989).

New York A supermarket chain entered into a lease for one of its stores. The terms included a base rent, plus 1.5 percent of gross sales if they exceeded a specified figure. The agreement was silent as to whether tenant had the right to assign the lease. When the chain tried to assign its lease to a rival chain, landlord sued to void the assignment, arguing that it had relied on the first chain's expertise in setting the percentage rental figure. *Held:*

The lease could be assigned. Recovery under the percentage rental clause was not one of the landlord's fundamental expectations. The base rent was not particularly low in comparison to other supermarket leases. Thus, landlord was not relying solely upon tenant's unique merchandising skills, and there was no reason to imply into the lease a covenant against assignment. *Rowe v. Great Atl. & Pac. Tea Co.,* 412 NYS2d 827 (1978).

New York Landlord rejected tenant's proposed assignee because landlord wished to rent the apartment to a person on a waiting list of prospective tenants. Tenant sued for summary judgment requiring landlord to consent to the assignment. *Held:* Summary judgment granted. In view of the housing shortage in New York City, where every landlord has a waiting list of tenants, legal recognition of a waiting list as a reasonable ground for withholding consent to an assignment would effectively render meaningless a tenant's right to assign as provided in N.Y. Real Prop. Law § 226-b. Landlord's withholding of consent was unreasonable and could not prevent the assignment. *Kreitman v. Einy,* 460 NYS2d 46 (App. Div. 1983).

31.10 —Lessor's Consent to Assignment

Arizona Lessee, who had a business in a shopping center, could not reassign the lease without written consent of lessor. Lessee found buyers who agreed to purchase his business for $96,000, provided lessor consented to assignment of the lease. Lessor refused to agree to the assignment unless the rental was renegotiated. Unable to sell his business, lessee sued lessor for unreasonably withholding consent. A jury awarded lessee $73,000. *Held:* The jury award was upheld. The appeals court imposed a standard of reasonableness on the landlord in withholding consent to a sublease, unless the lease expressly stated otherwise. It was unreasonable for lessor to refuse consent merely because he wanted a higher rent. The award was justified, since lessor's refusal constituted tortious interference with lessee's business. *Campbell v. Westdahl,* 715 P2d 288 (Ct. App. 1985).

California Subtenant arranged to sell his business and to assign the sublease to purchasers. A provision in the sublease required the sublessor's prior written consent to assignment. The sublessor refused permission to assign the sublease. Prospective purchasers sued, claiming sublessor's refusal to consent to assignment was unreasonable. *Held:* Prospective purchasers' complaint stated a cause of action. The California Supreme Court ruled that where a lease provided for assignment only with the prior consent of the lessor, such consent could be withheld only where the lessor had a commercially reasonable objection to the assignment, even in the absence of a provision in the lease that consent to assignment would not be unreasonably withheld. The court noted that this rule reflected trends toward greater freedom to alienate commercial space and increased recognition of the duty of good faith and fair dealing inherent in contracts. *Kendall v. Ernest Pestana, Inc.,* 709 P2d 837 (1985).

California A lessee sought to assign a lease on a retail store that called for percentage rentals. The lease, written 20 years earlier with no escalator clauses, called for a minimum monthly rental of $2,750, but lessee had actually been paying an average of nearly $4,000 a month over the past three years under the percentage rent formula. The lease also restricted lessee to operating a women's ready-to-wear shop and prohibited assignment without lessor's prior written consent. Lessee assigned the lease to a couple who intended to operate an antique store as a hobby. Expected gross sales would never generate rent over the minimum monthly rental. *Held:* Although it is settled that a lessor may not unreasonably withhold consent to an assignment, lessor here was justified in withholding consent. It is commercially reasonable for a lessor to refuse to consent to an assignment that would prevent the lessor from receiving at least the same rental income it would if the lessee were to continue operation. *John Hogan Enters. v. Kellogg,* 231 Cal. Rptr. 711 (Ct. App. 1986).

Connecticut Plaintiff sought declaratory relief and damages when landlord refused to consent to assignment of lease. Plaintiff leased an office building from landlord. The lease required landlord's written consent to assignment, which would not be unreasonably withheld provided the assignee was financially responsible. Plaintiff informed landlord of the proposed assignment and forwarded assignees' uncertified financial statement. Because of encumbrances on assignees' assets, landlord refused consent and asked for a certified financial statement. Plaintiff proceeded with the assignment without authorization and subsequently wrote to landlord, further detailing assignees' financial situation. Landlord then notified plaintiff that the lease was terminated. *Held:* Landlord's refusal to consent to the assignment was not unreasonable. The request for a certified financial statement followed prudent business practices. Plaintiff's failure to submit such a statement subsequent to the unauthorized assignment terminated the lease. *Robinson v. Weitz,* 370 A2d 1066 (1976).

Idaho Tenants leased an auto dealership from landlord. The premises were subleased to a corporation held by tenants. The sublease provided landlord would not unreasonably withhold his consent to assignment of the sublease. Subsequently, subtenant suffered financial setbacks and closed. Landlord sued to collect on his note. Tenants then obtained an offer from proposed assignee to take an assignment of the sublease from subtenant, contingent upon landlord's consent. Landlord received an unaudited financial statement from proposed assignee. When landlord filed an involuntary bankruptcy petition against subtenant, proposed assignee withdrew his offer. Tenants then counterclaimed for damages, alleging landlord had unreasonably withheld consent to the assignment. *Held:* Landlord did not act unreasonably by failing to consent within a four-day period to an assignment to a party whose financial status was unclear. A lessor of distressed commercial property was not required to accept a new tenant of unknown means merely because the prior tenant was a failure. *Fahrenwald v. LaBonte,* 653 P2d 806 (Ct. App. 1982).

Massachusetts Each time a dental laboratory changed ownership, lessors consented to assignment of the lease, which contained a clause prohibiting lessors from unreasonably withholding such consent. Subsequently, a new lease was entered into, providing for assignment only with the prior written consent of the lessor. Lessee then assigned the lease without the lessor's consent. Lessor held the lessee in default, and lessee sued for declaratory relief. *Held:* Failure to seek prior written consent to the assignment breached an express provision of the lease, rendering the lease voidable by the lessor, regardless of whether consent was unreasonably withheld. The lessor's prior consents did not waive its right to consent to further assignments, since the new lease contained no language about withholding consent unreasonably. *Healthco, Inc. v. E&S Realty Assocs.,* 511 NE2d 579 (1987).

Nebraska A commercial lease provided tenant could not assign or sublet without landlord's written consent. Tenant ceased operations and asked landlord's consent for a lease assignment, which was refused. Tenant nonetheless subleased without landlord's consent. Landlord filed a forcible entry and detainer action. *Held:* Where a commercial lease does not expressly permit lessor to withhold consent to assignment or subletting, consent may not be unreasonably withheld. In determining whether lessor has acted reasonably in withholding consent, the court will consider the financial responsibility of the proposed assignee, assignee's suitability for the property, legality of the proposed use, need for alteration of the premises, and nature of the occupancy. The lease did not expressly permit landlord to withhold consent to assignment of the lease. Therefore, the lessor was required to act in good faith and reasonably in withholding consent. Whether lessor reasonably withheld consent was a question of fact to be determined upon remand. *Newman v. Hinky Dinky Omaha-Lincoln, Inc.*, 427 NW2d 50 (1988).

New Jersey Shopping center tenant guaranteed the performance of all covenants under its lease if the landlord would agree to an assignment of the lease. Without investigating the financial solvency of the proposed assignee or finding it unsuitable, the landlord refused assignment but offered to enter into a new lease agreement at an increased rent. Considering this a breach of the lease, the tenant vacated, and the landlord's successor in interest brought suit for recovery of the rent. *Held:* Tenant had the right to terminate the lease. There has been a demise of the doctrine of independent covenants in commercial leaseholds. The assignment clause was a "significant inducement" to the making of the lease. Thus, landlord's unreasonable withholding of consent was sufficient to support the tenant's right to terminate on breach of a material covenant. *Ringwood Assocs., Ltd. v. Jack's of Route 23, Inc., 398* A2d 1315 (App. Div. 1979).

New York Tenant's prospective assignee mailed an application for assignment to landlord by certified mail on November 10. Having received no response from the landlord by December 5, tenant assigned the lease. On December 18, landlord sent a notice denying consent, and brought an action to take possession of the apartment from the assignee. Landlord contended that under N.Y. Real Prop. Law § 226-b, an assignment could not be made without the landlord's consent or prior to the end of 30 days after the assignment application was mailed. *Held:* The landlord's failure to act within thirty days after the request for consent was mailed amounted to consent. Although assignment could be effective only after 30 days from mailing of the request, the statute did not prohibit making an assignment prior to the expiration of the 30 days. *420 East Assocs. v. Kerner,* 438 NYS2d 316 (1981).

South Dakota The leased premises were acquired by defendant-corporation, an assignee for the benefit of creditors during bankruptcy proceedings of the prior tenant. Defendant assumed operation of the premises, a store, and paid rent to landlord. Landlord's president was a member of the creditors' committee that approved defendant's takeover of the assets of the prior tenant. Landlord and defendant began negotiations to expand their business relationship, which ultimately broke down, whereupon landlord informed defendant it was terminating the "oral month-to-month" lease. Defendant refused to vacate, and suit followed. Defendant contended the original lease was still in effect. Landlord argued it had never consented in writing to assignment of the lease to defendant. *Held:* The lease provision requiring written consent to assignment was waived by landlord when it accepted rent from defendant. Moreover, landlord was privy to the assignment of the earlier tenant's assets, including the lease, and did not object to the assignment at that time. *Taylor Oil Co. v. Contemporary Indus.*, 305 NW2d 854 (1981).

31.15
Covenant Against Assignment

U.S. District Court, New York The lease agreement between the landlord and the corporate tenant contained a no-assignment clause. However, when the tenant went bankrupt, the landlord took no action to prevent one of tenant's subsidiaries from moving into the premises. Landlord accepted rent from this new tenant and even changed the building directory to show the location of the subsidiary. When the subsidiary was sold at auction under the original tenant's bankruptcy reorganization plan, and the original tenant attempted to assign the lease, the landlord brought an action to enforce the no assignment clause. *Held:* The landlord may not enforce the no-assignment clause. The landlord had not taken prompt action when the new tenant occupied the premises even though there was evidence that the landlord knew of the tenant's financial instability. Therefore, the landlord would be barred from enforcing the no-assignment clause after the subsidiary had terminated its tenancy. *In re Duplan Corp.*, 473 F. Supp. 1089 (SD 1979).

California Lessees assigned their leasehold interest without consent of the lessors, as required by the lease. The lessors evicted the assignees without process, and notified the lessees that they considered the premises abandoned, and were therefore reletting as agents for the lessees. The lessees brought a forcible entry and detainer action. The trial court held that the assignment of the leasehold in violation of the lease amounted to an abandonment. *Held:* The act of assigning a lease in violation of a covenant against assignment was not an abandonment since the lessees did not leave the premises vacant with the avowed intention not to be bound by the lease. Instead, the lessees turned over the premises to an assignee, an act that affirmed the lessees' interest under the lease. *Kassan v. Stout,* 507 P2d 87 (1973).

New York Landlord and tenant executed a lease, which provided that the lease could not be assigned without the consent of the landlord. When the tenant was several months in default on his rent, he asked the landlord's consent to assign the lease. The landlord refused, unless the lease was modified to increase the rent. The tenant then sued the landlord, claiming damages for economic duress. *Held:* The tenant was not entitled to damages. The landlord was merely exercising his right under the contract to refuse to consent to the assignment. This was not economic duress. *Herlon Card Shop, Inc. v. Prudential Ins. Co. of Am.* 422 NYS2d 709 (1979).

31.20
Assignor's Rights and Obligations

Massachusetts Plaintiff-lessor consented to assignment of defendant lessee's lease, and at assignee's request, agreed to amend the lease to extend the term. Assignee defaulted on the rent, and plaintiff sued defendant. Defendant claimed that amendment of the original lease by plaintiff and assignee without his consent freed him from liability and that the amendment constituted either plaintiff's acceptance of the surrender of the lease or a release of defendant from a suretyship relation with assignee. *Held:* Both of defendant's contentions were incorrect. The lease assignment created a surety relationship between assignor and assignee as to debts for rent. Amendment of the lease term did not defeat this relationship, nor did plaintiff waive the lease provision holding defendant primarily liable on the lease once it was assigned. Amendment did not amount to a surrender or novation by plaintiff; the express language of the lease refuted this contention. *Net Realty Holding Trust v. Giannini,* 432 NE2d 120 (1981).

New York Landlord covenanted in a lease with his tenant that he would provide ten free parking spaces in a neighboring garage, which the landlord would construct. When the landlord sold the building and refused to provide the parking spaces, the tenant sued the original landlord and the new owner and successor landlord for the parking spaces specified in the lease. *Held:* The successor landlord was liable for the parking spaces. Even though the building was bought only "subject to" the existing lease, the purchaser assumed all the contractual obligations of the original landlord under the lease, freeing the original landlord of all covenants. *Bank of NY v. Hirschfeld,* 336 NE2d 710 (1975).

Utah Within a month of obtaining its lease, which included a right of first refusal on any sale of the premises, tenant agreed orally to lease the premises to its former manager, who represented to the landlord that he was a partner of the tenant-firm and had bought out its interest. Two years later, the landlord sold the property to the former manager without offering it first to the tenant, and the tenant alleged a breach of its right of first refusal. *Held:* Since a right of first refusal is transferred when a lessee assigns a lease, the case turned on whether the tenant assigned the lease to the former manager or merely subleased. The supreme court held that the oral transfer of the lease was an assignment, overturning the trial court's finding that tenant had merely sublet the premises. A sublease is a transfer of something less than the tenant's full interest, but the transfer of the tenant's entire term—the oral lease was for the entire remaining term of the original lease term—constitutes an assignment. *L&M Corp. v. Loader,* 688 P2d 448 (1984).

31.25
Assignee's Rights and Obligations

Idaho Lessor of a business establishment entered into a one-year lease with the original lessee which provided for three one-year renewable options. When the lease was later assigned, the lessor consented to permit the assignee to renew the lease under the first of the three one-year options. Thereafter, the lessor ordered subsequent assignees to vacate the premises when he found that liquor licenses had been improperly posted. The assignee sued the lessor for lost profits and return of the premises. *Held:* Since the first one-year option had already expired when the lessor ordered plaintiffs to vacate, he had the right to reenter and take possession of the premises. The assignee could not rely upon the agreement between the lessor and the original lessee in which the options had been exercised to support his claim to the premises, since he was not a party to that agreement. The court therefore held for the lessor. *Ringer v. Rice,* 540 P2d 290 (1975).

Maryland Tenant occupied a lot improved by an office and machine shop under a 40-year lease, which was not recorded. The tenant assigned its interest in the lease to a third party as security for a loan and gave the creditor the right to possession in the event of default. Upon default, the creditor sought specific performance of the lease against the original lessor. *Held:* An unrecorded lease for more than seven years is valid between the original parties and also may be enforced by an assignee claiming through an original party, if the interest was acquired with actual notice of the lease or the tenant was in such possession as to give reasonable notice to the assignee. The assignee can prevail only if it is shown that the assignor was in possession and had not breached any covenant of the lease or if the assignee had paid rent and was prepared to perform other covenants of the lease. *Layton v. Petrick,* 355 A2d 466 (1976).

Mississippi Tenant assigned the remainder of its lease to Weeks with the consent of landlord. Subsequently, Weeks notified landlord, but not tenant, that he intended to close his business. Landlord then leased the building to another party, who defaulted. Landlord sued tenant for past due rent. Tenant settled with landlord, then sued Weeks and landlord. *Held:* The assignment released Weeks from future rent obligations after the landlord accepted his surrender of the premises. Tenant had assigned its entire interest in the lease while agreeing to remain primarily liable, and Weeks thereby "stood in the shoes" of tenant. His surrender of the leased premises to landlord and the landlord's unqualified possession of the property released both Weeks and tenant from future rent obligations. However, Weeks was not released from rent that accrued prior to landlord's retaking of possession, and tenant could recover from Weeks any payment he owed prior to such surrender. *Weeks v. Cal-Maine Foods, Inc.,* 522 So. 2d 725 (1987).

Missouri To obtain Small Business Administration financing, owners of a restaurant agreed to assign their lease to the bank granting the loan. The landlord, restaurant owners, and the bank executed an assignment agreement, which provided the bank would assume all obligations of the lease including payments to be made thereunder. Several months later, restaurant owners vacated the premises, and landlord made written demand to the bank for the rent. The bank refused to pay, because it had not taken possession of the premises or exercised any of its rights under the lease. Landlord sued. *Held:* The bank was contractually bound to observe all the obligations of the lease, including the payment of rent. The assignment was absolute and unconditional. It was not a mortgage, although it was executed to serve as collateral for a loan. *South Lakeview Plaza v. Citizens Nat'l Bank,* 703 SW2d 84 (Ct. App. 1985).

32.00 SUBLEASES

32.05 Right to Sublease

6th Circuit Woolworth leased space in a shopping center owned by Joseph Bros. The lease ran until 1990, with options to extend, and called for a percentage rent based on gross annual sales as well as annual rent. In 1982, Woolworth gave Joseph Bros. notice it was closing the store. Woolworth entered into a sublease with Hills Department Store and then informed Joseph Bros. it was exercising its option to extend. Woolworth did not pay rent after making the sublease. Joseph Bros. filed an action for a declaratory judgment under its lease. *Held:* The agreement between Woolworth and Hills was a sublease not requiring the landlord's consent, and the percentage rent clause was not in effect after the tenant sublet the premises. The fact that Woolworth transferred less than the balance of its lease term, reserving a reversionary interest of one day, created a valid sublease. Woolworth's sublet to Hills Department Store did not require landlord consent, since the lease specified that consent was needed only for sublet to a bank, supermarket or grocery store. The court also found that when Woolworth closed and the landlord did not terminate the lease, the percentage rent clause was effectively deleted from the lease and Woolworth was responsible only for the fixed annual rental. *Joseph Bros. v. FW Woolworth Co.*, 844 F2d 369 (1988).

Alabama Homa-Goff Interiors filed a counterclaim against Cowden for Cowden's alleged interference with a contractual relationship and unlawful refusal to grant consent to a sublease between Homa-Goff and subtenants. *Held:* Where the lease contained an approval clause, the landlord could not unreasonably withhold consent to a sublease agreement. The landlord's rejection should be judged by reasonable commercial standards. *Homa-Goff Interiors, Inc. v. Cowden,* 350 So. 2d 1035 (1977).

District of Columbia Pursuant to a lease providing that landlord would not unreasonably withhold consent to sublease, commercial tenant exercised its option to rent additional space and requested landlord's consent to sublease the space. Landlord said it would consent only if it received half the increase in rent the tenant would charge the sublessee. Tenant refused, and landlord withheld consent to sublease, stating it intended to offer the same space to the subtenant at the increased rent. *Held:* It was unreasonable for the landlord to withhold consent to a sublessee for the purpose of extracting economic concessions. The original negotiations had established the balance of risks accepted by the landlord and tenant, and landlord could not now reasonably demand that the balance be altered in his favor as the price for his consent. *1010 Potomac Assoc. v. Grocery Mfrs.*, 485 A2d 199 (1984).

Idaho Pursuant to a lease providing that landlord would not unreasonably withhold consent to sublease the premises, farm tenants requested permission to sublet the land for the next crop year, promising to supervise the subtenant's operations and to furnish any additional information needed. Landlords refused permission to sublet unless the original lease was substantially rewritten. Tenants sublet a portion of the acreage without the landlord's permission, and landlords brought an action to terminate the underlying lease, contending that there were no restrictions in the lease on their right to withhold permission to sublet. *Held:* Regardless of whether a reasonableness requirement is contained in the lease, any refusal to consent to subleasing must be based on reasonable concerns in the particular circumstances. In this case, tenants had met their burden of proving that landlords had withheld consent unreasonably. *Funk v. Funk,* 633 P2d 586 (1981).

Louisiana Tenant leased two parcels of commercial property for a period of approximately 25 years. After 15 years, when the market value of the property had increased dramatically, tenant requested permission to sublease the premises. Landlord refused permission but offered to cancel the lease, whereupon tenant asked for a cash payment, and negotiations became stalemated. Tenant then sublet the premises without notifying landlord. When landlord found out and requested a conference, tenant refused, but continued to send the monthly rent, which landlord accepted. Landlord took no further action until two years later, when it started eviction proceedings. Tenant argued that landlord's long period of inaction, as well as the acceptance of rent, constituted implied consent to the sublease. *Held:* There was no implied consent to the sublease. Landlord's reasons for delay, including a change in corporate management, the large number of leases held by the company, and the desire to avoid a lawsuit, were valid enough to support the delay. *Illinois Central Gulf RR v. International Harvester Co.,* 368 So. 2d 1009 (1979).

New York Tenant, sole occupant of a three-bedroom rent-stabilized apartment, notified landlord he intended to sublet portions of the apartment to two other persons. Tenant was to remain in occupancy, with the subtenants occupying the two other bedrooms and contributing to the rent. Landlord rejected the requests, claiming there was a waiting list for apartments. *Held:* For tenant. N.Y. Real Prop. Law § 226-b can be invoked to permit a tenant to partially sublet his apartment. Because the statute was enacted to protect a tenant's rights during a housing shortage, the court saw no reason to construe it so as to restrict the alienation of space in underutilized apartments during a housing emergency. The court rejected landlord's reliance upon a waiting list as a reasonable basis for withholding consent, holding that the rights of tenants in possession took precedence over the mere expectancies of prospective tenants. *Lomax Holding Co. v. Calitri,* 461 NYS2d 152 (App. Term 1983).

New York Tenant, in violation of his lease, permitted a third party to occupy his apartment without landlord's prior approval. Upon discovering this, landlord refused tenant's request for consent to sublease to the occupant. The landlord asked for no information about the occupant. Tenant then assigned subtenant the remainder of his lease, and landlord commenced holdover proceedings. *Held:* For landlord. Landlord was not given an opportunity to exercise its right of reasonable refusal of sublease in advance of the transfer. Therefore it did not matter whether or not landlord's refusal was unreasonable. Tenant was not protected under N.Y. Real Prop. Law § 226-b, which prohibits landlords from unreasonably withholding consent to sublease, because tenant did not comply with its requirement of seeking landlord's approval before installing subtenant. *Brefries E. End, Inc. v. Platt,* 457 NYS2d 677 (App. Term 1982).

32.10 Covenant Against Subleasing

Arkansas A bank-tenant of a shopping mall built a drive-in facility in the parking lot. When the bank later merged with a bank in another location, it decided to sublease the drive-in facility to a savings and loan already in the mall. The lease stated that tenant could not sublet without landlord's consent. The landlord was asked to approve the sublease, but when landlord discovered the bank had vacated the premises, it terminated the lease. The bank sued, citing unreasonable failure to consent to a sublease. In support, the bank argued the savings and loan was an identical tenant. Landlord countered that if the savings and loan had a drive-in, fewer customers would enter the mall. *Held:* For landlord. Where the evidence indicated that the proposed sublease would be financially disadvantageous to the mall's tenants and to landlord, consent to sublet was not unreasonably withheld. *Warmack v. Merchant's Nat'l Bank,* 612 SW2d 733 (1981).

New York Landlord and tenant of commercial rental property entered into a renewal of their lease, under which landlord agreed to expand existing facilities; tenant agreed to pay an increased base rental plus a stated percentage of annual gross receipts. Following construction, the tenant's overall drop in profitability resulted in the closing of its store on landlord's property, and the premises were sublet to another concern. Landlord sued to recover possession, arguing that the tenant breached an implied covenant against assignment without the landlord's consent. *Held:* Although the agreement contained no prohibition against subleasing, an implied covenant can be said to arise where the landlord has entered into the base in reliance on some trait or ability of the lessee which has a material effect on fulfillment of the lessor's reasonable expectations. The percentage clause in the lease agreement is evidence of such an implied agreement, and if justified by other surrounding circumstances, the landlord will be entitled to reassume possession. *Rowe v. Great Atl. & Pac. Tea Co., Inc.,* 412 NYS2d 827 (1978).

North Dakota Tenant, who leased acreage from ranch owner under a lease that prohibited assignment of the farm or of the lease without written approval, entered into a pasturage and feeding contract to care for 200 to 250 pair of livestock on the ranch. The ranch owner sued to evict the tenant for default of the lease. *Held:* For the ranch owner. Generally, temporary pasturage contracts are not held to be assignments or leases. Here, however, because the tenant transferred the right to use almost all the grassland and cropland on the ranch, the pasturage arrangement was a subletting in violation of the lease. Further, because the lease entitled the ranch owner to a third of the gross sales of livestock, farm produce and rentals, the pasturage contract had the effect of changing the amount of rent and its method of calculation. *Hutton v. Janz,* 387 NW2d 494 (1986).

32.15
—Waiver of Covenant Against Subleasing

7th Circuit Tenant had sublet its premises in violation of its lease eight years previously. Lessor was aware of the sublease and accepted rent. When lessor attempted to sublease other premises to a competitor of tenant's, tenant attempted to enjoin the lessor in view of an exclusive use clause contained in the lease. Tenant's sublease incorporated by reference the exclusive use clause of the original lease. The lessor contended that it was not bound by the exclusive clause in view of tenant's previous subleasing of the premises. *Held:* By knowingly allowing the sublease and accepting rent for eight years, the lessor had waived the prohibition against subletting without permission and was obligated to comply with the exclusivity clause. However, an injunction could not be sustained, because tenant's loss, the amount of rent under its sublease, was calculable. Therefore, tenant had an adequate remedy at law. *American Dairy Queen v. Brown-Port Co.,* 621 F2d 255 (1980).

New York Plaintiff lived in apartment with tenant of record and remained there for four years after tenant of record moved out. The lease contained a nonwaiver clause providing that the landlord's failure to insist upon strict performance of any lease convenant would not constitute waiver of the covenant. Later, in a condominium conversion, plaintiff's apartment was sold. The new owner claimed that plaintiff's occupancy violated the lease. Plaintiff contended that the landlord's acceptance of rent for four years waived the landlord's right to object to plaintiff's occupancy. *Held:* For plaintiff. The nonwaiver clause did not preclude a finding of waiver. The landlord's knowing acceptance of rent without attempt to terminate the lease justified an inference that the landlord had waived any violation. *Lee v. Wright,* 485 NYS2d 543 (App. Div. 1985).

32.20
Rights of Tenant/Sublessor

10th Circuit Defendant assigned his lease for a tract containing coal to plaintiff for use as a tax shelter. Plaintiff was to pay royalties based on a minimum production level regardless of whether that amount was actually produced. After a tax law change, plaintiff made no efforts to mine and paid no royalties. Defendant took control of the property, and plaintiff sued for breach of the lease, claiming damages for the loss of coal stockpiled on the property. Defendant counterclaimed for unpaid royalties. *Held:* Defendant's sole remedy was repossession of the property. The transaction could be characterized as a sublease, for breach of which a sublessor had the remedy of recovery of possession and any monies due him under the sublease. Ordinarily, a sublessor could repossess the leased property and collect accrued royalties, which were regarded as rent. However, a provision in this sublease that defendant's remedy was repossession and retention of "all monies previously paid" defeated defendant's claim to additional money. *Cal-Am Corp. v. Spence,* 659 F2d 1034 (1981).

Connecticut After renewing a lease for a five-year term, the tenant learned that the landlord had leased the roof of the building to an advertising concern, which had commenced drilling holes in the roof to erect its signs and thereby allegedly damaged the safety of the structure. The tenant sued the landlord for damages, claiming that the landlord was unjustly enriched by rents from the advertising company. The trial court held that the future rent for the roof should be split between the landlord and the tenant. *Held:* The tenant alone would have the right to sublet the roof for advertising purposes. The court reversed the damage award, however, ruling that damages could not be prospective, but must be limited to rents already received, with future recovery, if any, to await a later date. *Monarch Accounting Supplies, Inc. v. Prezioso,* 368 A2d 6 (1976).

Iowa Tenant leased space in a shopping center and agreed to sublease part of this space to subtenant. Tenant sold fabrics and accessories, and subtenant sold women's apparel. When tenant vacated the premises, subtenant said it also intended to vacate, alleging that the sublease was based on tenant's continuing in business at the site. Tenant brought an action against subtenant for breach of the sublease. *Held:* Tenant, not subtenant, breached the sublease. The provisions of the sublease indicated a relationship of significant economic interdependence between the two businesses. It characterized subtenant as a department of tenant's store. The court recognized an implied covenant by tenant to continue its business on the leased premises during the term of the sublease. *Fashion Fabrics, Inc. v. Retail Investors Corp.,* 266 NW2d 22 (1978).

New Jersey Lease agreement provided that the tenant could not sublet without the landlord's written consent. The tenant, in violation of the agreement, sublet the premises without the landlord's knowledge. When the tenant subsequently went bankrupt, the original lease terminated. The sublessee refused, for two months after lease termination and the landlord's protests, to vacate the premises. The landlord brought action against the sublessee for trespass and for damages. *Held:* A clause in the lease providing for the landlord's consent constituted a condition subsequent and the sublessee took possession lawfully until avoided by the landlord. Therefore, the sublessee was not a trespasser, but a tenant at sufferance having entered lawfully, but retaining possession unlawfully. The landlord was entitled to damages. *Xerox Corp. v. Listmark Computer Sys.,* 361 A2d 81 (1976).

Texas The bank desired to buy a building occupied by a father and owned by a trust established for his children. The parties worked out a plan that called for the father to sublease space from the bank in another building when the bank acquired title to the father's building from the trust. The "termination agreement," but not the sublease, specified that the sublease could be terminated at any time upon 30 days' written notice. Tenant subsequently sent notice that he was terminating the lease, and the bank refused to assent to the termination. Tenant ceased rental payments and the bank sued for nonpayment of rent. *Held:* The parties intended for the two contracts to be read together; the right of termination upon 30 days' written notice was impliedly included in the sublease. The intent of the parties was that the sublease be temporary until the sublessee could find a permanent office. The termination agreement specifically referred to a lease of space in the bank's building, which was made through the sublease. The fact that the termination agreement anticipated and provided for an extension of the sublease until the bank completed its new building or until the five-year sublease expired is evidence that the parties intended the lease to be temporary. *Brown v. Republicbank First Nat'l Midland,* 766 SW2d 203 (1988).

Washington Defendant leased commercial premises for use as a retail grocery store. By the terms of the lease, defendant's rent was tied to profits, with a stated minimum monthly rental. In addition, the lease provided that defendant could freely assign or sublet the lease but would remain liable as surety for full performance. After a few years of operating from the premises, defendant moved to a newer location and sublet the store to an Asian food specialty concern. Landlord filed suit for damages, alleging that defendant's obligation under the lease was to operate a grocery generating the expected level of sales and that the right to assign or sublet was not "absolute." *Held:* The lease granted defendant the unconditional right to sublet the premises, subject only to the surety clause. There is no "implied" duty of defendant to insure production of certain levels of business activity, since no such implication arises under the language of lease, nor in any other pertinent document. *Brown v. Safeway Stores, Inc.,* 617 P2d 704 (1980).

32.25 Rights of Sublessee

5th Circuit A main lease required the lessee to return the premises in good order and in the condition in which they were demised, ordinary wear and tear excepted. The lessee in turn subleased the premises "as is," with the sublessee agreeing to return it at the end of the underlying main lease in a satisfactory condition pursuant to the terms of the main lease. Extensive damage to the premises occurred during the terms of both the lease and the sublease. The lessor brought suit for breach of the covenant to repair, and the lessee joined the sublessee as a third-party defendant, contending that the sublease obligated the sublessee to make any repairs sufficient to bring the premises into the condition required by the main lease. The sublessee asserted that the agreement was ambiguous, and did not reflect the intent of the parties. *Held:* The sublessee was only responsible for returning the property in the same condition as it received it—that is, its liability was for damages incurred during the term of its occupancy. *Freight Terminals, Inc. v. Ryder Sys., Inc.,* 461 F2d 1046 (1972).

Alabama Plaintiff landlord brought an action to recover the premises from the lessee and sublessee. Plaintiff was granted recovery against the lessee because of the lessee's insolvency. The sublessee argued that it would be inequitable to also force him to forfeit as he had recently made significant improvements to the property. The landlord was unaware of the improvements and had not given approval to the sublessee's tenancy since it was not required in the original lease. The court noted that some cases have not enforced a forfeiture against a sublessee where it would be inequitable to do so. However, the court noted that in these cases the lessor had always approved the sublessee's tenancy. *Held:* For the landlord, since to do otherwise would be to force the landlord into a contract not of his own making. The landlord had neither agreed to the amount of the subrental nor to the terms and conditions of the sublease. Absent proof of fraud, mistake, undue influence, coercion, or duress, this is not a proper case to grant relief from the forfeiture of the sublease. *USA Petroleum Corp. v. Jopat Bldg. Corp.*, 343 So. 2d 501 (1977).

California A sublease provided a right of extension for two successive 10-year terms, reflecting a similar provision in the overlease. The sublease also provided that if the overlease terminated for any reason, the sublease would also terminate. A new owner, objecting to the extensions provided under the sublease, obtained the sublessor's agreement that the overlease was terminated and that the sublease would not be extended. When the sublessee attempted to assert its rights to extend the lease, the new owner sued. *Held:* For the sublessee. The court applied a 1939 Oklahoma case involving a similar sublease provision, where the court had held that reservation by sublessor of a right to terminate the overlease for any reason was contrary to the tenor of the contract and should have been expressed clearly to be effective. Also, the sublease was found to contain an implied agreement that the sublessor would protect its sublessee by exercising its own option to renew. *Northridge Hosp. Found. v. Pic' n' Save No. 9, Inc.*, 232 Cal. Rptr. 329 (Ct. App. 1986).

Louisiana Sublessee sued his lessor and sublessor for the difference between rent paid and the actual fair market value of the leased premises when the lease was judicially canceled because the lessor failed to replace equipment and repair structural defects in the leased premises. The sublessee argued that it was entitled to a partial return of rent from the date the action was filed of 1965 to the date the lease was canceled in 1970. During the pendency of the suit, the sublessee continued to occupy the premises. *Held:* The sublessee was not entitled to a reduction of rent for the lessor's breach, since the sublessee continued its occupation of the premises. *Reed v. Classified Parking Sys.*, 324 So. 2d 485 (Ct. App. 1975).

Nebraska Tenant entered into a commercial lease with two renewal options. The lease provided that the options would expire if lessor sold the property. Defendant sublet the property for the balance of the original term plus renewal options. The sublease did not mention tenant's prime lease, although tenant represented it had the lessor's permission to sublease. When subtenant attempted to exercise the first renewal option, it was informed by tenant that the options were void since lessor had sold the building. Subtenant sued for a declaratory judgment. *Held:* For subtenant. Subtenant did not know or have reason to know of the cancellation clause; there was testimony that subtenant never saw the prime lease and tenant had kept subtenant from contact with the lessor. Subtenant reasonably construed tenant's representation that it had permission to sublease as consent by the lessor to the entire term plus renewals. *Occidental*

Sav. & Loan v. Bell Fed. Credit Union, 357 NW2d 198 (1984).

New York Tenant entered into a lease providing for additional rent to be paid if landlord's taxes or operating expenses in any lease year exceeded those prevailing in the base year 1978. Law firm entered into a sublease agreement with tenant. After landlord billed tenant for additional rent, tenant demanded that law firm pay the increase. When law firm refused to pay, tenant sued. *Held:* Boilerplate provision in sublease, providing that all provisions of the overlease applicable to the overtenant were binding on the sublessee, did not obligate law firm to pay the additional rent. This was especially true when sublease clearly defined law firm's rental obligations without referring to the additional rent. Law firm would not be put on clear notice by the boilerplate provision that it was assuming the obligation to pay additional rent. *NPS Eng's & Constructors, Inc. v. Underweiser & Underweiser,* 539 NE2d 100 (1989).

New York Building owner leased premises to tenant for a 21-year term with renewal options. Tenant subleased space to subtenant for a concurrent term with renewal options. The sublease provided that it was subject to the same terms and conditions as the master lease. Subtenant attempted to exercise its renewal option, but tenant had not renewed the master lease and took the position that the subtenant had no option to renew in that case. Subtenant failed to vacate the premises after the lease expired, and landlord brought a holdover proceeding. *Held:* Summary judgment for landlord. The sublease, including renewal options, was expressly made subject to the master lease. Subtenant could not compel tenant to renew the master lease so that subtenant could exercise its renewal option absent an agreement by tenant to do so or proof of special circumstances. *Minister, Elders & Deacons of the Reformed Protestant Dutch Church v. 198 Broadway, Inc.,* 451 NE2d 164 (1983).

New York Plaintiff, prime tenant of a rent-stabilized apartment, sought to regain possession after the expiration of subtenant's tenancy. Subtenant argued that he could not be evicted under the Rent Stabilization Code. *Held:* Subtenant could not be evicted except upon one of the special grounds set forth in the sections of the code, none of which were alleged in plaintiff's complaint. What especially startled the court was that plaintiff failed to establish the ground set forth in Section 54(b), that she wished to return to full time occupancy after the subtenancy had expired. The evidence established only that she wished to have the added convenience of an apartment in town. Therefore, the court could not allow her to amend her petition to allege Section 54(b) of the code. *Lindstrom v. Conte,* 448 NYS2d 636 (Civ. Ct. 1982).

Oklahoma Commercial tenant entered into an assignment, purporting to transfer all tenant's rights and responsibilities under the original lease and sublease, which provided that tenant would exercise the options to renew or to extend the original lease in favor of subtenant. The original lease provided that only tenant could exercise the option, and that tenant would remain liable if the lease were assigned. When subtenant notified landlord of its intent to exercise the renewal option, landlord sued for possession. *Held:* Subtenant had the right to exercise the original lease's option for an additional term. The court found that subtenant was in privity of estate with landlord, since the two documents effected an assignment; that the option ran with the land; and the option was not personal to the tenant. The option was to extend rather than to renew, which would have required a new lease, so that subtenant's exercise of the option did not effect an implied novation of tenant's liability in violation of the original lease. Tenant's rental liability during the option period had been set forth in the original lease, ensuring that tenant could be held liable as a surety during the extension. *Castle v. Double Time, Inc.*, 737 P2d 900 (1986).

Texas Sublessee of shopping center tenant complained of vandalism and harassment by patrons of an adjacent gameroom. The shopping center manager hired security guards, but refused to evict the gameroom, and sublessee was forced to close. Tenant sued sublessee for unpaid rent, and sublessee brought a third-party action against shopping center manager for violation of the Deceptive Trade Practices Act (DTPA), negligence, and breach of express and implied warranties. *Held:* For manager. An implied warranty under DTPA did not extend to services provided by the manager, which involved the exercise of professional judgment. The manager was not negligent in failing to enforce lease covenants since the manager owed no contractual duty to sublessee. Further, the manager acted reasonably to protect the public and was not required to evict the tenant. *Forestpark Enters., Inc. v. Culpepper,* 754 SW2d 775 (Ct. App. 1988).

32.30 Liability of Sublessee to Original Lessor

Arizona Tenant shared its space with a related corporation, without any formal sublease or assignment of the premises. When both tenant and the related corporation ceased doing business, landlord sought to impose a landlord's lien on $32,000 of computer equipment belonging to the related corporation, pursuant to Ariz. Rev. Stat. Ann. § 33-362, which provides that a landlord shall have a lien on all property of his "tenant" and shall have the same lien against a "sublessee or assignee." *Held:* Landlord was entitled to the lien, even though the premises were not formally subleased. The court resoned that the related corporation was liable for its pro rata share of rent under Section 33-323 as a "person in possession of land out of which rent is due." An entity that is liable for rent under Section 33-323 can be considered a "sublessee" under Section 33-362(D). Finally, landlord was entitled to the presumption of a legal tenancy based on possession and payment of rent. *State ex rel. Childers v. 2525 E. Ariz. Biltmore Circle Corp.*, 731 P2d 1239 (Ct. App. 1986).

California The vice-president of a corporate lessee signed a personal guarantee on a sublease, using his corporate title. After the sublessee defaulted, the lessee sued the vice-president to make good on the guarantee. *Held:* The vice-president was personally responsible for the default. The addition of the words "vice president" after his signature on the guarantee were merely descriptive, and did not change his personal liability. *Sebastian Int'l Inc. v. Peck,* 240 Cal. Rptr. 911 (Ct. App. 1987).

New York Plaintiff landlord's building was occupied by the tenant's sublessees, whose use of the premises violated municipal fire regulations. Shortly after the violations were reported, the building burned down. Plaintiff sued the tenant and the sublessees, alleging breach of a lease covenant obligating tenant to "comply with and execute" all rules and orders under the fire code. *Held:* The landlord cannot maintain suit against the sublessees since there is no privity of contract upon which to base the liability. The landlord's sole option is to seek recovery against the original subleasing tenant. *Tefft v. Pawnbroking & Jewelry Co.*, 428 NYS2d 52 (App. Div. 1980).

32.35 Tenant's/Sublessor's Liability for Acts of Sublessee

3d Circuit Tenant entered into a sublease with an automobile junkyard operator. After sublessee left the premises landlord brought an action against tenant for the costs of removing junk left behind by sublessee. *Held:* Under Pennsylvania law, landlord was entitled to reimbursement from tenant for removal of the junk left behind by, and reparation of unreasonable wear and tear inflicted by sublessee, especially in light of the fact that the costs incurred by landlord exceeded half the rent paid by sublessees in the course of the eight-year sublease. *United States Gypsum Co. v. Schiavo Bros.*, 668 F2d 172 (1981), cert. denied, 456 US 961 (1982).

Kansas Lessee sublet its leasehold interest to a third party who negligently caused a fire that damaged the building. Landlord sued lessee in tort for negligence, and lessee asked that summary judgment be granted in its favor because a third party had caused the fire. The trial court granted summary judgment, and plaintiff apealed. *Held:* Defendant lessee was liable to the landlord for the negligence of its sublessee. The lessee has an implied obligation to use reasonable diligence in treating the property demised so that no injury will result to it and to return it to landlord in the condition in which it was received. Where that general duty is violated, even when it arises from the terms of a contract and is caused by a third party, a tort is actionable on the theory of negligence. *Marcellus v. KOV, Inc.*, 615 P2d 170 (1980).

33.00 SALE-LEASEBACK

33.05 In General

4th Circuit In 1965, respondent purchased from seller a resort hotel in Florida for $2.5 million cash and assumed a $4.5 million mortgage. Respondent leased the property to seller's wholly owned subsidiary for a 21-year term with two 25-year renewal options, giving seller an option to repurchase for a stated price at designated intervals. In 1971, seller assigned the option contract to his Subchapter S corporation, which exercised the option. Respondent included the rental payments in its income and took a depreciation deduction for the property. To receive favorable tax treatment as a real estate investment trust, respondent distributed 90 percent of its taxable income to its shareholders. The Internal Revenue Service (IRS) determined that the sale-leaseback was really a secured lending arrangement and disallowed the deductions. Respondent sued for a refund, and the jury found that the sale-leaseback was a bona fide transaction. *Held:* The transaction was not merely to avoid taxation. Determination of the issue of bona fides was to be made as a matter of law, but there was evidence to sustain the jury's finding. The transaction was not a tax avoidance device merely because tax considerations entered into its planning. *American Realty Trust v. United States*, 498 F2d 1194 (1974).

7th Circuit Defendants had entered into similar sale and leaseback arrangements with plaintiff. Subsequent to defendants' becoming debtors in possession under Chapter XI of the Bankruptcy Act, plaintiff petitioned to terminate its leases and recover possession of the properties. Defendants asserted that the transactions were in substance mortgages; thus, defendants were owner-mortgagors and plaintiff a mortgagee. Plaintiff was therefore not entitled to the properties and improvements free of the equity of redemption that defendants would possess in mortgage foreclosure proceedings. *Held:* An instrument conveying real property is a mortgage if it appears to have been intended only as a security in the nature of a mortgage. Plaintiff was the fee simple owner of the lands by reason of absolute conveyance in the deed and termination of the lease without exercise of the repurchase option. Plaintiff was fee simple owner of the improvements by reason of forfeiture under the lease upon its termination. *Kassuba v. Realty Income Trust,* 562 F2d 511 (1977).

9th Circuit Overmeyer made a sale-leaseback of a warehouse with Bergin Way. Overmeyer was to pay a monthly rental plus taxes and expenses. Overmeyer took out lease guarantee insurance. When Overmeyer defaulted on the lease, defendant insurance company found new tenants, as the policy allowed. Tenants were not responsible to pay taxes and expenses, and defendant refused to do so. Bergin Way sold out to plaintiff, who sued for breach of the insurance contract, claiming that by becoming Overmeyer's successor in possession, defendant was liable for taxes and expenses. *Held:* For defendant. Defendant, by electing to take possession of the warehouse, did not assume all the benefits and burdens of the lease. Only part of the lease term was covered under the policy, and monthly payments were below the actual rent. These factors indicated that the insurance was intended to spread the risk of loss, not to completely shift it. *HKH Co. v. American Mortgage Ins. Co.,* 685 F2d 315 (1982).

Tax Court Taxpayer, a department store, entered into a sale-leaseback of land in a shopping complex. Prudential Insurance agreed to buy the completed building and the land thereunder for $4 million, and lease it back for 30 years at an annual rent of $360,000. Taxpayer built the store at a final cost of $4.3 million, and reported an ordinary income loss of $300,000 for the year. The IRS disallowed the loss on the ground that the sale-leaseback constituted a like-kind exchange within the meaning of Section 1031 of the Internal Revenue Code (IRC). Taxpayer argued the transaction was a sale for cash because the lease had no capital value. *Held:* The transaction was not a like-kind exchange, and taxpayer was entitled to an ordinary loss deduction. Whether the lease had capital value turned upon whether $4 million was close to fair market value and whether $360,000 was not less than fair rental value. The court, answering both questions in the affirmative, concluded the lease had no capital value. *Crowley, Milner & Co. v. Comm'r,* 76 TC 1030 (1981), aff'd, 689 F2d 635 (6th Cir. 1982).

Tax Court Taxpayers purchased a home and paid $7,000 ($100 cash down, $700 in maintenance work, and $100 per month until the purchase price was fully paid). Seller leased back the house at a rent well below the fair rental value. The IRS, declaring the transaction to be non-profit motivated under IRC Section 183, disallowed some of the deductions claimed by taxpayers. *Held:* The transaction was at arm's length, and taxpayers intended to profit from it. Taxpayers were expecting the seller, who was advanced in years, to remain in the house for a sufficiently short time to permit them to resell and realize the anticipated appreciation. Consequently, the Tax Court allowed the taxpayers to take loss deductions, which would not be subject to Section 183. *Langford v. Comm'r,* 42 TCM 1160 (1981).

Wisconsin Plaintiff and defendant exchanged their respective properties, a shopping center and an apartment complex, in a sale-leaseback. Plaintiff gave the apartment complex as a down payment on the shopping center. Defendant leased the shopping center back from plaintiff at a monthly rental that exceeded plaintiff's monthly payments on the shopping center purchase. When defendant terminated the lease, plaintiff sued for the unpaid rent and sought restitution of his purchase investment. *Held:* Plaintiff could recover his investment as remedy for breach of the lease. In most breach of contract cases, the remedy is the injured party's expected profit; in this case, where a losing contract was breached, restitution of the contract price was justified, because that price exceeded expected profit. In determining plaintiff's loss, the court declined to include plaintiff's tax benefits, since tax relief was not his sole purpose in acquiring the property. *Harris v. Metropolitan Mall,* 334 NW2d 519 (1983).

34.00 CONDEMNATION

34.05 Condemnation of Leased Premises

Alaska Lessee of state-owned airport property constructed a building on the property. Lessee exercised an option to renew, with an added provision for the state to require lessee to remove the building and accept substitute premises should the property be required for airport expansion. Lessee then assigned the lease and sold the building to Lathrop, which leased it back to lessee under a sublease. The sublease provided it would be terminated if the premises were taken by action of any public authority. The state then notified Lathrop it would require the building moved, as it needed the premises for expansion. Successor to lessee asserted the state's action terminated the sublease. Lathrop sued, contending the provision in the renewal agreement allowing the state to take the property was an amendment to the lease, and an exercise by the state of a contractual right, not an action of public authority. *Held:* The sublease was terminated. The addition to the renewal agreement allowing the state to take the property and provide substitute premises was an unenforceable agreement to agree, since the replacement property was not specified. Therefore, the act of the state in requiring the property was not done under the contract, but was a taking by action of public authority. *Western Airlines, Inc. v. Lathrop Co.,* 499 P2d 1013 (1972).

Illinois Tenants leased space in a building that was subsequently condemned. They defaulted on three months' rent, then vacated the premises, and landlord terminated the lease. Tenants sought part of the condemnation award based on their improvement of the property and landlord's failure to maintain the premises. *Held:* Tenants' failure to pay rent terminated their leasehold interest and extinguished their interest in the condemnation award. A tenant's obligation to pay rent could be discharged upon a constructive eviction, but there could be no constructive eviction unless the premises were vacated. If tenants remained on the premises, they were obligated to pay rent. Because they failed to do so for three months, landlord was justified in terminating the lease. Tenants therefore had no leasehold interest on the date of the condemnation award and had no interest therein. *City of Chicago v. American Nat'l Bank,* 408 NE2d 379 (App. Ct. 1980).

34.10 Right to Proceeds of Condemnation Award

Illinois Tenants leased space in a building that was subsequently condemned. They defaulted on three months' rent and then vacated the premises; landlord terminated the lease. Tenants sought part of the condemnation award based on their improvement of the property and landlord's failure to maintain the premises. *Held:* Tenants' failure to pay rent terminated their leasehold interest and extinguished their interest in the condemnation award. A tenant's obligation to pay rent could be discharged upon a constructive eviction, but there could be no constructive eviction unless the premises were vacated. If tenants remained on the premises, they were obligated to pay rent. Because they failed to do so for three months, landlord was justified in terminating the lease. Tenants therefore had no leasehold interest on the date of the condemnation award and had no interest therein. *City of Chicago v. American Nat'l Bank,* 408 NE2d 379 (App. Ct. 1980).

Missouri After an offer of compensation by the highway commission for taking a right-of-way was rejected by the property owner, a lessee on the property sued to enjoin the condemnation proceeding. When the lessee argued that it had not received an offer for the value of its billboard, the commission responded that the owner's rejection of the settlement offer precluded the necessity of further offers. *Held:* The condemning authority was required to separately consider the value of the tenant's structures, and any offer of compensation to the owner had to include an itemized summary of the structures affecting market value. Since the commission failed to follow the procedure, the condemnation was enjoined. *State ex rel. Weatherby Advertising Co. v. Conley,* 527 SW2d 334 (1975).

Oregon Lease provided that upon a default of rent payments for 10 days, the tenancy would terminate. When the rent had not been paid after 13 days, lessor commenced a forcible entry and detainer action. Tenant paid the rent that day, but the check was returned. Thereafter, the state filed a condemnation action, and the forcible entry and detainer suit was dismissed as moot. In proceedings supplemental to the condemnation action, lessor challenged the tenant's right to receive compensation for the market value of his lease. *Held:* Where tenant was clearly in breach of the lease, absent any showing of grounds for equitable relief, the tenancy terminated as per the terms of the lease; and tenant could not recover any part of the condemnation award for the market value of his lease. *State Highway Comm'n v. Demarest,* 503 P2d 682 (1972).

Virginia In the event of condemnation of the leased property, lessee had a right to receive a share of the condemnation award and the option to terminate the lease. When the property was condemned, lessee opted to terminate the lease, then later sought to recover the value of its leasehold interest from the award. The landlord argued that lessee had waived any right to a share of the award on exercising the option to terminate. *Held:* Lessee had a right to a share in the condemnation proceeds as provided in the lease. This right survived termination of the lease. Further, the leasehold, apart from improvements made to the property, had an ascertainable value. *Exxon Corp. v. M&O Holding Corp.,* 269 SE2d 371 (1980).

35.00 RENEWALS AND EXTENSIONS

35.05
Right to Renew or Extend

California A five-year lease for commercial property had a renewal option under which the rent for an additional five-year term would be "determined by mutual agreement." Through the term of the original lease, the monthly rate increased from $800 to $950. When the tenant tried to exercise the option, the landlord demanded a new rent of at least $2,500 per month, while the tenant insisted that $1,100 per month would be reasonable, based on changes in the local consumer price index. *Held:* The option here was essentially only an agreement to negotiate about the rent at a future date. An option agreement may specify that the new rent is to be "reasonable" or otherwise based on some objective standard which a court may determine and enforce. In this case, there was no such objectively ascertainable guide. *ETCO Corp. v. Hauer,* 208 Cal. Rptr. 118 (Ct. App. 1984).

Colorado Tenant's 25-year commercial lease contained an option to extend the term and expand the space exercisable within 90 days after the fifth, tenth, fifteenth, twentieth or twenty-fifth anniversary of the lease. When tenant requested additional space after the fifteenth anniversary, the owner claimed the expansion option violated the rule against perpetuities. *Held:* The rule against perpetuities did not apply to options given to tenant to purchase leased property or to extend the term, but did apply to options to purchase or lease additional premises. The 21-year perpetuities period ran from the date the lease was executed, not the commencement of the lease term, which was two years later. Therefore the options for the twentieth and twenty-fifth years violated the perpetuities rule. The court found the option clause was severable, so that the first three options, including that exercised by tenant, survived application of the perpetuities rule. *Crossroads Shopping Center v. Montgomery Ward & Co.,* 646 P2d 330 (1982).

Massachusetts A lease provided for a renewal option, with the rent for the renewal period to be established by negotiation, or in the event of a dispute, arbitration. Near the end of the lease term, the tenant exercised the option to renew, but then vacated the premises before expiration of the original lease. The landlord sued to recover rent for the renewal term. *Held:* For the tenant. The exercise of the option, without more, did not continue the lease relationship. The terms of the original lease were not to be extended automatically, but rather, required specific action for determining the rent for the additional term, which action the lessor did not initiate. *HLM Realty Corp. v. Morreale,* 477 NE2d 394 (1985).

Nebraska Tenant's lease contained an option for a 10-year renewal, which provided that the rental terms would be renegotiated for the renewal lease. When lessors refused to execute a new lease, tenants sued for specific performance of the option clause. *Held:* For lessors. The absence in the option clause of a rental price for the renewal period was significant. The record below indicated the parties were unable to agree on the renewal rent. When an agreement provides that certain terms will be settled later, such terms are not binding unless they are later agreed to. Since the law does not compel one to perform a duty one has not agreed to do, the landlord was not contractually bound by the terms of the option clause, which did not state a rental for the renewal period. *RAS Inc. v. Crowley,* 351 NW2d 414 (1984).

New York Lease between landlord and tenant included a renewal clause with "rentals to be agreed upon." Tenant sought to compel landlord to renew the lease in an amount proposed by its appraiser or by the court. Landlord argued that in order to be renewable, the lease had to contain an ascertainable rental agreement or the phrase "reasonable rent." *Held:* A lease renewal clause providing for "annual rents to be agreed upon" is too indefinite to enforce in that it constitutes merely an agreement to agree. The words provide for no method of determining rent and do not even bind the parties to a fair market value rental or "reasonable rent." In enforcing the lease renewal clause the court would be compelled to impose its own conceptions of a fair bargain rather than confining itself to the actual intent of the parties. Definiteness as to material matters is the essence of contract law. *Joseph Martin, Jr., Delicatessen, Inc. v. Schumacher,* 417 NE2d 451 (1981).

New York Tenant purchased a restaurant and received an assignment of an existing lease, with an option to renew for an additional term. Tenant was required to give six months' notice if he wished to exercise the option. Tenant failed to give timely notice of its intent to renew. Shortly before the lease expired, the landlord demanded that tenant vacate the premises and refused to accept tenant's belated attempt to exercise the option. The landlord sued to recover possession. *Held:* For tenant, providing there was no prejudice to landlord. Citing the repairs and improvements tenant made to the premises, the court concluded that tenant's failure to exercise the option was the result of "mere inattention." The case was remanded to determine whether landlord had suffered any damages from tenant's failure to exercise the option in a timely manner. *JNA Realty Corp. v. Cross Bay Chelsea, Inc.,* 397 NYS2d 958 (1977).

New York Landlord filed petition in summary proceeding to evict tenant. Tenant was given the option of renewing lease for the same terms and conditions except for the amount of future rent, which the renewal clause fixed at a "reasonable market value price." Landlord claimed renewal clause was unenforceable for indefiniteness. *Held:* Petition dismissed. The supreme court, appellate division, held that where a renewal clause fixes future rents at "a reasonable market value price," amount of rent is reasonably certain and the renewal agreement is enforceable. *Northrup v. Hushard,* 514 NYS2d 304 (App. Div. 1987).

New York Tenant was supposed to have contacted his landlord by October 1, 1989, if he wanted to renew his lease. The landlord wrote to the tenant about it on October 4. Tenant responded affirmatively on October 6, but on October 26 the landlord sent him a notice saying the option had expired. *Held:* As an equitable matter, tenant could still exercise the option. His failure to give timely notice was negligent or inadvertent, and he had made substantial improvements to the property that would be forfeit if he could not renew. Only if the landlord could show that he had changed his position when no notice was received would the letter of the lease be enforced in such a case. However, the landlord had not shown that he was prejudiced. *Niagara Frontier Serv., Inc. v. Thress,* 487 NYS2d 228 (App. Div. 1985).

Washington Plaintiff tenant entered into a lease with defendant-landlord's predecessor. Landlord bought the property and notified tenant of its intent to terminate the tenancy. When plaintiff refused to vacate, defendant brought an unlawful detainer action. The parties disputed whether the lease's renewal clause provided for a perpetual right to renew on a year-to-year basis, as plaintiff claimed, or whether it created a month-to-month tenancy. *Held:* The appeals court found the lease ambiguous as a matter of law, requiring a trial to determine the intentions of the parties. The strong presumption against perpetual leases could be overcome only by explicit language. The lease required plaintiff to take a positive act to renew rather than take a positive act to terminate the lease, indicating the parties did not have perpetuity in mind. *Oak Bay Properties, Ltd. v. Silverdale Sportsman's Center,* 648 P2d 465 (1982).

35.10 Notice of Renewal

Alabama A lease provided for extension on written notice by lessee at least 180 days before expiration. Lessee failed to give written notice, but continued to occupy the premises and pay rent. Nine months after the lease had expired, lessee and lessor met to discuss the prospect of a condemnation award. Lessor later asked for proof of written notice of the extension, which did not exist. Lessee sued, seeking a judgment that the lease had been extended by the actions of the parties. *Held:* By allowing lessee to remain in possession and accepting rent, lessor had waived the written notice requirement. Lessor did not inquire whether lessee had given written notice until the prospect of a condemnation award gave it a motive to cancel the lease. *Lott v. Douglas Oil Purchasing Co.,* 501 So. 2d 1195 (1986).

Illinois At the end of the term of a commercial leasehold, lessee conveyed its intent to renew the lease by sending regular mail notice to the lessor at the address provided. Lessor refused receipt of the letter, citing language in the lease that called for delivery by certified or registered mail. *Held:* Since the lease provided that notice could be made by "delivery" or by sending registered or certified mail, the regular mail delivery was constructive "delivery." Nothing in the lease excluded regular mail delivery, and, since the notice was timely and in other respects sufficient, the renewal option was exercised properly. *Liquorama, Inc. v. American Nat'l Bank & Trust Co.,* 408 NE2d 373 (1980).

Iowa Parties executed a lease that gave lessee an option to renew for a five-year period, provided that he give lessor six months' notice by mail of his election to renew. Lessee mailed his notice before the expiration of the notice period, but such notice was not received until the expiration of the notice period. Lessor brought an action to eject the lessee. *Held:* The option was properly exercised on mailing of the notice, not on receipt of the notice by the lessor. *White v. RCA Serv. Corp.,* 234 NW2d 153 (1975).

New Hampshire Plaintiffs leased premises from defendant with option to renew and an option to purchase the premises. The renewal option had to be exercised by written notice at least 90 days prior to expiration of the original term. Plaintiffs subleased the premises at a higher rent with a renewal option and an option to purchase at a higher price. Plaintiffs' notice of intent to renew the original lease was five weeks late, and defendant leased the premises to third parties. Plaintiffs sued for a declaratory judgment and an injunction. *Held:* Defendant was under no duty to renew plaintiffs' lease in view of the late notice. Plaintiffs were not entitled to equitable relief because the delay was substantial and there was no unconscionable hardship, notwithstanding their lost profits from subtenants. *Lemay v. Rouse,* 444 A2d 553 (1982).

New Hampshire Lessee purchased a laundromat, taking an assignment of an existing lease. Lessor then purchased the building where the laundromat was located, subject to the existing lease, which gave lessee an option to renew for two additional five-year terms, subject to giving notice at least 30 days prior to October 1, 1977. Because of an error by his attorney, lessee did not give notice until September 8, 1977. Lessor failed to recognize the exercise of the option and gave lessee a notice to quit. Lessee then brought an action seeking a declaratory judgment that he had effectively exercised the option. *Held:* Lessee had effectively exercised the option. The delay in exercising the option was slight and the damage to lessee would have been substantial if he had been forced to leave. Furthermore, the delay had been the result of an honest mistake. *Fletcher v. Frisbee,* 404 A2d 1106 (1979).

New York A commercial lease with an option to renew specified that the option was to be exercised by sending a written notice to the landlord within 90 days of the end of the lease term, along with an additional $1,500 security. Toward the end of the lease term, the tenant told the landlord verbally of his intent to renew. Allegedly, the landlord told the tenant not to bother with a written notice. However, when the term expired, the landlord sent a two-month termination notice. Only then did the tenant send an option to renew and the additional security. *Held:* The tenant would receive a preliminary injunction against termination of the tenancy. While a number of factual questions remained, it appeared that the tenant's default was excusable. Additionally, the equities were in his favor, since he had spent more than a quarter-million dollars in improving the leasehold. Any prejudice to the landlord arising the tenant's failure to give proper notice of renewal would be outweighed by the loss of the leasehold to the tenant. *Pepe's Shamrock, Inc. v. Vecchio,* 512 NYS2d 858 (App. Div. 1987).

South Carolina Under lease renewal clause, tenant could exercise option by tendering notice at a stated address 30 days before the end of the term, either by personal delivery or by mail. On the last day, tenant left written notice at the address; however, landlord had moved without informing tenant. On the next day, tenant mailed notice. *Held:* Tenant's failure to give timely notice was the fault of the landlord; therefore, the attempted personal delivery must be given effect. *Carmichael v. Dan Nance Corp.,* 264 SE2d 601 (1980).

35.15 Waiver of Notice

3d Circuit Lease ran for a period of two years from November 1966 through October 1968. The lessee was given the option to renew, but if he elected to renew he had to notify the landlord before September 1, 1968. On October 7, 1968, the tenant belatedly asked for a renewal; the landlord made no response to the request but accepted rent for November and then for December, without comment. Four and one-half months after the original term had ended the parties entered a separate lease for additional space next to the tenant's original premises. The new lease provided that it would not affect "our present lease" covering the original premises. Then, in November 1969, they entered into yet another agreement to revise the original lease. Despite all this, the landlord ordered the tenant to vacate in December 1969. For the first time, he asserted that the lease had expired on October 31, 1969, because of the tenant's failure to give timely notice of renewal. *Held:* The parties had acted as though the lease had been renewed; therefore, it had been. *HFD No. 26, Inc. v. Middletown Merchandise Mart,* 467 F2d 253 (1972).

Vermont When a tenant sent its notice to extend its lease, two weeks late, the landlord refused to extend the lease. The lower court found that the landlord orally waived the requirement of written notice. *Held:* Conversations between the landlord and tenant concerning repairs did not establish a waiver of the notice requirement. The import of the conversations was that the landlord sought assurance that the tenant would not terminate the lease. The conversations did not relate to the requirements for extending the lease. *Lynda Lee Fashions, Inc. v. Sharp Offset Printing, Inc.*, 352 A2d 676 (1976).

35.20 Perpetual Renewals

3d Circuit A lease had a term of 99 years, renewable forever, and an open-ended option to purchase after 20 years. The landlord sought a declaratory judgment that the lease was void under the rule against perpetuities. *Held:* The lease was not void. A lease and option agreement of this type was not an unreasonable restraint on alienation. Unlike an estate in fee simple, the lessee of property had a recognized need to be able to plan for the future to realize the benefits of the full use of land during the lease term. Similarly, the options in the 99-year lease were granted to the lessee and therefore tended to promote the use of the property, so they were valid irrespective of their perpetual nature. *Camerlo v. Howard Johnson Co.*, 710 F2d 987 (1983).

U.S. District Court, Virginia A one-year lease provided for renewal from year to year at the same rental. The use of the property was restricted, the lease could not be assigned, and the premises could be sublet only to "desirable tenants." The lease contained no covenants, undertakings, provisions, or conditions usually contained in a long-term lease, nor did it contain any language connoting "perpetuity." When the tenants asserted that they had the right to renew in perpetuity, the lessors sought a declaratory judgment that the option to renew extended only for a "reasonable" time. *Held:* As perpetual renewals are not favored in the law, the intent to create a perpetuity must appear in clear and unequivocal language. A perpetuity is not generally created by an ordinary covenant to renew. The provision here created a tenancy from year to year, which could be terminated by either party by giving notice. *McLean v. United States,* 316 F. Supp. 827 (ED 1970).

Alabama Tenant's lease for a campground provided an option to renew "as long as the camp is run for a profit." The parties orally agreed that tenant would pay owner half the monies received from boat rentals and launch fees. Five years later, owner sued to have the lease declared void for vagueness. *Held:* The renewal term was unenforceable. A renewal covenant does not create rights in perpetuity unless the parties have explicitly expressed such intention. The words "as long as the camp is run for a profit" did not satisfy this criterion. *Womack v. Hyche,* 503 So. 2d 832 (1987).

Georgia Tenant sued landlord for specific performance of a purchase option contained in a perpetually renewable lease. Landlord claimed that performance would be in violation of the rule against perpetuities. *Held:* While a perpetual option to purchase land violates the rule against perpetuities, a purchase option within a perpetually renewable lease does not violate the rule. *Rose v. Chandler,* 279 SE2d 423 (1981).

North Carolina A commercial lease contained a renewal clause that provided "this lease shall be automatically renewed for successive five-year terms. . . ." Lessor sought a declaratory judgment that this was not a perpetual lease. *Held:* The supreme court, addressing for the first time the validity of perpetual leases, held that in the absence of terms such as "forever," "in perpetuity," or words unmistakably of the same import, the lease did not grant tenant a right to perpetual renewals. The word "successive" in the agreement did not unmistakably convey unlimited duration. Perpetual leases are not favored in North Carolina absent express language or clear implication that the parties intended to create a perpetual lease. *Lattimore v. Fisher's Food Shoppe, Inc.*, 329 SE2d 346 (1985).

Texas Lessor and lessee executed an agreement granting the lessee an option to extend the lease for an additional year and thereafter on a year-to-year basis. It also provided that the lessee would have the use and benefit of the land as long as it was used for the purposes stated in the lease and the rent was paid. After a dispute, the lessor sued for a judgment, declaring the lease unenforceable because it was a perpetual lease not favored by law. *Held:* The lease was enforceable. Although the right of perpetual renewal is not favored, the lease provided clearly and unambiguously for such a right. *Hull v. Quanah Pipeline Corp.*, 574 SW2d 610 (1978).

35.25 Protected Tenancies

9th Circuit A rent control ordinance required mobile home park operators to give tenants leases of unlimited duration. Plaintiffs, owners of a mobile home park, claimed the ordinance was a taking of their property without just compensation by giving tenants the right to a perpetual lease at below-market rate that they could sell at a profit. Plaintiffs claimed that mobile homes in the park were selling for far above their value, reflecting the value of the property right to occupy the park at below-market rates. *Held:* Plaintiff's allegations, if proven, suggested that the ordinance constituted a taking without just compensation, because plaintiffs had lost the right to control transfers of their property. The court placed great weight on the claim that tenants' interest in the rented property was transferable and had an established market value. The court also questioned whether the ordinance advanced a legitimate state interest. The city intended to help low income families find affordable housing, but if the ordinance actually resulted in higher prices for mobile homes, it accomplished the opposite. *Hall v. City of Santa Barbara,* 813 F2d 198 (1986), cert. denied, 485 US 940 (1988).

U.S. District Court, California The city passed a commercial rental ordinance requiring landlords to renew leases to existing tenants except on one of eight grounds for eviction. No allowance was made for a landlord's desire to occupy the property himself. An affected landlord claimed that the ordinance, by failing to permit an owner personally to occupy the property at the end of a lease, unconstitutionally interfered with contract rights and deprived owners of property without just compensation or due process. *Held:* The absolute exclusion of owner occupancy from the enumeration of good causes for eviction violated landlord's rights under the contract clause of the Constitution. The ordinance significantly impaired the landlord's contract rights, potentially amounting to a permanent taking, since the tenant corporation's leasehold was potentially endless in light of the perpetual existence of corporations. Further, at the time he entered into the lease, landlord could not have reasonably expected the enactment of such an ordinance. The rationale of preserving a neighborhood shopping district's diversity and ambiance, while a legitimate subject for legislation, was not sufficiently compelling to justify severe impairments of contracts. Nor was the ordinance reasonable, since the city had not considered less restrictive alternatives to permanently prohibiting owner occupancy. However, the due process clause was not violated, since the ordinance served a legitimate purpose and did not completely deprive landlords of their property. *Ross v. City of Berkeley,* 655 F. Supp. 820 (ND 1987).

Hawaii Tenants who had built additions to their home on a residential lot leased in 1953 sought an order when the lease expired that landlords buy their residential improvements pursuant to Haw. Rev. Stat. § 516-70. This statute was amended in 1975 to require landlords to compensate tenants for on-site improvements at the end of the lease term if the tenant chose not to remove them. *Held:* The statute, as applied to leases existing at the time of the 1975 amendment, violated the constitutional prohibition against impairment of contracts, because had landlords known they would be obligated to purchase tenants' improvements at the termination of the lease, they may well have made a different bargain. *Anthony v. Kualoa Ranch, Inc.,* 736 P2d 55 (1987).

New York Tenant and his gay partner lived together in a rent-controlled apartment for over 10 years. When tenant died, landlord sought to evict the partner. *Held:* The term "family" in the city's rent control regulation, protecting the tenant's family members from eviction upon the tenant's death, is not rigidly restricted to people who have formalized their relationship by obtaining, for instance, a marriage certificate or an adoption order. A "family" may include two adult lifetime partners whose relationship is long-term and characterized by an emotional and financial commitment and interdependence. In this case, the partner demonstrated a likelihood of success in proving that he and the tenant enjoyed a "family" relationship, so he was entitled to protection from eviction under the city rent control law. *Braschi v. Stahl Assocs. Co.,* 544 NYS2d 784 (1989).

New York Tenant signed a renewal lease presented by his landlord, despite the fact the tenant was substantially in arrears on rent. Landlord thereafter attempted to refuse the renewal and to begin holdover proceedings, despite the fact that failure to pay rent was not one of the five circumstances named in the local rent stabilization law under which a renewal lease need not be offered. *Held:* Tenant could renew his lease. While landlord could have conditioned his original renewal offer on payment of the rent arrearage, he could not refuse to offer a renewal lease. In any event, once the offer was made, tenant's acceptance created a contract enforceable in equity. *Kips Bay Towers Assoc. v. Lander,* 466 NYS2d 628 (1983).

New York Tenants' rent payments were at least two months late throughout the terms of their lease; and when they did pay, their checks sometimes bounced. Landlord sought a declaratory judgment that the tenants would not be entitled to an automatic renewal of their lease on expiration because of chronic late payment. *Held:* The New York City Rent Stabilization Code, which governed the tenancy, provided only five grounds for nonrenewal of a lease, and tardiness in paying rent was not one of them. Thus, the lease would have to be renewed. *Gruen v. Patterson,* 446 NYS2d 253 (1981).

New York A university formerly had a policy of leasing apartments to scholars from other institutions, but now sought to regain control of these units in view of a shortage of housing. Tenant from another institution sued when the university refused to renew his lease. The lease gave the university the right to terminate the tenancy if tenant ceased to be an employee of the university. A provision of the Rent Stabilization Law permitted an educational institution to refuse to renew leases for affiliated tenants if (1) tenant received notice of possible nonrenewal at the time of execution; (2) tenant was affiliated with the institution before the lease began; and (3) the affiliation ended during the tenancy. *Held:* For tenant. The provision of the lease allowing the university to terminate should tenant cease to be a university employee did not apply, because plaintiff had never been an employee of the university. In addition, tenant did not receive the requisite statutory notice at the time of execution that the lease was subject to nonrenewal, so the university did not have the right to refuse to issue a renewal lease. *Cooper Union v. New York Univ.,* 500 NYS2d 984 (Sup. Ct. 1986).

New York Plaintiff, a rent-stabilized tenant, did not purchase her apartment under a "non-eviction" cooperative conversion plan presented in 1979. Instead, defendant had purchased the apartment as well as the shares allocable thereto. When plaintiff's lease expired in 1981, defendant refused to renew it stating that he sought possession of the apartment under Section 54(b) of the Rent Stabilization Code in order to permit his 82-year-old mother to reside there. Plaintiff then sought an injunction directing defendant to offer her a renewal lease and preventing him from attempting to evict her. *Held:* Plaintiff was granted injunctive relief. Plaintiff relied upon the fact that the conversion plan was "non-eviction" in her decision not to purchase the apartment. In addition, the code does not allow the eviction of nonpurchasing tenants unless at least 35 percent of the tenants in occupancy have consented to purchase. Since this was not the case with this particular conversion, defendant could not use Section 54(b) to evict tenants. *Tarman v. Rowe,* 447 NYS2d 648 (Sup. Ct. 1982).

36.00 OPTIONS TO LEASE

36.05 Damages for Breach

Nevada Renewal negotiations broke down between doctors and hospital from whom they rented space over the issue of rent for an additional term pursuant to a lease renewal option. Doctors remained on the premises several months past expiration of the original lease, then sued the hospital for breach of the renewal option. *Held:* The trial court's failure to instruct the jury that the renewal option was of finite duration required a new trial. The rule was that when parties could not agree on the rent for a renewal lease, the renewal option would be enforced and a reasonable rental imposed. The issue in this case was who, if anyone, breached the contract, for which it was first necessary to decide when the option expired. The court believed the jury, properly instructed, would have found the option lapsed when negotiations failed and doctors did not sue to have a reasonable rent imposed, and therefore no contract was left to breach. *Charter Medical Corp. v. Bealick,* 741 P2d 1359 (1987).

New York Plaintiff's lease contained a provision giving him "the first option to erect additional signs for advertising purposes with the consent of the Landlord which event would necessitate an additional lease upon terms to be agreed upon at such time." Before plaintiff moved in, however, the landlord entered into two leases for the erection of billboards with another party, without first offering plaintiff the opportunity to enter into leases on identical terms. Plaintiff, which was in the business of erecting billboards, sued the landlord for lost profits. *Held:* Regardless of how the option provision was interpreted, plaintiff was not entitled to damages. Under traditional rules of landlord-tenant law, a tenant not yet in possession of demised premises may not recover profits that allegedly would have been earned if not for a breach by the landlord preventing the tenant from taking possession. *Whitmier & Ferris v. Buffalo Structural,* 489 NE2d 1288 (1985).

37.00 TERMINATION

37.05 Expiration of Term

Arkansas An oil and gas lease provided that the lease was to remain in effect as long as production continued. Temporary breakdowns were not to void the lease. The system broke, but lessee did not attempt to fix it for four months. When the attempt was made, lessor refused lessee access and tried to void the lease. Lessee said lessor was estopped from terminating the lease, since its own actions prevented a return to production. *Held:* The lease could be terminated. The four-month delay before trying to repair the system was unreasonable under the circumstances. The breakdown was therefore not merely "temporary." *Wilson v. Talbert* 535 SW2d 807 (1976).

Maine Landlord leased office space to tenants under a lease agreement that expired in June 1970. In April 1970, tenants delivered a signed lease to landlord, but landlord refused to accept it because of a dispute over the amount of rent and other terms. After several months of unsuccessful negotiations, tenants sued landlord for failure to sign the lease. Landlord moved successfully for summary judgment, arguing that tenants' conduct constituted a revocation of the lease and that he had not renewed his offer. *Held:* Landlord is entitled to summary judgment. He had revoked his offer by a letter, which was introduced into evidence. This letter was sufficient to sustain the summary judgment. *Flavel v. Pacific Power & Light Co.,* 607 P2d 731 (1979).

Montana When lessor held rental payments tendered by lessee after the primary term ended, but refused to accept the payments as delay rentals and treated the lease as terminated, lessee argued that the term of the mining lease had been extended by lessor's actions. *Held:* When a mining lease obligated lessee to pay delay rentals in lieu of producing for the primary period or forfeit the lease, lessor was required to declare a forfeiture at the end of the primary term to terminate the lease. Where lessor held the rental payments tendered after the original term of the lease expired, there was a valid extension of the lease. *Carroll v. Eaton,* 541 P2d 64 (1975).

South Carolina City leased land and buildings to a fair association. The lease provided that "in the event of termination" of the lease, the assets of the association would become city property. When the term of the lease expired, the city sought a declaratory judgment that the association's assets belonged to the city. *Held:* The association's assets did not become city property. The language of the lease contemplated termination by breach, not by the normal expiration of the term. *Piedmont Interstate Fair Ass'n v. City of Spartanburg,* 264 SE2d 926 (1980).

37.10 Termination by Breach of Tenant

Alabama When tenant filed for bankruptcy, landlord demanded back rent but explicitly reserved whatever other remedies might be available under the lease. After receiving the back rent, landlord announced it was reentering the premises. Tenant claimed landlord had waived the right to reenter by accepting the back rent. *Held:* Landlord could reenter. Waiver of rights is a matter of intent, and landlord's letter to the tenant demanding the arrearage clearly expressed the intent to reserve any remedies. *USA Petroleum Corp. v. Jopat Bldg. Corp.,* 343 So. 2d 501 (1977).

Michigan Tenant continued to occupy her apartment after the lease expired, paying rent and necessary late charges, which landlord accepted. Twenty months after the lease expired landlord notified tenant the tenancy was terminated because of late payment, and landlord began summary proceedings. Tenant argued, first, that landlord waived notice to terminate by accepting rent, and second, that the lateness of some of the rent payments, which were made within a month of when due, was not grounds for terminating the tenancy. *Held:* Landlord waived notice to terminate by accepting rent subsequent to the date listed on the notice, because this led tenant to believe the tenancy had continued after the lease expired. Even in the absence of waiver, the lateness of tenant's rent payments was not reason to terminate the tenancy, because the lateness was not flagrant. *Park Forest of Blackman v. Smith,* 316 NW2d 442 (Ct. App. 1982).

New Jersey Plaintiff tenants' lease had a "no pets" clause, but tenants kept a dog in their apartment for 11 years, apparently with landlord's initial permission. Landlord had set certain conditions, such as keeping the animal chained up. Landlord announced one day that the no pets clause would be enforced and moved to dispossess plaintiffs when they did not comply. *Held:* Landlord's initial permission for the plaintiffs to keep a dog raised a promissory estoppel, especially since tenants had complied with the landlord's conditions for keeping the dog. *Royal Assocs. v. Concannon,* 490 A2d 357 (Super. Ct. App. Div. 1985).

Pennsylvania A petroleum company signed a renewable lease, under which it was to make substantial improvements to the property, which would revert to the lessor at expiration. The company began discharging sewage into an abandoned mine on the property. Lessors sued for ejectment on the ground that the dumping was illegal and lessors had been subjected to embarrassment and potential liability. *Held:* Lessors could not eject the company, since the lease was silent on dumping and the dumping statutes provided no remedy of ejectment. Unless the lease contemplates such a remedy, a tenant's violation of a law does not generally entitle a landlord to eject a tenant. *Ross v. Gulf Oil Corp.,* 522 A2d 97 (Super. Ct. 1987).

Utah Lessor sued to terminate a lease for nonpayment of rent. The trial court terminated both the lease and an option to purchase contained therein. The lease provided that no default of any provision should constitute a basis for forfeiture unless it continued for more than 45 days after written notice, and the default was not corrected within a reasonable time. *Held:* Since the lessee made no attempt to pay, during the 45-day grace period or for six weeks afterward, there was a reasonable basis for concluding that tender was not made within a reasonable time and was justifiably refused when made. *Russell v. Park City Utah Corp.*, 548 P2d 889 (1976), cert. denied, 429 US 860 (1977).

West Virginia Plaintiff leased land rich in coal deposits from a previous lessee, spending $6.5 million to modify a coal-processing plant on the site. The lease between plaintiff and defendant owner provided for renewal if plaintiff upheld its covenants, as well as for forfeiture in the event of default in performance of any covenant in the lease. Defendant refused to allow plaintiff to renew the lease, claiming it had not complied with contract terms regarding royalties and mining operations, and informed plaintiff that it was declaring a forfeiture and intended to take possession of the premises, including improvements. Plaintiff sought a declaratory judgment against forfeiture, and defendant counterclaimed for forfeiture and damages. *Held:* The supreme court refused to permit forfeiture given the "catchall, dragnet" nature of the forfeiture clause. Forfeiture would be not be allowed unless the lease clearly provided that breach of the specific covenants cited by defendants were ground for forfeiture. Plaintiff was required to pay damages and to give defendant an option to buy plaintiff's improvements at fair market value on termination of the lease. *Bethlehem Steel Corp. v. Shonk Land Co.*, 288 SE2d 139 (1982).

37.15
—Breach of "No Children" Condition

California During the term of tenants' lease, landlord adopted a no-children policy. When tenants had a child, landlord refused to renew. Tenants refused to vacate, and landlord sued in unlawful detainer. Tenants claimed that landlord was illegally discriminating against children. *Held:* Discrimination against children by the apartment complex was not beyond reach of the Unruh Civil Rights Act. The identification of particular bases of discrimination in the Act—race, color, sex, religion, nationality—was illustrative rather than restrictive. Nor was the policy of discrimination against children "reasonable" and "not arbitrary." The act provided equal access to business establishments, and did not permit exclusion of children. *Marina Point, Ltd. v. Wolfson*, 640 P2d 108 (1982).

37.20
Bankruptcy of Tenant

3d Circuit A lease with an option to purchase also provided for termination of the lease in the event insolvency proceedings were brought against the tenant. After an involuntary bankruptcy petition was filed against the tenant, the interim bankruptcy trustee sought a declaratory judgment that the tenant had the right to exercise the purchase option. *Held:* The case was remanded to determine whether the landlord had terminated the lease before or after the Bankruptcy Code went into effect on October 1, 1979. A termination provision of the type at issue would not be enforceable under the code, but would have been enforceable under the Bankruptcy Act of 1898, which preceded it. *In re Triangle Laboratories, Inc.*, 663 F2d 463 (1981).

Georgia Lessor sued defendants for breach of lease when they sought to vacate and remove property from the premises. Lessor recovered possession from a prior lessee after the lessee defaulted, rescinded the lease, and filed for bankruptcy. The bankruptcy court ordered the lessor to refrain from interfering with any building containing any property of the debtor. Defendants alleged that the bankruptcy order, which was subsequent to their lease, voided the lease. *Held:* The lessor was not affected by the bankruptcy order since rescission of the prior lease and his taking control and possession of the premises canceled that lease. Since the prior lessee was no longer liable for rent, the bankruptcy order did not affect the lessor's right to lease the property, and defendant's lease was valid. *Vineyard Village-Ga., Inc. v. RH Crum,* 221 SE2d 208 (Ct. App. 1975).

37.25
Surrender of Premises by Tenant

Colorado Subtenant abandoned its lease on a car wash, leaving the equipment in poor repair. Sublessor did not have the money to make repairs, without which the fair market value of the premises was less than the rent sublessor was paying under its lease with the owner. Sublessor therefore surrendered its lease and sued subtenant for the rent due under the sublease. *Held:* Subtenant remained obligated for the rent due for the remainder of the sublease term, less the rent sublessor saved by surrendering the premises. Recognizing the modern trend that a lease is a contract as well as a conveyance, the court ruled that, although a landlord who accepts the surrender of a lease cannot sue for rent due after termination of the lease, he can sue for contract damages caused by tenant's breach of the lease. The privity of estate between subtenant and sublessor was terminated by sublessor's acceptance of surrender of the premises, but sublessor remained personally obligated to pay rent. Sublessor also had an obligation to mitigate damages, which it met by its surrender of the prime lease. *Schneiker v. Gordon,* 732 P2d 603 (1987) (en banc).

Rhode Island Tenant leased business premises for a term to end on September 14, 1970. On September 2, tenant surrendered the keys to the general manager of a car dealership owned by landlord. Tenant's vacated premises were subsequently vandalized and damaged, and landlord sued to recover for damages during the September 2–14 period. *Held:* The landlord-tenant relationship can be terminated by surrender of the premises to an agent of the landlord. The evidence showed that the general manager worked for the landlord in several capacities and was in fact given keys to the leased premises so they could be shown to prospective tenants. The general manager was the landlord's agent, and a surrender of the keys to him terminated the landlord-tenant relationship. *Bove v. Transcom Elecs., Inc.,* 353 A2d 613 (1976).

Utah A warehouse under a lease suffered damage due to water leakage. Evidence indicated that lessor requested a key in order to inspect the damage and ascertain the cause. When lessor determined that the damage was lessee's fault, lessee refused to pay any more rent, and lessor initiated an action for rent. Lessee contended that acceptance of the key by lessor worked a surrender by operation of law. *Held:* A surrender by operation of law results from acts that imply mutual consent, independent of expressed intention. However, it will not be implied against the intention of the parties as manifested by their acts. The finder of fact found that the acts of the party manifested an intent to continue the lease, and that finding would not be disturbed. *Mariani Oil Prods. Co. v. Gill's Tire Market,* 508 P2d 808 (1973).

37.30
Frustration of Purpose

4th Circuit Plaintiff leased to defendant for 20 years under an agreement requiring lessee to make all improvements necessary to conduct its restaurant business. Upon finding that it would probably not be able to secure curb-cutting permits, lessee stopped paying rent and notified lessor that it considered the lease terminated. Lessor sued for breach of contract. The lower court held for lessor. *Held:* Affirmed. Lessor was under no duty to secure such a permit, nor was the tenancy conditioned on same. In addition, the evidence did not conclusively establish that the curb-cut permit would be denied. Therefore, defendant was guilty of an unjustifiable breach. *Ten Break v. Waffle Shops, Inc.*, 542 F2d 919 (1976).

Georgia A landowner leased his family farm for seven years in consideration of $250 per month rent and a covenant that the tenant would keep the farm under good husbandry, conserve the property, and keep buildings and other improvements in good repair. The lease did not provide specifically for termination, but did provide that in case of willful neglect or failure by either party to carry out substantial provisions of the lease, the other party would have the benefit of any proceedings provided by law. When tenant allowed the farm to deteriorate, landowner sued, seeking to terminate the lease. Tenant argued that the remedy, if any, should be limited to recovery of any damages, in the absence of an express termination provision in the lease. *Held:* For landowner. Tenant's failure to maintain the farm in a reasonable manner was such a substantial breach of the lease as to defeat the object of the lease. In such circumstances, lessor retains the inherent right to rescind or terminate the lease, even in the absence of an express provision in the lease. *Nunn v. Taylor,* 338 SE2d 453 (Ct. App. 1985).

Massachusetts Lease demised five areas of an airport facility to lessee for a "complete" fixed-base operation for general aviation. In the lease, each of the areas was subject to distinct words of demise, with the rental on each area separately stated. Subsequently, state law made it impossible for lessee to utilize one of the five areas. Lessor notified lessee that it considered the whole agreement terminated by the statute, as lessee could no longer provide a "complete" operation. Lessee, which was able to continue substantial services through the other four areas brought suit for declaratory judgment. *Held:* Since the conditions that rendered performance impossible as to the one area did not substantially abrogate lessee's ability to render services in the other areas, that part of the lease that had become impossible would be severed from the rest of the lease, and the lease would be enforced. *Van Dusen Aircraft Supplier, Inc. v. Massachusetts Port Auth.*, 279 NE2d 717 (1972).

37.35 Landlord's Right to Terminate on Notice

Colorado Defendant board of land commissioners leased state land to plaintiff to be used for agricultural purposes. Plaintiff sued for damages when the commission leased the property to another person for coal-mining and strip-mining purposes. A clause in the lease allowed the state to cancel upon 90 days' notice if it decided to lease the land for other purposes. *Held:* The board had the constitutional and statutory authority to reserve the right to cancel the lease. It could utilize any lease terms not prohibited by law to obtain maximum revenues. Any claim for incidental damages had to be submitted to the board, and the court did not have jurisdiction to enjoin the board or award damages. *Evans v. Simpson,* 547 P2d 931 (1976).

Georgia Landlord owned an office park in which tenant ran a restaurant pursuant to a lease with a five-year term and an option to renew for an additional five years. The lease provided landlord with the right of termination upon 90 days' prior written notice to tenant if, in landlord's sole and absolute discretion, tenant failed to conduct its business satisfactorily or exhibited gross negligence in the operation of its business. When tenant attempted to exercise the renewal option, landlord attempted to terminate the lease pursuant to the lease provision. *Held:* Landlord could enforce the termination provision only if its discretion as to the restaurant's operation was exercised honestly and in good faith. The evidence showed that its decision to terminate the lease was not made arbitrarily or capriciously. Other tenants had complained to landlord of the odors and roaches emanating from the restaurant, as well as the poor food and service. *A Cut Above Sandwiches v. Equitable Life,* 287 SE2d 241 (1981).

Minnesota Defendants had a month-to-month lease of plaintiff's mobile home. After the lease was signed, a law took effect converting existing month-to-month mobile home tenancies to year-to-year tenancies, and allowing lessors to terminate the tenancies upon 60 days' notice and to recover possession within 15 days of the end of the lease term. The statute also required lessors to give 30 days' written notice of alleged lease violations. Plaintiff did not send defendants written notice of their violation of park rules until it sent them a 60-day notice of termination pursuant to the lease. Plaintiff brought an unlawful detainer action against tenants and sought to have the year-to-year tenancy terminated. *Held:* The year-to-year tenancy was not terminated because plaintiff did not give 60 days' notice to defendants and did not seek to recover possession within 15 days of the end of the lease term. Plaintiff could not bring an unlawful detainer action because it failed to give defendants 30 days' written notice of alleged breaches of the lease as required by the statute. Although the lease allowed termination upon 60 days' notice, this was superseded by the statute. *Flamingo Terrace Mobile Home Park v. Scott,* 317 NW2d 697 (1981).

New York Plaintiff was a tenant in a public housing project operated by defendant housing authority, which notified plaintiff that charges of nondesirability had been made against her that, if proved, could result in termination of her tenancy. The charges alleged her son and grandson had engaged in violence and disruption of the neighborhood. Plaintiff presented evidence at the hearing that they had moved out months earlier. Nonetheless, the hearing officer recommended termination because of misconduct by another son and grandson when they visited plaintiff. *Held:* The termination recommendation denied plaintiff due process because the hearing officer relied on the misconduct of relatives who were not charged. Also, defendant violated its own procedures, which prohibited terminations where offenders have left the household. *Knox v. Christian,* 465 NYS2d 203 (App. Div. 1983).

Oklahoma When owner-lessor of a gas station in Oklahoma canceled a lease agreement and dealer franchise, tenant refused to vacate the premises. Lessor asserted the strict provisions of the lease, which provided for termination of the tenancy after one month's notice to tenant, and demanded immediate possession of the premises. Tenant asserted that the furnishing of a lease agreement and dealership agreement created a franchisor-franchisee relationship, which could not be terminated without good cause. Tenant relied primarily on the New Jersey decision of *Shell Oil Co. v. Marinello,* 63 NJ 402, cert. denied, 415 US 920 (1973), in which the court held that public policy dictated that franchisors could not cancel leases without good cause. *Held:* For the lessor. The Oklahoma Supreme Court rejected the reasoning of the New Jersey decision, citing cases from New York, Michigan, Montana, and the Ninth Circuit, all of which disclaimed any good-cause requirement. *Kerr-McGee Corp. v. Cutter,* 564 P2d 215 (1977).

37.40
—Judicial Stay to Allow Tenant to Cure Default

New York Tenant, a psychiatrist, was served notice his lease would be terminated if he continued to see patients in his residential apartment. He obtained a "Yellowstone" injunction staying further proceedings by the landlord until determination of the issues at trial. *Held:* Reversed. A new statute, N.Y. Real Prop. Acts. Law § 753(4), provided that in a summary proceeding the court shall, after adjudicating the merits, grant a losing tenant a 10-day period in which to cure the default. The court found that the statute provided full protection to tenants. The statute could be interpreted as tolling the running of the lease to prevent its expiration; otherwise tenants would have to keep going to court to obtain an adequate stay. *Post v. 120 E. End Ave. Corp.,* 464 NE2d 125 (1984).

37.45
Termination Due to Forfeiture by Landlord

Iowa A farmer rented land from a landlord who held the land under a land contract. The farmer was served with an eviction notice when the landlord defaulted on the contract. The farmer argued that he should retain the land through the next crop year, based on a statute (Iowa Code §§ 562.6 and 562.7) which extends the leases of farm tenants through the next crop year, unless written notice of termination is provided by September 1 (which had not been done in this case). *Held:* The tenant could retain possession through the next crop year. Although the common-law rule is that the tenant of a contract vendee has no higher right than the vendee, this principle had to give way to the legislature's policy of securing farm tenancies. *Ganzer v. Pfab,* 360 NW2d 754 (1985).

37.50
Landlord's Right to Repossess

Louisiana A commercial lease stated that the owners could reoccupy the premises if tenants abandoned the premises. When the tenants did so, ceasing to pay rent, owners reoccupied a portion of the premises and sued the tenants for breach of contract. *Held:* Owners had no right to future rentals, because they had occupied the premises themselves. Though the landlords may have intended to rerent the premises, in which case their rights under the original lease would have continued, their reoccupation physically and extrajudicially dispossessed the tenants. *Richard v. Broussard,* 495 So. 2d 1291 (1986).

Montana A tenant who operated a clothing store closed the store on the first of the month. Landlord entered the premises a week later and sent tenant a notice of delinquent rent and intention to relet. The locks were changed on the twentieth of the month. Tenant sued for illegal detainer. *Held:* Landlord had a right to relet. The lease agreement gave landlord the option to do so, without terminating the lease, in the event of unpaid rent or of tenant's vacating the premises. In any event, landlord did not repossess the property until he changed the locks. *LIC, Inc. v. Baltrusch,* 692 P2d 1264 (1985).

Oregon Landlord sent tenant an eviction notice. After landlord initiated an action to recover possession of the house, tenant moved out. In response to this action, tenant asserted two affirmative defenses, invalid notice and invalid service of notice. He also counterclaimed for injunctive relief and damages. The district court declared tenant's affirmative defenses moot, struck the counterclaim, and restored the premises to landlord. Tenant appealed. *Held:* The tenant's defenses were not moot. The district court never resolved the issue of whether landlord was entitled to possession. By moving out, tenant did not concede landlord's right to possession. Tenant had a statutory right, enforceable by counterclaim, to obtain an injunction or to recover damages for landlord's alleged noncompliance with the lease. *Edwards v. Fenn,* 775 P2d 1375 (1989).

PART D
CONDOMINIUMS AND COOPERATIVES

38.00 CONDOMINIUMS

38.05 In General

5th Circuit In response to abuses in its burgeoning condominium market, Florida enacted a law that prohibited condominium lease escalation clauses that were pegged to national commodity or consumer price indexes. The condominium industry challenged the statute's constitutionality, claiming a denial of due process and equal protection rights. *Held:* The statute was constitutional as it was rational on its face. The classification "furthers the legitimate objectives of curbing inflation and controlling abuses in the condominium trade." *Schlytter v. Baker,* 580 F2d 848 (1978).

California Condominium owners sought an order striking down defendant's condominium tax ordinance on the ground that it was inconsistent with state regulatory statutes. *Held:* Municipalities may impose a "license" tax on condominium transfers notwithstanding the state Subdivision Map Act. Statutory regulation of condominiums does not necessarily amount to preemption, and, therefore, a local revenue-raising measure that does not regulate condominium activity cannot be in conflict with state law. *Pines v. City of Santa Monica,* 166 Cal. Rptr. 649 (1980).

Colorado Condominium bylaws prohibited maintenance of pets in the units without written permission. A unit owner, defending against a suit for an injunction after her application for permission to keep her cats was denied, claimed that the condominium bylaws were improperly adopted and unreasonably applied. *Held:* Adoption of the bylaws 10 days before the articles of incorporation were filed was a technical defect that did not invalidate bylaws that were subsequently relied on and treated as valid by the condominium board. In addition, the unit owner was estopped from objecting to the manner in which the bylaws were adopted once she applied for relief under them. However, the association was not entitled to deny the unit owner's application for permission to keep her cats without considering the application on an individual basis in a reasonable manner. *Chateau Village N. Condominium v. Jordan,* 643 P2d 791 (Ct. App. 1982).

Florida Condominium association and certain of its members brought a suit against the original incorporators and directors of the association. Plaintiffs complained that defendants had contracted on behalf of the association a lease of recreational facilities while defendants were also officers and directors of the corporate lessors. Plaintiffs challenged the validity of the recreational lease. *Held:* Any officer or director of a condominium association may be liable to the association for that amount by which he was unjustly enriched if he contracts on behalf of association with himself, or with another corporation in which he has or later obtains a substantial interest, or with another for his personal benefit. The trial court is to determine the relief to be granted in its discretion based upon the circumstances of each case. The state supreme court also upheld the trial court's decision that recreational facilities may be linked with housing in a condominium, since the legislature and the courts have recognized such facilities to be part of the condominium concept. *Avila S. Condominium Ass'n v. Kappa Corp.*, 347 So. 2d 599 (1977).

Massachusetts When a condominium board of managers attempted to enforce a rule prohibiting pets, plaintiff claimed that she was free from the master deed encumbrances as a good-faith purchaser, since she had received her unit deed before the master deed containing the restrictions was recorded. *Held:* Plaintiff was subject to the master deed encumbrances since the unit deed contained a clause subjecting her property to terms in the master deed. In addition, she was fully aware of all the terms of the master deed and the bylaws at the time she received her unit deed. *Johnson v. Keith,* 331 NE2d 879 (1975).

New Jersey Plaintiffs, owners of single or double residential condominium units, sued the township's rent-leveling board seeking relief against the enforcement of a rent control ordinance. The issue was whether the ordinance that exempted housing units of two units or fewer applied to owners of two or fewer condominiums in one building. *Held:* Plaintiffs' units were exempt from the rent control ordinance. The ordinance did not intend to treat owners of single-dwelling units differently on the sole basis of whether their units were attached or unattached to other units. Landlords of two or fewer units were perceived as being more caring of tenants' needs, more equal in bargaining power to them, and less equipped to comply with burdensome rent control ordinances than landlords of three or more units. *AMN, Inc. v. South Brunswick Township Rent Leveling Bd.,* 461 A2d 1138 (1983).

New Jersey Plaintiff asked the township planning board if it could sell the ground underlying units of a planned development separately from the units themselves. They also proposed that the remaining common elements be held by a homeowners' association instead of by undivided interest as condominium owners. Membership in the association would arise in conjunction with the ownership of the residential units. The board denied the proposals as detrimental to the township for taxation and aesthetic reasons. *Held:* Ownership of the common elements would not be severed from ownership of the units, but individual owners could own their unit plots. Ownership of the common areas by a homeowner's association could cause their loss to the tax rolls, because the association's default would not threaten any unit owner with loss of the unit. The aesthetic objection to unit plot ownership was arbitrary, since the greater variety of appearance that may result would not differ from that in a condominium. *Bonner Properties v. Franklin Township Planning Bd.,* 449 A2d 1350 (Law Div. 1982).

Ohio Under Ohio statute the developer of a condominium has a right to designate members of the board, but the right is phased out over three years (five years for an expandable condominium) or sooner if 75 percent of the units have been sold.

Four years after filing the declaration, the developer had sold less than half the units, but could elect only a fraction of the board. To avoid foreclosure, the developer deeded the unsold units to the project lender. By voting its units as a block, the lender succeeded in electing a majority of the board and obtaining an amendment to the condominium declaration that was favorable to it. Unit owners sued, claiming the amendment was proposed by an improperly elected board. *Held:* A split court held that the amendment was improperly passed. The decision turned on whether the lender was a good faith purchaser for value or had assumed the status of a developer. Mere acquisition of title to the property through assertion of its security interest did not cast the lender in the role of a developer. Here, however, the lender went beyond a simple effort to recover its lending loss and ventured into dealings designed to produce a development profit. *McKnight v. Board of Directors,* 512 NE2d 316 (1987).

38.10 Conversions

3d Circuit Owners converted their apartment complex shortly before the New Jersey Senior Citizens and Disabled Protected Tenancy Act (Tenancy Act) took effect. The Tenancy Act entitled eligible tenants to a protected tenancy for 40 years from the date their rental apartments were converted. Rents were controlled either by the local rent control ordinance or by the Tenancy Act, both of which provided that the costs of conversion were not justification for a rent increase. In a unit not subject to rent control, the Anti-Eviction Act provided that no tenant shall be evicted for nonpayment of an unconscionable rent increase. The Tenancy Act had retroactive effect. Owners challenged the Tenancy Act's constitutionality. The district court held retroactive operation of the Tenancy Act was unconstitutional as an impairment of contract and an uncompensated taking. *Held:* Reversed. The court of appeals expressed doubt that any substantial impairment of contract had occurred, as the Tenancy Act merely enlarged rights already granted by the Anti-Eviction Act. Even if there was some impairment, it was justified by the broad remedial purposes of the act of preserving tenancies of senior citizens and the disabled. Whatever taking could be held to exist was not permanent, because, as to any given unit, it would last at longest for the remainder of tenant's life. Finally, the court held there was no taking for a public use, merely regulation of the use to which private property could be put. *Troy Ltd. v. Renna,* 727 F2d 287 (1984).

D.C. Circuit Owners sold a building to a tenant group under a contract that was terminable if the building was not converted to a condominium within a stated time. Tenants submitted forms to the District of Columbia showing that a majority had consented to conversion, but the District denied permission to convert because the forms had not been validated. Before the forms could be validated, the District enacted legislation that eliminated tenant-consent conversions. The owners of the building sued the District of Columbia, alleging that they had been illegally prevented from converting in violation of their constitutional rights. *Held:* For the District of Columbia. The delay was not such as to deprive owners of due process or equal protection. The District's actions, while not exemplary, were taken in pursuit of a legitimate governmental interest, i.e., the protection of the rights of both building owners and tenants. *Silverman v. Barry,* 845 F2d 1072 (1988).

U.S. District Court, Massachusetts A town had passed a bylaw amendment prohibiting condominium unit owners from evicting tenants who had been in possession prior to a conversion. Plaintiffs had entered into an agreement to buy their unit prior to the amendment's passage, but closed the sale after passage. The bylaw amendment gave the protected tenant a life estate that could be terminated only by death or voluntary departure, and provided that rents of rent-controlled units be established "at levels which would yield to landlords a fair net operating income for such units." Plaintiffs challenged the constitutionality of the bylaw amendment as a "taking" of their property in violation of the Fifth and Fourteenth Amendments. *Held:* Because plaintiffs closed the purchase agreement after the amendment had been passed and, therefore, should have reasonably expected that they could not evict any existing tenants, there was no taking. In addition, the amendment assured plaintiffs a fair return on their investment. The public need for an adequate supply of rental units at affordable rents far outweighed any harm to plaintiffs. *Loeterman v. Town of Brookline,* 524 F. Supp. 1325 (1981), cert. denied, 456 US 906 (1982).

U.S. District Court, Pennsylvania Plaintiffs, individual tenants and tenant associations residing in apartment buildings that were to be converted into condominiums, challenged the constitutionality of the Pennsylvania Uniform Condominium Act, which granted aged, blind or disabled tenants who had occupied their apartments for at least two years a two-year period of protection from terminations or rent increases. Plaintiffs claimed this violated the equal protection of tenants who were given only one-year protection. *Held:* Plaintiffs lacked standing to challenge the constitutionality of the act because they lacked a substantial personal stake in the outcome of the dispute. There were no allegations that aged, blind, or disabled tenants who lived in their apartments for less than two years were included among plaintiffs, nor that, if there were such tenants, that they were injured. *River Park Tenants Ass'n v. 3600 Venture,* 534 F. Supp. 45 (ED 1981).

California Appellants wished to convert an apartment building to a condominium. An amendment to the city charter was enacted requiring rent control board permission before a landlord could remove a rent-controlled unit from the rental housing market. After the amendment took effect, the city council approved appellants' final subdivision map. However, appellants' application for exemption from the removal permit requirement was denied. Appellants sued, contending they had acquired a vested right to convert the building free of rent control by allegedly spending $40,000 following a tentative subdivison map approval of their project before the amendment took effect. *Held:* Although approval of the tentative map gave rise to a vested right to subdivide their building, this right could not place appellants in a more favorable position than an owner of a single-family home who sold it before the effective date. Moreover, the amount of money expended by appellants in reliance on tentative map approval was actually only $1,709, an inadequate amount on which to predicate a vested right. *Santa Monica Pines, Ltd. v. Rent Control Bd. of the City of Santa Monica,* 679 P2d 27 (1984).

Connecticut Tenant occupied an apartment in a complex consisting of several groups of buildings with four apartments in each building. The owner of the complex, while converting the apartments to common ownership, put four apartment buildings up for sale, but not the individual dwelling units. Tenant was notified of the change and given the opportunity to purchase a modular group of four apartments, but not the exclusive right to purchase the apartments. The owner subsequently notified tenant that his oral lease had expired and ordered tenant to vacate the premises. When tenant refused, owner brought a summary proceeding. Tenant moved to dismiss because the owner had failed to provide a conversion notice as required by law. *Held:* Tenant was not a conversion tenant and did not have the right to receive a conversion notice. An exception to a conversion tenant's right to notice applied when the dimensions of a unit for sale substantially differed from those of the single dwelling units, as in the present case. *Nicota Wieler Inv. Management v. Grower,* 541 A2d 1226 (1988).

Illinois A mobile home park developer planned to sell "cubicles of air over pads," which would be independently owned units. The county sued to enjoin the implementation of the plan arguing that it violated the county's subdivision regulations. Developer argued that his plan was covered by the Condominium Property Act and not by the county's subdivision regulations. *Held:* The developer's plan of conversion was not covered by the Condominium Property Act because the plan was nothing more than a subdivision of the park by circumvention. Therefore, the plan was held to violate the county's subdivision regulations, and injunctive relief was granted to the county. *State of Ill. ex rel. County of La Salle v. Grundy County Nat'l Bank,* 422 NE2d 650 (1981).

Maryland In a challenge to local ordinances designated to restrict conversions of rental housing stock into condominiums, apartment project owners asserted unconstitutionality under state home rule provisions. The local measures, it was argued, conflicted with state law authorizing and regulating condominium developments. *Held:* Although the conversion "moratorium" had expired, thus rendering the case moot in part, the ordinances conflicted with state law. In requiring reimbursement of displaced tenants, and also in the effect of the first-right-to-buy requirements, the local laws were found to be improper usurpation of state powers. *Rockville Grosvenor, Inc. v. Montgomery,* 422 A2d 353 (1980).

Massachusetts City council amended the city's rental housing equity ordinance to make it unlawful to remove a housing accommodation from rental housing use without obtaining a permit. Under the amendment, permits would be denied, except in buildings in which a majority of tenants agreed to purchase their units as permanent residences. *Held:* The ordinance was invalid because the city lacked express or implied authority to enact it. The city's rent control enabling statutes did not specifically mention or regulate condominium conversions and the ordinance did not effectuate the purposes of the rent control enabling legislation. There was little if any rational relationship between the intention to preserve housing stock and an ordinance that barred investors (who by definition would be likely to offer their units for rent) from obtaining permits for condominium and cooperative housing transfers. *Greater Boston Real Estate Bd. v. City of Boston,* 494 NE2d 1301 (1986).

Massachusetts Plaintiff moved into an apartment in 1980, intending to remain in the unit as a tenant; however, two months later, she decided to buy the apartment. A local ordinance provided that an owner could not remove a controlled rental unit from the market without a permit, but the ordinance did not apply if the last previous occupant was a tenant who would continue to occupy the unit as its owner. Several weeks after plaintiff purchased the apartment, the rent control board passed a regulation defining "last previous occupant" under the ordinance as the last previous occupant prior to August 10, 1979, thus requiring plaintiff to apply for a permit, which was later denied. After she brought suit, another ordinance was passed in 1982, providing that only tenants who had occupied units before August 10, 1979 were eligible to own and occupy their units with a permit. *Held:* Plaintiff was entitled to occupy her apartment without applying for a permit. Retroactive application of the 1982 ordinance would interfere with plaintiff's expectation concerning the use of her property and therefore would entitle her to compensation, a result the rent control board did not intend. The 1980 regulation was also invalid because it was inconsistent with the plain terms of the earlier ordinance. *Polednak v. Rent Control Bd.*, 494 NE2d 1025 (1986).

Massachusetts Tenant lived in an apartment building that was converted into condominiums. Tenant's apartment was the only unsold unit in the building and was rent controlled. Landlord, after receiving late rent payments, filed a notice of eviction. *Held:* For tenant. Landlord's motive for seeking eviction was not late payment of rent, but to regain possession of the apartment in order to sell it as a condominium. Landlord had accepted chronically late rent payments without complaint, never initiating eviction proceedings. Although late payment of rent was grounds for eviction, the landlord's motive to gain possession in order to sell violated the bylaw restrictions applying to rent-controlled apartments. *Kahn v. Brookline Rent Control Bd.*, 477 NE2d 390 (1985).

Massachusetts Claimant owned an apartment complex that it wanted to convert into condominiums. While the claimant was in the process of selling units, the city enacted an ordinance restricting the right of owners to convert their property to condominiums. The central feature of the ordinance was a provision preventing the owner from regaining possession of the converted unit, regardless of the tenancy, for two years following the issuance of a conversion permit and five years in a hardship case. Claimant challenged the city's authority to enact the provision, alleging that the state constitution prohibited the enactment of a law governing civil relationships except as an incident to an exercise of municipal power. *Held:* For claimant. The ordinance, which directly affected the rights and duties of converting landlords, governed a civil relationship, and was not incident to an exercise of municipal power. *CHR Gen., Inc. v. City of Newton,* 439 NE2d 788 (1982).

New Jersey Tenant lived in an apartment building that landlord decided to convert to condominiums. Tenant declined to buy the apartment. Landlord brought a dispossess action. Tenant was given a one-year stay of eviction since landlord failed to provide comparable housing. During the stay period, landlord informed tenant that in lieu of comparable housing, tenant would receive hardship relocation compensation of five months' rent, as required by law and that he had until the end of the stay to vacate the premises. Tenant, however, claimed the relative statute required both comparable housing and waiver of the five months' rent and requested another stay. *Held:* For landlord. The statutory language clearly stated that after the imposition of the one-year stay, the owner may offer the tenant comparable housing or, in the alternative, waiver of five months' rent. Nor could the court authorize further stays. *Mountain Management Corp. v. Hinnant,* 490 A2d 381 (Super. Ct. Law Div. 1984), aff'd, 492 A2d 693 (Super. Ct. App. Div. 1985).

Rhode Island Owners of a parking lot planned to convert the lot into a parking condominium. The condominium declaration proposed to divide the lot into 47 parcels. The purchasers would own a fee simple interest in air space above the land that could be used to park vehicles. The land would constitute a common area that would be owned by the purchasers as tenants in common. After the owners attempted to file the condominium declaration, the clerk declared the conversion a subdivision of real property and refused to record the documents. The owners sued for a writ of mandamus directing the clerk to record the documents. *Held:* For the owners. Condominium conversion is not subject to regulation as a subdivision. The parking condominium satisfies the requisites of a condominium since the purchasers will own a fee simple interest in air space and an undivided interest in all common areas with other purchasers as tenants in common. The parking condominium constitutes a mere change in ownership form, not a subdivision of land. *McConnell v. Wilson,* 543 A2d 249 (1988).

38.15 Association's Standing to Sue

California A planned development association that owned all common areas, real property, and structures in a planned development, sued to hold the general contractor strictly liable for construction defects. The general contractor argued that the association lacked standing to sue. *Held:* The association had standing to sue, both as owner of the common areas and as a representative on behalf of its members, who effectively owned only the air space within their units. *Del Mar Beach Club Owners Ass'n v. Imperial Contracting Co.,* 176 Cal. Rptr. 886 (1981).

Florida A condominium association sought damages from the developer for negligent construction and breach of warranties to provide various common elements. The developer answered that the individual owners were the proper parties to bring suit and that the association could not collect damages for omissions in common elements. *Held:* Under Florida law, condominium associations may sue on behalf of all unit owners concerning matters of common interest. The association could recover damages for missing common elements. *Juno by the Sea Condominium Apartments, Inc. v. Juno by the Sea N. Condominium Ass'n,* 418 So. 2d 1190 (Dist. Ct. App. 1982).

Georgia Plaintiff condominium association was located on two tracts separated by a creek that passed through a culvert across which a road ran connecting the two tracts. The creekbed and culvert belonged to the condominium developer's predecessor. The creek overflowed onto the condominium property several times. Plaintiffs sued developer's predecessor for negligent construction and maintenance of the culvert, and also sued the developer and lending institution for damages and an injunction to prohibit a continuing nuisance. *Held:* Plaintiff, which did not own, lease, or have a legal interest in the property, lacked standing to sue for damages or injunctive relief. Such rights belonged not to plaintiff but to the individual unit owners. *Equitable Life Assurance Soc'y v. Tinsley Mill Village,* 294 SE2d 495 (1982).

Maryland A condominium unit owners association sued the condominium developer under a theory of breach of warranty for defects in some of the common elements. Developer moved to dismiss on grounds that no warranty as to the common elements ran to the association, which did not own the common elements. Developer relied on the leading statement in *Friendly Village Community Association v. Silva & Hill Construction Co.,* 107 Cal. Rptr. 123 (1973), of the minority rule prohibiting associations from suing for breach of warranty as to common elements. *Friendly Village* was, in turn, based on the real-party-in-interest rule. Reasoning that the real parties in interest were the unit owners, developer asserted that the action had to be prosecuted in their names, not the name of the association. *Held:* For the association. The case was governed by a Maryland statute granting a unit owners association power to sue and be sued on behalf of two or more owners on matters affecting the condominium. The statute was held to create an exception to the real party in interest rule. *Starfish Condominium Ass'n v. Yorkridge Serv. Corp.*, 458 A2d 805 (1983).

New Jersey Individual unit owners brought suit seeking to enjoin a settlement between the condominium developer and the condominium association with respect to defects in the common elements. The developer invoked the majority rule concerning permissibility of suits by unit owners associations to bar suits by individual unit owners. *Held:* For developer. The court held that the association was exclusively responsible for maintaining the common elements via lawsuits or any other means. It would be impractical, the court stated, for individual unit owners to bring suits in which their rights to damages would be but fractional shares of the total damages payable. Moreover, said the court, any sums recovered by a unit owner would only have to be turned over to the association anyway. The court noted, however, that such reasoning would not apply where individual owners brought actions based upon damages to their individual units, where associations failed to act, or where the developers retained control of the association. *Siller v. Hartz Mountain Assoc.*, 461 A2d 568, cert. denied, 464 US 961 (1983).

North Dakota When part of the retaining wall behind a condominium development collapsed, the condominium association sued the builder-developer of the condominium project. *Held:* The individual unit owners, rather than the condominium association, were the real parties in interest because the association did not have title to the common elements and was not specifically authorized by statute to sue on behalf of unit owners with respect to the common elements. Although the builder-developer was liable for damages because the wall did not meet engineering or building code standards, it was not required to pay the full cost of repairing the wall. Seven of the twenty-eight unit owners had purchased their units when they should have known of the defect, so, in essence, they consented to the defect, which barred them from sharing the recovery. *Jablonsky v. Klemm,* 377 NW2d 560 (1985).

Pennsylvania Association comprised of all unit owners of a residential condominium property brought an action against the developer for breach of warranty. The developer contended the association lacked standing to sue. *Held:* The association had standing to sue on behalf of individual condominium unit owners even though it alleged no injury to its status as their decision-making body. While ordinarily one may not claim standing to vindicate the rights of a third party, a condominium association may have standing solely as the representative of its members if, as here, it can allege an injury to any one of them. *1000 Grandview Ass'n v. Mt. Washington Assoc.*, 434 A2d 796 (1981).

Utah A management committee brought suit under Utah Code Ann. § 57-8-33 (1953) against the builders, designers, and sellers of a condominium project, based on alleged design and workmanship flaws in the common areas. The statute provides for actions to be brought by managers or managerial committees of condominiums on behalf of two or more unit owners with respect to any cause of action relating to the common areas or more than one unit. Defendants sought to have the action dismissed for lack of capacity or standing to sue. *Held:* The management committee had statutory authority to sue on behalf of two or more unit owners. At the same time, the individual unit owner retained the right to initiate suit on his own behalf. The committee's standing was derived from the statute, which authorized it to bring an action. The committee was not required, as defendants claimed, to initiate a class action or to join all unit owners to prevent multiple suits against the defendants. Res judicata would prevent unit owners from litigating the same issues later. *Brickyard Homeowners Ass'n Management Comm. v. Gibbons Realty Co.*, 668 P2d 535 (1983).

Virginia The unit owners association of a condominium sued the developer for violating the full disclosure provisions of state statute by labeling a parcel that the developer intended to sell for commercial development as a "park" on the plat attached to the public offering statement. The association and the developer reached a settlement in which the developer agreed to maintain part of the parcel as a park and to place certain restrictive covenants on the remainder of the parcel. At issue was whether the settlement bound unit owners who had intervened in the suit. *Held:* The intervening unit owners were bound. Since the Virginia statute gave the unit owners the power to assert a claim for the violation of a common right, the association also necessarily had the authority to compromise the claim. Even though the disputed parcel was not a common element of the condominium, the right claimed in that parcel, once established, would have been held in common by all the unit owners. *Frantz v. CBI Fairmac Corp.*, 331 SE2d 390 (1985).

38.20
Right and Powers of Association

Florida All 68 unit owners present at a meeting voted in favor of the condominium association's acquisition of an adjacent lot to provide additional parking. Defendants, nonvoting unit owners, refused to pay their proportional share of the purchase price when they were given notice of the vote. The association then filed lien claims against their units. Defendants argued that Florida law prohibited amendments to a declaration of condominium that "materially alter or modify the appurtenances to the unit" unless all unit owners approve the amendment. *Held:* The powers of a condominium association to purchase real property are limited by the Condominium Act, which fails to give an association authority to purchase any real estate other than the condominium units. Because the association lacked the power to purchase the lot, it held the lot in trust for the members of the association who provided funds for the purchase. *TowerHouse Condominium, Inc. v. Millman*, 475 So. 2d 674 (1985).

Florida The purchasers bought their condominium unit in part because of the exterior color scheme planned for their building. At the time, buildings were laid out in several different color clusters, with coordinated roof and trim. Five years later, without color being discussed, a regular meeting of the board of directors approved a $200,000 painting program. The board then arranged to have all the buildings painted light brown, without any notice to the unit owners. Purchasers sued, claiming that they had made improvements to their unit based on the original color scheme, including tile on the front walk and storm roll-ups. *Held:* Changing the color scheme from one of multicolor clusters to one uniform color was a substantial, material alteration that required a two-thirds vote of the unit owners under the terms of the declaration of condominium. If the board could not obtain the support of two thirds of the unit owners for the new color scheme, it would be required to repaint all the buildings in their original colors. *Islandia Condominium Ass'n, v. Vermut,* 501 So. 2d 741 (Dist. Ct. App. 1987).

Massachusetts Condominium development's master deed stated that the units were intended solely for "residential dwelling purposes." The condominium trust sought to stop a couple from operating a day care home in a condominium unit. *Held:* The couple was enjoined from operating the day care home. The "residential purposes" language in the condominium's master deed prohibited the conduct of business enterprises, including day care homes, in the condominium units. Day care home license requirements, state supervision, and the arrivals and departures of parents and children differentiate the operation of a day care home from other uses that are so homelike as to be indistinguishable from residence. *Woodvale Condominium Trust v. Scheff,* 540 NE2d 206 (App. Ct. 1989).

Michigan At the behest of the condominium association and pursuant to a court order, the sheriff's department conducted a warrantless inspection of a condominium unit owner's unit. The unit owner challenged the court order as an unreasonable search and seizure. *Held:* The order was reasonable. Inspections of common elements and limited common elements by private associations do not constitute unreasonable search and seizure. Under the Michigan Condominium Act a unit owner has fundamental property rights, but enjoys them coextensively with other members of the condominium. *Cohan v. Riverside Park Place,* 365 NW2d 201 (Ct. App. 1985).

38.25 —Restrictions on Use of Common Areas

Alaska Plaintiff bought a condominium unit that could be connected to a prewired central television antenna or an antenna-based cable system. Subsequently, the condominium association adopted a rule prohibiting antennae anywhere on the building. Plaintiff sought an injunction against enforcement of the rule. *Held:* The condominium association had the authority to ban antennae. The association's declaration of condominium authorized the association to adopt rules governing use of common areas and requiring unit owners to take action to preserve a uniform exterior appearance of the buildings. The ban was reasonable since it curtailed no significant interest of the owners, and the association had a legitimate interest in improving the building's exterior appearance, enhancing the units' marketability, and preventing roof leakage. *O'Buck v. Cottonwood Village Condominium Ass'n,* 750 P2d 813 (1988).

California The declaration of covenants of a condominium provided that "No truck . . . shall be parked on the . . . project, except temporarily and solely for the purposes of loading and unloading, without the prior approval of the Architectural Committee. . . . The carports shall be used for parking of passenger automobiles or nonpowered vehicles such as bicycles, only. . . ." One of the unit owners bought a new pickup truck and parked it in the carport. Management corporation sued to enjoin him from parking the pickup in the carport and to recover $2,600 in fines. *Held:* Although a condominium may impose covenants and restrictions on the use or enjoyment of any portion of the common area, the covenants and restrictions must be reasonable. The restriction at issue was unreasonable as applied to clean, noncommercial pickup trucks. Parking the pickup in the carport was not aesthetically unpleasant to reasonable persons and did not interfere with other owners' use and enjoyment of their property. *Bernardo Villas*

Management Corp. No. Two v. Black, 235 Cal. Rptr. 509 (Ct. App. 1987).

Colorado Condominium owners sued their condominium association for trespass. The owners had purchased the unit in question because of its panoramic view. However, the association, without permission of the owners, entered the unit and relocated a storage locker on the balcony, blocking a large part of the view. The association argued that the owners were not entitled to possession of the balcony because it was commonly held by all the unit owners. *Held:* The owners were in constructive possession of the balcony and could maintain the trespass action based on the association's use of it. *Plotkin v. Club Valencia Condominium Ass'n,* 717 P2d 1027 (Ct. App. 1986).

Hawaii An amendment to a condominium's declaration, changing the condominium association's club house area from a common element to a limited common element for one owner's exclusive use, was approved by 76.83 percent of the owners. Other owners challenged the amendment. *Held:* The amendment was invalid because it required the approval of 100 percent of the owners. Hawaii law allows 75 percent of the owners to approve a change in use of common elements. However, the conversion of a common element to a limited common element is distinguishable. A conversion that restricts or denies use significantly diminishes the benefits to all owners. The argument that a unanimous vote was unnecessary because Hawaii law requires such a vote only when the common *interest* is altered was rejected. Although each owner's percentage of undivided interest in the common element remained the same, for all intents and purposes, the common interest appurtenant to each apartment was diminished by the change. *Penney v. Association of Apartment Owners of Hale Kaanapali,* 776 P2d 393 (1989).

Illinois Plaintiff, owner of a condominium unit, sought defendant's permission to construct an addition to his unit converting a terrace into a bedroom. Although the terrace was part of the common areas, plaintiff had an easement entitling him to exclusive use of the terrace. Defendant rejected plaintiff's proposal. Plaintiff sued, arguing that its refusal to permit construction of the addition was arbitrary. Defendant argued that granting plaintiff's request would violate Section 8 of the Illinois Condominium Act, barring the partition or division of common elements. *Held:* Defendant's motion to dismiss denied. Construction of the bedroom did not violate Section 8, because physical division of common elements caused by an improvement did not constitute a "partition" or "division." Plaintiff was merely trying to build on a common element area as to which he already had an exclusive easement, without diminishing the common areas available to other unit owners. *Parrillo v. 1300 Lake Shore Drive Condominium,* 431 NE2d 1221 (1981).

Maryland The city, planning to construct a pedestrian bridge over a parkway, condemned a small part of a parking lot constituting a portion of the general common elements of a condominium. Condemnation proceedings were brought by the city against the common elements. The trial judge instructed the jury to award a lump sum to the council of unit owners of the condominium and deleted the names of the individual unit owners from the inquisition form submitted to the jury. Condominium unit owners contended that the trial judge erred in both of these actions. *Held:* Any unit owner whose unit suffered injuries separate from the whole was entitled to consequential damages as an individual. Trial judge should have included the names of individual unit owners in the inquisition form, even though it had already contained the names of council condominium members who were entitled to receive the condemnation award for general common elements. *Andrews v. City of Greenbelt,* 441 A2d 1064 (1982).

Michigan A unit owner appealed the board of directors' denial of his request to enclose his balcony with glass. *Held:* The board acted reasonably. The board's authority under the bylaws to approve alterations to the common elements extended only to alterations that did not impair the appearance of the condominium. The enclosure was a structural change that would have significantly changed the appearance of the balcony, a common element, and might therefore have disrupted the integrity of the common scheme. *Cohan v. Riverside Park Place Condominium Ass'n,* 333 NW2d 574 (Ct. App. 1983).

Missouri Unit owners appealed an injunction requiring them to remove concrete retaining walls at their expense. The unit owners had unsuccessfully sought the permission of the board of managers to erect the retaining walls to protect their unit from recurrent flooding, then had built the walls anyway at their own expense. *Held:* Order for injunction for removal affirmed. The flooding was not due to the board's negligence, but was caused by the city's approval of large-scale construction after installation of an undersized sewer. The board had no duty to maintain and protect condominium units from storm water damage not caused by the board or by another unit owner. Since by making improvements the unit owners had converted the common elements to their own personal use, the walls had to come down. *Westcott v. Burtonwood Manor Condominium Ass'n Bd. of Managers,* 743 SW2d 555 (Ct. App. 1987).

38.30
—Age Restrictions

California After moving into an adults-only condominium, plaintiffs had a child. Unable to find other housing, they brought an action challenging the condominium's age restriction. *Held:* For plaintiffs. California's Unruh Civil Rights Act protects all persons from arbitrary discrimination in "accommodations . . . in all business establishments of every kind whatsoever." Since the legislature clearly intended to define "business establishments" in the broadest sense possible, a homeowners association, with its responsibility for property management, is a "business establishment" subject to the act. *O'Connor v. Village Green Owners Ass'n,* 662 P2d 427 (1983).

California Ritchey purchased a condominium unit, subject to the condominium association's declaration and bylaws. At that time, there was no age restriction on residency, although the enabling declaration stated that the bylaws could be amended at any time by approval of a given percentage of unit owners. The association amended the bylaws to restrict occupancy to persons 18 years and older. Sometime therafter, Ritchey leased his unit to a woman with two children, and the association brought suite. After losing at trial, Ritchey argued on appeal that the amendment was unreasonable per se. *Held:* A condominium association bylaw restricting residency to persons over a certain age is not unreasonable per se. The court noted that some age restrictions on tenancies were legal under California law and that some federal housing programs have age limitations. It added that this age restriction was a reasonable recognition of the housing needs of older adults, that it was not unreasonable as it affected defendant, and that all buyers had had notice that the bylaws could be changed. *Ritchey v. Villa Neuva Condominium Ass'n,* 81 Cal. App. 3d 688 (1978).

Florida Two brothers bought half-interests in a condominium unit, with the intention to share it as a vacation home. The rules of the condominium association prohibited any child under 12 from living on the premises and restricted the use of the units to single-family residences. One of the brothers had children under 12, and the association soon brought suit to require him to convey his interest to his brother. He countered that the restrictions were a violation of his constitutional rights to equal protection and association. *Held:* The association was not entitled to enforce its rules against the brother. Although the rules themselves were constitutional, as enforced they were not, since other households in the condominium included children under 12. On the issue of the single-family use, the restriction was ambiguous and could include alternating use by two families. *White Egret Condominium, Inc. v. Franklin,* 379 So. 2d 346 (1979).

38.35
—Purchase and Leasing of Units

Florida Condominium unit owner entered into a lease with a prospective tenant but was denied approval by the condominium association. The association cited a rule that permitted those who had owned their units before a cut-off date to lease their apartments more frequently than other unit owners.The unit owner sued for damages. *Held:* The rule was invalid, since it violated a provision in the bylaws that all rules and regulations "shall be equally applicable to all members, and uniform in their application and effect." Since the association's actions constituted tortious interference with a contractual relationship, the unit owner was entitled to damages. *Barnett & Klein Corp. v. President of Palm Beach—A Condominium, Inc.,* 426 So. 2d 1074 (Dist. Ct. App. 1983).

North Dakota In 1974, plaintiffs purchased a condominium unit that they could lease without restrictions. In 1979, the condominium association amended the bylaws to prohibit leases of units for more than four months, but the bylaws as amended were not recorded as required by state law. After the amendment, plaintiffs were denied permission from the association to rent their unit. Plaintiffs then obtained a judgment that the restriction was invalid and should not be enforced. On the same day that judgment was entered, the association recorded the amendment. The association then appealed to the North Dakota Supreme Court on the issue of whether a condominium bylaw amendment restricting the use of a unit could be applied retroactively to an owner who obtained his unit prior to the promulgation of the amendment. *Held:* Under North Dakota law, a unit owner shall be bound only by those use restrictions in and on record prior to the conveyance of the unit to unit owner. *Breene v. Plaza Tower Ass'n,* 310 NW2d 730 (1981).

Illinois Plaintiff, an unwed mother, sought to acquire another unit in her condominium building, but was prevented when the association exercised its right of first refusal. She sued, claiming the association's action was an unreasonable restraint on alienation in violation of the bylaws of the association. *Held:* The association's exercise of its right of first refusal was an unreasonable restraint on alienation, because the plaintiff was a member of the association. Thus, its actions were not rationally related to the protection or proper operation of the property. The association's action was also within the scope of a local ordinance that barred discrimination on the basis of sex and marital status. *Wolinsky v. Kadison,* 449 NE2d 151 (App. Ct. 1983).

Massachusetts Plaintiff was denied the opportunity to purchase additional condominium units on the basis of a bylaw amendment that prohibited any person or entity from acquiring two or more units. He challenged the amendment on the grounds that it was an unreasonable restraint on alienation that violated his rights to due process and equal protection. *Held:* The restraint on alienation was valid because (1) it was of reasonable duration, since the bylaws could be amended at any time; (2) its purpose of encouraging occupancy by resident owners was worthwhile; (3) it prohibited an uncommon type of conveyance (few residents were likely to want to acquire more than two units); and (4) it was likely to affect only a few people. Since there was no state action involved, plaintiff's constitutional rights were not affected. *Franklin v. Spadafora,* 447 NE2d 1244 (1983).

38.40
—Assessments

Florida A corporate developer owned 65 units in a 254-unit condominium complex. The condominium association levied a special assessment against all unit owners to finance litigation against the developer. The developer sued, seeking a declaration absolving it from payment of the assessment. *Held:* A developer who owns condominium units is required to pay assessments levied by a condominium association as is any other unit owner, even when the purpose of the assessment is to finance legal action against the developer. *Brickell Biscayne Corp. v. Palace Condominium Ass'n,* 526 So. 2d 982 (Dist. Ct. App. 1988).

Florida Condominium's management agreement called for increases to be based on taxes, insurance, labor costs, and/or a specified consumer price index (CPI) formula. In practice, the CPI formula was used, until the Florida Condominium Act was amended to declare CPI-based escalation clauses in management contracts contrary to public policy. After the amendment, unit owners sued the management firm to recover the increases. *Held:* Because the management agreement incorporated by reference "the Condominium Act *as amended*," the management firm had waived its constitutional protection against state impairment of contract. The management firm would not suffer a loss, since the contract contained bases other than the CPI on which to increase assessments to recover costs of management. *Halpern v. Retirement Builders, Inc.,* 507 So. 2d 622 (Dist. Ct. App. 1987).

Florida A condominium association contracted to have another corporation provide bus transportation for its unit owners to areas outside the condominium property. A lump-sum payment permitted unit owners to ride the buses without paying a daily or trip charge. The lump sum was assessed against all unit owners as a common expense. Certain unit owners refused to pay, and the association placed a lien against their property and sued for a judgment on the lien. *Held:* The assessment for transportation was not permitted under the law. Under the Condominium Act, Fla. Stat. § 718.111 (1983), a condominium association may incur only those expenses that directly relate to the operation, maintenance, repair, or replacement of the condominium property. The only exception to this rule is that an association is granted the specific power to acquire possessory or use interests in recreational facilities, under Section 718.114. In this case, the bus transportaion service was neither condominium property nor a recreational facility; therefore, the association did not have the power to assess the cost against the unit owners. *Rothenberg v. Plymouth No. 5 Condominium Ass'n,* 511 So. 2d 651 (Dist. Ct. App. 1987).

Florida A condominium's declaration provided that no assessment would be made against units owned by the developer or condominium association unless the units were actually occupied by the developer or association. The unit owners sued, challenging this provision and seeking to recover the portion of the assessments the owners paid that should have been paid by the developer. *Held:* A developer cum unit owner is obligated to pay its proportionate share of assessments, regardless of any contrary provision in the condominium declaration. *Palm Bay Towers Corp. v. Brooks,* 466 So. 2d 1071 (Dist. Ct. App. 1984).

New Hampshire Residential condominium complex was set up as six separate condominium clusters. Each cluster had its own condominium association and the common expenses of a cluster were allocated among its members according to their units' percentage interest. Defendant was created as an umbrella organization for managing the community property and common areas of each cluster. Funding for managing the community property was provided by assessing each owner equally. The owners paid for defendant's servicing of the common areas via a common expense apportioned in accordance with their interests. When defendant lacked sufficient funds for its overall expenditures, it dipped into the surplus working capital raised by equal assessment. Several owners complained that this violated state condominium law because it resulted in the expenses of common area administration being paid in part by assessments of units equally, rather than proportionately. They also objected to the equal assessment of units for the purchase of maintenance equipment. *Held:* Defendant did not violate state law because it was not a condominium project. It was a corporate entity that stood in relation to the cluster condominium as an independent contractor. While routine maintenance fees must be allocated proportionately, the equipment purchase was an expense of defendant and not a common expense of any cluster. Defendant could use surplus working capital raised by equal assessments for the maintenance of common areas because it had been reimbursed for its outlay of capital by the clusters' proportionate assessment of unit members. *Hobson v. Hilltop Place Community Ass'n,* 453 A2d 841 (1982).

Ohio Unit owners refused to pay fees assessed them, claiming that the trustees of the condominium association had been improperly elected. The association filed a foreclosure suit to collect approximately \$2,500 in unpaid assessments, a late fee, and what eventually amounted to \$12,000 in attorney fees. *Held:* The unit owners were obligated to pay the assessments and the attorney fees. The court refused to consider the question of whether the assessments were imposed by a validly elected board, since the assessments were being paid by neighbors who were in effect "carrying" defendants. In a 4–3 decision, the Ohio Supreme Court allowed a contractual exception to the rule that litigants normally pay their own attorney fees; the exception applied here because of a "cost of collection" clause in the condominium declaration. *Nottingdale Homeowners Ass'n v. Darby,* 514 NE2d 702 (1987).

Virginia Defendant, a trash collection service, owned two units in an industrial condominium. A fleet of 11 trash-collection trucks operated from these units. The condominium was zoned in a region that permitted such activity, and regular health department inspections turned up no violations. Nonetheless, defendant's operations occasioned complaints from the unit owners association, which eventually decided to exercise a bylaw provision purportedly allowing it to fine defendant $25 per day per truck, with additional fines when compliance was not achieved within 10 days. When unpaid fines exceeded $20,000, the association sued for payment. *Held:* The fines were unlawful. Virginia's Condominium Act mandates that any private bylaws be consistent with the state and federal constitutions. The bylaw authorizing the summary imposition of $25 fines was inconsistent with constitutional provisions barring governments from imposing fines without due process of law. Although the Condominium Act authorized assessments by condominium associations, the fines levied were not assessments, which are nothing more than allocated payments for association expenditures. *Unit Owners Ass'n of BuildAmerica-1 v. Gillman,* 292 SE2d 378 (1982).

Washington Unit owners in a condominium development filed a petition for relief under Chapter 7 of the Bankruptcy Code. The homeowner's association received notice of the filing and was listed as a creditor. Owners resided in the condominium unit until the foreclosure sale and benefited from use of the common areas and amenities. The association sued to recover postpetition assessments, but the owners maintained their debt was discharged. *Held:* A Chapter 7 debtor who continues to reside in a condominium unit until the foreclosure sale remains liable for all assessments incurred from the date of bankruptcy until the property is abandoned or the unit is sold. *Mountain View Estates II Homeowners Ass'n v. Chapman,* 1988 Adv. No. 88-00490-HIH (Bankr. ED 1988).

38.45 Duties of Association

Florida Purchasers bought a condominium unit from a development association. Shortly after purchase they learned that litigation against the developer, represented to them as concerning only minor cosmetic repairs, was actually in regard to major structural defects. The purchasers sued, claiming that the association had a fiduciary duty to warn prospective buyers of defective conditions prior to sale. *Held:* The association had no duty to disclose structural defects to nonunit owners. Although the state condominium statute imposes a fiduciary relationship between the condominium association and a unit owner, the relationship does not extend to prospective purchasers. *Maillard v. Dowdell,* 528 So. 2d 512 (Dist. Ct. App. 1988).

Georgia Plaintiff purchased a condominium unit with an exterior wall that showed signs of previous repair efforts. The wall later developed a crack, caused by settling of the structure or movement of the underlying slope, that cost $50,000 to repair. Although the condominium association had previously repaired roofs, stoops, patios, and firewalls of individual units at its own expense, it took legal advice and refused to provide or pay for the needed repairs, although it did try unsuccessfully to persuade the developer to pay for the repairs. Plaintiff sued the association for the cost of the repairs. *Held:* The association was not liable. Under its bylaws and the then-current statute, the association was permitted, but not required, to make the repairs. Neither the bylaws nor the past actions of the association created a vested right in plaintiff to have the repairs performed. *Fleetwood v. Wieuca N. Condominium Ass'n,* 354 SE2d 623 (Ct. App. 1987).

Hawaii Condominium owners lent their unit to guests while they were away on their honeymoon. Late one night, two assailants passed through common areas of the development and entered the guests' apartment. The assailants shot one guest and raped another after robbing the apartment. The condominium project was in a high-crime area, and there had been previously unsolved cases of rape, robbery, and break-ins in the complex. There also were rumors that an extra master key was floating around. The victims sued the condominium association for negligence. *Held:* For the victims. When a condominium association performs all the traditional duties of a landlord, it also assumes the landlord's duty of care to protect resident condominium owners and their guests from foreseeable criminal acts of third parties. *Moody v. Cawdrey & Assocs., Inc.*, 721 P2d 707 (1986) (per curiam).

38.50
Liability of Developer

Illinois Condominium purchasers who complained of leaking roofs and other structural defects in the common elements of the condominium project sued the project's developers under several theories, including breach of an implied warranty of habitability and breach of trust. *Held:* Although the purchaser of a new condominium unit may rely upon an implied warranty of habitability,the doctrine does not apply to purchasers of converted units, when, as in this case, there was no significant refurbishing or renovation and the defects were not latent. The limitation on the board of managers' fiduciary duty in the declaration of condominium was effective and not in violation of public policy. In addition, under Illinois' Condominium Property Act, an exculpatory clause limits a developer's liability to acts of willful misconduct. *Kelley v. Astor Investors, Inc.*, 478 NE2d 1346 (1985).

38.55
Liability of Unit Owner

Texas A fire due to faulty wiring in condominium common elements caused extensive damage to the personal property of tenants in one of the units. Tenants sued the unit owner, relying in part on Texas case law, which holds each member of an association jointly and severally liable for association-induced damage to property submitted by the members to the control of the association. *Held:* The unit owner was liable only for 1.57 percent of the damages, based on the owner's pro rata undivided ownership in the common elements. The condominium association, not the individual unit owners, had control over the operations of the common area. Since the Texas Condominium Act provides for pro rata allocation of expenses, insurance, assessments, and taxes among unit owners, it can be inferred that the legislature intended that tort liability also be allocated on a pro rata basis. *Owens v. Dutcher,* 647 SW2d 948 (1983).

38.60
Time-Sharing

Florida Financier arranged with sellers of time-share units to advance $7,000 for each $5,000 in notes on sold time-shares they transferred to him. Financier was assigned six unsold units as collateral for the unpaid balance of the loan, which were to be traded for notes as they became available under the financing agreement. The project closed down, and some purchasers did not get their accommodations. The state sued the financier to compel him to assume the sellers' obligations. *Held:* Financier was liable under former Section 721.17 of Florida Statutes, which provides that "no seller shall sell, lease, assign . . . or otherwise transfer the seller's interest in the accommodations . . . of a time-sharing plan to a third party . . . unless the third party agrees to assume all obligations of the seller to purchasers. . . ." Financier was a seller of units for purposes of the act and an assignee required to comply with the act. *Smith v. Department of Business Regulation, Div. of Land Sales, Condominiums and Mobile Homes,* 504 So. 2d 1285 (Dist. Ct. App. 1986), appeal dismissed, 484 US 1052 (1988).

Virginia Condominium was developed as a time-sharing venture. Fifty-one single-week intervals were marketed in 39 units. Loans were guaranteed by the developer, with the lender holding the deeds until the loans were paid off. There were 25 defaults, and the developer paid off the loans, thereby reacquiring 25 unit weeks. A condominium bylaw provided that the developer was not liable for full assessments or maintenance charges for unsold units or unit weeks. The unit owners' association, however, assessed the developer for the 25 reacquired unit weeks on the theory that their having previously been sold took them outside the meaning of "unsold" as that word was used in the bylaws. When developer refused to pay, the owners' association sought a declaratory judgment. *Held:* The reacquired units were subject to assessments and maintenance charges. The original buyers had been given all the rights and responsibilities of an owner, but without a deed. Such transfer of beneficial interest was sufficient to make that transfer a sale, and once sold, a unit week could not be "unsold." *Colony Council Bd. of Directors v. Hightower Enters.*, 319 SE2d 772 (1984).

39.00 COOPERATIVES

39.05 In General

New York Prospective purchasers sued shareholder's wife, among others, under a civil rights law that prohibited discrimination in the sale of cooperative apartments. They charged that their purchase application was rejected because of their religion, and that the rejection was induced in part by the wife, who had made repeated derogatory remarks during an interview. The wife sought dismissal of the complaint on the ground that she was not a "cooperative tenant" subject to N.Y. Civ. Rights Law § 19-a. *Held:* The term "cooperative tenant" was meant to cover all individuals who reside in a building and are in a position to exert legitimate influence on the policies and practices of the corporation. Thus, the shareholder's wife was a cooperative tenant subject to the statute. *Sanders v. Winship*, 442 NE2d 1231 (1982).

39.10 Conversions

Massachusetts The Department of Housing and Urban Development (HUD) regulated the rents charged an apartment building's tenants until June 1, 1983, when HUD control of rents under the National Housing Act ended. When the building's owner converted the building to a cooperative, the city rent control board sued to block the sale of units and sought a declaration that the units were rent controlled and could not be removed from the rental market without a board permit. The owner claimed that HUD regulated the rents, excluding them from local rent control. *Held:* For the rent control board. HUD did not regulate rents on the building's units on November 15, 1983, the date the conversion took place. Under a regulation effective June 1, 1983, HUD intended that landlords of buildings on which it held mortgages would fix maximum rents without HUD involvement and in accordance with local rent control guidelines. Thus the units were subject to rent control and could not be removed from the rental market. *Rent Control Bd. v. Cambridge Tower Corp.*, 477 NE2d 1011 (1985).

39.15 —Right to Purchase

New York Corporate tenant of a residential apartment sought a judgment allowing it to purchase shares under a cooperative offering. Its application to purchase shares had been denied by the owner because tenant was not an individual seeking the apartment for its own use and personal occupancy. *Held:* For tenant. A corporate tenant that qualifies as a tenant in occupancy under the Rent Stabilization Code of New York City on the date a cooperative conversion plan is presented to tenants is entitled to purchase in its own name the shares allocated to its apartment. *Consolidated Edison Co. v. 10 W. 66th St. Corp.*, 462 NE2d 367 (1984).

New York Plaintiff sought a declaratory judgment that he, and not his wife, was entitled to purchase shares of the cooperative apartment in which his wife and children resided. He was the sole signatory of the lease, and he paid all the rent and utility charges connected with the apartment. The Rent Stabilization Law states that only an apartment's "tenant in occupancy" has the right to purchase the shares allocated to the unit under a plan for conversion to cooperative ownership. Plaintiff's spouse asserted that plaintiff could not be the "tenant in occupancy" because he did not physically occupy the apartment. *Held:* Plaintiff was the tenant in occupancy and, as such, was entitled to purchase the shares. Under the Rent Stabilization Law, one who signs the lease and pays the rent is the tenant in occupancy, even if he is not physically present, as long as members of his immediate family continue to occupy the premises. The wife, on the other hand, had no right to purchase the shares because she had not signed the lease. Her position with respect to her husband was no different from that of a subtenant. *Burns v. 500 E. 83rd St. Corp.*, 451 NE2d 475 (1983).

New York After a building converted to a cooperative, two estranged cotenants sought to purchase their jointly leased apartment separately. Each submitted a down payment within the allotted time period. One of the tenants brought an action for a declaratory judgment that he had the right to purchase the unit individually. *Held:* The landlord had to accept the separate offers as a joint offer and provide 30 additional days for a joint purchase. The right of the cotenants to purchase had to exist in some form. The mere fact that neither tenant was willing to withdraw in favor of the other did not destroy the right that was acquired with the unit lease. *Spitalnik v. Springer*, 450 NE2d 670 (1983).

New York During a cooperative conversion, a tenant arranged for her parents to acquire the rights to her own and to a second apartment, allegedly "outbidding" the individual who became president of the board of directors. When the board later refused to transfer the apartments from the tenant's parents to the tenant, the tenant sued and sought to conduct discovery to ascertain what influence the president of the board of directors had over the board's refusal to effect the transfers. *Held:* The tenant's claim of a "personal vendetta" entitled her to a hearing on the possible bad faith of the board in denying the requests for the transfers. *Boisson v. 4 E. Hous. Corp.*, 514 NYS2d 374 (App. Div. 1987).

New York Tenant was a not-for-profit corporation that had occupied an apartment and had run a group home for adolescent girls since 1955. In 1977, landlord decided to convert the premises to a cooperative. Tenant offered to purchase the apartment, but landlord refused on the ground that only "persons" were eligible to purchase. When the effective lease expired, landlord, who resided in the building, did not offer tenant a new lease, and subsequently purchased the shares allocated to the apartment. He then served a vacate notice on the tenant, claiming that the tenant was using the premises for commercial purposes. *Held:* For tenant. The court rejected landlord's argument that the apartment was used for commercial purposes, since tenant was a not-for-profit corporation. The group home was recognized in the lease as an extended family and as such was entitled to the rights accorded a family under the Rent Stabilization Code. *Koenig v. Jewish Child Care Ass'n,* 487 NYS2d 759 (App. Div. 1985), aff'd, 494 NE2d 86 (1986).

New York Defendants sought to convert a building to condominium ownership. After plaintiff failed to purchase the shares allotted to his apartment, defendants notified him that he would not be offered a renewal lease and that he would be evicted upon expiration of the lease term. Plaintiff argued that he was protected by the Rent Stabilization Law and the Emergency Tenant Protection Act because previously the building had six dwelling units; a temporary, unauthorized division of a duplex into two dwelling units had been made. *Held:* All applicable certificates of occupancy established a five-unit configuration for the building. The unauthorized division of the duplex could not be attributed to defendants, who had purchased the building without prior knowledge of the change. Because the temporary "sixth apartment" did not exist at the time plaintiff brought suit and conflicted with the certificate of occupancy when it did exist, defendants were not obligated to offer plaintiff a renewal lease and could evict him upon expiration of his lease. *Cooper v. Schube,* 449 NYS2d 32 (App. Div.), aff'd, 457 NYS2d 479 (1982).

New York Cooperative conversion offering plan restricted the opportunity to purchase apartments at an insider's price to tenants occupying apartments as their primary residences. A tenant, who used his apartment in his psychiatric profession and also as a secondary residence, sued for the right to subscribe to the offering plan. *Held:* The restriction to tenants occupying their apartments as primary residences violated the Rent Stabilization Code, which allows all tenants of record to purchase cooperative shares at an insider's price. *Payn v. Lyras,* 457 NYS2d 37 (App. Div. 1982).

New York The leases for a rent-stabilized building provided that the apartment was to be occupied by tenant or members of his immediate family for no other purpose than as a primary residence. Plaintiff had been using the premises as a professional office. Landlord never objected until plaintiff sought to purchase shares in the apartment at the 25 percent discount offered to rent-stabilized tenants when the building converted to a cooperative. Landlord claimed plaintiff was not a rent-stabilized tenant since he did not occupy the premises as his primary residence. *Held:* Landlord, who had been aware that plaintiff was violating a substantial obligation of his rent-stabilized tenancy, ignored three opportunities to deny plaintiff renewal leases and did not give plaintiff an opportunity to cure his default. Therefore, as of the date the conversion plan was presented, plaintiff was a rent-stabilized tenant entitled to the 25 percent discount. *Wissner v. 15 W. 72nd St. Assocs.,* 450 NYS2d 790 (App. Div.), aff'd, 444 NE2d 1003 (1982).

New York Plaintiff sought recognition as a tenant entitled to purchase shares during a cooperative conversion. Plaintiff had moved in shortly before the conversion and had signed a blank lease proffered by a realtor on behalf of the landlord. The lease was later returned to him signed on behalf of the landlord as owner and an employee of the realtor as lessor, as if the arrangement were a sublease. When the building was converted, landlord refused to sell shares to plaintiff, maintaining that the realtor's employee was the prime tenant, even though the employee had never occupied or paid rent on the apartment and had similar arrangements in other buildings owned by the landlord. *Held:*

Plaintiff was entitled to summary judgment. The facts made out an illegal arrangement between landlord and realtor to evade the laws governing cooperative offerings in rental buildings. *Yellon v. Reiner-Kaiser Assocs.,* 452 NYS2d 107 (App. Div. 1982).

39.20 Restrictions

Connecticut Plaintiffs, having contracted to buy stock in a cooperative corporation and to receive an assignment of the seller's proprietary lease, were unable to obtain approval from the board of directors or the shareholders, the defendants. Under the memorandum of offering for the stock, assignments were to be approved only for persons of suitable "character and financial responsibility." Under the proprietary lease, however, consent to assignments could be granted or withheld "for any reason or no reason." At issue was whether these provisions justified the withholding of consent. *Held:* The clause in the lease was an illegal restraint on alienation of property interests; it failed to recognize the legitimate interest of a leaseholder to enjoy reasonable access to the resale market. The clause in the memorandum of offering was valid, however, and it could justify the defendants' disapproval of the sale and assignment to plaintiffs. Defendants had several rational reasons for blocking the transaction. Plaintiffs already occupied one of the other six apartments in the cooperative, they allegedly misused property in the common areas, and their children were allegedly excessively noisy. *Jones v. O'Connell,* 458 A2d 355 (1983).

New York Cooperative corporation's standard form proprietary lease and bylaws each provided different procedures for amending the lease. Members whose maintenance charges had been reassessed pursuant to a lease amendment that satisfied only the amendment procedures contained in the lease sued. The cooperative, which prepared both documents, contended that the procedures set forth in the lease were intended for amendments proposed by management, while those set forth in the bylaws were intended to apply to member initiatives. *Held:* Changing the lease required compliance with both the procedures contained in the bylaws and those contained in the lease. Had the two procedures been intended as alternatives, both alternatives would have been contained in all the relevant documents. The maintenance charge amendment was therefore null and unenforceable. *Brennan v. Breezy Point Coop., Inc.,* 484 NYS2d 510 (1984).

Ohio A cooperative corporation sued to evict shareholder's sister. Shareholder had moved out and had sublet the apartment to the sister without the corporation's consent. *Held:* The sister was not entitled to the apartment, since, under the terms of the cooperative corporation agreement, she was not a member of the immediate family. A cooperative corporation retains the right to decide who may live with the shareholders, even to the extent of excluding immediate family members related by blood if they did not previously reside in the apartment with the shareholders. *Kohler v. Snow Village, Inc.,* 475 NE2d 1298 (Ct. App. 1984).

PART E
RECORD AND NOTICE OF OWNERSHIP

40.00
RECORDING AND REGISTRATION STATUTES

40.05
Operation and Effect

Alabama In 1939, the state acquired an additional 17-foot right-of-way along each side of an existing highway, but failed to record the acquisition. In 1965, a purchaser who had no actual knowledge of the extended right-of-way bought property along part of the highway and constructed a store on part of the state's right-of-way. When the state brought proceedings to remove the store, the purchaser argued that former Section 6887 of the Code of Alabama, later recodified as Section 35-4-90, applied to void the state's claim to the unrecorded extension of its right-of-way. That section provides that "[a]ll conveyances of real property . . . are inoperative and void as to purchasers for a valuable consideration . . . unless the same have been recorded before the accrual of the right of such purchasers. . . ." *Held:* The condemnation was a "conveyance of real property" within the meaning of the recording statute. The state's claim to the 1939 extension was therefore inoperable and void as to the purchaser. *State v. Abbott,* 476 So. 2d 1224 (1985).

Arizona When plaintiff sold his property, he orally reserved rights to take water from the land. When defendant purchased the property 14 years later, he was advised as to the oral reservation, but found that the alleged rights were not recorded. Plaintiff recorded his interest after defendant's purchase and sought to enforce his right and take water from the property. *Held:* Conveyance of lands, tenements, and hereditaments must be recorded to bind subsequent purchasers. Constructive notice was not sufficient to bind defendant where he complied with the recording statute and the water reservation rights were unrecorded. *Neal v. Hunt,* 541 P2d 559 (1975).

Colorado Lessee of oil and gas property sought to quiet title and assert priority of lease over remote transferor. *Held:* Where a party in the chain of title files an oil and gas lease containing a royalty reservation only in the Federal Bureau of Land Management and not in local land records, the interest of a subsequent purchaser is subject to such recorded lease under state constructive notice provisions. *Page v. Fees-Krey, Inc.,* 617 P2d 1188 (1980).

Florida Bank sued to quiet title to land in which it had acquired an interest through one of two prior co-owners (defendant was a descendant of the other co-owner). Only the name of the bank's predecessor in interest appeared in a tax deed from the state. *Held:* The deed was a root of title under Florida's Marketable Record of Title Act, so that no interest remained to the unrecorded co-owner. The 30-year statutory period in which the unrecorded co-owner could have filed a notice of interest had passed. *Allen v. St. Petersburg Bank & Trust Co.,* 383 So. 2d 1171 (1980).

Massachusetts A company leased a building for five years with a five-year option to renew in 1961. The lease was recorded, but subsequent unrecorded modifications gave the company options to renew until 1972. The purchaser of the building demanded that the company leave by 1970. When the lessee refused, the purchaser sued, claiming that the unrecorded modifications were invalid under a statute requiring that all leases for more than seven years must be recorded. *Held:* Although the original lease, with a possible term of 10 years, had to be recorded, the modified options lasted less than five years and did not have to be recorded to be valid. *Snyder v. Sperry & Hutchinson Co.,* 333 NE2d 421 (1975).

Michigan Owners of land zoned multiple-residential filed site plans for a multiple-residential development with the township planning commission. After numerous hearings and modifications, the township rezoned the land as single-family residential. The owners petitioned for a writ of mandamus to compel approval of their plans. *Held:* Where the rejection of the prior site plan was not based on competent, material, or substantial evidence, and where the township's conduct demonstrated bad faith, a subsequent amendment of the zoning ordinance was immaterial and the writ of mandamus should issue. *Keating Int'l Corp. v. Township of Orion,* 236 NW2d 409 (1975).

Mississippi When a landowner sued to cancel a mineral deed on the ground that the conveyance had been fradulently induced, the holder of the deed argued that the action was barred by the statute of limitations. *Held:* An action to recover land must be brought within 10 years after the cause of action accrues. Where the action was not commenced within 10 years after the mineral deed was filed, the action was time barred. *Cooley v. Cooley,* 328 So. 2d 56 (1976).

40.10
Constructive Notice

Florida In 1964, defendant conveyed a home by warranty deed to plaintiff's grantor, who conveyed to plaintiff in 1965. In 1974, the state began highway construction across plaintiff's yard. Plaintiff discovered that in 1950 the state had acquired a highway easement by quitclaim from an owner more remote in the chain of title than defendant. Plaintiff's suit for breach of covenant of warranty was dismissed for its failure to comply with the five-year statute of limitations. The court found that the statute of limitations began to run at the time of defendant's conveyance in 1964. *Held:* The statute of limitations against a grantee in possession who is unaware of the sovereign's undisclosed interest and of his own constructive eviction begins to run when the grantee becomes aware of the sovereign's theretofore undisclosed interest. Recording an otherwise undisclosed interest gives the grantee constructive awareness, but does not foreclose his reliance on the grantor's covenant of warranty. *Powell v. All,* 352 So. 2d 905 (Dist. Ct. App. 1977).

Maryland A substitution of property covered by a deed of trust was recorded but not indexed. The property substituted was in a county different from the one where the original property was located. The county clerk had returned the recorded agreement to the attorney who had handled the original deed of trust, asking him to supply the original document's liber and folio number. The trustors later sold the substituted property to a third party who had no actual notice of the deed of trust lien. The trustees eventually moved to foreclose on the substituted property, claiming that the third party had constructive notice. *Held:* The New Jersey Supreme Court held that the third party had constructive notice. The substitution agreement may have been unindexed, but it had still been recorded. *Frank v. Storer,* 517 A2d 1098 (1986).

Texas Vendor held lien on property subject to payment of a promissory note by the original purchasers. A warranty deed with reference to the lien was properly recorded. The land changed hands twice, and the original purchasers defaulted on the note. Vendor sued to foreclose. *Held:* The subsequent purchasers could not claim the "innocent purchasers" defense, because the warranty deed was within the chain of title and provided legal notice of the lien. *Cooksey v. Sinder,* 682 SW2d 252 (1984).

40.15 Parties Protected

Idaho Assignee of a lease sued lessor for possession of the premises and for damages for loss of profits when lessor ordered assignee to vacate the premises. The lease was for a one-year term and contained 3 one-year renewal options. Lessor consented to a renewal of the lease under the first of the 3 one-year options by assignee. After the one-year option had expired, lessor discovered that assignee was not in compliance with liquor authority regulations and ordered the assignee to vacate the premises. *Held:* Since the one-year option period had expired, the lessor had the right to reenter and take possession. The assignee was not a party to the lease and could not assert a right to the third-year option. The assignee therefore had no right to reenter. *Ringer v. Rice,* 540 P2d 290 (1975).

Washington Defendants, uneducated immigrants, were advised by the regular buyers of their berry crop to sell their farm to them. Some kind of tenancy for defendants was apparently to be arranged. Defendants entered into a land-sale contract with plaintiffs who accepted rent for a time and then notified defendants to vacate. When defendants refused, plaintiffs instituted an unlawful detainer action. Defendants asserted that a constructive trust in their favor should be placed on the land because of the questionable dealings of the buyers. Plaintiffs asserted that they were bona fide purchasers for value, not subject to defendant's defense. *Held:* Plaintiffs are no more than equitable owners under an executory land-sale contract. As such, they are not holders of legal title, and their right to assert a right to possession in an unlawful detainer action derives from whatever rights their vendor has. They are, therefore, not bona fide purchasers. *Snuffin v. Mayo,* 494 P2d 497 (Ct. App. 1972).

Wyoming Lessee of a tract of land sought a declaratory judgment that his lease was valid as against the claim of subsequent purchasers of the lessor's land. The purchasers contended that since the lease was not recorded, they took the estate free of the lease under Wyo. Stat. Ann. § 34-20. *Held:* A subsequent purchaser, in order to take free of unrecorded instruments, must prove that they purchased in good faith, for valuable consideration, and without prior notice. Here, evidence indicated that the purchasers had had actual notice of the lease, and they therefore could not avail themselves of the statute. *Suppe v. Breed,* 504 P2d 1077 (1973).

41.00 TITLE EXAMINATION AND INSURANCE

41.05 Construction of Title Insurance Policies

Missouri After plaintiff purchased a parcel of property, he obtained a $20,000 title insurance policy covering the entire parcel. Plaintiff thereafter discovered that he did not have good title to a part of the parcel. Plaintiff's title company contended that plaintiff was not entitled to recovery on the policy as he had not relied on the title policy when he purchased the property. *Held:* A present owner who insures his own title may, when his title subsequently proves to be defective, recover for the loss of the property he believed he purchased. Therefore, plaintiff was entitled to recovery because his lack of reliance on the title policy when making the purchase had no bearing on his right to a recovery. *Fohn v. Title Ins. Corp.*, 529 SW2d 1 (1975).

New Mexico Plaintiff purchased title insurance from defendant. The policy covered a 116,000-acre tract that plaintiff had purchased. Later, in a suit to quiet title, part of the property was declared to belong to a third party in possession of the property when plaintiff purchased it and whose ownership was recorded. Defendant refused to indemnify plaintiff under the policy of title insurance, and plaintiff then sued for breach of contract. Plaintiff argued that defendant had a duty to competently search the records before issuing a policy. *Held:* The court ruled for defendant, stating that "any duty on the part of defendant to search the records must be expressed in or implied from the policy of title insurance." The court then cited the policy language, which stated: "Nothing contained in this Policy shall be construed as insuring . . . against loss or damage by reason of the rights, titles or occupancies of parties in actual possession of any or all of the property herein described at the effective date of this policy. . . ." Thus, under the policy, defendant had no duty to search the records. *Horn v. Lawyers Title Ins. Corp.*, 557 P2d 206 (1976).

New York Landowner attempted to collect on title insurance policy when access roads to the property were condemned. Insurance company claimed that landowner's attorney knew of the condemnation, which was on file for two years at the county clerk's office, when the policy was taken out. *Held:* The insured would have had a duty to disclose the condemnation to the insurance company only if it had not been a matter of public record. *L. Smirlock Realty Corp. v. Title Guar. Co.*, 418 NE2d 650 (1981).

Pennsylvania Vendor sued buyer for the unsecured balance of purchase price, and buyer counterclaimed for vendor's failure to convey good title. Vendor then sued buyer's title insurer, claiming status as third party beneficiary of insurance policy. *Held:* Title insurer was not liable to vendor, because vendor was not a third party beneficiary. The policy did not indicate that vendor was intended by the contracting parties to be insured or entitled to policy benefits. *Logan v. Gam*, 419 A2d 772 (1980).

Texas Insured homeowners, after suffering a fire, sued to enforce a policy of insurance. Defendant insurer denied liability on the ground, inter alia, that plaintiffs had no insurable interest in the premises. *Held:* The parties had an insurable interest in the premises, even though they were in possession only by virtue of a written contract of purchase. The evidence established an enforceable oral contract of insurance; therefore, the insured were entitled to full recovery of proceeds. *First Preferred Ins. Co. v. Bell*, 587 SW2d (Civ. App. 1979).

41.10 —Risks Covered

California Land sold to purchasers had a recorded water easement, a fact that neither the title insurer's preliminary report nor the insurance policy itself mentioned. The policy did have a standard clause excluding loss or damage from water rights, claims, or title to water. Purchasers claimed damages under the policy when the easement holder moved to implement the easement. *Held:* The purchasers had a claim under the policy, since it was structured to give the impression that it insured against all easements of record. The purchasers also had a claim for negligence. *White v. Western Title Ins. Co.,* 710 P2d 309 (1985).

Colorado Plaintiff purchased title insurance from defendant in 1967. The policy was to protect plaintiff from all defects, liens, or encumbrances on the property insured. However, there was no coverage for "taxes and assessments not yet due." In 1969 and 1970, plaintiff was assessed for ad valorem district taxes totaling $4,407. Plaintiff sued defendant to recover damages for the diminution in value to his property and for any future district taxes. *Held:* The taxes were not liens against the property. The mere prospect of taxes in the future was not a lien, defect, or encumbrance as of the date of the issuance of the policy. While the value of the property is affected by the taxes, there is no effect on the title to the property or its marketability. *Edwards v. St. Paul Title Ins. Co.,* 563 P2d 979 (Ct. App. 1977).

New Jersey An estate's trustee, an attorney, used funds of the estate to invest in real estate. The trustee believed he was entitled to do this because the title insurer had told the trustee's secretary over the phone that the trust instrument gave the trustee the authority to invest in real estate. The estate's beneficiaries successfully sued him on the theory that he had no such authority. The trustee thereafter sued the title insurer, arguing that his incapacity to invest in real estate made the title unmarketable, and so covered by the insurance. He also argued that the insurer was estopped from denying liability, because the trustee had relied detrimentally on the insurer's advice. *Held:* The title was marketable, because it was without any defect. The trustee could not raise an estoppel against the insurer, because the trustee had had no right to rely on an ambiguous oral message relayed by a nonlawyer. *Keown v. West Jersey Title & Guaranty Co.,* 390 A2d 715 (1978).

Oregon Plaintiffs purchased a contract to buy property from a couple who were getting divorced. The property description in plaintiffs' title insurance policy included the whole tract. Following the divorce, however, the husband received a portion of the property, and plaintiffs acquired only the portion conveyed by the wife. A suit in ejectment was filed, and the title insurer refused to defend on the strength of a clause relieving it of liability in cases of title defects created by the insured. *Held:* A title insurer may not escape its obligation solely because the insured were innocent parties to a mutual mistake. Moreover, plaintiffs' actions did not create the adverse interest of the husband and therefore, by its terms, the nonliability clause did not apply. *Polsfoot v. Transamerica Title Ins. Co.,* 614 P2d 1173 (1980).

Washington Former part owner of property conveyed his interest to the other owners, but made an agreement with them for part of the proceeds of any sale of the property within his lifetime. Successor in interest to the property by inheritance received a preliminary report from the title insurer that failed to disclose this agreement. After the property was sold, the successor in interest was forced to pay part of the proceeds to the former part owner. The successor in interest then sued the title insurance company for indemnification. *Held:* The agreement in question was not a defect because it did not affect the title, and so the insurer had no duty to indemnify the successor in interest. *Klickman v. Title Guar. Co.,* 716 P2d 840 (1986).

41.15
—Exceptions From Coverage

Maryland Agent of purchaser converted money for purchase of real estate to his own use. The title insurance binder in effect excepted a vendor's lien from coverage by stating that the insured was obligated to pay the full consideration to the seller. A dispute arose as to whether the title insurance company was required to make payment. *Held:* Because of the vendor's lien exception, the title insurance company was not required to pay for the conversion. The parties were free to make their own agreement, within constitutional and statutory limits. *District-Realty Title Ins. Corp. v. Jack Spicer Real Estate, Inc.,* 373 A2d 952 (1977).

Missouri Property owner obtained a title insurance policy that did not cover defects, liens, encumbrances, and adverse claims known to the insured and not shown by the public records. When the insured attempted to have a sign removed from his property, he discovered that the sign's owner had valid title to the half-acre portion of property on which the sign was located. The insurance company refused to compensate the policy holder for his loss, alleging that the effectiveness of their policy was dependent on the written disclosure of the sign's existence. *Held:* The policy did not require written disclosure of the sign's presence. While the insured was aware of the signs, it was unreasonable to equate their presence with knowledge of a claim of title not reflected in public records. Therefore, the insured was entitled to recovery, as he had complied with the policy's requirements. *Fohn v. Title Ins. Corp.,* 529 SW2d 1 (1975).

New York A title insurance policy issued to plaintiff noted the existence of tax liens but did not specifically note or except an in rem proceeding to foreclose them. When the city foreclosed on the property, plaintiff sued the title insurance company for failing to disclose the pending in rem procedure. The title insurer moved for summary judgment, but an appeals court held that the insurer was not entitled to summary judgment. *Held:* For the insurer. The in rem proceeding on which the plaintiff's claim was based was not a separate incumbrance from the tax liens to which the defendant title insurance company had duly excepted. *Heidi Assocs. v. Lawyers Title Ins. Co.,* 495 NE2d 351 (1986).

Wisconsin Cobeneficiary of a fire insurance policy burned the property after being ordered to vacate the premises when the other beneficiary divorced him. The innocent beneficiary attempted to collect on the policy. *Held:* The innocent beneficiary could collect the proceeds, since she had a reasonable expectation that her interest would be protected. The court chose to avoid imputing the guilt of an arsonist to the innocent co-insured. *Hedtcke v. Sentry Ins. Co.,* 326 NW2d 727 (1982).

41.20
Responsibilities of Insurer

8th Circuit In researching title for land on which plaintiff wished to build a restaurant, title insurance company overlooked a covenant that would restrict such construction. The policy, which was issued under a priority service agreement between plaintiff and the insurer, had an integration clause limiting plaintiff's remedy to that set forth in the policy. Plaintiff, however, sued the insurer for consequential damages. *Held:* The integration clause in the policy did not supercede the remedy provisions of the priority service agreement. In addition, since the suit was in tort rather than contract, the insurer need not have "tacitly agreed" to be responsible for consequential damages in order to be liable for them. *Red Lobster Inns of Am., Inc. v. Lawyers Title Ins. Corp.*, 656 F2d 381 (1981).

Florida Buyer of land took out a mortgage with a bank and relied on the bank's law firm to investigate title. After closing, but prior to recording the title, the Internal Revenue Service (IRS) filed a lien against the land. The buyer then sued the bank's law firm for the allegedly faulty title search. *Held:* The law firm is not liable. The law firm's obligation was to its client, the builder, not to the buyer. The fact that the buyer relied on the law firm's expertise does not create a duty to him. *Amey, Inc. v. Henderson, Franklin, Starnes & Holt,* 367 So. 2d 633 (1979).

Florida Prior to a tax sale, a county tax collector gave one of the bidders an abstract of title, which failed to note an interest held by third persons in the property. After the bidder had successfully purchased the property, he discovered the error. He then sued both the tax collector and his title insurance company, which had prepared the abstract, alleging that he had relied on the information in the abstract in submitting his bid. *Held:* The suit against the tax collector was dismissed; the suit against the title insurance company was remanded. The tax collector did not proximately cause the injury, since it did not prepare the abstract. However, the title insurance company, which did prepare the abstract, may be liable for negligence if it is shown that the bidder relied on the abstract. *Kovaleski v. Tallahassee Title Co.*, 363 So. 2d 1156 (1978).

Montana Plaintiff acquired land crossed by irrigation ditches. Neighbors had easements to come on the land to maintain the ditches. Plaintiff bought title insurance from two companies, whose title search revealed a 20-year-old deed that recited only that the conveyance was made "subject to rights established by irrigation ditch." It was not clear when plaintiff learned of the easements. Plaintiff sued the title insurance companies when they refused to defend him in a suit brought by the neighbors to enforce their easements. *Held:* Plaintiff had a right to rely on the title report, and the title insurance companies should have defended him. *Lipinski v. Title Ins. Co.,* 655 P2d 970 (1982).

North Carolina The tenant held a 60-year lease on an undeveloped parcel of land, which lease included a clause for subordination of the title to any mortgage on the land to secure financing for construction and improvements. When the tenant obtained a loan commitment, the landlords executed a subordination agreement "for the purpose of erecting certain improvements." After the lender had secured title insurance, it authorized the release of a large portion of the loan to the tenant. When the tenant failed to start construction, the lender brought foreclosure proceedings against the landlord. The court ruled that the subordination agreement was void, and the lender then sued the title insurance company. *Held:* The lender may not recover. Although the subordination agreement was valid on the date when the insurance policy was issued, it became invalid when the tenant misappropriated the funds. The insurance company is not obligated to protect the lender from such misconduct. *National Mortgage Corp. v. American Title Ins. Co.,* 261 SE2d 844 (1980).

Texas Plaintiff mortgage investor brought suit against title insurer after discovering that the binder and an information letter prepared by insurer failed to disclose certain deed restrictions on mortgage property. *Held:* Judgment for title insurer affirmed. Plaintiff was party to a joint venture, and could not assert negligent misrepresentation where another party to the venture received information on the existence of restrictions prior to closing. The knowledge of one party was imputed to the others, thereby precluding reliance on the original binder and information letter. *Great Am. Mortgage Inv. v. Louisville Title Ins. Co.,* 597 SW2d 425 (Civ. App. 1980).

Texas Sellers conveyed land to buyer with the provision that if there was any residential subdivision of the property, the buyers would convey lots to the sellers. When the buyers had financial difficulty, they arranged for a loan. The lender obtained title insurance from a title company. In examining the title to determine its insurability, the title company discovered the seller's claim for ten lots. Buyers went bankrupt and lender foreclosed. Sellers claimed vested title to 10 lots. They argued that the title company, in conducting the investigation of title, was the agent of the lender; therefore, the lending company had constructive notice of their claim. *Held:* The sellers had no right to title. The title company was not the agent of the loan company when examining title prior to insuring the land; therefore, notice of the sellers' claim cannot be imputed to the lender company. *Tamburine v. Center Sav. Ass'n,* 583 SW2d 942 (Civ. App. 1979).

Washington Plaintiffs contracted with defendant to insure title to property against defects and encumbrances, with certain specified exceptions, including "right of way for existing roads." Plaintiffs were aware of a conspicuous county road across the property, but the policy did not identify that road. *Held:* Title insurance involves search and disclosure in Washington and so there is a duty to conduct a reasonable search. A policy holder has a reasonable expectation of being advised of such impediments even if he knows or should know of them. *Shotwell v. Transamerica Title Ins. Co.,* 558 P2d 1359 (Ct. App. 1976), aff'd, 588 P2d 208 (1978).

41.25 Subrogation

Indiana In an initial title insurance commitment to the seller, the insurer excepted part of the property that had been sold to another party but failed to include the exception in the final commitment. After the sale, the insurer discovered the error and asked the seller to reimburse the buyer for overpayment, without result. The insurer finally made the reimbursement itself, despite the fact that buyer had made no demand. The insurer then sued the seller under a theory of equitable subrogation. *Held:* The insurer was not entitled to subrogation, primarily because the error was its own. Also, the buyer might have sued the insurer, and the reimbursement could be considered a settlement. *Lawyers Title Ins. Corp. v. Capp,* 369 NE2d 672 (Ct. App. 1977).

Minnesota Owner of a substandard lot applied for a variance and a conditional use permit to allow construction of a single-family dwelling in a shorelands district. When the county board of adjustment issued a building permit, the owner of adjacent lot appealed to county board for a temporary restraining order on the construction. The county board found that appellant's use would be injurious to property values in the immediate vicinity and would not comply with sewage disposal statutes. *Held:* Appellant was not entitled to exemption from zoning ordinance where his lot and adjacent lot were not in separate ownership when the ordinance was adopted. Thus, appellant could have complied with the lot-size requirements at that time. In denying a conditional use permit and variance, the county board was furthering the purposes of county and state shorelands policy. The board had based its action on substantial evidence regarding the proposed sewage disposal system and did not act arbitrarily. Denial of the variance was affirmed. *Dedering v. Johnson,* 239 NW2d 913 (1976).

New Mexico In extending title insurance in favor of a mortgagee to property that had an IRS lien on it, title insurance company negligently failed to except the lien. When the IRS foreclosed, the title insurance company satisfied the lien and then claimed the right of subrogation under the policy. *Held:* The insurer's negligence precluded any right of subrogation. *US Life Title Ins. Co. v. Romero,* 652 P2d 249 (Ct. App. 1982).

41.30 Statutory Regulation

Iowa Nationally known title company launched an attack upon an Iowa statute that forbade the insurance of real estate titles. Instead of title insurance, lawyers' abstracts, which are transferred from owner to owner or from lender to lender, are used to protect titles. The title company charged that the statute violated the commerce, due process, and equal protection clauses of the U.S. Constitution. In appealing an adverse decision, the title company encountered staunch opposition from both the state bar association and the state land title association. *Held:* The statute is valid and all of the title company's claims were dismissed. The court noted possible abuses that would arise if title insurance were allowed, such as excessive premiums. Furthermore, since title insurance is different from other types of insurance, the state was not acting improperly in creating a separate and distinct classification for such insurance. Thus, no constitutional infirmities exist in the statute. *Chicago Title Ins. Co. v. Huff,* 256 NW2d 17 (1977).

Wyoming Title company sued certain individuals engaged in the business of preparing "photo transcripts of the records," claiming that these individuals were in the business of abstracting and were therefore in violation of the requirements of the Wyoming regulatory statute requiring the use of certain specified equipment and the filing of a bond. *Held:* The preparation of photographic reproductions of the entire instruments comprising the chain of title did not constitute "abstracts of title" within the meaning of the Wyoming regulatory statute. *Title Guar. Co. v. Belt d/b/a/ Petroleum Title Serv.,* 539 P2d 357 (1975).

42.00 LITIGATION TO ESTABLISH TITLE

42.05 Ejectment Action

Illinois An owner who inherited property long held by his father discovered for the first time that a city storm drain ran under it. The owner wanted it removed, but the city claimed it had had his father's permission to lay the drain. The owner sued in ejectment. *Held:* The owner could sue for ejectment despite the fact the entry had occurred before he acquired title. The statute did not say otherwise, and the owner had acquired all his predecessor's rights, including any right his predecessor might have had to sue for ejectment. The action was not time-barred, because a 20-year statute of limitations applies to ejectment claims. Finally, the city could not claim adverse possession, since the presence of a hidden underground drain could hardly be considered "open and notorious." *Rosenthal v. City of Crystal Lake,* 525 NE2d 1176 (Ct. App. 1988).

Nebraska Landowner conveyed property to a trust. When landowner defaulted on a promissory note to a bank, the bank succeeded in getting a court to set aside the conveyance as fraudulent, and the property was sold at a judicial sale. Two days later, landowner filed for bankruptcy, but the buyer obtained relief from the automatic bankruptcy stay that would otherwise have invalidated the sale. Then landowner's wife sued for ejectment of the buyer. *Held:* The wife had no title to sustain a petition for ejectment. She was incorrect in claiming that she had an interest in the land arising from her labor, services, materials, and investments in the property. At most, she had a lien, which is not a property interest that would support an action for ejectment. In a suit for ejectment, plaintiff has the burden to prove good title. *Nuttleman v. Julch,* 424 NW2d 333 (1988).

42.10
Action to Quiet Title

U.S. Supreme Court North Dakota brought action under the federal Quiet Title Act of 1972 regarding title to a riverbed within plaintiff's territory. Plaintiff also sought various forms of injunctive and equitable relief. The United States claimed the act's 12-year statute of limitation had run, because North Dakota had more than 12 years' notice of the United States' claim. *Held:* The act is an exclusive remedy for actions to challenge federal title to real estate. However, the claim under the act was time-barred. *Block v. North Dakota ex rel. Bd. of Univ. & School Lands,* 461 US 273 (1983).

Florida A city claimed some land on the strength of a 1919 statute that gave the city all the land in the area under navigable rivers. The land had been under water in 1919, but another chain of title to it went back to the last century and forward to 1944, when respondents' deed was recorded. Respondents argued that the city's claim was barred by the Marketable Record Title Act, which required unrecorded claimants to record their claim within six months of the law's effective date in 1941. *Held:* The city's claim was void. The Marketable Record Title Act was constitutional because it gave claimants a reasonable opportunity to file a claim. Further, although the act exempted the claims of the state and its agencies, this exemption did not include municipalities. *City of Miami v. St. Joe Paper Co.,* 364 So. 2d 439 (1978).

Florida In 1937, a widow conveyed a homestead property to herself and her son. Five years later, they conveyed it to plaintiff. In 1971, the widow's other three children filed record notice of their claims each to a vested, undivided one-quarter interest in remainder in the homestead lands that had existed at their father's death in 1935, subject only to the mother's life estate. Plaintiff brought suit to quiet title. *Held:* The 1937 deed was a valid "root of title" upon which could be established a marketable record title. The remainder interests of the children were not within any exception to the Marketable Record Title Act, which extinguished all interests in the estate predating the "root of title." *ITT Rayonier, Inc. v. Wadsworth,* 346 So. 2d 1004 (1977).

New Mexico Plaintiff brought suit to quiet title to three lots, claiming title through a 1974 deed. In 1964, the county treasurer conveyed the lots to the state for delinquent taxes of 1960. Neither plaintiff nor anyone in his chain of title made application to repurchase the property, and, in 1970, defendant applied to repurchase and was deeded the lots. *Held:* Plaintiff had no right in the property, since neither he nor his predecessors in title repurchased the property within the one-year preferential repurchase period, or in advance of defendant, and plaintiff did not contest defendant's deed from the state within the two-year period from the sale. The deed to the state stripped plaintiff of all rights to the lot except the preferential right to repurchase, but since that was not exercised, plaintiff was entitled to no relief. *Jackson v. Hartley,* 564 P2d 992 (1977).

Utah Plaintiff sought damages against defendant in an action to quiet title arising from defendant's refusal to release a security interest. *Held:* Damages are not available in actions to quiet title. *Jack B. Parsons Co. v. Nield,* 751 P2d 1131 (1988).

Utah Former wife of decedent brought suit to quiet title against him and those claiming title to and possession of the property by warranty deed from him. The property had been recorded in the husband's name alone and conveyed by him before the divorce decree was entered. The divorce decree did not vest any title to the property in the former wife. *Held:* Former wife was not entitled to have title to the property quieted in her. The divorce decree did not entitle her to one-half interest in the property, as the court has the discretion to make such orders in relation to property as may be equitable. Nor does state statute (Utah Code Ann. § 74-4-3 (1953)) entitle her to a one-third interest in the property, since that statute applies to a widow's right in the probate proceedings of a deceased husband's estate. As a divorced wife, plaintiff could not be her former husband's widow. *Hamilton v. Hamilton,* 562 P2d 235 (1977).

Wisconsin In 1918, land was sold to a school district, subject to a reversionary clause that would return the property to the seller (or his successors in interest) on repayment of the purchase price, in the event that land were ever used for anything besides school purposes. This reversion, however, was not recorded in any deed subsequent to 1922. In 1979, the land was sold to a municipality to be used for non-school purposes, and plaintiff, the original vendor's successor in interest, sued to regain title. *Held:* Plaintiff's suit was not barred by the provision of Wis. Stat. Ann. § 893.15 (West 1977), which prohibits suits affecting title to real estate based on instruments more than 30 years old, since that statute provides an exception for municipal corporations. *State Historical Soc'y v. Village of Maple Bluff,* 332 NW2d 792 (1983).

Wyoming A survey disclosed that the boundaries of certain adjoining properties did not match those recorded. The landowners affected agreed to move their fences to conform to the recorded lines. One of these landowners, however, having received more land when one neighbor moved his fence back, refused to do the same for the neighbor on the other side of his property. The offended neighbor sued to quiet title to the disputed strip, while the reneging landowner claimed the strip through adverse possession. *Held:* The offended neighbor was entitled to quiet title for equitable reasons, despite the fact the landowner could show adverse possession for the statutory period. An action to quiet title is an equitable remedy, and the landowner had acted inequitably toward his neighbors in light of the agreement they had reached to rectify their boundaries. *Harsha v. Anastos,* 693 P2d 760 (1985).

42.15
Notice of Lis Pendens

3d Circuit Plaintiff filed a notice of lis pendens incident to an action to enforce a lien against real property. Defendant, the owner of the property, challenged the New Jersey statute requiring the filing as an unconstitutional taking. *Held:* While the lis pendens notice is a partial taking, it is not unconstitutional. The state has an interest in preventing later litigation involving innocent purchasers who would otherwise not have been informed of the adverse claims to the property. *Chrysler Corp. v. Fedders Corp.*, 670 F2d 1316 (1982).

U.S. District Court, New York Plaintiff filed notices of lis pendens in two counties where property was located for which plaintiff intended to seek possession in federal court. Property owners in those counties obtained injunctions in state court, enjoining the indexing of the lis pendens notices by the counties in question. Plaintiff sought a counter injunction in federal court. *Held:* The federal court enjoined the state injunctions, holding that all questions relating to the plaintiff's land claims would have to be made in federal court. *Cayuga Indian Nation v. Fox,* 544 F. Supp. 542 (ND 1982).

Connecticut A dispute arose concerning the disposition of partnership property, and plaintiffs filed a notice of lis pendens for the real estate. Defendant attacked the constitutionality of the Connecticut lis pendens statute, arguing that it should have provided for a pre-trial hearing and an option for release from the lien through the substitution of security. *Held:* The Connecticut statute was not unconstitutional, because it did allow for a meaningful hearing, even if the hearing would occur after filing. The harm that might be suffered by defendant before a hearing could occur was minimal, while the potential harm to plaintiffs and the state through prejudgment transfers of property would be substantial. *Williams v. Bartlett,* 457 A2d 290 (1983).

Mississippi As part of a divorce settlement, the wife received the house, with the husband to receive a portion of the proceeds when it was sold. When a sale appeared imminent, the husband brought suit to secure a lien on the property. He filed a notice of lis pendens before filing the complaint, but the notice was not recorded for three days. The wife conveyed the property by warranty deed the day the notice was recorded. *Held:* The filing of the lis pendens notice did not create a lien in the property. Under state law, a lien is not created merely by filing a notice of lis pendens; the notice actually has to be recorded if it is to affect purchasers and encumbrancers. *Aldridge v. Aldridge,* 527 So. 2d 96 (1988).

Oregon When the buyer of an installment purchase land contract defaulted, the seller sued to foreclose. All parties with recorded liens and judgments on the property as of the commencement of the foreclosure action were joined as defendants. Thus, when the court ordered the sale of the property to pay off the seller's judgment, the interests of those other parties were foreclosed, except for the statutory right of redemption. However, three secured junior creditors had acquired interests in the property after the foreclosure action began. Another party bought those interests, and, wanting to redeem the property, intervened in the foreclosure proceedings. *Held:* The party who acquired the interests of the secured junior creditors had the right to redeem. The lis pendens put the unjoined creditors on the same footing as the joined ones: Their interests were foreclosed, but they retained the right of redemption. *Land Assocs. v. Becker,* 656 P2d 927 (1982).

Texas Plaintiff sued to impose a constructive trust on some property, and filed a notice of lis pendens. Defendant, acting under a Texas statute, moved to cancel the notice and instead post a bond in plaintiff's favor. *Held:* Defendant could cancel the notice and post the bond. The statute applied to any suit or action in which a notice of lis pendens has been filed and not, as plaintiff claimed, only to suits to recover money secured by real estate. The court also noted that, while the filing of a notice of lis pendens was privileged, this did not prevent the notice's cancellation. *Ransopher v. Deer Trails, Ltd.*, 647 SW2d 106 (Ct. App. 1983).

PART F
GOVERNMENTAL USE RESTRICTIONS

43.00
ZONING

43.05
Validity of Ordinances and Regulations

California Owners of five acres of unimproved land objected when the town, which wanted to preserve the property as open space, rezoned it. The zoning provided for single-family residential use with no more than one dwelling unit per acre. The owners sued the town for damages in inverse condemnation, alleging that the ordinance had completely destroyed the value of their land. *Held:* The action was dismissed. The owners may challenge the zoning ordinance only by way of declaratory relief or mandamus. They may not sue in inverse condemnation, and therefore convert the excessive use of the eminent domain power into a lawful taking that justifies compensation. *Agins v. Tiburon,* 24 Cal. 3d 266 (1979).

California A property owner discovered that a proposed subdivision on adjacent property had been approved by the county planning department without his notification. He sued the county, seeking to set aside the approval. His suit was dismissed, and he appealed. *Held:* Reversed. Whenever a proposed subdivision affects the rights of a private landowner, the landowner is entitled to reasonable notice and an opportunity to be heard. *Horn v. County of Ventura,* 596 P2d 1134 (1979).

Florida Mortgagee entered into a construction loan agreement providing that if construction ceased for 10 days, mortgagee had the right to enter and complete the project. During the construction period, the project's marketability was detrimentally affected by changes in the zoning ordinances. The mortgagor abandoned the project, and the original building permit expired. After mortgagee foreclosed and purchased the property at the foreclosure sale, the city required it to complete the project in compliance with the new zoning requirements. Mortgagee sued for equitable relief from having to meet those requirements. *Held:* The city was entitled to enforce the new zoning ordinance. Although mortgagee had relied on the original building permit, the city should not be stopped from enforcing the new zoning ordinances. Mortgagee was not merely a lienholder, but had the power to enter and complete the project. It could have requested court permission to extend the building permit or to renew construction earlier to prevent waste. Mortgagee's hardship was self-created by its inaction. *Gross v. City of Rivera Beach,* 367 So. 2d 649 (Dist. Ct. App. 1979).

Illinois Property owner's application to subdivide its land and to build a restaurant on it was refused by the planning board because of a moratorium on new restaurants. When the property owner brought a mandamus action, the board argued, for the first time, that the subdivision was denied because the intent to build two restaurants on one lot violated the one building–one lot ordinance. *Held:* The failure to raise the point at the hearing level prevented the property owner from amending its application or from contesting the objection. At trial, the property owner argued that the ambiguous ordinance did not apply to shopping districts. The trial court's acceptance of this interpretation was not disturbed. *People ex rel. JC Penney v. Village of Oak Lawn,* 349 NE2d 637 (App. Ct. 1976).

Georgia Developers argued that single-family zoning status of land in flood plain was an unconstitutional taking, because the land could not be developed profitably with that status in light of the work needed to make it habitable. *Held:* The zoning classification was confiscatory, since it made the land virtually worthless. *Mayor & Alderman v. Rauers,* 324 SE2d 173 (1985).

Maryland City ordinance provided that a landowner who conveyed a right-of-way to the city for highway construction could develop his remaining land at the density permissible to the entire tract prior to the conveyance. When a developer who conveyed land in accordance with the city's offer proposed construction in excess of ordinary density requirements, the city argued that the action constituted impermissible contract zoning. *Held:* The developers acquired a vested contractual interest derived form their acceptance and would be permitted to build accordingly. Because the ordinance was made applicable to anyone willing to convey land for the purposes specified, it was not contract zoning. *Mayor & City Council v. Crane,* 352 A2d 786 (1976).

Massachusetts Plaintiff claimed that a recodification of zoning laws was irrational. The new law permitted single-family residences on plaintiff's property and, depending on how it was read, required each building to be on a lot of at least either 87,000 or 200,000 square feet. Plaintiff also claimed that the recodification constituted spot zoning. *Held:* The new ordinance was to be read in the most reasonable way (i.e., requiring only the smaller parcels), in which case it was not irrational. Also, plaintiff could not claim that his land was being spot zoned, since the boundaries of the zoning district in which it was located were natural. *Marshall v. Town of Topsfield,* 433 NE2d 1244 (1982).

Massachusetts Town conservation commission denied plaintiff's application for a permit to build a road over marshland adjoining his property pursuant to a local bylaw designed to protect municipal foreshores (area of seashore between high-water and low-water marks) and wetlands. Plaintiff argued that the bylaw was an unlawful zoning ordinance. *Held:* The bylaw was an earth removal enactment, not a zoning law. It had neither the purpose nor the effect of a zoning regulation (e.g., regulation of land use, location of residences and businesses, or regulation of density). The purpose of the bylaw was to protect wetland values (e.g., water supply, groundwater, and flood control), and any effect on land use was incident to this purpose. *Lovequist v. Conservation Comm'n,* 393 NE2d 858 (1979).

Michigan A local zoning ordinance prohibited the construction of any structure within a given distance of the rear of the property. Defendants began to build a gravel tennis court within the setback area, arguing that the court was not a "structure." The city sought an injunction. *Held:* A tennis court is not a "structure" within the meaning of the statute. The word is usually taken to mean "any construction or any production or piece of work artificially built up or composed of parts joined together in some definite manner." *City of Bloomfield Hills v. Ziegelman,* 320 NW2d 49 (1982).

Minnesota Plaintiffs purchased a home on property bordered on one side by a lake and on the other by a road. Subsequent to the construction of the home, a zoning ordinance was enacted that specified minimum front-yard setbacks and rear-yard depths. Homeowners sought to build a detached garage on their property in the area between the road and their home. They claimed that the regulations specifying rear-yard requirements should apply to their planned construction. *Held:* The lakeside was the front yard of the property and the roadside the backyard. Since the property owners built and developed prior to the enactment of the zoning ordinance and considered the lakeside the front yard, and since a restrictive covenant adopted by the original owner identified the roadside as the rear, the zoning ordinance would be applied to those facts. *Girvan v. County of Le Sueur,* 232 NW2d 888 (1975).

New Hampshire Town officials attempted to limit the growth by enacting an ordinance that prohibited the issuance of more than four building permits per year to any one party. A developer sought a fifth permit for a subdivision project, but couldn't get it. The developer then sued the town. *Held:* The developer was entitled to the permit. Although municipalities have the right to control population expansion through detailed zoning plans, controls must be reasonable and nondiscriminatory. In this case, the ordinance was too broad and was, therefore, an invalid exercise of the police power. *Beck v. Town of Raymond,* 394 A2d 847 (1978).

New York Community residents brought action challenging zoning amendments that created a 14- to 20-block special district in the Chinatown section of New York City. The residents contended the amendments were unconstitutional and void because they failed to provide a realistic opportunity for the creation of low- and moderate-income housing. *Held:* The amendments were the product of a well-considered plan that took many factors into consideration, including the needs of Chinatown's low-income residents; and the plan was properly adopted. Further, community residents offered no legal authority holding that an area as small as this district, which was zoned, must contain specific provisions for construction of low-income housing. *Asian Ams. for Equality v. Koch,* 514 NYS2d 939 (App. Div. 1987).

Oklahoma State legislature passed laws authorizing the acquisition of property for use as community rehabilitation centers. The attorney general thereupon requested the state supreme court to assume jurisdiction to determine whether it was necessary for the state to submit its plans to the local city planning commission for approval of the centers. *Held:* Submission of plans is not necessary here. The sovereign is bound by a statute only when the statute expressly includes it; the general zoning statute does not do so. Furthermore, later specific statutes control earlier general statutes. In this instance, the laws authorizing land acquisition are subsequent to the zoning statute requiring plan submission and therefore control to the extent of any inconsistency. The rehabilitation of prisoners in an essential governmental function and is necessary for the good of the people. A local planning commission cannot be permitted an opportunity to thwart legislative goals by withholding approval of the state plans. *In re Suntide Inn Motel,* 563 P2d 125 (1977).

South Carolina Plaintiff challenged an amendment to the city's zoning ordinance extending a Class P–1 professional district into the surrounding Class R–12 residential district. Plaintiff argued that the amendment was arbitrary and unreasonable and constituted impermissible spot zoning. *Held:* The validity of the amendment to the zoning ordinance was affirmed. The Class P–1 district contained doctors' offices and a hospital that had recently been rebuilt and expanded to meet the needs of the public. The continued extension of the district was required for the hospital's related medical facilities. The amendment was deliberate, in full compliance with the zoning statute, and in the public interest. *Lurey v. City of Laurens,* 217 SE2d 226 (1975).

South Dakota Plaintiff property owners objected to defendant's expansion of his motel on property adjacent to their residence. A city ordinance, accompanied by an official zoning map, prohibited the expansion. The city building inspector originally issued defendant a building permit; however, after defendant began construction, he was informed that construction was in violation of zoning restrictions. Adjacent property owners sought an injunction prohibiting the commercial buildings, and defendant countered that the failure of the zoning commission to publish the map invalidated the city zoning ordinance. *Held:* The zoning ordinance was valid. In the absence of a statute providing otherwise, maps to an ordinance need not be published if the ordinance refers to the map, its place of filing, and its availability for public inspection. In this case, the map was displayed in the city council's meeting room and was available for inspection. When an ordinance is valid for all other present purposes, the failure to separately publish an official zoning map does not render it invalid, so long as the map is accessible to the public. *Crothy v. City of Deadwood,* 440 NW2d 525 (1989).

Virginia County board of supervisors adopted ordinance prohibiting the operation of privately owned debris landfills. Before the ordinance was adopted, plaintiffs applied for a permit to operate a debris landfill on their property. They challenged the validity of the ordinance. *Held:* County board of supervisors had the authority to enact the ordinance; state law authorizes the governing body of a locality to prohibit a specified land use. The Virginia Waste Management Act did not preempt the field of waste management regulation. The act displayed a legislative intent to permit active local involvement in waste management regulation. *Resource Conservation Management, Inc. v. Board of Supervisors,* 380 SE2d 879 (1989).

Washington Plaintiff landowners challenged approval of a shopping center project to be located on adjoining property. They sought to establish that the environmental impact statements were deficient and that the contemporaneous adoption of both a comprehensive plan and specific zoning regulations was improper. *Held:* The environmental impact statement prepared by local authorities was inadequate because it failed to consider the socio-economic effect of the shopping center and because it did not consider alternative sites. The comprehensive plan is only advisory and not binding under state law. As a result, zoning regulations that deviate from the comprehensive plan cannot be challenged on that basis alone. *Barrie v. Kitsap County,* 613 P2d 1148 (1980).

Wisconsin Owners of neighboring land challenged rezoning on the ground that the city zoning ordinance did not comply with state statutory requirements, because the city failed to adopt a comprehensive plan. Wis. Stat. § 62.23(7)(c) required that zoning regulations "be made in accordance with a comprehensive plan." The term "comprehensive plan" was not defined in the statutes. The trial court held that a formal comprehensive plan was not required for the enactment of a valid zoning ordinance. *Held:* Affirmed. Following rulings in other states that had adopted the Standard Zoning Enabling Act, the court held that a zoning ordinance itself may satisfy the requirement that zoning be in accordance with a comprehensive plan. *Bell v. City of Elkhorn,* 364 NW2d 144 (1985).

43.10 Constitutional Challenges

U.S. Supreme Court Commuters challenged the constitutionality of a county zoning ordinance that provided for issuance of parking permits only to residents and others in restricted areas and made unauthorized parking in such areas a misdemeanor. The state supreme court agreed with the commuters that the equal protection clause of the Fourteenth Amendment was violated. *Held:* The ordinance is constitutional. The equal protection clause demands only that distinctions between residents and nonresidents rationally promote the objectives of the ordinance. There is no prohibition against the social and environmental objectives of an ordinance like this, nor are all distinctions differentiating resident from resident necessarily invidious. *Arlington County Bd. v. Richards,* 434 US 5 (1977).

5th Circuit Plaintiffs owned property that was zoned to permit commercial use, including the operation of fast-food restaurants. A fast-food franchise company agreed to buy plaintiff's property for use as a restaurant consistent with existing zoning regulations. Upon announcement of the sale, the city council adopted an ordinance suspending issuance of permits for fast-food restaurants for one year to study the impact on land use in the area. The restaurant franchise then terminated its contract, and plaintiffs sued for an injunction against enforcement of the ordinance. *Held:* For the city. There was no procedural due process violation, since the city provided notice, a hearing, and an opportunity for plaintiffs to argue against adoption of the moratorium ordinance. There was sufficient showing that the ordinance was reasonably related to a valid governmental purpose, and plaintiffs were not deprived of property by the temporary suspension of the right to use land in a particular way. *Schafer v. New Orleans,* 743 F2d 1086 (1984).

5th Circuit Plaintiffs purchased a professional building and set it up for obstetric and gynecological services including legal abortion services. The building was in an area zoned "highway business district." Professional office uses were included in a list of permitted uses promulgated by the city. The city commission refused to grant plaintiffs an occupational license, despite a favorable recommendation by the zoning board. The reasons for denying the permit included the proximity of single-family residences, a church, and a general concern that the facility would pose a threat to the health and welfare of area citizens. *Held:* The denial of an occupational license to plaintiffs placed a significant burden on a woman's abortion decision by forestalling the availability of an abortion clinic in the city indefinitely and by discouraging any future efforts by other enterprises to locate an abortion facility in the city. The court found no legitimate basis for any of the city's objections; they were irrelevant to the declared commercial and professional purposes of the highway business district and were not listed in the city's own code as grounds for denial of an occupational permit. *Deerfield Medical Center v. City of Deerfield Beach,* 661 F2d 328 (1981).

7th Circuit City property owners and the board of realtors sought a preliminary injunction against the newly enacted Chicago Residential Landlord and Tenant Ordinance. *Held:* Motion denied. The ordinance did not destroy contract rights and bargained-for expectations created prior to its effective date. Landlords could have expected further regulation and the ordinance was supported by legitimate public purposes. The ordinance did not infringe procedural due process by delegating to tenants the power to redress their own repair grievances by withholding rent; it merely shifted some bargaining power to tenants. The ordinance was not impermissibly vague in its provisions for tenants' rights in case of a landlord's material noncompliance with a lease, in labeling a landlord's entry into leased premises as unlawful if accomplished in an unreasonable manner, or in establishing a presumption of retaliatory eviction. The ordinance was not irrational in its adjustment of the benefits and burdens of economic life, nor did it deny equal protection in exempting owner-occupied rental dwellings of six units or fewer. *Chicago Bd. of Realtors v. City of Chicago,* 819 F2d 732 (1987).

11th Circuit The city planning commission approved plaintiffs' building plans and issued a building permit to them for the construction of the first apartment complex in the city. In response to community opposition, the city council passed an ordinance prohibiting all apartment construction in the city after plaintiffs had already begun preparatory work on the complex. *Held:* The city acted unconstitutionally in enacting the ordinance and plaintiffs were entitled to damages. Plaintiffs held a validly issued building permit, which the ordinance attempted to revoke without rational justification. Thus, the ordinance was a confiscatory measure, arbitrarily and capriciously implemented, and violated plaintiffs' Fourteenth Amendment rights. *Wheeler v. City of Pleasant Grove,* 746 F2d 1437 (1984), applying the law of the case as set forth at 664 F2d 99 (5th Cir. 1981), cert. denied, 456 US 973 (1982).

California City adopted a rent control article in its city charter that required a landlord to obtain a permit before demolishing an apartment building. The article provided that a demolition permit would be denied for rental units that the landlord did not intend to replace unless removal of the units would not adversely affect the housing supply. One landlord challenged the ordinance on the ground that the city was forcing him to pursue the occupation of a landlord against his will. *Held:* While the Thirteenth Amendment prohibition of involuntary servitude limits the right of the state to force an individual to pursue a particular career, plaintiff was not forced to serve personally as a landlord. Rather, he could delegate responsibility to a property manager, sell the property, or withhold rental units from the market as they became vacant. Since the rental property offered plaintiff a fair return on his investment, the article imposed only an "indirect and minimal" burden on his liberty. *Nash v. City of Santa Monica,* 688 P2d 894 (1984).

District of Columbia Apartment complex owners, seeking to convert complex into condominium, challenged the city's Rental Housing Conversion and Sale Act, which prohibited condominium conversions unless 50 percent of the eligible tenants consent. *Held:* The tenant consent requirement was valid and did not constitute an improper delegation of legislative authority. When the city council made the finding that condominium conversion is contrary to the public interest and should be proscribed, it could constitutionally allow tenants, the prime beneficiaries of the proscription, to waive the act's benefits. Although the case was remanded to allow owners to present evidence concerning their uncompensated taking claim, the court asserted that proving the claim would be difficult. A land use regulation effects a taking only if it denies the owner any economically viable use for the property; diminution in property value, standing alone, does not amount to a taking. *Hornstein v. Barry,* 560 A2d 530 (Ct. App. 1989).

Maine Town ordinance prohibiting mobile homes outside of licensed mobile home parks contained a grandfather clause that exempted occupied mobile homes existing within the town. Plaintiffs, denied a permit to move their mobile home from another town to land they owned in defendant town, outside a mobile home park, sued the town. The trial court granted injunctive relief on the ground that the breadth of the grandfather clause rendered the ordinance unconstitutional. Under the interpretation of the clause by town officials, owners of mobile homes existing in town before the ordinance took effect had broad rights to move, sell or replace their mobile homes. *Held:* The state supreme court adopted a narrower interpretation of the grandfather clause, under which existing mobile homes could not be moved to another lot within town. A broader interpretation would have defeated the purpose of the ordinance, which was to protect the town's aesthetic character and property values. The narrower interpretation enabled the ordinance to meet these legitimate governmental concerns, while avoiding the danger of unconstitutionality. *Stewart v. Inhabitants of Durham,* 451 A2d 308 (1982).

Maryland Owner of a mobile home park restricted the size, quality, and type of mobile home that could be placed or retained after resale of the park. Several mobile home owners brought suit under the state's Mobile Home Park Act, which provides that a park owner cannot prevent the sale of a home already in the park or require it to be removed on resale. The park owner argued that the act was unconstitutional since it permanently deprived him of the right to use his land other than for a mobile home park. *Held:* The act is not unconstitutional. The park owner has not been permanently deprived of his property since he can terminate the landlord-tenant relationship by methods other than eviction; therefore, there has been no unconstitutional "taking." *Cider Barrel Mobile Home Court v. Fader,* 414 A2d 1246 (1980).

Massachusetts Owners rented an eight-bedroom house to eight unrelated tenants, all of whom signed a single standard lease containing an addendum that allowed the owners to give any one tenant 30 days' notice to vacate without affecting the tenancy of the rest. The owners were convicted of violating a zoning ordinance that prohibited the design, arrangement, construction, or use of a building in a single residence district for any purpose other than a dwelling for one family. *Held:* The ordinance was not unconstitutionally vague. It was unnecessary to define the term "one family" because the use of a house by eight unrelated adults with no evidence at all of communal living did not, when taken together with the lease addendum, fall within any reasonable judicial construction of the term "one family." *Commonwealth v. Jaffe,* 494 NE2d 1342 (1986).

Michigan City sued the owner of a mobile

home who located the home on a tract of land he owned. The local zoning ordinance restricted mobile homes to designated parks. The location of a mobile home outside a mobile home park was a nuisance per se. The owner argued the ordinance was arbitrary and vague, and that it unconstitutionally restricted a proper land use. *Held:* The ordinance was facially invalid. The per se exclusion of mobile homes not located in mobile home parks had no reasonable basis under the police power. Rather, a proper ordinance would ensure that such homes met the standards of site-built housing. *Robinson Township v. Knoll,* 302 NW2d 146 (1981).

New Jersey A borough adopted a zoning ordinance providing that, in certain residential districts, every one-family dwelling must have a minimum of two off-street parking spaces, one of which must be a garage. When plaintiff converted his attached garage, he was denied a variance from the garage requirement and so could not obtain a certificate of occupancy. Plaintiff sued, arguing that the ordinance was unconstitutional because it imposed excessive restrictions on property use. *Held:* The ordinance was constitutional. In the context of municipal land-use regulation, attention could be given to architectural structure as well as to uses of property. The statute conferring zoning power on municipalities authorized the establishment of reasonable standards for the "provision of adequate physical improvements including, but not limited to, off-street parking" for the purpose of promoting "the free flow of traffic and avoiding congestion." Although some garages would be put to other uses, many garages would house parked cars. Therefore, it was at least debatable that the means chosen by the zoning authorities to reduce street clutter would achieve their purpose. *Zilinsky v. Zoning Bd. of Adjustment,* 521 A2d 841 (1987).

New Jersey The Department of Environmental Protection (DEP) issued a permit to construct an apartment complex in a coastal area with a fair share housing condition of 10 percent low-income and 10 percent moderate-income housing. DEP asserted authority to impose such a condition under the state's Coastal Area Facility Review Act. Developer contended that the act was a purely environmental statute that could not be used to achieve fair housing goals. *Held:* DEP had the authority under the act to impose fair share housing conditions to create housing for the poor. Although the act's primary purpose is to protect coastal areas, it was also designed to ensure that coastal areas be dedicated to uses in furtherance of public health, safety, and welfare. The percentage requirements were not arbitrary or unreasonable. Nor was the fair share housing condition an unconstitutional taking; there was no evidence that the condition would prevent developer from realizing a reasonable rate of return. *In re Egg Harbor Assocs. (Bayshore Center),* 464 A2d 1115 (1983).

New York Lessors rented their four-bedroom house to four unrelated men in violation of a town ordinance that placed the house in a one-family housing zone. The ordinance defined "family" as any number of persons related by blood, marriage, or legal adoption, or any two persons 62 years of age or over. *Held:* The ordinance was a deprivation of property without due process. To be a valid exercise of police power, the ordinance must (1) further a legitimate governmental purpose and (2) have a reasonable relation between the end sought and the means used. The ordinance was enacted to further legitimate governmental purposes, including preservation of single-family neighborhoods, reduction of traffic and population, and prevention of noise. However, rather than limiting the number of occupants in a dwelling of a given type, the ordinance restricted occupancy based on genetic and legal relationships among occupants. The ordinance was both underinclusive, in allowing extremely large families, and overinclusive, in prohibiting young unmarried couples from living together in a one-family house. *McMinn v. Town of Oyster Bay,* 66 NY2d 544, 488 NE2d 1240, 498 NYS2d 128 (1985).

New York Town established a "Golden Age Residential District" to enable private developers to build multi-family housing for senior citizens. Plaintiffs sought to occupy housing in the district. They met the age requirement but did not meet the statutory requirement of at least one-year's legal residence in the town at the time of application. *Held:* The residence requirement was unconstitutional. Although zoning ordinances generally are limited to regulating and restricting the uses of property, rather than its users, ordinances that create special residence districts for senior citizens similar to the Golden Age Residential District are a special case. Because affordable housing for the elderly was not generally available within the town, plaintiffs and other similarly situated nonresident senior citizens would be effectively prevented from moving there if they could not obtain housing in a Golden Age Residential District. The ordinances were unconstitutional because they were enacted with an exclusionary purpose and ignored regional needs for housing for the elderly. *Allen v. Town of N. Hempstead,* 478 NYS2d 919 (1984).

North Carolina Plaintiff, an automobile dealership located beside a major thoroughfare, displayed a blimp with the name of the dealership printed in large red letters. The city enacted a zoning ordinance prohibiting the display of "windblown signs," such as blimps, except with a temporary permit, and then only for a maximum of 30 days. Permits were granted only for special events, i.e., activities not part of daily operations. Plaintiff challenged the ordinance on statutory and constitutional grounds. *Held:* The ordinance was valid. Regulations could be upheld on constitutional and statutory grounds if their aesthetic purpose outweighed the burden imposed on the private property owner. Plaintiff's failure to produce evidence of a correlation between sales and display of the blimp indicated that any burdens imposed by the statute were negligible. *Goodman Toyota, Inc. v. City of Raleigh,* 306 SE2d 192 (Ct. App. 1983).

Ohio Landowners of riverfront property located on a floodplain made a constitutional challenge to the city's rezoning of the property to a more restrictive riverfront classification. *Held:* The ordinance as applied to owners' land was unconstitutional. It denied them the economically viable use of their land without substantially advancing a legitimate government interest. Because the property was located on a floodplain, the uses permitted by the ordinance were not viable, because compliance with floodplain requirements would dramatically increase the construction costs. In addition, the city's stated goals of new riverfront business development and foreign trade were not achieved by the rezoning. *Karches v. City of Cincinnati,* 526 NE2d 1350 (1988).

Oklahoma Plaintiff built a carport without obtaining a city permit. The city later notified plaintiff that the carport did not comply with the zoning ordinance. Plaintiff applied for a variance, which was granted. The city appealed. *Held:* The ordinance was constitutional; the word "building" in the ordinance included the carport and was not unconstitutionally vague. Plaintiff was given fair warning that she was prohibited from constructing the carport. Plaintiff failed to prove that denial of the variance would cause her unnecessary hardship and that its grant would not cause substantial detriment to the public good. *In re Schrader,* 660 P2d 135 (1983).

Pennsylvania Landowners who sought to develop their land challenged the total prohibition of multi-family dwellings. *Held:* Where a zoning ordinance totally prohibits a legitimate use, the burden shifts to the municipality to establish that the prohibition promotes public health, safety, morals, and general welfare. Because the township failed to show that the total exclusion of apartments served a legitimate public purpose, the zoning ordinance was unconstitutional insofar as it failed to provide for apartments or other forms of multi-family housing. *Fernley v. Board of Supervisors,* 502 A2d 583 (1985).

Washington City enacted a zoning law that required a large percentage of privately owned lots be retained in, or restored to, a natural state. A group of landowners sued to have the ordinance declared unconstitutional. *Held:* The ordinance was invalid and constituted a taking of property without just compensation. While the ordinance advanced several legitimate public interests, it deprived some landowners of all profitable use of a substantial portion of their land. It would be inequitable to permit the city to preserve greenbelts without paying for the land taking under the guise of a zoning regulation. *Allingham v. City of Seattle,* 749 P2d 160, modified on other grounds, 757 P2d 533 (1988).

43.15 —First Amendment Issues

U.S. Supreme Court A city passed an ordinance prohibiting adult motion picture theatres from locating within 1,000 feet of any residential zone, single- or multiple-family dwelling, church, park, or school. Plaintiffs purchased two theaters in the city with the intention of exhibiting adult films and brought suit to challenge the ordinance's constitutionality. *Held:* The ordinance was constitutional. It served the valid governmental purpose of regulating the secondary effects of adult theaters on the surrounding community. Because the predominant motive was legitimate, the ordinance was not unconstitutional simply because restriction of certain types of free expression might have been another motivating factor in its passage. Plaintiffs were not effectively denied the opportunity to operate adult theaters in the city because of the lack of "commercially viable" adult theater sites. More than 5 percent of the city's entire land area was left open to their use under the ordinance. *City of Renton v. Playtime Theatres, Inc.,* 475 US 41, reh'g denied, 475 US 1132 (1986).

U.S. Supreme Court City enacted an ordinance restricting outdoor advertising. The ordinance permitted on-site commercial advertising but prohibited off-site commercial signs. It also prohibited most noncommercial advertising. Billboard owners challenged the ordinance on constitutional grounds. *Held:* Improving traffic safety and the appearance of the city were valid governmental goals. The city could reasonably distinguish between on-site and off-site commercial advertising because off-site advertising could create greater problems. However, the city's restrictions on noncommercial advertising in locations where it would permit commercial advertising violated the Fifth and Fourteenth Amendments; the city failed to explain how noncommercial billboards would obstruct the goals of traffic safety and aesthetics more than would commercial billboards. The city could not decide that the communication of commercial messages had more value than the communication of noncommercial messages. The ordinance, by in effect authorizing the city to choose appropriate subjects for public discourse, infringed on constitutional rights of free speech and was unconstitutional on its face. *Metromedia, Inc. v. City of San Diego,* 455 US 490 (1981).

U.S. Supreme Court The only area zoned for commercial activity in a borough was located next to a turnpike. Plaintiff operated an adult bookstore in the district, which bookstore, for a fee, permitted its patrons to watch a live nude dancer. The operation of the store and the services it provided were not uses of the district expressly permitted by the zoning ordinance. *Held:* Nude dancing, which was prohibited by the ordinance, is a form of expression protected by the First Amendment. The borough claimed that the commercial district was designed to provide only those services that were not provided in nearby areas, and that adult entertainment was not such a service. There was inadequate evidence to support that claim or the claim that adult entertainment was incompatible with permitted uses. *Schad v. Borough of Mt. Ephraim,* 452 US 105 (1981).

1st Circuit The city of Somerville passed an ordinance restricting billboards. Nonconforming signs were exempt from the regulations if they had carried on-site commercial messages or off-site noncommercial messages for at least a year before the effective date of the ordinance. Billboards that carried off-site commercial speech had to comply with the restrictions. Billboard owner challenged the ordinance. *Held:* The ordinance violated the First Amendment. The exemptions were invalid because they imposed an impermissible penalty on fully protected speech and the city failed to offer a rational basis for the penalty. The city was attempting to base the future right to engage in noncommercial or on-site commercial speech on whether the potential speaker had engaged in off-site commercial speech. The city could not deny the right to continue speaking by means of nonconforming signs because of the speaker's constitutionally protected prior speech. *Ackerley Communications, Inc. v. City of Somerville,* 878 F2d 513 (1989).

6th Circuit Sign company's applications to erect four billboards were denied under a village ordinance forbidding billboards in retail commercial districts. The ordinance allowed only on-premise signs with messages relating to the activities conducted on the premises in the retail district, and allowed only one billboard, which was to be located in the industrial district. Sign company challenged the ordinance on First Amendment grounds and charged that the ordinance exceeded the village's police powers. *Held:* The billboard regulations contained reasonable time, place, and manner restrictions, and were constitutional. The ordinance did not regulate the content of speech or make any distinctions between commercial and noncommercial speech. In addition, the regulations were tailored to serve important aesthetic interests, while minimizing traffic obstructions and possible visual hazards. *Rzadkowolski v. Village of Lake Orion,* 845 F2d 653 (1988).

6th Circuit Plaintiff was denied a certificate of occupancy for an adult bookstore under a zoning ordinance that restricted adult bookstores and theaters to a specific business district. Plaintiff challenged the ordinance as an infringement of free expression in violation of the equal protection clause. City officials cited the U.S. Supreme Court's decision in *Young v. American Mini-Theaters, Inc.,* 427 US 50 (1976) in favor of the constitutionality of the ordinance. The *Young* ordinance prohibited adult bookstores and theaters within 500 feet of a residential area and within 1000 feet of other regulated uses. *Held:* The *Young* ordinance was distinguishable from the city ordinance challenged here in that the former left room for adult businesses in the city, whereas the ordinance in this case restricted such businesses to a half-mile strip. Furthermore, unlike in *Young*, the city failed to justify the infringement of First Amendment rights by showing a compelling governmental interest. It presented no evidence that the ordinance would prevent urban blight. In fact, the ordinance could encourage it by concentrating all adult bookstores and theaters in a small area. Thus, there was no rational relationship between the statute's purpose and its effect. *CLR Corp. v. Henline,* 702 F2d 637 (1983).

6th Circuit Plaintiffs, a congregation of Jehovah's Witnesses, brought an action challenging the validity of a municipal zoning ordinance prohibiting the construction of church buildings and all other nonresidential buildings in any of the city's single-family residential districts. *Held:* The ordinance should be scrutinized under the "rational basis" rather than the "compelling interest" test because it did not infringe plaintiffs' right to free exercise of religion. Construction of a church building was not essential to plaintiffs' exercise of religious beliefs, which could be accomplished without undue burden on plaintiffs by worship in existing buildings, or in churches constructed in commercial or multi-family residential districts. The ordinance was constitutional under the "rational basis" test because it was based on the legitimate government interest in protecting residential districts from traffic congestion and noise. *Lakewood, Ohio Congregation of Jehovah's Witnesses, Inc. v. City of Lakewood, Ohio,* 600 F2d 303, cert. denied, 464 US 815 (1983).

U.S. District Court, Minnesota Plaintiff, owner and manager of adult bookstores and theaters, brought an action challenging the constitutionality of a city zoning ordinance restricting "adult" uses. Under the ordinance no "adult" use could be operated within 500 feet of a residentially zoned or office-residence zoned district, a church, a day-care facility, or a public educational facility serving persons age 17 or younger. In addition, no two "adult" uses could operate within 500 feet of one another. *Held:* The zoning ordinance was unconstitutional as applied to adult bookstores and movie theaters because it substantially restricted access to First Amendment protected materials. *Alexander v. City of Minneapolis,* 531 F. Supp. 1162 (1982), aff'd, 698 F2d 936 (8th Cir. 1983).

U.S. District Court, New York Plaintiff, purchaser of a restaurant, planned to install 40 dining tables in which coin video games were embedded. The city rejected the plan because it violated city licensing laws, under which licenses were only allowed to operators of up to four video games located in restaurants. An operator of five or more video games had to obtain an arcade license. Arcades were not a permitted use in the zone in which the restaurant was to be located. Plaintiff sued, challenging the constitutionality of the video game licensing laws on First Amendment and equal protection grounds. *Held:* Video games, which are not meant to inform and contain little in the way of particularized expression, cannot be characterized as a form of speech protected by the First Amendment. The licensing laws did not constitute a violation of equal protection merely because they distinguished between establishments with one to four video games and those with five or more. The classifications were rationally related to the city's interest in minimizing noise level, congestion and traffic. *America's Best Family Showplace Corp. v. City of New York Dep't of Bldgs.,* 536 F. Supp. 170 (ED 1982).

Alaska Municipality amended its sign ordinance to prohibit off-premise advertising signs, portable signs, and roof signs. Print shop operator was denied a permit to erect a roof sign and was cited for displaying a portable sign in an adjacent parking lot. Plaintiff claimed the ordinance was unconstitutional. *Held:* Ordinance did not violate plaintiff's First Amendment rights, because the incidental restriction on commercial speech was narrowly tailored to achieve the municipality's aesthetic goal of eliminating visual blight. Alternative means of communication were open to plaintiff; he could erect a permanent sign. The ordinance also did not deprive plaintiff of equal protection of the laws. Although the ordinance did not prohibit the display of aesthetically displeasing permanent signs, a statute is not unconstitutional, because it could have gone further. *Barber v. Municipality of Anchorage,* 776 P2d 1035 (1989).

Alaska A church was established in a rural residential subdivision of a city. The city made it clear that parochial schools were not permitted in the subdivision under zoning laws. Nonetheless, the church pastor decided to build the church, intending to operate a parochial school as well. The church challenged the zoning restriction on nonpublic schools. *Held:* The zoning law was valid under both the federal and state constitutions. The due process rights of the church were not violated because the city did not act arbitrarily or unreasonably when it concluded that a rural residential zone should be free of noise and traffic. Nor did the zoning law violate the free exercise clause of the U.S. Constitution. Church members' right to a religious education is not immune from government regulations that place reasonable restrictions on the time, place, and manner in which such right is exercised. The zoning law did not violate state constitutional protections of the right to religious education, because the law did not amount to a ban on parochial schools in any area and thus did not create an unreasonable burden on the exercise of religion. *Seward Chapel, Inc. v. City of Seward,* 655 P2d 1293 (1982).

Arkansas Zoning ordinance limited the location of billboards to commercial districts and a sign ordinance restricted the size of signs and prescribed minimum setback requirements. Plaintiff's billboards, erected before the latest ordinance was enacted, did not conform to the requirements. Plaintiff challenged the new restrictions on constitutional grounds. *Held:* The zoning and sign ordinances did not violate First or Fourteenth Amendments. The ordinances as applied to plaintiff, its advertisers, and its viewers were content neutral; they merely restricted the size, height, and location of billboards. The ordinances advanced the government's substantial interest in traffic safety, preservation of natural beauty, and the tourism industry. *Donrey Communications Co. v. City of Fayetteville,* 660 SW2d 900, cert. denied, 466 US 959 (1984).

Connecticut Because outdoor advertising signs violated department of transportation regulations prohibiting signs within 500 feet of highway interchange, the commissioner sought removal of signs erected on private property bordering an interstate highway exchange. Advertiser claimed the regulations were unconstitutional. *Held:* The regulations did not infringe on plaintiff's freedom of speech with regard to both commercial and noncommercial advertising. The state's interest in highway safety, especially at hazardous highway interchanges, is quite substantial and sufficient to justify prohibiting even noncommercial billboards near interchanges. The regulation's exemption for on-site signs did not indicate a preference for commercial messages; commercial or noncommercial signs may be erected as long as they have some reasonable connection to on-site activity. *Burns v. Barrett,* 561 A2d 1378 (1989).

Georgia The Outdoor Advertising Control Act of 1971 prohibited outdoor advertising within 660 feet of interstate and primary highways where they were visible from the road. The department of transportation ordered the removal of plaintiff's signs, which, according to the department, were in violation of the act. Plaintiff claimed the act unconstitutionally violated his freedom of expression. *Held:* The act was constitutional. It sought to implement a substantial government interest. The legislative determination that billboards near highways diminished safety and the recreational value of public travel was not manifestly unreasonable. No improper purpose of control of expression was shown by the subjective determination that billboards detract from natural beauty, nor was the remedy of removal more extensive than necessary to serve the interests involved. *Department of Transp. v. Shiflett,* 310 SE2d 509 (1984).

Georgia The city demanded removal of the satellite antenna that plaintiff set up in his front yard, because it violated a zoning ordinance providing that "structures shall be permitted only in rear yards. . . ." The antenna fell within the ordinance's definition of a "structure" as anything erected on the ground or attached to something on the ground. *Held:* The ordinance was constitutional. It concerned the noncommunicative aspects of the satellite, not the content of any satellite communications. Advancement of the city's aesthetic interests was a reasonable justification for any impingement on plaintiff's First Amendment rights. The ordinance did not amount to an unconstitutional taking of property, because it did not result in significant detriment to plaintiff, only in negligible inconvenience. The ordinance was not unconstitutionally vague, because the satellite, which was attached to the ground by concrete and iron supports, was clearly a "structure" within the meaning of the ordinance. The fact that other city residents had "structures" in their front yards did not establish that the ordinance violated equal protection, because plaintiff failed to establish that such "structures" were erected after the ordinance came into effect. *Gouge v. City of Snellville,* 287 SE2d 539 (1982).

Michigan Plaintiff owned land that had been zoned for general business use, and that excluded theaters as a permitted use. Plaintiff sought a waiver from the city that would allow construction of a four-theater complex. The city refused to grant the waiver, stating that there was already one theater on the site and that the new theater would overburden the area with traffic. Plaintiff challenged the constitutionality of the ordinance that barred additional theaters in the zone, alleging a First Amendment infringement. *Held:* The ordinance was constitutional. It was properly limited in its scope and served a compelling governmental need to deal with the existing traffic and parking problems in the area. In addition, the ordinance did not bar the existing theaters in the city, unlike the ordinance in *Shad v. Borough of Mt. Ephraim,* 452 US 61 (1981), which totally excluded any form of live entertainment in the borough. The ordinance was narrowly drawn to serve a significant government interest, leaving open adequate alternative channels of communication. *Jeffrey Lauren Land Co. v. City of Livonia,* 326 NW2d 604 (Ct. App. 1982), appeal denied, 338 NW2d 190 (1983).

New York Town sought to enjoin owners from operating adult bookstore that was in violation of town's zoning ordinance. The ordinance limited the operation of certain "adult" uses to areas zoned industrial. It required the termination of nonconforming adult uses and provided an amortization period depending on the amount of investment in the use. Owners claimed that the ordinance violated their constitutional right to free speech. *Held:* The ordinance was constitutional. Town's primary purpose in enacting the ordinance was to eliminate the secondary effects of adult uses and to control future development of business districts, not to regulate expression. The ordinance was predicated on town's own study as well as ordinances prepared by other municipalities. It provided adequate alternate locations in the town for adult use businesses. Amortization provisions that terminate nonconforming uses are constitutional if the period allowed to recapture the investment in the use is reasonable. In this case, owners had operated well beyond the maximum period and had presented no evidence of economic loss that would establish unreasonableness. *Town of Islip v. Caviglia,* 540 NE2d 215 (1989).

43.20 —Homes for the Mentally Retarded

U.S. Supreme Court Plaintiff sought to lease a four-bedroom house as a group home for the mentally retarded. Under the zoning ordinance, a special use permit was required; but after a hearing, the permit was denied. *Held:* The zoning ordinance violated the equal protection clause, but mental retardation was not a quasi-suspect classification justifying heightened scrutiny. The city did not require special use permits for boarding houses, hospitals, or other types of multiple dwellings. To support the distinction between homes for the mentally retarded and other uses, the city had to show a rational basis for believing that the home threatened legitimate interests in the city. The court concluded that the city's real reason for denying the permit was prejudice against the mentally retarded. *City of Cleburne, Tex. v. Cleburn Living Center,* 473 US 432 (1985).

9th Circuit Plaintiff operated a small group home that housed, among others, former mental patients. Under a zoning ordinance, group care homes in residential districts required a special use permit. Plaintiff applied for a permit but her application was rejected at a public hearing because of neighborhood opposition. Plaintiff challenged the ordinance as unlawful discrimination against former mental patients and as applied to plaintiff. *Held:* Because the class of former mental patients is not a suspect class for purposes of constitutional analysis, the test used to determine the ordinance's constitutionality was whether it was rationally related to the furtherance of some substantial goal of the city. The ordinance passed this test because it set forth criteria focusing on the health, safety, and general welfare of the public. However, the ordinance had been applied to plaintiff in an unconstitutional manner. The city had arbitrarily rejected plaintiff's application because of pressure from objecting neighbors, even though the group home satisfied all criteria set forth in the ordinance. *JW v. City of Tacoma, Wash.,* 720 F2d 1126 (1983).

Georgia Nonprofit organization requested that the county land planning and zoning commission amend its land development ordinance to permit homes for the mentally retarded in districts where such usages would otherwise be prohibited. The commission denied the application after a public hearing. The organization argued that the equal protection rights of the mentally retarded were violated. *Held:* The group homes for the mentally retarded did not constitute permissible uses within single-family zoning districts, not because the inhabitants of the house were mentally retarded, but because the inhabitants of the home did not fit within the zoning area limits of people related by blood or marriage, or of four unrelated people. Nothing on the face of this definition of "family" discriminated against mentally retarded individuals; this definition withstood equal protection analysis. *Macon Ass'n for Retarded Citizens v. Macon-Bibb County Planning & Zoning Comm'n,* 314 SE2d 218, appeal dismissed, 469 US 802 (1984).

43.25 Spot Zoning

District of Columbia Plaintiff challenged zoning board action approving construction of single-family row houses. *Held:* The amended classification was not illegal "spot" zoning. The board acted properly, because the affected area had no comprehensive zoning plan and because the change served the public need for new housing. *Lee v. Zoning Comm'n,* 411 A2d 635 (1980).

Massachusetts Plaintiff claimed that a recodification of zoning laws was irrational. The new law permitted single-family residences on plaintiff's property and, depending on how it was read, required each building to be on a lot of at least either 87,000 or 200,000 square feet. Plaintiff also claimed that the recodification constituted spot zoning. *Held:* The new ordinance was to be read in the most reasonable way (i.e., requiring only the smaller parcels), in which case it was not irrational. Also, plaintiff could not claim that his land was being spot zoned, since the boundaries of the zoning district in which it was located were natural. *Marshall v. Town of Topsfield,* 433 NE2d 1244 (1982).

Texas Plaintiffs and defendant owned land in an agricultural zoning district that restricted residential use to single-family homes on at least an acre. At the request of defendant, the city adopted an ordinance that amended the zoning of defendant's tract to allow for multi-unit dwellings. Defendant wished to build an apartment complex on his 5.98-acre tract. Plaintiffs sued the city and defendant, asking that the zoning amendment be declared invalid at spot zoning. *Held:* There were no changes in defendant's property, extension of services to the area, or public demand justifying the zoning amendment. The presumption of validity does not exist for spot zoning, which can be upheld only if changes occurred that justified treating a small area differently from the surrounding land. *City of Texarkana v. Howard,* 633 SW2d 596 (Ct. App. 1982).

43.30 Voter Zoning Initiatives

California The voters of the city adopted a growth control ordinance by initiative that limited the number of dwelling units constructed in the city. The Building Industry Association challenged the ordinance. The Supreme Court of California examined the validity of Cal. Evid. Code § 669.5, which established a presumption that growth control ordinances adversely affect regional housing needs and placed the burden of proof on the city to show a growth control ordinance is necessary to public health, safety, and welfare; and Cal. Gov't. Code § 65863.6, which required cities and counties to balance housing needs against public service needs before passing growth control ordinances. *Held:* Section 669.5 was applicable only to ordinances enacted by voter initiative after the effective date of the section. Application to all initiative measures would greatly impede the law's purpose of supporting construction of affordable housing. Section 65863.6 did not apply to growth control ordinances enacted by initiative. *Building Indus. Ass'n* *v. City of Camarillo,* 718 P2d 68 (1986) (en banc).

California After municipal authorities rezoned a tract of land to permit construction of a housing project, a neighborhood homeowners' association circulated a petition and placed an initiative on the local election ballot to rezone the property strictly for single-family residential use. After the initiative was passed, the developers sued to have it voided. *Held:* The initiative ordinance was invalid because it constituted arbitrary and discriminatory rezoning. It was passed in the absence of any significant changes in circumstances, since the rezoning permitting apartment development was enacted for the sole purpose of defeating plaintiff's proposed apartment development. The initiative ordinance was not rationally related to the general public welfare, especially in light of the region's acute shortage of moderate-income housing. At best, it was rationally related to conserving the interests of a few adjoining property owners. *Arnel Dev. Co. v. Costa Mesa,* 178 Cal. Rptr. 723 (1981), rev'g 620 P2d 565 (1980).

Hawaii Citizens' group sought to prevent housing development in beach area. The group circulated an initiative petition proposal to amend the site's zoning designation from residential to preservation. The initiative proposal was approved by the electorate. Developer challenged the initiative process as an improper procedure for changing the zoning of a tract of land. *Held:* The initiative proposal did not validly amend the city's zoning laws. When it enacted the Zoning Enabling Act, state legislature did not contemplate zoning by initiative, which is inconsistent with the act's emphasis on long-range comprehensive planning. City charter provision that permitted zoning by initiative was not superior to the Zoning Enabling Act. *Kaiser Hawaii Kai Dev. Co. v. City & County of Honolulu,* 777 P2d 244 (1989).

43.35
Exclusionary Devices

U.S. Supreme Court Woman convicted of a criminal violation of a city ordinance limiting occupancy of a single-family dwelling questioned the constitutionality of the ordinance, which defines "family" so as to exclude a household containing the woman, her two grandsons, and her son. The city argued that the due process clause was not violated, since the ordinance meets the standard of *Belle Terre v. Boraas,* 416 US 1 (1974). *Held:* The ordinance was unconstitutional. The U.S. Constitution provides protection for the sanctity of the family, an institution deeply rooted in our tradition. The history of the extended family living in a single household has roots meriting constitutional recognition. *Belle Terre* is distinguishable, since that ordinance affected only unrelated persons. *Moore v. East Cleveland,* 431 US 494 (1977).

U.S. Supreme Court Village composed of 220 one-family homes maintained its character by a zoning ordinance restricting land use to one-family dwellings. The word "family" as used in the ordinance meant "One or more persons related by blood, adoption, or marriage. . . ." One or two persons, "though not related by blood, adoption, or marriage shall be deemed to constitute a family." Despite the ordinance, six unrelated university students rented a house in the village. When the village ordered the owners of the house to remedy the violation, they and three tenants sought an injunction declaring the ordinance unconstitutional. *Held:* The ordinance was simply an effort to maintain a family neighborhood, a lawful objective. "A quiet place where yards are wide, people few, and motor vehicles restricted are legitimate guidelines in a land-use project addressed to family needs. This goal is a permissible one. . . . The police power is not confined to elimination of filth, stench, and unhealthy places. It is ample to lay out zones where family values, youth values, and the blessings of quiet seclusion, and clean air make the area a sanctuary for people." *Village of Belle Terre v. Boraas,* 416 US 1 (1974).

2d Circuit A nonprofit housing assistance corporation secured an option to purchase a 14.6-acre tract of land in an area zoned for single-family residences on one-acre lots. The corporation sought a zoning amendment to permit construction of a 162-unit low- and moderate-income housing project funded under the Section 8 federal housing program. The request for the zoning amendment was denied, so the corporation sued the town, alleging a violation of federal and state fair housing laws in its exclusionary zoning. Subsequently, Section 8 funding was effectively eliminated for that fiscal year. *Held:* The lack of Section 8 funding for the proposed housing project did not bar the suit. To allow a suit to proceed, all that is required is that plaintiff may improve its chances of avoiding an alleged injury. In this case, where funding might be restored and elimination of a zoning obstacle may improve the chances for obtaining financing, plaintiff must be granted its day in court. *Huntington Branch, NAACP v. Town of Huntington,* 689 F2d 391, cert. denied, 460 US 1069 (1982).

New Jersey Fair housing advocates and developers sued to enforce municipalities' compliance with earlier *Mount Laurel* decision requiring each "developing" municipality's zoning law to accommodate its fair share of low- and moderate-income housing. *Held:* The *Mount Laurel* obligation applies to communities specified as "developing" under a state development guide plan. All courts are authorized to order municipal cooperation with developers' efforts to obtain federal and state subsidies to fulfill the need for lower-income housing. The court proposed zoning that would increase the permitted density of housing where units are intended for low-income occupancy and would require a percentage of lower-income housing in new residential construction. Where extremely high land costs make lower-income housing impractical, a municipality must zone for the lowest-cost housing that can be built after removal of excessive restrictions. *Southern Burlington County NAACP v. Township of Mount Laurel,* 456 A2d 390 (1983).

New Jersey Dwelling units in a township's R-2 residential districts could be occupied only by a family, that is, "one or more persons occupying a dwelling unit as a single non-profit housekeeping unit, who are living together as a stable and permanent living unit, being a traditional family or the functional equivalent thereof." The purpose of this provision was to prevent students from living off-campus. The parents of a student set up a family partnership to purchase a home in the township for their son to live in and leased space to ten other students, with the leases renewable each semester. The township sued to prevent the use of the house in this manner. *Held:* The students were the functional equivalent of a traditional family unit, and their occupancy was therefore permitted under the ordinance. Their lifestyle was communal, and the relationship between the students showed stability and permanency. This was not a commercial use of the property requiring a rental license. *Borough of Glassboro v. Vallorosi,* 529 A2d 1028 (Super. Ct. Ch. Div. 1987).

43.40 Nonconforming Uses

Connecticut Essex Leasing acquired title to a building subject to a legal nonconforming commercial use in a residential zone. Plaintiff's application for a permit to continue the nonconforming use was denied. Plaintiff appealed the denial. *Held:* The regulation was valid. The zoning regulation allowed termination of a nonconforming use after a specified period of nonuse, without regard to the owner's intent to maintain that use. The court reasoned that the right to continue the use of property does not mean that the use cannot be forfeited by nonuse. *Essex Leasing v. Zoning Bd. of Appeals,* 539 A2d 101 (1988).

Connecticut Taxpayer appealed the issuance of a permit to a store owner to operate a liquor store. The premises were operated since 1933 as a drugstore that sold liquor under a drugstore liquor permit. In 1935, a zoning ordinance was adopted prohibiting liquor stores within 1,000 feet of each other. At this time, there were two liquor stores within 1,000 feet of the drugstore. In 1972, after the drugstore had vacated the premises, the owner applied for and received a permit to operate a liquor store. *Held:* After 1935, the use of the subject premises as an outlet for the sale of alcoholic beverages was a nonconforming use. However, the substitution of a liquor store permit for a drugstore liquor permit constituted an impermissible extension or expansion of the nonconforming use. *Macaluso v. Zoning Bd. of Appeals,* 356 A2d 885 (1975).

Georgia Plaintiff rented space in a condominium for use as a law office. When landlord applied for a writ of possession plaintiff claimed that this constituted a breach of the lease agreement. Landlord counterclaimed that the lease was in violation of the applicable zoning ordinance, which permitted multiple dwellings in buildings five stories and higher to provide only those services ordinarily furnished by hotels, such as drug stores, barber shops, and newsstands. Plaintiff's lease provided that premises "shall be used and occupied solely as an attorney's office by lessee." *Held:* Legal services are not included among those ordinarily furnished by hotels. An attorney's office would not ordinarily be established to serve such a limited market as customers of a given hotel rather than the public at large. Therefore, the use requirement in the lease violated the zoning ordinance. Since the usage requirement was central to the contract, and since the contract contained no severability clause, the entire lease was void and landlord was entitled to a writ of possession. *Merren v. Plaza Towers Ltd. Partnership,* 287 SE2d 771 (1982).

Maine Plaintiff was the owner of a single lot upon which three dwellings were occupied by tenants. The dwellings were nonconforming uses under the 1974 zoning ordinance; they did not meet the minimum frontage and set-back requirements. When plaintiff proposed to divide the land into four lots, she sought a determination that her proposal was not subject to the zoning ordinance or a variance. The commission denied her relief, and plaintiff appealed. *Held:* For plaintiff. The three dwellings continued to constitute a nonconforming use even after the land was divided. The mere change from tenant occupancy to owner occupancy in the proposed sale was not an extension or expansion of the preexisting nonconforming use. Thus, plaintiff could act on her proposal without violating the zoning ordinance. *Keith v. Saco River Corridor Comm'n,* 464 A2d 150 (1983).

Maryland A landowner operated sand and gravel equipment under rural-residential zoning. The land was subsequently rezoned to open space, single-family residential, so that sand and gravel, as well as wet-processing, which were permitted uses under the original zoning, became special exception uses. After the rezoning, landowner applied for a special exception for wet-processing. *Held:* The county denied the special exception, concluding that it would be an unwarranted extension of a nonconforming use, and contrary to the purpose of the county zoning ordinance of discouraging nonconforming uses. Although sand and gravel mining were legal nonconforming uses prior to rezoning, landowner was not automatically permitted to operate a wet-processing facility. Mining and wet-processing were separate and distinct special exceptions under the zoning ordinance, each with different standards and regulations. *County Council of Prince George's County v. EL Garner, Inc.*, 443 A2d 114 (1982).

Michigan A group store was open from 8:00 A.M. to 10:00 P.M. When the town rezoned the land to residential, the store continued operating as a nonconforming use. The grocery then leased the store building to lessee, who at first intended to operate from 7:00 A.M. to 11:00 P.M., but then sought to change its hours from 6:00 A.M. to 2:00 A.M. The town sought to limit the hours of operation from 7:00 A.M. to 11:00 P.M. *Held:* The town may restrain the operating hours of the store. Since the store was being operated as a nonconforming use, the town was entitled to deny an expansion of the nonconforming use. *Garb-Ko, Inc. v. Carrollton Township*, 272 NW2d 654 (1978).

New Hampshire When landowners placed a mobile home on their property in 1981, the town ordinance, which allowed only temporary location of these homes, was not in conformity with a new state law (N.H. Rev. Stat. Ann. § 31:119). The new law required municipalities to allow "manufactured housing to be located on individual lots . . . , or in mobile home parks and subdivisions created for the placement of mobile homes on individually owned lots. . . ." The town restricted the number of mobile home parks and denied individual ownership of land upon which to place mobile homes. *Held:* For landowners. Before the town ordinance was enacted, mobile home owners could place their homes anywhere in town. By moving their mobile home onto their lot before the town amended its zoning and mobile home ordinances, landowners had established a legal, nonconforming use that continued after enactment of the amended ordinance. *Town of Plainfield v. Sanville,* 485 A2d 1052 (1984).

New Hampshire Prior owner of land maintained a trailer on the property as a nonconforming use. The trailer was vacant for five years; and the town removed it upon acquiring a deed to the property at a tax collector's sale. The mortgagee of the trailer and property subsequently foreclosed and sold the property to plaintiff. Plaintiff, who had knowledge of the period of nonuse of the property, appealed from the denial of his application for a permit to put a trailer on the property. *Held:* Prior owner's abandonment of the trailer evidenced an intent to surrender the right of the nonconforming use and constituted an abandonment of that right. *Lawlor v. Town of Salem,* 352 A2d 721 (1976).

New York Petitioner owned a parcel of land on which a three-family and a one-family house stood. The prior owners lived in the one-family house and rented the other dwelling; such use was nonconforming under a zoning ordinance that permitted only one two-family house on the parcel. Both homes were occupied as nonconforming uses until 1969, when only the three-family house was occupied. Petitioner purchased the property in 1984 and applied for a permit to renovate the one-family house. The petition was denied on the ground that the use of the property for four families had been abandoned and that, under the village code, an abandoned nonconforming use could not be resumed. Petitioner asked the court to annul the zoning board's decision. *Held:* For petitioner. Abandonment does not occur unless there has been a complete cessation of the use, and there was no evidence the entire use was abandoned. *Marzella v. Munroe,* 509 NE2d 342 (1987).

Ohio A city adopted an ordinance that imposed design, size, location, and illlumination standards on all signs and required that nonconforming signs be removed within five and one-half years after the ordinance date. The ordinance was later amended to declare that nonconforming signs were a nuisance. The ordinance was challenged by an affected sign owner and the regional sign contractors association. *Held:* The ordinance bore a real and substantial relationship to the safety and general welfare of the public. The evidence demonstrated the existence of sign blight, which is the functional equivalent of a public nuisance, adversely affecting the aesthetics and vitality of the city's commercial areas, and creating a traffic hazard. Rejecting the owners' assertion that the city had to prove each sign was a nuisance, the court stated that the collective effect of the signs on the community could not be appreciated by considering the signs individually. *Northern Ohio Sign Contractors Ass'n v. City of Lakewood,* 513 NE2d 324 (1987).

Pennsylvania A landowner's use of part of his 40 acres for rental bungalows was an existing nonconforming use under the township's zoning ordinance. In 1976, he sold most of the acreage, including the land the bungalows occupied, to the federal government in lieu of condemnation, retaining salvage rights to the bungalows. He then moved the bungalows to eight acres he had retained. The town zoning board found that the move violated the zoning ordinance, and landowner went to court. *Held:* For the zoning board. Although the bungalows were a valid nonconforming use as long as they were in their original location, such use could not be transferred to another portion of the property. The exercise of eminent domain, which includes the sale of land under threat of condemnation, extinguishes a nonconforming use. Landowner could not initiate the nonconforming use elsewhere on his land once the use had been extinguished. *Bachman v. Zoning Hearing Bd.,* 494 A2d 1102 (1985).

Rhode Island Town sued to enjoin purchaser from subdividing a parcel of property purchased from the U.S. government containing a 32-unit, single-family housing development for military personnel. The complex did not comply with the local zoning ordinance establishing minimum lot sizes for single-family residences. When purchaser applied for a permit to install carports, it was informed that use of the property for single-family residences was in violation of the zoning ordinance. Although the government possessed a nonconforming use for the property, this use was discontinued by government deactivation of the property. *Held:* For purchaser. A nonconforming use of property is an alienable property interest. A mere change of ownership does not destroy such use, nor does discontinuance of the use constitute an abandonment absent proof by the asserting party of intent to abandon the use. *Town of Coventry v. Glickman,* 429 A2d 440 (1981).

South Carolina A zoning ordinance in a resort city allowed property zoned A-3 to be used for one-, two-, and multi-family dwellings for permanent occupancy. After consulting with the city director of zoning, the condominium owners invested in a short-term rental business in an A-3 district. Subsequently, the director changed his interpretation of the ordinance and held that short-term rentals were not permitted in an A-3 district. Condominium owners moved to enjoin the city from denying them the right to rent their units on a short-term basis. *Held:* For condominium owners. Although the doctrine of estoppel is not generally applied to deny a governmental agency the exercise of its police power, government agents, acting within the scope of their authority, can by their acts give rise to equitable estoppel against the municipality. To allow the city to repudiate its earlier interpretation of the ordinance would be "unconscionable." *Landing Dev. Corp. v. City of Myrtle Beach,* 329 SE2d 423 (1988).

43.45
Special Use Permits

Illinois City refused to issue a renewal license for the operation of a special care home in an area zoned for business. The original special use permit was subject to the condition that persons suffering from mental disorders apt to make them a burden to the neighborhood or other residents were not to be permitted. The city filed for an injunction when the home continued in operation. *Held:* The condition barred only individuals who were apt to be a burden on the community. Since the city had no evidence that any resident posed a threat of violence to the neighborhood and that the home had made substantial efforts to comply, the condition had not been violated. *City of Evanston v. Ridgeview House,* 349 NE2d 399 (1976).

Massachusetts A development agency sought to register title to a parcel of Boston waterfront, which had been conveyed by statute, in the nineteenth century, to the predecessor of the development agency. The Commonwealth refused to register title, arguing that the land was not conveyed in fee simple to the developer. *Held:* The Commonwealth must register title. The developer did own the property in fee simple. However, its ownership was subject to the condition subsequent that it must be used for the purposes for which it was granted. Title to the waterfront land is subject to the same public trust on which the Commonwealth originally held it, and may only be used for a purpose approved by the legislature as a public use. *Boston Waterfront Dev. Corp. v. Commonwealth,* 393 NE2d 356 (1979).

Minnesota Property owner's application for a special use permit to construct a retail store and automotive service facility was denied by the city council on the ground that it was not a permitted use under the neighborhood business zoning of the land. When the property owner sued to compel issuance of the permit, the city argued that the proposed use was not specifically included on the list of permitted uses. *Held:* Since both property owner's retail sales and automotive services operations were individually permissible in such a zone, the combination was also permissible, unless the city could show that the hybrid was in some way injurious to health, safety, or welfare. Since no citizen objected to the proposed use and the city offered no evidence of adverse effects, it was unreasonable for it to deny a special use permit. *NR Fairbanks Co. v. City of Blaine,* 242 NW2d 99 (1976).

Missouri Religious order appealed from the denial of its application for permission to use a single-family residence to house eight lay members of the order. The application was denied because a local ordinance prohibited the occupation of single-family dwellings by more than three unrelated persons. The order argued that the ordinance contained an exception that permitted the use of a single-family dwelling as a convent, rectory, or monastery. *Held:* The exception allowed fewer than ten unrelated persons to live in a single residence when such persons were priests, nuns, rabbis, or other generically similar members of the clergy. As the members of the order were laymen, the exception did not apply to them and their application was properly denied. *Association for Educ. Dev. v. Hayward,* 533 SW2d 579 (1976).

New York Plaintiff sought a special exception permit for a video game room. The zoning board rejected the application because the games were primarily used by young children and were in close proximity to sexually oriented magazines, and this could have an adverse effect on young children. Plaintiff sought review of this decision, arguing it was based on censorship and that video games were a protected form of free speech. *Held:* The zoning board did not abuse its discretion in acting to protect the well-being of minors in the community. The record supported the board's findings of fact. The board made no attempt to censor the magazines; rather, its intent was to shield children from sexually explicit publications. Plaintiff's First Amendment argument was rejected because he failed to contend either that the First Amendment required the issuance of a permit for all video games or that it mandated the issuance of a permit under these particular circumstances. *Wen & Liz Realty Corp. v. Board of Zoning Appeals,* 463 NYS2d 493 (1983).

Oklahoma Volunteer group applied to the city board of adjustment for a special exception to a zoning ordinance allowing establishment of a prison prerelease center in a district zoned "commercial high intensity." The board denied the application because of neighborhood opposition, and on appeal, the district court held that the center would adversely affect future development. *Held:* Reversed and remanded. The special exception could not be denied based on negative public perceptions of the proposed use and the potential of adverse effect on future development. The district court erred in denying the special exception based on testimony that expressed the belief that the center would affect area crime. Actual evidence must be presented to show that the prerelease center would injure the neighborhood or be detrimental to public welfare. *Application of Volunteers of Am., Inc.,* 749 P2d 549 (1988).

Virginia Plaintiff operated a national convenience store chain. The county zoning ordinance required quick-service food stores to obtain a special exemption in order to operate in certain commercial and industrial zoning areas. Plaintiff sued, seeking a judgment that the zoning ordinance was unconstitutional because it subjected quick-service food stores to a special exemption process in violation of the due process and equal protection clauses. *Held:* For the zoning board. The zoning board had the authority to subject certain uses to a special exemption process if it had reason to believe those uses would have greater impact upon neighboring property or the public than those uses permitted as a matter of right. The zoning board presented sufficient evidence of reasonableness, including traffic congestion, glare from night lighting, and runoff from storm drainage caused by convenience stores. *Board of Supervisors v. Southland Corp.,* 297 SE2d 718 (1982).

43.50
Conditional Use Exception

Arkansas A church was granted a conditional use permit authorizing construction of a church in a single-family residential zone. The planning commission denied use as a parochial school. A year later, the church opened a parochial school on the property. The commission obtained an injunction, and appellant church argued that the church was constitutionally guaranteed the right to operate a religious school as a tenant of religious belief, regardless of zoning restrictions. *Held:* Affirmed. It is religious beliefs, not religious actions, that must not be infringed. Religious actions are subject to reasonable laws designed to protect public health or welfare. The opening of a school is a religious action and subject to reasonable limits on time, place, and manner of operation. *Abram v. City of Fayetteville,* 661 SW2d 371 (1983).

District of Columbia The board of zoning appeals granted a child welfare organization a variance allowing it to use R-5-D property as office space, but imposed three conditions: only that organization would be able to use the premises; no more than twelve employees would be able to work in the offices; and if the building were offered for sale, the organization would be able to advertise it only for R-5-D use. The organization sought judicial review of the board's refusal to reconsider its restrictions. *Held:* The board must reconsider the restrictions. The board has the inherent power to adopt restrictions, but any such condition must run with the land to be valid. Thus a personal condition regulating the business conduct of the owner will generally be declared invalid—as opposed to a "generic" condition on the use of the property. Limiting use to the organization and imposing restrictions on any later resale were invalid personal conditions. The 12-employee limit was generic, but was unsupported by the evidence. *National Black Child Dev. Inst., Inc. v. District of Columbia Bd. of Zoning Adjustment,* 483 A2d 687 (App. 1984).

Maryland Developer bid for the right to develop property under the city's urban renewal plan. He was permitted to change the property's classification to allow construction of an office building and was granted a conditional use permit. The developer appealed additional conditions imposed after he sought to amend the conditional use, and the mayor and aldermen entered into a settlement with developer to receive a new conditional use permit upon the fulfillment of certain additional conditions. The amended conditional use was subsequently denied by the city council, and developer appealed, seeking to enforce the terms of the settlement. *Held:* Mayor and aldermen could not by agreement bind themselves to a future zoning or conditional use decision. As a general principle, a municipality cannot contract away the exercise of its zoning power. This principle applies not only to conditional zoning cases, but also to cases involving conditional uses. Just as the zoning authority is required to follow statutory procedure, so must the appropriate authority follow required procedures when deciding requests for special exceptions, conditional uses, or variances. The mayor and aldermen had no authority to agree to be bound to any conditions, and the agreement could not be enforced. *Attman v. Mayor,* 552 A2d 1277 (1989).

North Carolina A zoning ordinance restricted petitioner's property to single-family residential use. Although an accessory building was permitted on the property in addition to one main building, the accessory building could not "be inhabited or used by other than the owners . . . or their employees." When the zoning board of adjustment ruled that occupancy of the accessory building by petitioner's son, daughter-in-law, and grandchildren was a violation—she herself lived in the main building—petitioner appealed to the courts. *Held:* Use of the accessory building as a residence for petitioner's family was in compliance with the zoning ordinance. The term "owners," in the context of zoning ordinances such as the one in question, must be construed as including the holder of title to the property and members of the title holder's family, such as petitioner's son, daughter-in-law, and grandchildren. *Farr v. Board of Adjustment,* 349 SE2d 576 (1986).

Utah A county zoning ordinance allowed individuals related to or working for primary occupation farmers or dairymen to construct secondary dwellings on agriculturally zoned property without obtaining conditional use permits. The ordinance was challenged on equal protection grounds by individuals whose applications for a permit had been rejected. *Held:* The statute was constitutional because it was rationally related to legitimate public goals, including preservation of farmland and farm families, and preventing suburban encroachment. *Thurston v. Cache County,* 626 P2d 440 (1981).

43.55 Variances

Arkansas Plaintiff operated a laundromat, grocery store, drive-in restaurant, and filling station on his land, which was zoned C-1 for intensive commercial use. Plaintiff installed a mobile home on his land despite the denial of a variance for that purpose. The city sought an injunction to prevent plaintiff from keeping a mobile home on his land as an incompatible use in a C-1 district. Plaintiff argued that the mobile home was incidental and accessory to the commercial uses. *Held:* The city was entitled to an injunction. Under the zoning ordinance, "accessory use" is defined as "a use which is customarily incidental to the principal use. . . ." Although plaintiff argued that his use of the trailer as a residence and office was accessory to the business he operated, he offered no proof that the city council acted arbitrarily or capriciously in denying the requests. The city council simply followed the letter of the zoning ordinance, which prohibited any mobile home from being placed on C-1 property. *Ferguson v. City of Mountain Pine,* 647 SW2d 460 (1983).

Connecticut The Brunettos bought an industrial building where an aluminum casting business had operated as a nonconforming use in a light industrial zone for a period of years. When the Brunettos obtained variances to operate an auto repair facility on the premises, the landowner challenged the grant in court. *Held:* For the Brunettos. The court declined to overturn the lower court's determination that denial of the variance would likely render the subject property useless and effect an impermissible confiscation. The auto repair shop would be far less offensive in terms of air pollution than the foundry that it would supplant, and there was no finding that the use would have an adverse effect on property values in the zone. *Adolphson v. Fairfield Zoning Bd. of Appeals,* 535 A2d 799 (1988).

Connecticut After applying for a special exception in 1983, landowner was granted a variance of the zoning ordinance in order to sell a lot with less than the required area and frontage, but only on the condition that the property not be considered an approved building lot. In 1985, landowner sought area and frontage variances so the property could become an accepted building lot. She claimed a hardship existed since the lot's value would decrease unless it could be used as a building lot. A neighboring landowner challenged the grant of the variance. *Held:* (1) The restriction against building contained in the 1982 variance did not prevent the board from considering a new application on its merits because the applications did not seek identical relief. (2) Landowner failed to demonstrate a hardship entitling her to the variance. Her inability to use the parcel as a building lot was no different than the hardship affecting other properties in the same zoning district. *Grillo v. Zoning Bd. of Appeals*, 537 A2d 1030 (1988).

Delaware Owners of convenience stores sought a zoning variance permitting them to sell gasoline through self-service gasoline pumps. Although the county board of adjustments denied the variance, the superior court reversed, and the board appealed to the state supreme court. *Held:* The order granting the variance was affirmed. The superior court correctly distinguished "use" variances, which alter the character of a zoned district by permitting an otherwise proscribed use, from "area" variances, which concern only the practical difficulty in using the particular property for a permitted use. A lesser standard of owners' "exceptional practical difficulties" is appropriate for obtaining an area variance. The inability to improve one's business or to stay competitive as a result of area limitations may be a legitimate "exceptional practical difficulty" justifying the grant of a variance. *Board of Adjustment v. Kwik-Check Realty, Inc.*, 389 A2d 1289 (1978).

Florida City board of adjustment granted a property owner the right to convert an existing residence, situated in a multifamily residential dwelling zone, into a restaurant. Owners of land adjacent to the subject property sued on the ground that the board of adjustment did not have legal authority to grant use variances. The lower court declared the variance null and void, ruling that the statutory authorization to the board violated the constitutional prohibition on delegation of legislative authority to an administrative agency. *Held:* The statute did not represent an unconstitutional delegation, since it contained appropriate and meaningful standards to guide the administrative body. For example, a use variance could be granted only if not contrary to the public interest, and special conditions involving unnecessary hardship justified the changed use; and the variance would not become effective until reviewed by the county planning commission. *Clarke v. Morgan*, 327 So. 2d 769 (1975).

Kansas Before purchasing a piece of land, Metroplex obtained a variance that would allow it to build a 990-foot tower in a zone with a 75-foot height restriction. The zoning board's decision was reversed, however, after Metroplex purchased the property. Metroplex appealed, claiming hardship. *Held:* Metroplex failed to establish hardship. There was nothing about plaintiff's lot that made it uniquely suited for a 990-foot tower. Since Metroplex had bought the land knowing there was a 75-foot height restriction, the restriction was not an unnecessary hardship. And the tower departed substantially from established height restrictions since it exceeded the restrictions by over 900 feet, and, therefore, violated the general spirit and intent of the zoning ordinance. *City of Merriam v. Board of Zoning Appeals*, 748 P2d 883 (1988).

New Jersey In 1982, the owner of a nonconforming lot of about one-third the permitted size accepted an offer of $45,000 for the property, contingent on obtaining zoning variances. The zoning board granted the variances on hardship grounds despite the existence of a competing $45,000 offer by a neighboring landowner requiring no variances. The neighboring landowner challenged the variances, arguing that a property owner who refuses to sell at a fair and reasonable price cannot be said to suffer hardship. *Held:* The planning board acted within its discretion in granting the variance. Requiring a homeowner to sell to an adjoining owner as a condition for a hardship variance would generally seem to be unwarranted. Arguably, it would be better to eliminate substandard lots that do not conform to current zoning requirements. The function of a court, however, is to rule on the reasonableness of the zoning board's decision and not to substitute its judgment for the board's. *Davis Enter. v. Karpf,* 523 A2d 137 (1987).

New Jersey Developer was granted a use variance to construct garden apartments but, before he acted to begin construction, the zoning ordinance was amended to prohibit garden apartments in any zone. The developer sought approval of his site plan for the construction of the apartments on the basis of the variance. *Held:* Although the general rule is that a use variance does not expire and is not lost simply by the passage of time and its nonexercise, absent an express time limit in the ordinance, equitable principles required the denial of the application. The developers, without good cause, slept on their rights and, despite the claim that they spent $7,000 on a $3 million project, did not demonstrate sufficient reliance on the variance to justify their claim. *Dimitrov v. Carlson,* 350 A2d 246 (1975).

New York Petitioner applied to the board of zoning appeals for a variance to renovate and repair a preexisting, nonconforming, two-story garage-apartment. The board granted the variance but imposed four conditions. Petitioner brought suit to review the board's determination as to the four conditions. *Held:* Inasmuch as petitioner did not seek a change in the use of his garage-apartment, which was a nonconforming structure, but only to continue it as he was permitted or by repairing it, the conditions imposed by the board were arbitrary and capricious as being outside the scope of application. *Allen v. Hattrick,* 447 NYS2d 741 (1982).

New York Plaintiff maintained his chiropractic office in his residence under a zoning ordinance permitting a professional office as an accessory use provided the owner-professional resided on the premises. The village board of appeals denied a use variance to allow plaintiff to lease the residential portion of the premises while continuing his practice in the other portion of the house. Plaintiff sought judicial review of the board's decision, claiming hardship. *Held:* For the board of appeals. Plaintiff did not provide sufficient proof of unnecessary hardship or that the property could not yield a reasonable return as then zoned. Any hardship to plaintiff was self-created, because he was fully aware of the use restrictions in the zoning ordinance when he bought the property. Nor was the board acting arbitrarily in granting similar variances while denying that requested by plaintiff. *Solla v. Simonds,* 446 NYS2d 101 (1982).

New York Respondent-utility applied for an area and use variance in order to build a 565-foot cooling tower for its nuclear generating plant. The zoning board of appeals denied the application for a zoning variance, stating that the respondent-utility had failed to establish unnecessary hardship. The utility appealed. *Held:* To establish unnecessary hardship, the traditional approach has been to require the applicant to show that (1) the land cannot yield a reasonable return if used only for a purpose allowed in the zone; (2) the circumstances that cause the hardship are unique to the land and not to general neighborhood conditions; and (3) the requested use will not alter the essential character of the locality. When a public utility seeks a variance, however, although the land may be usable for a purpose consistent with the zoning, the uniqueness of the hardship imposed upon the utility by complying with the zoning law may be the result merely of the peculiar needs of the utility. Thus, the utility, in order to establish unnecessary hardship, need not show that the land cannot yield a reasonable return if used only for a purpose allowed in the zone. A failure to make such a showing cannot be the basis of a denial of the application for a variance. *Consolidated Edison Co. v. Hoffman,* 43 NY2d 598 (1978).

New York Owners of two adjoining parcels, one of which was substandard, applied for a special exception that would allow them to develop the land. The statute allowed an exception for a lot owned individually and separately from adjoining lots on the date of the statute's enactment. The zoning board claimed that the statute required individual ownership at all times after the statute's enactment, and that the exception must therefore be denied. *Held:* Zoning regulations must be strictly construed against the enacting municipality. The ordinance fails to provide that the adjacent parcels must continue to be separately owned to qualify for the exception. A merger is not effected merely because parcels come into common ownership. The property owners were therefore granted the special exemption. *Allen v. Adami,* 347 NE2d 890 (1976).

New York The petitioner owned an irregularly shaped parcel of land. The irregular configuration was the result of a prior partial condemnation by the state. While the parcel exceeded the minimum required lot area for a single-family dwelling, its irregular shape prevented it from meeting required front and width setbacks. The owner sought an area variance to permit construction on the lot. *Held:* The owner was entitled to a variance permitting construction and remitting front setback and width requirements. The parcel's irregular shape was the result of a partial condemnation and not from any conduct by petitioner. Additionally, since a residence cannot be built on the lot without violating applicable zoning restrictions, denial of the variance would result in infliction of "practical difficulty." *Cange v. Scheyer,* 536 NYS2d 836 (App. Div. 1989).

New York Homeowners constructed a deck behind their house that extended within one foot of the property boundary between themselves and the petitioner, in violation of a village ordinance. Defendants applied for an area variance on the grounds that compliance would result in "practical difficulties." The neighbors appealed the grant of the area variance. *Held:* The area variance ran counter to the standard for granting variances and constituted an abuse of discretion. Compliance with the original zoning ordinance would limit defendant's choice of a specific aesthetic style; however, it would not constitute a "practical difficulty." *Miller v. Messina,* 541 NYS2d 121 (App. Div. 1989).

Pennsylvania Landowners acquired a seven-unit apartment building. Although use of the structure as an apartment building did not conform to the zoning code, it was permitted because the apartment building existed prior to the code's enactment. Landowners subdivided the existing seven units to provide 14 units. The city refused to issue a final certificate of occupancy. The zoning appeals board granted landowners a variance after accepting their hardship claim that the subdivision was completed in reliance on city permits. The city appealed. *Held:* Landowners were not entitled to a variance. Any economic hardship was self-inflicted when landowners were aware of the zoning requirements. Landowners' claim that they subdivided in reliance on city permits was rejected because the permits were based on false information provided by landowners. *City of Pittsburgh v. Zoning Bd. of Adjustment,* 559 A2d 896 (1989).

Pennsylvania A local zoning ordinance permitted, as accessory to the single-family dwelling use, a home occupation customarily incidental to the residential use, provided that it occupy not more than 600 square feet. Plaintiff, already operating a hunting and fishing shop on the ground floor of his residence, sought a variance that would allow him to continue to operate the shop on the ground floor and open up a showroom in his 1,232-square foot basement. A variance was granted only for the ground floor, and plaintiff appealed. *Held:* Affirmed. A variance may be granted only where necessary to provide relief from unnecessary hardship uniquely and peculiarly imposed on the property by the letter of the zoning regulation. It may not be granted to provide relief from a regulation that affects the property no differently from other property in the zoning district. Economic hardship caused by the necessity of complying with a regulation similarly affecting property in the district is not the necessary hardship that will support a variance. *Van Horen v. Zoning Hearing Bd.,* 431 A2d 1168 (1981).

Rhode Island Property owner petitioned to obtain a variance to permit the use of a building that was subdivided into four separate dwelling units in violation of the zoning ordinance. The owner alleged that unless the use was permitted he would be unable to pay his mortgage. *Held:* Although denying the variance might deprive the owner of rental income that enabled him to pay off his mortgage, this was not the type of hardship that required the grant of a variance. A variance may be granted only if the property cannot be beneficially utilized or profitably operated if devoted to a permitted use. There was no showing that it could not be so utilized. *Worrell v. Del Sesto,* 357 A2d 443 (1976).

Vermont Plaintiffs appealed the granting of a variance on the ground that the property was subject to zoning restrictions at the time defendants purchased, and they therefore created their own hardship. *Held:* Where defendants or their predecessor in title did not create the physical characteristics of the lot, it could not be said that defendants created a hardship merely by purchasing the lot. Where an original owner would be entitled to a variance, any successor in title is ordinarily entitled to such a variance, provided that no owner in the chain of title since the adoption of the zoning restriction has done anything to create a condition for which relief by variance is sought. *Lewis v. Pickering,* 349 A2d 715 (1975).

Virginia Landowner proposed to divide her lot into two parcels, both containing more than the minimum square footage required, but violating a city ordinance that required residential lots to have a 125-foot width and direct access to a public street. The city council denied her application for a variance, and landowner sought judicial review. The trial court found the city council's action was legal, and landowner appealed. *Held:* Reversed. Financial loss alone does not amount to an "undue hardship" that would entitle a landowner to a variance to subdivide an existing lot into two nonconforming parcels. However, the court declined to decide whether the term "undue hardship" requires a showing of hardship approaching confiscation, or whether in a subdivision, rather than a zoning case, there is a lesser burden of proof. *Baum v. Lumsford,* 365 SE2d 739 (1988).

43.60 Moratoria

5th Circuit Developer of condominium complex sued after city council passed a moratorium on the establishment of time-share condominiums in residential areas and refused to grant developer an exemption. *Held:* Developer's constitutional rights were not violated. The moratorium and waiver refusal were legislative acts to which procedural due process rights do not apply. Substantive due process was not implicated, because the moratorium and waiver denial were justified by the city's concern that time-share arrangements in residential areas would increase noise, litter, and vandalism. Developer was not denied equal protection, because (1) city could deny the right to establish time-share condominiums in residential areas but allow other transient uses and (2) there was no evidence the city granted waivers to other time-share condominiums. Finally, the moratorium did not effect a taking of developer's property, because developer was not deprived of all viable economic use of its property. *Jackson Court Condominiums, Inc. v. City of New Orleans,* 874 F2d 1070 (1989).

Connecticut Five years after approving plaintiff's site plan for an office building, the zoning commission declared a moratorium on business development in the relevant area. Plaintiff appealed the moratorium. *Held:* The moratorium was valid. Although the statute (Conn. Gen. Stat. § 8-2) granting powers to local zoning boards did not specifically mention the power to declare a moratorium, the state supreme court found that other jurisdictions had construed similar statutes to include this power. The commission in this case had followed the correct procedures. In addition, the temporary regulations were reasonably limited in scope, since they did not prevent all development but applied only to business uses. *Arnold Bernhard & Co. v. Planning & Zoning Comm'n,* 479 A2d 801 (1984).

Connecticut Plaintiff filed an application for an office building site plan approval involving land zoned for commercial purposes. The zoning commission declared a zoning moratorium a few days after plaintiff's filing for an area including that covered by the application. The application was rejected during the moratorium. Just after the moratorium, the site in question was rezoned for residential purposes. Plaintiff sued to compel the zoning commission to consider his application under premoratorium rules. *Held:* The moratorium did not apply to plaintiff, and the application ought to have been processed under the former rules. The statute enacting the moratorium expressly referred only to applications made after the effective date of the moratorium. *Harlow v. Planning & Zoning Comm'n,* 479 A2d 808 (1984).

43.65
Rezoning

3d Circuit A township that had approved a condomium development for 12 units per acre later lowered the density allowance to four per acre while the units were being built. The condominium unit purchasers and the developer sued, alleging denial of due process and equal protection. *Held:* The amended zoning ordinance was valid. It was true that the developer was affected more harshly than those not in the midst of construction. However, the control of density is a valid purpose, so no equal protection or due process claim could be sustained. In addition, since the developer alleged a decline in the value of the property of only one third, there was no valid taking-without-compensation claim. *Rogin v. Bensalem Township,* 616 F2d 680 (1980), cert. denied, 450 US 1029 (1982).

9th Circuit Real estate developer obtained a permit to construct a high-rise apartment building under new interim height rules. After developer had commenced construction, the municipality reduced the height limit considerably, thus foreclosing any possible high-rise construction. The developer sued in federal court, alleging a taking of its property to the extent that its value dropped from $2 million to $100,000. *Held:* Summary judgment for municipality affirmed. Mere diminution in value does not constitute a state taking and does not entitle the owner to compensation. The zoning affected all neighboring owners equally and therefore was neither discriminatory nor unreasonable. *William C. Haas Co. v. City of San Francisco,* 605 F2d 1117 (1979).

11th Circuit Developer wished to build a low-income residential complex on land it owned in city. The land was zoned for general business so developer applied to have the land rezoned for residential use. Both the city and county refused to change the zoning to residential. Developer sued city, county, and local officials, alleging that they refused to change the zoning because they feared low-income housing would cause an influx of black residents. *Held:* Nonminority developers, such as developer in this case, have standing to challenge racially motivated zoning decisions by local governments. Developer was alleging its own injury, not an injury to be incurred by prospective tenants. Whether a nonminority developer can bring a suit alleging the latter injury is an issue still left open by the Supreme Court. However, the individual defendants had immunity because their decision to deny rezoning was a legislative function. Finally, developer's claim that the project was a taking without just compensation was dismissed. The property was not rendered worthless when defendants refused to rezone it for residential use. Because developer could not develop what it originally intended did not mean its investment-backed expectations were eradicated. *Baytree of Inverrary Realty v. City of Lauderhill,* 873 F2d 1407 (1989).

Arkansas Owners of three adjacent lots in a residential zone opposed a petition by other owners to have their lots rezoned from residential to commercial. The planning and zoning commission rejected the rezoning request; however, upon appeal to the city council, the rezoning request was approved. The chancery court upheld the council's action, and property owners appealed, stating that the holding was arbitrary and capricious and that they were entitled to damages as a result of the rezoning. *Held:* Affirmed. The city council had a reasonable basis for its decision to rezone. Petitioners sought rezoning in response to an offer to build a store on their lots. The rezoned area was surrounded by areas of commercial development, which existed when appellants purchased their lots. Appellants' knowledge that the rezoned area was one of potential commercial growth, and the fact that an unzoned county property abuts their lots, prevented a finding that the rezoning was arbitrary and capricious. Inverse condemnation did not result from the rezoning since the appellants still have use of their residential properties. *Cline v. City of Clarksville,* 746 SW2d 56 (1988).

California Property owners entered into a Williamson Act agreement with a municipality, binding them to put the land to open-space use for a minimum of 10 years in return for favorable tax treatment. After several years they sought to cancel their commitment, obtain rezoning, and sell the property to residential developers. The municipality granted the cancellation request, and plaintiffs, "environmental" groups, brought suit challenging the rezoning action. *Held:* The attempted cancellation is void. The statute specifies prerequisites for setting aside an agreement. The municipality failed to address each requirement and did not have sufficient evidence to conclude that the cancellation was "in the public interest." *Sierra Club v. Hayward,* 623 P2d 180 (1981).

Florida In 1969, a developer's 105-acre plot was rezoned to permit the construction of multiple-family dwellings. In 1970, the city granted the developer a building permit, which was to be effective as long as litigation continued. Extensive public opposition to the planned development resulted in delay, and, in 1972, the city commission enacted a new zoning ordinance that prevented the project's construction. The developer then sued to enjoin the city from rezoning its property. *Held:* The city's density and zoning ordinances were enjoined under the doctrine of equitable estoppel. In view of the developer's good faith reliance on the availability of multifamily use for the land and the considerable expenditure made on preliminary planning, the developer had acquired a vested right in the continuation of multiple-use zoning and the continued effectiveness of its building permit. *Hollywood Beach Hotel Co. v. City of Hollywood,* 329 So. 2d 10 (1976).

Georgia The city council denied the application by owners of property in a residentially zoned district for rezoning so that the property could also be used for offices. The surrounding areas were zoned for industrial or commercial purposes, such that noise and traffic made it difficult to keep residential units in the area rented. *Held:* The city council's refusal to rezone was unconstitutional, since owners suffered a serious deprivation that was not counterbalanced by significant public benefit. *City of Atlanta v. Standish,* 353 SE2d 489 (1987).

Minnesota Plaintiff developers applied to have land rezoned for planned development. They claimed that this application included a request for an underlying roadside business classification. The land was originally zoned agricultural, but showed as a roadside business district in the city's zoning plan. The planned development application was granted, but the city refused to grant the underlying roadside business classification on the ground that no application for that purpose was ever received. The developers appealed. *Held:* The requested underlying use should be granted. The city's denial of the request for an underlying roadside business use was arbitrary: Even the city's own plan showed that this use was appropriate for the property. It was certainly not suitable for agriculture. *Amcon Corp. v. City of Eagan,* 348 NW2d 66 (1984).

Mississippi Owner appealed the rezoning of commercial land to open land in September 1972. The city contended that the five-acre portion in question was accidentally zoned from open to commercial land in July 1972, when it rezoned 16 adjacent acres to commercial use for the construction of a hospital site at the behest of the appellant. Between the July and September rezonings, the appellant had contracted to sell three acres for $50,000 to a funeral home, but the sale was never completed because of the final change of classification to open usage. *Held:* Because the disputed property was not decribed in the notices for public hearings on the original rezoning, the evidence supported the city's contention that the land had been rezoned by mistake. The correction of a mistaken ordinance was not arbitrary, capricious, or confiscatory. *Dicks v. City of Natchez,* 319 So. 2d 214 (1975).

New Hampshire Between the period when the city council passed a motion to restrict high-rise residential construction and the actual rezoning of the district, a developer received a foundation permit for a high-rise residence in the proposed rezoning area. The city then refused to grant the developer a superstructure permit. The developer sued, arguing that adoption of the ordinance restricting property use during the zoning deliberation process was a retrospective application of the law. *Held:* The city's actions were valid. The rezoning had not been applied retrospectively, because it did not impair a vested legal right. At the time of the zoning change, the landowner had received only a foundation permit, which did not amount to a vested construction right. The court also ruled that the statute was not a zoning ordinance and therefore was not subject to the public hearing requirement. *Socha v. City of Manchester,* 490 A2d 794 (1985).

43.70 Subdivision Plans

Alaska Local property owners sued to stop a land lottery. The lottery itself went ahead, but the question remained whether the land could actually be transferred. *Held:* The land could not be transferred, because the state had not complied with the applicable rules regarding subdivisions. Specifically, the state ought to have submitted subdivision plats for borough approval. The state was in error in claiming that the intended disposition of the land was not a "sale" covered by the procedures of Alaska Stat. § 29.78.010(16). *State v. Weidner,* 684 P2d 103 (1984).

Arkansas A subdivision application that met minimum ordinance requirements was denied by the planning commission because of technical violations. The applicant appealed on the ground that the commission did not have the discretion to deny an application meeting minimum ordinance requirements. *Held:* The commission acted arbitrarily in denying approval of a subdivision plat meeting the commission's minimum standards. Once it enacted zoning regulations, the commission was bound by them and was required to enforce them in a predictable manner. *Richardson v. City of Little Rock Planning Comm'n,* 747 SW2d 116 (1988).

California Plaintiffs brought a mandamus action challenging approval of a subdivision map for real estate development. They charged, inter alia, that the decision to approve the map violated the fair hearing requirement of state law. *Held:* Members of city council are not disqualified from voting on proposed subdivision plan submitted to them by parties who have made political campaign contributions to such members. *Woodland Hills Residents Ass'n, Inc. v. City Council,* 609 P2d 1029 (1980).

Colorado Board of county commissioners petitioned to intervene in an action for specific performance of a contract to convey land. The board argued that the conveyance constituted a subdivision of land in violation of state and county laws since the board's approval of the plat prior to the sale had not been secured. *Held:* The board asked the authority to set aside a conveyance that was in violation of county and state subdivision laws. The board still could seek to enjoin the use of any land that was proposed to be used in violation of the subdivision laws. *Board of County Comm'rs v. Hinton,* 548 P2d 122 (1976).

Rhode Island Landowners planned to sell their land as parcels adjoining an already existing road; the parcels were to be used for single-family residences. The city claimed that this plan constituted an illegal subdivision, but the landowners said what they intended was not a subdivision at all. *Held:* The plan was a subdivision within the meaning of the ordinance. It was true that part of the statutory definition of "subdivision" involved the need for a new street to handle the new parcels, something that would not be required here. The court held, however, that the language referred simply to new municipal services that a subdivision would necessitate. It was within the intent of the act to characterize developments such as the one contemplated by the landowners as "subdivisions." *Sugarman v. Lewis,* 488 A2d 709 (1985).

Texas A municipal ordinance gave developers who wished to subdivide property the option either to dedicate land to the city to be used for parks, or to provide money that the city would have to use for parks within a specified time. A developer claimed the ordinance was an unconstitutional taking. *Held:* The ordinance was constitutional. The conditions put on the use of the money in the cash option were specific and reasonable. The statute required the city to use the developer's land or money for parks within a reasonable time. Also, the city could not initiate action that compelled dedication of park land, since the developer had to elect to develop land before the city could impose reasonable regulations on development. The case was remanded, however, to allow the developer to present evidence that the ordinance was unreasonable in its particular application. *City of College Station v. Turtle Rock Corp.*, 680 SW2d 802 (1984).

Utah Plaintiffs were duped into exchanging their homes for land that was falsely characterized by defendant as being in the process of subdivision. They sued under the Uniform Land Sales Act, Utah Code Ann. §§ 57-11-1 *et seq.* (1953). Defendant argued that it had not conveyed an interest in subdivided land to plaintiffs and therefore could not be held liable under the act, which dealt only with subdivided land. *Held:* The act applied. The act's definition of "subdivided land" included both land that had already been subdivided and land proposed for subdivision. The court defined "proposed" as having formed or declared a plan or intention. The intent of the defendant to subdivide could be proven by the elaborate documentation showed plaintiffs regarding the setup of the contemplated subdivision. *Wallis v. Thomas,* 632 P2d 39 (1981).

Virginia Two tenants in common of hunting land sought to partition it. One sought partition by sale, the other partition in kind (that is, the court would divide the property). The court granted partition by sale, noting that the land did not meet the usual criteria for subdivision, and was in any case shaped in a way that would make subdivision awkward. *Held:* Reversed on appeal. The land would be partitioned in kind. For partition by sale to be granted, the party seeking it must show that partition in kind could not be done conveniently. A mere decline in value of the partitioned land would not be a sufficient objection. The local subdivision statute created no bar to partition, since that law applied only to "persons," not to courts. Of course, the owners of the parcels created by the court were subject to use restrictions on the land. The use to which the land could be put was a factor in deciding whether partition was convenient. *Leake v. Casati,* 363 SE2d 924 (1988).

43.75
Administrative Review

Georgia Plaintiff owners appealed the county zoning board's dismissal of an appeal from a decision of the county planning commission. Plaintiffs owned land adjacent to a tract for which the planning commission granted approval of plans to build a unit development. State law (Ga. Code § 69-1211(1)) empowers the zoning board "to hear and decide appeals where it is alleged there is error in any order, requirement, decision or determination made by an administrative official in the enforcement of any ordinance or resolution." The state court of appeals held that the county planning commission was within the meaning of "administrative official," and directed the zoning board to hear plaintiffs' claim. *Held:* The state supreme court agreed that the planning commission may be viewed, under certain circumstances, as an administrative official, but held that its approval of the development plans did not constitute an enforcement decision as required in the statute. The court of appeals decision was reversed. *Royal Atlanta Dev. Corp. v. Staffieri,* 223 SE2d 128 (1976).

Massachusetts Planning board refused to approve a requested endorsement on the grounds that on the face of the proposed plan there were violations of local zoning bylaws. The owner of the property appealed to superior court, and the board was reversed. *Held:* Judgment affirmed. The planning board had no authority to refuse endorsement on the basis of possible zoning law irregularities in the plan. A planning board is limited to consideration of whether the plan shows a proper subdivision, and has no power to consider conformity with zoning laws. *Smalley v. Planning Bd.,* 410 NE2d 1219 (App. Ct. 1980).

West Virginia Planning commission refused to approve plaintiff's plat, citing, inter alia, the likelihood of traffic congestion and inadequate provision for schools and recreation. Developers appealed, arguing that the commission exceeded its statutory powers. *Held:* Judgment for developers. The statute that grants authority to the commission expressly limits the exercise thereof. Any action taken on subdivison platting applications must be derived from such statutory provisions and supported by credible evidence. *Singer v. Davenport,* 264 SE2d 637 (1980).

43.80 Judicial Review

9th Circuit When his application for a homestead entry was denied, plaintiff sued to have the property reclassified from suitable for retention to suitable for dismissal. *Held:* The department of the interior classified the property under the Classification and Multiple Use Act of 1964. The department had broad discretionary power under the act to evaluate the property. There was no judicial review of the administrative decision, since it was not clearly erroneous. *Strickland v. Morton,* 519 F2d 467 (1975).

Georgia Lessor and lessee of a granite quarry sought a variance from zoning restrictions. Neighbors appeared at a hearing before county board of zoning appeals to object, but the variance was granted. Neighbors then appealed, demanding a de novo jury trial pursuant to statute. *Held:* The statute providing for a de novo jury trial review of the zoning board of appeals decision empowered the courts to readjudicate questions that have already been committed to the administrative discretion of the board by state and county governing authorities. Thus, the statute is unconstitutional as a violation of the separation of powers doctrine and a burdening of the courts with a nonjudicial function. *Bentley v. Chastain,* 249 SE2d 38 (1978).

Maine Plaintiff, owner of a grocery superette, was granted a permit to install self-service gasoline pumps and an underground storage tank on its premises. When neighbors appealed the zoning board's grant of the permit, Superior Court reversed the grant. Plaintiff then appealed to the Supreme Judicial Court of Maine, arguing that the neighbors lacked standing to seek judicial review and that the sale of gasoline was an accessory use to the operation of a grocery superette, and was, therefore, permissible under local zoning law. *Held:* Neighbors, who appeared at the hearing on plaintiff's application, expressed their opposition to the zoning board and proved that the permit would injure their property. Therefore, neighbors were aggrieved parties with standing to seek judicial review of the board's decision. Also, the question of whether or not the sale of gasoline would be an accessory use to the operation of a grocery/superette and, therefore, would be permissible under local zoning law involved statutory interpretation and was a question of law for the court. *Singal v. City of Bangor,* 440 A2d 1048 (1982).

43.85
—Exhaustion of Administrative Remedies

9th Circuit A city passed an ordinance that generally prohibited co-op conversions, but allowed for special use permits. Before the ordinance went into effect, owners of a rental complex who planned such a conversion informed the city that the ordinance would violate state law if it were enacted without an exemption for their complex. The owners never filed for a special use permit, but took the question to state court. The state court ruled that plaintiffs' conversion was not affected by the ordinance. Plaintiffs then sued in federal court, alleging that the city's regulation of stock cooperative conversions was unconstitutional. *Held:* The constitutionality of the ordinance was not ripe for decision. An action on the constitutionality of a zoning or land use ordinance could not be judicially adjudicated until the owners had exhausted their administrative remedies by seeking a special use permit or requesting a variance. Although the state court held plaintiffs need not seek a permit, this holding was based on state law and was not applicable to the ripeness requirements under federal law. *Shelter Creek Dev. Corp. v. City of Oxnard,* 838 F2d 375, cert. denied, 109 S. Ct. 134 (1988).

Massachusetts Plaintiffs' construction permits for a concrete plant were revoked. The permits had originally been issued "as a matter of right" under the Boston Zoning Code, but were subsequently determined to be a "conditional use," and therefore required an application. Plaintiffs obtained an injunction from the land court permitting them to continue, but the city appealed, claiming that plaintiffs had not exhausted their administrative remedies. *Held:* Plaintiffs did not need to exhaust their administrative remedies. While exhaustion of remedies is the general rule, a statute (Mass. Gen. Laws Ann. ch. 240, § 14A) specifically states that suit may be filed in land court whether a permit has been applied for or not. The same exception applies when a permit has been applied for and denied. *Banquer Realty Co. v. Acting Bldg. Comm'r,* 451 NE2d 422 (1983).

New Hampshire When the building inspector denied the landowner's petition for a building permit, the landowner appealed to the zoning board. After the zoning board upheld the building inspector's decision, the landowner appealed to the superior court without petitioning the zoning board for a rehearing. The zoning board moved to dismiss the suit on the ground that the landowner had not exhausted his administrative remedies. *Held:* A party is not always required to exhaust his administrative remedies where the constitutionality of an ordinance is at issue. Since the question at issue, whether the road adjacent to the property was a public right-of-way, was a narrow legal one, the landowner could appeal directly to the superior court. *Metzger v. Town of Brentwood,* 343 A2d 24 (1975).

Virginia Plaintiff sought a judgment declaring a zoning ordinance unconstitutional. Plaintiff owned a 1.8-acre parcel that was originally zoned for all commercial uses; the land was rezoned as a two-acre planned industrial development classification. As originally zoned, the value of the property was estimated at between $160,000 and $200,000; the value under the new zoning, with a variance, was estimated at $40,000; and, without a variance, the land had little or no value. Plaintiff contended the rezoning was an unlawful taking because it denied practical utilization of the property. *Held:* The constitutionality of the zoning ordinance would not be considered until plaintiff exhausted all the adequate and administrative remedies open to him (that is, until he sought to obtain a variance). The function of the board of zoning appeals, which varies the terms of the zoning ordinance, affords some elasticity in the application of the zoning measures. This prevents the unconstitutional operation of the ordinance in an arbitrary or confiscatory manner. *Gayton Triangle Land Co. v. Board of Supervisors,* 222 SE2d 570 (1976).

43.90
—Standing

Connecticut A widow who held a life estate in her late husband's property appealed a decision to change the name of the street abutting the property. Under Conn. Gen. Stat. § 8-8(a), "any person owning land which abuts or is within a radius of one hundred feet of any portion of the land involved in any decision of said [zoning] board . . . may . . . take an appeal . . . ," but some question existed as to whether the widow was a "person owning land." *Held:* The widow was a "person owning land" within the meaning of the statute. Since her reserved life interest was subject to her direction and control as long as she lived, she was the owner of the property in every beneficial sense and entitled to the benefits of Section 8-8. *Smith v. Planning & Zoning Bd.,* 524 A2d 1128 (1987).

Florida Property owner sued to enjoin city from granting a variance from a base-elevation ordinance, thus allowing another property owner to build below the "100-year flood level." Plaintiff alleged that the variance threatened all property owners with loss of eligibility for the federal flood insurance program, and that he would suffer irreparable damages as a result. The trial court denied the city's motion to dismiss. *Held:* Plaintiff lacked standing to enjoin the operation of a municipal ordinance because he failed to allege any "special injury" different in kind from that suffered by the public generally. *Jack Eckerd Corp. v. Michels Island Village Pharmacy, Inc.,* 322 So. 2d 57 (1975).

Georgia Plaintiff husband and wife lived in a home that was legally owned by the wife. The area across the street from their home was rezoned, and defendant proposed to build a 269-unit apartment project on the property. The husband filed a complaint seeking injunctive relief, and defendants moved for summary judgment due to husband's lack of standing. The husband then moved to join or substitute his wife as a party plaintiff. *Held:* Husband lacked standing to challenge the rezoning; however, he was entitled to substitute his wife as plaintiff in the action. A two-step "substantial interest-aggrieved citizen" analysis is employed to determine if a neighbor has standing in a rezoning case. The husband's marital status does not entitle him to an equitable interest in the home where he resides since property rights are not created in marriage assets while parties are still married. Husband lacks any recognized legal or equitable interest in the property and does not have standing to challenge the rezoning. Husband may move to substitute his wife since she had been inadvertently omitted as a plaintiff. Husband promptly moved to correct the omission, and defendants would not be prejudiced by the substitution. *Miller v. Fulton County,* 375 SE2d 864 (1989).

Illinois Plaintiff municipalities brought suit against a neighboring village after the village had adopted zoning ordinances that would enable a developer to build an open-air music theater with a capacity of 20,000 persons and parking for 7,500 automobiles. The site chosen was far from the residential areas in defendant's municipality but close to plaintiff's residentially developed areas. The suit for injunction was dismissed for lack of standing. *Held:* Reversed. The effects of rezoning portend direct, substantial, and adverse effects upon plaintiff villages in the performance of their corporate obligations, thus giving them a real interest in the subject matter of the controversy. As plaintiff had argued, the court agreed that the theater would cause them to suffer a loss of revenues due to a diminution of property values, an increase in costs necessitated by additional police manpower and vehicles to control traffic, the increased expense of clearing litter from their roads, the degradation of air quality because of increased vehicular emissions, and an increase in noise levels because of electronic amplification in the theater and traffic. *Barrington Hills v. Hoffman Estates,* 410 NE2d 37 (1980).

Maryland Following a dispute between local zoning board and city council over a reclassification request, the department of state planning moved to intervene in the case after appeals were commenced. The lower court denied the motion. *Held:* Reversed. The motion was timely and, under state statute, the department has an unrestricted right to intervene in any proceeding concerning land use, development, or construction. *Department of State Planning v. Mayor & Council,* 415 A2d 296 (1980).

Mississippi The city granted a rezoning application to a church that wished to use a house it owned in a residential neighborhood for educational purposes. The rezoning was challenged by a neighborhood association. The church claimed the association could not appeal the decision because it was not a "person aggrieved" within the meaning of the statute authorizing appeals of zoning decisions. *Held:* The case was remanded for a factual assessment according to criteria set out by the state Supreme Court. In order to appeal the rezoning, the association would have to (1) allege an adverse impact on its members more specific than that which threatens the public at large and (2) show that its membership corresponded to the persons affected. That is, its membership criteria must not be so broad as to accept intermeddlers with no real stake in the controversy, or so narrow as to make the association a mere faction. *Belhaven Improvement Ass'n v. City of Jackson,* 507 So. 2d 41 (1987).

Nebraska A landowner contested the amendment to a zoning ordinance that would reclassify land adjacent to his own from residential to commercial. He claimed standing as a citizen, resident, taxpayer, and owner of neighboring land. *Held:* The landowner was not an "aggrieved" person within the meaning of Neb. Rev. Stat. § 15-1201, which allowed an appeal from an amendment to a city zoning ordinance. Landowner failed to demonstrate a special injury different in kind from that suffered by the general public. The possibility of an increase in business competition is not sufficient injury to confer standing to challenge a zoning amendment. *Copple v. City of Lincoln,* 315 NW2d 628 (1982).

New York Lessees of a car wash that operated under a variance appealed the grant of a similar variance to the owners of an adjacent parcel, who wished to open their own car wash. The only substantial objection presented was that the new car wash would cause the old one losses through competition. *Held:* Lessees of the existing car wash lacked standing. The problem was not that they were lessees, however. In order to be an "aggrieved" person entitled to challenge the variance, the lessees would need to have made a threshold showing of some special damage, different in degree and kind from that experienced by the general public. The threat of increased competition did not constitute such damage. *Sun-Brite Car Wash, Inc. v. Board of Zoning & Appeals,* 508 NE2d 130 (1987).

43.95
—Procedural Matters

U.S. District Court, Colorado Veterinarians used a lot in town to hold over 200 cattle in connection with their practice. A new ordinance limited the number to 36. Veterinarians were cited for violating the ordinance by the town building inspector, who also voted against their appeal of the citation in his capacity as zoning board member. The inspector was also among those who had brought a civil nuisance action against the veterinarians seeking abatement of their handling of livestock. The veterinarians alleged lack of due process in the hearing of their appeal of alleged violations. *Held:* The ordinance was valid, but the board's disposition of the veterinarians' appeal of the citation was not. The building inspector's financial interest in the civil suit, as well as the fact that he issued the citation being appealed, required that he should have recused himself from the matter. *Leverett v. Town of Limon,* 567 F. Supp. 471 (1983).

Connecticut Plaintiff sought approval of a plan from the zoning commission to convert an abandoned gas station into an office building. When the commission rejected plaintiff's plan, plaintiff appealed the decision. In his appeal he attacked the local zoning regulations as being unconstitutional per se for vagueness and for an impermissible delegation of legislative authority. *Held:* A party may not, in the same proceeding, request favorable treatment under a zoning regulation and raise the question of its constitutionality. The party could, however, raise the issue of constitutionality in a proper independent proceeding, in which all interested landowners are given notice and an opportunity to intervene. *Bierman v. Westport Planning & Zoning Comm'n,* 440 A2d 882 (1981).

Connecticut Property owner, found by zoning commission to have violated zoning regulations by maintaining an invalid nonconforming use on his property, brought suit to challenge the constitutionality of the ordinances. The provisions for regulation of nonconforming uses required of property owners "sufficient proof as the Zoning Commission may require to prove . . . the existence of a nonconforming use." The zoning commission argued that one cannot both attack the per se unconstitutionality of a zoning ordinance and argue compliance therewith. *Held:* Property owner was not estopped from raising the constitutional challenge by asserting that his use of the property was a valid nonconforming use under the ordinance. There was no estoppel because noncompliance could result in criminal liability, and the constitutional attack was made in an independent proceeding. The zoning ordinance violated the due process clause because it lacked sufficient guidelines and ascertainable standards for the zoning commission and those affected to know their rights and obligations. *Helbig v. Zoning Comm'n of Noank Fire Dist.,* 440 A2d 940 (1981).

Michigan When property owners sued to enjoin a city from interfering with their efforts to construct multi-family dwellings on property zoned single-family residential, neighboring property owners situated within 300 feet of the property petitioned to intervene as a matter of right. *Held:* Intervention is authorized where the petitioner's interests are not adequately represented by the parties, and the petitioner would be bound by the judgment. Where the city was primarily concerned with citywide zoning patterns, would not be guided solely by consideration of individual hardships, and might compromise the petitioners' interests, the petition should be granted. *D'Agostini v. City of Rosenville,* 240 NW2d 252 (1976).

Minnesota A subdivision application was denied by city council for environmental reasons. The trial court affirmed this decision in a summary judgment, holding that there was no need to try the case de novo because a verbatim record of the city council proceeding was available. The question of the necessity for a trial was eventually appealed to the state supreme court. *Held:* A trial was not necessary. Extensive documentation was available for the trial court to review, and the city council hearing was fairly conducted. In such a situation, there is no reason for the trial court to take new evidence into consideration, unless there was some good reason why it was not presented at the hearing. This rule encourages applicants to present all their evidence to the municipal body in the first instance, rather than to reserve some in the event of a later trial. *Swanson v. City of Bloomington,* 421 NW2d 307 (1988).

Missouri After a railroad received a judgment ordering that land in which it was interested be converted to commercial purposes, a city council member attempted to intervene, based on her status as a civil leader and the proximity of her residence to the land in question. The railroad claimed that the council member should have appeared at trial, at which she had been invited to testify. *Held:* The council member was precluded from intervening after judgment. While she might have been able to intervene as of right during trial, she waited too long to exercise her right. *City of Bridgeton v. Norfolk & WRR,* 535 SW2d 99 (1976).

Rhode Island Adjoining landowners sued to challenge the validity of a zoning amendment that classified a 33.5-acre tract from residential to limited business-multi-family use. On appeal, the property owners were required to post a $10,000 surety bond. *Held:* Because of the size of the apartment development and the delay in its construction due to the preliminary injunction, the trial judge did not abuse his discretion in ordering the bond. *Camara v. City of Warwick,* 358 A2d 23 (1976).

Vermont Electric company petitioned the public service board, seeking a declaration that it was not required to secure a zoning permit from the city for a facility covered by a certificate of public good issued by the board. After the petition was filed, the city sued in superior court to obtain a contrary ruling without attempting to stay the board order. *Held:* While the public service board and the superior court have concurrent jurisdiction for such declaratory actions, the company's resort to the board gave it exclusive jurisdiction. The validity of the city's zoning ordinance was not raised merely by seeking judicial review. *City of So. Burlington v. Vermont Elec. Power Co.,* 344 A2d 19 (1975).

43.100
Governmental Immunity

5th Circuit Plaintiff, owner of a tract of land zoned for single-family residential use, requested the city council rezone it for a medical office complex. While the planning commission was considering its recommendation on the rezoning, it was also planning to expropriate plaintiff's property by eminent domain for street realignment. Thereafter, plaintiff requested rezoning to multi-family residential. The commission delayed over three years in deciding both rezoning requests. Plaintiff sued the city and its mayor for deprivation of property without due process and just compensation resulting from the delay.

Held: Plaintiff did not have valid claims. The mayor had absolute immunity from federal damage claims arising from his conduct when acting in a legislative capacity, and exercise of his veto was clearly such an act. Although the city lacked absolute immunity, the court ruled that a taking had not occurred. "Mere fluctuations of value during the process of governmental decision-making" did not amount to a taking in violation of due process. *Hernandez v. City of Lafayette,* 643 F2d 1188 (1981), cert. denied, 455 US 907 (1982).

Georgia A nonprofit, government-funded organization asked the county zoning board to amend the county's comprehensive development resolution to allow for group homes in certain areas for the mentally retarded. The existing resolution did not allow these homes in the area where the organization had an option to build. The application was denied. The organization appealed, claiming immunity from zoning restrictions because the organization was carrying out a government function. *Held:* The resolution need not be amended to accommodate the group homes. While state entities are immune from zoning restrictions in their use of land, nonprofit organizations performing government functions generally are not, at least in the absence of clear legislative intent that such immunity be extended. *Macon Ass'n for Retarded Citizens v. Macon-Bibb County Planning & Zoning Comm'n,* 314 SE2d 218, appeal dismissed, 469 US 802 (1984).

Minnesota After landowner's building on his property was damaged by fire, the city issued him demolition and construction permits. After he demolished the building and began a new one, the city revoked the building permit because the building did not have four off-street parking spaces as required by the zoning ordinance. Landowner thought that spaces in a nearby parking facility would satisfy this requirement. The city refused to grant a variance to complete the structure. He sued for damages and the city claimed immunity. *Held:* City employees did not have the discretion to approve the construction permit in clear violation of the law, so the city had no discretionary immunity. Although the original building permit was wrongfully issued, landowner was justified in relying on it when he demolished the existing building, which did not meet the off-street parking requirement but which was grandfathered as a preexisting structure. Because landowner could not be charged with knowledge of the illegal nature of his proposed land use, he could recover in negligence against city. *Snyder v. City of Minneapolis,* 441 NW2d 781 (1989).

Ohio State determined that site of abandoned automobile plant in Cleveland was the most feasible site for a reformatory. Local zoning laws prohibited the construction on the site of a building for human habitation. City passed an ordinance prohibiting a zoning change in connection with the construction of a correctional facility. Plaintiffs sought to prevent the construction of the reformatory. Trial court held that state was required to comply with municipal zoning procedures. *Held:* In exercising its powers of eminent domain to condemn property for an essential state governmental function, state must make a reasonable effort to comply with local zoning laws, but is not required to follow a locally prescribed set of procedures to obtain approval of the local zoning agency. When reasonable efforts to comply with local land-use restrictions have been made to no avail, state may proceed with the proposed use unless enjoined by a court that determines state is not entitled to immunity from local zoning restrictions. *Taylor v. State,* 540 NE2d 310 (Ct. App. 1988).

44.00 BUILDING REGULATIONS AND PERMITS

44.05 Relation to Zoning Law

Alabama Landowner licensed to operate an automobile repair shop sought a declaratory judgment of his rights under a zoning ordinance that required repair work be done in buildings and that vehicles stored longer than 90 days be enclosed in a building. The landowner had a fenced lot where he stored wrecked and impounded cars upon which occasional repairs were made. He contended that he was not required to construct a building, because the statute required only those actively engaged in auto repair to enclose stored vehicles. *Held:* Under the ordinance, the word "shop" indicated that it was necessary to have a building and the landowner's fenced lot did not satisfy the requirements of the statute. *Parker v. City of Fultondale,* 319 So. 2d 669 (1975).

Maine Landowner of a tract zoned as a farm and forest district appealed the denial of his application to develop the tract as a campground. A campground was a permitted use in a farm and forest district, and the landowner complied with all the requirements of the zoning ordinance. The board of zoning appeals argued that the development was barred by an ordinance prohibiting dwellings on tracts of fewer than three acres. *Held:* Dwellings did not include tents and trailers intended for transient use by vacationers, and therefore the ordinance was inapplicable. The permit denial of the board of zoning appeals was ultra vires and void. The grant of such a permit is not discretionary, and neither the building inspector nor the board can deny a permit once the applicant has met all of the technical requirements of the ordinance. *Robinson v. Board of Appeals,* 356 A2d 196 (1976).

Massachusetts Landowners sued when their application for a permit to fill marshland and install a sewage system was denied by the zoning board. The board denied the permit on the ground that residential use of the land would not be permitted in any event, and that the marshland as it existed protected the ocean-food chain and prevented flooding and erosion. *Held:* Future possible requests for permits for residential use were not ground to deny the permit to fill. Where the harm to the ocean-food chain and the danger of flooding and erosion could be controlled by other limitations and safeguards, it was error to deny the permit. *MacGibbon v. Board of Appeals,* 340 NE2d 487 (1976).

Nevada A license was issued to operate a restaurant on the ground floor of an apartment building, despite the fact that the restaurant lacked a conditional use permit required under the local zoning ordinance. After the restaurant was in business, restauranteurs were cited for operating without a permit, for which they then applied. They were granted only a temporary permit. Restauranteurs sued, arguing detrimental reliance, or that the county had abused its discretion in not issuing a long-term permit. *Held:* The county was not estopped from enforcing its zoning ordinance because of restauranteurs' detrimental reliance on the county's mistaken issuance of a restaurant license. The protection of the public overrode the injury suffered by restauranteurs. The county had not abused its discretion in issuing only a temporary permit. The county had a rational motive in seeking first to determine the effect of smoke and grease from the restaurant on the neighborhood before issuing a long-term permit. *Board of County Comm'rs v. CAG, Inc.*, 654 P2d 531 (1982).

New Hampshire A zoning ordinance was amended to require additional square footage for certain units where the soil presented waste disposal problems. Shortly afterward, the town planning board approved a long-debated condominium development that did not conform to the amended ordinance. Neighbors challenged the approval, claiming that the soil at the site required the additional square footage, and that the board had erred in approving a site plan that violated a zoning ordinance. *Held:* The approval was invalid. Although the development had been under consideration long before the ordinance was amended, final approval did not come until afterward. The amended ordinance governs unless, prior to the amendment, a developer had acquired a vested right to complete the project, such as when developer had made expenditures relating to actual construction costs. *Cesare v. Town of Windham,* 430 A2d 1134 (1981).

New Jersey Landowners contracted to have a swimming pool constructed on their property, and the construction company was responsible for obtaining a building permit. The application for the permit, which was approved, incorrectly specified a different construction site from that contained in the contract. After the pool was built pursuant to the contract, the landowners were ordered to remove it since, as constructed, it violated a zoning ordinance. The landowners sued to recover for costs incurred in removing the pool. The company's defense was that the pool had been constructed in accordance with the contract. *Held:* The company had failed to exercise reasonable care in preparing the application for the permit. The landowner was entitled to recover for actual damages caused by the company's negligence. *Davi v. Cabana Pools, Inc.,* 343 A2d 478 (1975).

New York Developer bought land, over half of which was covered by a conservation easement. On the rest of the land, developer sought to build a hotel and condominium. Under local zoning law, no more than one residential unit could be built per acre. However, a "cluster" provision in the law permitted the units to be built close together. Environmentalists argued that the acreage covered by the conservation easement should not be included in determining the number of units permitted in the cluster. *Held:* The acreage of the burdened land could count toward setting the number of units permitted in the cluster. Use permitted by zoning and use permitted by easement are separate questions. The conservation easement was not an "applicable requirement" within the meaning of the zoning ordinance. *Friends of the Shawangunks, Inc. v. Knowlton,* 476 NE2d 988 (1985).

44.10 Constitutional Challenges

U.S. Supreme Court Coastal commission conditioned a construction permit for beachfront property on the owners granting a public easement across the portion of the property between two public beaches. The commission justified this condition on the need to counteract the psychological effect of restricting the use of the beach. *Held:* The easement requirement was an uncompensated taking forbidden by the Fifth Amendment. Permits may be conditioned or refused for valid public reasons, among which was the commission's desire to ensure the public visibility of the beach. However, the easement to cross the beach was not adequately related to this purpose. Thus, the majority rejected the commission's linkage of "visual access," i.e., the ability to see the beach, with physical access in the form of an easement. *Nollan v. California Coastal Comm'n,* 483 US 825 (1987).

2d Circuit A single-room occupancy property (SRO) renovation and demolition ordinance required certification that tenants had not been harassed in connection with the application. A waiver of certification was available where the SRO was purchased under a contract entered into and recorded before the date the bill was approved by legislative committee. Owners of vacant SROs bought but not recorded before the cut-off date sought an injunction against enforcement of the recordation requirement, claiming it was an uncompensated taking. *Held:* The recordation requirement was not a taking, but a reasonable measure to prevent collusive backdating of contracts by developers and purchasers. In determining whether there had been a taking, the court considered (1) the economic impact of the regulation, particularly whether the regulation interfered with investment-backed expectations; and (2) the character of the governmental action. Here, the fact that the owners would suffer financial hardship under the statute did not require a finding of a taking. As for interference with investment-backed expectations, owners knew they were taking a risk in making large investments in an enterprise clouded by regulatory uncertainty. *Sadowsky v. City of New York,* 732 F2d 312 (1984).

9th Circuit City adopted a growth policy that limited housing starts each year to approximately 6 percent of the existing housing stock, a figure substantially below the market demand for housing in the city. Additionally, it created a line intended to mark the outer geographical limits of expansion and refused to extend city facilities to land located beyond the line. The ordinance was challenged by a construction industry association. *Held:* The ordinance limiting housing starts was a reasonable exercise by the city of its police power and did not violate the due process clause. Nor was the ordinance unconstitutional as an unreasonable burden on interstate commerce, since the plan was rationally related to the environmental welfare of the city and did not discriminate against interstate commerce. *Construction Indus. Ass'n v. Petaluma,* 522 F2d 897 (1975).

Missouri Under local law, an apartment building or rooming house could be licensed only after the applicant presented a certificate of compliance with the building code and zoning law. Owners and tenants challenged the law's provision for judicial search warrants in connection with the licensing investigation. The law permitted municipal judges to issue these warrants, whereas the state constitution permitted only appellate judges or judges with original jurisdiction over an offense to issue a warrant in a criminal case. *Held:* The warrants were valid. The provisions of the state constitution regarding warrants in criminal cases did not directly or implicitly restrict the authority of municipal judges in a noncriminal context. *Frech v. City of Columbia,* 693 SW2d 813 (1985) (en banc).

New York New York City imposed a moratorium on the demolition or conversion of SRO properties. The law required that SRO owners rehabilitate and lease units at controlled rents for an indefinite period. Developers who owned SRO buildings objected to the law. *Held:* The law was invalid as both a physical and regulatory taking. It imposed on SRO owners more than their just share of the societal obligation to house the homeless, not only prohibiting conduct, but requiring that owners dedicate their property to a public purpose. The requirement that SRO owners rent their units constituted a physical taking because it compelled owners to subject their property to an undesired use. The city's argument that there was no taking because owners had some control over tenant selection and rental terms was rejected. It was the forced occupation by tenants, not their identity or lease terms, that deprived owners of their possessory interests. The law was invalid as a regulatory taking because it denied owners economically viable use of their property; and there was no clear relation between the law's restrictions and amelioration of the homeless crisis. *Seawall Assocs. v. City of New York,* 542 NE2d 1059 (1989).

Utah A county zoning ordinance allowed individuals related to or working for primary occupation farmers or dairymen to construct secondary dwellings on agriculturally zoned property without obtaining conditional use permits. The ordinance was challenged on equal protection grounds by individuals whose applications for a permit had been rejected. *Held:* The statute was constitutional because it was rationally related to legitimate public goals, including preservation of farmland and farm families, and preventing suburban encroachment. *Thurston v. Cache County,* 626 P2d 440 (1981).

44.15 Judicial Review

New Jersey A child was killed in a fire at a public housing project for which smoke detectors had recently been required by ordinance, but which had not yet been installed. The building long antedated the invention of smoke detectors. The housing authority raised the defense of design immunity, that is, that a court could not review the planning or design of an apartment building by public officials. *Held:* The housing authority's activities were reviewable. The housing authority had asserted that installation of smoke detectors was a design feature, its blueprints did not call for smoke detectors; therefore, the housing authority had immunity to suit with respect to smoke detectors. The court ruled that although smoke detectors may have been a design feature, the authority could not have claimed immunity for a feature that was not invented when the building was planned. Where, as here, a design feature is not set out in the plans, one claiming design immunity must show that the omission was deliberate and not the result simply of its having been outside the scope of consideration. *Thompson v. Newark Housing Auth.,* 531 A2d 734 (1987).

Virginia Municipality refused to grant developers' request for building permit, citing code prohibition of issuance in cases where the property abuts an unimproved street. Developers argued that the previous annexation decree obligated the municipality itself to make the necessary improvements. The lower court ordered municipal officials to issue the permits and undertake the improvements. *Held:* Judgment reversed. The annexation decree imposed a duty on the city to improve the streets but did not specify a time period within which such work was to be completed. As a consequence, it is beyond the power of a court to order municipal officials to act upon matters within their exclusive legislative discretion. *City of Stauton v. Cash,* 263 SE2d 45 (1980).

44.20 Right to Permit

Colorado Landowners petitioned to subdivide land outside the city limits for which the city was the only water and sewer servicing agency. The city refused to extend its utility services on the ground of growth control and land-use planning considerations. *Held:* The city could not refuse to extend its service to landowners for reasons unrelated to the utility program. The public has an enforceable right to demand services where there is no utility-related reason for failing to furnish such services. Since the city had not alleged a utility-related reason, such as an insufficient water supply, the city was ordered to provide service. *Robinson v. City of Boulder,* 547 P2d 228 (1976).

Illinois A three-phase condominium development site plan was approved by a village municipality. Phase one was completed and sold, but the municipality refused to issue building permits for phases two and three. The municipality argued that a height restriction that went into effect after phase one made approval impossible. *Held:* Permits for the later phases should be issued. After the original site plan was approved and permits issued for phase one, under which substantial development had occurred, the developer acquired a vested interest in completing the project that could not be nullified by the new ordinance. *Village of Palatine v. LaSalle Nat'l Bank,* 445 NE2d 1277 (1983).

Massachusetts Plaintiff sought to convert two-family houses used for summer rentals in a single-family zone into condominiums. (The houses at that time were valid, nonconforming uses.) Plaintiff argued either that the zoning law did not prohibit conversion, or that if a special permit were needed, one should be granted because the new nonconforming use was no more detrimental to the neighborhood than the old one. *Held:* A special permit was not needed for conversion to condominium ownership. A condominium conversion was merely a change in ownership, and the Massachusetts common-law rule is that a change in ownership does not destroy an existing nonconforming use. *Sullivan v. Board of Appeals,* 445 NE2d 174 (1983).

Nevada In granting plaintiff a variance for a hospital, the local planning commission required a 15-foot setback from an elementary school. One year later, however, the commission denied plaintiff's application for architectural supervision on the ground that the setback was inadequate. The architectural supervision ordinance authorized the commission to consider whether a project would "become unsightly, undesirable or obnoxious in appearance." The trial court ruled that the commission had exceeded its authority in denying plaintiff's application, because its sole authority under the ordinance was to make aesthetic determinations. *Held:* The ordinance authorized the commission to consider the general characteristics of the project, as well as its appearance. Plaintiff had no vested right to approval as a result of the initial permit issuance, because the commission possessed substantial discretion in the exercise of its functions. The commission, however, acted arbitrarily and capriciously in summarily denying the application without indicating how plaintiff could remedy any problems that might result from inadequate side setback. As a result, the case was remanded for a reprocessing of the application. *Board of County Comm'rs v. CMC,* 670 P2d 102 (1983).

New York Proceeding was brought in the state supreme court to challenge a determination of the respondent-zoning board of appeals directing the issuance of a building permit for a proposed group home. The proposed home, in a single-family residential district, would house 10 children with either two housemothers or a married couple, together with a social worker. The period of residency of a child in the group home would be at least two years. The court dismissed the petition, and petitioner appealed. *Held:* Affirmed. The proposed group home had an internal structure akin to a traditional biologically unitary family and an external appearance of a relatively normal, stable, and permanent family unit. It would therefore be regarded as a "family" for purposes of zoning requirements. Thus, the issuance of the building permit for the group home in a single-family residential district was proper. *Committee for the Betterment of Mount Kisco v. Taylor,* 404 NYS2d 380 (App. Div. 1978).

Washington Developer submitted proposed plan for a joint condominium, single-family residential development consistent with then-governing zoning ordinances. Prior to issuance of building permits, the municipality repealed the ordinances, leaving the developer's plans in violation of density requirements. *Held:* Under the minority rule in force in Washington, an applicant for a building permit has a vested right to approval if the property project conforms to the law then in force. The developer had envisioned construction in two phases, so that the overall project would be in compliance only after the second phase was completed. Even though the first phase did not conform to then-existing law, the developer is nevertheless entitled to building permits. *Mercer Enter. v. City of Bremerton,* 611 P2d 1237 (1980).

44.25 Revocation of Permit

Washington Plaintiff had a building permit vesting its rights under the prior zoning ordinance and enabling it to build a multi-family project in an area that had been downzoned for single-family use. The permit had been extended for one year, provided that plaintiff commence construction within 120 days of January 1, 1981. Despite an additional 180-day extension, plaintiff was prevented from beginning construction by financing difficulties, and the building permit expired. Plaintiff sued to compel the city to reissue the permit or respond in damages for what plaintiff termed an illegal downzone. *Held:* Because plaintiff failed to perform any permanent construction on the project for more than one year, the city was without authorization to renew its permit, and all vested rights under the prior zoning ordinance were lost. The building code required construction work to be performed in order to validate a building permit and provided that when work is not performed for one year, a permit cannot be renewed. *KSLW by Wells v. City of Renton,* 736 P2d 664 (Ct. App. 1986).

44.30 Development Fees and Requirements

9th Circuit A redevelopment agency sought to develop a parcel of land into a shopping center. A developer agreed to advance the deposit money provided that the agency would reimburse it if a development agreement was not reached. The deposit was to be repaid "to the extent legally permissible" out of the proceeds of an "assessment or development fee" to be levied on any subsequent developer of the project. The deal fell through, and the original developer sued to have the repayment agreement specifically enforced. *Held:* A subsequent developer may not be required to specifically perform an agency's alleged contractual obligation to reimburse an option deposit, absent a showing that a legally permissible method existed by which the agency could have imposed the assessment or development fee upon the subsequent developer. State law contains no provision allowing a redevelopment agency to levy an assessment on real property or on a developer of property for the purpose of reimbursing money to another developer. *Price Dev.*

Co. v. Redevelopment Agency, 852 F2d 1123 (1988).

California The city imposed a "transit impact development fee" of $5 per square foot of new office space to finance the development of public transportation. The fee was imposed on all owners of newly developed office buildings who had not yet received a building permit or certificate of occupancy. Local builders challenged the ordinance, arguing, inter alia, that the retroactive application of the ordinance to buildings under construction before its enactment was unconstitutional. *Held:* The tax was not retroactively assessed since all building permits contained a clause allowing the assessment. The resolutions that authorized the builders' permits contained a transit mitigation condition, and the challenged ordinance fell among the funding mechanisms envisioned by the resolution. Thus, application of the ordinance to owners of buildings already under construction was not an impairment of their vested right to complete construction in accordance with their building permits. *Russ Bldg. Partnership v. City & County of San Francisco,* 750 P2d 324, appeal dismissed, 109 S. Ct. 209 (1988).

New Jersey Township allocated 69 percent of the anticipated cost of roadway improvement for the next 20 years to new development, with the township paying for the remainder. A buiders' group challenged the validity of the ordinance by which the assessments were imposed. *Held:* The assessment was an "impact fee"—a charge against new development to defray the costs of basic services provided by local government. New Jersey law authorizes towns to require a developer to pay his pro rata share of the cost of providing only reasonable and necessary off-site improvements "necessitated or required by construction or improvements within a subdivision or development." This means a developer may be required to fund off-site improvements only when the need for them arises as a direct consequence of the development. Since the 20-year program of transportation improvements was not made necessary by any particular development, the ordinance was invalid. *New Jersey Builders Ass'n v. Bernards Township,* 528 A2d 555 (1987).

45.00 CIVIL RIGHTS LAW

45.05 Sales

U.S. Supreme Court Town ordinance banned the use of "For Sale" and "Sold" signs. Township officials were hoping to curtail white flight from an integrated neighborhood. The owner of some real estate in the town brought this action for declaratory and injunctive relief, claiming that the ordinance violated the First Amendment guarantee of freedom of speech. *Held:* The ordinance was unconstitutional and the owner may use such signs. The constitutional defect lies in the ordinance's preventing residents from obtaining information affecting their decision on where to live and raise a family. The township was concerned with the substance of the information conveyed, not with any commercial aspect of the signs. While the goal of the ordinance was commendable, government cannot have such sweeping power as to suppress data reflecting poorly on a locality. There was no indication that the ordinance was even needed to guarantee the township's remaining integrated. *Linmark Associates v. Willingboro,* 431 US 85 (1977).

7th Circuit The owner of a lot in a subdivision agreed to sell it to plaintiff, a black businessman, for $675,000. Covenants attached to every lot gave defendant community association rights of first refusal as to any proposed sale of a subdivision lot. Shortly before the closing, the community association voted to block the sale to plaintiff by invoking its right of first refusal. When plaintiff sued under the Fair Housing Act, the association argued that it had a legitimate interest in taking the challenged action. *Held:* The legitimacy of defendant's interest had no bearing where specific, intended discrimination was alleged. Plaintiff met his burden of proof by establishing that he was black, that he tried to purchase and was qualified to do so, that he was rejected, and that the house remained on the market. *Phillips v. Hunter Trails Community Ass'n,* 685 F2d 184 (1982).

U.S. District Court, Alabama Defendants refused to sell their motel under the installment plan to plaintiffs, who were of Indian origin. Defendants believed that Indian-operated motels were poorly operated and that the language barrier would prevent defendants from succeeding. Plaintiffs sued under the Fair Housing and Civil Rights Act. *Held:* For defendants. The Fair Housing Act was inapplicable to the dispute because the motel was neither designed nor intended for occupancy as a residency, as required by the statute. Furthermore, the Civil Rights Act does not apply when the sole basis of the claim is national origin. Discrimination based on skin color would state a claim under the act, but the record did not raise any genuine issue of fact that would establish that vendors' refusal to sell was based on anything but national origin. *Patel v. Holley House Motels,* 483 F. Supp. 374 (SD 1979).

U.S. District Court, Wisconsin After rejecting an $8,500 offer for their home by plaintiffs, who were black, homeowners sold the home to buyers, allegedly for $7,500. Eighteen days later, buyers allegedly offered the home to plaintiffs for $12,900, prompting housing bias suit against original homeowners, the realtor who sold to buyers, and buyers. Buyers moved to dismiss, disavowing any knowledge of plaintiffs' negotiations with homeowners. *Held:* For plaintiffs. Buyers may have exploited a situation tainted by racial discrimination. The price they demanded was far in excess of the property's fair market value. Plaintiff's allegations, therefore, made a prima facie case under Section 1982 of the Civil Rights Act. *Harris v. Wissert,* 514 F. Supp. 1153 (ED 1981).

Washington Buyers, who lived together without being married, sought to purchase seller's home on country club property. When seller proposed the sale to the club's board of directors, the board denied seller's application, citing the club's bylaws, which prohibited "immoral practices on club property." Buyers sued the club, alleging that its action violated the state's nondiscrimination statute, which made it an unfair practice for any person "to refuse to engage in a real estate transaction with another because of sexual or marital status." *Held:* The club did not violate the nondiscrimination statute. Although the proposed sale was a "real estate transaction" within the statute, the prohibition of discrimination on the basis of "marital status" does not apply to discrimination against unmarried couples living together. *McFadden v. Elma Country Club,* 613 P2d 146 (1980).

45.10
Mortgages and Other Credit Arrangements

7th Circuit The Southwest Community Congress (SCC) filed a class action suit charging the Veterans Administration (VA) with administering its home loan guarantee program in a manner that contributed to white flight and resegregation of the neighborhood. According to the SCC, the VA's "John Doe appraisals" speeded up housing turnover in a community-destabilizing fashion. The VA argued that the increase in the federal loan program activity was merely a symptom of resegregation. *Held:* Plaintiffs lacked standing to sue, because injury to plaintiffs from being forced to live under the threat of resegregation was not "fairly traceable" to the VA. The SCC failed to establish that different VA practices would have substantially decreased black housing demand in the target area or substantially increased the willingness of whites to remain. Moreover, there was no evidence that any specific sales were in fact accelerated by a John Doe appraisal. *Jorman v. Veterans Admin.*, 830 F2d 142 (1987).

D.C. Circuit An unmarried man and woman applied jointly for a mortgage loan from lender. Lender refused to grant the mortgage, claiming it had no duty to aggregate their incomes to determine creditworthiness, and it argued that it had the right to differentiate on the basis of marital status because the applicable state laws gave lenders greater remedies against married couples who default. The trial court agreed, saying that the lender could take note of "special legal ties" created by marriage. The couple appealed. *Held:* Lender must treat unmarried couples the same way as it considers credit applications from married couples. The federal Equal Credit Opportunity Act makes it illegal for a creditor to discriminate on the basis of marital status. Moreover, any "special ties" of marriage were irrelevant, since both the man and woman would have been jointly liable for the loan. *Markham v. Colonial Mortgage Serv. Co.*, 605 F2d 566 (1979).

U.S. District Court, Maryland A pro se plaintiff brought a class action against city officials on behalf of unemployed, black city residents living below the poverty line. The suit charged that defendants were unlawfully discriminating against the class by preventing its members from purchasing deteriorated buildings that the city owned and periodically sold for the purpose of renovation. Plaintiff sought an injunction and damages in the form of three buildings. *Held:* Relief denied. Plaintiff's cause of action had no constitutional or statutory basis. There was no violation of the Fourteenth Amendment's due process clause, since plaintiff failed to identify any entitlement he had to city-owned property that could have been infringed. Although plaintiff's complaint could be read as suggesting that he and his class were discriminated against on the basis of race, he failed to provide sufficiently specific allegations. *Allen v. Brodie,* 573 F. Supp. 87 (1983), appeal dismissed, 729 F2d 1451 (1984).

U.S. District Court, Michigan Plaintiff sued the city and the Department of Housing and Urban Development (HUD), seeking damages for discrimination under the Housing and Community Development Act of 1974 because she had been denied a housing repair loan under the community development block grant program. Defendants moved to dismiss. *Held:* For defendants. The statute does not expressly authorize a private right of action, and the court refused to imply one. The act has a specific antidiscrimination provision, and plaintiff was one of the class for whose benefit the act was passed. However, a damage remedy would be inconsistent with the purpose of the rehabilitation loan program in that it would divert program resources from the act's goal, which is to rebuild and revitalize urban areas. *Nabke v. United States Dep't of Hous. & Urban Dev.*, 529 F. Supp. 5 (WD 1981).

45.15 Leases

U.S. Supreme Court Petitioner brought suit on charges of violation of the fair housing provision of the Civil Rights Act of 1968, claiming she was denied housing by landlords because of her race. At issue was whether the Civil Rights Act or the Seventh Amendment requires a jury trial upon demand in an action for damages and injunctive relief. *Held:* The Seventh Amendment clearly gives a party a right to a jury trial in an action of this kind. Although the Civil Rights Act does not in itself explicitly grant a jury in this particular situation, there must be a jury trial if either party—plaintiff or landlord—demands one. *Curtis v. Loether,* 415 US 189 (1974).

11th Circuit A black woman, working as a "tester" for a fair housing group, was informed that no apartments were available, yet her white counterpart had been offered a one-bedroom apartment. She sued under Section 1982 of the Civil Rights Act of 1986, which provides, inter alia, that all citizens have the same right to lease real property. The management of the apartment complex argued that the woman had no standing to sue, since, as a tester who did not actually intend to rent the apartment, she suffered no personal injury. *Held:* The woman had standing to sue under Section 1982. The Eleventh Circuit agreed with *Meyers v. Pennypack Woods Home Ownership Assn.*, 559 F2d 894 (1977), in which the Third Circuit held that a black tester, motivated solely by the desire to challenge alleged discriminatory practices, had standing under Section 1982 to maintain a civil rights action. *Watts v. Boyd Properties, Inc.*, 758 F2d 1482 (1985).

Maine Tenants, recipients of public welfare, sought to enjoin their landlord and others from evicting them in violation of the state human rights act. *Held:* A violation of the statute can be shown only where a landlord seeks an eviction "solely" because the tenant receives welfare, and not merely because such status is a contributing or even the predominant reason. If tenant complaints, late rental payments, or other matters caused the landlord to seek eviction, the existence of such factors prevents application of the statute. *Vance v. Speakman,* 409 A2d 1307 (1980).

Michigan A landlord of a multi-unit apartment complex restricted families with children to certain designated buildings. In addition, the landlord denied the children of these tenants access to the swimming pool. When two families took their children to the pool, the landlord commenced eviction proceedings against them. On receipt of a complaint from these families, the state department of civil rights filed suit on behalf of the tenants, claiming discrimination in real estate transactions on the basis of age. *Held:* For landlord. The Michigan Supreme Court upheld a lower court decision that distinguished discrimination on the basis of chronological age from disparate treatment of families with children. In so doing, the court held that the designation of some buildings within a multi-unit complex for families with children does not per se violate the Michigan Civil Rights Act prohibition against age discrimination. Thus, the court ruled that a landlord has the right to restrict families with children to certain buildings within an apartment complex. *Department of Civil*

Rights v. Beznos Corp., 365 NW2d 82 (1984).

Minnesota In an unlawful detainer action against minority tenants, the landlord was awarded possession of the premises. Later, the tenants filed charges of bias against the landlord with the Minneapolis Commission on Civil Rights, and a finding of bias was affirmed by the district court. The landlord appealed, arguing that the commission was collaterally estopped from relitigating the issue of discriminatory eviction because of the verdict for the landlord in the unlawful detainer action. *Held:* The fact that no formal judgment was entered in the unlawful detainer action did not prevent an estoppel. By vacating the apartment before a formal judgment was entered, plaintiffs, in effect, acquiesced in the verdict. Plaintiffs had a full and fair opportunity to litigate the discrimination issue in the unlawful detainer action. Therefore, plaintiffs were collaterally estopped from relitigating the issue before the commission. *Ellis v. Minneapolis Comm'n on Civil Rights,* 319 NW2d 702 (1982).

45.20 Use of Property

U.S. Supreme Court Large anti-Semitic slogans, phrases, and symbols were sprayed in red and black paint on the outside walls of a synagogue. Members of the congregation brought suit, alleging that the defendants' desecration of the synagogue had violated 42 USC § 1982 and the Maryland common law of trespass, nuisance, and intentional infliction of emotional distress. The trial court dismissed the claims, holding that discrimination against Jews is not racial discrimination under Section 1982. *Held:* Jews can state a Section 1982 claim of racial discrimination, since they were among the peoples considered to be distinct races, and hence within the protection of the statute, at the time it was passed. *Shaare Tefila Congregation v. Cobb,* 481 US 615 (1987).

U.S. Supreme Court City council authorized the closing of a street located in a predominantly white community and heavily traveled by blacks. The closing was requested by white residents to decrease vehicular traffic, increase child safety, and reduce "traffic polution." A class action suit on behalf of Memphis blacks challenged the closing as a violation of the Thirteenth Amendment and Section 1982 of the Civil Rights Act. *Held:* The street closing was motivated not by racial factors but by an interest in protecting the safety and property values of a residential community. Although the closing was designed to benefit white residents, there was no reason to believe the city would refuse to grant black residents a similar benefit. *City of Memphis v. Green,* 451 US 100, reh'g denied, 452 US 955 (1981).

8th Circuit The county board of commissioners approved plaintiff's use of site in agricultural zone as a landfill. When a neighboring landowner succeeding in having that decision overturned in state court, plaintiff sought a rezoning from agricultural to industrial; but the board denied it. Plaintiff sued, charging that the refusal to rezone was arbitrary, capricious, and deprived them of property without due process. *Held:* Due process was afforded plaintiffs through the availability of state law procedures. It was an open question in the Eighth Circuit whether a substantive due process claim may arise from the denial of a zoning permit. In a concurring opinion, a majority of the court agreed that substantive due process claims should arise from the denial of a zoning application only if the board's decision was made in a truly irrational manner. Allegations that the decision was arbitrary and capricious did not suffice. *Lemke v. Cass County, Neb.*, 846 F2d 469 (1987).

New Jersey Plaintiff brought an action against borough alleging illegal and discriminatory practices in the operation and maintenance of its publicly owned beaches bordering the Atlantic Ocean. Plaintiff maintained that the dry beach area is subject to the public trust doctrine and should be available to the general public as well as residents so that there may be a proper enjoyment of public trust rights. *Held:* The public trust doctrine requires that municipally owned upland sand area adjacent to tidal water must be open to all on equal terms and without preference. All have the right to use and enjoy it, and the municipality cannot frustrate the public right by limiting its dedication of use to residents. *Van Ness v. Borough of Deal,* 393 A2d 571 (1978).

45.25
Indian Land

1st Circuit Plaintiffs, individual Indians, brought an action challenging past conveyances of Indian lands by their tribe and individual tribe members. They argued that the conveyances did not comply with the Indian Nonintercourse Act, because they were not made pursuant to a treaty or convention entered into pursuant to the U.S. Constitution. *Held:* Plaintiffs were not protected by the act, which grants relief only to tribes, because they sued as individual Indians, did not name the tribe as a plaintiff, and did not seek to represent the tribe. The court held that the same holding in *Epps v. Andrus,* 611 F2d 915, 917 (1st Cir. 1979), was stare decisis in the first circuit and would not be reexamined. Plaintiffs' motion to amend their complaint to include the tribe as a party plaintiff after they lost at the trial level was denied as untimely. *James v. Watt,* 716 F2d 71 (1983), cert. denied, 467 US 1209 (1984).

8th Circuit The Nebraska Public Power District sought to obtain, via condemnation proceedings, an easement over Indian lands for an electric transmission line. The concerned land was of two types: (1) lands allotted in severalty to individual Indians and (2) lands in which the tribe held future interests, with individual Indians holding a life estate. The district relied on a statute (25 USC § 357) allowing the condemnation of land allotted in severalty to Indians for any public purpose in the same manner as land is ordinarily condemned under the laws of the state in question. The Indians cited the 1948 Indian Right-of-Way Act, which bars the condemnation of easements on land allotted to individual Indians without the consent of each allottee and the United States as trustee. *Held:* The district could condemn the land allotted to individual Indians. Congress showed no clear intent to repeal Section 357 when it enacted the Indian Right-of-Way Act. The land in which the tribe held future interests was tribal land, however, which was not subject to the condemnation power of Section 357. *Nebraska Pub. Power Dist. v. 100.95 Acres of Land,* 719 F2d 956 (1983).

9th Circuit After applying for an Indian allotment of 160.42 acres with the Bureau of Indian Affairs under the 1887 General Allotment Act, plaintiff settled on the land and began to make improvements. Later, however, plaintiff's application was denied on the ground that the anticipated return from agricultural use would not support the residents. Plaintiff sued, claiming the land was suitable for agricultural use. *Held:* For the Bureau of Indian Affairs (BIA). There was substantial evidence that the land was unsuitable for grazing or growing cultivated crops; therefore, the denial was authorized. Furthermore, the BIA could not be estopped from denying the application on the ground that a government agent mistakenly represented that the land could be allotted or that similar land was mistakenly allotted to other Indians. *Saulque v. United States,* 663 F2d 968 (1981).

10th Circuit Plaintiff Indian tribe brought an action against the secretary of the interior and certain oil and gas lessees claiming that notices of the sale of leases on the reservation were inadequate under 25 CFR § 171.3. Plaintiff also alleged failure to comply with the National Environmental Protection Act (NEPA). *Held:* The notice regulation was not complied with, so plaintiff was entitled to damages for the loss of higher bids that proper notice would have attracted. But the court denied plaintiff equitable relief (i.e., lease cancellation) because the damage award was deemed sufficient. The NEPA claim for injunctive relief was barred by the doctrines of laches and unclean hands. The court also held that plaintiff was entitled to rentals on the leases while the action was pending because, although cancellation was denied, plaintiff could prove the secretary violated the notice regulation. *Jicarilla Apache Tribe v. Andrus,* 687 F2d 1324 (1982).

U.S. District Court, Connecticut An Indian tribe, seeking title to and possession of certain lands in Connecticut, brought suit against the state under the Indian Trade and Intercourse Act. Connecticut's defenses were that it received the lands via valid grants from private persons, that it enjoyed Eleventh Amendment immunity from the suit, and that the Tenth Amendment barred the application of the Indian Trade and Intercourse Act on these facts. *Held:* Where Connecticut received title to the land from private parties whose grant was void because the federal government did not consent to it, Connecticut's title was void. Connecticut waived its Eleventh Amendment immunity once it filed a counterclaim seeking the full value of any improvements made on Indian lands. Also, the Tenth Amendment did not bar application of the Indian Trade and Intercourse Act, since it addressed Connecticut in its capacity as a landowner, not as a sovereign state, and did not impair Connecticut's ability to structure integral operations in areas of traditional functions. *Mohegan Tribe v. State,* 528 F. Supp. 1359 (1981).

45.30
Racial Segregation in Public Housing

U.S. Supreme Court Uncontradicted evidence established that a public housing system was racially segregated and that there was need for corrective action. The question before the court was whether interdistrict relief could be granted in the absence of a finding of an interdistrict violation. *Held:* Since HUD was found to have violated the Constitution and federal statutes, remedies requiring corrective action beyond the city's boundaries could be taken. Local suburban governmental units would, however, retain the right to comment on proposals, reject programs inconsistent with their approved housing assistance plans, and require that zoning and land use instructions be observed by the builders. *Hills v. Gautreaux,* 425 US 284 (1976).

6th Circuit Minority individuals sued the housing authority, alleging that it engaged in discriminatory practices that led to segregation in the metropolitan area's public housing. They criticized a "three refusal" procedure that allowed applicants for public housing to decline the first two housing units offered them without being taken off the waiting list and also challenged the authority's failure to build public housing in the city's predominantly white suburbs. *Held:* Public housing in the city was seriously racially imbalanced. The court upheld the trial court's order that the housing authority submit an affirmative action plan to reduce racial segregation in the projects, including abandonment of the three refusal rule for new applicants and allowing earlier housing for applicants willing to move to a project where racial balance had not been achieved. Plaintiffs, however, lacked standing to challenge the housing authority's failure to build public housing in the suburbs. *Jaimes v. Toledo Metro. Hous. Auth.,* 758 F2d 1086 (1985).

7th Circuit Residents and a not-for-profit fair housing organization sued the county, alleging that it had intentionally pursued housing policies intended to exclude racial minorities and persons of low and moderate income from residing in the county. The county argued that plaintiffs lacked standing in that they had not established that the county's conduct, rather than the economics of the area housing market, was the substantial cause of the lack of housing. *Held:* Plaintiff had standing. They established that they were eligible for low- and moderate-income housing and that but for the county's policies, such housing would have been built. Plaintiffs alleged a distinct and palpable injury, in the form of deprivation of adequate housing, traceable to the alleged action, and inaction, of the county. *Hope, Inc. v. County of DuPage, Ill.,* 717 F2d 10612 (1983).

8th Circuit Low-income minorities eligible for public housing sued HUD for knowingly supporting a public housing authority that had engaged in discriminatory practices in violation of Titles VI and VIII of the Civil Rights Act and the Fifth Amendment. The local authority operated nine housing projects, and all were segregated in various ways. HUD moved for summary judgment based on a lack of discriminatory intent. *Held:* For plaintiffs. Because of HUD's long history of passivity and distribution of housing project funds despite the local housing authority's repeated failures to alleviate housing discrimination, HUD's actions had to be motivated in part by a discriminatory purpose. It is inconceivable that HUD would have so frequently acted to approve the housing authority's actions for so long unless its segregation and discriminatory policies were acceptable to HUD officials. *Clients' Counsel v. Pierce,* 711 F2d 1406 (1983).

45.35
Federal Fair Housing Act

U.S. Supreme Court A fair housing group and two of its investigators, one white and one black, sued a realty corporation for alleged violations of the Fair Housing Act. The defendant claimed plaintiffs lacked standing to sue. *Held:* The black investigator had standing; he was injured by being falsely advised as to the available housing, even though he may have expected such treatment. The fair housing group had standing because discriminatory practices impair its ability to provide housing counseling and referral services and drain its resources. The case was remanded for further proceedings on the issue of whether the white investigator was injured by deprivation of the benefits that result from living in an interracial community. *Havens Realty Corp. v. Coleman,* 435 US 363 (1982).

U.S. Supreme Court A village and six individuals brought suit against two real estate organizations for allegedly steering prospective black home buyers to one section of the village and prospective white purchasers to other parts of the village, in violation of the Fair Housing Act. The individuals conceded that they were not interested in buying a new house but had only tested the broker's steering practices. They argued that, as a result of these practices, they were denied the benefits of living in an integrated environment, and they suffered economic injury from a decline in value of their homes.

The brokers maintained that these individuals, and the village itself, could not bring the lawsuit beause they were not direct victims of discrimination. *Held:* The village and the individual parties could maintain the lawsuit under Section 812 of the Fair Housing Act, which permits direct access to the federal courts. The allegation of economic injury was sufficient for the petitioners to have standing to sue under Article III of the U.S. Constitution. *Gladstone Realtors v. Village of Bellwood,* 441 US 91 (1979).

2d Circuit Starrett City was the nation's largest housing development. The development sought to maintain a racial balance of 65 percent white, 22 percent black, and 8 percent Hispanic at the development, on the ground that the quotas were necessary to prevent white flight. The U.S. Attorney General challenged the policy as a violation of the Fair Housing Act. *Held:* Racial ceiling quotas violate the Fair Housing Act. The allocation of public housing units based on racial quotas denies an applicant access to a unit that is otherwise available solely because of that applicant's race and is, therefore, discriminatory. While quotas may promote the Fair Housing Act's integration policy, they contravene its antidiscrimination policy. Race is not always an inappropriate consideration in efforts to promote integrated housing. But the Fair Housing Act does not allow the use of rigid racial quotas of indefinite duration to maintain a fixed level of integration at Starrett City by restricting minority access to scarce and desirable housing. *United States v. Starrett City Assocs.,* 840 F2d 1096, cert. denied, 109 S. Ct. 376 (1988).

3d Circuit In response to community opposition, the city terminated the construction of a public housing project in a predominantly white area of the city in 1959. Various individuals eligible for low-income public housing and other organizations with a membership interested in such housing brought an action against the city, its housing authority, its redevelopment authority and HUD. The district court held that the city acted with discriminatory intent and thereby violated plaintiffs' constitutional and statutory rights. *Held:* Affirmed. In delaying and frustrating the construction of the project, the city acted with discriminatory intent. Additionally, the city's housing authority and redevelopment authority violated Title VIII of the Civil Rights Act of 1968 in failing to carry out construction of the project. The governmental defendants were ordered to proceed with construction of the planned project. *Resident Advisory Bd. v. Rizzo,* 564 F2d 126 (1977).

4th Circuit A black former insurance agent brought an action against his former employer alleging that its redlining practices violated 42 USC §§ 1981 and 1982 and the Fair Housing Act. Plaintiff accused the insurer of arbitrarily refusing to insure homes in predominantly black neighborhoods, thereby causing plaintiff economic harm because of his inability to sell insurance to black friends and business acquaintances. *Held:* Plaintiff lacked standing to challenge the alleged policy. Although plaintiff's loss of commission met the constitutional requirement of an injury in fact, he lacked standing because he was actually asserting the rights of others; there was nothing to prevent blacks who were denied insurance from bringing their own actions. Furthermore, the denial of insurance in minority neighborhoods does not "make housing unavailable" in violation of the Fair Housing Act. *Mackey v. Nationwide Ins. Cos.,* 724 F2d 419 (1984).

5th Circuit A landlord accused of discrimination claimed that he should not be required to comply with a HUD subpoena because Houston's Fair Housing Division had not finished its investigation of the complaint. Section 810(c) of the Fair Housing Act prohibits HUD from investigating a housing discrimination complaint if a local fair housing law provides substantially equivalent rights and remedies. *Held:* For HUD. Houston's fair housing law was not equivalent since it provided for fines rather than allowing actual and punitive damages, allowed only 60 days rather than 180 days for a complaint to be brought, and, most importantly, did not give the local Fair Housing Division any subpoena power or independent power to sue. *Pierce v. Winograd,* 757 F2d 714 (1985).

7th Circuit Property owners sued the county for failing to repair or remove dilapidated buildings acquired by the county through tax delinquency, allegedly decreasing the value of their property. They also charged that the city's failure to board up or demolish such abandoned buildings violated the Fair Housing Act and the Thirteenth and Fourteenth Amendments to the Constitution. *Held:* Plaintiffs failed to state a claim upon which relief could be granted. The causal nexus between the county's inaction and the effects alleged by plaintiffs was too tenuous to support a claim that plaintiffs' rights had been infringed upon. The county's action did not violate the Fair Housing Act in that it did not deny anyone the right to live where they chose. There was no constitutional violation in the absence of proof of unequal treatment of similarly situated persons for racial reasons or involuntary servitude that violated the Thirteenth Amendment. *Southend Neighborhood Improvement v. County of St. Clair,* 743 F2d 1207 (1984).

7th Circuit Plaintiffs sued their village to compel it to rezone their property to allow construction of federally financed low-cost housing. The village's refusal to rezone was racially discriminatory, plaintiff claimed. The U.S. Supreme Court, in a landmark decision, found that municipal zoning ordinances that have a racially discriminatory *effect* do not violate the equal protection clause of the Fourteenth Amendment, unless the ordinances' underlying *intent* is discriminatory. The Court sent the case back to the Seventh Circuit to decide whether the village's action was a violation of the Fair Housing Act. *Held:* The village had a statutory obligation to refrain from zoning policies that effectively foreclosed the construction of any low-cost housing within its boundaries, *regardless of intent.* The court based its decision on the congressional intent in enacting the Fair Housing Act to provide such housing and the need to construe the Fair Housing Act broadly to implement that goal. *Village of Arlington Heights v. Metropolitan Hous. Dev. Corp.,* 558 F2d 1283 (1977).

10th Circuit Agent of a black prospective tenant attempted to arrange housing through a real estate broker. The broker informed the agent that he could not rent to blacks. The prospective tenant brought an action against the broker for alleged violations of the Fair Housing Act of 1968. At issue was the type and amount of damages allowable. *Held:* The broker could be held liable for emotional distress even though he dealt only with the tenant's agent. However, where the broker did not own the property and had no record of bias or prejudice, punitive damages were not to be allowed. *Steele v. Title Realty Co.,* 478 F2d 380 (1973).

11th Circuit Class actions were brought under the Fair Housing Act alleging that the city had engaged in discriminatory practices contravening the intent of the Department of Housing and Urban Development's statutorily mandated policies to provide low-income housing. Plaintiffs asserted that HUD violated its obligation to "administer the programs and activities relating to housing and urban development'' in order to eliminate discrimination. *Held:* For HUD. That agency is subject to liability under the act only in two instances: (1) when HUD has taken discriminatory action itself, i.e., approving federal assistance to a project without considering the effect on the racial and socioeconomic composition of the area or (2) when HUD is aware of a grantee's biased practices and has made no effort to force it into compliance with the Fair Housing Act. Here, plaintiff's complaint did not fall into either category. *Anderson v. City of Alpharetta, Ga.,* 737 F2d 1530 (1984).

11th Circuit In 1976, plaintiffs, owners of 9.5 acres of property, entered into an agreement with a developer for the construction of a multi-family housing complex. By 1979, plaintiffs' plans for multi-family housing were dropped. In the same year, defendants rezoned their property from multi-family residential to single-family residential. As a result of the rezoning, the value of plaintiffs' property declined from $285,000 to $135,000. Plaintiffs brought suit to enjoin the rezoning on the ground that it violated the Fair Housing Act and was an unlawful taking without just compensation. *Held:* Plaintiffs, who had abandoned their plans to construct multi-family dwellings before they brought suit, were not injured parties and, therefore, lacked standing to sue under the Fair Housing Act. Nor did plaintiffs have a claim for a taking without just compensation. Neither deprivation of the most beneficial use of land, nor a severe decrease in its value measure up to an unlawful taking. A government could not persist if it had to pay for all declines in property values caused by its actions. *Nasser v. City of Homewood,* 671 F2d 432 (1982).

U.S. District Court, Michigan Suit was brought against a city for violating the Fair Housing Act by intentionally obstructing the development of a racially integrated low-income family and senior citizen project. The city claimed that it acted not out of racially discriminatory intent, but out of a desire to protect private property values. *Held:* The city's motivation was found to be based, at least in part, on racial discrimination. The court stated that its finding was based upon much more than the bigoted comments of a few affected property owners. Rather, its finding was based on a showing that members of the city commission who chose to block the project were motivated to do so by a desire to effectuate the wishes of the affected property owners, and that such wishes were based upon racial considerations. The evidence also showed that the commission members were fully aware of the motivations of the property owners. *United States v. City of Birmingham,* 538 F. Supp. 819 (ED 1982), modified on other grounds, 727 F2d 560 (6th Cir.), cert. denied, 469 US 821 (1984).

U.S. District Court, Ohio Black homeowners living in predominantly black neighborhood sued insurance company for refusing to write policies covering houses in their area (a practice commonly known as redlining). The homeowners alleged that the company had violated Section 3604(a) of the Fair Housing Act, which prohibits racial discrimination in the sale or rental of housing. The company argued that the section did not apply to insurance companies, which are not in the business of selling or renting housing. *Held:* The companies are prohibited from "redlining" by Section 3604(a). Although the Fair Housing Act does not expressly prohibit insurance redlining, insurance is a prerequisite to decent housing, and a discriminatory denial of insurance effectively prevents a person from buying a house. In accordance with Congress' intention to eliminate housing discrimination, and citing a broad interpretation in analogous contexts, the court stressed that the Fair Housing Act must be given a very expansive reading. *Dunn v. Midwestern Indem. Co.*, 472 F. Supp. 1106 (1979).

46.00 PUBLIC HEALTH AND SAFETY LAWS

46.05 Validity

U.S. Supreme Court A 20 percent tax imposed by the city on gross receipts from all nonresidential parking places was challenged by operators of private, off-street parking facilities on constitutional grounds. *Held:* The tax was valid. The Court wrote: "The City was constitutionally entitled to put the automobile parker to the choice of using other transportation or paying the increased tax." *City of Pittsburgh v. Aleo Parking Corp.*, 416 US 903 (1974).

U.S. District Court, District of Columbia Zoning Commission down-zoned a portion of the downtown area to prohibit many types of office and business structures in order to make the area primarily an area of residences and small shops. About 50 percent of the existing structures became nonconforming in their use, but the area contained vacant land and land occupied by condemned buildings. Many property owners in the area, including one which had planned to build an office structure, attacked the commission's action. At issue was whether an environmental impact statement was required. *Held:* No environmental impact statement was required because the action of the commission was essentially local, not federal. *Ruppert v. Washington*, 366 F. Supp. 686 (1973), aff'd, 543 F2d 416 (1976).

California City prohibited the erection of outdoor signs in certain locations, asserting that Cal. Gov't Code § 38774 authorized cities to regulate the placement of such signs and billboards by enacting an ordinance adopted by the procedure prescribed for the adoption of ordinances generally. Plaintiff claimed that the ordinance could be enacted only when the procedure for enacting zoning ordinances was followed. *Held:* The city had the power under Section 38774 to enact the ordinance regulating the use of signs. *City of Escondido v. Desert Outdoor Advertising, Inc.*, 505 P2d 1012, cert. denied, 414 US 828 (1973).

Colorado Property owners brought an action for declaratory judgment, seeking to have a town ordinance declared unconstitutional. The ordinance required the construction of two types of fencing for multi-family dwellings. The statute required the erection of board fences around trash collection areas and wood fences around sides or rearlot boundaries. *Held:* A city may, in the exercise of its police power, restrict the use of property in a manner that is not arbitrary or unreasonable and that bears a substantial relationship to a legitimate governmental concern. Where the object of the ordinance is the protection of health, safety, and welfare of the community (i.e., refuse and litter control), the matter is within the scope of legitimate governmental concern. Where the object of the ordinance is the protection of health, safety, and welfare of the community (i.e., refuse and litter control), the matter is within the scope of legitimate municipal concern. Nor were the property owners denied equal protection under the laws where multi-family dwellings were required to provide fences, but single-family dwellings were not, in view of the fact that the multi-family property classification has a rational basis in that litter control becomes correspondingly more acute in proportion to population density. *Mosgrove v. Town of Federal Heights,* 543 P2d 715 (1975).

Iowa When a town sued to enjoin a wrecking and excavating company from operating a landfill, on the ground that the company failed to obtain a required permit, the company argued that the ordinance requiring the permit was invalid. *Held:* A municipality has the right to regulate the disposal of garbage and landfill to prevent the creation of public nuisances. Where defendant offered no evidence to rebut the presumption that the ordinance was valid, the ordinance was presumed to be reasonable. The ordinance was not unreasonable merely because a better means might exist. *Incorporated Town of Carter Lake v. Anderson Excavating & Wrecking Co.,* 241 NW2d 896 (1976).

Massachusetts Defendant challenged the constitutionality of a city traffic regulation that permitted only residents of the city to park in certain areas. The areas were in congested neighborhoods near the court house and other public facilities, and they were accessible by public transportation. *Held:* The regulation did not deny nonresidents equal protection. The regulation bore a rational relationship to furthering legitimate state interests of reducing highway congestion and air pollution and of encouraging public transportation. *Commonwealth v. Petralia,* 362 NE2d 513 (1977).

Minnesota Village ordinance prohibited persons from dwelling in trailers for periods in excess of three days, unless they applied for and obtained a permit. Owner of mobile home challenged the constitutionality of the ordinance on the ground of vagueness and lack of ascertainable standards but at trial admitted that he understood its requirements. *Held:* A public regulation to promote public health and safety is presumptively valid. Where plaintiff admits at trial that he understands its requirements, no clear showing of vagueness has been established to overcome the presumption of validity. Although ordinance lacked express guidelines for the issuance of permits, implied limitations and accepted common-law standards designed to promote the public health, safety, and welfare would be applied. *Paal v. Village of Wells,* 232 NW2d 808 (1975).

Missouri Local ordinance required that all shopping centers with parking areas in excess of a stated minimum provide security for the protection and safety of shoppers. A shopping center contended that the locality,which had a home-rule charter, lacked the authority to enact such an ordinance. *Held:* A home-rule charter carries with it an implied grant of such powers as are reasonably necessary to the exercise of the power granted. Such a charter may not invade the province of general legislation involving the public policy of the state as a whole. Therefore, since compelling owners of private property to provide police protection for shoppers was a matter of state-wide concern, the locality lacked the authority to enact the ordinance. *Flower Valley Shopping Center, Inc. v. St. Louis County,* 528 SW2d 749 (1975).

46.10 Enforcement

U.S. Supreme Court A real estate management company operated nine apartment and office buildings under contract with the buildings' different owners. The management company obtained tenants, signed leases, collected rents, and employed maintenance workers. At issue was whether the management company was an "enterprise" so as to be subject to the wage and overtime provisions of the Fair Labor Standards Act (FLSA). The FLSA provides that an enterprise within its jurisdiction must have "annual gross volume of sales made or business done" of at least $250,000. The management company claimed that its commission were less than the statutory minimum, and it therefore was not subject to the FLSA. *Held:* The management company was an "enterprise" within the meaning of the FLSA definition because it engaged in related activities under common control for a common business purpose. Gross rentals, rather than commissions, were the proper measure of "annual gross volume of sales made or business done" under the statute. *Brennan v. Arnheim & Neely, Inc.*, 410 US 512 (1973).

District of Columbia Landlord was convicted of housing code violations involving the use of lead paint in one apartment. He contended that he lacked the mens rea to be found guilty, and that the burden of correcting the condition was excessive. *Held:* Where reasonable regulations create public welfare offenses for the purpose of maintaining the health and safety of those ill-equipped to protect themselves, the defenses of good faith or lack of mens rea are unavailable. A property owner may not avoid compliance with safety standards merely because it is expensive or difficult. Where the cost of removing the paint was only $800, the repairs were simple in nature, and the prosecution was not started until four months after notice of the violations was given, the obligations were not unreasonable. *Holmes v. District of Columbia,* 354 A2d 858 (1976).

New York Developer of discotheque dance hall was denied a liquor license because the immediate neighborhood could not accommodate the expected traffic and parking congestion. The developer appealed. *Held:* Reversed. Matters such as parking and traffic congestion are the exclusive province of city zoning authorities and cannot be considered by liquor licensing officials in ruling on otherwise proper applications. *Circus Disco Ltd. v. Liquor Auth.*, 409 NE2d 963 (1980).

47.00 FEDERAL ENVIRONMENTAL PROTECTION LAWS

47.05 National Environmental Protection Act

U.S. Supreme Court After the serious nuclear accident at Three Mile Island, the Nuclear Regulatory Commission (NRC) decided to permit the renewed operation of an undamaged reactor. The NRC did not take evidence from neighboring residents showing that the restart would cause both severe psychological harm to persons living in the area and serious damage to the well-being of surrounding communities. For this reason, respondents contended that the NRC failed to comply with the National Environmental Policy Act (NEPA). *Held:* Under NEPA, the NRC need not assess every impact of its proposed action; it is required only to study the restart's effect on the physical environment. Moreover, the causal connection between the change in the physical environment, the operation of the reactor, and the effect at issue (the alleged psychological harm) was too far removed for NEPA to apply. *Metropolitan Edison Co. v. People Against Nuclear Energy,* 460 US 766 (1983), rev'g by unanimous decision 678 F2d 222 (DC Cir. 1982).

1st Circuit City residents sued to enjoin the financing and construction of a federally subsidized housing project on the ground that the Department of Housing and Urban Development (HUD) had failed to comply with NEPA requirements. At the time of the suit, the work on the project was well underway. *Held:* Since plaintiffs failed to show that the federal government planned to participate in future projects involving the neighborhood site and since federal participation in the present development of the site was complete, compliance with NEPA was not required. *Chick v. Hills,* 528 F2d 445 (1976).

5th Circuit HUD approved funding for the construction and operation of a proposed low-income housing project after following its own guidelines and finding the proposed project would have no significant environmental impact. Plaintiffs claimed HUD's preconstruction clearance procedures to be defective and in deliberate disregard of NEPA because the agency did not consider the project's adverse impact on existing noise and crowding problems. However, plaintiffs did not seek to set aside the approval and enjoin further funding of the project until after construction and occupancy were completed. *Held:* Plaintiffs' demands were deemed moot and inappropriate. In the absence of blatant bad faith violations of NEPA-mandated preconstruction procedures, NEPA does not contemplate relief after the challenged project has been substantially or wholly completed. HUD substantially complied with NEPA procedures and acted reasonably in considering the environmental consequences of its decision. *Richland Park Homeowners Ass'n, Inc. v. Pierce,* 671 F2d 935 (1982).

9th Circuit City sued to enjoin the construction of a highway interchange by the state highway department on the ground that the project violated NEPA. The department alleged that the city lacked standing to challenge the project under NEPA. *Held:* Although the immediate purpose of the new interchange was to provide access to a limited number of local motorists, the long-range objective was to stimulate industrial development in the area. Therefore, the city had standing to challenge construction of the interchange on the ground that NEPA had been violated. Pursuant to NEPA, an environmental impact statement must be prepared and public hearings conducted before construction of interchange could proceed. *City of Davis v. Coleman,* 521 F2d 661 (1975).

U.S. District, Georgia In June 1968, the Federal Aviation Administration (FAA) approved the city's plan to construct a fourth runway at its international airport. However, the FAA was still required to install navigational aids and adopt flight procedures to make the runway operational. Construction had not yet begun when, in January 1970, NEPA went into effect. Under the new law, the FAA viewed its remaining duties as major federal actions requiring environmental assessment before any construction could be undertaken. The city contended that NEPA did not apply since the FAA had already approved the plan before NEPA became law. *Held:* NEPA applied to the FAA's obligation to install navigational equipment and adopt flight procedures regardless of when the runway project was approved. These were major federal actions significantly affecting the environment, for they made possible substantially increased air traffic with its attendant increases in noise and air pollution. *City of Atlanta v. United States,* 531 F. Supp. 506 (ND 1982).

47.10
—Necessity of Environmental Impact Statement

U.S. Supreme Court The U.S. Navy planned to construct weapons storage facilities in Hawaii. It prepared several environmental assessments for a particular site, concluding that the new construction, as well as the storage, handling, and transport of nuclear weapons, would have no significant environmental effect. Petitioners, concerned about the impact a nuclear accident at the proposed site would have on the population and environment of Hawaii, claimed that the Navy violated NEPA by not issuing and disclosing an environmental impact statement (EIS). *Held:* An EIS was not required, since Congress intended that the public's interest in the Navy's compliance with NEPA yield to the government's need to preserve military secrets. The information relating to the Navy's weapons storage facilities was classified as secret under executive order, and, therefore, was exempt under the Freedom of Information Act from the public disclosure requirements of NEPA. *Weinberger v. Catholic Action of Hawaii/Peace Educ. Project,* 454 US 139 (1981).

U.S. Supreme Court Environmental organization sued to enjoin the sale of lots in a 3,000-lot development, claiming that an EIS was required by NEPA. The lots were along a state-designated scenic river, and the developer had filed documents with the HUD pursuant to the Interstate Land Sales Act (ILSA). *Held:* NEPA's EIS does not apply to such a case. NEPA must yield because there is a clear and unavoidable conflict in statutory duty; the secretary of HUD cannot comply with his statutory duty to allow the developer's statement of record to go into effect within 30 days of filing and simultaneously prepare impact statements on the proposed development. *Flint Ridge Dev. v. Scenic Rivers Ass'n,* 425 US 902 (1976).

3d Circuit The NRC approved the proposal of a nuclear generating plant to expand its spent fuel storage capacity. The NRC determined that an EIS was unnecessary, in that the expansion did not "significantly affect the quality of the human environment." The township-petitioner contended that this determination was unreasonable and in violation of NEPA. *Held:* The NRC did not err or act unreasonably in approving the plan without first issuing an EIS. Petitioner failed to meet its burden under NEPA to furnish evidentiary support for its contention that the expansion of the plant's spent fuel capacity was "significant" for NEPA purposes. Moreover, the NRC conducted an adequate environmental review, which petitioner failed to address. *Lower Alloways Creek Township v. Public Serv. Elec. & Gas Co.,* 687 F2d 732 (1982).

9th Circuit HUD determined that an EIS was not required when it approved plans for the interior conversion of a building into low-income housing units, because the proposal would have no significant environmental impact. Plaintiffs, a group of local artists and residents of the building, contended that this determination violated NEPA, in that HUD failed to consider the irreparable damage to the cultural character of the area caused by the proposed rehabilitation. *Held:* HUD acted reasonably in finding no significant impact on the physical environment, and therefore, no EIS was required. Under NEPA, the cultural and esthetic effects of proposed actions do not, by themselves, require an EIS. It is appropriate for HUD to consider potential cultural effects only when an EIS is generated because of a proposed project's primary impact on the physical environment. *Goodman Group, Inc. v. Dishroom,* 679 F2d 182 (1982).

9th Circuit Plaintiffs sued to enjoin the construction of extensive improvements to an airport until a satisfactory EIS was submitted. The airport's commission had adopted a 15-year plan for the extensive expansion and improvement of the airport, and the project was to be supported in part by federal funds. The work on parking garages and the terminal under construction at the time of the suit was financed by state funds. *Held:* Approval of an airport layout plan by the FAA does not require an EIS. Pursuant to NEPA, an EIS is required for federally funded projects entailing federal action. Where state-funded, locally funded, and federally funded projects are not functionally interdependent an EIS is required only for that portion of the project to use federal funds. *Friends of Earth, Inc. v. Coleman,* 518 F2d 323 (1975).

D.C. Circuit The U.S. Forest Service and the Department of the Interior (appellees) issued oil and gas leases on lands within two national forests. The leases provided that the appellees could not preclude surface-disturbing activities; they could not deny a permit to drill but could only impose reasonable conditions designed to mitigate the environmental impacts of drilling operations. Appellees determined that since this stipulation would prevent significant adverse environmental impact, no EIS was required prior to the leases' issuance. Plaintiff contended that the issuance of the leases alone, without the preparation of an EIS, violated NEPA. *Held:* Under NEPA, appellees must either prepare an EIS prior to leasing or retain the authority to preclude surface-disturbing activities until the appropriate environmental analysis is completed. The lease stipulation, by itself, put appellees in violation of their duty under NEPA to evaluate all significant environmental impacts of their actions before the point of commitment or leasing. *Sierra Club v. Peterson,* 717 F2d 1409 (1983).

U.S. District Court, New York HUD issued a final loan commitment for a senior citizen housing project of 111 units. Under HUD regulations, an EIS was required only for projects of 500 units or more. Therefore, its environmental impact was evaluated under the agency's lowest level of scrutiny, and HUD found the building not to be a major federal action significantly affecting the environment. Plaintiffs, concerned about the project's impact on the area's existing sewage systems, contended that HUD acted arbitrarily in making this determination and in fixing the 500-unit cutoff point for filing an EIS. *Held:* It was not arbitrary for HUD to rely on its own regulations to fix 500 units as the EIS cutoff point, or for it to rely on its own procedures when it found no major, significant federal action. This finding was reasonable, and therefore entitled to great deference. *United Neighbors Civic Ass'n v. Pierce,* 563 F. Supp. 200 (ED 1983).

U.S. District Court, Pennsylvania A multi state river basin commission approved revised plans for a river water diversion project primarily because the amount of water to be withdrawn from the river was reduced from 150 to 95 million gallons per day. This was the only substantial change from the originally approved plans, which had already generated at least three prior EISs. After following its own regulations, the commission issued a final environmental assessment (FEA), which found that the decreased water usage would have no significant adverse environmental impact, and, therefore, a new, updated, EIS was not required. Plaintiffs claimed the commission's actions to be arbitrary, capricious, and an abuse of discretion. *Held:* No new EIS was required. The commission's determinations were reasonable and in compliance with law; at least three prior EISs were prepared, the project had been under constant study from its start, and the FEA sufficiently provided details of the only significant change in circumstances. *Delaware Water Emergency Group v. Hansler,* 536 F. Supp. 26 (ED 1981), aff'd, 681 F2d 805 (3d Cir. 1982).

Minnesota Petitioner, a watershed district, was requested by landowners to repair a ditch that had not been repaired since its construction in 1917. Opponents of the repair petitioned the environmental quality board, asking for the preparation of an EIS. The board, finding that "although a ditch repair is generally not considered to be the type of action requiring an EIS, [this ditch] is distinguished by its length of 8.2 miles." It concluded that an EIS was necessary because the repair would have significant environmental impact. Petitioner appealed the board's determination arguing that the repair was mandated by statute. *Held:* An EIS can be required for a statutorily mandated repair of a county ditch. The EIS requirement did not delay necessary repairs in violation of the drainage ditch statute, as the statute imposes no time limit for making repairs. In fact, no repairs had been made since the ditch was constructed in 1917. *Coon Creek Watershed Dist. v. State Envtl. Quality Bd.,* 315 NW2d 604 (1982).

New York The town board adopted three resolutions authorizing the establishment, construction, and financing of a new sewer district. The resolutions were then submitted to, and approved by, the voters in a special election authorized by the town board. An EIS was not prepared prior to either of these events. Plaintiffs contended that since the establishment of a sewer district was an action that might have an environmental impact, the town board violated the State Environmental Quality Review Act (SEQRA) by failing to issue an EIS. *Held:* SEQRA required the town board to prepare and make available to board members and to the public an EIS before the board adopted the resolutions, and before it held the special election, as these actions were determinative in establishing a project which might have a significant environmental impact. Therefore, the resolutions and the election were declared null and void. *Tri-County Taxpayers Ass'n v. Town Bd.,* 432 NE2d 592 (1982).

47.15 —Sufficiency of Environmental Impact Statement

1st Circuit An interstate highway extension was proposed that would cross a 900-acre tract containing farmland, a wildlife sanctuary, and a riding school. The owners of the farmland sought to convince federal and state officials that a different route across its property would be preferable because it would protect more fully the farm's unique resources, while providing an adequate alignment for the highway. Their proposed route was studied by the Federal Highway Administration (FHWA) and was found to be more costly, as well as possibly interfering with water well fields. It was, therefore, rejected, and the owners, still dissatisfied, submitted the analysis of their own experts, which supported their contentions. While both the FHWA and the Massachusetts Department of Public Works rejected that analysis, the analysis by the government agencies and their conclusions never became part of the final EIS and, consequently, never received widespread circulation through the federal government and the requisite comment that it should have received. The owners sought a preliminary injunction under the NEPA. *Held:* The construction was enjoined. The requirement of NEPA that a federal agency prepare a detailed statement discussing alternatives to proposed agency action is not satisfied when pertinent information is found in the administrative record but is not incorporated in an EIS. *Grazing Fields v. Goldschmidt,* 626 F2d 1068 (1980).

1st Circuit Citizens' environmental conservation group sued to enjoin the FAA from constructing a radar facility and paved access road on the ground that the EIS it filed did not satisfy the requirements of NEPA. Plaintiff claimed that the EIS failed to discuss the possibility of future development at or near the proposed site, or the presence of alternative locations both within and without the immediate area of the proposed site. *Held:* Where the district court determined that the EIS was sufficient, review on appeal was limited to clear error. Where the EIS's discussion of future development and of alternative sites was less than fully satisfactory but was minimally adequate, it satisfied NEPA requirements. *Commington Preservation Comm. v. FAA,* 524 F2d 241 (1975).

9th Circuit Public interest group sued to enjoin the National Forest Service from logging activities in a wilderness area under the grant of a timber easement, until an environmental impact statement was filed. *Held:* Although, normally, activities are suspended until the NEPA requirements are satisfied, where it appears that greater injury will ensue if the activity is enjoined, an injunction suspending the activity is not granted. The forest service established that the logging activities were necessary to preserve the wildlife area. *Alpine Lakes Protection Soc'y v. Schlapfer,* 518 F2d 1089 (1975).

U.S. District Court, New York In connection with a highway project in Manhattan, an EIS was prepared, describing the portion of the Hudson River scheduled to be filled as a "biological wasteland" that contributed nothing to the river's productivity. The Environmental Protection Agency (EPA), which questioned the EIS, ordered a more thorough biological study to focus on fish. The new study showed the landfill area to be an important source of striped bass and other fish species. The Corps of Engineers granted the landfill permit after both studies were concluded and published. *Held:* The landfill permit was invalid because the Corps of Engineers failed to consider the landfill's impact on the fish in the Hudson River as shown by the newer study. The permit clearly violated NEPA, the Clean Water Act, and the Rivers and Harbors Act; and its grant was based on an unjustified reliance on the earlier EIS. *Action for Rational Transit v. West Side Highway Project,* 536 F. Supp. 1225 (SD 1982).

47.20
—Injunction Pending Compliance

1st Circuit The district court enjoined the Department of Interior from auctioning rights to drill oil in a North Atlantic fishing area off the New England coast. The court based this finding on a likelihood that the department violated NEPA when it failed to supply an EIS supplement reflecting its downward revision of the estimate of oil likely to be found on the tracts it intended to lease. A mere likelihood of a NEPA violation, argued the government, was not a sufficient basis for the grant of a preliminary injunction. *Held:* The department's failure to supplement the EIS after it lowered the oil estimate by 97 percent was unreasonable and a probable violation of NEPA. Setting aside a lease sale if it were found to be unlawful would become progressively harder with the passage of time, even if new NEPA statements were subsequently requested. The resulting harm to plaintiff would significantly outweigh any harm to the government caused by the injunction, so the likelihood of a NEPA violation was a sufficient basis for the injunction. *Commonwealth v. Watt,* 716 F2d 946 (1983).

2d Circuit The Westway Project, which contemplated the creation of landfill for an interstate highway to be built in Manhattan, was approved by the FHWA. The approval was based on a final environmental impact statement (FEIS), which concluded that the project's impact on air quality, noise, and water quality would be minimal. Appended to the FEIS was a report stating that the project would have no adverse impact on the Hudson River fish population. After the approval, the EPA and other environmental agencies questioned the findings as to the fish population. A further study concluded that the landfill site served as a major nursery ground for striped bass and other species. The district court held that the FEIS inadequately considered the fishery impact. Accordingly, FHWA's funding approvals were declared void and it was permanently enjoined from reimbursing the state for the right-of-way acquired from the city. *Held:* The permanent injunction was reversed because plaintiffs failed to establish irreparable injury. Their claim that any federal funding of the project would jeopardize impartial review under NEPA was rejected. Any threat to impartial review flowed, not from reimbursement to the state, which was revocable, but from acquisition of the right-of-way, which had already been accomplished by the state. On the other hand, harm to the city and the state from a permanent injunction far outweighed the potential benefits to plaintiffs. *Sierra Club v. Hennessy,* 695 F2d 643 (1982).

8th Circuit Landowners and an ecology group sued to enjoin construction of high-voltage lines across the landowners' properties on the ground that the requirements of NEPA had not been satisfied. The corporation constructing the lines had previously instituted a state condemnation proceeding, claiming that a federal court could not enjoin the construction over lands subject to the state condemnation proceeding. *Held:* The anti-injunction statute (28 USC § 2283) prohibits the interference of a federal court with state court proceedings except where expressly authorized by acts of congress. NEPA requires the preparation of an environmental impact statement as to any federal action that may affect the environment. To preserve the objectives of NEPA, the federal court could enjoin the offending state proceeding. *Stockslager v. Carroll Elec. Coop. Corp.,* 528 F2d 949 (1976).

47.25
Endangered Species Act

U.S. Supreme Court In 1967, Tennessee Valley Authority (TVA) commenced construction on a dam and reservoir project on the Little Tennessee River. In 1973, a new species of perch, the snail darter, was discovered in the river. About four months later Congress passed the Endangered Species Act. In 1975, the secretary of the interior listed the snail darter as an endangered species and in 1976 filed an action against TVA to enjoin completion of the project on the ground that the project violated the act by directly causing the extinction of the snail darter. Thereafter, TVA's budget for the completion of the project was passed by Congress. *Held:* The Endangered Species Act has no exceptions, and thus applies to projects under construction at the time of the passage of the act. Furthermore, continuing congressional appropriations do not constitute an implied repeal of the act insofar as the instant project is concerned. *Tennessee Valley Auth. v. Hill,* 437 US 153 (1978).

47.30
Clean Air Act

U.S. Supreme Court The EPA adopted a "bubble concept" regulation under which stationary sources of air pollution were to be defined on a plant-wide basis, rather than an individual equipment basis, for areas in which air quality does not meet federal standards (nonattainment areas). EPA promulgated this regulation under the Clean Air Act to cut back substantially its review coverage. Several environmental organizations challenged the application of the bubble concept to a discrete Clean Air Act scheme. *Held:* The EPA bubble regulations were based on a reasonable construction of the term "stationary source" in Section 172(b) of the 1977 amendments to the Clean Air Act. Congress did not have a specific intention as to the applicability of the bubble concept; the EPA's interpretation of the statute represented a reasonable accommodation of manifestly competing interests. Moreover, the EPA had considered the matter in a detailed and reasonable fashion. In view of these factors, the EPA's determination was entitled to deference. *Chevron USA v. Natural Resources Defense Council, Inc.*, 467 US 837 (1984).

U.S. Supreme Court Petitioner was indicted for violating the Clean Air Act of 1970. While demolishing a building, petitioner allegedly failed to comply with an EPA regulation concerning emission standards for asbestos. The regulation specified the procedures to be followed in connection with building demolitions, but did not by its terms limit emissions of asbestos that occur during the course of a demolition. *Held:* A defendant charged with a criminal violation under the act may assert the defense that the emission standard it is accused of violating is not a standard that Congress contemplated when it used the term. It is clear that Congress intended to limit "emission standards" to regulations of a certain type and did not intend to empower the EPA to make a regulation an "emission standard" by mere designation. The regulation in this case did not constitute an emission standard. *Adamo Wrecking Co. v. United States,* 434 US 275 (1978).

3d Circuit Steel company was served with notice from the EPA of a violation of the Clean Air Act. The company asked EPA to withdraw the notice, arguing that EPA had exceeded its powers under the act and its own regulations. EPA refused to withdraw the notice, and ordered a hearing to decide whether the company was violating emission limitations. Steel company chose to bypass administrative proceedings and brought suit to have the notice of violation withdrawn. EPA requested dismissal, claiming that the company had to first exhaust its administrative remedies. The company argued that the exhaustion doctrine should not apply to these facts, because the dispute was purely legal in nature and immediate judicial review was necessary to protect it from irreversible and undue hardship. *Held:* The dispute was factual, as well as legal, in nature. Determinations of compliance or exemption turn on whether the company's operations exceeded the act's emission limitations and, if so, to what extent. Nor did these facts fall within the hardship exception to the exhaustion requirement. The company's choice between yielding to coerced compliance and risking accumulating fines created no undue hardship. In fact, the company's hardship was minimal, because the penalty was equal to the economic value gained from continuing noncompliance. *Bethlehem Steel Corp. v. EPA,* 669 F2d 903 (1982).

U.S. District Court, California In 1979, the EPA listed radionuclides as a hazardous air pollutant. However, the EPA failed to publish proposed regulations establishing national emission standards for radionuclides within 180 days after the listing as required by the Clean Air Act. An environmental organization and several individuals brought suit for the EPA's alleged failure to perform its duties under the act. EPA claimed that it would need at least nine years after the statutory deadline to issue proposed regulations for some emission sources. *Held:* EPA failed to meet its heavy burden of demonstrating that it was unfeasible to issue the proposed regulations by the 180-day deadline or by the time the action was brought in 1982. EPA should have had enough knowledge to at least issue tentative proposed regulations that could be revised from time to time. The act's purpose was to regulate hazardous air pollutants on an expedited basis. The thorough, time-consuming study of radionuclides that EPA envisioned was not within the contemplation of Congress when it passed the act. *Sierra Club v. Gorsuch,* 551 F. Supp. 785 (ND 1982).

U.S. District Court, New Jersey Defendant operated a landfill that served as a disposal site for solid and liquid municipal, industrial, and chemical wastes. After numerous fires occurred at the landfill and the receipt of numerous citations from the New Jersey Department of Environmental Protection Agency, defendant was sued by the U.S. Government under the federal common law of nuisance for air and water pollution. Defendants moved to dismiss that claim. *Held:* The Clean Air Act preempted federal common law for nuisance and, therefore, the claim based on common law was not available. When Congress occupies the field through the establishment of a comprehensive regulatory program supervised by an expert administrative agency, there is no need for federal common law. *United States v. Kin-Buc, Inc.,* 532 F. Supp. 699 (1982).

47.35 Water Pollution Control Act

U.S. Supreme Court When a developer placed fill materials on low-lying, marshy land near a Michigan lakeshore, the Corps of Engineers filed for an injunction on the ground that the land constituted an "adjacent wetland" that fell within the Clean Water Act's prohibition against dredging or filling "navigable waters" without a permit. *Held:* For the Corps of Engineers. The inclusion by the Corps of Engineers of wetlands not subject to frequent flooding within the Clean Water Act's definition of navigable waters was reasonable, because such wetlands could affect the water quality of adjacent lakes, rivers, and streams. For example, wetlands could drain into adjacent waters, serving as a filter and helping prevent flooding and erosion. Thus, the developer was required to have a permit. *United States v. Riverside Bayview Homes, Inc.,* 474 US 121 (1985).

3d Circuit A county utilities authority sought to construct a sewage treatment plant to be used by many municipalities. EPA funding was sought under the Clean Water Act, which required that the applicant adopt a system of sewer use charges. Funding was granted but was suspended after 80 percent of the funds were disbursed, because the borough where the plant was to be located had not adopted a user charge ordinance. The borough claimed that the funding requirement impermissibly infringed on state sovereignty, in contravention of the Tenth Amendment. *Held:* The requirement of a user fee ordinance did not impermissibly infringe on state sovereignty. Specifically, the requirement did not directly impair the state's ability to structure its integral operations in areas of traditional state government functions. *Middlesex County Utils. Auth. v. Borough of Say-*

erville, 690 F2d 358 (1982), cert. denied, 460 US 1023 (1983).

7th Circuit As a condition for permitting plaintiff, the operator of a petroleum refinery, to dump certain pollutants into an adjacent river, the EPA required plaintiff to regularly test water samples taken at a point in the waste streams "representative of discharge" and to report the results to the EPA. Because plaintiff treated its wastes before dumping them, the point in the waste streams "representative of discharge" occurred after the waste had been treated. After the EPA was refused permission to collect untreated samples, it obtained a warrant, and plaintiff moved to quash it. *Held:* The warrant was proper. Section 308(a) of the Federal Water Pollution Control Act gave the EPA a right of entry upon any premises "in which an effluent source is located" and to "sample any effluents which the owner or operator is required to sample." In order to assess the operator's treatment of waste water, it was necessary for the EPA to evaluate both treated and untreated water. *Mobil Oil Corp. v. EPA,* 716 F2d 1187 (1983), cert. denied, 466 US 980 (1984).

7th Circuit Section 107(d) of the Clean Air Act required states to submit to the EPA a list of areas that had attained air quality standards, nonattainment areas, and areas that could not yet be classified. Four years after Indiana designated one county as unclassifiable, the EPA reclassified part of the county as a nonattainment area and required the state to submit a new implementation plan. Petitioner, a steel company, sought to set aside the reclassification, arguing that Section 107(d) does not authorize the EPA to modify a state's list after promulgation. *Held:* For the petitioner. The scheme of cooperation between state and federal regulations would be destroyed if the EPA had the power to change a state's classifications long after the EPA promulgated them. Thus the EPA was required to verify classifications within the 60 days provided for in the statute. *Bethlehem Steel Corp. v. EPA,* 723 F2d 1303 (1983).

10th Circuit The EPA sought to regulate discharge of pollutants from uranium mining into two gullies. The mining companies contended that the gullies were not "waters of the United States" under the Clean Water Act and that the EPA lacked jurisdiction to sue. *Held:* The gullies were subject to regulation by the EPA. The goal of the Clean Water Act was to eliminate discharge of pollutants into navigable waters, defined as "waters of the United States." Although the gullies did not ordinarily flow, they did flow for a period after pollutants were discharged into them by passing through underground aquifers into navigable-in-fact streams; or via a surface connection formed between gullies and navigable streams after intense rainfall. *Quivira Mining Co. v. United States Envtl. Protection Agency,* 765 F2d 126 (1985).

U.S. District Court, Michigan Shipowners were polluting the waters by the emission of raw and treated sewage. They brought suit against the efforts of the state of Michigan to prohibit the pollution as a violation of the Michigan Watercraft Pollution Control Act and the Federal Water Pollution Control Act Amendments. *Held:* Michigan's authority to prohibit the emission of raw or treated sewage into waters was not in violation of the uniformity implicit in the constitutional grant of admiralty jurisdiction to federal courts. The Pollution Control Act is not inconsistent with the equal protection clause, nor do the Control Act Amendments violate the constitutional reservation to the federal government of treaty-making powers in relation to foreign nations. *Lake Carriers' Ass'n v. Kelley,* 527 F. Supp. 1114 (ED), aff'd, 456 US 985 (1982).

U.S. District Court, New York Landowner sued developer for discharging pollutants into a stream leading to landowner's property, and the state department of environmental conservation for failing to enforce state environmental standards. *Held:* The department had constitutional immunity from suit in federal court. Also, the Federal Water Pollution Control Act imposed no liability on the state for the failure of third parties to comply with its standards. *Love v. New York State Dep't of Envtl. Conservation,* 529 F. Supp. 832 (SD 1981).

U.S. District Court, Pennsylvania Defendants discharged pollutants from their mushroom compost operation into navigable waters without a permit, in alleged violation of the criminal provisions of the Federal Water Pollution Control Act. Defendants claimed that they did not require a permit, because they fell under the exemption for agricultural activities provided for in the act's implementing regulations. *Held:* The agricultural exemption did not apply. First, defendants did not show that they even knew about the exemption at the time of the discharge. Second, defendant's compost operation, which constituted most of their business, was not an "agricultural activity," but was manufacturing in nature. Third, even if the compost operation were an agricultural activity, it was in any event an "agricultural point source," to which the exemption did not apply. *United States v. Frezzo Bros.,* 546 F. Supp. 713 (ED 1982), aff'd, 703 F2d 62 (3d Cir.), cert. denied, 464 US 829 (1983).

47.40 Resource Conservation and Recovery Act

4th Circuit Waste buried during operation of a landfill began leaching through sandy soil and into the groundwater aquifer below. A successor water system initiated to improve the situation and tests by the EPA indicated that no improvement in water quality was expected. The EPA sued the landfill operator and the property owners under Section 7003 of the Resouce Conservation and Recovery Act of 1976 (42 USC § 6973) to compel defendants to develop a plan to prevent further contamination, take remedial action, and to reimburse the EPA for its expenditures. Defendants argued that Section 7003 did not apply to its past conduct, which had terminated before enforcement was sought. *Held:* Permanent injunctive relief under Section 7003 was appropriate. The legislative history of the 1980 amendments to the statute expressly indicated that it could be used for events that took place at some time in the past but that continued to present a threat to public health or the environment. *United States v. Waste Indus., Inc.,* 734 F2d 159 (1984).

47.45 Asbestos Hazard Emergency Response Act

D.C. Circuit The Asbestos Hazard Emergency Response Act of 1986 required the EPA to issue regulations to identify and control asbestos in school buildings. Manufacturers of asbestos-containing materials challenged EPA regulations promulgated under the act, contending that the EPA improperly allowed school officials to ascertain the least burdensome abatement method based on reports from inspectors and management planners. *Held:* Petition for review denied. EPA regulations, which allowed schools to choose from a list of approved responses, were within the act's mandate. Congress impelled the EPA to act within 360 days to address existing hazards, and in doing so, granted the EPA considerable leeway in determining how to deal with asbestos problems in the schools. Under the circumstances, the EPA's regulations were a reasonable interpretation of the act's command to define a response sufficient to protect human health and environment. *Safe Bldgs. Alliance v. EPA,* 846 F2d 79 (1988).

48.00 STATE AND LOCAL ENVIRONMENTAL PROTECTION LAWS

48.05 State Laws in General

Georgia Landowner's tract bordering the river fell within a corridor that was subject to a comprehensive land and water use plan under the Metropolitan River Protection Act. When the landowner began construction of a tennis court on the land, the city obtained a stop-work order. Landowner appealed, asserting that the act unconstitutionally appropriated private property for public use without compensation. *Held:* The stop-work order was upheld. This case did not involve eminent domain by which private property was appropriated, but involved the state's police power to regulate the use of private property in the public interest. Applying a balancing of interests test, the court concluded that the state's interest in preventing flooding, halting land erosion, and protecting the water supply outweighed the landowner's interest in building a tennis court beside the river. *Pope v. City of Atlanta,* 249 SE2d 16 (1978).

Maryland Residents near a proposed site for sewage disposal sought to enjoin a bicounty sanitation commission from purchasing the site. The residents alleged that no environmental impact report that had been prepared as required by the state Environmental Protection Agency (EPA). *Held:* The county commission did not have to prepare an environmental effects report to purchase the proposed sewage site with its own funds because no "state action" was taken. A report would have been required if legislative requests for appropriations had been made. *Pitman v. Washington Suburban Sanitary Comm'n,* 368 A2d 473 (1977).

Michigan Landowners shared a boundary in a heavily wooded area. When defendant landowner removed four face cords of wood from plaintiff's property, plaintiff sued for an injunction against defendant's continued trespass. In addition, plaintiff alleged that defendant violated Section 3 of the Michigan Environmental Protection Act (MEPA), which provides for injunctive or declaratory relief if defendant's conduct "has, or is likely to pollute, impair or destroy the air, water or other natural resources or the public trust therein." The trial court dismissed the MEPA claim, stating that the act did not apply, because no public trust was involved in this situation. *Held:* Section 3 protections are not limited to natural resources affecting land in which there is a public trust. Plaintiff could establish a prima facie case under the MEPA claim by establishing that (1) a natural resource is involved and (2) the impact of defendant's activity on the environment rises to a level of impairment justifying injunctive relief. Since a natural resource—the destroyed trees—was clearly involved, the court remanded the case for a determination of environmental impact. *Steven v. Creek,* 328 NW2d 672 (1982).

Minnesota Landowners brought suit against the state, challenging a scenic river ordinance that contained a setback and minimum lot size requirement. The enforcement of the ordinance was enjoined, and the state appealed. *Held:* Reversed. Despite the fact that the dominant purpose of the ordinance was aesthetic, it did not constitute an unconstitutional taking since the landowners could not establish immediate, irreparable harm. *County of Pine v. State,* 280 NW2d 625 (1979).

New York The town planning board approved plaintiff's plan to develop a tract of land for two motels although no assessment form accompanied its application. Subsequently, when construction was substantially complete, plaintiff submitted an application to modify the site plan, which had an assessment form and was approved. During construction, adjoining landowners successfully sued to prevent implementation of the modified site plan. Plaintiff resubmitted a modified site plan, and a new board ordered an environmental impact statement. Ultimately, the board approved the modified plan subject to several conditions to which plaintiff objected. *Held:* For plaintiff. The board could not be estopped from placing additional conditions on the development of the site. This was its legislatively granted prerogative. However, the board exercised its power in an arbitrary and capricious manner when it used the modified site plan approval to impose additional burdens on plaintiff that were unrelated to the completed portion of the development, and required changes to accommodate environmental problems that had been previously reviewed and approved. *EFS Ventures Corp. v. Foster,* 520 NE2d 1345 (1988).

Washington The Department of Social and Health Services approved the environmental impact statement (EIS) for the planned construction of a prison as in compliance with state laws. The county in which the prison was to be located sued to enjoin construction on the ground of noncompliance with local zoning ordinances. *Held:* For the state. Where local zoning law, as here, was in conflict with state law, the local law would have to be superseded because prison location was a state decision. The court noted that if counties were to decide the location of prisons, it was conceivable that state prisons would not be permitted in any county. *Snohomish County v. State,* 648 P2d 430 (1982).

48.10 —Enforcement Proceedings by State Agency

New Jersey The New Jersey Department of Environmental Protection sued defendants, former mercury processors and landowners, for the cost of cleanup of mercury pollution. Defendants were each charged with nuisance, violation of the New Jersey Water Quality Improvement Act and, on appeal, the Spill Act. Contributors to the Spill Compensation Fund intervened to seek a declaratory judgment that the Spill Act not be applied retroactively. The Supreme Court of New Jersey granted certiorari to consider the retroactive effect of the Spill Act and the liability of a parent company for the acts of its subsidiary, a former processor that had dumped waste on land owned by the parent. *Held:* The retroactive application of the Spill Act and liability of the parent were affirmed. The 1979 amendment to the Spill Act made it applicable to pre-1972 discharge and imposed retroactive strict liability if a substantial public threat and damage to the environment exist. The court held the landowners strictly liable for the conduct of an abnormally dangerous activity, mercury processing, discarding former distinctions between "ultrahazardous" and "inherently dangerous" activities, the latter of which would require proof of negligence. The parent was strictly liable under the 1979 amendment to the Spill Act as one "in any way responsible for any hazardous substance." The parent's employees were involved in the subsidiary's daily operations and had permitted the dumping of wastes on the parent's property. All defendant mercury processors were found jointly and severally liable for cleanup costs without regard to fault. *State Dep't of Envtl. Protection v. Ventron,* 463 A2d 893 (1983).

New Jersey Condominium developer was denied a construction permit under the Coastal Area Facility Review Act when the environmental board concluded that a 10-story high-density structure in the midst of low-lying and low-density buildings would be an abrupt invasion upon existing land use and would result in the degradation of the aesthetic attributes of the area. The developer appealed, alleging that these considerations were beyond the scope of the act. *Held:* The legislature authorized the consideration of aesthetic impact on an application involving a housing facility. The statute directed the commissioner to consider existing aesthetic attributes at the site and within the surrounding area. The board's conclusion was supported by the record. *Toms River Affiliates v. Department of Envtl. Protection,* 355 A2d 679 (Super. Ct. App. Div. 1976).

New York In 1962, defendant owner obtained an excavation permit to mine lime from land he owned. The permit incorporated by reference a town ordinance prohibiting any excavation that could not be leveled to provide adequate drainage. After the excavation ceased, owner backfilled portions of the land and continued the backfilling operation for 20 years. During that time, the premises became wetlands subject to the Freshwater Wetlands Act. Owner appealed a misdemeanor conviction of altering a freshwater wetlands area without a permit by continuing the backfilling of his land after the Wetlands Act went into effect. *Held:* The backfilling was not authorized by the town excavation permits and did not fall under the Wetlands Act's "grandfather clause" exempting owner from the act's permit requirement. The act provides an exemption for any land use that had final approval prior to the act's effective date. The town excavation permit neither required nor authorized owner to restore the premises to their original level. The town had never taken any action to compel restoration of the premises. In this case, the record was devoid of evidence to support the assumption that backfilling was expected or contemplated by the ordinance or permits. *People v. Genesee Lime Products, Inc.,* 533 NE2d 664 (1988).

Pennsylvania When the Department of Environmental Resources ordered the planning and construction of a wastewater-treatment facility, the borough contended that it was economically depressed, and could not comply with the order. *Held:* Where there was uncontradicted evidence that raw sewage flowed into a stream of the Commonwealth, the department had adequate factual basis for issuing the order. The alleged financial inability of the municipality to comply with the order was not a basis to challenge the validity of the order. *Ramey, Borough v. Commonwealth,* 351 A2d 613 (1976).

48.15 —Right to an Injunction

6th Circuit Construction project designed to remedy a dangerous traffic intersection was subtantially completed when a public-interest group sued to enjoin further construction on the ground that the project would have an adverse impact on the environment. *Held:* Since the project was substantially completed, and since the possible adverse impact on the environment was negligible as compared to the obvious need for improvement of the intersection, preliminary injunction was properly denied. *Public Interest Research Group v. Brinegar,* 517 F2d 917 (1975).

California "Citizens' group" sued municipality to prevent a street-widening plan. The trial court issued a writ requiring the municipality to submit an EIS but refused to enjoin the project. *Held:* The municipality clearly abused its discretion under the circumstances in adopting a negative zoning declaration in lieu of preparing an EIS. The trial court was correct in issuing the writ but erred in concluding that it had no power to enjoin the municipality's activities under governing statutes. *Friends of "B" St. v. City of Hayward,* 165 Cal. Rptr. 514 (1980).

48.20 —Validity of State Wetlands Acts

Florida Plaintiff planned to develop a new community with dwelling units, commercial centers and recreational facilities on 6,500 acres it had purchased. The county commissioners rejected plaintiff's plan on the ground it would cause ecological damage to the local waters in violation of Florida wetlands regulations. Plaintiff brought suit seeking damages for an uncompensated taking of its property. *Held:* The court, invoking the principal that a regulation serving to prevent a public harm rather than to grant the public a benefit was more likely to be an exercise of police power, found a valid exercise of police power and not a taking requiring compensation. An act to prevent public harm could be deemed a taking if it rendered property worthless, but since plaintiff knew what it was getting into, the commission's act did not amount to rendering the property worthless. *Graham v. Estuary Properties, Inc.,* 399 So. 2d 1374 (1981), cert. denied, 454 US 1083 (1982).

New York To comply with the Freshwater Wetlands Act in 1975, the Department of Environmental Protection (DEP) prepared a tentative map designating wetlands in the state. Under the act, DEP regulated the use of designated wetlands and could prohibit landowners from certain activities unless a permit was obtained. Five years later, DEP issued a second tentative map that doubled the designated areas. Owners, whose property did not appear on the first tentative map, had commenced development and were now advised that permits were necessary in view of the second map. Owners challenged DEP's attempt to regulate their property. *Held:* DEP's failure to designate freshwater wetlands in the first tentative map did not exempt the properties from DEP jurisdiction and regulation. The plain language of the act proscribes activity on wetlands as of the act's effective date and prior to promulgation of the final map unless a permit has been issued. Moreover, tentative designation as wetland does not amount to a deprivation of property without compensation, since it does not prohibit development or convert ownership from private to public; owners may continue to develop if a permit is obtained. *Wedingner v. Goldberger,* 522 NE2d 25 (1988).

Rhode Island When property owners were ordered not to proceed with the relocation of a river running through their property, they challenged the Fresh Water Wetlands Act as authorizing unconstitutional deprivation of property without compensation. *Held:* The act was constitutional on its face. Two remedies are provided to a landowner whose application to relocate a river is denied. The landowner may appeal and, if his contention is upheld, he may proceed with the project, since the director of the Department of Natural Resources does not have the power of condemnation. A landowner may also elect to proceed with a de novo review of the director's decision, and, if the director is found to have overestimated the impact of a proposed alteration, the landowner may either proceed with the project or be compensated for the denial of the beneficial use of his property. *JM Mills, Inc. v. Murphy,* 352 A2d 661 (1976).

48.25
Municipal Ordinances

Illinois Defendants contended that a municipality did not have the authority to enact a noise control ordinance because the regulation of noise pollution was preempted by the state of Illinois under the noise regulation adopted by the Illinois Pollution Control Board. Municipality contended that, as a home rule municipality, it has the power to regulate any function pertaining to its government and affairs including, but not limited to, the protection of health, safety, and welfare. *Held:* Noise pollution is a matter of regional or statewide concern because certain categories of noise pollution extend beyond the boundaries of a single municipality. Therefore, any attempt by municipal ordinance to regulate noise pollution emission was not within the municipality's home rule power. *City of Des Plaines v. Chicago & NWRR,* 357 NE2d 433 (1976).

Massachusetts Plaintiff applied to town conservation commission for a permit to build a road over marshland adjoining his property, which he subsequently planned to subdivide. The commission denied the application under the authority of a town bylaw protecting municipal foreshores (area of seashore between high-water and low-water marks) and wetlands. Plaintiff argued that the denial was unlawful because state law had preempted the town's bylaw. *Held:* The town bylaw was lawful: A local law is preempted by a state law only if the laws are inconsistent. The local bylaw was not inconsistent with state zoning law because it had neither the purpose nor the effect of a zoning law. Nor was the bylaw inconsistent with the state law regulating wetlands, which was less stringent than the bylaw. The state law mandated only minimum standards, and local governments were free to legislate stronger measures to further the general purpose of the state law. *Lovequist v. Conservation Comm'n,* 393 NE2d 858 (1979).

49.00
LANDMARK PRESERVATION

49.05
Validity

U.S. Supreme Court Under New York City's Landmarks Preservation Law, the Grand Central Terminal, owned by plaintiff Penn Central, was designated a "landmark" 'and the block it occupies a "landmark site." Thereafter, Penn Central entered into a lease with plaintiff UGP, whereby UGP was to construct a multistory office building over the terminal. After the Landmarks Preservation Commission rejected plaintiff's plans for the building as destructive of the terminal's historic and aesthetic features, plaintiffs brought suit in state court claiming that the application of the statute had "taken" their property without just compensation in violation of the Fifth and Fourteenth Amendments. The trial court's grant of relief was reserved on appeal. *Held:* Affirmed. The statute did not interfere here with continuing the terminal's past uses, permitted the owners a "reasonable return" on their investment, did not completely prohibit occupation of the terminal's air space, and granted the owners the valuable right to transfer the terminal's air rights to other parcels suitable for office building construction. Under these circumstances, the application of the statute to the terminal property did not constitute a "taking" of appellants' property within a meaning of the Fifth Amendment as made applicable by the states to the Fourteenth Amendment. *Penn Central Transp. Co. v. City of New York,* 438 US 104 (1978).

District of Columbia When a zoning commission approved a planned unit development, a citizens' association challenged the plan, arguing that the preservation of historical landmarks was not a valid purpose for zoning. *Held:* The Zoning Act authorizes the commission to promote the general welfare of the District of Columbia and its planning and orderly development as the nation's capital. Preservation of historical areas is within the concept of "general welfare." *Dupont Circle Citizens Ass'n v. District of Columbia Zoning Comm'n,* 355 A2d 550 (1976).

49.10 Operation and Effect

District of Columbia The purchaser of property designated for preservation under the District's Historic Landmark and Historic Preservation Act sought a review of the designation of his property as a historic landmark, complaining that he was entitled to a full trial-type hearing under the due process clause. *Held:* Plaintiff was not entitled to a trial-type hearing prior to the designation of his property; therefore, the court did not have jurisdiction to reexamine the designation on its merits. Moreover, an owner of designated property may still obtain a permit to demolish it if he can show that the permit would be necessary in the public interest or that denial of the permit would cause him to suffer unreasonable economic hardship. Full procedural protection under the due process clause is generally reserved for people who are deprived of the very means by which to live or are put out of busines. *Donnelly Assocs. v. District of Columbia Historic Preservation Review Bd.,* 520 A2d 270 (1987).

District of Columbia Building owner appealed from an order entered by an agent of the District of Columbia government denying a permit to demolish a building pursuant to the Historic Landmark and Historic District Protection Act of 1978, D.C. Code §§ 5-821 et seq. He asserted that the decision was an unconstitutional taking because it placed an unreasonable economic hardship on the property owner with regard to the best use of the land. Evidence showed that the building could be rented "as is" or with minimal renovation, and that a full renovation would have cost much less than claimed by the owner. *Held:* Denial of permit affirmed. If there is a reasonable alternative economic use for the property after the imposition of a restriction on that property as a historical landmark, there is no taking, and hence no unreasonble economic hardship to owners, regardless of how much the property may be diminished in cash value and no matter what "higher" or "more beneficial use" of the property may exist. *900 G. Street Assocs. v. Department of Hous. & Community Dev.,* 430 A2d 1387 (1981).

Missouri Townhouse property within the limits of a historic district was purchased by appellant, who intended to replace it with a parking lot. The board of adjustment denied appellant a wrecking permit on the ground that the building had not deteriorated structurally beyond all possibility of renovation and that it deserved to stand because of its architectural and historic significance. The purchaser appealed the denial of the wrecking permit. *Held:* The board applied an improper standard by considering only technological and not economic feasibility; it must reconsider its denial of the permit. This is the first Missouri case dealing with a historic district ordinance. *Lafayette Park Baptist Church v. Scott,* 553 SW2d 856 (Ct. App. 1977).

New Jersey The township passed a statute empowering a seven-member landmarks commission to determine and designate historic properties. When an eighteenth century farmhouse property was designated historic, the owner brought an action to have the designation declared invalid on the ground that only a planning board or board of adjustment could make such a designation. *Held:* For the owner. New Jersey's Municipal Land Use Law (N.J. Stat. Ann. § 40:55D-20), which served as the state enabling statute for municipal preservation efforts, provided unequivocally that the powers it authorized not be exercised by any body other than a planning board or board of adjustment. Historic designation ordinances are, in essence, zoning ordinances, and New Jersey has endeavored to avoid fractionalization of planning and zoning functions by adopting unitary controls. *Estate of Neuberger v. Township of Middletown,* 521 A2d 1336 (Super Ct. App. Div. 1987).

50.00 URBAN RENEWAL

50.05 Acquisition of Property

Alabama As part of an urban renewal plan, the city condemned a commercial block in the downtown area consisting of 22 lots, which included three vacant buildings that were found to have numerous minor violations of the building, fire, electrical, and plumbing codes. Nonetheless, the buildings were in good condition for their age and a number of merchants on the block were well-respected firms that had been in the same location for many years. A merchant on the block sued to have the redevelopment resolution declared invalid. *Held:* For the city. The applicable standard for court review was that the court would defer to the city council's decision as long as it was based on a "fairly debatable rationale." Although the block was clearly not a slum, it did contain some blighting factors. Further, the block occupied a key location in a larger blighted area that was being redeveloped, and it is the condition of the entire redevelopment area, not plaintiff's property, that determines whether redevelopment is warranted. *City of Birmingham v. Tutwiler Drug Co.,* 475 So. 2d 458 (1985).

Minnesota Owners of property located in an urban renewal area sued to compel a government agency to acquire their property. They alleged that the agency's activity in the neighborhood had caused their property to decline in value. The agency answered that a shortage of funds prevented them from acquiring the property. *Held:* Decreases in value caused by the changed character of the neighborhood due to normal activities in connection with an urban renewal project do not, without more, constitute a taking by the agency. The agency was not required to acquire the owners' property. *Orfield v. Housing & Redev. Auth.,* 232 NW2d 923 (1975).

Utah Property owner sued to obtain a declaratory judgment that the Neighborhood Development Act, establishing an agency to redevelop the inner city area, was unconstitutional. The property owner contended that (1) the agency was a special commission and therefore lacked the authority to issue bonds and taxes; (2) taxing authority given to the agency interfered with the authority of the city to tax;

and (3) the bonds would create a debt requiring approval of the electorate. *Held:* The agency was not a special commission, but rather a quasi-municipal corporation established by the legislature to remedy urban blight. As a quasi-municipal corporation, it was within the authority of the legislature to give it the power to issue bonds and assess taxes. *Tribe v. Salt Lake City Corp.*, 540 P2d 499 (1975).

50.10 Rights of Parties

U.S. Supreme Court Respondent telephone company was required to relocate some of its telephone transmission facilities by reason of a street realignment resulting from federally funded urban renewal projects carried out by petitioner. Respondent sought reimbursement for its relocation expenses, claiming it was a "displaced person" within the meaning of the Uniform Relocation Assistance and Real Property Acquisition Policies Act of 1970 (42 USC § 4622(a)(1)). *Held:* The Supreme Court reversed the Fourth Circuit's holding that respondent was a "displaced person" entitled to compensation under the act. The legislative history convinced the Court that the act was passed to meet the needs of residential and business tenants and owners, and did not deal with the separate problem posed by the relocation of utility service lines. The act did not expressly repeal the long-established common-law principle that a utility forced to relocate from the public right-of-way must do so at its own expense. *Norfolk Redevelopment & Hous. Auth. v. Chesapeake & Potomac Tel. Co.*, 464 US 30 (1983).

4th Circuit Housing act provided that an urban renewal project, which demolished or removed residential structures, must provide sufficient standard housing units for displaced low- and moderate-income families. Tenants and owners of housing to be demolished for construction of a park sued on the ground that the housing authority failed to comply with the provisions of the act. The housing authority claimed that there were sufficient vacant housing units in the area. *Held:* The housing act did not impose on local agencies the duty to build or rehabilitate substitute standard housing for low- or moderate-income families displaced by the urban renewal project. The obligation was satisfied where there were substitute federally supported private housing units for displaced persons. *Barton v. Lynn*, 529 F2d 189 (1975).

U.S. District Court, California When a city filed a community development block grant application for federal aid for a proposed regional shopping center, civil rights groups challenged the application. They claimed that more funds should have been allocated to increase low- and middle-income housing and that the community groups were improperly excluded from drafting of the plans. *Held:* The use of the grant for development of a regional shopping center was not illegal, nor was the application inappropriate, even though it did not allocate a greater percentage of funds to low- and middle-income housing. Title I did not compel the participation of community groups in the drafting of applications. *NAACP–Santa Rose–Sonoma County v. Hills*, 412 F. Supp. 102 (ND 1976).

U.S. District Court, New York Urban renewal project to rehabilitate a city's downtown area proposed the demolition of an old courthouse. The city's urban renewal agency and the Department of Housing and Urban Development (HUD) contracted in 1965 for federal grants and loans to effectuate the project. A city agency thereafter purchased the courthouse and proceeded with its plans for demolition. After a contractor for the demolition had been selected, a citizens' group sued to enjoin the demolition on the ground that the city agency and HUD failed to satisfy the requirements of the National Environmental Protection Act (NEPA). *Held:* NEPA is applicable to ongoing projects begun prior to its enactment, provided that a federal agency has been meaningfully involved in its implementation. Such involvement was present where HUD was involved by its approval of new grants and loans. The demolition of the courthouse was enjoined until the project complied with NEPA. *Save Courthouse Comm'n v. Lynn,* 408 F. Supp. 1323 (SD 1975).

U.S. District Court, Pennsylvania When the landowners' home was destroyed by a flood before construction was completed, they were compensated under a federally assisted urban renewal program but were denied a relocation allowance. The landowners argued that the denial of the allowance on the basis that they had not occupied the building before its destruction violated their equal protection and due process rights. *Held:* The policy granting relocation assistance only to those who had occupied their homes prior to the disaster did not violate the owners' rights, since there was national basis for the distinction. *Seeherman v. Lynn,* 404 F. Supp. 1318 (MD 1975).

California The chairman and president of the state housing finance agency refused to print and issue revenue bonds for a housing project, on the ground that to do so would violate Article XXXIV of the California Constitution. The article in question requires a local referendum before any low-income housing project may be developed, constructed, or acquired in any manner by any state public body. An interpretative statute declared that a "low-income housing project" did not include any development that is privately owned, not exempt from property tax, and rents no more than 49 percent of its available units to persons of low income. *Held:* Since the language of Article XXXIV was ambiguous, the interpretative efforts of the legislature should be upheld. Therefore, the project in question did not require voter approval; the bonds could be issued. *California Hous. Fin. Agency v. Patitucci,* 148 Cal. Rptr. 875 (1978).

Maryland City urban renewal ordinance required the removal of certain advertising structures. No compensation was provided under the ordinance, but the proximity of several signs to federal highways prompted the question of compensation under the federal Highway Beautification Act. Owners of the structures and the land on which they were located challenged the constitutionality of the ordinance. *Held:* The ordinance was constitutional. The prohibition was not based on the content of the signs, so there was no First Amendment violation. Equal protection rights were not violated. The ordinance was a proper exercise of the police power, and no compensation was necessary. Since the removal of the signs was not required by the federal Beautification Act, compensation under that act was not available. *Donnelly Advertising Corp. v. City of Baltimore,* 370 A2d 1127 (1977).

PART G
PRIVATE USE RESTRICTIONS

51.00 RESTRICTIVE COVENANTS

51.05 Validity

Arkansas Homeowners appealed a judgment in favor of the property owners' association foreclosing the members' delinquent and unpaid assessments. Homeowners contended, among other things, that the provision of the homeowners' association agreement that members would be differentially assessed, depending upon the extent to which their property was improved, rendered the entire agreement invalid. *Held:* (1) Although the differential assessment was invalid since all property owners had the same rights to use community facilities, the remainder of the agreement was enforceable because the agreement contained a severability clause; (2) the assessment covenant, though it provided it would remain outstanding for a period of 26 years, and then for 10-year periods, until such time as two thirds of the members voted to terminate it, did not create an invalid perpetuity, because the agreement contained adequate provision for termination at a specific date; (3) granting sole veto power to the developer over any increase in annual assessments was a valid delegation of voting power based on class distinctions; and (4) the provision allowing assessments to be made for capital improvements upon the approval of 51 percent of the members did not constitute an invalid restraint in alienation, because the provisions related only to improvements that benefited the community. *Kell v. Bella Vista Property Owners Ass'n,* 528 SW2d 651 (1975).

Connecticut A builder filed a declaration of covenants and restrictions upon a 64-lot subdivision. One of the covenants, which expressly ran with the land as to bind all subsequent purchasers, required any grantee who wished to sell or lease the property to give exclusive sales and leasing rights to the builder for a period of three months. Thereafter, defendant broker was assigned the builder's rights and a homeowner in the subdivision listed her property for sale with a competing broker. The state brought an action for a declaration that the restrictive covenant operated in restraint of trade as proscribed by the state antitrust statutes. *Held:* The court ruled that the restrictive covenant amounted to an illegal tying arrangement, unlawful in and of itself. Defendant's advantage, not shared with its competitors, unfairly restrained trade. *State v. Hossan-Maxwell, Inc.,* 436 A2d 284 (1981).

Florida Plaintiffs purchased a residence under a contract that bound them to pay rent for recreational facilities. The contract did not provide that the duty to pay would be secured by a lien, but prior to closing, the developer filed a declaration of restrictions stating that the obligation to pay recreational rents would be enforceable by a lien and providing that it was a covenant running with the land. Subsequently, the developer executed a deed conveying to plaintiffs the property subject to restrictions of record. Five years later, the developer's successor in interest sued to foreclose the lien against plaintiffs' property for nonpayment of recreational rents. *Held:* An affirmative covenant can be entered into by acceptance of a deed embodying the same, even if by reference. Thus, a valid contractual lien was created upon passage of the deed and creation of the lien related to the date of the filing of the declaration. The lien therefore arose prior to plaintiffs' possession of their residence, and the lienor's right, being prior in time, prevailed over their homestead interest. *Bessemer v. Gersten,* 381 So. 2d 1344 (1980).

Idaho Plaintiff, a county highway district, condemned a major portion of a vacant, unimproved residential lot that defendant had purchased as a site for a future office. The land carried restrictive covenants preventing use other than for residential purposes, but was surrounded by major thoroughfares and office buildings. When the trial court set its figure for the condemnation award, it took into consideration the likelihood of rezoning to "limited-office" use and removal of the restrictive covenants. Plaintiff contended that the trial court erred in admitting testimony as to the value of the lot if it were rezoned and that a zoning change was not probable. *Held:* The trial court's award was upheld. The possibility of rezoning would be taken into consideration by a prospective buyer, and so was properly taken into consideration by the trial court. However, plaintiff's assertion that the restrictive covenants were unenforceable was incorrect. If the subdivision subject to the covenants remains unchanged, changes in the surrounding areas do not invalidate the covenants, nor does the fact that the property would increase in value if used for a different purpose. *Ada County Highway District v. Magwire,* 662 P2d 237 (1983).

Kentucky Landlord entered into a lease agreement with tenant for space in a mall. The lease provided that tenant would use the premises solely for the sale of medium-to-better men's and boy's clothing, furnishings, and accessories. In addition, the lease provided that landlord would not lease or cause to be occupied any other space in the mall for the sale of anything that would compete with tenant's business. During the lease term, landlord leased other space in the mall to another company for the purpose of conducting the "retail sale of men's and boys' clothing, furnishing, apparel, accessories, and footwear of all types." When tenant brought suit for a permanent injunction against breach of the restrictive covenant in the lease, landlord contended that the covenant was invalid as a per se unreasonable restraint of trade. *Held:* The restrictive covenant applies to only one line of business, men's and boys' clothing, and not every kind of business that might be conducted in the mall. Therefore, the covenant does not constitute an unreasonable restraint of trade. *Mendell v. Golden-Farley of Hopkinsville, Inc.,* 573 SW2d 346 (1978).

Maine Owners of land previously devised to a hospital sought a declaratory judgment that their commercial use of the land did not violate restrictions imposed by the devise to the hospital. The testatrix owned no land other than the lot she attempted to restrict, and her interest terminated at the time of the attempted imposition of the servitude at her death. *Held:* Where the restriction was not imposed to effect a general development scheme and was not an agreement between adjoining landowners to restrict the property for their mutual benefit, the restriction was not effective. A restriction that benefits only land owned by a stranger to the transaction will not be enforced as an equitable servitude. *Brown v. Heirs of Fuller,* 347 A2d 127 (1975).

Massachusetts Town desired to build a skating rink on a parcel that had been deeded to it in 1917 "to be kept and used as a Public Park in perpetuity for the public good. . . ." Descendents of grantor objected that the proposed rink would use most of the parcel and would require the destruction of many trees. The lower court ruled that the language of the deed constituted a restriction on the land. *Held:* The language of the deed was not a mere restriction, but, instead, created a public charitable trust that had been accepted by the town. Neither the town nor the legislature could impair the obligations to keep the land as a public park without destroying the trust. *Dunphy v. Commonwealth,* 331 NE2d 883 (1975).

Michigan Defendants entered into a binding lease agreement to use land contracted for to establish a residential facility for mentally impaired persons. Subsequently, the restrictive covenant that had been in effect at the time the contract was executed was amended to specifically prohibit the use of any subdivision lots for a state-licensed group residential facility. Plaintiffs, residents of the subdivision, sued, alleging that defendants' proposed use of subdivision land violated the amendment. *Held:* The court granted defendants summary judgment, holding that the amendment was unenforceable because it was retroactive and violated public policy. The amendment was enacted after defendants committed themselves to a particular use of the land. To comply with the amendment would force defendants to be in breach of contract, which would be manifestly unfair. Moreover, Michigan's public policy of providing facilities for the mentally handicapped was more compelling than its public policy on the power to impose restrictions on the use of land. *McMillan v. Iserman,* 327 NW2d 559 (1982).

New York Original grantee of land covenanted in their deed to accept and pay for a seasonal water supply from their grantor. It was expressly provided that the covenant should run with the land. The successor in interest of the original grantor sought to enforce the covenant against the successor in interest of the original grantee. *Held:* The covenant creates a burden in perpetuity binding all owners, regardless of the use to which the land is put. Such a ground militates strongly against its enforcement. Affirmative covenants are disfavored in the law. *Eagle Enters., Inc. v. Gross,* 349 NE2d 816 (1976).

North Carolina Purchaser sought to rescind the conveyance of property that was subject to various restrictive covenants that limited the use to single-family residences. Purchaser contended that he was unable to construct a home on the lot since the property would support neither a septic tank nor an on-site sewage disposal system. The deed contained no covenant of warranty that the lot was suitable for single-family homes, and neither the purchaser nor defendant vendor had known of the defects. The vendor asserted the doctrine of caveat emptor as a defense. *Held:* When a vendor sells land subject to a restrictive covenant, an implied warranty arises that the land is suitable for the use limited by the restrictive covenant. Rescission was granted because the vendor breached this implied warranty when defects arose that were both unknown to and not reasonably discoverable by the purchaser at the time of purchase and that rendered the property unusable for its specific purpose. *Hinson v. Jefferson,* 215 SE2d 102 (1975).

Texas Plaintiffs purchased a lot in a subdivision that was subject to an architectural control covenant requiring that plans for construction be approved by the developer and owners' committee before implementation. Plaintiff submitted a plan to build a house that complied with all recorded restrictive covenants. In spite of this, the developer rejected the plan on the stated grounds that the proposed placement of the house was inconsistent with the general plan of the subdivision. Plaintiffs subsequently began construction without approval, and defendants sued to enjoin construction. *Held:* Injunctive relief was denied because plaintiffs did not have notice of any covenant that would place restrictions on their plan. Restrictions imposed on a discretionary basis are required to be part of a general scheme of which notice must be given to a party who is made to comply with the scheme. The general scheme of mutually compatible dwelling locations within the subdivision was not provided for in any of the covenants recorded prior to the sale of the lots to plaintiffs. Thus, plaintiffs were not bound by the scheme. *Davis v. Huey,* 620 SW2d 561 (1981).

51.10
Who May Impose Restrictions

Alabama Subdivision was governed by a set of restrictive covenants imposed by the original developer. A principal restriction limited construction to single-family private dwellings or residences of not less than 900 square feet. Subsequently, the original developer transferred its interest in the subdivision to another developer, which planned to build a condominium project within the subdivision featuring 40 single-family residential units. Several subdivision owners sued to block the project, pointing to the restrictive covenants. *Held:* Condominium development in the subdivision was denied. The court observed that standing alone, the word "dwelling" embraced not only types of houses being built at the time but also structures developed later for residential use in accordance with changing conditions such as condominiums. However, the word "private" was included in the restriction. A private dwelling or residence was completely inconsistent with the multi-family nature of a condominium. *Orange Beach Marine, Inc. v. Warner,* 500 So. 2d 1068 (1986).

Nebraska When buyers made the down payment on their land and signed the purchase agreement, the land was free of any restrictive covenants. The vendor executed a warranty deed conveying the land to the buyers free and clear of any encumbrances and put the deed into escrow to await final payment. While the deed was in escrow, the vendor imposed restrictive covenants on buyers' land and recorded it in the registry office. After voluntarily complying for the first few years, buyers sued to clear their title of the covenants. *Held:* The property was not subject to the covenants. Where a land contract has an escrow provision providing that the deed will be held in escrow until payment of the purchase price, the vendor of the deed loses control over it so long as the vendee does not default. The vendor may not further encumber the land without the consent of the vendee. *DeBoer v. Oakbrook Home Ass'n,* 359 NW2d 768 (1984).

51.15
Construction

Illinois Buyers purchased a four-acre parcel of land from seller, who owned the surrounding acreage. Prior to the sale, seller stated that his land was restricted and that he intended to use his property for fine residential homesites. The contract contained an assurance that these restrictions "shall be included in the sale by the seller of any adjacent property owned by him." Seller subsequently sold land 190 feet south of buyers' property to a mining company for use as a sand and gravel pit. Buyers sued, seeking, among other things, a permanent injunction for breach of a plan of development. *Held:* There was no general plan of development. Factors that negate the existence of a general plan include the absence of notice of restrictions in the recorded subdivision plat, absence of a common grantor, and the failure of the deeds to state that the restrictions run with the land. In this case, no general plan of development that would prevent operation of a gravel pit existed in the area surrounding buyers' land. There was no recorded subdivision, since the plat that was shown to the buyer did not include the gravel pit area, and other deeds conveyed by seller did not contain uniform restrictions. *Pasulka v. Koob,* 524 NE2d 1227 (App. Ct. 1988).

Illinois The Catholic Bishop of Chicago took conveyance of a subdivision lot subject to a restrictive covenant that provided that all lots shall be used for single-family residence purposes except the lot purchased by the Bishop, which lot shall be designated a church site. After conveyance of the lot to the Bishop, developer recorded a second document providing that the lot could be used for single-family residences only if the Bishop decided not to use the entire lot for a church. The Bishop elected to use only a portion for church purposes and conveyed part to plaintiff, who proposed to use his property for a medical office. When neighboring residents objected, plaintiff sued, seeking a declaration that the covenant did not bar his proposed use. *Held:* For plaintiff. The covenant in place when the Bishop conveyed the property was ambiguous. The second document filed by developer was legally impotent where the Bishop did not expressly adopt it in the chain of title. As the first covenant was ambiguous, it had to be construed in favor of unrestricted use of the land as a matter of public policy. *Cimino v. Dill,* 439 NE2d 980 (App. Ct. 1982).

Kansas A business engaged in engineering and constructing modular homes purchased a lot in a subdivision and obtained permission from the seller to construct a modular home on the site. Neighboring lot owners filed suit, alleging that the subdivision's restrictive covenants prohibited construction of a modular home. They cited a covenant providing that no buildings could be moved into the subdivision. *Held:* The covenant did not bar the construction of a modular home on the lot. The court found that the word "building" in the covenant clearly imported some kind of assembled or completed structure rather than various component parts. The use of modular construction is a modern building technique that in no way resembles the usual concept of the mobile home and has not been shown to be inferior to total on-site construction. *Kennedy v. Classic Designs, Inc.*, 722 P2d 504 (1986).

Massachusetts Defendants resided in a home in a subdivision, holding their property under a deed subject to a restrictive covenant recited in a common subdivision plan duly recorded. The covenant stated, "only one one-family house shall be erected hereon and no structure so erected shall be used for commercial purposes." Plaintiffs, neighboring homeowners, sued to enjoin defendants' practice of renting rooms to unrelated college students. *Held:* For defendants. A restrictive covenant must be strictly construed in favor of limiting the restraint on the use of the premises. The language "one-family house shall be erected hereon," strictly interperted, deals only with the type of structure that may be built on each of the lots of the subdivision. Using the same rule of construction, the court interpreted "commercial purposes" as meaning used for business purposes as opposed to residential purposes. The fact that residential use of the property by tenants may produce income did not change the character of the use to that of a business nature. *Brennan v. Kos,* 446 NE2d 1082 (1983).

Missouri A developer recorded an indenture that placed covenants and restrictions on the original development property. Subsequently, the owner added property to that already subject to the covenants. The new property had not been approved by the community association and was unplatted. The community association filed a petition stating that the purchasers of the unplatted lots were not entitled to the use of amenities until the covenants and restrictions were properly placed on the new property. *Held:* The trial court's dismissal was affirmed. In this case, it was clearly the intent of the covenantor-developer to add property subject to the covenants and restrictions. Covenants and restrictions refer to "land" to be added, and not to "platted lots." The court interpreted the document to mean that once property is added, its development character is established and subject to the indenture. Likewise, when the land is developed, it may be used only if it complies with the terms of the indenture. *Lake Saint Louis Community Ass'n v. Ravenwood Properties, Ltd.,* 746 SW2d 642 (Ct. App. 1988).

Minnesota Homeowner sued a neighbor to enforce a restrictive covenant in the deed preventing rental of parts of the house to non–family members. *Held:* The restrictive covenant was enforced. The finding that the original grantor's intent was to restrict development to single-family dwellings was not erroneous. Rental of the basement of the house to strangers violated the grantor's intent to restrict the development to single-family housing. *Lavalle v. Kulkay,* 277 NW2d 400 (1979).

Nebraska A covenant in a condominium sale contract required "alterations" to townhouses to be approved by a majority vote of the owners. When a townhouse owner installed a skylight without permission, the other owners sought to enforce the covenant. *Held:* The covenant was unenforceable. In the absence of language in the covenant explaining the meaning of "alterations," the covenant was too vague to be enforceable. *Ross v. Newman,* 291 NW2d 228 (1980).

Utah In 1947, certain "building restrictions" were filed in county recorder's office limiting properties in a subdivision to single-family residences. The restriction was for 25 years and would automatically be extended for successive periods of 10 years, unless a majority of the owners decided otherwise. The restriction also provided that anyone with an interest in the land could bring an action to enforce the covenant within 25 years of its execution. Defendant commenced alterations on her property to create a duplex dwelling in 1975, and plaintiff brought an action to enforce the restrictive covenants. *Held:* The provision for bringing an action within 25 years made the covenant ambiguous as to whether it was enforceable for more than 25 years. Evidence was required to determine the intent of the parties. *Leaver v. Grose,* 563 P2d 773 (1977).

Washington Owners of a home in a subdivision that was subject to a set of restrictive covenants that provided "no building shall be erected . . . on any lot other than one detached single-family dwelling not to exceed two and one-half stories in height. . . ." put a swimming pool in their yard and began construction of an enclosure for the pool. Their neighbors brought suit for an injunction against construction of the enclosure, claiming it constituted a violation of the restrictive covenant and was a separate building within the meaning of the restriction. *Held:* The court ruled that the swimming pool enclosure was built to be an addition to and part of the house, rather than a separate and distinct structure. Accordingly, it did not violate the restrictive covenant.

The enclosure was attached to the house, was to be sided with cedar siding, windows, doors and trim similar to the house, and was to be painted the same color. *White v. Wilhelm,* 665 P2d 407 (1983).

West Virginia Restrictive covenants prohibited the construction of a "main foundation of any permanent structure" beyond an established setback. A portion of a house, consisting of a column structure, roof, and room, extended beyond the setback line, and neighbors sued. The trial court ordered that only the column be removed. *Held:* The supreme court rejected a narrow interpretation of the covenants in favor of one that best expressed the intent of the parties. It directed the trial court to order the part of the roof and room extending beyond the setback line removed as well. Modern construction techniques and materials, which permit permanent structure support in ways radically different from those traditionally feasible, may not be utilized to undermine the purpose of restrictive covenants prohibiting the construction of main foundations beyond a prescribed setback line. *Allred v. City of Huntington,* 331 SE2d 861 (1985).

Wisconsin Plaintiffs sought to enforce a mutual restrictive covenant against defendants, arguing that use of property as a public park was a prohibited purpose. *Held:* Judgment for defendants. A restrictive covenant prohibiting any use other than construction of single-family dwellings is not violated by dedication of a lot as a public park. The term "residential" in this context is used in contradistinction to "business" or "commerce." A park serves a residential purpose, and therefore would not frustrate the intent of the restrictive covenant. *Ziemann v. Village of N. Hudson,* 298 NW2d 233 (Ct. App. 1980), vacated for mootness, 307 NW2d 236 (1981).

51.20 Covenants Running With the Land

Alabama By a vendor's lien deed, a grantor conveyed 220 acres out of a much larger tract. A clause requiring the grantee to use not less than 50 acres of the property for construction of a golf course was inadvertently included among the boilerplate provisions, which were effective only until the purchase price was paid. Four years later, the purchase price having been paid and the vendor's lien cancelled, the grantee transferred 67 acres of the property to an intermediary who in turn sold them to the city. The conveyance to the city contained the same language, obligating it to construct a golf course. The new city government sued, seeking equitable relief from enforcement of the covenant to build a golf course. The original grantor intervened in an attempt to enforce the covenant. *Held:* The grantor had a legal right to enforce the covenant. That the covenant was intended to enhance the value of the grantor's remaining property was strong evidence that it was intended to run with the land. The scrivener's error in placing the covenant among the numbered boilerplate provisions was obvious and self-correcting. *Lowenburg v. City of Saraland,* 489 So. 2d 562 (1986).

Alabama Brother sued to set aside a conveyance from his sister to a third-party. The deed to the sister from their mother contained language granting a fee simple, but also included a restrictive provision requiring the sister to provide a home for her brother upon his request. The brother contended that the sister's conveyance violated the restrictive clause in the deed. *Held:* While it was the mother's intention to provide a permanent home for her son, the deed restriction should be construed as a covenant rather than a condition subsequent. As a personal obligation, the covenant did not run with the land, and the sister's conveyance was valid. *Schaefers v. Apel,* 328 So. 2d 274 (1976).

Arkansas Under a homeowners' association agreement, members were assessed in order to maintain the common property of a planned community development. Homeowner appealed the enforcement of the lien on the ground that the covenant contained in the agreement did not run with his land. *Held:* The covenant ran with the land since the maintenance of common properties increased the value of each member's property. *Kell v. Bella Vista Property Owner's Ass'n,* 528 SW2d 651 (1975).

Iowa Grantor deeded land to a grantee, reserving "recreational rights" for himself. When a successor owner "clearcut" the timber on the property, the grantor sued for a loss of recreational rights, primarily hunting and fishing. A jury found for the grantor, and the owner appealed. *Held:* Absent a showing of bad faith, the grantor may not recover. The grantor knew at the time of the conveyance that the land would be used for extensive logging. If he wished to more specifically limit the conveyance, he could have done so at the time. *Mikesh v. Peters,* 284 NW2d 215 (1979).

Montana In 1970, property owners signed an agreement that their premises would not be used for the sale of beer or liquor after January 1, 1981. In 1979, the new owners brought an action to have the agreement voided, arguing that the agreement did not constitute a "grant," and therefore was not a covenant running with the land. *Held:* The agreement is enforceable. The agreement was expressly intended to constitute a covenant running with the land and was binding on subsequent owners. *Reichart v. Weeden,* 618 P2d 1216 (1980).

New Jersey Township conveyed 25 acres to the Board of Education in 1949. The deed included a restrictive covenant that limited the use of the land to solely "public school purposes, athletic, recreation and accessory public uses." In 1983, the board adopted a resolution authorizing the public sale of 12 acres. Purchaser, who intended to use the land for residential development, was the sole bidder, and a contract of sale was executed. The township attempted to obtain a judicial invalidation of the sale. *Held:* The contract of sale was illegal because it violated N.J. Stat. Ann. § 18A:20-10 of the New Jersey Statutes and because it abrogated the dedication to public use effected by the covenant. The court stated that even if the contract was not illegal, the board would be entitled to rescission on the ground of mutual mistake of both fact and law, since both the board and the purchaser were mistaken in believing that the land could be conveyed free of restriction. *Springfield Township v. Board of Educ.,* 526 A2d 714 (Super. Ct. App. Div. 1987).

New York Original grantees of land covenanted in their deed to accept and pay for a seasonal water supply from their grantor. It was expressly provided that the covenant should run with the land. The successor in interest of the original grantor sought to enforce the covenant against the successor in interest of the original grantee. *Held:* For a covenant to run with the land, there must be three conditions: (1) intent that it run with the land; (2) privity of estate between the parties; and (3) requirement to touch and to concern the land. Here, the obligation to receive water resembles a personal contractual promise, rather than a significant interest attaching to the property, and therefore does not run with the land. *Eagle Enters., Inc. v. Gross,* 349 NE2d 816 (1976).

Texas Private utilities company agreed with a subdivision developer that it would be granted the exclusive right to furnish water and sewer service to the eight-acre subdivision. The contract stated that it inured to the benefit of the company and the developer and to their respective heirs, legal representatives, successors, and assigns. The contract further provided that the agreement constituted a covenant running with the land. After the developer conveyed the subdivision to plaintiff, it contended that it was not required to use the company's services, as the agreement did not constitute a valid covenant running with the land. *Held:* The contract did not meet the requirements necessary to make it a covenant running with the land, enforceable at law so as to bind the developer's successors in title. Such a covenant must be made between parties who are in privity of estate at the time the covenant is made, and must be contained in a grant of land or in a grant of some property interest in the land. As the service contract did not contain these elements, it was not enforceable against the developer's grantee. *Clear Lake Apts., Inc. v. Clear Lake Utils. Co.,* 537 SW2d 43 (Civ. App. 1976).

51.25 Amendment

Missouri Covenants applicable to the lots surrounding Lake Tishomingo, a manmade lake, allowed for a maximum assessment of $0.55 per foot of lake frontage to maintain the lake. Though this had become inadequate, the covenants made no provision for amendment. An earlier dispute had resulted in a court-approved settlement decree authorizing changes in the subdivision restrictions and setting forth a voting procedure that was followed in this case. Lot owners voted for a one-time special assessment of $2.60 per square foot of lake frontage to pay for some necessary dredging. A minority of the lot owners refused to pay the special assessments, arguing that the court had no authority to allow the covenants to be amended. *Held:* Reformation of covenants is permissible only upon proof of fraud or error, neither of which was alleged here. However, the court felt compelled to enforce the clear equitable obligation of appellants to bear their share of the costs necessary for preserving the common property essential for the continuation of the subdivision. The assessment, while not enforceable as part of a restrictive covenant, was enforceable in equity. *Lake Tishomingo Property Owners Ass'n v. Cronin,* 679 SW2d 852 (1984) (en banc).

52.00 DURATION

52.05 Abandonment and Waiver

Georgia Lots in a subdivision contained restrictive covenants stating that "no building shall be located on any lot nearer than fifty (50) feet to the front lot line, unless approved in writing by [the developer]." A prospective second purchaser of the last lot sold in the subdivision obtained a written waiver permitting him to build 35 feet from the front lot line. Adjacent lot owners sought to enjoin construction. *Held:* Injunction denied. The court adopted the rule exemplified in New York and Illinois cases holding that developers lacked authority to waive setback restrictions after divesting themselves of their interests in these subdivisions. However, balancing the equities, the court took note of the fact that much of the construction was completed before the injunction was sought, of the lack of evidence to suggest that second purchaser's request for a waiver was unreasonable or that the developer acted arbitrarily or capriciously in granting the waiver for an "awkward lot layout," and of adjacent lot owners' awareness of the developer's authority to waive setback restrictions. *Armstrong v. Roberts,* 325 SE2d 769 (1985).

Kansas Developer of residential area sued to enforce restrictive covenants against property owners subject to restrictions against mobile homes, campers, and tents. Property owners had erected no buildings on their lots, but, from time to time, they or guests camped out in tents or mobile homes. They argued that since they had used the property for recreational camping for seven years, the developer's right to enforce the restrictions had been lost by laches, waiver, or acquiescence. *Held:* While it is true that a right to enforce a restriction may be lost by laches, waiver, or acquiescence, mere acquiescence will not bar enforcement so long as a restriction remains of any value. Where there was no evidence of general and continuous violations of the several restrictions which would constitute waiver or acquiescence, and no evidence that property owners had changed their position or that it would be inequitable to enforce the restrictions, the restrictions were not waived. *South Shore Homes Ass'n v. Holland Holidays,* 549 P2d 1035 (1976).

Massachusetts Plaintiffs, owners of beach property, sued to enjoin defendants, owners of neighboring property, from constructing a house thereon. The deed by which plaintiffs had acquired their property contained (1) a covenant by grantor not to build on the beach property that was assigned to defendants; (2) a reservation by grantor to build bath houses on an area where defendants' house was built; and (3) beach rights to areas including the building site. Although plaintiffs were fully informed that substantial work had been done toward construction of the house, they waited at least two years to bring their action to enforce the covenants. *Held:* Plaintiffs were guilty of laches with respect to construction of the house. Their delay in bringing suit caused defendants significant harm. However, the defense of laches was not available with respect to plaintiffs' beach rights because there was no evidence that the construction and exercise of the beach rights interfered with one another in any substantial way. *Myers v. Salin,* 431 NE2d 233 (1981).

Missouri Pursuant to a covenant in the declaration of restrictions for the homeowners association, which provided that no structure be built until the subdivision's original owners had approved plans in writing, the association brought suit to enjoin the building of a prefabricated home on a new resident's lot. Before purchasing the lot, the new owners had made their plans known to one of the original owners who continued to exercise his authority on his behalf and as agent for the other original owners. He orally gave his approval to the plans, as was customary, and defendants purchased the land. After the new owners started building, the association got a temporary injunction to stop them. The trial court issued a permanent injunction against defendants. *Held:* Reversed. While the declaration did require written submission and approval of plans, the unbroken practice of allowing all necessary approvals in oral form, without any reduction to writing, constituted a waiver and abandonment of the requirement that approval be in written form. *Ashelford v. Baltrusaitis,* 600 SW2d 581 (1980).

North Dakota Plaintiffs built a shopping center that was covered by an unrecorded principal lease limiting the use of the shopping center to specified commercial uses. Subsequently, plaintiffs agreed between themselves to allow one building to operate as a movie theatre, a use not expressly authorized by the principal lease. Defendant purchased the theatre building and was granted a deed that incorporated the restrictive covenant included in the principal lease; nevertheless, both parties understood the property was to be used as a movie theatre. Defendant later sold the property to a church over the objection of plaintiffs, who then sued to enjoin use of the property as a church, citing the restrictive covenant. *Held:* Clearly the defendant and the church had constructive knowlege of restrictions of record, and defendant knew that plaintiffs, in agreeing to allow theater operations, had expressly stated that they were not waiving any of their rights. Since no substantial change of the shopping center had come to pass, the purpose of the restrictive covenant was still viable and use of the site as a church was prohibited. *Allen v. Minot Amusement Corp.*, 312 NW2d 698 (1981).

South Carolina Purchasers bought four adjacent lots in a subdivision and invested $43,000 in adapting the property for use as a day care center. Lots 50 and 51 were reserved for exclusively residential use under a restrictive covenant recorded by the developer. However, the former owner of the lots had used a portion of the building on Lot 50 to conduct his business. Neighbors sought to enjoin the new owners from operating any commercial enterprises on the restricted Lots 50 and 51. *Held:* The defense of laches applied so that the neighbors could not enforce the covenant with respect to Lot 50. Lot 51, however, had never been used for commercial purposes, so the purchasers were enjoined from using it commercially. *Rabon v. Mali,* 344 SE2d 608 (1986).

Texas Plaintiffs, property owners in a single subdivision, sued defendant, a property owner in the same subdivision, to enforce restrictive covenants against trailers and buildings with less than 1,200 square feet. Defendant, who had moved a mobile home onto his property, argued that the covenants should not be enforced because other owners in the subdivision had moved recreational trailers onto their property and a few had erected metal outbuildings smaller than 1,200 square feet. *Held:* Because no other property owners lived in trailers, and because there was no evidence that small outbuildings materially affected the other owners, defendant failed to show that the restrictions had been abandoned. It is true that the courts will not enforce restrictive covenants where property owners have acquiesced in substantial violations or where conditions have changed in the surrounding area. However, failure to complain of covenant violations that are trivial or that do not materially affect him does not prevent a property owner from enforcing a covenant restriction when its violation does materially affect him. *Witmer v. McCarty,* 566 SW2d 102 (Civ. App. 1978).

52.10 Changing Neighborhood Conditions

Massachusetts Landowners sued to void a restrictive covenant in their deeds limiting their property to residential use for 30 years. While some industrial uses were now allowed nearby, the general character of the neighborhood was residential. *Held:* The landowners failed to support their claim that the restriction be discontinued. The neighborhood had not changed to such an extent that enforcement would fail to serve the grantor's purposes or impede desirable uses. There was a public interest in keeping the area residential. *Caglians v. Lyman,* 348 NE2d 765 (1976).

Nebraska Defendant sought to construct a convenience store and service station on property adjacent to plaintiffs'. Plaintiffs sought injunctive relief, claiming such use violated protected covenants of the subdivision enacted in 1955 that prohibited commercial development. Surrounding subdivisions permitted convenience stores. Defendant claimed the neighborhood had become significantly more commercial since 1955 and thus, the restriction was no longer of value to the land. *Held:* For plaintiffs. The character of the neighborhood had not changed so drastically as to render the restriction valueless. The fact that the surrounding area had become increasingly commercial did not destroy the covenant's purpose of protecting the residential character of the subdivision itself. *Plumb v. Ruffin,* 328 NW2d 792 (1983).

New Mexico Defendants sold beer and wine at their restaurants. The land titles of the parties contained covenants prohibiting sale of alcoholic beverages in public places. Plaintiffs sued to enjoin violation of the covenants. *Held:* For plaintiffs. The doctrine of changed circumstances provides that obligations in a covenant will not be enforced where conditions have changed so radically as to frustrate the original intentions of the parties to such restrictions. Changes in condition must be of such a material nature that it is impossible to secure the benefits sought to be obtained through the covenant. There was not substantial evidence that the changes in the community were of such a magnitude as to support a refusal to enjoin enforcement. Defendants' claim that enforcement of the covenant made restaurants within the town less competitive was insufficient to justify withholding relief. *Whorton v. Mr. C's,* 687 P2d 86 (1984).

52.15 Effect of Zoning Laws

Nevada Developer subdivided a tract and placed a restriction thereon limiting its use to residential purposes. Approximately 30 years later, the developer attempted to construct a shopping center on a parcel in the tract, and homeowners in the area sought to enjoin construction. The developer attempted to show that the restrictive covenants had outlived their usefulness by referring to a city council resolution to the effect that it intended to reclassify the property from residential to commercial. *Held:* A zoning ordinance cannot override privately placed restrictions, and a court cannot be compelled to invalidate restrictive covenants merely because of a zoning change. *Western Land Co. v. Truskolaski,* 495 P2d 624 (1972).

South Carolina Plaintiff sought a declaratory judgment that a zoning ordinance was unconstitutional when applied to property the rezoning of which would be contrary to restrictive covenants imposed upon the property. *Held:* When restrictive covenants and zoning ordinances were in conflict, the more restrictive of the two will prevail. Here, the zoning ordinance was more restrictive. *Byrd v. City of N. Augusta,* 201 SE2d 744 (1974).

Texas Plaintiffs sued to enjoin defendant from using certain lands for church purposes, contending that such use violated a restrictive covenant limiting the use of land to residential purposes. *Held:* That the city had zoned the land in a manner that would have permitted defendant's proposed use was unimportant; and even assuming there was some evidence of changed conditions outside the subdivision since its dedication, the covenants were still enforceable because there was no evidence that the benefits of the original plan could not still be realized for the protection of the interior lots. *Ireland v. Bible Baptist Church,* 480 SW2d 407 (Civ. App. 1972).

53.00
TYPES

53.05
Residential Use Only

Alabama Defendant, developer of a residential subdivision, recorded and was enforcing restrictive covenants providing for the maintenance of the subdivision's residential character and requiring building plans to be approved by an architectural committee. When purchaser bought two lots in the subdivision, the committee annulled the residential restrictions that applied to those two lots. Purchaser began construction of a convenience store on the lots. Plaintiffs, owners of other lots in the subdivision, sued to enjoin construction of the store on the ground that the covenants continued to restrict all lots to residential use. *Held:* Plaintiffs were granted injunctive relief. The court found an inconsistency between an elaborate set of restrictive covenants designed to provide for residential development and a covenant clause conferring the right to abandon unilaterally and arbitrarily any or all of the restrictions. It concluded that a requirement of reasonableness had to be read into the power to modify or terminate, and that it could be exercised only to further the general scheme of development. *Wright v. Cypress Shores Dev. Co.,* 431 So. 2d 1115 (1982).

Michigan Homeowner leased his home in a subdivision for use as a home for elderly women. The landowners' association sued to enforce a restrictive covenant providing for exclusively residential use of the property. Defendant argued that the occupants of the house were a single-family unit. *Held:* The restrictive covenant was enforced. Under the contract rights created by the restrictive covenant, the use of the house as a home for elderly women is not single-family use. *Jayno Heights Landowners Ass'n. v. Preston,* 271 NW2d 268 (1971).

South Carolina A high-rise residential condominium was barred by covenants limiting a subdivision to "residential purposes" when the subdivision contained mostly single-family dwellings. The court thought that the phrase, "residential purposes," was ambiguous so far as condominiums are concerned because in 1941, when the restriction was imposed, condominiums were unheard of in South Carolina. To clear up the ambiguity, the court looked to the history of the subdivision and found that the overwhelming majority (181) of purchasers had erected single-family dwellings, although there were three two-family dwellings and one five-unit building. Thus, ruled the court, the restriction was intended to limit the subdivision to single-family homes and to exclude a 16-story condominium of 62 units. In addition, the court noted that such a large condominium, even if it were residential, would result in congestion typical of commercial enterprises as hotels. For this reason, too, the condominium was inconsistent with the residential restriction. *Hoffman v. Cohen,* 202 SE2d 363 (1974).

53.10
—Definition of "Family"

Colorado The United Cerebral Palsy Association purchased a residence in a subdivision for use as a group home for eight developmentally disabled adults. Neighboring homeowners alleged that the group residence violated a private restrictive covenant, since it did not constitute a "single family" as required by the covenant. The homeowners sought a permanent injunction to prevent the development of the residence. *Held:* The association's use of the property did not violate the restrictive covenant. The group home contemplated was a single-family residence for purpose of the covenant. The living arrangements were similar to those found in other typical family units and were compatible with the single-family character of the neighborhood. *Turner v. United Cerebral Palsy Ass'n,* 772 P2d 628 (Ct. App. 1988).

Michigan A nonprofit corporation sought a license to operate a small group home for six or fewer developmentally disabled adults. Residents sought denial of the license, arguing, inter alia, that restrictive covenants limited the use of the lot to residential purposes and allowed only a single-family dwelling on the lot. *Held:* The group home was a permitted use under the covenant. The adults living in the group home functioned as a fixed housekeeping and social unit and were a "family" using the home for appropriate residential purposes. Homes of this nature are not permitted to provide continuous nursing or psychiatric care and are thus not institutional in nature. The fact that adults might be required to pay for certain items and services would not of itself change the nature of the activities conducted in the home from residential to commercial. *City of Livonia v. Department of Social Servs.,* 378 NW2d 402 (1985).

Michigan A subdivision restriction provided that no structure could be erected on a particular lot except "one detached single dwelling not to exceed two stories in height." Residents alleged that occupancy of a house on the premises as a permanent supervised residence for five mentally regarded women violated the restriction. *Held:* The restriction was not violated. For purposes of the restriction, the five women constituted a family, particularly in light of the fact that the public policy of the state was to foster and support programs and services for the mentally handicapped. *Malcolm v. Sharmik,* 290 NW2d 101 (1980).

New York Defendant organization, acting pursuant to N.Y. Mental Hyg. Law § 41.34, notified a village of its interest in setting up a community residence to be used by eight mentally disabled adults. Plaintiff homeowners sued to enjoin the establishment of the community residence, arguing that it would violate a restrictive covenant affecting the premises that barred construction and maintenance of "any building other than single-family dwellings." *Held:* The court rejected plaintiffs' narrow definition of "single-family dwelling" as a dwelling occupied by a group of persons united by blood or marriage. It cited New York case law construing the term "family" in a broad sense and a provision of Section 41.34 stating that a "community residence established pursuant to [the statute] . . . shall be deemed a family unit for purposes of local laws and ordinances." The court held that the narrower interpretation of "family" would render the restrictive covenant in violation of the public policies in favor of the unobstructed use of real property and the transfer of mentally disabled persons from institutions to less restrictive environments. *Crane Neck Ass'n v. NYC/Long Island City Serv.,* 460 NYS2d 69 (App. Div. 1983), aff'd, 460 NE2d 1336, cert. denied, 469 US 804 (1984).

Virginia Property owners had obtained permanent injunctions against construction and operation of a group home for mentally retarded adults. The homes would each have four residents and one counselor, and the residents would be employed elsewhere during the day. The homes would operate like typical suburban households, with no training or medical attention on the premises. The non-profit corporation that sought to run the home appealed. *Held:* Issuance of the injunction affirmed. The relevant subdivision covenant limited the use of lots to single-family dwellings used for residential purposes. The Supreme Court of Virginia agreed with the lower court that "[a] single family use does not include occupancy by unrelated persons who live in the home with a counselor." While unrelated adults could live together as a family unit, it was the constant surveillance by counselors, employees qualified to care for the handicapped, that the court found antithetical to the notion of family. Such presence converted what might otherwise be a single-family use into a "facility" for the mentally retarded. *Omega Corp. v. Malloy,* 319 SE2d 728 (1984), cert. denied, 469 US 1192 (1985).

53.15
—Units Per Lot

Alabama Homeowners' organization sued to enjoin proposed construction of a 43-unit townhouse project on a 13-acre tract in their residential development. Homeowners argued the development violated restrictive covenants in their deed, limiting density to five units per acre. *Held:* The townhouse development was within the contemplation of the parties and did not violate the covenant. Restrictive covenants are strictly construed in favor of the free use of property. The restrictive covenant mentioned only single-family and condominium or other multi-family use, but did not define these terms and did not mention townhouse use. The area's master development map referred to in homeowners' deeds, showed the area of proposed townhouse development as a site for high-density use. Therefore, the townhouse development was within the intent of the parties to the deed. *Riverchase Homeowners v. City of Hoover,* 531 So. 2d 645 (1988).

Maryland Village covenants prohibited subdivision of lots without approval of an architectural committee. Owners of a lot attempted to subdivide it into four parcels despite the architectural committee's opposition. The village sought an injunction ordering the four parcels to be rejoined. *Held:* For the association. Owners had attacked the covenant as unenforceable due to a lack of criteria explaining how an application to subdivide would be evaluated. The court disagreed, citing *Kirkley v. Seipelt,* 128 A2d 430 (1957), which held that covenants lacking criteria for evaluation of applications were enforceable provided that refusal to approve was based on the relation to other buildings or the general plan of development. The architectural committee had found the original design for the community to be viable and successful, and along with environmental factors, these were valid reasons for limiting development. *Souza v. Columbia Park & Recreation Assoc., Inc.,* 522 A2d 1376 (Ct. Spec. App. 1987).

Mississippi A residential subdivision was subject to a restrictive covenant that provided that no lot was to be used other than for construction of a dwelling and that each dwelling was to be placed on a lot no less than 50 feet wide or 20,000 square feet. Two large lots were sold to developers who further divided them into 15 new lots, each of which was of the required dimensions. The owners' association sued to enjoin construction of single-family homes on the new lots under the theory that the covenant's restriction of construction to one dwelling per lot referred to the two original large lots, not to the 15 new lots. *Held:* The word "lot" was ambiguous; thus the court applied the rule that ambiguities in a restrictive covenant are resolved in favor of the party being restricted. Since "lot" did not clearly refer only to those lots originally created, the court applied the one-dwelling-per-lot limitation to each of the new lots. The court noted in support that the new lots each met the covenant's minimum acreage requirements. *Andrews v. Lake Serene Property Owners' Ass'n,* 434 So. 2d 1328 (1983).

Nebraska Property owners in a subdivision sued for an injunction against property owners who moved an older house onto their land and constructed additional apartment units in connection therewith. Plaintiff property owners contended this violated restrictive covenants limiting the kind and usage of structures. *Held:* Defendant's house violated the covenant limiting the height of structures to two stories. The construction of apartments was in violation of a covenant limiting the use of the lots to a "private dwelling house." The latter had been interpreted to mean a single dwelling used by one family. Defendants also violated a covenant prohibiting the transfer of previously constructed buildings to the property. *Pool v. Denbeck,* 241 NW2d 503 (1976).

Wyoming The Dices acquired four 20,000-square-foot lots in a subdivision subject to a restrictive covenant permitting only one single-family dwelling on each lot. The lots were also governed by additional restrictions adopted by CDS, the owner of some of the lots, one of which provided for a minimum lot area of 9,000 feet, providing the lot area was at least three times the floor area of the building. The Dices halved each lot and constructed single-family homes on one half of each of the four lots. The county sevice district obtained a judgment enjoining the Dices from building more than one home per lot. *Held:* Affirmed. The Dices' argument that they were permitted to subdivide their lots into lots of 9,000 feet was erroneous, since the covenants referred to lots as originally platted. The failure by CDS to elect a supervising committee in accordance with CDS restrictions was not material to the disposition of the case. Finally, the court could grant injunctive relief even in the absence of proof of irreparable harm. *Dice v. Central Natrona County Improvement & Serv. Dist.,* 684 P2d 815 (1984).

53.20
Covenants to Pay Money

New York Defendants knew when they purchased homes in the community that the community association assessed property owners for the costs of providing maintenance and recreational services. Defendants did not join the association and refused to pay the assessment. The association sued to recover unpaid assessments. *Held:* A contract to pay the assessments was implied in defendants' purchases of houses with knowledge of the nature of the community and the conditions imposed on ownership there. The implied-in-fact contract includes the obligation to pay a proportionate share of the full cost of maintaining facilities and services offered, not merely the reasonable value of the services actually used. *Seaview Ass'n v. Williams,* 510 NE2d 793 (1987).

Vermont Plaintiff, owner of four lots in defendant's vacation home complex, was billed for expenses of the water system, with a threat to cut off water service for nonpayment. Plaintiff brought a declaratory judgment action to prevent curtailment of water and for a declaration of his rights with respect to the water system, which was owned by defendant. The deed gave grantees the right to connect to the water main, and provided for the lot owner to bear a proportionate share of the cost of maintaining the system. Plaintiff claimed that his right to take water from the system was a grant that could not be revoked by defendant grantor's successor in interest. *Held:* The grant to plaintiff was subject to an obligation to share in the expense of maintenance of the system. Defendant was entitled to recover the expenses of maintenance of the water system from lot owners. *Kelly v. Alpstetten Ass'n,* 303 A2d 136 (1973).

53.25
Restrictions on Commercial Uses and Structures

Connecticut Two commercial food corporations applied for a permit to build a restaurant on three parcels of land. Lot 3 contained an abandoned gas station, and the remaining two lots had no structures except a billboard. The building permit application indicated that the proposed restaurant would be situated on commercial Lot 3, and Lots 1 and 2 would be used for a parking lot, memo board, and trash enclosures. The parcels were located within a zone that ordinarily permitted this type of construction, but Lots 1 and 2 were part of a subdivision that maintained deed restrictions allowing only quality residential structures. The community association sought an injunction to prevent the construction of the restaurant and to uphold the restrictions. *Held:* A common scheme of development existed in the subdivision, but the proposed commercial use of the land would not violate the deed restrictions. The restrictions did not prohibit the building of these types of structures, but limited the quality and type of dwellings being constructed. *5011 Community Org. v. Harris,* 548 A2d 9 (1988).

Wyoming Defendants, owners of an undeveloped parcel in a subdivision, commenced construction of a metal building on their lot intended as a shop and garage. They announced that they intended to build a residence on the property within the year. Plaintiffs, property owners in the subdivision, sued to enjoin construction on subdivision property. *Held:* For plaintiffs. The restrictive covenant provided that only residential buildings could be erected, "and outbuildings incidental to the use and occupancy of property for residential purposes only." The shop could not be incidental to residential property without there first being a residence on the property. The court noted that an outbuilding cannot legally be constructed independent of a residence. *Sutherland v. Bock,* 688 P2d 157 (1984).

53.30
Restrictions on Trailers

California Three adult sisters entered into a contract to purchase a mobile home in which the three intended to live with the minor child of the eldest sister. The sale was conditioned on the mobile home park owner's acceptance of the sisters' application. Defendants rejected the application on the basis of a park policy requiring new park residents to be at least 25 years old. The sisters sued contending that the age limit was in violation of the Unruh Civil Rights Act and various constitutional provisions. *Held:* The private mobile home park rule permitting the exclusion of persons under age 25 was valid and enforceable. A state statute, which permits a mobile home park owner to enforce a rule excluding those under age 25 from the park, does not violate the petitioner's rights of familial privacy and equal protection. The state Mobilehome Residency Law is not limited to permit a mobile home park owner to adopt a rule excluding children only when the facilities are reserved for senior citizens. *Schmidt v. Superior Court,* 769 P2d 932, 256 Cal. Rptr. 750 (1989).

Ohio Original grantor, owner of two adjoining lots, conveyed one lot to plaintiff's predecessor. The deed from the original grantor contained a covenant that grantor would restrict the use of the second lot from use for sale of petroleum products by anyone other than grantee. The second lot was subsequently sold by grantor, but its deed did not contain a covenant restricting the sale of petroleum products. The buyer of the second lot began selling diesel fuel. Owner of the first lot sought to enjoin owner of the second lot from further fuel sales. *Held:* The deed to the first lot created a restriction enforceable against the owner of the second lot. A land restriction may be enforced against one who takes property with notice of the restriction, although the restriction is not within his chain of title. The language in the original deed was a restriction on the land. Both parties to the original conveyance intended to place a limitation on the use of the surrounding property. The purchaser of the second lot, therefore, had actual notice that the property was so burdened, and that adjacent landowners had relied upon the restriction. *Hi-Lo Oil Co. v. McCollum,* 526 NE2d 90 (Ct. App. 1987).

Illinois Plaintiff sued to obtain removal of defendant's mobile home, contending it violated restrictive covenant prohibiting structures of a temporary nature, such as trailers or mobile homes, on the property. Defendants contended that although the structure might have originally been considered a mobile home, its placement on a concrete foundation and removal of its running gear converted it to a prefabricated sectional home, making it immobile except for delivery purposes. *Held:* The removal of the running gear and placing the home on a concrete foundation does not convert a mobile home to a permanent structure, therefore the restrictive covenant has been violated. *Brownfield Subdivision, Inc. v. McKee,* 334 NE2d 131 (1975).

New Mexico Plaintiffs sued to enforce a restrictive covenant against trailer houses on land they had sold to defendants. The covenant prohibited trailer houses or modular homes on the premises, except that grantors were allowed such structures for three years or less. Defendants claimed that their mobile home was not specifically prohibited. *Held:* Judgment for plaintiffs affirmed. Using principles of construction favoring free enjoyment and free alienability of land, as well as the principle favoring the ordinary meaning of words, the court found no distinction between a mobile home and a trailer house. The defendants' structure, 10 feet wide and 40 feet long and designed for residential habitation, was the type of structure the covenant's drafter wished to exclude. *Heath v. Parker,* 604 P2d 818, a 1980 decision of the court and apparently contra the instant decision, was concerned with different language in the dedicating instrument; the court overruled it to the extent that it was inconsistent with this decision. *Cain v. Powers,* 668 P2d 300 (1983).

New Mexico Buyer purchased two lots in a subdivision. The purchase agreement contained a restrictive covenant against placing a "trailer" on the property. Buyer then bought a mobile home, removed the wheels and axles, and placed it on a concrete foundation on the property. He also constructed sidewalks, a patio, and other permanent structures. Other subdivision lot owners sued to enforce the restrictive covenant, arguing that the mobile home was a "trailer." *Held:* Buyer had not violated the restrictive covenant. Restrictive covenants should be construed in favor of free use of property. Here, the purpose of the covenant was to prevent temporary structures from undermining the residential character of the subdivision. However, the purchaser's mobile house was clearly not a temporary structure. *Heath v. Parker,* 604 P2d 818 (1980).

New York Tenants in a mobile home park brought an action against the operator of the park, challenging a park rule that conditioned the tenants' right to install window air conditioners on the prior approval of management and the written consent of their next-door neighbors. Although all of the park's tenants consented to the regulation before taking occupancy, plaintiffs contended that the rule violated N.Y. Real Prop. Law § 233, which forbids mobile home park owners from restricting the installation of any electric or gas appliance. *Held:* The statute forbidding mobile home park owners from restricting the installation of any electric or gas appliance, when read in context, is directed against efforts to foster park monopolies by obstructing outside servicemen hired by the tenant to install a competitive appliance. The rule here, however, to which all of the tenants consented before taking occupancy, operated to the mutual welfare of all tenants rather than to the economic advantage of the park owner. Thus, the rule did not violate the statute forbidding restrictions on the installation of electrical appliances. *Miller v. Valley Forge Village,* 43 NY2d 626 (1978).

South Carolina The developer of a subdivision purchased a double-wide mobile home and towed the structure to his lot in the subdivision. The structure was connected to a water line, an electrical line, and septic tank, and its wheels and tongue were removed and the lot was landscaped. The developer intended to use the structure as his residence. However, a restrictive covenant governing the use of the subdivision provided that no structure of any temporary character, trailer, tent, shack, or garage shall be used on any lot, either temporarily or permanently. Homeowners in the subdivision sought an injunction compelling removal of the structure. *Held:* For the owners of the subdivision. The term "trailer" in the covenant was determined to include "mobile home" within its meaning. *Heape v. Broxton,* 360 SE2d 157 (Ct. App. 1987).

South Dakota A restriction in a subdivision allowed for the use of modular homes as permanent residences but prohibited the use of mobile homes as permanent residences. A mobile home was built at a factory and purchased by owner who removed its wheels after placing it on the subdivision and cementing it down. The owner claimed that he could use the home as a permanent residence on the subdivision because he had converted it from a mobile home to a modular home. *Held:* Owner's home was still a mobile home after its wheels were removed. A home that is not movable is a mobile home if it was designed to be moved. The wheels could readily be reattached to owner's home to make it movable again. A temporary hiatus of mobility does not convert a mobile home into a modular home. *Farnam v. Evans,* 306 NW2d 228 (1981).

Texas Although restrictive covenants in their subdivision prohibited "tents, house trailers or temporary structures," landowners purchased a 24 feet by 48 feet manufactured home and installed it on their property. Neighbors sued, seeking to enforce the covenants. The trial court held that the structure was a house trailer and ordered its removal, but the appeals court reversed. *Held:* The manufactured house was a "house trailer" and prohibited by the covenants. *Wilmoth v. Wilcox,* 734 SW2d 656 (1987).

53.35 Other Restrictions

Arkansas Homeowners' association agreement provided for periodic assessment for the stated purposes of promoting the residents' health, safety, and welfare, and improving properties and services. The assessments were used for the payment of taxes, insurance, and repairs, plus the costs of labor, equipment, material, and management. A homeowner appealed the enforcement of the lien created by the agreement on the ground that the stated purposes were so vague as to constitute a restraint on alienation. *Held:* The agreement provided that assessment would be levied according to a readily ascertainable formula and was therefore valid. The homeowner's remedy was not to challenge the assessment, but rather to challenge the expenditures as improper. *Kell v. Bella Vista Property Owner's Ass'n,* 528 SW2d 651 (1975).

California Mobile home park adopted an "adults only" rule permitting only adults age 25 and over to live in the park. Two sisters who did not meet the age requirement brought an age discrimination suit. The California Mobile Home Residency Law permitted mobile home park managements to limit residence to adults. *Held:* For the mobile home park. The issue was the intention of the legislature in authorizing mobile home park operators to restrict residence to adults. The legislature had defined adults in other contexts as those age 18 or older. The sisters contended that "adults" should be read to mean "senior citizens" in the mobile home context. The court disagreed, holding that the adults-only option for mobile home parks constituted an exception to the Unruh Act. Plaintiffs argued that if the adults-only authority was not limited by the Unruh Act, it was unconstitutional as a denial of equal protection and right to privacy. The court declined to view age classifications as "suspect" and thus demanding strict scrutiny. On the privacy issue, plaintiffs argued that the adults-only rule created an invidious distinction for purposes of exercise of the fundamental right to live together as a family between people with children and those without. The court, however, found that the adults-only rule did not directly regulate the family. The rule did not restrict who lived with whom, aside from requiring that all be of a certain age. The court concluded the rule need bear only a rational relationship to a legitimate state goal, a test easily passed in light of the small size of mobile homes and their close proximity in parks, rendering them of questionable suitability for children. *Schmidt v. Superior Court,* 742 P2d 209 (1987).

Florida Two brothers bought half-interest in a condominium unit, with the intention to share it as a vacation home. The rules of the condominium association prohibited any child under age 12 from living on the premises and restricted the use of the units to single-family residences. One of the brothers had children under age 12, and the association soon brought suit to require him to convey his interest to his brother. He countered that the restrictions were a violation of his constitutional rights to equal protection and association. *Held:* The association was not entitled to enforce its rules against the brother. Although the rules themselves were constitutional, as enforced they were not, since other households in the condominium included children under age 12. On the issue of the single-family use, the restriction was ambiguous and could include alternating use by two families. *White Egret Condominium, Inc. v. Franklin,* 379 So. 2d 346 (1979).

Florida Owners purchased a lot in a planned development and planned for a flat-roofed home. Recorded restrictions imposed extensive building requirements, including that each owner obtain the approval of the architectural control board before commencing construction. The board rejected owners' plans. The owners argued the board did not have authority to prohibit flat roofs. The recorded restrictions did not mention such a prohibition, and some houses in the development had flat roofs. The board obtained an injunction requiring the owners to replace their roof. *Held:* Reversed. The court cited the rule that restrictive covenants should be construed narrowly where they limit an owner's free use of land. In the absence of an existing scheme of architecture that puts a prospective purchaser on notice that only one style will be allowed, either in the recorded restrictions or de facto from the unified building scheme in a subdivision, a board empowered to approve building plans does not have the power to impose one style over another, based purely on aesthetic considerations. An architectural control board is not limited to enforcing only recorded restrictions, but the right of approval cannot be exercised arbitrarily. *Young v. Tortoise Island Homeowner's Ass'n,* 511 So. 2d 381 (Dist. Ct. App. 1987).

Florida Appellant owned and operated a mobile home park where it both leased space and sold mobile homes to prospective park residents. Appellant sued mobile home owners and real estate brokers who had placed "for sale" signs in front of mobile homes. Appellant conceded that Fla. Stat. § 83.765(1) precluded a mobile home park owner from enforcing a rule prohibiting "for sale" signs by mobile home owners. However, appellant argued that the statute did not apply to a rule prohibiting real estate brokers' signs. *Held:* The statute in question was designed to prevent park owners from unreasonably restricting mobile home owners from selling their homes. To bar brokers' signs prevents mobile home owners from utilizing an effective way of selling a mobile home, and therefore is inconsistent with the purpose of the statute. *Old Bridge Corp. v. Dugan,* 463 So. 2d 1200 (Dist. Ct. App. 1985).

Louisiana Restrictive covenants of a subdivision required that proposed structures be approved "as to the harmony of external design and location in relation to surrounding structures and topography." Owners of a property submitted building plans that were disapproved by the association board because the plans for a house, shop, and garage created a commercial appearance not in harmony with surrounding buildings. The owners began construction without approval, and the association sued for an injunction. *Held:* The building restriction was enforceable, provided the association could prove that it was enforced reasonably and in good faith. The standard for approval of a building based on whether it was in harmony with other structures and the topography was not ambiguous and was enforceable. *Oakbrook Civic Ass'n v. Sonnier,* 481 So. 2d 1008 (1986).

Maryland Defendants purchased a lot in a subdivision upon which a restrictive covenant existed that prohibited the construction of any "building, fence, wall, hedge or other structure" without the developer's prior approval. When defendants later constructed an above-ground swimming pool without permission, they were notified of the violation and told to remove the pool. They refused, and the developers brought suit asking the court to require the removal of the pool. The court so ordered, and defendants appealed. *Held:* The above-ground swimming pool erected in this case was a "structure" as contemplated by the restrictive covenant in the deed and required the approval of the developer before it could be erected. The order directing that the pool be removed was not too broad. This did not, however, preclude defendants from submitting the plans and specifications for the pool to the developer. The developer would then be required to approve or disapprove in accordance with previously enunciated principles. *Lindner v. Woytowitz,* 378 A2d 212 (1977).

Massachusetts When a condominium board of managers attempted to enforce a rule prohibiting pets, plaintiff claimed that she was free from the master deed encumbrances as a good faith purchaser, since she had received her unit deed before the master deed containing the restrictions was recorded. *Held:* Plaintiff is subject to the master deed encumbrances since the unit deed contained a clause subjecting her property to terms in the master deed. In addition, she was fully aware of all the terms of the master deed and the bylaws at the time she received her unit deed. *Johnson v. Keith,* 331 NE2d 879 (1975).

Michigan Owner of land reserved two lots for the use of subdivision residents to access a lake for recreational purposes. Owner also reserved the right to make reasonable rules and to exercise police power over the subdivision. Sixty years later, adjoining landowners physically prevented the subdivision association's attempts to make improvements to the lots. The association filed an action to restrain defendants from interfering with the improvements. Defendants asserted the association did not represent them as adjacent lot owners and, even if it did, the improvements planned were not within the purposes described by the grantor. *Held:* For the association. While the grantor never granted the association police powers that he had reserved for himself, the grantor had anticipated the need for the association to manage the lots. Thus, residents could act to sustain and improve the lots for their stated purposes through the association, which represented 79 to 85 percent of affected property owners. Additionally, the proposed improvements were within the scope of the grantor's dedication since the association did not intend to change the use or topography of the lots. Instead, the improvements were to ensure better and safer access to the lake and to make the lots more appropriate for their intended use. *Wisniewski v. Kelly,* 437 NW2d 25 (Ct. App. 1989) (per curiam).

North Carolina Plaintiff bought a home in a residential development that was subject to restrictive covenants. The recorded restrictive agreement provided that all homes in the subdivision must have a minimum square footage and that all building plans be approved by the developer or owners' association. Plaintiff's proposed plans for a geodesic dome house were rejected by the review commission because the home was a marked departure from existing home styles. Plaintiff instituted a declaratory judgment action challenging enforcement of the restrictive covenant. *Held:* Evidence supported the trial court's finding that plaintiff's proposed house plans were 30 to 50 feet short of the minimum square footage requirement. The trial court could make an independent finding of fact that the house plans violated minimum square footage restrictions, even though evidence showed that the association did not reject the plans under that restriction. Restrictive covenants running with the land may be varied or discharged by a properly executed release signed by all affected property owners; however, plaintiff may not modify the restrictions without the agreement of the others. The restrictive covenant in this case is valid and enforceable against plaintiff. *Smith v. Butler Mountain Estates,* 375 SE2d 905 (1989).

North Carolina Plaintiffs' successors in interest sold realty subject to a 20-year restrictive covenant granting them a preemptive right of first refusal on subsequent sales of the property. Ten years later, owners of record sold the land to a third party without first offering it to plaintiffs. The trial court ruled against plaintiffs, citing an 1892 case as authority for the proposition that a preemptive right is per se an impermissible restraint in alienation. *Held:* Reversed. Only such preemptive rights as are unreasonable in terms of repurchase price or duration are prohibited. Since the parties set the price at market levels, the owner was assured of receiving a fair return. As to the timing element, the court adopted the 21-year limit of the rule against perpetuities as the measure of reasonableness in such cases. On this basis the case was remanded to trial court for a determination of damages. *Smith v. Mitchell,* 269 SE2d 608 (1980).

Oregon Homeowners placed satellite dishes in their yards. The homeowners' association claimed that this practice violated a restrictive covenant, which provided that "No dwelling house, garage, fence, wall or other structures . . . shall be erected or constructed . . . unless a complete set of plans therefore . . . shall have been submitted to and approved by the homeowners association. . . ." It sued for an injunction ordering removal of the satellite dishes. *Held:* The satellite dishes were in violation of the covenant. Although the term "structure" was not defined, numerous restrictions limited homeowners' rights to erect structures that had not been approved or that were inharmonious with the general plan, with the residential nature of the property, or with structures erected on neighboring sites. The satellite dishes, which were eight and one-half to ten feet in diameter and bolted to concrete bases, were "other structures" within the meaning of the covenant. *Shoreline Estate Homeowner's Ass'n v. Loucks,* 733 P2d 942 (Ct. App. 1987).

54.00 ENFORCEMENT

54.05 Who May Enforce

Arkansas When a homeowner attempted to construct a carport less than 30 feet from the curb, an adjoining landowner sought to enforce a restrictive covenant prohibiting the construction of any building improvements within 30 feet of the curb. The homeowner seeking to build contended that the restriction could be enforced only by the common grantor, since the restrictive covenant was not present in all the deeds of the subdivision. *Held:* The applicable test of enforcibility of a restrictive covenant is whether or not the grantor has reserved any portion of the conveyed subdivision to himself. If he has not, then his failure to include a restrictive covenant in all subdivision deeds does not preclude a finding that the covenants were intended for the benefit of one purchaser against another. *West v. Anthony,* 533 SW2d 518 (1976).

California Property owner in a subdivision filed a class action on behalf of himself and other owners against various others who allegedly were violating the uniform deed restrictions. The trial court sustained demurrers to the class action counts, and property owner appealed. *Held:* The action did not fulfill the requirements for a class action, because there were no common questions of law or fact; liability and damage issues would have to be decided individually. However, the alleged violations did give rise to an individual cause of action for damages against the defendants. Therefore, plaintiff's individual suit was allowed to proceed. *Knox v. Streatfield,* 145 Cal. Rptr. 39 (Ct. App. 1978).

Nebraska Plaintiff purchased property in a district he believed was restricted to one-family use. He knew at the time of purchase that an adjoining property was under construction, but believed a residents' group would prevail in its suit to restrain construction. Two weeks after purchasing, plaintiff sued to force alteration or removal of the neighboring structure, arguing the property was subject to a reciprocal negative easement. *Held:* Without reaching the question of whether Nebraska would adopt the doctrine of reciprocal negative easements, the court found that plaintiff had waived the right to enforce any restriction, since he knew before he purchased the property that a new structure was being built on the adjoining property. Although a party who purchases property after a nuisance comes into existence may still sue to enjoin the nuisance, there is no comparable right to sue to enforce a restrictive covenant. The law does not tolerate a nuisance, but it disfavors restrictions on use of land. *Egan v. Catholic Bishop,* 363 NW2d 380 (1985).

New York Restrictive covenants imposed by the former owner restricted building on certain tracts to one-family homes. A property owner sued to enforce the restriction against nearby property owners. Defendant owners argued their properties had no common plan or scheme. Both plaintiff and defendants had chains of title descending from the original grantor. *Held:* Plaintiff was entitled to enforce the restrictive covenants. To establish privity necessary to enforce a restrictive covenant, a party need show only that its property derives from the original grantor who imposed the covenant and whose property benefited thereby and that the party to be burdened derives his property from the original grantee, who took the property subject to the restrictive covenant. Once this vertical privity has been established, a common plan or scheme is not necessary. It is sufficient that the circumstances manifest the original grantor's intent that the covenant run with the land. *Malley v. Hanna,* 480 NE2d 1068 (1985).

New York Original grantees of land covenanted in their deed to accept and pay for a seasonal water supply from their grantor. It was expressly provided that the covenant should run with the land. The successor in interest of the original grantor sought to enforce the covenant against the successor in interest of the original grantee. *Held:* For a covenant to run with the land, there must be the intent that it run with the land, there must exist privity of estate between the parties, and it must touch and concern the land. Here, the obligation to receive water resembles a personal contractual promise rather than a significant interest attaching to the property and therefore does not run with the land. *Eagle Enter., Inc. v. Gross,* 349 NE2d 816 (1976).

54.10 Against Whom Covenant May Be Enforced

D.C. Circuit Plaintiff homeowners held deeds containing racially restrictive covenants. They brought suit to enjoin the recorder of deeds from accepting for filing any instrument that contained a racially restrictive covenant and to require him to give certain kinds of notice that such covenants were void and unenforceable. The trial court ruled that there was no authority for the requested relief, and that the correct parties to sue would be the real estate brokers and title insurance companies that perpetuate such covenants in deeds. *Held:* The appellate court reversed and granted the relief. *Mayers v. Ridley,* 465 F2d 630 (1972).

Florida Owners of mobile park lots sued mortgagee, who had purchased the developer's interest at foreclosure, to require it to maintain the common areas. The developer of the mobile home park had recorded restrictive covenants obligating it to maintain the common areas until 825 lots were sold, after which the lot owners would assume the responsibility. The mortgagee did not consider it feasible to develop more than 600 lots on the property. It argued that its mortgage had priority over the declaration and that the lot owners lacked privity with it. *Held:* For the mortgagee. A mortgagee should not be deprived of a valuable potential right that it enjoyed when the mortgage was executed, even if the mortgagee had actual notice of recreational facilities on the property on which it foreclosed. The mortgagee had no duty to investigate the chain of title, and was not bound by the declaration. *Mortgage Investors v. Moore,* 493 So. 2d 6 (Dist. Ct. App. 1986).

Missouri Grantor sold a portion of his property in 1962 with a covenant that no additional buildings would be placed on his remaining property. Grantor conveyed the remaining property in 1978 without mentioning the 1962 covenant. The 1978 purchaser built on his tract, and the 1962 buyer's successor sued, alleging breach of the covenant. *Held:* The covenant was not enforceable against the 1978 buyer, who purchased without actual or constructive notice. The 1978 purchaser was not bound by an instrument lying outside his chain of title, as was the 1962 deed. Although the 1962 tract shared a common grantor and a common boundary with the 1978 tract, the 1962 deed was the sole instrument on which the restrictive covenant was recorded. *Basore v. Johnson,* 689 SW2d 103 (Ct. App. 1985).

54.15 Existence of Common Scheme or Plan

D.C. Circuit Written declaration of covenants imposing restrictions on subdivided properties made no mention of a servitude on one lot for vehicular parking. The annexed copy of the revised subdivision plat, however, bore within the boundaries it marked for that lot an inscription reading "to be graded and cinder covered for car parking." Subsequently, that lot was conveyed to the appellee who planned to develop it for parking for tenants of a complex on adjacent land which was never part of the subdivision. The appellant, a subdivision resident, brought an action for declaratory judgment that the inscription on the revised plat gave rise to a right appurtenant to other properties in the subdivision and for an injunction compelling the appellee to use the lot as specified for parking for subdivision residents. At issue was whether an equitable servitude could be created by the mere inscription on a subdivision plat. *Held:* Easements and equitable servitudes may arise from the plat inscription. *Case v. Morrisette,* 475 F2d 1300 (1973).

Massachusetts In 1957, the housing authority approved a redevelopment plan that divided the relevant area of the city into two zones, General Commercial A and B. Gulf was the owner of a gas station in Area A, and its deed provided that the land was subject to all restrictions and covenants in the original contract between Gulf's predecessor and the authority. The original deed contained a covenant that restricted the construction of a gas station in Area B if one had previously been built in Area A. Gulf sought to enforce this covenant and prevent the continued operation of a gas station in Area B. *Held:* The court upheld Gulf's request, on the basis that every property owner, regardless of the order of purchase, has a stake in the plan and has standing to sue on a violation of the common scheme; a common scheme does not require physical uniformity, but exists when each property owner understands the nature of the whole plan before purchase. For the covenant to run, it must touch the land, and the land must be land which the parties intended to benefit by the covenant; intent is to be determined by the circumstances of the transaction, with considerable weight given to the fact that a common scheme existed. *Gulf Oil Corp. v. Fall River Hous. Auth.,* 306 NE2d 257 (1974).

South Carolina Plaintiffs sued several neighbors, asking the court for injunctive relief upon a theory that certain restrictions contained in all deeds conveyed out of common grantor amounted to enforceable mutual covenants. The deeds contained various restrictions such as "no limitation on the size of dwellings . . . ; no trailer home or mobile home will be allowed . . . ; no pigs or swine . . . ; farm animals will be permitted on lots consisting of two acres or more." The court noted that one defendant had built what was in shape and appearance a mobile home, but in actuality could not operate as one. *Held:* Because the "restrictions" were often not restrictions at all (for example no minimal building standards), no common scheme or plan could be found that would logically support the implication of enforceable mutual covenants. Therefore, enforcement of particular restrictions would inequitably encumber the land for no justifiable reason. *Vickery v. Powell,* 225 SE2d 856 (1976).

PART H
CONSTITUTIONAL RIGHTS ON PRIVATE PROPERTY

55.00
CONSTITUTIONAL RIGHTS IN GENERAL

55.05
Shopping Centers

California High school students entered upon defendant shopping center premises during business hours and set up a card table for the purpose of gathering signatures for a political petition. They were expelled by security guards and admonished not to return. In their suit, plaintiffs sought injunctive relief to prevent further denials of access to the shopping center for political activities. *Held:* Although the federal constitution under Supreme Court rulings does not protect speech and petitioning at privately owned shopping centers, the court determined nevertheless that public rights must yield to private interests in this case under the state constitution. The "public character" of shopping centers, coupled with the power of government to regulate private property, requires that peaceful circulation of petitions be protected against restrictions that are not "responsive to the needs of the social whole." *Robins v. Pruneyard Shopping Center,* 592 P2d 341 (1979).

Massachusetts Plaintiff entered defendant's private shopping center to obtain signatures and distribute pamphlets in behalf of his nomination as a political candidate. The shopping center had a policy of prohibiting the solicitation of signatures, but permitted candidates already on the ballot to campaign. Asked to leave, plaintiff did so, and he obtained elsewhere sufficient signatures for his candidacy. Plaintiff then sued, challenging the shopping center's policy. Defendant claimed plaintiff had no constitutional right to solicit signatures in the shopping center and that the issue became moot once plaintiff had obtained the necessary signatures. *Held:* The court rejected defendant's claim of mootness. The issues raised in the action were of substantial public interest and were likely to arise again. The court also rejected defendant's claim that plaintiff had no constitutional right to solicit signatures and distribute pamphlets in a private shopping center. Although the federal constitution provided no such right, the courts held that such a right was found in Article 9 of the Massachusetts Declaration of Rights, concerning freedom of elections. No "state action" requirement was expressed in Article 9, and the court held that no such requirement should be found when private property held open to the public is involved. Finally, the court noted that defendant's policy, while not affecting the economic interests of defendant or its tenants, could substantially impair a candidate's access to voters. *Batchelder v. Allied Stores Int'l, Inc.,* 445 NE2d 590 (1983).

New York A group opposed to the building of nuclear power plants attempted to distribute leaflets at a shopping mall. The mall prohibited leafleting and political activities on its premises. The group was informed of the mall's policy and was directed to cease its activities. The group sued, arguing that the New York Constitution's guarantee of free speech entitled it to distribute leaflets expressing its viewpoint and advertising a demonstration. *Held:* The court of appeals upheld the mall's right to ban leafleting. The court noted that the bill of rights is designed to protect individual rights against the government, and its free speech provisions apply only to governmental actions curbing free expression. Since the mall's ban on leafleting was a private action by a private entity, it was permitted under the state constitution. *SHAD Alliance v. Smith Haven Mall,* 498 NYS2d 99 (1985).

Pennsylvania Plaintiffs, leaders of a political organization, sought a mandatory injunction requiring a shopping mall to cease interfering with their political activities on mall premises. The mall had a uniform policy of forbidding all political solicitation. Plaintiffs argued they had the right under the Pennsylvania Constitution's guarantees of free speech and petition to collect signatures for their candidate's nomination in the private shopping mall. *Held:* Dismissal of plaintiffs' suit affirmed. Although privately owned shopping malls serve a similar societal function as main streets and town marketplaces as gathering places, they do not have the same legal status. The court distinguished *Commonwealth v. Tate,* 432 S2d 1382 (1981), in which a private college that sponsored a symposium was held to have made itself a private forum. The shopping mall was operated solely as a marketplace for goods and services, and not for the exchange of ideas. As long as the owner uniformly applied the policy of prohibiting political solicitation, he was not required to provide a political forum for views on public issues. *Western Pa. Socialist Workers 1982 Campaign v. Connecticut Gen. Life Ins. Co.,* 515 A2d 1331 (1986).

55.10 Picketing

Maryland State statute prohibited picketing residential property, except in a labor dispute. Defendants were convicted under the statute and challenged its constitutionality. *Held:* The statute violated the free speech and the equal protection clauses of the First and Fourteenth Amendments of the U.S. Constitution. *State v. Schuller,* 372 A2d 1076 (1977).

New Jersey Defendants, dissatisfied with the construction of their home, sued the home builder for damages and, in addition, commenced picketing and distributing leaflets at another housing project under construction by plaintiff. Although plaintiff company did not build defendants' house, it shared common officers and shareholders with the company that did the actual construction. Plaintiff sought to enjoin the picketing, contending that defendants sought to pressure plaintiff to settle the lawsuit against a related company. *Held:* Defendants' informational picketing was protected by the First and Fourteenth Amendments of the U.S. Constitution; therefore the injunctive relief sought was not justified since plaintiff had a remedy at law for monetary damages. *Pebble Beach v. Smith,* 356 A2d 48 (Super. Ct. Ch. Div. 1976).

New York Plaintiffs, who had previously expressed views against adoption of a so-called gay rights bill, sought injunction relief to prevent picketing and demonstrating in front of their suburban residence. *Held:* The interests of a homeowner in the peaceful enjoyment of his property, when combined with the coercive and intimidating effect of residential picketing, outweigh the rights of picketers publicly to express their views. The right to privacy in one's home must outweigh First Amendment protections, particularly where alternative sites are available.

Walkinsky v. Kennedy, 404 NYS2d 491 (Ct. App. 1977).

55.15 Other First Amendment Rights

U.S. Supreme Court A resolution adopted by the Board of Airport Commissioners stated that the Los Angeles airport's central terminal was "not open for First Amendment activities by any individual and/or entity." A minister, prevented from distributing religious literature in the terminal, challenged the constitutionality of the resolution. *Held:* The resolution was facially unconstitutional as a violation of the First Amendment overbreadth doctrine. The resolution prohibited all protected expression, not merely expression that could create specific problems of congestion or disruption. Even if the airport were not considered a public forum (an issue the Court did not resolve), no conceivable governmental interest would justify such an absolute prohibition of speech. In addition, the resolution's vagueness presented serious constitutional difficulties. *Board of Airport Comm'rs v. Jews for Jesus, Inc.,* 482 US 569 (1987).

California After having contracted with appellant for the installation of a satellite antenna system in its apartment complex, respondent wanted to remove the cable system supplied by appellant. Appellant sought an injunction preventing the removal, claiming its First Amendment rights had been violated. *Held:* Denial of injunction affirmed. The First Amendment's prohibitions against interfering with speech generally apply to interference by government, and not by private individuals on private property, except in limited circumstances when the individuals or property are the functional equivalent of a municipality or public forum, and the medium is transitory trespass by leafletters and speakers. The record did not suggest that the apartment complex had the attributes of a quasi-municipality, nor was appellant's medium transitory. Attaching cable equipment to a building involves a nontransitory physical invasion of private property, which denies the owner his right to possess and use the space himself and to exclude others. *Cox Cable San Diego, Inc. v. Bookspan,* 240 Cal. Rptr. 407 (Ct. App. 1987).

Texas Defendant was arrested for protesting against taxes on a private church-owned street. He appealed his conviction of criminal trespass, claiming it was unconstitutional. *Held:* Defendant was properly convicted. Under the First Amendment, freedom of expression is not protected on a privately owned street. The street, which was bordered on both sides by church property and controlled by the church, was not the functional equivalent of a public street. Although church permitted general public access to the street, there was no evidence that it had ever been open for public expressive activity. *Gibbons v. State,* 775 SW2d 790 (Ct. App. 1989).

56.00 LABOR UNION ACTIVITY

56.05 Right to Organize

Washington Migrant workers, housed in a labor camp owned by a farm corporation, paid $2.75 a day for room and board. Defendants, a legal aid bureau attorney and a labor organizer, were convicted for trespassing on the private property of the farm corporation when they attempted to visit the camp, after working hours, to consult with the workers. *Held:* The workers paid for the right to live in the camp and enjoyed the status of tenants. They had a right to invite others onto the premises. The First and Fourteenth Amendments rights include the right to counsel. The attorney merely went on the premises and waited for the arrival of the workers who wanted to talk to him; he was, therefore, lawfully there. A union organizer has a right to go where necessary to meet with workers so long as the exercise of the right is reasonable. The visit of the union organizer after working hours but still in daytime was reasonable. Thus, the two men had a lawful right to be at the labor camp when they were arrested. *Washington v. Fox,* 510 P2d 230 (1973), cert. denied, 414 US 1130 (1974).

56.10
Picketing

10th Circuit Under civil rights laws, plaintiff members challenged city ordinance making it unlawful to picket on certain private property. *Held:* Although picketing is a valid exercise of constitutional rights, a municipality may exercise its police power to protect private residential property owners from the nuisance and potential harm from pickets and demonstrators. *Garcia v. Gray,* 507 F2d 539 (1974).

U.S. District Court, New York Union brought suit for injunction to prevent defendants from interfering with peaceful picketing outside an airport. The union pickets were directed toward an independent janitorial concern, which performed services at the airport. *Held:* Injunction denied. Whether the union picketed inside the terminal building or outside upon a paved area used by the public for access to the building is of no consequence, since both areas are private property and "not the functional equivalent of a municipality." There is no constitutionally protected right to picket on private property, and even where such property is leased from the port authority, it is still to be regarded as private. *Local 32B-32J v. Port. Auth.,* 462 F. Supp. 852 (SD 1978).

PART I
ADJOINING LANDOWNERS

57.00
RIGHTS AND LIABILITIES IN GENERAL

57.05
Boundary Lines

U.S. District Court, Virginia When a dispute arose over the boundary line between properties, the parties signed a boundary line agreement, which was recorded. In an action to resolve the dispute, one of the signers claimed it was invalid as a product of fraud, duress, and coercion, and that title to the land could not be determined by a written agreement of the parties. *Held:* Since the individual repudiating the agreement was 28 years old, familiar with the property, and well educated, the written boundary agreement was not invalid as a product of fraud, duress, or coercion. The written boundary line agreement was effective to resolve the dispute. *Williamson v. Williamson,* 407 F. Supp. 370 (ED 1976), aff'd, 547 F2d 811 (4th Cir. 1977).

Alabama An ejectment action was brought to resolve a boundary dispute between adjoining landowners. A jury determined that plaintiff owned all land "in SE corner except the eight acres in the North East corner as shown in Allen survey." On appeal, judgment was remanded to establish the true line. On remand, the trial court determined that the jury had ascertained the true boundary line of the property and amended its judgment, adding a metes and bounds description. Appellant argued the jury verdict was not sufficiently complete to allow the trial court to amend its judgment to fix the true boundary line. *Held:* Affirmed. The jury verdict that referred to a survey as establishing the true boundary could be amended by the trial court to fix the true boundary line by the use of metes and bounds descriptions and references to the survey. Although mere reference to a survey may render a verdict technically incomplete, the verdict may be amended by the trial court to definitely fix the true boundary line, as happened in this case. *Knox v. Criddle,* 529 So. 2d 969 (1988).

Alabama In 1926, adjacent landowner's predecessors in title drew up a metes and bounds deed, which established their respective boundaries on either side of a common line. The deed grantor subsequently subdivided his property into various-sized lots and recorded the plat, whose description of the common boundary differed from the description found in the deed. A subsequent survey by plaintiff revealed two separate northern boundary lines: one according to the deed and the other according to the plat description. The owner of the southern lot sued the adjacent landowner to determine ownership of the land. *Held:* Error of plaintiff's predecessor in title through his subdivision of property south of the common boundary could be charged only against plaintiff, and not against the adjoining landowner whose southern boundary was fixed by a prior deed. The evidence indicated that the subdivision plat erroneously depicted distances by omitting the width of a street shown on the plat. A landowner cannot use his own or his predecessor's error in the subdivision of land to increase his holdings at the expense of an adjoining landowner with whom he shares a common boundary. *Sandefer v. Fairchild,* 538 So. 2d 3 (1988).

Georgia Vendor sought to establish boundary lines on a tract of property that he sold to defendant. Plaintiff neighbor had handdrawn a plat and stepped it off on the ground, but did not place any markers on the property. The land was conveyed and defendant had it surveyed. The surveyor, to obtain the measurements, called for a change in an angle referred to as 90° to 79.9°. Plaintiff contended that this change as well as one involving defendant's road frontage was an encroachment on his adjoining property. *Held:* The surveyor was correct in placing the boundary lines as he did since they complied with the description given in the deed. Plaintiff could not contest the surveyor's assessment when the iron pins in the ground he provided for measuring did not exist. *Duncan v. Frye,* 223 SE2d 713 (1976).

New Hampshire In a boundary dispute, the master found that the remains of a wire fence and stone wall were sufficient monuments to establish the boundary line. Plaintiff alleged that the monuments were part of an old fence intended to restrain cows rather than to mark the boundary. There was additional disagreement as to the location of a roadway. *Held:* The location of a boundary line was a question of fact for the master. Where the evidence was in dispute and there were gaps in the evidence presented, the findings were warranted by substantial evidence. *Starvish v. Farley,* 347 A2d 175 (1975).

New Mexico Plaintiff brought suit to quiet title to a parcel of land that was the subject of a boundary dispute. In suit to quiet title, defendant, who owned land adjacent to plaintiff's, sought to prove acquiescence by showing that an old fence line had been accepted as the dividing line by plaintiff and his predecessors in title. *Held:* Defendant failed to prove mutual acquiescence. The area in question was the site of a gulch, in which fenceposts could not have been placed because of the rocky terrain. Without evidence establishing acceptance by plaintiff's actions or statements, defendant's claim could not be sustained. *Tresemer v. Albuquerque Pub. School Dist.,* 619 P2d 819 (1980).

North Dakota A landowner attempted to establish a boundary between his land and that of an adjoining landowner according to the doctrine of acquiescence. The disputed line was "marked" by a trail between three rock piles, one of which was removed and two of which varied in size with time. The landowner who claimed that his neighbor acquiesced to the boundary erected a fence one foot to his neighbor's side of the survey line, and the neighbor brought suit. *Held:* For the neighboring landowner. In order to establish a boundary line by acquiescence, the claimed line must be recognized not just as a barrier, but as a boundary. The court ruled that in this case, the "border line" in dispute was merely a barrier for farming purposes and not a true boundary. The trail that supposedly constituted a boundary by acquiescence moved from side to side with field usage, and the rock piles changed in diameter in the same way. Hence, the court held that insufficient evidence existed to establish a boundary by acquiescence. *Manz v. Bohara,* 367 NW2d 743 (1985).

Rhode Island Landowners sued to enjoin a town from widening a roadway that adjoined their property, and sought to quiet title to a section of the road's untraveled portion that they claimed was part of their land. They contended that without a recorded plan showing the dedication of a public highway or a declaration of public use by the town, the road was a common-law highway by prescription, and its width was limited to its traveled portion. The town maintained that the road was a duly created public highway, and even if it were a public highway by prescription, its width extended to a line marked by stone walls at one edge of the property. *Held:* Regardless of whether the road was a public highway by prescription rather than dedication, its width could not be limited to its traveled portions where there was evidence that width had otherwise been established. Under Rhode Island law, once a highway has been dedicated and its boundaries defined by a wall or other physical barrier, the right-of-way cannot be lost by nonuse. *Anderson v. Town of E. Greenwich,* 460 A2d 420 (1983).

Utah Plaintiffs, owners of residential property, built their home and made improvements on the erroneous belief that the boundary line of their lot extended 17 feet beyond the point where markers had been placed years before in the original subdivision survey. The lower court quieted title in plaintiffs, finding a boundary by acquiescence. *Held:* Reversed. The elements that must be proven to establish a boundary by acquiescence include occupation up to a visible line definitely marked by monuments, fences or buildings. Here, the alleged markers had long since been removed and the driveway and line of trees had been placed within the boundary. Consequently, without a visible line, there can be no boundary by acquiescence. *Monroe v. Harper,* 619 P2d 323 (1980).

57.10
—Encroachments

New Mexico Property owner brought a suit against the owner of adjacent property, claiming that a fence constructed by defendant encroached upon her land. Although plaintiff had been on the property numerous times, she had been unaware that an encroaching fence had been built, since the view of the fence from her side was obscured by brush and terrain. Defendant counterclaimed, seeking to quiet title on alternative grounds of either adverse possession or acquiescence. *Held:* State law required payment of taxes on the disputed land to sustain a claim of adverse possession, regardless of whether any other element was present. The absence of evidence of payment defeated defendant's claim on this theory. Moreover, plaintiff was unaware of the existence of the fence, making acquiescence inapplicable. While "mutual intent" to establish a certain line as a common boundary is not essential to a finding of acquiescence in that line as the true boundary, there must be some knowledge from which "consent by silence" will spring that indicates the property owner knows of the existence of the line. Such knowledge was not present in this case. *Platt v. Martinez,* 563 P2d 586 (1977).

Rhode Island Plaintiffs sought an order requiring defendants to remove a portion of a driveway that encroached on their property. Plaintiffs built their house in 1969, but did not receive the deed to the property until the house was completed. Meanwhile, defendants built their adjacent house in 1967 and installed the encroachment before plaintiffs built their home. Plaintiffs' deed contained an easement in favor of defendants. In a suit against plaintiffs' grantor plaintiffs were awarded a reformed deed. Defendants argued they were entitled to the encroachment because plaintiffs delayed taking action to oust them. *Held:* For plaintiffs. The fact that defendants were in possession of their property before plaintiffs received their deed did not prove that plaintiffs were ousted. The first deed was invalid; the reformed deed established the correct boundary between the lots. In addition, plaintiffs were not guilty of laches, as defendants were aware of plaintiffs' action against grantor and that plaintiffs were attempting to end the encroachment. *Adams v. Toro,* 508 A2d 399 (1986).

57.15 Construction and Excavation

5th Circuit Plaintiff alleged that the seawall built by defendant had caused his property to erode and that the wall was illegally constructed because it was below the mean high-tide line and thus within the territory owned by the state sovereign. Defendant answered that it had relied on a survey undertaken by a registered surveyor and that the property line should be determined by this survey because of its innocent reliance. *Held:* For plaintiff. Reliance on a private survey is done at the purchaser's risk. *Rhoads v. Virginia Fla. Corp.,* 476 F2d 82 (1973).

Florida A downstream blockage of a stream crossing defendant's property was causing the property to flood. Defendant obtained permission from someone it thought was the owner to clear the waterway, during which several trees were destroyed on the property. Plaintiff sued for trespass, seeking compensatory and punitive damages. The court vacated a jury award of punitive damages. *Held:* Affirmed. The usual measure of damages for trespass to real property is the difference in value of the property before and after the trespass. Plaintiff did not offer evidence that the value of the property diminished after the trespass. Thus plaintiff was not entitled to compensatory damages. As to punitive damages, the court below correctly vacated the jury award, because the trespass was committed by mistake and not by willful and wanton misconduct. *Horn v. Corkland Corp.,* 518 So. 2d 418 (Dist. Ct. App. 1988).

Nevada Plaintiff sued to recover damages arising from the rotation of a sidewalk allegedly resulting from negligent excavation work performed by defendant construction company on an adjoining lot. *Held:* Where the contractor had notice of the deteriorated condition of plaintiff's building and where there was evidence that the excavation caused heavy vibrations and that the damage claimed by plaintiff there was sufficient evidence to support a jury conclusion that the contractor had been negligent. *Lyon v. Walker Boudwin Constr. Co.,* 503 P2d 1219 (1972).

South Dakota A crack had appeared in defendant's wall four months before excavation by an adjoining landowner. The wall collapsed two days after completion of excavation. *Held:* Defendant could not rely on the right to lateral support between coterminous owners, since this right refers only to situations where the adjoining land is removed causing the contiguous land to fall or sink. The right is not applicable to improvements; thus, defendant's only ground, which he was unable to prove, was plaintiff's failure to use ordinary care during excavation. *Grady v. Felkner,* 186 NW2d 509 (1971).

Texas Defendants entered onto plaintiff's property and undertook grading work in order to conform the level of plaintiff's property to that of defendants' private street. Plaintiff sued for damages but was denied recovery since there was no actual diminution in the value of his land. *Held:* Reversed. Although as a general rule the measure of damages is the lower of diminution of market value and cost of restoration, it is inequitable to deny recovery altogether in the face of clearly wrongful conduct. Consequently, the trial court on remand must assess reasonable damages to reflect proper compensation under the circumstances. *BA Mortgage Co. v. McCullough,* 590 SW2d 955 (Civ. App. 1979).

57.20 Drainage

Arizona A group of 219 homeowners sued a water users' association, which operated a canal that burst during a severe rainstorm and flooded their property. The association contended that it had no flood-control duties. *Held:* Once the flood waters entered the canal system, the association was under a duty to exercise reasonable care in disposing of the water. The failure to have at least a few spillways in this natural drainageway constituted negligence. There was not, however, sufficient evidence of recklessness that would warrant the imposition of punitive damages. The fact that the canal's permanent character resulted in its being treated as a natural watercourse for some purposes did not mean that the association did not have the duty to operate, maintain, and repair. *Salt River Valley Water User's Ass'n. v. Giglio,* 549 P2d 162 (1976).

California After his house was severely damaged by a landslide, plaintiff sued the owner of undeveloped property lying upslope from him, alleging negligence in permitting conditions to exist that encouraged the landslide. Defendant cited the common-law rule that a property owner has no duty to remedy a natural condition of the land in order to prevent harm to adjacent property. *Held:* The California Supreme Court decided to end the common-law distinction between merely failing to act on a risky natural condition and creating a risky artificial condition on one's property. Property owners may be liable for harm caused by natural, as well as artificial, conditions depending on the foreseeability of harm to others, the proximity between their conduct and the harm, and the extent of the burden of preventing the harm. *Sprecher v. Adamson Cos.,* 636 P2d 1121 (1981).

District of Columbia Property owners brought suit to compel the District of Columbia to repair water service pipes joining the main water pipes with the property owners' private plumbing systems. The district appealed from a permanent injunction granted by the superior court enjoining the district from enforcing certain rules regarding water-pipe repair and declaring the district liable for the cost of future repairs. *Held:* The injunction was improperly granted. The district had the power to compel property owners to repair the connecting pipes, and the district was not liable to tort for any damage or breakage of these pipes. While the cost of repairs may be substantial to the individual property owner, this inequity is best corrected by legislative, and not judicial, action. *District of Columbia v. North Wash. Neighbors, Inc.,* 367 A2d 142 (1977).

Iowa Owner of a servient estate sued the owners of dominant estate for relief from an alleged nuisance resulting from a flow of surface waters from dominant estate, and for damages. Defendants counterclaimed, asking that plaintiff be ordered to construct a retaining wall. The trial court awarded plaintiff half the damages proved and ordered that one third of the costs of a wall be paid by plaintiff and two thirds by defendants. *Held:* A service estate had to accept surface waters that drain from a dominant estate, but there was no right to alter the drainage system so as to substantially increase the burden on servient estate. A modified judgment for two thirds instead of one half of the cleanup cost and pipe-extension expense incurred by plaintiff was entered. Joint participation was required in construction of a proper retaining wall, with costs to be shared as determined by the trial court. *Braverman v. Eicher,* 238 NW2d 331 (1976).

Louisiana Defendant, while constructing a warehouse on his property, created channels that caused water to drain from his property into a catch basin near the neighboring property of plaintiff. Some of the water fell directly behind plaintiff's home, and plaintiff claimed this water caused substantial flooding on his property. In a suit for damages, plaintiff offered evidence that defendant violated the local building code in constructing the warehouse higher than plaintiff's property without making adequate drainage arrangements. Defendant presented evidence that most of the drainage was due to extreme rainfall. *Held:* For defendant. Plaintiff, seeking damages based on defendant's use of adjoining land, had the burden of proving causation between defendant's acts or omissions and the damage to plaintiff's property. Since only defendant had addressed the issue of causation, plaintiff could not recover. *Patterson v. Garic,* 411 So. 2d 1091 (Ct. App. 1982).

Montana Flood resulting from a heavy rain followed the topography and contours of the land causing damage to plaintiff's property. *Held:* An uphill property owner owes no duty to his downhill neighbor to prevent the encroachment of vagrant or surface waters from his property onto that of his neighbor. *Roope v. Anaconda Co.,* 494 P2d 922 (1972).

Nebraska Plaintiff sued to permanently enjoin defendants from discharging waste irrigation upon plaintiff's adjoining land. The district court ruled that all waste irrigation would be barred. Defendants appealed. *Held:* Reversed and remanded. An injunction that absolutely prohibited the discharge of waste irrigation onto plaintiff's land at any time, in any quantity, whether injurious or not, was too broad. Thus, defendants had the right to discharge only such waste irrigation waters as could be done without injury to the adjoining land. *Peters v. Langrehr,* 197 NW2d 698 (1972).

Nebraska Relief was needed to prevent the discharge of irrigation water into the drainways in injurious quantities; otherwise, the possibility would have existed for the formation of a prescriptive right to discharge waste irrigation water onto plaintiff's land. However, an injunction that absolutely prohibited the discharge of waste irrigation onto plaintiff's land at any time, in any quantity, whether injurious or not, was too broad. *Peters v. Langrehr,* 197 NW2d 699 (1972).

Rhode Island Property owner sued for damages when a neighbor developed his lot without providing adequate drainage for surface water. The neighbor answered that he had used reasonable care in developing the property and had not unnecessarily injured plaintiff. *Held:* The decision of the trial court denying recovery under the "common enemy" doctrine, which permits each landowner unlimited privilege to deal with surface water, was reversed. The case was remanded to apply the rule of reasonable use, which requires consideration of the need for drainage, the care taken to avoid injury, and the benefits to the party whose land is drained. *Butler v. Bruno,* 341 A2d 735 (1975).

Utah When the canal of an electric utility company overflowed because of heavy rain, causing damage to a nearby home, the homeowners sued for damages. *Held:* Whether the occurrence was an act of God that precluded the imposition of liability depended on its severity and unforeseeability. Where the trial court rejected the utility's contention that the storm was an act of God, the utility was liable for damages to the homeowner's property if it was negligent in any way.

Dougherty v. California-Pacific Utils. Co., 546 P2d 880 (1976).

58.00 LATERAL AND SUBJACENT SUPPORT

58.05 Right to Support

Colorado Some buildings were damaged by subsidence when a creek channel was relocated, so the buildings' owner sued the creek owner and the predecessor in interest who had actually relocated the channel. The creek owner argued that there cannot be strict liability for removal of support to land containing manmade structures. *Held:* The creek owner could be held strictly liable for damage to the buildings. The question is whether an artificial condition on the affected land was a proximate cause of the damage. If the fact finder finds that the mere weight of the buildings could not have caused the subsidence, the party who removed the lateral support can be held strictly liable. In addition, the creek owner was liable in negligence, since it knew of the dangerous artificial condition of the land it acquired and knew or should have known that this condition was without the consent of those put in peril. *Gladin v. Von Engelin,* 575 P2d 418 (1978).

North Carolina Excavation by a local government agency removed lateral support from a neighboring building and damaged it. The agency had posted a public notice of its proposal to build on the property, but had begun excavation without any notification to owners of adjacent property. The owner of the adjacent property sued. *Held:* For the plaintiff. The agency was liable for damages resulting from the excavation because it had negligently failed to warn the plaintiff. Notice of excavation affords adjacent landowners the opportunity to underpin or shore up a wall, or relieve it of extra weight. *Waters v. Biesecker,* 305 SE2d 539 (1983).

South Dakota In 1949, a retaining wall was built at the edge of an upslope lot that, as a result of excavation, rose above the lower lot in the manner of a terrace. Plaintiffs purchased the upper lot in 1972 and built a house thereon. In 1973, defendant purchased the lower lot from the prior owners who had built the wall. In 1976, when the retaining wall collapsed, plaintiffs sued defendant for damages caused by a breach of an alleged duty to provide lateral support. Undisputed testimony established that the wall was poorly constructed. *Held:* Defendant was liable because the obligation of providing lateral support was not personal, but ran with the land. If the Massachusetts rule were otherwise, original owners could be liable for damages occurring as a result of subsequent owners allowing the wall to fall into disrepair. The dissent noted that the opposite rule should apply as, in this instance, the original owner had inadequately constructed the wall. *Salmon v. Peterson,* 311 NW2d 505 (1981).

Washington Defendant contractor dug ditches 25 feet from plaintiff's house. The house started to tilt. Plaintiff sought summary judgment on the ground that the excavation obviously removed lateral support from his house. *Held:* A material issue of fact existed as to the cause of the tilt. It had not been established that the soil settled by its own weight because of the loss of lateral support rather than because of the weight of plaintiff's building. In any event, defendant was indemnified by its contract with the city. *Simons v. Tri-State Constr. Co.*, 655 P2d 703 (1982).

West Virginia A house built on a slope began to collapse when a retaining wall further down the slope fell into disrepair. The owner of the house sued the owner of the wall for failure to provide lateral support. The house had been built long after the wall, but the house owner claimed the wall had been built to support both his land and the buildings on it. *Held:* The wall owner was liable for damage to both the house owner's land and his building. While adjacent landowners are not generally liable for damage caused by the added weight of buildings, adjacent landowners *are* liable for their acts of commission or omission affecting lateral support where the land in its natural state can support the weight of the building. *Noone v. Price,* 298 SE2d 218 (1982).

58.10 Remedies for Withdrawal of Support

Kansas Plaintiff brought suit on a theory of inverse condemnation for damages sustained when a large portion of his yard subsided into an area of highway excavation. *Held:* For plaintiff. The common-law right to lateral support is absolute; the right to lateral and subjacent support accompanies the land itself and cannot be taken by the state without payment to the owner. *Sanders v. State Highway Comm'n,* 508 P2d 981 (1973).

New York A developer sued an adjoining landowner to compel landowner to build a retaining wall (at a cost of $25,000) to protect developer's property after he had done extensive excavation. He based his action on provisions of New York City's Administrative Code requiring lateral support between adjoining landowners (Section C26-1903.1, Subdivision a, Paragraph 2). *Held:* The adjoining landowner was not required to build a retaining wall. The record did not indicate whether a retaining wall was necesary or whether the developer could have improved his land without excavation. In any event, enforcement of the code provision would impose a disproportionately heavy burden of compliance. *Tilbro Home Builders, Inc. v. Leidel,* 361 NYS2d 895 (1974).

Rhode Island When defendant raised the grade of his lot 12 to 14 feet, loose fill, gravel, and dirt washed onto plaintiff's adjoining lot. Defendant appealed an injunction ordering him to erect a retaining wall without compensation from plaintiff. *Held:* A landowner who alters the grade of his land has an affirmative duty not to permit his land to fall or slide onto an adjoining parcel. A landowner who fills his lot above the level of the lot of an adjoining landowner has no right to lateral support from the latter, and the latter cannot be compelled to contribute to the cost of a retaining wall. *Tortolano v. DiFilippo,* 349 A2d 48 (1975).

59.00 FENCES AND PARTY WALLS

59.05 Fences

10th Circuit Landowner had fenced his own land in such a way as to enclose federal and state land that he leased for grazing, thereby impeding the movement of antelope across federal land. The federal government sued under the Unlawful Inclosures of Public Lands Act (43 USC § 1061) to have the fence removed. *Held:* The fence had to be removed. The statute, which protects access to public lands, declares such fences to be nuisances that must be abated. The restriction on fences is not a taking, and does not imply any easement for the antelope. *United States v. Lawrence,* 848 F2d 1502 (1988).

Nebraska The landowners wanted to repair and replace a division fence between their tract and that of another landowner. They tried to get the adjoining landowner to share the expense, but he refused. The landowners brought suit for damages, which the district court awarded. This court also ruled that the adjoining landowner was responsible for maintenance of half of the fence. *Held:* Reversed and remanded. In the absence of an agreement between the adjoining landowners, there is no presumption of responsibility for maintaining any portion of a division between them. There was no recorded document regarding a division fence between the tracts. Although there had been a long-standing oral agreement between the landowners' predecessors and those of the adjoining landowner, there was no evidence that the adjoining landowner had notice of any such agreement. Hence, the Nebraska Supreme Court overturned the judgment against the landowner. *Schnakenberg v. Schroeder,* 367 NW2d 692 (1985).

New Mexico Homeowners abutting a municipal golf course objected to city plans to build a seven-foot fence around the facility. After compromising with homeowners, the city decided to breach the agreement and build a five-foot fence. The trial court granted homeowners' request for an injunction and ordered the city to honor its earlier commitment. *Held:* Judgment affirmed. The contractual agreement is not void as a bargaining away of legislative powers but involves proprietary functions of local governments. The state governmental immunity statute has no application, because it does not apply to municipalities. *Spray v. City of Albuquerque,* 608 P2d 511 (1980).

59.10 Party Walls

Louisiana Purchaser sued vendor to recover deposit on property, claiming lack of marketable title in vendor. A survey had revealed that building walls encroached on adjoining property. At issue was whether the existence of party wall servitudes constituted an encumbrance sufficient to render title unmarketable. *Held:* Return of deposit denied. There was no evidence the wall was a party wall. A state statute provided that the first party to build on urban property could rest half of his wall on adjoining land. A wall so constructed remained a private wall until the adjoining landowner acted to make it a party wall. The record did not show who built the wall and whether there was contribution by the neighboring property owner. Therefore insufficient proof was present that litigation was seriously threatened so as to impair marketability. *Langford Land Co. v. Dietzgen Corp.,* 352 So. 2d 386 (Ct. App. 1977).

Ohio In 1978, plaintiff and defendant were adjoining landowners. Each owned a series of row houses on their respective parcels connected by a common brick wall erected on the property line. Defendant hired a contractor to raze the row houses on his property and soon after conveyed his property to purchaser. Plaintiff sued the former owner and purchaser, alleging that portions of the razed structures attached to the party wall had gradually damaged it. *Held:* The complaint constituted a cause of action in continuous trespass against the former landowner as well as the subsequent purchaser. Adjoining landowners owe a duty to each other to use due care in removal of structures attached to a party wall and to protect the legal interest, akin to an easement, in the party wall. *Boll v. Griffith,* 535 NE2d 1375 (Ct. App. 1987).

PART J
TRESPASS AND NUISANCE

60.00
TRESPASS

60.05
Nature of Trespass

U.S. Supreme Court Owners of apartment buildings sought damages for trespass by defendant in the installation of cable television equipment in the buildings. Defendants relied upon Executive Law No. 828, which prohibits landlords from interfering with the installation of cable television equipment that services their own tenants. *Held:* The U.S. Supreme Court, reversing the New York State Court of Appeals, found for the owners. The Court held that when the character of the government action is a permanent, physical occupation of private property, a taking has occurred even if the public benefits or there is only a minimal economic impact on the owner. The Court then remanded the case to the state for a determination of the amount of compensation due the owners. *Loretto v. Teleprompter Manhattan CATV Corp.,* 458 U.S. 419 (1982).

U.S. District Court, Colorado Defendant lived in a house constructed on national forest land, where he extracted and sold minerals and timber belonging to the United States. The government claimed that he was trespassing, noting that he had no deed and paid no taxes on the property. Defendant argued that he should be permitted to remain as a matter of equity, since his predecessor in interest had constructed the house on a patented mining claim at a time when the boundary of the national forest was ill-defined. Indeed, the government did not seek to recover the property until 15 years after the boundary was fixed. *Held:* Defendant was a trespasser. The once-valid mining claim was of no use to defendant since he did not operate a mine, and he could show no other evidence of title. In addition, defendant's equitable argument failed, because the rights of the government are not defeated by the negligent passivity of its officials. *United States v. Osterlund,* 505 F. Supp. 165 (1981), aff'd, 671 F2d 1267 (10th Cir. 1982).

Alabama Defendant in a criminal prosecution was convicted of disturbing an assemblage of people meeting for religious worship. Evidence in the case showed that defendant entered a church at noon on a Sunday carrying a placard proselytizing his private religious views. On appeal, defendant argued, inter alia, that he should have been tried under the state trespass statute. *Held:* The conviction was proper under the statute charged. Since defendant had been specifically invited to enter onto church premises and had been told that he would be welcome as a visitor, a worshiper or an observer, his entry could not constitute criminal trespass. *Ex parte Hill,* 381 So. 2d 206, cert. denied, 381 So. 2d 213 (1980).

California Defendants discovered from a survey that plaintiffs' chain link fence and foilage was actually across the true boundary line and encroaching on their property. Defendants had the fence removed, and plaintiffs sued in an action of trespass, claiming damages. *Held:* Inasmuch as the boundary line claimed by defendants was not in dispute and since plaintiffs did not seek restitution of possession, the action for trespass cannot be maintained. Plaintiffs have no possessory interest to be vindicated and therefore no trespass can be said to have occurred. *Allen v. McMillion,* 147 Cal. Rptr. 77 (Ct. App. 1978).

North Carolina An apartment building was built accidentally one foot onto plaintiff's land. After nine years, plaintiff sued for continuing trespass, seeking to have the building removed. However, N.C. Gen. Stat. § 1-52(3) requires that actions for continuing trespass be brought within three years of the original trespass. *Held:* Plaintiff's action was timely, since the most important limitations period was the 20 years in which an action may be brought for adverse possession. The three-year period merely barred plaintiff from seeking damages for the original trespass. Defendant did not have the option of paying monetary damages for the continuing encroachment; the building would have to be removed. *Williams v. South & S. Rentals, Inc.*, 346 SE2d 665 (Ct. App. 1986).

Ohio Defendant was arrested for walking on and standing upon the lawn in front of a building that had "no trespassing" signs clearly posted. According to a city code section, "No person, without privilege to do so, shall . . . knowingly enter or remain on the land or premises of another." Defendant was accused of trespassing on the "premises," not specifically on the "land." He did not deny entering on the land; but claimed that since he did not enter the building, he did not trespass on the "premises." *Held:* Defendant was guilty of criminal trespass. The phrase in the pertinent section, "land or premises," is a redundancy, because "premises" includes both land and buildings. Thus, defendant did not actually have to enter the dwelling to commit criminal trespass. *City of Columbus v. Hagwood,* 475 NE2d 195 (Ct. App. 1984).

Washington Plaintiff, a business invitee at a skiing area operated by defendant, was injured while attempting to board a ski lift. The evidence showed that the lift was not open for public use but was nevertheless in operation at the time of the accident. No notice was posted to warn passersby that the lift was closed, nor were any employees on hand to supervise. The trial court entered judgment for the plaintiff. *Held:* Reversed. The determinative issue in the case is the status of plaintiff. Defendant argued that plaintiff's status changed when she attempted to board the lift from that of public invitee, to whom a broad duty of reasonable care is owed, to a trespasser to whom no duty of reasonable care is owed. The court refused to abandon the traditional common-law categories and adopt a unified standard of care. The case was sent back to the trial court on the basis of erroneous jury instructions which presumed that plaintiff was, in fact, an invitee. *Egede-Nissen v. Crystal Mt. Inc.*, 606 P2d 1214 (1980).

60.10 Right to Maintain Action

Alabama A landowner sought damages under a theory of trespass, to which a six-year statute of limitations applied, after the one-year statute of limitations for action on the case had expired. The damages had been caused when a construction firm working on adjacent property owned by the city blocked a walkway leading to landowner's building, withdrew water from the underlying water table causing subsidence, and drove piles into the neighboring property, causing structural damage. *Held:* Landowner could not maintain an action for trespass, because the property was leased at the time the damage occurred. The gist of an action for trespass to realty is injury to plaintiff's possession. Having granted possession to its tenant, landlord had only a reversionary interest in possession. The remedy for injury to landowner's reversionary interest would have been an action on the case, which was time barred. *AmSouth Bank, NA v. City of Mobile,* 500 So. 2d 1072 (1986).

California Plaintiff's land was subleased to a lumber company without plaintiff's knowledge. The lumber company ordered tons of broken concrete from defendant, who left it on plaintiffs' land. Plaintiffs sued in trespass. *Held:* However plaintiffs' claim was styled, they were entitled to recover either the land's lost market value, or the cost of removing the concrete. While a recovery in trespass may be available only for injuries to the right to possession (which the plaintiffs did not have while their property was leased), they were in any event entitled to compensation for injury to their ownership rights. *Smith v. Cap Concrete,* 184 Cal. Rptr. 308 (Ct. App. 1982).

Louisiana A state highway department began work on disputed land after having obtained the right to do so from the owners of record, while ignoring plaintiffs' claim to ownership by inheritance. Plaintiffs sued for trespass and related claims. *Held:* Plaintiffs were not estopped from suing, since they had often warned the department of their (eventually successful) claim to the property. In fact, the state's wanton pursuit of the construction project entitled plaintiffs to damages for some losses to be calculated according to replacement value and to damages for mental distress. *Pearce v. LJ Earnest, Inc.,* 411 So. 2d 1276 (Ct. App. 1982).

Pennsylvania Construction work on private land bordered by a county road resulted in two landslides, which damaged the road and caused continuing erosion of its subjacent and lateral support. The limitations period for trespass was two years; but the county sued the construction company only when the road was repaired, more than three years after the original landslide. The county alleged continuing trespass for the period until the repair work had begun, less than two years before the commencement of the action. *Held:* The construction company had committed a permanent trespass to the road, since its actions had permanently injured the road. This damage was caused by the two landslides, so the limitations period began to run with the occurrence of the later of them. *County of Allegheny v. Merrit Constr. Co.,* 454 A2d 1051 (Super. Ct. 1982).

60.15
Measure of Damages

Alabama Owner of woodlands sued for compensatory and punitive damages arising from a trespass and the taking of 52 pine trees when defendant directed the employees of a woodyard to remove all surface timber from his own leased land and they mistakenly cut plaintiff's trees. Defendant's land had been surveyed and marked, but the trees taken were clearly beyond these boundaries. *Held:* The award of punitive damages by the jury was proper since the taking of trees beyond the boundary lines implied that cutting was intentional and deliberate or was done with gross negligence. *Sibley v. Adams,* 324 So. 2d 287 (Civ. App.), cert. denied, 324 So. 2d 291 (1975).

California Defendants, believing they had a valid easement, cleared a strip nearly a mile long through plaintiffs' property. In the process, they damaged 225 trees and nearby undergrowth, and plaintiffs sought damages to compensate for the cost of their replacement. However, the resulting road improved access to the property, resulting in an increase in value of plaintiffs' land. *Held:* Plaintiffs were entitled to damages. Although as a general rule the measure of damages is the lesser of the cost of restoration and the diminution of market value, a property owner who can show a "personal reason" for restoring the land may be awarded reasonable damages. In the present case, however, the cost of complete restoration was unreasonably high in relation to the vlaue of the land. The lower court was required to determine on remand the extent to which partial damages were reasonable under the circumstances. *Heninger v. Dunn,* 162 Cal. Rptr. 104 (Ct. App. 1980).

Florida A downstream blockage of a stream crossing defendant's property was causing the property to flood. Defendant obtained permission from someone it thought was the owner to clear the waterway, during which effort several trees were destroyed on the property. Plaintiff sued for trespass, seeking compensatory and punitive damages. The court vacated a jury award of punitive damages. *Held:* Affirmed. The usual measure of damages for trespass to real property is the difference in value of the property before and after the trespass. Plaintiff did not offer evidence that the value of the property diminished after the trespass. Thus, plaintiff was not entitled to compensatory damages. As to punitive damages, the court below correctly vacated the jury award, because the trespass was committed by mistake and not by willful and wanton misconduct. *Horn v. Corkland Corp.,* 518 So. 2d 418 (Dist. Ct. App. 1988).

Illinois Defendant township widened a road and made improvements to a drainage system. When flooding occurred on the property located on the side of the road, homeowners of the flooded land sued defendant, alleging trespass, nuisance, and negligence. The trial court dismissed the negligence count, but found for plaintiffs on the trespass and nuisance counts. *Held:* On appeal, the court affirmed the damage award for nuisance, but reversed the award for trespass damages. There was sufficient evidence that defendant's engineers were aware that the changes to the drainage system would increase the flow of water to plaintiffs' land and that in fact an increased flow of water resulted from the changes. The appropriate method of determining whether there is compensable injury from the increased water flow is to balance the benefit to the dominate estate against the harm to the servient estate. Since no evidence was presented as to the cost of property damage from the trespass, the award of damages for trespass was improper. As to damages for nuisance, the evidence supported a finding that plaintiffs had suffered loss of use of land, discomfort, annoyance, and inconvenience as a result of defendant's actions. Thus, the damage award for nuisance was proper. *Dovin v. Winfield Township,* 517 NE2d 1119 (App. Ct. 1987).

Mississippi Defendant was held liable for removing $1,400 in timber from plaintiff's tract and for $2,000 in punitive damages. While defendant claimed the land by adverse possession, the trier of fact found that his grazing of animals and repairing of a fence failed to demonstrate open, notorious possession where he was in daily contact with the neighboring owner and had never claimed the property as his own. Defendant contended that his trespass was under a bona fide mistake in fact on the advice of counsel and that punitive damages should be set aside. *Held:* There was no evidence in the record to support defendant's contentions, and testimony indicated that defendant had ill feelings toward plaintiff arising from a prior boundary dispute. Where a trespasser acts in a malicious and oppressive manner, punitive damages may be awarded. *Woodall v. Ross,* 317 So. 2d 892 (1975).

Washington Defendant built a road on plaintiff's undeveloped property without first securing permission. The trial court awarded timber damages but refused to permit recovery for destruction of slate deposits, finding that plaintiff had not shown that the parcel's value had diminished because of defendant's actions. *Held:* Judgment reversed. Plaintiff is entitled to actual compensation for slate damage because it is a mineral resource that is commercially valuable and severable from the property. *Wilson v. Brand S Corp.*, 621 P2d 748 (1980).

61.00 NUISANCE

61.05 Essential Elements

California Defendant, operator of a major commercial airport, appealed a trial court's award of damages in plaintiff homeowners' nuisance claim. Defendant argued that federal jurisdiction over in-flight aircraft preempted state and local control over the level of permissible noise from low-flying aircraft. *Held:* Judgment affirmed. Local airport authorities retain control over noise and related nuisances notwithstanding federal government participation in the operation of an airport and jurisdiction over aircraft flights. *Greater Westchester Homeowners Assoc. v. City of Los Angeles,* 603 P2d 1329 (1979).

Colorado The owner of a vacant lot scraped and leveled it with heavy machinery, leaving the soil loose and sandy. When a series of heavy windstorms blew a substantial amount of soil onto a neighboring property, the neighbors sued for damages. The owner of the lot argued that it was not liable for any damage caused by windstorms. *Held:* The owner of the lot was liable for damage to the neighbor's property. The drifting soil did interfere with the neighbors' enjoyment of their property; and the owner's conduct was intentional, in that it should have known the consequences of the scraping. Since the owner had not taken precautions against the risk of damage, it was ordered to pay damages to the neighbors. *Lowder v. Tina Marie Homes, Inc.,* 601 P2d 657 (Ct. App. 1979).

Georgia Plaintiff condominium association was located on two tracts separated by a creek that passed through a culvert across which a road ran connecting the two tracts. The creekbed and culvert belonged to the condominium developer's predecessor. The creek overflowed onto the condominium property several times. Plaintiffs sued developer's predecessor for negligent construction and maintenance of the culvert, and also sued the developer and lending institution for damages and an injunction to prohibit a continuing nuisance. *Held:* Plaintiff, which did not own, lease, or have a legal interest in the property, lacked standing to sue for damages or injunctive relief. Such rights belonged not to plaintiff but to the individual unit owners. *Equitable Life Assurance Soc'y v. Tinsley Mill Village,* 294 SE2d 495 (1982).

Rhode Island When an explosion erupted into 50-foot flames on property defendants used as a hazardous waste dump site, plaintiffs, neighbors of defendants, sued to enjoin further disposals and burials of the chemical wastes on the ground of nuisance. *Held:* Evidence of defendants' disposal activities causing threats in the forms of cancer and liver disease to the well-being of persons and aquatic life was sufficient to establish the requisite injury for public and private nuisance. Plaintiffs were not required to establish negligence, since under Rhode Island law, liability in nuisance is predicated upon unreasonable injury rather than upon unreasonable conduct. *Wood v. Picillo,* 443 A2d 1244 (1982).

61.10
Public Nuisance

California Defendants owned and operated farmland, a commercial cattle feedyard, a cotton gin, and a restaurant, the operations as a whole being known as the Harris Ranch. A sign that read "Harris Ranch 7 Miles" was erected on a water tank owned by defendants and was visible from an interstate freeway. The Department of Transportation claimed that the sign violated the Outdoor Advertising Act and brought suit for injunctive relief. *Held:* The purpose of the sign was to be determined not by defendants' subjective intent, but by an objective reading of the sign in light of the existing physical circumstances. The words "7 Miles" called the public's attention to a site precisely seven miles away—the restaurant. Thus, at least the "7 Miles" portion of the sign was advertisement in violation of the act, constituting a public nuisance. *People v. Harris,* 180 Cal. Rptr. 148 (Ct. App. 1982).

Iowa Mobile home park was located on a floodplain below a dam. State found the park to be a nuisance subject to abatement. Owner of the park brought suit to compel state and county to institute condemnation proceedings. *Held:* Generally, the use of police power to abate a nuisance does not give rise to a compensable taking, because there is no vested right in a nuisance. The collective benefit of the regulatory action to the state outweighed the restrictions on owner. The park adversely affected the utilization of state's water resources to the extent that either the park or the dam had to go. State was not equitably estopped from resisting condemnation proceedings when (1) owner failed to obtain necessary state permits for development in floodplain and (2) state allowed only the park to occupy its site in the floodplain until the final adjudication of the nuisance action and the additional five years allowed for abatement. *Easter Lake Estates, Inc. v. Polk County,* 444 NW2d 72 (1989).

Michigan Plaintiffs owned a parcel of land they leased to an automobile dealership. Defendants owned an abutting parcel, which they had allowed to grow in a wild and uncultivated state, creating soil and erosion problems on plaintiffs' land. Because defendants' land was elevated 10 to 15 feet, it impaired the view of people exiting from plaintiffs' parking lot, causing an increase in theft and vandalism. *Held:* Plaintiffs did not have a cause of action for public nuisance. In Michigan, an act of man must have contributed to the existence of a public nuisance. Ill results that flow exclusively from natural causes do not constitute a nuisance no matter how extensive the results or how easily avoidable. *Ken Cowden Chevrolet, Inc. v. Corts,* 316 NW2d 259 (1982).

Missouri Defendant executed a "contract for deed" for the sale of property under which the buyers took possession while defendant retained title. The city subsequently determined that debris on the premises was a public nuisance. The debris only increased after notice of violation was sent, and defendant was convicted of violation of the city public nuisance ordinances. Defendant appealed, stating that he was not an "owner" as used in the public nuisance ordinance, since the contract for deed made the buyers the "true owner" and himself only a trustee with bare legal title. *Held:* Defendant had sufficient control of the premises to abate the nuisance and therefore was an owner chargeable under the public nuisance ordinance. "Owner," as used in the ordinance, includes any owner, legal or equitable, who has the right to control the premises so as to abate the nuisance thereon. In this case, the contract for deed specified that a general warranty deed would be conveyed only upon payment in full of the purchase price. It also contained a clause protecting defendant from the consequences of certain city ordinances relating to the condition of the premises by allowing him to correct conditions on the premises as directed by a governmental authority if the purchaser failed to do so. *City of Webster Groves v. Erickson*, 763 SW2d 278 (Ct. App. 1988).

Rhode Island In an action to enjoin a dump operation, plaintiff alleged, inter alia, that a public nuisance was created by the unreasonable amount of noise produced by vehicles hauling refuse to the site. *Held:* Noise in and of itself can be a nuisance if it unreasonably interferes with the use and enjoyment of property. Although noise may have a detrimental effect on others, it will constitute nuisance only if the risk of harm is greater than it ought to be under the circumstances. Because of failure to prove that the noise complained of was unreasonable, nuisance was found not to exist on the issue of noise. *Citizens for Preservation of Waterman Lake v. Davis,* 420 A2d 53 (1980).

61.15 Private Nuisance

3rd Circuit Electric company bought land containing a pond that leaked resinous materials into a river. The chemical producer that had polluted the land had sold the land to a third party that, in turn, sold it to the electric company. The polluter then merged with another firm, Hercules. After spending $300,000 cleaning up the pond, electric company sued Hercules for the cost of the cleanup on a private nuisance theory. *Held:* Electric company had no cause of action. The relationship between a vendor and a remote vendee of land is governed by the rule of caveat emptor. Private nuisance, "a nontrespassory invasion of another's interest in the private use and enjoyment of land," has historically been concerned with conflicts between neighboring, contemporaneous land uses. It should not be extended to the relationship between a vendor and purchaser, since the purchaser has the opportunity to protect himself by inspecting the land and negotiating for a lower price. *Philadelphia Elec. Co. v. Hercules, Inc.,* 762 F2d 303, cert. denied, 474 US 980 (1985).

Kentucky Landowners complained that droppings from a tree, planted by a neighbor along the boundary line between the two properties, had damaged their roof. The damages were the result of normal droppings of leaves and debris from the tree. *Held:* Noting that the tree was healthy and not in danger of falling, the court elected to apply the "Massachusetts Rule," which holds that an owner of land is at liberty to use his land, and all of it, to grow trees, the growth of which will naturally lead to the extension of boughs and roots over and into adjoining properties. The neighbor's remedy for such growth is to cut off any offending boughs and roots. The court reasoned that failure to adopt the "Massachusetts Rule" would have led to innumerable lawsuits and would have imposed liability upon landowners for the natural processes and cycles of trees. *Schwalbach v. Forest Lawn Memorial Park,* 687 SW2d 551 (Ct. App. 1985).

Massachusetts Defendants maintained a large willow tree on their premises whose branches overhung the driveway of plaintiff, the adjoining landowner. Leaves, branches, and sap fell onto plaintiff's driveway as a result of the natural characteristics of the tree, which was not diseased. When plaintiff accidentally fell on her driveway because of the slippery nature of the sap and leaves, she sued defendants for private nuisance for the personal injuries she sustained. *Held:* Plaintiff was not entitled to damages since defendants were not unreasonable in failing to prevent the dropping of leaves, branches, and sap from their healthy tree, and thus did not commit a private nuisance. *Ponte v. Da Silva,* 446 NE2d 77 (1983).

New Hampshire Plaintiffs had been selling modular and mobile homes on their property when defendant neighbor completed the construction of a dog kennel that came within four feet of a home on which plaintiffs had just spent $6,000 for renovations. Plaintiffs were unable to attract prospective tenants to the home and sued defendant on private nuisance grounds for injunctive relief and damages. *Held:* The dog kennel constituted a private nuisance because it substantially, unreasonably, and tangibly interfered with the use of plaintiffs' property. Plaintiffs were granted injunctive relief because defendant failed to take reasonable steps to prevent or minimize the substantial harm done to plaintiffs. Money damages were also granted in the amount of rental income lost by plaintiffs. *Dunlop v. Daigle,* 444 A2d 519 (1982).

New Jersey Plaintiffs and defendants were owners of neighboring single-family homes. Defendants constructed a windmill in an effort to conserve energy. When the windmill operated, it produced offensive noise levels. *Held:* Noise can constitute an actionable private nuisance if it causes an injury, unreasonable under the circumstances to the health and comfort of ordinary people in the vicinity. The court decided that the operation of the windmill harmed human health and well-being to an unreasonable extent, and the intrusiveness of the noise was heightened by the quiet nature of the neighborhood. Furthermore, defendants could have devised less harmful ways to conserve energy. Plaintiffs were clearly "interested parties" entitled to injunctive relief because their proximity to the mill caused them greater injury than that suffered by the general public. *Rose v. Chaikin,* 453 A2d 1378 (Super. Ct. Ch. Div. 1982).

North Dakota Plaintiff, who operated a motor vehicle dealership, and defendant, who operated a feed plant, were adjoining property owners. When plaintiff's costs in keeping its display cars clean increased owing to dust from defendant's operations, it sued defendant, alleging that defendant's operations constituted a private nuisance. *Held:* Plaintiff failed to establish that defendant's operations constituted a private nuisance. Where, as here, plaintiff had "come to the nuisance," it had a heavy burden of proving liability. As plaintiff failed to identify any law that imposed a duty upon defendant to refrain from doing what it did, and since common law on nuisance did not apply where the state, as here, had enacted a nuisance law, the court concluded that defendant's operations were not a private nuisance. *Jerry Harmon Motors, Inc. v. Farmers Union Grain Terminal Ass'n,* 337 NW2d 427 (1983).

South Carolina Plaintiff and defendant constructed adjacent homes in a subdivision developed by a development company. The development's declaration of restrictions required minimum setback restrictions of 15 feet to any side boundary; however, it also provided the developer with the right to vary the setback lines at will. After receiving developer's permission, defendant erected a dog pen and basketball goal near his property line. Plaintiffs sought an injunction commanding removal of the structures, contending that the constructions were a nuisance and violated the setback requirements. *Held:* The constructions did not violate the setback limits since the declaration permits the developer to vary setback requirements at will for any construction in violation of the restrictive covenant. Defendant also had the developer's permission to build the structures. However, a private nuisance may be ordered removed. In this case, no evidence was presented supporting a conclusion that the basketball goal was a nuisance. The dog pen constituted a nuisance since it was poorly maintained and odorous. *Blanks v. Rawson,* 370 SE2d 890 (Ct. App. 1988).

Wisconsin Plaintiff sued to enjoin construction of defendant's home that would block the sunlight from the rooftop collectors of plaintiff's solar heater. *Held:* Under English common law, landowners had a right to enjoy sunlight across adjoining land under the "doctrine of ancient lights." The states later repudiated this doctrine on the basis of three policy considerations: the landowner has a right to use his land as he wishes; sunlight is of little economic value; and society should not interfere with land development. The court, however, found that these policies were no longer applicable at a time when society was increasing its regulation of land uses and sunlight was becoming a major alternative source of energy. Therefore, plaintiff had the right to file a private nuisance claim. *Prah v. Maretti,* 321 NW2d 182 (1982).

61.20 Right to an Injunction

1st Circuit Plaintiffs, landowners living in the vicinity of an airport, sought injunctive relief and damages in a suit against the Federal Aviation Administration (FAA) and the Massachusetts Port Authority (Massport). Plaintiffs alleged the two agencies conspired to maintain a nuisance condition through the operation of the airport. *Held:* The First Circuit upheld the district court's dismissal of the complaint for failure to state a claim. The Federal Aviation Act empowers the FAA in its discretion to provide for the control of aircraft noise. However, a related statute gives citizens the right to sue where there is an alleged failure to perform a duty that is nondiscretionary. Since any noise control regulations are discretionary, the branch of the statute granting such discretion to the FAA is an insufficient basis for a private suit. The other branch of the Act is concerned primarily with safety and not noise. Finally, the local proprietor (in this case Massport) has traditionally been viewed by the courts as the party liable for nuisance claims. *DiPerri v. FAA*, 671 F2d 54 (1982).

7th Circuit Landowners brought a nuisance action against the operators of a junk-automobile-shredding-machine business, claiming that the machines emitted pollution and noise, and endangered the public health and safety. They sought a permanent injunction and compensatory and punitive damages. *Held:* A legitimate business will not be restrained unless the injury is material. A permanent injunction of the junk-automobile-shredding-machine operator's business was denied where injury to health, safety, or welfare were not shown. Plaintiffs were not entitled to compensatory or punitive damages. *Harrison v. Indiana Auto Shredders Co.,* 528 F2d 1107 (1976).

U.S. District Court, New York Residents of communities adjacent to a park sued to compel the National Park Service to abate the practice of nude sunbathing on federally protected lands. Plaintiffs asserted that federal question jurisdiction existed because a "federal common law" interest was involved, or alternatively, that jurisdiction could be based on "federalized" state law in a federal enclave. *Held:* There was no federal jurisdiction under either theory. The federal court refused to apply substantive state rules and deem them "federal." No federal interest existed, especially with regard to a matter that was historically judged by reference to local community norms. *Sylvane v. Whelan,* 506 F. Supp. 1355 (ED 1981).

California The county obtained an injunction against defendants, owners and operators of a restaurant and bar, that prohibited them from allowing noise emanating from their facilities to be audible outside the boundaries of their property. *Held:* The injunction was too broad. It should have been worked so as to permit some noise to escape defendants' facilities, except for that which unreasonably interfered with residents' use and enjoyment of their property. *People v. Mason,* 177 Cal. Rptr. 284 (1981).

61.25 Damages

Missouri Plaintiff was the grantee of an easement of access from his landlocked property to a state highway. Defendant sewer company commenced the construction of sewer lines adjacent to plaintiff's property and upon the access road. During the course of construction, defendant cut down and removed trees and shrubbery, failed to properly seed construction areas, created holes in the road, placed equipment on the road so as to obstruct plaintiff's access thereto, and removed a retaining wall in a creek running alongside the road. Plaintiff brought suit against defendant, alleging temporary damage from defendant's interference with the easement of access. *Held:* Plaintiff was entitled to damages for interference with his easement because it constituted a nuisance. However, because the interference was temporary in nature, plaintiff was not entitled to the difference in fair market value of his property before and after the interference occurred. The proper measure of damages was the reduction in rental value of the property during the period of interference. *Mondelli v. Saline Sewer Co.,* 628 SW2d 697 (Ct. App. 1982).

New York State took over a private airport for operation by the transit authority. The state appropriated airspace and imposed height limitations on buildings in the surrounding area. Two property owners sued the state, contending that they were entitled to damages for the cost of soundproofing their homes and for the decline in property values as a result of increased noise and the new height restrictions. *Held:* As a matter of law, damages could be assessed against the state for aircraft noise. Aviation easements do not give the state the right to make whatever noise is necessary and incidental to overflights by whatever type of aircraft. In this case, however, the court denied the property owners damages because they failed to prove that the market value of their properties had actually declined after the state began running the airport. *Kupster Realty Corp. v. State,* 404 NYS2d 225 (Ct. Cl. 1978).

PART K
WATER AND WATERCOURSES

62.00
NATURAL WATERCOURSES

62.05
Rights and Liabilities of Riparian Owners

U.S. Supreme Court The Vermejo River, which originates in Southern Colorado but is located primarily in New Mexico, was at the time of this suit fully appropriated by users in New Mexico. When a Colorado corporation obtained a conditional right to divert water from the river, the New Mexico users sued to enjoin any diversion by the Colorado corporation that would violate their senior rights. *Held:* The Special Master's criteria in recommending that Colorado be permitted a diversion under the doctrine of equitable apportionment was upheld. When, as in this case, both states recognized the doctrine of prior appropriation, priority becomes the guiding principle in an allocation between competing states. However, the issue of just apportionment is a question of federal, not state, law. Under federal law, priority is considered along with such factors as the efficiency of current uses in the user state and the balance of benefits and harms to the competing states. *Colorado v. New Mexico,* 459 US 176 (1982).

7th Circuit Drainage district was responsible for maintaining a stretch of river in an agricultural region. Company owned land north of the river and, under the terms of a contract with the district, pumped millions of gallons of water from wells on its land into the river. South of the district, the company drew water from the river for use in its plant and sold the rest as drinking water. After a dispute, the district terminated the contract, but the company continued to pump water into the river. The district sought to enjoin the pumping, claiming that the added flow of water eroded riverbanks, damaged drainage ditches, and impeded drainage by raising the level of the water. *Held:* An injunction against the pumping of water into the river was denied. A riparian owner may use a river as a conduit for water pumped into the river for its use downstream. The riparian owner does not lose its rights merely because part of the river is under the control of a drainage district. The contract in this case could not be read as a commitment by the company to stop using the river when the contract was terminated. Even if the district faced increased costs because of the pumping, an injunction was not justified when damages would remedy the district's injury. *Okaw Drainage Dist. v. National Distillers & Chemical Corp.,* 882 F2d 1241 (1989).

9th Circuit Landowners sued a power company for negligently operating a flood-control system and flooding their property. The power company alleged that the dam was constructed primarily to control the flow of water from a lake to a river, to provide water for irrigation, and to generate hydroelectric power. It argued that the plan to use the facility to control spring runoffs was only secondary. *Held:* Even though flood control was not a primary duty of the power company, the power company undertook flood-control efforts in its operation of the system and altered the natural waterflow patterns of the area. Since the landowners relied on the system, the power company was responsible for exercising reasonable care to avoid flood damages. The power company could be liable for damages caused by its negligence to downstream landowners. *Kunz v. Utah Power & Light Co.,* 526 F2d 500 (1975).

California Defendant constructed a dam without a permit, and the state sued 20 years later for an injunction. Defendant contended that he had established a prescriptive right to divert and capture the water. *Held:* The state water code permit procedure applies to all affected uses and rights that have arisen since its effective date of 1914. Public rights generally cannot be lost to prescriptive rights, and, therefore, defendant is subject to governing restrictions under law. *People v. Shirokow,* 605 P2d 859 (1980).

California Owners of property along an isolated stream system sought an adjudication from the State Water Resources Control Board to determine the extent to which they could apply the scarce waters that flowed seasonally through the area. After conducting an investigation, the board issued an order establishing the rights of various parties. One party brought this action challenging the order insofar as it awarded him the right to extract and apply enough water to irrigate 89 acres of property being cultivated. The board's action had the effect of barring any future claim to exercise riparian rights to the remaining acreage not being farmed. *Held:* By setting up the special adjudication procedure, the legislature did not intend to empower the board to extinguish future rights without considering whether less drastic limitations could be adopted to achieve the goal of ensuring reasonable and beneficial water use. Although an unexercised riparian right will lose priority to active rights, there is no constitutional authority for the state summarily to declare that such unused rights are forever extinguished. *In re Waters of Long Valley Creek Stream Sys.,* 599 P2d 656 (1979).

Florida The Department of Transportation moved to condemn land adjoining a lake, while reserving the riparian rights to the precondemnation owners of the land. The owners claimed that they were entitled to severance damages and argued that the reservation of riparian rights was not meaningful, since riparian rights could not be enjoyed by nonriparian landowners. *Held:* For the landowners. A condemnor should not be permitted to reserve the riparian rights to the condemnee without an express bilateral agreement to do so. The court reasoned that the ability to enjoy riparian rights was dependent upon the opportunity to enter upon the riparian lands. The court also resolved, in dicta, the question of whether riparian rights are severable at all from the riparian land, ruling that a Florida tax statute, Section 197.228, does not apply to property law, and that, accordingly, riparian rights may be severed from riparian land by bilateral agreement or transferred by a voluntary act of the upland owner. *Belvedere Dev. v. Department of Transp.,* 476 So. 2d 649 (1985).

Indiana Natural accumulations of water on plaintiffs' farm drained into a channel that emptied into defendant's farm by way of a culvert. The water had flowed in that direction by way of the waterway for over 50 years. When defendants erected several dams to obstruct the flow of water, causing water to back up onto plaintiffs' farm, plaintiffs sued to permanently enjoin defendants from obstructing the flow of water. *Held:* Plaintiffs were granted permanent injunctive relief. The court ruled that the water was not surface water, but that it flowed through a natural water course. If the water had been surface water (i.e., not flowing through a definite channel), defendants would have won under the common enemy rule, which permits a lower tenant to protect himself from the flow of water any way he can. *Birdwell v. Moore,* 439 NE2d 718 (Ct. App. 1982).

Mississippi An upstream timber company used pentachlorophenal to treat wood. The poisonous biproducts of the treatment were funneled off into a waste pond, and heavy rainfall caused the pond to drain into a stream that fed plaintiff's lake. *Held:* There was not sufficient proof of damage to require a restoration of the lake to its previous unpolluted state. However, plaintiff had established an invasion of his property and a nuisance, and was entitled to damages and to an injunction against further pollution. *Phillips v. Davis Timber Co.,* 468 So. 2d 72 (1985).

New Jersey When a landowner's property was flooded several times by heavy rains after the county constructed a bridge across the offending brook, the landowner sued to require the county to abate the flood-making changes in the bed of the stream. The landowner alleged that under the Bridge Act the county has a duty to maintain bridges and that property owners had a cause of action for damages suffered by wrongful neglect in connection with the construction or repair of a bridge. *Held:* The Bridge Act did not create an action against the county for damages caused by the condition of the bed of a stream other than where it passed under the bridge. *Ades v. Mayor & Council,* 351 A2d 14 (1976).

South Carolina A riparian landowner mined sand from part of the bed of an adjacent stream. The state sued the landowner, claiming that title to riverbeds vested in the state. Although the landowner could not show a clear chain of title, it was not disputed that its land was originally conveyed by Crown Grant in 1767. There was no evidence that the state had regained title to the land or reconveyed it at any time. *Held:* For the riparian owner. The landowner's rights in the streambed were controlled by the common law as it existed in colonial South Carolina in 1767. The English common-law rule that gave owners of adjacent riparian land title to the beds of nontidal, fresh water streams to the center of the stream applied, since no changes had been made to this 1767 rule. The state could not rely on a postcolonial break in title to claim ownership of the riverbed; the state, like any other litigant, could recover only on the strength of its own title, not the weakness of the opposing party's. If the state's "perfect chain of title" argument were accepted, few private titles would be secure against the state. *State ex rel. McLeod v. Sloan Constr. Co.,* 328 SE2d 84 (Ct. App. 1985).

Wisconsin Department of Natural Resources prevented the diversion of waters by riparian landowners for irrigation by enforcing a statute that required a permit before any water could be diverted. Landowners sued, alleging that the statute violated procedural due process. Plaintiffs appealed the judgment for defendant. *Held:* The legislature abrogated the riparian right of irrigation and substituted a permit procedure. The statute was not unconstitutional in failing to provide a hearing to adjudicate the right of irrigations.

Omerick v. Department of Natural Resources, 238 NW2d 115 (1976).

62.10
—Right to Natural Flow of Stream

4th Circuit Plaintiff sued a power company for flooding of her property caused by company's downstream hydroelectric dam. Plaintiff alleged that opening of the dam had caused a narrow lake to form that resulted in increased upstream water, resulting in flooding on plaintiff's property. *Held:* For plaintiff. A state statute prohibited making a dam so as to overflow the lands of another without prior consent. The court found that plaintiff's action could be maintained under this law, even though the dam had not caused the river to overflow its natural banks. *Cooley v. Clifton Power Corp.,* 747 F2d 258 (1984).

California A state water authority granted a municipal water authority the right to almost all the flow of water into an ecologically important lake. When municipal diversion of this flow damaged the lake, the state authority sued to stop it, on the theory that the area surrounding the lake was protected by a public trust. *Held:* The public trust doctrine protects navigable waters, such as the lake, from damage caused by diversion of inflow. The court ordered the state to reconsider its original appropriation of the public trust land and to perform an environmental study. *National Audubon Soc'y v. Superior Court,* 658 P2d 709, cert. denied, 464 US 977 (1983).

Kansas Upper landowners sued to recover for crop damages caused by an alleged obstruction of a water course by the lower landowners. The lower landowners answered that the action was barred by the statute of limitations since the crops were destroyed more than two years before the suit was commenced. *Held:* The obstructions were not permanent, but, rather, temporary. Since the obstructions were temporary, the two-year statute of limitations applicable to permanent damages did not bar the action. The statute of limitations begins to run when the crops were actually harmed, and each injury constituted a new cause of action. *Goving v. McCandless,* 547 P2d 338 (1976).

Louisiana Defendant, while constructing a warehouse on his property, created channels that caused water to drain from his property into a catch basin near the neighboring property of plaintiff. Some of the water fell directly behind plaintiff's home, and plaintiff claimed this water caused substantial flooding on his property. In a suit for damages, plaintiff offered evidence that defendant violated the local building code in constructing the warehouse higher than plaintiff's property without making adequate drainage arrangements. Defendant presented evidence that most of the drainage was due to extreme rainfall. *Held:* For defendant. Plaintiff, seeking damages based on defendant's use of adjoining land, had the burden of proving causation between defendant's acts or omissions and the damage to plaintiff's property. Since only defendant had addressed the issue of causation, plaintiff could not recover. *Patterson v. Garic,* 411 So. 2d 1091 (Ct. App. 1982).

Texas Vendor sued to obtain specific performance of a contract that stated that the property conveyed included an area shaded green on an attached map. This shaded area did not totally conform to the otherwise specific contract description. The vendor contended that it had been mutually understood that the property contained in a specific survey was part of the 600 acres, and, further, that the shaded area represented the results of this survey. The vendee argued that specific performance could not be required, since the contract failed to mention this survey.

Held: Before a court requires specific performance of a contract for the sale of land, the written agreement must be found to contain the essential elements of a contract, expressed with such clarity and certainty that it may be understood without resort to parol evidence. Although an agreement's reference to an attached map may provide such a sufficient description, where the agreement failed to indicate that the shaded area represented the results of a specific survey and that this survey's results represented the property to be conveyed, specific performance could not be ordered. *US Enters. Inc. v. Pauley,* 535 SW2d 623 (1976).

Vermont A drainage culvert on defendant's land, which was on a plateau, increased the flow of water onto plaintiffs' property below. Claiming that this increased flow caused flooding of their house, plaintiffs sued for damages and injunctive relief. Heavy rainfall was admittedly a factor. *Held:* Where only the amount of the artificially altered flow from the higher property is in question and not its location, the injured party must show that the increase was the proximate cause of the damage. A factual determination would have to be made on this question. *Swanson v. Bishop Farm, Inc.,* 443 A2d 464 (1982).

62.15
—Acquisition of Water Rights by Prescription

Montana Two neighboring ranches, one upstream from the other, had been using stream water for irrigation for almost a century. Then the downstream user blocked the upstream user's ditches and obtained a temporary order restraining the upstream user from irrigating from the disputed creeks. The upstream user claimed a right to the water by prescription. *Held:* The upstream user failed to establish a prescriptive right. The Water Use Act eliminated the right to acquire water by prescription in 1973. Before that point, the evidence showed that the water had been shared by accommodation. For instance, at one point the manager of the upstream ranch was guardian to the minor children who had inherited the downstream ranch. Prescriptive rights could not be acquired while such a relationship was in effect, and no notice was ever sent thereafter stating that the upstream ranch's water use had become adverse. *Hill v. Merrimac Cattle Co.,* 687 P2d 59 (1984).

Wyoming The holders of junior water rights had, for periods of more than 25 years, used water from the tributaries to a creek to the detriment of a downstream appropriator. Failure by state officials to regulate the appropriation of water by the upstream users meant that the downstream user often failed to receive the full amount of water to which it held a state permit. The upstream users claimed to have acquired rights to the downstream user's appropriation by viture of adverse possession. *Held:* Water rights may not be acquired by adverse possession or prescription in Wyoming. Article 8, Section 1 of the Wyoming Constitution provides that the water of all natural streams, springs, lakes, or other collections of still water, within the boundaries of the state, are the property of the state. Water rights may be acquired only by state permit. *Lewis v. State Bd. of Control,* 699 P2d 822 (1985).

62.20
—Developed Water Rights

Colorado A resort owner applied for a developed water right, based on his plan to develop a marshy meadow so as to increase water flow in the stream. The plan involved steps to minimize seepage, evaporation, and transpiration from plants. *Held:* The resort owner was not entitled to the increase of the flow. The court acknowledged having held in the past that one who increases the flow of a natural stream is entitled to the use of the water to the extent of the increase. However, since seepage belongs to the river, a project that reduces it is not regarded as increasing the river's flow. The court also refused to grant any right to an increase of the flow from transpiration, since this would encourage the destruction of plant life. *RJA, Inc. v. Water Users Ass'n of Dist. 6,* 690 P2d 823 (1984) (en banc).

62.25 —Water Rights on Federal Reserve Lands

California The U.S. Forest Service asserted claims in the Hallett Creek Stream System: a reserved water right under federal law for primary national forest purposes (firefighting and road watering) and a riparian water right under state law for secondary national forest purposes (wildlife enhancement). The state water board upheld the United States on the reserved rights claim but rejected the request for riparian water rights; the United States filed a notice of exception. *Held:* The federal government has the same riparian rights on federal lands reserved for national forest purposes as any other landholder. The federal government's property rights were not defined exclusively by federal law; thus, state law could determine water rights on federal lands. Under California law, the federal government's interest in public domain waters was subordinated to the rights of subsequent appropriators. *State Water Resources Control Bd. v. United States,* 749 P2d 324 (1988).

62.30 Pollution

Florida Riparian landowners brought a class action on behalf of such owners and all other persons who owned property bordering on a creek, seeking to recover for damage resulting from alleged pollution by defendant corporations. *Held:* Although the action was dismissed as inappropriate for a class, the court stated that the complaint was sufficient as to an individual cause of action. When a landowner's common-law riparian rights are violated by the acts of another individual, he is not limited to seeking relief from public authority, but may bring action on his own behalf. *Harrell v. Hess Oil & Chem. Corp.,* 287 So. 2d 291 (1973).

Massachusetts Plaintiff sought an injunction against the Commonwealth, which was polluting the corporation's water supply by storing salt in open piles on state property near plaintiff's wells. The Commonwealth successfully demurred on the basis of the doctrine of sovereign immunity. *Held:* The Commonwealth is not immune from liability for damage caused by its maintenance of a private nuisance. *Morash & Sons v. Commonwealth,* 296 NE2d 461 (1973).

New York Defendants accidentally spilled landfill into a pond jointly owned with plaintiffs. The pond was filled with silt, rendered temporarily unusable, and some of plaintiffs' trees were destroyed. Plaintiffs sued for damages. *Held:* Plaintiffs were entitled to damages only for the cost of removing the silt. Plaintiffs would have been entitled to damages for the decline in fair market value of the property if that amount was lower than the cost of restoration, but the duty to prove the lesser measure fell within defendants' duty to mitigate damages. However, the awards for tree loss and loss of pond usage were set aside because plaintiffs had not sufficiently established the degree of loss. *Jenkins v. Etlinger,* 432 NE2d 589 (1982).

63.00 SURFACE WATERS

63.05 Rights and Liabilities

Arkansas Rainwater and drainage from nearby fields overflowed and ran through landowners' field. Landowners built a levee on their property to ward off drainage. The county sued for injunctive relief, alleging the levee blocked a natural watercourse. The trial court held that a watercourse existed on the land. Under state law, no one may obstruct the flow of an existing watercourse. If no watercourse existed, an affected landowner had the right to defend himself against surface water unless this would cause unnecessary injury to another. *Held*: No watercourse ran across landowners' land. In this case, the flow of water was mere surface water not flowing in a definite channel with a bed and banks. The water flowed onto landowners' land only because it was the low ground. The case was remanded to determine whether landowners, in protecting their land, had unnecessarily caused damage to others. *Boyd v. Greene County,* 644 SW2d 615 (1983).

Idaho A mine produced an open flow of water from a mine portal. Neighbors claimed an entitlement of 100 gallons a day for domestic use. The mine owners objected to the allocation eventually made by the state, claiming that the mine water was nonappropriable private water. *Held*: The water was public groundwater subject to appropriation. Appropriable waters include all waters flowing in their natural channels, even those waters brought to the surface by artificial means. *In re General Determination of Rights to Payette River Drainage Basin Water Use*, 687 P2d 1348 (1984).

Utah Purchaser argued that when he bought the seller's house, he acquired the water rights to springs on the property. The contract made no mention of water rights. *Held*: The grantee of land has the statutory right to the use of water appurtenant to that land. Where the water right had been used to irrigate different parcels at different times, the water conveyed was the amount of water that was being used for the conveyed land before and at the time of sale. *Stephens v. Burton,* 546 P2d 240 (1976).

Wisconsin Water routinely collected on defendants' low-lying parcel of land, frequently flooding plaintiff's neighboring parking lot. Plaintiff sued for damages. *Held*: Defendants were liable because the flooding from their land was an unreasonable and intentional invasion of plaintiff's lot. That is, the damage was serious, but fixing the problem would not interfere with the development of the offending parcel. Defendants had already spent over a quarter of a million dollars on their land, while repairing plaintiff's lot and connecting defendants' property with a storm sewer would cost only $16,000. *Crest Chevrolet-Oldsmobile-Cadillac v. Willemsen*, 384 NW2d 692 (1986).

63.10 Drainage and Diversion

California Plaintiff and defendant were neighboring landowners along a creek. Defendants placed boulders along the creek's banks to stop ongoing erosion. As a result, the flow of the creek was altered, resulting in erosion damage to plaintiff's property. Plaintiff sued defendants for strict liability for diversion and obstruction of a natural stream. *Held*: For defendants. The reasonable use doctrine applies when one landowner seeks damages for another owner's installation of erosion control materials. In this case, defendant was reasonably acting to protect his land so as to prevent its loss. Each owner has a right to protect his own land, and an owner who fails to do so cannot prevent others from protecting their land. *Weaver v. Bishop*, 254 Cal. Rptr. 425 (Ct. App. 1988).

Illinois Defendant township widened a road and made such improvements to the drainage system that the property to the west of the road was routinely flooded. Property owners sued for trespass, nuisance, and negligence. *Held*: The property owner could recover only for nuisance. The landowner's lower, servient estate was required to accept only the quantity of water that would flow naturally from the township's higher, dominant estate. The changes made by the township greatly increased this flow, and the landowner had shown damages from inconvenience, loss of use of the land, annoyance, and discomfort. However, while the township's actions also satisfied the elements of trespass, plaintiff could not recover because it could not be shown that the damage from the township's work outweighed the benefits. *Dovin v. Winfield Township*, 517 NE2d 1119 (1987).

Minnesota Neighboring farmers constructed a field drainage system to benefit their farms. Subsequently, defendant, whose farm adjoined the farms in the drainage system, purchased from one of the farmers the right to connect his farm's drainage to the neighboring system. The other neighboring farmers claimed their crops were damaged after the hookup because of poor drainage and brought suit to enjoin defendant from using the system. *Held*: Defendant's use of the drainage system was reasonable when (1) his land naturally drained onto the neighbors' land, (2) there was no evidence that neighbors' crops were damaged, and (3) farmer had the right to sell defendant the right to hookup. If neighboring farmers wished to prevent interlopers like defendant from using their system, they should have put an express limitation on the right to sell hookups. *Evers v. Willaby*, 444 NW2d 856 (Ct. App. 1989).

Nebraska The lower-lying property to the east of plaintiff's land was protected from the flooding of a bordering river by a levee system. When the river flooded, a floodgate leading to the lower region was closed, and plaintiff's property suffered severe damage. Plaintiff sued for damages from the flood and for an injunction. *Held*: Plaintiff was entitled to an injunction but failed to establish damages caused by the closing of the floodgate. The floodgate obstructed a natural drainageway from plaintiff's property, however, and the water district had no right to block the natural movement of surface water from plaintiff's land. *Holman v. Papio Natural Resources Dist.*, 421 NW2d 430 (1988).

Nebraska A concrete drainageway carried off the surface water from the residences of plaintiffs onto defendant's golf course. Defendant built an earthen structure to prevent flooding from what defendant claimed was increased runoff. Alleging that defendant's structure caused their drainageway to back up, plaintiffs sued for an injunction to have the earthen structure removed. *Held*: Plaintiffs had a right to seek relief, because their concrete drainageway simply channeled water through a natural watercourse. The owner of the lower property had no right to dam, divert, or repel the rainfall or melted snow from plaintiffs' property. *Fink v. O'Neill Country Club*, 352 NW2d 166 (1984).

Virginia Landowner appealed the denial of injunctive relief to remedy the flow of rainwater that allegedly resulted from defendants' construction of a drainage pipe.

Defendants had erected buildings, hard-surfaced a portion of their land, and installed a drainage pipe. Plaintiff alleged that he suffered damage caused by the pipe and introduced evidence to show erosion, flooding, and damage to its septic tank. Defendants showed that water from other property also drained onto plaintiff's property, that the septic tank repairs were part of normal maintenance, and that plaintiff's property was not damaged by the water. *Held*: Where no greater surface water damage occurs than would naturally result from the reasonable development of an upper landowner's property, liability will not be imposed merely because of the presence of an artificial drainage system. The chancellor's report that defendants had not willfully channeled their water onto plaintiff's property was affirmed. *McCauler v. Phillips*, 219 SE2d 854 (1975).

Wisconsin Condominiums were built on pilings above wetlands separated from a lake by a roadway. Culverts connected the wetlands with the lake. The state sought to have the condominiums removed. The state argued that the wetlands were really a lake bed, and that title to the beds of navigable lakes rests in public trust. *Held*: The court used the standard of whether an area was above or below the lake's ordinary high-water mark to determine which parts of the wetlands were a lake bed. Those that were a lake bed were held in public trust; those that were not a lake bed were floodplain, subject to normal county zoning ordinances. *State v. Trudeau*, 408 NW2d 337 (1987).

64.00 NAVIGABLE WATERS

64.05 Navigation in General

6th Circuit A local conservancy district sued the Army Corps of Engineers to determine whether the Great Miami River was "navigable," and so within federal jurisdiction. *Held*: Only a portion of the river was navigable. It is sufficient for a river to be considered navigable if it was used historically as a commercial highway, even if it is now too blocked or obstructed to be used for that purpose. Part of the river was judged navigable on the basis of its use between 1800 and 1830. *Miami Valley Conservancy Dist. v. Alexander*, 692 F2d 447 (1982), cert. denied, 462 US 1123 (1983).

9th Circuit The State of Oregon sought a declaratory judgment that when the state was admitted to the Union the McKenzie River was navigable and therefore vested in the state at that time. An association of landowners with real property riparian to the river, many who held title derived from federal land patents, claimed that the river was not navigable and therefore belonged to the United States. *Held*: The river was navigable under federal law because it was used and susceptible of use in its ordinary condition as a highway for trade and travel conducted in the customary mode of commerce on water. Use of the river need not be easy, long, or continuous in order for the river to be deemed navigable, nor need use be possible during all times of the year. Therefore, the riverbed was vested in the state when it was admitted to the Union. *State v. Riverfront Protection Ass'n*, 672 F2d 792 (1982).

64.10 Riparian and Littoral Rights

Alabama The owner of an easement across a stretch of beach sought to build a pier appurtenant to the easement. The owner of the beach objected. At trial, testimony by the grantor regarding his intent for the extent of the easement was admitted, since the language of the easement was ambiguous. *Held*: The owner of the easement could not build a pier, since the easement was granted with the intent that it be used solely for pedestrian access. *Fouts v. Beall*, 518 So. 2d 1236 (1987).

Louisiana In the 1830s, the Red River created a peninsula on which a plantation was located. In the early 1900s, the course of the river changed and the southern section of the peninsula was cut off. Sand bars in the area stopped the flow of the river and created the oxbow lake. The river abandoned its former bed and created a new bed, which meandered eastward. At issue was ownership of the bed of the oxbow lake. The state contended that since the Red River was navigable in 1812, it was deemed navigable thereafter. Therefore, the bed of the oxbow lake was navigable in law and not susceptible to private ownership. *Held*: When the river abandoned its bed and created the oxbow lake and opened a new bed, the private owners of the land on which the new bed was located were privileged to claim the abandoned bed of the river. The private landowner who loses the new bed takes the abandoned bed as indemnification. It does not matter that the oxbow lake is navigable; as a matter of law, the bed loses its identity as a public entity and becomes privately owned. The bed of the oxbow lake is privately owned by owners of land on which the new bed is located by virtue of 30 years' acquisitive prescription. *State v. Bourdon*, 535 So. 2d 1091 (Ct. App. 1988).

New Hampshire Plaintiff and defendant, owners of adjoining shorefront property, sought a determination respecting the proper placement and use of defendant's dock. The trial court determined that the location of the dock, although within the boundary line of defendant's property, constituted a nuisance and an encroachment on plaintiff's littoral rights. In its order, the court required that defendant remove his dock beyond a 30-foot "buffer zone" established as a fixed limitation on littoral rights. *Held*: The trial court erred in ruling that the parties have fixed shoreline rights. In any case of nuisance occurring on navigable waters, an equitable remedy must be reasonable and sufficiently flexible to suit the requirements of the particular situation. *Heston v. Ousler*, 398 A2d 536 (1979).

Texas When the state billed plaintiff $.25 per cubic yard of material dredged by plaintiff from a navigable river adjacent to its property, plaintiff challenged the state's right to recover. When plaintiff obtained approval of the project from the state, this cost was not mentioned. The state contended that it was statutorily empowered to sell marl, gravel, sand, shells, or mudshale, and that it had authority to condition approval of a dredging permit on the applicant's future purchase of the material dredged. *Held*: Since plaintiff's operations were necessary and incidental to navigation and were done under federal authority, plaintiff was excepted from the statutory permit requirement. Therefore, the state Park and Wildlife Department did not have statutory authority to require plaintiff to pay for the spoil. *Amdel Pipeline, Inc. v. State*, 541 SW2d 821 (1976).

64.15 Tidewater

U.S. Supreme Court Record titleholders of Mississippi land underlying nonnavigable bayous and streams that were influenced by the Gulf Coast tide brought suit to quiet title after the state issued oil and gas leases on the property. The state argued it had acquired title to the property at the time of statehood and that all land lying under any waters that are influenced by the tide, whether navigable or not, are held in public trust. *Held*: Mississippi took title to lands lying under nonnavigable waters that were influenced by the tide running in the Gulf of Mexico when the state entered the Union. The Court stated that it had held since *Shively v. Bowlby*, 152 US 1 (1894) that the original states reserved title to soils under the tidewater, and that new states admitted to the Union have the same rights as the original states in the tidewaters and underlying lands located in their jurisdiction. Further, the Court noted that it has recognized in the past that states have an interest in lands beneath tidal waters having nothing to do with navigation. Thus, the Court rejected petitioner's argument that state ownership of lands beneath tidewaters rested on the navigability of the waters, rather than on the ebb and flow of the tide. *Phillips Petroleum Co. v. Mississippi*, 484 US 469 (1988).

65.00 SUBTERRANEAN AND PERCOLATING WATERS

65.05 Wells, Springs, and Percolating Waters

Arizona The city had been pumping groundwater from wells on property of a nearby town to serve its municipal customers. The town, but not the city, was located within a critical groundwater area. The town subsequently sued the city to enjoin it from pumping groundwater within this area. While the lawsuit was pending, the Groundwater Management Act was enacted, as a result of which both town and city became part of a single management area, which included the basin from which town and city drew water. The town asserted that the act, which permitted the city to draw groundwater from the basin, constituted a taking of property without due process and just compensation. *Held*: The act was not an unjust taking of property. Under Arizona common law, there is no right of ownership of groundwater before it is captured and withdrawn. The right of the owner of underlying land is to the usufruct of the water and not to the water itself. *Town of Chino Valley v. City of Prescott*, 638 P2d 1324, (1981), appeal dismissed, 457 US 1101, reh'g denied, 459 US 899 (1982).

Florida Condominium corporation erected units on land with the intention of using fresh water from a shallow aquifer for the complex. A municipality that owned a well field near the property depleted the fresh water in the aquifer, causing an influx of saltwater that rendered the aquifer unfit as a water supply. The condominium, forced to obtain water at much greater cost from a deeper aquifer, sued the municipality, claiming inverse condemnation. The court of appeals ruled that a shallow aquifer is a form of private property that could not be taken without compensation. *Held*: The Florida Supreme Court reversed. The municipality could not be held liable. The diversion of water was not a taking requiring compensation or a condemnation hearing. *Village of Tequesta v. Jupiter Inlet Corp.*, 371 So. 2d 663 (1979).

Nevada Cattle from adjacent ranches had historically shared water from springs located on appellants' land. Before there were fences, the cattle had intergrazed. In 1957, predecessor owners of the ranches agreed in writing to build a fence and divide the spring's water. Appellants' predecessor owner built a fence and pipeline to land on respondents' ranch. Appellants became aware of the fence and pipeline two years after purchase and removed them. The state engineer issued an order of determination giving each party a vested annual watering right for 50 head of cattle. *Held:* the order was affirmed. Respondents had a vested right to share in the spring's water. The continuous sharing of the water by both ranches' cattle constituted sufficient appropriation to beneficial use to establish a vested right; actual diversion was not necessary. Appellants were not, however, bound by the written agreement. At the time they purchased the ranch, appellants had no actual knowledge of the fence and waterworks on their property. *Waters of Horse Springs v. State Eng'r,* 671 P2d 1131 (1983).

Ohio Landowners sued a quarry for dewatering and polluting the wells located on their properties, which adjoined the quarry. They claimed that pumping by the quarry removed underground water they all used and that the mining process spoiled the common water supply. *Held:* For landowners. A proprietor who pumps water from beneath his land is liable for interference if he (1) unreasonably lowers the water table or pressure of his neighbors, (2) takes more than his share of the common store, or (3) causes harm to a person also entitled to use of the water through his conduct. In the instant case, it was clear that the pumping of underground water by the quarry had an adverse effect on the common source of water for adjoining landowners; thus, the quarry had unreasonably caused harm to landowners. *Cline v. American Aggregates Corp.,* 474 NE2d 324 (1984).

65.10 Artesian Wells

Nebraska Existing owners of land supplied with water from artesian wells lost their water when new owners of an adjacent tract drilled a deep irrigation well. The existing owners sued for damages and injunctive relief. *Held:* Under state law, a landowner is entitled to appropriate subterranean waters under his land, but he cannot extract them in excess of a reasonable and beneficial use, especially if such use is injurious to others who have substantial rights to the waters. If the natural underground supply is insufficient for all owners, each is entitled to a reasonable proportion of the whole. The rule, however, had to be construed in light of a Nebraska statute that provides that preference in the use of underground water shall be given to those using the water for domestic purposes. Since the existing owners used the water for domestic purposes and the new owners used the water for irrigation, the new owners were entitled to reimbursement for expenses incurred in drilling new and deeper wells to restore their water supply. *Prather v. Eisenmann,* 261 NW2d 766 (1978).

PART L
ROADS, HIGHWAYS, AND STREETS

66.00
ESTABLISHMENT

66.05
By Prescription or Use

Iowa Plaintiff purchased real estate lying east and north of a road. Defendants purchased land on the south and west sides of the road. After the city filed a condemnation proceeding to acquire a portion of plaintiff's land, plaintiff discovered that the road was not in the location approved when it was dedicated and that change of location resulted in his loss of over four acres of land. Plaintiff brought suit to establish the proper location of the road and to require the city to either remove the road or compensate him for his loss. *Held*: Plaintiff's requests for relief were refused. The road, which was originally located by mistake, was established by a prescriptive easement between the servient property owner and the city. *Murrane v. Clarke County*, 440 NW2d 613 (1989).

Louisiana In a boundary action between the owner of property separated by an untraveled road that defendant had fenced and was using for pasture, plaintiff sought to have the center of the roadbed declared as the dividing line between the properties. Neither party had record title to the road. Defendant opposed this action on the ground that he had obtained title to the road through adverse possession. *Held:* Because there was never a dedication of the road property to the public, the greatest right that the public could have over the roadbed was a servitude of passage obtained through use or maintenance of the road. Whatever rights the parties to this suit may have in this property could be acquired only from or adversely to the record owners thereof. Since neither party so claimed, the case had to be dismissed. *Dodds v. Manning*, 316 So. 2d 907 (Ct. App. 1975).

Utah Property owner constructed two gates across a road, barring access to other property owners' land. The neighbors sued, alleging a prescriptive easement to use of the road or, alternatively, that the road was a public thoroughfare and could not be blocked by the landowner. *Held:* The landowner may not block the road. The existence of a public roadway is supported by evidence and by the decree of the court in a previous case. *Condas v. Condas*, 618 P2d 491 (1980).

66.10
By Map Plat

West Virginia Plaintiffs sued to enjoin defendants from denying them the use of Mountain Vista Drive. The plat of the subdivision showed the drive as a public way, but it had never been developed. Plaintiffs also claimed that a private right-of-way acquired by defendants' predecessor in interest had become public. *Held:* Plaintiffs had an easement to the drive, but not to the access road. The access road was never taken by condemnation or adverse possession, nor did the owners dedicate the land to public use. Plaintiffs did have a right to use Mountain Vista Drive, however. Since plaintiffs' lot was conveyed by reference to a map plat showing the road, title carried with it the right to an easement in the drive. *Reger v. Weist*, 310 SE2d 499 (1983).

66.15
By Dedication

Alabama Property owner sought to open a road by clearing the timber from a strip of land that ran between plaintiffs' land and led to owner's property. The strip of land was designated in the parties' deeds as a road. Adjoining property owners sought a temporary restraining order to prevent the land from being cleared. *Held:* Strip of land was designated as a "public road" under common-law dedication and could be cleared of timber to make it a usable road. A common-law dedication results when the owner of property expresses an intention to dedicate property and the public or an authorized body indicates acceptance of the dedicated property. The common grantors of the parties indicated in their deeds an intention to dedicate the land for use as a road. Except for the disputed portion, the road was employed for public use, implying acceptance. Adjoining property owners were estopped from denying the existence of the road since they knew the land had been dedicated as a public street when they purchased their lots. *Stapler v. Hicks,* 530 So. 2d 230 (1988).

Missouri Property owner agreed to the establishment of a gravel road across his property, which road was paid for by neighboring landowners. The neighbors used the new access route until the underlying property was sold. The new owner objected to his neighbors' use of the road and blocked the road with vehicles claiming that its users lacked the right to access the route across his land. The neighboring owners brought an action to enjoin the landowner from blocking the road. *Held:* The access road was a public road established by common-law dedication. A common-law dedication is found where there is a clear intent to dedicate land for public use and the land is accepted and so used by the public; acceptance by the governmental authority is not needed so long as the public accepts the dedication through its use. In this case, landowner's predecessor in title dedicated to the public the access route when he allowed its construction. Evidence showed that he intended the route to be public and route users testified they used the route to access their property. *Moon Equip. Co. v. Hess,* 761 SW2d 742 (Ct. App. 1988).

66.20
Title to Fee

Washington A landowner filed a plat dedicating for public uses a park and certain streets that intersected the park. The park was later annexed to the city, which later vacated portions of the streets. The successor in interest of the grantor claimed ownership of the vacated streets. *Held:* The fee in a public street or highway remains in the abutting landowner. The public acquires only a right of passage. However, in this case the fee was subject to two easements. The abandonment of the easement for a public street did not result in the reversion of the fee to the abutting landowner because the land was further burdened by the dedication of the land for a public park. The city was entitled to continue to exercise dominion over the land as a park. The vacated streets, therefore, could not revert to the grantor and his successors in interest. *Rainier Ave. Corp. v. City of Seattle,* 494 P2d 996, cert. denied, 409 US 983 (1972).

66.25
Right of Access

New Hampshire Plaintiff, owner of a gas station, sued the state seeking compensation for the alleged taking of his right of access. The state, in order to improve traffic safety at an intersection, decided to construct a median strip along the road in front of plaintiff's station. The strip would prevent eastbound traffic from turning left into the station and, plaintiff claimed, take away his vested right of access. *Held:* Plaintiff was not entitled to compensation. A landowner's vested right of access consists only of access to a general system of highways, not to a particular means of access. Construction of the median strip would not deprive plaintiff of that vested right. It would merely alter the flow of traffic. Plaintiff's claim involved only a change in traffic patterns rather than a deprivation of access. *Merit Oil, Inc. v. State,* 461 A2d 97 (1983).

67.00 CONSTRUCTION AND MAINTENANCE

67.05 Duty to Construct

Nebraska Rural property owners sought a writ of mandamus compelling county commissioners to exercise their statutory power to undertake improvements on certain rural highways. *Held:* The court denied the writ, finding that the decision of whether to create and/or improve public thoroughfares is vested by statute in the sound discretion of the county commissioners, and is not a purely ministerial act. The only mandatory duty upon such local officials is to hold an open hearing and consider all proposed resolutions. *State ex rel. Stansbery v. Schwasigner,* 289 NW2d 506 (1980).

67.10 Obligation to Repair and Maintain

Minnesota The city council approved plains for improvements to a street in front of owner's apartment building. Owner objected to the council's assessment of 73 percent of the cost of improvements. The trial court found that the owner's property received no benefit from the improvements and the assessment was void. *Held:* Reversed. State statute specifies that the cost of any improvement may be assessed upon benefited property, the benefit to be determined by the increase in fair market value. The record showed an appreciable increase in the fair market value of the apartment complex as a result of the improvements. In addition, evidence was presented that the street had a poor surface prior to improvements; appraisers agreed that the new street was an improvement and a benefit. Remanded to determine whether the assessment exceeded the increase in market value and amounted to a taking. *Schumacker v. City of Excelsior,* 427 NW2d 235 (1988).

New York A new village ordinance required owners of private roads open to public use to comply with upgraded maintenance standards. If after 10 days' notice the owner failed to comply, the village could repair the road and recover the cost from the owner in a civil suit. The village notified plaintiff that his road was improperly maintained; when he failed to correct it, the village made repairs at a cost of over $8,000. Plaintiff sued, arguing the ordinance violated due process under the federal Constitution and exceeded state enabling legislation. The village counterclaimed for the cost of the improvements. *Held:* The ordinance did not violate due process, because it bore a reasonable relation to public health, safety, and welfare. The ordinance was nonetheless illegal because it authorized proceedings in personam, in violation of the state enabling law, which authorizes the collection of costs in an in rem proceeding only after an assessment and levy. In addition, the village could not collect from plaintiff, because the repair contract was not submitted to competitive bidding. *D'Angelo v. Cole,* 490 NE2d 819 (1986).

Tennessee The gravel base of the roads in a residential subdivision was not compacted in accordance with planning commission regulations. The commission waived the rule when developers agreed to maintain the roads for 18 months to check for settling of the road surface. At the end of that time, a municipal employee found the roads satisfactory. Believing they had discharged their commitment and the municipality would assume the duty to maintain, developers made no further effort to keep the roads in repair. Naturally, the roads fell apart. Homeowners sued developers and the planning commission. *Held:* Responsibility for maintaining the roads lay with homeowners, not the municipality, since the planning commission never accepted dedication of the roads. However, developers had an "implied" obligation to owners. Approval of the subdivision plat by the planning commission did not signify acceptance of the roads. The court found a legislative intent to protect the public by requiring a second level of official action beyond the steps connected with plat approval. Without such action in this case the municipality had never incurred a duty to maintain. The case was remanded as to developers for a decree that they make all necessary repairs and take steps to obtain the county's acceptance of the road. *Foley v. Hamilton,* 659 SW2d 356 (1983).

68.00 REGULATION AND USE

68.05 Power to Regulate

U.S. Supreme Court San Diego enacted an ordinance restricting outdoor advertising. The ordinance permitted on-site commercial advertising but prohibited off-site commercial signs. It also prohibited most noncommercial advertising. Billboard owners challenged the ordinance on constitutional grounds. *Held:* Improving traffic safety and the appearance of the city were valid governmental goals. The city could reasonably distinguish between on-site and off-site commercial advertising because off-site advertising could create greater problems. However, the city's restrictions on noncommercial advertising in locations where it would permit commercial advertising violated the Fifth and Fourteenth Amendments; the city failed to explain how noncommercial billboards would obstruct the goals of traffic safety and aesthetics more than would commercial billboards. The city could not decide that the communication of commercial messages had more value than the communication of noncommercial messages. The ordinance, by in effect authorizing the city to choose appropriate subjects for public discourse, infringed on constitutional rights of free speech and was unconstitutional on its face. *Metromedia, Inc. v. City of San Diego,* 453 US 490 (1981).

Connecticut Because outdoor advertising signs violated Department of Transportation regulations prohibiting signs within 500 feet of highway interchange, the commissioner sought removal of signs erected on private property bordering an interstate highway exchange. Advertiser claimed the regulations were unconstitutional. *Held:* The regulations did not infringe on plaintiff's freedom of speech with regard to both commercial and noncommercial advertising. The state's interest in highway safety, especially at hazardous highway interchanges, is quite substantial and sufficient to justify prohibiting even noncommercial billboards near interchanges. The regulation's exemption for on-site signs did not indicate a preference for commercial messages; commercial or noncommercial signs may be erected as long as they have some reasonable connection to on-site activity. *Burns v. Barrett,* 561 A2d 1378 (1989).

Florida Plaintiff, a real estate developer, relied heavily on off-site billboard advertising. The city enacted an ordinance allowing only one off-site billboard per subdivision. Plaintiff, alleging the ordinance was an unconstitutional exercise of police powers, sued to enjoin its enforcement. *Held:* The appellate court reversed the trial court's judgment that the ordinance was unconstitutional. Citing the U.S. Supreme Court in *Metromedia, Inc. v. City of San Diego,* the appellate court rejected the trial court's finding that protection of aesthetic interests is not a substantial government goal. It held that the ordinance was not more extensive than necessary to serve that goal, and further held that a municipality could separately classify on-site and off-site signs solely on the basis of aesthetics. *City of Sunrise v. DCA Homes, Inc.,* 421 So. 2d 1084 (Dist. Ct. App. 1982).

New York Town ordinance required nonconforming billboards to be removed by June 1, 1975, but allowed owners to apply for an extension of the amortization period prescribed by the ordinance. The town denied petitioner's application for extension. Plaintiff sued for compensation of the value lost from its billboards under two theories: (1) The Surface Transportation Assistance Act (23 U.S.C. § 131), requiring compensation in plaintiff's situation, invalidated the amortization provision of the ordinance and (2) the amortization provision resulted in an unconstitutional taking. *Held:* The amortization provision of the ordinance was valid. The Surface Transporation Assistance Act does not forbid removal of billboards through amortization; it withholds highway aid from a state that does not pay compensation. The amortization period was reasonable as applied to petitioner's billboards because petitioner had fully recouped its investment and had depreciated its billboards for tax purposes. *Suffolk Outdoor Advertising Co. v. Southampton,* 455 NE2d 1245 (1983).

North Carolina Plaintiff, an automobile dealership located beside a major thoroughfare, displayed a blimp with its name printed in large red letters. The city enacted a zoning ordinance prohibiting the display of "windblown signs" such as blimps except with a temporary permit and then only for a maximum of 30 days. Permits were granted only for special events, i.e., activities not part of daily operations. Plaintiff challenged the ordinance on statutory and constitutional grounds. *Held:* The ordinance was valid. Regulations could be upheld on constitutional and statutory grounds if their aesthetic purpose outweighed the burden imposed on the private property owner. Plaintiff's failure to produce evidence of a correlation between sales and display of the blimp indicated that any burdens imposed by the statute were negligible. *Goodman Toyota, Inc. v. City of Raleigh,* 306 SE2d 192 (Ct. App. 1983).

68.10 Encroachments and Obstructions

Vermont Landowner appealed the order requiring him to remove part of a wall found to be within a public highway on the ground that the finding as to the location of the highway was in error. The landowner alleged that the traveled portion of the highway had shifted over the years toward his wall and therefore the wall was not within the limits of the highway. *Held:* The legislature created a presumption that the center line of the traveled portion as it presently existed was the center line of the highway as originally laid out. Where landowner introduced evidence to show the shift in location, he rebutted the presumption and the trial court's finding was erroneous. *Town of Dorset v. Fausett,* 346 A2d 200 (1975).

68.15 Liability for Injury From Defects

Connecticut Plaintiff slipped on ice and injured herself on a highway on the University of Connecticut campus. She sued the commissioner of transporation, claiming he had breached his duty to maintain all highways in the state. Defendant argued that the statute imposing this obligation applied only to highways within the "state highway system," which did not include the highway in question, although it was property of a state institution. *Held:* The statute included highways on the property of state institutions even if they were not within the statutorily defined "state highway system." Since a dangerous accumulation of snow or ice would make a highway defective within the meaning of the statute, the commissioner breached his statutory duty to maintain the highway. *Cairns v. Shugrue,* 441 A2d 185 (1981).

Utah Homeowners whose properties were damaged by flood water and debris sued the state for negligently constructing a highway in the area. *Held:* The state was not immune from suit by homeowners under the Utah immunity statute, which provides immunity for negligent acts unless such acts are in the discharge of a discretionary function. Although the decision to build a highway and specifying its general location was discretionary, the preparation of the plans and specifications and the supervision of the work was not. Whether the state had created a dangerous condition by its design of the highway was a jury question to be determined on remand. *Andrun v. States,* 541 P2d 1117 (1975).

Wisconsin After a motorist was paralyzed in an automobile accident, he sued the city, alleging that the city's failure to keep the highway in good repair caused the accident and resulting injuries. At issue was the amount that motorist could be awarded in light of the $25,000 statutory limit on liability. *Held:* For the motorist. Statute that established a $25,000 limitation on a municipality's liability for injuries caused by negligent street repair and maintenance was unconstitutional. Inasmuch as the statute set different monetary limitations for different acts of negligence without regard to the severity of injury, they created improper distinctions within the class of "victims of public tortfeasors." This was held to amount to an unreasonable and arbitrary exercise of the power to restrict state liability. *Sambs v. City of Brookfield,* 289 NW2d 308 (Ct. App. 1979).

PART M
SALES CONTRACTS

69.00
REQUISITES AND VALIDITY

69.05
Capacity of Parties

Alabama McAllister entered into a contract to purchase real estate from Deatherage. Subsequently, McAllister sought to set aside the purchase, claiming he was suffering from a mental defect at the time of entering into the contract and therefore lacked capacity. *Held:* Deatherage was not entitled to summary judgment. In Alabama, contracts of insane persons are void. To avoid a contract, a party must show that his insanity caused a loss of reasonable perception rendering him incapable of understanding the nature and terms of the contract. The evidence showed that McAllister was a manic-depressive and was on medication. His psychiatrist testified that three days prior to signing the contract he was off his medication and was psychotic, and that manic-depression is characterized by buying sprees. The court found that under these circumstances, McAllister lacked capacity to understand the effect of his act or the nature and terms of the contract. *McAllister v. Deatherage,* 523 So. 2d 387 (1988).

District of Columbia A voluntary, unincorporated association of tenants sought to purchase the apartment complex in which they lived, arguing that Section 602(b) of the Rental Housing Act of 1979 gave them a right of first refusal to purchase. *Held:* The tenants' association was not entitled to first refusal, because it was unincorporated and was voluntary; it had no legal capacity to hold title to real estate. *Rock Creek Gardens Tenants v. Ferguson,* 404 A2d 972 (Ct. App. 1979).

Florida During the course of a lawsuit concerning the partition of certain property, one attorney made a written offer to purchase the property on behalf of his client for $600 per acre. The offer was accepted by written response for which plaintiff claimed, in a suit for specific performance, that a valid contract for sale existed. *Held:* The attorney's offer in correspondence to plaintiff's attorney cannot be construed as a binding contract for the sale of an interest in land upon which a judgment for specific performance can be entered. The court cited cases from other jurisdictions holding that there is no presumption that an attorney has authority to bind his client to convey real estate. Such authority must be proven through parol evidence by the person asserting that it existed. *Rushing v. Garrett,* 375 So. 2d 903 (Dist. Ct. App. 1979).

Minnesota Sellers (husband and wife) sold their home to buyers and received check made out to both of them as earnest money. Only the husband had executed the earnest-money contract and the warranty deed. When the sellers refused to convey the house, the buyers sued. The sellers argued that the wife's failure to sign any document, other than to indorse the earnest-money check, rendered the contract void. *Held:* The contract was void. Under Minnesota law, the contract for sale or deed must be jointly signed

(Minn. Stat. § 507.02 (1978)). *Dvorak v. Maring,* 285 NW2d 675 (1979).

Missouri Plaintiffs sued for specific performance of a contract for sale of real estate. Defendant, guardian of a mental incompetent, contended that his ward was mentally infirm on the contract day. *Held:* A contract made by an incompetent under guardianship is void; a contract made prior to adjudication, but at a time when the person is mentally disabled, is merely voidable. In order to avoid a contract on grounds of preadjudicated incompetency, it must be shown that the other party was aware of the mental defect and took advantage of it. Failing this, the contract can be rescinded only if, short of inadequacy of consideration, there are other inequities in the bargain. *Cohen v. Crumpacker,* 586 SW2d 370 (Ct. App. 1979).

Nebraska Agent for landowners entered into a listing contract with a real estate broker for sale of property. The broker signed an agreement with the purported buyer for the sale of the property. The agent refused to consummate the sale, and the buyer sued the agent for specific performance. Plaintiff appealed from a judgment for defendants. *Held:* In order to authorize a broker to enter a contract for sale of land, the listing contract must have indicated unequivocably that the owner of the land had intended that the broker have that authority. The listing contract could not be construed to grant that authority, and the language in question merely sought to protect the broker on the commission. *Brezina v. Hill,* 238 NW2d 903 (1976).

South Dakota At age 85, vendor executed a contract for sale of lands under which the land was to be sold for $70 per acre with 5 percent interest on the unpaid balance. After the vendor's death, buyers agreed to pay the unpaid balance in return for conveyance of the property by the estate's executor, and the court allowed the conveyance. Contestants of the will argued that the court erred, because decedent was not competent to execute the contract. *Held:* Since the trial court made no findings of fact as to the mental competence of the decedent on the date of deed execution and since no separate evidentiary hearing was ever held on the compentency question, the case was reversed and remanded for presentation of evidence and findings of fact. *Jones v. South Dakota Children's Home Soc'y,* 238 NW2d 677 (1976).

69.10 Meeting of the Minds

Delaware After several discussions, a buyer sent a "contract" to a seller for his signature. The "contract" was a one-page letter stating that buyer wished to purchase seller's nursing home subject to inspection of the books and records for $3.5 million. The document was signed by an officer of the buyer, a corporation with no assets. Seller signed it, although it contained no mention of tax-free industrial revenue bond (IRB) financing, which he had insisted was a condition of sale. Although further negotiations broke down, buyer recorded the "contract." Seller sued to quiet title. *Held:* The document was a letter of intent, not a contract. A contract is not formed until all points the parties regard as essential have expressly or implicitly been resolved. Buyer could not reasonably have concluded that the recorded document represented a complete negotiation, especially since he was aware of the seller's insistence on IRB financing. Moreover, it would be extraordinary to make a binding contract to sell a $3.5 million business on a document of one page. *Leeds v. First Allied Constr. Corp.,* 521 A2d 1095 (Ch. 1986).

North Carolina Prospective purchasers prepared a written offer to purchase a property that required acceptance before 5:00 P.M. the following day. The same day, seller returned the offer, signed but with several changes in the terms. Prospective purchasers, believing no one else could make an offer for the property while they had this "counteroffer," decided to wait before deciding what to do. At 2:00 P.M. the next day, seller revoked her counteroffer, having accepted another offer to purchase. Prospective purchasers delivered an initialed copy of the purchase form and counteroffer with earnest money to the broker's office by 5:00 P.M. that day and sued for specific performance. *Held:* The counteroffer was not an option to purchase. Where a seller accepts a buyer's offer but changes the terms, the effect is a counterproposal upon which the parties have not yet agreed. Since prospective purchasers failed to accept or reject seller's counteroffer before she revoked it, there was no meeting of the minds between the parties and hence no contract. *Normile v. Miller,* 326 SE2d 11 (1985).

Virginia Plaintiff sued for specific performance of an alleged contract for the sale of land. Plaintiff offered in evidence a series of letters exchanged by plaintiff and defendant and their respective attorneys that represented the offers and counteroffers on the price, down payment, leasing arrangements, and closing date arrangements. The final letter from defendant rejected plaintiff's offer made two weeks earlier. Defendant's lawyer telephoned plaintiff's counsel and informed him that defendant had rejected the offer. Plaintiff and his counsel then telegraphed defendant, agreeing to terms set earlier by defendant, and then executed and sent the contract, which defendant never signed. *Held:* In order to establish a binding contract, there must be a mutual meeting of the minds. The exchange of letters did not evidence such an accord, but merely evidence of negotiations. *Chittum v. Potter,* 219 SE2d 859 (1975).

69.15 Consideration

California An agreement to sell land contained a liquidated damages clause that provided that seller's sole remedy for buyers' failure to perform would be possession of all plans and reports. Seller expressly waived the right to specific performance. Buyers expressly promised to pursue their obligations diligently and refrain from unreasonably withholding their approval. Buyers sued seller for specific performance when seller refused to proceed under the terms of the agreement. Seller argued the agreement was void because it imposed no legal obligation on buyers, and that seller's waiver of specific performance precluded either party from seeking specific performance. *Held:* Buyers were entitled to specific performance. There was mutuality of obligation, since buyers had an express obligation to proceed in good faith and diligence. As to remedy, the fact that specific enforcement is not available to one party is not reason to refuse it to the other. *Bleecher v. Conte,* 698 P2d 1154 (1981) (en banc).

California Purchaser sued defendant for specific performance to sell land. The trial court ruled the contract was unenforceable because it lacked mutuality of obligation, granting purchaser sole discretion whether to proceed with the sale. The court also found that its terms were ambiguous. *Held:* Reversed. Taking extrinsic evidence into consideration of the parties' intentions regarding development of the land, the court ruled that the terms of the contract did not lack mutuality of obligation, because they were within the intentions of the parties when drafted. The court should not interfere with a transaction where it appears the parties intended to make a contract, even if the court must choose among conflicting meanings of terms and fill gaps left by the parties. *Larwin–So. Cal., Inc. v. JGB Inv. Co.*, 162 Cal. Rptr. 62 (Ct. App. 1979).

69.20 Effect of Fraud

1st Circuit After a series of negotiations fell through, prospective purchaser brought an action for deceit, negligent misrepresentation, and violation of state consumer protection law. Purchaser charged that he had relief on an oral statement by vendor that committee approval for the sale was a mere formality if purchaser met vendor's price. *Held:* Summary judgment for vendor affirmed. Purchaser's reliance on the oral statement was unreasonable. Vendor had sent a letter to purchaser stating that the decision to accept or reject the offer was in the sole discretion of the committee. Purchaser acknowledged in writing that he understood committee approval was required. Given these facts, purchaser could not assert that he reasonably relied on the oral statement. In addition, the conflict between the oral and written statements should have put purchaser on notice that he could not rely on either statement. *Trifiro v. New York Life Ins. Co.*, 845 F2d 30 (1988).

Colorado The seller of an apartment house fraudulently misrepresented income projections by not acknowledging the number of vacant apartments or disclosing agreements with some tenants for rebates or concessions. The buyer sued, seeking damages measured by the difference between the actual market value of the property and its value had the representations been true. The buyer sought to establish the latter value on an income-capitalization basis. *Held:* The basis for determining market value if the property had been as represented required a determination of what the property in that condition would bring on the open market, assuming a voluntary sale to a willing buyer. In determining such market value, there must be taken into consideration such factors as market conditions generally and the location and condition of the particular property, and not alone a capitalization of income based on a fully leased building. *Sorenson v. Scurr*, 490 P2d 88 (1971).

Illinois Plaintiff purchaser alleged that defendant sellers had fraudulently misrepresented and concealed material information about water and flooding conditions on the property sold. After the closing, the basement and garage flooded on at least 10 occasions to depths of 30 to 50 inches. During the negotiations, the sellers had made no mention of prior floods. In fact, shortly before the closing, they washed off and painted over all of the water marks left by prior floods. Although the purchasers never inquired directly as to whether the house flooded, they did ask whether the drain outside was adequate, and they received an affirmative answer. *Held:* Fraud can comprise anything calculated to deceive, including acts of omission and concealment involving a breach of duty. What is determinative is not what the sellers said, but what they left unsaid. There was a duty on their part to reveal a condition that was within their knowledge and that obviously they had deliberately concealed from the purchasers. *Russow v. Bobola*, 277 NE2d 769 (1972).

Kansas Purchasers brought an action against the developer, alleging fraudulent concealment of a soil defect. Each homeowner had selected sites in the development and had entered into agreements with contractors, who in turn purchased lots from the developer. After the homes had been constructed, it was discovered that the land had a high salt content, and nothing would grow. *Held:* Lack of privity will not bar an action for fraud where the purchasers are essentially the class of persons that the developer intended to reach. A duty to disclose extends not just to persons with whom the developer immediately deals, but to all those who would be expected to act or refrain in reliance on the misrepresentation. *Griffith v. Byers Constr. Co.*, 510 P2d 198 (1973).

New Mexico Defendant builder bought lots backed by an unpaved road at a discount to offset the cost of assessments that might be levied against the property. After homes were built and sold to plaintiffs, the city levied a street-paving assessment on the lots. Plaintiffs sued on the ground of defendant's failure to disclose the possibility of the assessment. *Held:* Summary judgment for defendant. Fraud is actionable where a party to a transaction knows material facts, has a duty to disclose them, but remains silent. Defendant was not in direct contact with plaintiffs, who bought their homes through an agency; no fiduciary relationship existed; nor was there reliance on affirmative acts or statements of defendant. The most that could be shown was that defendant knew of the possibility of assessment when plaintiffs purchased their homes. However, defendant had no duty to disclose the discount he had received, nor to pass along the benefit of it, since it was based on unknown contingencies. *Krupiak v. Payton*, 561 P2d 1345 (1977).

Oregon Defendants sold two contiguous units of land to plaintiffs. The land, however, had not been legally partitioned. Plaintiffs sued, claiming defendants had fraudulently misrepresented that the land was partitioned before sale. The trial court granted summary judgment to defendants, and the court of appeals affirmed. *Held:* Reversed. Oregon law (Or. Rev. Stat. § 92.016(2)) prohibits the sale of a parcel before a tentative plan for partitioning is approved. A contractual promise to convey land that violates this provision is enforceable by the purchaser against the seller if purchaser can prove that there was a breach of contract, that the land was unpartitioned, and that damages were caused by breach of the implied promise of lawful partitioning. The purchaser may sue for rescission and recover any monies paid, affirm the transaction and sue for breach of contract, or maintain an action for fraud. *Ogan v. Ellison*, 682 P2d 760 (1984).

Texas At the time of signing a contract for sale of agricultural property, the parties orally considered the question of whether the standing wheat crop would belong to the buyer or to the seller at harvest time. A dispute later arose over what was promised, and suit was commenced shortly thereafter. The buyer counterclaimed under the state Deceptive Trade Practices Act, alleging fraud on the part of seller. *Held:* Judgment for sellers on the counterclaim. The act applies to real estate contracts regardless of whether the purchase was consummated. However, the court concluded that the evidence was insufficient to compel compensable damages. *Anderson v. Havins*, 595 SW2d 147 (Civ. App. 1980).

69.25 Sufficiency of Execution of a Written Contract

California Seller and buyer agreed to the transfer of seller's house, which was jointly owned by seller and his wife. The parties prepared a sales agreement, which was signed by seller and buyer. Seller's wife failed to sign the document. Subsequently, buyer experienced difficulty in selling his former residence and had to renege on the agreement. Seller sued buyer for damages for breach of contract. Buyer argued that the sales agreement was invalid because seller's wife had not signed it. *Held:* Seller was entitled to damages. The validity of the contract was dependent upon the intention of the parties to the agreement. Buyer could offer no proof that he did not intent to be bound unless seller's wife signed the document. Thus, buyer was bound by the agreement. *Angell v. Rowlands,* 149 Cal. Rptr. 574 (Ct. App. 1978).

Kansas Buyer sued for specific performance of a real estate contract that the seller had written out in longhand and that was signed by the parties. The formal contract drawn up by the buyer's attorney was rejected by the seller, who then sold to other buyers. *Held:* Whether parties to an informal agreement become formal prior to the drafting and execution of a contemplated formal writing is largely a question of intent. The fact that the parties contemplated the execution of a formal document was some evidence, not in itself conclusive, that they intended not to be bound until it was executed. Where the buyer immediately went to his attorney to work our additional details and have a formal contract drafted, neither party began performance under the informal agreement; and where the buyer withheld the earnest money set forth in the agreement, he was not entitled to specific performance. *King v. Wenger,* 549 P2d 986 (1976).

Minnesota When co-owners sued to recover possession from a purchaser, they alleged that the purchaser did not establish that the original contract was delivered. Purchaser alleged that the original and copies were either lost or destroyed and introduced a photocopy of the contract. *Held:* The delivery requirement was fulfilled by a photocopy. Delivery is ordinarily an essential element of the execution of a written contract. Where the original and copies were lost, delivery to the purchaser of a photocopy signed by six of eight co-owners satisfied the delivery requirement, since it evidenced an intention to complete the transaction. *Nodland v. Chirpich,* 240 NW2d 513 (1976).

Oregon Buyer and sellers executed an earnest money agreement for the sale of land and agreed that a more formal land sales contract would be drawn up subsequently. The buyer made several late payments under the earnest money agreement; the sellers accepted them. Finally, sellers notified buyer that they were foreclosing on the property. The buyer then tendered payment and, when sellers refused the payments, sued for specific performance of the earnest money agreement. The sellers argued that the failure of the buyer to make prompt payments and his failure to sign a formal contract entitled sellers to forfeiture. *Held:* Buyer was entitled to specific performance of the earnest money agreement. It contained the essential terms of the agreement and was definite enough to be enforced. The failure to sign a more formal contract did not entitle sellers to forfeiture. *Pittman v. Thompson,* 608 P2d 1223 (1980).

70.00 STATUTE OF FRAUDS

70.05 Necessity of a Written Contract

6th Circuit When the purchaser of property at a public auction refused to accept the deed, the mortgagee sued for specific performance. When the bid for the purchase of the property was accepted, no written contract of sale or memorandum was executed. *Held:* The Statute of Frauds applied to the sale at public auction. Therefore, where there was no contract or memorandum signed by the party to be charged, the contract for the sale of the land was unenforceable. *Watson v. McCabe,* 527 F2d 286 (1975).

Maine Buyer negotiated the purchase of real property from owners-trustees. One trustee signed the final draft of a purchase and sale agreement; but before the second trustee could sign, a higher offer was received, and the second trustee refused to sign. Buyer sued for specific performance of an oral contract for sale of real estate. *Held:* The draft purchase and sale agreement satisfied the Statute of Frauds. Although a final written agreement was not yet completed, a valid oral contract for sale of real property existed, since the parties had a meeting of the minds on all essential terms of an oral contract. A memorandum that satisfies the Statute of Frauds must be signed by the party to be charged or by an authorized person. In this case, the signing trustee had both actual and apparent authority to deal with the property on behalf of himself and the co-trustee. Therefore, a single trustee signature was sufficient to satisfy the Statute. *Rulon-Miller v. Carhart,* 544 A2d 340 (1988).

Michigan Landowners and developer negotiated for the sale of landowners' property. At a meeting, developer gave landowners a check for $5,000. On the back of the check, developer had written that the check was a deposit for the purchase of the property. Developer also gave landowners a tax receipt indicating that the check was a deposit. Before formal documents were executed, landowners received a higher offer and they told developer the deal was off. Developer sued for specific performance. *Held:* Developer was not entitled to specific performance. The check and tax receipt failed to set forth all essential terms of the parties' agreement and so did not satisfy the Statute of Frauds. They did not contain a designated payment period or interest rate. There was no evidence that the parties discussed, let alone agreed to, payment terms. *Kojaian v. Ernst,* 442 NW2d 286 (Ct. App. 1989).

Minnesota Beach and Anderson entered into an oral partnership to own and operate an amusement park. After Beach filed for dissolution of the partnership, the partners resolved the suit by entering into an oral stipulation agreement before a court reporter that gave Beach possession of the amusement park, for which he was to pay Anderson $85,000. Anderson refused to abide by the settlement, claiming it was invalid under the Statute of Frauds. *Held:* The stipulation did not fall within the Statute of Frauds and was thus binding on Anderson. The agreement, although oral, did not involve the transfer of real property. Under state law, a partnership interest is considered personal property, so the stipulation involved the transfer of personalty, not realty. Realty acquired by a partnership with partnership funds becomes personal property, and its transfer along with a partnership interest is considered merely ancillary to the partnership transfer. *Beach v. Anderson,* 417 NW2d 409 (1988).

South Carolina Purchaser sought specific performance of a contract for the sale of land. The only written evidence of the contract was a check mailed by the purchasers that stated: "15 acres in Pichens, S.C., land binder, 30 days from date of check." Sellers refused to convey, contending there was no written contract to satisfy the Statute of Frauds. *Held:* The check was not a sufficient writing to satisfy the Statute of Frauds. The statement on the check did not adequately identify the property and was not described sufficiently to enable a court to render a decree for its performance. In order to satisfy the Statute of Frauds, a writing must contain the essential terms of the contract without resort to parol evidence. *Cash v. Maddox,* 220 SE2d 121 (1975).

Texas The parties entered into a purchase agreement for the sale of land, providing for financing by both the owners and the Veterans Land Board. Two earnest money contracts were drawn up, each describing the location of the land as being "out of" a certain survey. After the contracts were executed, the survey referred to therein was prepared, and an ownership affidavit was filed with the Veterans Land Board. The owners subsequently refused to sell on the ground that the land descriptions in the earnest money contracts did not satisfy the Statute of Frauds. *Held:* The owners were ordered to perform the contracts. The contracts, read together, adequately described the land and its location. The court also found that the survey and ownership affidavit could be treated as parts of the contract, although they were drafted after the contracts were executed. *Jones v. Kelley,* 614 SW2d 95 (1981).

Texas Seller agreed to convey property to buyer, and described it as a "Brick Home owned by Effie Cowart—Location 2½ miles on left on Airport Road (Lost Scott Rd.) west of U.S. 96." When sued for specific performance, defendant asserted the Statute of Frauds as a defense. *Held:* Under the Statute of Frauds, the description was too vague; the purported contract was consequently unenforceable. *Sessions v. Cowart,* 601 SW2d 82 (Civ. App. 1980).

Vermont Plaintiff, through an agent, arranged for a client to purchase a lot and introduced him to defendant, a dealer in modular homes. The parties agreed that plaintiff would receive a 10 percent commission upon the client's purchase of a modular home. This agreement, however, was not formally reduced to a writing. When the home was erected and paid for, neither party received a commission. Plaintiff brought suit to recover its commission. When the trial court found for plaintiff, defendant appealed, claiming that state Real Estate Commission Rule 16 required that a listing agreement be in writing before the contract would be enforceable. *Held:* Rule 16 does not apply and the absence of a written listing agreement or other written agreement does not preclude enforcement of the contract. The better view is that the agreement between the parties was not a sales transaction but rather was in the nature of a finder's agreement. Its purpose was to bring a prospective buyer and a seller together concerning property as yet unattached to the land, hence personal property. An agreement for the procuring of personal property is not an agreement for the sale of goods. Thus, the Statute of Frauds did not apply, and the contract was unenforceable. *Selected Listings Co. v. Humiston,* 370 A2d 1297 (1977).

70.10 Part Performance

Oregon Purchaser sued to recover payments made pursuant to an oral contract for the sale of land. He was to make monthly installment payments, but the payments stopped after six months because of a dispute. The vendor sought to introduce evidence of the oral agreement and the loss suffered as a consequence of the purchaser's breach. *Held:* Although the purpose of the Statute of Frauds is to prevent the enforcement of oral land sale contracts, the statute is not operative when evidence of the oral contract is used, not to enforce the contract, but to obtain other relief. Since the vendee introduced evidence of the oral contract to recover the amounts already paid, it was proper for vendor to introduce evidence of the oral contract to show his loss as a setoff. Since the vendor could not perform the oral contract following purchaser's breach, the vendor was entitled to a setoff for the losses he suffered as a result of the breach. *Golden v. Golden,* 541 P2d 1397 (1975).

Tennessee Seller orally agreed to convey property to buyer and then sent a letter to buyer's bank verifying the agreement. When the seller refused to convey, buyer sued for specific performance. The seller argued that the letter, which did not specifically describe the property to be conveyed, did not satisfy the Statute of Frauds. *Held:* The agreement violated the Statute of Frauds. However, because of partial performance by the seller, the doctrine of equitable estoppel applied. *Baliles v. Cities Serv. Co.,* 518 SW2d 621 (1979).

Utah Plaintiffs sought specific performance of an oral contract to buy defendant's undivided one-half interest in real property. After hearing the evidence, the trial court granted the relief. *Held:* Affirmed. The evidence clearly established part performance of the oral contract, and therefore the Statute of Frauds could not bar the sale. Plaintiffs made extensive improvements, they paid valuable consideration, and their possession of the property was open and known to defendant and not without his consent. Such indicia of reliance on the oral contract was not referable solely to the fact that plaintiffs had purchased the other one-half interest prior to negotiations with defendant. The court found that payments made to defendant established reliance on the oral contract and not merely the exercise of rights under plaintiffs' one-half interest. *Ryan v. Earl,* 618 P2d 54 (1980).

Virginia Landowner promised to convey land to plaintiff in exchange for her promise to work on his farm one day each week. Plaintiff did so for two years; but when landowner died, he left all his estate to the bank. Plaintiff sued for specific performance of the oral promise. *Held:* The oral agreement was barred by the Statute of Frauds; and part performance did not render it enforceable, because the agreement was not sufficiently definite. To escape the Statute of Frauds rule invalidating oral agreements for the sale of land, an oral agreement must be definite in all its terms; acts establishing part performance must be consistent with no theory other than the existence of an oral contract. In this case, the consideration of one day's labor per week was too indefinite to establish an oral contract to convey land, as neither the work required nor a time period for performance was specified. Since the owner did not convey the property even two years after the agreement, two years' labor was not enough to satisfy the purchase price. *Beach v. Virginia Nat'l Bank,* 367 SE2d 516 (1988).

70.15
—Improvements

Pennsylvania Seller entered into a written agreement to sell a lot and house. Buyers occupied the premises prior to the settlement date, paid a monthly rental, and made substantial improvements. The parties orally agreed to extend indefinitely the time for settlement, and buyers continued to occupy the house. Five years later, they tried to arrange for settlement and were told the price had more than doubled. Buyers sought to enforce the purchase price established in their original agreement. *Held:* For buyers. Buyers' possession and substantial improvement of property subject to a contract of sale was sufficient to take the contract out of the Statute of Frauds. An exception to the Statute of Frauds permits specific performance of an oral contract for sale of real estate when the buyer has continuous, exclusive possession of the property and has made improvements. Seller was estopped from asserting that the action was barred by the statute of limitations or laches since seller engaged in intentional acts calculated to induce buyers not to pursue their rights diligently. *Hostetter v. Hoover,* 547 A2d 1247 (Super. Ct. 1988).

South Carolina Buyer, under a written contract to purchase, asserted that the contract was subsequently orally modified to reduce the acres to be purchased with a proportionately reduced purchase price. Buyer sued to enforce the oral contract to convey real estate, arguing that part performance took the oral contract from the reach of the Statute of Frauds. *Held:* Buyer failed to prove part performance; therefore, the Statute of Frauds barred enforcement of the oral contract. Evidence of part performance includes improvements to, or possession of, the property, or payment of the purchase price. Evidence that buyer improved real estate by moving a large ranch house to the property and by clearing and grading the property could not be used as evidence of part performance since the acts were done at the direction of a third party and not by buyer with his own means and upon the faith of the vendor's promise. Evidence that buyers picked up trash and cut wood on the property was likewise insufficient to show part performance since the improvements were not permanent and did not substantially enhance the value of the property. Evidence that buyer lobbied the city council to extend a road through the property did not establish part performance since the act was not solely on behalf of the buyer. Finally, buyer failed to show that payments he made clearly referred to the oral contract. *Bradshaw v. Ewing,* 376 SE2d 264 (1989).

South Carolina Plaintiff brought an action for specific performance against his brother, contending that there was an enforceable oral contract between them. Defendant was to purchase plaintiff's note to a bank secured by land and bid on the land at the foreclosure sale. He was then to hold the land for plaintiff until such time as plaintiff was able to reimburse defendant for his expense. Defendant, who had purchased the land, denied the oral contract. Plaintiff had made extensive improvements on the property after the acquisition by defendant. *Held:* Plaintiff's part performance by making improvements on the land was sufficient to take the case out of the Statute of Frauds. *Cloniger v. Cloniger,* 193 SE2d 647 (1973).

70.20
Oral Modification

Delaware Plaintiffs agreed to purchase a lot from defendant with the date for final settlement specified contingent on their obtaining financing. Defendant orally agreed to several extensions of time "for financial reasons." When plaintiffs obtained financing and attempted to close the deal, defendant informed them that the lot was no longer for sale. They sued for specific performance. *Held:* Judgment for plaintiffs with specific performance ordered. A time-of-the-essence clause was implied in the original agreement. However, no authority was found to support the position that a clause making time of the essence may not be altered by subsequent agreement of the parties. Although oral, the agreement to extend the closing date was not barred by the Statute of Frauds. The prior rule permitting an admission of an agreement and the simultaneous assertion of the Statute of Frauds as a bar to its enforcement should no longer be recognized. *Wolf v. Crosby,* 377 A2d 22 (1977).

Pennsylvania Seller entered into a written agreement to sell a lot and house. Buyers occupied the premises prior to the settlement date, paid a monthly rental, and made substantial improvements. The parties orally agreed to extend indefinitely the time for settlement, and buyers continued to occupy the house. Five years later, they tried to arrange for settlement and were told the price had more than doubled. Buyers sought to enforce the purchase price established in their original agreement. *Held:* For buyers. Although oral contracts for the sale of real estate are generally unenforceable, an oral modification as to time of settlement relates merely to manner of performance and does not change the character of the written agreement, which remains enforceable. In addition, an exception to the Statute of Frauds permits specific performance of an oral contract for sale of real estate when the buyer has continuous, exclusive possession of the property and has made improvements. *Hostetter v. Hoover,* 547 A2d 1247 (Super. Ct. 1988).

Texas Plaintiff and defendant entered into a sale and lease of an apartment project, whereby defendant sold to plaintiff the improvements and leased the land on which the improvements were located. At the end of the lease, the improvements would revert to defendant. Plaintiff agreed to pay, in addition to rental for the lease of the land, the balance of a first lien note to mortgagee. When plaintiff defaulted in the payment of the first lien note and mortgagee foreclosed upon the land and improvements, plaintiff brought an action to rescind the sale and lease, on the ground that there was an oral agreement, which was not expressed in the documents, that plaintiff would have no personal liability on his agreement to pay the first lien note. *Held:* A written agreement contains an accurate expression of prior oral negotiations, and unless trickery or artifice is shown, a party cannot avoid the consequences of the written agreement on the ground that he did not know what he was signing. *Farina v. Calvary Hill Cemetery,* 566 SW2d 650 (1978).

West Virginia Plaintiff sought specific performance of a contract for the sale of real estate. The contract for sale was a handwritten agreement signed by the parties, wherein a specified parcel of land was to be sold for $6,000. Defendants contended that the execution of the contract was predicated on their obtaining a release from a deed of trust on the land held by a bank to secure a debt. Defendants offered in evidence the bank's written refusal to release its security. Plaintiff stated that this evidence was inadmissible as parol evidence. *Held:* The evidence was properly admitted since it represented an oral agreement of a condition precedent to the efficacy of the contract. The parol evidence rule applies to evidence that, if admitted, would vary or contradict the terms of the contract. There was nothing in the oral agreement that was inconsistent with the terms of the written contract. *Harrow v. Akers,* 222 SE2d 822 (1976).

70.25 Admissibility of Parol Evidence

Nebraska Parties to an installment sale of property used a preprinted standard form contract that contained a blank space in the clause calling for interest to be paid on the outstanding balance. They neglected to fill in the blank indicating the agreed-upon rate of interest, and vendor eventually brought suit claiming to be entitled to reasonable interest. *Held:* Over dissent, the court found that the parties intended that no interest was to be paid on the balance. The contract was neither ambiguous nor vague; therefore, parol evidence was inadmissible. *Lovelace v. Stern,* 297 NW2d 160 (1980).

71.00 CONSTRUCTION AND OPERATION

71.05
General Rules of Construction

Alabama Moore, unable to obtain mortgage approval, entered into an 18-month lease-sale contract with Akin, owner of the property, after which Moore was to reapply to assume Akin's mortgage. Moore was again denied approval, but continued to occupy the property, making monthly payments. When Moore fell behind. Akin sent a notice of default pursuant to the contract. Akin discovered Moore had tax liens attached to the property, and sued to quiet title. Moore counterclaimed for specific performance, arguing that Akin had waived the contract's cancellation provision by accepting monthly payments in lieu of assumption of the mortgage. *Held:* For Akin. Mere acceptance of payments in default under a lease-sale contract does not waive future defaults. The purpose of the lease-sale contract was to give Moore additional time to gain approval to assume the mortgage. Akin's allowance of Moore as a holdover tenant did not constitute a waiver, particularly in view of Akin's statements to Moore that he intended to enforce strictly the terms of the contract. *Killen v. Akin,* 519 So. 2d 926 (1988).

Utah Plaintiff purchaser entered into a written contract for the sale of eight parcels of land within a subdivision. The contract provided that payments on two lots were to be completed on the first of each month, for four months. Plaintiff defaulted on the first month's payment, and defendant responded with notice to repossess if the total amount due under the contract was not paid within five days. Plaintiff complained that certain improvements had not been made, and defendant thereafter sold the lots to third parties. Plaintiff then commenced suit, arguing that the contract was severable and that defendant was in breach as to the remaining six lots. *Held:* Judgment and damages for plaintiff. The contract was ambiguous regarding the severability of the purchase; consequently, parol evidence was admissible to show intent. *Management Serv. Corp. v. Development Ass'n,* 617 P2d 406 (1980).

West Virginia Grantors deeded a remainder interest in their home to grantees. There was no stated consideration for the transfer but several witnesses testified that there had been discussions about grantees' supporting grantors. After a dispute, grantors sued to cancel the deed, on the ground that grantees had failed to support them. Grantees contended that the deed did not obligate them to support grantors. *Held:* The deed was cancelled. Under a theory of equitable relief, the failure of grantees to support grantors justified cancellation even though the support obligation was not expressed in the contract. *Frasher v. Frasher,* 249 SE2d 513 (1978).

71.10
Variance Between Property Owned by Seller and Property Described in Contract

11th Circuit Several members of a family sold land that was later discovered to be fewer acres than represented. The court found the sale was by the acre rather than by the tract and ordered the family to refund the overpayment. The trial court further held that each family member was liable only for the portion of the sales price he received. One family member had failed to pay her share of the overpayment and the others refused to pay it for her. *Held:* The family was jointly and severally liable for the full amount of the overpayment. Under Georgia law, when two or more persons sign a deed containing a general warranty without limitation or exception, both signers become liable to the grantee as joint warrantors. *Canal Indus., Inc. v. Childs,* 832 F2d 460 (1987).

Maine Responding to an advertisement for the sale of three fourths of an acre of land, buyer signed an agreement to purchase. Prior to the closing, the broker notified them that the lot might be less than three fourths of an acre. Seller refused to reduce the purchase price but offered to terminate the agreement. Purchaser proceeded with the closing and then sued the broker for misrepresentation and fraud. *Held:* Purchaser cannot recover from the broker. He was not entitled to reformation of the contract, because the purchaser had contracted to purchase the buildings and land in gross; the price was not determined on a per-acre basis. His remedy was to rescind the contract and obtain the return of his deposit. *Bartner v. Carter,* 405 A2d 194 (1979).

Maryland A contract of sale described the property as 16,000 square feet more or less but stated that the contract was contingent upon completion of a survey. After the contract was signed, a survey showed an area of 22,047 square feet. The vendor demanded an increase in the purchase price, and buyers sued, asking that the sales agreement be declared valid and enforceable. *Held:* Buyers were entitled to specific performance of the sales contract that incorrectly stated the square footage of the property. The sale was one in gross since the property was described by definite boundaries, and the contract used words of qualification. Thus, the statement of square footage was mere description and not of the essence. The buyer's estimate of square footage gained by pacing off the lot did not give rise to fraud justifying rescission since buyers did not know with certainty that the lot contained more than 16,000 square feet. Nor was there mutual mistake, since buyers did not make a knowing or negligent misrepresentation as to size of the lot. *Steele v. Goettee,* 542 A2d 847 (Ct. App. 1988).

North Carolina Seller listed his house with broker, who advertised the structure as having 1,700 heated square feet. Purchaser, after inspecting the house, signed a sales contract that contained no reference to the total square footage. Subsequently, purchaser discovered that the house contained only 1,410 heated square feet and sued both broker and seller for the difference between the value of the home as represented and as it actually was. *Held:* The average buyer should have the mathematical skills to determine the number of square feet in a house. Since the purchaser had a full opportunity to inspect the structure, he could not recover for the alleged misrepresentation. *Marshall v. Keavney,* 248 SE2d 750 (Ct. App. 1978).

Oregon Buyers, after expressing an interest in purchasing a motel, walked around the premises and inspected each unit. Several months later, they stayed at the motel for 20 days, talked to local townspeople, and generally educated themselves about the enterprise and its problems. Subsequently, they signed a sales contract that described the boundaries of the property and that stated that buyers were accepting the property based on their own examination and not in reliance on seller's statements. One year later, a survey revealed that buyers owned only 1.3 acres, rather than the 13 acres that they claimed seller represented to them they were buying. Buyers sued seller for $25,000 in damages resulting from the seller's false representation. *Held:* For seller. The deed accurately described the boundaries of the property. Moreover, buyers had ample time to inspect the land, and even if it were true that the acreage was misrepresented, they should have realized the substantial difference between 1.3 and 13 acres. The contract clearly indicated that buyers had made their own examination, and so seller could not be held liable for any damages. *Schulz v. Peake,* 583 P2d 425 (1978).

Texas Seller brought an action for specific performance of a contract for the sale of land; buyer counterclaimed for the return of his deposit. The land involved was approximately 20 acres, and there was a dispute as to whether the property description contained in the contract was sufficient to fulfill the Statute of Frauds. Seller appealed an order granting summary judgment for buyer. *Held:* The description of the land was insufficient to comply with the Statute of Frauds. Conflicting affidavits of surveyors did not create a question of fact, where other writings referred to were useless in identifying the land, and no adequate metes and bounds description was included. None of the four corners could be established on the ground, and certain undescribed lands were excepted from the purported conveyance. The contract was void and buyer's deposit should be returned. *Barham v. Powell,* 554 SW2d 826 (Civ. App. 1977).

Virginia A contract providing for a sale in gross of "463 acres more or less" gave the purchaser the right to survey the property prior to closing. If a survey was performed, the sale price was to be adjusted by $1,000 per acre, up or down. The purchaser, unwilling to pay for a full survey, asked a surveyor to estimate the acreage without determining the exact bounds of the property. The surveyor estimated that the contract acreage was very close to accurate. Seller, however, learning of the surveyor's activity, refused to perform without a complete survey. A complete survey showed six to seven additional acres, which purchaser offered to pay for. When seller still refused to close, purchaser sued for specific performance. *Held:* For purchaser. The purchaser made a proper tender of performance before the closing date, and was willing to perform in accordance with the contract for a sale in gross. Purchaser was not obligated to convert a sale in gross to a sale by the acre by supplying a complete survey. *Scott v. Sutherland,* 327 SE2d 78 (1985).

71.15 Conflicting Descriptions

Oregon Land sale contract contained two descriptions of the property. One was in terms of distances from a certain building. Under the other, which was a courses and distances description, the property conveyed would include a portion of a building owned by the vendor. *Held:* Where there are irreconcilable descriptions in a conveying instrument, the court must choose the description that best comports with the intention of the parties. The self-evident fact that the parties would not have intended the building to encroach on the grantee's land justified the adoption of the description that would not establish the encroachment. *McCoshum v. Hoselton,* 543 P2d 657 (1975).

South Carolina A buyer and seller entered into negotiations for the sale of a specified lot of property. The buyer made a $1,000 deposit on the purchase price, but no formal contract was signed. During the negotiations, the buyer had also expressed interest in an adjoining piece of property. When the buyer made a written offer for both pieces of property, accompanied by an additional deposit of $1,000, the seller accepted the offer and cashed the check. Subsequently, a dispute arose and the seller claimed that the sale covered only the first lot that was offered for sale. The buyer argued that the sale covered both properties, and he sued to have them both conveyed to him. He also sued for damages, arguing that the delay caused by the lawsuit resulted in increased construction costs for him. *Held:* The buyer was entitled to transfer of both properties, and damages for the delay. The actions of the parties indicated that there was a valid and binding contract for sale of both properties. Furthermore, the seller was aware of the buyer's construction plans and, therefore, was liable for damages when it failed to perform the contract in full. *Goodwin v. Hilton Head Co.,* 259 SE2d 611 (1979).

71.20 Risk of Loss

California Plaintiff leased with option to buy property of defendant. Plaintiff exercised the option and placed a deposit in escrow along with note for the balance of the purchase price. Under the terms of the contract, plaintiff was to buy fire insurance payable to defendant, but failed to do so. Prior to closing, the property was destroyed by fire. Defendant attempted to rescind the contract; plaintiff sued for damages in the amount received by defendant on his own fire insurance policy. *Held:* Rescission of the contract affirmed. Under the Uniform Vendor and Purchaser Risk Act, since plaintiff was in possession of the property, she was bound by the contract and bore all risk of loss if the premises were destroyed without fault of vendor. The vendor retained an equity interest in the property until the transaction was completed, was entitled to the insurance proceeds, and could elect to rescind the contract. *Long v. Keller,* 163 Cal. Rptr. 532 (1980).

South Carolina A home builder had a risk insurance policy on a house he was building. When the house was almost finished, it burned down, and the owner employed another contractor to restore the house. The builder sued the insurance company for the balance the owner owed him under the construction contract. *Held:* The builder is not entitled to recover against the insurance company. By the time of the fire, the risk of loss had passed from the builder to the owner, and the builder had no insurable interest. *Baker v. Aetna Ins. Co.,* 262 SE2d 417 (1980).

South Carolina Nelson conveyed .55 of an acre of land to Durant, but the parties agreed that the conveyance did not include a house that was to be moved to another piece of property. Before the house could be moved, it was destroyed by fire. Nelson maintained fire isurance on the house, but the insurance company refused to pay because it contended that the insurable interest in the land and its improvements terminated upon the conveyance of the property. The trial court ruled in favor of the insurance company. *Held:* Reversed. Even though he had transferred the property beneath it, Nelson retained an equitable interest in the house that maintained his insurable interest therein. *Nelson v. United Fire Ins. Co.,* 267 SE2d 604 (1980).

Texas Where property was damaged by a storm subsequent to the execution of the purchase contract and the taking of possession by the purchaser, but prior to closing of the transaction. Seller sued for specific performance. *Held:* For seller, because when property contracted to be sold is damaged by fire, storm, or other cause not the fault of either party, the loss will fall on the party who, at the time, owned the beneficial interest. *Smith v. Warth,* 483 SW2d 834 (1972).

71.25 Right to Insurance Proceeds

7th Circuit Fire insurance policy contained a standard provision requiring the insurer's consent to any transfer or assignment of the policies. The insured sold the property but agreed to continue its management. Assignments of the fire insurance policies were executed with an agreement to obtain approval of the assignments from the insurers. The insured failed to deliver the assignments, and a fire subsequently destroyed the buildings on the property. The insurer denied liability, alleging that the insured's insurable interest in the property had terminated at the time of the sale of the property. *Held:* Neither legal title nor possession is necessary to claim an insurable interest in property. The contingency that an individual might suffer a loss is sufficient to create an insurable interest. The insured had agreed to arrange for the assignment of the insurance policy to the purchaser of the property. Its failure to do so and potential liability gave rise to an insurable interest in the property. *Prince v. Royal Indem. Co.,* 541 F2d 646 (1976).

Minnesota Insured, a company in the business of selling fire protection equipment, purchased an insurance policy covering "completed operation and products liability." The terms of the original policy protected against loss caused by the negligent installation of insured's products. Shortly after receiving the original policy, however, insured received an indorsement to the policy that excluded coverage of both negligent manufacture and installation. A fire subsequently destroyed premises in which insured's equipment had been installed but had failed to operate. When insured was sued, it turned the matter over to the insurer. However, the insurer, reciting the provisions of the indorsement, disclaimed liability. *Held:* The indorsement constituted a change of coverage, and there are California and New Jersey decisions requiring insurers to notify insureds of such modifications. When an insurer substantially reduces coverage by way of a new policy or indorsement, it must notify the insured, in writing, as to the specifics of the change being made. *Canadian Universal Ins. Co. v. Fire Watch, Inc.,* 258 NW2d 570 (1977).

New York Tenants had a one-year lease on a motel and restaurant with an option to buy. With 23 days left on the lease, a fire totally destroyed the premises, including $15,000 worth of improvements that tenants had made. Tenants sued their insurance company for reimbursement for the full value of the improvements. *Held:* The purchase option did not give tenants a full insurable interest in the property; therefore, they were entitled to recover only a portion of the improvements, prorated over the unexpired term of the lease ($^{23}/_{365}$ of their loss, since only 23 days remained in the term). *Vendriesco v. Aetna Casualty & Surety Co.,* 414 NYS2d 64 (App. Div. 1979).

South Dakota Seaman sought to obain Lawrence Co. property via tax-free exchange for his Sully County property. Seaman's friend, Vetter, purchased the Lawrence County property. Pursuant to an agreement with Seaman, Vetter purchased comprehensive insurance on the property in his own name. The agreement was silent as to who would receive the proceeds of the policy. Vetter subsequently entered into an agreement to sell the property to a third party who would then transfer it to Seaman in exchange for his Sully property. This agreement was also silent as to insurance. Before the sale and exchange took place, the Lawrence house burned down. However, purchaser paid Vetter the full purchase price and completed the exchange with Seaman. The insurer claimed Vetter was not entitled to indemnification since he suffered no loss. *Held:* Although Vetter was not entitled to the insurance proceeds, the insurer could not escape paying because the insured had received the undamaged value of the property. Citing the principle that "insurance money belongs to him on whom falls the loss," the court ruled that

Seaman was entitled to the proceeds. *New Hampshire Ins. Co. v. Vetter,* 326 NW2d 723 (1982).

71.30
Effect of Vendor's Death

Maryland Calvin and Cecelia held a farm as tenants by the entirety. Carlton paid $100 for a written option to purchase the farm, which was extended without additional consideration. Calvin died and Carlton wrote Cecelia accepting the offer to sell. Cecelia refused to convey the property, and Carlton sued. *Held:* Under the Maryland Statute of Frauds, the written extension of the option was insufficient because of absence of consideration. Therefore, the issue became whether there was an offer to sell the property, which Carlton accepted by his letter. The general rule is that the death of an offeror revokes the offer or causes it to lapse. The continued vitality of the offer depended on the continued assent of both Calvin and Cecelia. Since upon Calvin's death his assent was no longer possible, the offer lapsed. Therefore, no outstanding offer existed and Carlton's letter was a mere offer to buy, which Cecelia refused. *Beall v. Beall,* 434 A2d 1015 (1981).

Maryland Realtor assigned his interest in a land sale contract to a husband and wife, who agreed to pay the realtor $9,000 above the purchase price. The husband died one day prior to closing, and the wife did not attend this or subsequent closings. The realtor then brought suit against the wife, both individually and in her capacity as representative of her husband's estate. The wife argued that she should be relieved from the agreement because of a clause allowing breach in the event the sale was not completed through no fault of the purchasers. *Held:* The wife was bound by the contract terms. Since the obligation of the parties was a joint undertaking, each party was jointly and severally liable. The death of one party, therefore, could not excuse performance by the other absent a provision to the contrary. *Burka v. Patrick,* 366 A2d 1070 (1976).

Texas Just prior to his death, an owner of property executed a deed that was placed in escrow. When grantee complied with the terms of the sales contract and obtained delivery of the deed after grantor's death, grantor's son sought to have the conveyance set aside. *Held:* The death of grantor, while grantor's deed is held is escrow, does not invalidate the instrument upon its subsequent delivery. Where grantee performs the conditions of the escrow agreement after grantor's death, grantee is entitled to delivery of the deed, and his title relates back to the date of the original deposit of the instrument in escrow. Therefore, grantor's death did not divest grantee of title to the property, since grantee had complied with the conditions of the escrow agreement. *Fuqua v. Fuqua,* 528 SW2d 896 (Civ. App. 1975).

71.35
Implied Contracts

New York Association whose membership consisted of owners of parcels of land that included a beach area sued to recover the cost of maintenance of the communal beach facilities from nonmembers. The group argued that defendants were liable although they had not agreed to make payments to the association, did not use the facilities, and were willing to surrender any rights they had to the beach. *Held:* The owners of land in the subdivision containing communal beach facilities were liable in quasi-contract and implied contract for maintenance expenses for the communal beach facilities to the extent they enjoyed their use and benefit. Further, nonmembers would be held to have benefited even if they did not use the beach, where the value of their parcels increased due to maintenance of the beach area. *Mohegan Colony Ass'n v. Picone,* 402 NYS2d 40 (App. Div. 1978).

72.00 PERFORMANCE

72.05 Conditions Precedent

8th Circuit Plaintiff sold defendant housing authority 250 low-rent housing units. The contract called for seven installment conveyances, wherein defendant was to make payments at each closing with "water, rent, operating charges and current taxes . . . adjusted to the date of settlement." At the first six closings, none of the payments were prorated to cover the taxes incurred. However, at the seventh closing, defendant withheld part of the payment to cover plaintiff's prorated share of the taxes due. Plaintiff sued for the money withheld, claiming it had no tax liability. Since the actual payment of the taxes was not due until after full title had been transferred to defendant, plaintiff argued that there were no "current taxes" for him to be responsible for. *Held:* The plain meaning of the contract, under the "current taxes" clause, made plaintiff liable for the taxes incurred even though defendant had failed to prorate at each closing. Defendant's conduct was not a waiver of the provision as the contract did not set a specific date for payment of the taxes by plaintiff. *Ithaca Corp. v. Housing Auth.,* 541 F2d 1317 (1976).

Idaho Seller of plant agreed to make improvements and sell it to a buyer under a land contract in which seller was to retain title until the purchase price was fully paid. The contract also called for buyer to take possession upon making a down payment. Buyer took possession without making the full down payment, but seller agreed to accept the remainder in two installments. When buyer failed to pay the second installment on time, seller gave notice of default and sued for foreclosure. The buyer counterclaimed that seller had breached the contract by not furnishing marketable title, since there was a mortgage on the property. *Held:* The existence of an encumbrance does not excuse the buyer from performing the contract. Seller, who informed buyer of the mortgage, did not breach the contract by failing to furnish marketable title, since under the contract seller retained title until full payment was made by the buyer. *Jensen v. Bledsoe,* 593 P2d 988 (1979).

72.10 —Financing Clauses

Georgia A real estate sales contract called for the purchaser to provide the seller with a letter of approval for a $700,000 loan in the form of a 25-year adjustable rate loan at 10.75 percent within two weeks of the date the contract was executed. On the last day, the vice-president of the bank delivered a handwritten letter stating that the purchaser had been approved for a loan of $700,000. The terms of the loan were not mentioned. The seller terminated the contract, claiming the purchaser had failed to comply with the financing clause, and purchaser sued for specific performance. *Held:* Seller was entitled to summary judgment. The seller could not determine from the information in the letter whether the purchaser had been offered the loan on terms that would bind her to the sales contract. The letter from the bank was not adequate assurance of that information. *Brown v. Morris Real Estate Consultants,* 347 SE2d 563 (1986).

Louisiana The sale of a house for $142,000 was contingent upon the buyer's obtaining a mortgage for $92,000. Buyer intended to make the down payment with a gift of $50,000 from his father. However, when the father rescinded the gift, a bank that had agreed to lend the money refused to make the loan. Buyer sought the return of his deposit, arguing his inability to obtain financing rendered the contract void. *Held:* For seller. The agreement presupposed that buyer could furnish a $50,000 down payment apart from the financed portion of the purchase price. It was because of purchaser's inability to tender the down payment that the financing commitment was revoked. A condition is regarded as fulfilled if it is not fulfilled because of the fault of a party with an in terest contrary to the fulfillment. *Farnsworth/Samuel Ltd. v. Cervini,* 492 So. 2d 1245 (Ct. App. 1986).

Maine Purchasers sued to recover monies paid under a contract for the sale of land that was contingent on their securing a $140,000 mortgage on the property. A bank rejected the purchasers' plan to obtain long-term financing and use the property as a boy's camp, but offered a one-year loan requiring that the land be subdivided and sold. *Held:* The purchasers made reasonable efforts to secure financing and were awarded recovery of the moneys paid under the contract. The short-term loan that was offered did not satisfy the financing contingency. *Rand v. BG Pride Realty,* 350 A2d 565 (1976).

New York A contract of sale for real property was conditioned on issuance by "a lending institution" of a conventional first mortgage loan on the premises on specified terms. Buyer applied to a savings bank, and was rejected. When buyer requested the return of his deposit, seller instead insisted buyer assume two existing mortgages on the property and agree to a seller-financed mortgage loan for the balance. Buyer instead sued for the return of his deposit. *Held:* Buyer was required neither to apply to more than one institutional lender nor to accept private seller financing. *Macho Assets, Inc. v. Spring Corp.,* 513 NYS2d 180 (App. Div. 1987).

New York A purchase and sale agreement was conditioned on vendee's ability to obtain a mortgage. Failure to meet the condition was to result in return of the down payment. Vendee obtained a Veterans Administration (VA) loan, which provided that vendee could cancel the agreement without penalty if the purchase price exceeded the reasonable value of the property as determined by the VA. Vendor refused to execute the mortgage on the ground that it modified the sales contract and asked vendee to apply for a conventional mortgage. Vendee sued after vendor refused to return vendee's down payment. *Held:* Summary judgment for vendee affirmed. A purchaser is generally entitled to refund of his deposit where the contract calls for cancellation should purchaser be unable to obtain a mortgage within a specified time. Two issues remained for the trial court: (1) whether the parties intended the vendee to apply for a conventional mortgage and (2) whether vendee satisfied the implied condition of good faith by making only one mortgage application, and was the VA mortgage the type contemplated by the parties. *Johnson v. Werner,* 407 NYS2d 28 (App. Div. 1978).

72.15
Time of Performance

Colorado Sellers entered into an exclusive listing with a real estate brokerage to sell their home. A salesperson with the firm prepared a contract, which the parties signed, for an offer to buy the property. A provision of the contract required sellers to deliver to purchasers a commitment for title insurance by July 10,

1981. The closing was July 20. The salesperson was notified of the brokerage's receipt of title insurance on July 7, but purchasers did not receive the commitment until July 15. By that time, purchasers had stopped payment on their $20,000 deposit and refused to proceed with the purchase. Sellers sued for breach of contract. *Held:* For purchasers. Salesperson was not the agent of purchasers, but of sellers, and delivery of the title commitment to the salesperson did not fulfill the terms of the contract requiring delivery to purchasers. In a multiple listing transaction, the selling salesperson is an agent of the listing broker and is thus within a chain of agency to the seller. *Rohauer v. Little,* 736 P2d 403 (1987) (en banc).

District of Columbia Buyers entered into contract with an oil company for sale of a combination gas station and liquor store in May 1976. The purchase price was $100,000, payable in full by June 1, 1976. Buyers furnished a down payment of $10,000, to be forfeited if they defaulted on the contract. Because of a delay in getting a liquor license, buyers requested, on July 5, an extension until October 1 to complete payment. On October 1, when buyers had still not made payment or contacted the company, the company gave them until October 15 to make payment or the contract would be voided and the down payment forfeited. On October 27, the company notified that the contract was void; and on November 5, the down payment was returned. Buyers then sued for specific performance of the contract, claiming that the 15-day extension from October 1 to October 15 was unreasonable. *Held:* Buyers' suit for specific performance was dismissed. In light of the extension of a period of four months, the 15-day limit was not unreasonable. *Drazin v. American Oil Co.,* 395 A2d 32 (1978).

Georgia A commercial real estate sales contract originally called for closing no later than July 1983. An addendum postponed the closing, and provided that it would occur within 10 days after final approval of the subdivision plat by the county planning commission. When the plat was approved on November 9, 1983, the seller refused to close, arguing that the contract expired July 12. The buyer sued for specific performance. Reasoning that the absence of a specific date for closing left the contract open for more than 21 years, the trial court granted summary judgment to the seller. *Held:* Reversed. The failure to include a time limit for the nonoccurrence of a contingency meant only that the contract was missing a term specifying time for performance. A reasonable time for performance would be implied under Georgia common law. As 21 years would be unreasonable, the contract did not create a perpetuity. *Read v. GHDC, Inc.,* 334 SE2d 165 (1985).

Illinois In a land installment contract, buyer and seller agreed that time was of the essence in payment, and an acceleration clause was inserted in the contract. However, beginning with the first payment, buyer was consistently late; but seller accepted payments without protest. Finally, when buyer failed to make two monthly payments, seller wrote a letter to buyer, notifying him that the payments would be accelerated. When the letter was returned unclaimed, seller brought a forfeiture action. *Held:* Seller was not entitled to forfeiture. Seller had consistently accepted late payments and therefore had waived the right to strict compliance with the "time of the essence" clause of the contract. *Aden v. Alwardt,* 394 NE2d 716 (App. Ct. 1979).

New Hampshire An agreement to purchase property provided that if buyers did not close within a reasonable time after September 15, 1975, the down payment would be forfeited to sellers. In addition, the agreement was conditioned on the buyers' obtaining Farmers Home Administration (FmHA) financing. Buyers applied for an FmHA loan in March 1975, but were turned down on September 23, 1975. They then applied to a bank, which agreed to a loan and a closing date of December 17. However, sellers notified the bank they considered the contract void because closing was not effected by September 15. Buyers sued for specific performance, claiming the delay in financing was not their fault. *Held:* For buyers. Time was not of the essence in the contract and the delay was not willful, nor did it harm sellers. The time limitation was formal rather than essential and should not defeat the contract. *Leavitt v. Fowler,* 391 A2d 876 (1978).

New Jersey Buyer and sellers entered into a modification agreement of their contract of sale that scheduled the closing for a specified date and time and that provided time was of the essence. When plaintiff failed to appear at the closing at the designated time, sellers declared the contract terminated, despite the fact that plaintiff's attorney explained plaintiff's absence as a scheduling mix-up and closing could occur later in the day. *Held:* Sellers were entitled to the full benefit of the time of the essence provision. Such provisions are effective tools of contract administration, providing certainty and objectivity in defining the rights and obligations of the parties. A negotiated agreement requiring performance on a specified date and time will be strictly enforced. Judicial tampering to determine whether a default should be excused would merely promote litigation. Moreover, the equities were on the side of the sellers. *Gorrie v. Winters,* 518 A2d 515 (Super. Ct. App. Div. 1986), cert. denied, 562 A2d 184 (1987).

New Mexico A contract to purchase a home provided for buyer to assume the mortgage, plus make additional monthly payments. Buyer's failure to make any missed payment within 15 days after written demand was mailed gave seller the option to terminate the contract. Buyer missed a payment on February 1, seller mailed a written demand on February 4, and on February 19 seller terminated the contract. On February 20, buyer tendered payment but was refused. Seller brought an unlawful detainer action against buyers. *Held:* For buyer. A summary proceeding cannot be used to oust an equitable owner under a real estate contract; nor can a real estate contract transform a vendor-vendee relationship into one of landlord-tenant. Further, the effective date of the seller's notice was when buyer received it. If notice was received the day after mailing, buyer's tender on February 20 was timely. *Ott v. Keller,* 558 P2d 613 (1976).

Pennsylvania Buyers signed a contract to acquire a tract of land from sellers, who were at the time negotiating for purchase of the property from the owner. A closing date was set, but it had to be rescheduled because one of buyers refused to supply certain financial data. Because of this delay and a disagreement among buyers, sellers had owner transfer the property to them rather than to buyers. Buyers sued owner, arguing that the transfer violated the sales contract. Owner contended that buyers' delays constituted a breach of the contract. *Held:* Buyers' delays were not a breach of the contract since time was not "of the essence" in closing the deal. There was no specific language in the contract stating that time was essential, nor was there any indication from the surrounding circumstances that time was considered of the essence by the parties. *Tanenbaum v. Sears, Roebuck and Co.,* 401 A2d 809 (Super. Ct. 1979).

Virginia Purchaser and vendor executed a contract of sale that gave purchaser the "sole option" to declare the contract void. The contract provided that sale would close within 120 days. The sale date was extended twice with vendor's approval. When vendor died prior to the sale date, his widow extended the contract for an additional three months, but later refused to consummate the sale and returned purchaser's deposit, stating the property had increased in value. Purchaser sued for specific performance. *Held:* The actions of the parties indicate that time of the closing was not essential to performance of the contract. All extensions of time were readily agreed to by vendor. Purchaser's option to cancel did not create an option contract out of what was clearly intended to be a contract of sale. *Wood v. Wood,* 224 SE2d 159 (1976).

Washington Sellers' lessee had made improvements that encroached on another part of the property, which was being offered to prospective purchasers. Sellers negotiated a lease amendment with lessee, but it was not signed by the closing date. Purchasers refused to close because sellers could not deliver title, but accepted an extention. Sellers then declared the earnest money agreement null and void. Purchasers sued to recover lost profits and earnest money. *Held:* Both parties defaulted. The agreement provided that "purchaser and seller shall deposit with closing agent all instruments, documents and monies necessary to complete the sale. . . ." Nothing in the agreement suggested that either party was to perform first. Since purchasers could not have known that sellers were not ready to submit a marketable title for closing, they were not excused from tendering the purchase price. *Willener v. Sweeting,* 730 P2d 45 (1986) (en banc).

72.20 Payment by Check

Minnesota Plaintiff sued for breach of an option contract. For four years, plaintiff had been renewing the option annually by check. In the fifth year, plaintiff tried to renegotiate the date of payment for renewal, but defendants refused. Plaintiff then paid on time by check, but when defendants presented the check to plaintiff's bank, it was dishonored for insufficient and uncollected funds. Defendants returned the check to plaintiff and declared the option had lapsed. Plaintiff argued that timely tender of the check was sufficient to extend the option for one year. *Held:* The option lapsed when plaintiff tendered a check that was dishonored by the bank. Delivery of a check is not payment unless the parties expressly so agree. The fact that defendants had previously negotiated plaintiff's checks by deposit in their own account rather than by presentation to plaintiff's bank did not imply a course of dealing tantamount to such an agreement. Furthermore, the general rule with regard to time of performance in option contracts is that time is of the essence. *Merriman v. Sandeen,* 267 NW2d 714 (1978).

New York General contractor tendered a check to subcontractor for work on a construction project, deducting expenses incurred due to allegedly defective materials supplied by subcontractor. The subcontractor certified the check and deposited it with the endorsement "without prejudice and under protest." The subcontractor argued its certification did not constitute acceptance of the check resulting in an accord and satisfaction, and he sought to recover the amount deducted. *Held:* For the general contractor. Under UCC § 1-207, endorsement of a check "without prejudice and under protest" reserves the right to demand the balance allegedly due. However, in this case, payee's certification of the check was equivalent to acceptance and therefore resulted in an accord and satisfaction. *Lange-Firm Constr. Co. v. Albany Steel & Iron Supply Co.,* 403 NYS2d 1012 (Sup. Ct. 1978).

Oregon A land-sale contract provided that time was of the essence and that purchaser would be in default if he failed "to make any payment at the time required, or within ten (10) days thereof." Purchaser made several late payments and received notice from seller's attorney that subsequent checks must be *received* by the tenth of each month to avoid foreclosure. After this, the purchaser sent the May payment on May 10, and the escrow agent received it on May 14. Seller requested the agent to return the check and then sued for specific performance. *Held:* A split appellate court held that the payment was "made" on the date it was received by seller, and was therefore not timely. The court cited an Oregon case approving the rule stated in 48 CJ *Payment* § 8 that "a debt is payable at the place where the creditor resides, or at his place of business. . . ." *Gordon v. Schumacher,* 733 P2d 35 (Ct. App. 1987).

Utah Plaintiff buyer offered and defendant vendor accepted an "earnest money receipt and offer to purchase" property for $500 down, with the balance due June 6, 1975. On June 6, buyer paid the balance by personal check to the escrow agent; vendor was not told of the form of payment. Vendor signed the closing documents and deed. On June 11, vendor learned the money was not available because purchaser had paid by a check that would not clear. Vendor rescinded the agreement and directed the escrow agent not to release the closing documents. Buyer sought specific performance. *Held:* Vendor's objection was timely, and he was entitled to rescind without giving buyer additional time to perform. To make a valid tender or offer to pay, purchaser of real property must tender lawful money. When he fails to do so, as here, vendor may refuse to accept the tender. Buyer had been told to replace the worthless check but had not done so. *Griffith v. Zumbrennan,* 577 P2d 129 (1978).

73.00 SELLER'S DUTY TO DELIVER MARKETABLE TITLE

73.05 What Constitutes Marketable Title

10th Circuit Plaintiff brought an action for enforcement of contract with defendants for a sale of real property. Plaintiff was to deliver a warranty deed and furnish merchantable title at closing. The property had been purchased by plaintiff at a foreclosure sale and had not yet been redeemed, plaintiff contending it would use the sale proceeds from defendants to discharge the obligation and lien. Defendants were aware of these facts at the time they entered into the contract. Nevertheless, defendants refused to complete the transaction, arguing that the unpaid lien rendered the title unmerchantable since it would not be removed prior to closing. *Held:* A lien that is to be paid off from proceeds of the sale is not to be regarded as a failure or inability to furnish a marketable title. Defendants were fully aware of the lien and the foreclosure, and it appeared that plaintiff intended to pay off the loan from the sale proceeds. *Lone Star Dev. Corp. v. Miller,* 564 F2d 921 (1977).

Illinois Purchasers bought a piece of property without any access. Vendor and purchasers had been afforded access across the property of adjoining landowners, but this practice was discontinued by the surrounding landowners before purchasers received title to the property. Purchasers sued vendor, alleging that title to the property was not merchantable. *Held:* For vendor. The fact that land is inaccessible due to the lack of a public road does not make the property legally not merchantable. The responsibility to inspect the property to ensure access before purchase belongs to prospective purchaser, because a lack of access is not usually disclosed in an abstract. While the inaccessible property may have been of questionable marketability before its sale, the land was merchantable under the law. *Sinks v. Karleskint,* 474 NE2d 767 (App. Ct. 1985).

Massachusetts To prevent the state from taking their property by eminent domain, defendants executed an agreement with a land conservation trust restricting the use of their property so as to preserve its natural state. Sixteen years later, defendants entered into an agreement with plaintiff to sell the property; in this agreement, defendants promised to convey clear and marketable title free of encumbrances. When plaintiff learned of the restrictive agreement, she sued for return of her deposit. *Held:* Summary judgment for plaintiff affirmed. The restrictive convenant was an encumbrance preventing clear record of title. The relevant statute, St. 1961, ch. 579, § 3, provided preemption from eminent domain to property "encumbered by restrictive agreements . . . which will limit the use of such marsh or land." *Coons v. Carstensen,* 446 NE2d 114 (1983).

Minnesota A contract for sale of land for a restaurant was contingent upon purchaser's obtaining rezoning at his own expense. The city granted approval, with the condition that $28,000 be dedicated for public parks. When seller refused to pay, purchaser paid and sued to recover the money from seller. The trial court granted summary judgment to the purchaser, reasoning that seller could not grant marketable title without paying the assessment and that seller, as owner of the property, was the one required to pay. *Held:* Reversed. Seller had conveyed marketable title to purchaser. As to who was obligated to pay the assessment, either party could be considered the owner, since the purchaser of property in an executory contract for the sale of land is the equitable owner. The question of who was obligated to pay the assessment turned on the intentions of the parties; a trial was needed on this issue. *Glaser v. Minnesota Fed. Sav. & Loan,* 389 NW2d 763 (Ct. App. 1986).

New Jersey A purchase and sale agreement provided for conveyance of marketable title. When vendees discovered that vendors' title to part of the parcel was grounded upon adverse possession, vendees refused to close and sued for rescission and return of their down payment. Defendant argued that the agreement called for marketable title and not perfect record title; therefore, the adverse claim did not violate the title provisions of the agreement. *Held:* Vendors are entitled to judgment if they can prove, on remand, title by adverse possession. Title by adverse possession, once clearly established, is marketable. The court noted that where marketability of title is at issue, "marketability" is to be determined according to the title vendee will get at the close of the lawsuit, not the title that vendor had at its commencement. *Conklin v. Davi,* 388 A2d 598 (1978).

South Dakota Purchasers agreed to buy a gold-mining operation consisting of a deeded parcel, a mill, and an unpatented placer mining claim. Purchasers did not request an examination of title to the claim. Before closing, the parties learned that the Bureau of Land Management had cancelled the claim and a third party had filed an intervening placer claim to the property. Purchasers accepted sellers' assurances that the bureau was not entitled to cancel the claim. However, purchasers were unable to raise the purchase price, and agreed to relinquish their earnest money and their rights in the agreement. Later, purchasers sued for return of the earnest money on the ground that sellers did not have good title. *Held:* Sellers were entitled to retain the earnest money. Where time is not of the essence, a vendor has a reasonable time to provide good title. Here, vendors took measures to clear their title and, in fact, cured the defect. Even if the defects had been incurable, purchasers could not prevail, since by agreeing to accept title without examination, they waived the right to rescind. *Wolken v. Wade,* 406 NW2d 720 (1987).

73.10 Purchaser's Remedies

10th Circuit Buyer and seller executed a contract for the sale of a large parcel of land. Buyer was informed that seller was in bankruptcy and that the property had been sold at a foreclosure sale prior to the contract date. Seller, however, retained a right of redemption and could regain title to the land by paying off a debt out of the closing proceeds. Buyer refused to go through with the deal, contending that the unpaid lien rendered the title unmerchantable, since it would not be removed prior to closing. Seller was unable to redeem the property, and he sued buyer for damages. *Held:* Buyer had no right to rescind the contract, and seller was entitled to sue for damages. Almost all the 50 states recognize the principle that a seller may use closing proceeds to satisfy outstanding liens. Furthermore, sufficient safeguards exist to ensure that sellers pay liens from the closing proceeds. *Lone Star Dev. Corp. v. Miller,* 564 F2d 921 (1977).

Alabama Plaintiffs bought a home based on a title search by Realty Title for Lawyers Title Insurance, which issued a policy. Realty Title missed an agreement by plaintiffs' predecessor in title releasing the city from any damage caused by flooding. When a flood heavily damaged their home, plaintiffs discovered they could not recover from the city. They sued Realty Title for fraud in failing to inform them of the release agreement. *Held:* Plaintiffs had a cause of action. The fraud claim was based on Alabama law regarding the suppression of a material fact the possessor thereof is obligated to communicate. The title examination was performed at least partly for the benefit of plaintiffs. The existence of the release agreement was a valuable fact in connection with plaintiffs' decision to acquire the property, to which fact Realty Title had superior access. Therefore, Realty Title had a duty to disclose the release agreement. *Hopkins v. Lawyers Title Ins. Corp.,* 514 So. 2d 786 (1986).

Arkansas Grantors conveyed certain acreage to grantees by general warranty deed. A third party then informed grantees he had acquired 2.72 acres of the land by adverse possession. Grantees sued the third party for possession and grantors for breach of warranty. Grantees prevailed against the third party, but were denied litigation costs from grantors. *Held:* Reversed in favor of grantees. Grantors had warranted the title and covenanted that they would defend the title against all claims. The court found that the third party's possession of the 2.72 acres was a breach of the covenant of seisin. A covenant of seisin implies that the covenantor is in possession of the land conveyed. If anyone is actually in possession claiming adversely to the covenantor, the covenant of seisin is broken, and the grantee is entitled to recover the costs incurred in vindicating its rights. *Bosnick v. Hill,* 731 SW2d 204 (1987).

New Jersey Seller unwittingly sold property to plaintiffs to which it did not have clear title. The sale was financed in part by a 30-year note secured by a mortgage. When a title search revealed that seller was not the record owner, plaintiffs sued for damages. Prior to trial, plaintiffs purchased another home with a mortgage bearing 13.25 percent interest. They claimed the difference in interest as part of their damages. Seller argued that under the "English rule," which was applied in New Jersey, plaintiffs were entitled only to their out-of-pocket losses. *Held:* The New Jersey Supreme Court ruled that New Jersey would henceforth follow the American rule, under which plaintiffs could recover the benefit of the bargain they would have enjoyed had the sale been consummated. However, the court did not agree that the interest difference was an element of damage. Although the transaction between the parties amounted to a purchase money mortgage, seller's motive was to sell a house, not to lend money. The proper measure of damages was the difference between the contract price and the fair market value of property that could be acquired with a purchase money mortgage in the amount and at the interest rate and term offered by the seller. *Donovan v. Bachstadt,* 453 A2d 160 (1982).

74.00 ASSIGNMENTS

74.05 Purchaser's Right to Assign

8th Circuit Sellers sold their apartments to buyer under two sales contracts. The contracts provided that an assignee must make an express written assumption of the obligations of the contract. Buyer assigned all his rights in the contracts to two limited partnerships. Sellers objected to the assignment, and the sale fell through. Partnerships sued sellers for breach of contract and tortious interference. At issue before the court of appeals was whether there had been a true assignment, in the absence of written assumptions of duties from the assignee partnerships as required by the contracts. *Held:* A contractual prohibition against assignment is presumed to bar only the delegation of duties and not the assignment of rights. Since buyer remained liable on the original contracts, the "assignments" did not violate the contract prohibitions and so the partnerships had standing to sue the sellers on the contracts. A de facto assumption of buyer's duties could be inferred from the partnerships' conduct, despite buyer's failure to obtain written assumptions from the partnerships. *Cedar Point Apartments, Ltd. v. Cedar Point Inv. Corp.,* 693 F2d 748 (1982), cert. denied, 461 US 914 (1983).

Idaho Real estate purchasers agreed not to assign their purchase agreement "without first obtaining the written consent of Sellers." The purchasers later sought to sell the property and requested sellers' consent to assignment of the contract. Sellers refused. *Held:* A nonassignment clause conditioned on the consent of seller necessarily implies that seller will act reasonably and in good faith in exercising his right of approval. Since sellers had no objection to the proposed assignee's credit, assignee's reputation, or assignee personally, sellers' refusal was not given in good faith and was totally unreasonable. The court justified its ruling as an extension of the principles it applied in *Funk v. Funk,* 633 P2d 586 (1981), in which it held that a lessor may not unreasonably withhold his consent to a prospective sublease. The court expressed no opinion with respect to real estate sales contracts that absolutely prohibit assignment. *Cheney v. Jemmett,* 693 P2d 1031 (1984).

New Mexico A land sale contract contained a clause prohibiting assignment without consent. Purchasers, without vendor's approval, transferred their interest in the property to a subpurchaser. Vendor claimed that purchasers had violated the anti-assignment clause and were therefore in default. *Held:* The transfers were not assignments, and thus did not violate the contract. A subcontract by a purchaser to sell his interest under a contract of sale is a separate contract between purchaser and subpurchaser. It does not meet the definition of "assignment," since subpurchaser assumes no obligations toward the original vendor and is not in privity with him. A provision prohibiting assignment of a contract bars only delegation of duties, not the assignment of purchaser's rights. *Paperchase Partnership v. Bruckner,* 693 P2d 587 (1985).

Washington Seller of real property agreed to convey it to the buyer, who agreed to pay the purchase price in monthly installments over a period of years. The contract did not permit prepayment nor could it be assigned or conveyed without seller's consent. When buyer contracted to sell it without seller's consent, seller sued to forfeit the contract. *Held:* Seller is not entitled to forfeiture of the contract. The provisions in the contract prohibiting assignment or conveyance without seller's consent constituted an unreasonable and unenforceable restraint on alienation, unless seller could prove that it was necessary to protect his security. *Terry v. Born,* 604 P2d 504 (1979).

74.10
—Rights of Purchaser's Assignee

Rhode Island Plaintiffs appealed an order granting the motion of Downing, codefendant, to quash a notice of lis pendens that had been filed by plaintiffs. Plaintiffs had entered into a contract with Oakhurst Realty, defendant, to convey certain unimproved land for $4,000. The land was to be to be conveyed to plaintiffs as soon as it was platted and approved by the town. Subsequently, plaintiffs received a letter from Oakhurst requesting that they execute an accompanying release of the agreement. In the interim, Oakhurst had conveyed the land to Downing. Plaintiffs filed the notice of lis pendens at issue here. Downing argued that because plaintiffs asserted neither contractual nor equitable rights against it with respect to Downing's interest in the disputed property, plaintiffs did not have a right to specific performance against Downing. Therefore the application of lis pendens, which is limited to actual litigation involving title to real property, was improper against Downing's interest in the land. *Held:* For plaintiffs. It is well established that an executory purchase and sale agreement vests in vendee, plaintiff in this case, equitable title to the land involved. Therefore a third party who purchases such land with notice of vendee's interest under a preexisting contract takes title subject to such interest, and may have to convey the land to the aggrieved vendee. Thus, the order of lis pendens was reinstated. *George v. Oakhurst Realty, Inc.,* 414 A2d 471 (1980).

Wisconsin Purchaser's assignees appealed a deficiency judgment against both purchasers and themselves after a default and judicial sale. Assignees had taken the contract under a bare assignment without assumption or the obligations of the contract or a novation. *Held:* For purchaser's assignees. Assignees under a bare assignment of a contract were not in privity of contract with vendors and were under no contractual obligation to pay the purchase price or make up any deficiency. *Peterson v. Johnson,* 201 NW2d 507 (1972).

74.15
—Rights of Seller Against Purchaser's Assignee

Oregon Contract assignees made payments to sellers, mortgaged the land, rented out pasture, and listed the property for sale. They also received lot releases from sellers and sold the released parcels. However, they never expressly assumed the liabilities of the contract. Assignees subsequently defaulted; and when sellers sued them for the balance due, assignees claimed they were not obligated to pay, because they had not assumed the contract. The court of appeals held for contract sellers, stating that, although as a general rule, an assignee assumes no liability to vendor on the contract, an assignee may become liable if he claims the benefits of the contract. Here, assignees not only possessed and paid for the property, but also received lot releases and threatened to use the courts to enforce the original contract. Assignees had claimed the contract's benefits and were bound by it. *Held:* Affirmed. An assignee claims the benefits of a land sale contract when he exercises the rights conferred upon vendee by the contract. Where an assignee of a land sale contract "steps into the shoes" of assignor and asserts the interests the contract conveys, the presumption arises that assignee intended also to assume the duties the contract imposes. *Kunzman v. Thorsen,* 740 P2d 754 (1987).

74.20
Successive Assignments

Indiana Three successive vendees of real property, each of whom acquired his interest by assignment of a single land contract, were held liable upon default by the last assignee. On appeal, the questions arose as to whether, under all the circumstances, the first two vendees were discharged under the doctrine of novation and whether the first vendee could be liable in the absence of consent to the successive assignment. *Held:* Judgment affirmed. A simple assignment with the consent of vendor does not operate as a novation and thereby does not discharge the assignor's liability. The original assigning vendee remains liable as surety regardless of subsequent assignments. *Boswell v. Lyon,* 401 NE2d 735 (Ct. App. 1980).

74.25
Seller's Right to Assign

9th Circuit A son assigned all his expectancy in the estate of his father, and the assignee brought an action to enforce the assignment. *Held:* Such assignments were void at common law, but are enforceable in equity when the expectancy develops into a right. Here, however, the father's entire estate passed to the mother by the laws of intestate succession. The real property, which was the subject of the litigation, was acquired by the son as a gift by a deed from his mother. Therefore, the son took the property free of the assignment. *Sgambellini v. Nelson,* 480 F2d 619 (1973).

California Plaintiff, deceased's adopted son, brought an action to impose a constructive trust on the proceeds from the sale of property that the deceased had promised to devise him. Deceased had subsequently sold the property and assigned the proceeds to defendant, but plaintiff contended that the assignment was not supported by valuable consideration. *Held:* The consideration was adequate. The amount of consideration necessary for one to be a bona fide purchaser is the legal consideration adequate to sustain an action for damages rather than the amount of consideration required in an equitable action for specific performance. Here, the evidence indicated that assignee had cared for the deceased until his death, as well as had paid his medical and burial expenses. *Walters v. Calderon,* 102 Cal. Rptr. 89 (1972).

Iowa Purchaser of property instituted an action against defendant insurer for an insured loss, and vendor's assignees intervened in the action. The contract required purchaser to secure insurance on the property and designate vendor as owner. *Held:* Vendor's interest was like that of a mortgagee, giving him an interest in the policy and an independent right to sue. Vendor's assignment of all his interest in the contract and any causes of action accruing thereunder was an assignment of a chose in action, not a nonassignable personal contract, since the loss had occurred prior to assignment. Transfer of the chose in action to assignees carried with it the right to any remedies available to assignor without the consent of insurer. *Kintzel v. Wheatland Mut. Ins. Ass'n,* 203 NW2d 799 (1973).

Washington An assignment of the right to receive payments under a real estate contract is subject to the provisions of UCC Article 9. Such a contract right is personal property and not within the exception in Section 9-104(j) relative to interests in the realty itself. If an assignment of contract rights is coupled with a conveyance of an interest in the realty, assignee must file under Article 9 as well as in the real estate records to insure priority. *In re Freeborn,* 617 P2d 42 (1980).

75.00 INSTALLMENT CONTRACTS

75.05 Seller's Rights and Duties

Illinois Buyer sued to recover amounts he paid under an installment agreement when the property was sold at a tax sale. Seller was supposed to pay the taxes for that year. *Held:* Buyer was entitled to rescind the contract and recover payments made, since seller, owing to his own fault, was unable to convey good title. To restore both parties to their positions when the contract was executed, purchaser was chargeable with the reasonable rental value of the land plus interest thereon, and seller was chargeable with a restoration of the payments made and taxes paid by purchaser plus interest thereon. *Williams v. Dunas,* 352 NE2d 266 (App. Ct. 1976).

Minnesota A contract for deed provided that the purchase price consisted of $200,000 cash and a purchase money promissory note, and the "unpaid balance of the purchase price," which was to be paid in monthly installments over ten years. The promissory note, due one year after closing, was secured by an irrevocable letter of credit. The agreement also provided that seller's first recourse for nonpayment on the note was to draw on the letter of credit. When buyer became delinquent on payments, seller cancelled the contract and sought to collect on the promissory note, characterizing it as part of the down payment. *Held:* Whether the note was in fact a down payment and survived cancellation of the contract was a question of fact. There is a rebuttable presumption that a promissory note is not a down payment. However, the evidence strongly suggested the note was a down payment, since the contract referred to the note as separate from the "unpaid" balance of the purchase price. *Novus*

Equities Corp. v. EM-TY Partnership, 381 NW2d 426 (1986).

Utah A long-term sales contract provided that upon default by purchaser, vendor could rescind, keeping all payments as liquidated damages, or accelerate the contract to make all payments immediately due and payable. Vendor, however, was required to give 30 days' notice before rescinding, so that purchaser might remedy the default. Purchaser defaulted, and without notifying purchaser, vendor demanded the entire contract price. Purchaser deposited the late payments with an escrow holder, but vendor instituted action for the full contract price. Vendor was awarded summary judgment upon his contention that since the notice provision referred to rescission, he retained the option of accelerating the contract without notice or providing an opportunity to remedy the default. *Held:* The interpretation of the clause raises a material issue of fact as to the intention of parties, precluding summary judgment. Since contracts are most strictly constued against the drafter, which is especially true where there is a danger of a forfeiture, an equitable interpretation is to be preferred. *Wingets, Inc. v. Bitters,* 500 P2d 1007 (1972).

75.10 Purchaser's Rights and Duties

California Purchaser made monthly payments for 10 years pursuant to a land contract that also provided that no timber be removed without seller's consent. In 1963, finding that some timber had been taken from the property, purchaser accused seller of being responsible and refused to make further payments. Three years later, seller brought action to quiet title. Purchaser offered to pay the balance of the purchase price, but seller refused to accept the offer, claiming purchaser had forfeited all rights because the contract provided that time was of the essence as to each payment. *Held:* For purchaser. A land contract must be treated like a mortgage. The court will not enforce a forfeiture when the result would be unjust enrichment of the vendor. *MacFadden v. Walker,* 488 P2d 1353 (1971).

Maryland Purchasers of real property executed a contract with the vendor on April 9, 1973. Vendor acquired title to the land on August 7, 1973, and later conveyed to the purchasers on September 16, 1974. Plaintiff obtained a money judgment against vendor on July 31, 1974, and sought to recover from the property in question, maintaining that his rights are prior to purchasers'. *Held:* Affirmed for purchasers. "A contract purchaser holds the equitable title under the contract of sale and has a superior claim to that of a creditor of a seller who obtains a judgment after the date of the contract." *Clarence M. Bull, Inc. v. Goldman,* 353 A2d 661 (Ct. Spec. App. 1976).

Nebraska Developer sued to recover allegedly usurious interest charged on a loan obtained to pay for land on which developer intended to construct an apartment building. The loan was secured by a mortgage on the land. The general rule in Nebraska is that usury is a defense when a lender attempts to collect illegal interest, but it does not permit the borrower to sue to recover the interest once it is paid. However, Nebraska's Installment Loan Act provides an exception and permits a borrower to sue to reclaim usurious interest paid under an "installment loan." Developer argued that all loans payable in installments were governed by the act, and that he could accordingly sue to recover usurious interest from the mortgagee. *Held:* The only loans that were "installment loans" within the meaning of the act were small, high-risk loans of $3,000 or less, where the relatively high interest rate permitted by the act was justified. The act did not control large loans made in connection with a real estate development at a normal interest rate and secured by a mortgage. *Seldin v. Northland Mortgage Co.*, 202 NW2d 174 (1972).

Washington Plaintiff sold forest lands to vendee under a land contract that prohibited logging activity until half of the purchase price had been paid. Vendee promptly sold the timber to a lumber company, using the proceeds to make the down payment. Plaintiff discovered the deception and commenced suit against vendee and the lumber company, seeking, inter alia, treble damages against the latter under the state timber trespass statute. *Held:* The lumber company is not liable under the statute. Plaintiff has a remedy under the statute against purchaser both for the tort of conversion vis-a-vis the timber, as well as for quiet title. The lumber company's liability is limited, however, to reasonable damages under the circumstances. *Bremerton Cent. Lions Club, Inc. v. Manke Lumber Co.*, 604 P2d 1325 (Ct. App. 1979).

75.15 Acceleration of Installments

Colorado Plaintiff purchased defendant's property, which was to be paid for in monthly installments. After 43 payments, plaintiff tendered defendant the total unpaid principal. Defendant refused and demanded instead the total principal plus total remaining interest, and plaintiff paid under protest. At trial, verdict for defendant. *Held:* Affirmed. A purchaser may not compel a seller to accept tender of payments prior to their becoming due and there is no right to prepay in the absence of an express contractual provision. *Carpenter v. Winn*, 566 P2d 370 (Ct. App. 1977).

Michigan A land contract provided that the entire balance could be accelerated, at the option of vendors, if purchasers were in default for 45 days or more. As of January 1, 1984, purchasers were delinquent on five monthly installments. Vendors' lawyer advised purchasers that vendors would foreclose unless the delinquent installments were paid. Purchasers found a buyer for their interest. On January 17, 1984, they closed with the buyer, to whom they assigned their interest, and tendered the delinquency to vendors. Vendors refused to accept the late payment and commenced a foreclosure action. *Held:* Vendors could not exercise their option to accelerate the balance due and foreclose after purchaser made a valid tender of the delinquent installments. It is the rule that a tender of arrears due on a mortgage containing an acceleration clause, made before the holder of the mortgage has exercised his option to declare the entire balance due, prevents the exercise of the acceleration option. This rule, which applies to mortgages, should also apply to foreclosure of a land sale contract. *Sindlinger v. Paul*, 404 NW2d 212 (1987).

Montana Plaintiffs asked the court for a declaratory judgment that would relieve them of any responsibility to accelerate their payments to defendant seller. Plaintiffs entered into a contract for sale of property, one provision of which prevented plaintiff from assigning his interest in the contract without defendant's prior consent. Failure to obtain prior consent would result in a "default" which would automatically acelerate payments. *Held:* The prior consent provision was not an unlawful restraint upon alienation; and plaintiffs, by assigning their contract rights without defendant's consent, committed a "default" allowing defendant to demand acceleration. *Dobitz v. Oakland*, 561 P2d 441 (1977).

Wisconsin Vendors under a land sale contract brought an action for specific performance of the contract pursuant to a clause expressly making time of the essence and providing for acceleration of the indebtedness upon default. Vendee missed one payment, failed to pay real estate taxes, and lost the liquor license on the property. *Held:* The default on one payment was substantial enough to justify an equitable remedy of specific performance for vendor. Any equitable relief otherwise available to vendee was precluded by the failure to pay taxes and loss of the liquor license. *Huntoon v. Capozza,* 204 NW2d 649 (1973).

75.20 Prepayment

California Seller of property wanted to report capital gains by the installment method under IRC § 453. The contract limited payment to 30 percent of the sale price per year and further provided for a penalty in the event of prepayment. Buyers subsequently refinanced the purchase and challenged the validity of the prepayment penalty. *Held:* The clause is valid, and the 50 percent penalty is reasonable considering the increased tax liability that would result. *Williams v. Fassler,* 167 Cal. Rptr. 545 (1980).

Minnesota Parties entered into an earnest money contract that provided that payment would be made under a contract for deed at "not less than" $223.84 per month. When purchasers tendered the full balance and demanded a deed, which vendors declined to deliver, purchasers sued for specific performance. *Held:* Since the terms of the earnest money contract were merged into the contract for deed, the contract for deed governs. The words "not less than" confer upon purchasers an unqualified right to prepay the entire balance. *Peters v. Fenner,* 199 NW2d 795 (1972).

New Mexico Buyers purchased a log cabin designed for single-family use but located in a commercial district. Buyers used it as a recreational second home. Soon after entering into an installment sale contract to purchase the property, buyers notified sellers that they wished to prepay the outstanding balance. Prepayment was not allowed under the contract; however, Section 56-8-30 of the Residential Home Loan Act rendered unenforceable any provision in a loan requiring a prepayment penalty. Buyers sued to have the prepayment provision declared invalid. *Held:* For the buyers. The property was within the scope of the statute, despite its location and the fact that it was not the buyers' primary residence. The contract's complete prohibition of prepayment was an extreme penalty and, thus, forbidden by the statute. *Naumburg v. Pattison,* 711 P2d 1387 (1985).

75.25 Assignments

Tax Court Taxpayer, a partnership, sold real estate for cash and an installment note for $788,000 secured by a deed of trust. On the same day, taxpayer obtained a loan equal to the obligation evidenced by the installment note. The loan was secured by assignment of the installment obligation. The bank loan and installment payments were scheduled to be made at the same times and in approximately the same amounts. Moreover, taxpayer advised its obligor to make payments directly to the bank, which would apply them to the bank loan. The Internal Revenue Service (IRS) argued that taxpayer's transaction effected a sale or other disposition of the installment obligation, and that the gain should be recognized from the sale of real property under Section 453B. The taxpayer contended it merely pledged the obligation as security. *Held:* For taxpayer. The assignment of the installment obligation was not a sale; thus, taxpayer realized no gain. The court relied on previous decisions defining a sale or disposition as the relinquishment of incidents of ownership. The mere entrustment of collateral that occurred here did not fit that definition. Additional evidence that taxpayer did not dispose of the obligation was the structuring of the transaction as a loan and the payment of state income tax by the taxpayer on interest received on the installment obligations. The court rejected the IRS argument regarding the similarity of face amount and payment schedule of the installment obligation and bank loan as indications the installment obligation was sold. *Schaeffer v. Commissioner,* 41 TCM 752 (1981).

Illinois Contract purchasers of commercial real estate assigned their interest in an installment contract to a bank in order to secure certain loans. Purchasers declared bankruptcy and defaulted on the contract and bank loans. The bank obtained an order of abandonment from the bankruptcy trustee, obtained insurance on the property, collected rent, and made payments on the installment contract. Then, apparently deciding to cut its losses, it ceased making payments or collecting rent. Contract sellers sued the bank for the balance due. *Held:* The bank was obligated to pay the balance in return for a warranty deed to the property. Although the assignment did not contain language by which the bank expressly agreed to assume the duties of contract purchasers, it provided that if the bank paid installments without reimbursement from contract purchasers, the bank would be deemed the vendee. This language and the parties' conduct demonstrated that the assignment was intended to transfer assignors' rights and duties under the installment contract to the bank upon default by assignors. *Pelz v. Streator Nat'l Bank,* 496 NE2d 315 (Ct. App. 1986).

Iowa Installment land sale contract contained a provision forbidding purchaser from assigning without the prior written consent of vendor. After the contract was signed, vendee married and executed a written instrument purporting to assign his entire interest to himself and his wife as joint tenants. The instrument was signed and notarized, but never recorded. Vendor did not consent to the assignment in writing, and the testimony was in conflict as to whether vendor had knowledge of the assignment. When vendee defaulted, vendor sent him a notice of forfeiture, but did not name his wife. Vendee claimed that such failure, in light of the assignment, made the notice invalid. *Held:* Since vendor had neither actual nor constructive notice of the assignment, the notice of forfeiture was valid, despite its failure to name the wife. *Hansen v. Chapin,* 232 NW2d 506 (1975).

Kansas Parents agreed to sell real estate to their son and daughter-in-law. The installment contract contained a clause prohibiting assignment of the contract without sellers' written consent. Subsequently, the children took out a loan from a bank secured by delivery of a conditional assignment and transfer of their interest in the land and a mortgage, deed, and security agreement. The bank did not obtain the parents' consent to the assignment. The mortgage and assignment were recorded. When the children filed for bankruptcy under Chapter 7, the bank brought an action to determine the validity of the mortgage. *Held:* The deed to the parents was void and the bank could foreclose. The assignment was valid despite the lack of consent. The court stated that a purchaser under a real estate contract has a property interest that is assignable as security for a debt, despite a provision prohibiting assignment without seller's consent. The court found the contract restriction was solely against assignment of the contract, not against its use as security for a loan. A restriction against assignment is a restraint on alienation, which is strictly construed against the party urging the restriction. *First Bank & Trust v. Novak,* 747 P2d 850 (Ct. App. 1987).

North Dakota The Striegels sold a campground to Bilby under a contract that Bilby later assigned, without obtaining the required consent, to Hillside Trust. Subsequently, the Striegels sought to foreclose and cancel the contract owing to delinquent payment. Bilby claimed he had no interest in the property, having assigned it. Bilby then filed for Chapter 11. A trial court cancelled the deed and awarded the property to the Striegels, leaving the fraud counterclaims to be addressed in further proceedings. Hillside appealed. *Held:* The Striegels were entitled to summary judgment. The pendency of Bilby's bankruptcy was irrelevant, because only property in which Bilby had an interest under state law was affected by the automatic stay. Bilby had disclaimed all interest in the property after the assignment, and did not list it on his schedules. Further, a vendee cannot assert the invalidity of his own assignment against his assignee. *Striegel v. Dakota Hills, Inc.,* 365 NW2d 491 (1985).

75.30 Rescission

Georgia Purchaser who sought to recover a down payment paid pursuant to a land sale contract contended that the contract financing terms were so vague and indefinite as to render the contract void and unenforceable: Purchaser was to arrange permanent financing; if this was not done within 60 days, vendor would attempt to arrange financing with purchaser's cooperation; and if this was not done, purchaser was to begin liquidating the balance of the purchase price at a rate of $1,000 a month with interest at 8 percent per year. *Held:* Judgment for vendor affirmed. Even though purchaser would not acquire legal title until all the deferred payments were made, he would increase his equitable interest in the property with each payment. The legal title to the property would be held by vendor in trust for purchaser, who acquired natural equity in the property with each installment payment. *Horner v. Savannah Valley Enters., Inc.,* 216 SE2d 113 (1975).

Idaho Parties entered into land sale contracts of a substantially identical nature concerning two farms. The contracts stated that vendors would provide title insurance within a reasonable time. Four years later, while title policies were in preparation, purchasers defaulted on the contracts and vendors declared forfeitures pursuant to contract terms. Purchasers then sought rescission, based on the alleged breach of contract due to the failure of vendors to provide title insurance within a reasonable time. *Held:* A precondition of rescission is prompt action on the part of the party seeking rescission to state his intent and treat the contract as no longer in existence. Where a party treats a contract as valid after the appearance of facts that would establish the right to rescind, that right is waived. Since purchasers themselves delayed well beyond a reasonable time in attempting to rescind, they waived their right to do so. *Blinzer v. Andrews,* 485 P2d 157 (1971).

Oregon Purchaser alleged that vendor had breached the agreement by failing to provide a title insurance policy within 10 days of execution as provided in the contract. *Held:* Rescission requires a breach of contract that is "substantial," and that impairs the objects of the parties. The failure to supply title insurance within 10 days was not such a breach. *Shopping Centers of Am., Inc. v. Standard Growth Properties, Inc.,* 509 P2d 1189 (1973).

75.35 Forfeiture

9th Circuit Trustee in bankruptcy sought to quiet title to a building that was allegedly fraudulently transferred to a transferee. The transferee then sold the building to a buyer, who again sold the property by a land sale contract, while still making payments on its own contract with transferee. Trustee was granted summary judgment by the district court, based on the California rule that a purchaser under a land sale contract cannot be a bona fide purchaser until he pays the full purchase price and obtains legal title. *Held:* Reversed. Finding a "gradual erosion of the rigid distinction between legal and equitable title" in California, the court rejected an 1888 California precedent in favor of a 1955 appellate ruling that a purchaser holding equitable title to property is a bona fide purchaser (*Utley v. Smith,* 134 Cal. App. 2d 448 285 P2d 986 (1955)). The former rule would lead to an unfair result, since one who paid all but the last installment under a land sale contract would lose the property, although he had no notice of the prior interest, while a mortgagor under identical circumstances would keep the property. *Perry v. O'Donnell,* 749 F2d 1346 (1984).

Alabama A restaurant was sold under a lease-purchase agreement that provided for purchasers to make monthly rent payments. The rent was due on the first of the month, with a 15-day grace period; and the agreement stated time was of the essence. If purchasers defaulted, all payments, including a $25,000 advance, would be forfeited as liquidated damages. Purchasers missed a payment, and seller declared the lease null and void, demanding return of the premises. Purchasers sued for equitable relief from forfeiture. The trial court denied the requested relief. The agreement, which purchasers' attorney had drafted, made clear that delinquent rent payments would subject lessor to foreclosure. The penalty of forfeiture was not disproportionate to damages suffered as a result of the breach, nor was it unconscionable. *Held:* On appeal, the supreme court quoted extensively from and affirmed the trial judgment. *Taylor v. Jones,* 486 So. 2d 1281 (1986).

California Landowner sold her granddaughter six acres of unimproved land for $9,000, payable at $50 per month. Buyer was free to prepay, and there was no provision making time of the essence or specifying remedies in case of default. Granddaughter missed a number of payments, then ceased paying entirely, although the grandmother depended on the payments financially. Two years after ceasing payments, she sent a check for $250, which the landowner's attorney returned, stating that the landowner elected to terminate the contract. The granddaughter's children, as assignees, sued for specific performance, tendering the entire balance due. *Held:* The granddaughter and her assignees had an absolute right of redemption and exercised it timely. The court stated that where the seller of land retains title as security for amounts payable under an installment sale contract, a vendee who willfully defaults on one or more payments after having paid a substantial part of the purchase price nonetheless retains an absolute right to redeem the property by paying the entire balance due. This right may be exercised as soon as the seller gives notice of election to terminate the contract on account of the default. *Petersen v. Hartell,* 707 P2d 232 (1985).

Illinois Vendor, faced with vendee's default under installment contract for the sale of commercial property, exercised its right to declare forfeiture of the contract. Vendor thereafter sought to recover against defendants as guarantors. Defendants argued that the termination of the sales contract by plaintiff's exercise of forfeiture rights also put an end to their guarantor liability. *Held:* For plaintiff. The contract provided for the guarantors to be liable "notwithstanding any forfeiture'' declared by plaintiff. This clause constituted a waiver of the effect of forfeiture as to the guarantors, and preserved liability regardless of the enforceability of the rest of the contract. At the same time, guarantors' liability is not foreclosed simply because the creditor resold the property at a figure greater than the original sale price. The present action is based solely upon the contract of guaranty, and was not brought to recover damages on the default itself. *Illini Fed. Sav. & Loan Ass'n v. Childers,* 411 NE2d 110 (App. Ct. 1980).

Iowa Buyer, under an installment contract, agreed to pay all real estate taxes accruing against the property, and contract provided for forfeiture, or voiding the contract, if its terms were not met. When buyer defaulted in payment of taxes and seller was required to pay in his stead, seller demanded reimbursement plus interest and served a notice of forfeiture on buyer. Buyer then paid the back taxes, but refused to pay $10.48 in interest and fees for service of the forfeiture notice, despite numerous attempts by seller to collect. *Held:* Seller was entitled to regain possession of the property. Buyer's contention that he should not be penalized for a ''trifling amount'' was beside the point where there were several ''flagrant and deliberate actions'' by buyer that had the effect of voiding the contract. *Miller v. American Wonderlands, Inc.,* 275 NW2d 399 (1979).

Kentucky Buyer agreed to purchase seller's house, and they signed an installment sales contract. The contract contained a forfeiture clause that provided that if buyer failed to make a monthly payment and remained in default for 60 days, seller could terminate and retain all payments as rent and liquidated damages. Buyer missed seven installments during the first 21 months, and seller sued for the money owned plus compensation for taxes and insurance. He also sought enforcement of the forfeiture clause. *Held:* Seller is not entitled to enforce the forfeiture clause. When an installment land contract is used as a means of financing the purchase of property, seller's interest, being bare legal title, constitutes a lien on the property to secure payment. The forfeiture clause was intended simply as security for payment, and the proper remedy for seller is to seek judicial sale of the property if buyer defaults. *Sebastian v. Floyd,* 585 SW2d 381 (1979).

Michigan Plaintiff, seller of property under land contract, gave notice of default to defendant purchaser and commenced a forfeiture action. The case took some six months to come to final judgment, and defendant remained in possession during the entire time. Plaintiff then sought to recover rent for the period of occupancy following the effective date of notice. *Held:* Under the terms of the contract, defendant had no right to possession after forfeiture, and consequently plaintiff was entitled to fair rental value of the premises. Once defendant received notice, any continuing possession amounted to wrongful possession. *Durda v. Chembar Dev. Corp.,* 291 NW2d 179 (1980).

New Mexico Ranch owner sold land to a partnership, which then assigned its interest to borrower. The purchase price was payable in annual installments due April 15. The contract provided that seller could terminate the contract if a default was not cured. Prior to April 15, borrower asked for a postponement. Seller agreed to an extension to July 31, conditioned on borrower's immediate payment of an extra $4,900. Seller's proposal provided that if borrower did not comply at once, seller's letter would serve as notice of default. On May 27, borrower sent a check for $3,132, with a statement that collection of the check would constitute seller's agreement to the extension. By July 31, seller neither approved any extension nor cashed the check. Subsequently, seller attempted to exercise its right of forfeiture, and the escrow agent sought judicial determination of the rights of the parties. *Held:* For seller. The court noted that under the doctrine of accord and satisfaction, retention for an unreasonable time of a borrower's check tendered subject to conditions constitutes an acceptance of the conditions if creditor does not notify borrower of his rejection of the tender. However, in this case no accord and satisfaction took place, because the conditions attached to the check did not provide for full satisfaction of borrower's contractual obligations. *Albuquerque Nat'l Bank v. Albuquerque Ranch Estates, Inc.*, 654 P2d 548 (1982).

Oklahoma Seller sued for a judgment declaring land forfeited under contract of sale when the buyer failed to make the annual payments. The buyer had gone into possession prior to the written contract. Two payments of $1,000 were made before the contract was signed. The day of the contract, buyer paid $1,800 to the seller. On the first annual installment date, buyer paid $1,500 instead of $1,000 as agreed. *Held:* The sellers were entitled to recover the property and retain moneys paid as liquidated damages. The two $1,000 payments were rent or interest on the purchase price. These credits along with the $1,800 constituted the down payment. The first annual payment was made, but with an overpayment credited to the next annual payment. The balance of that payment was never made. *Crowell v. Whitmere*, 548 P2d 221 (1976).

Utah Purchaser under installment land contract fell into default and promptly received written notice, as required under the agreement, giving him 15 days within which to cure the delinquency. After 15 days had passed, seller delivered a second notice, and after yet another notice purchaser tendered a check in the full amount of the arrearage, including 18 percent interest. However, seller claimed to be entitled to foreclosure and also asserted that interest was due on the unpaid balance of the purchase price, citing language in the agreement calling for interest to be paid on "amounts unpaid under the contact." *Held:* Case remanded for further proceedings. Although contract gave seller a clear right of forfeiture that matured 15 days after the first notice, the subsequent renotifications revived the purchaser's right to cure default with timely payment. The court also found that the disputed language was ambiguous and ordered the trial court to consider whether it refers solely to interest on delinquent amounts or on the entire amount of the debt. *Grow v. Marwich Dev., Inc.*, 621 P2d 1249 (1980).

Washington Installment contract prohibited prepayment and assignment or conveyance without seller's consent. When buyer contracted to sell it without seller's consent, seller sued for forfeiture of the contract. *Held:* Seller is not entitled to forfeiture. The provisions in the contract prohibiting assignment or conveyance without the seller's consent constituted an unreasonable and unenforceable restraint on alienation, unless the seller could prove that it was necessary to protect his security. *Terry v. Born*, 604 P2d 504 (1979).

76.00 BUILD-TO-SUIT CONTRACTS

76.05
In General

California The contract to build a home specified a completion date of April 17, 1973, and provided time was of the essence, except for "excusable delays." The home had to be completed by the stated date so that buyers could save capital gains tax on the sale of their former home. The new home was not finished until September, and buyers sued developer. *Held:* The court refused to overturn a jury's verdict that construction delays could not be excused, and allowed compensatory damages of $8,414. Developer had repeatedly assured buyers that the house would be completed on time, but then failed to satisfactorily account for delays. In view of this, the award of $215,000 in punitive damages, based on the wealth of the developer, was justified. *Walker v. Signal Cos., Inc.,* 149 Cal. Rptr. 119 (Ct. App. 1978).

Indiana Lumber company entered into an agreement with owner to provide a floor package at cost if it could also supply all materials necessary for construction of the owner's residence. Owner employed contractor at lumber company's suggestion. The lumber company understood that it would be paid when the job was completed. In fact, the owner made partial payments to the contractor; however, lumber company did not receive any payments. The contractor subsequently filed for bankruptcy and owner completed the project on his own. Lumber company sued for compensation for materials provided for the home construction. *Held:* Lumberyard was entitled to payment from owners, on the theory of unjust enrichment, for materials used in home after owners took over from bankrupt contractor, but not for materials previously used for which property owner had paid contractor. Unjust enrichment was justified because the owner dealt directly with lumber company, promised to pay lumber company, and owner stepped into the shoes of the contractor. Lumber company reasonably expected owner to pay for the materials and therefore made no effort to prevent owner from using materials already delivered to the site but not yet built into the structure. *Stafford v. Barnard Lumber Co.,* 531 NE2d 202 (1988).

Minnesota Construction company contracted with landowner to build townhouses on its property. Following the completion of the first phase of construction, a dispute arose concerning company'sworkmanship.Arbitrators,aspartof their award, ordered the company to purchase the property on which the buildings were located. Company argued that the arbitration award exceeded the arbitrators' power and violated the Statute of Frauds. *Held:* Arbitrators who fashioned the award, which was equitable in nature, did not exceed the powers delegated to them by the arbitration clause. The extent and magnitude of the construction defects, the repeated noncompliance with contractual obligations, and numerous building code violations combined to produce a building of little value and exposed landowner to future liabilities, justifying the novel remedy. The arbitration award did not violate the Statute of Frauds, because it ordered the conveyance of the property clear of liens by landowner, upon company's payment of damages. *David Co. v. Jim W. Miller Constr., Inc.,* 444 NW2d 836 (1989).

Oregon Several condominium unit purchasers complained that their lots were severely damaged by erosion from the ocean. They argued that the developers were liable for the damage because they had represented themselves as highly skilled and competent in establishing resort communities. Developers maintained that they could not be held responsible for the wearing away of the land, since this was something they were powerless to control. *Held:* Although developers could not guarantee the property against latent defects, they could be held liable for negligence in their site selection for the development. The erosion was in no sense the result of developers' work on the property. Purchasers' problem had to do with the inherent nature of the land. There was no implied warranty concerning the nature or quality of the lots themselves. However, developers, who represented themselves as resort experts, could be liable for their negligence in failing to take reasonable precautions to make sure the lots were suitable for residential condominium units. The case was sent back to the lower court for trial on that issue. *Beri, Inc. v. Salishan Properties, Inc.*, 580 P2d 173 (1978).

Texas Developer of apartment project entered into a contract under which the builder was to construct and, for a short period of time, to manage the property. The agreement stipulated that the builder was to assume all operating expenses during the management period and to retain the net earnings. The contract provided for proration of taxes. A dispute arose over the taxes and the proper treatment of forfeited security deposits. *Held:* Under the terms of the contract, taxes were treated separately from other items of expense; however, seller was liable to pay taxes for the management period. The security deposit issue was resolved in favor of the developer, the court holding that forfeited deposits were neither income nor "cash flow," since they were subject to outstanding contingencies under the contracts. *Skyland Dev., Inc. v. Sky Harbor Assoc.*, 586 SW2d 564 (Civ. App. 1979).

76.10 Builder/Vendor's Warranties

Alabama Buyer purchased a new house constructed by builder. The septic system for the house was built by a subcontractor and conformed to applicable guidelines set by the Farmers Home Administration, which financed the house. Almost six years after the purchase, the septic tank malfunctioned and buyer brought an action against builder, alleging breach of the implied warranty of fitness and habitability. Builder argued that no such warranty existed since it would make him, in effect, an insurer of the house against any future unforeseen problems. *Held:* The failure of the sewage system was a breach of an implied warranty. The court overruled previous Alabama cases and applied the general rule for the implied warranty of fitness and habitability. The house was sold in a defective condition that the buyers were neither aware of nor could have reasonably discovered and that adversely affected the value of the house. *Sims v. Lewis*, 374 So. 2d 298 (1979).

Illinois Buyers contracted with a builder to construct a new house for them. After completion of the construction, buyers became dissatisfied and refused to accept the house, asserting a number of defects. Builder, invoking a contract forfeiture provision, notified buyers that they had forfeited both their deposit and $9,000 spent on labor and materials. Buyers sued under the contract, but builder argued that the defects did not render the house unfit for habitation and buyers must accept it. *Held:* Buyers are entitled to recover their deposit and the value of labor and materials. Under the implied warranty of habitability, a house must reasonably be suitable for its intended use and not merely fit for habitation. *Petersen v. Hubschman Constr. Co.*, 389 NE2d 1154 (1979).

New Jersey Purchasers of a new house discovered that the water supply was impure and brought suit against the builder-vendor for breach of an implied warranty of habitability. The builder-vendor argued that, as a "small-scale" developer, he should not be held to the same standard as a mass developer, and furthermore, the impure water supply was not due to any substandard construction on his part. *Held:* Where a builder-vendor constructs a new house, the implied warranty of habitability applies whether or not he is a mass developer. A potable water supply is included in the implied warranty, whether or not it was due to builder's substandard construction. *McDonald v. Mianecki,* 398 A2d 1283 (1979).

West Virginia Builder constructed a home and sold it in 1975. In 1979, builder acted as the real estate agent for homeowners and sold the home to second purchaser. Shortly after purchasers moved in, heavy rains flooded the house and significantly damaged the property. Efforts to solve the flooding problem proved fruitless because of how and where the house was constructed. Purchasers sued builder for breach of the warranty of habitability and fitness. *Held:* A builder's implied warranty of habitability and fitness is extended to a second purchaser. Subsequent purchasers are protected by the warranty for latent defects for a reasonable length of time after construction. Latent defects are those that appear after purchase and are not discoverable through reasonable inspection. *Sewell v. Gregory,* 371 SE2d 82 (1988).

76.15 Builder/Vendor's Liability for Fraud

Kansas Purchasers brought an action against developer, alleging fraudulent concealment of a soil defect. Each homeowner had selected sites in the development and had entered into agreements with contractors, who in turn purchased lots from the developer. After the homes had been constructed, it was discovered that the land had a high salt content, and nothing would grow. *Held:* Lack of privity does not bar an action for fraud where the purchasers are essentially the class of persons that developer intended to reach. A duty to disclose extends not just to persons with whom developer immediately deals, but to all those who would be expected to act or refrain in reliance on the misrepresentation. *Griffith v. Byers Constr. Co.,* 510 P2d 198 (1973).

South Carolina Purchasers of land brought suit against developer when the houses they bought began to sink. Upon investigation, it was discovered that developer had filled a large gully with debris and capped it with clay so that the land appeared level and had not informed the purchasers of this. *Held:* Seller's nondisclosure of a latent defect that he knew the purchasers could not discover is actionable fraud. *Lawson v. Citizens & So. Nat'l Bank,* 193 SE2d 124 (1972).

Texas Purchaser of residential housing counterclaimed against contractor alleging, inter alia, violation of the state Deceptive Trade Practices Act. *Held:* No claim under the act is cognizable where the contractor has effected substantial performance. Substantial performance negates the claim of deceptive practices where such performance of essential conditions under the contract has been done in a workmanlike manner. *Baldwin v. Smith,* 586 SW2d 624 (Civ. App. 1979).

76.20 Interstate Land Sales Full Disclosure Act

5th Circuit Purchasers of properties in a development sued developer's agent to rescind their contracts and recover the purchase price on the ground that the sale violated the Interstate Land Sales Full Disclosure Act. The master plan of the development described extensive recreational facilities, and the project report distributed to prospective buyers stated that completion of the project depended on satisfactory land sales and the ability of developer to obtain adequate financing. *Held:* The Interestate Land Sales Full Disclosure Act authorizes suits against developers of projects, and not against developers' agents. Also, purchasers' suit could not be maintained, because purchasers did not show that the property report lacked factual substance or that it misrepresented the facts. *Paquin v. Four Seasons, Inc.,* 519 F2d 1105 (1975).

U.S. District Court, Illinois A group of 328 buyers joined in a lawsuit against developer of an Illinois subdivision and developer's lender, alleging misrepresentations in violation of securities laws and the Interstate Land Sales Full Disclosure Act. Buyers contended that the bank went beyond mere financing of the project and actually actively aided and abetted developer. The bank moved to dismiss the suit, arguing that it was merely acting in the normal course of its business in lending money to developer. *Held:* Purchasers were entitled to try to show by evidence at a trial that the bank exceeded normal financing practices, actively participated in a fraudulent scheme, or otherwise assisted in the luring of buyers for a dubious project. *Timmreck v. Munn,* 433 F. Supp. 396 (ND 1977).

Texas Plaintiff brought action to rescind contract to purchase modular home, alleging that defendants had fraudulently misrepresented the cost of building the home and, also, had violated the Interstate Land Sales Full Disclosure Act by stating in their property report that no special foundation work was needed when, in fact, the ground had to be leveled by the use of piers and beams in order to build the house. *Held:* In order to prove that a promise for the future, i.e., estimated cost to build a home, constituted fraud, one must be able to show that at the time of the representation there was intention to misrepresent. Plaintiff presented no evidence that defendant had intentionally misrepresented cost at the time when the contract was signed. There was no violation of the act. (See Section 43.31.) *NRC Inc. v. Huckabee,* 539 SW2d 375 (Civ. App. 1976).

76.25
Contractor Licensing Requirements

Arizona An unlicensed subcontractor who performed stucco work on residential structures being built on a Navajo reservation sued the contractor to recover money allegedly due him. The contractor argued that an unlicensed subcontractor lacks standing to sue to recover for work performed, citing Ariz. Rev. Stat. Ann. § 32-1153. *Held:* For the subcontractor. The U.S. Supreme Court held in *White Mountain Apache Tribe v. Bracker,* 448 US 136 (1980) that when the state seeks to assert authority over the conduct of non-Indians on an Indian reservation, an inquiry must be made into whether the exercise of state authority would unduly impinge on some federal purpose. Here, application of state licensing requirements to reservation construction would interfere with the Navajo Housing Authority's attempt to secure work at the lowest cost. Further, it was not clear that the statute applied to construction on Indian reservations. *Kenyon v. Karber Constr. Co.,* 698 P2d 1295 (Ct. App. 1985).

South Carolina Contractor sued to recover payment for its construction of an indoor swimming pool and surrounding sunroom added to a residence. The contractor had only an out-of-state license when construction began; however, he obtained the proper state license before construction was finished. *Held:* The contractor violated S.C. Code Ann. § 40-59-130 by entering into a contract for home construction without the required license, and could not enforce the contract. Construction of a swimming pool and sunroom was properly classified as residential home building for purposes of the statute. *Columbia Pools, Inc. v. Moon,* 325 SE2d 540 (1985).

77.00 SPECIFIC PERFORMANCE

77.05 Purchaser's Right to Specific Performance

California After accepting a purchase offer from the Grimsgaards, seller accepted a "back-up offer" from the Meadowses, contracting to sell his house to them for the same amount in case of termination or novation of the contract with the Grimsgaards. The original contract allowed for closing as late as March 21, 1978, to allow purchasers to sell their property. In January, the contract was altered to remove the condition that the Grimsgaards' property be sold first. In April, seller entered into a "hold harmless" agreement with the Grimsgaards and agreed to accept their property and a note and deed of trust in place of the sale price. After the sale-exchange closed, the Meadowses sued the seller for specific performance of the back-up agreement. They alleged that the contract with the Grimsgaards had expired when closing did not occur by March 21 and that execution of the hold harmless and exchange agreements in April constituted novations. *Held:* For seller. At issue was whether the Grimsgaards and seller intended to terminate and/or novate the original contract, or merely to modify it. Since the original parties never intended to cancel their agreement, and there was no showing of fraud or collusion against third parties, the court upheld the trial court judgment. *Meadows v. Lee,* 221 Cal. Rptr. 22 (Ct. App. 1985).

Connecticut Parties entered into an agreement concerning a piece of property. When defendants refused to convey the property, plaintiff sued for specific performance. Defendants claimed they had no obligation to convey because the agreement was merely an option, not a bilateral purchase and sale contract. *Held:* Plaintiff was entitled to specific performance. The following factors indicated that the agreement was a purchase and sale agreement: (1) The agreement referred to the parties as purchaser and seller rather than as optioner and optionee; (2) it included a provision obligating plaintiff to purchase the property; (3) it was devoid of any language granting plaintiff an option; (4) plaintiff rarely took options on property; (5) letters exchanged by the parties' attorneys indicated that the agreement was for purchase and sale; and (6) closing documents were attached to the agreement. The fact that the agreement was titled "Option Agreement" did not mandate a determination that the agreement was an option contract; the heading did not reflect the actual intent of the parties and the title was the only place the word "option" appeared. *Cutter Dev. Corp. v. Peluso,* 561 A2d 926 (1989).

Connecticut Plaintiff shopping center developer sued defendant for specific performance of an option contract for a corner parcel of land, without which the latter could not construct a planned shopping center. Defendant refused to sell the land, because the value had risen substantially above the exercise price of the option; but both parties knew when entering into the contract that if developer got the required change in zoning, the land would have a substantially higher value. *Held:* Specific performance was the appropriate remedy where the corner parcel was essential for building the shopping center, and without which the value of the contiguous parcels purchased would be diminished by almost twice the amount of damages to which plaintiff would be entitled. *Robert Lawrence Assocs. v. Del Vecchio,* 420 A2d 1142 (1979).

Florida Restauranteur sought to purchase rented premises from lessor, a cooperative association of residential tenants. The association agreed to sell the property provided that the Department of Housing and Urban Development (HUD), which guaranteed the cooperative's mortgage, agreed to release the restaurant premises from the mortgage. HUD rejected the application. The restauranteur negotiated on his own with HUD and presented several alternative means of obtaining the requisite approval. When the association refused to pursue the alternatives, restauranteur sued for specific performance. *Held:* For the restauranteur. Members of the board of the association had information at the time the proposal was formulated that it would not meet HUD requirements. In addition, outvoted members of the association had mounted a letter-writing campaign against the transaction that the board had done little to counter. These circumstances raised doubt as to whether the application was pursued diligently. The court concluded that the board's refusal to consider alternatives established a failure to make a good faith effort to obtain consent. *Galt View Apartments, Inc. v. Fazio,* 490 So. 2d 1005 (Dist. Ct. App. 1986).

Florida Contract for purchase of condominium unit provided that, in the event of a default by developer, purchasers' only remedy would be to terminate the agreement and receive a refund of their deposit. Developer, however, in the event of a default by purchasers, had the right to retain the deposit or to pursue any other legal or equitable remedies. Developer defaulted, and purchasers sued for specific performance. *Held:* Purchasers were entitled to specific performance. The contract limitation on purchasers' remedy was unreasonable and unenforceable. The contract effectively provided no reasonable remedy for its breach by developer. Developer's obligations under the contract were illusory, since it could opt to sell the unit to any new buyer willing to pay a higher price than the existing contract with no harmful consequences. Merely returning purchasers' deposit after depriving them of the use of the money for several years did not constitute damages and was unconscionable. *Ocean Dunes v. Colangelo,* 463 So. 2d 437 (Dist. Ct. App. 1985).

Georgia Transaction for the sale of land included a security deed to secure buyer's debt. One provision of the security deed required seller to release 20 percent of the property from the deed at the time of the closing. Nearly two years after closing, buyer demanded a release under this provision; seller refused. Buyer then sued seller for specific performance of the release provision. At the time of the suit, buyer defaulted on a substantial interest payment. The trial court entered a directed verdict against buyer as to the prayer for specific performance. Arguing that the release provision was part of a severable contract that he had fully performed on his part, buyer appealed. *Held:* Buyer is not entitled to specific performance. Although the land was to be released from the security deed in proportion to the amount of principal paid, the court found that the contract was entire, not severable, because its subject was a single, undivided tract of land. However, the court also held that buyer was entitled to a jury verdict on the issue of damages caused by seller's breach of the release provision. *Dozier v. Shirley,* 239 SE2d 343 (1977).

Hawaii Defendants agreed to sell their land to the Brauns, evidenced by a standard form executory contract. The contract stated time was of the essence in closing, scheduled for October 1, 1977. Because of a disagreement, the contract never closed. Plaintiffs then offered to purchase the property. The parties signed a contract, but with an addendum stating that defendants had a prior contract with the Brauns and plaintiffs could not bring an action for specific performance if the Brauns prevented closing. Closing was set for January 1, 1978. The second contract did not contain a time-of-the-essence clause. The Brauns now threatened to sue if their contract was not closed. Defendants refused a requested extension by plaintiffs of the closing date to August 1, and refused to proceed with closing. Plaintiffs sued for specific performance. *Held:* For plaintiffs. The absence of a time-of-the-essence clause in the second contract clearly showed the parties chose not to make performance by the stated date essential. To hold defendants to their agreement for several months was not unreasonable, and to deny plaintiffs the benefit of their bargain would be inequitable. *Freeman v. Boyce,* 661 P2d 702 (1983).

Illinois Plaintiff sought to purchase defendant's building. The parties agreed on a purchase price to be paid over 10 years with interest. A handwritten statement was added to the offer-to-purchase form, stating that the offer was subject to seller's approval of buyer's credit report. Realtors present at the negotiations later testified that defendant indicated he would convey the property at contract terms if he received a favorable credit report on plaintiff. This was forwarded, but defendant refused to convey and sought to raise the purchase price. Plaintiff sued for specific performance. *Held:* For plaintiff. Where a satisfaction clause is added as an inducement for seller to sign a contract, seller must be allowed a free, subjective evaluation of buyer's credit. The personal judgment standard, however, must be exercised in good faith. Defendant's attempt to renegotiate the contract after receiving a favorable credit report demonstrated that his ultimate rejection, based on the satisfaction clause, was in bad faith. *Forman v. Benson,* 446 NE2d 535 (1983).

Indiana A Veterans of Foreign Wars post that listed property for sale informed the broker that post trustees were authorized to sell the property. Plaintiff and two trustees had entered into a contract when the parties were informed that the corporation, not the post, held title. The corporation's board of directors, several of whom were also trustees, authorized the sale. Plaintiff had ordered a survey, retained architects, and begun work when he was told the contract had to be approved by the general membership. Floor approval was not obtained, the property never conveyed, and plaintiff sued for specific performance. The post and corporation argued no enforceable contract was made, because the trustees had no authority. *Held:* For plaintiff. The court described this as a "classic situation that equitable estoppel was designed to redress." Plaintiff negotiated with post trustees for three months with no mention of a corporation, trustees made express assurances they were authorized to sell, and trustees had apparent authority to do so. The corporation's board ratified the contract, and floor approval was not disclosed. In reliance, plaintiff changed his financial position. *Kokomo Veterans Inc. v. Schick,* 439 NE2d 639 (Ct. App. 1982).

Iowa Sellers listed their land with Davitt Realty to be sold at $750 per acre, firm.

The listing agreement provided that the property could be multiple-listed. Buyers learned of the property from a broker who was not a member of the multiple-listing service. A member had illegally told the broker of the sellers' land. The broker obtained an offer from buyers to purchase the land for $500 per acre. Sellers, who mistakenly assumed broker was from Davitt Realty and that the contract price was $750 per acre, signed the agreement. When sellers refused to convey the land, buyers sued for specific performance. *Held:* Buyers' motion for specific performance denied, because the balance of equities was in sellers' favor. Under Iowa law, one who signs an agreement is bound by it, and is precluded from claiming he did not read it. However, if he was induced to sign without reading owing to a misrepresentation, he is not estopped from denying the agreement's validity. The broker's conduct toward sellers was wrongful and fraudulent; such conduct was attributable to buyers with whom broker had an agency relationship. Sellers were therefore granted the right of rescission so as to restore the status quo. *Bauman v. Nutter,* 328 NW2d 354 (Ct. App. 1982).

Maryland A contract of sale described the property as 16,000 square feet more or less but stated that the contract was contingent upon completion of a survey. After the contract was signed, a survey showed an area of 22,047 square feet. Vendor demanded an increase in the purchase price, and buyers sued, asking that the sales agreement be declared valid and enforceable. *Held:* Buyers were entitled to specific performance of the sales contract that incorrectly stated the square footage of the property. The sale was one in gross since the property was described by definite boundaries, and the contract used words of qualification. Thus, the statement of square footage was mere description and not of the essence. The buyer's estimate of square footage gained by pacing off the lot did not give rise to fraud justifying rescission since buyers did not know with certainty that the lot contained more than 16,000 square feet. Nor was there mutual mistake, since buyers did not make a knowing or negligent misrepresentation as to size of the lot. *Steele v. Goettee,* 542 A2d 847 (Ct. App. 1988).

Montana Purchasers of subdivision parcels sued owner-developer to specifically enforce promises made in the subdivision plat that roadways be constructed. *Held:* For purchasers. The fact that vendor's sales agents had made representations that roads would be built and the plat designated roadways was sufficient to require vendor to perform specifically. Mere designation of roadways in plats does not give rise to a promise to build. In this case, sales agents had made actual representations that the roads would be constructed by vendor. The obligations generated by the sales contract were sufficiently definite to support specific performance since the plats designated the route, location, and width of the roadways. *Majers v. Shining Mountains,* 750 P2d 449 (1988).

Nebraska Seller agreed to sell an unimproved tract for $14,875. As part of the purchase agreement, he promised to obtain the release of a "right-of-way" easement across the lot, to arrange at his own expense to relocate a buried gasline that crossed the property, and to pave a street abutting the lot. On learning that the cost of relocating the gasline alone would be $10,050, seller sought to persuade buyer to accept another lot. Buyer sued for specific performance. *Held:* Buyer was entitled to specific performance. Real estate is considered to be unique by law, and the availability of similar or superior land is not a defense to specific performance. An imprudent or bad bargain is not of itself an excuse for nonperformance of a contract. While hardship due to unforeseeable circumstances might excuse a party from performance, in the instant case, complete information about the cost of relocating the gasline was available to seller when he entered the contract. Seller's belated realization of the financial burden imposed was not hardship. *Mohrlang v. Draper,* 365 NW2d 443 (1985).

Nebraska Defendant entered into an agreement to sell a certain parcel of land. Buyer assigned the contract to a new purchaser, who then executed an amendment fixing the closing date for February 25, 1977. Shortly thereafter, seller entered into a contract to sell the same parcel to a different buyer in the event that the first transaction did not close on or before February 25, 1977. On that date, the first buyer's assignee appeared, but the transaction was not closed; seller claimed that assignee lacked sufficient funds, while assignee claimed that seller's title was defective. The second buyer demanded enforcement of the second contract. Both purchasers went to court, each demanding specific performance of his contract. *Held:* Because all parties knew of the second contract, the first deal was required to close on February 25, 1977 or a reasonable time thereafter. Because assignee had not tendered the purchase price within a reasonable time, the court ordered specific performance of the second buyer's contract. *Tedco Dev. Corp. v. Overland Hills, Inc.,* 266 NW2d 56 (1978).

New York A limitation-of-liability clause of a contract became effective only if seller was unable to convey in accordance with the terms of the contract. The contract provided that purchaser could declare the contract null and void if seller could not make the second floor available by May 15, 1979. Purchaser was also given the right to extend the May 15 date at its sole option without rending the contract null and void. Nothing in the contract made time of the essence. Thus, the second floor's unavailability would not make seller unable to convey in accordance with the contract if purchaser exercised its option to extend the date for second floor vacancy. In that event, the limitation-of-liability clause would offer seller no protection. Purchaser indicated in a letter that it intended to sue for specific performance if the second floor was not vacated by September 6, 1979. *Held:* Purchaser was entitled to sue for specific performance. Its suit did not constitute a refusal to close title, nor did it make time of the essence. An action for specific performance was in affirmation of the contract. Purchaser was simply insisting upon what it contracted for. *Judnick Realty Corp. v. 32 W. 32nd St. Corp.,* 462 NE2d 131 (1984).

New York Seller claimed she could rescind a real estate sales contract, since purchasers had not accepted a firm commitment from a bank for an option to take a mortgage within the time required by the sales contract. Purchasers, in an action for specific performance, claimed that they had arranged with seller for an extension of the time for acceptance. *Held:* Purchasers had a right to specific performance of the sales contract because they had obtained the commitment within the extension period agreed upon by both parties. Seller would not be allowed to rescind the contract because of purchasers' reliance on an extension of time for acceptance given by seller herself. *Livoti v. Mallon,* 438 NYS2d 81 (1981).

North Carolina A developer orally promised to construct a paved access road and dredge a channel for boat access. Restrictive covenants provided for purchasers to take over maintenance of the road and boat channel when four lots had been sold, and plats showed a road built to state specifications. Developers finished most of the work on the road and the channel, but neither was completed. Purchasers sued for specific performance. *Held:* For purchasers. A developer may not, by use of recorded plats and restrictive covenants, create the illusion of a high-quality subdivision and then shield itself from responsibility for constructing such amenities. Developer was required to construct the road as described in the plats and to dredge the channel to the depth at which the restrictive covenants required purchasers to "maintain" it. *Lyerly v. Malpass,* 346 SE2d 254 (Ct. App. 1986).

Oregon Buyer and seller executed an earnest-money agreement, which included clauses covering purchase price, interest rate, annual payments, and other items. An addendum provided that a land sale contract would be prepared by seller's attorney; buyer could then sign the agreement or reject it and have his deposit refunded. Buyer later rejected the sale contract as prepared by seller's attorney because many items contradicted the express provisions of the earnest-money agreement. Buyer sued for specific performance of the sale based on the terms of the earnest-money agreement, rather than on the sale contract. *Held:* The earnest-money agreement was a preliminary document only and could not be enforced. The court said that an earnest-money document could represent the complete agreement or could be merely a "bargain in rough form." The court went on to find that because these parties had stated that the final agreement would be prepared by seller's attorney, the first document was merely preliminary and unenforceable. *Higgins v. Bonnett,* 580 P2d 180 (1978).

Pennsylvania Appellant purchased a lot adjacent to a proposed lake and built a cottage overlooking the yet unconstructed lake. Developer filed for bankruptcy and reached a settlement with other property owners in the appellant's community to substitute a recreational area for the proposed lake. Appellant sued for specific performance of the original agreement and to enjoin performance of the settlement agreement. *Held:* The balance of equities did not require specific performance of the agreement. The agreement to build the lake was collateral to the sale of appellant's lot and was analogous to an affirmative real covenant between a common grantor and a purchaser of a single lot in a subdivision. Appellant had no estate in developer's retained land, merely a beneficial right that was contractual in nature. The trial court's refusal of specific performance was justified in view of the facts of the case. *Petry v. Tanglewood Lakes, Inc.,* 522 A2d 1053 (1987).

Texas Buyers and sellers executed an earnest-money contract for the sale of property, and buyer deposited $10,000 as a down payment. The agreement provided that buyers were to assume the sellers' first lien mortgage or, if they were unable to obtain approval for assumption, then the parties would enter into a contract for a deed. After failure to consummate the sale, buyers sued for specific performance or, alternatively, the return of their $10,000 down payment. *Held:* Buyers were not entitled to specific performance or return of the down payment. Buyers had not even attempted to secure approval for assumption of the first lien mortgage; therefore, they had breached the contract and were entitled to no relief. Sellers were entitled to keep the $10,000 down payment in liquidated damages under the contract. *McDaniel v. Kudlik,* 598 SW2d 350 (1980).

Utah Purchasers sued for specific performance of an oral contract, and vendor answered that the contract could not be enforced on the ground that it was too indefinite. Purchasers had made a down payment, assumed the mortgage, and made payments for 12 years. *Held:* Specific performance was awarded. A court of equity will not allow a party to accept performance over a period of years and then defeat a suit for specific performance on an assertion of indefiniteness. *Woolsey v. Brown,* 539 P2d 1035 (1975).

Virginia A contract providing for a sale in gross of "463 acres more or less" gave purchaser the right to survey the property prior to closing. If a survey was performed, the sale price was to be adjusted by $1,000 per acre, up or down. Purchaser, unwilling to pay for a full survey, asked a surveyor to estimate the acreage without determining the exact bounds of the property. The surveyor estimated that the contract acreage was very close to accurate. Seller, however, learning of the surveyor's activity, refused to perform without a complete survey. After attempts at conciliation failed and seller still refused to close, purchaser sued for specific performance. *Held:* For purchaser. Purchaser made a proper tender of performance before the closing date and was willing to perform in accordance with the contract for a sale in gross. Purchaser was not obligated to convert a sale in gross to a sale by the acre by supplying a complete survey. *Scott v. Sutherland,* 327 SE2d 78 (1985).

77.10
Seller's Right to Specific Performance

Louisiana Seller accepted $500 from purchaser and, in a document that only seller signed, agreed in return to sell his interest in a well and a lease for $70,000 cash. He also promised to return the $500 if title proved defective. Purchaser later refused to complete the sale because of an alleged error in the description. Seller sued for specific performance, which a trial court granted. *Held:* The agreement was a conditional agreement to sell, not a contract of sale. Under Louisiana law, any deposit made pursuant to a contract to sell is earnest money. The giving of earnest money is equivalent to a stipulation for liquidated damages, barring the remedy of specific performance. In the absence of a provision in the contract to sell, which would reserve the right to specific performance, seller had no right to specific performance. *Bounds v. Makar,* 493 So. 2d 268 (Ct. App. 1986).

Minnesota Buyers had defaulted on a payment due under a contract of sale. When sellers sent a 60-day statutory notice of cancellation, buyers sued, claiming their down payment entitled them to a release of acreage under the contract. Judgment was obtained that buyers were not entitled to a release of acreage and had 15 days to cure the default; otherwise the contract would terminate. Before the 15 days elapsed, however, sellers notified buyers that they were revoking the notice of cancellation and would hold buyers to the contract. Buyers sued to terminate the contract. *Held:* For sellers. The contract did not preclude revocation by seller, since it was silent as to sellers' rights to revoke the notice of cancellation, merely stating that the contract would terminate unless the default was cured. Nor did the doctrine of election of remedies bar revocation, since buyers failed to show that they had detrimentally relied on sellers' earlier election of termination or that sellers had pursued that remedy to a conclusion. *Kosbau v. Dress,* 400 NW2d 106 (Ct. App. 1987).

Montana Nicholson purchased real property from Hidden Valley Ranches under a contract for deed that was subsequently purchased by Aveco. When Nicholson missed an installment payment, Aveco sent a notice of default, but Nicholson failed to cure within the default period. A year later, Aveco notified Nicholson that it intended to declare the principal balance and accrued interest due and payable. Aveco sought specific performance of the contract, compelling Nicholson to pay the full amount due. *Held:* Specific performance affirmed. The contract for deed was not a mortgage under Montana law and did not require mortgage foreclosure procedures. Since a contract for deed and a mortgage are different legal concepts under Montana law, a contract for deed need not be treated as a mortgage for purpose of foreclosure. Aveco was entitled to acceleration of payments, sale of the property if Nicholson failed to pay the remaining balance, and a deficiency judgment if the sale proceeds were insufficient to pay the monies owed. *Aveco Properties, Inc. v. Nicholson,* 747 P2d 1358 (1987).

South Dakota Buyers agreed to purchase a house, contingent upon their obtaining a "13 percent conventional loan." Buyers learned that local lenders were not offering 30-year fixed-rate loans at 13 percent interest, as they interpreted the phrase. Nonetheless, buyers assured the broker that they intended to go through with the purchase. When their application for a 13 percent state housing authority loan was denied, buyers told the broker they did not intend to close. Buyers refused a loan from a bank for a 13 percent mortgage with a term of less than 30 years. Buyers then bought another home at 11.75 percent with a seven-year term. Sellers sued for specific performance. *Held:* For sellers. The phrase "13 percent conventional loan" was not too ambiguous to award specific performance. Local bankers testified that a "conventional loan" was a loan from a local lending agency not guaranteed by a governmental agency. Buyers' contention that a long-term loan was implied was belied by their obtaining a seven-year loan two months later. *Wiggins v. Shewmake,* 374 NW2d 111 (1985).

77.15 Mutuality of Remedy

California An agreement to sell land contained a liquidated damages clause that provided that seller's sole remedy for buyers' failure to perform would be possession of all plans and reports. Seller expressly waived the right to specific performance. Buyers expressly promised to pursue their obligations diligently and to refrain from unreasonably withholding their approval. Buyers sued seller for specific performance when seller refused to proceed under the terms of the agreement. Seller argued that the agreement was void because it imposed no legal obligation on buyers and that seller's waiver of specific performance precluded either party from seeking specific performance. *Held:* Buyers were entitled to specific performance. There was mutuality of obligation, since buyers had an express obligation to proceed in good faith and diligence. As to remedy, the fact that specific enforcement is not available to one party is not reason to refuse it to the other. *Bleecher v. Conte,* 698 P2d 1154 (1981) (en banc).

Georgia Plaintiff sought specific performance of a contract that provided that there was a defect in the title to the property because the U.S. government held a reservation of mineral interest and that the closing date would be 30 days after the government reported whether it would release its interest. The parties later agreed in writing that the closing would take place 10 days following receipt of the government report. After receiving a quitclaim deed for the mineral interest, defendant refused to convey, contending that the contract was unenforceable due to lack of mutuality. *Held:* The meeting of the condition precedent (i.e., the quitclaim deed from the government) cured any lack of mutuality that might have existed. Plaintiff had no right to specific performance prior to the government's release, but the right matured after the conveyance. *Moore v. Buiso,* 221 SE2d 414 (1975).

Missouri Contract for the sale of real property was contingent on vendee's obtaining a $22,500 loan on terms acceptable to him, at an interest rate not to exceed 7.5 percent for a period of not less than 25 years. When vendee attempted to obtain specific performance, vendor contended that the contract was void for want of mutuality of obligation, since the "buyer approval" clause rendered the contract illusory. *Held:* If a controversial provision is susceptible of a fair and reasonable construction, then it must be so construed in an action for specific performance. The language "on terms acceptable to vendee" was susceptible of being fairly and reasonably construed as subjecting buyer to residual loan terms in conformity with those prevailing in the marketplace for comparable loans. So construed, "acceptable" loan terms were capable of being measured by extrinsic facts and were not dependent on the whim or fancy of the vendee. Therefore, vendee could require specific performance. *Solberg v. Kane,* 536 SW2d 885 (Ct. App. 1976).

77.20 Conditions Precedent

Alabama Provision of an option contract conditioned the sale on purchaser's ability to have the property rezoned. Although purchaser was unable to obtain a zoning variance, it notified sellers in writing that it was exercising the option to purchase. Sellers refused to convey the property and returned purchaser's down payment. Purchaser brought an action for specific performance. *Held:* The provision was inserted in the contract solely for purchaser's benefit. Purchaser was entitled to specific performance. *La Grave v. Jones,* 336 So. 2d 1330 (1976).

Connecticut An agreement to purchase a home called for a financing commitment to be obtained by April 23, 1975, "or this agreement shall become null and void and deposit money returned to buyer." On April 23, plaintiff obtained loan approval, and notified defendants by letter on April 24. Defendants withdrew from the deal, based on the financing condition. Plaintiff then obtained a comparable home elsewhere for an additional $1,000. Plaintiff sued for specific performance, and the trial court decreed the house be sold to plaintiff. However, by this time the value of the house had increased far beyond the agreed purchase price. *Held:* Time was not of the essence, and the slight delay in plaintiff's performance was not valid ground for termination. The court rejected defendant's argument that inflation made specific performance inequitable, because events subsequent to the time of performance were irrelevant to the equity of ordering performance. *Kakalik v. Bernardo,* 439 A2d 1016 (1981).

Florida Buyer contracted to purchase real property. Title to two acres of the property was disputed by a third party. The contract made closing contingent upon "successful termination" of the action challenging seller's title to the disputed acres. The contract also provided that if the action were not terminated and title resolved by August 1, 1982, buyer would be free to terminate the contract. On July 30, seller entered into a settlement with the litigant, which provided for a stipulation of dismissal to be filed with the court after closing. Buyer, however, refused to close on the ground that the action was not formally dismissed by August 1. Seller sued for specific performance. *Held:* For seller. The issue on appeal was whether the contract required that marketable title be clear as of August

1. The contract did not expressly require marketable title by that date. Buyer's claim that the litigation was not "terminated" was dismissed on the ground that the terms "resolved" and "terminated" were not defined in the contract and were subject to differing interpretations. *Brinson v. Luley,* 448 So. 2d 583 (Dist. Ct. App. 1984).

Maine When purchaser sued for specific performance, vendor contended that purchaser had paid the manager of their corporation, rather than their attorney as required by the contract, and therefore had not fully performed. *Held:* The provision in the contract referring to the attorney as the person through whom the exchange of money and deed was to be accomplished was not an absolute contractual requirement. The clause merely specified the method by which the transaction could be consummated. Therefore, purchaser's payment was in conformance with the contract. *Morton v. Tuck,* 345 A2d 891 (1975).

Oregon Sellers agreed on sale of land subject to buyer's securing a "satisfactory report for subdivision purposes" from zoning authorities. Buyer did not have to provide down payment, but was obligated to pay purchase price from funds received from future buyers of subdivided lots. Buyer could not obtain approval for subdivision by the closing date, and sellers, who had found another buyer at a higher price, refused to grant him an extension of time. Buyer sued for specific performance of the contract. *Held:* Buyer was not entitled to specific performance. Sellers were entitled to cancel the contract, since the contingency provision for subdivision approval benefited the sellers, and, without approval, there was no assurance that sellers would be paid. *Dan Bunn, Inc. v. Brown,* 590 P2d 209 (1979).

Utah Plaintiff submitted an offer to purchase defendant's land. Defendant crossed off plaintiff's conditions and wrote in that marketable title was to be the only condition imposed on defendant, stating the price and giving plaintiff 48 hours to accept the counteroffer. The counteroffer retained the offer's provision for a $5,000 earnest-money deposit. Plaintiff accepted the counteroffer by mailing a signed copy to defendant and sent $5,000 to the title insurance company. Defendant refused to convey the land to plaintiff because it did not receive the deposit nor notification of acceptance within the 48-hour period specified in the counteroffer. *Held:* Plaintiff was not entitled to specific performance, because it did not effectively accept defendant's counteroffer. Plaintiff's offer, which provided for a "deposit with you as earnest money the sum of $5,000" was incorporated into the counteroffer. Therefore, the money should have been deposited directly with defendant within the 48-hour period specified in the contract. Plaintiff's tender of earnest money to the title company did not constitute tender to defendant. Plaintiff's acceptance by mail was not reasonable where the offer and counteroffer were delivered personally. *Parks Enters. v. New Century Realty,* 652 P2d 918 (1982).

Wyoming Purchasers sued a seller's heirs for specific performance of a written contract for the sale of kind. During the administration of the estate, purchasers filed no claim and did not petition the court for a conveyance under available statutes. *Held:* Unless the statute specifically provided that the proceeding in a probate was the exclusive remedy, chancery could not be deprived of its powers in causes of actions brought for specific performance of contracts to convey land. Nor was it necessary for the prospective purchaser to file a claim with the decedent's personal representatives in order to assert his contractual rights. *Crockett v. Lowther,* 549 P2d 303 (1976).

77.25
Financing Conditions

Alabama A contract for the purchase of a home that seller was to build contained a financing clause that made the sale subject to purchasers' obtaining a conventional adjustable rate mortgage loan. Purchasers applied for the loan but withdrew their application after the husband learned that he would be transferred to another state, since his current job was being eliminated. To obtain an adjustable rate mortgage loan, borrower or a relative of borrower must occupy the property to be financed. Seller sued purchasers for breach of contract, and the trial court granted summary judgment in seller's favor. *Held:* Reversed. Purchasers did not breach the real estate contract, since the condition precedent to their performance under the contract (their obtaining financing) did not occur owing to circumstances beyond their control. Although there may be a general rule that difficulty, expense, or hardship does not excuse a promisor's performance under a contract, equity did not require the husband to give up his employment to obtain the mortgage. *Carmichael v. Lambert Constr. Co.,* 487 So. 2d 1367 (Civ. App. 1986).

Connecticut Buyers entered into a purchase agreement with sellers to purchase their home for $74,000, with a 10 percent down payment. The agreement was contingent upon buyers' obtaining a conventional mortgage loan by March 12, 1979. The agreement also required sellers to remove tenants from the house by May 1. On March 14, buyers obtained a loan commitment for an amount lower than required. Buyers notified sellers and asked them to remove tenants. On April 9, after the bank denied them a commitment increase, buyers notified sellers that they could not perform the purchase agreement. Buyers sued for return of the down payment. *Held:* Buyers forfeited the down payment by failing to perform under the agreement and waiving their right to be excused from such performance under the financing contingency. Buyers' argument that sellers had waived the contingency was rejected because the contingency was for buyers' benefit. Evidence of waiver was seen in buyers' request to remove tenants, and their failure to tell sellers to relist the property after March 12. *Loda v. HK Sargent & Assocs.,* 448 A2d 812 (1982).

Missouri Unknown to sellers, a couple sought to purchase two houses at the same time. One was for their own use, the second for a relative who might have had trouble obtaining financing on her own. Each contract was contingent on the couple obtaining financing, but did not mention they would need financing for two properties. After the second contract was signed, the couple told sellers they would not be buying the house because no bank was willing to finance a second house. Sellers sued for breach of contract. *Held:* Buyers were not obligated to purchase the house. The financing contingency clause was a condition subsequent, providing for an ipso facto cancellation on the nonoccurrence of a stipulated event—qualifying for a loan. Although sellers argued that the couple had placed themselves in a position making financing impossible, buyers executed the contract in the good faith belief that they could obtain financing for both houses and did not intentionally disqualify themselves for the second loan. *Maynard v. Bazazzadegan,* 732 SW2d 950 (Ct. App. 1987).

New Jersey The parties entered into a contract for sale of a house, which provided that buyer had 60 days to obtain a mortgage loan commitment. The 60 days expired on August 28. Buyers obtained a commitment on August 25, but buyers did not notify sellers until three days after the expiration date. However, sellers declared the contract void, and buyers sued for specific performance. The issue on appeal was whether the 60-day period applied only to obtaining a commitment or whether it also included notification to sellers. *Held:* For buyers. The court declined to imply a requirement of notice within the 60-day period. The purpose of the contingency clause was to protect buyers against the consequences of inability to obtain financing. Once buyers received that commitment, the parties were bound by the contract. Buyer's notification within three days was reasonable as a matter of law. *Schultz v. Topakyan,* 475 A2d 91 (Super. Ct. App. Div. 1984).

New York A real estate contract contained a mortgage contingency clause providing that the contract would be binding on the purchaser only if he were able to obtain a conventional mortgage loan, that purchaser would apply for such a loan within four business days after seller accepted the contract, and that purchaser would apply at two lending institutions if necessary. Purchaser promptly applied to three banks, none of which would grant a mortgage. He then sought to be excused from performance based on the mortgage contingency clause. Sellers refused to release purchaser, instead offering purchaser a purchase money mortgage. *Held:* For buyers. The contingency clause did not allow sellers an option to substitute themselves as mortgagees in the event no bank agreed to extend a mortgage loan. Good faith does not require buyers to accept a mortgage from sellers if conventional financing was unavailable. If this was the parties' intent, the contract should have expressly so provided. *Senese v. Litz,* 471 NYS2d 401 (App. Div. 1984).

77.30 Defenses

5th Circuit Sellers entered into an agreement to buy a mobile home park. The contract called for refinancing and buyer's assumption of an FHA loan. Sellers, however, were behind in their payments, and the FHA does not refinance delinquent loans. Buyer then orally offered to pay the full purchase price in cash. Sellers refused. Buyer sued for specific performance. Sellers contended that a cash payment would cause them adverse tax consequences. *Held:* No inequity would result from a grant of specific performance. The cash payment would grant the sellers a benefit equivalent to that called for in the contract: the discharge of their obligation to the FHA, and a return of their equity, for which they contracted. However, the court conditioned specific performance upon compensation to sellers for any adverse tax consequences incurred as a result of a cash payment. *Horner v. Bourland,* 724 F2d 1142 (1984).

9th Circuit Seller entered into a sales contract to sell her house to buyers. Buyers tendered full performance on the date of closing, that is, a combination of cash and a loan commitment. Seller refused to convey title, and buyers sued for specific performance. Seller then filed a Chapter 13 bankruptcy petition and elected to reject the sale contract as executory. Buyers filed an adversary proceeding alleging the contract was nonexecutory in that they had tendered full performance. *Held:* The Ninth Circuit ruled that the contract was still executory and thus subject to rejection in Chapter 13. Although "executory contract" was undefined by the Bankruptcy Code, the case law established that tender of performance alone did not constitute full performance by buyers. Only full payment of the purchase price would make the contract nonexecutory. The seller therefore had a right to reject the contract under Chapter 13. *In re Alexander,* 670 F2d 885 (1982).

Alaska Buyer, through a broker, entered into an agreement to purchase land for a residential development. Because sellers had doubts about buyer's financial strength, the name of another contractor was added as co-buyer. The agreement provided that broker was the sellers' agent. The broker falsely represented to sellers that buyer's financial problems were resolved and that the cobuyer was a well-known developer. When sellers discovered the truth, they refused to close with plaintiff, who was buyer and co-buyer's assignee. Plaintiff sought specific performance. *Held:* The court rejected plaintiff's theory that the broker's representations could not be attributed to buyers, because the broker was sellers' agent. The recital of agency in the agreement was not controlling; the actual situation was shown by the evidence to be otherwise. The court also rejected plaintiff's claim that assignment cured the misrepresentations. Following assignment, a seller retains a right of recourse against the assignor, which may be impaired by misrepresentations concerning the buyer's position. *Foster v. Cross,* 650 P12d 406 (1982).

Montana Landowner offered to sell a parcel of land to defendant. Defendant arranged to purchase the property with plaintiff, who would provide the $60,000 down payment, with defendant making installment payments. Plaintiff would have a half interest and had the right to "control any contractual arrangements" until defendant had paid $60,000 in monthly installments. Before that point was reached, plaintiff received an offer for the property, and plaintiff drew up a contract for sale. However, defendant would not agree to the sale. After defendant's installments had exceeded $60,000, plaintiff sued for judgment entitling him to control contractual arrangements for one year. Defendant argued that plaintiff was not entitled to relief, because he failed to arrange the sale of the parcel before defendant's payments reached $60,000. *Held:* The court characterized the remedy sought as a valid one that returned the parties to the status quo as of the time plaintiff claimed defendant refused to agree to the sale. It remanded the case for a determination of whether plaintiff's control authorized him to sell the property over defendant's objections. *Downs v. Smyk,* 651 P2d 1238 (1982).

Texas Parties entered into separate contracts for the sale of real estate. Two weeks later, buyer indicated that he was having trouble obtaining financing and through his attorney sent written notice repudiating the contracts. Seller demanded performance. Several weeks later, buyer secured financing and sought to arrange for closing. Seller refused to close, and suit followed. *Held:* Judgment for seller. The buyer's initial repudiation would not have justified seller's refusal to perform, because seller failed to treat it as an anticipatory breach, thereby enabling buyer to retract his repudiation. However, the attempted retraction was made after the contract time for performance had passed; therefore, seller no longer had a duty to perform. Because the demand for performance was made after the date specified, time became of the essence as a matter of law. *Glass v. Anderson,* 596 SW2d 507 (1980).

Washington Defendant contracted to construct a home for plaintiffs. Plaintiffs were to provide power and water. To get a building permit, plaintiffs represented that there was a water supply on their property. The bank furnishing a loan to plaintiffs said it was withholding funds until plaintiffs procured a state-approved water supply or proved the existence of their well. Defendant halted construction, and plaintiffs sought the return of a payment made. Plaintiffs refused to locate the well or to provide one. *Held:* Plaintiffs had breached the contract, and defendant was entitled to damages. Just because performance became more difficult or expensive for plaintiffs, they were not justified in setting the contract aside. Plaintiffs were bound to perform if possible, notwithstanding an unexpected, yet foreseeable event. Impossibility of performance, which excuses a party from performing, is not the same as subjective inability to perform. *Liner v. Armstrong Homes of Bremerton, Inc.*, 579 P2d 367 (Ct. App. 1978).

77.35 Delay in Bringing Action

Kansas Delay of five months between vendor's breach of a land sales contract and purchaser's commencement of a specific performance action did not constitute laches. Laches does not arise from mere delay alone, but requires some change in the condition or relations of the parties or property which would prejudice the rights of the adverse party. *Darby v. Keeran,* 505 P2d 710 (1972).

Maryland A son brought an action against his father, seeking to assert rights as a third-party beneficiary to a property settlement between his parents wherein the father was to convey a one-half interest in certain property to his son. The action was brought about 15 years after the date on which the transfer was to take place. *Held:* Even assuming that the son was a donee beneficiary of the settlement, his 15-year delay barred his suit by reason of the statute of limitations. *Spates v. Spates,* 296 A2d 581 (1972).

New Hampshire Would-be purchasers obtained and recorded a letter acceptance of their purchase offer. Agreement was never reached, however, as to the nonmonetary terms of the agreement. When sellers learned their acceptance letter was recorded, they informed purchasers the deal was off and returned the deposit check. The property was later sold to other purchasers, who made improvements and sued to quiet title. The would-be purchasers challenged this petition, claiming the letter was a binding contract. A year later, they sued for specific performance. *Held:* Specific performance was barred by laches. Would-be purchasers' failure to bring their action for specific performance until two years after negotiations with sellers broke down, and over a year after the property was sold to other purchasers, constituted unreasonable delay. This delay, coupled with the prejudice successful purchasers would suffer by a grant of specific performance, supported a finding of laches. *Estate of Younge v. Huysmans,* 506 A2d 282 (1985).

Oregon Purchaser sued vendor for specific performance of a contract to purchase real property. Purchaser had agreed to construct a house and shop for vendor on separate property of the vendor as part of the consideration for the sale. The contract provided that purchaser could be excused for not starting construction by the date called for in the contract if a zoning change could not be secured. *Held:* Specific performance denied. Despite an excusable delay in obtaining a zoning change, purchaser was unreasonably dilatory in preparing plans and specifications and in starting construction for the house and the shop. Such a failure constituted a material breach and excused performance by vendor. *Trachsel v. Barney,* 503 P2d 696 (1972).

78.00 RESCISSION AND REFORMATION

78.05 Rescission

Arizona An agreement for the sale of real property provided for escrow to close by July 31, 1974. Escrow instructions were signed by the parties. Escrow did not close on July 31, and seller orally agreed to postpone closing to August 15. On August 15, seller learned the necessary funds were not deposited in escrow. Seller advised purchaser that he would not sell since the contract had expired on July 31. Seller then signed a letter at the title company to cancel the escrow if purchaser did not comply with the escrow instructions within 13 days. Purchaser complied within 13 days and claimed compliance with the contract. Seller sued for rescission of the contract and escrow instructions. *Held:* Escrow instructions cannot modify a sales contract unless that intention is clearly stated by the parties. When the contract was terminated, the escrow instructions became unenforceable because there was no longer a binding contract as the subject. Thus, when the purchase price was not paid by the agreed date, seller had the right to cancel the contract. *Allan v. Martin,* 574 P2d 457 (1978).

Illinois Under a contract of sale, sellers were to deliver possession of a house to purchasers in the same condition it was in on the contract date, ordinary wear and care excepted. Purchasers learned shortly before closing that items had been removed and the house damaged. When this was brought to sellers' attention, they refused to close without granting a release. Purchasers executed a release, as a clause added to the closing statement, and were given a $500 credit on the purchase price. Purchasers sued for damages under the contract and to set aside the release agreement, claiming duress. Sellers argued that to rescind the release would require rescission of the contract in toto. *Held:* The release was rescinded and the sales contract upheld. The rule that rescission must be in toto does not apply to a contract whose parts are severable. The price paid as consideration for the release was apportioned to the release and so was easily separated from the sales contract. Duress existed, because purchasers would have had no place to move to while enforcing their claim in the courts. *Kaplan v. Keith,* 377 NE2d 279 (1978).

Louisiana After contracting to buy a house and putting down a 10 percent deposit, prospective purchaser discovered a crack one sixteenth of an inch wide and more than eight feet long under a bedroom carpet, and a dip in the kitchen floor. He sued for the rescission of the contract and return of his deposit. At trial, the expert for the prospective purchaser testified that these and other defects he found in the house were serious, and that he would not have purchased the house. *Held:* The prospective purchaser was entitled to rescission. It was not necessary to prove that the slab was faulty, only that a reasonable buyer would not have signed the agreement knowing the facts about the house. *Sigsworth v. Gernon,* 465 So. 2d 705 (1985).

New Jersey A contract for the sale of property contained a clause providing it would not become legally binding should one party's attorney notify the other party of rejection within three days. On the third day, seller's attorney notified buyer's broker of disapproval. Seller's attorney then enlisted the broker to sell the property to a new buyer. Original buyer refused to accept the rejection. Seller sought a judgment that the contract was terminated by notice to the broker, whom seller characterized as buyer's agent. *Held:* Notice to the broker alone was insufficient. The broker was the listing broker, chosen and paid by seller. The broker's interest was in negotiating a contract and obtaining a commission, an interest at odds with that of buyer, since the broker stood to gain a higher commission from cancellation of the contract. *Denesevich v. Moran,* 512 A2d 505 (Super. Ct. App. Div. 1986).

New Jersey Former owner of a motel sold it to Hilton Hotels for $3.25 million. Hilton gave former owner a letter stating that Hilton would give it 30 days' written notice prior to negotiating for the sale of the property to anyone else. The letter was recorded. Six years after the sale, Hilton negotiated a sale of the property to a third party, but notified the former owner 30 days prior to sale, rather than prior to negotiations. Former owner never tendered an offer, and Hilton proceeded with the sale. When the former owner refused to discharge from record the letter agreement, Hilton filed suit. The former owner countersued for rescission of the original sale. *Held:* Rescission was impossible, since to return the parties to the position they held six years earlier would be unrealistic and unfair. Hilton had occupied the premises and had been deprived of the $3.25 million purchase price for six years following the sale. Former owner had no interest in the motel property, either through rescission or under the letter agreement, since the letter explicitly did not create a right of first refusal. *Hilton Hotels Corp. v. Piper Co.,* 319 A2d 368 (Super. Ct. Ch. Div. 1986).

Pennsylvania Plaintiffs, purchasers of real estate, and sellers agreed to share the cost of a realty transfer tax. Fourteen months later, plaintiffs, alleging misrepresentations or mutual mistake of fact as to profitability, sued to have the deed declared null and void. The parties settled, and the property was returned to seller. To avoid paying a second transfer tax and to obtain a refund of the original tax, the parties drew up a consent decree, approved by the court, stating no transfer tax was required and the deed was null and void. The state board of finance and revenue denied them a refund. *Held:* The Pennsylvania Supreme Court held that although plaintiffs stipulated the existence of the consent decree, they failed to stipulate as to the conclusion of the decree that the deed was null and void. The parties therefore failed to present independent evidence of the voiding of the deed. The consent decree was binding on the parties, not on the state. *Sabatine v. Commonwealth,* 442 A2d 210 (1982).

Texas Purchasers sought to rescind their contract to buy realty, alleging that the lakefront lot was unfit for residential purposes because it was below a flood easement owned by the state. *Held:* By failing to disclose such material fact, seller is estopped to demand performance. The defect was not discoverable by the exercise of ordinary care and diligence; accordingly, purchasers are entitled to rescission and to interest on the purchase price from the date of payment. *Smith v. National Resort Communities, Inc.,* 585 SW2d 655 (1979).

Wyoming Buyers entered into agreement with contractor for sale of yet unbuilt condominium units. The contract contained a clause stating that the bank providing interim financing for seller required that two thirds of the condominium units be sold prior to construction. If seller did not sell a sufficient number of units by June 1, 1981, seller could terminate the agreement. Seller did not sell two thirds of the units before it began construction. Buyers notified seller they wished to terminate the contract. They alleged the contract was void for lack of mutuality of obligation in the cancellation clause; and that failure to sell two thirds of the units amounted to breach. *Held:* Buyers' contentions rejected. The cancellation clause did not make seller's promises illusory. It was based on an objective event, seller's failure to obtain financing, a common limitation in business contracts. The contract recitation that the bank required two-thirds sale of units was incidental to the financing condition. Where seller was able to build and obtain financing without presale of two thirds of the units, it had performed as promised and sellers could not allege breach. *Jackson Hole Builders v. Piros,* 654 P2d 120 (1982).

78.10
—Unilateral Mistake

5th Circuit Interim lender on a construction contract entered into a " take out" agreement with a long-term lender, which was to purchase the note secured by a mortgage. The contract itself contained reference to certain attachments that were not attached when the long-term lender executed the contract. When the interim lender tendered the note to the long-term lender for purchase, the long-term lender refused. The interim lender sued for breach of contract, to which the long-term lender pleaded mistake of fact, because it had been unable to examine the missing attachments. *Held:* A mistake under Texas law is limited to unconscious ignorance or mistake as to a question of fact. Here, the long-term lender was put on notice of missing attachments by the references to them in the contract. Where a party has actual or constructive notice of other documents, but proceeds without attempting to examine them, it is not a legal mistake. *Southern Nat'l Bank v. Crateo, Inc.,* 458 F2d 688 (1972).

Idaho Seller, who made a unilateral mistake in including a cafe in the sale of a garage property, sought to rescind the sale. Seller argued that, regardless of knowledge of buyers, the unilateral mistake of seller in including the legal description of the cafe property in the documentation was sufficient to justify summary judgment rescinding the sale. *Held:* Seller's motion denied. Where the record raised factual issues regarding buyers' knowledge of seller's mistake, such questions of fact could not be resolved on a motion for summary judgment. A seller who makes a unilateral mistake cannot rescind or modify the agreement absent knowledge or reason to know on the part of buyer. *Cohen v. Merrill,* 503 P2d 299 (1972).

New York Parties entered into a sublease with an option to purchase the lease, building, and equipment of a car wash. The option, which was exercised, contained reference to purchasers' intention to alter the premises. Seller knew that no building permits were being issued in the area. Purchasers brought an action for rescission of the contract. *Held:* Rescission is granted for a unilateral mistake when the mistake is known to the other party, who stands silent. *De Meo v. Horn,* 334 NYS2d 22 (Sup. Ct. 1972).

78.15
—Mutual Mistake

Arizona Lease purchasers began to develop desert land for commercial jojoba production. After spending $229,000 to drill wells, they concluded there was inadequate water and sued to rescind the contract. *Held:* Purchasers were entitled to rescission based on mutual mistake of fact. They had made clear they were interested in the property only for jojoba production and required adequate water supplies, and the sale would not have taken place had not both parties believed it was possible to grow jojoba on the land.

However, purchasers were not entitled to $229,000 in consequential damages awarded to them by the trial court for development costs. Absent proof of fraud or misrepresentation, one who rescinds a contract may not recover consequential damages. However, to avoid unjust enrichment, sellers were obligated to pay purchasers the amount by which their property had been enhanced in value by purchasers' efforts. *Renner v. Kehl,* 722 P2d 262 (1986).

Kansas Buyer purchased a lot on which he intended to build a house. Subsequently, he learned that a zoning change enacted just before the closing made it impossible for him to build the kind of structure he wanted, so he sued for rescission of the contract. *Held:* Buyer was entitled to rescind the contract. Seller knew or should have known about the zoning modification and should have told buyer. With the issue treated as a "mutual mistake," rescission is permitted. *Garrison v. Berryman,* 594 P2d 159 (1979).

Maine Defendant, owner of two parcels of land with apartment buildings, as well as a third parcel across the street, hired a real estate broker to find a purchaser for the two buildings. The broker was told not to sell the third parcel. The broker found plaintiff, who signed a contract to purchase the two apartment buildings. There was no mention during negotiations or at the time of signing regarding land to go with the respective buildings. After signing the contract, plaintiff discovered that drainage servicing one of the buildings was located on the parcel of land that broker was told not to sell. Plaintiff refused to buy the buildings without the drainage parcel. Plaintiff sued for specific performance and damages, alleging breach of contract. *Held:* The sales contract was entered into under mutual mistake with respect to a material term, i.e., whether plaintiff was purchasing buildings together with drainage area or not. Therefore, there was no meeting of the minds, and neither damages nor equitable relief was warranted. *Oullette v. Bolduc,* 440 A2d 1042 (1981).

New Hampshire The parties entered into a contract for the purchase and sale of a house. Approximately one month after the closing, buyers discovered that the center chimney and fireplaces were unsafe and would have to be rebuilt. They hired a mason to commence repairs on the chimney. Subsequently, they sued sellers for restitution of the purchase price for alleged mutual mistake as to the condition of the chimneys. *Held:* Relief denied. A buyer seeking restitution for entering into a contract based on mutual mistake is expected to rescind the contract by returning what he has received from the seller. It is well settled under New Hampshire law that before granting the remedy of rescission, the court must determine whether the parties can be returned to the status quo. The court found that rescission, and thus restitution, was not possible because buyers had incurred substantial expenditures for reconstruction of the fireplaces and chimney; therefore, the property could not be returned in the same condition in which it was received. *Derouin v. Granite State Realty, Inc.,* 459 A2d 231 (1983).

New York Plaintiff agreed to purchase defendants' apartment building, which was subject to two mortgages. After a binder was executed, defendants discovered that an earlier extension they had obtained of their second mortgage provided that if defendants sold the building, the balance would become due. The second mortgagee offered to waive the due-on-sale clause for a payment of $22,000, but defendants refused. Plaintiff sued for specific performance. Defendant demanded rescission of the contract based on mutual mistake. *Held:* For plaintiff. Specific performance must be granted if the mistake was due to defendant's own carelessness, unless performance would cause defendant undue hardship. Although defendants would, under the due-on-sale clause, have to pay off the second mortgage before conveying the building to plaintiff, they would still receive the consideration they bargained for and would be compensated for having to finance the second mortgage. The court noted that the second mortgagee was prepared to leave its loan outstanding if defendants paid $22,000. *DaSilva v. Musso,* 428 NE2d 382 (1981).

Virginia Purchasers sued to rescind a conveyance on the ground of mutual mistake. The sales contract was contingent on plaintiffs' obtaining a building permit and percolation of a septic tank. Defendant assured plaintiffs that the land was suitable for building, relying on a board of health report and their having obtained a building permit for the adjacent parcel. When plaintiffs applied for the building permit, they were denied and were advised that the standards and requirements for sewage systems had changed from the time they had received title. *Held:* Plaintiffs were entitled to rescission since both parties had bargained on plaintiffs' obtaining the necessary permit to build a house. Since the parties did not intend the sales contract to merge in the deed, the contingency of obtaining a permit was still in force. *Miller v. Reynolds,* 223 SE2d 883 (1976).

78.20
—Fraud

California After plaintiff purchased a home, she discovered it had been the site of a multiple murder 10 years earlier. She sued the seller and real estate agent for failing to disclose this fact and sought rescission of the contract and damages. Defendants knew of the murder, but represented to plaintiff that the premises were fit for her, an elderly lady living alone. Defendants also asked a neighbor prior to closing not to inform plaintiff of the murder. The trial court held that no cause of action existed unless the property was currently the object of notoriety. *Held:* Reversed. Plaintiff had a cause of action in fraud. Her complaint alleged concealment of a material fact made with knowledge of its falsity with intent to induce plaintiff to act in reliance on the concealment to her detriment. Defendants had a duty to disclose the information because it was sufficiently material to affect the value of the property. *Reed v. King,* 193 Cal. Rptr. 130 (Ct. App. 1983).

Oklahoma Seller sold property to buyer for a down payment and mortgage. After two years, buyer notified seller it was rescinding its purchase of the property owing to discovery of material oral misrepresentations made by the seller regarding market value. Seller sued to foreclose the mortgage, and buyer counterclaimed for rescission. *Held:* The rule of *Onstott v. Osborne,* 417 P2d 291 (1966) states that fraud in real estate cases may not be predicated on alleged false statements if the party making the allegations could have ascertained the truth with reasonable diligence. The court found that buyer could have ascertained the truth or falsity of the alleged misrepresentations regarding market value of the property. Since means of knowledge were at hand and buyer failed to avail itself of these means, it could not now claim it was deceived by the representations of seller. *Sokolosky v. Tulsa Orthopaedic Ass'n Pension Trust,* 566 P2d 429 (1977).

Pennsylvania Plaintiff contracted to purchase land from defendant. Later, defendant refused to convey and plaintiff sued in equity for specific performance. Defendants, who had contracted to sell only part of their property while retaining a historical colonial farmhouse, argued that plaintiff misrepresented the use to which the property would be put. Plaintiff had assured defendant that he intended to build a "colonial village" type of development consisting of single-family homes. Defendants later discovered that plaintiff planned to build a nursing home, a medical center, and a high-rise building. *Held:* Even though the misrepresentation did not cause defendant pecuniary injury, plaintiff's fraudulent misrepresentation was ground for rescission. The court noted that at the same time plaintiff made his representations to defendant, he appeared before the local planning commission in an attempt to rezone the land for his actual intended uses. Defendant had shown fraudulent misrepresentation, and a rescission of the contract for sale was granted by the court. *Brentwater Homes, Inc. v. Weibley,* 369 A2d 1172 (1977).

South Carolina A condominium developer executed purchase agreements with several purchasers of units. The agreements provided financing at 8.25 percent interest. After the agreements had been signed, the developer informed purchasers that financing would be at the prevailing market rate (more than 8.25 percent). The purchasers then sued for breach of contract, and the developer offered to arrange for financing at the original 8.25 percent. Several closings were then made on individual units, but some purchasers pursued the suit, seeking rescission. *Held:* Purchasers can rescind the contract. Since the fraud was discovered while the contract was executory, purchasers were not required to wait until the time of the performance to seek rescission. *O'Quinn v. Beach Assocs.,* 249 SE2d 734 (1979).

78.25 —Material Misrepresentation

2d Circuit Shopping mall's representative told plaintiff, a prospective tenant, that 65 percent of the space in the shopping center had already been rented and estimated that taxes would be $1.25 per square foot and common charges for heating and lighting would be $0.65 per square foot. Encouraged by these figures, plaintiff signed a lease. After entering the premises and making substantial improvements, plaintiff learned that only 32 percent of the shopping center space had been rented. Plaintiff also discovered that the taxes and common charges were 200 to 300 percent greater than had been represented. Plaintiff vacated the premises and sued for rescission of the lease and damages. Defendant contended that finding of fraud could not be based on future expectations and projects. *Held:* Rescission of the contract was ordered. An intent to deceive was inferred from defendant's awareness of internal figures, which indicated that the estimates were quite inaccurate. *Magnaleasing, Inc. v. Staten Island Mall,* 563 F2d 567 (1977).

Delaware Seller owned an industrial park zoned M-1 for light industry, including storage of petroleum. Seller retained a broker to sell the property, and broker advertised it as zoned M-1. Buyer, looking for a site suitable for his petroleum business, contacted the broker. Buyer told broker and seller of his need for petroleum storage. Seller and broker never supplied buyer with a copy of a recorded list of restrictions requiring approval of an industrial park building committee for many uses permitted by M-1 zoning, including petroleum storage. After the contract was signed, a title search disclosed the restrictions. The committee denied approval for buyer's required uses, and buyer refused to close. Seller sued for specific performance, and buyer counterclaimed for rescission based on misinterpretation. The contract was contingent on the M-1 zoning, but expressly subject to restrictions of record. *Held:* For buyer. The advertisement indicating the property was zoned M-1 amounted to an innocent misinterpretation that the property could be used for all purposes permitted by the zoning code. If buyer could establish at trial that this misinterpretation was material, that it induced him to execute the contract, and that his reliance on the misinterpretation was justified, he was entitled to rescission. *Norton v. Poplos,* 443 A2d 1 (1982).

Georgia McKnight entered into a contract to purchase a condominium unit that was yet to be constructed. The floor plan stated the unit would be 1,420 square feet. Eighteen months later, McKnight sued, alleging the contract was voidable because the unit had only 1,394.7 square feet. *Held:* Defendant's motion for summary judgment affirmed. Georgia law provides that one who relies on a false material statement published by seller in purchasing a condominium unit has an action for damages, and may rescind the contract prior to closing. The standard method of measuring heated space is to measure the exterior surface of exterior walls to the center of common walls. Plaintiff measured the interior surfaces of interior walls. Therefore, the plan contained no false statements that would make the contract voidable. *McKnight v. Golden Isles Marina, Inc.,* 366 SE2d 830 (Ct. App. 1988).

Georgia Seller knew of serious defects in his property that could not be discerned by the buyer even with the exercise of due diligence, and the seller withheld this information. *Held:* In a possible modification of caveat emptor, the court held this constituted a suppression of facts supporting the buyer's suit for fraud. *Wilhite v. Mays,* 232 SE2d 141 (Ct. App.), aff'd, 235 SE2d 532 (1977).

Massachusetts Purchaser bought a building and land subject to a lease he believed ran until 1970. He was shown the lease and a modification showing that the lease would terminate in 1970. In fact, a new agreement had been entered into that extended the lease until 1972. When purchaser sued seller for the misrepresentations, the claim was not allowed because there was no proof of an intent to deceive by the seller. *Held:* Intention to deceive is not a prerequisite for recovery when there was proof of numerous false representations of the fact that the lease expired in 1970. *Snyder v. Sperry & Hutchinson Co.,* 333 NE2d 421 (1976).

Mississippi Landowner sold land to an agent for a church. A month later, the church sold half the land to landowner's neighbor. Owing to a zoning dispute, landowner was unwilling to sell any property to this neighbor. Landowner sued to rescind the conveyance to the church, claiming the church's agent had fraudulently failed to disclose that he was acting in part for the neighbor. *Held:* Landowner stated a claim for rescission based on material misrepresentation. The identity of a vendee is a material matter. Where a vendor would not have made a conveyance of land had he known of a prior agreement by the vendee to convey to another vendee that vendor finds objectionable, vendor is entitled to rescission of the conveyance. Even if the resale will not cause the vendor any pecuniary loss, the vendor has the right to refuse to sell to the third party for any legally permissible reason. *Gray v. Baker,* 485 So. 2d 306 (1986).

Oregon Sellers listed property with a broker, but allegedly failed to inform him that the well on the property was dry. Subsequently, sellers executed an installment contract with purchaser that provided that the land had been purchased without any representations made by sellers and with knowledge that the well was not guaranteed. Later, after beginning work for the construction of a road on the land, purchaser discovered that the well was dry and that no functioning well could be drilled. Purchaser sued for rescission of the contract and for damages in the amount of money expended for construction of the road. Sellers claimed to have informed the broker of a prior lawsuit concerning the well, but both the broker and the purchaser denied having been told of the problem. The trial court granted purchaser rescission of the contract, but denied any damages for the cost of the road. *Held:* The deliberate withholding of information constituted a material misrepresentation allowing rescission. The lower court was upheld. *Bodenhamer v. Patterson,* 563 P2d 1212 (1977).

Texas Buyers purchased a lot in a subdivision located on a lake. They were given a document entitled "Declaration of Reservations," which referred to an overflow easement held by the Lower Colorado River Authority. The overflow easement was also mentioned in the title insurance policy, but developer's sales personnel never referred to the restriction in their dealings with buyers. Subsequently, buyers learned that their lot could be flooded and sued to cancel the sales contract. Buyers argued that developer had concealed or failed to disclose the easement. *Held:* Buyers were entitled to rescission. A seller of real estate is under a duty to disclose material facts that would not be discoverable by the exercise of ordinary care and diligence on the part of a buyer. The declaration contained only a general reference to the overflow easement. A careful reading of the declaration would not have reasonably alerted buyers to the possibility that the mentioned easement encumbered the lot they were purchasing. Nor did photographs of the lot provide visible evidence that the lake had risen above the level of the lot purchased by past buyers. *Smith v. NRC, Inc.,* 585 SW2d 655 (1979).

78.30
—Economic Duress

New York Plaintiff was ground lessee of a blockfront except for a small building owned by defendant. Plaintiff wished to build a 31-story building, and agreed to purchase air rights from defendant. Plaintiff agreed to deliver to defendant a down payment, promissory note, letter of credit, and architectural drawings. Defendant agreed to deliver in escrow on the closing date a declaration of zoning lot restrictions and an easement agreement. Plaintiff alleged that defendant refused to deliver the declaration or easement agreement unless plaintiff agreed to modify the agreement. Plaintiff charged that this constituted economic duress, because defendant knew construction delays would cause irreparable harm. Plaintiff sued for rescission of the modified contract. *Held:* For defendant. Under the agreement, plaintiff was required to perform the conditions for transfer of air rights on the date construction commenced. Since plaintiff failed to perform the conditions at that time, seller had no duty to transfer the air rights. As plaintiff was not entitled to performance, it had no cause of action for economic duress. *805 Third Ave. Co. v. MW Realty Assocs.,* 448 NE2d 445 (1983).

78.35
—Interstate Land Sales Full Disclosure Act

5th Circuit Buyers executed an agreement to purchase property from seller prior to receiving a property report as required by the Interstate Land Sales Full Disclosure Act (ILSA) (15 USCA § 1701). However, buyers did receive the report from seller before seller executed the agreement. About a year later, buyers asked to rescind the agreement, but sellers refused. Buyers sued for rescission, claiming the contract was invalid since seller had not furnished them with a property report before they executed the agreement as required by Sections 1703(a) and 1703(b). Seller argued that the contract did not come into existence until after it had signed, and that buyers were barred by laches from asserting the claim. *Held:* Buyers were entitled to rescission. Section 1703(b) unambiguously gives buyer the right to rescind "where the property report has not been given to the purchaser in advance or at the time of his signing." Furthermore, seller could not invoke the doctrine of laches since it could not establish that it had been prejudiced by buyers' delay in raising the claim. *Law v. Royal Palm Beach Colony, Inc.*, 578 F2d 98 (1978).

5th Circuit Purchasers of properties in a development sued developer's agent to rescind their contracts and recover the purchase price on the ground that the sale violated ILSA. The master plan of the development described extensive recreational facilities, and the project report distributed to prospective buyers stated that completion of the project depended on satisfactory land sales and the ability of the developer to obtain adequate financing. *Held:* ILSA authorizes suits against developers of project, and not against developers' agents. Also, the purchasers' suit could not be maintained, because purchasers did not show that the property report lacked factual substance or that it misrepresented the facts. *Paquin v. Four Seasons, Inc.*, 519 F2d 1105 (1975).

Arizona Purchaser agreed to buy a lot and executed a promissory note and mortgage. Pursuant to ILSA, however, the purchaser rescinded the transaction two days later and received the down payment previously paid. Earlier that same day, the seller had discounted the promissory note and assigned it to a third party. When the third-party assignee sued on the note, purchaser claimed that rescission of the sale made the note void by operation of law. Assignee, on the other hand, argued that he was a "holder in due course" and not subject to any defenses that purchaser might have against seller. *Held:* Assignee had not acted in good faith and was not a holder in due course. The assignee had purchased the note for less than full value and, had the assignee examined the contract, he would have ascertained that the underlying transaction was still voidable. *Steward v. Thornton*, 568 P2d 414 (1977).

Colorado Purchaser enterd into a contract to buy two condominium units from builder for $185,000 in earnest money. A year later, purchaser had insufficient funds to close on both units, and builder allowed him to pool his earnest money and delay closing on one unit, subject to conditions. When the conditions were not met, builder retained the deposits as liquidated damages under the original purchase agreements. Purchaser sued to revoke the contracts under ILSA and to recover his earnest money. *Held:* Summary judgment for purchaser affirmed. ILSA applied to condominium units which were "lots" within the definition of ILSA. ILSA exempted the sale or lease of land on which there is a building or the sale or lease of land under a contract to build thereon within two years. The date of the proposed substitute agreement was not controlling. It was contingent on performance of conditions that purchaser failed to fulfill; therefore, the parties did not enter into a substitute agreement. The exemption for an agreement covering land on which there was a building at the time of the original agreement also did not apply. The project was uncomplete at the time the contracts were executed and was therefore not a "building" at the time of sale. *Giralt v. Vail Village Inn Assocs.*, 759 P2d 801 (Ct. App. 1988).

Delaware Purchaser of condominium unit sued to rescind his contract under ILSA on the ground that he never received a printed property report as required under ILSA. Defendant argued that ILSA by its terms did not apply to "the sale or lease of any improved land." *Held:* Condominium units carry all the indicia of real estate and are within ILSA, which should be liberally interpreted in order to attain its stated goal of preventing land development fraud. ILSA applied here, since the land in question was not "improved"; rather, the contract called for the property to be improved. *Nargiz v. Henlopen Developers,* 380 A2d 1361 (1977).

Florida Purchasers sought to rescind their agreement to purchase a home on the ground that seller failed to comply with certain disclosure requirements of ILSA. Seller claimed that the transaction was exempt under Section 1702(a)(2) of ILSA because the purchase agreement obligated it to build a house on the land within two years. *Held:* Purchasers could rescind. A seller is "obligated" within the meaning of Section 1702(a)(2) only if the contract contains an unconditional commitment by the seller to complete construction within two years. A seller is not "obligated" if the purchaser's only remedy is rescission. Here, purchasers had waived their right to specific performance unless specific performance of the obligation to complete the unit within two years was an "absolute condition" for seller to take advantage of the provisions of Section 1702(a)(2). The court found that the agreement made the remedy of specific performance available to purchasers solely to allow seller to evade ILSA's disclosure requirements. Section 1702(a) expressly prohibits any method of disposition adopted for the purpose of evasion of the disclosure requirements. *Arvida Corp. v. Barnett,* 502 So. 2d 11 (Dist. Ct. App. 1986).

Texas Plaintiff brought action to rescind contract to purchase modular home, alleging that defendants had fraudulently misrepresented the cost of building the home and also had violated ILSA by stating, in their property report, that no special foundation work was needed when, in fact, the ground had to be leveled by the use of piers and beams in order to build the house. *Held:* In order to prove that a promise for the future, i.e., estimated cost to build a home, constituted fraud, one must be able to show that at the time of the representation there was intention to misrepresent. Plaintiff presented no evidence that defendant had intentionally misrepresented cost at the time when the contract was signed. There was no violation of the act. (See Section 43.31.) *NRC, Inc. v. Huckabee,* 539 SW2d 375 (Civ. App. 1976).

78.40 Reformation

Alaska A real estate agent purchased a 12-unit apartment house from a 73-year-old seller. The sale terms called for buyer to assume an existing $90,000 deed of trust, to pay a $10,000 down payment, and to execute a second deed of trust for $153,000, with 8.5 percent interest, payable at the rate of $500 per month, with payments to begin over a year after the sale, with a balloon payment of $15,000 also due at that time. At the suggestion of buyer's attorney, the term was set at 30 years. Seller sued for reformation 14.5 years later. *Held:* The agreement was reformed to provide for larger payments from the date of sale that would amortize the principal and interest over the 30-year term. The original contract was unconscionable: It would have resulted in a large balloon payment of $311,000 that would not be paid until the elderly seller was 103 years old; the value of the security would have decreased over the 30-year term, even as the amount secured increased; seller was not to receive any interest on the deferred interest payments; and seller was far less knowledgeable than buyer, who was a real estate agent represented by counsel. *Vockner v. Erickson,* 712 P2d 379 (1986).

Idaho Real estate contract between seller and buyer reserved 10 acres enclosed by a fence surrounding seller's house for seller, and allowed buyer an easement over the property. Buyer sought to reform the contract, alleging that the fence enclosed fewer than 10 acres. *Held:* Since it was the intent of the parties at the time the contract was made to reserve only the land enclosed by the fence, the contract should be reformed so as to reserve only the property enclosed by the fence. *Suitts v. McMurtrey,* 546 P2d 62 (1976).

Minnesota Plaintiffs defaulted on $20,000 in business loans from defendant bank and entered into negotiations for refinancing the amount owed. The bank extended additional credit of $10,000 and took a $30,000 mortgage on plaintiffs' home. Plaintiffs sued for reformation, arguing that the parties had agreed to create only a $10,000 mortgage as security for the last extension of credit. *Held:* In spite of probative evidence supporting plaintiffs' assertions of their good faith beliefs, reformation is not available where there has been unilateral mistake. Neither mutual mistake nor bank misrepresentation was established; therefore, equity does not interfere to rewrite a contract that plaintiffs negligently had failed to read before signing. *Nichols v. Shelard Nat'l Bank,* 294 NW2d 730 (1980).

Washington Vendors represented in an earnest-money agreement that the parcel of land that they were putting up for sale consisted of about 70 acres. The price was based upon a figure of $2,200 per acre, which was explicitly mentioned during negotiations. When vendors signed the agreement, they deleted with red ink a clause providing for a reduction in the purchase price should the acreage be less than 70 acres. When a subsequent survey revealed that the tract contained only 50.99 acres, purchaser sued to reform the contract. *Held:* Where vendors fraudulently misrepresented the quantity of land, price abatement was the appropriate remedy. It should have been awarded based upon the deficiency in acreage and the agreed-upon price per acre. *Alexander Myers & Co. v. Hopke,* 565 P2d 80 (1977).

79.00 REPUDIATION

79.05 Anticipatory Repudiation

Michigan Landowner sold real estate under a land sale contract as well as his bar business, conducted on the same property, to the same purchasers on an installment note. The bar later burned. Purchasers paid the former owner a third of the insurance proceeds and agreed to add the balance of the installment note to the balance of the contract and to rebuild the bar. Purchasers failed to make further payments under the contract or to rebuild the bar, and former owner moved for foreclosure and a deficiency judgment. *Held:* For former owner, based on the doctrine of anticipatory repudiation. Purchasers stated they had no intention of fulfilling their contractual obligations. They failed to make payments, repairs, pay taxes; and arranged to sell the liquor license. These actions amounted to complete repudiation of the contract. *Carpenter v. Smith,* 383 NW2d 248 (Ct. App. 1985).

Virginia Husband and wife contracted to purchase realty from sellers. Three weeks prior to closing, the husband advised sellers he was unable to close and requested a return of his deposit. Sellers sued two days before closing, alleging anticipatory repudiation. The trial court granted a defense motion to dismiss on the ground that if only one of two joint obligors anticipatorily repudiates, there is no breach of contract because the remaining obligor is bound to perform at closing. *Held:* Affirmed. Where two or more parties jointly contract to do a single act, each is bound for the whole performance. Though the husband repudiated, his repudiation could not serve as the basis for a breach of contract claim because his co-obligor did not join the repudiation. Seller should have waited until the closing date to determine if the wife would fulfill her contractual obligation. *Link v. Weizenbaum,* 326 SE2d 667 (1985).

80.00 DAMAGES FOR BREACH

80.05 Purchaser's Damages

11th Circuit Vendor, planning to create a lot on an island by dredging and filling underwater land, contracted with buyer in 1971 to deliver marketable title to the lot on or before May 1980. However, because of vendor's difficulties in seeking dredge and fill permits from the Army Corps of Engineers for comparable sites, vendor never requested such permission for buyer's site. Buyer sued for breach of contract and vendor raised the defense of impossibility because of the increased regulation. *Held:* The defense of impossibility was not open to vendor. The issue was whether the increase in regulation was "foreseeable," and the court concluded that this change was not beyond vendor's contemplation in 1971, even if the extent of the increase was not foreseen. *Cook v. Deltona Corp.,* 753 F2d 1552 (1985).

California The contract to build a home specified a completion date of April 17, 1973, and provided time was of the essence, except for "excusable delays." The home had to be completed by the stated date so that buyers could save capital gains tax on the sale of their former home. The new home was not finished until September, and buyers sued developer. *Held:* The court refused to overturn a jury's verdict that construction delays could not be excused, and allowed compensatory damages of $8,414. Developer had repeatedly assured buyers that the house would be completed on time, but then failed to satisfactorily account for delays. In view of this, the award of $215,000 in punitive damages, based on the wealth of the developer, was justified. *Walker v. Signal Cos.,* 149 Cal. Rptr. 119 (Ct. App. 1978).

Colorado A condominium developer presold several condominium units to contract purchasers. The contracts of sale were contingent on purchasers' obtaining financing within 30 days from the date of execution of the agreements. When developer defaulted on its construction loan, leaving itself unable to close in accordance with the terms of the contracts of sale, the contract purchasers sued for breach of contract. *Held:* The contract purchasers were entitled to return of their earnest money but not to loss of bargain damages. None of the contract purchasers had obtained financing, nor had any of them sufficient funds from other sources to close. Since each party's duty to render performance was conditioned on the other party's performance or readiness to perform, developer's duty to pay damages was discharged by the failure of performance by the contract purchasers. *Daybreak Constr. Specialties v. Saghatoleslami,* 712 P2d 1028 (Ct. App. 1985).

Florida Purchasers of a house to be built by defendant sued when the house was not completed until four months after the date contracted for. Purchasers incurred expenses in renting an apartment and losing a mortgage commitment at a low interest rate. The trial course dismissed the complaint because the contract stated that the contractor would not be responsible for damages for delay under any circumstances. Purchasers contended the completion date was fraudulently represented to them because contractor intended to use their lot as a roadway to carry supplies and equipment from defendant's construction yard to other home lots in the development. *Held:* Although a "no damages for delay" clause is ordinarily valid, it will be ineffective to protect a party from active interference, fraud, or concealment. *McIntire v. Green-Tree Communities, Inc.,* 318 So. 2d 197 (Dist. Ct. App. 1975).

Georgia Sellers, associates of a realty company, agreed to sell plaintiff a renovated house under the company's name. Sellers certified to the Farmers Home Administration (FmHA) that the house was free from termite damage, so that plaintiff could receive a mortgage loan from the agency. Shortly thereafter, plaintiff discovered substantial termite damage and sued sellers, the realty company, the exterminator, and the renovator, alleging conspiracy to defraud. Plaintiff was awarded actual and punitive damages. On appeal, defendants contended that punitive damages could not be assessed unless each individual defendant was fould liable of the requisite conduct to justify punitive damages. *Held:* The court permitted the award to stand in full. Defendants were not sued jointly per se but were found liable under a conspiracy theory. The law allows punitive damages to be assessed against all defendants found liable either individually or as part of a conspiracy. *Mercer v. Woodard,* 303 SE2d (1983).

Iowa Buyers and sellers entered into a contract for the sale of a lot and warehouse building and a lease agreement allowing buyers to rent the property until closing. Buyers refused to close until disputes over the cost of paving and an easement were resolved. Seller, claiming buyers' refusal to close rescinded the contract, served buyers with a notice to terminate tenancy. Buyers sued for breach of contract, and were awarded actual and punitive damages. *Held:* The compensatory damages award was upheld, since there was evidence of loss of bargain. Between the date performance became due and the date of the verdict, purchasers lost the equity they would have built in their property had the contract been performed. However, the award of punitive damages was not justified. A breach of contract alone is an insufficient basis for punitive damages; the breach must also constitute an intentional tort, or other wrongful act, committed with malice. *Berryhill v. Hatt,* 428 NW2d 647 (1988).

New Hampshire Dissatisfied with plaintiff's performance, defendant buyer of a new house to be built by plaintiff ordered him off the project. Defendant then spent $50,000 over the contract's stated allowances for cabinets, carpets, and a heating system. Plaintiff sued for the value of his labor and materials, and defendant counterclaimed for the difference between the contract price and defendant's cost of completion, plus consequential damages for delays and inconvenience caused by builder's breach. *Held:* Defendant was denied a credit for amounts exceeding the contract's stated allowances. To allow such amounts would place defendant in a better position than he would have been in under the contract. However, defendant was allowed consequential damages for delay and inconvenience that the parties could have reasonably anticipated as a likely result of plaintiff's breach. Since plaintiff's work had a negative value to defendant, the court refused to offset the value of his labor and materials from consequential damages. *Martin v. Phillips,* 440 A2d 1124 (1982).

New Hampshire Plaintiffs, who leased part of a building owned by defendant where they operated their business, entered into an oral agreement with defendant for a one-year option to buy the property. Plaintiffs exercised the option, and the parties signed a sales agreement. In reliance on the sales agreement, plaintiffs spent $7,000 on improvements, which defendant was aware of. At closing, defendant tendered a deed with new conditions that plaintiffs refused to accept. As a result, plaintiffs were evicted four months before the lease terminated. Plaintiffs sued for breach of the oral lease and written sales agreement, seeking lost profits and an award for unjust enrichment based on the cost of improvements. *Held:* For plaintiffs. Consequential damages were warranted because lost profits were reasonably foreseeable by defendant as a result of breach of the agreement. Such losses were greater than plaintiffs would have incurred had they simply been required to relocate at lease termination. Plaintiffs were entitled to quantum meruit, but only to the extent of defendant's unjust enrichment, which was the value differential between the property unimproved and the property with improvements, i.e., $5,000. *Petrie-Clemons v. Butterfield,* 441 A2d 1167 (1982).

New Mexico Homebuyer brought suit against appraiser, with whom homebuyer had had no direct contact, when the valuation proved erroneous. Appraiser made an error in the square footage of the property, and then used this mistaken figure in calculating the total value. Homebuyer's suit against appraiser was summarily dismissed by the trial court, because the appraisal report was ordered and paid for by seller. Homebuyer appealed. *Held:* The case should not have been summarily dismissed. Appraiser should have known that the valuation report would be relied on by prospective purchasers. Even though homebuyer was not a party to the contract between appraiser and seller, he had a right to recover damages, if he could show that the contract was intended to benefit prospective purchasers and that he was harmed by relying on a negligently made appraisal. *Stotlar v. Hester,* 582 P2d 403 (Ct. App. 1978).

Oregon Purchasers sued to recover damages against vendor for misrepresentations involving the sale of property. Vendor sold his ranch with a representation that the ranch had an appurtenant right to take water from the adjoining stream for irrigation purposes. Vendor, however, had not exercised his water rights for a number of years; and, a couple of years after the sale, the state canceled a portion of the water rights. *Held:* Vendor who represented that he had water rights, but had actually abandoned them by nonuse for five or more consecutive years, acted recklessly, as a matter of law, when he represented that the ranch had the right to take water from the adjoining stream for irrigation of all 27 acres of the conveyed premises. Purchasers were therefore entitled to recover damages for misrepresentation. *Bausch v. Myers,* 541 P2d 817 (1975).

Utah Purchaser sued seller for breach of a real estate contract that provided that seller would construct a sewer line. Seller argued that under the contract he was not required to supply sewer disposal service. Owing to the inadequacies of the public sewage system, the sewer line could not be connected to the public line, and purchaser had to construct a temporary holding tank and had to pay to haul the sewage away. *Held:* Purchaser failed to show a breach of contract. Seller was obligated only to construct a sewer line and not to provide sewer service. *Price v. Research Indus. Corp.*, 548 P2d 618 (1976).

80.10
—Measure of Purchaser's Damages

8th Circuit Assignees of buyers were awarded damages for breach of contract to sell two apartment complexes. The court set damages as the difference between the contract price and the price for which the apartments were eventually sold to a third party. It added an "interest rate differential" equal to the difference between loan payments under buyers' mortgage (at 8.5 percent interest) and those due under the third party's mortgage (at 9.5 percent). *Held:* The interest rate differential should not have been used, and damages were reduced accordingly. The issue was whether, in determining damages, the value of the third-party contract should be enhanced because its interest rate was higher than the rate under the buyer's contract. Under Missouri law, a disappointed buyer cannot recover for an increase in interest rates that he has neither paid nor committed himself to pay. *Cedar Point Apartments v. Cedar Point Inv.*, 756 F2d 629 (1985).

Nebraska When commercial lessee-buyer tried to exercise a purchase option, lessor-vendor refused to comply. Lessee-buyer remained as a holdover tenant before vacating the premises two months early. Lessee sued for specific performance of the option and thereafter appealed the court's order adding an additional amount to the purchase price, alleging error in the damage computation. *Held:* Lessor was obligated to pay taxes and other expenses that accrued during the delay in performance of the contract; to allow otherwise would permit lessor to benefit from his own failure to convey the property. Lessee was properly denied lost profits caused by the delay, owing to insufficient evidence. Lessor was not entitled to interest on the unpaid purchase price, because the delay in performance was caused by the lessor-vendor and the lessee-buyer was not in possession during the delay. *III Lounges v. Gaines,* 419 NW2d 143 (1988).

Nebraska Buyers-mortgagors made all payments to seller-mortgagee on a purchase money mortgage in connection with the sale of a number of acres of farmland, until it was discovered that seller had previously conveyed 18.5 acres to a third party. Buyers calculated their loss based on the average cost per acre and deducted this amount from the next installment of the mortgage debt. Seller refused the tender and commenced foreclosure. The trial court decreed foreclosure and awarded buyers an abatement for the missing acres; buyers appealed. *Held:* Affirmed. Under Nebraska law, foreclosure is an available remedy for a mortgagor's breach despite mortgagor's right to an abatement of part of the unpaid mortgage debt owing to a deficiency in the quantity of land contracted to be sold by the mortgagee. The abatement is measured by the value of the land lost relative to the purchase price of the entire tract, not the average cost per acre. The evidence showed that the missing 18.5 acres had the least value of any of the other land. Therefore, the amount of abatement awarded was proper. *Kuhlman v. Grimminger,* 327 NW2d 104 (1982).

New Jersey A contract for the sale of a house called for a purchase money mortgage at 13 percent interest. This was reduced, in an earlier suit, to 10.5 percent, because seller was unable to deliver marketable title. Buyers then purchased another home, obtaining a new mortgage at 13.25 percent interest. They sought the difference between the 10.5 percent and 13.25 percent loans as compensatory damages. *Held:* For buyers. Although the accepted damages for vendor's inability to convey marketable title is return of deposit plus expenses, with only nominal damages for loss of bargain, the court stated that there was no sound basis why loss of bargain damages should not be available in a case such as this. The purchase money mortgage was clearly of great consequence to buyers under current market conditions. Damages were calculated as the difference between the original purchase price and the fair market value of a home that could be acquired with a purchase money mortgage in the contract amount but at 10.5 percent interest. *Donovan v. Bachstadt,* 453 A2d 160 (1982).

Texas Purchaser sued seller of real property for breach of contract, and lower court awarded damages for the plaintiff purchaser's loss of the "benefit of his bargain." Seller appealed, arguing that the measure of damages was incorrect. *Held:* Reversed. When a buyer of realty cannot perform because of a bank's refusal to release lien money, the proper amount of damages for the aggrieved seller is the escrow deposit plus interest, not the difference between the contract price and the market value. *Long v. Brown,* 593 SW2d 371 (Civ. App. 1979).

80.15 Seller's Damages

Indiana One condition of a contract for the sale of residential real property was that buyers obtain a mortgage for not less than $35,000 within 30 days. Buyers could not obtain a mortgage and sellers retained a $1,000 earnest-money/liquidated damage deposit required by the contract. Buyers argued that the failure to obtain a mortgage relieved them from performance. *Held:* Sellers recovered. The condition in the contract was a "subject to financing" clause. Such clauses imposed an implied obligation to make a reasonable and good faith effort to satisfy the condition. Buyers did not make such effort. *Billman v. Hensel,* 391 NE2d 671 (1979).

Maryland Plaintiffs, sellers of 65.5 acres of land, entered into a contract in which defendant, a limited partnership, agreed to fully develop the first section of the property within 18 months of the date of the record of plat. Default on any contract provision by defendant would result in the reconveyance of the remaining unsold lots to plaintiffs. After 18 months, development of the first section was still uncompleted, and plaintiffs sued for reconveyance of the unsold lots. Even after the complaint was filed, defendant expended large sums of money for site improvements. Although the trial court found defendant in default, it held reconveyance to be too harsh a remedy and entered judgment for defendant. *Held:* Reversed. The contract unambiguously provided for reconveyance in the event of defendant's default, and this was plaintiffs' entire legal remedy. Defendant was a limited partnership of persons skilled in law and business who had agreed to these terms. Moreover, defendant created additional hardship for itself by expending large sums for improvements after the complaint had been filed. *Stueber v. Arrowhead Farm Estates Ltd. Partnership,* 519 A2d 816 (Ct. Spec. App. 1987).

Pennsylvania Contract for the sale of a home included a provision allowing the seller to retain "sum or sums paid on account'' in the event of buyer's failure to complete the purchase. The amount was to be ''on account of the purchase price, or as compensation for damages and expenses'' of seller, at seller's election. Buyer paid $100 as a deposit on the home, for which the contract price was $60,000. Buyer then breached. Seller sold the home to a third party for $54,000 and sued buyer for the $6,000 difference. One issue was the effect of the deposit clause. *Held:* The deposit clause barred seller from any recovery beyond the $100 deposit. The court concluded that the parties had intended that seller could apply the deposit to the purchase price or accept it as liquidated damages. Although this was an unjust result, the court refused to redraft the clause for the benefit of one party. *Harris v. Dawson,* 388 A2d 748 (1978).

Texas Contract to sell real property stated that the subject property was sold free and clear of all encumbrances, except those named in the contract. The contract did not list any encumbrances, but it did state that the property conveyed was that property described in a specific deed. The deed stated that the property was subject to a recorded mineral and gas reservation. When vendor attempted to recover earnest money that had been paid in escrow, vendee contended that vendor was not entitled to such recovery, since the property sold was not free and clear of encumbrances. *Held:* Where an earnest-money contract makes only general reference to a deed, purchaser is not charged with notice of any reservations contained in those instruments, unless the contract itself specifically mentions them. Therefore, since the contract contained only a general reference to the reservations-containing instrument, vendor was not entitled to recover. *Fajkus v. Bland,* 535 SW2d 398 (Civ. App. 1976).

80.20
—Measure of Seller's Damages

10th Circuit Seller sued realty company for breach of a contract to purchase a house. The district court awarded consequential damages equal to 10 percent interest on the adjusted appraised value of the house, less the adjusted rental seller received. *Held:* Reversed. When a seller of land seeks damages, as opposed to specific performance, seller is not entitled to the interest on the unpaid purchase price. Seller is entitled to loss of bargain damages, or the difference between the contract price and the fair market value of the house at the time and place of breach, plus consequential damages, such as costs incurred in attempting to resell and property taxes incurred between time the contract was breached and resumption of residency by seller. Seller was not, however, entitled to interest payments on loans, the additional mortgage she took to pay off the loans, and legal fees paid to avoid foreclosure, since she informed realty company's agent that she had ''full equity'' in the house. *Van Moorlehem v. Brown Realty Co.,* 747 F2d 992 (1984).

Oregon Developer contracted to construct and sell homes on 231 lots. After building 17 homes and selling only three, developer breached the contract and reassigned his interest to vendor. Vendor resold the remaining lots and sued to recover damages including (1) the interest payments on the purchase price of the lots, (2) property taxes until the lots were resold, (3) excess interest paid by vendor for short-term notes, (4) refinancing charges, and (5) resale expenses. *Held:* Only the interest payments on the purchase price, property taxes, and resale expenses were recoverable. Excess interest paid by vendor and refinancing charges were consequential damages that were found not to have been within the contemplation of the parties at the time of contracting. *Senior Estates, Inc. v. Bauman Homes, Inc.,* 539 P2d 142 (1975).

Utah Purchaser defaulted on a uniform real estate sales contract and brought an action to recover part of $34,596.10 that he had paid under the contract. Vendor sought to retain the entire sum purchaser had paid, arguing that the forfeiture clause of the uniform real estate sales contract was valid and should be enforced. *Held:* To allow vendor to retain the entire $34,596.10 would have been unconscionable; the forfeiture provision within the contract was not enforceable, since it was grossly excessive and disproportionate to any possible loss to vendor. And the trial court, in computing vendor's equitable damages, did not err in using a factor consisting of 8.5 percent interest on the unpaid balance of contract instead of using what may have been a speculative fair market value. *Johnson v. Carman,* 572 P2d 371 (1977).

80.25
Election of Remedies

New Hampshire Buyers, advised by a broker that the septic system in the house they were purchasing was in good working order, moved in and rented the house for one month before closing with the permission of the bank that foreclosed the property. After moving in, buyers discovered that the septic system did not work and demanded that the bank fix it. The bank refused, but offered to cancel the contract and return their down payment. Buyers refused this offer, closed the deal and sued the bank for damages. The bank contended that buyers waived their right to damages by closing with "full knowledge" of the defective septic system. *Held:* The bank was liable for damages. Since buyers had already moved out of their previous home, they were well within their right to close the deal and sue for damages. The bank was responsible for the broker's representation, although it had no knowledge of the defective septic system. *Mertens v. Wolfeboro Nat'l Bank,* 402 A2d 1335 (1979).

Texas Contract for the sale of realty provided for a $200 down payment and stated that in the event of default, seller would retain the deposit as liquidated damages for the contract breach. Purchaser breached the contract and seller, who had retained the original deposit, brought action for additional moneys. Seller contended that the contract clause did not preclude him from seeking actual damages, but merely gave him the right of electing between liquidated or actual damages. *Held:* Seller, by agreement, bound himself to accept the stipulated sum ($200) as compensation for the breach of contract and could not now elect to sue purchaser for actual damages. *Brewer v. Myers,* 545 SW2d 235 (Civ. App. 1976).

Washington First purchasers bought an apartment house from owners under a contract calling for monthly interest payments and a balloon payment in three years. Before the balloon payment was due, first purchasers sold the property to second purchasers who assumed the first contract. The second contract called for second purchasers to pay first purchasers a deposit, monthly interest, and a balloon payment. Second purchasers abandoned the property and ceased making payments under both contracts. Owners successfully sued to declare the interests of both sets of purchasers forfeited under the first contract; first purchasers successfully cross-claimed against second purchasers. *Held:* First purchasers were entitled to damages from second purchasers consisting of the balloon payment plus unpaid interest. First purchasers were entitled to the benefit of their bargain with second purchasers. In addition, a clause in the second contract providing that first purchasers, as sellers, "may elect" to seek liquidated damages against second purchasers gave the first purchasers the option of suing for actual damages instead. *Smith v. King,* 722 P2d 796 (1986).

80.30
Recovery of Purchaser's Deposit and Expenses

Maryland Contract for the sale of real property was conditioned upon purchaser's ability to arrange special financing within 10 days. Purchaser gave a 10 percent deposit on the price of the home at the signing of the agreement. Two days later, purchaser wanted to terminate and so ceased negotiating for the proper financing. Sellers appealed a lower court decision returning the deposit to purchaser. *Held:* By voluntarily ending her efforts to seek financing, purchaser waived her right to terminate the contract. Purchaser was not entitled to her deposit. *Bushmiller v. Schiller,* 368 A2d 1044 (1977).

New York Purchasers entered into a contract for a new home and gave sellers a 10 percent down payment. The contract gave buyers the right to cancel "upon written notice to the seller within three days" if real estate taxes were found to be higher than $3,500. The taxes were higher, and buyers' written notice was not received in time. Nonetheless, buyers stopped payment on their down payment check. Sellers sued to recover the down payment. *Held:* For sellers. Buyers' cancellation was ineffective, since it was not received by sellers on time. Purchasers' refusal to perform was therefore a breach. The court noted a modern trend toward substituting actual damages as the amount a seller can recover where purchaser breaches a contract after partially performing. However, the court unanimously concluded that with respect to down payments of 10 percent of the purchase price, it would not depart from the long-settled rule that a purchaser who defaults on a real estate contract cannot recover the down payment. *Maxton Builders, Inc. v. Lo Galbo,* 502 NE2d 184 (1986).

New York Buyer signed a sales contract for purchase of property from seller, and gave seller a down payment with the balance payable on closing. Buyer was to take the property subject to an existing mortgage, and the contract required seller to produce an estoppel certificate certifying the balance due, interest rate, and other pertinent provisions of the mortgage. At closing, seller could not produce the estoppel certificate and offered to prove the outstanding balance by producing canceled checks. He also produced a letter from the lender that stated that the mortgage was not "in good standing." Buyer refused to accept seller's proof and refused to complete the closing. When buyer sued for return of the down payment, seller argued that buyer had wrongfully refused to close. *Held:* Buyer was entitled to return of down payment. Seller's substitute offers were inadequate, particularly since the lender considered the mortgage not in good standing. Buyer had a right to good title. *Grace v. Nappa,* 389 NE2d 107 (1979).

New York The parties entered into a contract to purchase real estate. The contract stipulated that the purchasers had 60 days from the date of the contract was executed to secure a mortgage. In order to rescind, however, the purchasers had to notify sellers within 35 days after learning of their inability to secure a mortgage. Purchasers notified sellers that they were unable to obtain a mortgage; however, they had never submitted a mortgage application. Purchasers sued to recover the down payment on the canceled contract. *Held:* Purchasers' failure to apply for a mortgage before canceling the purchase contract caused a breach of contract and prohibited recovery of the down payment. *Hendel v. Scheuer,* 541 NYS2d 40 (App. Div. 1989).

80.35 Recovery for Purchaser's Improvements

Louisiana Prospective purchasers signed a purchase agreement with vendor to buy a condominium unit. Purchasers began to decorate and improve the unit before their loan application had been approved. Purchasers were unable to obtain financing within the time specified by the contract through no fault of their own and decided against making the purchase. Purchasers sued for compensation after vendor refused to reimburse purchasers for the improvements or to return their purchase deposit. *Held:* For purchasers. Under the state law of accessions, installation of carpet, flooring, wallpaper, ceiling fan, and a burglar alarm constitute "component parts" of a condominium. Purchaser may file a claim against vendor for reimbursement of "component parts" if a sale is not completed. The sale was conditioned on purchaser's ability to obtain financing; therefore, under the terms of the agreement, return of the deposit was required. *Berot v. Norcondo Partnership,* 544 So. 2d 508 (Ct. App. 1989).

Pennsylvania Parties entered into an agreement for the sale of a business and appurtenant real property. Prior to settling, with the vendor's consent, purchaser entered upon the premises and expended money on improvements. When purchaser was unable to settle on the specified date, the vendors sought equitable relief—an injunction from occupancy and an accounting. Purchaser sought to compel settlement, having since obtained financing. *Held:* It would be inequitable to compel settlement. However, since purchaser occupied the property and made improvements with the vendor's consent, equitable principles required that purchaser be reimbursed for the improvements. *Ruggieri v. West Forum Corp.,* 282 A2d 304 (1971).

80.40 Right to Deficiency Judgment

Indiana When purchasers of property from a corporation defaulted on their payments, the corporation foreclosed. The corporation was the only bidder at the sheriff's sale, where it regained the property for less than half the price of the previous sale, and considerably below the market price. Despite the fact that purchasers had already made payments for property about the size of the corporation's sheriff's sale bid, the corporation sought a deficiency judgment against the previous purchasers for the difference between the sheriff's sale price and purchasers' outstanding debt to the corporation. *Held:* The corporation was not entitled to a deficiency judgment, since in this instance it would have constituted a windfall. A deficiency judgment is appropriate only where the real estate's value is less than the total remaining deficiency. *Arnold v. Hall,* 481 NE2d 409 (Ct. App. 1985).

Nebraska Purchasers defaulted on an installment purchase agreement. Sellers foreclosed on the contract, which provided for the entire balance on default, and recovered just over half of the amount owed them. They then commenced a separate action seeking a deficiency judgment for the balance owed. Purchasers appealed, contending that a deficiency judgment may not be entered following a foreclosure on an installment sales contract. They pointed to Neb. Rev. Stat. § 25-2139, which provides that "[w]hen a petition shall be filed for the satisfaction of a mortgage, the court shall have the power only to decree and compel delivery of the premises to the purchaser thereof.'' *Held:* The right of a vendor to a deficiency judgment after a foreclosure has been recognized by Nebraska courts since 1897. Section 25-2139 operates only to separate the deficiency action from the foreclosure action and requires that a separate action be brought to collect a deficiency after a foreclosure. In Nebraska, a vendor in an executory land contract has the right to foreclose on the executory land contract as if it were a mortgage. *Carman v. Gibbs,* 371 NW2d 283 (1985).

PART N
OPTIONS TO PURCHASE

81.00
CREATION AND VALIDITY

81.05
Elements of a Valid Option

Connecticut Parties entered into an agreement concerning a piece of property. When defendants refused to convey the property, plaintiff sued for specific performance. Defendants claimed they had no obligation to convey because the agreement was merely an option, not a bilateral purchase and sale contract. *Held:* Plaintiff was entitled to specific performance. The following factors indicated that the agreement was a purchase and sale agreement: (1) The agreement referred to the parties as purchaser and seller rather than as optioner and optionee, (2) it included a provision obligating plaintiff to purchase the property, (3) it was devoid of any language granting plaintiff an option, (4) plaintiff rarely took options on property, (5) letters exchanged by the parties' attorneys indicated that the agreement was for purchase and sale, and (6) closing documents were attached to the agreement. The fact that the agreement was titled "Option Agreement" did not mandate a determination that the agreement was an option contract; the heading did not reflect the actual intent of the parties and the title was the only place the word "option" appeared. *Cutter Dev. Corp. v. Peluso,* 561 A2d 926 (1989).

Georgia When plaintiff sued for specific performance of a purchase option agreement, defendant contended that the option was too indefinite to be specifically enforced. The description of the land in the lease was shown by the militia district and showed the adjoining property owners on two sides, a state highway on the third, and a river on the fourth. The agreement specifically referred by date and record to two deeds, containing "200 acres more or less." *Held:* The option agreement was sufficiently definite in reference to the tract of land and as boundaries to be enforced. The terms "more or less" did not render the agreement indefinite where there were other descriptions that could sufficiently describe the property. *Saine v. Clark,* 219 SE2d 407 (1975).

Idaho Defendants owned a 440-acre tract of land, some of which plaintiffs were interested in purchasing. The parties executed a "receipt and agreement" to purchase 360 acres. Four days later, the parties signed an option agreement for another 40 acres, which inaccurately stated that $20 had been paid. Neither contract was made contingent upon the execution of the other and neither referred to the other. Subsequently, plaintiffs gave notice of their intention to exercise the option, but defendants resisted and plaintiffs sued for specific performance of the option agreement. The trial court found that the purchase agreement and option agreement were two separate contracts and that, standing by itself, the option agreement thus failed for lack of consideration. *Held:* Affirmed. A signed option contract that contains a false recital of payment of consideration and acknowledgment of its receipt is unenforceable. *Lewis v. Fletcher,* 617 P2d 834 (1980).

Massachusetts As part of a leasing arrangement, guardians granted an option to purchase property owned by their ward. The lease, with option, was authorized by judicial decree. Fifteen years later, lessees sought to exercise the option. A panel of three appraisers was selected as provided for in the lease, but the value they arrived at was unacceptable to the guardians. *Held:* A fiduciary's authority to sell real estate does not normally include authority to grant an option to purchase. Even if there is court approval and the option price is not fixed but is left to be determined by appraisers when the option is exercised, option clauses should not be included in leases made by guardians on behalf of wards. The option clause would only be enforceable if its inclusion in the lease was clearly necessary to make the most advantageous arrangement for the ward. Statutory provisions governing the sale of a ward's property would otherwise apply. *Nelson v. Maiorana,* 478 NE2d 945 (1985).

Mississippi An option contract indicated the property to be purchased and the purchase price, but left the manner of payment, the type of deed to be delivered, and other terms to be provided by later agreement. When optionee sued to enforce the contract, the trial court determined that the contract was unenforceable because it did not contain all the essential and material terms. *Held:* On appeal, the option was held to be sufficiently definite, since it contained enough information for the court to ascertain the contract's terms under the proper rules of construction. These rules allow for consideration of the general circumstances of the parties and, where necessary, relevant extrinsic evidence. The contract was ambiguous but not unenforceable. *Busching v. Griffin,* 465 So. 2d 1037 (1985).

Pennsylvania Buyers sued for specific performance of a portion of a sales agreement for the sale of a building providing for an option to purchase the adjoining property. Sellers alleged that the option portion was vague, indefinite, ambiguous, and unenforceable. The provision provided that "[b]uyers have first option to purchase adjoining or remainder of this plot to be conveyed subject to survey and to owner terminating operations." *Held:* Although the agreement did not provide a date or time limit, buyers were entitled to a reasonable time following the termination of operations in which to exercise the option. The agreement sufficiently described the parcel covered by the option where there was no doubt it constituted the adjoining remainder of the plot. Although the agreement failed to describe the operations to be determined, parol evidence may be admitted to determine what operations were contemplated. *Trapuzzano v. Lorish,* 354 A2d 534 (1976).

Utah A lease and option to purchase agreement for a "single family dwelling" described the property only as "residence 106 Pacific, aka 106 Lumber Yard." When a third party bought the property from the landlord, the third party claimed that the option was unenforceable because the description of the property was too vague and uncertain. *Held:* The use of a street address to describe the property was sufficient. The property, which included a residence, garage, and yard, was well-defined by fences and surrounding streets; so there was no serious question about the boundary. *Park W. Village, Inc. v. Avise,* 714 P2d 1137 (1986).

Wyoming In 1957, lessor executed an agreement with lessee, an oil company, for the lease of property. The lease was for a term of 10 years, with an option to extend the lease for two successive five-year terms. The rental for the lease term and the option period was to be $250 per month. The lease also gave lessee the option of purchasing the property for

$45,000. In 1977, after the lease had been transferred to a subsequent lessee, this lessee notified lessor of his desire to exercise his option to purchase the property for $45,000. When lessor refused because the price was too low, lessee sued for specific performance of the option clause. Lessor argued that the lease and the option, which were fixed in price over a 20-year period, were unconscionable. *Held:* Lessee was entitled to specific performance of the option clause. At the time of the agreement, the property was worth $35,000, and, at the time of the exercise of the option, with improvements, was worth $80,000. However, the risks of inflation are inherent in any contract, and the mere increase in the value of the land does not invalidate an agreement. *In re Estate of Frederick,* 599 P2d 550 (1979).

81.10
—Consideration

Georgia A mother conveyed all her interest in her brother's-in-law estate to her sons, but later the parties agreed to a second contract that gave the mother the option to require her sons' to reconvey to her their interest in the estate. When the mother tried to enforce this option 25 years later, the sons claimed that the second contract lacked consideration. *Held:* The contract's recital of "ten dollars and other valuable consideration" made the contract enforceable, despite the sons' claim that the $10 was never paid. The contract was under seal, and, in any event, the parties' natural affection for each other was adequate consideration. In addition, there was no evidence that the contract was unjust. *Warthen v. Moore,* 366 SE2d 666 (1988).

Illinois Defendants were approached to sell their house by an oil company that wished to expand an adjacent service station. Defendants refused to sell until oil company offered as part of the transaction an adjoining parcel of land. Defendants agreed, and oil company obtained and exercised an option to purchase the land from plaintiffs, who in turn deeded the property to defendant. The deed contained recitations that the property was transferred for $1 and other good and valuable consideration and also contained an option to repurchase by the seller within 15.5 years of the sale for $11,500. Nearly 15.5 years after the transaction, when the house had a fair market value of $37,500, plaintiffs notified defendants that they desired to exercise their repurchase option. Defendants refused to sell and sued for specific performance. Defendants asserted inadequate consideration for the conveyance. *Held:* For plaintiffs. Nominal consideration, given in exchange for both the conveyance and repurchase option, was sufficient. If a bargain was intended, the mere fact that the price exacted for the promise was $1 or less will not defeat the contract on ground of lack of consideration. *McMillan v. Ingolia,* 410 NE2d 162 (App. Ct. 1980).

Massachusetts Plaintiff's uncle gave defendant housing authority an option to purchase land for $20,000 for six months. Two months later, the uncle died; and the following month, defendant took the land by eminent domain. Following a probate court decision that the land passed to plaintiff under her uncle's will, plaintiff petitioned the trial court for an assessment of damages. Defendant agreed to pay plaintiff the $20,000, but the jury found plaintiff was owed $53,100 in damages. The judge overturned that verdict, finding that as the option agreement was binding on plaintiff, she was entitled only to the $20,000. She appealed, contending that the option was made without consideration and was therefore unenforceable. *Held:* The option was enforceable and binding on plaintiff. The option agreement was made in consideration of the sum of $1, which was not even paid, casting doubt as to whether there was any consideration. However, the agreement was signed under seal, and no consideration is necessary to make a sealed instrument binding on the parties. *Johnson v. Norton Hous. Auth.*, 375 NE2d 1209 (1978).

North Dakota Purchaser signed an option agreement to buy certain hotel properties. The agreement required the seller to convey "merchantable title free of all liens and encumbrances." Both parties were aware of an existing tenancy in the property when the agreement was signed. When purchaser attempted to exercise the option and seller offered to convey title subject to the outstanding lease, buyer protested, asserting that the lease made the title unmerchantable. After the option period expired without a sale, seller brought an action to remove the option, and purchaser countersued to enforce the option. *Held:* The option was void and unenforceable. The purchaser signed the option agreement with full knowledge of the existing tenancy. When purchaser refused to exercise the option subject to this lease, the agreement became null and void. *Alumni Ass'n v. Hart Agency, Inc.*, 283 NW2d 119 (1979).

Oklahoma Buyer sued seller for specific performance of a real estate option contract. Seller claimed that no consideration for the option had been received. *Held:* In an action for specific performance of a contract executed on a U.S. Department of Agriculture Farmers Home Administration form, if the $1 specified as consideration was actually paid and was considered adequate, the consideration was binding on the option. Parol evidence should have been admitted by the trial court to show failure of consideration. *Bobo v. Bigbee*, 548 P2d 224 (1976).

81.15
Options in Leases

Arizona Plaintiff leased property with an option to purchase that was to be exercised by payment to an escrow account. To the first set of escrow instructions, plaintiff added a provision that seller pay any existing mechanic's liens. Seller then prepared a new set of instructions requiring purchaser to take subject to the liens. When plaintiff failed to comply with the terms contained in the instructions, seller canceled the escrow, and plaintiff sued for specific performance of the first escrow instructions. *Held:* Although there was a general intent to sell the property, the parties did not have a mutual understanding as to all terms. Since plaintiff added the condition with respect to payment of liens, the first escrow instructions were not a valid exercise of the option to purchase and could not be specifically enforced. *Gifford v. Makaus*, 540 P2d 704 (1975).

Georgia Two parties made an agreement to lease a nursing home, with a five-year option to buy. When they actually signed the lease and exchanged money 10 days later, however, they signed only a lease giving lessee the right of first refusal. Toward the end of the five-year period, lessee tried to exercise the option under the earlier agreement. *Held:* The option in the first agreement did not survive the execution of the actual lease. The lease contained a merger clause that stated that the lease contained the entire agreement between the parties and superseded all prior agreements between them. Under the merger rule, prior agreements on the same subject are merged into the final contract. The option and the right of first refusal dealt with the same subject, acquisition of the nursing home. *Health Serv. Centers, Inc. v. Boddy*, 359 SE2d 659 (1987).

Idaho Leasing agreement provided for an option to buy and contained covenants concerning lessee's duty to care for the leased property. Lessee duly exercised the option in writing, but lessor refused to tender the documents of title and sued to terminate the lease for lessee's alleged failure to perform the lease covenants. Lessee counterclaimed for specific performance of the lease option. *Held:* Specific performance of the option was granted. The alleged covenant violations occurred after exercise of the option, and exercise of the option terminated the lease and all covenants therein. *Ford v. Lord,* 586 P2d 270 (1978).

Montana Lease between owner of ranch and tenants gave a right of first refusal to tenants if owner decided to sell. After expiration of lease, the parties concluded a modified lease agreement, providing for a year-to-year extension of the tenancy. Thereafter, owner offered to sell the ranch to tenants but canceled the sale; however, he also canceled sale to a third party when tenants objected. Tenants brought action for order requiring owner to set a price and give them first refusal, contending that he had formed the requisite intention to sell under the original lease. Meanwhile, owner had served a notice of determination of tenancy. *Held:* Tenants were not entitled to enforcement of the first refusal provisions of the original lease. The year-to-year tenancy had created a new agreement without the first refusal provision. *Nevala v. McKay,* 583 P2d 1065 (1978).

New York A lease contained both an option to renew and an option to buy for a fixed sum within a specified period. Exercise of the option was predicated upon "faithful performance by the Lessee of all the covenants, conditions and agreements" of the lease. When lessee attempted to exercise the option, lessor claimed that lessee had been a few days late with the rent at various times in the past and had thus forfeited the right to exercise the option. While lessor did not dispute that lessee was entitled to renew, it urged that any breaches by the lessee mandated forfeiture of the option to purchase, no matter how minor. *Held:* Lessee was not entitled to summary judgment. Lessor's allegation that lessee had not performed under the lease was sufficiently particular to impose upon lessee the burden of providing performance, which burden lessee had failed to meet. *1014 Fifth Ave. Realty Corp. v. Manhattan Realty Co.,* 499 NYS2d 936 (1986).

New York Landlord brought suit to enforce a lease provision that landlord would obtain a percentage rent between the time when tenant exercised the option to purchase and when title to the property was conveyed. *Held:* Landlord was entitled to the percentage rent due under the lease where there was no evidentiary proof that the closing was unreasonably delayed by landlord and where there was no showing of extrinsic evidence to resolve any ambiguity with respect to tenants' obligation to pay rent after exercising the option to purchase. Landlord was also entitled to attorney fees under the lease. *WA Olson Enters. v. Agway, Inc.,* 431 NE2d 289 (1981).

Washington The parties entered into a three-year lease of a house. At the same time, they executed an option agreement with no termination date allowing lessees to purchase the property for a set price, less any monthly payments after the first 12 rental payments. The option price was to increase 10 percent for each of the three years of the lease. A week after the lease expired, plaintiffs sought to exercise the option. Defendants refused to sell plaintiffs the house, claiming that the option had expired simultaneously with the lease. *Held:* Because it is commonly accepted that two contracts executed simultaneously and involving the same subject matter should be construed as one, the option agreement had the same duration as the lease. Plaintiffs, therefore, could no longer exercise the purchase option. *Beaudry v. Harman,* 626 P2d 50 (1981).

81.20 Duration

Alaska A purchase option did not contain a time limit for its exercise. Some 10 years after the option was granted, grantee invoked the option. Grantor's widow refused to honor it, claiming that the option violated the rule against perpetuities. *Held:* The option was valid. The Alaskan court, having never invoked the rule against perpetuities, opted to adopt a modified form of the rule that it concluded was more enlightened: the "wait and see" approach. Under this approach, an interest does not violate the rule against perpetuities if actual events cause it to vest within 21 years after the death of all lives in being at the creation of the interest, even if at the time the interest was created there was no foreseeable time limit in which the interest would vest. The modified rule already applied to post-1983 creations of interests by virtue of a statute passed in 1983. *Hansen v. Stroecker,* 699 P2d 871 (1985).

Georgia Two timber leases for 60 years contained options allowing lessee to purchase the land during the term of the lease. Lessor sued for a judgment declaring the options void as a violation of the rule against perpetuities. In this case, the maximum allowable period for vesting under the rule was only 21 years (instead of lives in being at the time of creation plus 21 years) because the future estate created in the lease (i.e., the option) was not tied to any lives in being at the time of execution of the lease. The trial court agreed with lessor and granted summary judgment. An appeals court affirmed. *Held:* Reversed. The rule against perpetuities does not apply to an option to purchase contained in a lease of the optioned property. Upon execution of the lease, an interest in the leased property vested in lessee; any eventual exercise of the option would only be the ripening into a larger interest of the existing leasehold interest. In addition, lessee was in possession of the property from the date of execution. *St. Regis Paper Co. v. Brown,* 276 SE2d 24 (1981).

Maryland After an option agreement had been signed, the giver of the option died and her heirs accepted a bid for the property without regard for the option holder's rights. The agreement had included the phrase "heirs and assigns" only with regard to the option holder's right to purchase. *Held:* The asymmetry of language in the option contract indicated that while the option to purchase was not personal, the obligation to convey was, and as such it terminated upon the death of the one giving the option. *Iglehart v. Jenifer,* 371 A2d 453 (1977).

Mississippi Walker conveyed a tract of land to Culpepper, with an option to purchase additional land. Under the option, the Walkers and their heirs, executors, administrators, or assigns would give the Culpeppers, their heirs, executors, administrators, or assigns first option to purchase the land. Walker conveyed the land to his daughter, who conveyed an undivided one-half interest to her brother. Daughter and brother brought an action to set aside the option on the ground that it violated the rule against perpetuities. *Held:* The option violated the rule against perpetuities because it might not have vested within the time required by the rule. The option was not personal to the optionees but created a preemptive right to purchase of indefinite duration. *Pace v. Culpepper,* 347 So. 2d 1313 (1977).

Missouri Defendant had an option to purchase property and granted an option to plaintiff to purchase the same property. When plaintiff told defendant that he did not intend to exercise the option, defendant obtained bank financing and exercised his option. When plaintiff sued to enforce his option before it expired, defendant argued that plaintiff had waived its right. *Held:* An option is irrevocable for the period stated; and once an option has been purchased for a valuable consideration, the rights of the option holder are not terminated unless the optionor has materially changed his position prior to a timely acceptance. Therefore, since the initial rejection did not cause any detrimental change of defendant's position, plaintiff could exercise the option, despite his initial rejection. *Ryder v. Westcoat,* 535 SW2d 269 (1976).

New York A sale contract for a tract of land intended to be used for a shopping center provided for a large payment to be made either when the land was rezoned for a shopping center or a year after signing of the contract, whichever was earlier. Several smaller initial payments were also contemplated and made. The land was never rezoned, and the payment was tendered a week later; seller refused to accept it. When purchaser sued for specific performance, seller claimed that purchaser had essentially agreed to an option to purchase, which had expired after a year. *Held:* The agreement was both a contract and an option, and the latter had expired. Since seller was obligated to keep the property off the market for a year, the payments made were similar to option payments. The payment provisions were, therefore, governed by rules applicable to options; time was of the essence in making the large payment. Seller could cancel the deed and retain the payments already made. *TIP Holding Corp. v. Wicks,* 407 NYS2d 709 (App. Div. 1978).

South Carolina Successors in interest sued in 1981 to repurchase land condemned in 1941 in connection with a hydroelectric project. The authorizing statute provided that owners of condemned lands that were not covered with water or dams five years after the state acquired the land would have the absolute right for a year to repurchase the land for the condemnation price. The state could extinguish the repurchase right after the one-year period by giving 90 days' notice. Successors in interest bought the repurchase right from the heirs of the original owner. *Held:* The repurchase right could not be exercised because of laches, stale demand, and presumption of grant. The failure to exercise the right within a reasonable time was negligent. *Gray v. South Carolina Pub. Serv. Auth.,* 325 SE2d 547 (1985).

Utah Grantor, in 1966, conveyed three mining claims to grantee, subject to an agreement that provided that grantee would pay grantor a percentage of the gross receipts from any ski lift built on land conveyed. This recorded agreement was to be binding upon any successors in title of grantee. In 1969, this agreement was amended to provide that grantee or his successors could acquire grantor's interest for a certain specified sum. In 1973, after ski lifts were installed, grantee tendered the sum required for the purchase of the grantor's interest, but grantor refused to sell. Grantor then sued to collect his royalty payments when grantee refused to make payments. *Held:* The amendment to the contract was an option, or a continuing offer, which had to be accepted within a reasonable amount of time to create a binding contract. Where the option was not exercised in a reasonable time, grantee could not enforce the agreement, and the grantor was entitled to a percentage of the gross receipts attributable to the ski lift. *Catmull v. Johnson,* 541 P2d 793 (1975).

82.00
EXERCISE

82.05
In General

U.S. District Court, Pennsylvania Tenant signed a lease and separate option agreement with landlord for the same piece of property. Pursuant to the option agreement, tenant notified landlord of his intention to purchase the property. The agreement provided that notice must be given "within 45 days" of the end of any five-year period. Tenant had give notice over a year prior to the end of one such period; and landlord, claiming that this violated the agreement, refused to sell. Landlord also charged that tenant had improperly assigned the lease to a third party. Tenant sued for specific performance of the option agreement. *Held:* Tenant was entitled to specific performance. The requirement of notice "within 45 days," meant only that tenant had to give notice at least 45 days before the end of a lease period, so tenant had not violated the option agreement. Since the option agreement was separate from the lease, default under the lease was no defense to an action to enforce the option agreement. *Owens-Illinois, Inc. v. Lake Shore Land Co.,* 457 F. Supp. 896 (WD 1978), aff'd 610 F2d 1185 (3d Cir. 1979).

Georgia Optionee, having decided to exercise an option to purchase land, deposited notice of such intent in the mail within the time allowed for proper exercise of the option. However, optionor had not received the notice by the last day for exercise of the option. *Held:* The notice was not timely. Although in some jurisdictions notice becomes effective upon its delivery, in the state of Georgia it does not become effective until receipt. *Musgrove v. Long,* 287 SE2d 23 (1982).

Idaho A contingent sale option clause read ". . . should [owners] desire or propose to sell or dispose of, or create any outstanding interest of any kind or nature in all or any part of said real estate property, . . . they shall give notice, in writing, to [optionee] of that intention . . . [and] . . . within a period of thirty-days, [optionee] may exercise the option. . . ." Optionee claimed that this clause would invoke by any devise to family members on the death of the owners of the property. *Held:* A devise would not trigger the option. Under optionee's interpretation, the option clause would have been essentially a land sale with a life estate to optionor. The option gave optionee only a right of first refusal at an agreed price should the owners, their heirs, or their assigns decide to sell or otherwise encumber the property. *Brooks v. Terteling,* 688 P2d 1167 (1984).

Illinois Lessee of farmland attempted to exercise his option to purchase under the lease by sending notice to lessor. Lessor died before acting on the notice, and his successor in interest let the option lapse, claiming that lessee's notice contained terms different from the option agreement. *Held:* Lessee was entitled to specific performance on the option, because the notice was clearly intended to invoke the option agreement. It was not decisive that the notice mischaracterized the size of the land in question, the computation of the tender offer, and the estate to be retained by the grantor. *Birkmeier v. Herget Nat'l Bank,* 468 NE2d 1220 (1984).

Massachusetts A lease for a store signed in 1950 provided for a perpetual tenancy from year to year, with an option to purchase at any time on written notice. The store was a family business, and the building was family owned. The store closed in 1970, and the premises were leased to another business. Former lessee then wrote to lessor to ask when he would receive his share of the rent from the new business. In 1976, former lessee informed lessor that he was exercising his option to purchase. In 1982, lessee sued for breach of contract and a constructive trust for rents. *Held:* There was insufficient evidence that lessee had exercised his right to purchase, and the statute of limitations prevented enforcement of a resulting trust for rents. To exercise the option to purchase, lessee was required to comply strictly with its terms, one of which provided for exercise only upon written notice. Only contradictory evidence was offered on the question of whether written notice had been provided. *Stapleton v. Macchi,* 519 NE2d 273 (1988).

Nevada Two leases were assigned to Summa Corporation, which brought suit for specific performance of an option to purchase contained in the leases. Defendant contended that the option was not assignable because the lease stated that lessee could assign an option only after giving written notice and making a deposit. The lease, though, was assignable without lessor's consent. *Held:* Reversed and remanded. The option was assignable to Summa. The lease provision was merely an antiseverability clause that prevented lessee or its assigns from transferring the option before its exercise independently of the leasehold interest. *Summa Corp. v. Richardson,* 564 P2d 181 (1977).

New Hampshire A business leased a building with an option to purchase from the local chapter of a national lodge. When the business tried to exercise the option, the local lodge refused, however, because consent could not be obtained from the national lodge. A copy of the bylaws was recorded under "Grand Lodge" in the registry of deeds, but the lease was recorded under the name of the local lodge. The business sued for specific performance. *Held:* The business was not entitled to specific performance, because it was not a bona fide purchaser without notice of the national lodge's interest. No purchase had yet been made; the monthly payments under the lease were rental charges separate from the option agreement. The local lodge could not act without the approval of the national lodge, which had no notice of the matter. *Continental Cablevision v. Osgood Lodge No. 48,* 459 A2d 263 (1983).

New York Defendant bought a classical music station under a contract that stipulated that plaintiff would withdraw a competing FCC application for the station's license. Defendant agreed to execute an option agreement in plaintiff's favor. The option agreement stated defendant would operate the station as a classical music station for at least five years; however, plaintiff would have the option of acquiring the station if defendant decided to sell it within that time. Shortly before expiration of the option, defendant decided to sell the station and plaintiff attempted to exercise its option. Defendant refused the option and plaintiff sued for specific performance. *Held:* Plaintiff was not entitled to specific performance of the option. In this case, plaintiff was adequately compensated by the legal remedy of damages. Specific performance was not necessary to effectuate plaintiff's intent in entering into the option agreement to assure continuance of classical programming, since defendant had operated the station as a classical station for 12 years. Additionally, defendant would sustain considerable losses if specific performance were awarded. *Concert*

Radio, Inc., *v. GAF Corp.*, 532 NE2d 1280 (1988).

North Dakota An option to buy land was renewed yearly from March 1 to March 1, until optionor died in July. Later that year, his estate informed optionee that the estate was not bound by the option. Optionee nevertheless then sent the estate notice that it intended to exercise the option. The estate rejected optionee's terms. Optionee sued for specific performance. *Held:* The option was never properly exercised. The agreement had called for the option to be exercised either by a 5 percent down payment or a contract for a deed. Optionee's notice had tendered neither money nor terms of a contract. The estate's alleged repudiation of the option did not relieve optionee of the obligation to comply with the option's terms. *Wessels v. Whetstone,* 338 NW2d 830 (1983).

Vermont Landowners granted the state two options to purchase land. Thereafter, the legislature passed a land gains tax. When the state exercised its option, the commissioner determined a tax was due from landowners. Landowners contended that it was the grant of the option that constituted the "taxable event," and that therefore no tax was due since the grant occurred before enactment of the tax statute. *Held:* The taxable event was the transfer of title to the state, and, therefore, landowners were subject to assessment at the time the state exercised the option. The grant of the option did not give the state any title or estate, legal or equitable, in the optioned property. *Harden v. Vermont Dep't of Taxes,* 352 A2d 685 (1976).

82.10 Right of First Refusal

3d Circuit In 1965, with assistance from the Department of Housing and Urban Development (HUD), defendant housing authority acquired and planned to redevelop an 80-acre tract bordering the Atlantic City boardwalk. Plaintiff, a private redevelopment corporation, was selected by defendant to carry out the plans. In 1969, both parties and HUD executed a contract calling for the immediate conveyance of a small parcel and final conveyance of the balance of the tract to plaintiff within five years. The contract entitled plaintiff to right of first refusal, but did not provide for the duration of this right. In 1976, a third party entered into a new redevelopment contract with defendant. At this point, plaintiff asserted an intent to exercise the right of first refusal. *Held:* The right of first refusal, which had no explicit expiration date, was to last only for a commercially reasonable period of time. The court concluded that the right of first refusal expired along with the expiration of the five-year period originally allotted for redevelopment of the land. It based its conclusion on a provision of the contract that incorporated a HUD policy of prohibiting developers from speculating in subsidized redevelopment by holding property without building in hopes that it would increase in value as the result of the efforts of others or of market inflation. *Barco Urban Renewal Corp. v. Housing Auth.*, 674 F2d 1001 (1982).

Colorado Tenant's lease contained a right of first refusal to purchase the property and an option to renew that did not require express notification to landlord. When the agreement expired, neither landlord nor tenant discussed the renewal option. However, tenant continued to occupy the premises and pay rent. Subsequently, landlord sold the property to buyers, advising them that tenant did not have a lease and was only a month-to-month tenant. Buyer did not examine the original lease and made no inquiries as to tenant's rights. Tenant subsequently brought suit to have the sale set aside and the right of first refusal enforced. *Held:* Tenant's continued occupancy constituted a renewal of the lease. Thus, all the provisions of the agreement were still in effect, including the right of first refusal. Since tenant remained on the premises, buyers were deemed to have constructive notice of all the terms of the tenancy, and they therefore took title subject to the right of first refusal. *Cohen v. Thomas & Son Transfer Line, Inc.*, 586 P2d 39 (1978).

Georgia Two brothers had received equal undivided interests in land from their late father in return for a note, and divided the land in kind. Each brother gave the stepmother, who had inherited the note, a new note and security deed covering his half. Each brother also gave the other a right of first refusal. After one brother defaulted on his note, his stepmother exercised her power of sale under the security deed and auctioned the property, purchasing it for the amount due on the note. The other brother then sought to exercise his right of first refusal. The stepmother argued that the right of first refusal applied only to an election to sell, not to an involuntary sale under a security deed. *Held:* The brother was entitled to buy defaulting brother's property for the amount bid by his stepmother. In executing the security deed, defaulting brother could not convey more than the interest he owned, which was a fee simple interest subject to a right of first refusal. Further, the involuntary nature of the sale did not defeat the right of first refusal. The security deed empowered the stepmother to sell the land as defaulting brother's attorney in fact if he defaulted. An owner may not avoid a right of first refusal by allowing land to be sold by an attorney in fact. *Hornsby v. Holt*, 359 SE2d 646 (1987).

Georgia Grantor conveyed property subject to a right of first refusal in the grantor. After grantee died, his estate arranged to sell the property, along with four other tracts, for a total price of $400,000. The purchase price was not allocated among the five tracts. The estate notified grantor of the impending sale and offered to sell him the tract that was subject to his right of first refusal for $200,000, without explaining how the $200,000 figure was determined. Grantor sued. *Held:* A preemptive right of first refusal may not be defeated by a third party offer to purchase the land in question as part of a package transaction, even if the purchase price is allocated among several tracts. *Hinson v. Roberts*, 349 SE2d 454 (1986).

Idaho Plaintiff had a right of first refusal as to a lot in a subdivision owned by defendant. Subsequently, defendant agreed to sell the seven remaining lots in the subdivision to a third party in exchange for the construction of a house worth over $200,000. Under this purchase agreement, the lot subject to plaintiff's right of first refusal was priced at $50,000, which price plaintiff could not meet. Subsequently, plaintiff obtained a copy of an agreement between defendant and third-party purchaser, indicating that the true cost of each lot was $30,000 in labor and materials spent on the residence. Plaintiff sued for the right to exercise its first refusal right for $30,000. *Held:* Plaintiff did not receive notice of an offer to purchase that would trigger his decision as to exercise of his right of first refusal. He was never presented with a writing of the full terms of the purchase offer, including the fact that its true cost to offeror was $30,000, not $50,000. The court enjoined the sale of the lot to the third party but did not order its sale to plaintiff for $30,000, holding that defendant should not be compelled to sell the lot when he had not received an offer to purchase it separately from the larger parcel. *Gyurkey v. Babler*, 651 P2d 928 (1982).

Iowa When grantors sold a lot adjacent to their property, they covenanted that should they "elect to sell" a portion of their property for erection of a residence to anyone other than their son or daughter, the owners of the neighboring lot would be notified and have a right of first refusal. Grantors' property was later divided into two parcels, the front with a residence, the rear vacant. Owners of the rear parcel defaulted on a mortgage, and the property was sold at foreclosure sale. Owners of the neighboring lot sued to quiet title, claiming the covenant gave them the option of purchasing the rear parcel for the amount bid at foreclosure, since the foreclosure purchaser had bought the land intending to build a residence. *Held:* The option was not triggered by the sale. The neighbors' right of first refusal was to be triggered only if the grantor's successors *elected* to sell the property; complying with a foreclosure judgment was not an "election" by defaulting property owners. The foreclosure purchaser, however, who had actual and constructive knowledge of the option did not have a right to build a residence on the property. *Henderon v. Millis,* 373 NW2d 497 (1985).

Kansas Plaintiff tenant's lease had an option to purchase the leased property from defendant owners for $25,000 and a right of first refusal if defendants received a bona fide offer to purchase the property. The right of first refusal provided that if tenant failed to exercise its preemptive right and the proposed sale to a third party fell through, the preemptive right continued. The provision was silent as to whether the option continued under similar circumstances. The city offered to purchase the parcel leased to plaintiff for $60,000, as well as an adjoining parcel. Plaintiff did not exercise its option or right of first refusal but expressed its intention to rely on its claimed continuing right to exercise the option. Ultimately, the city purchased both parcels. Afterwards, plaintiff made an offer to exercise its option for $25,000, and was refused. Plaintiff sued to enforce the option. *Held:* The city's offer triggered plaintiff's right of first refusal even though it was greater than the amount of the option and was a combined offer to purchase the leased premises and the adjacent lot. Where, as here, the lease did not specify whether the option provision or the right of first refusal provision took precedence, the rule of *Tarrant v. Self,* 387 NE2d 1349 (Ind. Ct. App. 1979) applied, that is, if landlord notified tenant of a bona fide purchase offer and tenant refused to exercise his option to purchase under the terms of such offer, then tenant forfeited his right to purchase under the fixed price option. *M&M Oil Co. v. Finch,* 640 P2d 317 (1982).

Maine Two parcels of land were leased to lessee with an option to buy both parcels but a right of first refusal (if lessor "had an opportunity to sell") only on the second parcel. When a offer was made for the second parcel, lessee gave lessor a $50 down payment. Thereafter, lessor refused to sell all of the second parcel, because he would then be left with a substandard area for zoning purposes. Lessee insisted on buying all of both parcels. Lessor claimed that lack of specificity in the option agreements, in addition to the fact the purchase price was never tendered, invalidated the options. *Held:* The options were enforceable, and lessee was entitled to specific performance. Tender of the purchase price was not necessary to exercise the options. Though the options were silent on the matter, lessor was required to deliver marketable title in fee by deed of quitclaim, with covenants of special warranty against encumbrances created by lessor. *Littlefield v. Brown,* 394 A2d 794 (1978).

New Hampshire Defendants and two other families acquired and held a tract of land as tenants in common. A portion of the land was conveyed separately to defendants, who built a house thereon. Tenants in common then sold another portion of the land to plaintiffs. In the deed to that parcel, tenants in common also granted plaintiffs a right of first refusal to be enforceable upon receipt by tenants of any offer to purchase the remaining tenancy property. Subsequently, tenants decided to transfer their undivided interests to defendants. Plaintiffs sued, claiming that defendants' offer to purchase triggered the right of first refusal. *Held:* The right of first refusal was inoperative in the transaction among tenants in common. The language in the deed's right of first refusal, which used the plural in each reference to tenants in common, showed that tenants intended the right of refusal to be operative only if a purchase offer were made to them as a whole group and not individually among themselves. *Baker v. McCarthy,* 443 A2d 138 (1982).

New York The Metropolitan Transportation Authority (MTA) bought a freight yard from the Pennsylvania Railroad. Delbay Corporation, a subsidiary of Pennsylvania Railroad, was given an option to purchase lots in the freight yard if the MTA deemed the property "no longer necessary for transportation operations." Years later, the MTA notified Delbay that six of its lots were for sale. Delbay assigned its rights to two of the lots to defendant, Bruken Realty, who notified the MTA of its election to purchase them. However, the parties reached an impasse in negotiations. The MTA then sued to declare the option agreement void for violation of the rule against perpetuities. *Held:* Delbay had a preemptive right, or right of first refusal, to buy the freight yard property, although the agreement was called an option. This did not mean optionee could compel the MTA to sell. The MTA instead activated Delbay's rights by notifying it that the property was for sale. Although unlimited preemptive rights violate the rule against perpetuities, they do so only marginally, and strict application of the rule would nullify an agreement that enabled the parties to maximize the productive use of their property. The court therefore assessed the validity of the preemptive right by the common-law rule prohibiting unreasonable restraints, rather than by the rule against remote vesting. *Metropolitan Transp. Auth. v. Bruken Realty,* 492 NE2d 379 (1986).

Rhode Island Vendors sold two lots to purchasers, subject to a restrictive covenant giving vendors a right of first refusal to repurchase the lots. Purchasers transferred title for tax reasons to a corporation they controlled. Purchasers sued to determine the validity of vendors' right of first refusal. *Held:* The right of first refusal applied only where purchasers sold the property to a third party for residential purposes, not where the property was sold for tax purposes to purchasers' corporation. Utilizing the language of the covenant, the court found that preemptive rights were intended for a conveyance to another resident. The conveyance in this case was not of the type intended to trigger defendants' right of first refusal. First, it was made solely for tax purposes, and second, the coveyance resulted in no significant transfer of ownership interest within the meaning of the restrictions. Transferor-purchaser was an owner of transferee, the corporation, and therefore the transfer did not effect a change in control to a third party. The court concluded it would be inequitable to allow vendors to exercise their first refusal rights in this situation. The conveyance was allowed with the requirement that the corporation take the property subject to vendors' preemptive rights. *Belliveau v. O'Coin,* 557 A2d 75 (1989).

Rhode Island The purchase and sale agreement between Elizabeth P. Firestone and David W. Sawyer gave Sawyer an unrestricted right of first refusal on Firestone's ocean front property. After execution of the agreement and the payment of a "nonrefundable" deposit, Firestone insisted that she did not understand such a right of first refusal was contained in the agreement and asked if Sawyer would agree to delete the right of first refusal provision. Sawyer declined. Firestone then proposed draft deeds limiting the right of first refusal to a sale of the lot as a separate parcel. According to Firestone, the right of first refusal provision of the original agreement did not preclude her from including the lot in a larger tract of land and selling it to a third party. Sawyer terminated negotiations and sought rescission of the purchase and sale agreement plus the return of his deposit. *Held:* Sawyer was entitled to rescission. Firestone breached the agreement by attempting to restrict Sawyer's right of first refusal to sale of the lot as a separate parcel. The holder of such a right, contrary to Firestone's argument, may enjoin the proposed sale of a larger tract that includes the parcel. *Sawyer v. Firestone,* 513 A2d 36 (1986).

Utah Landlord leased an unimproved parcel of land to tenant and granted tenant the right of first refusal to purchase the parcel if it was offered for sale during the lease term or within a year following the lease's termination date. While the lease was still in effect, landlord decided to develop the parcel and, for that purpose, formed a partnership with another developer. Under the partnership agreement, landlord was to contribute the parcel to the partnership and take 51 percent of the partnership in return. The other developer, in exchange for the remaining 49 percent of the partnership, agreed to finance, construct, and manage an office building on the premises. When landlord refused to offer the parcel to tenant, tenant sued for specific performance of the right of first refusal. *Held:* The Supreme Court of Utah held that the landlord's contribution of its parcel to the partnership in which an outsider took a substantial ownership interest constituted a sale and was subject to the right of first refusal provision. It then remanded the case for further proceedings on the issue of whether the particular nature of the partnership precluded matching the acquisition offer of tenant. *Prince v. Elm Co.,* 649 P2d 820 (1982).

Wyoming When Whitlock purchased a tract of land in 1960, he executed an agreement by which plaintiff and defendant would each purchase a 20 percent undivided interest in the tract. The agreement provided each party with a right of first refusal should one of the other two parties desire to sell his interest to an outsider. The right of first refusal was to be "for the mutual benefit of and binding upon the parties signatory, their respective heirs and assigns." In 1965, Whitlock conveyed his 60 percent interest to defendant. Plaintiff did not learn of this transaction until 1970. The value of the lots continued to rise until 1976, when another party offered to purchase the remaining lots. Plaintiff sued for payment for the share he claimed should have been offered to him in 1965 pursuant to the right of first refusal. Defendant argued that the right of first refusal was a violation of the rule against perpetuities. *Held:* The right of first refusal was valid. Whereas the rule of perpetuities was designed to prevent restraints on the alienation of real property, rights of first refusal do not impose such restraints. A right of first refusal merely gives certain purchasers a preference in the event a landowner decides to sell his property. *Hartnett v. Jones,* 629 P2d 1357 (1981).

82.15
Fixed-Price Option

Connecticut Golart owned property on which he operated a service station. Golart entered into lease agreements with Texaco that gave Texaco an option to purchase the property for a fixed price. In both leases, Texaco's representative indicated that the option clause had to be accepted or there would be no agreement. When Texaco sought to exercise the purchase option, Golart refused to convey. Texaco sued, seeking specific performance of the fixed-price purchase option. Golart claimed the option was unconscionable. *Held:* For Texaco. The court utilized the test of Official Comment 1 to UCC § 2-302 in examining the claim of unconscionability: whether in light of the general commercial background and of the particular needs of the trade or case, the clause is so one-sided as to be unconscionable under the circumstances. Given the circumstances of the case and the relative bargaining power of the parties, the lease was found not unreasonably favorable to Texaco. *Texaco, Inc. v. Golart,* 538 A2d 1017 (1988).

North Carolina Texaco's lease for a lot contained a fixed-price option clause which gave lessee the right to purchase the property for $50,000 at any time during the lease or extension, as well as a right of first refusal, giving lessee the right to buy the property ". . . (on) the same terms and at the same price as any bona fide offer . . . which lessor desires to accept." Defendant lessors received an offer from a third party to purchase the property for $217,000. Texaco tendered $50,000; defendants, believing the lease required Texaco to meet the highest offer for the property, refused to convey. Texaco sued for specific performance. *Held:* For Texaco. The court examined for the first time the interpretation of a fixed-price option accompanied by a right of first refusal option. The court chose to follow the line of authority that deems the two options separate and distinct so that lessee may exercise his option to purchase for a fixed price without regard to the provision for first right of purchase. Lessee's rights under a fixed-price option have been held to be continued and not extinguished by lessee's failure to exercise a first right to purchase after notice of an offer from a third person. This interpretation comported more closely with the language of the lease. *Texaco Inc. v. Creel,* 314 SE2d 506 (1984).

South Dakota A lease on a filling station contained two option clauses: an option to purchase for a fixed price at any time during the lease term and a right of first refusal, under which lessee, on 30 days' notice, could purchase the station by meeting an offer made to lessor. Lessor gave notice of such an offer, but lessee failed to respond until the 30 days had passed. Lessee then notified lessor that it elected to exercise the purchase option for a fixed price, which was less than the outside offer. *Held:* Lessee could exercise the fixed-price option. The two options were independently valid, and the purchase option survived the expiration of the right of first refusal. *Crowley v. Texaco, Inc.,* 306 NW2d 871 (1981).

Vermont Lessee-optionee sought specific performance of a fixed-price purchase option, one of two options contained in a lease. The other option gave lessee a right of first refusal to meet bona fide offers to purchase the property. Lessee-optionee refused to exercise either of these options when original lessor sold the property. Subsequently, when purchaser received an offer more than three times greater than the fixed-price option, lessee-optionee sought to exercise the fixed-price option. *Held:* Where lessee-optionee has an opportunity to exercise either option but has refused to do so, equity does not allow lessee-optionee to exercise the fixed-price option after the property has substantially appreciated in value. *Shell Oil Co. v. Jolley,* 296 A2d 236 (1972).

PART O

PURCHASER'S REMEDIES FOR PROPERTY DEFECTS

83.00 SELLER'S OR BUILDER'S WARRANTIES

83.05 Implied Warranties in General

4th Circuit Hotel guest injured in a fall on a spiral staircase inside his suite of rooms sued the architect, alleging breach of an implied warranty of safe design. *Held:* The court, citing *Surf Realty Corp. v. Standing,* 78 SE2d 901 (Va. 1953), stated that under Virginia law, in the absence of a special agreement, an architect is not liable for fault in construction resulting from defects in the plans, because he does not imply or guarantee a perfect plan or a satisfactory result. The court also pointed out that any duty owed by the architect was owed to his employer rather than to the general public. The court affirmed judgment for the architect. *Gravely v. Providence Partnership*, 549 F2d 958 (1977).

Alabama Plaintiff contracted to buy defendant's home, contingent upon obtaining a 33-year Farmer's Home Administration (FmHA) mortgage. Defendant applied for the mortgage and an FmHA inspector checked the premises. The loan was approved and the sale closed. After taking possession, plaintiffs discovered severe fire damage in the attic. Plaintiff sued for damages, alleging the true value of the home to be well below the purchase price. Plaintiff argued that the contract contained an implied promise the house would meet minimum FmHA structural standards. *Held:* The court refused to read implied terms into the contract, ruling the contract clear and unambiguous. Further, the contract contained the standard statement "buyer has examined this property and agrees to accept same in its present condition, except as may be specified herein." The mortgage clause merely incorporated a financial contingency and did not amount to a covenant by defendant to deliver the home in a condition meeting FmHA standards. *Holloway v. Jackson*, 412 So. 2d 774 (1982).

Colorado Builder began construction on a home, intending to occupy it with his family. Upon encountering financial difficulties, he decided to sell it. Buyer requested express warranties of habitability and workmanlike construction; they were not given. When defects appeared, buyer sued on the theory of implied warranties. *Held:* Implied warranties of habitability and workmanlike construction arose in the sale of a new home by builder-vendor even though vendor had commenced construction of the home with the intent of residing there with his family. The sale to buyer was a "commercial sale" in that the builder, who was in the business of building, sold a new home to a member of the general public. *Sloat v. Matheny*, 625 P2d

1031 (1981), rev'g 605 P2d 71 (Ct. App. 1980).

Florida Unit owners of a condominium sued developer for breach of implied warranties of fitness, of merchantability, and of compliance with plans approved by local governmental authorities. Developer argued that the unit owners were not in privity with him and could not, therefore, sue. *Held:* Suit dismissed. Owners were not in privity with the developer. The privity doctrine should be upheld because many unforeseen ramifications could arise if developers were held liable to remote purchasers. *Strathmore Riverside v. Paver Dev. Corp.*, 369 So. 2d 971 (1979).

Illinois Plaintiff entered into a contract for the construction of a home with defendant builder. After substantial completion of the home, plaintiff refused to accept it, citing various construction defects. Defendant appealed the trial court's award of damages in the amount of earnest money paid, plus the value of labor and materials provided by plaintiff. *Held:* Affirmed. The high court ruled that there is an implied warranty in such construction contracts that the premises will be reasonably suited for its intended purpose, much like the Uniform Commercial Code (UCC) warranty of merchantability and fitness for a particular purpose. The construction warranty is a separate covenant, independent of the covenant to convey. *Petersen v. Hubschman Constr. Co.*, 389 NE2d 1154 (1979).

Texas Plaintiffs contracted with defendant to design, provide materials for, and build a house for plaintiffs. The contract contained no express warranties. A promissory note signed by plaintiffs provided that there were "no . . . warranties, express or implied, in addition to said written instruments." Defendant refused to repair the house's sagging roof, noting that plaintiffs had waived all warranties. Plaintiffs sued for damages, arguing that the language of the promissory note was not sufficient to waive the home builder's implied warranties of workmanship and habitability. *Held:* The language of the promissory note was a clear waiver of implied warranties that plaintiffs had an opportunity to object to prior to signing the contract documents. Plaintiffs' reliance upon UCC§ 2-316(b) was inappropriate. The UCC applies to the sales of goods, while the construction contract was primarily a sale of services. Using the same rationale, the court held that the UCC implied warranty of merchantability was also inapposite. *G-W-L v. Robichaux*, 643 SW2d 392 (1982).

83.10 —Implied Warranties of Fitness and Habitability

Alabama Buyer purchased a new house constructed by builder. The septic system for the house was built by a subcontractor and conformed to applicable guidelines set by the FmHA, which financed the house. Almost six years after the purchase, the septic tank malfunctioned and buyer brought an action against builder alleging breach of the implied warranty of fitness and habitability. Builder argued that no such warranty existed since it would make him, in effect, an insurer of the house against any future unforeseen problems. *Held:* The failure of the sewage system was a breach of an implied warranty. The court overruled previous Alabama cases and applied the general rule for the implied warranty of fitness and habitability. In this case, the house was sold in a defective condition that buyers were neither aware of nor could have reasonably discovered and adversely affected the value of the house. *Sims v. Lewis*, 374 So. 2d 298 (1979).

Arkansas A house built by defendant was

purchased by plaintiffs after having been occupied by the initial purchaser and several purchasers in succession. Soon after occupying the house, plaintiffs noticed the odor of formaldehyde, which they traced to the carpet and pad installed by defendant. Plaintiffs sued defendants, alleging both breach of the implied warranty of habitability and of strict liability. *Held:* Defendant's motions to dismiss both counts were denied. Privity of contract is not required for the implied warranty of habitability under Arkansas law. Instead, the relevant considerations are whether the building was altered so as to produce the defect subsequent to the initial sale and whether the defect was discoverable upon reasonable inspection by subsequent purchasers. If neither consideration applies, then privity between seller and purchaser is not a prerequisite to recovery under the implied warranty theory in Arkansas. *Blagg v. Hunt Co.*, 612 SW2d 321 (1981).

Florida Plaintiffs purchased undeveloped residential waterfront lots abutting a seawall. The seawall collapsed, and plaintiffs sued seller on a theory of breach of implied warranty of fitness. Plaintiffs relied heavily upon *Gable v. Silver*, 258 So. 2d 11 (Dist. Ct. App. 1972), which recognized an implied warranty of habitability in the sale of new residences. *Held:* The Florida Supreme Court refused to extend *Gable* to these facts. *Gable* involved purchase by consumers, without special expertise in real estate or the ability to spot flaws in construction of new homes purchased for personal use. Here, plaintiffs purchased an empty lot as investors, not consumers. Purchasers of unimproved lots may more reasonably be expected to inspect them knowledgeably before purchasing them, and may be more likely to request an express warranty than would consumers purchasing homes. *Conklin v. Hurley*, 428 So. 2d 654 (1983).

Idaho Buyers purchased apartment complex from developer. Subsequent investigation of the foundation, which had been constructed on fill dirt using improper techniques, revealed that it was cracking. Buyers sued both developer and builder on several theories, including breach of implied warranty of habitability. The trial court entered summary judgment in builder's and contractor's favor. *Held:* For buyers. On issues of first impression, the court ruled that a subsequent, non-occupying purchaser of income-producing residential property that suffers a purely economic loss from latent defects manifesting themselves within a reasonable time may maintain an action against a builder or builder-developer based on the implied warranty of habitability, even if no privity of contract exists between the two. *Tusch Enters. v. Coffin*, 740 P2d 1022 (1987).

Illinois Plaintiff, who was not original purchaser of his home, alleged that his home was not fit for residential use in a suit against builder. Plaintiff claimed that builder breached his implied warranty of habitability and that the warranty extended to plaintiff regarding all latent defects in the home that manifested themselves within a reasonable time after the purchase. The public policy behind habitability warranties, which is to protect purchasers of new homes upon the discovery of latent purchasers of new home defects, has nothing to do with privity of contract, especially if, as in these facts, a short period of time elapsed between the original and subsequent purchases. Subsequent purchasers, like original purchasers, usually lack knowledge of construction practices and have little opportunity to inspect the costruction process. They must, therefore, place great reliance upon the builder's expertise and should not be forced to live with his mistakes. *Redarowicz v. Ohlendorf*, 441 NE2d 334 (1982).

Maryland Buyers of a home sued seller for misrepresentation, breach of express warranty, and breach of implied warranty because of an insufficient water supply from a well that had failed two weeks after settlement. The lower court gave seller summary judgment. *Held:* An implied warranty of habitability requires an adequate water supply. A genuine question of material fact concerning whether or not the water supply was adequate precluded summary judgment. *Krol v. York Terrace Bldg., Inc.*, 370 A2d 589 (1977).

Montana Plaintiff contracted to purchase, for $90,000, a home to be built by seller. Settling caused by water in the moisture-sensitive soil under the house, and the "pooling" of water at the north end of the house, resulted in damages that required extensive, costly repairs. Plaintiff sued builder-vendor seeking damages for breach of implied warranty of habitability. *Held:* The doctrine of caveat emptor no longer barred an implied warranty action against builder-vendor of a new residence. Builder-vendor impliedly warranted that the home was constructed in a workmanlike manner and was suitable for habitation. The home's defect was within the implied warranty even though it was not structural, and involved instead the moisture-sensitivity of the soil and water "pooling." *Chandler v. Madsen*, 642 P2d 1028 (1982).

New Jersey Purchasers of a new house discovered that the water supply was impure and brought suit against builder-vendor for breach of an implied warranty of habitability. Builder-vendor argued that, as a "small-scale" developer, he should not be held to the same standard as a mass developer, and furthermore, the impure water supply was not due to any substandard construction on his part. *Held:* Where a builder-vendor constructs a new house, the implied warranty of habitability applies whether or not he is a mass developer. A potable water supply is included in the implied warranty, whether or not it was due to builder's substandard construction. *McDonald v. Mianecki*, 398 A2d 1283 (1979), aff'd, 398 A2d 1283 (1979).

North Carolina Buyers purchased house from builder more than four years after its completion. The central air conditioning system lacked sufficient capacity to cool the house, and buyers sued builder for breach of warranty of habitability. Builder moved for summary judgment, claiming the warranty of habitability did not apply because the house was not recently completed and an inadequate air-conditioning system was not a major structural defect. *Held:* Motion denied. Defendant's claims were questions of fact for a jury to resolve. In determining whether the dwelling was "recently completed," the jury should use a reasonableness standard, weighing such factors as the age of the building, the use to which it had been put, the nature of the defects, and the expectations of the parties. In determining whether a defect was a major structural defect, the test for the jury was whether there was a failure to meet the prevailing standard of workmanlike quality, not whether the defective fixture was an essential utility. *Gaito v. Auman*, 327 SE2d 870 (1985).

North Dakota Defendant contracted with plaintiff to design, manufacture, and install an electrical system in plaintiff's plant. After the work was completed, a fire destroyed a substantial part of the property. The fire was caused by a defect in the electrical system. Plaintiff sued defendant for breach of implied warranties of fitness. *Held:* Judgment for plaintiff affirmed. The court applied the rule of *Dobler v. Malloy*, 214 NW2d 510 (1973), which extended an implied warranty of fitness to construction contracts where the contractor holds himself out as competent to undertake the contract, and the owner has no expertise in the type of work contemplated, furnishes no plans, and relies on the experience and skill of the contractor. The installation of an electrical system was part of the construction process; therefore the warranty of fitness defined in *Dobler* applied here. *Air Heaters, Inc. v. Johnson Elec., Inc.*, 258 NW2d 649 (1977).

Virginia Buyer purchased a home that was surfaced with a veneer of concrete bricks. Shortly after taking possession, buyer discovered cracks in some of the bricks. Alleging breach of implied warranty, buyer sued seller to recover damages incident to the repair and replacement of the defective bricks. *Held:* The common-law rule of caveat emptor applies in Virginia, and the decision as to whether the rule should be changed is a matter for the legislature and not for the courts. Under the common law, a conveyance of real estate carries no covenants except those expressly made. Thus, the sale here did not carry an implied warranty of fitness for intended use, and buyer could not recover. *Bruce Farms, Inc. v. Coupe*, 247 SE2d 400 (1978).

West Virginia Plaintiffs retained defendant contractor to select a site and build a residence on their steeply sloped lot. A year after plaintiffs moved into the new home, a slip developed in the front yard, causing seepage from the septic system defendant had installed. Plaintiff charged defendant with breaching the implied warranty of habitability and fitness implicit in the home building contract. *Held:* The implied warranty does not extend to soil conditions of which builder is unaware or could not, with the exercise of reasonable care, discover. Evidence demonstrated that the slippage was due to an undisclosed, preexisting natural movement of the land. The fact that builder selected the site and positioned the home did not extend the implied warranty of habitability to such conditions, absent express provision to the contrary. *Gamble v. Main*, 300 SE2d 110 (1983).

Wyoming Homeowners brought actions in negligence and breach of warranty against land developer and builders to recover damages to their homes from seepage of water. *Held:* The evidence showed that developer had employed an engineering firm that conducted a drilling program, soil analysis, and determination of the depth of water table and drainage for the subdivision. Developer advised builders of the areas described in the engineering firm's reports and further advised them that they should stay two feet above the water table in building the homes. Builder alone decided whether to build homes with or without a basement and neither sought out nor made inquiry of the developer. Here, where developer furnished lots suitable for construction of dwellings, his duty to purchaser was satisfied. However, the court described the evidence of builder's liability as "overwhelming." *Anderson v. Bauer*, 681 P2d 1316 (1984).

83.15 —Implied Warranty of Workmanlike Construction

New Hampshire Buyers of a newly constructed home sued for damages caused by water seepage into the basement and sewage backup from a defective septic tank. *Held:* Vendor breached the implied warranty of workmanship, since the drainage and septic tank systems were not constructed in a workmanlike manner. There was substantial evidence to support the finding that the damage was caused by the defective construction. *Norton v. Burleaud*, 342 A2d 629 (1975).

New Jersey Restaurant owners contracted to purchase a new building from seller. Seller agreed not only to erect the structure but also to finance a portion of the purchase price through a second mortgage. After moving in, buyers discovered several instances of poor workmanship; they stopped their mortgage payments and demanded that repairs be made. In response, seller foreclosed on the second mortgage. *Held:* Seller was not entitled to foreclose since it breached the implied warranty of merchantability because of the major defects in the construction. Despite the lack of precedent, the court applied the rule of implied warranties of reasonable workmanship and fitness to a commercial construction. Those factors making implied warranties appropriate for residential construction are equally applicable in the commercial setting. Buyers were dependent on knowledge of seller, who was a builder, concerning the construction of the premises. *Hodgson v. Chin*, 403 A2d 942 (App. Div. 1979).

83.20 Express Warranties

U.S. District Court, Texas Plaintiffs bought a four-year-old home from the Department of Housing and Urban Development and executed a one-year warranty against defects. The agreement disclaimed liability for any injury or damage to persons or property by reason of any defects and limited seller's responsibility to the correction of the defect. During the first night in their new home, plaintiffs were overcome by gaseous fumes caused by a clogged ventilation pipe, and they sued the government under the federal Tort Claims Act. *Held:* The validity of the disclaimer was upheld. Although under state law contractual disclaimers limiting liability for personal injury in the sale of consumer goods are prima facie unconscionable, the rule does not extend to real estate transactions. Seller would be liable only if seller knew or had reason to know of the defect at the time of the sale, which was not the case here. *Graham v. United States*, 441 F. Supp. 741 (ND 1977).

Illinois Contractor entered into a contract with defendant to repair a leaking roof on defendant's building. After completion of the construction, the roof still leaked and defendant refused to pay. Contractor alleged full performance and filed suit against defendant, seeking contract price plus an agreed extra. Contractor maintained that defendant's failure to pay excused contractor from compliance with an express warranty. *Held:* Where the sole purpose of a contract is a leakproof roof, failure to attain that purpose raises no obligation of payment. Therefore, defendant's failure to pay contractor did not excuse contractor's noncompliance with the warranty. *Miller v. Racine Trust*, 382 NE2d 41 (1978).

Nebraska Purchasers of a home brought an action against sellers, alleging breach of warranty based on a clause of the sales contract that provided that the heating would be maintained until the time of closing in "working condition." The subsequent purchase agreement stated that all representations concerning the condition of the premises were based on purchasers' personal inspection and did not constitute any warranties of condition. The boiler in the home had been serviced annually prior to purchase and provided adequate heat despite a leak in the system. Prior to the purchase, the boiler had been inspected by purchasers and appeared to be in fine condition. *Held:* The clause in the sales contract relied upon by purchasers did not constitute a warranty. The phrase "working condition" pertains to the condition of the boiler at the time of the purchase, there being no allegation that the condition of the boiler had worsened from the time of purchase to the time of closing. *Gunset v. Mossman*, 243 NW2d 783 (1976).

North Carolina Home buyers, having signed a sales agreement containing a merger clause, could not rely on vendor's oral assurances made prior to signing the agreement. Therefore, on appeal, buyers relied on the theory that vendor's agent made a parol warranty respecting flooding after the contract was signed. After buyers' first flooding experience, vendor's agent had assured them the home was "warranted" and made unsuccessful efforts to correct the flooding condition. *Held:* Vendor's agent's assurance that the home was warranted was too vague to create a warranty. Nor could a warranty be inferred from the fact that vendor made attempts to remedy defects. Even if vendor had made a parol warranty after the contract was signed, it would be unenforceable under the Statute of Frauds, since an agreement to modify the terms of a contract must be based on new consideration or on evidence that one party intentionally induced the other party's detrimental reliance. *Clifford v. River Bend Plantation, Inc.*, 323 SE2d 23 (1984).

83.25
—Sale of Used Structures

Colorado Defendants built and sold a house, bought it back from purchasers, and later resold it. After discovering several defects, the second purchasers sued defendants for breach of the implied warranty of habitability. Defendants argued that this warranty applied only to new housing. *Held:* Builder-vendor is obligated to purchaser of a new home by an implied warranty of habitability, which traditionally does not extend to used housing. However, the rule is meant to protect home buyers from overreaching by more knowledgeable builder-vendors, and a brief intervening ownership by a third party does not affect the warranty. Here, the parties occupied the same respective positions as the builder-vendor and the purchasers of a new home; thus, defendants were held liable. *Duncan v. Schuster-Graham Homes, Inc.*, 578 P2d 637 (1978).

Indiana Builder constructed a home for buyers, who sold it five years later. Subsequent purchasers discovered a defect in the construction of the septic tank and sued builder for breach of the implied warranty of habitability, without notifying him or asking him to remedy the defect. *Held:* Subsequent purchaser cannot recover. Although subsequent purchaser may generally sue for breach of the implied warranty of habitability, he must first notify builder of the defect and give him an opportunity to remedy it. *Wagner Constr. Co., Inc. v. Noonan*, 403 NE2d 1144 (1980).

Missouri The second owner of a home brought a negligence action against the contractor who built the house and sold it to the first owners. Plaintiff alleged that builders have a duty, enforceable by an action in tort, to protect purchasers from damage consisting of deterioration or loss of bargain. *Held:* Plaintiff could not recover in a tort action for negligence. The implied warranty theory provides an adequate and appropriate remedy to a first purchaser who seeks damages from a builder for deterioration as a result of latent structural defects in the house purchased. A second theory of recovery based on failure to use ordinary care should not be authorized. *Crowder v. Vandendeale*, 564 SW2d 879 (1978).

South Carolina Subsequent purchaser of home sued contractor for damages allegedly caused after extensive settlement of the foundation. Contractor argued that there was no privity of contract and, therefore, no basis for imposing liability. *Held:* Summary judgment for contractor reversed. A subsequent purchaser of residential housing may sue the contractor for defects under implied warranties as well as in tort regardless of whether privity of contract exists. *Terlinde v. Neely*, 271 SE2d 768 (1980).

South Dakota A builder constructed a house for buyer. After buyer moved in, he discovered settling problems and complained to builder, who corrected the problem at his own expense. Second buyer purchased the house without knowing of the previous defects. When he discovered structural problems he contacted an engineer who found that the house had not been built in conformance with local building criteria. Second buyer then sued builder for damages to the basement. *Held:* Second buyer was entitled to receive damages. The court found that builder owed a duty of proper construction to second buyer, even though that buyer had not purchased the house directly from him. *Brown v. Fowler*, 279 NW2d 907 (1979).

83.30
—Measure of Damages for Breach of Warranty

Alabama During the construction of a $37,000 home, builder told buyers not to worry about a hairline crack in a concrete slab extending from the front porch through the den. After they moved in, however, the crack widened, and builder could not repair it. Buyers sued for breach of warranty and demanded damages for "mental anguish of having to live in the defective house." The jury awarded $25,000 in damages, and builder appealed. *Held:* Buyers were entitled to the jury award. Although such damages are not usually recoverable, in this case the builder should have reasonably foreseen that buyers, who had made a large investment in the house, would suffer mental anguish from the defects, which testimony had established made the house virtually worthless. *B&M Homes, Inc. v. Hogan*, 376 So. 2d 667 (1979).

Missouri A home purchaser sued builder-vendor for cutting and installing floor joists in an unworkmanlike manner. Plaintiff charged builder-vendor with breach of warranty and willful and malicious violation of the city building code. The trial court refused to submit the issue of punitive damages to the jury, and plaintiff appealed. *Held:* For plaintiff. While punitive damages are ordinarily not recoverable in a case arising from breach of contract, there are exceptions where the breach amounts to an independent willful tort and where there are proper allegations of malice, wantonness, or oppression. Here, there was evidence from which a jury could have found a willful, deliberate, and malicious violation, so the jury should have been allowed to consider punitive damages. *Sands v. RG McKelvey Bldg. Co.*, 571 SW2d 726 (Ct. App. 1978).

Utah A contract for the sale of a building stated that seller would "keep the premises in good condition and repair until possession is delivered to Buyer and Seller shall pay . . . all necessary maintenance, repair, and replacement costs, if any [until] possession is delivered to Buyer. . . ." Buyer later discovered defects in the air-conditioning system and sued the seller for the $6,000 he spent to correct them. The trial court awarded the buyer $1,297, holding that the system's condition had to be qualified by its age, 13 years. Buyer appealed. *Held:* For seller. Normally, the sale of a used building does not carry any implied warranty of fitness of an air-conditioning system. The parties may vary this rule by contract. Here, however, the agreement did not require seller to restore the air conditioning to its original condition, but merely to keep it in good condition until turning over the premises to buyer. *Utah State Medical Ass'n. v. Utah State Em-*

ployees' Credit Union, 655 P2d 643 (1982).

Vermont When the lower court awarded damages in an action for breach of warranty based on the reasonable cost of repair, vendor argued that the measure of damages should be the difference in market value between the house as built and as it should have been built. *Held:* When damage is permanent and beyond repair, the difference in market value affords the better guide to a just award. But where the defects are curable by repair or replacement, the cost of repair rule provides adequate compensation. *Bolkum v. Stabb*, 346 A2d 210 (1975).

83.35
—Contractual Limitations

Washington Condominium buyers sued developer for breach of warranty, negligent construction, misrepresentation, and violation of the Consumer Protection Act. The sale and warranty agreements required that suits for negligence or breach of warranty be brought within one year of occupancy or delivery of a certificate of occupancy, and four years had passed since plaintiffs' occupancy. The trial court granted developer partial summary judgment on negligence and breach of warranty claims. *Held:* Affirmed. The contract limitation of one year to commence an action was valid. It appeared in various documents, and not all warranties or remedies were excluded. *Southcenter View Condominium Owners' Ass'n v. Condominium Builders, Inc.*, 736 P2d 1075 (Ct. App. 1986).

84.00
SELLER'S OR BUILDER'S TORT LIABILITY

84.05
Negligence

Colorado Plaintiffs, the fourth owners of a house, brought a negligence action against the home builder for cracking in the foundation that occurred subsequent to their purchase. The builder argued that negligence actions, like actions for breach of the implied warranty of habitability, should be available only to first purchasers. *Held:* For plaintiffs. The obligation to act without negligence in the construction of a home is independent of contractual obligations such as an implied warranty of habitability. The builder had a duty of care to plaintiffs because he was in a far better position to determine the house's structural condition and could reasonably foresee that, in light of the mobility of most potential homeowners, the house would be sold to subsequent purchasers. *Cosmopolitan Homes, Inc. v. Weller*, 663 P2d 1041 (1983).

Missouri Second owner of a home brought a negligence action against the contractor who built the house and sold it to first owners. Plaintiff alleged that builders have a duty, enforceable by an action in tort, to protect purchasers from damage consisting of deterioration or loss of bargain. *Held:* Plaintiff could not recover in a tort action for negligence. The implied warranty theory provides an adequate and appropriate remedy to a first purchaser who seeks damages from builder for deterioration as a result of latent structural defects in the house purchased. A second theory of recovery based on failure to use ordinary care should not be authorized. *Crowder v. Vandendeale*, 564 SW2d 879 (1978).

North Carolina Condominium's architect was sued by the condominium association for noncompliance with building codes and negligent supervision, inspection, and testing of the complex's water pipes. The architect denied any obligation of supervision and inspection, and moved for dismissal on the ground that he had no contract with or obligation to the condominium association. *Held:* An architect who contracts to perform professional services is liable for damages proximately caused by his negligence to anyone who reasonably could be foreseen to rely upon the architect's performing services in a reasonable manner. Plaintiffs, as members of an association of condominium purchasers, were persons to whom harm may result as a consequence of negligent performance of services by the architect. *Quail Hollow E. Condo Ass'n v. Donald J. Scholz Co.*, 268 SE2d 12 (1980).

Ohio Plaintiffs, the second owners of a home, sued builder for negligence in the placing, grading, and compacting of the fill material used to level their property. Builder argued that the suit should be dismissed for lack of privity. *Held:* Privity is no longer a necessary element of a negligence action by a buyer of real property against builder-seller. No sound policy reason exists not to extend a builder's duty of care in performing work and selecting building materials to all subsequent vendees. In many cases, defects may be undetectable even after reasonable investigation by vendee, so caveat emptor must give way to the negligence standard of liability. *McMillan v. Brune-Harpenau-Torbeck Builders, Inc.*, 455 NE2d 1276 (1983).

Oregon Several condominum unit owners sued developers for damages caused when their lots were injured by beach erosion. They argued developers were liable because they had represented themselves as highly skilled in establishing resort communities. Developers maintained that they could not be held responsible, because they were powerless to control the wearing away of the land. *Held:* Developers could be held liable for negligence in site selection for the development. The erosion was in no sense the result of developers' work on the property; the problem was in the inherent nature of the land. There was no implied warranty concerning the nature or quality of the lots themselves. However, developers, who represented themselves as resort experts, could be liable for their negligence in failing to take reasonable steps to make sure the lots were suitable for residential condominium units. *Beri, Inc. v. Salishan Properties, Inc.*, 580 P2d 173 (1978).

Wyoming After heavy rains resulted in the collapse of walls in their home, plaintiffs sued the original contractor for breach of warranty and negligence. The trial court dismissed the suit under state statute that barred the bringing of such actions involving real property more than 10 years after substantial completion of construction. *Held:* The statue was unconstitutional. The court ruled that the statute was not one of limitation but, rather, a grant of immunity from suit conferred upon a "narrow spectrum of defendants" with no rational or reasonable justification. In violation of the state constitution, the statute operated to close the courts to individuals who have had dealings with the protected class. The court asserted that myriad circumstances may occur where defects might not be discovered, nor suit filed, against the class of defendants protected by the statute within the arbitrary time period set therein. *Phillips v. ABC Builders, Inc.*, 611 P2d 821 (1980).

84.10 Strict Liability

Arkansas Plaintiffs, the second owners of a house, sued builder over an improperly installed carpet, seeking to recover for breach of the implied warranty of habitability and under the theory of strict liability. *Held:* Privity of contract is not a precondition for recovery for breach of the implied warranty of habitability if the defect was the result of a post-sale alteration and (b) the defect was not discoverable upon reasonable inspection by subsequent purchasers. A cause of action in product or strict liability was available to plaintiffs. The product liability theory applies to property damage as well as personal injury, and the concept of "product" includes homes. *Blagg v. Hunt Co.*, 612 SW2d 321 (1981).

California Plaintiff, a planned development association created to acquire and hold title to property in a planned development, brought a strict liability action against the general contractor who constructed the living units, clubhouse, and recreational areas. Construction defects allegedly caused $2 million in damages. The contractor argued that plaintiff lacked standing to sue and could not state a cause of action in strict liability. *Held:* Plaintiff had standing to sue as owner of all common areas, real property, and structures and as representative of its members. There is authority in cases involving the mass production of homes to support application of the strict liability theory to the facts of this case. Defendant was found strictly liable for defects in grading, paving, design, surveying, and construction of improvements. *Del Mar Beach Club Owners Ass'n v. Imperial Contracting Co.*, 176 Cal. Rptr. 886 (1981).

District of Columbia Tenant-shareholder in a housing cooperative sued the company that marketed the cooperatives and the cooperative itself for damages flowing from the breach of express and implied warranties. The cooperative's sponsor did not sell units directly to the consumer, but rather transferred title to the cooperative and marketed the units as proprietary leaseholds. The trial court ruled for defendants, holding that plaintiff failed to show any contractual obligation on the marketing company's part. *Held:* Reversed. The law of products liability applies not only to the sale of goods, but also to the sale of newly constructed homes. Although there was no contract between plaintiff and the marketing company, each of the involved entities was an integral part of the enterprise that placed the allegedly defective product in the stream of commerce, and so each may be held liable to plaintiff. *Berman v. Watergate West, Inc.*, 391 A2d 1351 (1978).

New Mexico Plaintiff landowners brought suit against defendant developer after quantities of runoff water drained onto their property and caused flooding and silting. The evidence showed that in the course of construction defendant had built dams and drainage devices that collected surface waters and periodically discharged them in large quantities. Defendant appealed the trial court's judgment, arguing that its instruction on strict liability was erroneous. *Held:* Case remanded for new trial. Strict liability under state law is not available unless there is an "ultrahazardous activity," which previously had been restricted to cases involving storage or use of explosives. Collection and dispersement of surface waters in rural areas simply do not amount to an "ultrahazardous activity." Accordingly, plaintiffs must proceed under negligence principles on remand. *Gutierrez v. Rio Rancho Estates, Inc.*, 605 P2d 1154 (1980).

84.15 Fraud and Misrepresentation

4th Circuit Purchasers contacted realtors, who showed them Maryland waterfront property that they decided to buy.

The sales contract provided that all improvements to the property, including the septic system, were sold "as is." After purchasing the property, purchasers began to install a new septic system. However, the Maryland Department of Health told them to stop because the property's soil was not suited for an on-site septic system. Purchasers learned that sellers knew of the soil's condition before they sold the property. Purchasers sued realtors and sellers. *Held:* The "as is" clause did not bar all claims against defendants, because it referred only to *improvements* on the property, not to the property's natural features, such as soil condition. Purchasers' claims against realtors were dismissed because realtors did not know of the soil problem. Even if the relationship between purchasers and realtors gave rise to a duty of care, this duty would not encompass an obligation by realtors to make an independent investigation of hidden defects. The case was remanded to determine whether sellers intended to mislead purchasers and whether they owed them a duty of care in making representations about the property. *Herber v. Saffell*, 877 F2d 267 (1989).

Florida Buyers of an apartment building claimed that seller had misrepresented the rent roll and the duration of the leases of the existing tenants. Seller denied the allegations and also argued that buyers should have verified the financial particulars before signing the contract. A lower court found that buyers should have exercised "reasonable diligence" and dismissed their case. Buyers appealed. *Held:* Buyers were entitled to a full hearing on their allegations. Although buyers could not sue for statements that are obviously false or incredible, they had no reason to doubt seller's representations and were therefore under no duty to check on their accuracy themselves. *Upledger v. Vilanor*, 369 So. 2d 427 (Dist. Ct. App. 1979).

Massachusetts Surveyor's report furnished to plaintiffs, potential land buyers, indicated in technical jargon the presence of surface water, but not in layman's terms. Plaintiffs did not ask about wetness problems, and nothing was volunteered on the subject. Following the sale, plaintiffs discovered the problem and sued seller, broker, and, in a separate suit, surveyor for fraud and violation of the consumer protection statute. *Held:* For defendants. Mere nondisclosure does not constitute fraud, and sellers had no duty to cure plaintiffs' ignorance. None of defendants was liable under the consumer protection statute. Sellers were selling their own home and so were not "engaged in trade or commerce." There was no evidence that the broker knew the significance of surveyor's report. Surveyor had no legal relationship with plaintiffs, and had played only a minor role in the transaction. *Nei v. Burley*, 446 NE2d 674 (1983); *Nei v. Boston Survey Consultants, Inc.*, 446 NE2d 681 (1983).

Missouri Fairmont Foods Co. purchased a parcel of land from Skelly Oil Co., taking a warranty deed conveying the property subject to easements and restrictions. Later, Fairmont learned of a limitation of access to the site due to the condemnation of access rights by the highway department. Fairmont sued Skelly, arguing that Skelly had a duty to disclose the condemnation since Skelly had superior knowledge of the facts. *Held:* There was no duty to disclose. Both parties were large corporations acting through their attorneys. To establish fraud, nondisclosure as between business equals must be of facts not within the fair and reasonable reach of the party alleging fraud. Here, the information in question was part of the public record to which Fairmont had access. In addition, Fairmont's acceptance of a warranty deed subject to easements and restrictions qualified the deed's warranty so as to preclude recovery on that basis as well. *Fairmont Foods Co. v. Skelly Oil Co.*, 616 SW2d 548 (Ct. App. 1981).

Nevada On buyers' initial tour of the house they were to buy, the listing agent told them the house had an operating solar heating system. In fact, the solar panel was simply a piece of corrugated metal, painted black, that was part of the roof and had numerous holes. Buyers sued vendors for fraud and breach of contract. The trial court granted summary judgment to defendants. *Held:* Reversed. Buyers' acceptance and occupation of the house did not constitute a waiver of their rights under contract. A jury was entitled to hear evidence as to whether buyers knew or should have known of the defect prior to the closing of escrow. In addition, buyers were entitled to argue to a jury that the statements of the agent were calculated to mislead them into believing that the house had a fully operative solar heating system. *Epperson v. Roloff*, 719 P2d 799 (1986).

North Carolina Buyers agreed to purchase a new home from builder. When builder advised them that their residence was finished, buyers moved, only to find that the new structure was not completed. Builder told them, however, that all remaining work would be done promptly. Buyers relied on these assurances and moved in. Builder never made any of the promised repairs and, within six months, buyers discovered that their house had been built on vegetable fill and had a variety of defects. Buyers sued for breach of express and implied new home warranties and for fraud. A jury awarded buyers $16,000 damages for breach of warranties and $3,500 damages for fraud. Both sides appealed. *Held:* The award as to breach of warranties was not in error. However the award for builder's actual fraud should be tripled, pursuant to the North Carolina antifraud statute (N.C. Gen. Stat. §75-16). The judgment was modified accordingly. *Stone v. Paradise Park Homes, Inc.*, 245 SE2d 801 (Ct. App. 1978).

North Dakota Buyers purchased a home from its owners after viewing the property for an hour. On occupying the home, buyers learned that the sewage and water systems, which they had not inspected or inquired about, were defective. The tap water was contaminated and polluted, and the sewage system backed up on several occasions, flooding the basement. Four months after buying the house, buyers sought rescission of the contract. *Held:* Buyers were entitled to rescission. Seller has a duty to disclose material facts that he knows or should know and that buyer would not be able to discover by exercising ordinary care and diligence. Passive concealment by seller of defects in real property is an exception to the rule of *caveat emptor*. The defective sewage and water systems were material facts, not discoverable by buyer, and seller's concealment of these facts constituted constructive fraud. *Holcomb v. Zinke*, 365 NW2d 507 (1985).

Oregon John Herbert bought a house that defendant had recently built. Two years later, Herbert sold the house to plaintiff. Owing to "adverse soil conditions," the foundation settled, causing damage to the house and fixtures. Plaintiff discovered that, contrary to representations made by defendant to the original owner, the footing and foundation inspections required by law were never made. Plaintiff brought suit for fraud. *Held:* Affirmed for defendant. Plaintiff admitted that defendant had made no direct representations to him. Plaintiff's fraud count did not even state a cause of action, because there was no allegation that defendant intended his "indirect" representation be communicated to plaintiff. *Sponseller v. Meltebeke*, 570 P2d 974 (1977).

Texas Purchasers of a home sued a real estate agent under the Texas Deceptive Trade Practices Act. They complained that the real estate listing contained inaccuracies concerning the amount of air-conditioned and heated space. Defendant argued that the act did not apply, because he was merely an agent of seller and home purchasers were not consumers to whom he provided goods and services. *Held:* Defendant could be held liable under the act. The court, construing the act liberally to promote consumer protection, held that the act intended to define "consumer" more broadly than as a person seeking or acquiring goods or services from the person being sued. In other words, privity between the parties is not required for a cause of action under the Texas Deceptive Trade Practices Act. *Cameron v. Terrell & Garrett, Inc.*, 618 SW2d 535 (1981).

84.20
Consumer Protection Laws

Texas Buyers sued builder for breach of implied warranties with respect to construction and repair of their modular home. Discretionary damages of $5,000 were awarded under Texas's Deceptive Trade Practices—Consumer Protection Act. Builder appealed, arguing that buyers were not "consumers" with respect to repairs as they were not charged for the work. *Held:* The repairs were a continuation of the original purchase transaction as to which buyers were definitely consumers. It would be inequitable to penalize buyers for deferring a possible lawsuit and attempting a repair solution by denying them consumer status. The court also ruled that repair services carry an implied warranty that they will be performed in a good and workmanlike manner. The public interest in protecting consumers from inferior services overrides any concern for the monetary impact of damage awards on the providers of the services. *Melody Home Mfg. Co. v. Barnes*, 741 SW2d 349 (1987).

Texas Builder warranted construction of house for one year. When cracks appeared in the foundation and bricks, owners sued under the Texas Deceptive Trade Practices Act. A jury found that builder breached its express and/or implied warranty and awarded homeowners triple damages under the statute. Builder appealed. *Held:* There was sufficient evidence to support the jury's finding, and builder failed to prove that it was not given a reasonable opportunity to cure the defects in the house before the suit was filed. Had builder established that it made a good faith offer to repair the building, the cost of the repairs builder was willing to make could have been deducted from the damages owners could claim under the statute. *Roy E. Thomas Constr. Co. v. Arbs*, 688 SW2d 916 (Ct. App. 1985).

85.00
LENDER'S LIABILITY

85.05
Lender's Liability to Purchaser

U.S. Supreme Court Home buyer's contract with builder required work to conform to plans approved by the Farmer's Home Administration (FmHA), and granted FmHA the right to inspect and test all materials and workmanship and reject any that were defective. An FmHA official made such an inspection and reported no defects. When defects were later found, buyer sued FmHA under the Federal Tort Claims Act (FTCA), arguing that the defects were partly due to the negligence of the FmHA inspector. The Sixth Circuit held that buyer had a cause of action under the FTCA. Once the FmHA agreed to supervise construction of the house, it had a duty to supervise with due care. Second, plaintiff's claim did not fall within the exception for a claim "arising out of . . . misrepresentation" (28 USC §2680(h)) because negligence, rather than deceit, was involved in FmHA reports of no defects in the house. The Supreme Court addressed the question of whether plaintiff's claim arose out of misrepresentation. *Held:* The "misrepresentation" exception to the FTCA did not bar the action. Plaintiff's complaint focused not on the FmHA's communication of misinformation on the quality of construction, but on its lack of due care in supervising the construction. The duty to use due care to ensure that builder adhered to approved plans was distinct from any duty to use due care in communicating information to the buyer. *Block v. Neal*, 460 US 1089 (1983), aff'g, *Neal v. Bergland*, 646 F2d 1178 (6th Cir. 1981).

10th Circuit Home buyers received financial assistance from the FmHA to construct a house on their property. FmHA inspected the premises and found no defects in heating system. Later, however, buyer's son was asphyxiated by carbon monoxide from the heating system, which was negligently installed. Claiming reliance on the FmHA inspector's approval of the residence as constructed, buyers sued the FmHA under the FTCA. *Held:* Buyers could not recover, because the FmHA's conduct fell within the FTCA's misrepresentation exception. FmHA had no duty of care to buyers, but only to the United States to ensure the repayment of all loans. The faulty appraisal of the house based on a negligent inspection amounted to a misrepresentation, so buyers suit was barred. *Reynolds v. United States*, 643 F2d 707 (1981), cert. denied, 454 US 817 (1982).

Alaska When construction defects prevented closing of home buyers' contemplated Veterans Administration loan, buyers sued developer. Concerned about these problems, developer's bank declared its short-term construction loan to developer to be in default when the due date for payment arrived. Buyers sought to enjoin foreclosure of developer's loan, arguing that the bank was liable for developer's failure to perform. *Held:* The bank, which had merely extended a short-term construction loan to developer and whose activities did not go beyond the normal actions of a bank to protect its investment, was not liable to buyers. It owed no duty of care to buyers by operation of law, nor was there an express or implied agreement that would inure to their benefit. *Wierzbicki v. Alaska Mut. Sav. Bank*, 630 P2d 998 (1981).

Florida Condominium purchasers sued lender, alleging construction defects in common areas and individual units. Lender, who had acquired title from original builder through foreclosure following substantial completion by builder, argued that it had no duty to inspect the progress of construction. *Held:* By taking title, completing construction, and holding itself out as developer and owner of the project, lender stands in the place of developer and is liable for breach of all applicable warranties. *Chotka v. Fidelco Growth Inv.*, 383 So. 2d 1169 (App. Ct. 1980).

South Carolina A construction lender, seeking to protect its loan, formed its own corporation to take title to 25 condominium units and to the common elements for the purpose of selling them. Prompted by owners' complaints about structural defects in roofs and balconies, lender arranged for stopgap repairs, but vetoed replacement of roof. Corporation later obtained a verdict against lender for negligence and reckless construction, and lender appealed. *Held:* Lender could not be held liable for faulty construction, since it was not an active participant in the building enterprise during the initial construction. However, when it formed the corporation to market the units and undertook to make repairs, a common-law duty to use due care arose. Lender could therefore be held liable for any damages proximately caused by the alleged negligent repairs. *Roundtree Villas Ass'n v. 4701 Kings Corp.*, 321 SE2d 46 (1984).

85.10 Lender's Rights Against Seller or Builder

5th Circuit Partnership formed to construct apartment complex violated provisions of loan agreement requiring loan proceeds to be used solely for construction costs and requiring architect to certify the draw requests as progress payments. After the general contractor became insolvent, one of the partners sought to avoid foreclosure by taking over the project, but failed to complete it. Subsequently, he sued his former partners, including the lending bank, for fraud and breach of conduct even though he had participated in some of the alleged misconduct. The trial court granted defendants summary judgment. *Held:* Affirmed. The partnership's misuse of the loan proceeds was a material violation of the loan agreement, and the bank owed no duty to plaintiff to ensure the architect's proper conduct in certifying the draws. That provision of the agreement was for the bank's protection, and any benefit to the project owners was merely incidental. *Henslee v. Houston*, 566 F2d 475 (1978).

California U.S. Financial, the beneficiary of a second trust deed on lots in a subdivision under development, foreclosed and purchased the lots, not knowing that a differential earth settlement had damaged the houses. U.S. Financial subsequently made some repairs and sold some of the houses. The beneficiary of the first trust deed, joined by U.S. Financial, sought damages from original developers, who had been responsible for engineering, grading, and excavation, in an impairment of security theory. The first deed beneficiary claimed developers were liable to it under a strict liability theory. *Held:* Lender could not recover under this theory. A mass-producer/seller of homes is strictly liable for defects where purchaser cannot reasonably be expected to make a thorough inspection. However, lender is not as vulnerable as individual purchaser and additionally is in a position to spread the cost of the risk. *U.S. Financial v. Sullivan*, 112 Cal. Rptr. 18 (Ct. App. 1974).

Florida Builder entered into a $6 million standby permanent loan commitment with lender to be disbursed only upon completion of the building. Builder paid a $30,000 commitment fee and furnished an irrevocable letter of credit for $60,000; the letter was to be returned to builder if the loan was funded and kept by lender if it was not. After the project fell through, builder sought an injunction to prevent lender from cashing the letter of credit because lender had not earmarked funds for the loan and its financial condition would have precluded lender from closing the loan had the building been completed. *Held:* The commitment fee represented expenses incurred by lender, while the $60,000 was to be compensation for lender's readiness to make the loan or liquidated damages in the event the borrower failed to proceed. Lender should not recover if it was unable to perform, but it did not have to earmark funds for completion of each particular loan. *Lev-*

enson v. Barnett Bank, 330 So. 2d 192 (Dist. Ct. App. 1976).

86.00 LIABILITY OF OTHERS

86.05 Attorney

Massachusetts Home buyer signed a mortgage application stating that bank's attorney represented bank's interest and that buyer would retain his own attorney. Nonetheless, buyer sued bank's attorney for damages, claiming he had detrimentally relied upon the latter's defective title examination. *Held:* Buyer had no cause of action. The strong exculpatory language in the mortgage application made it clear that buyer was not to rely exclusively on bank's attorney. The latter's contract to examine title was exclusively for the bank's benefit and protection. The court distinguished its earlier decisions recognizing that tort liability could exist in the absence of privity of contract. This was not a case where defendants should have been on notice that plaintiffs would rely on their actions. *Page v. Frazier*, 445 NE2d 148 (1983).

86.10 Appraiser

North Carolina Home buyers paid mortgagee $100 to retain an appraiser, who submitted a report citing "no visible major problems." The mortgage loan was approved, but numerous defects surfaced after buyers took possession of the premises. Buyers sued the appraiser, charging negligent performance of his contract with the mortgagee amounting to a breach of a contract intended for their benefit. *Held:* Buyers could not sue as third-party beneficiaries, but could sue on negligence grounds. Any benefit flowing to them from the contract between the appraiser and the mortgagee was incidental; they were not intended beneficiaries. Buyers could sue in tort, however. Their reliance on the appraisal could reasonably be expected by defendant, whose failure to discover defects in buyers' house, if negligent, was a proximate cause of their injuries. *Alva v. Cloninger*, 277 SE2d 535 (Ct. App. 1981).

86.15 Local Authorities

Florida A condominium association sued the city for negligence in inspecting the condominium building and certifying it for occupancy. The city contested its liability under Fla. Stat. § 768.28, which provides that governmental entities "shall be liable for tort claims in the same manner and to the same extent as a private individual under like circumstances." *Held:* The city was not liable. The power to enforce the building code flows from the police power of the state. The purpose of Section 768.28 is to waive the immunity that prevents recovery against the state for breaches of common-law duties of care. There has never been a common-law duty to individual citizens for the enforcement of police power functions, and adoption of the building code did not create one. A contrary ruling would make a city's taxpayers insurers of all building construction within the city. *Trianon Park Condominium v. City of Hialeah*, 468 So. 2d 912 (1985).

Illinois A home was built in such a way that the house was subject to flooding. Owners claimed that this flooding occurred because the foundation grade level was too low, and sued the village in which the house was located, as well as the civil engineer who designed the surface water drainage system. *Held:* For the village and the civil engineer. The court ruled that the village bore no responsibility to set foundation drainage levels on the property in question. The house was custom-built on a lot in a subdivided tract, which met the village's minimum height requirements as a whole. The civil engineer, who had been hired by land developer and not by builder of the house, also was not liable since he had no contractual duty to establish adequate foundation grade levels. He merely had to comply with the legal minimum. The court stated that it was the responsibility of architect and builder to establish the proper foundation level and to construct functional drainage channels. *Ferentchak v. Village of Frankfort*, 457 NE2d 822 (1985).

86.20 Contractor Other Than Builder

Maryland Plaintiff built and sold a house in 1979 after obtaining a use and occupancy certificate of approval. In 1983, buyers complained to the county about roof leaks, and the county ordered plaintiff to take corrective action. Plaintiff contested the directive, arguing that his responsibility had ended because the certificate of occupancy showed that his work had been approved. *Held:* Plaintiff was not responsible for the defects. The building code sets up the use and occupancy certificate as a prerequisite to consummation of the sale of a new dwelling. Thus, the code imposes on the seller responsibility for notices of violations issued at the time of the closing. The responsibility of seller terminates at the closing, however, and buyer assumes responsibility for correction of building code violations noticed thereafter. *Passnault v. Board of Admin. Appeals*, 535 A2d 222 (1987).

New Jersey In 1974, homeowners paid contractor $5,000 to build a patio. A year later, they sold their home. When defects in the patio became apparent, purchasers sued contractor for breach of an implied warranty of good workmanship. *Held:* For purchasers. The law implies a promise to construct the patio in a good and workmanlike manner, and this warranty was transferred to purchasers of a home. A contractor should not be immunized from his contractual obligations in the absence of a nonassignability clause in his contract simply because a property was transferred. Purchaser's right to recover for defects in workmanship is limited, however, to defects that were not readily apparent or discoverable at the time the property was purchased. It may also be limited by contract. *Aronsohn v. Mandara*, 484 A2d 675 (1984).

87.00 STATUTE OF LIMITATIONS

87.05 In General

Nebraska Homeowner sued architect, general contractor, and engineer for damages from burst water pipe. The pipe was installed more than 10 years before the suit was brought, but the house was completed less than 10 years before the suit. Defendants sought dismissal under statutes mandating 10-year limitation period for actions charging breach of warranty involving real property or professional negligence. *Held:* Owner's suit was time-barred with respect to the engineer only. The act giving rise to the claim against the general contractor was the failure to erect the house in a good and workmanlike manner. That occurred at the completion of construction—within the 10-year period. A similar theory applied with respect to the architect, who was engaged to design the house and inspect its construction as it progressed. The engineer's work, however, ended on or before the date the pipe was installed, which was not within the 10-year period. *Witherspoon v. Sides Constr. Co.*, 362 NW2d 35 (1985).

Wisconsin The owner of a silo was injured in a fall and sued the silo's builder. The action was dismissed pursuant to a statute requiring that actions for injury resulting from real estate improvements be brought within six years of the completion of construction. Owner appealed, challenging the constitutionality of the statute. *Held:* State statute setting a six-year limitation period for actions resulting from injury from improvements to real property violated equal protection. Unlike the usual statute of limitations, this statute does not discourage state suits. Instead, it acts as an immunity statute which, in actual practice, may bar an action before the injury is ever sustained or before any right to bring suit arises. The legislature cannot abrogate legal rights that have not vested. No rational basis exists for including suppliers and builders in the protected class, while denying protection to owners and tenants. As such, the statute makes a meaningless distinction between classes and is unconstitutional on equal protection grounds. *Funk v. Wollin Silo & Equip., Inc.*, 435 NW2d 244 (1989).

PART P
BROKERS AND BROKERAGE AGREEMENTS

88.00
CREATION OF BROKER-CLIENT RELATIONSHIP

88.05
Creation by Express Agreement

9th Circuit Sullivan, not a real estate broker, learned of a ranch for sale and upon seller's agreement to pay him a 5 percent commission, undertook to find a buyer. He did find a buyer, introduced the parties, and was present during negotiations but did not actually take part in them. He made himself helpful to the parties—all experienced real estate people—by obtaining papers from public records, etc. All parties understood he was to receive a commission but all were under the impression he was a broker. When the contract of sale was signed, it provided specifically that the buyer (rather than the seller) would pay Sullivan his commission in consideration of a reduced purchase price. When buyer refused to pay on the ground that Sullivan was not a licensed broker, Sullivan sued. *Held:* There is sufficient evidence to support the finding that Sullivan played no more than a finder's role and so he is entitled to the commission. The key finding of fact was that the parties were in fact brought together by Sullivan, but afterwards neither party expected or relied upon Sullivan's further participation in negotiations. *Sullivan v. Hopkins*, 435 F2d 1128 (1970).

California Seller listed his property for sale with a local real estate broker. When the broker discovered that the property had already been sold to the state for nonpayment of taxes, he purchased the property for himself at the public sale. When seller sued the broker for breaching his fiduciary duty, the broker argued that there was no agency and therefore no breach of duty. *Held:* The broker was seller's agent. The agency does not begin only with the execution of an agreement with a ready, willing, and able buyer, nor is the authority to exercise discretion essential to the creation of an agency. *Skopp v. Weaver*, 546 P2d 307 (1976).

Texas Plaintiff broker sued to recover a commission he alleged he earned by procuring a ready, willing, and able buyer. The parties had entered into a listing agreement whereby vendor agreed that the broker would earn his commission by procuring a purchaser at the asking price. Vendor sought to avoid the contract by alleging it insufficient to satisfy the Statute of Frauds requirement that real property involved in the contract be sufficiently identified. The lower court held that the writing was sufficient under the Statute of Frauds. The property was described as Deluxe Model, 1302 East Central, Comanche, Comanche County, Texas, and was signed by Joy Jones, "owner." Such a description, said the court, is sufficient if extrinsic evidence demonstrates that the party to be charged and who has signed as owner in fact owns only one parcel of land which could answer the written description in the memorandum. *Held:* Judgment for broker was reversed. A fact issue existed as to whether broker produced a ready, willing, and able buyer. The code imposes a requirement that broker *must* advise purchasers in writing that they should either examine the abstract or obtain title insurance. Without that advice, no commission can be paid. Since the broker failed to advise, he couldn't collect. *Jones v. Del Anderson & Assocs.*, 539 SW2d 348 (1976).

88.10
Creation by Implied Agreement

New Jersey In an attempt to redevelop certain blighted areas, the city commenced a promotional campaign to induce businesses to locate in the development area. The promotional literature bore the phrase "brokers protected." Several brokers interested a corporation in purchasing a 180-acre tract at a price of $33,000 per acre. The city refused to pay the brokers a commission, asserting that there was no contract. Two lower courts ruled that the brokers could not recover any money based on an oral agreement, and the brokers appealed. *Held:* The city's advertisements with the phrase "brokers protected" constituted a written offer, which the brokers accepted by locating a buyer. "Brokers protected" is a commonly used term of art meaning that seller will pay a commission at the established rate to any broker who produces a buyer. Thus, the brokers were entitled to a commission of 10 percent of the sale price. *National Newark & Essex Bank v. Housing Auth.*, 384 A2d 138 (1978).

New York A real estate broker procured buyer for a property, but the sale fell through, and the property was sold to another party. Broker sued for its commission. *Held:* Because broker had a signed agreement to act as *purchaser's* agent in the transaction, it was not entitled to prove that it also had an implied contract with seller. Seller was entitled to summary judgment. *Julien J. Studley, Inc. v. New York News, Inc.*, 512 NE2d 300 (1987), aff'g 505 NYS2d 419 (App. Div. 1986).

Washington Two parties entered into a contract for the sale of a building. The contract stipulated that the commission was to be split between two brokers. Before the sale was completed, seller rejected the contract. Subsequently, seller asked purchaser's broker to assist in renegotiating the contract. The broker solicited offers from purchaser, but no contract resulted. Seller later signed a listing agreement with a third broker, which led to the sale of the building to the original purchaser. The two original brokers sued seller for commissions. *Held:* The appellate court rejected the claim. An employment agreement, either express or implied, is necessary for a broker to collect commission, and there was no evidence of such an agreement in this case. *Haskell v. Raugust*, 745 P2d 535 (Ct. App. 1987).

88.15
Creation by Oral Agreement

California Shapell Industries was in the housing construction business and had a real estate license; but rather than locate suitable land itself, Shapell contacted Phillippe, a licensed real estate broker and proposed that Phillippe work as the front man in Shapell's land acquisition efforts. Phillippe agreed, on the condition that his commission would be paid by Shapell. Shapell orally agreed. On one property, Shapell submitted a written offer to purchase that included the statement that Shapell would pay 6 percent commission to the broker. On another property, a deal was held up by zoning problems, but a year and a half later, negotiations were resumed directly between Shapell and the owner, resulting in a sale. Phillippe sued for commission. *Held:* For Shapell. The court rejected Phillippe's contentions that his agreement with Shapell for a commission was not subject to the Statute of Frauds, which invalidated oral commission agreements, or that it satisfied the statute in any event. The court did not regard Shapell's prior written acknowledgment of its commission obligation as a writing satisfying the Statute of Frauds, because it related to a property different from the one finally purchased. Phillippe then argued that equitable estoppel prohibited Shapell from asserting the Statute of Frauds. However, the court found that licensed brokers are not subject to equitable protection, because their reliance on an oral promise to pay a commission cannot be reasonable in view of their knowledge of the laws governing the real estate business. The increasing complexity of the business world argued in favor of written contracts, the court concluded. *Phillippe v. Shapell Indus., Inc.*, 743 P2d 1279 (1987), cert. denied, 486 US 1011 (1988).

Massachusetts Landowners sought to lease their property for approximately $25,000 per year and orally agreed with a real estate broker to pay a commission of 6 percent of the rent for the first year, 5 percent of the rent for the second year, and 4 percent of the rent for the third and any subsequent years. The broker located a tenant that contracted to pay $83,000 per year over a three-year-term. The landowners interpreted their agreement with the broker as requiring them to pay commission on only the first $25,000 of the yearly rental. The broker sued, seeking commission on the full $83,000. The landowners successfully asserted the Statute of Frauds, and the broker appealed. *Held:* The oral contract was unenforceable because it fell within the Statute of Frauds. The contract was not capable of being fully performed within one year, since the parties apparently intended the payment of commission to take place each year for three or more years of the lease. *Richard Tucker Assocs., Inc. v. Smith*, 481 NE2d 489 (1985).

Virginia A real estate broker publicized a flyer describing a property for sale by his son, and stating that the agent's commission would be "7% (50/50 split)." In reliance on this, a second broker produced a buyer and brought about the sale. The sales contract acknowledged that the second broker, along with the seller's father, were the sales agents, but the commission was stated to be $5,000, half to the second broker and half to the seller's father. The second broker sued, claiming as commission one half of 7 percent of the $365,000 purchase price. Seller and father raised the Statute of Frauds as a defense. *Held:* The court refused to apply the Statute of Frauds. The sales contract, which stated that "seller agress to pay the agent a commission on the sales price" satisfied the requirement of a writing evincing the brokerage agreement. However, to hold plaintiff to the $5,000 commission unilaterally imposed therein by sellers would be unconscionable. Parol evidence supported plaintiff's claim to half the 7 percent commission. *Murphy v. Nolte & Co.*, 307 SE2d 242 (1983).

89.00 BROKER'S DUTIES

89.05 Fiduciary Duties

8th Circuit Plaintiff developer enlisted defendant to act as mortgage broker for a large construction project. Defendant secured financing under a complex schedule, serving as loan correspondent to lender. When construction was delayed, plaintiff again approached defendant and asked it to renegotiate the loans and, if possible, to avert certain penalty provisions. The defendant was successful in its attempt, and, as a part of the deal, made a separate arrangement with lender to split the prepayment penalty. When plaintiff learned of this, it filed suit alleging breach of fiduciary duties. The district court awarded judgment for plaintiff and included punitive damages. *Held:* Judgment affirmed. By agreeing to renegotiate the loan, defendant served as plaintiff's gratuitous agent and was bound to place the interests of the principal ahead of its own. This duty was clearly breached when defendant conspired to share in the prepayment penalty. *Armstrong v. Republic Realty Mortgage Corp.*, 631 F2d 1344 (1980).

Arizona Defendant broker received an offer for plaintiff owners' residence consisting of a cash down payment and an unsecured promissory note. The broker presented the offer to owners without advice as to the contents, and owners accepted. The note had the words "[t]his note is secured by a mortgage on real property" stricken. After default and bankruptcy by obligors, owners sued the broker for breach of duty and negligence. *Held:* Brokers in Arizona have the duty of explaining the implications of documents for sale of real property to the parties. The broker should have advised seller to require security from buyer on the note. *Morley v. J. Pagel Realty & Ins.*, 550 P2d 1104 (1976).

Illinois Buyer was informed by seller's brokers that the property buyer had previously offered to purchase had been sold, and buyer's earnest-money deposit was returned. However, they failed to tell buyer that the ultimate purchasers were some of the brokers themselves, who paid less than what buyer had offered. The issue was whether buyer had a private right of action for harm caused by brokers' violation of the Illinois Brokers Licensing Act and regulations requiring brokers to disclose "any and all material knowledge [they] may have" to all parties. *Held:* A private right of action was found to exist because the statutory remedies were not expressly limited, buyer was within the class of individuals the act was designed to protect, the alleged injury was one that the act was designed to prevent, and recognition of this right of action was consistent with the act's policy of protecting the public from incompetent and dishonest brokers. Brokers violated the regulations by occupying a position of trust with buyer while, at the same time, acting adverse to his interests. The previous rule that a broker's duty to disclose ran only to his principal was no longer viable. *Sawyer Realty Group, Inc. v. Jarvis Corp.*, 432 NE2d 849 (1982).

Kansas A real estate developer offered to locate sites and landlords for restaurants in Mexico for a restaurant franchise builder-operator. Builder agreed to pay developer $4,000 plus one percent of the gross revenue from each site for the original lease terms. Developer secured a site with the help of a developer in Mexico and they purchased the site for $56,000 and then sold it to the builder for $88,000, not informing the builder of the markup. Developer secured a total of four sites, and was paid $16,000, but did not receive any percentage of profits. When developer sued for a percentage, builder counterclaimed for breach of fiduciary duty. At trial, developer revealed the $32,000 markup, but claimed that he was an independent contractor rather than agent of the builder and therefore owed him no fiduciary duty. *Held:* Developer is neither entitled to a percentage of the profits nor to the $16,000 compensation he received. Developer acted as broker for the builder, and therefore had a fiduciary duty to him, which he breached when he took the secret illicit profits. By virtue of this breach, he must forfeit not only the compensation for the one site but for all four of the transactions, since they were permeated by unfaithfulness. *Henderson v. Hassur*, 594 P2d 650 (1979).

Louisiana Brokerage agent was contacted by a publishing company whose warehouse had just been damaged by fire. The company urgently needed a new location for storage of its inventory. The broker had a client who was seeking to sublet suitable property, and in view of the emergency, the broker moved the publisher into the building without first notifying the owner as required in the sublease. Upon learning of this development, owner demanded an unconditional one-year lease. The publisher was not willing to make the commitment without a 120-day cancellation clause. The impasse was broken by the intervention of another broker, who negotiated a lease on behalf of owner upon substantially the same terms originally proposed. In a subsequent suit, the first broker sued owner for a fee. *Held:* Judgment for owner. The original broker breached its duty to owner by moving the publisher into the premises without owner's permission. As a result of the publisher's occupation of the property, owner lost a powerful bargaining advantage and was justified in seeking further negotiations using a different agent. *Latter & Blum, Inc. v. Richmond*, 388 So. 2d 368 (1980).

Minnesota Sellers agreed to sell an apartment building for $1,425,000, a price proposed by a real estate salesman, to a purchaser whom the salesman had previously arranged to represent in the purchase. The agreement provided for the salesman to receive a commission. Sellers had previously rejected another buyer who was willing to pay more for the building. Before the closing, purchaser sold his rights to the building for $1,445,000 to the salesman's corporation, which then resold those same rights for $1,505,000 to a partnership in which the salesman owned an 18.5 percent interest. *Held:* Sellers were entitled to cancel salesman's commission for the sale to purchaser and to recover the $80,000 difference between the price at which they sold and the price paid by the partnership. The salesman had a fiduciary duty to fully disclose to sellers his role in the transaction and his relationship with the buyers; for after obtaining such a disclosure, sellers would probably not have agreed to sell to purchaser at the proposed price of $1,425,000. *Handy v. Garmaker*, 324 NW2d 168 (1982).

Nebraska Seller was forced to sell his bar to a close relative of broker for $1,950 less than if he had sold it to another offeror. He reported the broker to the state real estate commission, which suspended broker's license for six months. Broker appealed the suspension order. *Held:* Broker breached his fiduciary duty to seller by not adhering faithfully to seller's instructions to revoke the sales agreement with broker's sister; this justified the six-month suspension of broker's license. The suspension order was supported by substantial evidence, the real estate commission acted within the scope of its authority, and its action was not arbitrary or capricious. *Abboud v. State ex rel. State Real Estate Comm'n*, 316 NW2d 608 (1982).

New Mexico After exclusive listing agreements between a real estate salesman and his clients had expired, the salesman continued attempting to sell the listed properties for them. At the same time, he negotiated with them to purchase a parcel on his own behalf, which he intended to sell in segments. However, he never advised his clients of the potential value of their property if they were to sell it in segments. The sale fell through, and the salesman sued for breach of contract. *Held:* The salesman's failure to disclose material facts such as the property's value if sold in segments and the value of associated water rights was a breach of his fiduciary duty, rendering the sales contract void as against public policy. Given the course of conduct between the parties and the reliance by clients on the salesman for real estate advice, the fiduciary relationship continued even after the listing agreements expired. *Swallows v. Laney*, 691 P2d 874 (1984).

New York Buyer bid on an improved residential lot after being told by the brokers that it was owned by a third party. When buyer expressed interest in an unimproved lot nearby, the brokers told him that the same third party owned that lot as well but would not sell it. At closing, buyer discovered that a few days before he executed a binder for the improved lot, the brokers had themselves purchased both lots as one purchase from the third party and intended to subdivide them into the two lots. *Held:* No cause of action existed for fraud or for breach of brokers' fiduciary duty to buyer. The brokers were not acting for buyer, and even if they undertook to purchase property for themselves, brokers owed a fiduciary duty only to the third-party seller. Buyer's contentions that his bargaining position suffered owing to brokers' misrepresentations and that he otherwise could have negotiated for the unimproved lot as well, did not constitute the next cause of buyer's damages, which were speculative at best. *Weissman v. Mertz*, 512 NYS2d 865 (App. Div. 1987), appeal dismissed, 517 NYS2d 940 (1987).

Utah Earnest-money agreement executed by seller contained a "subject to" clause, stating that the "possession date [is] subject to relocation of seller." Seller asserted he had told the agent, before the agent filled out the agreement, that he did not want to sell his house until he had located another. When seller failed to locate another house, he refused to complete the sale. Buyer sued and obtained a ruling that the "subject to" clause made only buyer's *possession* of the house, not its sale, subject to seller's relocation. Seller sued broker and agent for indemnification on the ground that the agent erred in phrasing the agreement. *Held:* For broker and agent. Seller knew the words used by the real estate agent, and by signing the agreement, seller approved and ratified the acts of the agent and was bound by them. The language at issue was nontechnical and readily understandable, and there was no hint of fraud or sharp dealing. *Kidd v. Maldonado*, 688 P2d 461 (1984).

Virginia A prospective buyer complained to the Virginia Real Estate Commission of broker's failure to promptly communicate buyer's offer to the owner of a tract of land. Broker made his own offer to owner and did not learn of buyer's offer until he returned from out of town, and after the owner had orally accepted broker's own offer. Broker never told owner of buyer's offer, because he believed it was not to her advantage. The commission ruled that, by failing to transmit the offer to owner, the broker represented his own interests to the detriment of owner and any prospective buyers. *Held:* The court upheld the commission's ruling. Broker should have known of the buyer's offer on the day he returned to the office. A broker's duty to disclose an offer is absolute and independent of his evaluation of the offer. It was for seller alone to weigh an offer. *Virginia Real Estate Comm'n v. Bias*, 308 SE2d 123 (1983).

Washington Through broker's efforts, seller and purchaser entered into an agreement for the sale of land. Seller agreed to pay broker a $19,000 commission on closing. Before closing, purchaser assigned his rights (as the contract permitted) to broker's client, Allied. Allied retained broker as its exclusive agent, agreeing to pay a $20,000 commission. Allied then requested a 30-day extension of the closing date in order to arrange for financing, to which seller agreed. The extension cost seller an additional $660 in interest on unpaid taxes. Seller was not told the reason for the extension, nor of the agency relationship between broker and Allied and their commission arrangement. Seller subsequently sued broker for breach of fiduciary duty. *Held:* For seller. Broker breached its duty by failing to disclose to seller its other commitments. Further, broker's failure to disclose the reason for the extension request was viewed as a representation that the extension was in seller's best interests. Seller might not have agreed to it had he known the full extent of broker's role. *Cogan v. Kidder, Matthews & Segner, Inc.*, 648 P2d 875 (1982).

89.10 Liability for Fraud and Misrepresentation

4th Circuit Purchasers contacted realtors, who showed them Maryland waterfront property that they decided to buy. The sales contract provided that all improvements to the property, including the septic system, were sold "as is." After purchasing the property, purchasers began to install a new septic system. However, the Maryland Department of Health told them to stop because the property's soil was not suited for an on-site septic system. Purchasers learned that sellers knew of the soil's condition before they sold the property. Purchasers sued realtors and sellers. *Held:* The "as is" clause did not bar all claims against defendants, because it referred only to *improvements* on the property, not to the property's natural features, such as soil condition. Purchasers' claims against realtors were dismissed because realtors did not know of the soil problem. Even if the relationship between purchasers and realtors gave rise to a duty of care, this duty would not encompass an obligation by realtors to make an independent investigation of hidden defects. The case was remanded to determine whether sellers intended to mislead purchasers and whether they owed them a duty of care in making representations about the property. *Herbert v. Saffell*, 877 F2d 267 (1989).

Alabama Purchasers of a used home sued seller's broker, alleging that the broker had fraudulently misrepresented the extent of problems stemming from water damage. After the contract was signed, seller's broker arranged for a contractor to repair visible water damage. The contractor stated there was no serious problem. At closing, a termite report and repair bill were presented to purchasers. *Held:* Purchasers were legally obligated to purchase the home, even if structural damage was present. Seller's broker made no express warranties, and he told purchasers all he knew about water damage. Purchasers had ample opportunity to inspect the home prior to closing. Since broker's representation did not induce the purchasers to do anything more than they were obligated to do, purchase the home, no injury was shown and there was no actionable fraud. *Reeves v. Porter*, 521 So. 2d 963 (1988).

Alaska Buyers entered into an earnest-money agreement with sellers for the purchase of a house. A subsequent survey showed that the property encroached on neighboring land. Buyers entered into a rescission agreement providing for the return of their deposit. Broker, however, on advice of counsel, refused to execute the agreement; the attorney believed the encroachment was a curable defect not rendering title unmarketable. Buyers filed a claim for reimbursement with the real estate commission. The examiner concluded that the broker had innocently misrepresented the boundaries but that the Real Estate Surety Fund allowed recovery for innocent misrepresentations. Broker appealed. *Held:* Reversed. The surety fund does not allow recovery for innocent misrepresentations, only for loss due to fraud or intentional misrepresentation. *State Real Estate Comm'n v. Johnston*, 682 P2d 383 (1984).

California Broker represented to plaintiffs that the house they agreed to purchase was worth much more than the contract price, that it had a minor, easily correctible pest control problem, and that the house was free of dry rot and infestation. The evidence showed that all representations were intentionally false, and the uninhabitable condition of the house caused plaintiffs severe emotional distress. Plaintiffs sued for fraudulent misrepresentation, fraudulent concealment, and emotional distress. Broker moved to dismiss the mental distress cause of action. *Held:* Victims of a fraudulent sale of real property are entitled to actual and punitive damages for emotional distress when broker's conduct has been outside tolerable bounds. Conduct of broker was sufficiently outrageous to give plaintiffs a cause of action for emotional distress, to which contributory negligence was not a defense. *Godfrey v. Steinpress*, 180 Cal. Rptr. 9 (1982).

Illinois Buyers purchased a church, which both owners and real estate agent had represented to be connected to the city's sanitary sewage system. Upon discovering the lack of such a connection, buyers sued owner and real estate agent for negligent misrepresentation. Agent defended on the ground that he relied on the church's representations. *Held:* Agent was not liable. An agent is not liable unless he knows or should know that fraudulent misrepresentation of a principal is indeed a misrepresentation. *Lyons v. Christ Episcopal Church*, 389 NE2d 623 (1979).

Illinois After purchasing a house, buyers discovered it was subject to severe flooding and was situated on a lot substantially smaller than they thought they had purchased. Buyers charged broker with common-law fraud, negligence, violation of the Consumer Fraud Act, and violations of the Broker Licensing Act. *Held:* For plaintiffs on all four counts. Since the broker had lived next door to the house for five years and had worked for developer of the subdivision, she could have been expected to know of the flooding and the lot size. Broker's concealment of these material facts was fraudulent, and a violation of the duty imposed on realtors under the Real Estate Brokers and Salesmen License Act to disclose material facts. Since broker was in the business of supplying information for others in business transactions, plaintiffs could also recover their economic losses in tort. Finally, broker's legal duty to disclose material facts overrode an exculpatory clause in the sales contract. *Zimmerman v. Northfield Real Estate, Inc.*, 510 NE2d 409 (App. Ct. 1986).

Kansas Broker relied on information provided by sellers to assure buyers that the house for sale was connected to a public sewer system. The contract of sale stated that all plumbing was connected to a sewer. Subsequently, buyers discovered that the plumbing was connected to a septic tank. Buyers sued broker and sellers. The jury found sellers not at fault, as they never had sewer problems and believed their prior owner's assurances; but the jury held the broker liable, assessing actual and punitive damages. *Held:* The broker was liable for actual damages, but not punitive damages. The Kansas Real Estate Brokers and Salespersons' Act, Kan.

Stat. Ann. § 58-3062(a)(31), requires a broker to disclose material information relating to the property that the broker knows or should have known. There were indications on the property that would lead an experienced broker to conclude that the house was not served by a public sewer system. The act placed a higher duty on the broker than on seller because of the public reliance on a broker's expertise. *Johnson v. Geer Real Estate Co.*, 720 P2d 660 (1986).

New Hampshire Before buying, purchasers of a house asked seller's real estate agent about the condition of the well, plumbing, wiring, and septic system, and the agent replied that they were "okay." After discovering that the septic system was defective, purchasers sued the real estate agent and sellers for fraud. The agent and sellers, who had never occupied the house, argued that they were unaware of defects in the system and therefore were not liable. *Held:* The agent and seller were liable. By representing that the septic system was "okay," the agent misrepresented the extent of his knowledge and was therefore liable for fraud. *Mertens v. Woffleboro Nat'l Bank*, 402 A2d 1335 (1979).

Ohio Broker represented both buyers and sellers in a home sale. During negotiations, broker's employee represented that buyers could tap into newly built sewers for an estimated cost of $500. Buyers had asked about the sewage project because additional costs would prohibit the purchase of the house. After closing, the town notified buyers that the new sewer tap-in was mandatory and would cost $1,166; in addition, buyers incurred an assessment fee of $2,200 with interest of $1,300. Buyers sued sellers and broker for fraud, and recovered compensatory and punitive damages. Broker appealed, claiming buyers had a duty to make further inquiry. *Held:* Sellers and broker had a duty to disclose any material, nonvisible facts about the property, such as the sewer system; and nondisclosure was a material misrepresentation. Buyers were entitled to rely upon broker's statement because he represented both buyers and sellers and had a fiduciary duty to disclose material facts known to him. Sellers had informed broker of the mandatory assessment, and broker's employee had notice of the assessment; therefore, the punitive damage award against broker was appropriate. *Foust v. Valleybrook Realty Co.*, 446 NE2d 1122 (1982).

Ohio Real estate broker told buyers that seller's house was a "good solid home." Although she had been informed of termite infestation and damage, the broker did not inform buyers of this fact until after the closing. When buyers discovered the infestation, they sued the broker for fraud. *Held:* The broker was liable. The broker had a duty to disclose the termite infestation at the time it was discovered. The hidden nature of the infestation entitled buyers to rely on the broker's representations. *Miles v. McSwegin*, 388 NE2d 1367 (1979).

Virginia Broker's agreement with sellers gave him the exclusive right to sell their house for 120 days; and the agreement provided that if the house was not sold within that time, broker would purchase the home. Broker, unable to sell the house, requested an extension of the listing time to obtain funds for its purchase, which sellers refused. Sellers sold the house a year later for less than broker had promised. They sued broker for fraud and deceit, and were awarded $1 compensatory and $15,000 punitive damages. *Held:* Reversed. State law requires clear and convincing evidence of fraud and deceit. Fraud cannot be predicated on unfulfilled promises or statements as to future events. An exception exists where a promise is made with present intent not to perform; however, the evidence failed to prove that broker did not intend to perform at the time he made the promise to purchase. The evidence merely showed breach of contract, which does not support a punitive damage award. *Patrick v. Summers,* 369 SE2d 162 (1988).

Washington Soon after purchasing property, buyers discovered that many of sellers' improvements encroached upon adjoining property. Moving the improvements would cost $6,000. Prior to the purchase, sellers had informed broker that the improvements were located inside the property line, and showed brokers markers and boundary lines. Broker gave buyers this information and showed them the markers and boundary lines. The issue was whether broker was liable for innocently and nonnegligently conveying sellers' misrepresentations to buyers. *Held:* Broker was not liable. Brokers, like other professionals, should be held to a standard of reasonable care and cannot be turned into guarantors. Broker had no reason to think that anything was wrong with the boundaries as represented by sellers, and because boundary checks are not the norm in real estate business, broker did not breach the standard of reasonable care. *Hoffman v. Connall,* 736 P2d 242 (1987).

Washington Buyers sued seller and broker for damages stemming from a misrepresentation that the property had the required permits for the installation of a septic tank. Buyers claimed that seller had misrepresented the permit information and that the broker was liable for damages for failing to exercise due care in the capacity of seller's agent. *Held:* The broker was liable for damages to buyer. As a professional, the broker, even though not engaged by buyer, had a duty to verify critical information given him by seller that he knew or should have known was pivotal to the transaction from buyers' point of view. *Tennant v. Lawton,* 615 P2d 1305 (1980).

Wisconsin Two years after buyers purchased a resort hotel, they discovered that the total acreage was significantly less than the figures they were shown on a specification sheet provided by their broker. The figures on the sheet were given by the former hotel owners to owners' real estate agent. Former owners approved the accuracy of the figures. Buyers' broker obtained the figures from the former owners' agent. Both brokers were found strictly liable for misrepresentations to buyers. The brokers appealed, claiming strict liability did not apply because they could not normally be expected to know the property's dimensions without an investigation. *Held:* The actual source of brokers' knowledge is not relevant to strict liability for misrepresentation. State policy is to place the loss on the innocent defendant speaker, rather than on the innocent plaintiff, where the broker, as in this case, had the means to ascertain the pertinent facts or where his position made complete knowledge possible. *Gauerke v. Rozga,* 332 NW2d 804 (1983).

Wisconsin After purchasing residential property from seller, buyers ordered a survey that showed buyers' lot was substantially smaller than represented. The jury awarded judgment to buyers for misrepresentation based on strict responsibility and negligence. Broker appealed. *Held:* Broker is strictly responsible for misrepresentations made to buyers concerning lot size. State policy is to place the loss caused by the misrepresentation on the innocent defendant rather than on the innocent plaintiff who has been misled. Buyers were not required to prove that broker "ought to have known" the lot size, because the broker represented that he had personal knowledge of the property's dimensions. Broker's liability could not be reduced by seller's purported negligence, since contributory negligence is not a defense to a strict responsibility claim. *Reda v. Sincaban*, 426 NW2d 100 (Ct. App. 1988).

89.15 —Vendor's Liability for Broker's Fraud

South Carolina Vendor brought an action against purchaser to foreclose a purchase-money second mortgage he had taken back when the house was sold. Purchasers counterclaimed, accusing vendor of fraud arising from misrepresentations by vendor's broker when the transaction was consummated regarding the physical condition of the house, its improvements, and its appurtenances. The trial court entered judgment for vendor and refused to grant relief on the counterclaim. *Held:* Reversed. Where broker had made false representations concerning the physical condition of property, purchaser could maintain his counterclaim against vendor, who as a principal would be liable for the misrepresentations of broker, his agent. *Byrn v. Walker*, 267 SE2d 601 (1980).

89.20 Liability for Negligence

California Shortly after buyers purchased a luxury home, massive earth movement caused a substantial diminution of the home's value. Buyers purchased the home unaware of soil problems or that there was a history of slides. However, seller's agents were aware of certain "red flags," which should have indicated to them that soil problems existed. However, they did not request soil stability tests and did not inform buyers of potential soil problems. The trial court instructed the jury that a real estate broker has a duty to investigate and disclose defects in property he lists for sale. *Held:* Affirmed. A broker is requried to disclose not only facts known to him, but also facts that are reasonably discoverable. The duty of seller's broker to disclose includes the affirmative duty to conduct a diligent inspection of the property and inform prospective purchasers of all facts materially affecting the property's value. *Easton v. Strassburger*, 199 Cal. Rptr. 383 (Ct. App. 1984).

Montana Defendant subdivided a ranch and contracted with its codefendant to serve as selling broker. The broker found prospective buyers but showed them the wrong property. A year after sale, buyers discovered the mistake and sued defendants. Seller unilaterally settled and sought reimbursement on its cross claim against the broker. *Held:* Judgment for seller. The court rejected the broker's argument that, since his liability to buyer had never been proven, he could not be liable on the cross claim. Although there was no evidence in the record concerning applicable real estate standards, the majority concluded that showing the wrong property constituted negligence under any reasonable standard. By the same reasoning, the court rejected the broker's contention that the complete investigation clause would have insulated him from liability. *McCarty v. Lincoln Green, Inc.*, 620 P2d 1221 (1980).

Nebraska Owners of ranchland retained broker to sell the land for cash only. However, broker prepared a standard form contract making the sale subject to buyer's obtaining a bank loan. The agent assured seller that the contract obligated buyer to complete the sale and that a correct form could be prepared later. When the sale fell through because buyer could not obtain financing, sellers sued broker for negligence. They recovered the difference between the sale price under the negligently prepared contract and the fair market value of the property at the time the sale should have been completed.

Held: Affirmed. The brokerage agent breached his duty to use reasonable care, skill, and diligence to bring about the results sought by sellers. The formula for calculating damages correctly followed the Nebraska rule, under which losses incurred owing to negligence are determined as of the time the sale should have been completed. *Tetherow v. Wolfe*, 392 NW2d 374 (1986).

89.25 Practice of Law

Iowa Relying on their broker's advice, buyers purchased a new house that had substantial defects. Buyers sued broker for malpractice, claiming that broker failed to inspect the house and disclose defects to them, gave them improper and erroneous legal advice as to the likely effects of failure to close, failed to insist on an adequate escrow fund, and failed to advise them of building code requirements or to inform them that the house had failed a building inspection. *Held:* For buyers. Although violation of the National Association of Realtors' Code of Ethics was evidence only of negligence, and not negligence per se, the trial court's rejection of the association's ethical standards was reversible error. A broker who undertakes to render professional services is required to exercise the skill and knowledge normally possessed by members of that profession under like circumstances. The realtors' code of ethics was the accepted standard in the profession. *Menzel v. Morse*, 362 NW2d 465 (1985).

New Jersey A licensed real estate broker negotiated a sale of real property, prepared a form contract of sale, and submitted it to the parties for signature. The broker was charged with the crime of engaging in the unlawful practice of law. *Held:* The New Jersey Supreme Court ruled that the broker had not committed a crime within the meaning of the statute, but it reserved judgment on whether he had practiced law without authority. At the court's suggestion, the New Jersey State Bar Association filed suit against licensed realtors as a class, seeking a declaratory judgment and injunctive relief. A settlement was reached and approved by the court. It provided that brokers could prepare for the sale of residential real estate containing not more than four dwelling units and unimproved single-family lots. The attorney for buyer or seller had three days to disapprove the contract before it became binding. Brokers were also given the right to prepare residential leases not exceeding one year's terms. *New Jersey State Bar Ass'n v. New Jersey Ass'n of Realtor Bds.*, 461 A2d 1112, modified, 467 A2d 577 (1983).

Utah Earnest-money agreement executed by seller contained a "subject to" clause, stating that the "possession date [is] subject to relocation of seller." Seller asserted he had told the agent, before the agent filled out the agreement, that he did not want to sell his house until he had located another. When seller failed to locate another house, he refused to complete the sale. Buyer sued, and obtained a ruling that the "subject to" clause made only buyer's *possession* of the house, not its sale, subject to seller's relocation. Seller sued broker and agent for indemnification on the ground that the agent erred in phrasing the agreement. *Held:* For broker and agent. Seller knew the words used by the real estate agent; and by signing the agreement, seller approved and ratified the acts of the agent and was bound by them. The language at issue was nontechnical and readily understandable, and there was no hint of fraud or sharp dealing. *Kidd v. Maldonado*, 688 P2d 461 (1984).

Washington Broker's agent prepared a real estate earnest-money agreement for buyer by filling in the blanks on a standardized form drafted by an attorney. When buyer noted that the agreement lacked a clause allowing her to withdraw her offer on the basis of an inspection, the agent added a standardized, attorney-drafted, structural inspection contingency clause. When the inspection revealed damage to the roof and exterior siding, buyer demanded the return of her earnest money. Seller refused, interpreting the added clause to mean that the report had to reveal real structural defects based upon an objective standard. *Held:* Broker was liable for negligence because he undertook to practice law and prepared the contract at variance with client's instructions. Although a real estate broker or salesperson may complete printed standardized lawyer-approved forms to be used in simple real estate transactions, when he does so, the broker must comply with the standard of care demanded of a practicing attorney. *Cultum v. Heritage House Realtors, Inc.*, 694 P2d 630, cert. denied, 105 SCt. 2345 (1985).

89.30
Duty to Explain

Virginia Seller told broker that she would accept a first deed of trust as part of the sale price for her house but that she would not accept a second trust. Broker obtained a land sales contract from a prospective purchaser containing a clause subordinating seller to a construction loan. Seller signed the contract on broker's urging, after broker assured her the clause would make the property more valuable. When seller learned the meaning of subordination, she had the sale renegotiated to eliminate the clause. *Held:* The broker breached her duty to explain the terms of the sales contract to seller. As a result, seller suffered damages equal to the difference between the value of the note she bargained for in the first contract and the value of the note she actually received. *Long & Foster Real Estate, Inc. v. Clay*, 343 SE2d 297 (1986).

89.35
Duty of Full Disclosure

California Plaintiffs purchased and occupied a single-family residence. Sometime after moving in, they began to notice cracks, distress, and deterioration of the home. They submitted a claim to their homeowner's insurance carrier, who reported that the foundation was inadequate for the type of surface the structure was constructed on. The homeowners sued their real estate broker, claiming that he had an affirmative duty to inspect the premises and disclose material defects affecting the value of the purchase. The broker moved to dismiss the complaint. *Held:* For the broker. Purchaser's broker owes no duty to inspect the premises. Seller's broker, who has much easier access to the property, has a duty to inspect and evaluate the premises. A duplication of effort would result if the same duty were imposed upon the purchaser's broker. *Murray v. Haden*, 259 Cal. Rptr. 257 (1989).

Hawaii Broker entered into an exclusive listing agreement with seller for the sale of hotels, under which the broker would receive a percentage of the sale price as commission. Subsequently, broker entered into an agreement with prospective buyer of the hotels, with broker to receive an additional commission. Prospective buyer made an offer through his attorney but stipulated that seller pay the broker the commission specified in their listing agreement. The broker had no knowledge of this offer. *Held:* Any right the broker had to a commission from seller was barred by its undisclosed dual representation. While buyer knew of broker's agreement with seller, seller did not know of or consent to the dual agency. Even though the broker may have merely acted as a middleman or finder, such distinctions are not exceptions to the broker's duty of full disclosure and consent. *Property House, Inc. v. Kelley*, 715 P2d 805 (1986).

Montana An agent of seller's brokers found a buyer who proposed making a down payment on seller's farm and securing the balance of the purchase price with bonds bought on margin loan. Eventually a deal was struck and sellers' attorney drafted a sales agreement. However, the bonds provided inadequate security for the loan because they were subject to margin loans. After margin sales liquidated the bonds, sellers were left with less than a quarter of the value of their security interest in the purchase price. Sellers sued, alleging that brokers should have informed them that the bonds provided inadequate collateral. *Held:* Summary judgment for brokers' agent affirmed. While a realtor has an affirmative duty to disclose all material facts to sellers, the brokers' agent did not breach this duty, because sellers and their attorneys already knew, from the buyer's initial proposal, that the bonds were held on margin. Moreover, neither broker was aware that the bonds were subject to margin loans. *Bills v. Hannah, Inc.*, 749 P2d 1076 (1988).

Texas Principal signed a listing agreement with broker for the sale of her property, which was subject to a mortgage debt and liens. During the agency relationship, broker became aware that principal was delinquent in payments and that the note holder intended to foreclose on the property. The property was sold at trustee's sale, and principal learned of the foreclosure in a telephone conversation with broker. Principal sued broker for negligence and breach of fiduciary duty in failing to disclose facts and for damages under the Deceptive Trade Practices Act. The trial court granted the broker's motion for summary judgment. Principal appealed. *Held:* Reversed and remanded. Broker was obligated to inform client of all information that might affect her decision about the listing property including the fact that foreclosure proceedings were pending against the property. State real estate commission regulations provides that a broker is obligated to convey all information of which he has knowledge and that may affect the principal's decision about the property. A valid agency regulation has the force and effect of law. Since the regulation exised at the time the listing agreement was formed, it was incorporated by law into parties' agreement. *Kinnard v. Homann*, 750 SW2d 30 (Ct. App. 1988).

90.00
LISTING AGREEMENTS

90.05
Validity of Listing Agreements

Connecticut Real estate broker's client purchased 25 units in a condominium complex and, in accordance with the broker's agreement, broker requested the appropriate commission. Developer of the complex refused to pay anything to broker, arguing that the agreement did not conform to state law because it failed to identify the location and price of the specific units sold. *Held:* Broker was entitled to the commission. The broker's agreement did not need to specify the particular location and sales price of units within the complex to satisfy the statutory requirement that it set forth the "conditions of such contract authorization." Based on the nature of the premises and the failure of the agreement to contain the purchase price of individual units, it was evident that developer intended to reserve to itself the right to determine which units to sell and the price of each; broker's primary obligation was to find potential buyers for developer rather than to sell the units himself. *Sticklor v. Woodland House Condominium, Inc.,* 518 A2d 949 (App. Ct. 1986).

Idaho Partnership entered into an exclusive listing agreement with plaintiff. Three of seven partners signed the agreement for the partnership. One of the three partners, also an agent for plaintiff brokerage, signed the agreement on behalf of plaintiff as well. Defendant, an outside broker, knew of a prospective purchaser for the property, and unsuccessfully approached plaintiff regarding a commission-splitting arrangement. Subsequently, one of the four nonsigning partners gave defendant a verbal listing. After negotiating the sale and getting all partners to sign the sales documents, defendant received a commission. Plaintiff sued defendant for interference with contract rights. Defendant challenged the validity of the agreement. *Held:* Plaintiff failed to establish the validity of the listing agreement and therefore the tort of interference with contract. There was never a meeting of the minds between plaintiff and all seven partners before or after the signing of the listing agreement. *Southern Idaho Realty, Inc.—Century 21 v. Larry J. Hellhake & Assocs.,* 636 P2d 168 (1981).

Illinois Broker and owner entered into an exclusive listing agreement for the sale of owner's condominium. The agreement provided that the term would continue for 90 days, after which time the agreement would continue until terminated by either party and would automatically terminate one year from the date of execution. After owners had terminated the listing agreement, a party who had originally been shown the property by broker purchased the condominium. Another brokerage received the commission, and plaintiffs demanded that, under the terms of the listing agreement, they were entitled to the commission. *Held:* The listing agreement was void. The state licensing act provides that a listing contract that does not provide an automatic expiration within a definite period of time is void. In this case, the term of the agreement was 90 days, to be automatically extended until a written notice of termination was sent. Brokers cannot obtain listing agreements that contain a clause automatically extending the listing period. An interpretation that the listing agreement automatically terminated in one year would allow brokers to circumvent the intent of the licensing act by merely adding a provision that the agreement shall terminate after an extended period of time. *Grayway Real Estate Corp. v. Dickey*, 533 NE2d 100 (Ct. App. 1988).

Nevada Real estate broker was authorized to sell a certain hotel. A document labeled "offer for sale" was signed by broker and one of the potential buyers. A clause in the document stated that any negotiations for the hotel would be handled through broker. Buyers' offer, made through broker, was rejected. They then reached a favorable lease-purchase agreement for the hotel through another broker. Broker brought an action for breach of contract against buyers, claiming that they had a contract to deal exclusively with him. *Held:* The agreement between broker and buyers was not sufficiently definite to be enforceable as an exclusive dealing agreement because it (1) did not disclose broker's fees or commissions, (2) did not specify the services to be performed by broker, and (3) was deceptively labeled as an offer for sale rather than an exclusive dealing agreement. *Chung v. Atwell*, 745 P2d 370 (1987).

90.10
Scope of Broker's Authority

New Mexico Purchasers sought specific performance of a swap agreement that would have allowed them to trade their commercial parcel for any equivalent parcel of residential land within a proposed development. They had been shown the land by developer's sales agent and would not have purchased the property without the swap agreement. Developer refused to effect the swap and tendered back to purchasers their down payment, contending that the sales agent lacked authority to enter the agreement. *Held:* Developer's performance was enforced. A principal is bound by the apparent authority of its agent, whether or not the agent actually has such authority, if the agent is placed in a position that would lead a reasonably prudent person to believe the agent has such authority. In this case, developer did nothing to indicate to prospective buyers that the agent's authority was limited prior to the transaction's consummation. Additionally, the cashing of the down payment check created an inference of ratification of the agent's actions. *Vickers v. North Am. Land Dev., Inc.*, 607 P2d 603 (1980).

North Carolina Seller entered into an exclusive listing agreement with broker for the sale of certain real property. Broker, without the consent of seller and without specific authorization, entered into a contract for sale with buyer and accepted an earnest-money deposit as consideration for the contract. Seller refused to deliver a deed to buyer, and the latter sued for specific performance. Seller asked that the lawsuit be dismissed for failure to state an actionable claim, and the trial court granted the motion. Seller appealed. *Held:* Affirmed. Without the authorization of seller (either express or implied), an exclusive listing agreement does not give the broker authority to enter into a contract. *Forbis v. Honeycutt,* 268 SE2d 247 (1980).

Pennsylvania Seller entered into a listing agreement with broker, giving broker the "sole and exclusive right to sell" a property for $32,000. Broker then executed two proposed sale agreements for the property: one with prospective purchasers for $32,000 and another, several days later, with other purchasers for $40,000. Seller signed only the high bid agreement. The first prospective purchasers sued to quiet title. After the trial court entered an order quieting legal title in the first prospective purchasers and equitable title in the high bidders, the first prospective purchasers argued that the listing agreement constituted an offer to sell the property. *Held:* The listing agreement was not a general solicitation, but rather, an apparent agreement between the seller and a single real estate broker that did not even give the broker apparent authority to sell. Even if the listing agreement were considered to be directed towards the general public, it could be viewed only as an invitation to bid and not as an offer. *Roskwitalski v. Reiss*, 487 A2d 864 (Super. Ct. 1985).

90.15
Exclusive Agency

Illinois Defendant couple had originally borrowed $20,000 from the wife's parents for the down payment on a house they were now seeking to sell. They signed an exclusive listing contract with a broker for a six-month period providing for a 6 percent fee if the property were sold by the broker, defendants, or anyone else during the contract period. Two days after the contract expired, defendants conveyed the house to the wife's parents, in return for which the parents extinguished the debt and assumed the mortgage. *Held:* The broker was entitled to commission. Although the agreement to sell was not put in writing until after the exclusive period expired, evidence indicated the agreement had been reached during the exclusive period. Further, the transfer met the definition of a sale as a contract whereby property is transferred from one person to another for valuable consideration. *Hammel v. Ruby,* 487 NE2d 409 (App. Ct. 1985).

Oregon In April 1976, broker and seller signed an exclusive listing agreement that called for commission to be paid to broker if, within a 30-day period, broker found a buyer ready and willing to buy the property at terms agreeable to the seller. It also called for commission to be paid if, during that period, broker introduced seller or placed seller "in contact with a buyer to or through whom" a sale was made within a year. During the 30-day period, broker showed the property to a prospective buyer, who made an offer that seller rejected. Seven months later, the prospective buyer's son bought the property. Broker had never had any dealings with the son, but claimed that the sale was made "through" the prospective buyer, so that broker was entitled to a commission. *Held:* No commission was due. The exact meaning of the phrase "to or through whom" was unclear. Since the listing agreement was a form contract provided by broker, any ambiguities in the document would be interpreted against him. *Bob Secolo Realty, Inc. v. Dunnigan,* 583 P2d 1154 (1978).

Texas Purchaser brought suit for specific performance for sale and leaseback of a corporation's property. The real estate broker, who had an exclusive listing to sell the property, had signed the contract as corporation's "principal agent." When the corporation received the contract, it refused to perform because of its attorneys' numerous objections. Purchaser agreed to sign the contract if certain modifications were made but found the suggested modifications unacceptable and brought suit. The trial court ruled in favor of purchaser, finding that the broker was the corporation's general agent with power to sell the property by virtue of their listing agreement. *Held:* Reversed. A broker is a special agent limited to showing the property and finding a purchaser and, as a general rule, has no authority to contract on the principal's behalf. Thus, a contract signed by the broker as "principal agent" did not bind seller. *UTL Corp. v. Marcus,* 589 SW2d 782 (Civ. App. 1979).

90.20
Multiple Listing

Colorado Plaintiffs listed their home for sale with one of Foremost Realty's broker-associates and asked her to help them find a new house. The broker located a house, which was listed for sale with Olthoff Realty under an agreement that specifically authorized Olthoff to market the house through the multiple-listing service (MLS). With the broker's assistance, plaintiffs bid $105,000. Property owner made a counteroffer for $110,000, which was transmitted to plaintiffs by Olthoff through the broker. Shortly thereafter, another couple bid $112,000, which Olthoff accepted on behalf of the owner. Before Olthoff contacted the broker with the news, she had already received plaintiffs' acceptance of the counteroffer. Plaintiffs claimed to have purchased the property on the theory that the broker was property owner's agent. *Held:* The arrangement established by owner's listing agreement and the use by Olthoff of information furnished by owner required the broker to be regarded as a subagent of owner. Even if there were indicia of an agency relationship between plaintiffs and the broker, there was ground for refusing to accord agency status to the relationship. The dual agency that would result, with its potential for conflicts of interest, was unacceptable. It would be inconsistent with the ethical responsibilities of brokers to characterize a selling broker in a multiple-listing scenario as an agent for both seller and buyer. Moreover, it might not be to buyer's advantage to be in an agency relationship with the selling broker because this could deprive the buyer of certain remedies. *Stortroen v. Beneficial Fin. Co.*, 736 P2d 391 (1987).

Connecticut An organization of real estate brokers instituted a plan under which each member would assist the others in finding buyers for individual listings. Under the listing agreement, owner was permitted to grant nonexclusive listings to other brokers but was prohibited from granting exclusive listings. The organization sought a ruling from the state realty commission to determine whether it could negotiate a sale where owner later gives an exclusive listing in violation of the agreement. The commission ruled that its regulation forbidding brokerage activity on property subject to a competing exclusive listing would be violated in such a case. *Held:* Ruling struck down. Under contract law, the original nonexclusive listing constitutes a bilateral contract with mutual obligations. To permit a competing buyer to obtain an exclusive listing and cut off the other broker's interest would be to authorize the second broker to induce and aid in the breach of a contract. Consequently, the organization cannot be prevented from continuing to sell its listed property. *Real Estate Listing Serv., Inc. v. Real Estate Comm'n*, 425 A2d 581 (1979).

Pennsylvania Real estate brokers sued the Delaware County Board of Realtors on the ground that the denial of their applications for membership constituted an unlawful restraint of trade. The board argued that its membership was limited to brokers in Delaware County and plaintiffs had no offices in the county. *Held:* Under the ruling in *Collins v. Main Line Board of Realtors*, 452 Pa. 342, 304 A2d 493 (1973), multiple-listing practices of an organization of brokers that operated to exclude a licensed broker were per se unreasonable. Where the brokers maintained offices in the county adjacent to Delaware County, the suit should not be dismissed solely on the basis of an artificial boundary unrelated to business practices. *Suburban Fair Hous., Inc. v. Delaware County Bd. of Realtors*, 344 A2d 481 (1975).

90.25 Expiration and Revocation

7th Circuit A broker's contract with developer of a shopping center provided that the broker would receive a substantial bonus if 90 percent of the stores were leased by a given date and other conditions were met. The broker sued for bonus commission, even though leases had not been signed for 90 percent of the stores, on the theory that it had found ready, willing, and able buyers for 90 percent of the stores. *Held:* For the client. The policy reasons behind Illinois' "procuring broker" approach, which entitles a broker who has produced a ready, willing, and able buyer or lessee to basic commission, do not apply with the same force to bonus provisions. The client's inclusion of a deadline in a bonus provision suggests that time is of the essence to the client, who is likely facing his own deadlines, and that the client is far less likely to delay signing a lease to avoid paying the bonus. The deadline was not an arbitrary date, but presumably had independent importance to the client, meriting its strict enforcement. In the absence of contrary indications, it would be wrong to extend the Illinois doctrine of the ready, willing, and able buyer to override contract provisions controlling bonus commissions. *Harry F. Chaddick Realty, Inc. v. Maisel*, 762 F2d 534 (1985).

Florida In 1979, property owner entered into a verbal listing of his property with a real estate broker. The broker produced a potential purchaser in 1980, but his offer was refused. In 1983, owner finally sold the property to the same purchaser who made an offer in 1980. When the broker learned about the sale he brought suit for the commission, contending that the listing agreement was still valid and that he was responsible for the sale. *Held:* For property owner. When a listing contract does not specify the time period in which performance must occur, a reasonable time is implied. In this case, the two and one-half year period during which the broker failed to communicate with seller was beyond a reasonable period. Therefore, seller had the right to asssume that the broker had abandoned the sale. *Richland Grove & Cathe Co. v. Easterling*, 526 So. 2d 685 (1988).

Mississippi Sellers listed land for sale with a real estate broker. After the listing expired without a response, the broker interested a prospect in the property and received permission from sellers to negotiate on their behalf. Before the purchase agreement was executed, sellers were approached by another prospect who proposed to lease all mineral rights in sellers' land. To take advantage of this proposal, sellers attempted to bring the prospective purchaser in on the deal, but the broker would not cooperate. After learning that the broker cosigned a loan application with prospective purchaser to finance the land purchase, sellers filed a complaint against the broker. The Mississippi Real Estate Commission revoked the broker's license, and he appealed. *Held:* The agency relationship between sellers and defendant terminated when the listing agreement expired. Once the broker went back to sellers to advise them of prospective purchaser's interest, he revived the listing agreement and all his fiduciary obligations to sellers. The broker breached his obligation not to represent another principal in the same matter without informing sellers. Thus, license revocation was the proper penalty. *Smith v. Sullivan*, 419 So. 2d 184 (1982).

South Carolina Broker contracted in an "Exclusive Listing Agreement" with an 80-year-old landowner to make all reasonable efforts to sell certain property. The listing was to be for 15 years and the price agreed upon after a feasibility study for future development by a real estate consultant. The contract contained a provision making it binding on landowner's heirs and assignees. After the feasibility study was completed, a new exclusive listing agreement was signed fixing the selling price and shortening the term to five years. The agreement did not include the provision binding the heirs and assigns. Landowner died, and the executor sold the property through another broker. *Held:* The executor was bound by the listing agreement, and the broker was entitled to his commission. The second agreement supplemented the first and did not supersede it. Although a listing agreement normally ends with the death of the property owner, given landowner's age, the parties intended that the agreement be binding on the estate. *Wilber Smith & Assocs. v. National Bank,* 263 SE2d 643 (1980).

Utah A partnership owned an historic building. Because of tax considerations, they had not decided whether to lease, sell, or exchange it, and had not set a price on it. However, the president of the partnership executed an exclusive listing agreement with a broker, which stated that broker would receive a 6 percent commission whether the building was leased, sold, or exchanged. The listing agreement did not state a definite term and did not set a price on the property. The partnership sold the building without notice to broker. When broker sued for commission, the partnership claimed that the absence of a specific time period made it impossible to say that the agreement was still in force when the property was sold. *Held:* Broker was entitled to commission. In the absence of a specific time period, an exclusive listing agreement is revocable at will; the partnership never revoked broker's agency to market the building. The absence of a specified price also was not fatal to the enforcement of the agreement. *Gump & Ayers Real Estate, Inc. v. Domcoy Investors V*, 733 P2d 128 (1987).

91.00
BROKER'S COMMISSIONS

91.05
Necessity for a Broker's License

Colorado Owner of a radio station offered to pay a 5 percent fee to finder if he obtained a buyer. After a buyer was found and the station was sold, owner refused to pay the finder's fee, arguing that the finder did not have a real estate broker's license. The finder argued that the mere act of finding a buyer does not require a license. *Held:* The finder is not entitled to his fee. Under the Colo. Rev. Stat. § 12-61-101(2)(i) (1973), a finder is required to have a broker's license if the sale of a business includes the transfer of any interest in real estate. In this case, the sale of the radio station included the transfer of a leasehold interest in the land where the station was located. Although the value of the leasehold may have been slight, it falls within the statute. Nor could the contract be severed based on that part of the sale not involving real estate, since that would frustrate the purpose of the statute. *Broughhall v. Black Forest Dev. Co.*, 593 P2d 314 (1978).

Maryland Sybert and Nippard were partners in law firm that was not in the business of dealing in real estate as a broker. Sybert was retained by ARCO to help it obtain a variance on property it wished to buy. Nippard was separately retained by Citadel in an unrelated matter to help it buy land in the area. When ARCO indicated it might wish to sell a parcel of land, the partners arranged a meeting between their clients. After ARCO sold Citadel the parcel, it refused to pay Sybert a commission, claiming he was not a broker and had not been employed as a broker. *Held:* Sybert was entitled to the commission. The ARCO executives with whom the partners dealt had apparent authority to dispose of corporate property and discussed compensation with the partners. The fact that Sybert was not a licensed real estate broker did not bar his claim to a commission, because attorneys not in the brokerage business are exempt from the Maryland licensing statute. The partners' efforts caused the sale, entitling Sybert to a commission by either express or implied contract. *Atlantic Richfield Co. v. Sybert*, 441 A2d 1079 (Ct. Spec. App. 1982), aff'd, 456 A2d 20 (1983).

Montana Defendant owner hired plaintiff, a real estate broker, to sell his ranch. Plaintiff incorrectly represented himself to defendant as a licensed real estate broker. The parties orally agreed to a nonexclusive listing and that plaintiff would be paid a 5 percent commission. No written contract was executed. Plaintiff found a purchaser and a sales contract was executed, with the 5 percent commission provided for in the contract. By then, plaintiff had obtained a real estate license. At closing, defendant disputed plaintiff's claim to a commission because of plaintiff's misrepresentation as to his license status. *Held:* For plaintiff. Under Montana law, an action for a commission can be maintained if plaintiff was a real estate broker at the time the action arose. Here, the action arose at the time of contract execution. Further, plaintiff's misrepresentation was not material. *Deimler v. Ostler,* 651 P2d 41 (1982).

Nebraska Corporation asked consultant to approach hospital about a possible acquisition or merger. The consultant alleged that the corporation orally agreed to pay him one percent of the consideration paid if the acquisition was consummated. The corporation entered into a "lease and agreement" arrangement, but refused to pay consultant any commission. *Held:* The consultant was not entitled to a commission. The Nebraska Real Estate License Law bars an unlicensed business consultant from recovering a fee for a business transaction involving real estate. The consultant's activities in negotiating a fee for the sale, purchase, or lease of hospital put him within the statute's orbit. His contention that the transaction was not a real estate transaction, but a transaction for the acquisition of an ongoing business, which put his activities outside the statute, was rejected. The court declined to follow the "New Jersey rule," which permits an unlicensed business broker to recover a fee on the portion of the sale attributable to personal property. *Ford v. American Medical Int'l, Inc.*, 422 NW2d 67 (1988).

Vermont Plaintiff, who was in a business unrelated to real estate, learned about a prospective purchaser for a residence listed with broker. Plaintiff offered to disclose the prospective purchaser's name to broker in exchange for a third of any commission broker might receive from a sale to the purchaser. The offer and broker's acceptance were not reduced to writing. After broker sold the residence to the purchaser, broker refused to pay plaintiff one third of the commission, claiming the arrangement with plaintiff represented an agreement to engage in real estate brokerage without a license, in violation of state law. *Held:* Plaintiff was entitled to one third of broker's commission. His agreement to act as a "finder" did not represent an engagement in real estate brokerage, because it did not entail any action that could be characterized as negotiation. Plaintiff had neither knowledge of, nor contact with, seller, nor was he involved in the events that culminated in the sale. His efforts did not proceed to the point where the prospect would be reasonably considered a realistic prospect for the purchase of the property. *Garfano v. Wells*, 458 A2d 1122 (1983).

Washington Plaintiff, president and chief shareholder of defendant's supermarket, was asked by defendant to find a purchaser for the stock of the supermarket. It was implied by defendant and understood by both parties that plaintiff, upon finding a ready, willing, and able purchaser, would receive either a reasonable fee or a share in defendant's business. After plaintiff found such a purchaser, defendant terminated him as president, refused the purchase offer, and did not pay plaintiff a commission. Plaintiff, who failed to allege he was a duly licensed real estate broker, sued defendant for a commission. *Held:* Not only was plaintiff not entitled to a commission, but what he did violated Washington's real estate statute. The fact that the transaction was isolated and that plaintiff was defendant's employee did not exempt him from the licensing requirement of the statute. Nor was plaintiff entitled to a reasonable fee or quantum meruit, quasi contract, or unjust enrichment grounds because his contract with defendant was illegal and, therefore, unenforceable. *Springer v. Rosauer*, 641 P2d 1216 (1982).

91.10 Construction of Contractual Provisions Concerning Commissions

Georgia In November 1972, landlord executed a three-year lease with a corporation. The lease provided that if the tenant purchased the property during the term of the agreement, landlord was to pay a sales commission to broker. In January 1974, landlord sold the property to the corporation's president and to a witness to the agreement. Broker tried to collect a commission, but landlord refused to pay. In the subsequent lawsuit, purchasers executed an affidavit stating that they were purchasing the premises as individuals. *Held:* The lease provision applied only if the tenant purchased the property. The corporation was a separate and distinct legal entity and the only tenant specified in the agreement. There were no allegations that purchasers had acted fraudulently or in collusion with landlord. Accordingly, the corporate veil would not be pierced, and there was no commission due. *DeKalb Realty Co. v. McColgan,* 250 SE2d 29 (1978).

Minnesota Brokers sued for their commission under an exclusive right to sell listing agreement. Owners conceded that they signed the agreement; but they alleged that they subsequently told brokers to increase the asking price and told them that the purchase contract on which brokers sought their commission did not reflect this increase in price. Owners terminated the agreement when brokers submitted the purchase contract. *Held:* As an agent, a broker is under a duty not to act except in accordance with the principal's directions. Once broker undertakes his performance, the principal does not have the right to modify the terms of the agreement. When owners changed the terms of the prospective sale, brokers were entitled to damages for any loss suffered although they were bound by the modification and no longer could act under the original agreement. Brokers' cause of action was for breach of contract and not for commission. The case was remanded to allow brokers to show the reasonable likelihood of producing a buyer under the original terms. *Klawitter v. Billick*, 242 NW2d 588 (1976).

Nebraska Plaintiff brought an action to recover a commission allegedly due under the terms of an exclusive real estate listing agreement. Defendant conveyed real estate to the corporate parent in relinquishment of claims against it by the parent. Defendant claimed the conveyance was not a "sale" within the terms of the agreement. *Held:* A sale had taken place, and plaintiff was owed a commission. There had been a transfer of property from one company to another for consideration, so the essential elements of a sale were present. *Dial Realty v. Cudahy Co.*, 254 NW2d 421 (1977).

Wisconsin Owners listed their resort for sale with a broker. The listing agreement included an override clause calling for a commission to be paid to broker if within the year following the contract's expiration, the resort was sold to someone with whom the broker negotiated during the term of the contract and whose name the broker had submitted in writing prior to the contract's expiration date. Before the end of the listing period, broker submitted in writing the name of prospective purchasers. After the listing expired, a deal was consummated in which prospective purchasers acquired a one-half interest in the property, with the other half acquired by a couple with whom broker had no contact. Owners refused to pay broker a commission under the override clause. *Held:* Broker was entitled to a commission. The override clause was clear and sufficiently broad to include a likely purchaser who purchased in combination with other parties. Even if the clause were ambiguous, it need not be construed against broker, because it was drafted by the Wisconsin Real Estate Examining Board. *United Farm Agency, Inc. v. Klasen*, 334 NW2d 110 (1983).

91.15
—Ready, Willing, and Able Buyer

7th Circuit Owner retained broker to sell his farm and signed an exclusive listing agreement stating that he would pay a commission if the broker procured a purchaser ready, willing, and able to purchase at the stated price of $80 million or at any other price and terms agreeable to owner. The broker's agent introduced owner to a prospective purchaser, which made an offer to the agent, who conveyed it to the owner. Purchaser bought the farm for under $40 million. Owner excluded broker's personnel from all final negotiations and refused to pay a commission. *Held:* Broker was entitled to the commission. The object of the listing agreement was achieved; broker produced a purchaser ready, willing, and able to buy. By selling the farm to purchaser, owner accepted broker's performance. His argument after the fact that a higher price might have been obtained was immaterial; a broker cannot be held responsible for a seller's poor judgment in accepting a low offer. *Coldwell, Barker & Co. v. Karlock*, 686 F2d 596 (1982).

Alaska A broker produced a group of buyers who signed a purchase and sale agreement providing that a closing would occur "within ten days of clear title." Seller wanted the closing to take place on April 11 so ex-wife's judgment encumbering the property could be paid by then. Whether broker agreed to an April 11 closing was disputed. Buyers were not able to produce the money until April 12. Seller withdrew his offer on April 11 and sold his property through another broker. The first broker sued for the commission. *Held:* Although a real estate broker does not earn a commission unless the contract is performed, broker is still entitled to a commission if improper or frustrating conduct by the owner prevents title from passing. Even if broker had agreed to an April 11 closing, he was not the buyers' agent, and lacked authority to modify their contract. Buyers met their obligation to tender the down payment within 10 days of receiving the title report. *Drake v. Hosley*, 713 P2d 1203 (1986).

Montana Owners listed their ranch for sale with broker. Under the listing agreement, broker would be entitled to a commission if it found a buyer within the listing period or if it placed the owners in contact with someone who bought the ranch by December 22, 1980. Prospective purchasers decided to buy the ranch and signed a buy/sell agreement that was contingent upon the sale of their own house. Immediately thereafter, they moved into the ranch as tenants. Their house was not sold until December 31, 1980, and the ranch purchase was closed on January 29, 1981. The owners refused to pay broker a commission, pointing out that the events that enabled purchasers to buy the ranch occurred after December 22, 1980. *Held:* Broker was not entitled to a commission, because the purchase price was not paid, title was not conveyed, and the sale was not completed within the time frame of the listing agreement. Purchasers did not become ready, willing, and able until they sold their house after the listing agreement had expired. *Property Brokers, Inc. v. Loyning*, 654 P2d 521 (1982).

Nebraska Broker and seller executed a "farm listing contract" providing for the payment of a commission for the sale of a farm, including its bee colonies, or production of a ready, willing, and able purchaser by broker. After the listing contract was made, broker procured a prospective buyer who executed a purchase agreement with an option to cancel by a certain date. Subsequently, buyer notified seller that he would not purchase, and the sale was not completed. Broker sued for his commission, arguing that buyer did not purchase the farm because he counted only 860 beehives, although the seller had stated in the contracts that the farm contained 1,800 beehives. *Held:* Despite this allegation, buyer was not entitled to a commission, because there was no evidence that seller prevented buyer from exercising his purchase option. A broker is not entitled to a commission for producing a prospective buyer willing only to execute an option. *DaLee Realty v. Kuhl*, 305 NW2d 891 (1981).

New York Broker sued to recover his commission after he had located a prospective purchaser who provided a binder and good faith deposit. *Held:* The real estate broker was not entitled to the commission. Absent an agreement to the contrary, the broker is deemed to have earned his commission when he produces a buyer who is ready, willing, and able to purchase at vendor's terms. The burden lies with broker to establish that prospective purchaser is financially able to meet the purchase price. The binder and good faith deposit did not constitute sufficient evidence of purchaser's financial ability to complete the transaction, *O'Connor Realty Servs. v. Higgins*, 539 NYS2d 975 (1989).

New York Plaintiff sued to recover broker's commission. The trial court had instructed the jury, in response to its request on the issue, that they were not to be concerned with prospective buyer's' financial capability to purchase, because that was not an element in this case. The verdict for broker was affirmed by the appellate court. *Held:* Reversed and remanded. Unless agreed otherwise, a commission is earned by a real estate broker when he produces a buyer who is not only ready and willing to purchase but able to do so as well. Prospective buyer's financial ability was indeed an element that broker had to prove in order to recover. The instruction to the jury was error. *Rusciano Servs., Ltd. v. Griffler*, 465 NE2d 33 (1984).

Tennessee Defendants listed their business for sale with plaintiff, a real estate brokerage. Plaintiff found prospective buyers ready and willing to agree to defendants' terms. Defendants, however, were uncertain of buyers' ability to carry the mortgage payments and asked plaintiff for more information about their finances. When plaintiff failed to supply this, defendants called off the deal. Plaintiff sued for commission. *Held:* For defendants. Defendants had reason to refuse to close the sale. They faced substantial economic risk in allowing buyers to assume their mortgage and acted reasonably in demanding assurances that the risk could be safely accepted. The duty to pay a brokerage commission arises not simply when a ready, willing, and able buyer is produced, but when such readiness, willingness, and ability is communicated to the seller by objective indicators. *Gatlinburg*

Real Estate Co. v. Booth, 651 SW2d 203 (1983).

91.20
—Procuring Cause

Alabama Property owners signed an open listing agreement with a brokerage firm. The agreement covered a parcel with a house on it and a larger parcel of farmland. The brokerage agent brought prospective purchasers to look at the larger tract of land and spent two hours showing it to them. As they passed the house, the agent mentioned to them that it was also listed with his firm. The property owners sold the properties directly to the purchasers without notifying the broker. The brokerage sued for its commission on the sale of both properties. *Held:* The broker was entitled to a commission on the larger property but not on the house. In the case of the larger parcel, the agent showed the purchasers the land and was the source of their knowledge about it. In the case of the house, the agent neither showed the property nor conducted negotiations. It could be inferred that broker was not the procuring cause of the sale. *United Farm Agency v. Green*, 466 So. 2d 118 (1985).

Illinois A listing agreement between broker and seller of a house provided for a six-month exclusive listing and another two-month grace period entitling broker to his commission if he sold the property to anyone with whom he negotiated during the six-month period, as long as he informed seller. Broker had shown the property to prospective purchasers, whose offer was rejected by seller. Negotiations continued but no agreement was reached. Shortly thereafter, seller orally requested that broker continue to try to sell the property to prospective purchasers but refused to sign another listing agreement. Nine days after the two-month grace period expired, seller entered into a real estate sale contract with purchasers. Seller refused to pay broker a commission. Broker argued that although he was not entitled to a commission based on the express terms of the contract, he had "procured" the buyer and thus deserved the commission. *Held:* Even though the listing agreement limited his right to a commission, broker could recover his commission since a buyer had been procured through his efforts. The case was remanded to determine whether there was a "meeting of the minds pertaining to the purchase of the property during the time period of the brokerage contract." *Pilson v. Roush*, 402 NE2d 906 (1980).

Nevada Broker contracted with defendants to procure lessees for an office development. Broker began negotiations with state agencies and with a state official whose approval was required in order for any agency to consummate a lease outside of state-owned buildings. With broker's permission, defendants took over and completed the negotiations on similar terms. Broker then sued for his commission. *Held:* Broker was entitled to commission because he was the procuring cause of the consummation of the leases. In nonexclusive situations, "procuring cause" means more than "merely trifling" conduct. Here, broker's dealings with the state official constituted considerable efforts, entitling him to commission. *Schneider v. Biglieri*, 581 P2d 8 (1978).

91.25
Amount of Compensation

6th Circuit Limited partnership decided to sell airport hotel and entered into a brokerage contract. Through brokers, a purchaser was found. The partnership agreed to sell the hotel, but the mortgagee refused to waive a due-on-sale clause, and a waiver was a condition of the sales contract. Instead of purchasing the hotel, an entity controlled by the purchaser bought a 49 percent share in the partnership. Brokers argued that they were entitled to commission. The district court awarded brokers treble damages from the purchaser for inducing the partnership to breach the brokerage contract. *Held:* Brokers were entitled to treble damages. Tennessee common and statutory laws prohibits persons from inducing parties to valid contracts to breach their contractual obligations. The evidence supported the district court's finding that purchaser acted with malice, a necessary element for recovery. *Continental Motel Brokers v. Blankenship*, 739 F2d 226 (1984).

Florida A $5 million sales contract provided that if buyer failed to perform, broker would be entitled to half of any retained deposits, up to the amount of its fee. An addendum to the contract provided for buyer to pay $50,000 per month as a "monthly fee" for the granting of a six-month extension between completion of a feasibility study and closing. Buyer paid the fee directly to seller rather than into escrow, and seller had unrestricted use of the money. When buyer failed to perform, broker sued seller seeking half of the $300,000 in extension fees. *Held:* Broker was not entitled to the money. The $300,000 was not a deposit, nor was it purely a payment for an option to purchase. *John F. Doran, Inc. v. Oldham NV Corp.*, 501 So. 2d 743 (Dist. Ct. App. 1987).

Maryland A real estate broker sold real estate parcels on a regular basis for a partnership. In one instance, the partnership asked him to market an unimproved parcel, which then proved difficult to sell. Finally, broker located a buyer who offered to buy half the parcel at half the asking price. The partnership agreed to accept the proposal if broker would reduce his commission from 8 percent to 4 percent. Broker did not agree but did not express his objection to the partners. When they sold the property, broker demanded a full 8 percent commission. When they refused to pay, he sued. *Held:* The broker was entitled only to the 4 percent commission. Because of their history of prior dealings, broker knew that the partners would act on the assumption that he would accept a half-rate commission, and therefore he had a duty to clarify the situation. *Ganley v. G&W Partnership*, 409 A2d 761 (Ct. Spec. App. 1980).

91.30
—Quantum Meruit

Delaware Broker contacted a prospective tenant for defendant Marta's shopping center, and negotiations were held. Marta's agreement to pay broker was in dispute. Negotiations broke off when tenant's offer was rejected, but, subsequently, broker informed Marta that tenant had agreed to Marta's terms. No action was taken by Marta until after broker's death, when Marta and the tenant entered into a lease agreement. Broker's executor brought suit for a broker's commission. *Held:* Broker was entitled to a recovery based on quasicontract. The lack of agreement as to compensation and the indefiniteness of the terms did not bar recovery where the party performing services expected to be paid for them and where circumstances would notify the recipient of the services of this expectation. The amount of quantum meruit recovery is not necessarily the prevailing real estate commission rate, but rather the worth of the specific services rendered by broker and the reasonable compensation he deserved for such services. *Marta v. Nepa*, 385 A2d 727 (1978).

District of Columbia Seller-bank authorized agent to procure a buyer for seller's building and to acquire new office space for bank. Broker contacted buyer, who proposed to lease space to seller and purchase seller's building. The parties agreed that broker would serve as intermediary for both parties during negotiations. After the contracts were signed, broker sued buyer for commission, claiming that there was an implied-in-fact contract between the parties. *Held:* No agency relationship could be implied. One seeking payment under an implied-in-fact contract theory must show that services were performed under such circumstances as to give the recipient reason to know the services were rendered for the recipient and not for someone else. Here, broker began the transaction in the role of seller's agent, and nothing in the record indicated that broker did anything to change buyer's impression that broker was acting for seller alone. *HG Smithy Co. v. Washington Medical Center, Inc.*, 374 A2d 891 (1977).

91.35 Buyer's Failure to Complete the Sale

2d Circuit Plaintiff attorney sued purchaser for real estate brokerage commissions on sale of land in Florida and on the option price of other Florida land. The agreement for the optioned land did not close, because of the failure of a zoning change, which was an express condition. Plaintiff sued for 10 percent of the price of the land actually sold and also of the optioned parcels. *Held:* Applying the law of New York, the situs of the brokerage agreement, plaintiff was entitled to a commission on the transaction that closed. As to the optioned property, broker, in the absence of an express agreement to the contrary, was not entitled to a commission on a contract subject to a contingency that did not occur through no fault of buyer. *Geller v. New England Indus., Inc.*, 535 F2d 1381 (1976).

Arkansas When vendee reneged on a contract to purchase land, which contract included commission for the broker, broker sued vendee for commission. Broker did not attempt to collect from vendor, who had originally retained him. *Held:* Broker could not recover under the contract, because he was not in privity with the parties nor did vendee intend to make the contract for broker's benefit. An agent may not sue on a contract in his own name merely because he is entitled to part of the proceeds as compensation for bringing it about. *Hopkins v. Ives*, 566 SW2d 147 (1978).

New Jersey Broker and buyers entered into a contract for the purchase of a house that was contingent upon broker's securing for buyers a $60,000 mortgage. Plaintiff broker completed his part of an agreement, but defendants were unable to do so because of a drastic drop in the market value of certain stocks they had intended to use for obtaining the necessary financing. Plaintiff sued for damages due to loss of his commission, but the trial court found against him. The appellate division, relying on the *Ellsworth Dobbs* rule of purchaser liability, held that plaintiff was due the commission irrespective of defendants' inability to complete the contemplated transaction. *Held:* The *Ellsworth Dobbs* rule of liability is not applicable where purchaser is an individual buying a residence. Defendants' implied promise to broker to complete the transaction did not encompass a failure to close where they had acted in good faith and the inability to consummate the deal was due to a circumstance beyond their control. Under these circumstances, defendants were not obligated to pay broker damages measured by the commission loss. *Rothman Realty Corp. v. Bereck*, 376 A2d 902 (1977).

Wisconsin Plaintiff broker brought this action for commission allegedly due under an exclusive listing contract entered into with defendant. Plaintiff had procured a written offer that contained a "subject to financing" clause for a first mortgage. Prospective buyer obtained a mortgage, but the mortgage lender's commitment contained an interest escalation clause. Prospective buyer notified plaintiff that since the escalation clause would not assure that the mortgage rate would stay within the amount specified in the "subject to financing" clause, the offer to purchase was null and void. *Held:* Plaintiff did not procure a purchaser in accordance with the listing contract. The inclusion of an interest rate escalation clause was a material deviation from the terms of the "subject to financing" provision that kept purchasers from becoming ready, able, and willing purchasers and thus prevented a valid and enforceable contract. The court observed that a "subject to finance" clause in an offer acts as a condition precedent to buyer's performance. *Woodland Realty, Inc. v. Winzenreid*, 262 NW2d 106 (1978).

Wisconsin A real estate broker's contract contained a standard provision, stating that "[i]f buyer of the Property should fail to carry out the buyer's agreement, and SELLER elects to take as liquidated damages all money paid by the buyer, then such money shall be applied first to reimburse BROKER for cash advances . . . and one-half of the balance, . . . shall be paid to broker." The broker produced a ready, willing, and able buyer, who signed a written purchase agreement, paid seller $50,000, and then defaulted. The purchase agreement provided for liquidated damages of $1,000 should either party default, but broker claimed his full commission. *Held:* For broker. The contractual provision at issue did not apply to all cases where seller accepted liquidated damages, but only to cases where seller retained *all money paid* by the buyer as liquidated damages. Since seller did not retain the $50,000, the broker was entitled to a full commission. *Menard v. Sass*, 379 NW2d 344 (Ct. App. 1985).

91.40 Seller's Failure to Complete the Sale

U.S. District Court, District of Columbia An association decided to move its corporate headquarters and signed a listing agreement with a real estate broker. The agreement provided that no commission was payable unless a sale took place. Broker then provided two buyers, and the association agreed to accept sealed bids whereby the highest bid would be unanimously approved by the board of directors. Soon after the bid was accepted, however, a change of leadership occurred in the organization, and the contract of sale was rejected, along with broker's commission. When broker sued, the new leadership group argued that no commission was payable since it was contingent on actual sale of the property. *Held:* Broker was entitled to his commission. A party to the contract could not prevent the sale from occurring and at the same time benefit from its action by denying broker his commission. In this case, broker had properly relied on the promise that the highest bid would be unanimously affirmed. *Shear v. National Rifle Ass'n*, 606 F2d 1251 (1979).

Arkansas Sellers employed broker to find a buyer for their land. The broker produced a buyer who signed an "offer and acceptance" form, which included a provision for a 6 percent commission. The land was described in the form as "10 acres more or less. . . . " Although the form recited that a legal description would be attached, sellers never produced the description. Prior to closing, sellers alleged the form was void due to insufficient description of the land and repudiated their desire to sell. Broker sued for commission. *Held:* For broker. Sellers' failure to provide a legal description, as agreed, would not inure to their benefit. All parties knew exactly what land was the subject of the contract. Broker was entitled to a commission because he had produced a buyer ready, willing, and able to buy at sellers' terms. *Whitefield v. Haggart*, 615 SW2d 350 (1981).

Georgia Broker and seller entered into an exclusive listing agreement whereby broker was promised a 10 percent commission on any sales contract accepted by seller whether procured by broker or seller. During the 180-day period in which the exclusive listing was in force, broker procured a prospective purchaser; and seller entered into a contract of sale with him. Under the contract of sale, purchaser agreed to pay the 10 percent commission if seller lowered the sales price from the listing price. Subsequently, seller refused to close the sale. Broker then sued for his commission. Seller contended in the alternative that (1) broker never earned the commission and (2) it was purchaser's duty to pay the commission. *Held:* Broker was entitled to a commission of 10 percent of the sales price from seller. Once broker procured a purchaser ready, able, and willing to buy on seller's terms or on terms acceptable to seller, he had earned his commission. Seller's subsequent refusal to close the sale could not defeat that right. Nor could seller's duty to pay the commission be abrogated by the provision in the contract of sale obligating purchaser to pay the commission, since broker was not a party to that contract. *Jones v. Trail Cities Realty, Inc.*, 287 SE2d 588 (1981).

Minnesota According to terms of an exclusive listing agreement, plaintiff broker would receive a commission of 5 percent of the sales price upon the sale of defendant's farm. Plaintiff found a purchaser who initially made an offer that differed from the terms of the agreement, but who subsequently made a second offer that complied with those terms. The listing agreement expired before defendant seller acted on either offer. Plaintiff then sued for his commission. In defense, defendant claimed he was relieved of paying the commission because a defect in his title that was known to plaintiff in advance of the agreement rendered the farm unmarketable and the broker had merely assumed the risk of good title. *Held:* The listing agreement made no reference to the determination of title. Under these circumstances, it was defendant's duty to cure the possible defect in his title or to inform plaintiff immediately. He chose to allow plaintiff to provide his services and could not later refuse to pay for them on this basis. *Klawitter v. Strauman*, 255 NW2d 407 (1977).

New York Broker entered into an agreement with vendor that provided for commission to be paid if and when title passed on a piece of property. Commission was also payable on demand in the event of willful default by seller. Broker found a buyer who was ready, willing, and able to purchase the property, but vendor did not sign a sales contract with prospective buyer. Vendor subsequently received a better offer and sold the property to new buyer. Broker sued for commission, charging default on the part of vendor. *Held:* For vendor. The agreement between vendor and broker explicitly stated that commission would be due when "title passes" on the property, and title never in fact passed between vendor and broker's buyer. Vendor's refusal to sell his property to broker's buyer did not constitute willful default of the brokerage agreement, since no sales contract was ever entered into by vendor and broker's buyer. *Graff v. Billet*, 487 NYS2d 733 (1984).

Oklahoma Broker sued to recover its commission and alleged that it had secured a ready, willing, and able purchaser, but that seller had refused to close. Seller argued that the commission was to be paid only upon the closing of the sale and her children had advised her not to sell. Seller owned the property in common with her children, who had not signed the brokerage contract. *Held:* Where a real estate broker, at the time it makes a contract, knows of any defects in the title or is aware of facts sufficient to put a reasonable person on inquiry, it is not entitled to its commission if the sale fails because of the defect. Where broker knew prior to the execution of the contract that the children would have to agree to the sale, it was not entitled to a commission. *Eastern Okla. Land & Cattle Co. v. Dorris*, 549 P2d 78 (1976).

Oregon Seller agreed to an exclusive listing of 180 days with a real estate broker. Their agreement provided that broker would be entitled to a 10 percent commission if broker produced a "ready, willing, and able" buyer or if the seller withdrew the property from the market during the listing period. After five months, broker produced a buyer, but seller refused to accept the deal and withdrew his property from the market. Broker sued for a commission, claiming that the money was due under their agreement. *Held:* Since the offer differed in several material respects from the terms of the listing agreement, seller had a right to reject it. Furthermore, broker, who had provided only the one listing in 27 weeks, had failed to prove actual damages, and probably could not have sold the property anyway. *Dean Vincent, Inc. v. Krimm*, 591 P2d 740 (1979).

91.45
Direct Sale by Seller

3d Circuit Sellers signed an "exclusive" listing agreement with a brokerage firm providing that the firm would be entitled to a commission "in the event that the realtor . . . procures a prospect." Subsequently, sellers procured a buyer without the firm's assistance and refused to pay it a commission. *Held:* The contract was ambiguous concerning the firm's right to a commission. The term "exclusive right to sell" did not clearly indicate whether it excluded only other brokers or the sellers as well. To add to the ambiguity, the contract contained no clause dealing with sellers' right to sell the property through their own efforts. *Lockhart v. Holiday Homes of St. John, Inc.*, 678 F2d 1176 (1982).

Alaska Landowner and broker entered into a listing agreement for the sale of a commercial building. The listing agreement provided broker with the exclusive right to sell the property and the right to a commission upon his finding a purchaser. After landowner sold the building himself, he refused to pay a commission and broker sued. Broker presented landowner's deposition testimony, which indicated that landowner believed he was liable for the commission. The trial court refused to admit the testimony and held that broker was not entitled to a commission. Broker appealed. *Held:* The trial court's reliance on the parol evidence rule to bar the introduction of landowner's deposition testimony was mistaken, because the rule applies only to antecedent understandings, not to subsequent statements regarding a party's understanding of an agreement. Admission of the parol evidence was necessary because it established a mutual understanding of the listing agreement's effect. Furthermore, the agreement's language did not clearly rule against construing the agreement as an "exclusive right to sell" contract. *Dahl v. Griffin*, 652 P2d 84 (1982).

District of Columbia Broker, the agent for landlord's apartment building, arranged for the lease of two floors to tenant. The lease provided that broker was to be paid a commission of one-half month's rent for each year of tenancy. The leases also gave broker a 6 percent commission if the building was sold or offered for sale during the term of the lease or renewal. Tenant and landlord entered into negotiations regarding purchase of the building, and the sale to tenant was accomplished. Broker played no role in the negotiations or sale, but sued for 6 percent commission. *Held:* Generally, the broker would not be entitled to a commission if the sale was made directly by seller to buyer. However, broker was entitled to commission on these facts where the lease clearly waived landlord's right to make a sale without liability to pay a brokerage commission. *Kendrick v. Kennedy*, 444 A2d 960 (1982).

91.50
Effect of Sale on Different Terms

Arizona Broker and seller entered into an exclusive listing agreement, which provided that broker was entitled to a commission if the property was sold, exchanged, rented, or leased during a specified period, whether or not through broker's efforts. During the listing period, the U.S. Department of Interior, Bureau of Reclamation, pursuant to the Uniform Real Property Acquisition Policy Act of 1970 (1970 Act) notified seller of its intent to acquire fee title to the land in order to construct an aqueduct thereon. Seller accepted the government's terms, and no formal condemnation proceedings were ever instituted. Broker then sued for a commission. *Held:* The 1970 Act directs that an agency involved in land takeovers make every reasonable effort to acquire real property by negotiation rather than by formal condemnation. The 1970 Act was intended to provide a substitute for condemnation, but an agency's actions under the statute nevertheless represent formal taking. Since the government's acquisition was the practical equivalent of a condemnation, broker was not entitled to a commission. *Mealy v. Orlich*, 585 P2d 1233 (1978).

Florida A real estate broker agreed with a property owner to find a buyer, and they agreed on a minimum sales price. Broker was to receive a 6 percent commission if he found a ready, willing, and able purchaser. Broker found a buyer and entered into negotiations. Owner broke off the negotiations and sold at less than the minimum agreed price. Owner then refused to pay broker's commission, and broker sued. *Held:* Broker was entitled to his commission. Since broker found a ready, willing, and able purchaser pursuant to an agreement, broker was entitled to his commission. *Fearich v. Smugglers Cove, Inc.*, 379 So. 2d 400 (1980).

91.55
Sale by Another Broker

New Mexico A broker entered into an exclusive right to sell agreement with landowners. This contract was later modified into an "exclusive agency" agreement to sell the property. Broker advertised the property and found a buyer for it. Nonetheless, owners contracted with another broker, who subsequently sold the property. First broker then brought suit to recover commission. *Held:* For first broker. An "exclusive agency" provision of a brokerage contract does not preclude the owner from selling the property himself without the aid of any broker, but it does preclude the owner from selling through the agency of another broker. In the instant case, owners did not in fact sell the property themselves, but contracted with a second broker who sold it for them, regardless of the agreement with the first broker who had fulfilled his performance requirement. This was a clear breach of contract, ruled the court, which awarded commission to the first broker. *Clodfelter v. Plaza Ltd.*, 698 P2d 1 (1985).

Ohio Vendor retained broker to sell his farm under a three-month exclusive listing contract. The instrument contained an extension clause that stated that if the property "is sold within three months after the period of this listing to anyone with whom you [broker] have negotiated with respect to a sale during the period of this listing and of whom I have notice, I agree to pay you a commission of 6%." Vendor's neighbors had negotiated with broker during the period of the listing but never came to terms with vendor. However, within three months after the expiration of the exclusive listing contract, vendor sold the property to his neighbors, through a different realtor. Broker then claimed a 6 percent commission was due him by the terms of the exclusive listing agreement. *Held:* After construing the above language, the court, over vigorous dissent, ruled that the clause was ambiguous on whether it was to have effect if a sale was made by another broker or only by vendor. Broker, who had drafted the agreement, could have prevented confusion on this issue with more explicit phraseology. The doubt thereby created must be resolved against broker. *Central Realty Co. v. Clutter*, 406 NE2d 515 (1980).

91.60 Sale After Expiration of Broker's Authority

Alabama A broker signed an exclusive listing agreement to sell owner's lounge. The agreement provided for payment of the commission if the property was sold by broker or anyone else during the listing period, or if it was sold to a prospect introduced by broker. During the listing period, a prospective buyer went to another broker who had previously listed the property and made an offer that the owner rejected. When the same buyer made another offer after the expiration of the listing period, owner accepted. When no commission was paid to either broker, they both sued. *Held:* Both brokers are entitled to a commission. The first broker had done more than "merely introduce" the prospective buyer and was therefore entitled to a commission. The second broker, by virtue of the exclusive listing, was entitled to a commission because he had negotiated with the prospective buyer. *Mellos v. Silverman*, 367 So. 2d 1369 (1979).

Connecticut Broker entered into an exclusive listing agreement to sell and/or lease landowner's property. If no transaction had occurred by the end of two months, broker was to notify landowner in writing of all prospects. Broker then would be entitled to a commission if a deal was made with one of its prospects within 120 days. Broker registered a food market as a potential buyer. Negotiations between landowners and the market continued at the end of the listing period, but broker failed to provide the written notice to landowner called for in the listing agreement. Ninety days later, the market leased the property. When broker sued, claiming a commission was due, landowner argued that broker's failure to provide written notice barred the extension of the listing agreement beyond the original two-month term. *Held:* Broker was entitled to a commission. The purpose of written notice is to protect an owner from unknowingly entering a transaction in which an unexpected claim for a commission would be asserted. No written notification was necessary in this case, because broker had procured a buyer with landowner's knowledge. *DeForest Indus. v. Gaetano*, 461 A2d 453 (1983).

Maine Broker entered into an agreement with a lumber company to sell its industrial property. The agreement was to expire in March 1983, but an extension clause provided that "if a prospect with whom the said Broker or associates *have been negotiating* purchases the said property within six months after the agreement's termination, the commission shall be due and payable." In February 1983, an associate of broker showed the property to a prospective buyer. Buyer did not pursue its interest until late March. Although the company had not renewed the listing agreement with broker, it permitted the associate to show the property to the buyer five days after the agreement had expired. In April, the company entered into a listing agreement with another broker and four days later entered into an agreement with buyer. Commission was paid to the second broker, and the original broker sued. *Held:* For company. The record did not support a finding that broker had been negotiating with buyer before the original agreement's expiration date. Before that date, there was one routine, preliminary showing and certain information was provided to buyer. Buyer had merely expressed an interest in seeing the property again, which was insufficient to support a finding of negotiation. In the context of the agreement, "negotiation" denoted a dialogue aimed at striking a bargain. *Gendron Realty v. NJ Gendron Lumber Co.*, 519 A2d 723 (1987).

Massachusetts Vendor enlisted broker to provide a buyer for vendor's property. When broker found a prospective buyer, vendor objected to the terms of buyer's offer and refused it. Vendor subsequently revoked broker's authority. Approximately six months later, the same buyer made a better direct offer to the vendor, who accepted the new terms and sold the property to him. Broker then sued vendor for a commission. *Held:* For vendor. Broker was not entitled to a commission, because he had not found a ready, willing, and able buyer on vendor's terms before his authority was revoked. The court ruled that the eventual sale of the property was not effectuated through the efforts of broker; and since vendor had acted in good faith, broker was not entitled to commission. *Sordillo v. Putnam*, 477 NE2d 380 (1985).

New Mexico Owner held unimproved land and, in an exclusive listing contract, gave brokers the right to sell 26 lots for a 10 percent commission. During the exclusive listing period, owners contacted developer and granted it an option to purchase any lots that brokers did not sell. This contract specified that the option was subject to brokers' prior rights in the listing agreement. After the exclusive listing period, developer exercised its option to buy. Brokers sued, claiming that owner owed them a commission on the 26 lots. *Held:* Brokers were not entitled to a commission. The sale to developer did not relate to the date owner granted the option when there was no evidence of collusion between owner and developer to defraud brokers; indeed, the contract was made subject to broker's rights. Owner did not sell the property during the 180-day period, brokers did not find developer, and owner did nothing adverse to brokers' rights under the listing agreement. *Talley v. Security Serv. Corp.*, 663 P2d 361 (1983).

Pennsylvania Owner of a motel signed a listing agreement with brokers that provided for a commission "when a legally binding and enforceable sales agreement shall be executed." A buyer contacted owner, who referred him to brokers. Buyer made an offer that the owner rejected and then proposed to rent the property. Owner agreed, and they signed a rental agreement with an option to purchase. After the listing agreement had expired, owner sold the motel to tenant because it was failing and no other buyer could be found. Brokers sued for their commission, arguing that the purchase option was an agreement to sell. *Held:* Brokers are not entitled to a commission. Generally, a broker is entitled to commission when an optionee exercises a purchase option. However, in this case, the motel was not sold pursuant to the purchase option; it was sold, in effect, by default to the buyer-tenant when no other purchaser could be found and the motel was failing. *In re Estate of Baldwin*, 400 A2d 1297 (1979).

Rhode Island Broker entered into an agreement which granted him the exclusive right to sell a corporation's real estate until March 1981, with the appointed receiver of the corporation. Before the end of the exclusive selling period, broker was dismissed. The property was purchased in 1982. Buyer leased the restaurant to tenants who later exercised an option to purchase contained in the lease. Broker sued to recover commission. *Held:* Broker was not entitled to a commission, because the sale occurred outside the exclusive selling period and broker was not instrumental in bringing about the sale. The receiver had refused to include a clause in the agreement providing for a fee if a tenant provided by the realtor subsequently purchased the property. Although broker had shown the tenants the property during the term of the agreement, they were not ready, willing, or able to purchase the property. It was actually sold after the agreement's expiration date to another party that had not dealt with broker. *Brenner Assocs. v. Rousseau*, 537 A2d 120 (1988).

West Virginia Although the written listing agreement had expired several months earlier, realtor showed clients a house with sellers' permission. Sellers later sold the house to the clients but refused to pay realtor a commission. *Held:* Realtor was entitled to commission. The fact that realtor showed the house three or four times after the written agreement expired and that the clients made an offer almost immediately after seeing the house corroborated realtor's claim that, after the agreement had expired, sellers encouraged him to sell the property on the same terms set forth in the agreement. Sellers deliberately misled realtor into believing that the terms of the original written contract would continue to be binding and were therefore estopped from asserting the Statute of Frauds. *Everett v. Brown*, 321 SE2d 685 (1984).

91.65
Date Commission Due

Montana Seller and broker entered into two listing agreements under which broker was to find purchasers for two parcels of land owned by seller. Broker found two purchasers, and written contracts of sale were executed. One of the agreements collapsed at the last minute when purchaser attempted to substitute his wife as contract purchaser. The other agreement collapsed when seller failed to obtain a required easement. Broker sued seller for commissions for both sales. *Held:* The court held that broker was entitled to recover a commission only when the sale of the property was completed. Where real property is involved, "completing a sale" means payment of the purchase price and conveyance of title, not merely finding a purchaser to sign the buy/sell agreement. *Diehl & Assocs., Inc. v. Houtchens*, 567 P2d 920 (1977).

Oregon As an inducement to encourage purchasers to buy certain land, broker told purchasers "that if within six months [purchasers] notified [broker] that they were not satisfied with the property, [broker] would, at the same price paid by the [purchasers], sell the property to another purchaser." Purchasers then bought the land, but become dissatisfied and informed broker of a desire to sell. Broker then resold the land to a third party under an installment land contract, but the new purchaser defaulted after only two payments and returned the property to the first purchasers, who then sued the original owner of the property and broker. Essentially, purchasers sought rescission of the contract, which would have meant no commission for broker. *Held:* Broker fulfilled his agreement with the first purchasers by reselling the property to another buyer at the same price. Citing *Setser v. Commonwealth*, 476 P2d 142 (1970), the court concluded: "Thus if the buyer has done everything necessary under the contract to close the sale and there remains only the payment of future installments, broker need not wait until the future installments are paid before he is entitled to his commission." *Engelking v. Boyce*, 563 P2d 703 (1977).

South Carolina Broker brought action to recover commission where he had procured a buyer for seller and a contract of sale was executed, but the sale was never consummated. Seller contended that the contract, which provided "undersigned will pay to the listing broker on or [word "before" stricken] settlement the sum of, . . ." precluded broker from collecting commission until purchase was concluded. *Held:* Broker was entitled to a commission. The general rule is that a broker is entitled to a commission after procurement of a customer and execution of a contract of sale. The specific language of the contract between the parties referred to the time of payment of the commission and not to when broker's right to the commission vested. *Thomas-McCain, Inc. v. Siter*, 232 SE2d 728 (1977).

Wisconsin Seller entered a real estate listing contract with broker, which obligated broker to find a purchaser for the property at $430,000 in return for a 5 percent broker's fee. Broker procured an offer of $412,000, which seller agreed to, after convincing broker to modify his commission to a flat $15,000. However, when buyer sent the check, seller changed his mind and refused to acept the offer. When broker asked for his fee of $15,000, seller refused to pay and broker sued. *Held:* Broker is entitled to his $15,000 fee. The general rule is that a broker employed to procure a purchaser is entitled to his commission when he produces a ready, willing, and able buyer. In this case, since there was a valid contract of sale between buyer and seller, broker was entitled to his commission. *Mansfield v. Smith*, 277 NW2d 740 (1979).

91.70 Cobrokers

Maine A corporate licensed broker had a written house policy whereby commissions were divided 50 percent to the corporation and 50 percent between the listing salesperson and the selling salesperson. An employee sued the corporation for his share of a commission, which the corporation refused to pay. The corporation maintained that, notwithstanding the house policy, it had made a separate oral agreement with the employee that no commission was payable on the sale in question and that the employee had not really been the selling salesperson. *Held:* There was insufficient evidence to establish the existence of any changes in the basic house policy. Furthermore, the employee had participated not only in consummating the purchase and sales contract, but also in closing the transaction. Thus, the employee was entitled to his commission under the express terms of the house policy. *Milliken v. Coastal Acreage, Inc.*, 395 A2d 1169 (1979).

New Jersey Seller listed home with broker. Another broker learned of the property through a multiple-listing service and found a buyer. Seller signed a sales contract and gave a $3,000 deposit to the second broker pending closing. After closing, seller found that broker had converted the deposit money to his own use. Seller sued, among others, the original broker, charging that it was liable as a joint venturer with the second broker. *Held:* The original broker had no duty to oversee the conduct of the second broker. The use of multiple-listing services does not create a joint venture. *Sullivan v. Jefferson, Jefferson & Vaida*, 400 A2d 836 (App. Div. 1979).

New Mexico One broker sued another for payment under an alleged oral contract to divide a commission earned when certain premises were leased. Defendant broker argued that there was no contract and that, even if they were, it could not be enforced because it was not in writing. A lower court found for defendant on the basis of a state law requiring an agreement "authorizing or employing an agent or broker to purchase or sell lands . . . or any interest in or concerning them" to be in writing. Plaintiff appealed to the state supreme court. *Held:* The statute was enacted to regulate the owner-broker relationship and therefore does not require written agreements between brokers. The case was remanded for trial on the issue of whether an oral contract in fact existed. *Hapsas Realty, Inc. v. McCain*, 579 P2d 785 (1978).

Virginia A corporate landowner gave broker who habitually handled its land transactions in southwestern Virginia an exclusive listing agreement covering its land in the area. Later, it entered into an open listing agreement with an out-of-state firm for the sale of all its assets in all states. The out-of-state firm attracted a buyer who purchased the corporate landowner's stock and merged with it. Landowner refused to pay the in-state broker anything beyond the commissions he had earned from selling individual parcels in southwestern Virginia. The in-state broker claimed commissions on the value of the remaining unsold southwestern Virginia parcels that had passed to buyer by virtue of the stock purchase and merger. *Held:* The stock sale and merger did not amount to a "sale of land" on which the in-state broker was entitled to commissions. The in-state broker was not employed to sell all landowner's assets. Thus the transfer of the landowner's assets by corporate merger was not "substantially the equivalent" of the limited sales the in-state broker was authorized to make. *Burruss Timber Co. v. Frith*, 324 SE2d 679 (1985).

91.75
Waiver or Loss of Commission

Iowa Broker advised sellers to make an installment sale of their property to obtain favorable tax treatment of capital gains. To this end, broker found a buyer who was willing to pay in installments over a 15-year period. However, the contract for sale drawn up by seller's attorney included a prepayment provision suggested by broker that would nullify the tax benefits of the installment sale. Broker rushed the attorney to prepare the contract and did not notify sellers of the provision's effect. Furthermore, he had lent money to buyer to make the installment payments and had acted as broker for buyer in the sale of another property. Buyer was required to prepay his obligation to sellers before the other transaction could be completed. Sellers refused to pay broker a commission. *Held:* Broker was not entitled to a commission. An agent has the duty not to act on behalf of an adverse party in a transaction connected with the agency without the principal's knowledge. Broker's loan transaction with buyer and potential resale transaction may have influenced him to advise the seller improperly by suggesting the prepayment provision. *Miller v. Berkoski*, 297 NW2d 334 (1980).

Nebraska Broker produced a ready, willing, and able buyer for land, but seller refused to convey the land, saying he had received a better offer. Broker signed the sales contract on seller's behalf anyway, thus putting a cloud on seller's title. *Held:* In broker's action for commission against seller, broker was entitled to commission even though title to the land was not actually conveyed to buyer. However, broker breached his fiduciary duty to seller by signing the contract on the seller's behalf, contrary to seller's instructions, and broker was therefore entitled to no financial recovery since seller's damages by reason of the cloud on the title exceeded the amount of the commission. *Brezina v. Hill*, 277 NW2d 244 (1979).

New Jersey After being approached by purchasers, broker arranged a deal whereby purchasers would buy a new home to be constructed at a price of approximately $135,000. Broker's 4 percent commission was to be paid at closing, out of the proceeds of the sale. Pursuant to the terms of the contract, a mortgage was to be obtained for $60,000, with the balance paid in cash from purchaser's existing assets, which consisted primarily of stock in one company. Less than two weeks short of closing, the stock dropped sharply, leaving purchasers short of funds to complete the deal. Broker then sued purchasers for the deposit. The lower court ruled in favor of purchasers, and the broker appealed. *Held:* Although a buyer who fails to complete a transaction without valid legal reason would be liable for commissions that would have been paid, purchasers in this case had acted reasonably without malice and should not be held responsible for events beyond their control. *Rothman Realty Corp. v. Bereck*, 376 A2d 902 (1977).

Pennsylvania Brokers signed a listing agreement with bank for sale of motel. During the listing period, bank leased property to tenant for a 10-year term, with an option to purchase at a price of $900,000. After eight years, tenant had difficulty paying rent and intended to vacate. However, bank could not find a new tenant and agreed to sell the property to tenant for $428,000. Brokers demanded a commission on this sale since the original lease contained a purchase option, which operated as a contract of sale. *Held:* Brokers were not entitled to a commission. The sale was made under a "new" agreement and did not come under the purchase option. The reduced sales price and the bank's inability to find a new tenant were evidence of the existence of a new agreement. *In re Estate of Baldwin*, 400 A2d 1297 (1979).

Utah Developer entered into an exclusive listing agreement with real estate agent regarding one of developer's houses. Agent showed the house to buyer who expressed an interest but felt the purchase price was too high. Agent suggested that buyer make his own deal with developer and did not object to developer's statement that an exchange of properties would eliminate the commission. Subsequently, developer and buyer arranged for such an exchange without agent's assistance. Developer refused to pay agent a commission. *Held:* Agent waived her right to a commission. Her argument that any oral waiver did not comply with the Statute of Frauds was rejected. Developer would not have exchanged properties without an oral waiver because the exchange did not generate cash from which a commission could be paid. A repudiation of agent's oral modification of the listing agreement clearly would be inequitable. *White v. Fox*, 665 P2d 1297 (1983).

Vermont Broker and seller entered into two listing agreements for the sale of real estate and a business located on the property. Seller ultimately decided to sell the business and keep the real estate, and a new listing agreement was signed to this effect. Broker sold the business to buyer who obtained a lease of the premises with an option to purchase. Five years later, seller executed a tax-free exchange of the property with buyer. Broker sued, claiming he was entitled to a commission upon the exercise of the purchase option. *Held:* Broker was not entitled to a commission for sale of the real estate. Broker was obliged to prepare the final contract to comport with the seller's desires. Once broker learned of seller's change of mind, he was obligated to draft the second agreement to accurately reflect the seller's intent to sell only the business. Broker's failure to comply with seller's intent to terminate the real estate listing and the broker's entitlement to a commission upon its sale caused broker to forfeit any commission due. *Janes & Jacob Real Estate, Inc. v. Dave's Automotive, Inc.*, 552 A2d 380 (1988).

Virginia Broker found buyers to purchase estate property but by the closing date buyers had not obtained financing. The estate executor instructed broker to delay the closing and to collect 7 percent interest from buyers until they closed. At the closing, buyers paid the interest under written protest. Broker disbursed the sales proceeds and interest minus his commission to the executor but never notified him of the protest letter. Shortly after closing, buyers sued the estate for the interest. In its successful defense, the estate incurred $3,800 in legal fees and costs. The executor then sued broker for the legal costs and the commission. *Held:* Broker was ordered to pay the costs of the suit and repay his commission. He breached his fiduciary duty to the executor when he failed to disclose all information that might have influenced the executor's decision whether to proceed with the closing. It could be inferred that broker was more interested in securing his commission than in protecting his client. *Owen v. Shelton*, 277 SE2d 189 (1981).

91.80
Commissions on Leases

Mississippi Insurance agency leased office space. The lease provided for payment of a brokerage commission to the procuring agent. When the building was sold, purchaser continued to pay the commission for the duration of the lease; but after the lease was renewed, purchaser refused to continue paying commission. *Held:* For purchaser. A successor in title is not liable to pay brokerage commissions in the absence of an express agreement to do so. Mere assignment of a lease does not obligate assignee to assume assignor's obligations thereunder. *Coggins v. Joseph*, 504 So. 2d 211 (1987).

92.00
BROKER'S RELATION WITH LICENSING AUTHORITY

92.05
Applicability and Validity of Licensing Statutes

US. Supreme Court Home buyers brought suit under the Sherman Antitrust Act against a number of organizations and individuals, including real estate associations, real estate firms and others, charging that they had committed antitrust violations by conspiring to (1) systematically use fixed commission rates, (2) engage in widespread fee-splitting, (3) suppress market information, and (4) engage in other anticompetitive practices. Plaintiffs alleged that these practices resulted in higher prices for housing and affected interstate commerce because (1) there was a movement of residential buyers and sellers across state lines, (2) there was interstate movement of home mortgage funds, and (3) title insurance was often procured from out-of-state sources. Defendants contended that they functioned at an entirely local level and had nothing to do with interstate financing, title insurance, or other services. *Held:* There were sufficient effects on interstate commerce to bring the case under the antitrust laws. The Court, citing its earlier decision in *Goldfarb v. Virginia State Bar*, 421 US 773 (1975), found that there were sufficient allegations of the interstate effects of brokers' activities to send the case back to the lower court for trial on price-fixing charges. *McClain v. Real Estate Bd.*, 444 US 232 502 (1980).

5th Circuit Brokers operated a real estate agency and were members of the county board of realtors, which operated a multiple-listing service (MLS). Brokers withdrew from the board, alleging that its members changed the fee schedule in a way that significantly increased brokers' agency dues. Brokers sued for, among other things, a violation of the state antitrust laws, alleging that defendants boycotted the agency by refusing it access to the MLS and by refusing to allow the agency to use the term "realtor" unless brokers again became board members. *Held:* The board could reasonably exclude nonmembers from the MLS or from using the term "realtor." Antitrust violations are viewed under the rule of reason. Membership dues that are related to expenses and the recouping of costs of the MLS, and that assess greater fees on firms that will presumably make the greatest use of the MLS, are reasonable. The board's activities were not "plainly anticompetitive" or lacking in "any redeeming value" to warrant application of the per se rule. The county fee schedule, which required greater fees of firms employing the most agents, did not pose any entry barrier to the MLS. *Pope v. Mississippi Real Estate Comm'n.*, 872 F2d 127 (1989).

Colorado Broker was charged with professional misconduct by state real estate commission for alleged violations of state real estate licensing laws. The commission recommended broker's license be suspended; and broker appealed, challenging the constitutionality of the licensing statute. *Held:* Affirmed. Licensing statute giving commission power to discipline broker for "unworthiness" or "incompetence" was not unconstitutionally vague. A statute is not void for vagueness if it fairly describes the conduct forbidden, and its meaning can be readily understood by persons of common intelligence. The terms "unworthiness" and "incompetence" as used in the statute were sufficiently precise to meet this standard. The term "unworthiness" referred to the prohibition against unethical conduct. Brokers governed by the statute and the enforcing authority were familiar with acceptable standards of real estate practice; therefore, the potential for misunderstanding was minimized. *Eckley v. Colorado Real Estate Comm'n*, 752 P2d 68 (1988) (en banc).

Georgia Plaintiff out-of-state realty broker brought suit to collect a broker's fee allegedly due from the in-state sale of listed property. *Held:* Under statute barring suit for collection of brokerage fees by unlicensed parties, the enforceability of claims made by out-of-state brokers depends upon whether the brokerage services were performed within the state. When broker undertakes all acts essential to the recovery of a commission outside of the state, the statute has no application and a suit for collection may proceed. When, however, broker performs services in Georgia without a proper license, such a suit is prohibited. *Krizan v. Newman & Co.*, 271 SE2d 135 (1980).

New Jersey An out-of-state bank proposed to provide mortgage financing for transactions arranged by New Jersey brokers. Brokers would sell the mortgages at a discount to the out-of-state bank. Domestic bankers claimed the arrangement violated N.J. Stat. Ann.§ 45:15-17(i), prohibiting brokers from representing different parties in conflict of interest. The real estate commission ruled that as long as buyers were informed of other financing opportunities and brokers did not engage in "steering," brokers could operate as mortgage bankers. On appeal, the superior court rules that brokers could not both receive compensation for placing mortgages and also for selling the properties to be mortgaged, and that the sale and mortgage were effectively parts of the same transaction, with potential for conflict of interest and self-dealing. *Held:* Reversed and remanded. The supreme court was concerned that the lower court had not adequately addressed the distinction among the methods by which brokers might participate in and be compensated by a mortgage transaction, particularly the distinction between placing loans and issuing them. The court affirmed the right of brokers to act as mortgage bankers, but pointed out that by performing mortgage-related functions, they came under the jurisdiction of the Department of Banking rather than the real estate commission. *Mortgage Bankers Ass'n v. New Jersey Real Estate Comm'n*, 506 A2d 733 (1986).

New Mexico Contract sellers engaged broker to sell their contract interest and authorized broker's real estate firm to act as their exclusive agent. Broker was appointed attorney in fact and sold the contract interest. He forwarded the sale proceeds to sellers, less his commission, plus an additional sum withheld pending a signed statement from sellers that the property was not subject to outstanding liens. Sellers sent the statement, but broker claimed the check for the withheld sum was lost in the mail. Another check bounced. The real estate commission brought disciplinary proceedings against broker and suspended his license for a year. Broker appealed, arguing that the commission lacked authority to regulate the sale of real estate contracts and that the licensing statute did not apply to one acting as attorney in fact under a power of attorney from the owner. *Held:* For the commission. A majority of the court found that plaintiff was a real estate broker. The contract indicated he was employed in a broker's capacity. Further, he was paid a commission. Under these facts, broker's participation in the sale of a contract interest was subject to the licensing restrictions imposed on real estate brokers. As to the attorney in fact exclusion, broker was in a fiduciary relationship to sellers, and his attorney in fact status was secondary to his primary obligations as a fiduciary. *Elliot v. New Mexico Real Estate Comm'n*, 705 P2d 679 (1985).

North Carolina A licensed real estate broker negotiated the sale of a house owned by a corporation of which she was a shareholder. When the real estate licensing board sought to revoke her license for providing false information, she contended that she was not acting as real estate broker in the transaction but as "owner" and was therefore exempt from the licensing statutes (N.C. Gen. Stat. §§ 93A-1 et seq., 93A-2(a), 93A-2(c)). *Held:* Her license could be revoked. The shareholder of a corporation owning real property is not an owner for the purposes of the licensing statutes. *Cox v. North Carolina Real Estate Licensing Bd.*, 266 SE2d 851 (1980).

Rhode Island Plaintiff, a business intermediary, contacted buyer about a nursing home for sale. Buyer instead expressed interest in another nursing home but said that plaintiff would have to collect any fee for his services from owner of that home. Plaintiff negotiated a fee with owner, and the sale was consummated. However, owner refused to pay the fee, arguing that plaintiff did not have a real estate broker's license until two days before the transaction was completed. *Held:* Plaintiff was entitled to a finder's fee; a broker's license was not necessary. Plaintiff acted as a finder rather than a real estate broker. The transaction was primarily the sale of a business and plaintiff found, introduced, and brought together both sides. The parties then negotiated and consummated the transaction themselves. A broker does more; he attempts to bring the parties to agreement on his principal's terms. Typically, a broker procures a buyer for a property; here, plaintiff found a seller. *Bottomley v. Coffin*, 399 A2d 485 (1979).

Texas Buyer executed a promissory note in payment of a broker's commission. Buyer made three payments and then advised broker that it would not make further payments because of broker's misrepresentations about the property. Broker sued, and buyer argued that broker could not recover because it had not pleaded or proved that it was a duly licensed broker under Texas law (Tex. Rev. Civ. Stat. Ann. art. 6572a, § 20(a)). *Held:* Broker was not entitled to a commission and was required to plead and prove that it was a duly licensed real estate broker in order to recover on the note. *Henry S. Miller Co. v. Treo Enters.*, 585 SW2d 674 (1979).

Utah Salesman was employed by a company that was a licensed broker. Salesman knew that IBM was looking for office space in Salt Lake City, and knew that John Price Associates had a building available for rent. He contacted Price, which informed him that he would receive a commission if IBM leased the building. Subsequently, salesman left his job at the real estate broker, and some time thereafter IBM did rent space from Price. When salesman requested his commission, Price refused to pay because salesman was not a licensed broker. Salesman, joined by his former employer, sued Price. *Held:* Although salesman, who was not a licensed broker, could not sue for commission, his company could and was entitled to the money, since salesman had been an employee when initial contact was made. *Morris v. John Price Assocs., Inc.*, 590 P2d 315 (1979).

92.10 Revocation or Suspension of License

Nebraska A broker licensed by the state real estate commission sold his house. The contract provided broker would use the purchase money to pay off a first mortgage, but broker failed to do so. Purchasers only learned of the broker's breach of contract when they tried to resell the house. They filed a complaint against broker with the real estate commission. Although broker eventually paid off the mortgage, the commission revoked his license pursuant to the licensing statute, which provides disciplinary measures for unfair trade practices, specifically, "unworthiness or incompetency to act as a broker." The broker appealed, arguing that the sale of his own house was irrelevant to his competency as a broker. *Held:* Affirmed. A broker's competency and character for licensing purposes should be determined by acts performed out of, as well as within, his official capacity. The court could not at the same time find broker dishonest as a property owner and honest as a broker. *Wright v. State ex rel. State Real Estate Comm'n*, 304 NW2d 39 (1981).

North Carolina Buyer filed a complaint

with the state real estate licensing board alleging that defendant broker failed to properly explain the terms of a sales contract. The licensing board, under authority of state law (N.C. Gen. Stat. § 93A-6), suspended defendant's license, finding there was "substantial evidence" that defendant acted in violation of the code's standards. *Held:* Section 93A-6, which permits revocation of a broker's license, is penal in nature and therefore should be strictly construed. The statute requires a finding of guilt to warrant a revocation, which was not satisfied by the determination that there was "substantial evidence" of a violation. *North Carolina Real Estate Licensing Bd. v. Weedard*, 219 SE2d 271 (Ct. App. 1975).

92.15 Criminal Liability

New Jersey A licensed real estate broker negotiated a sale of real property, prepared a form contract of sale, and submitted it to the parties for signature. Broker was charged with the crime of engaging in the unlawful practice of law. *Held:* The New Jersey Supreme Court rules that the broker had not committed a crime within the meaning of the statute, but it reserved judgment on whether he had practiced law without authority. At the court's suggestion, the New Jersey State Bar Association filed suit against licensed realtors as a class, seeking a declaratory judgment and injunctive relief. A settlement was reached and approved by the court. It provided that brokers could prepare contracts for the sale of residential real estate containing not more than four dwelling units and unimproved single-family lots. The attorney for buyer or seller had three days to disapprove the contract before it became binding. Brokers were also given the right to prepare residential leases not exceeding one year's term. *New Jersey State Bar Ass'n v. New Jersey Ass'n of Realtor Bds.*, 461 A2d 1112, modified, 467 A2d 577 (1983).

Washington Defendant broker, planning to close her real estate brokerage business, failed to renew her license when it expired at the end of 1977. In January, 1978, she assisted in the sale of a home and as a result of that transaction was convicted of acting as a real estate broker without a license. She testified at trial that she believed her license did not expire until 30 days after its stated expiration date. Other testimony established that the license expired on its stated expiration date. The issue on appeal was whether knowledge is an element of the crime of acting as a real estate broker without a license. *Held:* No intent is required for conviction under the statute if it is not so specified therein. The commission of the prohibitive act constituted the crime. *State v. Waymire*, 614 P2d 214 (1980).

92.20 Right to Advertise

Illinois A brokerage, to induce potential customers to use its services, provided such customers a coupon booklet for discount merchandise, and gave brokerage employees commission discounts on the sale or purchase of homes. The director of the Department of Registration and Education alleged these inducements violated a state statute prohibiting using valuable consideration conditioned on purchase or lease of property to secure customers. The brokerage contended the statute violated the First and Fourteenth Amendments of the U.S. Constitution and similar clauses of the Illinois Constitution. *Held:* For the brokerage. Although the state has a right to regulate business and professional activities where a public interest, such as consumer protection, is involved, the statute did not directly advance the state's interest in consumer protection. *Coldwell Banker Res. Real Estate v. Clayton*, 475 NE2d 536 (1985).

Missouri Coldwell, a national brokerage firm owned by Sears, Roebuck, developed a promotional sales program under which those who purchased a home through Coldwell would receive a booklet of Sears discount coupons after closing. Mo. Rev. Stat. § 339.100.2(12) (1978) provides that licensed real estate brokers shall not condition the award of prizes, money, or gifts on the purchase, lease, sale, or listing of real property. Coldwell brought an action for declaratory judgment against the Missouri Real Estate Commission, claiming that the statute and implementing regulation unconstitutionally deprived it of due process of law, equal protection of the laws, and the right to free speech in violation of the First and Fourteenth Amendments. *Held:* The statute was constitutional. The court rejected Coldwell's contention that economic regulation is subject to rather close scrutiny and that the proponents of legislation must convince the courts that the regulation is reasonable and arguably effective. *Coldwell Banker Residential Real Estate Servs. v. Missouri Real Estate Comm'n,* 712 SW2d 666 (1986) (en banc).

92.25 Right to Solicit

7th Circuit A 1973 antiblockbusting statute prohibited any individual or corporation from contacting residential property owners to solicit sale of their homes after the owner gave notice he had no desire to sell. Plaintiff realtor was charged with criminal violations under the statute. Realtor claimed the statute violated his First Amendment rights and sought an injunction against the statute's enforcement. *Held:* The statute did not violate the First Amendment. The speech involved was commercial speech, to which First Amendment protections apply. The court, using a four-part analysis, determined the speech was protected under the First Amendment, but the state's interest in protecting a homeowner's right of privacy was sufficient to justify curtailment of plaintiff's right to speak to homeowners. The regulation advanced the goal of ensuring privacy in the home, and the reach of statute was appropriate to the interest served. Thus, the court concluded, the statute properly limited a realtor's right to engage in commercial speech. *Curtis v. Thompson*, 840 F2d 1291 (1988).

New York When residents in Bronx County complained of excessive solicitation and aggressive activities by local real estate brokers, the secretary of state of New York issued an order prohibiting brokers from soliciting listings of properties for sale in any manner within certain areas of Bronx County. Twelve years later, broker, who had relocated her office to the Bronx, challenged the nonsolicitation order, contending the secretary of state lacked the authority to issue the order. *Held:* The order prohibiting solicitations of realty was in excess of the authority granted the secretary of state by statutes proscribing blockbusting activity. The secretary of state is empowered to prohibit blockbusting activity under a state regulation that prevents brokers from representing that a change has occurred in the neighborhood's composition owing to an influx of peoples of different race, creed, or color, and that this change will have undesirable consequences. The nonsolicitation order in this case went beyond the regulation's ban and interdicted all broker initiated solicitation, not merely illegal solicitation. *Campagna v. Shaffer*, 536 NE2d 368 (1989).

PART Q
TRANSFER BY DEED

93.00
REQUISITES AND VALIDITY

93.05
Grantor's Capacity to Convey

Alabama State statute limited the right of a married woman to alienate or mortgage her land without her husband's consent. A married man, however, could convey his land without his wife's consent, although his grantee would take subject to the wife's dower interest. The constitutionality of the state statute was questioned. *Held:* The statute violates the state constitution in denying to one class of adult landowners the rights guaranteed to all other adult landowners by the constitution and laws of the state. *Peddy v. Montgomery*, 345 So. 2d 631 (1977).

Oklahoma Four brothers who were joint tenants petitioned to terminate their joint tenancy after the death of one joint tenant. Their four sisters filed cross-petitions to set aside the joint tenancy deed on ground of lack of mental capacity. The deed was executed after decedent, 79 years old, had become ill and was moved to a nursing home. *Held:* The test of capacity to make a deed is that grantor had the ability to understand the nature and effect of the act in which he engaged. There is a presumption that the maker of the deed had requisite mental capacity. The burden is upon the person attacking its validity. The testimony of forgetfulness or wandering of grantor's mind was not sufficient to prove lack of capacity. The law does not require grantor of a deed to be completely competent. A person may be old, enfeebled, erratic, and irrational at times, yet still execute a valid deed. *In re Woodward*, 549 P2d 1207 (1976).

93.10
—Intention to Convey

Florida Seeking to dissuade his wife from divorce, husband conveyed his interest in the marital residence to her with the understanding she would reconvey to him when the husband rehabilitated himself so they could reconcile. No time was specified. Without husband's knowledge, the wife conveyed title to the residence to her brother. The husband filed suit seeking to have the deed to the wife's brother set aside. *Held:* For the husband. The agreement to convey property on the basis that it would be reconveyed at some future date was legally unenforceable because the time for performance was indefinite. The court also found that the husband had no intention to convey his interest in land, but was only making a good faith gesture to his wife. The wife's subsequent deed to her brother was therefore, void, since she attempted to transfer her husband's interest, which was not legally vested in her at that time. *Smith v. Smith*, 375 So. 2d 1138 (Dist. Ct. App. 1979).

Maine Grantee was given title to a parcel of land with a cottage on it. When grantor died, her children retained possession, arguing that their mother did not intend to convey the cottage lot. Successor to the original grantee then brought an action at law to establish title to the cottage lot. *Held:* Successor established title, but grantor's children were permitted to amend their answer for the purpose of counterclaiming for equitable relief. The intent of grantor was clear, as was the description of the property; however, grantees were entitled to equitable relief if there was a mutual mistake. *Sargent v. Coolidge*, 399 A2d 1333 (1979).

South Carolina Plaintiffs sued to invalidate a deed, which they contended lacked the words necessary to convey a fee in that it contained no words of inheritance in the granting clause and had no completed habendum clause. *Held:* Words of inheritance in the granting clause or a habendum clause are necessary to convey a fee, and words of inheritance appearing only in the warranty clause are not enough to supply the deficiency. This rule applies irrespective of the intention of the grantor; the deed in question, therefore, did not convey a fee simple title. *McLaurin v. McLaurin*, 217 SE2d 41 (1975).

93.15
—Undue Influence

Alabama In 1974, defendant's parents conveyed 40 acres of land to their son for consideration of $10. The deed contained a clause admonishing defendant to keep the property and not dispose of it. In 1978, defendant's father, then 90 years old, filed a complaint against defendant, alleging that defendant unduly influenced his parents so as to have them execute the deed to him. Defendant filed an answer alleging that the deed was valid. During the proceedings, defendant's father died, and a motion to substitute the parties was granted in favor of the heirs at law, the plaintiffs. After the trial court upheld the deed, plaintiffs moved for reconsideration, which was denied. Plaintiffs presented evidence that defendant's parents were senile, in poor health, and had been dependent on their son to transact their business. *Held:* The state supreme court affirmed the trial court's determination of no undue influence, finding that there was sufficient evidence on the record for such a holding. The record supported a finding that defendant, while he influenced his parents' actions, did not substitute his will for their will. For this reason, the court refused to impose a constructive trust on the land. *Seals v. Seals*, 423 So. 2d 222 (1982).

Idaho Two months before his death, a father made a gift of real property to his son. At the time the deed was made, the father was suffering the effects of cancer and a recent stroke. Upon submission of the father's will to probate, other will beneficiaries sued to invalidate the gift on the bases of diminished mental capacity and/or undue influence. *Held:* The father had the mental capacity to understand the nature and effect of the act of signing the deed, and no undue influence was exerted on grantor. In this case, the father's doctor, language pathologist, and nurse testified that owing to the effects of cancer and the stroke the father could not have understood the complex language of the deed. Defendant and two witnesses, who were not present at the signing, testified that the father understood what he was doing when he signed the deed. While the court found it difficult to express why the jury could have concluded that decedent was competent to make the deed, the jury's resolution of the case was not disturbed since there appeared to be substantial and competent evidence to support the verdict. *Montgomery v. Montgomery*, 768 P2d 787 (1989).

Missouri Plaintiff sued to set aside a conveyance from decedent to decedent's attorney on the ground that the deed was obtained through undue influence. The attorney alleged that he conferred with decedent at the hospital after decedent suffered a stroke and suggested that the conveyance be made to defray the expenses of administering the estate. When plaintiff, who was also at the hospital, objected, the attorney told plaintiff to wait in the hospital chapel. Ten minutes later, defendant returned with the deed conveying the property. *Held:* A conveyance of real property from a client to an attorney is presumptuously fraudulent. Therefore, in the absence of any explanation by the attorney to indicate that his signature was not the result of undue influence, the conveyance was invalid. *Flanagan v. DeLapp*, 533 SW2d 592 (1976).

Montana Son transferred to his mother certain real property in settlement of a debt. From the date of conveyance, the mother paid all property taxes. The estate of the deceased and his heirs at law sued to compel a reconveyance to the estate. The trial court ordered the mother to reconvey the property. *Held:* Trial court's imposition of a resultant or constructive trust was erroneous where the records failed to reveal any fraud, deceit, mistake, or undue influence on the part of the would-be constructive trustee. The existence of a confidential relationship (mother and son) was not enough, standing alone, to support a finding of undue influence on the part of grantee. *Mahaffey v. DeLeeuw*, 542 P2d 103 (1975).

Tennessee An elderly widow conveyed her home to a friend in return for the friend's promise to care for her for the rest of her life, to continue to pay rent, to pay insurance and property taxes, and to keep the property in good repair. After the deed was recorded, the widow sued her friend, alleging the conveyance was the result of fraud and duress. *Held:* Insufficient evidence existed to establish that a confidential relationship between the parties existed or that undue influence was exerted over the widow. Proof of a confidential relationship, by itself, does not give rise to a presumption of invalidity; plaintiff must also show that the dominant party exercised dominion or influence over the weaker party. In this case, the friend did not exercise sufficient dominion over the widow to enable her to influence the widow's decisions concerning the property; therefore, a confidential relationship was not evident. The widow maintained her own accounts, paid her own bills, and spent her money as she pleased. Additionally, suspicious circumstances were absent from the record; the parties did not conceal the conveyance, reasons existed for the conveyance, and substantial consideration was present. Rescission was not required since there was no proof that fraud or duress existed, that the friend repudiated or was unable to fulfill her obligations to the widow, or that rescission would restore the parties to their status quo. *Williamson v. Upchurch*, 768 SW2d 265 (Ct. App. 1988).

93.20 —Fraud

3d Circuit Petitioner's broker obtained a judgment against petitioner for debts on a trading account. Shortly thereafter, petitioner filed for bankruptcy. Two years earlier, he had executed a deed placing the house in his wife's name. The deed was not recorded until three months prior to the bankruptcy. The broker complained that petitioner should be denied a discharge because the transfer of the house had been fraudulent. The issue before the court of appeals was whether the house was transferred with intent to defraud creditors less than one year prior to filing for bankruptcy and, in particular, whether the transfer occurred on the date the deed was executed or the date it was recorded. *Held:* Denial of discharge affirmed. Under the Bankruptcy Code, a transfer is complete when it is perfected so that no one can acquire an interest in the property superior to that of the transferee. Under

Pennsylvania law, a transfer by deed is effective as to third parties when it is recorded. Therefore, petitioner's conveyance to his wife did not become final for creditors until the deed was recorded, which was less than one year before filing of the bankruptcy petition. Thus, petitioner's interest in the home was reachable by creditors. *In re MacQuown*, 717 F2d 859 (1983).

5th Circuit Property owners transferred their ranch to a corporation whose sole shareholder was their daughter. The daughter allowed the owners to continue living on the ranch. At the time of the sale, owners were in debt to a credit association. Two years after the sale, the ranch was sold to a third party for substantially below market value. Owner later filed for bankruptcy. Trustee sought to set aside the real property transfers. The bankruptcy court, applying Louisiana law, found the transfer to the daughter void as a simulation. *Held:* Affirmed. Creditor could revoke the real property transfers. A transaction may be void as a "simulation" under state law if the parties lacked genuine intent to transfer property. A rebuttal presumption of a simulation arises if the circumstances create reasonable doubt as to the validity of the sale. In this case, the evidence showed the sale to the daughter was funded by the parents. Therefore, the sale to the third party was actually by owners, not by the daughter's corporation. The transaction could be revoked by a creditor if he could show insolvency of the debtor, injury to the creditor, intent to defraud, and existing indebtedness. The third party's good faith would not prevent revocation of the sale, although creditor could recover the consideration paid. *Matter of Lenard*, 849 F2d 974 (1988).

Pennsylvania Husband, who joined with his wife in conveying property held as tenants by the entireties to her alone for consideration of $1, sued to set aside the conveyance. The husband alleged that the conveyance was induced by threats and misrepresentations by the wife. *Held:* Where the wife induced the husband to transfer the property to protect it from a judgment in a threatened lawsuit against the husband for adultery, the evidence supported a finding that the conveyance was fraudulently induced. *Stauffer v. Stauffer*, 351 A2d 236 (1976).

Texas Builder began construction of a condominium project on a stretch of beach. Construction was postponed until a judicial determination was made as to whether the project's location violated the state's Open Beaches Act. The builder and the state entered into a settlement under which builder agreed to convey a nearby piece of land to the state in return for the state's forbearance on construction of the condominium project. After builder finished and sold the condominiums, it sued to have the conveyance of land set aside on the basis that the deed was obtained by fraud and duress. *Held:* For the state. Under the Open Beaches Act, the state may sue to remove any structure erected seaward of the vegetation line. Generally, fraud cannot be established based on representations concerning matters of law. Any assertion by the state that the condominium was constructed on an "open beach" is a legal position that cannot form the basis of actionable fraud. Additionally, the state had not acted in fraud by negotiating away the public's easement over the beachfront since it had the power to settle the dispute by agreed judgment. Since the attorney general of Texas has a duty to enforce the Open Beaches Act, the threat to institute a civil suit over the dispute does not constitute duress. *Executive Condominiums, Inc. v. State*, 764 SW2d 899 (Ct. App. 1989).

Utah Officers of plaintiff corporation conveyed to plaintiff a ranch property. Two officers of plaintiff who were also officers of defendant church conveyed to church by warranty deed a part of the property. At the same time, officers of plaintiff conveyed the entire property to one Fain, who later discovered defendant's adverse claim. The warranty deed was then rerecorded by plaintiff's grantors, the date changed, and a recital of consideration added. Plaintiff sued to set aside the deed on the ground that recordation was fraudulent. *Held:* The deed was valid and binding on plaintiff corporation. A conveyance of real property is valid and binding even without recordation. Plaintiff, regardless of who owned a controlling interest, could not rely upon insufficient recordation to overturn a conveyance it had made. The fact that grantors were officers of both plaintiff and defendant at the time of conveyance did not defeat their right to record. Absent evidence of fraud in the rerecordation, the deed could not be set aside. *Bekins Bar V Ranch v. Beryl Baptist Church*, 642 P2d 371 (1982).

Virginia Grantor agreed to donate a lot to an itinerant evangelist for the building of a church, but she stated that she wanted the lot back if the church ever ceased and requested that a right be reserved for her restaurant customers to continue to park on the lot. Grantee hired an attorney, who drafted a deed of gift conveying the lot to the evangelist as tenant by the entirety. The deed reserved a right-of-way for parking but failed to include a reversionary clause. Grantor signed the deed under the mistaken belief that it contained the reversion clause. Subsequently, grantee sought to sell the lot and sued to have the parking easement removed owing to mistake and fraud. Grantor made a cross claim for rescission of the deed. *Held:* Failure of grantee's attorney to disclose that the deed transferred property directly to grantee without providing for a reversion amounted to actual fraud, which justified rescission. When the deed was executed, grantor was anxious to return to her business. She trusted grantee as a preacher and his attorney as an attorney and was assured that the deed was as she wanted it. Since grantee induced grantor not to read the deed, grantor's failure to read the deed before she signed it did not prevent her recovery. Grantee's nondisclosure was the equivalent of a fraudulent assertion of material fact made with an intent to mislead. *Spence v. Griffin*, 372 SE2d 595 (1988).

93.25
—Estoppel by Deed

Arkansas In 1960, husband and wife agreed to sell land to their daughter. The contract provided that royalties would be paid to grantors and the deed would be delivered to the daughter after 10 years. The executed, but undelivered, deed did not contain a reservation of any kind. When the wife died and the husband remarried, the husband and his new wife executed a new deed to the daughter in 1969, reserving royalties and mineral rights for the life of grantors. In 1984, the husband died, and the daughter began receiving royalties from the land. Lessee, however, refused to make payments to the daughter because of the reservation contained in the 1969 deed. In 1986, the daughter sued to quiet title to the mineral rights. *Held:* Petition dismissed; the second wife was entitled to all proceeds from the mineral lease. The doctrine of estoppel barred the daughter from objecting to the deed's reservation of a life estate in the mineral proceeds. As a general rule, property cannot be conveyed by reservation and a reservation in favor of a stranger to the deed is void. But the 1969 deed was in the daughter's possession for 16 years, during which she made no objection to the reservation executed by her father and stepmother. *Haynes v. Metcalf*, 759 SW2d 542 (1988).

North Dakota The Moravecs executed a contract for a deed conveying property, which they did not yet own, to the Lambourns. Twelve days later, they obtained a limited warranty deed that conveyed only 50 percent of the mineral interest. The deed was recorded five minutes before the contract with the Lambourns was recorded. Before the property was conveyed, the Moravecs obtained a quitclaim deed for the remaining 50 percent mineral interest. Later, they conveyed the real property to relatives, subject to the contract for deed. Ten years later, the Lambourns made their final payment on the contract and received a warranty deed, without reservation of mineral rights, from the Moravecs' relatives. The Moravecs' heirs brought a quiet title action against the Lambourns, claiming ownership of the 50 percent mineral interest conveyed in the quitclaim deed. *Held:* The doctrine of estoppel by deed protects an unwitting grantee who takes conveyance in reliance upon the title of grantor when in fact grantor does not possess legal title to the property. A grantor is liable for damages if, after conveying property with a warranty of title, he asserts against grantee any right or title in an attempt to defeat the deed. Estoppel by deed depends upon four factors: was the party to be estopped apprised of the true state of his title; did he act with intent to deceive or with such negligence as to constitute constructive fraud; was the party asserting estoppel without means of ascertaining the true state of title; and did the party asserting estoppel rely on the conduct of the party to be estopped. The trial court's finding on those facts was not clearly erroneous, and estoppel by deed was therefore applicable. *McLaughlin v. Lambourn*, 359 NW2d 370 (1985).

93.30 Consideration

Florida An elderly woman transferred title to her home to an unrelated young man by a quitclaim deed that stated it was given with consideration of "love and affection." Grantor subsequently sued for cancellation of the deed on the ground of lack of consideration, arguing that a deed not supported by valuable consideration is valid only if the parties are related by blood or marriage, under the so-called English Rule. *Held:* Grantor could not have her deed set aside. The court rejected the English Rule, finding that Florida's Statute of Uses, Section 689.09, does not expressly require that a deed of land be supported by consideration. In addition, the court noted that the constitutional law of homestead protection had been changed in 1968 to eliminate the requirement of valuable consideration as a condition of a conveyance of homestead property. Allowing a grantor to convey land without consideration to any person the grantor chooses is more in keeping with modern practices of land conveyances. *Chase Fed. Sav. & Loan Ass'n v. Schreiber*, 479 So. 2d 90 (1985), cert. denied, 467 US 1160 (1986).

Georgia Grantor sued to cancel a deed on the ground that he had received no consideration. Defendant had agreed that in consideration for the conveyance, grantee would assume grantor's indebtedness that the land was subject to. Defendant's grantee later conveyed the deed and denied any liability for the debt. *Held:* Defendant's promise to pay the consideration constituted consideration. Failure to pay the consideration did not render the conveyance invalid but did give rise to a cause of action for breach. *Barrett v. Simmons*, 221 SE2d 25 (1976).

Louisiana Plaintiffs, six siblings, alleged that sales of certain real property by their parents to two other older brothers amounted to illegal donations, since the donors failed to reserve enough interest for subsistence. The alleged sale of the 95-acre tract was for $1,120 as recited in the deeds. However, one brother admitted to paying no consideration and the other could produce no receipt or other evidence to support his claim of payment. The state court of appeals held that the sales contract was void, since the father did not reserve a subsistence interest, and so subsequent transfer to third-party purchasers could be set aside. *Held:* The state supreme court reversed. The rights of the third-party purchasers were protected, since they purchased on the basis of a public record, evidencing an apparently valid sale. Since the third-party purchasers had not participated in fraud, the sale to them could not be voided. *Owen v. Owen*, 336 So. 2d 782 (1976).

Utah Homeowner had a judgment against him in the amount of $28,000 when he deeded his house, worth $38,000, to his wife as part of a divorce settlement. The judgment creditors sought to set aside the conveyance as a fraudulent transfer, also arguing that it was made without fair consideration. *Held:* The conveyance was valid. Based on 20 years of marriage, the parties had jointly participated in working to acquire the house. In addition, the equity in the house was only $10,000, and the statutory exemption was more than the equity, leaving nothing available to judgment creditors. *Road Runner, Inc. v. Merrill*, 605 P2d 776 (1980).

93.35 Formalities

Florida State department of revenue appealed a decision holding that a deed did not require a documentary tax stamp. The deed was given by a corporation to its sole shareholder subject to a mortgage, which the shareholder did not assume but which he paid. *Held:* The conveyance was taxable. Although grantee did not assume the mortgage, there was, in fact, a shifting of the burden of paying the mortgage from corporation to grantee. This constituted a "reasonably determinable consideration," so as to make grantee a purchaser under the statute (Fla. Stat. Ann. § 201.02). *Florida Dep't of Revenue v. DeMaria*, 338 So. 2d 838 (1976).

Louisiana Plaintiffs asserted an interest in land on the basis of a deed recorded in 1970 and in the hands of the proper municipal authorities at the time of the suit. Plaintiffs relied on the presumption that the deed was genuine and properly executed at the time it was recorded. Other evidence indicated that (1) the name was merely written in ink over another legible name, (2) the inserted name was the same as a deputy clerk in the recording office at the time that the deed was recorded, and (3) the handwriting of the deed was not similar to the handwritten name. *Held:* Although the presumption of authenticity may be rebutted by those attacking the document, defendants did not meet this burden since innocent explanations for the alteration were equally possible. *Osborn v. Johnston*, 322 So. 2d 112 (1975).

North Carolina Plaintiff grounded his claim to title on a deed, which described the land as "the following real estate in Chowan County, to wit: A certain tract of Pocosin Land adjoining the lands of the late Henderson Luton and others, containing, by estimation, three hundred and nineteen acres." Defendants contended that this deed was void since it lacked a sufficient description to identify it. *Held:* The conveyance was invalid since the description in the deed was patently ambiguous and referred to nothing extrinsic by which the land could be identified. The description left in doubt the exact area of the tract, which side of the Henderson tract was intended, the boundaries, and whether the tract was all or part of a single Pocosin area. *Overton v. Boyce*, 221 SE2d 347 (1976).

94.00 ESCROW

94.05 Action for Breach of Escrow Conditions

Arizona Plaintiff, a judgment creditor of Smith, had a prejudgment writ of garnishment served on a title company acting as escrow agent for Smith, who was selling property. A written escrow agreement signed by Smith and his purchaser stated that the title company was to hold funds in escrow that would be used to pay the broker's commission and that the company should pay the commission only to the broker. When the writ of garnishment was served on the title company, it informed plaintiff that it held the sum of $3,360 free of claims of creditors. Title company paid the funds in escrow to the real estate broker pursuant to the escrow instructions. Plaintiff was granted summary judgment against title company for the amount it held in escrow. *Held:* Reversed. An irrevocable assignment of the funds took place upon execution of the escrow instructions prior in time and right to the writ of garnishment served on the title company. Since the funds were to be used to pay the broker and seller-debtor had no right to them after they were placed in escrow, the funds were not subject to garnishment. *Webster v. US Life Title Co.*, 598 P2d 108 (1979).

Delaware Defendant escrow agent received checks as advances on a pending sale of property but did not cash them even though it informed the seller that the funds had been "deposited." Purchaser went bankrupt, and seller sued the escrow agent for breach of fiduciary duty. The escrow attempted to escape liability by placing its own money into the account of the bankrupt and thereafter asserting his right to unilateral cancellation. *Held:* Judgment for seller. The purchase agreement required cash deposits into escrow, and the failure to reduce the checks to cash placed the buyer in breach. Consequently, the escrow cannot assert a greater claim to cancellation than that held by purchaser. Apart from this, the court found that the misrepresentations of the escrow led seller to hold its property off the market for a considerable period of time and that to permit execution of the agreement under such circumstances would be unjust. *Countrywide Realty Corp. v. Albani*, 420 A2d 1181 (1980).

Mississippi Grantor by quitclaim deed transferred all oil, gas, and mineral rights, specifically reserving one-half thereof. It later came to light that grantor held only a one-half mineral interest, and grantee argued that the entire half interest had been conveyed. *Held:* Grantor's express reservation of the one-half portion must be given effect, with the result that the parties each hold a one-quarter interest in the whole. Since a quitclaim deed—not a warranty deed—was used, the conveyance could be effective only as to the interest actually held by the grantor. The court rejected several other grantee arguments, including the doctrine of estoppel to assert an after-acquired title, as well as ambiguity in the language of the instrument. *Rosenbaum v. McCaskey*, 386 So. 2d 387 (1980).

95.00 CONSTRUCTION OF DEEDS

95.05 General Rules of Construction

New Hampshire Landowner's association sued to require successors in interest to the original developers to convey beach property to the association. The members of the association alleged that at the time they purchased their lots, developer's broker represented that the lots would be conveyed to the association. *Held:* Where landowner's deeds granted the association the right to use the beach area in common with others, the master correctly ruled that testimony of a possible oral agreement could not be considered. *Sargent Lake Ass'n. v. Dane*, 351 A2d 54 (1976).

North Carolina Plaintiffs sought to have their church declared the sole owner of a one-acre lot. Defendants, as heirs of grantors, claimed ownership under a reverter clause that followed the description in the deed. The clause stipulated that the land would revert if the church changed its name or failed to occupy the space with a church for three years. Defendants stated that the church had changed its name from the Second Advent Baptist Church to the Second Advent Christian Church and had failed to occupy the land with a church for three years. *Held:* The reverter clause was not valid nor effective since it appeared at the end of the description and was not referred to elsewhere in the deed. The court followed a line of cases that held that when the granting of a fee is absolute and the habendum clause contains no limitation on the fee, any additional clause repugnant to the grant that was not incorporated into the body of the deed is deemed mere surplusage without force or effect. *Whetsell v. Jernigan*, 223 SE2d 397 (Ct. App.), aff'd, 229 SE2d 183 (1976).

South Carolina Action was brought to settle the legal effect to be given the words "more or less" in a deed conveying an eight-acre tract. The deed contained a description of the property by noting the boundaries of the acres and stating that it began 700 feet from the road. The petitioner contended that the intent of the original grantor was to convey a tract that consisted of four acres of old cleared land and four acres of newly cleared land; to do this the land's boundary would have to begin 1,100 feet from the road. *Held:* The words "more or less" in the conveyance had no legal effect since the description included the amount of land to be conveyed and clearly stipulated the limits by reference to established boundaries. The intent of grantor could not be introduced when it was not included as part of the deed and conflicted with the description of the deed. *Kirven v. Bartell*, 223 SE2d 597 (1976).

Vermont Purchasers sued to claim title of six acres of a twelve-acre tract. The contract of sale and the deed described the land as approximately six acres, but the purchasers alleged that the southern boundary was intended to be a certain stream. The deed made no reference to the stream. *Held:* Where the description in the deed was vague except as to the number of acres, that quantity controlled despite the contention that the brook was the only "reasonable" boundary to the parcel. If the parties wished the brook to be a boundary, they could have clearly so provided in the deed. *Downer v. Gourlay*, 349 A2d 707 (1975).

95.10 Merger

Georgia Vendor sued to reform a deed based on alleged mutual mistake as to description and quantity of land. The sales contract contained a metes and bounds description of one lot, and the deed conveyed two adjoining lots with different addresses. Defendant contended that the sales contract merged in the deed and the deed correctly reflected the intention of the parties. *Held:* When the description of the land in the sales contract differed from the land conveyed by the deed and the evidence as to the intent of the parties was in sharp dispute, the contract of sale did not, as a matter of law, merge in the deed. *Rasmussen v. Martin*, 223 SE2d 663 (1976).

Illinois Contract for deed called for purchasers to pay $85,000 in $12,000 annual installments. It made payment a condition of the conveyance and delivery of the deed. Nonetheless, sellers delivered a warranty deed the next day. Six years later, when sellers died, purchasers recorded the deed and ceased making payments. The executor of seller's estate sued for the unpaid balance, and purchasers argued that sellers had expressly waived the contractual condition of payment for conveyance by delivering the deed. *Held:* For the estate. Generally a deed in full execution of a contract for sale of land merges the provisions of the contract into the deed. However, if there are provisions in the contract that delivery of the deed does not fulfill, the contract is not merged in the deed and remains open for performance of such terms. Here, the facts of the case showed purchasers were trying to take advantage of sellers' deaths to evade their contractual responsibilities. *Biehl v. Atwood*, 502 NE2d 1234 (App. Ct. 1986).

Minnesota Sellers agreed to sell a house, in which they retained an office, to buyers with closing scheduled for November 1, and buyers to take possession "not later than November 1." After the purchase agreement was signed, the parties amended it, moving the closing up to October 7 to accommodate buyer, but not specifying any change in the date of possession. The closing was acrimonious, but sellers ultimately signed a warranty deed conveying the property. However, they told buyers they were using the house to meet clients and would not surrender possession until November 1. Buyers did not accept this and eventually took possession on October 10 by brandishing a court order and breaking in through a window to get around barricaded doorways. They pursued this action seeking damages. *Held:* Buyers were entitled to immediate possession on October 7 and to any damages incurred because of the delay. The purchase agreement merged into the deed as to the date of possession. Delivery of possession is normally essential to the transfer of good title. A move-in move-out agreement or similar collateral agreement would not have merged into the deed, but no such agreement was reached. *Sullivan v. Eginton*, 406 NW2d 599 (Ct. App. 1987).

Mississippi Developer of real estate subdivision transferred a deed of property as collateral for a loan from an attorney. When the loan was not paid, the attorney viewed the property as his own, but there was an oral understanding that developer could repay him any time and buy the land back. Developer began negotiating to sell the property to buyers, intending to use the down payment to repurchase the property from the attorney. Buyers agreed to purchase the property from developer, who represented himself as owner. The contract provided that if the county did not issue a building permit, all monies paid would be refunded. Buyers gave attorney a deposit. The developer died soon after and attorney completed the sale, not disclosing his connection with the property. Attorney promised buyers that if a building permit were denied, he would refund any payments. Buyers were denied a permit, and attorney began foreclosure proceedings when buyers ceased payments on the property. Buyers sued for breach of contract, seeking a refund of monies paid and cancellation of the deed. *Held:* Buyers could obtain a refund. The independent and collateral agreement that buyers secured from developer regarding refund of their purchase price if a building permit were not obtained survived the deed and was enforceable. Generally, the doctrine of merger would cause previous negotiations or contracts to be merged into a deed of conveyance. Here, the court adopted the collateral agreement exception to the merger doctrine, that is, that certain preliminary stipulations that were independent and collateral would survive the deed and confer independent causes of action. *Knight v. McCain*, 531 So. 2d 590 (1988).

Texas Buyer purchased a tract of raw land under a contract that provided the seller would convey title free of all restrictions and specified that seller would furnish buyer with a current title commitment setting forth title to the property, including all exceptions. The contract failed to disclose the existence of a restrictive covenant prohibiting any building on the property over 30 feet in height. Both seller and his broker knew of the height restriction prior to the sale; however, buyer was never told of the restriction, and the title policy commitment did not disclose the height restriction. Buyer sued seller and broker upon learning of the restriction. Seller argued that the deed was expressly subject to any outstanding interests, and any contrary representations made prior to the deed were extinguished under the doctrine of merger. *Held:* Buyer's claims were not barred by the doctrine of merger. The doctrine of merger does not bar claims of fraud, accident, or mistake in transactions leading up to the deed. If the doctrine could be so used, there could never be a cause of action for fraud in the sale of real estate unless the misrepresentation were contained in the deed itself. *ECC Parkway Joint Venture v. Baldwin*, 765 SW2d 504 (Ct. App. 1989).

Washington Landowners filed an action to determine right to oil and gas deposits on their property in light of a mineral reservation in their deed. Original sale contract for their land included a reservation of only iron and coal, but the deed referred to all minerals. Original seller's successors and lessees argued that they were entitled to the oil and gas deposits. *Held:* The sale contract merged into the subsequently issued deed so terms of deed, including the reserved right to all minerals, controlled. A deed made in full execution of a sale contract merges the provisions of the underlying contract, including all prior negotiations and agreements leading up to the deed's execution. However, the mineral reservation in the deed, which included the authority to explore and extract, unambiguously excluded mineral rights to oil and gas from the grant. *Kunkel v. Meridian Oil, Inc.*, 775 P2d 470 (Ct. App. 1989).

Wisconsin Purchasers sued seller and its agent when the property was foreclosed for nonpayment of real estate taxes. Although the agreement of purchase and sale provided that the seller was to pay taxes until payment was complete and that the property was to be conveyed free and clear, the deed was executed subject to taxes for the previous two years. *Held:* When the deed was accepted by purchasers, the agreement of purchase and sale merged into the deed. Where the taxes were specifically provided for in the deed, purchasers could not argue that it was a collateral matter for which the contract controlled. *Miles v. Mackle Bros.*, 242 NW2d 247 (1976).

95.15 Reservations and Exceptions

Alabama In 1929, Holloway deeded property to Minor, reserving a one-half interest in mineral rights. In 1946, Minor conveyed the property to Taylor by warranty deed, expressly covenanting that grantor had full rights to convey title and a reservation for grantors of a one-half interest in mineral rights. The deed did not mention the reservation by Holloway. Taylor's successor in interest sued Minor's successor in interest to construe the mineral rights reservation in the deed. *Held:* The Alabama Supreme Court held that grantee was entitled to a full one-half interest. Where a warranty deed is supported by consideration and grantor has insufficient interest to give effect to both a grant and a reservation, the grant must take precedence over the reservation. Thus, in this case, the reservation of one-half interest failed, and the risk of title loss fell on the grantor. In addition, since the grant purported to transfer 100 percent of right, title, and interest, except for the 50 percent reservation of mineral rights, grantee was entitled to 50 percent of such rights. *Cole v. Minor*, 518 So. 2d 61 (1987).

Mississippi Miller, appellant, conveyed land to the Paces that the Paces later resold. Miller included a clause making the conveyance "subject to" the reservation of oil, gas, and mineral rights by prior grantors. There were, however, no reservations by prior grantors. Miller later executed a lease of the mineral rights. The lease was declared invalid by the chancellor, and Miller appealed. *Held:* Affirmed. Miller had inadvertently conveyed mineral rights that she later sought to lease. The words "subject to" are not the functional equivalent of "reserving." The court refused to reform the conveyance to reflect the intent of the parties, as bona fide purchasers without notice would be affected by any correction of the agreement, since a search of county records would not reveal any prior reservations. *Miller v. Lowery*, 468 So. 2d 865 (1985).

Mississippi Grantee of land under a warranty deed sued to obtain a judicial determination that it was the owner of certain mineral rights previously held by his grantor. The deed was subject to "prior reservations and conveyances of all the oil, gas and other minerals . . . under said lands." Grantor had conveyed all the oil, gas, and mineral rights prior to the deed but repurchased one-eighth interest in all the rights prior to the sale of the surface land to grantee. Grantee contended that the deed conveyed his grantor's one-eighth mineral interest since it was not reserved or conveyed to anyone else. *Held:* Property that is excepted is not granted; when not outstanding in another, it remains with grantor. Tthe deed thus excepted all mineral rights from sale to grantee. *Pfisterer v. Noble*, 320 So. 2d 383 (1975).

95.20 Ambiguities in Description

Maine Deed conveying certain land contained a course and distance description formulated from an inaccurate municipal tax map. Plaintiffs contended that the deed conveyed only the three acres described within, while defendants claimed that they held title to the entire parcel of grantor, since the description referred to abutting landowners without exception for retained lands. *Held:* Proper deed construction requires that available monuments control over courses and distances, even where the resulting bounds are grossly inconsistent with that description. The boundary line should follow the recognized line of the abutting landowners even though they are incorrectly identified. There is a strong presumption that grantor's entire parcel has been conveyed if the deed description runs between abutting landowners without express reservation for land retained by grantor. *Hedberg v. Wallingford*, 379 A2d 126 (1977).

South Carolina State sued to settle a dispute between itself and corporations concerning title to certain tidelands. The state contended it never parted with title to the tidelands, and defendants claimed they were owners by virtue of grants from the state that described the property granted as being bounded by an "inlet" and a "sound or creek." *Held:* Descriptive language of the type used was insufficient to convey tidelands. Since the "inlet" and "sound or creek" referred to were arms of the Atlantic Ocean and subject to the ebb and flow of tides, they were tidelands, and the grant was insufficient to convey title. Under settled rules of construction, naming such boundaries will convey only to the high-water marks in the absence of specific language, either in the grant or upon a plat showing that it was intended to convey the land below the high-water mark. *State v. Yelsen Land Co.*, 216 SE2d 876 (1975).

96.00 DELIVERY AND ACCEPTANCE OF DEED

96.05 Delivery of Deed

Alabama Deceased parents of plaintiffs and defendant conveyed to one another individual one-half interests for life in 270 acres of land with a remainder in fee simple to their son, defendant. The deed conveying these interests was held by a bank for safekeeping. It was the policy of that particular bank to permit the retrieval of all documents deposited there for safekeeping. Several years after both parents had died, plaintiffs, being six of defendant's siblings, brought an action to set aside the deed because of lack of legal delivery. Plaintiffs contended that there was never a delivery to defendant because the father did not place the deed beyond his control, and thereby kept the right of revocation. *Held:* The fact of delivery rests in grantor's intention, not in the safekeeper's policy of permitting those who leave papers with it to retrieve those papers. The evidence established that the father, in instructing the bank to deliver the deed to defendant after the death of both parents, and in not expressly reserving in himself a right of revocation, intended delivery of the deed. *Chandler v. Chandler*, 409 So. 2d 780 (1981).

Georgia Plaintiffs, the heirs of G.W. Johns, sought to have title to land willed by J.W. Johns to his legatees declared in them. The deed to the land from G.W. Johns to J.W. Johns offered into evidence by defendants was dated 1924, recorded in 1969 (long after the death of grantor), and discovered in 1972 after the death of grantee. Plaintiffs contended that the deed was a forgery and had not been delivered. *Held:* There was ample evidence to support the jury's verdict for defendants. There is a presumption that a deed is delivered when it is found in the custody of grantee who is in possession of the land. This presumption overcame the presumption that plaintiffs relied on, namely, that there was no delivery of a deed when recorded after grantor's death. *Corley v. Parson*, 223 SE2d 708 (1976).

Illinois Contract for deed called for purchasers to pay $85,000 in $12,000 annual installments. It made payment a condition of the conveyance and delivery of the deed. Nonetheless, sellers delivered a warranty deed the next day. Six years later, when sellers died, purchasers recorded the deed and ceased making payments. The executor of seller's estate sued for the unpaid balance, and purchasers argued that sellers had expressly waived the contractual condition of payment for conveyance by delivering the deed. *Held:* For the estate. Generally a deed in full execution of a contract for sale of land merges the provisions of the contract into the deed. However, if there are provisions in the contract that delivery of the deed does not fulfill, the contract is not merged in the deed and remains open for performance of such terms. Here, the facts of the case showed purchasers were trying to take advantage of sellers' deaths to evade their contractual responsibilities. *Biehl v. Atwood*, 502 NE2d 1234 (App. Ct. 1986).

Kansas Husband and wife executed two deeds giving 80 acres each to their two sons. The deeds were not recorded during grantors' lifetime. The deeds were placed in a safe deposit box and the father gave one son the key to the box, saying he was delivering the deed to him. The father died in 1962; the mother in 1967. After her death, the deeds were recorded. The other son predeceased the mother, and his share passed to his heirs. The surviving son claimed the entire property on the theory that the deed was a nullity because it had never been delivered. *Held:* Delivery is largely a matter of grantor's intention to divest himself of title. To be effective, a deed must be delivered during grantor's lifetime. However, delivery of the safe deposit key to one son who was living nearby was constructive delivery to both sons. Delivery of the key was evidence of grantors' intention to divest themselves of title. *Agnelius v. Moheskey*, 494 P2d 1095 (1972).

96.10
Acceptance by Grantee

Missouri Plaintiff brought an action for partition, contending she and defendants were co-owners of 100 acres of land. Plaintiff claimed she and defendants were residual devisees under the will of the deceased owner, which will granted the land to decedent's brother's children after his death. Defendants, the brother's children, claimed ownership under a deed that provided a life estate from decedent to her brother, with the remainder in fee to defendants, his sons. Testimony showed that decedent attempted to give the deed to her brother, but, angered that the deed granted the remainder only to his sons and not to his daughters, he tore it up. He did retain half the deed, which was never recorded. *Held:* The deed was invalid because the facts did not establish proper delivery and acceptance. Where grantor's brother, named grantee, tore up the deed when it was initially handed to him, his retention of half of the deed did not establish that he thereafter accepted it. No presumption of delivery arises by possession of half a deed earlier rejected. *Underwood v. Gillespie*, 594 SW2d 374 (Ct. App. 1980).

97.00
REFORMATION

97.05
Ground for Reformation

Delaware Defendants purchased a parcel of three quarters of an acre of land. Several years after the conveyance, plaintiff realized that, according to the legal description, the parcel ran through the rear of his barn on an adjacent parcel of land. The lower court ordered reformation of the legal description of the deed, changing defendants' rectangular parcel to an L-shaped parcel. *Held:* Reversed and remanded. Because defendant had intended to purchase a rectangular parcel of land and because the error in description was made by the surveyor through no fault of defendant, the lower court was instructed to reverse the description to exclude the barn but to maintain the parcel in rectangular shape. *Collins v. Burke*, 418 A2d 499 (Super. Ct. 1980).

Iowa Plaintiff deeded a life estate to his mother in 1956. Plaintiff brought an action for reformation of the deed based on the doctrine of mutual mistake. He claimed that he had intended only to create a joint right of occupancy. *Held:* The claim for reformation was upheld. Plaintiff received no consideration from his mother for the conveyance. The court treated the conveyance as unilateral and reformed the deed to express the intent of grantor. *Westcott v. Westcott*, 259 NW2d 545 (1977).

Kansas Landowners sought to sell property bordering a lumberyard. The owner of the lumberyard agreed to buy the property but added to the contract and warranty deed the phrase "this proposal includes all land owned by sellers in above NW ¼, whether described herein or not." The lumberyard owner secretly intended by adding this language to include in the sale a larger property in which landowners owned a reversionary interest. He led landowners to believe he merely intended to clarify the description of the smaller property. When the lumberyard owner's claim to the larger property was revealed, landowners sued for reformation of deed. *Held:* The deed was reformed to exclude the larger property. A written instrument may be reformed where there is ignorance or mistake on one side and fraud or inequitable conduct on the other, a situation exemplified by this case. *Andres v. Claassen*, 714 P2d 963 (1986).

Maine Property owner appealed judgment that established the boundaries of her land by reforming her deed and that of adjoining landowner. Both had filed actions seeking to quiet title to their properties based on a boundary dispute. The Toussaints originally owned all the land in question, but had deeded out a parcel to the Perraults' predecessors in title. There was a discrepancy in the description of the property in the parties' deeds. In determining the disputed southern boundary line, the court reformed the deed and established the western end of the southern boundary line through extrinsic evidence, essentially redrawing the location of the property. *Held:* While the use of extrinsic evidence was valid to determine the eastern end of the southern boundary line as requested by the parties, the trial court erred in reforming the deeds contrary to the intention or desire of the parties. *Perrault v. Toussaint*, 419 A2d 1009 (1980).

Massachusetts City manager agreed to sell to a hospital a tract of land except for a small parcel, which the city was to retain for recreational purposes. The city council authorized the sale of the entire parcel for $300,000, which the hospital paid. The hospital argued that the deed should be reformed to convey the entire tract since the city never used the land for recreational purposes and that the city manager was bound to sell the whole parcel pursuant to the city council authorization. *Held:* There was no contract for the sale of the entire parcel. The intention of both parties was for the sale of the land minus the small parcel. *Sancta Maria Hosp. v. City of Cambridge*, 341 NE2d 674 (1976).

North Carolina Suit was brought for reformation of deeds to effectuate the true intention of the parties. *Held:* Reformation of a deed will be granted when clear and convincing evidence shows that owing to mutual mistake the deed does not express the actual agreement made between the parties. Grantor receiving no consideration from grantee is entitled to reformation when the deed fails to express the actual intent of the parties because of grantor's unilateral mistake. *Nelson v. Harris*, 232 SE2d 298, cert. denied, 235 SE2d 62 (1977).

Oregon Seller of timberland sued to reform a warranty deed that failed to contain a reservation of 60 old-growth Douglas fir trees contained in the contract of sale. The grantee of all rights to merchantable timber not subject to prior right of removal by seller appealed from a decree reforming the deed. *Held:* The meaning of the term "old-growth Douglas fir" could be ascertained from the circumstances surrounding the sale and was therefore not ambiguous. Where grantee was a purchaser with notice, it could not defeat the prior claim of seller, since a purchaser with notice of a prior right takes subject to that right. *Benton v. Medicine Rock Land Co.*, 549 P2d 1122 (1976).

Vermont Seller agreed to sell 220 acres of her farm, 160 acres of which were to be tillable. Seller was to retain 30 acres. The sales agreement described the conveyance. Buyers received a warranty deed that was made subject to the sales agreement. However, the deed failed to include the 30 retained acres. Buyers refused to execute a corrected deed, since a survey they had prepared showed less acreage than the town records showed; if seller were allowed to retain 30 acres, buyers would receive nine acres less than they bargained for. Seller sued, seeking reformation of the deed in accordance with the sales agreement. *Held:* If the deed could be reformed without depriving buyers of the nine acres for which they bargained, the proper standard of reformation was the sales agreement. Reformation was appropriate since the parties executed and accepted a faulty deed. The sales agreement was the proper standard for reforming the deed, since it represented the parties' agreement. However, if reformation would deprive buyers of nine acres and if on remand the deficiency could not be satisifed, the deed should be rescinded. *Bourne v. Lajoie*, 540 A2d 359 (1987).

98.00 COVENANTS OF TITLE

98.05 Seisin

5th Circuit After purchasing a tract of coastal land, buyer surveyed the property. The surveyance revealed that only 3.16 of the 14 acres sold were above the mean high water line. Seller had obtained title to the land from a patent issued by the United States in 1883. Buyer maintained that Florida acquired title to all land below the mean high water mark when it was admitted to the Union in 1845, that the patent was therefore void and the seller was never seized of fee simple title to 10.84 acres of the 14 acres, and that the seller therefore breached the covenant of seisin contained in the warranty deed. *Held:* Ancient conveyances of sovereign lands in existence for more than 30 years, when the state has made no effort of record to reclaim same, clearly vests marketable title in grantees, their successors, or their assigns under the Florida Marketable Record Title Act (Fla. Stat. § 712.02). Thus, the land may be recovered by the state only by direct purchase or eminent domain proceedings. Accordingly, judgment in favor of seller. *Starnes v. Marcon Inv. Group*, 571 F2d 1369 (1978).

98.10 Encumbrances

Alabama At a closing of sale of real property, purchaser received a warranty deed that stated the property was free of encumbrances. He executed a mortgage containing a statement that this was a second mortgage and was subject to a first mortgage. Purchaser purportedly did not read the statement. When he subsequently learned of the prior mortgage, he sued for breach of covenant. The trial court granted defendants summary judgment. *Held:* Reversed. Although purchaser was given notice of the prior emcumbrance when he signed the mortgage, such notice was not sufficient to overcome the covenant in the deed, which warranted there were no encumbrances on the property. A covenant of freedom from encumbrances is indemnity against known, as well as unknown, encumbrances. *Lockhart v. Phenix City Inv. Co.*, 488 So. 2d 1353 (1986).

Illinois Property owners appealed a dismissal of their action to recover damages for breach of the covenant against encumbrances in a warranty deed. The title search indicated that there were five judgment liens totalling $10,500 against the property. The property owners had not paid the liens and no actions were pending to enforce the liens. *Held:* Under the statutory warranty against encumbrances, grantor in the warranty deed warranted against more than failure of title; it also warranted "the quiet and peaceable possession of such premises" and that it would "defend the title thereto against all persons who may lawfully claim the same." The existence of judgments that may have been encumbrances on the property caused the possibility of more than nominal damages, even though grantees had not yet been disturbed in the title and had paid nothing to remove the encumbrances. Accordingly, the court reversed the dismissal and remanded to give the property owners an opportunity to plead and prove the nature and extent of such damages. *Fechtner v. Lake County Sav. & Loan Ass'n*, 361 NE2d 575 (1977).

New Jersey Owner of property wanted to build a new access road over a stream on the property. He asked the state bureau of water for permission to build a culvert nine feet in diameter. The bureau said that only a 16-foot culvert could handle the stream in flood condition; however, the owner ignored this recommendation and installed the nine-foot culvert. Ten years later, he sold the land, giving a warranty deed for "quiet possession of paid land, free of all encumbrances." After a few years, when the buyer attempted to resell the land, it discovered that the culvert had never been approved and did not meet state or local requirements. Buyer sued seller for the cost of a new culvert, arguing that seller had breached the covenant of the warranty deed. *Held:* Buyer was not entitled to recover the cost of a new culvert. Although the culvert was in violation of local regulations, this defect did not constitute an interest in the land and therefore was not an encumbrance that affected title to the land. Since the defect did not affect the title, buyer could not collect. *Fahmie v. Wulster*, 408 A2d 789 (1979).

New York Plaintiff purchased land from defendant and was promised "good title to the property free of all liens and encumbrances." Later, plaintiff discovered the existence of an easement and demanded return of his down payment. *Held:* Plaintiff purchaser was entitled to the return of his deposit. It was settled that an easement is an encumbrance. Purchaser need not accept title even though there was no showing that the encumbrance diminishes the market value of the property. The encumbrance breached the covenant for title. *Rhodes v. Astro-Pac, Inc.*, 394 NYS2d 623 (1977).

North Carolina Buyers of a house discovered after the sale that the house violated certain city building requirements because it was too close to the property lines. Buyers sued seller for breach of the warranty against encumbrances; summary judgment was granted to seller. Buyer appealed. *Held:* Reversed. The existing violation of the city's minimum side lot requirement constituted an encumbrance under the warranty deed. *Wilcox v. Pioneer Homes, Inc.*, 254 SE2d 214 (1979).

Oregon Plaintiffs purchased land from Hinnenkamp, defendant's deceased predecessor. Hinnenkamp had conveyed the property by statutory warranty deed. Plaintiffs later learned that the Lees claimed a large part of the land by adverse possession and their claim had allegedly matured before Hinnenkamp's conveyance. Plaintiffs brought an action in ejectment against the Lees and a claim for damages against defendants, alleging that Hinnenkamp had breached the warranty of title. The Lees' adverse possession claim was established at trial. Hinnenkamp claimed that the Lees' occupation was an exception to the warranty against encumbrances in a statutory warranty deed. Under. Or. Rev. Stat. § 93.850(2)(c), such a deed convenanted that the property "is free of encumbrances except as specifically set forth on the deed." *Held:* For plaintiffs. An adverse possession claim is not an encumbrance on title; it is a denial of title and is inconsistent with the passing of the fee by conveyance. Hinnenkamp had nothing to convey to plaintiffs, because the Lees were the fee owners of the land. Hinnenkamp had breached Or. Rev. Stat. § 93.850(2)(c)(A), the covenant that at the time of delivery of the deed the grantor was seized of the estate and had the right to convey it. *Wright v. Hinnenkamp*, 687 P2d 163 (1984).

Oregon Property owners were sued by a neighbor who sought to establish his right to use and maintain a spring on the property. Property owners, in turn, joined grantor of the property as third-party defendant, suing the neighbor for breach of warranty because of the encumbrance. The trial court granted relief to the neighbor, but entered judgment for grantor. The property owner appealed the judgment for grantor. *Held:* There was no breach of warranty by grantor. When they bought the property, the owners were aware that the neighbor used water from the spring, and therefore it was a jury question whether an irrevocable license for the spring was an encumbrance. *Leach v. Gunnarson*, 604 P2d 419 (1979).

Washington The Chamberlins sold land improved with two office buildings to plaintiff Mellor. The adjoining property was owned by Buckman, and prior to the sale, the Chamberlins leased this property for use as a parking lot. This use was continued by Mellor, although the lease was not mentioned in the real estate contract. In 1974, Buckman informed Mellor that his building encroached on her property and that she owned the parking lot used by his tenants. In the first action filed in 1975, Mellor alleged the Chamberlins had misrepresented the parking lot as included in the sale of the office buildings. The lawsuit was settled in 1976. Meanwhile, Mellor received a warranty deed to the property. In 1977, Buckman and Mellor settled the encroachment matter. In 1979, Mellor brought a second lawsuit against the Chamberlins for breach of covenants of title. The Chamberlins appealed from a damages judgment, claiming the action was barred by res judicata by the settlement of the prior lawsuit for misrepresentation. *Held:* The second action was not barred by res judicata. Subsequent litigation must be identical to prior litigation in four respects to be barred by res judicata: subject matter, cause of action, parties, and quality of persons. Although both lawsuits arose out of the same transaction, the sale of property, their subject matter differed. The first lawsuit involved misrepresentation of the parking lot as part of the sale. The second raised the claim that the encroachment breached the covenant of title. *Mellor v. Chamberlin*, 673 P2d 610 (1983).

98.15
Warranty

Nebraska Vendor conveyed to purchaser a hotel by deed containing covenants of warranty and title. Purchaser leased the premises to plaintiff under a lease containing no specific covenant of quiet possession. Subsequently, it was discovered that a beauty shop on the premises held a valid unrecorded lease. Plaintiff brought suit against both purchaser and vendor of the hotel. The trial court dismissed plaintiff's cause of action against vendor based on its covenants in the deed, since plaintiff was not a party to the deed. *Held:* By statute (Neb. Rev. Stat § 76.208 (1943)), covenants of title run with the land and are enforceable by assignees. Since the lessee here took all of the possessory interests and title of the lessor, "and the rights, privileges and appurtenances thereunto . . . for and during the term of 25 years . . . ," it is an "assignee" within the meaning of the statute and may enforce covenants of title involving possessory rights contained in a prior conveyance of the real estate to his lessor. *Grand Island Hotel Corp. v. Second Island Dev. Co.*, 214 NW2d 253 (1972).

Washington Vendor sought a declaration of rights against purchasers as to certain monies remaining on account. Purchasers were divested of title in a successful action for specific performance by prior purchasers, and counterclaimed, alleging breach of covenant of warranty and of quiet enjoyment. *Held:* The decree of specific performance obtained by prior purchasers of the land was an eviction and constituted a breach of the covenants of warranty and quiet enjoyment in the deed. Knowledge by purchasers of a potentially superior claim did not bar their suit for breach of the covenants of warranty and quiet enjoyment when they were later evicted from the property by judicial action. *Foley v. Smith*, 539 P2d 874 (Ct. App. 1975).

PART R
EMINENT DOMAIN

99.00
EXERCISE OF POWER

99.05
Precondemnation Right of Survey

Georgia Utility attempted to conduct field inspections and surveys on properties of prospective condemnees to determine placement of a transmission line. The proposed survey work involved removal of some trees and underbrush in wooded areas. Prospective condemnees denied access to utility. The trial court granted prospective condemnees an injunction on the ground that no public necessity existed for placement of the transmission line in this area. *Held:* Reversed. "A condemning body has the right, incidental to its power of eminent domain, to enter private property in order to survey, inspect, and appraise the property." A prospective condemnor does not have to begin condemnation proceedings before exercising its right of entry. The permissible scope of entry for preliminary survey and inspection, however, was limited by constitutional restrictions on taking of property without just compensation. Thus, the cutting of trees could be authorized only if it was an unavoidable incident of preliminary surveyiing. *Oglethorpe Power Corp. v. Goss*, 322 SE2d 887 (1984).

Missouri Appraisers conducted precondemnation appraisals of property for the Missouri Highway and Transportation Commission. The results were not revealed to the owner, who suspected that the appraisers had been generous in their appraisals and that the state was burying the results. The owner moved for document discovery in connection with appraisals. *Held:* Denial of motion affirmed. The state argued such discovery would be pointless because the amount offered by the state and the market value had no bearing on the good faith of the state in making the offer. The owner maintained that the state's failure to offer an amount commensurate with its own appraisers' opinion might establish bad faith. The court took the position that the all-important condemnation function could not be delayed at the preliminary hearing stage by discovery with respect to sufficiency of an amount offered by the state. *Missouri Highway & Transp. Comm'n v. Anderson*, 735 SW2d 350 (1987).

Missouri KAMO, an electric cooperative engaged in rural electrification, held a statutory grant of eminent domain in connection with construction and operation of transmission lines in its service area. KAMO proposed construction of a transmission line through landowners' property. Landowners refused to allow surveyors access to the property to determine the placement of transmission lines, and KAMO petitioned for an injunction granting access to surveyors. An injunction was issued. *Held:* Affirmed. The court noted that the issue, precondemnation right of survey, was first impression in the state. The eminent domain statute contemplates that the condemning authority designate the land to be taken with sufficient particularity that the owner can determine what is being taken. Therefore, precondemnation surveying is a necessary part of eminent domain; to hold otherwise would result in the anomaly of the legislature granting the power to condemn, yet denying the condemning entity the means by which to utilize the grant. *State ex rel. Rhodes v. Crouch*, 621 SW2d 47 (1981) (en banc).

99.10
Power to Condemn

4th Circuit Landowners owned parcels that were annexed by city. Landowners claimed the annexation was for the purpose of increasing city's tax base and shares of state revenue-sharing funds, in violation of the due process clause of the Fourteenth Amendment. Plaintiffs also alleged that only wealthy areas were annexed, while similarly situated poor areas were not. *Held:* For the city. While historically issues of municipal annexation have been deemed state political matters by the federal courts, racially motivated redefinitions of municipal limits have been struck down. Likewise, annexation by voting referendum has been held valid absent infringement of fundamental rights or creation of a suspect classification. Plaintiffs' allegations that only wealthy sections were annexed did not, if true, create a suspect classification. And there is no fundamental right to be free of additional local taxation. *Baldwin v. City of Winston-Salem*, 710 F2d 132 (1983), cert. denied, 464 US 1012 (1983).

5th Circuit Property owner sought injunctive relief and damages from Army Corps of Engineers, alleging that its decision not to locate a hurricane protection levee on property owner's land constituted a taking. *Held:* Army Corps' decision not to locate the hurricane protection levee on property owner's land did not amount to a taking, because it was based on a desire not to enclose a certain tract of wetlands within property owner's land. The fact that the Army Corps' decision denied property owner the business opportunities it would have enjoyed had the levee been located where owner desired did not make such decision a taking without due process or just compensation. Owner was still free to contract with the local levee district. *Allain-Lebreton Co. v. Department of Army*, 670 F2d 43 (1982).

5th Circuit Plaintiff, owner of a tract of land zoned for single-family residential use, requested the city council rezone it for a medical office complex. While the planning commission was considering its recommendation on the rezoning, it was also planning to expropriate plaintiff's property by eminent domain for street realignment. Thereafter, plaintiff requested rezoning to multi-family residential. The commission delayed over three years in deciding both rezoning requests. Plaintiff sued the city and its mayor for deprivation of property without due process and just compensation resulting from the delay. *Held:* Plaintiff did not have valid claims. The mayor had absolute immunity from federal damage claims arising from his conduct when acting in a legislative capacity, and exercise of his veto was clearly such an act. Although the city lacked absolute immunity, the court ruled that a taking had not occurred. "Mere fluctuations of value during the process of governmental decision-making" did not amount to a taking in violation of due process. *Hernandez v. City of Lafayette*, 643 F2d 1188 (1981), cert. denied, 455 US 907 (1982).

7th Circuit Plaintiffs, displaced residents, sued to enjoin the Department of Housing and Urban Development (HUD) and the city from funding a commercial development project. They alleged the city failed to afford them "reasonable opportunity" to relocate in the area, as required by the Housing and Community Development Act (42 USC § 5304(c)(1)(C)(i)). *Held:* The statute applied only when housing was available in the neighborhood. To interpret the "reasonable opportunity" requirement as absolute would frustrate development. Congress could not have intended to foreclose HUD funding for projects in areas where relocation housing did not exist; the more blighted the area, the less likely such housing was available. The language of the statute did not require the city to subsidize private development of replacement housing, as plaintiffs argued, when such housing was lacking in the neighborhood. Plaintiffs could be relocated to comparable housing elsewhere. *Mejia v. HUD*, 688 F2d 529 (1982).

U.S. District Court, Nebraska Plaintiff, a utility, sought to obtain by condemnation an easement over Indian lands to build an electric transmission line. The lands were allotted in severalty to Indians by the United States. Plaintiff cited a federal statute, 25 USCA § 357, providing that land allotted in severalty to Indians may be condemned for any public purpose under the applicable laws of the state. However, the 1948 Indian Right-of-Way Act (1948 Act) prohibited condemnation of easements across land allotted to individual Indians without the consent of each allottee. The access statute cited by plaintiff was not expressly overridden by the 1948 Act. *Held:* Construing the 1948 Act, the court considered three long-standing principles: (1) Indians should not be denied property rights without their consent; (2) statutes passed for the benefit of Indian tribes are to be liberally construed in favor of Indians; and (3) when a later statute conflicts with an earlier one, the later act prevails. The court held that the 1948 Act superseded 25 USCA § 357. *Nebraska Pub. Power Dist. v. 100.95 Acres of Land*, 540 F. Supp. 592 (1982).

U.S. District Court, North Carolina Defendant challenged the condemnation of his land for use in an Army Corps of Engineers navigation project. Defendant argued the federal condemnation statute provided that the cost of any water development project be less than $15 million, and the final project cost in this case exceeded $15 million. Second, defendant argued that the North Carolina constitution required a voter referendum on the condemnation agreement between the county and the United States. *Held:* The United States was authorized under both statutory and constitutional grounds to condemn the property. The $15 million limit applied to the initial cost estimate and not to the final actual cost, and the original cost estimate of the project was only $6 million. Defendant's constitutional argument failed because the provision he relied upon had been amended to narrow the restriction on local government's contracting powers. *United States v. 30.60 Acres of Land*, 535 F. Supp. 33 (ED 1981).

U.S. District Court, Texas An engineer designed a cement liner for a creek as part of a county flood control project, which extended onto Stearns' adjoining property. No easement existed for the proposed route. Stearns sued to enjoin construction, and it was decided to end the liner at Stearns' property line so as to avoid delay. However, this configuration caused accumulation of water upstream and resulted, Stearns alleged, in undue settling of his property. He spent $10,000 on anti-erosion measures. Stearns alleged an unconstitutional taking. *Held:* Relief denied. Stearns had not demonstrated any additional erosion of his property due to construction of the liner. If the liner had been built as originally designed, a taking would have occurred if a right-of-way was not acquired over Stearns' property. The liner having ended at his property line, however, recovery was barred based on the proof submitted. *Stearns v. Smith*, 551 F. Supp. 32 (SD 1982).

Colorado The Board of County Commissioners negotiated with property owner to obtain office space. When a price could not be agreed upon, the board filed a petition to condemn the building. The board argued that the county had a duty to provide offices for county officials, and the power to acquire property to effectuate this public purpose must be implied by necessity. *Held:* Dismissal of petition affirmed. The power of eminent domain is vested in the state, and may not be exercised by a governmental subdivision unless the power has been delegated by the legislature to the local authority. Historically, the courts have been reluctant to allow condemnation of private property where the authority to do so is not expressly implied by statute. Here, the legislature must have intended that counties obtain property for office space through the real estate marketplace. *Board of County Comm'rs v. Intermountain Rural Elec. Ass'n*, 655 P2d 831 (1982) (en banc).

Colorado Plaintiff held oil and gas leaseholds that lacked access to a public road. Plaintiff filed a condemnation petition seeking an easement of necessity across defendant's property. *Held:* Plaintiff did not have a cause of action because the Colorado constitutional and statutory condemnation provisions allowed only owners of a fee interest to seek condemnation. The provisions were construed against lessees to protect the owners of adjacent servient estates from repeated condemnation litigation each time an estate changed hands. In contrast, a taking by a fee owner was permanent. Even if lessees were permitted to seek condemnation, plaintiff could not do so, because a property owner could not create the necessity for an easement across the property of a third party by subdividing its land into "landlocked" leaseholds. *Coquina Oil Corp. v. Harry Kourlis Ranch*, 643 P2d 519 (1982).

Connecticut In February 1974, the local planning commission rejected plaintiff's plans for subdividing seven acres of its property. At the same time, it was considering a redevelopment plan for the town, which became effective in December 1974. The plan resulted in a revision of subdivision regulations and the condemnation of part of plaintiff's seven acres for the purpose of extending Lindeman Drive. So, when plaintiff resubmitted the same subdivision plan for its seven acres in April 1976, it was rejected. Plaintiff sued for subdivision approval, contending that the planning commission's actions constituted a taking without due process or just compensation. *Held:* Because the planning commission's actions were shown to be reasonable and impartial, their actions did not constitute a taking without due process of law or just compensation. The planning commission was authorized by state and municipal law to take all reasonable steps necessary to the implementation of the redevelopment plan, because such plan was designed to protect the health, safety, and welfare of inhabitants of the town. *Raybestos-Manhattan, Inc. v. Planning & Zoning Comm'r*, 442 A2d 65 (1982).

Florida Plaintiff purchased 6,500 acres of wetlands on which it planned to develop a new community with dwelling units, commercial centers, and recreational facilities. The county commissioners rejected plaintiff's plan on the ground that it would cause ecological damage to the local waters in violation of Florida wetlands regulations. Plaintiff brought suit seeking damages from the Florida Land and Water Adjudicatory Commission for what plaintiff alleged to be an uncompensated taking of its property. *Held:* The court found a valid exercise of police power and not a taking requiring compensation for the party whose private property had been encroached upon. It invoked the principle that a regulation serving to prevent a public harm rather than serving to grant the public a benefit was more likely to be an exercise of police power. The court then said that an act to prevent public harm could be deemed a taking if it rendered owner's property worthless; and since plaintiff knew what it was getting into, the commission's act did not amount to rendering the property worthless. *Graham v. Estuary Properties, Inc.*, 399 So. 2d 1374 (1981), cert. denied, 454 US 1083 (1982).

Georgia Public subway authority constructed a commuter line under defendants' condominium property. The resulting vibrations caused severe structural cracking in the building. When efforts to correct the problem proved unsatisfactory, the subway authority instituted a condemnation action to obtain a noise and vibration easement. *Held:* Eminent domain is not available where the condemning authority seeks only to damage the property and not to take an interest in it. The term "damage" as used in the statute refers to the type of compensable injury and does not authorize the state to buy a right to damage property. The court dismissed the case to await further action by defendants when the nature and extent of their injuries had been fully ascertained. *Metropolitan Atlanta Reg. Trans. Auth. v. Trussell*, 273 SE2d 859 (1981).

Iowa The city began condemnation proceedings to acquire an easement to build a waterway for surface drainage over the Thompson's property. The city identified a permanent easement, as well as a temporary easement for construction and maintenance of the waterway. The Thompsons challenged the city's authority to condemn a temporary easement over their property. *Held:* The city had authority to condemn permanent and temporary easements to build and maintain a waterway for surface drainage. The Thompsons had failed to prove the city acted illegally in taking the temporary easement. Iowa Code § 471.4 confers on cities the right to take private property for public use if the use is reasonable and necessary. The general rule is that where an easement is sufficient to satisfy the purpose of the taking, no greater interest than easement is presumed to be taken. Damages could be determined because the easements were clearly described and their purpose clearly stated. *Thompson v. City of Osage*, 421 NW2d 529 (1988).

Maine The Maine Land Use Regulation Commission, defendant, restricted plaintiff, owner of a large tract of timberland, from harvesting timber on approximately two thirds of the land. Plaintiff could apply for additional cutting rights in the future to avoid economic loss due to deterioration of trees. Plaintiff sought review, arguing its property had been taken without just compensation. *Held:* No "taking" had occurred. To be a taking, a regulatory scheme must extinguish a fundamental right of ownership that would render the property substantially useless. As to plaintiff's argument that the land's profitabilty had been reduced to zero, the court noted that the expectation of future profits may be considered in taking cases only to the extent it affects present market value. In light of the temporary and limited nature of the restrictions, plaintiff did not demonstrate that its land had been rendered useless. *Seven Islands Land Co. v. Maine Land Use Regulation Comm'n*, 450 A2d 475 (1982).

Maryland A landowner applied to the Maryland-National Capital Park and Planning Commission for approval of his preliminary plan to subdivide 104 acres. The commission denied the request and, in accordance with a county ordinance, placed the property in reservation for public use for up to three years. The ordinance further prohibited the use of such reserved land without written approval of the commission's planning board. Landowner filed suit, seeking the issuance of a writ of mandamus directing the commission to approve the subdivision plan and for a declaratory judgment that "reserving" the land without consent of the owner unconstitutionally deprived him of the use of his property without just compensation. The trial court ruled for the landowner, and the commission appealed. *Held:* Affirmed. The commission's actions reserving the property for up to three years without permitting any reasonable use thereof constituted a taking, and since no compensatory payment was made, the reservation was unconstitutional and null and void. The commission was required to approve the preliminary plan. *Maryland-Nat'l Capital Park & Planning Comm'n v. Chadwick*, 405 A2d 241 (1979).

Minnesota In a condemnation proceeding initiated by a municipality to acquire land for highway use, a state-sanctioned regional waste disposal authority intervened to assert its equitable interest in the subject properties. The waste authority showed that it had exercised options to purchase the property for use in its disposal operations. *Held:* The waste authority had acquired an equitable interest in the land and was thus a proper party to the action. By operation of such interest, the land is no longer private property in the strict sense. Accordingly, the municipality cannot proceed with condemnation since it has no statutory authority to exercise eminent domain over public property. *In re Shakopee*, 295 NW2d 495 (1980).

Pennsylvania Mazzaro acquired title to a tract of land from Cosgrove Coal, which reserved all mineral rights. The county later condemned the land "in fee simple" for an airport, and a condemnation award was issued to Mazzaro. Cosgrove Coal was not notified of the proceeding, and the award did not mention mineral rights. Cosgrove Coal subsequently conveyed its mineral rights under the tract to Mazzaro. Fifteen years later, the county began improvements to the tract. Mazzaro's estate learned that coal had been removed from the tract and sued in trespass. *Held:* The question presented was what was meant by condemnation "in fee simple." In Pennsylvania, three separate estates in land can be held in fee simple: surface, mineral rights, and right of support. Absent evidence the court knew of a separate mineral estate, the condemnation in fee simple for airport purposes must have been intended to condemn all estates in land. The case was remanded to determine if notice requirements to Cosgrove Coal were satisfied. *Captline v. County of Allegheny*, 459 A2d 1298 (Commw. Ct. 1983), cert. denied, 466 US 904 (1984).

South Carolina The city of Columbia, as part of its downtown development project, removed the sidewalks and support adjoining plaintiff's store building and excavated trenches to the basement for the purpose of installing and relocating water meters and pipes. Heavy rains that evening and resulting floods filled the excavations, which were not backfilled, and entered plaintiff's basement. Plantiff alleged the floodwater caused extensive damage to the basement and to the merchandise stored there. The city's demurrer to plaintiff's complaint was sustained, the court ruling that plaintiff had failed to allege an affirmative, positive, aggressive act on the part of the city and also had failed to show a taking with some degree of permanence. *Held:* On appeal the case was reversed. The removal of the sidewalk and building support in the course of the redevelopment project constituted an affirmative, positive, aggressive act by the city. Also, destruction of personal property and damage to the structure were "of a permanent nature," sufficient to preclude a demurrer. *Berry's On Main, Inc. v. City of Columbia*, 281 SE2d 796 (1981).

Utah Plaintiff commenced an action to condemn certain outdoor advertising signs owned by defendants pursuant to the Utah Highway Beautification Act. The Department of Transporation received permission to take immediate occupancy of the property. The judge granting the request did not give any reason as the basis for his decision other than the state's right, under its power of eminent domain, to take immediate occupancy of property it condemned. Defendants appealed, claiming that the court erred because it did not base its decision to grant immediate occupancy on the prerequisites set down by Utah law; namely, that immediate occupancy is granted only after an evidentiary hearing before the court to determine the value of the property condemned, the damages resulting from the immediate occupancy of the property, and the pertinent reasons for requiring the speedy occupancy of the premises. *Held:* The trial court erred by not holding an evidentiary hearing on the issue of immediate occupancy and by basing its memorandum decision solely on the notion of the state's right to immediate occupancy. *Utah Dept. of Transp. v. Hatch*, 613 P2d 764 (1980).

99.15 Necessity for Valid Public Purpose

U.S. Supreme Court The Land Reform Act was enacted in 1967 to prevent concentration of land ownership by a few people. The act permitted the Hawaii Housing Authority to hold a hearing to determine whether acquisition of property by residential tenants accomplishes the purposes of the act. If so, the housing authority could acquire the property by negotiation or condemnation, and would then sell the land to tenants. Plaintiff landlords refused to participate in negotiations or compulsory arbitration to set acquisition prices for their lands, challenging the constitutionality of the act. *Held:* The aim of the act, to prevent concentrated ownership of land in Hawaii, was a legitimate public purpose. This purpose could be accomplished by use of police power, via eminent domain. The legislature's approach to solving the land oligopoly problem was rational. *Hawaii Hous. Auth. v. Midkiff*, 467 US 229 (1984).

Georgia The city brought condemnation proceedings, seeking to obtain a right-of-way to build an underground passageway linking a banking operations center to a commuter train station across the street from the bank center. The condemnees challenged the action, claiming that it served only the private purpose of the bank. *Held:* There was evidence that many of the banking center's 1,500 employees would use the train station and that the absence of the passageway would cause them to cross the street against traffic. The avoidance of the congestion caused by such crossings was a sufficient public purpose to remove the actions of the city from the category of bad faith. *City of Atlanta v. Petkas*, 321 SE2d 725 (1984).

Idaho Plaintiff, a water and sewer district, commenced a project to rehabilitate the city sewer system. Respondents owned unincorporated land over which new sewer lines were to pass. After failing to obtain easements over respondents' land through negotiation, plaintiff instituted a condemnation action. The trial court denied the motion for possession based on Idaho Code § 7-701, which it held implied a legislative intent to exclude unincorporated areas. *Held:* The trial court's reading of Section 7-701 was too narrow, and contradicted language in the Idaho constitution authorizing the state to make any use of private land necessary for preservation of the health of state residents. Further, the broad language of Section 7-701(2), which authorized "all other public uses for the benefit of the state or of any county, incorporated city or inhabitants thereof," indicated an intent to include public uses not enumerated. Therefore, plaintiff's proposed use of respondents' land was public within the meaning of the statute and authorized under the state constitution. *Payette Lakes Water & Sewer Dist. v. Hays*, 653 P2d 438 (1982).

Kentucky The Bureau of Highways condemned a strip of land belonging to the Knieriems in order to widen Interstate 65. The strip of land had an easement running to adjoining land owned by the Bluegrass Saddle Club. To avoid landlocking Bluegrass, the Commonwealth condemned a contiguous second strip of the Knieriems' land as part of a plan to replace the easement to Bluegrass that had been destroyed in the taking of the first strip, but the Knieriems objected. The trial court found that the second strip of land was taken for Bluegrass's private use and stated that eminent domain can be exercised only where the property is taken for a public use. On appeal, the Commonwealth argued that they should be allowed to condemn land in order to provide access to property landlocked by proposed highway construction. *Held:* Affirmed. The court found that the Commonwealth condemned property over which it would not maintain control but that it would transfer to a private interest. The taking of private property for a private use is unconstitutional. *Commonwealth of Ky. v. Knieriem*, 707 SW2d 340 (1986).

Minnesota The city determined that a deteriorating area of the city would be suitable for a paper mill and spent a number of years seeking a company interested in building the mill. The search was finally successful, and the city council passed a resolution creating a 156-acre development district, 92 acres of which were to be used for the mill. Plaintiff's land was then condemned, and plaintiffs appealed, arguing that the taking was not for public use. *Held:* The taking was justified. The mill was expected to provide employment in an economically distressed area and would revitalize an area that was previously inadequate for development because of a deteriorating and obsolete infrastructure. These are public purposes, and therefore met the "public use" standard, even though the land was to be turned over to a private entity. *City of Duluth v. State*, 390 NW2d 757 (1986).

Nebraska Landowner, who had sued unsuccessfully for the right to flow water over a neighboring irrigation district, formed his own irrigation district, which moved to condemn the neighboring district's land. He formed the irrigation district by transferring land, without consideration, to relatives who would form the board of the new irrigation district. Landowner acknowledged that his purpose in forming the new irrigation district was to exercise the power of eminent domain for his own benefit. A Nebraska statute provided that land necessarily taken to benefit an irrigation district is taken for a public use (Neb. Rev. Stat. § 46-128). *Held:* The new irrigation district's condemnation proceeding was dismissed on the ground that it was an attempt to obtain private property against the will of the owners for a private purpose under the guise of an exercise of the power of eminent domain. Substance, rather than form, was controlling. A private use is not converted into a public one merely because a number of individuals band together to do what a single individual could not. *Chimney Rock Irrigation Dist. v. Fawcus Springs Irrigation Dist.*, 359 NW2d 100 (1984).

New Mexico Under a contract of sale with the state, defendants purchased forty acres of land, which the local school district sought to condemn for the construction of a new school. Defendants objected to the taking of the land. The trial court found in favor of defendants and condemned only 15 acres. The school board appealed, claiming that it needed all 40 acres of land and that the court could not condemn only a portion of land under contract for sale by the state. *Held:* The trial court was affirmed. A condemnor may take no greater interest than is reasonably necessary for the contemplated public use. A court may approve the condemnation of land even though it involves less than the entire tract held by third parties under contract with the state. *Hobbs Mun. School Dist. v. Knowles Dev. Co.*, 606 P2d 541 (1980).

Washington The city approved an ordinance adopting a project to improve a block consisting of several retail stores and the terminal of a passenger monorail. The project was one of many in the city designed to forestall the decay experienced in retail areas. Petitioners, owners of property that the city was planning to condemn under the ordinance, brought suit to block the project on the ground that the city's eminent domain power could not be exercised to promote private retail business. Their claim was based on a provision of the Washington Constitution proscribing the taking of private property for private use. The city contended that the taking would be for a public use because the public would benefit from the improvement of a business district. *Held:* The court conceded that the project would serve public interest, but held that public interest was not tantamount to public use. It held the project to be strictly private and noted the absence of statutory authority for the city to involve itself in a retail shopping center. The court rejected the city's view of the project as basically a public one with the retail uses merely incidental to the public uses. *Petition of Seattle*, 638 P2d 549 (1981).

99.20
Repurchase Right

Florida Upon abandonment of the Cross-Florida Barge Canal project, property owners sought to reacquire lands taken from them in condemnation proceedings. Property owners claimed that the canal authority had represented to them that the value of their remaining lands would be enhanced by the canal project and that because the project was abandoned the consideration for the conveyance to the canal authority had failed. *Held:* The canal authority was not required to reconvey land to which it had acquired in fee simple title. Once land has been acquired in fee simple for public use, the former property owner retains no interest in the land. The public use can be abandoned or the land devoted to a different use without impairment of title, absent fraud or bad faith at the time of conveyance. Under Florida law, enhancement to remaining lands can be used by a condemning authority only to offset severance damages to remaining land. Property owners had not, however, offered any evidence that they were entitled to severance damages. *Mainer v. Canal Auth. of State*, 467 So. 2d 989 (1985).

Massachusetts The city entered into eminent domain proceedings pursuant to the Riverfront Urban Renewal Project. The renewal plan envisioned a park, a parcel designated for educational and recreational use, which Emerson College agreed to purchase from the redevelopment authority. Plaintiffs commenced actions seeking to enjoin the taking of their land claiming, among other things, that the taking was void owing to the bad faith of local authorities in providing a private college with a favorable location on advantageous terms. *Held:* Local authorities did not act in bad faith, because the proposed taking benefited a private college. A taking pursuant to a valid development plan is not void merely because disposition of the land indirectly benefits private individuals, especially if disposition to private redeveloper may be necessary to achieve the public purpose. In this case, the project had a valid public purpose since substantial evidence supported a finding that the predominant motive behind the project was the elimination of a blighted open area. Any benefit to the redeveloper was incidental to the main purpose of the plan and did not warrant a finding that local authorities acted in bad faith. *Lodge No. 65 v. Planning Bd.*, 531 NE2d 1233 (1988).

New York The city condemned owner's property with the purpose of building a new courthouse. The courthouse was never constructed; instead, the city attempted to lease the property to private tenants. Owner sued to prohibit the city from leasing the property, claiming it had the right of first refusal to purchase the property under state law. State law provides that the condemning authority may not dispose of the property without providing the former fee owner the right of first refusal if the condemned property had not been "materially improved" and is abandoned for the project with which it was acquired. *Held:* Attempts by the city to lease the condemned property were not a "disposition" that triggered operation of the statute. The term "dispose of" used in the statute referred only to a sale or transfer of title to the property to a private party, and not to a short-term lease. Since the purpose of the statute is to give a former owner a right of first refusal to purchase property, that remedy would be disproportionate if it were triggered by an effort by the condemning authority to enter into a short-term lease. *Mary Chamberlain Trust v. Litke*, 534 NE2d 33 (1988).

South Carolina The city acquired a building under threat of condemnation for the purpose of widening a street. Subsequently, the city, encountering financial problems, changed its plan to widen the street, and instead decided to transfer the building to a private developer. Original owners of the building sought and were granted an injunction ordering the city to reconvey the property for the original purchase price. *Held:* For the city. South Carolina adheres to the common-law rule that there is no reversion when a fee simple is acquired by purchase on eminent domain and the original use is abandoned. The subsequent abandonment of the original purpose for which the property was taken did not affect the validity of the condemnation. The validity of title was determined by the conditions existing at the time of the taking. The court was not willing to place a cloud on the title of property obtained through eminent domain by creating an equitable right of repurchase. *Indigo Realty Co. v. City of Charleston*, 314 SE2d 601 (1984).

99.25
Procedural Matters

1st Circuit Landowner sued to challenge the state's condemnation procedure under which a pro tanto payment is offered to the condemnee pending the outcome of judicial proceedings that finally determine the amount of damages in the event the state's offer is rejected. He claimed that a landowner should be entitled to a judicial determination of fair value before losing possession of his land.

Held: The taking of property for public use by a state need not be accompanied or preceded by payment. The requirement of just compensation is satisified when the public faith and credit are pledged to a reasonably prompt ascertainment and payment and when there is adequate provision for enforcing the pledge. Statutes requiring a pro tanto payment after the taking are constitutional. Such payment need not be equal to the fair value of the property, but, rather, must not be so low as to cause substantial and irreparable injury. *Vazza v. Campbell*, 520 F2d 848 (1975).

5th Circuit Plaintiffs claimed title to property in front of their home solely by virtue of adverse possession. The town claimed an easement by prescription in the disputed strip of land. With knowledge of plaintiffs' claim but without attempting to determine or settle the competing claims, the town knocked down fences plaintiffs had constructed around the strip and built a road. Plaintiffs sued the town under 28 USC § § 1331 and 1343 and 42 USC § 1983 for damages, for taking property without due process of law. *Held:* Judgment reversed because of an erroneous jury charge. On the merits of the case, the court found that, despite a clear legal defense to plaintiffs' claim of adverse possession, plaintiffs had alleged a significant property interest in the land sufficient to entitle them to a hearing. The town's failure to grant such a hearing was an actionable wrong independent of the uncompensated taking in that it denied plaintiffs due process of law. *McCulloch v. Glasgow*, 620 F2d 47 (1980).

8th Circuit Out-of-state property owner was never personally notified of the condemnation of his property by the United States, owing to a mistaken belief by the government that he only held certain mineral interests within the tract condemned. On learning of the condemnation 19 years later, the condemnee brought an action pursuant to the Quiet Title Act, claiming that the apparent acquisition of title by the government was void because he never received notice of the taking. *Held:* Following the holding of the majority in *Fulcher v. United States*, 632 F2d 278 (4th Cir. 1980) (en banc), the Eighth Circuit held that once the government filed the declaration of taking and deposited estimated compensation pursuant to the Declaration of Taking Act, it acquired indefeasible title to condemnee's property, subject to the equitable interest in condemnee to receive just compensation. An unnotified condemnee does not retain title but does retain an equitable lien on the land sufficient to give him a disputed property interest under the Quiet Title Act. The condemnee was entitled to the fair market value of the property as of the date of taking, with interest as compensation. *United States v. Herring*, 750 F2d 669 (1984).

Maryland Property owners sued the state highway administration for extending a highway in such a manner that their access was cut off when the property flooded. The property owners alleged that the highway administration was aware that their land was regularly flooded and testified that they received assurances that access would not be cut off. The lower court dismissed the complaint for failure to state a cause of action, since the flooding was temporary and resulted from acts of God. *Held:* Where the complaint alleged arbitrary and capricious acts by the highway administration, it was sufficient to state a cause of action. The property owners were entitled to a determination of their allegations that the administration was aware of the flooding, made assurances, and reneged on them. *Zion Evangelical Lutheran Church v. State Highway Administration*, 350 A2d 125 (1976).

Oklahoma State highway department sued to condemn property leased by a drive-in food service. The major elements of damages were the loss of access to the expressway and the inconvenience of the new access. The state witness set the total damages at $15,000 but did not consider the loss of access. Owner's witnesses appraised the damages at from $91,000 to $108,000. The jury verdict was $45,000. Owner and lessee filed motions for a new trial, which were granted. The state appealed the order granting a new trial. *Held:* Since an order granting a new trial only restores the parties to their positions before the trial, the trial court could not be said to have abused its discretion in sustaining the motion. The motions were correctly granted where there was some question as to the effect of the testimony of the state's witness on the jury. *State ex rel Department of Highways v. Owen*, 548 P2d 212 (1976).

Pennsylvania Plaintiff bought a property at a tax sale. When the taxpayer did not redeem the property within a year, the deed was delivered to plaintiff and recorded. Meanwhile, city inspectors noted building code violations at the property and, prior to the conveyance, decided to condemn the building. Notice of condemnation was sent to the former owner. Shortly after the city transferred title to plaintiff, the building was demolished. The inspection bureau was routinely advised of properties that had been sold for taxes. Plaintiff sued for negligent demolition, claiming he should have been personally notified of the condemnation. Plaintiff argued he acquired a legally protected interest when he bought the property at the tax sale. *Held:* For plaintiff. Plaintiff was likened to a private purchaser to whom the doctrine of equitable conversion applied. A private purchaser of realty is deemed the owner for all beneficial purposes even before closing. Equitable conversion principles were equally applicable to tax sales. The purchaser at a tax sale can enforce his ownership rights, including the right not to have his property interest divested by government action without notice. *Pivorotto v. City of Pittsburgh*, 528 A2d 125 (1987).

Rhode Island Landowner sued to challenge the validity of a redevelopment plan when his property was taken, on the ground that he did not receive sufficient notice. Hearings on the proposed project were held after notice was published in several newspapers, but no individual notice was provided to area residents. *Held:* There is no right to a hearing prior to the taking of property by eminent domain. Where the hearings are for the purpose of determining legislative facts relating to the proposed project and not for the purpose of adjudicating the rights in the property under consideration, notice to each person affected is not required. *Paiva v. Providence Redev. Agency*, 356 A2d 203 (1976).

Virginia Condemnor appealed a commissioner's award of $5,000, alleging that it was arbitrary and capricious. The condemnor's appraiser evaluated the land taken to be worth $575 and estimated no damage to the residue in excess of the enhancement. The condemnee's witness placed the value of the land at $434 and the damage resulting from the condemnation at $2,500. *Held:* The commissioners are required to consider both the evidence offered at the condemnation hearing and their own evaluation of the site upon viewing. The award bore a reasonable relationship to the testimonial evidence. The condemnee's witness testifed that the taking reduced the land to a nonconforming lot size, violated the 60-foot setback, and might provide nuisance road traffic. Other property in the vicinity had been sold for sums comparable to the award. This testimony, coupled with the commissioner's view, did not make the decision capricious. *State Highway Comm'r v. Foster*, 222 SE2d 780 (1976).

99.30
—Parties

3d Circuit Plaintiff succeeded by intestacy to his father's real property, which then became the subject of condemnation proceedings. The district court appointed three commissioners to value the land. The commissioners accepted the government's valuation of the property and did not allow plaintiff to participate in the hearing. Plaintiff's motion for relief was denied by the district court, with the explanation that plaintiff could not participate in the hearing unless he appeared as the legal representative of the estate, as an adjudicated heir of decedent, or as an attorney for any other adjudicated heir. Plaintiff, who did not appear in any of those capacities, appealed. *Held:* Reversed. Both Federal Rule of Civil Procedure 71A and Virgin Islands law gave plaintiff the right to participate in the valuation proceedings, even though his status was that of a putative heir. A contrary reading of the laws would lead to a manifestly unjust result, for those who have the greatest stake in the determination of a property's value would be barred from protecting their interest by the mere fortuity that the condemnation coincided with an intestate succession. *Government of the VI v. Certain Parcels of Land*, 713 F2d 53 (1983).

7th Circuit When the government condemned two tracts of land, each legally held in the names of many different members of the same family, it failed to name each owner in the pleadings. Owners sued to vacate the condemnation proceeding on the ground that the unnamed owners were indispensable parties. *Held:* Since an eminent domain proceeding is in rem, there are no indispensable parties. The failure to name all the owners did not defeat condemnor's title or owners' right to compensation. *United States v. 416.81 Acres of Land*, 525 F2d 450 (1975).

Colorado When a city instituted a condemnation proceeding against a mutual ditch corporation, stockholders petitioned to intervene in the action. *Held:* The right of the corporation to hold title to the water rights and other property and to manage the affairs of the corporation is independent from the right of the shareholders who have the benefit of use of the water for their lands. The water rights of the shareholders of the corporation constituted a specific property right to use the water. Thus, the corporation was not a trustee of the water rights, but, rather, the shareholders were the real parties in interest and were indispensable parties to the proceeding. *Jacobucci v. District Court*, 541 P2d 667 (1975).

99.35
Immediate Title

Alaska An Alaska statute authorized "quick-take" condemnation, in which title passed upon the filing of a declaration of taking and issues such as the necessity for a taking and fair market value were left for later determination. The condemning authority was required to declare that the property was taken by necessity for the public good. If this proved to be untrue, the court was empowered to divest the condemnor of title or possession. Case law required individual consideration of the private injury a public project would cause each private landholder. In this case, Ship Creek Hydraulic Syndicate petitioned the court to set aside the "quick taking" of its property for a highway project. On appeal, the issue was whether condemning authorities should be required to summarize their decisions in a "decisional document." *Held:* The court had the power to require decisional documents, and this would not prove unduly burdensome to condemning authorities. However, in this case, the court declined to require the Department of Transportation to issue such a document, because it would inevitably express post-taking rationalizations. Since a decisional document was most useful if it separated an agency's reasons for making a decision from the legal arguments it later advanced to justify it, the court would require such a document only for declarations of taking filed after this opinion. *Ship Creek Hydraulic Syndicate v. State of Alaska*, 685 P2d 715 (1984).

California The city filed a complaint seeking to condemn a portion of defendant landowner's property. On the same date, the city invoked the "quick-take" provision, which permits a condemning agency to take possession prior to trial and judgment by filing an ex parte application. Landowners objected to the order and disagreed with the city's request for immediate possession due to necessity. The city was granted immediate possession under the provision, and landowners filed notice of appeal. *Held:* Appeal dismissed. An order of immediate possession entered pursuant to the "quick-take" provision of eminent domain law is not appealable. Landowners had several prior opportunities to challenge the order but failed to do so. *City of Morgan Hill v. Albuti*, 260 Cal. Rptr. 42 (1989).

99.40
What Constitutes Condemnation

U.S. Supreme Court Coal mining that causes subsidence to public buildings and dwellings is prohibited by Pennsylvania's Bituminous Mine Subsidence and Land Conservation Act. Regulations required that 50 percent of the coal beneath protected structures remain in place to provide surface support. Owners of coal reserves sued, alleging the act and regulations violated the Fifth Amendment takings clause and the contracts clause. *Held:* The Act did not effect a taking. There was no evidence that plaintiffs' mines had become unprofitable since the act was passed. Although plaintiffs claimed the coal they would have to leave in the ground had been appropriated, this estimated 2 percent of their interests did not constitute a separate segment of property for taking purposes; and there was no showing that plaintiffs' reasonable investment-backed expectations had been materially affected. To the extent the act did impair miners' contracts with surface owners, it was a legitimate exercise of the police power, since the act served legitimate public interests in health and environment by minimizing damage to surface areas. *Keystone Bituminous Coal Ass'n v. DeBenedictis*, 480 US 470 (1987).

2d Circuit A city ordinance governing single-room-occupancy buildings (SROs) required certification that no harassment of tenants had occurred in three years preceding application for permits for renovation or demolition. A waiver of the certificate requirement could be granted for SROs purchased under contracts entered into and recorded before the date the bill was approved. Appellants, owners of two vacant SROs, allegedly entered into a contract to purchase the SROs before the cutoff date but did not record the contract. They sought a preliminary injunction against enforcement of the recordation requirement, contending that the law effected a taking without just compensation. *Held:* The law was a valid exercise of the city's police powers. The recordation requirement was designed to avoid collusive backdating of contracts and was not arbitrary or capricious. Among the significant factors in deciding whether there had been a taking were (1) economic impact of the regulation and the extent to which it interfered with investment-backed expectations and (2) the character of the governmental action. As to the economic factor, prohibition of the most profitable or beneficial use would not necessitate a finding that a taking had occurred. Nor was financial hardship to appellants dispositive on the taking issue. With respect to interference with investment-backed expectations, the investors knew at closing there would be obstacles to developing the property. *Sadowsky v. City of New York*, 732 F2d 312 (1984).

6th Circuit A bank was the successor in interest to developers of a tract of land, which it acquired through foreclosure. After acquiring the property, the bank submitted preliminary plans for development of the land by building 476 dwelling units, which plans the planning commission disapproved. The bank sued the planning commission, claiming a taking of property without just compensation. *Held:* A taking had occurred, and the jury's award of $350,000 damages was upheld. Expert testimony established that if the commission's objections were allowed to determine development, only 67 sites could be sold and the net loss would be $1 million. The evidence supported a finding that the property had no remaining economically viable use. The court utilized the standard of "interference with investment-backed expectations" outlined in *Loretto v. Teleprompter Manhattan CATV Corp.*, 458 US 419 (1982). The bank had a reasonable expectation that development could be completed, in light of evidence that the commission had approved preliminary plats with the knowledge that a total of 736 units was intended. This was the developers' expectation concerning use of the land, and was backed by considerable investment. *Hamilton Bank v. Williamson County Regional Planning Comm'n*, 729 F2d 402 (1984), rev'd on other grounds, 473 US 172 (1985).

9th Circuit Developer owned tracts of land in the city that contained geothermal wells. On one tract, developer planned to build an apartment complex that would be heated by a geothermal well. Developer sought zoning variances and the vacation of certain platted streets. The city required the dedication of a certain 20-foot strip of developer's property, because fee ownership would give the city rights to the geothermal wells on the tract. Developer refused to convey the property, and the city denied the street vacation. Developer sued, claiming the city required it to choose between street vacation and its right to just compensation for its geothermal wells. The city was granted summary judgment. *Held:* Reversed and remanded. The issue was whether the condition imposed by the city was rationally related to the benefit sought by developer. Developer had offered to pay the city for the vacated streets, and the record suggested that the city was using its power to withhold street vacation to compel developer to dedicate the property for little or no compensation. No rational relationship existed between this condition and the act of street vacation. The city's actions therefore constituted a taking of developer's property without just compensation. *Parks v. Watson*, 716 F2d 646 (1983).

Illinois Builders sought to construct two office buildings on property adjacent to a village. The village sued to enjoin issuance of a county building permit, alleging that the neighboring county's zoning ordinance permitting construction of buildings over 65 feet (like the proposed project) was invalid. Builders answered by filing suit alleging various state and federal causes of action. *Held:* For the county. The damage to private property for public use necessary to a state taking claim is any direct physical disturbance of a right an owner enjoys in connection with his property. The village's injunction action did not constitute a direct physical disturbance of builder's property. Interference with the right to develop property did not constitute damage justifying compensation. Any hardship plaintiffs suffered in this case was due to their own decision to postpone construction during pendency of the village's challenge of the county zoning ordinance and was not due to the village's own zoning laws. Builders' failure to establish a state taking claim precluded a federal taking claim. *Equity Assocs. v. Village of Northbrook*, 524 NE2d 1119 (Ct. App. 1988).

Indiana Landowner's property, which was currently used as farmland, sat atop a large quantity of coal. A small portion of the land contained archaeological deposits with substantial historic and scientific value. The Indiana Department of Natural Resources determined that the area was not suited for surface coal mining. Landowner argued that the department's order amounted to an unconstitutional taking. *Held:* There was no unconstitutional taking because (1) protecting the state's heritage through the preservation of archaeological sites was a legitimate government interest; (2) the department provided a mitigation plan by which the designation could be removed; (3) the land could still be farmed; (4) landowner could strip-mine virtually all the coal from its property; and (5) landowner could remove the coal under the archaeological site by means other than strip mining. *Department of Natural Resources v. Indiana Coal Council, Inc.*, 542 NE2d 1000 (1989).

Iowa The city, defendant, planned to acquire some of plaintiffs' land to create a "green belt." Defendant instituted three successive condemnation suits, but dropped each suit after receiving widely varying property valuations. Finally, defendant commenced condemnation proceedings to acquire an easement over plaintiffs' land. Plaintiff maintained that their land was as good as taken because no prospective purchaser would buy it. *Held:* Defendant's repeated initiation of condemnation suits substantially interfered with plaintiffs' use and enjoyment of their property. As a result of the continuous threat against the property, a public taking of private property had occurred. *Osborn v. City of Cedar Rapids*, 324 NW2d 471 (1982).

Louisiana Ferry service across the Intercoastal Waterway had been discontinued by the Police Jury. Owners of property south of the waterway were greatly inconvenienced and sued to enjoin the Police Jury from discontinuing the service. *Held:* Discontinuance of ferry service did not result in taking of any property. Even though termination of ferry service made the use of the southern portion of the road inconvenient, discontinuance of service did not prevent the road's use or show an intent by the jury to abandon the roadway leading to and from the Intercoastal Waterway. *Odom v. Calcasieu Parish Police Jury*, 540 So. 2d 560 (Ct. App. 1989).

Maine In November 1987, the city approved an order to take plaintiff's property. The city recorded a certificate with the Registry of Deeds in late November and delivered an award check to plaintiff in December. In mid-February, plaintiff appealed the compensation award. He argued that the 60-day statutory period for appeal of the award had not lapsed, since the taking did not occur until he received the check. The city argued that taking occured when the condemnation order was filed. *Held:* For the city. The statutory period to appeal a compensation award begins when title passes. Title passes upon service of the condemnation order, award of the compensation check, or upon proper recordation, whichever comes first, regardless of whether the owner had actual notice of the taking. *Luce v. City of Portland*, 556 A2d 656 (1989).

New Jersey The Department of Environmental Protection (DEP) issued a permit to construct an apartment complex in a coastal area with a fair share housing condition of 10 percent low-income and 10 percent moderate-income housing. DEP asserted authority to impose such a condition under the state's Coastal Area Facility Review Act (CAFRA). Developer contended that CAFRA was a purely environmental statute that could not be used to achieve fair housing goals. *Held:* DEP had the authority under CAFRA to impose fair share housing conditions to create housing for the poor. Although CAFRA's primary purpose is to protect coastal areas, it is also designed to ensure that coastal areas be dedicated to uses in furtherance of public health, safety, and welfare. The percentage requirements were not arbitrary or unreasonable. Nor was the fair share housing condition an unconstitutional taking; there was no evidence that the condition would prevent developer from realizing a reasonable rate of return. *In re Egg Harbor Assocs. (Bayshore Center)*, 464 A2d 1115 (1983).

New York After operator of a nursing home died, executors of his estate determined that the nursing home was unprofitable and attempted to close it. The state brought an action to enjoin the closing and a receiver was appointed to manage the nursing home until alternative arrangements could be made for continued patient care. Executors argued that this amounted to a taking of their property without compensation. *Held:* The prevention of the precipitous closing of the nursing home in contravention of state regulations did not constitute a taking of property. Executors' investment-backed expectations were not affected when regulations existed preventing a nursing home from immediately discontinuing services. In any event, executors could recover their investment by selling the nursing home later. Although the state could not force executors to operate the nursing home at a loss indefinitely, there was no evidence in this case that state unreasonably delayed the closing. *Birnbaum v. State*, 541 NE2d 23 (1989).

99.45 Federal Preemption of State Condemnation Law

U.S. Supreme Court Chicago and Northwestern Transportation Company (Company) filed an application with the Interstate Commerce Commission for permission to abandon a 44-mile rail line. Shippers in Minnesota opposed abandonment of a segment of the line. After administrative proceedings pursuant to the Staggers Rail Act, the commission issued a certificate of abandonment. The shippers then formed the Hayfield Northern Railroad Company (Hayfield), appellant in this case. Hayfield planned to use the eminent domain authority vested in it by Minn. Stat. § 227.27 to condemn the segment that appellee had abandoned. Hayfield obtained a temporary restraining order preventing the company from removing track from the Hayfield segment. The Company sued in federal court, alleging that the Staggers Rail Act preempted the Minnesota condemnation statute. *Held:* For Hayfield. Condemnation under Minn. Stat. § 227.27 was not preempted by the Staggers Rail Act. Moreover, the commission's jurisdiction ended once the abandonment was authorized, and the subsequent disposition of railroad property was subject to state law. *Hayfield N. Ry. v. Chicago & NW Transp. Co.*, 467 US 622 (1984).

2d Circuit When the railroad discontinued service, owners of adjacent property claimed a reversionary interest in the right-of-way under Vermont law. The state and railway sought a class exemption under federal statute, which would allow unused railroad rights-of-way to become recreational trails and prevent a reversionary interest from vesting in adjacent owners. The Interstate Commerce Commission granted the exemption allowing the railway to discontinue service, approved use of the line for recreation, and dismissed landowners' petition for a certificate of abandonment. Landowners challenged the constitutionality of the federal statute. *Held:* Petition denied. The purposes of the statute, to preserve corridors for future railroad use and to permit public recreational use of trails, are legitimate Congressional goals under the commerce clause; and the law was a reasonable means of achieving these goals. There was no taking without compensation. State law usually determines the interest of a property owner whose land is subject to a railroad right-of-way. However, under the commission's authority to regulate railroad abandonments, the property is subject to the commission's jurisdiction until the commission issues a certificate of abandonment. *Preseault v. Interstate Commerce Comm'n*, 853 F2d 145 (1988).

99.50 Reversionary Interests

8th Circuit Landowners owned property next to a railroad line that was no longer in use. The property was subject to easements or rights-of-way for railroad use. Landowners challenged as unconstitutional the National Trails System Act of 1968 (16 USC § 1247(d)), which preserved for possible future railroad use rights-of-way on lines not currently in service and allowed interim use of rail corridors as recreational trails. Landowners argued that, by operation of state law, once the rights-of-way were no longer used for rail purposes, they automatically dissolved. *Held:* Section 1247(d) violated neither the commerce nor the takings clauses. The statute, as part of a comprehensive federal scheme regulating railroads, was subject to the rational basis test for commerce clause analysis. Congress acted rationally in enacting the section; it elected to postpone railroad abandonment and encourage interim trail use to further its rail-banking purpose. Section 1247(d) also was not an unconstitutional taking of landowners' property without just compensation. Even if there was a taking of the landowners' reversionary interests in the rights-of-way, landowners had an available legal remedy under the Tucker Act in claims court so were not entitled to equitable relief. *Glosemeyer v. Missouri-Kansas-Texas RR*, 879 F2d 317 (1989).

New York New York City imposed a moratorium on the demolition or conversion of SROs. The law required that SRO owners rehabilitate and lease units at controlled rents for an indefinite period. Developers who owned SROs objected to the law. *Held:* The law was invalid as both a physical and regulatory taking. It imposed on SRO owners more than their just share of the societal obligation to house the homeless, not only prohibiting conduct but requiring that owners dedicate their property to a public purpose. The requirement that SRO owners rent their units constituted a physical taking because it compelled owners to subject their property to an undesired use. The city's argument that there was no taking because owners had some control over tenant selection and rental terms was rejected. It was the forced occupation by tenants, not their identity or lease tems, that deprived owners of their possessory interests. The law was invalid as a regulatory taking because it denied owners economically viable use of their property; and there was no clear relation between the law's restrictions and amelioration of the homeless crisis. *Seawall Assocs. v. City of New York*, 542 NE2d 1059 (1989).

Washington A state statute, Wash. Rev. Code § 64.04.190, declared that railroad properties on which railroad operations had ceased constituted "public utility and transportation corridors" if they were acquired by the state or a public utility and that such corridors retained their public use character as long as they were owned by a public agency or utility and were not subject to reversion on cessation of railroad operations. Owners claiming reversionary interests in an abandoned right-of-way that the county sought to use as a hiking and biking trail challenged the constitutionality of the statute, on the ground that it was an uncompensated taking. *Held:* The statute was unconstitutional because it allowed the county to acquire existing reversionary interests without payment. Although Washington common law allowed a railroad easement to be used for public transportation without a finding that the easement had been abandoned, recreational use was not consistent with the transportation purposes of the easement. *Lawson v. State*, 730 P2d 1308 (1986) (en banc).

100.00 JUST COMPENSATION

100.05 Precondemnation Awards

10th Circuit The U.S. government instituted eminent domain action to subordinate all oil, gas, and other mineral rights in four tracts of plaintiff's land to the government's right to flood the tracts as necessary for the construction or operation of a reservoir project. A federal court-appointed commission found no evidence that the government intended to plug the existing wells or that all producing reserves could not be recovered. The commission awarded plaintiffs nominal damages. *Held:* Affirmed. Plaintiffs could not collect damages for the plugging of their wells, as such plugging had not taken place and there was insufficient evidence that plugging would occur in the near future. If the government subsequently plugged the wells, plaintiffs could claim damages. *United States v. 1,606.00 Acres of Land*, 698 F2d 402 (1983).

California The city, planning to develop its air terminal, notified plaintiff homeowners in November 1973 that it would acquire their homes. Because of delays in obtaining sufficient funding for the project, purchase offers were not made to plaintiffs until November 1976. Plaintiffs sued the city for precondemnation delay damages, contending that the long delay between the city's decision to acquire their homes and its condemnation action caused plaintiffs a loss of use and enjoyment of their homes. Specifically, plaintiffs sought the decrease in rental value during the course of the delay resulting from the city's notification of condemnation. There was no evidence that plaintiffs had ever intended or attempted to rent their homes at any point in time. *Held:* Plaintiffs were entitled not to precondemnation delay damages, but only to the fair market value of their homes once actual condemnation occurred. Because plaintiffs had not lost any actual or anticipated rental income during the delay, they were not entitled to an award, no matter how unreasonable the delay might have been. *City of Fresno v. Shewmake*, 181 Cal. Rptr. 451 (1982).

Missouri The Washington University Medical Center Redevelopment Corporation was given condemnation power under state law to acquire property to expand the university medical center. Upon condemnation, landowner's property was appraised at $45,000 by court-appointed commissioners. The redevelopment corporation brought suit to have the appraisal reduced. Landowner counterclaimed for damages allegedly caused during a three-year blight designation. The redevelopment corporation moved to dismiss the counterclaim, citing a Missouri rule of procedure that provided that the trial of a condemnation case is restricted to the consideration of objections made to the appraised value of the condemned property. Landowner argued that the rules of procedure required him to bring his counterclaim. *Held:* When a provision of general application conflicts with a provision of specialized application, the former shall give way to the latter. Thus, landowner was precluded from counterclaiming. *State ex rel. Washington Univ. v. Gaertner*, 626 SW2d 373 (1982).

100.10
Valuation in General

8th Circuit Plaintiff, a Sioux Indian, was awarded damages for the loss of an allotment of Indian land selected by his great-grandfather. The award was based on the allotment's value at the time the certificate for land was delivered to his ancestor, plus interest. On appeal, plaintiff contended that the judgment was inadequate because it was not based on the present value of the tract, did not compensate for the loss of income from the land and interest on the lost income, and it computed interest at only 5 percent over nearly 100 years. *Held:* Affirmed as to all issues except interest. Compensation for lost income was properly denied under the reasoning of *Vicenti v. United States*, 470 F2d 845 (10th Cir. 1972). Owner of property taken by the government is entitled to its value at the time of the taking plus an amount sufficient "to produce the present full equivalent of that value paid contemporaneously with the taking." A sum equal to the value of the property at the time it was taken plus interest at a reasonable rate complies with this rule. A 5 percent rate for all the years involved was unreasonable. The court remanded for an examination by the district court of the prevailing interest rates over the years. *Antoine v. United States*, 710 F2d 477 (1983).

10th Circuit Government began condemnation proceedings against ranch. At the first trial, the jury valued the condemned ranch property based on insufficient evidence, and the government was granted a new trial. At the second trial, the court refused to permit landowner to testify to value of the condemned property unless he complied with standards required of an expert appraiser, and ranch filed a motion for a new trial. Motion was denied. *Held:* It is reversible error to refuse to allow landowner to testify as to the value of his own ranch. A landowner is presumed to have special knowledge of his property, and may testify to its value without further qualification. However, offering price of replacement properties cannot be used to show the fair market value of condemned land; therefore, landowner's testimony had no probative value and could not sustain a jury award. *United States v. 10,031.98 Acres*, 850 F2d 634 (1988).

10th Circuit In November 1969, plaintiffs' dwellings were condemned by the

U.S. Army Corps of Engineers. Plaintiffs were permitted to continue occupying their former homes as tenants beyond January 2, 1971, the effective date of the Uniform Relocation Assistance and Reacquisition Policies Act. The government then awarded plaintiffs tenant relocation benefits under Section 204 of the act, but refused more comprehensive homeowner relocation benefits under Section 203. Plaintiffs sued the government for Section 203 relief, arguing that Section 203 provided benefits for all individuals who had been displaced from dwellings they had owned and occupied more than 180 days prior to the initiation of negotiations for its acquisition. *Held:* The act should not be applied retroactively to those persons whose property was sold before the act existed. Plaintiffs remained in possession of their condemned dwellings as priority tenants. Retroactive application to former homeowners was not contemplated by Congress. *Jensen v. United States*, 662 F2d 664 (1981).

Florida Plaintiff owned five adjoining canal front lots and sold two of them. When the state built a bridge across the canal, one of the lots was completely cut off from independent access to the public road, although it retained indirect access through one of the other lots landowner still held. Plaintiff brought an inverse condemnation action, seeking damages for the loss of direct access. *Held:* Plaintiff was entitled to damages. The court expressly disapproved a 1967 ruling from Florida's fourth district court of appeals, *Di Virgilio v. State Road Department*, 205 So. 2d 317, which had held that contiguous lands that are only nominally divided are presumed to be one unit unless actually devoted to such divergent uses that they take on the character of separate properties. Instead, it ruled that vacant city property constitutes presumptively separate units if platted into lots, although the presumption is rebuttable. The decision recognized that platting requires considerable time and expense and cannot be easily changed without government approval. *Department of Transp. v. Jirik*, 498 So. 2d 1253 (1986).

Illinois When a restaurant parking lot was condemned, owner's experts testified to the value of the land as a whole. The state objected to the fact that the land was appraised in this manner rather than by valuing the tract before and after the taking with an allowance for improvements. *Held:* The proper method of valuation was the market approach, without regard to speculative improvements. The contention that the remainder could still be used as a restaurant was too speculative. *People ex rel. Department of Transp. v. Quincy Coach House, Inc.*, 356 NE2d 13 (1976).

Massachusetts After the state built a highway near property owner's land, a drainage problem developed. The state took drainage and slope easements to remedy the problem. Owner then sued the state for compensation, not only for the taking of the easements, but also for incidental damages due to traffic noise from the highway. The state argued that the property owner was entitled to incidental damages only to the extent that they resulted from the drainage and slope easements, but not from traffic noise. *Held:* The owner was entitled to incidental damages. State law requires compensation for all incidental damages from public improvements, whether or not the taking actually caused the damage (Mass. Gen. Laws Ann. ch. 79, § 612). *Roman Catholic Bishop v. Commonwealth*, 392 NE2d 829 (1979).

Minnesota Plaintiffs owned land surrounded by a residential neighborhood. After plaintiffs submitted a proposed development plat to the city, defendant county passed a resolution authorizing acquisition of the property by negotiation or condemnation. Plaintiffs and defendant agreed that the land's highest and best use was for residential development. However, defendant's award was based on the comparable sales approach to valuation. Plaintiffs' experts proposed to present valuation opinions using the development cost approach. The value opinions of plaintiffs' experts ran as high as $1,635,000. The trial judge admitted these opinions into evidence but refused to permit the experts to discuss their use of the development cost approach, arguing that it was speculative. *Held:* Evidence pertaining to the development cost approach may be admitted. Two qualifications were stated: (1) some showing of a current potential for subdivision and sale was necessary and (2) the hypothesis for development had to display some minimal practicality. *County of Ramsey v. Miller*, 316 NW2d 917 (1982).

Mississippi The city expanded its city limits and, in doing so, condemned two water and sewer systems. At a trial to determine the purchase value of the systems, the city's expert witness testified to two different methods of valuation. He first outlined the depreciation replacement costs plus going-concern value method and arrived at a total value of $109,750. The expert then used the return-on-investment method and arrived at a value of $58,683. He averaged the two values and stated that the ultimate figure, $84,217, was the fair market value. *Held:* The averaging of two separate and totally different approaches to value was error. The expert must reconcile the two indications of value using his expertise and offer his opinion as to the true value of the property in question. *Times Square Realty, Inc. v. City of Granada*, 421 So. 2d 1053 (1982).

New Hampshire In proceeding to determine just compensation for a housing authority taking, trial court allowed expert testimony on the fair market value at the time of the taking based on a modification of the reproduction cost method. On appeal, housing authority asserted error in the admission of expert testimony and the jury instruction on reproduction cost evidence. *Held:* The jury may properly consider evidence of reproduction cost in the determination of fair market value of property damaged by fire. The appraiser determines the value of the land without buildings, then adds the depreciated current cost of reconstructing the buildings to determine the value of the property as a whole. Admission of reproduction cost evidence and the jury instruction was proper since owner's appraiser used the method only after determining that other methods could not be used, and confined the method to determining the value of the building "shells." *Manchester Hous. Auth. v. Reingold*, 547 A2d 219 (1988).

New Mexico County tax officials began a comprehensive reassessment of property values but stopped the program after two years. Owners whose properties were revalued and taxed at the higher rates brought suit, contending that they were paying taxes unfairly at full market value, while the majority of properties were taxed at the previous rates. *Held:* Judgment for defendant affirmed. The property owners have no cause of action without evidence that the county had established a discriminatory taxation scheme or was engaged in fraud. The mere fact that one's taxes are higher than one's neighbor's does not create an actionable wrong as long as the tax rate does not exceed the legal limit. *Appelman v. Beach*, 608 P2d 1119 (1980).

New York In an eminent domain proceeding, the condemnee contended that financing costs that would have had to be expended in the course of reproducing a building situated on a taken parcel should be included in the award properly calculated in accordance with the summation method. *Held:* Implementation of the summation method requires the inclusion not only of payments for material, equipment, labor, and other obvious physical ingredients that go directly into construction, but also of those charges that may be termed indirect or less direct, such as architects' fees, contractors' profits, interest and taxes on land value during the period of construction, cost of procuring necessary licenses, and other essential overhead or incidental expenses. A fair and realistic appraisal of reproduction costs must embrace in its reckoning all expenditures that reasonably and necessarily are to be expected in the re-creation of a structure so idiosyncratic as to leave no alternative method by which to measure fair compensation. Financing costs are such an expenditure, and therefore must be included in the award. *City of New York v. Salvation Army, Inc.*, 373 NE2d 984 (1978).

Pennsylvania The Department of Transportation (DOT) condemned part of plaintiffs' property for the purpose of constructing a state road. Entry upon plaintiffs' land did not occur until more than four years later. During the period between DOT's condemnation and entry, plaintiffs continued in the normal use of their condemned property. Plaintiffs argued that their condemnation award should have included delay compensation computed from the date of DOT's condemnation, which constituted a taking. *Held:* The court held that DOT became owner of the property upon its condemnation, and that plaintiffs became lessees of the property at that point until the time of DOT's entry. It applied Pennsylvania law, which is that the condemnee shall not be entitled to compensation for delay in payment during the period he remains in possession after the condemnation. The court also rejected plaintiffs' argument that the property's market value should have been calculated at the 1976 level rather than at the lower 1971 level, again stating that DOT acquired ownership rights in 1971. *Demeno v. Commonwealth Dep't of Transp.*, 443 A2d 429 (1982).

Texas The state, in connection with a highway construction project, condemned a parcel of land on which a truck stop was operated. The owner of the truck stop sought not only compensation for the value of the land taken, but also damages for impaired access to the truck stop. The trial court awarded damages for the value of the condemned land, but not for the impairment of access. The appeals court reversed and remanded, stating it was an error to exclude evidence of damages for impairment of access. Both parties appealed. *Held:* Judgment reversed, and trial court judgment affirmed. Evidence of damages due to inconvenience suffered by condemnee as a result of circuity of travel are inadmissable in eminent domain proceedings and are not compensable as a matter of law. It is a question of law whether there has been a material impairment of access or whether there merely exists circuity of travel. *State v. Wood Oil Distrib. Inc.*, 751 SW2d 863 (1988).

Washington Landowners brought an inverse condemnation action contending that state surveys, press releases, and hearings amounted to a taking. The state subsequently filed a condemnation action. Compensation was awarded by the trial court based upon the value of the property at the time of the trial of the condemnation proceeding. *Held:* Although property is generally valued as of the date of trial, the rule is modified where it would be grossly unfair to the property owner. Any decrease in value attributable to the condemnation activities or the project itself is to be disregarded. Since the state's actions before the condemnation proceeding were brought substantially impaired the marketability of the land, compensation should be determined as of the date the state issued its formal notice of the proposed highway project, nearly two years before the condemnation action was filed. *Lange v. State*, 547 P2d 282 (1976).

West Virginia Taxpayers contested municipality's tax valuation of certain mineral interests. Their claims were dismissed after the lower court found they had no standing. *Held:* Reversed. To have standing to challenge a property tax assessment, a party need not be the owner of the property in question, but need only show that he is a resident or taxpayer. Discriminatory assessment affects every taxpayer, since every taxpayer has a financial interest in fair and equal valuation. *Tug Valley Recovery Center, Inc. v. Mingo County Comm'n*, 261 SE2d 165 (1979).

100.15 —Replacement Cost

U.S. Supreme Court The federal government condemned 50 acres of land used as a sanitary landfill. The city replaced the condemned landfill with a larger and better facility, and claimed that the condemnation award should encompass its entire cost for the better facility. The trial court awarded the city $225,000, representing the fair market value of the site, rather than the reasonable cost of replacement. The Fifth Circuit reversed, reasoning that the city's loss attributable to the condemnation was the amount reasonably spent to create a functionally equivalent facility. *Held:* The federal government is not required to compensate a public condemnee for the cost of acquiring a substitute facility, even where the condemnee has a duty to replace the condemned facility, as long as the market value of the condemned property is ascertainable. The Court criticized the substitute facilities approach to valuation as being difficult to implement, lacking in objectivity, and tending to add complexity and uncertainty to the valuation proceeding. *United States v. 50 Acres of Land*, 469 US 24 (1984).

Pennsylvania Owners were unable to purchase comparable replacement property for the $53,000 paid to them as general damages in this eminent domain case. The owners occupied an apartment on the property, and used the premises for their management and leasing business. They paid $57,000 for comparable replacement property. The trial court awarded owners $4,000 replacement damages and $10,000 business relocation damages. *Held:* Affirmed. Special damages were justified to provide for economic loss where the owners were unable to find a comparable dwelling for under $57,000. The business relocation damages were upheld under Section 201(7) of the Eminent Domain Code, which allows such damages in an amount 40 times the fair monthly rental value of the unit. The monthly rental of the apartment was $250, which multiplied by 40 equaled $10,000, the amount of the award. *Carlynton School Dist. v. Hays*, 526 A2d 843 (Commw. Ct. 1987).

Texas When one half of a property owner's half-acre tract was condemned, he alleged that the remaining portion was too small for his farm-implement business. Owner constructed a new building on a nearby parcel and contended that the cost to construct this building established the market value of the condemned property. *Held:* The construction cost of a building other than the one condemned was not relevant to the market value of the condemned structure, especially where the new structure was on property wholly removed from the condemned property. *State v. Schaefer*, 530 SW2d 813 (1975).

100.20
—Comparable Sales

California City condemned 773 acres of land to expand Los Angeles International Airport. The city appealed judgment of $14 million for landowner. *Held:* The trial court did not err in permitting owner's appraiser to testify as to the trend of sales prices of noncomparable neighboring properties, since the trend could possibly shed light on the subject property's appreciation. The testimony was limited to percentage increases in sale prices, and no dollar amounts were mentioned. The trial court had discretion to consider the relevancy of such data balanced against its possible prejudicial effects on the jury. The trial court did not mislead the jury by telling it that there is no requirement in establishing fair market value that any specific person by ready, willing, and able to buy the property, nor even that there is any active demand for the property. *City of Los Angeles v. Retlaw Enters., Inc.*, 546 P2d 1380 (1976).

Missouri The local board of public buildings instituted eminent domain proceedings to acquire a building. The court entered judgment for $300,000 to the owner after a jury verdict. The board appealed, arguing that the court had erred by admitting evidence of prices paid by a developer of another piece of downtown property. *Held:* Affirmed. The sale of the other property was voluntary and evidence of the price paid was admissible in fixing damages. *Board of Pub. Bldgs. v. GMT Corp.*, 580 SWd 519 (1979).

Montana When the state condemned a parcel of property upon which a very lucrative gas station was built, the jury awarded both the owner and the lessees $50,000. *Held:* Although it is generally held that the best method to determine market value is recent sales of comparable property, when comparable sales cannot be shown, the income capitalization method is permissible if, compared to alternative methods, it provides the least conjecture and uncertainty. *Department of Highways v. HyGrade Auto Court*, 546 P2d 1050 (1976).

100.25
—Loss of Business

Connecticut Defendant, the local transit district, took by eminent domain the property of plaintiff, a public bus company, and valued it at $532,000. Plaintiff appealed the assessment, and a state referee found damages for taking of the realty, tangible personalty, and intangible personalty to be $1,272,182. Defendant claimed error in the referee's valuation of the real estate and intangibles. *Held:* The referee's judgment was upheld as to the valuation of the realty, but set aside as to the valuation of the intangibles. The $425,000 value placed upon the real estate fell well within the broad range of trier discretion. Where, as here, the condemnation award for tangible personalty at its prevailing market value greatly exceeded the property's value for the production of income, the franchise to operate the business was worthless. Thus, no award should have been granted for its taking. Plaintiff, however, was entitled to damages for the reasonable cost of training personnel and installing business systems that benefitted defendant when it took over operation of the bus lines. *Gray Line Bus Co. v. Greater Bridgeport Transit Dist.*, 449 A2d 1036 (1982).

Delaware State condemned a concrete mixing plant, consisting of land, building, machinery, and equipment, for a highway right-of-way. Testimony by the owner established that the property had a value of $750,000, $463,000 of which represented the value of the business to the owner as a going concern. *Held:* It was improper to admit testimony of loss-of-the-business value that was personal to the owner and not shown to be related to the fair market value of the real property taken. In determining constitutional just compensation, the owner is not entitled to recover for the destruction of a business on the land taken, and therefore the value of the business is not relevant except as it may tend to establish the market value of the real property. *State v. Davis Concrete, Inc.*, 355 A2d 883 (1976).

Florida Texaco constructed an automotive service station on property on which it held a long-term lease. Texaco subleased the service station to a dealer-operator, who agreed to buy its supplies wholesale from Texaco. The property was partially taken by eminent domain, and the dealer was awarded business damages. At issue was the right of a lessee to receive business damages in an eminent domain case. *Held:* Lessee of property taken by eminent domain may not receive business damages where lessee acts as wholesale supplier of products to sublessee who operates a business on the premises. State statute requires that a business have a physical existence for more than five years on the partially taken property to be entitled to business damages. In this case, although Texaco derived some income from sale of gas at the station, its employees did not operate the business. The dealer, and not Texaco, would suffer the business losses if any occurred. Texaco acted only as a passive wholesaler and was not licensed to do business at the location. Under these facts, Texaco did not have the requisite physical existence on the condemned property to be entitled to business damages. *Texaco, Inc. v. Department of Transp.*, 537 So. 2d 92 (1989).

Michigan Defendant operated and leased a gas station, which DOT sought to condemn in order to construct a highway. Plaintiff sought to bar defendant's evidence concerning the going-concern value of his business. *Held:* The station operator was permitted to introduce evidence concerning the going-concern value of his business for purposes of the condemnation proceedings. In a condemnation, the business's value is determined by its transferability to another location. If the business can be transferred, nothing is taken and compensation is not required. Evidence of the station's going-concern value was admissable to determine the property's uniqueness. *Department of Transp. v. Campbell*, 438 NW2d 267 (Ct. App. 1988).

100.30
—Goodwill

California Plaintiff owned land on which stood the veterinary hospital where he practiced. He leased the hospital to a professional corporation consisting of himself and two colleagues. On learning that the hospital was to be condemned, plaintiff spent $502,000 to build a new facility a mile away. The new facility was leased to the corporation for $54,000 a year. His colleagues, concerned that income from the practice would not cover increased costs at the new location, left the practice. Plaintiff was unable to sell the practice. Plaintiff brought an action under Section 1263.510 of California's Eminent Domain Law, which provides compensation for loss of goodwill. The jury awarded plaintiff $96,000 for the value of the goodwill taken by the condemnation. *Held:* Plaintiff's loss came within the statutory defintion of "compensable goodwill." The statute authorizes compensation for a loss of "benefits" of "location." Here, the old location carried the manifest benefit of a cheap rent in an older building. *People ex rel. Department of Transp. v. Muller*, 681 P2d 1340 (1984).

California City redevelopment authority sued to condemn property of a pharmacist. The judgment awarded compensation for certain drugs on the condemned property, but denied compensation for loss of business goodwill. The condemnee argued that he was unable to relocate his pharmacy for age and health reasons and that prescription drugs could not be resold because of regulations making it unduly expensive. He argued that he was thus entitled to compensation for the value of the drugs and business goodwill lost. *Held:* Compensation was not constitutionally required for loss of goodwill sustained due to the exercise of the power of eminent domain. However, the court erred in awarding compensation for the drug inventory. Condemnee's personal circumstances that prevented him from relocating his business did not justify a departure from the rule denying compensation for movable personal property on condemned realty. *Community Redevelopment Agency v. Abrams*, 543 P2d 905 (1975).

100.35
—Effect of Zoning

Idaho Plaintiff, a county highway district, condemned a major portion of a vacant, unimproved residential lot that defendant had purchased as a site for a future office. The land carried restrictive covenants preventing use other than for residential purposes, but was surrounded by major thoroughfares and office buildings. When the trial court set its figure for the condemnation award, it took into consideration the likelihood of rezoning to "limited-office" use and removal of the restrictive covenants. Plaintiff contended that the trail court erred in admitting testimony as to the value of the lot if it were rezoned and that a zoning change was not probable. *Held:* The trial court's award was upheld. The possibility of rezoning would be taken into consideration by a prospective buyer, and so was properly taken into consideration by the trial court. However, plaintiff's assertion that the restrictive covenants were unenforceable was incorrect. If the subdivision subject to the covenants remains unchanged, changes in the surrounding areas will not invalidate the covenants, nor does the fact that the property would increase in value if used for a different purpose. *Ada County Highway District v. Magwire*, 662 P2d 237 (1983).

Illinois In a condemnation proceeding, the state appealed a condemnation award that was based on the probable value of the property for a commercial use. The state argued that such valuation was improper since there was no direct testimony that rezoning was reasonable probable. The property owner's witnesses had testified as to the property's value given a future commercial use. *Held:* It is proper to base value upon the highest and best use permitted under other than existing zoning classifications where the court feels that there is a reasonable probability of the granting of such zoning in the near future. While defendant has the burden of proof regarding the probability of a rezoning, he may not present an expert witness to testify solely on this issue. Since there was sufficient evidence to indicate that a rezoning was probable, the property's valuation as a commercial use was proper. *Department of Transp. v. Western Nat'l Bank*, 347 NE2d 161 (1976).

New York Owners of property zoned for residential development petitioned town for a variance to erect a small office building on the site. They contended that this was the only appropriate use of the property because the site was only slightly larger than an acre, irregular in shape, and surrounded by public thoroughfares, restaurants, small businesses, professional offices, and residences. When the petition was denied and condemnation effected, the property was still zoned residential. The town contended that just compensation for the property should be limited to its value for residential development. *Held:* The court found owner's contentions correct. While as a general rule in matters of compensation, value of property taken should be limited to the highest use permitted by existing zoning, in this case, given the probability of rezoning, an award should be on the next increment. *In re Town of Islip*, 402 NE2d 1123 (1980).

100.40
—Effect of Condemnation

5th Circuit State, acting through the river authority, instituted condemnation proceedings to acquire land adjacent to a dam for recreational purposes. In assessing damages, the land was valued in reference to its best and highest use as timberland. Landowners appealed, claiming that they were entitled to compensation based on the enhanced value of the land attributable to the project that made condemnation necessary. *Held:* A landowner is not entitled to any enhanced value to his property attributable to the project that makes condemnation necessary. *Louisiana v. Lindsey*, 524 F2d 934 (1975).

Kansas City condemned a portion of a tract of land, used to manufacture concrete products, for highway improvements. Landowners argued that the purchase price of adjoining property should have been admitted into evidence. *Held:* The purchase price of adjoining property, which is subject to condemnation, but transferred by deed, is not admissable in evidence. It is not an arm's-length transaction since the threat of condemnation affects the price. There was no assurance it was a sale between a willing buyer and a willing seller. *In re Condemnation of Land for Controlled Access Highway Purposes*, 548 P2d 756 (1976).

Nebraska An easement for a river channel and drainage works was taken by eminent domain over plaintiff's land. When plaintiff's property remained on county rolls at the same valuation, leaving taxes unchanged, he protested. The County Board of Equalization reduced the actual value of the land subject to the easement by 50 percent. Plaintiff claimed the land should be valued at zero and not taxed. *Held:* An easement is not an estate in land; therefore plaintiff's fee in the land was not reduced. The only question here was the actual value of the property. The burden of proof remained on the contesting party to prove that the board's valuation was incorrect. The easement was a burden borne by the whole tract. That burden was to be considered in arriving at the fair market value (actual value) of the whole tract. Plaintiff's theory for separate valuation of easement and non-easement property was invalid. *Voltmer Family Farms, Inc. v. Board of Equalization*, 343 NW2d 755 (1983).

Utah A property was condemned as part of a neighborhood redevelopment plan. Owners maintained that the condemnation award should have taken into account the increased value of the property due to the redevelopment project, particularly a zoning change adopted as part of the project. The trial court refused to consider any increase in value resulting from the redevelopment project. *Held:* Affirmed. Disavowing several decisions to the contrary as "dubious antecedents" and "confusion in the law," the Utah court decided to adopt the majority rule, which disregards any enhancement or decrease in value attributable to the purpose for which the property is being condemned in determining the fair market value of condemned property. It cited also Utah Code Ann. § 57-12-13(3), which, while not controlling, expressed a clear legislative policy to similar effect. *Rede-*

velopment Agency v. Grutter, 734 P2d 434 (1986).

100.45
—Effect of Fear

Florida Plaintiff initiated condemnation proceedings for a perpetual utility easement across landowner's property to build a 500,000-volt transmission line. Defendant's argued that they were entitled to severance damages, contending that public fear of the adverse health effects of living close to high voltage power lines would reduce market value of their properties. Plaintiff moved to exclude testimony of scientific experts concerning the adverse health effects of the transmission lines. The trial court denied plaintiff's motion. *Held:* The impact of public fear on market value is admissible in an eminent domain case without independent proof of the reasonableness of the fear. However, in this case, the introduction of scientific testimony as to adverse health effects was irrelevant and unnecessary, since the issue in eminent domain is to determine full compensation for property taken and damages for the remaining property. *Florida Power & Light Co. v. Jennings*, 518 So. 2d 895 (1987).

100.50
—Assemblage Doctrine

Wisconsin Truck terminal property was condemend. The potential profitability of the terminal had been diminished by the prior condemnation of an adjacent parcel. But for the adjacent condemnation, the terminal's owner could have purchased an adjacent 25-foot strip for about $15,000 and integrated it with his parcel to obtain full use of the terminal. The circuit judge awarded the value of the integrated parcel, less than $15,000 cost of acquisition. *Held:* The supreme court concluded that allowing a court to consider a prospective, integrated use with the land of another in determining the fair market value of a parcel was consistent with its standards for valuation of condemned land in settings where potential assemblage of lands does in fact affect the fair market value. The integrated approach would be suitable where it is the only way to achieve the "most advantageous" use of the land and the prospective combination of parcels is "reasonably probable." *Clarmar Realty v. Redevelopment Auth.*, 383 NW2d 890 (1986).

100.55
Leasehold Interests

U.S. Supreme Court State executed a 10-year grazing lease of lands that had been granted to the state in trust. The United States instituted a condemnation proceeding to acquire the leased tracts for a flood-control project. The condemnation award included an amount of the lessee's interest at the time of the taking and its prospective leasehold interest. The state claimed that lessee was not entitled to compensation for its leasehold interest. *Held:* If the lessee possesses a compensable leasehold interest upon condemnation, it is entitled to just compensation. The case was remanded for a determination of whether the lessee had a compensable leasehold interest under the lease and state law. *Alamo Land & Cattle Co. v. Arizona*, 424 US 295 (1976).

7th Circuit Tenants required by city to vacate their homes when their condition violated local housing code, sued under Fifth Amendment and the Uniform Relocation Assistance and Real Property Acquisition Policies Act (Relocation Act) for compensation. The city's relocation assistance program provided benefits only to tenants evicted from homes that required razing, which tenants' homes did not require. *Held:* The evictions amounted to takings of property rights in exercise of the city's police power. The takings benefitted the public by protecting them from substandard housing. Meanwhile, tenants were deprived of their homes and of all property rights thereto. Therefore, just compensation to tenants was warranted under the Fifth Amendement. Tenants were not entitled to Relocation Act benefits as they were not "displaced persons," since the city did not acquire affirmative property rights to the building, but merely restricted the property rights of tenants. *Devines v. Maier*, 665 F2d 138 (1981).

Connecticut The state leased plaintiff a parcel of land at a local airport, upon which tenant was to construct an air freight terminal that would belong to the state. The lease contained a condemnation clause, which set damages at the unamortized investment of the tenant in the lease allocated over the original lease term. Subsequently, the state notified plaintiff that its leasehold interest would be suject to condemnation at the end to the period. Accordingly, defendant filed a certificate of taking and assessed damages under the condemnation clause of the lease at $1. Plaintiff appealed the assessment of damages. *Held:* The condemnation clause of the lease was determinative of damages. The U.S. Constitution prohibits the impairment of contract; however, an award made pursuant to an agreement cannot be regarded as an impairment of contract, even if the amount of damages arrived at through the stipulated formula appears to be inadequate when compared to the amount to be received in the absence of such an agreement. The state has the power of eminent domain and may exercise this power at any time during the term of the agreement, provided that the owner is fairly compensated. Where the parties to a lease agree beforehand to an award calculation formula, the resulting sum is deemed fair compensation since it is in accordance with their agreement. *Bradley Facilities, Inc. v. Burns*, 551 A2d 746 (1988).

Kansas A city condemned property owners' land and they sued for just compensation. An appraiser awarded them $109,138, but a jury verdict gave them $205,192.36. The city appealed, arguing that the verdict was speculative and that property owners' evidence was premised on usage of the property as a motel site, which the city claimed was unrealistic. *Held:* The jury verdict was proper. Property owners were entitled to introduce evidence of the highest and best use of the condemned land, and it was proper for the jury to consider such evidence. *Cain v. City of Topeka*, 603 P2d 1031 (1979).

Louisiana Restaurant operators leased premises under an unrecorded written lease. When they learned that some of the land adjacent to the restaurant would be expropriated to build a highway, they became concerned that their business would not withstand the impact and they sued. The state asserted that, because the lease was not recorded, lessees had no right to assert a claim for damages. *Held:* The lease was clearly a property interest, even if unrecorded. The constitutional requirement that property not be taken by the state without just compensation entitled the lessees to damages. *State Dep't of Transp. & Dev. v. Jacob*, 483 So. 2d 592 (1986).

Maryland Before condemnation, lessor's two properties had been combined into a single, large department store complex by lessee. The lease (which expressly bound successors and assigns of the parties) required lessee to restore or rebuild the premises at its own expense. The city refused to take the lease covenant into consideration in its condemnation award, on the ground that the covenant did not run with the land but was merely a personal right of lessor. *Held:* The covenant was a compensable right. The covenant ran with the land because it was to be performed on the land, related to the physical condition of the land, burdened the covenantor and benefited the covenantee, and bound successors and assigns. Had the covenant not bound and benefited successors and assigns, it would not have been compensable. *Mercantile-Safe Deposit & Trust Co. v. Mayor of Baltimore*, 521 A2d 734 (1987).

Washington The question certified to the Supreme Court of Washington was whether, under the Mobile Home Landlord-Tenant Act (Wash. Rev. Code § 59.20), mobile homes owned by tenants of a mobile home park and located on rented lots within the park become part of the real property so that, upon condemnation of the lands within the park for public use, the condemnor also acquired the mobile homes within the park. *Held:* It is implicit in the Mobile Home Act that mobile homes on rented lots in such parks do not lose their identity as personal property belonging to tenants and do not become part of the real estate. Nonetheless, a mobile home owner who is a tenant for years under a written lease has an estate in the leased land that would require condemnation and compensation, as would outbuildings and other improvements made by the tenant on the leased land. *United States v. 19.7 Acres of Land*, 692 P2d 809 (1984).

100.60 Severance Damages

9th Circuit Petitioners owned easements over a condemned tract to gain access to their property. They sought severance damages for the reduction in value of the properties served by the easements. The district court denied petitioners severance damages on the ground that each owned only an easement over the condemned tract, and not the underlying fee. *Held:* The court cited U.S. Supreme Court decisions that the owner of a condemned access easement is entitled to compensation for the diminution in value of the property that it serves. The law established by these cases applied even though the condemned tracts were not contiguous to the tracts that the easements served and even though one petitioner held only a leasehold interest in one such tract. Furthermore, the unity of ownership in the use of the easements and the tracts required for a grant of severance damages were present. *United States v. 57.09 Acres of Land*, 706 F2d 280 (1983).

Alaska Plaintiff operated a nightclub on a leased parcel of land that abutted a highway. The state, planning to improve the highway, blocked off the driveway that gave drivers direct access from the nightclub to the highway and took four fifths of an acre of the rented parcel for purposes of widening the highway. A condemnation proceeding in the local court resulted in a judgment for plaintiff of $1,680 as compensation for the four fifths acre taken. The court ruled, however, that plaintiff was not entitled to compensation for the loss of direct access to the highway resulting from the blockage of the driveway. Plaintiff appealed the ruling to the Supreme Court of Alaska. *Held:* Plaintiff, whose property abutted a public way, had no right to direct access. His right was limited to reasonable access, defined as a means of access that does not substantially interfere with ingress or egress. The necessity of traveling an extra one-half mile to reach the highway from the nightclub, which resulted from the blockage of the driveway, was held not to be unreasonable access. Therefore, the court found that there had been no compensable taking of access. *Triangle, Inc. v. State*, 632 P2d 965 (1981).

Arizona Buchanan owned a tract lying along a highway. The state decided to condemn an 80-foot strip of the tract lying closest to the highway. Buchanan argued that the strip taken was more valuable by itself than as part of the whole parcel. He also presented evidence that the remaining part of the tract decreased in value. A jury awarded damages based on the strip having a separate value and also awarded severance damages. *Held:* The court affirmed the compensation award but disallowed severance damages. As long as the parcel taken was of such size and shape as to have a separate and independent use in the market, it could be valued in its own right. An owner must be consistent in the valuation method used with respect to the part taken and to the remainder. Although an owner is not precluded from offering alternative valuation methods, the methods are not to be combined. If the remainder were regarded as a separate and independent unit, its "before" value would have to be the same as its "after" value, because the taking of the strip would not affect frontage rights of the separate parcel existing before and after taking. Evidence of the severance damages of a separate, independent unit should not have been admitted. *State ex rel. Ordway v. Buchanan*, 741 P2d 292 (1987).

Colorado Landowner, part of whose land was condemned to provide an easement for a power line, sought additional compensation for aesthetic damages to the remainder of his property and loss of view. *Held:* For landowner. Overruling an earlier case, a split Colorado court held that a landowner, part of whose property is condemned, should be compensated for all damages that are the natural, necessary and reasonable result of the taking, including damages to the remainder of his property that would not have been compensable if a landowner who had not suffered a partial taking suffered the same damages. The court found that this new approach was endorsed by a significant majority of other state courts and that it was fairer and more economically realistic: A landowner selling a piece of his property to a private party will fix a price that will compensate him for any diminution in value to the remaining property. *La Plata Elec. Ass'n v. Cummins*, 728 P2d 696 (1986) (en banc).

New Jersey Plaintiffs owned two contiguous parcels of land along a highway. The state condemned a 45-foot-wide strip on the frontage of each parcel. Condemnation commissioners fixed separate awards for each parcel, and both parties sought judicial review. The trial court ordered separate trials for each parcel and granted separate awards, and the appellate court affirmed. *Held:* Reversed and remanded. Evidence regarding the potential assemblage of two parcels should have been presented to the trier of fact. Where there has been a partial taking, the prospective as well as the current use of the condemned property can be relevant to a determination of severance damages. The court remanded the case for a valuation determination by a single jury. Separate trials would be unnecessary because of the strong connection between the parcels and the overlap of the proofs regarding the after-taking value of each. *State v. Silver*, 457 A2d 463 (1983).

New York City appealed the size of a fee and fixture award given to owners of partially condemned property. The city argued that costs for restoring the parcel were wrongfully granted since property owners had been fully compensated for the property's decrease in value by an award based on the reduced rental value of the lot. *Held:* The measure of damages for a partial taking is the difference between the value of the whole parcel before the taking and the value of the remainder after the taking. Capitalization of income is generally a valid method of determining valuation for income-producing property.

Since the loss of the condemned portion of the lot and the associated improvements were reflected in the lot's reduced rental value, no additional award for these items was proper. However, the additional restoration award was proper since owners were required to make expenditures, not reflected in the lower rent, to restore the property to working order. *In re City of New York*, 348 NE2d 878 (1976).

Oregon Two parcels used together in a gravel-mining operation were owned by different corporations that had substantial, but not complete, unity of ownership. The state condemned one of the parcels, and owners of the other parcel sought severance damages. *Held:* Severance damages were denied because the two parcels lacked the requisite unity of ownership. Noting that Oregon has been especially reluctant to disregard the corporate form unless exceptional circumstances exist, the court ruled that Oregon courts will not look to the identity of individual shareholders in order to determine unity of ownership in eminent domain cases, even where there is complete identity of record title holders at the date of a taking. A condemning body is not required to go beyond the public record title. *City of Salem v. HSB*, 733 P2d 890 (1987) (en banc).

Texas To facilitate the laying of a pipeline, a utility company built a dirt road across a condemnee's lake, and the condemnee was compensated for the 13.5-acre strip needed for the pipeline right-of-way. When heavy rains washed out the road and filled the lake with mud, the condemnee demanded additional compensation to restore the lake to its prior condition, alleging that the washout had caused a reasonably forseeable diminution of the market value of property that had not been condemned. The utility company defended on the ground that the condemnee had already been compensated for the taking. *Held:* Compensation for diminution in value of the remainder is properly awarded when damages accrue as a result of the employment of condemned property for a condemnation-related purpose. Since damage to the lake was a foreseeable consequence of building a dirt road across it and since the damage caused was a factor that would be taken into consideration by a prospective purchaser of the remainder, the condemnee was entitled to additional compensation. *Spindor v. Lo-Vaca Gathering Co.*, 529 SW2d 63 (1975).

Virginia Condemnor appealed an award by the commissioners for $11,000 on the ground that it was excessive and bore no reasonable relationship to the evidence. An expert appraiser for the condemnor estimated that the value of the condemnee's land taken and the damages to the residual land totaled $5,020. The condemnees' appraiser set the figure at $6,902. *Held:* The award by the commissioners was not so grossly excessive or unreasonable that it bore no relationship to the evidence presented and therefore was upheld. The commissioner's report was entitled to great weight and was prima facie correct and must be confirmed unless there was a showing of good cause to overturn it. *State Highway Comm'r v. Carter*, 222 SE2d 776 (1976).

100.65 Consequential Damages

Georgia In a condemnation proceeding, landowner appealed the compensation of $14,900 for the taking of a portion of its lot by DOT. A jury trial was held with regard to consequential damages, and evidence showed that the project necessitated condemnation of an adjacent lot, which had become landlocked. The court instructed the jury on the right of a landlocked property owner to condemn an easement across the land upon payment of compensation and consequential damages to the property after the taking. The jury awarded $42,900. The state appealed. *Held:* Reversed. If a condemnee's remaining property is damaged owing to a taking of an adjacent tract, such damages must be asserted in a separate action and may not be directly recovered in the condemnation proceeding. Only those damages that rise proximately to the remainder of the tract as a result of a taking are consequential damages recoverable in a condemnation action. *Department of Transp. v. Simon*, 261 SE2d 710 (Ct. App. 1979), aff'd, 265 SE2d 777 (1980).

New York Claimants owned a 6.662-acre tract of land. The state took 2.008 acres, which consisted of the 343 feet of frontage on Maple Road closest to the highway, to the full depth of the parcel. Claimant owners sought and won direct damages for the taking and consequential damages for the effect on the remainder parcel. *Held:* Affirmed as to direct damages. However, the court of claims verdict for consequential damages was reversed by both appellate courts. No change in the use of claimants' remaining land was caused by the taking of that portion of it close to Millersport Highway, nor did evidence show compensable damages because of the increased distance from the remaining land to the highway. *Forest City Enters. v. State*, 452 NE2d 1262 (1983).

100.70 Attorney Fees and Costs

5th Circuit Owner objected to the United States' compensation offer to defendant landowner for easements over its property, and was awarded a larger amount at trial. Landowner sought attorney fees from the government under the Equal Access to Justice Act (EAJA), 28 USC § 2412(d)(1)(A), which provides that a court "shall" award attorney fees to a "prevailing party" against the United States in a civil action "unless the court finds that the position of the United States was substantially justified or that special circumstances make an award unjust." *Held:* The EAJA by its terms applies to eminent domain cases brought by or against the United States. The purpose of the EAJA is to award litigants the costs of seeking review of unreasonable government action. The legislative history indicated that Congress intended to help small litigants, such as defendant, challenge agency action without being burdened by the costs of federal litigation. The government also claimed that landowner had not prevailed, because the government had obtained the easements it wanted and had therefore itself prevailed. Landowner argued that it had prevailed in establishing the value of just compensation to be greater than the government's offer. The court agreed; under the EAJA, a prevailing party was one who prevailed by a favorable settlement or decision on central issues. *United States v. 329.73 Acres of Land*, 704 F2d 800 (1983).

8th Circuit At issue was the applicability of the EAJA to condemnation proceedings in cases in which condemnees pursuing litigation were ultimately awarded many times the amount originally offered by the government, but were denied attorney fees and costs. EAJA provides that a prevailing party in a civil action against the United States shall be awarded attorney fees, "unless the court finds the position of the United States was substantially justified." *Held:* The court followed the Fifth Circuit (*United States v. 329.73 Acres of Land*, 704 F2d 800 (1983)) in holding that the EAJA applied to condemnation proceedings. However, it defined differently the terms "prevailing party" and "substantial justification," narrowing the chances for recovery of attorney fees and expenses by a condemnee. It held that property owners are prevailing parties "when they win either by judgment or settlement more than the government offered . . . as just compensation,'' since such property owners ''succeed on a significant issue in litigation which achieves some of the benefit the parties sought in bringing suit,'' thus declining to require a threshhold level of difference between the award and the offer. However, the court held that the government's position was ''substantially justified,'' preventing successful litigants in such cases from recovering fees and costs if the government's offer is consistent with qualified appraisals. *United States v. 341.45 Acres of Land*, 751 F2d 924 (1984).

Mississippi State highway commission deposited a substantial sum with the court under a Mississippi law permitting a condemning authority to obtain immediate possession of property in an eminent domain proceeding upon making such a deposit. The case was settled, and the court ordered the highway commission to pay the clerk a commission of half a percent on the sum deposited. *Held:* Affirmed. Mississippi law permits the clerk of the circuit court to charge a commission ''on all monies coming into his hands,'' including a deposit in an eminent domain proceeding. In addition, state statute required the condemning authority to pay court costs. *Mississippi State Highway Comm'n v. Herban*, 522 So. 2d 210 (1988).

100.75 Interest

U.S. Supreme Court District court, in determining a condemnation award, granted interest from the date the complaint was filed to the date the government deposited the value of the land with the court. The court justified its award of interest on the ground that the date of institution of condemnation proceedings ''effectively denied [petitioner] economically viable use and enjoyment of its property.'' The Fifth Circuit reversed the interest award, holding that the date of taking should be deemed the date on which the compensation award was paid. Thus, no interest was due on the award. The Supreme Court granted certiorari to resolve the conflict in the circuits regarding the date on which the taking in a ''straight condemnation'' proceeding is deemed to occur. *Held:* Affirmed. In a condemnation proceeding under 40 USC § 257, the taking occurs upon termination of the proceedings. The provision of 40 USC § 258a, permitting peremptory appropriation prior to judgment in certain situations, would have been superfluous if a taking occurred upon filing of the complaint. In this instance, the interference with defendant's property rights prior to the award was not severe enough to give rise to a taking. Defendant failed to demonstrate that its interests were constitutionally impaired before the government tendered payment. *Kirby Forest Indus., Inc. v. United States*, 467 US 1 (1984).

9th Circuit In November 1977, a condemnation judgment was entered in favor of the United States. The judgment decreed title vested in the government upon deposit of the sum awarded. In November 1978, the government deposited the amount plus 6 percent interest from date of entry of judgment. Thereafter, the government's motion to disallow the interest on the judgment was granted by the district court. Plaintiff appealed, noting that he had remained liable for all land-related expenses from the date of judgment until the date of deposit without enjoying any use or income from the land. *Held:* In a condemnation case involving vacant, unimproved land, the taking occurred on the date of judgment. Condemnees were entitled to interest from that date, since judgment forced them to hold property that generated expenses but no benefits. *United States v. 156.81 Acres of Land*, 671 F2d 336, cert. denied, 459 US 1086 (1982).

California The Burbank Redevelopment Agency condemned land under the "quick-take" provisions of the Eminent Domain Law, which allowed an order for possession of property prior to trial by a deposit in court of the "probable" compensation. Condemnees were ultimately awarded amounts far in excess of the "probable" compensation. They were statutorily entitled to only 7 percent interst on the difference between the final award and the probable compensation. They appealed, arguing that a statutory interest rate far below the market interest rate did not meet the constitutional requirement of just compensation. *Held:* Citing *Phelps v. United States*, 274 US 341 (1927), for the proposition that if the government pays for condemned property after taking and using it, the owners "are entitled to have the *full* equivalent of the value of its use at the time of the taking paid contemporaneously with the taking," the court held that application of a legal interest rate substantially below market did not meet the "just compensation" requirement. The court left it for trial courts to determine the appropriate rates. *Redevelopment Agency v. Gilmore*, 700 P2d 794 (1985).

New York After the amount of a condemnee's award had been fully litigated and the city offered to pay it, the condemnee learned of a court decision awarding interest above the statutory amount and appealed the interest part of the award. *Held:* The court of appeals held that the condemnee's failure to litigate the interest issue in the original condemnation proceeding barred it from maintaining an independent action for additional interest. The statutory rate of interest is presumptively reasonable and will be applied unless the condemnee rebuts the presumption of reasonableness at the condemnation trial. The condemnee's claim to additional interest, due to delay between judgment and receipt of the award, was not relevant, since postjudgment interest is not constitutionally required and thus does not have to meet the "just compensation" test. Postjudgment interest is awarded merely by way of penalty or incidental interest and is always at the statutory rate. *Adventurers Whitestone v. City of New York*, 479 NE2d 241, appeal dismissed, 474 US 935 (1985).

New York In June 1972, the city condemned private property. Property owners filed claims between April 1974 and January 1975. The trial court rendered a compensation award, with interest at the statutory rate of 6 percent from the date of taking to the date of payment. Claimants objected to the interest rate. Expert testimony was introduced that market interest rates during the relevant period exceeded 6 percent. The trial court held that claimants were entitled to interest of 9 percent from January 1, 1978, to the date of payment, and 6 percent from June 1972 to December 31, 1977. The parties appealed. *Held:* Affirmed. The statutory interest rate, although presumptively reasonable, may be rebutted by evidence that a higher rate must be paid to afford a property owner just compensation. The interest rates set by the trial court were consistent with findings as to interest rates during the relevant periods. *In re City of New York*, 449 NE2d 399 (1983).

100.80
Right to Share in Proceeds

8th Circuit In 1979, the federal government condemned certain land in Arkansas with a stipulated value of $192,000. A woman claimed an interest in the property and entitlement to a portion of the condemnation proceeds under her late mother's will. The will devised the property in fee simple to decedent's son, subject to the condition that upon sale or other disposition of the property, the proceeds were to be divided equally among decedent's surviving children. The district court denied the claim. *Held:* Affirmed. If claimant's rights were construed as a possibility of reverter or other future interest, the rule is that compensation for condemnation must be paid to the owner of the defeasible fee without apportionment to the holder of a reversionary interest. An exception exists where the event on which the defeasible fee is to terminate is imminent. On these facts, the court concluded claimant had no recognizable basis for asserting a right to the award. *United States v. 726.23 Acres of Land*, 746 F2d 1363 (1984).

10th Circuit A brother and two sisters each had undivided one-third interests in a tract of land in Oklahoma. In 1956, the sisters contracted to sell their interests to their brother. The contract provided that, in the event of condemnation, each sister was to receive one-third of the award. In 1975, the government commenced condemnation proceedings to acquire the land. The brother and sisters attacked the sufficiency of the award, and the sisters filed a cross claim against the brother, asserting their rights to a portion of the condemnation award. At issue before the Tenth Circuit was whether the sisters were entitled to a portion of the final award and whether the sisters should pay part of the brother's attorney fees if they did obtain part of the award. *Held:* For the sisters on both issues. The promise to pay a portion of the award to the sisters did not violate the rule against perpetuities, as the brother maintained. The rule does not apply to personal contracts to pay upon the happening of a contingency such as federal condemnation. The brother's fee simple title was not encumbered by any restraint or alienation. Nor was the promise to pay an illegal "quarter sale," in which a conveyee of land is required to pay a portion of the sales price to conveyor upon a later conveyance of the land. Therefore, the brother was required to pay part of the condemnation award to the sisters. However, the court rejected the brother's claim for attorney fees. Although the brother's attorneys had convinced the court to raise the award, they had insisted throughout that the sisters had no right to share in the fund. *United States v. 397.51 Acres of Land*, 692 F2d 688 (1982).

Nevada A portion of a $3 million, 20-building apartment complex was condemned to build a freeway. The deed of trust on the property, which secured a debt of $700,000, provided that the beneficiary of the deed of trust was entitled to receive any condemnation award, and to apply or to release it at the beneficiary's discretion. The property owners argued that they were entitled to the award, since the beneficiary had not shown that the value of its security was impaired. *Held:* The effectiveness of such an assignment clause is limited to the extent to which a mortgagee or beneficiary can demonstrate that its security has actually been impaired. The ratio of the property's worth to the debt secured, which was $4.73 to $1 before the taking and $4.38 to $1 after the taking, had to be restored to the precondemnation ratio. The ruling had the effect of requiring that the condemnation proceeds be applied so as to reduce the secured debt by the same percentage as the taking had reduced the value of the property and that the remainder of the award be turned over to the property owners. *First W. Fin. v. Vegas Continental*, 692 P2d 1279 (1984).

South Carolina Landowners sued to enjoin defendants from trespassing on a 30-foot street that ran through their property. Defendants contended that the originally recorded plat gave them an easement for their use of the street. Plaintiffs asserted that a subsequent recutting and a resubdivision of the property destroyed the easement in the earlier plat. *Held:* When the original grantor subdivided and platted his property into lots and streets, and conveyed the lots with reference to the plat, the purchasers and those claiming under them acquired an appurtenant easement in the 30-foot street as delineated on the plat. An appurtenant easement passes with the dominant estate, and the subsequent resubdivision of plaintiff's property did not destroy the easement created by the original plat. *Carolina Land Co. v. Bland*, 217 SE2d 16 (1975).

100.85 Setoffs Against Award

Missouri State highway commission condemned part of landowner's tract to improve a roadway intersection. The work severed a part of landowner's property and left it adjoined to an executive park that had been rezoned from residential to commercial use. At condemnation proceedings, state highway experts testified that the severed parcel would probably be rezoned to commercial use and hence its value would increase significantly. The jury set off this benefit to landowner against the value of the condemned land in its condemnation award. Landowner contended that the severance of its parcel created no special benefit and that evidence as to benefit should have been excluded. *Held:* The evidence was admissible as the basis of a setoff award because it established special benefit to landowner. The benefit to landowner was special, not general, because it accrued directly to its land to increase its market value, and was beyond the benefit landowners usually derive from neighboring public works projects. *State ex rel. State Highway Comm'r v. Koziatek*, 639 SW2d 86 (Ct. App. 1982).

100.90 Temporary Takings

U.S. Supreme Court A church operated a retreat and campground located in a canyon. When the camp was completely obliterated in a flood, the county adopted an ordinance creating a flood protection in the canyon and prohibiting any construction in the area. The church filed an inverse condemnation suit, seeking compensation for loss of use of the campground. The suit was dismissed; California law did not authorize an inverse condemnation action based on a regulatory taking. The court ruled that the regulation must be overturned in a prior action before compensation could be allowed, and that no damages were due for temporary loss of the use of private property before the regulation was invalidated. *Held:* Temporary takings due to a regulation that is later invalidated must be compensated if they result in total loss of use of property. Temporary regulatory takings are no different from permanent takings for which the Constitution requires compensation. No subsequent government action invalidating an unconstitutional land use regulation relieves the government of the duty to provide compensation. *First Lutheran Evangelical Church v. County of Los Angeles*, 482 US 304 (1987).

11th Circuit A development company contracted to purchase a parcel of land for the purpose of building an apartment complex. After strong community opposition to the project, the city council enacted an ordinance outlawing construction of apartment complexes. Development company and landowner sued on constitutional grounds. The district court held the ordinance was unconstitutional and granted injunctive relief, but refused plaintiffs' request for damages. *Held:* Plaintiffs were entitled to compensation for the temporary regulatory taking. Landowner's loss was the injury to the property's potential for producing income or expected profit. Landowner's compensable interest was the return on the portion of fair market value that was lost as a result of the regulatory action. Landowner should be awarded the market rate return computed over the period of the taking on the difference between the property's fair market value with and without the regulatory restriction. *Wheeler v. City of Pleasant Grove*, 833 F2d 267 (1987).

Arizona A city zoning ordinance prohibited development in mountainous areas vulnerable to landslides and erosion, declaring these areas conservation zones. The ordinance compensated affected landowners with "density credits," permitting greater development in adjacent areas where they owned land. One landowner sued. Most of her land fell within the affected area. Appraisers agreed that the mountainous part of her tract would have no monetary value under the ordinance. An appeals court ruled the zoning was confiscatory and that density credits did not constitute just compensation. The appeals court, however, denied damages for the temporary taking. *Held:* Where a regulation effects an unconstitutional taking, landowner is entitled to monetary damages from the time the regulation was protested or challenged. The court stressed that an award must be only for actual damages, and provable to a reasonable certainty; and the court noted that an owner who had no development plans for property at the time of the taking may have difficulty proving actual damages. *Corrigan v. City of Scottsdale*, 720 P2d 513, cert. denied, 107 S. Ct. 577 (1986).

Georgia DOT filed to condemn construction easements for a 13-month period for road work. After receiving $50 for a temporary easement on the property, owner sought to introduce evidence that the value of the remaining land was diminished by the easements. The trial court refused to admit the evidence, ruling that consequential damages from construction must be shown as a permanent result of the improvement. Owner appealed, citing the Georgia Constitution, which states that "private property shall not be taken *or damaged* for public purposes" without just compensation. *Held:* For owner. Consequential damages in condemnation do not have to be permanent to be compensable. Consequential damages must only be special to the condemnee rather than suffered by the public in general. If the taking of a temporary easement could be shown to have diminished the fair market value of the land not taken, the owner was entitled to compensation. *Hillman v. Department of Transp.*, 359 SE2d 637 (1987).

Kansas Landowners owned property on corner of two streets upon which they operated a gas station. City moved to acquire by eminent domain a five-foot-wide permanent easement to widen one of the streets fronting the gas station. The city also requested a temporary construction easement on both streets. City permanently closed one of the gas station's entrances because it would be unsafe after street was widened. Compensation to landowners was based on city's right to block all of gas station's driveways during the temporary easement. City argued that compensation should be lower because at least one of the driveways remained open during the term of the easement. *Held:* Landowners were entitled to full compensation for the right the city acquired to block all access to the gas station even though the actual use was less. City's eminent domain petition did not have to specifically claim the right to close all driveways to allow compensation to landowners for city's right to block access; the temporary easement encompassing all three driveways gave city the right to deny access. But city did not have to compensate landowners for the permanent closing of one entrance for safety reasons; no compensation is required for a taking under the exercise of police powers unless that taking results in complete deprivation of access. *Hudson v. City of Shawnee*, 777 P2d 800 (1989).

101.00 DE FACTO AND INVERSE CONDEMNATION

101.05 De Facto Condemnation

5th Circuit Plaintiff, owner of a 16.7-acre tract of land zoned for single-family residential use, requested rezoning from the city council for use as a medical office complex. The planning commission staff, while considering the request, was also planning to expropriate the property by eminent domain, an act that would compel the city to pay more money if the land was reclassified according to plaintiff's request. Thereafter, plaintiff requested rezoning to multi-family residential use. It took three and one-half years for the city council and planning commission to decide on both requests. Plaintiff sued the city and its mayor for deprivation of property without due process and just compensation resulting from the delay in granting either request. *Held:* No taking by the city occurred, for "mere fluctuations of value during the process of governmental decision-making" do not amount to a taking in violation of due process. The mayor, as a local legislator, was entitled to absolute immunity from federal damage claims arising from his conduct when acting in a legislative capacity. *Hernandez v. City of Lafayette*, 643 F2d 1188 (1981).

Georgia Landowners sought to restrain the city from constructing a transit station and a pedestrian mall on a public street. The city had acquired an easement of public right-of-way over plaintiffs' property. Landowners contended that the city's action amounted to a taking for which just and adequate compensation must be paid. The city argued that the limiting of the street for pedestrian use did not constitute an abandonment of the easement. *Held:* The right of access to a public road is a property right that arises from ownership of land contiguous to a public right-of-way. A landowner cannot be deprived of such right without the payment of just and adequate compensation. An action that impedes a landowner's ingress and egress constituted a taking that entitled the landowner to damages. Construction of a transit station constituted an additional servitude on the landowners' fee and required the payment of just and adequate compensation. *Metropolitan Atlanta Rapid Transit Auth. v. Datry*, 200 SE2d 905 (1975).

Massachusetts Town conservation commission denied plaintiff's application to build a road on marshlands adjoining his property, which he then planned to develop. Plaintiff argued that the denial was a taking of his property requiring compensation because his property could not be developed without the road. *Held:* Although plaintiff was deprived of one profitable use of his property, there was no taking. A compensable taking exists only if all practical value of the property is destroyed. Several profitable alternative uses remained, even without the road. *Lovequist v. Conservation Comm'n* 393 NE2d 858 (1979).

Oklahoma Landowners sued to recover damages from the state when a 19-gun salute at the governor's inauguration injured their home. The state submitted that sovereign immunity barred the action. Landowners contended that the interference was so substantial as to constitute a taking. *Held:* A single, unintentionally destructive act does not amount to a taking.

The firing of the cannons did not constitute an abnormally dangerous activity so as to support a strict liability theory of recovery. *State ex rel. Coffey v. District of Okla. City*, 547 P2d 947 (1976).

Pennsylvania In 1975, the state Department of Transportation (DOT) placed stakes on a small triangular portion of owners' backyard required for a new road's right-of-way. Owners tried selling their home, but could find no buyer even after lowering their price. Owners sued DOT for a de facto taking, contending that, because the highway might pass above their property, generating noise, there was a substantial interference with their use and enjoyment of the property. *Held:* No de facto taking had occurred. There was no evidence owners had lost the use of their property as a residence; and, since neither the highway nor the noise had come to pass, there could be no present de facto taking. Merely having a somewhat less desirable house to live in, or having difficulties in selling, did not constitute the type of exceptional circumstances needed to prove de facto taking. *Pennsylvania Dep't of Transp. v. Steppler*, 542 A2d 175 (Commw. Ct. 1988).

South Dakota Owner purchased 11 acres of land next to the municipal airport, intending to construct commercial buildings. However, he abandoned his efforts to obtain a building permit upon learning of plans to acquire his land for airport expansion. Four years later, the city began condemnation proceedings, but the owner won his counterclaim for delay damages for a de facto taking, which he claimed had occurred four years earlier. *Held:* Reversed. Owner did not meet the two-pronged test for a de facto taking by failing to show either that condemnation had become inevitable as of a certain date before it actually took place or that the land had lost its value and could not be sold or rented. Four years was not a remarkably long time for the city to start condemnation proceedings for an airport expansion. Owner's failure to apply for a building permit was his own business decision, and in the absence of coercion by the city, the city would not be held responsible. *City of Brookings v. Mills*, 412 NW2d 497 (1987).

Washington Railroad sued an irrigation district when an irrigation canal broke and the escaping water washed away their railroad tracks. The railroad alleged that the damage constituted a taking and required compensation. *Held:* A constitutional taking is a permanent or recurring invasion of private property. Where the railroad tracks were repaired, there was no constitutional taking. *Northern Pac. Ry. v. Sunnyside Valley Irrigation Dist.*, 540 P2d 1387 (1975).

101.10 Inverse Condemnation

9th Circuit Plaintiffs acquired an option to purchase land from seller, in exchange for a loan by plaintiffs. The option agreement provided that during its term, seller would not transfer the parcels to any third party. Before the expiration of the option, the governor of Hawaii announced that, under threat of condemnation, seller had agreed to sell the parcels to the state, and that the state was to take the land subject to plaintiffs' option. As a result of this announcement, plaintiffs were unable to obtain the financing necessary to exercise their option. They sued the state and seller, claiming they had conspired to announce the state's purchase of the land so as to prevent plaintiffs' obtaining purchase financing. *Held:* Loss of opportunity to exercise an option to purchase real property was not a compensable property interest. The announcement of an intent to condemn is not, by itself, inverse condemnation in the absence of a more direct and substantial interference with the use and enjoyment of the property. *Windward Partners v. Ariyoshi*, 693 F2d 928 (1982) cert. denied, 461 US 906 (1983).

9th Circuit Landowner owned two contiguous parcels, A and B, both of which he intended to develop. Meanwhile, the county rezoned Parcel A to allow four multiple residential units per acre; and Parcel B, as with all water-edge lowlands, was rezoned "urban open space" to allow one multiple residential unit per five acres. Landowner sought damages for inverse condemnation of Parcel B. Landowner appealed a summary judgment ruling that there was no taking, arguing Parcel B should be considered a separate parcel for purposes of inverse condemnation. *Held:* For landowner. There was a question of fact as to whether both parcels or Parcel B alone should be examined to determine if a taking occurred. The ordinance, by adopting different zoning designations for the two tracts, may have created two separate parcels for "taking" purposes. Landowner should have submitted a development plan to the county for the parcels to determine whether the county would treat them separately at the development stage. If that was the case, then Parcel B must be analyzed as a separate parcel. *American Sav. & Loan Ass'n v. County of Marin*, 653 F2d 364 (1981).

D.C. Circuit As part of a navigational project, the Army Corps of Engineers dredged and widened portions of certain riverbeds, knowing it would increase erosion of adjoining property. Ultimately, the work undermined a house, causing it to collapse. The court of claims ruled the government was immune from suit under its navigational servitude. *Held:* Construction on the riverbed was a compensable taking despite the government's navigational servitude. Navigable waters are considered public property under the exclusive control of the federal government. There is no compensable taking if the government improves navigation within the boundaries of the navigational servitude. The government argued that since all construction occurred within the riverbed, any damage outside it was indirect and noncompensable. However, the court ruled that a taking may result when improvements to navigation result in erosion to land located outside the bed of the stream. *Owen v. United States*, 851 F2d 1404 (1988).

Federal Circuit Plaintiff claimed compensation for a six-year period when the United States denied it the opportunity to mine its goldfields because of a title dispute with the government, which plaintiff eventually won. The court of claims granted summary judgment to the United States, holding that there had been no taking, because it had not physically barred plaintiff from using the mine. *Held:* Reversed and remanded. The basic factual issue of whether a taking had occurred was decided on an incomplete record. The government's action had the effect of eminent domain taking; it was an inverse condemnation. The government's interference with plaintiff's use of its property may have been so burdensome that a constitutional taking could be implied; a physical taking and possession were not required. An absence of good faith on the part of the United States was found in its denial to plaintiff of mining rights for six years. *Yuba Goldfields, Inc. v. United States*, 723 F2d 884 (1983).

Alaska Plaintiff operated an air taxi service from his waterfront property on a lake. The state built a bridge in the vicinity, and as a result plaintiff had to relocate his business. He brought suit claiming damages in condemnation, arguing that his riparian rights were destroyed. *Held:* Plaintiff has no right of compensation. Although state policy, as expressed in prior cases, is to construe broadly the right of condemnation recovery in instances of shoreline interference, there was no true property interest at stake in this case. The bridge did not prevent access to the lake from plaintiff's property, but merely prevented the enjoyment of purported airspace easement. *Classen v. Department of Highways*, 621 P2d 15 (1980).

Arkansas In 1983, the Arkansas General Assembly passed Act 166, giving county judges the discretion to designate roads used as school bus routes as county roads and obligating the county to maintain and repair roads so designated. As a result, Road 244, a privately owned gravel road that had been used as a school bus route for at least ten years and had been maintained by the county, was declared a county road. An additional factor in the county judge's decision was the complaints of members of the public who had been verbally abused when they sought to use the private road. Owners of part of the road sued, arguing that the judge had abused his discretion and that Act 166 was unconstitutional, since it allowed the taking of private property for public use without compensation. *Held:* There was no taking in the sense contemplated by the Constitution. Where an owner permits what might otherwise have been a private road to be used as a school bus route for upwards of 10 years and permits the county to repair and maintain the road for a comparable period, he cannot be heard to complain that his property has been taken without compensation. *Johnson v. Wylie*, 679 SW2d 198 (1984).

California Plaintiffs, owners of 30 acres of vacant land, applied to the county for a zoning change from agricultural to commercial and were rejected. The taxes and assessments on plaintiffs' land had always been based on its highest and best use as an area of commercial and industrial development. Plaintiffs sued the county for inverse condemnation, claiming that under the Fifth and Fourteenth Amendments, the refusal to rezone was an unlawful taking of property without just compensation. *Held:* The remedy of inverse condemnation was not available where plaintiffs never submitted a specific plan to use their property according to the manner permitted by the zoning regulations; the controversy required for a judgment of inverse condemnation therefore did not exist. The zoning regulations, whose purpose was to reduce the density and noise level in a particular region of the county, constituted a valid exercise of police power and was not a compensable taking. *Gilliland v. County of Los Angeles*, 179 Cal. Rptr. 73 (1981).

California Plaintiffs sued the Bay Area Rapid Transit District (BART) in inverse condemnation, alleging that excavation by BART alongside their property resulted in damages to the property and required them to make extensive repairs to prevent their building from settling. *Held:* The subject of the litigation was damage caused by the BART excavation to the right of lateral support, which plaintiffs' property enjoyed. This right constitutes an interest in real property. Thus, the costs reimbursement was upheld. Under California law, the interest is theorized as a right incident to the land itself and part of the owner's right to enjoy his land. Furthermore, no actual physical "taking" is required in order to justify the award of costs; it is sufficient if a public entity encroaches upon some lesser property interest. *Holtz v. San Francisco Bay Area Rapid Transit Dist.*, 552 P2d 430 (1976).

Connecticut Plaintiffs' land abutted an unimproved public highway, which the town lawfully discontinued. Claiming this deprived them of access to the public road system, plaintiffs sued the town. *Held:* The statute authorizing discontinuance of public highways did not violate plaintiffs' constitutional rights, and the diminished right of access was not an inverse condemnation entitling plaintiffs to compensation. Under Conn. Gen. Stat. § 13a-55, owners of land abutting a discontinued highway continue to have a right-of-way over it to the nearest highway. Before the statute was enacted, discontinuance of public highways extinguished the private easement of access and entitled abutting landowners to compensation. The statute, by allowing a town to impose an easement on private land, did not unconstitutionally authorize a taking of private property without compensation. The court rejected plaintiffs' argument that the discontinuance so impaired their access rights as to constitute a taking. Plaintiffs had the right to improve the road or to use it in its unimproved state. *Luf v. Town of Southbury*, 449 A2d 1001 (1982).

District of Columbia Building owner appealed an order entered by an agent of the District of Columbia government denying a permit to demolish a building pursuant to the Historic Landmark and Historic District Protection Act of 1978, D.C. Code 1980 Supp., §§ 5-821 et seq. He asserted that the decision was an unconstitutional taking because it placed an unreasonable economic hardship on the property owner with regard to the best use of the land. Evidence showed that the building could be rented "as is" or with minimal renovation, and that a full renovation would have cost much less than claimed by the owner. *Held:* Denial of permit affirmed. If there is a reasonable alternative economic use for the property after the imposition of a restriction on that property as an historical landmark, there is no taking, and hence no unreasonable economic hardship to owners regardless of how much the property may be diminished in cash value and no matter what "higher" or "more beneficial use" of the property may exist. *900 G. St. Assocs. v. Department of Hous. & Community Dev.*, 430 A2d 1387 (1981).

Florida The Florida Department of Agriculture burned 300,000 of growers' citrus trees and budwood despite tests that showed growers' stock was not infected with citrus canker that had been found at a neighboring nursery. Growers brought an inverse condemnation suit. At issue was whether the state had the authority to destroy healthy, but suspect, citrus trees without compensation. *Held:* When the state destroyed the healthy trees pursuant to its police power and for a public benefit, a taking occurred, and the growers were entitled to full and just compensation. A taking may consist of an entirely negative act such as the trees' destruction, and does not depend on the state's taking a proprietary interest in the property. It was also immaterial that no statute specifically authorized recovery for the loss of healthy trees, since the Fifth Amendment requirement that just compensation be paid upon a taking is self-executing. *Department of Agric. & Consumer Servs. v. Mid-Florida Growers*, 521 So. 2d 101, cert. denied, 109 S. Ct. 180 (1988).

Florida Plaintiff planned to develop submerged shallow flatlands, and applied to the Department of Environmental Regulation (DER) for a permit. DER denied the permit because it found the project would obliterate aquatic life in the area. Plaintiff, bypassing the administrative appeal process, went directly to court, claiming DER's denial was a taking of its property by inverse condemnation. The Florida Supreme Court addressed, first, whether plaintiff could omit an administrative appeal, and second, what judicial remedies plaintiff could claim following an adverse administrative decision. *Held:* An administrative appeal could have been dispensed with only if plaintiff had challenged the constitutionality of the statute on which DER had based its denial. Since plaintiff made no such claim, administrative review was required. As to judicial remedy, however, plaintiff could concede the correctness of an administrative denial and still claim compensation for a taking. *Key Haven Assoc. Board of Trustees of the Internal Improvement Fund*, 427 So. 2d 153 (1982).

Illinois Landowners sought compensation in an inverse condemnation action for the destruction of their means of access to a public highway when the township road was closed. The state contended that the taken property rights should be valued as of the filing date of the condemnation petition. *Held:* Where there is no actual taking of land and where the damage suffered results solely from the elimination of direct access to a public road, the proper valuation date for the purpose of assessment of damages is the date of the physical closing of the township road. *Department of Transp. v. Shaw*, 369 NE2d 884 (1977).

Maryland Maryland Port Administration (MPA) leased land near the Baltimore harbor to plaintiff, a chemical processor. Another MPA parcel was leased for use as a hazardous waste dump. Plaintiff filed an inverse condemnation suit against the MPA, claiming it was forced to close its plant owing to contamination caused by carcinogens released into the atmosphere from the hazardous wastes. *Held:* There was no governmental taking. First, it was alleged, under a theory of a taking by physical invasion, that the air over plaintiff's plant was occupied by a contaminant. The court rejected this theory; the presence of microscopic airborne particles did not amount to a physical taking in the constitutional sense. Under a theory of a taking without physical invasion, i.e., an adverse effect on plaintiff's property of state activity elsewhere, the consequences did not support an inverse condemnation claim. The effect must be severe and specific to the property to support damages. The landfill did not have a greater impact on plaintiff's property than on other properties in the area. Finally, the court rejected the theory of a "regulatory taking," based on the effect of state activity on use of the property, as there was no evidence plaintiff's product was actually contaminated. *Maryland Port Admin. v. QC Corp.*, 529 A2d 829 (1987).

Massachusetts Plaintiff threatened to curtail services and dismiss patients in his nursing home. In response, the governor declared a public health emergency, thereby empowering the Department of Public Health to operate the nursing home (which it did for the duration of the emergency). Plaintiff claimed that the department's appropriation and operation of his nursing home was a taking of his property under the state's eminent domain power. *Held:* There was no taking of plaintiff's property for which he was entitled to compensation. The department's operation of the nursing home was a lawful exercise of the state's police power because its purpose was to prevent plaintiff from using his property to the public detriment. Only when an owner's property is appropriated and used for a beneficial public use is there a compensable taking. Moreover, the state's interference with plaintiff's property was minimal; the operation was temporary, and plaintiff at all times retained title. *Davidson v. Commonwealth*, 395 NE2d 1314 (1979).

Minnesota Owners of land abutting an interstate highway claimed that the state's construction of sound barriers along both sides of the road blocked their light and view. They also claimed the barriers acted as traps for auto exhaust, inhibiting airflow and creating a greater health risk than without the barriers. They sued for inverse condemnation of their implied easements for light, air, and view, and sought just compensation. *Held:* The easements, which were limited property interests, remained subservient to the public right to travel on the roadway. Any interference with owners' light, air, and view easements as a result of a proper street use by the public was not compensable. The sound barriers, constructed to comply with federal noise pollution regulations, were themselves a proper street use. Since there had been no additional servitude placed upon landowners' easements, there had been no taking of those easements. *Haeussler v. Brown*, 314 NW2d 4 (1981).

New Hampshire Landowner owned three contiguous parcels, amounting to several hundred acres. All three parcels had frontage on a road, and the third parcel had frontage on the road exclusively. The town decided to discontinue the road, and landowner sued. The superior court dismissed her action insofar as she sought damages, and the supreme court accepted her interlocutory appeal concerning the damages. *Held:* The court held that landowner was entitled to damages if she could persuade the court or jury that she did not have reasonable access to her property after the road was discontinued. The court limited its earlier finding in *Wolfe v. Windham*, 327 A2d 721 (1974), that a landowner whose property has frontage on a public road cannot recover damages for the road's discontinuance if there remains a means by which the landowner retains access to his property, by requiring that the alternative access be reasonable. The court did not offer guidance on what would constitute "reasonable" access to the public highway system. *Orcutt v. Town of Richmond*, 517 A2d 1160 (1986).

New Mexico Plaintiff entered into a contract to purchase land from the state of New Mexico. The contract contained a provision reserving all of the minerals to the State. The state land commissioner then authorized the removal of sand and gravel, having a value over $20,000, from the land. Plaintiff brought suit seeking damages for the removal of sand and gravel in breach of the sales contract. The state counterclaimed that the land contract was void under the New Mexico Enabling Act and, therefore, should be declared void. *Held:* The court held that, in the absence of a specific reservation in the contract, common sand and gravel are not "minerals" under a mineral reservation clause, because they lack exceptional characteristics. It then held that nothing in the Enabling Act or the New Mexico Constitution prohibited the state or land commissioner from selling lands and the sand and gravel contained thereon. The contract with plaintiff was held to be a valid conveyance of land, sand, and gravel. *Jensen v. State Highway Comm'n*, 642 P2d 1089 (1982), cert. denied, 459 US 838 (1984).

Oklahoma Landowner sued in inverse condemnation, contending that municipality's floodplain ordinance was in effect a taking of his land without due process. Plaintiff alleged in his complaint that the ordinance reserved his land for drainage purposes, and that, given the diversion of streams and inadequate drainage channels, flooding would ensue repeatedly. The trial court dismissed the complaint on the ground that the ordinance was a valid exercise of the city's police power. *Held:* The constitutional validity of a municipality's exercise of its police powers does not foreclose a suit in inverse condemnation. The complaint states a cause of action and must be heard. *Mattoon v. City of Norman*, 617 P2d 1347 (1980).

Oregon Plaintiff brought an inverse condemnation action against the state highway commission to recover damages for alleged taking of property in the process of freeway construction by placing a "cloud of condemnation" over the property, resulting in a "condemnation blight" and a de facto taking, not of actual possession, but of the use and benefit of the property. The highway commission's acts consisted of posting notices that the land was being taken for highway purposes; dismantling surrounding homes; creating noise, dust, decay, and confusion; posting a notice to tenants of property that they would be required to leave and that their moving expenses would be paid if they vacated promptly. Since plaintiff's property was not actually taken, the highway commission demurred to the complaint. *Held:* A landowner's rights in the land and not the land itself are taken in an inverse condemnation proceeding. The state need not benefit in order to find a taking. Where the complaint stated facts whereby the state led the tenants to believe that the property was being condemned, and plaintiff's property declined in value and its rental income was decreased, the complaint stated a cause of action in inverse condemnation. *Lincoln Loan Co. v. State*, 545 P2d 105 (1976).

Tennessee Landowners sued the county for closing a road and thereby interfering with their direct access to an interstate highway. The county alleged that since there had been only an impairment of access to the property, damages should be computed on a different basis than when property is condemned. *Held:* The impairment of the right of ingress and egress to a public way involves a deprivation of a landowner's property right. The measure of damages is the difference between the fair market values before and after the taking. This is the same measure used in condemnation proceedings. *Shelby County v. Barden*, 527 SW2d 124 (1975).

Texas A sidewalk and street improvement project undertaken by the city temporarily impaired access to a restaurant along the street and generated noise and dust inside the restaurant. The restaurant owners sued for inverse condemnation, claiming that they had lost profits because of the noise, dust, and reduced access. The court of appeals found for the restaurant, holding that an action for damages will lie even though all reasonable access has not been disrupted if access is materially and substantially impaired. *Held:* Reversed. In order to show a material and substantial interference with access to one's property, it is necessary to show that there has been a total but temporary restriction of access, a partial but permanent restriction of access, or a temporary limited restriction of access brought about by an illegal activity or one that is negligently performed or unduly delayed. The facts of this case did not fit any of these categories. Therefore, the restaurant owners were not entitled to a condemnation award. *City of Austin v. Avenue Corp.*, 704 SW2d 11 (1986), rev'g 685 SW2d 453 (Ct. App. 1985).

Washington Property owners who had lived near the Seattle Airport since it opened in 1948 brought an inverse condemnation suit against the port authority for compensation for the diminished value of their property resulting from noise at the airport. The port authority argued that plaintiffs' claim was barred by the 10-year statute of limitations for suits in adverse possession since it had acquired a prescriptive avigational easement over the property well before 1964. *Held:* While a 10-year period of time, together with the requisite elements of adverse possession, would vest defendant with a prescriptive avigational easement that would not be compensable, the increase in airport activity following such acquisition would be compensable. However, a prescriptive avigational easement did not exist because, prior to 1964, aircraft then being used did not generate enough noise to have caused any diminution of the value of plaintiffs' property. Furthermore, even if defendant had acquired some kind of pre-1964 prescriptive easement, it would not bar plaintiffs' action for increased damages caused by the more recent uses. *Petersen v. Port of Seattle*, 618 P2d 67 (1980).

PART S

OTHER METHODS OF TRANSFER AND RESTRAINTS ON ALIENATION

102.00 JUDICIAL PROCESS

102.05 Transfer by Judicial Process

9th Circuit Relying on prior law in which the Hawaii Supreme Court had held that the common-law doctrine of riparian rights was not in force in Hawaii with respect to "surplus" waters of a stream and that a landowner could use such water collected on his land, plaintiffs spent millions of dollars improving property irrigated by the Hanapepe River. In 1973, the Hawaii Supreme Court adopted the common-law doctrine of riparian rights and declared the flow of the Hanapepe River to be the sovereign property of the state. Plaintiffs sought to enjoin enforcement of the new law. *Held:* Plaintiffs, having acquired through judicial process a de jure right to divert water from their lands within the river watershed to other lands outside the watershed, could not be divested of that right without just compensation. The Supreme Court of Hawaii could not interfere with rights that were vested before the change in law was announced. The case was vacated and remanded for consideration in light of *Williamson County Regional Planning Commission v. Hamilton Bank*, 473 US 172 (1985). *Robinson v. Ariyoshi*, 753 F2d 1468 (1985), vacated, 474 US 1018 (1986), reaffirmed, 676 F. Supp. 1002 (D. Haw. 1987).

Alabama Plaintiff purchased property at a tax sale and obtained a tax certificate from the commissioner of revenue that was later destroyed by fire. He sued to obtain a duplicate of the certificate from the circuit court, alleging that he had never transferred or assigned the certificate. The trial court dismissed the complaint on the ground that the tax certificate was plaintiff's private property. *Held:* Plaintiff made out a prima facie case for restoration of his lost tax certificate. The tax certificate is the equivalent of a deed and it is within the court's equity jurisdiction to establish lost, and execute new, deeds. *Wilkerson v. Moore*, 318 So. 2d 241 (1975).

Illinois Original owner of property sold at a tax sale sought to vacate a tax deed issued to assignee of the tax sale purchaser and held by a subsequent grantee. Original owner claimed that the tax deed was fraudulently obtained and that grantees were not bona fide purchasers, because they knew the original owner was regularly using the property. The lower court held that grantees were bona fide purchasers and that the two-year statute of limitations, which would have been tolled if there were fraud, barred the complaint. *Held:* Grantees could not claim status as bona fide purchasers, since they had constructive notice that the original owner had a claim to the property. *Application of County Treasurer v. Ex-Officio County Collector*, 332 NE2d 557 (App. Ct. 1975).

Michigan When owner failed to pay county and city taxes for a two-year period, property was sold to the state and, after the expiration of the redemption period, was sold at public auction. Owner had paid unpaid city taxes during the redemption period and sued to set aside the deed by the state, claiming that by paying the city taxes she had redeemed the property. Owner sought damages on the ground that the state was unjustly enriched by the amount received at public auction in excess of the amount of taxes due. *Held:* The action for unjust enrichment was directed at vacating the deed. It was, therefore, barred by the six-month statute of limitations for challenging the validity of such deeds. The six-month statute of limitations did not apply to the action for restitution, and the court consequently reversed and remanded to allow proceedings on that action. *Dean v. Michigan Dep't of Natural Resources*, 247 NW2d 876 (1976).

Nevada Former wife brought a suit in equity against the estate of her deceased former husband for an implied trust with respect to an interest in land that had been conveyed to decedent alone. Friends of the wife and decedent promised to give them a two-acre parcel of land if they assumed the management duties of a certain trailer park. When decedent died, it was discovered that the land was deeded only in the name of the husband. The trial court found that the consideration for the deed was provided by services rendered principally by the wife. *Held:* Where consideration is provided by one party, but title is taken in another, and the circumstances negate the possibility of the consideration being a gift, equity intervenes to protect the rights of the first party. Thus, when the land was deeded erroneously to the husband as sole grantee, he took title to the land in trust for the wife, creating a resulting trust based on the presumed intention of the parties. *Cummings v. Tinkle*, 539 P2d 1213 (1975).

New Hampshire When a property owner failed to pay taxes for the years 1968 to 1971, the property was sold at a tax sale. In a suit to set aside the tax deed held by purchaser, the trial court excluded evidence concerning the inadequacy of the purchase price and the experience of purchaser. *Held:* The evidence was properly excluded. The inadequacy of the purchase price given at a tax sale did not constitute a valid objection to that sale. Nor was the purchaser's experience in buying at tax sales relevant to the issue of the validity of the sale. *Cross v. Linski*, 354 A2d 409 (1976).

103.00
NATURAL CAUSES

103.05
Accretion

U.S. Supreme Court The construction of jetties on Coast Guard property at the entrance of a bay in California caused 184 acres of formerly submerged lands to become uplands. A dispute arise as to ownership of the 184 acres. California sued to quiet title. *Held:* For the United States. Under California law, accretion caused by artificial means does not result in a change in the upland boundary. Under federal law, however, accretion, whatever its cause, belongs to the upland owner. Under the Submerged Lands Act, the United States has title to all accretions to coastal lands that it has acquired; therefore, the dispute was controlled by federal law. *California ex rel. State Lands Comm'n v. United States*, 457 US 273, reh'g denied, 458 US 1131 (1982).

Alaska State gave the owner of an island in a navigable stream a contract to bail gravel from the bed of the river. As a result of the bailings, a gravel bar was formed. The island owner was given a second contract to bail gravel, which he stockpiled upon the bar. The state then demanded that the gravel be removed, subsequently bringing an action to quiet title of the gravel bar and enjoin owner's trespass. *Held:* Since the state failed to impeach owner's testimony that the gravel bar had accreted above the high-water mark, owner was entitled to the land. Under federal law, the state title reaches to the bed of its navigable rivers as far as the ordinary high-water mark, as modified by accretion. The high-water mark is determined by several factors including shelving, change in soil, absence of litter, and destruction of terrestrial vegetation. The burden of proving accretion remains with the party claiming it, and although accretion may result from artificial causes, the claiming party cannot himself be the cause. Since the state could not disprove the accretion above the high-water mark, nor prove that owner was the cause, owner was entitled to claim the land. *State v. Pandratz*, 538 P2d 984 (1975).

Georgia Oceanfront subdivision was originally owned by family who sold lots along an avenue fronting the ocean. The family retained title to the beach but granted lot owners recreational and access easements. Over the years, the beach area underwent extensive accretion. Family argued that lot owners easement rights over the newly accreted land should be limited to extensions of the side streets that ran into the oceanfront avenue. *Held:* Lot owners' easement extended over the entire beach, including the accreted area. As the rights of family expanded with the accreted land, so did the easement rights of lot owners. Even if the lot owners' recreational rights could be confined to the original beach area, they still would have unlimited access over the accreted area. *Bruce v. Garges*, 379 SE2d 783 (1989).

Mississippi Riparian landowner brought an action to confirm title in 100 acres of land claimed by accretion. The state answered the action and claimed that it was the owner of the accretions. The land had formed from an island in the middle of the river owned by the state; the island gradually attracted soil and eventually connected with the landowner's dike. *Held:* The accretions to or extensions of an island become the property of the owner of the island. *HK Porter Co. v. Board of Supervisors*, 324 So. 2d 746 (1975).

Nebraska Owner of land on the Nebraska side of a river sought an action to quiet title to accretion lands against the owners of land on the Iowa side. The river had originally abutted defendants' land and later moved to the Nebraska side of the state line. In moving, it left an island on the original Nebraska bank and accretion formed downstream from this island. A substantial chute was left on the Iowa side of the island, with additional accretion forming on the Iowa bank east of the chute. *Held:* Defendants acquired title to the land east of the chute. Where accretions to the island and the mainland meet, owner of each owns the accretions to the line of contact. *Valder v. Wallis*, 242 NW2d 112 (1976).

South Carolina Defendant's land lay between plaintiffs' land and the oceanfront. Over the years, by a natural process of accretion, defendant's acreage increased substantially. Plaintiffs, who would lose their ocean view and access across the accreted land, sued to prevent development of the land by defendant. *Held:* Plaintiffs had a right of access to the ocean across the accreted land, but defendant had the right to develop the land. In the court's view, plaintiffs' claim amounted to a prescriptive right to ocean view and breezes, which does not exist under South Carolina law. Plaintiffs' reliance on a case containing similar facts, *Eppes v. Freeman*,

200 SE2d 3235 (1973), was misplaced. Unlike *Eppes*, no public dedication of the accreted land could be proved by plat or other written instrument. Further, lack of implied dedication was proved by evidence that private citizens and public entities would customarily seek defendant's permission to use the accreted land. *Hill v. Beach Co.*, 306 SE2d 604 (1983).

103.10
Reliction

U.S. Supreme Court Ejectment action was brought by the state of Oregon against a corporation that had been digging without a lease for over 40 years in two sections of riverbed of a navigable river that was not an interstate boundary. The first section had been riverbed since the state's admission to the Union, but the second had become so somewhat later, owing to changes in the river's course. The state courts awarded the first part to the state under the equal footing doctrine. This doctrine gives new states the same sovereignty, jurisdiction, and rights as the original states; upon admission, new states acquire title to lands underlying navigable waters within their boundaries. The courts then cited *Bonelli Cattle Co. v. Arizona*, 414 US 313 (1973), as requiring the application of federal common law to the question of ownership of the second part, and they awarded that section to the corporation. The U.S. Supreme Court granted cross-petitions for certiorari. *Held:* Once equal footing gives title to the riverbed to the state upon its admission to the Union, changes in the course of the river are not subject to a reapplication of the doctrine. The thesis of *Bonnelli* was that equal footing required the effect of such changes to be decided under federal common law. *Bonnelli* is overruled. Title to the land is to be decided solely by state law. *Oregon v. Corvallis Sand & Gravel Co.*, 429 US 363 (1977).

Alaska Plaintiffs owned homestead lands in a wetlands region. Since the time of the original federal surveys, 95 acres of land had emerged on the seaward side of plaintiffs' property. Plaintiffs contended the ninety-five acres were created by accretion, and that the land should inure to their benefit as shoreline owners. The State of Alaska argued that the land was formed by glacio-isostatic uplift and was not subject to the common-law doctrine of accretion. *Held:* For plaintiffs. The court first held that state, not federal, law governed. Under Alaska common law, accretion is an expansion of land along a waterway by the gradual deposit of soil due to the movement of contiguous waters. Reliction, involving the expansion of land by the emergence of existing soil, was subject to the same rule as accretion regarding title; the benefit accrues to the shoreline owner. Glacio-isostatic uplift was a form of reliction and therefore subject to the doctrine of accretion. *Honsinger v. State*, 642 P2d 1352 (1982).

North Dakota Landowners brought a class action suit to determine the ownership of a lake bed. The state claimed title to all land up to the ordinary high-water mark represented by the meander line, despite recession of the lake's waters. Landowners claimed ownership of land exposed by recession of the lake's waters under the doctrine of reliction, using a fluctuating ordinary high-water mark. *Held:* For landowners. The doctrine of reliction, using an ambulatory ordinary high-water mark, may be applied to determine the boundary of the state's ownership in the lake bed. The water line, and not the meander line, is ordinarily used to determine the boundary of a tract of land abutting a navigable body of water. The test to determine the high-water mark is the point where the presence of water is so continuous that it destroys the value of the land for agricultural purposes. In this case, evidence based upon vegetation and strand lines was sufficient to show an ordinary high-water mark. *In re Ownership of Bed of Devils Lake*, 423 NW2d 141 (1988).

103.15
Erosion

Washington Meander lines were established by government surveys along banks of navigable rivers. Subsequent to the surveys there were accretions and erosions at certain points of the rivers. An action was brought for a declaratory judgment by upland owners, claiming title through federal grants, to quiet title to disputed riverbeds, and to determine the rights of their lessees. A counterclaim sought that the state be declared the lawful owner of the riverbeds and that leases issued under its claim of ownership be declared valid. *Held:* Owners of land abutting navigable rivers acquired from the federal government by owners' predecessors and lessees of such owners were entitled to accreted lands lying between current lines of ordinary high water and original meander lines to the landward; but the state and its lessees were entitled to beds of navigable rivers that lay between original meander lines in the rivers and the current lines of ordinary high water to which rivers had eroded. *Smith Tug & Barge Co. v. Columbia-Pacific Towing Corp.*, 482 P2d 769 (1971), cert. denied, 404 US 829 (1971).

103.20
Effect of Waterlines on Boundaries and Titles

8th Circuit Along a bend of the Arkansas River, defendants owned land on which the river encroached steadily. The Army Corps of Engineers straightened the river, making fertile land of the riverbend. The United States acquired title to the land northeast of the former riverbed and set boundary markings in the thalweg of the bend, marking the boundary of a wildlife refuge northeast of the bend. Defendants farmed the riverbed northeast of the boundary, and the United States brought suit to quiet title. *Held:* The land northeast of the thalweg belonged to the United States. The defendants' contention that a shift in the river in the early 1950s was an avulsion, entitling them to restoration of their 1951 boundaries, had no merit. Since the change in the river's course was due to erosion and since defendants could not identify land formerly belonging to them that had shifted to the other side, the shift was an accretion. Title to the riverbed vested in the riparian owners at the time of the diversion, with the boundary between the owners at the thalweg. *United States v. Keenan*, 753 F2d 681 (1985).

Oklahoma Property owners asserted claim of title to land that had undergone surface changes after a river altered course and created new acreage. The lower court ruled, inter alia, that surface and mineral interests were fixed, notwithstanding the migration of natural waters. *Held:* Reversed. Once they have been severed, mineral interests may be diminished by natural forces such as erosion and accretion. The movement and change of surface characteristics are controlling in such cases, since any other rule would introduce gross inequity in treatment of owners who have severed their property and those who have not. *Nilsen v. Tenneco Oil Co.*, 614 P2d 36 (1980).

Wisconsin Proceeding was brought by the state to compel riparian landowner to remove fill that he had allegedly deposited onto the bed of a navigable lake. *Held:* For landowner. Although the state's claim ran to the ordinary high-water mark, the riparian owner had a qualified right to the land between the actual water level and the ordinary high-water mark. Landowner could exclude the public but could not interfere with navigation. *State v. McFarren*, 215 NW2d 459 (1974).

104.00 ADVERSE POSSESSION

104.05 Open, Notorious, and Visible Possession

Alabama In a boundary action, defendant appealed from a decision fixing a boundary line based on plaintiff's adverse possession of the property up to a fence constructed in 1920. Defendant argued that the mere grazing of cattle on the land from time to time did not constitue adverse possession. *Held:* The fence had been used openly and notoriously to contain cattle for over 40 years and thus amply supported the trial court's ruling. *Kimbrell v. Allred*, 317 So. 2d 487 (1975).

Arkansas Stahl's property was bisected by a public road. Thompson owned a house north of Stahl's property. Two dirt roads were created by constant use, leading from the public road on Stahl's property to the Thompson house. Stahl's property north of the public road was wild and unimproved. Stahl claimed the roads were used by permission; Thompson claimed a prescriptive easement over the roads. *Held:* A prescriptive easement was acquired. The use of wild, unimproved land is presumed to be permissive until those using the land demonstrate their claim by open and notorious conduct. Here, witnesses testified that the roads had existed for 30 years. Stahl's predecessor in title testified that the use of the land was without permission. Under the circumstances, open, hostile, and adverse use was established. *Stahl v. Thompson*, 641 SW2d 721 (1982).

Louisiana Record title owners brought a petitory action against a neighboring landowner for recognition of their ownership of disputed four-and-a-half-acre tract. Defendant claimed ownership based on adverse possession for more than 30 years. Defendant had lived there with his four children since 1922, and had fenced and cultivated the land since 1925. Most of the property had been used for pasture for defendant's horses, cattle, and hogs. *Held:* Partial fencing and use of property amounted to sufficient enclosure and possession of land to support defendant's claim of title by adverse possession. *William T. Burton Indus., Inc. v. Cook*, 322 So. 2d 880 (Ct. App. 1975), aff'd, 326 So. 2d 372 (1976).

Mississippi Landowner sued for damages when defendant cut all the timber on his lands. Defendant claimed that he owned the land by adverse possession under state law (Miss. Code Ann. § 15-1-17), which sets a two-year period as the time in which possession of "wild lands" ripens into ownership. While defendant had cut firewood on the land and had grazed cattle there during the past two winters, he had not paid taxes on the property, nor had he told plaintiff, with whom he was in daily contact, that he claimed the property as his own. *Held:* Although possession need not include actual occupation and cultivation, defendant had failed to demonstrate that his possession was exclusive, open, and notorious, and that the lands were wild lands. *Woodall v. Ross*, 317 So. 2d 892 (1975).

Montana Party claiming title to two lots by adverse possession brought an action to quiet title against successors of the titleholders. The claimant based his adverse possession upon the acts of his grantor whose land abutted the lots in question. The grantor had continuously occupied the land and, for at least 15 years, had cultivated it yearly, had paid the property taxes, leased the land, and, finally, had conveyed it to the claimant. *Held:* The burden of proof rests with the party claiming adverse possession. Since the evidence was conflicting and legal title had at all times remained with defendants, the evidence would be reviewed in a light most favorable to defendants who were the prevailing party. *Horacek v. Hudson*, 538 P2d 1019 (1975).

Nebraska Plaintiff sued to quiet title to a disputed tract of land based on a claim of adverse possession through farming the land. Plaintiff objected to the admission of aerial photographs to show that the possession was not adverse. *Held:* The trial court did not err in admitting evidence of aerial photographs supporting defendant's contentions without interpretation by an expert witness and not provided for in the pretrial conference. Plaintiff did not sustain his burden of showing actual, open, exclusive, and continuous possession for 10 years; and the decision for defendants was affirmed. *Mousel v. Ten Bensel*, 238 NW2d 632 (1976).

New York In 1954, portion of property was sold, together with a nonexclusive easement over seller's retained property affording access to a street. In 1970, the dominant parcel was sold to plaintiff. Landlord leased the servient parcel to defendant. In 1977, plaintiff demanded that defendant remove obstructions blocking the easement. When defendant refused, suit followed. *Held:* The easement had been extinguished through adverse possession after 10 years of continuous and exclusive use by defendant. Defendant had erected locked gates across the easement and parked wrecked cars over it. No one, including plaintiff, had used the easement after defendant leased the property and erected barriers over easement in 1966. There was no requirement that plaintiff demand the removal of the obstructions before the easement could be extinguished when defendant's adverse possession was exclusive, open, and notoriously hostile to the interests of plaintiff. Defendant did not lack standing to assert adverse possession because it was a tenant rather than the owner of the servient parcel. Its use was hostile to plaintiff, not the owner, who would enjoy the benefit of the extinguished easement when the tenancy expired. *Spiegel v. Ferraro*, 541 NE2d 15 (1989).

Pennsylvania Landowners owned property on street dedicated for public use on a recorded plan, but the street was never accepted by the city for public use and never opened to the public. To permit access to their lots, landowners created a roadway on the street. Neighbors owned lots adjacent to landowners and had used a portion of the street as part of their yards. They objected to landowners' access road, claiming that the right of access had been extinguished by their adverse possession. *Held:* Neighbors failed to prove adverse possession of the disputed portion of the street when they had not (1) erected barriers to obstruct the street or (2) erected any structures or planted any trees, shrubs, and so forth to give the impression that access to the right-of-way was restricted. Neighbors' maintenance of the disputed portion of the street as extensions of their yards was not inconsistent with the access right and could not be used to prove adverse possession. *Estojak v. Mazsa*, 562 A2d 271 (1989).

Vermont In an action by the record owner to quiet title to a parcel of land, the trial court found that the record owner had used the disputed parcel for logging, pasturing, and grazing, while the adverse claimant had cut some hay and timber from the land. *Held:* Occupancy and use by the record owner during the 15-year period both interrupted the continuity of possession necessary and rendered such possession nonexclusive. The doctrine asserted by the adverse claimant that continuous possession is not necessary in certain cases was not relevant, since the land was not unoccupied. *Rueda v. Kuban*, 349 A2d 907 (1975).

Virginia When plaintiffs sued to ascertain and designate the true boundary between adjoining parcels of property, defendant argued that he acquired title by adverse possession. Defendant, after purchasing his lot, used the land in question for water and lumber and later enclosed it with a fence. Plaintiffs offered to buy the parcel from defendant, but investigation revealed that title to the land was in the hands of a third party, who later conveyed title to plaintiffs. After conveyance, defendant continued to cut firewood, graze cattle, and maintain a junkyard and an outdoor toilet, and he ran plaintiffs' surveyor off the land. *Held:* Defendant established ownership through adverse possession. Defendant had used the land in an open and notorious manner, had enclosed it and exercised dominion and had claimed superior title by right over that of plaintiffs for the statutory period. *Walton v. Rosson*, 222 SE2d 553 (1976).

104.10 Hostile Possession

Illinois For more than 20 years, plaintiffs used a driveway strip that they believed was part of their property. Then defendants, owners of neighboring property, discovered that the driveway strip was actually part of their property. Claiming they had occupied the strip beyond the 20-year statutory time when defendants could maintain an action for possession, plaintiffs brought suit to enjoin defendants from taking the strip into their possession. Defendants argued that plaintiffs' possession did not qualify as adverse possession since plaintiffs were not even aware that defendants owned the strip. *Held:* Possession can be hostile even though it is innocent and without an intent to possess property belonging to another. All that is required to meet the hostility requirement is the act of possession itself. *Joiner v. Janssen*, 421 NE2d 170 (1981).

Maine Plaintiffs were record owners of woodlands that defendants claimed by adverse possession. The trial court ruled that wild land could not be the subject of adverse possession and that defendants failed to prove adverse use by evidence of frequent wood cutting, hunting, and fishing. *Held:* Reversed and remanded for judgment in favor of defendants. The sole issue was whether defendants lacked the requisite intent to hold adversely to plaintiffs. Under state law, whether contested property was entered by mistake, as the lower court held, should not be determinative of the issue of intent. The law requires only that the adverse party intend to hold the property against all other claims, regardless of whether he knew he was an adverse user. The court found no evidence of conduct inconsistent with the exercise of full possessory and ownership rights by defendants. *McMullen v. Dowley*, 483 A2d 698 (1984).

Michigan Adjacent landowners' property shared a common boundary line and was separated by a fence. Landowners believed the fence represented the boundary line. A survey, however, showed the fence was four feet within one owner's property line, and owner moved the fence to reflect the actual boundary. Adjacent owner sued, claiming he had obtained title by adverse possession. *Held:* For defendant. Possession of the disputed land was not hostile, since adjacent owner believed the fence represented the true boundary line. Under Michigan law, one who takes possession of another's land with the intent of holding to the true boundary line, rather than to possess the property adversely, does not show hostile possession necessary to an adverse possession claim. *McQueen v. Black*, 425 NW2d 203 (Ct. App. 1988) (per curiam).

Oregon In 1951, plaintiffs gave neighbors permission to use their driveway to access a public road. The neighbors sold their property in 1964, and the assignees mistakenly believed they had easement rights in the driveway. Plaintiffs and assignees used the driveway and shared maintenance expenses, but never discussed its use or ownership. In 1978, assignees sold the property to defendants, who also mistakenly believed they had an easement to use the driveway. Plaintiffs sued to enjoin defendants' use; defendants claimed an easement by prescription. *Held:* For defendants. Plaintiffs had granted neighbors a nonassignable license to use the driveway, which was revoked when neighbors sold the property in 1964. The use of the driveway by defendants and their assignees was adverse in that it was open, notorious, and continuous for over 10 years. The fact that defendants' and assignees' use of the driveway was based on a mistaken belief was sufficient to prove the element of hostile intent. *Hanscam v. Sousa*, 641 P2d 86 (1982).

Pennsylvania Interloper filed complaint seeking title to a strip of land by adverse possession. On appeal, the superior court found that the use was not hostile, so interloper could not obtain title through adverse possession. *Held:* Reversed and remanded. If all other elements of adverse possession are established, hostility is implied if the true owner fails to eject interloper within the allotted time for an action in ejectment, regardless of trespasser's subjective state of mind. Pennsylvania follows the majority view that hostility is implied if all other elements of adverse possession are present. Attempting to learn the mental state of the adverse possessor involves guesswork; the objective test promotes the use of the land against abandonment. *Tioga Coal v. Supermarkets Gen. Corp.*, 546 A2d 1 (1988).

Rhode Island In 1928, plaintiff conveyed a parcel of land with warranty covenants to buyer. In 1975, buyer's son began building a baseball field on a subdivision of the parcel, conveyed to him by his father. Plaintiff brought an adverse possession action, claiming that since 1928 she had kept the parcel as a cattle farm. She alleged that she had built a fence separating the property from buyer's lots. *Held:* Where grantor retains possession of land, such possession presumably remains subordinate to grantee. The presumption may be rebutted by a showing that grantor, by affirmative action, indicated to grantee that grantor was holding the land in hostility to grantee's title. Such a rebuttal of the presumption appeared to exist in this case. However, a grantor that extends warranty covenants is obligated to protect grantee against any future rightful claims. By granting warranty covenants in the 1928 deed, plaintiff was precluded from asserting a claim to the field by adverse possession, even if rightful. *Lewicki v. Marszalkowski*, 455 A2d 307 (1983).

104.15
Exclusive Possession

Kentucky Plaintiff's parents offered him half their farm if he would work the farm and care for them. He did so for 20 years, until his parents died. During this time, plaintiff had managed the farm, paid taxes and insurance, and claimed ownership of the farm on tax returns and loan applications. No interest was ever deeded to plaintiff. The father's will gave the entire estate to plaintiff and his four sisters in equal shares. Plaintiff sued for the promised half interest. *Held:* For plaintiff. The general rule of nontransferability of real property by parol gift was subject to an exception that possession ripens into title after 15 years. Although plaintiff's possession was not exclusive, and therefore would not strictly satisfy an adverse possession claim, the majority characterized plaintiff's possession as concurrent ownership. Entry on land by permission is fatal to a claim of adverse possession. Entry by gift, however, is adverse to the donor's exclusive title because the donee's possession under the gift is coupled with an assertion of title. In addition, adverseness is not required in the case of concurrent ownership, since the owners are expected to share in the possessory aspects of ownership. *Humphrey v. Harrison*, 646 SW2d 340 (1982).

Nebraska After defendant erected a fence on his land, plaintiff used the south tract for cattle grazing and hunting. Defendant ceased using the tract for cattle grazing but continued using it for hunting. *Held:* Plaintiff did not have exclusive possession of the tract and thus was denied title by adverse possession. *Hutson v. Rush Creek Land & Livestock*, 294 NW2d 374 (1980).

Oregon Defendants bought land from a man who incorrectly told them that the north fence marked the boundary. They maintained the fence often in order to keep their animals on the property, including a triangular area adjacent to the fence, which they assumed to be theirs. However, cattle belonging to others occasionally strayed beyond the fence onto the disputed triangular area. *Held:* These occasional wanderings by cattle belonging to others did not prevent defendants from claiming exclusive possession of the disputed property since they actively maintained the fence in the interest of keeping the area exclusive. *Terry v. Timmons*, 578 P2d 405 (1978).

Washington Since 1972, houseboat owner had moored his houseboat on landowner's property. Landowner sued to quiet title to the property and for trespass damages. Owner claimed the property by adverse possession. *Held:* Owner failed to establish exclusive possession of the property. He shared the use of the property with other owners of houseboats and did not use the property continuously for the full 10-year statutory period for adverse possession. Owner's subjective belief regarding his true intent to dispossess landowner was irrelevant to a determination of adverse possession. *ITT Rayonier, Inc. v. Bell*, 774 P2d 6 (1989).

Washington Husband and wife separated in 1943 but were never divorced; their subsequent conduct was found to establish that they had renounced their marriage. Prior to his death in 1972, husband made a gift of one half of property acquired by the couple before their final separation. Husband had solely controlled the property for almost 30 years after the separation. The trial court held that, since the marriage was a nullity after the final separation, the husband had obtained sole title to the community property by adverse possession and his gift of one half of the property was valid. Wife appealed, seeking to set aside the deed as an unauthorized gift of community property. *Held:* Affirmed. While possession of community property by a spouse can never be hostile to the interests of the other spouse, the termination of the marriage relieves the managing spouse of his duty to act for the benefit of the lapsed community. The evidence showed that the separation in 1943 was meant to be permanent and that after that time there was no union. Thereafter, there was no legal barrier preventing husband from claiming adversely to wife in the property. *Peters v. Skalman*, 617 P2d 448 (1980).

104.20 Actual Possession

Alabama A landline dispute arose between owners of coterminous land. Defendants owned record title to the disputed tract, and plaintiffs claimed title by adverse possession. At the trial, plaintiffs produced numerous witnesses to support their claim that they and those in privity with them plowed and cultivated portions of the tract for a continuous period of 56 years. Although defendants testified that they saw no evidence of adverse possession, they acknowledged that portions of the tract had been plowed and cultivated. The court found for defendants, and plaintiffs appealed. *Held:* Reversed as to those portions of the tract cultivated by plaintiffs. Under Alabama law, cultivation by a coterminous landowner is a sufficient possessory act to constitute adverse possession by actual possession. In light of the uncontroverted testimony of plaintiffs' activities on the land, the trial court's decision was clearly erroneous. However, there was no evidence that plaintiffs ever adversely possessed 400 feet of wooded area. Thus, the trial court's decision was affirmed as to the wooded portion of the tract. *Hayes v. Cotter*, 439 So. 2d 102 (1983).

Alabama Plaintiffs' father bought a parcel in 1917 and dug a ditch that established the boundary line with defendant's adjoining property. The strip was cultivated by the family until 1944. Thereafter, they used the strip sporadically. Defendant purchased his property in 1958 and was told by the previous owner that he owned the strip. In 1981, a survey confirmed that the strip was owned by defendant. Plaintiffs claimed the land by adverse possession. Defendant claimed that even if plaintiffs acquired title, he divested them of it through his adverse possession following his purchase of the adjoining property. *Held:* For plaintiffs. Cultivation of the strip for 27 years was a sufficient possessory act to meet the requirements of adverse possession. Once plaintiffs had proved title to the strip by undisputed evidence of adverse possession, subsequent sporadic use thereafter was insufficient to divest them of title. Defendant's use failed to divest plaintiffs of title, because it was not exclusive, in that he failed to act when plaintiffs planted hedges on it. *Roberts v. Mitchell*, 437 So. 2d 512 (1983).

Georgia After growing crops for two years, landowner converted use of the disputed parcel to tree farming. He planted trees in rows that were visible from an abutting public road. After 20 years, a deed revealed that the parcel was included in land recently bought by plaintiff, who sued to enjoin the trespass. *Held:* Defendant owned the land by adverse possession. Defendant had actual possession for the first two years when he cultivated crops. Whether defendant had actual possession for the remaining years depended on whether the use of the land was so notorious as to attract attention of adverse claimants. Trees planted in rows along a public road gave clear and lasting notice that someone was exercising possession. Changing the nature and appearance of the land contributed to such notice. The court agreed that mere cutting of timber does not constitute actual possession, but noted that tree farming went far beyond occasional removal of trees from wild land. *Cheek v. Wainwright*, 269 SE2d 443 (1980).

Missouri Evidence demonstrated that for the statutory period, intervenor-appellant had the disputed parcel mowed weekly, that she regularly walked across the land, and she planted trees on it. She treated the parcel in all respects as part of her front yard. She paid no taxes and was told that the city owned it. Eleven years after intervenor-appellant began caring for the land, defendant unknowingly bought the land along with his residence. He discovered that his boundaries included this parcel only six years later when he had a survey done. He then built a fence and began maintaining the parcel. Intervenor-appellant did not contest his actions from the time they began in 1971 until the city filed a petition to have the fence removed. *Held:* For appellant. She had actual possession for the statutory period required for adverse possession. She alone exercised the incidences of possession normal to a residential front yard for the statutory period and thus satisfied the actual possession requirement. *City of South Greenfield v. Cagle*, 591 SW2d 156 (1979).

Wyoming Plaintiff had received an overriding royalty interest in mineral rights through an assignment by the original lessee. Plaintiff failed to file the assignment with the county clerk's office. Subsequently, defendants claimed an interest in the lease through an assignment from a bankruptcy receiver. Plaintiff filed a complaint alleging ownership of the overriding royalty and asked for an accounting. The trial court granted summary judgment to defendants on the basis of adverse possession, and plaintiff appealed. *Held:* Reversed and remanded. Adverse possession grants title to real property to one who asserts ownership in the property by actual possession. However, for the owner to have actual possession, the interest in real property must be possessory, that is, the owner must have a degree of physical control over the land. The court stated that while an overriding royalty is an interest in real property, it is a nonpossessory right that entitles the owner to only a share of production. As such, it is not capable of being adversely possessed. *Connaghan v. Eighty-Eight Oil Co.*, 750 P2d 1321 (1988).

104.25
Period of Possession

Arizona Strip of land was acquired through adverse possession by a company that deeded the land to appellee. Appellants had been in possession of the strip of land for eight months when adverse possessor brought an action to quiet title to the property, but appellants were not served. Appellants claimed that they were indispensable parties to the action and sought a declaratory judgment of their rights. *Held:* Appellants were trespassers on the land and were not indispensable parties to the action to quiet title. The adverse possessor acquired title at the end of the 10-year adverse possession period. The title action made the title marketable, but it was not necessary in order to perfect the title. *Babo v. Bookbinder Fin. Corp.*, 551 P2d 63 (1976).

Arkansas Defendant acquired title by adverse possession to a house and two lots that his mother had purchased in 1945. Defendant occupied the house until 1964, when it was destroyed by fire. In 1972, plaintiff asserted that he had acquired title by adverse possession to the property since he had paid property taxes on the property from 1949 until 1972, and since the property had been unimproved and unenclosed for the seven years following the fire. *Held:* Where a taxpayer is without color of title, he can gain title to wild and unimproved land by adverse possession for 15 years. However, "wild and unimproved" is not the equivalent of unimproved and unenclosed land. Once land has been improved, it cannot be wild or unimproved unless it is allowed to return to its natural state. The fact of a fire on the property did not indicate such a return, and the fact of the tax payments did not result in plaintiff's acquisition of title. *Schuman v. Martin*, 531 SW2d 26 (1975).

Mississippi Mother conveyed land to her daughter in 1959, reserving a life estate for herself. She lived with her daughter until she died in 1966. More than 10 years later, the claimant sued, attacking the daughter's title through the original grant to the mother. The daughter claimed title by adverse possession, beginning with the conveyance from her mother in 1959. *Held:* The daughter owned the land. The hostile and adverse possession by the mother and daughter, beginning in 1959, were sufficient to create adverse possession from that date. The possession of the mother/life tenant could be tacked on to the possession of the daughter/remainderman. *Williams v. Woodruff*, 374 So. 2d 232 (1979).

Nebraska Landowners sued to quiet title by adverse possession and alleged that their predecessor in title possessed the premises adversely. *Held:* Where the premises were originally owned by the predecessors as tenants in common and there was no evidence that the landowners' predecessors in title had ousted the defendant's predecessors in title, there was no basis for tacking the landowners' alleged adverse possession onto that of their predecessor in title. *Bartlett v. Kloepping*, 240 NW2d 592 (1976).

Vermont Plaintiff sued to quiet title to a disputed parcel on which it maintained a logging road. Plaintiff claimed record title by intervening conveyances from McCullough in 1902. Defendant also claimed record title from McCullough, claiming that the parcel was reserved when McCullough sold the land to defendant's grantor, the state. The trial court held that plaintiff had record title, but defendant had acquired title by adverse possession. In 1936, the state had acquired the land from McCullough by quitclaim deed. The state conveyed the property to defendant in 1948, reserving a 100-foot strip for a highway. Defendant claimed the benefit of the state's holding period under the doctrine of "tacking"—that the state held the property under claim of right and defendant's subsequent occupancy was also under claim of right and constituted constructive possession. *Held:* There was no adverse possession. Constructive possession is presumed to be with the legal title and will not be disturbed by the claim of one who has a poorer claim of title. Plaintiff had record title and thus constructive possession. The state, and subsequently defendant, had only a claim of right under an ineffective deed. Moreover, plaintiff had actual occupancy by its use of the logging road. The state's minimal actual occupancy of the strip along the highway during construction did not constitute actual possession of the entire parcel. Defendant's "tacking" claim therefore failed. *Laird Properties New Eng. Land Syndicate v. Mad River Corp.*, 306 A2d 562 (1973).

104.30 Continuous Possession

Colorado Plaintiffs sued to quiet title to certain property bordering two reservoirs owned by defendant. The evidence showed that defendant entered on the disputed property for the limited purpose of spraying weeds and removing trash. *Held:* Occasional entry by defendant's employees on disputed property for a limited purpose was not an entry that interrupted plaintiff's occupancy of the disputed property for pasturing livestock and farming. To disrupt adverse possession, the record owner must assert a claim to the land that would reinstate him in possession. Where defendant was on notice from 1946 that plaintiff's use of the disputed land was adverse to its record title, the finding that plaintiff's use of land was adverse, not permissive, was proper. *Bushey v. Seven Lakes Reservoir Co.*, 545 P2d 158 (Ct. App. 1975).

Louisiana Property owner sought to restrain his neighbor from disturbing his peaceful possession of a tract of land. The neighbor threatened to build a chain link fence at what he asserted was the boundary. Plaintiff contended that an old white wooden fence represented the actual boundary, that his garage was located on this area, and that he mowed the area. Defendant alleged that the action could not be maintained, since his grantor had surveyed the property and removed a portion of the wooden fence in 1973. Defendant asserted that these acts interrupted plaintiff's peaceful possession more than one year before the action was brought and barred the action under state law (La. Code Civ. Prov. § 3658 (2)). *Held:* The survey and removal of fence portion did not amount to a disturbance of possession, and the action could therefore be maintained. *Dunn v. Pipes*, 325 So. 2d 349 (Ct. App. 1976).

Pennsylvania Plaintiffs claimed record ownership of a tract of land under a 1973 deed. They inherited the tract in 1957, and had not made any use of it since. Eight to ten years before the trial, plaintiffs stopped to see the property, finding it occupied by defendant. Defendant claimed that when he purchased some property in 1946, his surveyor assured him (incorrectly, the trial court decided) that the tract in question was included in defendant's purchase. In support of his adverse claim, defendant stated that he had cut timber from the disputed tract since 1946, put up "No Trespassing" signs during hunting seasons on what he believed to be the boundary of his property since 1950, expanded the driveway in 1970, installed a garden patch in 1974, and put up a shed in 1979. *Held:* Defendant's only continuous use of the tract was the timber cutting. Most other use of the property was sporadic, and did not even begin until after 1970. There was no adverse possession because there was no actual, continuous, exclusive, visible, notorious, distinct, and hostile use for a 21-year period. *Bigham v. Wenschhof*, 441 A2d 391 (1981).

104.35 Payment of Taxes

Alabama Defendant's ex-husband conveyed property to plaintiff by warranty deed on February 2, 1977. Defendant's ex-husband subsequently conveyed the same property to defendant by quitclaim deed. Plaintiff sued to quiet title. Defendant claimed the land by adverse possession. She alleged that the land was originally from her parents' estates, and although she had conveyed it to her ex-husband, she had paid taxes and remained in possession since 1961. *Held:* Payment of taxes alone does not establish adverse possession. There must also be adverse, actual possession and occupancy that is clear, notorious, continuous, and exclusive for the statutory period under claim of right. This was not the situation here as defendant and ex-husband occupied the property together after it was conveyed to ex-husband. *Reed v. Ray*, 409 So. 2d 814 (1982).

California Defendants habitually crossed to their land over a portion of a neighboring plot that they mistakenly believed to be their own. However, they never paid taxes on the plot. When plaintiff sued to quiet title, defendants counterclaimed for adverse possession and a prescriptive easement. *Held:* Possession by defendants was hostile and adverse for purposes of title by adverse possession or establishing a prescriptive easement. Defendants' failure to pay taxes on the plot precluded a claim of adverse possession, but it did not bar a claim of easement by prescription. *Gilardi v. Hallam*, 636 P2d 588 (1981).

Nevada A landowner claimed some of his adjacent neighbors' land under the doctrine of adverse possession. Because two surveys were made of the tracts, the first in 1881 and the second in 1934, the claimant landowner was confused about the dimensions of his own property, and when he built a house, it inadvertently encroached on his neighbors' land by about 35 feet. The neighbors, record owners according to the official survey, brought suit to remove the landowner from the tract. *Held:* For the record owners. In order to establish adverse possession, a claimant must pay all taxes assessed on the disputed land for a statutory period. In the instant case, the claimant paid taxes only on the value of improvements he made on the disputed land. He was never assessed, and thus never paid, any taxes on the assessed value of the strip in question, which by survey was included in the piece of land belonging to the record owners. Taxes were thus assessed against and paid by the record owners. *Biasi v. Leavitt*, 692 P2d 1301 (1985).

104.40
Possession Under Color of Title

Montana Disputed land was erroneously included in a land inventory by a probate administrator. The purchaser of the estate lands paid taxes on it and used it to drive cattle between two tracts he owned. He granted an easement to a power company, offered to sell it to the record owner, and subsequently had the boundary surveyed and resold it to another party who fenced it and built a home on it. *Held:* Although the land was not originally fenced, the record owner had sufficient notice that the land was adversely possessed, and the actual fencing later was incidental to the possession. Further, record owner, who had offered to purchase the land, showed that he thought the adverse possessor owned the land. The administrator's deed was an adequate basis for a claim under color of title, since the claim was in good faith and the defect would not have been apparent to a claimant. The use of the tract to drive cattle, along with other indicia of ownership, was sufficiently continuous for purposes of adverse possession. *Brown v. Cartwright*, 515 P2d 684 (1973).

North Carolina A deed conveying land to daughter from her parents contained less road frontage than daughter believed she was entitled to. Unknown to daughter, her brother's deed gave the disputed strip to his successors in title. Daughter remained in possession of the disputed land for 30 years in the mistaken belief that the land was deeded to her. Possession was actual, open, hostile, exclusive, and continuous. The brother's successors in title, learning they had record title to the strip, sued to quiet title. The rule in North Carolina was that possession by mistake did not meet the test of adverse possession. *Held:* Reversing the position it had taken since the 1950s, the state supreme court held that one may acquire title by adverse possession even if the claim of title is based on a mistake, if all other elements are met and possession continues for the statutory period. Therefore, daughter had acquired title to the land by adverse possession. *Walls v. Grohman*, 337 SE2d 556 (1985).

104.45
Possession Under Claim of Right

5th Circuit Defendant took title to property subject to a condition subsequent that it would revert to grantors if used for nonresidential purposes. This condition was referred to as a covenant running with the land. Defendant applied the land to a prohibited use, but asserted ownership by adverse possession. The Fifth Circuit held that defendant could not be an adverse possessor under Texas law unless he could claim the entire interest held by grantor, which claim the court found to be impossible where grantor retained a contingent right of reversion. On remand, the district court held that ambiguities in language that would effect a forfeiture are to be resolved against forfeiture. The case was again appealed. *Held:* For defendant. A forfeiture of property should be ordered only if provided for in clear and unambiguous language. The word "covenant" to describe the condition created an ambiguity as to whether the breached restriction was a condition subsequent or a covenant, for which injunctive relief restraining nonresidential use is available. Plaintiff's use of the word "covenant," and his failure to request injunctive relief, was fatal to his cause of action. *Humphrey v. CG Jung Educ. Center*, 714 F2d 477 (1983).

Arkansas Appellants in a quiet title action sought to establish that their occupation of land was adverse, alleging they entered into a swap of lands with appellees' predecessor, and therefore occupied under a claim of right. *Held:* The exchange of lands was sufficient to establish adverse possession under claim of right. For possession to be adverse, as distinguished from permissive, it is only necessary that it be hostile in the sense that it is under a claim of right, title or ownership, rather than possession in recognition of the superior right of the owner, which is permissive. The evidence clearly showed that appellants entered into possession of the disputed tract under a claim of right by reason of the exchange. Claim of ownership, even under a mistaken belief, is nonetheless adverse. *Barclay v. Tussey*, 532 SW2d 193 (1976).

Wyoming Where the evidence showed that a fence between two pieces of property was a party-line fence, and not a "fence of convenience," and that plaintiff's possession of land on her side of the fence had been actual, open, notorious, hostile, and under a claim of ownership for the prescribed period, the court ruled plaintiff had acquired title by adverse possession and would prevail in an action to quiet title. *Mader v. Stephenson*, 501 P2d 1253 (1972).

104.50
Possession by Government Entities

Ohio Two streets dedicated in 1913 encroached on private land. A firm that purchased property in 1980 learned these streets encroached on its property. It filed a reverse condemnation suit against the city, seeking compensation. *Held:* For the city. The city acquired title to the land by adverse possession, the public having used the streets adversely under claim of right continuously for more than 21 years. Plaintiff had no constitutional right to compensation for the "taking" of its land. The court cited analogous reasoning by the Supreme Court in *Texaco, Inc. v. Short*, 454 US 516 (1982), a case involving unused mineral rights that passed to the state: "It is the owner's failing to make any use of the property—and not the action of the State—that causes the lapse of the property right; there is no 'taking' that requires compensation." *State ex rel. AAA Invs. v. City of Columbus*, 478 NE2d 773 (1985).

Tennessee The city built a sewage treatment plant and, without a survey, surrounded the property with a fence. It later built a new plant and constructed an interceptor line across property claimed by plaintiffs, who filed an inverse condemnation action. They subsequently learned that land belonging to their predecessor in title had been enclosed by fencing of the original plant. The land had since been leased to a private oil company. Plaintiffs amended their complaint to bring an ejectment action with respect to the leased property. The city claimed title to the leased property by adverse possession. *Held:* The city had acquired title to the fenced-in area by adverse possession. The court rejected as an erroneous interpretation of Tennessee law the Sixth Circuit's holding in *United States v. 371.94 Acres of Land*, 431 F2d 975 (6th Cir. 1970) that a government entity cannot acquire title by adverse possession. It also rejected plaintiff's arguments that the city held only a possessory right or easement, which lapsed when it ceased to use the land for public purposes. This argument was inapplicable here, where the city had mistakenly claimed ownership of plaintiff's property and over which it exercised complete dominion. *Johnson v. City of Mt. Pleasant*, 713 SW2d 659 (Ct. App. 1985).

104.55 Proof of Location

Illinois In 1980, defendants purchased land adjoining plaintiffs' property. An old fence had formed a boundary between the two tracts for several years. From 1919 to 1979, plaintiffs and their predecessors in title had used the property up to the fence line to pasture farm animals. Defendants, based on the results of a survey, constructed a new fence north of the old fence line. Plaintiffs sued for a declaration that they owned the property up to the old fence line by virtue of adverse possession. *Held:* For plaintiffs. There was no requirement in adverse possession cases that plaintiffs prove the location of the disputed property by exact legal description. Rather, plaintiffs were required to establish the boundaries with reasonable certainty. The court found the evidence was sufficient to identify the property. Plaintiffs' witnesses, who had lived in the area since childhood and were familiar with the old fence, testified to its location. *Crowell v. Parrish*, 512 NE2d 382 (Ct. App. 1987).

105.00 DEDICATION

105.05 Methods of Dedication

4th Circuit Landowners filed a subdivision plat that showed land designated as "park." Seventy years later, owners' descendant gave grantee a special warranty deed to use the land designated as a park for a residence. Neighboring property owners sued to enjoin grantee from restricting use of the park by residents, claiming an easement over the land. *Held:* The park was dedicated to public use by the filing of the subdivision plat and the sale of lots referring to the recorded plat; neither the grantee nor adjoining landowners had an enforceable interest in the land. The fact that the park was taken off county tax rolls when the plat was recorded and remained off the tax rolls until grantee recorded his deed showed sufficient dominion and control over the property to constitute an acceptance of the dedication as a park. In addition, the public had used the land as a park for 70 years without any act of dominion by the family of the original owners. *Laughlin v. Morauer*, 849 F2d 122 (1988).

Alaska In 1970, plaintiffs purchased an unsubdivided parcel of land. Subsequently, vendors obtained approval of a subdivision plat, including plaintiffs' parcel. A portion of their land was shown as dedicated to public use as a right-of-way. In 1977, plaintiffs sold part of the parcel to a third party, identifying the land by reference to the recorded plat. The land affected by the right-of-way was not included in the sale. Plaintiffs were unaware of the dedication until 1979, then sued the borough for damages resulting from inverse condemnation. The trial court granted the borough summary judgment based on the argument that plaintiffs had adopted the legal description contained in the plat when they sold a portion of their land in 1977. *Held:* Reversed and remanded. There was no clear evidence that plaintiffs intended to make a dedication. Reference to a recorded plat may be for description purposes only, without intent to dedicate. The borough failed to prove a dedication by estoppel, because the land conveyed by plaintiffs with reference to the plat was not affected by the dedication. Nor was there a showing that the borough or the public had relied on the purported dedication. *Creary v. Kenai Peninsula Borough*, 671 P2d 1286 (1983).

Arkansas A developer sued another developer for intentional trespass and encroachment. Defendant had mistakenly connected his sewer line to plaintiff's sewer line and installed a manhole cover on plaintiff's property. Defendant pleaded that his sewer hookup had been lawfully installed within a sewer easement dedicated to the general public. Although she claimed she had never dedicated the sewer line to the city, her line connected to the city's main sewer line and was maintained by the city. Thus, plaintiff had expressly dedicated her subdivision's utility easements for the use of the general public. Also, the line had been tapped by the city for another development in the past. *Held:* The hookup was lawful within the easement contained in plaintiff's plat. Although the plat did not specifically show any defined utility easements, plaintiff had constructed the sewer easement along its present lines immediately after filing the plat. Plaintiff had dedicated the sewer line by her actions, and the dedication could not be revoked or limited so as to preclude its use by a competing development. *Harvey v. Bell*, 732 SW2d 138 (1987).

California Owner of a beach front parcel that straddled two towns filed plans for an apartment complex. It was approved by one town, but the other town denied permission and sued to prevent construction. The town argued that public recreational use of the beach had created an implied dedication for such use. Owner argued that several deeds of trust were outstanding on the property, and the holders would be adversely affected by implied dedication for public use. *Held:* The town was entitled to preserve implied dedication. The use of the property by the public for recreation imparts knowledge of an implied dedication to all the world. Holder of security interests were therefore on notice and were bound by their inaction. *County of Los Angeles v. Berk*, 605 P2d 381 (1980).

Georgia During a land registration trial between claimants to beach land and the county, evidence was adduced that some public use of the land had occurred over many years. The county had sporadically stationed lifeguards, removed trash, and posted warning signs. Nonresidents testified they had used the beach as members of the general public for 60 years. By a 1914 plat, duly recorded, an express offer of dedication of the beach to the public had been made. The lower court directed a verdict that the offer of dedication had not been accepted by the county. *Held:* The directed verdict was in error. An express offer of dedication had been made, and the issue was whether acceptance by the county could be implied from the evidence of public use. Where an express offer of dedication exists, public use consistent with the character of the land, such as occasional recreational use of a beach by the public, would be sufficient to imply acceptance of a dedication. *Smith v. State*, 282 SE2d 76 (1981).

Illinois Village accepted a dedication of property for public purposes, with no other stated restrictions on use of the land. For years, the village kept the lot vacant, using it only to access a drainage ditch. The village subsequently decided to sell the land to a private builder for a residence. Adjoining landowners opposed sale of the lot. *Held:* Village could not sell the property under the theory of cy pres. A dedication of land as "public ground" is an unrestricted dedication to public use, with the municipality acting as trustee for the benefit of the public. Once the dedication is accepted, the city acquires legal title to the land upon an express charitable trust. The city may not dispose of the land for its own benefit and has no power to convey the property. Only if literal execution of a charitable trust is impossible or impractical, may the court apply the doctrine of cy pres. *Petition of Village of Mount Prospect*, 522 NE2d 122 (Ct. App. 1988).

Minnesota During discussions among neighboring landowners of plans to plat their properties, it became clear that the construction of access roads would not affect everyone's property equally. Plaintiff discussed having everyone compensate each other for property lost to street construction. The others reached agreement on this issue, and defendants, who were present, did not object. Plaintiff dedicated 10,000 square feet to build a road, and defendants gave up 3,400 square feet. Plaintiff claimed she would not have dedicated so much land had there not been a common plan with defendants. She sued for compensation for the land dedicated under the oral agreement. *Held:* Defendants had entered into an implied-in-fact agreement to compensate plaintiff for the 6,600 square foot difference between the land she dedicated and the land defendants dedicated. The cul-de-sac created directly served defendants' needs and was not plaintiff's choice. Although ordinarily silence does not amount to acceptance, here it did. *Gryc v. Lewis*, 410 NW2d 888 (Ct. App. 1987).

Mississippi Corporation, which owned a cemetery, and 11 purchasers of cemetery plots sued to cancel deeds given by a former sole shareholder of the corporation to developers of an apartment building. Plaintiffs alleged that the entire acreage owned by the corporation had been represented to the public as perpetual-care cemeteries and that the land, having been dedicated as a cemetery, could not now be used for residential purposes. The land was exempt from taxation for three years as a cemetery until the deeds conveying a portion of the land to developers were executed. *Held:* Common-law dedication occurs when there is an intent to donate the land for use of the public at large. In this case, there was no intent to donate to the public at large since the corporation was acting for profit, and since the use of the cemetery was restricted to members of the white race. The corporation was therefore free to convey the land to whomever it chose. *Magnolia Memorial Gardens, Inc. v. Denton*, 317 So. 2d 38 (1975).

Nevada Residents of city brought an action to cancel deeds conveying a part of certain real property that had been given to the city in trust as a public park. The city had deeded the land to acquire other property needed for a proposed bridge and street widening. *Held:* The city breached the trust agreement by trading the property to private persons for their nonpublic use. The municipality was without power to use the property for any purpose other than that stated in the trust agreement. *City of Reno v. Goldwater*, 558 P2d 532 (1976).

New Jersey Plaintiff was a nonprofit corporation whose members were builders in defendant township. Members of the corporation had to receive approvals from the township planning board in order to build and sell homes. Approvals were often conditioned upon dedication of improvements to the township. A performance bond was required to insure completion according to specifications. If approval was granted, the performance bond was released and a two-year maintenance bond posted. The township required developer to continue paying taxes and costs generated by the dedicated, improved street until the maintenance bond was released. Plaintiff sought a judgment that release of the performance bond constituted defendant's acceptance of the improvements and dedication. *Held:* Defendant's release of the performance bond did not constitute its acceptance of the improvements and dedication. Such acceptance could be accomplished by adoption of an ordinance, or by exercise of control over the dedicated property. *Home Builders League, Inc. v. Township of Evesham*, 440 A2d 1361 (Super. Ct. App. Div. 1981).

Virginia Landowner sued to enjoin the city from interfering with his property. The city had ordered owner to remove improvements, stating that they were located on a dedicated public street. Plaintiff contended that the property was his own since the predecessor in title's offer of dedication was never accepted by the city. *Held:* Recordation of a subdivision plat manifested an intent to allow public access to platted streets and constituted a common-law offer of dedication. Intent to accept the offer may be manifested expressly or by implication. Improvements made by the city are acts of dominion and control that constitute acceptance of the offer. Where a governing body accepted part of a dedication and no intention to limit the acceptance was shown, the partial acceptance constituted acceptance of all streets in the subdivision. *Ocean Island Inn v. City of Va. Beach*, 220 SE2d 247 (1975).

Washington Irrigation district sued to be reimbursed by the county for the cost of relocating its water pipes, hydrants, and valves, in connection with a road-improvement project. The original dedicators of the street had reversed the right to maintain water pipes, and the irrigation district had acquired all the assets of the dedicator's water company. *Held:* The county's acceptance of the dedication created an easement in favor of the district's predecessor. The city was required to compensate the district when it interfered with the easement. The reservation in no way restricted the county's use and control of the streets, and was therefore valid. *North Spokane Irrigation Dist. No. 8 v. County of Spokane*, 547 P2d 859 (1976).

West Virginia Plaintiffs sued to enjoin defendants from denying them the use of a drive. The plat of the subdivision showed the drive as a public way, but it had never been developed. Plaintiffs also claimed that a private right-of-way acquired by defendants' predecessor in interest had become public. *Held:* Plaintiffs had an easement to the drive, but not to the access road. The access road was never taken by condemnation or adverse possession, nor did the owners dedicate the land to public use. Plaintiffs did have a right to use the drive, however. Since plaintiffs' lot was conveyed by reference to a map plat showing the road, title carried with it the right to an easement in the drive. *Reger v. Weist*, 310 SE2d 499 (1983).

West Virginia The town sued to enjoin mobile homeowners from blocking a street alleged to be a "public way." The town presented evidence that the street had been used adversely by the public for more than 10 years prior to the placement of the mobile home, that the town incurred expenses in improving and maintaining it, and that the homeowners had been told by the town that the street was a public way before placing their trailer on the property. *Held:* The evidence was sufficient to establish a dedication of the street as a public way by continuous and adverse possession by the public coupled with official town recognition. *Town of Bancroft v. Turley*, 287 SE2d 161 (1981).

106.00 RESTRAINTS ON ALIENATION

106.05 Validity of Restraints on Alienation

Florida In certified questions presented upon stipulated facts by the U.S. Fifth Circuit Court of Appeals, the court was asked to determine whether a covenant in a deed was void as an unreasonable restraint on alienation. The facts showed that the owner had purchased a large parcel of property in 1959 for a total cash consideration of $10. Grantor had retained, by a covenant running with the land, an option consisting of the right of first refusal for an unlimited period to repurchase the property for the same $10 consideration, plus the cost of improvements. *Held:* The covenant was invalid as an unreasonable restraint on alienation. A grantor cannot enforce a repurchase option of unlimited duration unless the option price is based upon market or appraised value. Such fixed-price options, when they inhibit the use and improvement of property, are unreasonable. The court concluded that inasmuch as the option was a primary part of the consideration and understood by all parties, the deed would not be subject to rescission or cancellation under state law. *Iglehart v. Phillips*, 383 So. 2d 610 (1980).

Montana Plaintiffs asked the court for a declaratory judgment that would relieve them of any responsibility to accelerate their payments to defendant seller. Plaintiffs entered into a contract for sale of property, one provision of which prevented plaintiff from assigning his interest in the contract without defendant's prior consent. Failure to obtain prior consent would result in a "default" that would automatically accelerate payments. *Held:* The prior consent provision was not an unlawful restraint upon alienation. Further, plaintiffs, by assigning their contract rights without defendant's consent, committed a "default" allowing defendant to demand acceleration. *Dobitz v. Oakland*, 561 P2d 441 (1977).

North Carolina Plaintiffs' successors in interest sold realty subject to a 20-year restrictive covenant granting them a preemptive right of first refusal on subsequent sales of the property. Ten years later, owners of record sold the land to a third party without first offering it to plaintiffs. The trial court ruled against plaintiffs, citing an 1892 case as authority for the proposition that a preemptive right is per se an impermissible restraint on alienation. *Held:* Reversed. Only such preemptive rights as are unreasonable in terms of repurchase price or duration are prohibited. Since the parties set the price at market levels, owner was assured of receiving a fair return. As to the timing element, the court adopted the 21-year limit of the rule against perpetuities as the measure of reasonableness in such cases. On this basis the case was remanded to trial court for a determination of damages. *Smith v. Mitchell*, 269 SE2d 608 (1980).

106.10 Effect of Mortgage Acceleration Clause

California Defendant, a veteran, and the Department of Veterans Affairs entered into an installment contract for the purchase of a home. The contract provided that if defendant transferred the property without the department's consent, the balance would become immediately due. When defendant conveyed the property without the department's consent, the department demanded full payment and canceled the contract. In a suit to quiet title, defendant argued that the rule of *Wellenkamp v. Bank of America*, 21 Cal. App. 3d 943 (1978) applied, which invalidated due-on-sale clauses unless lender can prove impairment of security. *Held:* The department had authority to cancel the contract. The *Wellenkamp* rule is based on Civil Code § 711, which is a general prohibition against restraints on alienation. The department, however, had specific statutory authority under the Veterans' Farm and Home Purchase Act to restrain alienation in ways an ordinary lender could not. *Department of Veterans Affairs v. Duerkson*, 187 Cal. Rptr. 832 (Ct. App. 1982).

Washington A promissory note on a 15-year loan prohibited prepayment during the first seven years of the loan. The note also contained a due-on-sale clause. Borrowers sought to refinance the loan two years later. Lender refused prepayment unless borrowers paid an additional sum. Borrowers sued, seeking a declaration that a due-on-sale clause together with a prepayment restriction in a commercial loan constitutes an invalid restraint on alienation. *Held:* For the bank. Due-on-sale and prepayment restrictions, separately or in combination, are not an unreasonable restraint on alienation in a commercial real estate loan. A seven-year prepayment restriction was not unreasonable since borrowers had notice of the restrictions, there was no allegation of fraud, the provisions were stated in the loan documents, and borrowers were not restricted from selling the property. The combination of a due-on-sale clause and a prepayment restriction was not an unreasonable restraint because the provisions do not operate simultaneously, and are each used for differing purposes. They serve to protect a lender's long-term loan portfolio and allocate risk in a period of fluctuating interest rates. *McCausland v. Bankers Life Ins. Co.*, 747 P2d 941 (1988).

PART T
LIENS AND ENCUMBRANCES

107.00
MECHANIC'S AND MATERIALMAN'S LIENS

107.05
Creation and Perfection

Connecticut Plaintiff contractor served a copy of a certificate of mechanic's lien upon codefendant condominium developer but not upon the 31 codefendant unit owners. A new statute, passed before plaintiff served the certificate upon the developer, conditioned mechanic's liens upon the serving of notice to each owner in the case of two or more owners. However, the contractor argued that the legislature did not intend to impose such a broad requirement upon mechanics and materialmen and that the legislature's use of the term "owner" should be limited to the contracting owner. The lower court disagreed and discharged the lien. *Held:* Each unit owner was entitled to notice of the lien. The previous law had been declared unconstitutional because it violated property owners' due process rights. Since the new law was designed to remedy this defect and protect property owners' rights, it was comprehensive, not restrictive, in scope. This constitutional consideration outweighed the inconvenience for mechanics in serving notice. *Papa v. Greenwich Green, Inc.*, 416 A2d 1196 (1979).

Connecticut Under their lease, lessees were permitted to make certain improvements, but were specifically barred from subjecting the leased property to an encumbrance or mechanic's lien. However, soon after they engaged contractor to make the specified improvements, they were evicted from the premises. Thereafter, contractor filed a mechanic's lien on lessor's property for completed work not paid for by lessees. *Held:* Contractor failed to establish the lien's validity by way of implied contract with lessor. Lessor did not take any action causing contractor to conclude that lessor's agent was authorized to undertake financial liability for the entire project; he did not give his agent apparent authority. Also, lessor clearly did not consent to performance of work for lessees, because of the specific lease provision barring liens on the property. Moreover, lessor specifically noted the charges he would pay and gave no indication that he would pay for any others. *Newtown Assocs. v. Northeast Structures*, 546 A2d 310 (Ct. App. 1988).

Idaho Contractor successfully foreclosed his materialman's lien on a house belonging to two owners and straddling the line between the north halves of two lots. Subsequently, however, it was discovered that the description of the property in the lien, complaint, judgment and deed was inadequate. The reformed sheriff's deed was effective against one owner only, because of defective service of process on the other. Subsequently, the owner who was effectively served with the reformation petition died, and the surviving owner moved to set the execution sale aside. *Held:* Since the reformed lien and decree were limited in application to the deceased owner only, the surviving owner still possessed an undivided one-half interest in the northern half of one of the lots, thereby making contractor and surviving owner tenants in common. The court ordered the sale of the northern halves of both lots, including the house, with 75 percent of the proceeds to the surviving owner, and 25 percent to contractor. *Ketterer v. Billings*, 683 P2d 868 (1984).

Illinois Subcontractor sought to foreclose a mechanic's lien for work done under an agreement between the Peoria Housing Authority and a developer to building scattered-site housing. The housing authority would purchase the homes built from the developer using interim financing from a local lender. The last two phases of the project were placed in receivership and sold at auction. Both plaintiff subcontractor and lender sought to recover the proceeds. The trial court held that subcontractor's claim of lien was defective, since he had failed to send the lending agency notice of lien as required by the mechanic's lien statute. In addition, the lien was against multiple noncontiguous tracts and did not set forth date of work and amount claimed against each tract as required by the lien law. *Held:* Affirmed. The subcontractor had not complied with the mechanic's lien law for work on separate, noncontiguous parcels; and he had filed his claim after the statutory filing time had lapsed. *Dougherty-Janssen Co. v. Danage Enters.*, 400 NE2d 1023 (1980).

Iowa General contractor performed preliminary excavation on a shopping center project when the project failed. The contractor asserted that his mechanic's lien had priority over the financing bank's mortgage, because his work preceded the mortgage recordation date. *Held:* For contractor. Examining contractor's preparatory activities, the court found one was essential to actual construction—the moving of concrete pads with a front-end loader so a utility could relocate a stream line. This work, commenced prior to the mortgage recordation date, established a mechanic's lien with priority over the bank's mortgage lien. *Northwestern Nat'l Bank v. Metro Center, Inc.*, 303 NW2d 395 (1981).

Kansas Defendant supplied materials to a subcontractor on plaintiff's construction project. The subcontractor failed to pay defendant for its last delivery of materials, and, approximately eight months later, defendant filed a mechanic's lien against plaintiff. Plaintiff, in turn, brought an action to have the lien canceled and to recover damages for clouding the title of the property. Plaintiff contended that the lien was not timely filed in that it was not filed within the three-month statutory limit after the date that the equipment or labor was last furnished. Defendant asserted that additional materials were still needed to complete the job, which would thus extend the time for filing the lien. *Held:* The test for whether a lien has been timely filed is whether it is filed within three months of when the work contracted for has been completed. Plaintiff had no contract, therefore it had completed all work on the construction site that it was required to do. The lien was not timely filed. *Holiday Dev. Co. v. JA Tobin Constr. Co.*, 549 P2d 1376 (1976).

Montana Contractor agreed to install water and sewer lines for defendant, with payment monthly per linear foot of completed lines minus 10 percent holdback. Approval by a licensed engineer of defendant would be required. At the completion of the job, defendant refused to pay the holdback. Plaintiff filed a mechanic's lien and brought an action to foreclose the lien. Defendant alleged defective work and counterclaimed for the cost of repairing same. The lower court held for defendant. *Held:* Affirmed, but damages were modified. The court stated: "A contractor cannot successfully assert a mechanic's lien where there has been only partial performance or a lack of substantial performance of the work for which the party claims the lien." Substantial performance is a condition precedent to the liability of defendant. *Olson v. Westfork Properties, Inc.*, 557 P2d 821 (1976).

Nevada Subcontractor recorded a lien on defendant's land for materials he supplied to the general contractor and used on defendant's construction project. When subcontractor sought to serve notice, he found no one present at defendant's place of business with whom he could leave a copy of the lien. He therefore posted one copy on defendant's business premises and mailed another to the same place. Defendant learned about the lien but on foreclosure contended that service was defective under Nevada law, because a copy was not posted at the construction site. *Held:* Subcontractor's attempt to comply with Nevada's notice requirement was sufficient to perfect his mechanic's lien. His method of posting the notice of lien was in substantial compliance with Nevada law, for defendant had actually received notice of it. *Las Vegas Plywood & Lumber, Inc. v. D&D Enters.*, 649 P2d 1367 (1982).

New Hampshire Plaintiff did dry-wall work for defendant builder, who later sold the property to Richey. Plaintiff, after the sale to Richey, was not paid in full and attached the property, asserting a statutory mechanic's lien. Richey argued that plaintiff, as a subcontractor to the builder, had failed to give him (the owner) notice as required by the Mechanic's Lien Act. *Held:* When plaintiff contracted to do the work, the builder was the owner and, as between parties who are in privity, no notice or filing was required. It was Richey's failure to record his contract of purchase that was the fatal error. Plaintiff, as a lien claimant, had the right to rely on record title, and Richey had failed to protect himself by not recording his contract. *James Drywall Inc. v. Europa Dev. Corp.*, 365 A2d 1047 (1976).

Oregon After plaintiff completed work on defendant's property, it filed a lien claim for the value of the labor and materials furnished but unpaid for. Upon discovering that the claim contained the incorrect name of the restaurant, tax lot number, and address, plaintiff filed a corrected lien notice and delivered a copy to defendant. In the foreclosure action, defendant contended that the inaccurate information in the first claim invalidated the lien, because plaintiff's description of defendant's property was not "sufficient for identification" under the lien statute (Or. Rev. Stat. § 87.035(2)(d)). *Held:* Plaintiff's lien was valid. Despite errors in plaintiff's property description, it was "sufficient for identification" under Oregon law. The lien notice was sufficient for defendant to identify the property covered, he was not misled or prejudiced by the inaccuracies, and he had actual notice of plaintiff's lien. *C-3 Builders, Inc. v. Krueger*, 642 P2d 344 (1981).

Utah Contractor recorded a notice of mechanic's lien to secure past due payments, but failed to make an oral averment as to the truthfulness of the contents of the notice to a notary public. Seven months later, contractor commenced an action to foreclose the lien, and owner defended that the lien was invalid since it was not verified by oath. *Held:* The notice of lien was properly verified. State statute requires that the contents of the claim "must be verified by the oath of [the claimant] or of some other person." For a valid verification, there must be a correct written oath, signed by affiant in the presence of a notary and the notary must affix a proper jurat. There is no requirement that the oath must be administered to the affiant or that the affiant must speak an oral oath or raise his hand. In this case, the notice of lien was properly verified where the verification contained in the notice was worded so that plaintiff swore to its truthfulness by signing the notice, the verification was signed in the presence of a notary, and the notary fixed a proper jurat. *Mickelsen v. Craigco, Inc.*, 767 P2d 561 (1989).

Virginia Plaintiff alleged in its claim that it had entered into separate contractual agreements with defendant to improve certain real property and to perform masonry work on 132 apartments and a clubhouse. Plaintiff further alleged that he had performed but had not been paid, and he claimed a blanket mechanic's lien against the property. Defendant demurred on the ground that the lien must be apportioned among the various condominium units. The trial court sustained the demurrer, and plaintiff appealed. *Held:* Under these circumstances, where work had been done and materials furnished under two separate and distinct contracts that added disproportionate values to the properties liened, a memorandum that failed to apportion the amounts due between the several properties benefited was defective and the lien void. Two separate liens should have been recorded: one upon the 132 units and their common elements and another against the entire project. The decision to sustain the demurrer and declare the lien void was affirmed. *United Masonry Inc. v. Jefferson Mews, Inc.*, 237 SE2d 171 (1977).

107.10 Expiration

Alaska Contractor recorded a mechanic's lien on defendant's property. With an extension, the duration of the lien was one year. The day before the lien expired, contractor filed suit to enforce it. Contractor did not actively prosecute the suit for a year and a half. Meanwhile, defendant's bank took a deed of trust from defendant on the same property. The lien failed to appear on the bank's title report because the one-year period had expired, and the land records contained no notice of the suit. The bank received actual notice of the lien only when it was served with contractor's complaint. The issue was whether the lien's recordation would have lead a reasonable person to inquire whether the lien's normal one-year period had been extended by the lawsuit's commencement. *Held:* The contractor's mechanic's lien was still valid, and the bank's deed of trust was taken subject to it. The bank was not an innocent purchaser, for it necessarily knew that a suit could have been started. This knowledge should have impelled it to inquire whether any court papers had been filed. *First Nat'l Bank v. Dent*, 683 P2d 722 (1984).

Tennessee House builder executed deeds of trust to the bank. Builder abandoned the properties, which were subject to a materialman's lien. The bank foreclosed on the properties, and the materialman filed suit to enforce its lien and to share in the proceeds of the sale of the improved properties. *Held:* The materialman was not entitled to assert its lien against the bank. The statute providing for the filing of a notice of lien within 90 days after a building is demolished, altered, or completed also includes a partially completed building that is abandoned. The lien had not been perfected within the 90-day period, and all lien rights had expired. *Tindell Home Center, Inc. v. Union Peoples Bank*, 543 SW2d 843 (1977).

Utah A general contractor invested in the development of a condominium project. In return, developer agreed that the contractor would receive a share of the profits from the sale of the development and would also be paid for his labor and services. After the project was completed, the contractor was paid for his labor and services but did not receive his share of the profits. The contractor stated that he intended to file a timely mechanic's lien. Developer asked that he withhold the lien until they refinanced and promised to pay contractor his share of the profits within two weeks. Months later, payment had not been made; however, contractor agreed to make further repairs and inspections. After proceeding with the work, the contractor filed a mechanic's lien against the project, listing his last day of labor as being the time spent making repairs. *Held:* The contractor failed to timely file the mechanic's lien. A contractor must record a lien within 100 days after completion of the contract. Completion is marked by the end of a related series of tasks required for substantial performance. Minor adjustments that alter the main work cannot be used to extend the filing deadline. *Daniels v. Desert Fed. Sav. & Loan*, 771 P2d 1100 (Ct. App. 1989).

107.15 Property Subject to Mechanic's Lien

Indiana Plaintiff materialman provided, but was not paid by, another materialman for cement beams used in the construction of a parking garage built through the issuance of municipal revenue bonds. Plaintiff filed a mechanic's lien against the real property underlying the garage, which had been conveyed by the owner to the city as security for the bonds' issuance and then leased back to the owner. The city, in opposing foreclosure, argued that the Indiana lien law protected only those suppliers who furnished materials to owners of private, not public, property. *Held:* Although this was by nature a private project, with the city not liable on the bonds' indebtedness, plaintiff was still not protected. Under Indiana's lien law, a materialman is protected only if he supplies a contractor or subcontractor, not when he merely supplies another materialman. *City of Evansville v. Verplank Concrete*, 400 NE2d 812 (1980).

Maine A contractor agreed to build a pipeline connecting two separate parcels of land of owner, who had obtained right-of-way for the pipeline over land he did not own. The contractor subcontracted the work to subcontractor who in turn hired a supplier to obtain equipment. When the supplier was not paid, he sued the other parties to enforce his mechanic's lien. The owner of the property argued that the lien could not be enforced against owner's property. *Held:* Even though most of the pipeline was not physically on owner's property, it benefitted the property and therefore the lien could attach to the property. *Newell v. Carlow, Newell & Smith, Inc.*, 403 A2d 1209 (1979).

Maryland A condominium developer contracted with an out-of-state manufacturer to build modules for a project. The manufacturer went bankrupt after supplying the units. The materialmen who supplied the manufacturer moved for mechanic's liens under Maryland law. *Held:* The materialmen were entitled to liens. Under Md. Real Prop. Code § 9-102, "[e]very building erected . . . is subject to establishment of a lien for the payment of all debts . . . contracted for work done for or about the building and for materials furnished for or about the building." The court interpreted this statute as applying to materials supplied in Delaware that were incorporated into the Maryland project. Even if the modules were completely built in Delaware, there was work to be done in Maryland within the meaning of the statute. *5500 Coastal Highway v. Electrical Equip. Co.*, 505 A2d 533 (1986).

Minnesota Developer contracted for architectural services to help obtain approvals from the city council for the commercial development of owners' property, on which developer held various options. Although owners were not party to the architect's contract, they were aware of the services being rendered for developer. Subsequently, architect was not paid by developer, and he filed a mechanic's lien on owners' property. *Held:* Architect was entitled to enforce his lien against owners' property, because while they were aware of his services, they failed to issue the required statutory disclaimer. Under Minn. Stat. § 514.06, the type of architectural services performed, although invisible, were "contributions to the improvement of real estate." Owners could have prevented attachment of the lien by serving written notice on the architect, declaring that his services were not being made at owners' request. *Korsunsky Frank Erickson Architects v. Walsh*, 370 NW2d 29 (1985).

New York A general construction contractor entered into a contract to renovate a tenant's cooperative apartment. After completion of the renovations, tenant failed to pay the outstanding balance. The contractor filed a mechanic's lien for the unpaid balance against the cooperative apartment corporation. Corporation defended on the basis that it was not a party to the contract and would not benefit from the performed work. *Held:* The contractor could file the mechanic's lien against the cooperative corporation, since a corporate representative actively supervised and consented to the improvements. Furthermore, the corporation would reap the benefits of the renovations owing to the common ownership of the building. *Dash Contracting Corp. v. Slater*, 537 NYS2d 736 (1989).

Oklahoma Tenant hired contractors to perform work on leased commercial premises and failed to pay them. Landlord had not consented to having the work done. The contractors and materialmen sought to enforce liens on the premises. *Held:* The liens were not enforceable. Under a state statute, if the labor performed and material furnished resulted in the erection of a new building, the liens could attach. Here, only repairs to an existing structure were made. When repairs or alterations to an existing structure are made under an agreement with someone other than the title owner, no lien may encumber the structure. *Dieterle Plumbing & Heating v. Green*, 605 P2d 1335 (1980).

Oregon Plaintiff sued to foreclose a mechanic's lien for materials furnished to defendant for the construction of a condominium. Defendant regularly purchased materials from plaintiff, and, as payments were made, plaintiff applied the money to the oldest outstanding sales. Approximately 50 percent of the amount claimed by plaintiffs on the lien foreclosure represented purchases by defendant for construction projects other than the condominium. *Held:* Fifty percent of the materials on the condominium project for which the lien had been filed had already been paid for by defendants. The filing for a larger amount than was owed will not destroy plaintiff's lien for the amount still outstanding if negligence, and not fraud or gross negligence, was responsible for the filing error. The portion of the amount due that is interest is not lienable. *JW Copeland Yards v. Phillips*, 550 P2d 438 (1976).

Pennsylvania Appellant claimed that a mechanic's lien should be levied on land for work it performed strip mining and backfilling, unconnected with the construction of a building or other permanent structure. *Held:* A mechanic's lien cannot attach to land for work unconnected with the construction of a building or other permanent structure even though the land has been improved. While the Mechanic's Lien Act included a mine in its definition of a structure to which a mechanic's lien may attach, land from which coal has been removed by surface stripping does not constitute a mine for purposes of a mechanic's lien. *Yellow Run Coal Co. v. Yellow Run Energy Co.*, 420 A2d 690 (Super. Ct. 1980).

South Dakota Supplier of glass for the construction of a motel brought foreclosure proceedings against a corporation that owned part and leased part of the land on which the motel was built. The building was owned by a partnership of which the corporation was a member. *Held:* The mechanic's lien was valid as to the interest that the corporation holds in the entire physical structure. It was valid as to the real property owned by the corporation, but not as to the real property leased. Improvements built on leased land were subject to a lien, although the leased land itself was not. *Schubloom v. Donavon & Assocs., Inc.*, 241 NW2d 710 (1976).

Wisconsin Contractor and landscaper sued to foreclose a construction lien against the owners of eight of 35 purchased condominium units and the mortgagee bank. They appealed a judgment concluding that the unit owners were entitled to a lien release upon payment of a proportional share of the amounts still due claimants. *Held:* Since a blanket lien cannot equitably be enforced against less than all of the parcels making up a property, the amount of the lien should be apportioned among the individual parcels. Where unit owners did not receive full payments allocable to the unsold units, it would be inequitable for the eight owners to have to pay off the lien for the benefit of the other 27 units. *Stevens Constr. Corp. v. Draper Hall, Inc.*, 242 NW2d 893 (1976).

107.20 Persons Entitled to Mechanic's Lien

Alaska After engineering firm supplied preliminary and detailed plans and drawings to developer for a proposed project, it filed and recorded a lien against developer's property for the unpaid work, and commenced foreclosure. At the time the lien was filed, the statute then in effect (Alaska Stat. § 34.35.050) provided that an engineer who furnished design services preliminary to site preparation or construction has "a lien on it for work done." The issue was whether "it" referred only to the visible product of labor, such as a building or structure, therefore precluding a lien's creation before "it" materialized. *Held:* The engineering firm was not entitled to the lien. "It" referred only to visible improvements on the land, which, in this case, had not yet been constructed. This view was consistent with legislative intent that a visibility requirement was necessary to protect the rights of third-party purchasers, by putting them on notice that liens may exist. *Torkko/Korman/Eng'rs v. Penland Ventures*, 673 P2d 769 (1983).

Georgia Under an oral agreement with developer, architect was to perform design work on a project in return for a 5 percent ownership interest. When architect began work, developer had not yet acquired the land, but a purchase was subsequently concluded. Eventually, architect sued developer for the reasonable value of his services, but his suit was stayed while lender successfully foreclosed on the property and conveyed portions of it to unrelated parties. New owners sought to declare their interests superior to any lien architect had. *Held:* Since an owner cannot create a lien against his own property, the architect had no lien on the property as against the interests of subsequent transferees. On the basis of his oral agreement, the architect had a 5 percent equitable interest in the property, even though developer never actually conveyed it to him. *Murray v. Chulak*, 300 SE2d 493 (1983).

Illinois Contractor retained plaintiff to haul away the debris from a building he had contracted with defendant to demolish. When contractor went into bankruptcy, plaintiff did not receive his fee. He then sued for foreclosure of a mechanic's lien against defendant. When the trial court dismissed the suit, plaintiff appealed. *Held:* The demolition and hauling away of debris are not lienable items under the state Mechanics' Lien Act. Demolition does not fall within the express language of the act and therefore must be excluded. A lien attaches only where a house is moved onto the land, not, as here, where it is moved from the land. Thus, plaintiff was not entitled to a mechanic's lien. *Robinette v. Servite Fathers*, 364 NE2d 679 (1977).

Iowa Plaintiff architect was employed to provide architectural, engineering, and planning services for a proposed real estate development. Plaintiff, in fact, did the surveying and marking, and drew up plans to be used for subcontractor bidding; but the project was abandoned. The plans were not used, and construction was never begun. Plaintiff filed a mechanic's lien and sought to foreclose. *Held:* The architect's lien was invalid; plaintiff did not furnish labor on the property resulting in its improvement, as required by the mechanic's lien statute. A lien for preparing plans that are actually used is allowed because, in that case, there is visible evidence to put the world on notice that the lien exists. *Gollehon, Schemmer & Assocs., Inc. v. Fairway-Bettendorf*, 268 NW2d 200 (1978).

South Dakota Supplier of glass for the construction of a motel brought foreclosure proceedings against the corporation that owned the land on which the motel was built. The corporation argued that plaintiff was not entitled to the protection of the lien law since he was merely a supplier to the materialman. *Held:* Plaintiff was within the statute because he was requested by the owner to provide materials and labor. *Schubloom v. Donavon & Assocs., Inc.*, 241 NW2d 710 (1976).

Wyoming A manufacturer of prefabricated buildings, under an agreement with the property owner, sold several buildings to a dealer. The dealer, in turn, sold the buildings to the property owner, who then erected them. Owner paid dealer, but dealer failed to pay manufacturer. The manufacturer filed a mechanic's lien against the property on the theory that it was a materialman, and sought to foreclose. *Held:* Enforcement of the lien denied. One who merely supplies materials without installing them is a materialman, and one who merely supplies materials to a materialman is too remotely related to the property owner to be protected by the lien statute. This conclusion, previously reached in other jurisdictions, is necessary for the protection of property owners. *American Bldgs. Co. v. Wheelers Stores*, 585 P2d 845 (1978).

107.25 Enforcement

D.C. Circuit Developers defaulted in repaying a bank's construction loan that was secured by a deed of trust on the property. A subcontractor filed a notice of mechanic's lien. Later, the trustees of the deed of trust foreclosed and sold the property free and clear of mechanic's liens. The trustees paid the bank the entire proceeds of the sale. The subcontractor sued, claiming its lien should have been paid from the interest on loan advances made before the filing of the lien but accrued after the lien had been filed. *Held:*

The subcontractor was not entitled to priority as to the interest on loan advances made prior to the filing of its mechanic's lien. D.C. Code § 38-109 grants a mechanic's lien priority over a deed of trust securing a construction loan that is recorded prior to commencement of work, only as to advances made after the mechanic files a notice of intention to assert a lien. *Electrical Equip. Co. v. Security Nat'l Bank*, 606 F2d 1357 (1979).

U.S. District Court, Maine Subcontractor, who had not been paid for materials he supplied to a job site on land leased to the United States, sued in state court to enforce a mechanic's lien on the property, naming the United States as a defendant. The government had the case removed to the federal district court. At issue was whether or not the federal court had the requisite jurisdiction to enforce the lien. *Held:* Removal of the action by the United States was invalid. Subcontractor based his case upon Maine's mechanic's lien laws; no federal statute was invoked. The defense asserted by the United States, that the property was invulnerable to lien because it was owned by the federal government, did not confer federal question jurisdiction. *New England Explosives Corp. v. Maine Ledge Blasting Specialists Inc.*, 542 F. Supp. 1343 (1982).

Alabama Owners told lumber company that after their new home was completed, company would be entitled to any funds remaining in the construction account established to pay their contractor's unpaid invoices to materialmen. After all the other workmen had been paid, the amount remaining in the account was not enough to satisfy the company, and it filed a lien against owners' property and against any unpaid balance due the contractor. The lumber company recovered only 64 percent of this unpaid balance. Owners appealed, contending that the entire unpaid balance of the construction account was depleted by payments for work left uncompleted by contractor. *Held:* The lumber company's lien was enforceable. The company's claim was subordinated by the owners' right to use the remainder of the account to complete construction and pay the materialmen according to the original contract. However, since owners failed to meet their burden of proof regarding proper disbursement of these payments, they could not argue that the construction account was depleted by payments for uncompleted work. *Justice v. Arab Lumber & Supply, Inc.*, 533 So. 2d 538 (1988).

Georgia Materialman sued property owner to foreclose a lien for materials he had allegedly supplied to a contractor working on the property. Plaintiff offered direct proof of two deliveries of materials to the site and produced delivery tickets containing the signature of a person on the premises. He contended that the trial judge incorrectly charged the jury concerning the burden of proof. The court of appeals held that the materialman was not entitled to a presumption that the materials delivered to the site were used in the construction of the dwelling, but rather had to prove the point at trial. *Held:* The state supreme court reversed that decision. Presumption of the use of materials in a building arises from the fact of their delivery thereto for that purpose, and the burden is on the property owner to prove that the materials were not used that way. *Bankston v. Smith*, 222 SE2d 375 (1976).

Idaho Subcontractor who sued to foreclose a mechanic's lien sought to enforce the judgment personally against property owner. *Held:* Lien foreclosures are in rem, not in personam, proceedings. There is a charge against the property to the extent of its value, but no personal charge against owner of the property. A personal judgment could not be sustained against owner on a contract theory because he had not assumed the general contractor's contract. *Pierson v. Sewell*, 539 P2d 590 (1975).

Illinois Fifteen months after subcontractor filed a lien claim against contractor and homeowners for work performed on owners' house, subcontractor was automatically stayed from issuing process against contractor when contractor filed for bankruptcy. However, 133 days after the stay, the bankruptcy court permitted subcontractor to enforce his lien, and he filed suit against contractor after the two-year limitation period had expired under Illinois lien law. The issue was whether the automatic stay tolled the two-year limitation period for filing foreclosure actions. *Held:* The two-year limitation period was tolled. Section 108(c)(1) of the Bankruptcy Code provides for suspension of time to sue where the applicable period has not expired at the time of bankruptcy filing. Therefore, subcontractor should have been allowed an extra 133 days to file suit after the two-year limitations period expired. *Garbe Iron Works, Inc. v. Priester*, 457 NE2d 422 (1983).

Illinois Subcontractor brought a foreclosure action to enforce a mechanic's lien arising from agreement to supply lumber and other materials to contractor. Contractor had an oral contract with owner to construct a barn on owner's property. Subcontractor's suit was filed more than two years after completing his agreement with contractor, but less than two years after contractor completed his contract with owner. The issue was whether the two-year limitation period for filing a foreclosure suit began running on the date the subcontractor's agreement with contractor was completed or on the date the contractor completed his contract with owner. *Held:* Subcontractor's action to enforce his mechanic's lien was time-barred. Under the Illinois Mechanic's Lien Act, the two-year limitation period began running on the date of completion of the agreement between contractor and subcontractor, which date was more than two years before subcontractor filed his action. *Mixer v. Billingsley*, 442 NE2d 275 (1982).

Oklahoma In a foreclosure action brought by defendant bank, plaintiff cross-petitioned, alleging that defendant, as lender, had a fiduciary duty to insure that loan funds be distributed properly to satisfy lienable claims. Defendant's demurrer was sustained, and plaintiff appealed. *Held:* Judgment affirmed. There is no authority for the proposition that a mortgage lender, the source of the mortgage funds delivered to the owner engaged in construction of a building, has some special responsibility to mechanics or materialmen with lienable claims. That special responsibility is defined in Okla. Stat. tit. 42, § 152 (1971). The court declined to apply New York law, upon which plaintiff's position was grounded, because that law was derived from a statutory scheme so different from that existing in this state. *Shankle Equip. Co. v. Liberty Nat'l Bank*, 569 P2d 965 (1977).

Utah The Olsens contracted separately with a number of contractors to build a house. The ground was broken on August 4, 1980. The Olsens obtained a construction loan from a bank secured by a deed of trust on the property, recorded in November 1980. The contractor who broke the ground was paid in full by the bank. The remaining contractors began work in December 1980. When the house was completed, the Olsens filed for bankruptcy, and the bank and unpaid contractors sued to enforce their liens on the property. *Held:* For the contractors. Where two contractors perform work in connection with what is essentially a single project performed under a common plan carried out with reasonable promptness, the one contractor's lien relates back to the commencement of work or supplying of materials by the other contractor. Therefore the other contractors could date their liens back to the August 4 ground breaking. *Duckett v. Olsen*, 699 P2d 734 (1985).

Utah Subcontractor sued for the balance due for materials and labor furnished to build defendants' home. Defendants counterclaimed that the work was unsatisfactory and the lien was wrongfully imposed. Defendants alleged that because plaintiff did not release the lien within 10 days after the demand, they were entitled to damages of $120 per day for 21 days. *Held:* A party seeking to invoke a penalty statute must demonstrate with particularity that he comes within the specific terms of the statute. The statute limited the penalty to a lienor who refused to remove his lien after the property owner paid the amount of the lien. *K&P Plumbing & Heating, Inc. v. Winterton*, 543 P2d 1352 (1975).

107.30
Priorities

U.S. District Court, South Carolina Subcontractor asserted the priority of his mechanic's lien in an action by the United States to foreclose mortgage insured by the Department of Housing and Urban Development. *Held:* In determining the priority between federal and state liens, the ruled applied is first in time, first in right. For a nonfederal lien to be entitled to priority, it must be "choate" at the time the federal lien arises. Since the mechanic's lien was a nonfederal lien that was recorded after the federal lien, the federal lien must take priority. *United States v. Chesler Heights Assocs.*, 406 F. Supp. 600 (1976).

Arkansas Hill agreed to purchase building to be built by construction company on its land. The following day, materials were delivered to the construction site. Bank agreed to loan money to construction company to be used in the erection of the building. Construction company received and signed a deed of trust securing the total sum of construction loan and received a draw for two thirds of the amount to begin work. The following month, Hill delivered materials for construction. Later, he brought action against bank and construction company to establish a materialman's lien and to foreclose the same. *Held:* The materialman's lien related back to the first delivery of materials to the construction site, i.e., the commencement of the building. Since the first delivery occurred before the construction mortgage was signed and recorded, all materialmen had liens higher in priority than the construction lender. This result was reached because the construction lender was in the best position to inspect the premises to determine whether construction had started, therefore insuring that his lien had priority over all others. *Bank of Cave City v. Hill*, 587 SW2d 833 (1979).

California Defendant, a public utility district, provided sewage service for a mobile home park, which had been encumbered by a $550,000 lien of a savings and loan association. When the mobile home park was delinquent on the payments due both defendant and savings and loan, defendant threatened to discontinue services. The county sought an injunction to prevent the district from discontinuing services. Purchaser at the foreclosure sale intervened on the government's side. *Held:* When the lien on the mobile park home was created in the bank, a bona fide encumbrance for value, the lien created by virtue of the delinquent sewer charges, did not attach. Thus, purchaser's acquisition at the foreclosure sale was free and clear of liability for accrued service charge delinquencies. The district's only remedy was against other property of the parties who failed to pay the delinquent charges. *Butte County v. North Burbank Pub. Util. Dist.*, 177 Cal. Rptr. 282 (1981).

Colorado Dovenmuehle, Inc., beneficiary of a deed of trust, executed and recorded the deed on March 15, 1974. Later, a lien claimant filed to foreclose his lien, which had been perfected prior to March 15, 1974. *Held:* Dovenmuehle's interest was junior to that of the lien claimants. On February 11, 1974, a surveyor had prepared a certified boundary survey and several days later had staked the perimeter lot boundaries. The applicable statute states: "All liens established by virtue of this article shall relate back to the time of the commencement of work under the contract between the owner and the first contractor. . . ." Thus the survey and staking by the surveyor constituted commencement of the work for purposes of determining the date to which mechanic's liens relate back. *Weather Eng'r & Mfg., Inc. v. Pinon Springs Condominiums, Inc.*, 563 P2d 346 (1977).

Illinois Plaintiff bank challenged the validity of defendant's mechanic's lien filed against three buildings on which the bank held prior mortgages. The filing statement claimed a blanket lien against all three buildings without apportionment of the total contract price to each. It also stated that all work under the contract had been completed by a specified date, but did not specify a separate completion date for each building. The issue was whether the filing statement covering multiple parcels provided sufficient notice of the lien as required by the Illinois Mechanics' Lien Act. *Held:* The defendant's blanket mechanic's lien had priority over the bank's mortgages. The filing statement gave bank sufficient notice of the lien, because it was timely filed and gave an adequate description of each building and the work performed therein. The Illinois Mechanics' Lien Act specifically authorizes the filing of a single-claim statement covering multiple parcels, and nothing in its language requires the filing statement to contain different information for each parcel. *First Fed. Sav. & Loan Ass'n v. Connelly*, 454 NE2d 314 (1983).

Louisiana Construction of an apartment complex was divided into two phases, performed on separate but adjacent lots. When work had clearly begun on the first phase, but before any visible work was performed on the second phase, the mortgage of the second-phase construction site was recorded. Mortgagee brought an action to have that mortgage recognized as superior to the liens of materialmen. *Held:* Mortgagee had rights as to the second-phase site superior to those of the materialmen. There were separate phases of development under separate construction contracts. Construction on the second phase was based on plans not drafted until first-phase construction was under way. And the second-phase site occupied a separate parcel of land clearly identified in a separate mortgage. Thus, materials furnished in the first phase could not provide liens on the second-phase site superior to the second-phase mortgage. Moreover, work on the second job site was not visible on inspection so as to warn prospective lenders of possible materialmen's liens. *Louisiana Nat'l Bank v. Triple R. Contractors, Inc.*, 345 So. 2d 7 (1977).

Michigan Plaintiff engineering firm filed a foreclosure suit to enforce its mechanic's lien on developer's property for off-site feasibility studies performed before developer purchased the property. Actual on-site construction began eight months after the firm performed its services, and one month after purchase and two mortgages were recorded. The issue was whether, for purposes of priority, "commencement of improvements to the property" under Michigan's Mechanic's Lien Law referred to when engineering services were first performed or to when construction began. The engineering firm contended that construction began on the day it provided services, and therefore the lien related back to that date. *Held:* Mortgagee, which recorded its mortgage before actual on-site construction had begun, had priority over engineering firm's mechanic's lien. Off-site engineering services, although made lienable by the legislature, did not signal the "commencement" of a building, structure, or improvement for purposes of fixing priority under Michigan Mechanic's Lien Law. Rather, "commencement" begins with the providing of visible, on-site construction. *Williams & Works, Inc. v. Springfield Corp.*, 293 NW2d 304 (1980).

Mississippi Unpaid contractors filed mechanic's and materialman's liens on developer's lots. However, financing banks foreclosed and purchased the lots for 5 percent of their fair market value. Contractors sued to enjoin the foreclosure sale, contending their liens had priority. The banks claimed that the recording of their liens before contractors filed their liens was conclusive on the issue. *Held:* For contractors. While normally the banks would have priority under the state's construction lien statute, the equities of the situation ran against them. The banks had failed to perform their obligation to supervise use of the loan proceeds and ensure payment to contractors, so as to prevent developer's diversion of funds. Contractors could not seek satisfaction from the sale proceeds, as the bank had argued, because the proceeds were negligible, leaving contractors with no remedy but an injunction of the sale and grant of priority. *Peoples Bank & Trust Co. v. L&T Devs., Inc.*, 434 So. 2d 699 (1983).

Mississippi Tenant, with landlord's approval, sought interim construction financing from mortgagee to build a shopping center. A loan was made, secured by a deed of trust binding the fee simple ownership of the land. Construction was undertaken and disbursements were made by tenant from its own account of commingled construction funds held by mortgagee. Funds were distributed by tenant with the knowledge of mortgagee without control, supervision, or limitation. During the course of construction, tenant experienced financial difficulty. After materialmen filed notice of their materialmen's liens, mortgagee instituted proceedings to foreclose on its deed of trust, claiming that the deed took priority over the materialmen's and mechanics' liens. *Held:* The lien of a deed of trust securing a construction loan has priority over mechanics' and materialmen's liens only to the extent that (1) the funds disbursed actually went into the construction or (2) the construction lender used reasonable diligence in disbursing the construction loan. Since mortgagee did not use reasonable diligence in disbursing funds to tenant, mortgagee was entitled to a lien superior to the materialmen only in the amount that went into the construction project. *Guaranty Mortgage Co. v. WM Seitz*, 367 So. 2d 483 (1979).

Nevada Workmen performed work consisting of land surveyance, soil testing, and drafting architectural plans prior to the recordation of the deed of trust and the commencement of construction. Workmen contended that this work caused their liens to attach and take priority over the deed of trust. *Held:* The deed of trust had priority over the mechanics' liens. Mechanics' liens did not relate back to preparatory work done prior to commencement of construction, and the deed of trust was recorded before construction began. Otherwise, prospective lenders inspecting the premises would not be informed that liens could exist. *Aladdin Heating v. Trustees, Cent. States*, 563 P2d 82 (1977).

New Mexico Savings & loan association

(S&L) recorded a mortgage, the proceeds of which were used to construct a home. The S&L relied on its inspector's assurance that the site was unimproved, thus believing it had priority over any subsequent liens arising from work on the site. However, the inspector failed to notice preliminary foundation work performed by two subcontractors. After the S&L began foreclosure proceedings, the contractor, who did no work on the site before the mortgage was recorded, claimed that it shared lien priority with the two subcontractors. The contractor argued that, under the state's lien statute, if the S&L's lien arose after any work was commenced, regardless of by whom, then it was junior to every mechanic's and materialman's lien. *Held:* The contractor shared lien priority with the two subcontractors. The lender's inspector could have been more thorough; the S&L could have also required all contractors to submit their invoices directly to it for payment, assuring proper allocation of loan proceeds; and lender could have demanded contractor execute a waiver that contractor would subordinate his claim to the proceeds of a foreclosure sale to that of lender. *Valley Fed. Sav. & Loan Ass'n v. T-Bird Home Centers, Inc.*, 741 P2d 826 (1987).

Oklahoma Engineering company filed a mechanic's and materialman's lien on landowner's property in August 1975 for surveying and site inspection work performed between May 1971 and April 1975 under an oral agreement with landowner. Mortgagee filed its mortgage on the same property in January 1974. During mortgagee's foreclosure action, the engineering firm cross-claimed to have its lien declared superior to the mortgage. *Held:* The engineering firm's lien had priority. Surveying work constituted an improvement of the realty and was therefore lienable. Under the state's mechanic's and materialman's statute, the first work that the firm performed on the project preceded the filing of the mortgage and therefore was superior to all subsequent liens that could attach after the date of the first labor on the land. *Midland Mortgage Co. v. Sanders Eng. Invs.*, 682 P2d 748 (1984).

Utah After morgagor executed a purchase money mortgage on his property, but before it was recorded, he hired first contractor to paint his building and perform some gardening tasks. No mechanics' liens were filed as a result of this work. After the mortgage was recorded, mortgagor then hired a second contractor to resurface the parking area and supply all materials. A mechanics' lien was filed as a result of this work. Mortgagee successfully brought a foreclosure action. The second contractor appealed, contending that its lien priority was established when the first contractor's work began, before the mortgage's recording. *Held:* The second contractor's lien did not have priority over the recorded mortgage, because it did not relate back to the beginning of first contractor's work. The tacking of second contractor's lien date onto an earlier time, when work was performed by first contractor, would be permitted only if both projects were performed under the same improvement plan. Since no evidence of such a common plan existed, both projects were simply ordinary maintenance work. *Calder Bros. v. Anderson*, 652 P2d 922 (1982).

107.35 Termination

5th Circuit Subcontractor sought, in an interpleader action brought by plaintiff, to enforce its claim against contractor for building materials supplied on a construction project. Prior to the contractor's declaring bankruptcy, the subcontractor, who had supplied materials valued at $740,000, had received $50,000 in cash and a promissory note for the balance.

The subcontractor had indicated on his books "payment" with reference to these two items. Contractor's trustee in bankruptcy, filing a motion for partial summary judgment, contended that the notation "payment" was evidence that the outstanding balance had been previously satisfied. *Held:* The acceptance of a promissory note does not automatically extinguish a mechanic's lien unless the intent to do this is clear. The notation in the subcontractor's accounts did tend to prove that the subcontractor intended the promissory note to constitute payment, but since this was an issue of fact, summary judgment would be inappropriate, and was denied. *Scott Paper Co. v. Adair Truck & Equip. Co.*, 542 F2d 1257 (1976).

Florida When general contractor abandoned work on a construction project, subcontractor filed a timely lien claim on owner's property for unpaid materials. Eight months later, owner hired a new general contractor at a higher cost and resumed work on the project. Subcontractor then sued to foreclose its statutory and equitable liens against owner and to recover the monies owed by the former contractor. Owner argued that under Florida case law and statute, its liability to subcontractor was limited by subtracting the cost of the project's completion from the amount remaining unpaid on the original contract. *Held:* For subcontractor. The Mechanics' Lien Act was designed to protect the innocent lienor who faithfully performed and properly perfected its lien. Owner could not limit its liability to subcontractor, because it did not strictly comply with the statute. Moreover, the costs of completing the project were higher than usual, since construction had ceased for eight months. *Florida Steel v. Adaptable Devs.*, 503 So. 2d 1232 (1986).

Kentucky General contractor was having difficulty meeting its schedule to build housing units for a developer, and the original contract was renegotiated. Unpaid materialmen who had furnished materials to general contractor prior to the renegotiation filed liens against the property. Developer argued the liens were invalid because (1) general contractor had failed to perform satisfactorily under the original agreement; (2) as a result of the renegotiation, general contractor entered into a new agreement; and (3) movement of a modular unit from the construction site to its ultimate destination extinguishes a materialman's lien. *Held:* The liens were valid and enforceable. A materialman's right to assert a lien is not affected by any defect in contractor's performance. The status of the parties is determined as of the time the material is furnished, according to the contracts in effect at that time. Kentucky lien law (Ky. Rev. Stat. § 376.010) extends protection to materialmen who furnish material to a contractor away from a job site, as long as the material is ultimately used to improve the property. *Woodson Bend, Inc. v. Masters' Supply, Inc.*, 571 SW2d 95 (Ct. App. 1978).

107.40 Waiver

Connecticut Architects sought to foreclose a mechanic's lien against a bank. The bank contended that an arbitration clause between the parties precluded the action to foreclose. *Held:* The mere existence of an arbitration clause does not waive the right to foreclosure of a lien absent language expressly so providing or conduct that unambiguously implies such a waiver. *Meyer v. Lafayette Bank & Trust Co.*, 377 A2d 861 (1977).

Minnesota In an action to foreclose a mechanic's lien, defendant asserted as affirmative defenses three lien waivers. Two of the waivers were form agreements expressly waiving "all rights acquired to date." A third waiver consisted of a check stamped with a statement purporting to waive all past and future rights in consideration for the payment represented by the check. *Held:* A mechanic's lien waiver that waives "all rights acquired to date" does not waive rights subsequent to the date of the agreement. Further, a lien waiver must be based on valuable consideration. Payments made for a preexisting obligation could not constitute consideration. Therefore, the lien waiver on the check was unenforceable. *Sussel Co. v. First Fed. Sav. & Loan*, 232 NW2d 88 (Sup. Ct. 1975), aff'd, 238 NW2d 625 (1976).

Pennsylvania A foundation contractor waived, for himself and his subcontractors, the right to file any mechanic's liens in connection with the construction of a commercial building. After "visible commencement" of the excavation work began, the bank recorded a construction mortgage from the owner. Thereafter, two new contractors, neither of whom were connected with the foundation contractor, performed work on the building, but were not paid. Each filed a mechanic's lien against owner. When the bank sought to foreclose on its mortgage, the two contractors claimed lien priority. *Held:* The foundation contractor's waiver of lien did not waive priority as to all contractors; therefore the two subsequent liens had priority over the bank's recorded mortgage. Also, under Pennsylvania mechanic's lien statute, the contractor's lien claims had priority because they were filed after "visible commencement" of the excavation work. The bank, which had relied upon the waiver before recording its mortgage, was left defenseless against mechanic's liens arising thereafter. *Security Bank & Trust v. Pocono Web Press*, 441 A2d 1321 (1982).

Utah Plaintiff brought action to foreclose on lien for concrete and labor supplied to the defendant. Defendant contended that plaintiff had executed a lien waiver to him signed in blank that released defendant from any claim plaintiff might have on the property. The parties had worked together previously and plaintiff regularly signed blank lien waivers. *Held:* The blank lien waiver held valid where it had been a common business practice between the parties. *Le Grand Johnson Constr. Co. v. Kennedy*, 541 P2d 1038 (1975).

107.45 Constitutionality of Lien Statutes

3d Circuit Plaintiff, seeking to enforce a lien on owner's property, filed a notice of lis pendens. Under New Jersey law, constructive notice of any pending actions involving the property described is attributed to all potential purchasers. Owner challenged the New Jersey law as an unconstitutional taking. Plaintiff contended the opposite, because that the notice of lis pendens did not affect owner's possession, use, or enjoyment of the property. *Held:* Although there was a taking, the New Jersey law did not violate due process. The lis pendens notice impaired the property's marketability, and was a deprivation of owner's free use and enjoyment. However, it was a taking necessitated by a valid state interest in minimizing litigation that would otherwise arise from transfers to purchasers who had no notice of adverse claims to the property. Moreover, the notice did not amount to a total taking, for owners who did not intend selling or mortgaging their property would not be affected. *Chrysler Corp. v. Fedders Corp.*, 670 F2d 1316 (1982).

U.S. District Court, Pennsylvania Plaintiffs, owners of property encumbered by mechanics' liens, brought action to have the Pennsylvania mechanic's lien law declared unconstitutional in that it violated the due process requirements of the Constitution because it did not require notice and a hearing before a mechanic's lien could be filed. *Held:* The state law is constitutional where there has been no actual deprivation of property. The court cited *Speilman-Fond, Inc. v. Hanson's Inc.*, 379 F. Supp. 997 (D. Ariz. 1973), aff'd, 417 US 901, as the leading case in the area. *B&P Dev. v. Walker*, 420 F. Supp. 704 (WD 1976).

U.S. District Court, Virginia Petitioner challenged Virginia's mechanic's lien statute on the grounds that it violated due process and the equal protection clauses of the Fourteenth Amendment of the Constitution because it failed to provide for notice and a hearing prior to a lien being recorded. *Held:* The statute is constitutional. Citing numerous decisions in other states upholding the constitutionality of similar statutes, the courts have stated that although outstanding liens cloud the title to property, the owner's rights to possession, enjoyment, and alienation remain unrestricted. *In re Thomas Carey, Inc.*, 412 F. Supp. 667 (ED 1976), aff'd, 562 F2d 48 (4th Cir. 1977).

Georgia Plaintiff, owner of property on which improvements had been made, sued for injunctive relief from a materialmen's lien that had been filed against the property and for a declaratory judgment that the statute providing for the creation, recording, and notice of materialmen's liens was unconstitutional. Plaintiff argued that the lien was an unconstitutional interference with property by use of the facilities of the state without an opportunity for immediate hearing. *Held:* The materialmen's lien statutes are not unconstitutional, because owner is not deprived of a significant property interest without notice and hearing. While there may be some interference with the use of property, the owner is "not legally prevented from . . . dealing with his property as he chooses." In addition, the imposition of materialmen's liens serves an important public interest. *Fayetteville-85 Assocs., Ltd. v. Samas, Inc.*, 243 SE2d 887 (1978).

Maryland Hotel owners hired a construction company to renovate the hotel. The construction company hired a subcontractor, which, through an oral agreement, purchased materials from supplier. The supplier was only partially compensated by the subcontractor for the purchases before the subcontractor walked off the job. Supplier gave owner written notice of its intent to claim a mechanic's lien, as required by state law, and filed a petition for the lien. Owners asserted the mechanic's lien law unconstitutionally deprived an owner of property without due process of law. *Held:* Mechanic's lien law is constitutional. The lien law does not provide that a lien attach automatically once materials are supplied; instead, if a subcontractor has no direct contract with the owner, he must provide the owner with written notice of his intent to claim a lien. Due process does not require that the subcontractor inform the owner of its involvement with a project before any work is performed; it requires only that the defendant be notified in writing of any claim against him and that he be provided with a hearing before deprivation of his property occurs. The lien law is not a state scheme to take private property for a nonpublic use for the benefit of materialmen who have no contractual privity with the owner. In this case, the state was not taking property; instead, it was creating an orderly process for the satisfaction of a debt that had a basis in law and that had been found by a court to be due and owing. *AMI Operating Partners Ltd. Partnership v. JAD Enters.*, 551 A2d 888 (Ct. Spec. App. 1989).

107.50 Defenses

Florida When general contractor abandoned work on a construction project, subcontractor filed a timely lien claim on owner's property for unpaid materials. Eight months later, owner hired a new general contractor at a higher cost and resumed work on the project. Owner, relying on Florida statute and prior case law, asserted the defense that its liability to subcontractor was limited by subtracting the cost of the project's completion from the amount remaining unpaid on the original contract. *Held:* For subcontractor. Owner's defense of limited liability was rejected. Owner was not entitled to statutory protection, because, unlike the situations in the cited cases, this project had been interrupted for a significant period, making the completion costs higher than they would have been if construction had resumed immediately. Moreover, owner failed to comply with the statutory provision requiring it to file certain notices, and to pay or make prorated payments to all lienors before restarting work. *Florida Steel v. Adaptable Devs.*, 503 So. 2d 1232 (1986).

108.00
JUDGMENT LIENS

108.05
Scope and Extent

10th Circuit Colorado home buyers bought an improved lot from previous purchasers, who had purchased the lot from a judgment debtor under an unrecorded installment land contract. Five months before the judgment debtor gave previous purchasers a warranty deed to the lot, judgment creditors obtained a lien against debtor's property, including the unimproved lot, of which he was then record owner. Previous purchasers recorded the warranty deed, built a home on the lot and sold it to home buyers. When judgment creditors sought to execute against the lot, buyers invoked the "good faith improver" doctrine, which they claimed gave them an equitable lien on the home. *Held:* For judgment creditors. Under Colorado law, record notice of a judgment lien constitutes constructive notice and is tantamount to actual notice. Previous purchasers were charged with constructive notice of the recorded lien at the time they built on the lot and were not "good faith improvers." *Mooring v. Brown*, 763 F2d 386 (1985).

Florida Bankrupt petitioned to discharge a judgment obtained by a creditor prior to bankruptcy. The bankrupt was not personally liable for the judgment, but it constituted a lien on real property. The bankrupt relied on a state statute allowing such cancellation of judgments upon petition after one year from a bankrupt's discharge. *Held:* The statute did not affect a lien that arose prior to bankruptcy and that attached to the bankrupt's exempt property. The statute was designed to clear the record of liens arising prior to bankruptcy on subsequently acquired real property. *Albruton v. General Portland Cement Co.*, 344 So. 2d 574 (1977).

Minnesota Seller sold his home, which he occupied as his homestead, to buyers. After the sale, five judgment liens were docketed against seller. Buyers resided in the home before the judgment liens were docketed but did not record the contract for deed until after the judgment liens were filed. Subsequently, seller received a discharge in bankruptcy. Buyers discovered the existence of the liens when they attempted to refinance their home. Buyers sued to remove the judgments from the record due to seller's subsequent discharge in bankruptcy. *Held:* Since seller homesteaded the property prior to its sale, buyers acquired it free of grantor's creditors and were entitled to discharge of grantor's judgment liens. Under state law, a judgment lien cannot attach to homestead property, which is exempt from seizure, and any such liens would be destroyed by a discharge in bankruptcy. The fact that the judgments were docketed before buyers recorded the contract did not make the liens enforceable against the property, since possession by vendee under a contract for deed operates as constructive notice to creditors, preventing creditors from gaining priority by virtue of the recoding act. *Hentges v. PH Feely & Son*, 436 NW2d 488 (Ct. App. 1989).

Utah Wilkinson sold land to Themy under an installment contract and retained title pending completion of payments. Themy's creditors obtained liens against the property, and Wilkinson and Themy sought to sell the parcel to Christensen. Themy quitclaimed to Wilkinson his interest in the property. Christensen gave Wilkinson a $25,000 down payment, which Wilkinson loaned to Themy, protecting it from reach of creditors. Themy's creditors sued. *Held:* For creditors. The court examined whether Themy's relinquishment of rights under the installment contract was a forfeiture that extinguished liens attaching to Themy's interest. A land contract seller's security interest was analogous to that of a purchase-money mortgagee whose rights were protected from creditors, but only to the extent of the indebtedness. To the degree the property had appreciated since inception of the loan, the installment contract seller's position was vulnerable unless termination of buyer's interest in the property was by forfeiture. Creditors contended that the test of a forfeiture was the voluntariness of buyer's relinquishment of his interest. The court viewed Themy's role in the Christensen transfer as that of a coseller. The termination of Themy's contract was thus not a bona fide forfeiture, and judgment creditor's liens survived to the extent of the "inflation equity," or the appreciation of the property. The Christensen sale cut off the liens. However, the court found the transfer to Wilkinson was for the purpose of hindering creditors and was fraudulent. Judgment creditors were awarded against Wilkinson the difference between Themy's debt and the sale price to Wilkinson. *Butler v. Wilkinson*, 740 P2d 1244 (1987).

108.10 Interests Subject

Georgia Employee sued his employer for breach of contract and demanded specific performance. When plaintiff filed a notice of lis pendens against certain property in which he claimed an interest, defendant employers argued that no lis pendens could be filed as the employee only had a personal property interest at stake in the litigation. *Held:* Plaintiff was not entitled to file a notice of lis pendens where the action did not involve any interest in real property. Even if successful in his action, plaintiff would receive only damages and a limited partnership interest, both of which are personal property interests. *Hill v. L/A Management Corp.*, 216 SE2d 97 (1975).

New Mexico Buyer and sellers of a house signed a sales contract, which was recorded two years later in the county clerk's office. Several months after the contract was recorded, the city in which the property was located obtained a judgment against sellers and filed a lien on the property. During this period, a bank had been holding the deed to the property in escrow. It was not delivered to buyer until almost a year after the lien was filed, and the city maintained that buyer acquired the property subject to the lien, since sellers still had title when the lien was filed. *Held:* The city did not have a lien on the property. Under state law, buyer who has signed a sales contract is considered the "equitable owner" of the property, and seller holds the legal title only as a trustee for buyer. The city could not attach a lien since sellers did not have the sort of interest to which the liens could attach. *Marks v. City of Tucumcari*, 595 P2d 1199 (1979).

New York A town leased property to a recovery resources corporation to build a waste disposal system. The corporation then hired a subcontractor to make improvements on the property. The subcontractor later filed mechanics' liens against the leasehold interest of the corporation in the land. The corporation sought to vacate the liens. *Held:* The subcontractor cannot assert a lien; real property owned by a municipality cannot be attached. To attach the leasehold would be to attach the land. *Hempstead Resources v. Peter Scalamandre*, 428 NYS2d 146 (1980).

Pennsylvania Davidson defaulted on a loan from Jefferson Bank. The bank obtained judgment, which it attempted to execute by sheriff's sale of certain real property. The property was held by a partnership set up by Davidson until two months after the judgment (but before the sheriff's sale), when it was transferred to Davidson. He then sold it to a third party, McCurdy. McCurdy petitioned the court to stay the sale. The bank was present and silent at the closing of the sale to McCurdy. One year later, the bank appealed to the superior court, asserting a theory of fraud. It argued (1) Davidson was true owner of the property and the partnership was a sham and (2) McCurdy knew of the claim against Davidson and was obligated to inquire further. *Held:* Although the partnership was a sham, McCurdy was a bona fide purchaser. The bank waited too long to reveal its theory of fraud to permit the bank's knowledge to be imputed to McCurdy. Mere knowledge of the existence of another's claim against seller does not obligate a purchaser to investigate further. *Jefferson Bank v. Davidson*, 512 A2d 658 (Super. Ct. 1986).

108.15 Exemptions

8th Circuit The Stevenses lived on and operated a farm. They fell behind on loan payments and sought relief under Chapter 13. The debtors, joint owners and joint debtors in the bankruptcy, each claimed a state homestead exemption under Section 522(b)(2)(A) of the Bankruptcy Code. Arkansas permits debtors to exempt 80 acres of land. By claiming separate exemptions, the Stevenses sought to protect their entire 120-acre farm. *Held:* Double exemption was disallowed. Although Section 522(m) provides for separate federal homestead exemptions in a joint case, the subsection had no force if a state alternative was available under Section 522(b)(2)(A). The court rejected debtors' claim that state law permits separate homesteads. The Supreme Court of Arkansas had stated that while husband and wife are living together, there can be no separate homestead of the wife, apart from her husband. *Stevens v. Pike County Bank*, 829 F2d 693 (1987).

10th Circuit Pruitt's business failed, and he filed a voluntary bankruptcy petition, although it meant his home would have to be sold. Pruitt's wife was a joint owner of the house but was not a party to the petition. Therefore, she was entitled to receive her share prior to distribution to creditors. Pruitt had a $20,000 homestead exemption under Colorado law made applicable by Section 522(b)(2)(A). Pruitt argued the bankruptcy court wrongly ordered the homestead exemption be applied prior to dividing the remaining proceeds of sale between his wife and the trustee. He argued that Section 522(m) requires exemptions be applied "separately with respect to each debtor," and therefore the exemption should be applied only to his interest. *Held:* Affirmed. Pruitt mistakenly regarded the homestead exemption as a personal rather than a real property interest. The homestead exemption attached to the dwelling and did not follow one occupant to the exclusion of others. *In re Pruitt*, 829 F2d 1002 (1987).

Minnesota Plaintiffs sued to recover the amount due them for remodeling work on defendant's building. They were awarded the full amount plus interest. Defendant moved for a release of the lien on his home, arguing it was not enforceable on his homestead under state law. *Held:* Plaintiffs' lien fell under the labor and services exception to the general rule that a lien cannot be enforced on a homestead. The labor and services exception is for manual work done on a homestead. In this case, plaintiffs had performed the remodeling personally and the work was manual labor as required by statute. Although the work was performed on another piece of property, the lien was enforceable against defendant's homestead. Plaintiffs were entitled to the amount initially awarded. *Luna v. Edel*, 417 NW2d 308 (1988).

Texas A subdivision was established by the recording of covenants and restrictions, including a homeowner's association for management of common areas. The association was empowered to impose assessments on members to pay for maintenance and improvements. The covenants and restrictions provided that the assessments were "a charge on the land" secured by a lien on the land assessed. When several homeowners stopped paying assessments, the association sued. *Held:* The association could foreclose its liens. In Texas, a homestead is protected from forced sale for payment of most debts. Nonetheless, this exemption could not override preexisting rights. The central issue was, when did the association's lien for unpaid assessments attach to the subdivision lots—before or after their acquisition by purchasers? If the covenants were found to run with the land, the lien attached before owners took possession and established homesteads, and therefore, owners and their lots were subject to the lien. This result was in accord with the rule in other jurisdictions that creation of a lien by acceptance of a deed is deemed to relate back to the time of recording of the covenant containing the lien. The court concluded that the property interest, which homestead claimants acquired by purchasing in the subdivision, was a fee simple less the interest vested in the association by virtue of purchaser's acceptance of the requirement to pay assessments and the lien attendant to failure to make such payment. Foreclosure was necessary to enforce the property right inherent in the system of assessments. *Inwood N. Homeowners' Ass'n v. Harris*, 736 SW2d 632 (1987).

108.20 Priorities

Connecticut Holder of a first mortgage brought a foreclosure action, and, after payment of the mortgage, the balance of the proceeds were held pending the resolution of the claims of subsequent creditors. The holder of the second mortgage contended that certain attachments against the property were invalid since they were made without prior notice to debtor and thereby violated his due process rights. *Held:* Creditor did not have standing to challenge the constitutional validity of the attachments on the basis of the due process rights of another person, since the creditor's own rights were not violated. *Shaskan v. Waltham Indus. Corp.*, 357 A2d 472 (1975).

New Jersey Husband and wife sold their marital home after their divorce. The divorce judgment created a lien of $3,000 in favor of the wife on the basis of monies she spent for improvements, payments on the mortgage, interest, taxes, and insurance. When the house was sold, the parties disagreed as to how the proceeds were to be divided and the lien satisfied. *Held:* Liens on particular property should be satisfied prior to the distribution of the proceeds to the property owners. In this case, where one of the property owners is also a lien creditor, the proceeds from the sale should first be divided equally between the parties and the lien then satisifed out of the husband's share. *Phillips v. Phillips*, 350 A2d 504 (1975).

108.25
Vendor's and Vendee's Liens

Missouri After prospective purchasers had paid $12,300 in earnest money to a construction firm, the firm applied to a bank for a "presold" construction loan of $84,000. The sale contract executed by prospective purchasers was attached to the loan application, which the bank approved. One construction delay followed another. Before the final closing could take place, the bank foreclosed. Prospective purchasers sued, seeking an equitable lien on the property. The trial court rendered a money judgment only, and prospective purchasers appealed. *Held:* Prospective purchasers were entitled to a vendee's equitable lien against the real estate. The bank's claim that it was an innocent purchaser for value was untenable, since when it made the loan the bank knew of the sale to prospective purchasers. *Stanovsky v. Group Enter. & Constr. Co.*, 714 SW2d 836 (Ct. App. 1986).

109.00
GOVERNMENTAL LIENS

109.05
Creation and Perfection

3d Circuit City residents were denied water and sewer services by the city owing to unpaid service charges incurred by prior occupants. The liens for unpaid utility bills were recorded in "lien books" for the properties, but were not recorded in the court judgment index. Residents sued, alleging the service shut-off denied them due process and equal protection. *Held:* The city was authorized to deny water and sewer services based on delinquencies in payment by prior occupants. The liens were enforceable and followed the property through subsequent transfers. Where occupants of affected residences were not intervening purchasers or mortgagees protected from attachment of the lien, but mere occupants or inheritors of property, a municipal lien for unpaid service is perfectible even though it was not filed in the judgment index. In addition, a municipal ordinance allowed the water department to disconnect services for residences with delinquent charges. This remedy is authorized by state law and applies to premises in which the service customer did not personally incur the charges. Absence of personal liability had no bearing, since the remedy does not impose personal liability, but affects the property and makes payment a condition of continued service. *Ransom v. Marrazzo*, 848 F2d 398 (1988).

9th Circuit The state of California filed a tax deed against already encumbered property on which taxes were delinquent. Owner of the property sold half of his interest (in effect, half his right to redeem). The Internal Revenue Service (IRS) then placed a lien against the property for nonpayment of federal employment taxes. When the original encumbrance on the property was foreclosed on, the IRS attempted to redeem the property under 26 USC § 7425. The objection was raised, however, that the portion of the right to redeem that had been sold did not rise to the level of an interest in property to which a federal tax lien could attach under 26 USC § 6321. *Held:* Under California law, the right to redeem is a valuable, transferable pecuniary asset to which a lien could attach. This was supported in this case by the fact that valuable consideration had been given for it and indeed by the fact that it was the subject of a suit. *Little v. United States*, 704 F2d 1100 (1983).

Georgia Banks foreclosed on security deeds and purchased apartment properties. County, pursuant to an ordinance, refused to provide water, sewer, and sanitary services to the properties until past bills for such services were paid. Banks protested, arguing that it was unconstitutional to apply the ordinance to them, since they weren't responsible for the arrearages, and that the security deeds were superior liens to the county's service charges. *Held:* Although banks may not have had personal liability for the delinquent accounts, as property owners their properties were subject to liability where the county's liens were valid and superior to the security deeds. The county's liens were valid, since they were created by an ordinance that was a valid exercise of the police power and that was properly applied to property owners who take title subject to prior liens. The county's liens had the same priority as ad valorem taxes and were thus superior to the security deeds and not extinguished by the banks' foreclosures. Consequently, the bounty could refuse service to the properties until its liens were satisfied. *Bowery Sav. Bank v. De Kalb County*, 242 SE2d 50 (1978).

109.10 Priorities

U.S. Supreme Court A supermarket borrowed $27,000 from a grocery wholesaler, secured by the supermarket's equipment and merchandise. The agreement also provided that the collateral would secure all future advances. The supermarket also borrowed $300,000 from a bank, secured by the same collateral, and guaranteed by the Small Business Administration (SBA). The supermarket used this loan to pay the grocery wholesaler, but continued to make purchases from it on credit. When the supermarket failed to pay, the wholesaler sued for the amount of credit purchases and recovered a judgment. Meanwhile, the supermarket sold its assets and put the money in escrow pending resolution of the competing claims of creditors. The wholesaler brought an action to foreclose its lien, claiming that its interest was superior to the SBA's, which had a lien after honoring its commitment to the bank. *Held:* The relative priority of the liens must be determined by state law. Federal law governs the priority of liens stemming from federal lending programs, and a uniform national policy is unnecessary to protect the federal interests underlying these programs. The relative priority of private liens and consensual liens arising from the federal loan program must be determined, absent a congressional directive to the contrary, under nondiscriminatory state laws. *United States v. Kimbell Foods, Inc.*, 440 US 715 (1979).

1st Circuit Housing project developer defaulted on a mortgage insured by the Department of Housing and Urban Development (HUD) and lender assigned the mortgage to HUD. Title insurance company warranted as to the mortgage's priority over subsequently recorded liens. Subcontractor claimed its mechanic's lien had priority over the mortgage since it was executed first. Under federal common law, the first to record has priority. The bank and title insurance company sued for a declaration that the government's mortgage lien was entitled to priority over subcontractor's mechanic's lien. *Held:* The mechanic's lien had priority. Applying the balancing test set forth in *United States v. Kimbell Foods, Inc.*, 440 US 715 (1979) with respect to choice of law in the absence of federal statute, the court held that a national rule was unnecessary to protect the interests of the federal government and to prevent commercial disruption and adopted Maine law as the federal rule of decision. *Chicago Title Ins. Co. v. Sherred Village Ass'n*, 708 F2d 804 (1983).

9th Circuit The SBA sued to enforce a lien that it alleged had priority over state and county tax liens. The SBA had acted as servicing agent for a loan to a business that later failed to pay real estate taxes. The property was deeded to the state; and, on foreclosure, the amount realized was placed in the registry of the court pending a determination of the priority of the liens. The SBA claimed that their lien, being first in time, should have priority over state and county tax liens. *Held:* The principle of first in time, first in right did not control in determining the priority of the SBA lien. The federal lien is subordinate to state and county tax liens notwithstanding the fact that the federal lien was created prior to the local tax liens. *United States v. California-Oregon Plywood, Inc.*, 527 F2d 687 (1975).

110.00 TAXES AND TAX LIENS

110.05 Validity of Tax or Assessment

U.S. Supreme Court West Virginia, by its constitution, established a principle of uniform taxation so that all property is taxed in proportion to its value. For a ten-year period ending in 1986, the county tax assessor valued petitioners' real property on the basis of its recent purchase price, while neighboring properties were subject to only a minor modification in their assessment. Petitioners appealed their assessments, and review was granted. *Held:* Assessment of property that created gross disparities in the assessed value of generally comparable property based on whether the property had been recently transferred violated the equal protection clause. Generally, an assessment scheme that bases values on recent arm's-length purchase price and uses a general adjustment as a transitional substitute for individual reappraisals is constitutionally adequate. However, the general adjustment must be accurate enough over a short period of time to provide rough equality in tax treatment of similarly situated property. In this case, the general adjustment did not provide transitional equality since petitioners' property was assessed at eight to 35 times more than comparable neighboring property for a period of more than 10 years. *Allegheny Pittsburgh Coal Co. v. County Comm'n,* 488 US 336 (1989).

U.S. Supreme Court State statute authorizes an annual use or property tax on possessory interests in improvements on tax-exempt land. Certain federal employees are required to live in federally owned housing, and their occupancy of the homes is considered partial compensation. When two counties imposed the use tax, these employees paid it under protest and sued for a refund. They contended that the tax violates the supremacy clause of the U.S. Constitution by interfering with a federal function and discriminating against federal employees. They relied on McCulloch v. Maryland, 4 Wheat. 316 (1819), which prohibited a tax on a federal institution on the ground that such a tax could be exercised to destroy the institution. *Held:* The state statute is constitutional. As long as such a tax is imposed equally on all similarly situated constituents of the state, the economic burden on the federal function does not render the tax unconstitutional. The legal incidence of this tax did not fall on or discriminate against federal property or the federal government; it was imposed only on private citizens working for the federal government. *United States v. County of Fresno,* 429 US 452 (1977).

California After the city electorate adopted a charter amendment that nullified the city's real property transfer tax, certain taxpayers filed a class action suit to recover taxes previously paid. The trial court held that the taxes constituted a tax on real property and that their imposition and collection were in violation of the charter limitation on real property taxes. The court ordered that the taxes illegally collected be returned to the class members. The city appealed. *Held:* Reversed. The transfer tax is not a property tax: Liability for the tax arises only when the property is conveyed; transferor and transferee become jointly and severally liable for the tax upon delivery of the instrument of transfer, and the tax is a debt collectible by an action against the persons liable. The tax is, therefore, on the exercise of one of the incidences of property ownership and, as such, in an excise tax. Thus, the class is not entitled to recover the imposed and collected taxes. *City of Huntington Beach v. Superior Ct.,* 144 Cal. Rptr. 236 (1978).

California Owners of an apartment building agreed to sell the property to a purchasing corporation. Purchaser made a down payment and received a deed of trust. Efforts to convert the building into a cooperative failed, and purchaser fell behind in payment. Owners initiated foreclosure proceedings and received a quitclaim title. Owners disputed a property tax reassessment, contending that there had never been a change of ownership, since the initial transfer lacked a beneficial use and purchasers were only granted an option to purchase the property. *Held:* The initial transaction between the parties constituted a change of ownership, permitting a reassessment for property tax purposes. The parties' agreement did not create an option to purchase or condition acquisition of title upon payment since the documents are absolute on their face and contain no conditions, exceptions, or reservations regarding transfer. *Cal-American Income Property Fund II v. County of Los Angeles,* 256 Cal. Rptr. 21 (Ct. App. 1989).

California In 1980, the city leased real property to a properties company. At the time the lease was executed, the maximum term permitted under the city's charter for leasing real property was 40 years. However, the company and city were aware of a proposed amendment to extend the maximum lease period to 66 years. The lease adopted by the parties provided for an extension equal to the period allowed by the amendment once the amendment was approved. The amendment was passed and the parties entered into an extended lease. The property was reassessed at a higher value because of the increased term of possession. The properties company paid the increased taxes but sued for a refund of the additional taxes on the basis that no change of ownership had occurred as a result of the amendment. *Held:* For the properties company. The original lease created rights to a 66-year term through an automatic extension. Therefore, the automatic extension did not involve a subsequent change of ownership, which would allow revaluation of the property for property tax purposes. *Wrather Port Properties Inc. v. County of Los Angeles,* 257 Cal. Rptr. 266 (Ct. App. 1989).

Colorado A class action was instituted by property owners against an ordinance imposing a service expansion fee as a condition of issuance of a building permit. The amount charged was based on the square footage of improvements. Property owners claimed the fee was constitutionally invalid as a property tax. If the fee was a property tax, it would violate the constitutional mandate of uniformity in property taxes. *Held:* The fee was an excise tax not subject to the restrictions on property taxes. Property taxes were computed based on the value of the property involved, whereas excise taxes were levies on the right to exercise a privilege and were measured by the extent of the exercise of the privilege. The fee was imposed only on the expanded use of property, without regard to value of the property. The fee, a tax on the privilege of improving the property by construction, was therefore an excise tax. *Cherry Hill Farms, Inc. v. City of Cherry Hills Village,* 670 P2d 779 (1983).

District of Columbia Trial court made a reduced assessment binding "until another valuation is made according to law." The District of Columbia appealed on the basis that each tax year is a distinct entity and that jurisdiction over the housing company does not extend for succeeding years. *Held:* The jurisdiction of the court to make a valuation extends until a lawful substitute superseded that valuation. Any other scheme would result in a multiplicity of litigation on the same issue. *District of Columbia v. Burlington Apartment House,* 375 A2d 1052 (1977).

Maryland Tax assessment for all residential property in Annapolis except condominiums was made on a front foot basis. Assessment of condominiums was made on a square-foot basis, pursuant to statute. A lower court held the different method for condominiums improper. The only question presented to the appellate court was the propriety of the method of assessment. *Held:* The lower court decision was reversed. There was no evidence of discrimination or of a deliberate violation of the essential principle of uniformity. No overvaluation of the property in question had occurred. The method of valuation of condominiums, although different, was proper. *Supervisor of Assessments v. Southgate Harbor,* 369 A2d 1053 (1977).

Missouri An electric cooperative corporation constructed, maintained, and operated electric distributing facilities. The corporation maintained power lines, meters, poles, and transformers across public thoroughfares and private lands. The state tax commission directed local assessing officers to classify the corporation's equipment as real property for taxing purposes; and the corporation sought both a declaratory judgment prohibiting the classification and a declaration that the classification order exceeded the commission's authority. *Held:* The commission's order did not exceed its authority; however, the electric corporation's equipment could not be taxed as real property. Instead, the equipment was taxed as tangible personal property, since it did not constitute structures or fixtures, did not form part of the real property, and did not become an integral part of it. *Cuivre River Elec. Coop. Inc. v. State Tax Comm'n,* 769 SW2d 431 (1989).

New York Respondents, owners of a single-family residence, occupied the residence solely as a home until 1986 when, with the permission of the town planning board, respondents remodeled part of the house to be used in their practice of psychiatry. The office consisted of 17.5 percent of the gross first floor space. Following an assessment, respondents filed a complaint alleging that, as owners of a structure "used exclusively for residential purposes," they qualified for a small claims assessment review. *Held:* The single-family residence containing the professional office was qualified for the small claims assessment review. The legislature did not intend the term "used exclusively for residential purposes," contained in the simplified tax assessment review statute, to prevent *any* nonresidential use from disqualifying a structure from eligibility. Residential taxpayers who occasionally use their home for business are permitted use of the simplified procedure. In this case, taxpayers who used their home for ten hours in the preceding seven-month period for business use are eligible for small claims assessment review. *Town of New Castle v. Kaufmann,* 536 NYS2d 37 (1988).

New York In response to a state law permitting cities to adopt a dual-rate tax structure, a city adopted a new tax rate structure under which nonhomestead properties paid twice as much tax as homestead properties of similar value. Unequal fractional assessments were used to compute both city and county taxes, even though other localities in the county did not use fractional assessment. An owner in the city sued, claiming that by taxing his property at rates higher than similar homestead property in Rochester, and higher than similar property elsewhere in the county, he was denied equal protection. *Held:* The New York Court of Appeals held that the new state law (Section 305 and Article 19 of the Real Property Tax Law) and the local statute passed in reliance on it were unconstitutional, insofar as they resulted in similar property in the county being taxed at different rates. Homestead and nonhomestead properties arguably received different services, justifying the dual-rate structure. However, the county's reliance on different assessment structures used by different localities within the county constituted impermissible discrimination among properties of the same type and value receiving the same county services, and violated equal protection guarantees. *Foss v. City of Rochester,* 480 NE2d 717 (1985).

New York Defendant, the town assessor, exempted from property tax any owner who registered with the Universal Life Church. Many property owners signed up and were exempted from property tax under a state statute covering religious property. The Universal Life Church was apparently a tax dodge. As a result, the tax burden fell on property owners who did not register with the church. Plaintiff, one such owner, sued to enjoin defendant from assessing in this fashion and challenged the assessments of neighbors' property. Defendant argued that New York law prohibits suits seeking review of assessments on property in which plaintiff has no ownership interest. *Held:* Plaintiff could challenge defendant's assessments. The rule defendant referred to, that plaintiff's sole remedy was political—to elect a better assessor—was set aside. The court stated that a political solution would be inadequate, as the majority would be expected to side with the assessor. *Dudley v. Kerwick,* 421 NE2d 797 (1981).

New York When company went bankrupt, one of the buildings it owned was sold to plaintiff corporation for $25,000 plus assumption of liability of unpaid property taxes amounting to $150,000. Plaintiff, contending that the amount of taxes was based on an incorrect assessment of the building, refused to pay them. The city then took the property by tax deed. Plaintiff sued for a lower assessment on the property. The appellate division reduced the assessment to a level beneath that claimed by plaintiff. The city appealed, relying on the then current New York law that relief in a tax review proceeding was limited to the amount requested in the petition. *Held:* This was overturned by the New York Court of Appeals for the reason that tax review proceedings should be conducted in a manner that facilitates a fair and realistic valuation of property. Such a valuation should not be precluded by taxpayer's pleading for an inadequate reduction of an assessment. *WT Grant Co. v. Srogi,* 420 NE2d 953 (1981).

South Carolina Defendant-landowners sought to have tax statutes (S.C. Code § 65-1620.4(1) (1962)) declared unconstitutional. The statute provided that every new building, renovation, or other improvement in Charleston County would be taxable during the year of initial occupancy. The landowners contended that the statute violated Section 34 of Article 3 of the South Carolina Constitution because other landowners in the state were not required to pay taxes on their property during the initial year of occupancy. *Held:* The statute is unconstitutional as it directly contravenes Section 34 of Article 3 of the state constitution, which prohibits special laws from being enacted where a general law could be made applicable. *Thorne v. Seabrook,* 216 SE2d 177 (1975).

Tennessee Nonresident owners of duplex apartments attacked as discriminatory a property tax classification that taxed them at the commercial rate, while owners of rented single-family units and owner-and-tenant-occupied duplex apartments were taxed at the more favorable residential rate. *Held:* While there was some discrimination in favor of those taxed at the residential rate, such discrimination was minimal and insignificant when measured against the reasonable state purpose of providing preferential tax treatment for the owners of single-family residences and owner-occupied dwellings. As the rental of single-family units was considered a generally poor investment, it was reasonable to differentiate such units from the type of income-producing property associated with taxation at the commercial rate. *Snow v. City of Memphis,* 527 SW2d 55 (1975), reh'g denied, 423 US 1083 (1976).

Vermont Property owner challenged the real estate tax assessments of two parcels that failed to consider the effect of restrictive covenants on the fair market value of the property. The trial court found that the valuations were proper where the property owner offered no evidence on how the value was effected. *Held:* Even though no evidence was submitted as to the effect on market value, the existence of the covenants established that the property was incorrectly categorized as real-lot property and evaluated on that mistaken basis. *Lantman v. Town of Hinesburg,* 349 A2d 888 (1975).

Virginia A golf course built as the centerpiece of a recreational community was burdened with easements in favor of residents of the surrounding subdivision. The golf course had been transferred by the subdivision developer to the subdivision owners' association for a nominal sum. Although some outside memberships were sold, the golf course, heavily burdened by the easements, was never economically sufficient. County tax assessors ignored the easements in valuing the golf course for tax purposes, and the owners' association sued. *Held:* For the owners' association. Where a servient estate is burdened by an easement for the benefit of dominant estates, for tax purposes, the value of the servient estate is to be reduced and the value of the dominant estate is to be increased in accordance with the corresponding burden and benefit.

The rule in Virginia, as announced in *Bank v. Amherst County,* 132 SE2d 721 (1963), is that the taxpayer pays taxes in accordance with the benefit derived from the property in question. *Lake Monticello Owners' Ass'n v. Ritter,* 327 SE2d 117 (1985).

Virginia A tax assessor of the city of Richmond updated appraisals of apartment complexes based on information from questionnaires, including income statements. Petitioner failed to respond to a 1973 questionnaire, and produced the 1974 figures after the deadline. The assessor set the 1974 and 1975 assessments based on available information to the city and later testified that the assessments would have been lower if the income information had been available when requested. Petitioner contested the assessments for 1974 and 1975. *Held:* The assessor acted properly in basing appraisals on information available to the city, such as rents charged. An assessment based on such data need not be set aside when shown to be at variance with an appraisal using data generated by actual experience. The court upheld the assessor's appraisals because the assessor considered all available information in fixing the assessment figures; any procedural flaw in the assessments was attributable to petitioner's untimely submission of tax information. *Richmond v. Gordon,* 294 SE2d 846 (1982).

110.10 Priority of Tax Liens

9th Circuit Buyers bought real property at a tax sale. Because the Internal Revenue Service (IRS) had no notice of the sale, the sale did not affect a $200,000 federal tax lien on the property. The IRS levied upon and was paid a $19,000 surplus remaining after local taxes were paid. The IRS then obtained a district court ruling that buyers' interest in the property was subordinate to the IRS lien and allowing it to exercise its rights of distraint and sale to satisfy the lien. Buyers appealed, citing an IRS agent's statement that if they purchased the property, at worst the IRS would exercise its right of redemption and buyers would be reimbursed the purchase price. *Held:* Affirmed. The government was not equitably estopped from asserting the lien because of the agent's statement. It was buyers' responsibility to ascertain the legal requirements surrounding the sale. Buyers were not entitled to be equitably subrogated to the rights of the government to the extent of the surplus because it did not meet the prerequisites of subrogation under California law. Nor was the IRS unjustly enriched by the surplus proceeds, since they were applied to reduce a legitimate federal tax lien. *Simon v. United States,* 756 F2d 696 (1985).

9th Circuit Contract purchasers of real property fell behind in installment payments several times. Finally, when purchasers were seven months behind, sellers filed an action seeking termination of purchasers' rights under the contract. Sellers, unaware of a recorded federal tax lien on the property, did not join the United States as a party. The court granted sellers relief. Three years later, the government brought a foreclosure action. *Held:* Under federal law, a federal tax lien is not affected by actions to quiet title if the government was not joined as a party. Having waived strict performance by accepting late payments, sellers, under Washington law, could have elected to declare a forfeiture for purchasers' failure to perform. Had sellers declared a forfeiture, Washington law would have allowed the tax liens to be extinguished as is the rule where a seller had no actual notice of lien. But because sellers sought a quiet title action and failed to join the United States, the tax lien was unaffected by the judgment. *United*

States v. Winterburn, 749 F2d 1283 (1984).

D.C. Circuit Insurance company acted as surety for a contractor on federal contracts. Contractor had defaulted on payments in the past, and insurance company incurred a deficit in fulfilling contractor's obligations. Insurance company bonded a contract for contractor to repair the Navy Museum. Contractor completed performance, but defaulted on payment obligations. Insurance company paid subcontractors under its payment bond. The IRS claimed a retainage held by the Navy on the contract, because of contractor's failure to pay federal taxes. Insurance company sued, seeking the retained contract proceeds. *Held:* Insurance company's status as performance bond surety on other federal contracts gave it no right to retainages held under the Navy contract. The surety could recover retained funds only from the contract generating the claim. Insurance company's power to defeat the government's right of setoff is limited to the specific contracts on which it fulfilled its performance bond obligations. It was not entitled to be subrogated to rights to retained funds on contracts where it fulfilled payment bond obligations. *Dependable Ins. Co. v. United States,* 846 F2d 65 (1988).

Federal Circuit The IRS foreclosed a tax lien on a parcel of land in North Dakota. Holders of a second mortgage on the land sought to redeem the property. The IRS would not permit the redemption, alleging that the second mortgage was given by an individual shareholder of the corporation that owned the parcel to secure a personal debt. The second mortgagees brought a Fifth Amendment claim before the Claims Court, seeking compensation for the taking of their property interest. When the claim was dismissed, the second mortgagees appealed. *Held:* Vacated and remanded. Under North Carolina law, a mortgagee possesses a lien on the subject property. Such a mortgagee's lien is a property interest within the meaning of the Fifth Amendment. The alleged "destruction" of the second mortgage lien for which the second mortgagees received no compensation stated a claim on which the mortgagees were entitled to a hearing. *Murray v. United States,* 817 F2d 1580 (1987).

U.S. District Court, Vermont Landowner sued to quiet title to a parcel of property he had purchased at a foreclosure sale. The IRS filed a notice of tax lien against the property after the foreclosure proceeding was commenced, but failed to intervene in the action. The IRS contended that the judgment order of foreclosure did not discharge its tax lien against the property. *Held:* Since the IRS had notice of judicial foreclosure proceedings and failed to intervene, its tax lien against the property was discharged by the judgment of foreclosure. *Gacesi v. United States,* 406 F. Supp. 623, aff'd, 544 F2d 606 (1976).

110.15 Taxation of Leasehold Interests

Maryland In 1962, Sears, Roebuck built a warehouse and leased it to a company for an initial term of 20 years. The annual rent, $22,500, was then the going rate. By 1979, rentals were twice as high for comparable properties. For 1979, the tax assessor assessed the property at $169,425. Owner challenged the assessment on the ground that it was based on fair rental value and not on the existing rent. The tax court reduced the assessment to $123,425 to reflect the lease terms. An assessment statute provided that real property must be assessed at "full cash value." *Held:* The court rejected the assessor's argument that the statute required consideration of fair rental value. The statute did not compel total disregard of contract rent in assessing property. No standard of valuation was expressed; thus the statute did not prohibit the tax court from considering the actual rent in its reassessment. The court noted that the 1962 lease was a bona fide transaction and the parties agreed at the time that the rent was reasonable. *Supervisor of Assessments v. Ort Children Trust Four,* 448 A2d 947 (1982).

Missouri Airlines contesting the use of a "possessory interest" formula for the taxation of their leasehold interests attempted to establish the value of their leasehold interests in city-owned airport property by comparison to the rental amounts paid at comparable airports for similar space. *Held:* In determining the value of airlines' leasehold interest, it was proper to consider the depreciated replacement value of leased buildings and to compare the premises' rental amounts with amounts paid for similar facilities at other comparable airports. *Frontier Airlines, Inc. v. State Tax Comm'n,* 528 SW2d 943 (1975).

Tennessee Lessee objected to the assessment of his leasehold interest on the ground that it did not separately value the interest of his sublessee and the municipality's reversionary interest. The annual rental for the lessee was $25,000, the rent for the sublessee was $25,300 per month, and the title to the building was to vest in the municipality in 25 years. *Held:* The valuation of the leasehold interest was proper where the fair market value of the building was not in excess of the rent the lessee received and where the municipality derived no value from the building, except rent, until the title would vest. *Metropolitan Gov't v. Schatten Cypress Co.,* 530 SW2d 277 (1975).

Washington Corporation formed to provide parking facilities for an urban renewal project filed a writ of prohibition to enjoin the county tax officials from laying and collecting ad valorem taxes on its interest. The corporation claimed that it did not own the land, but rather leased it from the city; was not a profit-making corporation; and did not exercise management control over the facility. *Held:* The leasehold interest held by the corporation was not exempt from the tax since one of the primary purposes of the tax was to collect "taxes on leasehold interests in publicly-owned tax-exempt land." The court concluded that the facts presented by the corporation affected the valuation of its taxes, as opposed to its taxable status, and remanded the case to determine the correct valuation. *New Tacoma Parking Corp. v. Johnston,* 538 P2d 1232 (1975).

110.20
Interest on Tax Refund

Delaware Taxpayer brought an action against city to recover interest on overassessed property taxes paid for the period prior to entry of judgment awarding him a tax refund. *Held:* The city was not exempt from the payment of interest. Interest runs from the date taxpayer gives notice that the tax was improper. However, the courts have discretion in determining the amount of interest when there has been an undue delay in the prosecution of the lawsuit. The case was remanded to determine when the taxpayer first gave notice to the city and whether the taxpayer or his attorney was responsible for a 14-year delay in prosecution of the lawsuit. *Moskowitz v. Mayor of Wilmington,* 391 A2d 209 (1978).

110.25
Exemption From Taxation

Delaware By amendment to the state constitution, the general assembly gave the local taxing authority the exclusive right to grant exemptions from real estate taxation. Previously, however, the general assembly had given such exemption to certain specified organizations by statute. The issue presented to the court was whether the local taxing authority was empowered under the amended constitution to repeal the previously granted exemptions. *Held:* The amendment granted local government its powers prospectively only. The exemptions already granted by the general assembly could not be repealed. *Board of Assessment v. Silverbrook Cemetery Co.,* 378 A2d 619 (1977).

Michigan Plaintiff, a nonprofit corporation of the United Methodist Church, constructed and operated a retirement apartment complex with apartment units that were to be rented to persons over age 65 who provided their own regular medical care. The fees paid monthly by residents covered utilities, operating expenses, and amortization of construction costs over a 20-year period. Applicants for residence were accepted on the basis of financial ability to pay the monthly fee and their ability to live independently. A dispute soon arose with the local township over exemption of the apartment from real property taxes. Plaintiff claimed that the apartment complex qualified for a charitable property-tax exemption. *Held:* The exemption was denied on the ground that the apartment complex was not a true charity but was, instead, a self-supporting operation. It did not serve the general elderly population, but rather furnished comfortable housing to a limited number of persons who could pay for it and had the health to enjoy it. To grant the exemption, the court held, would be to confer unfairly a tax benefit on the relatively few affluent elderly who could afford retirement apartments. *Retirement Homes, Inc. v. Sylvan Township,* 330 NW2d 682 (1982).

Maine Operator of a turnpike service area, leased from the turnpike authority, sued to challenge the assessment of real estate taxes. The authority was owner of the land and buildings at all times. The operator argued that under a statute providing that the authority was not "required to pay any taxes or assessments on any property acquired or used by it for the purposes provided in this act," he was exempt. *Held:* The property was exempt from taxation since the operation of turnpike restaurant facilities is a public use as contemplated by the act. The legislative intent was that the umbrella against liability of the authority for tax payments should also protect the authority's lessee as user of the property for a public purpose. *Howard D. Johnson Co. v. King,* 351 A2d 524 (1976).

Maryland State statute grants a property tax exemption to educational institutions. The court was asked whether the exemption applied to property undergoing remodeling for educational purposes. *Held:* The exemption applied. The test is whether, under the given circumstances, the property is being used to its fullest extent for educational purposes. *Montgomery County v. Meany,* 368 A2d 1107 (Ct. App. 1977), aff'd, 377 A2d 1184 (1977).

Massachusetts School was denied a real estate tax exemption as a charitable organization because out-of-state corporations were not entitled to such exemptions under a state statute (Mass. Gen. L. ch. 59, § 5). The school argued that the statute violated its right to equal protection under the Fourteenth Amendment. The tax board contended that the state did not have the same regulatory power over out-of-state charitable corporations and could therefore deny the exemption. *Held:* Once the state allows a foreign charitable corporation to enter, it cannot discriminate against it in property taxation. Massachusetts had sufficient statutory authority to regulate all charitable organizations operating within its borders. *Mary*

C. Wheeler School, Inc. v. Board of Assessors, 331 NE2d 888 (1975).

Minnesota Company petitioned commissioner of taxation to review an assessment of real estate taxes on land in which company claimed a leasehold interest and to determine that the tract was exempt from taxation. The company contended that payment of the property tax and the gross earnings tax resulted in double taxation. The corporation appealed the denial of relief, and, when the tax court reversed, the commissioner appealed. *Held:* The lease agreement evidenced the intention of the parties that no leasehold estate would come into existence until the building was constructed and ready for occupancy. Thus, taxpayer did not have a leasehold interest on the assessment date and could not properly assert its claim of double taxation. The court reversed for commissioner. *Railway Express Agency, Inc. v. Commissioner of Taxes,* 239 NW2d 245 (1976).

Missouri National church governing body, a pro forma corporation, owned several residential parcels that were used by its various executives. The state sought to collect taxes on the properties, and the church argued that they were tax exempt. *Held:* Judgment for the state. Tax-exempt status for religious organizations is unavailable where the property is not used as the residence of a pastor of a particular church. Since no church activities were conducted on the premises, the use thereof did not relate to religious affairs, and no tax-exempt treatment was available. *Pentecostal Church of God v. Hughlett,* 601 SW2d 666 (Ct. App. 1980).

New Jersey City parking authority, which leased property from private persons for use as public parking lots, appealed a determination that the land was subject to taxation by the city. The city argued that since the parking project constituted only a leasehold interest, the exemption for land used for a public purpose did not apply. *Held:* The statutory section providing the exemption referred to property that the parking authority "held" rather than "owned." Therefore, the leased property was within the exemption for as long as the lease continued and the property was used for a public purpose. *Jersey City v. Jersey City Parking Auth.,* 351 A2d 377 (Super. Ct. App. Div.), aff'd, 366 A2d 648 (1976).

Oklahoma Nonprofit corporation was incorporated by a religious organization that had tax-exempt status as a church. The corporation was to provide low-cost housing on a nonprofit basis to families displaced by governmental urban renewal. The families were allowed to apply to the Department of Housing and Urban Development (HUD) for "rent supplements," and the corporation collected from each tenant the amount of rent less the amount of the supplement. In the event of profit after operating expenses and mortgage payments, the surplus was to be returned to HUD as credit against rent supplements. The court was asked only to decide whether the property and housing were subject to the state ad valorem tax. *Held:* The ad valorem tax was applicable. The corporation's property was not used exclusively and directly for charitable purposes and was therefore not exempt from the tax. Since each tenant was required to pay for accommodations, the property was not exclusively charitable. *London Square Village, Inc. v. Oklahoma County Equalization & Excise Bd.,* 559 P2d 1224 (1976).

110.30 Deduction of Taxes

Tax Court Taxpayers entered into a cost-plus contract with a contractor to build their new home. The contract provided that contractor would provide labor and materials, and taxpayers would pay him $20,000 plus the cost of labor and materials. Taxpayers reimbursed contractor for purchase of materials and sales tax. Claiming contractor was their agent for the purchase of materials, taxpayers deducted $3,500 in sales taxes on their income tax return. The IRS disallowed the deduction. North Carolina law provides that a sales tax imposed on a seller with the intent it be passed on to a consumer is deductible by the consumer. *Held:* Here the contractor, not taxpayers, was the consumer. He purchased the materials and used them in the job. Taxpayers' argument that contractor was their agent was rejected, as there was no agency agreement or evidence of an agency relationship. *Jerry M. Petty,* 77 TC 482 (1981).

110.35
Homestead Exemption

U.S. Supreme Court The federal government sought to enforce a tax lien against a deceased taxpayer's estate. The widow objected, citing her homestead rights under Texas' constitution. In Texas, each spouse has a separate and undivided possessory interest in their homestead that may not be compromised by the other spouse. However, the government cited IRC § 7403, which authorizes a federal district court to order the sale of a home in which a delinquent taxpayer had an interest at the time he incurred his indebtedness, even if the taxpayer's spouse also has an interest and does not owe any taxes. *Held:* Because of the supremacy clause, the Texas Homestead Law could not immunize the property from the reach of Section 7403. Thus, the district court was authorized to order the sale and give the widow her share of the proceeds. However, the language of Section 7403 permitted, but did not require, the court to authorize a forced sale, permitting the court to balance the equities. *United States v. Rodgers,* 461 US 677 (1983).

110.40
Validity of Tax Deed

Illinois State statute (Ill. Rev. Stat. 1971 ch. 120, § 744) required owners residing on real estate to be served with personal notice before a tax deed could be granted to a purchaser in a tax foreclosure. The trial court granted the tax deed even though it found that the process server did not personally and directly serve notice to one of the owners. *Held:* The trial court had jurisdiction to order the issuance of the tax deed, since a tax sale proceeding is in rem and not in personam. The court acquired jurisdiction over the land when the county collector made his application for judgment and order for sale. Having acquired jurisdiction, the court retains it and is competent to make all necessary findings and enter all necessary orders. The question of whether a party has received the required notice goes to the propriety of the court's issuance of the tax deed, not to its jurisdiction in the proceeding. *Smith v. DRG, Inc.,* 344 NE2d 468 (1976).

Missouri Plaintiff brought an action to set aside tax deeds on the basis of inadequacy of consideration. The tracts had been offered for sale twice wherein, under the statute, bids were required to equal taxes, penalties, interest, and costs, and were subject to a right of redemption by the owner. No sufficient bids were received and none of the tracts had been sold. The properties were offered a third time and sold to the highest bidder. Under the statute, when properties are offered a third time, there is no statutory requirement that the amount bid equal taxes, penalties, interest, and costs. However, a line of cases held that there was a right to have such a sale declared void for fraud, based on inadequacy of consideration. *Held:*

This line of cases was inapplicable here, because the practical effect was to make it almost impossible to consummate a valid sale of land for delinquent taxes until the accrued taxes, penalties, interests, and costs exceeded a level of "gross inadequacy," a level not yet defined. *Powell v. County of St. Louis,* 559 SW2d 189 (1977).

Nebraska Owners purchased a building in 1974 and failed to record the deed until 1981. The federal government filed tax liens against the property in 1977 for taxes owed by former owners. In 1982, the government sold the property at tax sale. Purchaser sued to quiet title. *Held:* Purchaser did not have good title. The ruling in *Mingus v. Bell,* 29 NW2d 332 (1947) that "a purchaser, having notice of a previous outstanding title in land, who purchases from one without notice, will be protected in his title by the want of notice in his vendor," did not apply to purchaser, who did not prove lack of notice in himself or in the government. The fact that at the time the government liens were filed owner had been paying taxes on and remodeling the property was constructive notice to the government of owners' interest. *Mader v. Kallos,* 365 NW2d 408 (1985).

New York Plaintiff sought to void a tax deed granting a six-acre parcel of land to defendant purchaser. The six-acre parcel was located within a larger parcel conveyed to plaintiff in 1971. The smaller parcel was excepted from the conveyance, but plaintiff claimed ownership by adverse possession. Defendant had acquired the deed via tax sale by the county. Plaintiff alleged the county failed to assess the parcel to its owner or occupant and failed to give personal notice to plaintiff of the tax sale. *Held:* Citing *Mullane v. Central Hanover Trust Co.,* 339 US 306 (1950) and *Mennonite Bd. of Missions v. Adams,* 462 US 103 (1983), the New York Court of Appeals noted that personal notice of a tax proceeding is required only when the owner's name and address are reasonably ascertainable from public records. Here, the tax assessor could not discover the owner of the six-acre parcel from tax records. The records showed that the 1971 conveyance excluded the six-acre tract, and taxes were paid until 1973 by the transferor, not by plaintiff. The assessor had no duty to look beyond public records for the true owner or occupant. *Congregation Yetev Lev D'Satmar, Inc. v. County of Sullivan,* 452 NE2d 1207 (1983).

Tennessee Property owned by a nonresident of the county was sold at a tax sale. The only notice given was notice by publication. Plaintiff purchased the property from owner after the tax sale but before the tax sale deed was executed and recorded. Plaintiff sued to remove the cloud from its title. *Held:* Notice by publication is adequate notice to a nonresident owner of property in a tax sale situation. However, the tax sale deed here was a nullity, since it was not executed until after plaintiff bought the property. Plaintiff's title was clear. *Marlow v. Kingdom Hall of Jehovah's Witnesses,* 541 SW2d 121 (1976).

Virginia In 1877, Harding conveyed land to the Rush family. Their name was mistakenly recorded as "Bush." Tax records showed the land was assessed to Reanna Rush from 1895 through 1955. Taxes were unpaid for years. After 1955, the land was assessed to George and Reanna *Bush*, and taxes continued unpaid. In 1964, the land was sold for unpaid 1958 taxes and bought by the Sternes, who conveyed the land to the Fergusons. In 1978, the Pruitts acquired deeds to the tract from the Rush heirs. The Pruitts argued the tax sale to Ferguson was void because the assessment was made against nonexistent persons named Bush and no notice was given to true owners. They argued that title remained in the Rush family and the Rushes conveyed it to them in 1978. *Held:* The tax deed to Ferguson was valid because the assessors had the right to rely on the tax records in assessing 1958 taxes against George and Reanna Bush. Adequate notice of the sale was given, in accord with Virginia law, to the person in whose name the land stood at the time of sale, i.e., the "Bush" name. *Pruitt v. Ferguson,* 297 SE2d 714 (1982).

110.45
Rights of Purchaser at Tax Sale

Indiana Prior to *Mennonite Board of Missions v. Adams,* 462 US 103 (1983), Indiana lenders had to request notice of tax sales of mortgaged property by filing annually with the county auditor. *Mennonite* held that mortgagees had an absolute right to notice. At a time when a lender still had to request notification, Kokomo Bank took a mortgage on unimproved land. The borrower defaulted and failed to pay taxes. The bank did not learn of the tax delinquency because it never filed a request for tax sale notification. The county sold the land for taxes shortly after the bank held a foreclosure sale. Neither purchaser knew of the other because Rushville Bank, the foreclosure purchaser, did not record its interest on time. At the end of the redemption period, the tax sale purchaser, Calhoun, tried to obtain a tax deed. Rushville Bank, in a suit to quiet title, argued, based on *Mennonite,* that the auditor should have given prior notice of the tax sale to Rushville Bank's predecessor in interest, Kokomo Bank. *Held:* Rushville Bank lacked standing to raise the right of Kokomo Bank to notice of the tax sale. Rushville Bank then argued, based on *Mennonite*, that it was entitled to notice of the impending issuance of the tax deed, because such a proceeding adversely affects the property interest of a reasonably ascertainable party. The court noted that while a tax sale decided property rights, issuance of a tax deed merely carried out rights previously decided. It would be an unwarranted expansion of *Mennonite* to hold that interested parties are entitled to notice of expiration of the redemption period. *Calhoun v. Jennings,* 512 NE2d 178 (1987).

Washington Restrictive covenants, recorded as part of a planned unit development, called for four tracts in the development to be maintained for at least 25 years as greenbelts and be preserved in their natural condition to beautify the development. When developer failed to pay property taxes on the four tracts, the county treasurer sold them at a tax foreclosure sale, and a developer eventually acquired part of the property. The city then sued to rescind the sales and declare them void. *Held:* Although the sales presumably were not void, the property remained subject to the restrictive covenants. Wash. Rev. Code § 84.64.460, enacted in 1959, provides that tax deeds issued pursuant to a tax foreclosure sale shall be subject to any easements that were established of record before the tax year for which the tax was foreclosed. Although the statute did not explicitly refer to restrictive covenants, restrictive covenants in planned unit developments are the same as negative easements, because they curtail the rights of the owner of the servient tenement in favor of the owners of all the dominant tenements. *City of Olympia v. Palzer,* 728 P2d 135 (1986) (en banc).

111.00
SPECIAL ASSESSMENTS

111.05
Validity of Assessment

Michigan Property owners abutting a road brought a class action to enjoin a city from levying an assessment of $4 per front foot to cover a portion of the cost of widening and paving the road. The trial court found that the primary beneficiary of the improved road was the motoring public and that no special benefit was conferred upon the property owners. The city appealed a judgment for plaintiffs. *Held:* While plaintiffs benefited by the elimination of ditches, there was no reasonable basis for concluding that plaintiffs were specifically benefited as to the street widening. The purpose of the project was to benefit the county as a whole, and the judgment for plaintiffs was affirmed. *Tack v. City of Roseville,* 239 NW2d 752 (Ct. App. 1976).

North Dakota When a city levied a special assessment against plaintiff's property, plaintiff contended that the formula for assessing the property throughout the district based on square footage did not comply with the state law relating to property specially benefited by local improvement. Plaintiff appealed from the district court judgment confirming the assessment. *Held:* There was substantial evidence to support the assessment of benefits made by the special assessment commission, which personally viewed all the lots within the district. The commissioner was not mistaken as to the applicable law, and its action was not oppressive or unreasonable. Judgment was affirmed for defendant city. *Buehler v.City of Mandan,* 239 NW2d 522 (1976).

Washington Defendant owned several unoccupied homes in a housing development. Plaintiff brought a lien foreclosure action for accumulated sewer charges that had been assessed against the homes. A state statute permits such assessment of charges against those "to whom such service is available." *Held:* Because of the way in which sewers are financed and maintained, the mere physical connection between the side sewer connecting the flow from a parcel of property and the trunk sewers of the district constitutes "availability." Such availability is interpreted as tantamount to actual use. The assessment against the unoccupied homes was therefore valid. *Lake Stevens Sewer Dist. v. Village Homes, Inc.,* 566 P2d 1256 (1977).

111.10
Enforcement of Lien

Delaware A county council resolution undertook to levy delinquent sewer-service charges as an assessment on the subject mortgaged premises and to authorize a monition sale of those premises. The successful bidder at a sheriff's sale at which the property was sold moved to vacate the default judgment for mortgagee as to him. *Held:* Monition sale for collection of sewer-service charges was invalid since the Delaware Code required county to properly levy the sewer-service charge as an assessment before enforcement of the lien by monition proceedings. A county council resolution was insufficient as it failed to meet the statutory formality of an ordinance. *Wilmington Trust Co. v. Caratello,* 385 A2d 1131 (Super. 1978).

Louisiana When a city sued to enforce a lien arising from a sewage assessment, the trial court dismissed the lien on an exception of prescription. By statute, the assessment is conclusively presumed to be payable in equal annual installments if it is not paid by a specified date, and, if an installment is not paid, the entire amount is accelerated. Since the owner had made no payments, he contended that a suit brought three and a half years after default was prescribed by state law (La. Rev. Stat. Ann. § 33:3746), which provided that an action could be maintained only within three years "after the date when the final installment . . . shall become due." *Held:* The prescriptive period was not accelerated, but began to run at the end of the extended period for payment, not the date determined by the taxpayer's default. Since the acceleration clause is for the benefit of the town and is not self-operative, upon default, the town may either institute foreclosure proceedings or waive the acceleration provision without starting the running of the statute of limitations. *City of Lafayette v. Marks Constr. Co.,* 317 So. 2d 232 (Ct. App.), aff'd, 320 So. 2d 563 (1975).

PART U
MORTGAGES AND DEEDS OF TRUST

112.00
CREATION AND VALIDITY

112.05
Validity in General

Alabama Original owners attempted to convey property on which mortgages were executed to purchaser by a warranty deed. Subsequently, one of the mortgages on the property was assigned to assignees who foreclosed and received a mortgage foreclosure deed. Purchaser sued to eject assignees and to quiet title. He argued that the mortgage through which assignees claimed title did not correctly describe the property. *Held:* For assignees. Plaintiff was not a bona fide purchaser because he had constructive notice of the mortgages on the property. Even though the description of the property in assignees' mortgage was incorrect, other mortgages on the property had the correct description and it should have been obvious that the same property was intended to be conveyed in assignees' mortgage. *Perine v. Jackson,* 545 So. 2d 1318 (1989).

California A mortgage company conducted an extensive television campaign to attract borrowers. Responding to the advertisements, borrowers discussed a loan with an officer of the company, who orally advised them about a "small" balloon payment at the end of the mortgage period and other charges. However, when borrowers signed the agreement, it contained several provisions that were contrary to his oral assurances. When borrowers were assessed a balloon payment that was more than the original loan principal, they brought suit against the company for misrepresentation. *Held:* The mortgage company was liable for the misrepresentation and for punitive damages. The company must fully disclose the provisions of its loan agreements. The company had breached its fiduciary duty to the borrowers by its misleading advertisements and misrepresentation. *Wyatt v. Union Mortgage Co.,* 598 P2d 45 (1979).

Florida Property owners mortgaged their land to an investment corporation for $150,000. Shortly thereafter, owners deeded the property to a third party in payment for legal services. The third party was aware of the mortgage but alleged that the owners told him it was invalid at the time of the conveyance. The third party sued to quiet title, claiming that the mortgage was invalid for lack of consideration. The investment corporation counterclaimed for foreclosure. *Held:* A purchaser cannot obtain property subject to a mortgage and then challenge the validity of the mortgage. When a purchaser takes title to property without actual notice of prior mortgage, he will be charged with constructive notice and will take title subject to any duly recorded mortgage. Consequently, a subsequent purchaser taking title to property subject to a mortgage does not assume any personal liability to satisfy the mortgage. *Eurovest v. Segall,* 528 So. 2d 482 (Ct. App. 1988).

Nevada Plaintiff loaned money to defendant for use in making a down payment on land to be used in a housing development. Defendant subsequently entered into a mortgage with an institutional lender. When defendant defaulted in its payments, plaintiff recorded a lien and caused defendant to enter into an agreement in which defendant purported to mortgage the property as security for the unpaid loan. The institutional lender later foreclosed and plaintiff brought suit to have her interest declared a mortgage. *Held:* No particular language or form of instrument is required to create a mortgage. Where the parties disclose an intent to convey an equitable interest and where the terms are unambiguous, the agreement is treated as a valid mortgage. *Nee v. LC Smith, Inc.,* 624 P2d 4 (1981).

New Jersey Finance companies sued to foreclose real property mortgages given as additional collateral in connection with the purchase of an automobile by mortgagors. *Held:* A real property mortgage may not be taken as additional security under the Retail Installment Sales Act. The mortgage in question was thereby null and void, and was ordered discharged of record. *Girard Acceptance Corp. v. Wallace,* 388 A2d 582 (1978).

North Dakota In a document entitled "Security Agreement," Elevator agreed to grant Cargill a continuing "security interest in and mortgage of" certain real property. The document also provided that Elevator, upon request, would evidence the security interest and mortgage by providing Cargill with properly executed financing statements, real estate mortgages, leasehold assignments, and other documents. No real estate mortgage was ever recorded. In a dispute with a competing lienholder, Cargill contended that the "security document" gave it a mortgage on the subject property. *Held:* The agreement was a valid mortgage. There is no requirement that a mortgage be created by a separate instrument or observe a standard form. The promise to execute real estate mortgages on request was merely a promise to evidence, in recordable form, the legal relationship that was created between the parties by the document's language. *Poyzer v. Amenia Seed & Grain Co.,* 381 NW2d 192 (1986).

South Dakota A father sold his son a lot and building under an oral contract for deed. No down payment was made, and the son was to make payments whenever he could. Few payments were made. The son gave a mortgage to Erck in 1979 to secure a $15,000 loan, but Erck never checked title either by ordering title insurance or examining an abstract. The son allegedly reconveyed the property to the father in 1984. In October 1984, Erck was requested to release the mortgage on the premises. When he refused, the father commenced a quiet title proceeding. *Held:* The son had no estate or interest in the property since with the exception of a few quarterly rent payments, he made no other payments to the father. Therefore, the son had no equity upon which the mortgage lien could attach. Moreover, there was no basis to estop the father from contesting Erck's mortgage. The father did not know about the mortgage until after the fact, so he could not be charged with fraud when he sold the building to the son nor when the son executed the mortgage. Although the son may be guilty of bad faith, that cannot be imputed to the father. *Ainsworth v. Erck,* 388 NW2d 886 (1986).

112.10
—Defenses Against Enforcement

2d Circuit Plaintiff, a corporation, claimed as a defense in foreclosure proceedings that its mortgage was obtained under duress and was therefore void. *Held:* Plaintiff's claim was dismissed. In order to prevail on such a claim, plaintiff would have had to show, inter alia, that it had available no legal remedies to avoid the duress and that it acted promptly to repudiate the contract. Plaintiff showed neither. There was no basis for inferring that, if the bank's conduct was indeed improperly coercive, plaintiff could not have resorted to legal process to enforce enforceable agreements or fend off unwarranted punitive actions by the bank. Furthermore, not having resorted to legal process, plaintiff did not promptly repudiate the mortgage agreement, but instead made payments on the mortgage for over a year and did not bring suit for several more years. *Durante Bros. & Sons, v. Flushing Nat'l Bank,* 755 F2d 239, cert. denied, 473 US 906 (1985).

Illinois Mortgage provided that any default of its provisions would subject mortgagor to a one percent charge above the original rate on the unpaid balance. Mortgagee attempted to enforce this provision when mortgagor conveyed the land without mortgagee's consent, as required in the mortgage agreement. Mortgagor claimed that this charge was unconscionable and inequitable as a penalty. *Held:* The increase in the rate was valid as reasonable liquidated damages for breach of a covenant. *Baker v. Loves Park Sav. & Loan Ass'n,* 333 NE2d 1 (1975).

South Carolina Defendant gave a note secured by an open-end mortgage on his house and lot, then deeded the house and lot to his wife. Defendant satisfied the original note, but the mortgage was left on record to secure future advances. Defendant and his wife executed a subsequent note, and mortgagee required that the wife execute a mortgage on the house and lot. When mortgagee brought action to foreclose both mortgages, the wife, who was a minor, repudiated the latter mortgage. *Held:* The first open-end mortgage did not die when initial debt was paid. It remained viable to secure payment of additional notes, and was not extinguished by the subsequent invalid mortgage. *Central Prod. Credit Ass'n v. Page,* 231 SE2d 210 (1977).

112.15 Sufficiency of Execution

Alabama In April 1981, a husband and wife mortgaged real estate they owned as tenants in common as security for a loan. The note was renewed once. When the note again came due, the husband executed another note that combined the $16,000 debt with a debt for $56,000 owed by him alone. The combined note was secured by the mortgage on the property and by collateral from the husband's debt. After the bank foreclosed on the property, the wife sued to quiet title to her undivided one-half interest. *Held:* For the wife. The trial court was justified in finding that the bank had created a new contract by which the old debt owed by the wife and husband became extinguished and a new debt between the bank and the husband came into being. The mortgage in question did not contain a clear and express provision securing future indebtedness. Furthermore, the bank treated the combined note as a new note, with different collateral and a higher interest rate. *First State Bank of Franklin County v. Ford,* 484 So. 2d 407 (1986).

Indiana A mortgage was executed on a family farm owned in tenancy by the entirety. On default and suit to foreclose, the wife testified that she never signed the mortgage or authorized her husband to do so. *Held:* The mortgage was valid since the husband signed for his wife as her agent. An implied agency will be inferred based upon the circumstances and the parties' actions. There was a long history of the husband conducting the family business with the wife's tacit approval. Additionally, she failed to revoke his implied authority by objecting to his signing her name on an earlier note and mortgage. *Moehlenkamp v. Schatz,* 396 NE2d 433 (1979).

Minnesota A few days after taking a loan out with plaintiff bank, defendants were asked to sign another document, which they were unable to identify. The document was a second mortgage granted to plaintiff as security for the loan. In plaintiff's action to foreclose, defendants disputed plaintiff's contention that defendants had signed the second mortgage only after the document had been appropriately explained. *Held:* There was sufficient evidence to support the finding that plaintiff did not possess a valid second mortgage. Plaintiff's president testified that he could not remember if standard procedures were followed or if the mortgage was discussed with defendants. The mortgage was not recorded until eight years after closing, and defendants testified that they had no recollection of signing or discussing the mortgage. *State Bank of Hamburg v. Stoeckmann,* 417 NW2d 113 (1987).

Ohio At the time defendant's father executed a mortgage in favor of plaintiff bank, the legal description of the land was omitted from the mortgage document but was supplied later. Defendant obtained title to the property and subsequently defaulted. When plaintiff began foreclosure proceedings, defendant argued the mortgage was defective because it was signed with blank portions to be filled in later. *Held:* The mortgage was valid. A mortgage is not fatally defective when parties knowingly and voluntarily leave portions of the document blank, with the understanding that the missing information will be filled in at a later date, as long as this is done within a reasonable time. The rule that a deed executed in blank is void does not apply to mortgages because a mortgage does not establish title, but equity in the grantor. *Security Bank v. Hawk,* 517 NE2d 886 (1988).

Virginia A bank loaned a husband $13,000 on the strength of his signature on a deed of trust that purported to encumber his home, which he owned with his wife as tenants by the entirety. The deed of trust was recorded on March 27, 1981. The marriage was dissolved on June 24, 1981. In an action to partition the marital home, the chancery commissioner held that a child support judgment had priority over the bank's lien, and the bank appealed. *Held:* For the wife. Prior to the divorce judgment, neither spouse could convey the property held as tenants by the entirety by either's sole act. Thus, the bank's lien was not effective when recorded on March 27. The lien did become viable, however, after the divorce decree pursuant to Virginia law (Va. Code § 55-52), but the statute did not prejudice the rights of third parties, such as husband's wife and children. *Hausman v. Hausman,* 352 SE2d 710 (1987).

112.20 Equitable Mortgages

Alabama To secure a bank loan for his business, the owner of the business obtained an accommodation mortgage on a commercial building from his parents and their business associate. However, the notary who attested to the signatures did not witness the signing of the document. When the bank brought foreclosure proceedings, the trial court ruled that the mortgage was invalid because the acknowledgement was defective. It also ruled that the doctrine of equitable mortgage was not available to the bank because there was no obligation due from mortgagors to mortgagee. *Held:* The supreme court reversed, ruling that an accommodation mortgage can form the basis for an equitable mortgage, thus refusing to follow its own dicta in *Murphy v. Carrigan,* 116 So. 2d 568 (1959). It noted that the doctrine of equitable mortgage does not always operate in favor of mortgagee and that it would be anomalous if an accommodation mortgagor unintentionally conveyed a fee interest to a mortgagee and the doctrine of equitable mortgage were not available to correct the mistake. *Central Bank v. Dinsmore,* 475 So. 2d 842 (1985).

New Mexico City purchased land from a developer, leased it back, and financed construction of an ethanol-processing facility with industrial revenue bonds. Title to the projects was to remain in the city while the bonds were outstanding, but developer had an option to buy the properties once they were completed. Following developer's default, the court issued a decree terminating the interests of the partnerships that had purchased from developer the right to possession and use of the properties. The partnerships appealed, claiming that the original conveyance and leaseback with right of repurchase constituted an equitable mortgage with rights of redemption. *Held:* There was no equitable mortgage. The partnerships presented no evidence that the city and the developer ever intended the transaction to be a loan and a mortgage. Unlike *Palmer v. City of Albuquerque,* 142 P. 929 (1914), where the city needed to obtain funds without exceeding its debt ceiling, the instant transactions were governed by the Industrial Revenue Bond Act, which expressly promoted municipal ownership with leaseback to encourage industry, and were also structured to enable the city to pass along tax benefits. *Sunwest Bank, NA v. Clovis IV,* 740 P2d 699 (1987).

112.25 Statute of Frauds

1st Circuit A corporation that owned a restaurant wrote a promissory note for $120,000 and issued a mortgage on the restaurant to secure the note, both of which were eventually assigned to CLIC & Company for $1. The corporation, however, did not then borrow the money. Later, Paramount agreed to lend FFSI $30,000 for the restaurant, which it did by writing checks to CLIC. The corporation later became insolvent, and the Small Business Administration erroneously paid the full amount of the promissory note ($120,000) to CLIC. One issue to be decided was whether Paramount was entitled to the $30,000 it had paid the corporation despite the lack of a writing evidencing the transaction. *Held:* Paramount could recover. Since Paramount intended to advance the money to the corporation against the previously executed promissory note and mortgage, Paramount was an assignee of the mortgage. The note and mortgage issued by the restaurant constituted a promise to repay any money CLIC or its assignees advanced to the corporation. Pursuant to Rhode Island law, such an assignment need not be in writing, since it is not an interest in land. *CLIC & Co. v. Goldfarb,* 838 F2d 32 (1988).

5th Circuit Plaintiff sued for alleged breach of loan agreement to develop a condominium project, based upon two letters it had received from defendant during the course of negotiating a loan, which plaintiff contended constituted a contract. The letters, when read together, did not clearly indicate how the initial interest rate was to be determined, when the interest was to be paid, when the loan was to be disbursed, the terms of repayment, or who the contemplated corporate borrower was. The letters also referred to a future commitment and additional conditions. *Held:* The terms encompassed in the two letters were too vague to constitute an agreement or indicate that there had been a "meeting of the minds" between the parties. The letters reflected that the parties were still in the negotiation process and that a formal commitment in writing was contemplated to consummate the loan agreement. *Willowood Condominium Ass'n v. HNC Realty Co.,* 531 F2d 1249 (1976).

9th Circuit Plaintiffs and debtors orally agreed that debtors would pay plaintiff $5,000 and deliver a new note for $20,000 secured by a new mortgage on debtors' Buena Park property. In return, plaintiff reconveyed to debtors one of two original mortgages on the property. Debtors paid the $5,000, but failed to execute and deliver the new $20,000 note. Debtors declared bankruptcy shortly thereafter. The trustee in bankruptcy asserted the Statute of Frauds in defense to plaintiff's claim of an equitable lien on the property. *Held:* Plaintiff had an equitable lien. Equity will recognize a valid mortgage when the parties have manifested an intent that the real property of one shall secure the payment of an obligation due to the other. Plaintiff, who fully performed his duties under the oral agreement, took the agreement out of the California Statute of Frauds under the doctrine of partial performance. In addition, the trustee was estopped from raising the statute as a defense because plaintiff relied upon debtors' promise to his detriment, and would suffer an unconscionable injury if the promise were not enforced. *In re Destro,* 675 F2d 1037 (1982).

Florida Mortgagors gave mortgagee a second mortgage on their home to secure indebtedness on a promissory note. The mortgage was not signed in the presence of two witnesses, and the trial court declared the mortgage invalid for that reason. On appeal, mortgagee argued that under the new constitution, there is no longer any requirement that a mortgage or homestead realty be signed in the presence of two attesting witnesses. *Held:* The omission of the words "duly executed" in the new constitution must be given effect: The signatures of two attesting witnesses is no longer required. Therefore, the mortgage was valid. *Moxley v. Wickes Corp.,* 356 So. 2d 785 (1978).

Michigan Plaintiff and defendant were brothers. Plaintiff, allegedly out of concern for defendant's family, offered defendant 53 acres of the family farm for $9,000. A warranty deed was executed, transferring the 53 acres to defendant "forever" and "without exception." When defendant refused to reconvey the land for $9,000, however, plaintiff brought an action alleging that the warranty deed was executed pursuant to an oral mortgage agreement. The value of the land at that point was between $10,600 and $13,000. *Held:* Plaintiff was not entitled to relief under an equitable mortgage doctrine. The Statute of Frauds would not prevent a court from declaring a deed absolute on its face to be an equitable mortgage, especially when the parties were in a fiduciary relationship. Here, however, such relief was not warranted. This was not a case where a guardian was abusing a ward or a creditor oppressing a debtor, and defendant paid a fair price for the property. *Schultz v. Schultz,* 324 NW2d 48 (1982).

112.30 Consideration

Maine West executed a promissory note to the bank, secured by a mortgage on the home he owned in joint tenancy with his wife. Both husband and wife signed the mortgage deed, but only the husband signed the note and security agreement. The husband defaulted, and the bank sought to foreclose. The husband argued that the wife's interest in the home was not subject to foreclosure, because she did not sign the note and did not receive the loan proceeds. *Held:* Summary judgment for bank affirmed. No consideration had to flow directly to the wife for her to be liable on the mortgage, which she had jointly executed with her husband. Consideration supporting a mortgage can be either a benefit to promisor or a detriment to promissee. Consideration may consist of a benefit to a third party, in this case, a loan to the husband. *Kennebunk Sav. Bank v. West,* 538 A2d 303 (1988).

Minnesota When plaintiff's business was in financial straits, the bank threatened to call the company's outstanding notes unless plaintiff executed a second mortgage on his farm property. Plaintiff did so on December 16. The company's notes were nonetheless called by the bank on December 23. Plaintiff and his wife sued the bank to have the second mortgage declared invalid for lack of consideration. *Held:* The mortgage was invalid. The company's preexisting debt was not consideration. A promise to forbear from exercising a legal right of the creditor's can be sufficient consideration to make any return promise of guaranty enforceable, but only if the promise is coupled with actual forbearance. Where no time of forbearance is stated, a reasonable time is implied. In the present case, the seven-day period of forbearance was clearly unreasonable. Thus, there was no consideration for the second mortgage. *Baker v. Citizens State Bank,* 349 NW2d 552 (1984).

112.35 Usury

9th Circuit A California partnership sought financing for a condominium to be built in Los Angeles. It applied for and received a loan commitment from a real estate investment trust (REIT), which was organized under the laws of Massachusetts and had no offices or employees in California. The California firm signed a commitment letter that provided that the loan would be governed by the laws of Massachusetts. All subsequent accounts and disbursements were made in Boston. When the California company brought suit for recovery of usurious interest under California law, the REIT argued that the loan agreement was governed by Massachusetts law, and therefore was not usurious. *Held:* Massachusetts law governs, and the loan was not usurious. The court, applying the rules for a federal court in a diversity case, found that California law respects the contractual choice of law unless (1) the chosen state has no substantial relationship to the parties or the transaction or (2) the application of the law of the chosen state would be contrary to fundamental policy of the state. Here, Massachusetts, the chosen state, had significant contact with the transaction, and the public policy of California was not offended by the adoption of Massachusetts law. *Sarlot-Kantarjian v. First Pa. Mortgage Trust,* 599 F2d 915 (1979).

9th Circuit Corporation, which sold four ranches subject to an option to repurchase, sued to recover the property after it allowed the option to expire. Corporation alleged that the sale with repurchase option was in fact a loan secured by a mortgage and that it violated usury and redemption statutes. *Held:* Whether a sale subject to an option to repurchase is a disguised loan intended to avoid a seller's right of redemption or to circumvent the usury laws is a question of fact. The parties negotiated for a sale from the outset, buyer paid taxes and used the greater portion of the land, and the purchase price was not significantly less than fair market value. Thus the transaction was properly characterized as a sale. The complaint was therefore dismissed. *Swallow*

Ranches, Inc. v. Bidart, 525 F2d 995 (1975).

10th Circuit After a transaction of common stock for total assets involving a Texas corporation, borrower became indebted to lender, and a note was executed. The note provided for interest payable quarterly at 1.25 percent above the prime interest rate set by the First National Bank of Chicago. After a substantial rise in the prime rate, borrower refused to pay further interest, citing a Texas law declaring rates above a stated maximum, which had been exceeded by the prime rate, to be usurious. Lender argued that the note was not usurious on its face, and therefore he was entitled to recover the interest at the agreed rate. *Held:* Under Texas law, the note is usurious and lender may not collect interest in excess of the legal rate. The court found that although the note was not usurious on its face, lender did show an intent to commit usury by charging rates in excess of Texas law after the prime rate climbed. The fact that the excess interest was the result of uncontrollable economic factors did not change the result. *Kin-Ark Corp. v. Boyles,* 593 F2d 361 (1979).

11th Circuit Two federally chartered savings and loan associations (S&Ls) granted loans to home buyers at rates one quarter below the legal maximum. In each case, the home was sold to a subsequent purchaser, who entered into a loan assumption and modification agreement with lender. The interest rate on each loan was raised above the maximum in force at the time of the original loan but within the maximum current at the time of assumption. Each agreement stated that the assumption was not a novation. Subsequent purchasers sued claiming that because there was no novation, the interest ceiling at the time of the original loans was controlling, and the loans to them were usurious. *Held:* For lenders. Under Georgia law, the fact that an agreement is not a novation does not prevent its being a new contract. Looking at the substance of the assumption agreements, the court found they were new contracts. Moreover, although Federal Home Loan Bank Board regulations providing that assumptions were new loans took effect after the making of the original loans, the regulations were merely intended to preempt conflicting state law. *Lindenberg v. First Fed. Sav. & Loan,* 691 F2d 974 (1982).

Arkansas Lender sued on usury grounds to cancel two construction loans with defendant. *Held:* In a decision overruling precedent of long standing, the state supreme court held that "discounting" loans by means of advance interest deduction from loan proceeds can result in violation of state usury laws where the effective rate of interest exceeds the statutory limit of 10 percent. The court also upheld previous decisions that treat "service charges" as essentially equivalent to interest. *Fausett & Co. v. G&P Real Estate, Inc.,* 602 SW2d 669 (1980).

California During the month before a loan repayment was due, mortgage company, licensed as a real estate broker, charged plaintiff interest at a rate exceeding the limit imposed by Article XV of the state constitution. More than five years later, the state electorate amended the constitution to exempt licensed real estate brokers from liability for usury in making or arranging loans and to repeal the 10 percent rate limit on nonconsumer loans, including real estate loans. The trial court relied upon dicta to hold that the interest rate was not usurious, and plaintiffs appealed. *Held:* Affirmed as to decision but not as to reasoning. Even if the loan was usurious when made, it was not so under the amendment, which the court held to apply retroactively. The court cited two widely recognized cases establishing that there is no liability under the penalties of a repealed usury law for usurious loans made before repeal. *Orden v. Crawshaw Mortgage & Inv. Co.,* 167 Cal. Rptr. 62 (1980).

California Landowners brought a class action against a mortgage banking company, alleging that transactions involving defendant's purchase of installment contracts to finance the construction of mobile homes, vacation homes, and home improvements on landowners' properties constituted usurious loans to landowners. Defendant, after passing upon landowners' credit reliability, would agree to be the financing agent and have the builders assign to it the construction contracts at a prearranged discount. Included among these terms was the finance charge to be paid by landowners. Landowners argued that this kind of participation by defendant made it a "lender" of money within the meaning of the usury laws. *Held:* Mere participation by defendant in the financing of sales by builders to landowners did not operate to convert what would otherwise be regarded as bona fide credit sales into "loans" subject to the usury laws. Characterization of the transactions as bona fide credit sales did not have to be altered by reason of the assignments of the contracts from the builders to defendant. *Boerner v. Colwell Co.,* 145 Cal. Rptr. 380 (1978).

Florida Borrowers agreed to borrow \$4.25 million at a rate of interest equal to 3.5 percent per annum above the prime rate with a ceiling of 15 percent. The agreement also included a commission for lender's agent and an additional interest fee for extension of the loan. During the extension period of the loan, borrowers brought suit for a declaratory judgment that the loan violated usury laws by charging more than 15 percent per annum (Fla. Stat. Ann. §§ 687.01 et seq., 687.03.) *Held:* The loan violated usury laws. The extension fee and the commission for lender's agent must be considered as interest for the purpose of the usury laws. *North American Mortgage Investors v. Cape San Blas Joint Venture,* 378 So. 2d 287 (1979).

Florida Owners of a condominium offered buyer a wraparound mortgage of \$58,000 at 13 percent interest, remaining liable themselves on the underlying first mortgage on the property, which amounted to approximately \$34,000 at the time of sale. Later, buyer sued sellers for usury. She charged that sellers had not extended \$58,000 in credit to her, but had only extended \$24,000, the difference between the wraparound and underlying mortgages, with an effective interest rate of 19.04 percent. The applicable usury ceiling was 18 percent. *Held:* Sellers had in fact advanced the entire \$58,000 as credit to buyer, meaning the effective interest rate was a legally permissible 13 percent. The court distinguished seller's wraparound in this case from the refinancing wraparound in *Mindlin v. Davis,* 74 So. 2d 789 (1954). In a refinancing wraparound, borrower already possesses the advantages of a low-interest underlying loan; in a seller's wraparound, seller has, and is entitled to retain, the advantages of a low-interest loan. *Hool v. Rydholm,* 467 So. 2d 1038 (Dist. Ct. App. 1985).

Georgia Plaintiff was awarded judgment for nonpayment of a promissory note executed as partial payment of the purchase price of real estate but not secured by any interest in real estate. Defendant claimed that the note, bearing an interest rate of 9.5 percent per annum, violated the state usury ceiling of 9 percent for unsecured loans. The trial court found that the transaction was governed by a different statute, which governs interest rates on real estate loans and allows a maximum interest charge of 10 percent. *Held:* The trial court erred in holding that the note was governed by the usury ceiling for real estate loans since the note was not secured by real estate. The note was accordingly usurious, and all interest should have been forfeited on it according to the usury statute. *Peterson v. Newton,* 261 SE2d 763 (1979).

Idaho Plaintiff arranged a $35,000 loan with defendant, who charged a 5 percent finder's fee and a 5 percent loan payment guarantee fee. Among the financing papers was a deed of trust on plaintiff's lounge and a $48,750 promissory note payable in monthly installments with 10 percent interest on deferred payments and a final balloon payment to pay the note in full. Plaintiff argued that the loan violated the usury statute requiring lenders to disclose the total amount of interest charged if it exceeds 10 percent per year. *Held:* The loan violated the statute. The $48,750 note, which secured a basic loan of only $35,000, could not have possibly constituted a valid disclosure of the rate of interest charged. The interest charged exceeded the statutory maximum. Finally, the 5 percent finder's fee and loan payment guarantee constituted disguised interest. *Howes v. Curtis,* 661 P2d 729 (1983).

Minnesota In 1973, borrower executed agreement for loan of $2.3 million from lender and an interest rate of 9.5 percent. In 1974, the Minnesota legislature enacted a law (Minn. Stat. § 334.01(2), as amended by L.1974, c.238 § 1) that exempted transactions of $100,000 or more from the usury laws, which forbade interest rates of more than 8 percent. When borrower defaulted and lender brought suit in 1976, borrower claimed that the loan was usurious and argued that the 1974 statute could not be applied retroactively to the 1973 transaction. *Held:* Lender may recover. The 1974 exemption may be applied to the 1973 transaction, since the law was a repeal of a penalty that applies to all legal actions initiated after the law was passed. *United Realty Trust v. Property Dev. & Research Co.,* 269 NW2d 737 (1978).

New York Mortgagor obtained a loan of $35,000 from mortgagee with a three-year term at an interest rate of 24 percent. At the closing, only $32,900 was paid to mortgagor; the remaining $2,100 went to mortgagee corporation's secretary treasurer as a "commission." Mortgagor then signed an estoppel certificate stating that there were no defenses to the mortgage; and 10 days later, the mortgage was assigned to plaintiff. When plaintiff brought a foreclosure action, mortgagor moved to dismiss, asserting criminal usury as an affirmative defense. *Held:* If the estoppel certificate was executed by mortgagor in the absence of coercion or duress and plaintiff acted in good faith in relying on it, then it was an effective bar to the usury defense. If on remand, the trial court found this to be the case, then mortgagor's use of the usury defense would give it an unconscionable advantage at the expense of an innocent party. Whether the $2,100 commission was a cover for even more usury would also be determined on remand. *Hammelburger v. Foursome Inn Corp.,* 431 NE2d 278 (1981).

New York Plaintiffs entered into two mortgage agreements with defendant bank, which agreements provided that mortgage payments were to be made on the first day of each month. When plaintiffs' December 1978 payments were received on January 2, 1979, defendant imposed late charges pursuant to the provisions of the loan agreements. After plaintiffs paid the late charges, they brought suit against defendant for a return of the late payments, which plaintiffs alleged were improperly imposed, and for a return of all interest payments on the ground that the assessments for late payments rendered the contract usurious.

Held: Where December 31 fell on a Sunday, and January 1 was a legal holiday, payment on January 2 was timely, making imposition of the late charges improper. However, the imposition of late charges, which defendant believed in good faith was in accordance with the provisions of the loan agreement, did not render the contract usurious. There was no evidence of intent on defendant's part to exact a usurious rate of interest on the loans. *Li v. Astoria Fed. Sav. & Loan Ass'n,* 438 NYS2d 865 (1981).

New York Developer paid a $150,000 commitment fee to a federal S&L to reserve some $7.5 million for future mortgage loans. Subsequently, the S&L made such loans to 66 individual unit purchasers, charging them 8.5 percent interest, the maximum then permitted under New York law. The state attorney general brought suit on the ground that the commitment fee, when added to the 8.5 percent interest, rendered each of the loans usurious. The attorney general argued that the S&L was effectively collecting more than the law allows, and demanded that it repay to borrowers twice the amount of interest it had already collected. *Held:* The state usury law barred excessive payments to lenders only if paid "to or for the account of the lender in consideration for making the loan. . . ." In this case, the commitment fee was not paid by developer in consideration for making loans to any particular purchaser. Rather, the money was paid so that $7.5 million in mortgage funds would be kept in reserve. The S&L could keep the fee regardless of whether it ever made any loans to individual buyers. Since merging the commitment fee with the interest charged on the mortgage loans would be ignoring the "economic realities" of the situation, the court rejected the attorney general's argument. *People v. Central Fed. Sav. & Loan Ass'n,* 412 NYS2d 815 (1978).

Texas A corporation borrowed money at 10 percent per year. The loan was secured by real property owned by a partnership. The partnership sued the lender, charging the loan was usurious because it was actually made to a partnership not a corporation. *Held:* The loan was not usurious. Although the security was owned by the partnership, the loan was executed by the corporation and, therefore, was not usurious. *Prestonview Co. v. State Mut. Investors,* 581 SW2d 701 (1980).

Texas Parties entered into a loan arrangement whereby debtor was charged 10 percent "interest" as a commitment fee prior to actual dispersal of funds for construction project. Debtor argued that the "fee" was in reality a cloak to conceal usurious interest. *Held:* The loan commitment was bona fide, since it was a true option to borrow funds at a future time, and not an obligation binding on the parties. Although the charge was styled as "interest" in the instrument, it was clearly intended to serve as a permissible accruing charge and could not result in a usury violation. *Stedman v. Georgetown Sav. & Loan Ass'n,* 595 SW2d 486 (1979).

Washington Plaintiff, a widowed school teacher with no knowledge of usury laws, made real estate investment loans to defendants, one of whom was an auditor. Plaintiff agreed to his suggestion that she receive interest ranging from 18 percent to 36 percent on the loans. Defendants refused to repay the loans, contending that the interest rates were illegal. Plaintiff argued that defendants should be estopped from asserting a usury defense. *Held:* The usury defense could be estopped if, upon remand, it could be proven either that defendants breached a fiduciary duty to disclose the illegality of the agreement or a contractual duty to deal in good faith by withholding that knowledge. A breach of either duty would meet the estoppel requirement of justifiable reliance on defendants' actions. *Liebergesell v. Evans,* 613 P2d 1170 (1980).

Washington Decedent loaned borrower $35,000 in return for a promissory note. The note was originally due in 1968, but had been extended three times, the last extension continuing until 1982. The personal representatives of decedent's estate claimed that borrower owed $26,128.85 plus 12 percent interest, and $2,000 in attorney fees on this note, and as plaintiffs, they accelerated the debt and sued to collect. Borrower counterclaimed under the usury statute. Plaintiffs contended that the usury statute did not apply to the suit on the original debt, because the original contract was valid and was not affected by a subsequent usurious transaction. *Held:* The nonusurious original promissory note and the usurious extension agreement were not separable. The entire transaction was considered one contract and was thus subject to the usury statute. *Bakke v. Buck,* 587 P2d 575 (1978).

Wisconsin Two individuals signed a note on which their corporation was principally liable. *Held:* The two were guarantors of the debt and could not interpose a usury defense that was unavailable to the corporation itself. This was the first Wisconsin case on this point. *Sundseth v. Roadmaster Body Corp.,* 245 NW2d 919 (1976).

112.40 Loan Commitment

5th Circuit Defendant issued a permanent loan commitment to a borrower to build a housing project. Defendant, borrower, and plaintiff then agreed that plaintiff would provide interim construction financing for the project. The loan was for 12 months, but obligated defendant to purchase the loan at any time at plaintiff's option. Eleven months later, defendant defaulted on its agreement to purchase. Borrower then defaulted on the loan agreement with plaintiff. Rather than sue borrower, plaintiff sued defendant for its failure to purchase the construction mortgage. *Held:* The trial court's grant of specific performance was reversed, because there was a remedy at law. Plaintiff could have sued borrower on the note and foreclosed the mortgage, then sued defendant for the deficiency. In the alternative, plaintiff could have proved injury by showing the value of the mortgage and the property at the time of the breach. *American Bancshares Mortgage Co. v. Empire Home,* 568 F2d 1124 (1978).

5th Circuit Developer sued to enforce what it claimed was a loan agreement. Two letters were sent to developer; the first was from a mortgage broker setting forth the terms upon which a loan would be made, and the second letter said that its parent REIT's loan committee had acted favorably on the loan. The developer never filed a written acceptance, and the loan was never consummated. *Held:* There was no binding agreement since essential terms were left open for future negotiations. The interest formula, the disbursement and the identity of the borrower, and the repayment schedule were unclear and unspecified. *Willowood Condominium Ass'n v. HNC Realty Co.,* 531 F2d 1249 (1976).

U.S. District Court, New York Developers entered into a permanent loan commitment with a lender. The closing was to occur 17 months later. In the interim, however, interest rates declined, and developer began negotiating with other lenders to obtain better terms. Developer refused to close on the original loan, allegedly objecting to the inclusion of a default prepayment clause in the proposed mortgage. Lender sued, seeking damages equal to the difference between the mortgage loan of 14.25 percent and the rate prevailing on the date of breach. *Held:*

For lender. Developer breached the duty of fair dealing and good faith implicit in every New York contract by failing to negotiate in good faith. The clause allegedly objected to by developer was needed to protect lender against deliberate defaults by borrowers seeking lower rates, was standard industry practice, and was invariably included in lender's mortgages. Moreover, developer later agreed to even more punitive default prepayment fees in return for lower interest-rate financing from another lender. *Teachers Ins. & Annuity Ass'n of Am. v. Butler,* 626 F. Supp. 1229 (SD 1986), appeal dismissed, 816 F2d 670 (2d Cir. 1987).

Florida Builder borrowed $2.25 million for construction of a high-rise office building. Approximately two years later, lender advanced an additional $450,000 to complete the project. Two months later, however, it became apparent that more money would be needed to finish the building. Lender refused to supply extra funding and, instead, brought an action to foreclose on the two notes. Borrower objected, claiming that lender, by advancing the additional $450,000, had impliedly agreed to finance completion of the building. *Held:* Lender advanced the additional $450,000 on the understanding that the amount would be sufficient to complete the project. When advised of the additional cost overruns, lender had the right to cease funding the project and exercise its rights under the notes and mortgage. *Walter Harvey Corp. v. O'Keefe,* 346 So. 2d 617 (Dist. Ct. App. 1977).

Pennsylvania A tenant and landlord contracted to build a movie theater according to specifications proposed by tenant within 60 days of the execution of the lease. Under the lease, landlord was obligated to agree to any reasonable mortgage commitment obtained by tenant. On two occasions, tenant obtained mortgage commitments, but the landlord rejected them, claiming the terms of the commitments contravened the terms of the lease. Tenant sued for specific performance of the lease, and landlord countered that tenant had breached the agreement by failing to submit final plans within 60 days and by refusing to furnish the landlord with certain financial information. *Held:* Tenant was entitled to specific performance. Tenant was not obliged to submit final plans and furnish financial information as a condition to the landlord's agreeing to the mortgage commitments. *Easton Theatres v. Wells Fargo Land & Mortgage Co.,* 401 A2d 1333 (Super. Ct. 1979).

112.45
Absolute Conveyance as Mortgage

Nebraska Landowner contracted to give his relative a warranty deed for a farm. The relative was to have full control over the farmland, pay off debts of landowner, and pay future taxes. Landowner had the right to remain on the farm and was to receive credit for one third of income from the sale of crops. Landowner also had the option, exercisable within 10 years, to offset the crop credit against relative's expenditures and reclaim the deed to the property. The option was not exercised within the 10-year period. After the relative died, landowner sued for return of the deed, arguing that the deed was actually a mortgage given to secure personal loans. *Held:* A mere option to purchase, under any conditions, does not transform an absolute sale into a mortgage. A deed is not considered a mortgage unless it was given to secure a debt; here, there was no evidence of any loan. Furthermore, the repurchase option had to be exercised within the required period. *Cizek v. Cizek,* 266 NW2d 68 (1978).

Oklahoma When the first mortgage holder began foreclosure proceedings on the Mize's ranch, Mize entered into a financial arrangement with Republic, the second mortgage holder, to prevent foreclosure. The arrangement involved a voluntary surrender agreement, a quitclaim deed, and contract for sale of real estate. Mize was released from neither the first nor second mortgage. The surrender agreement specified that the transfer of title to Republic was not intended to merge Republic's second mortgage on the property with the title, but was intended solely to permit Republic to satisfy the first and second mortgage indebtedness to the extent possible. The agreement stated that Mize was not released from any deficiency should Republic sell the property. Mize was given the right to repurchase the property on or before March 5, 1980. When Mize attempted to sell the property to a third party on March 5, 1980, Republic sued to quiet title. *Held:* The transaction constituted a mortgage, and foreclosure was the only means by which Mize's right to redeem could be extinguished. Okla. Stat. tit. 46, § 1 provides that "every instrument purporting to be an absolute or qualified conveyance of real estate or any interest therein, but intended to be defeasible or as security for the payment of money, shall be deemed a mortgage and must be recorded and foreclosed as such." Thus, an absolute deed, executed together with a separate instrument, wherein the grantee agrees to reconvey, upon payment of a certain sum of money within a specified time, makes the deed a mortgage. *Republic Fin. Corp. v. Mize,* 682 P2d 207 (1984).

Texas A landowner executed a general warranty deed to a local bank and its director, along with a one-year lease agreement, in exchange for $120,000 in cash and an option to repurchase the land for $132,000. When landowner failed to make the second semiannual payment of $12,510, the bank sought to evict him. He sued, claiming the transaction was an illegal and usurious loan. *Held:* Whether an instrument written as a deed is actually a mortgage is a question of fact, and parol evidence was admissible to show that the parties actually intended even a seemingly unambiguous instrument to be a mortgage. The purported "deed" executed by landowner was in fact a mortgage. The property had been "sold" for less than half its $320,000 worth, landowner had refused a local realtor permission to list the property before the transaction, and the annual rent of $25,020 was far in excess of the property's market rental value of at most $4,500 a year. *Johnson v. Cherry,* 726 SW2d 4 (1987).

113.00 TRUTH-IN-LENDING REQUIREMENTS

113.05 Disclosure Under Federal Law

U.S. Supreme Court Magazine subscriber sued subscription service to recover civil penalty for failure of company to make disclosures required by the Truth-In-Lending Act (TILA). At issue was the statutory authority of the Federal Reserve Board to issue Regulation Z since the regulation required disclosure where no finance charge was imposed, but where consumers were required to pay in four or more installments. *Held:* The "Four Installment Rule" of Regulation Z was a valid exercise of the Federal Reserve Board's rule-making authority under TILA and was reasonably related to the goal of preventing merchants from evading the reporting requirements of TILA by concealment of credit charges. Congress gave the Federal Reserve Board broad rule-making power to enact rules to deal with the practice of merchants of concealing finance charges in the cash price of merchandise. The fact that TILA mentions disclosure only in regard to transactions in which a finance charge is imposed while the disclosure requirements of Regulation Z often apply where there is no finance charge is not a conflict, because the rule clearly implements the objectives of TILA. The regulation did not create a conclusive presumption in violation of due process by imposing a disclosure requirement on all members of a defined class to discourage evasion by a substantial portion of that class. *Mourning v. Family Pub. Serv., Inc.,* 411 US 356 (1973).

2d Circuit Home improvement corporation brought an action for an injunction challenging Federal Reserve Board regulation allowing a consumer to rescind a home improvement contract within three days where the contract is secured by the consumer's home. Creditor argued that the right of rescission of Section 125(a) of TILA was improperly extended by the regulation to cover statutory liens. *Held:* The regulation validly extended the right of rescission to statutory liens. In enacting Section 125(a), Congress intended to extend the protections of TILA to all consumer credit transactions involving a home improvement contract regardless of whether the lien was consensual or nonconsensual. The legislative history indicates the goal was to provide uniform protection on a nationwide basis, regardless of the different state lien laws. To achieve TILA's objectives of meaningful disclosure, it was necessary to treat all statutory liens uniformly under TILA. *NC Freed Co. v. Board of Governors,* 473 F2d 1210, cert. denied, 414 US 827 (1973).

5th Circuit Developer of a subdivision financed the down payment on a home in return for two notes and a second mortgage. There was no interest charge, provided the loan was paid timely. Purchaser defaulted, then sought to rescind the loan transaction, claiming that developer had violated TILA. Developer argued that TILA was not applicable, since the transaction was not an extension of credit for which the purchaser could readily compare other credit terms. Few, if any, financial institutions would have loaned money at no interest. *Held:* TILA was nonetheless applicable. A subjective lack of awareness of credit terms does not insulate a creditor from the provisions of TILA. The purchaser therefore had a right to rescind the loan transaction. *Arnold v. WDL Invs., Inc.,*703 F2d 848 (1983).

9th Circuit Real estate broker who extends credit to a purchaser of land or arranges the extension of credit to a purchaser by a third party should provide the purchaser with a statement containing all the disclosures required by the Truth-in-Lending Act and Regulation Z. A broker who sells land of his own three times within a period of a year and a half and takes a first or second mortgage to cover part of the purchase price is a "creditor" within the meaning of Truth-in-Lending and must make disclosures like any other mortgage lender. *Eby v. Reb Realty, Inc.,* 495 F2d 646 (1974).

11th Circuit In 1980, plaintiffs obtained a loan of $37,000 from lender. The loan application stated that the proceeds would be used to build a barn for and to operate a horse ranch. The loan was secured by a second mortgage on the ranch (which also served as plaintiffs' home). After missing some payments, plaintiffs sought to rescind the mortgage, claiming that the lender violated the disclosure provisions of TILA. Lender moved to dismiss, arguing that, pursuant to 15 USC §§ 1603(1) and 1603(5), TILA did not apply to transactions primarily for agricultural purposes involving more than $25,000 nor to transactions for business purposes. *Held:* Complaint dismissed. Although the loan was secured by a mortgage on plaintiffs' principal residence, it is the purpose of a transaction, not the nature of the property on which a security interest is retained, that controls. The loan had clearly been obtained for agricultural purposes, and therefore was not subject to TILA. *Sherrill v. Verde Capital Corp.*, 719 F2d 364 (1983).

U.S. District Court, Ohio Homeowners borrowed $16,000 in return for a mortgage against their home. The note provided for a three-year term, with amortization based on a 20-year maturity. It also authorized an interest rate increase when the loan matured. Some four years after the maturity date, lender called the loan, but allowed homeowners to continue it at the increased rate provided in the note. Six years later, in 1980, lender notified the homeowners of yet another rate increase, but did not provide TILA disclosure statements for the increase. Homeowners sued to rescind the loan because of lender's failure to provide disclosure statements. *Held:* Lender's act of calling the loan and increasing the interest rate in 1980 constituted a new transaction within the meaning of Regulation Z, which would entitle plaintiffs to disclosures under TILA. For that violation, homeowners were awarded a civil penalty of $1,000. However, homeowners were not entitled to rescission, since the mortgage was a first lien. TILA and Regulation Z exempt first liens from the requirement that lenders notify borrowers of their right to rescind. *Sutliff v. County Sav. & Loan Co.*, 533 F. Supp. 1307 (ND 1982).

113.10
—Sufficiency of Disclosure

5th Circuit In return for home improvements, a homeowner signed four documents: a contract, a blank deed of trust containing only a property description, and two disclosure statements. One disclosure statement was the required right-of-rescission form, indicating that homeowner had three business days to rescind the transaction, but not giving the date on which the third business day fell; the other indicated that homeowner was giving the improver a deed of trust securing the improvements. Homeowner later sued under TILA to rescind the transaction. *Held:* For homeowner. The Fifth Circuit strictly applied the requirement of Regulation Z that the rescission form include the date up to which the consumer may cancel. Also, disclosure that the improver would take a security interest in homeowner's property was not made, because the request to execute a deed of trust, containing no information other than a property description, did not put homeowner on notice that a security interest was being created in her home. *Williamson v. Lafferty*, 698 F2d 767 (1983).

5th Circuit The disclosure statement prepared in connection with the refinancing of a loan on which borrowers had defaulted stated that "this loan is also secured by a Deed of Trust on real property identified as follows: . . . " The bank failed to fill in the blank. However, all parties understood that borrowers' home was the collateral. Borrowers, who had signed a waiver of their right to rescind, sued to rescind the loan agreement because of incomplete disclosure. *Held:* The disclosure of the collateral was immaterial to borrowers, who fully understood when they signed the deed of trust that they were encumbering their home. Since the omission could not have influenced borrowers' decision to refinance, borrowers were entitled to money damages only, not to rescission. *Jones v. Fitch*, 665 F2d 586 (1982).

7th Circuit A lender increased the interest rate on an adjustable rate mortgage loan on two occasions. On both occasions, lender notified borrowers four months in advance of the increase by letter. Neither letter used the term "annual percentage rate" in disclosing the new rate to borrowers and neither mentioned borrowers' right under the original loan agreement to prepay the loan without penalty at any time during the four-month notice period. Borrowers claimed that the lender's failure to provide full TILA disclosures was a violation of TILA. *Held:* For borrowers. The letters were new transactions requiring separate TILA disclosures. They therefore should have disclosed that the new rates were annual percentage rates, themselves subject to change, and that a prepayment penalty waiver existed. Whenever a loan's rate is about to be increased significantly and the note waives the prepayment penalty during the requisite notice period, borrower must choose between obtaining new financing and facing a dramatically altered financing obligation to existing lender. *Brown v. Marquette Sav. & Loan Ass'n*, 686 F2d 609 (1982).

U.S. District Court, Florida Borrowers brought suit, alleging a number of minor violations of TILA. For example, the term "annual percentage rate," although printed in capital letters, italicized, and made conspicuous by isolation from other terms, was not printed more conspicuously than the term "amount financed." Also, the terms of the prepayment penalty were not set forth in exactly the words of the note, although the penalty and the explanation of its computation were disclosed in understandable terms. *Held:* For lender. Lender's compliance with TILA was "strict compliance" even though lender may have deviated slightly from required language. Lender's disclosures were sufficient, since they were clear and accurate representations of all the essential financing information and fulfilled the purpose behind the legislation. *Schroder v. Suburban Coastal Corp.*, 550 F. Supp. 377 (SD 1982).

U.S. District Court, Kentucky Contract for the sale of a lot provided that the down payment "received" was $600, with $200 due "today" and $400 due at a later date. No provision specified the total down payment. Purchasers sued to rescind alleging that the down payment provisions violated TILA. *Held:* Since the down payment provision was confusing and failed to itemize the total down payment due, the intent of TILA and Regulation Z was violated in that seller had failed to provide meaningful disclosure. *Glover v. Doe Valley Dev. Corp.*, 408 F. Supp. 699 (WD 1975).

U.S. District Court, Mississippi Homeowners contracted for installation of aluminum siding. The truth-in-lending disclosure statement did not mention a deed of trust, but stated that homeowners were "giving a security interest" in "other" property, listing their home address. Homeowners claimed they did not know of the deeds of trust, that their signatures were forged, and that they did not realize creditor was to receive a security interest in their home. *Held:* Homeowners were entitled to rescission but were required to repay creditor in reasonable installments. TILA allows a debtor three years to rescind a transaction if a creditor omits a material disclosure. Regulation Z requires a creditor to disclose the fact that it will acquire a security interest in borrower's property. In this case, the disclosure did not specify that a security interest was being taken in the home. If homeowners acknowledged signing the deeds of trust, this nondisclosure would be immaterial. Since the evidence indicated homeowners did not know of or sign the deeds of trust, the nondisclosure was material, entitling homeowners to rescission. *Smith v. Capital Roofing Co.*, 622 F. Supp. 191 (1985).

Illinois Bank, giving a home purchaser a mortgage, ordered a title policy and paid the fee. On settlement at closing, the fee was charged to buyer. Later, the bank received from the title company a rebate on the fee. At issue was whether the bank's undisclosed receipt and retention of the rebate was a violation of the disclosure provisions of TILA and the Federal Reserve Board's Regulation Z Section 221.4. The bank argued that the rebate was a "prompt payment" allowance. The title company pointed out that the rebate was dependent on the bank's payment before the tenth of the month following the billing, and further, it was in compensation for the bank's assumption of personal liability for the policy costs. The title company also maintained that the bank's services in assembling documents saved it bookkeeping costs, and that it saved money by billing the bank instead of the individuals involved. *Held:* The case was remanded to determine whether the rebate was for bona fide services and, if so, whether the charges were reasonable, or the rebate merely disguised as a fee for the purpose of circumventing Regulation Z. The trial court was directed to explain why the bank's services were not compensated for by "the $35 'service fee' separately disclosed to and authorized by the buyer." *James v. First Fed. Sav. & Loan Ass'n,* 312 NE2d 605 (1974).

113.15
—Effect of Noncompliance

9th Circuit Purchaser bought a home financed by seller, made a down payment, assumed an existing mortgage, and gave seller a second mortgage for the balance of the purchase price. After she had paid interest of $239.41 on the purchase price, purchaser canceled the purchase of the home under TILA and sought damages and attorney fees. *Held:* Purchaser could recover as damages twice the amount of interest paid, $478.82. When a consumer uses Section 125 of the TILA to cancel a credit transaction involving a home mortgage, consumer may recover the down payment, closing costs, installments made, and finance charges paid. The rental value of the house while purchaser had use of it must be deducted. The consumer is also entitled to damages of twice the finance charges, up to $1,000, if creditor has failed to make full TILA disclosures. In this case, the purchase agreement would have required interest of several thousand dollars had the sale been completed; nevertheless, the court did not award purchaser the maximum damages of $1,000. Rather, it awarded her twice the interest actually paid prior to rescission of the sale because this is all purchaser had requested. *Eby v. Reb Realty, Inc.,* 495 F2d 646 (1974).

10th Circuit Purchasers sought to rescind under TILA a purchase of real property used as a residence after the one-year statute of limitations contained in 15 USC § 1640(e). The purchasers sued under 15 USC § 1635, which gives a consumer three days to rescind a consumer credit transaction secured by the consumer's residence. Creditor failed to make the required disclosure to purchaser of his right to rescind. The question was whether a Section 1635 claim could be barred by Subsection 1640(e). *Held:* For purchasers. The Section 1635 rescission claim was not barred by Section 1640(e), which provides for civil liability for failure to make TILA disclosures. Section 1640(e) applies by its express terms only to actions to enforce Section 1640 rights. Section 1635 has no provision limiting the time for suit. TILA is remedial and must be liberally construed to effectuate the intent of Congress. Purchasers brought suit six weeks after they learned of their right to rescind. What detriment might be suffered by defendants was brought on by their violation of the statute. *Littlefield v.*

Walt Flanagan & Co., 498 F2d 1133 (1974).

D.C. Circuit Appellant, a home improvement company, challenged the Federal Reserve Board's promulgation of Regulation Z permitting a consumer to rescind within three days any credit transaction in which a security interest is acquired in the consumer's residence. Appellants argued that the language of Section 125(a) of TILA should permit rescission only where the property was encumbered by a second mortgage or other consensual lien, not when the property was encumbered by a mechanic's lien or statutory lien. *Held:* The Federal Reserve Board's construction of the statute as promulgated in Regulation Z was consistent with the legislative purpose of TILA and was a reasonable use of its authority. Congress intended to require disclosure of all consequences flowing from the signing of a home improvement contract, not just those spelled out in the contract, but those necessarily inherent therein, such as liens arising by operation of law. Since the purpose of the legislation is remedial, to protect the homeowner, it must be broadly construed to effectuate its purpose. *Gardner & North Roofing & Siding Corp. v. Board of Governors,* 464 F2d 838 (1972).

U.S. District Court, Kentucky Purchaser sued to recover a deposit and alleged that a forfeiture and liquidated damages clause placed on the reverse side of the acquisition agreement violated the disclosure requirements of TILA. *Held:* Forfeiture and liquidated damage clause is a charge within the meaning of TILA. The method of computing the potential charge must be disclosed, and such provisions must appear on the same side of the sheet with other default provisions and above or adjacent to the purchaser's signatures. *Glover v. Doe Valley Dev. Corp.*, 408 F. Supp. 699 (WD 1975).

Florida Two years after a home improvement contract had been signed, debtor defaulted and the contractor sued to foreclose his mortgage. The consumer alleged that the contractor had violated the disclosure provisions of TILA at the time the home improvement contract was concluded. Therefore, the mortgage was a nullity that could not be enforced; moreover, the consumer was entitled to damages. *Held:* Breach of the disclosure provisions of TILA does not affect the legality of the transaction involved. Consequently, the mortgage was enforceable by the contractor, even if he had failed to make the required disclosures. The consumer's remedy for a breach of the disclosure provisions was an action for damages. However, it was too late for the consumer to claim damages in the foreclosure action because the foreclosure action was commenced two years after the contractor should have made the disclosures. A claim for damages must be made within the year following the date the disclosures should have been made. *Gillis v. Fisher Hardware Co.*, 289 So. 2d 451 (Dist. Ct. App. 1974).

114.00 RIGHTS AND LIABILITIES OF PARTIES

114.05
Nature of Mortgagor's or Trustor's Rights

Michigan Defendant investment company, planning to build several hotels, obtained two mortgages from defendant bank. The bank was sole mortgagee for both projects. The investment company and landowner were mortgagors for the first project. The investment company was sole mortgagor for the second project. The mortgage for the first project contained a "dragnet" clause indicating that the first property secured all other debts or liabilities that might become due from mortgagor. When the second project failed, the bank attempted to have a default declared on the first mortgage because of the dragnet clause. *Held:* The second mortgage was not included in the dragnet clause of the first mortgage because the mortgages did not involve identical parties. Mortgagor of the first project was the investment company and landowner, whereas mortgagor of the second project was the investment company alone. The court pointed out that the result would have been different had the dragnet clause referred to debts "of the mortgagors or either or any of them." *Holiday Inns v. Susher-Schaefer Inv. Co.*, 259 NW2d 170 (Ct. App. 1977).

Texas Mortgagees sued mortgagors to recover delinquent property taxes after foreclosure. The deeds of trust provided, first, that the mortgaged property would be the only source of funds for repayment of the loan, and mortgagors would not be personally liable. The deed of trust also provided that if mortgagors did not pay property taxes, mortgagee could pay them, add the amount paid to the principal of the note, and accelerate the obligation. *Held:* Mortgagees were not entitled to recover. Under the mortgage contract, mortgagor's liability for unpaid taxes was enforceable as part of the mortgage debt, but the deed created no personal liability for taxes on the part of mortgagors. Thus, mortgagees' remedy for recovery of delinquent taxes was foreclosure against the property. Since mortgagees had not recovered unpaid taxes as part of the foreclosure proceedings, they could not now assert an additional right to a personal judgment. *Wood v. Henry S. Miller Co.*, 597 SW2d 332 (1980).

114.10
—Liability of Guarantor

4th Circuit Defendant, a corporate president, personally guaranteed his company's loans with the bank. The guaranty agreement stated that in case of default, the bank could institute proceedings to enforce payment without first having recourse to any other available security or remedy. The company defaulted on its loan, and the bank took possession of its security and sued defendant to recover under the guaranty agreement. Defendant alleged that the bank's failure to take commercially reasonable steps by collecting the corporate accounts receivable that it held as collateral prevented it from collecting on his personal guaranty. *Held:* The guaranty agreement waived any entitlement defendant had to a commercially reasonable disposition of the collateral. Defendant expressly agreed that the bank could institute legal proceedings against him to enforce payment without first having recourse to other security or pursuing other remedy. Section 9-501(3) of the Uniform Commercial Code (UCC) prevents a debtor from waiving his entitlement to a commercially reasonable disposition of his collateral, but it is silent as to a guarantor's capacity to do so. Under Maryland law, a guarantor may waive his entitlement to a commercial reasonable disposition of debtor's collateral under UCC § 9-504. *National Bank of Wash. v. Pearson,* 863 F2d 322 (1988).

7th Circuit Defendant guaranteed a mortgage, through an individual agreement and as one of five signers of an unlimited joint and several guaranty. Both guaranties authorized lender to extend or renew the indebtedness without guarantors' consent and provided that the guaranty was to continue until guarantors sent written notices of revocation. Several years later, defendant notified mortgagee of his intention to rescind his guaranties as to any new or additional loans. After receiving this notice, mortgagee extended the loan term without notifying defendant. (The other four guarantors were notified and executed new guaranties.) After mortgagor defaulted, the Federal Deposit Insurance Corporation, as receiver for the insolvent mortgagee, sued defendant on the note. It argued that the guaranty was irrevocable as to extensions on the note. *Held:* Defendant was not liable on the note. Under Wisconsin law, a material alteration in a guaranty contract made after the contract has been executed and without a guarantor's consent discharges guarantor. The loan extension agreement was such a material alteration. The court also held that defendant's notice of revocation was effective, since the bank's failure to request defendant to execute a new guaranty while it requested this of other guarantors showed that the bank believed the revocation was effective. *FDIC v. Manion,* 712 F2d 295 (1983).

U.S. District Court, Illinois Guarantor guaranteed two installment notes that were secured by mortgages. When borrower defaulted on the notes, assignee of the notes instituted foreclosure proceedings. Although guarantor was named in the proceedings, he did not receive notice or make an appearance. Assignee purchased the property at a judicial sale, and then sued guarantor for the balance due on the notes. *Held:* Guarantor was liable for the balance due. Under Illinois law, an individual who gives an unconditional and absolute guaranty is liable for amounts due on installment notes even though the properties securing the loans may be worth more than the amount outstanding. Guarantor could have placed limits or conditions on his guaranty, but instead voluntarily gave an absolute guaranty. The fact that guarantor was not present at the judicial sale and was not informed of the default would not change the result, unless there was a showing of fraud or other wrongful conduct on the part of assignee. *Marathon Fin. Co. v. Disharoon,* 671 F. Supp. 12 (ND 1987).

California Guarantor of a note raised as a defense the fact that the acceleration clause was set forth only in the mortgage and not in the note and deed of trust that guarantor signed. *Held:* The several documents constituted a single integrated transaction, and therefore the holder's acceleration was effective against all parties. At the same time, the clause does not fail under the rule against restraint of alienation, but is fully within applicable provisions of the UCC. *Guild Wineries & Distilleries v. Land Dynamics,* 163 Cal. Rptr. 348 (1980).

Delaware A bank loaned money to a corporation, with the obligation individually guaranteed by the principals, a married couple. The guaranty was secured by a second mortgage on their Delaware residence. Defendants claimed that the guaranty was unenforceable, because the bank had extended credit on the security of a second mortgage loan on residential property that, according to the state Secondary Mortgage Act, was outside the authority of a banking corporation doing business in Delaware. The bank argued that the residence merely served as collateral and guaranty for a corporate loan. The trial court ruled that the bank should forfeit the principal it had loaned, since the act protected state residents from predatory second mortgage practices regardless of the status of the loan recipient. *Held:* Affirmed in part. The obligation of the individual guarantors clearly arose "out of a secondary mortgage loan" as defined in the act. Nonetheless, the bank might be entitled to restitution of the principal amount of the loan on some equitable basis independent of the loan contract. *First Nat'l Consumer Discount Co. v. Fuller*, 419 A2d 440 (1980).

Nebraska Parents executed a personal guaranty on two deeds of trust to secure a bank loan for their son. The son defaulted on the loan, and the bank began to foreclose the land under the deeds of trust. The parents sued to rescind, vacate, and set aside their personal guaranties. *Held:* For the bank. Sufficient consideration to support the guaranty and the trust deeds exists where evidence shows that the bank, to its detriment, paid out all of the loan amount and the money was used for the benefit of the son, his parents, or the son's business. A finding of duress cannot be supported where evidence showed that parents had pledged their farm for the son's benefit in the past, that they had sufficient business sense to contact a certified public accountant regarding the tax consequences of the deal, and that they had knowledge of the terms of the agreement. Additionally, the bank had no duty to disclose the son's financial situation to the parents, since the parents did not ask for information regarding their son's financial condition and since the financial history of the son's business indicated that it had in the past generated sufficient profits to service the loan. *Bock v. Bank of Bellevue,* 434 NW2d 310 (1989).

South Dakota Landowners who wished to develop a shopping mall executed a 99-year lease in which they agreed to join in any mortgage necessary to finance such a mall. They obtained a $3 million mortgage from a state investment board (mortgagee) and joined lessee in execution of the mortgage and security agreement. On the lessee's default, the mortgagee and the lessee entered into a modification agreement without owners' knowledge, which eventually caused the outstanding principal to increase by $25,000. When the mortgagee foreclosed, owners appealed, claiming that they had signed the mortgage as sureties rather than as principals, and that the modification without their consent exonerated them. *Held:* Because they cosigned the mortgage to promote their personal financial interests, owners were principals, rather than sureties, and remained liable under the mortgage. Although owners appeared to fit within the definition of "suretyship" in Chapter 56-2 of the South Dakota Code, case law indicates that one who receives the benefit of a contract cannot be a surety. Here, owners looked to have unimproved land produce rent for 99 years and then be turned over to their heirs in improved condition. *Wisconsin Inv. Bd. v. Hurst*, 410 NW 560 (1987).

Virginia A real estate investment trust (REIT) entered into an agreement with two developers to build a condominium using land and construction money provided by the REIT. The REIT obtained a commitment from a bank for $10 million and agreed in writing to indemnify developers against personal loss and to guarantee the loan. On default, the bank sued the REIT as guarantor. The REIT claimed to be liable only to the extent of its interest in the condominium property, based on a statement in the deed of trust that the REIT was not liable to the bank beyond its interest in the property. The bank had drafted conflicting liability provisions in the deed of trust and guaranty. *Held:* The REIT was held to its unconditional guaranty. Although the maxims for contract interpretation favored the REIT, a mechanical interpretation would have been inappropriate. Evidence of assurances by developers that the REIT would answer for any liability of the joint venturers showed that the REIT itself interpreted the loan closing documents to provide for an unconditional guaranty. *American Realty Trust v. Chase Manhattan Bank*, 281 SE2d 825 (1981).

114.15
—Right to Rent and Profits

9th Circuit Mortgage loan, including an assignment of rents, was followed by borrower's default. Then borrower became a bankrupt and, still later, the mortgage was foreclosed, leaving a deficiency of $360,000. Between the time of borrower's default and the foreclosure sale, tenants paid $75,000 in rent to the bankruptcy court. The trustee in bankruptcy argued that the rents belonged to borrower and, hence, to the trustee for the benefit of all the borrower's creditors. *Held:* As a result of the assignment, lender was owner of the rents, and the entire amount had to be turned over to it in partial satisfaction of the deficiency. *In re Ventura-Louise Properties,* 490 F2d 1141 (1974).

Kansas The holder of a second mortgage appealed a trial court's refusal to award it rents collected from mortgaged property after mortgagors' default. The property in question was subject to two mortgages, both of which conveyed the real estate along with all the rents of the property and provided for the appointment of a receiver upon default. Mortgagors defaulted on both notes and, while foreclosure proceedings were pending against them, sold the property to a third party, who took it subject to the mortgages. At the sheriff's sale, first mortgagee purchased the property for the amount of its debt. The trial court affirmed the sale and awarded rent proceeds, which were collected by a receiver prior to the sale, to the third party purchaser. *Held:* Second mortgagee was entitled to the rents collected by the receiver. The third party purchaser took the property subject to the mortgages and was bound by the rent conveyance in the second mortgage. The second mortgagee did not lose its right to share in the rents upon extinguishment of the mortgage at the sheriff's sale. *Missouri Valley Inv. Co. v. Curtis*, 745 P2d 683 (1987).

South Carolina Borrower defaulted on a $30,000 mortgage. The mortgage provided that the property be transferred to mortgagee until the mortgage was repaid and that, in case of default, the mortgagee would have "the immediate right, in his sole discretion, to make said delinquent or defaulted payments and to sell the property at a price to be agreed upon between [the parties]" with the purchase price being applied to the costs of closing, satisfaction of mortgages, and reimbursement to mortgagee for payments made by him, with the remainder payable to borrower. While mortgagee was in actual possession of the property, he received $15,000 of rental income. Borrower brought action seeking, inter alia, to recover the rental income received. *Held:* Since the contract was silent about who should receive any rental income derived from the property and since the right to possession of land, coupled with possession in fact, carries with it the right to rent the property and collect the rents, mortgagee was entitled to the rental income. *JTM Co. v. Vane,* 323 SE2d 794 (Ct. App. 1984).

114.20
—Duty to Account

Massachusetts Mortgagors of property sought an accounting of profits realized by mortgagee from its investment of municipal real estate taxes that mortgagors had paid to mortgagee in escrow. *Held:* Mortgage agreements that require payment of taxes to the bank do not mean that the bank must invest the money for mortgagor's benefit. Because the mortgage instruments were integrated documents that made no mention of the interest on these tax payments, no trust in favor of mortgagor was created, and the bank did not need to pay mortgagors any of the return on the investment of the money. *Carpenter v. Suffolk Franklin Sav. Bank,* 346 NE2d 892 (1976).

Wisconsin Mortgagors sought an accounting of the profits made by the savings and loan association (S&L) from the investment of property tax and insurance premium deposits made by mortgagors pursuant to their mortgage notes. Mortgagors maintained that the notes created a fiduciary relationship with respect to the deposits. *Held:* No such relationship was created, for any possible loss on the investments must be borne by the S&L. The terms of the note constituted only bare agency, which would not sustain an action for an accounting in equity. *Richman v. Security Sav. & Loan Ass'n,* 204 NW2d 511 (1973).

114.25
—Liability for Waste

4th Circuit When its tenant closed a rented store for business reasons, plaintiff sued seeking the balance of rent due under an unexpired 25-year lease. Tenant successfully argued that it was constructively evicted, because for 10 years it had been complaining about a leak that plaintiff had failed to correct. Meanwhile, mortgagee of the property entered the case, seeking judgment against plaintiff for waste. *Held:* Because of a large crack in the roof, judgment for waste was granted in the amount of $499,000, which was the value of the outstanding mortgage. Mortgagee's failure to bring an action for foreclosure did not preclude its recovery for waste. *Jaffe-Spindler Co. v. Genesco,* 747 F2d 253 (1984).

9th Circuit A limited partnership acquired title to a housing project; as part of the consideration for the purchase, the partnership agreed to assume and be bound by a Federal Housing Administration (FHA) note, deed of trust, and regulatory agreement. The regulatory agreement required owners to maintain the project in good repair and keep books and accounts of operations. The limited partnership defaulted, and FHA paid the note and received an assignment of the replacement fund, deed of trust, and note. Later, the Department of Housing and Urban Development sued to foreclose, and a judgment of foreclosure was entered. The government brought in the general partners as defendants and sued for damages for waste and other violations of the regulatory agreement. *Held:* The partners were liable for damages; the specific remedies provided by the regulatory agreement were to be used against owners before the property was sold, and, after a sale, only a damage claim remained. *United States v. Haddon Haciendas Co.,* 541 F2d 777 (1976).

U.S. District Court, Michigan Stevens leased a service station to Mobil Oil Corp. in 1956, which lease was subsequently extended to 1976. In 1972, the city passed an ordinance stating, in essence, that any service station not open for business for 120 consecutive days would be deemed abandoned and an order for its demolition would be summarily issued. Mobil sought to convert the station to an auto reconditioning center, but Stevens vetoed the idea. Mobil then boarded up the station and left it, claiming refusal to consent to a sublease, a breach of the lease. Under the city ordinance, a demolition order was entered. Stevens sued, alleging that Mobil's abandonment of the property constituted waste and entitled him to double damages under the appropriate Michigan statute. *Held:* The court disagreed and entered summary judgment for Mobil. Liability for waste is based upon physical injury to the land committed by one rightfully in possession. Assuming that all of Stevens' allegations were true, there was no basis for a finding of waste because no physical injury had been done by Mobil to the premises. *Stevens v. Mobil Oil Corp.*, 412 F. Supp. 809 (ED 1976), aff'd, 577 F2d 743 (6th Cir. 1978).

Utah Plaintiffs purchased a house and property from defendants, who remained in possession as month-to-month tenants. Plaintiffs brought an action alleging that defendants had failed to take proper care of the property and had committed damage. The lower court awarded damages to plaintiffs, but not attorney fees. *Held:* The provision in the contract allowing attorney fees did not extend to implied covenants or obligations not expressly included therein, only to express covenants. Since the covenant not to commit waste was implied, attorney fees were not allowed. *Cluff v. Culmer,* 556 P2d 499 (1977).

114.30
—Nature of Mortgagee's or Trustee's Interest

6th Circuit Pioneer had made a first mortgage loan to building owners and recorded its mortgage. Approximately a year later, the city notified property owners that the building was in violation of the housing code provisions and would be demolished if the violations were not corrected. Pioneer was not notified, and the building was subsequently demolished. Shortly thereafter, Pioneer filed for foreclosure and was notified by the receiver that the building no longer existed. Before conclusion of the foreclosure proceedings, owners were declared bankrupt. Following the foreclosure sale, Pioneer filed an action against the city for deprivation of property rights without due process. *Held:* The city had notice of Pioneer's interest by recordation, and was obligated to furnish Pioneer notice of condemnation. Pioneer was entitled to recover from the city the value of property taken without compensation, since Pioneer could not recover the deficiency from mortgagors. *Pioneer Sav. & Loan Co. v. City of Cleveland,* 479 F2d 595 (1973).

New York A restaurant owner gave his meat supplier a mortgage to secure a $100,000 debt in March 1973. The mortgage made no mention of future indebtedness. However, a second, unrecorded agreement provided that the mortgage would cover "all sums . . . to become due and owing." The meat supplier asserted on the basis of the unrecorded agreement that credit advanced by him after the original $100,000 was repaid had priority over two subsequently recorded mortgage loans extended by third parties. *Held:* Since no mortgage for future advances was ever recorded, and since the mortgage as reflected in the recorded agreement was extinguished by payment, the meat supplier was denied priority. The subsequent mortgagees were bound only by recorded disclosures and were under no duty to search out unrecorded agreements. *First Nat'l City Bank v. Tara Realty Corp.*, 423 NYS2d 923 (1979).

114.35
—Extension of Time for Payment

9th Circuit Defendants signed an installment note in both their individual capacities and as officers of a corporation that they owned. They also signed an accompanying mortgage, but only as corporate officers. The note did not refer to the mortgage or require defendants to perform the mortgage covenants. The mortgage payments were current when defendants sold their stock in the corporation. Soon after, the note went into default, and the corporation was subsequently reorganized. Promisee agreed to "extend" the note (including capitalized interest, taxes, and insurance paid by promisee) and an additional loan. The note again went into default, and promisee foreclosed on the mortgage and sued defendants for the deficiency. Defendants claimed that the note extension was a material alteration that relieved their obligation as sureties and that they were not obligated under the mortgage. *Held:* The original debt was not released and a new one substituted. Hence, there was not a novation of the note. Although defendants did not sign the mortgage individually, the security they had given for the note was "gradually depleted" by a transaction they set in motion, and they were personally liable for a money judgment to promisee. *United Am., Inc. v. Perillo,* 462 F2d 254, cert. denied, 409 US 1008 (1972).

New York The parties by their actions waived the time periods for repayment under the loan agreement and option agreement. The option agreement provided that time was of the essence only as to the last payment due September 1, 1980, a legal holiday. Defendant tendered the June and final payments on September 2, and lender obtained a declaratory judgment that it was the sole owner of the mortgage. *Held:* Tender of both payments on September 2 was timely. Under the circumstances, where the covenant was simply for the payment of money and lender showed no change in his position by the delayed tender, equity may intervene to prevent a forfeiture of a substantial interest despite a technical breach. *Hirsch v. Lindor Realty Corp.,* 472 NE2d 1024 (1984).

114.40
—Prepayment

7th Circuit A realty company operating under Chapter 11 bankruptcy protection fell behind in payments on a mortgage-secured debt. Mortgagee petitioned the bankruptcy court to allow it to proceed with foreclosure of its lien, or to dismiss the bankruptcy action or liquidate the debtor. The issue on appeal was whether, having requested foreclosure, the bank was entitled to prepayment premiums. *Held:* The bank was not entitled to prepayment premiums. When a lender elects to accelerate a debt, it waives its right to a prepayment premium. When a lender has the option to accelerate, "[i]t is only necessary to show an unmistakable intention to exercise the option, and this may be done by taking steps for foreclosure. . . ." *In re LHD Corp.*, 726 F2d 327 (1984).

9th Circuit The loan document for a 15-year commercial construction loan provided that borrower could not repay the principal in whole or in part for the first 12 years. In the event of default during the first 12 years, lender had the option of accelerating the note and adding a 10 percent prepayment fee. Four years later, borrower sued, seeking to prepay the note subject to a 10 percent prepayment fee. *Held:* Under the terms of the loan document, borrower was not entitled to prepay the loan. However, under California law, borrower was entitled to an opportunity to present extrinsic evidence to vary the terms of an otherwise unambiguous loan document. *Trident Center v. Connecticut Gen. Life Ins. Co.*, 847 F2d 564 (1988).

California The terms of an installment sale of land provided that seller was to receive no more than 30 percent of the sales price in the first year after purchase, and there were to be no balloon payments or extra monies paid for the first five years. Such payments, if made, were subject to a 50 percent prepayment penalty. Purchasers specifically agreed to the penalty. Seven months later, purchasers learned that it would be necessary to pay off the note to obtain construction financing for a home they wished to build on the property. They sued, seeking a declaration that the prepayment penalty was invalid. *Held:* Summary judgment for seller. While a prepayment penalty may be unenforceable if it is unreasonable and unconscionable, in this case the 50 percent penalty was reasonably related to seller's anticipated risk of incurring increased tax liability upon prepayment. *Williams v. Fassler*, 167 Cal. Rptr. 545 (1980).

Oregon Insurance company sued mortgagor to collect payments due on mortgage loan. Mortgagor admitted nonpayment but claimed that mortgage was void since it barred full prepayment for first 10 years of the term and therefore unreasonably restrained his right to alienation of the property. *Held:* The mortgage was valid, since the provisions barring full prepayment did not really restrain alienation. Mortgagor could easily have sold his equity interest in the property for a form other than cash, such as a purchase money mortgage. *Hartford Life Ins. Co. v. Randall,* 583 P2d 1126 (1978).

Pennsylvania Mortgagor defaulted, and proceedings by mortgagee against mortgagor progressed to the point where the mortgaged property was listed for sheriff's sale. However, another creditor of mortgagor intervened. Creditor brought the loan account payments up-to-date and arranged for a buyer to purchase the mortgaged property and pay off the entire mortgage. When mortgagee demanded payment of the prepayment penalty included in the mortgage, mortgagor paid under protest and sued to recover the payment. The trial court found for mortgagor, since the circumstances made the prepayment involuntary and thus did not trigger the prepayment penalty. *Held:* Reversed. While a prepayment penalty may not be enforceable where the mortgage loan is paid off because of fire or condemnation, mortgagor's lack of control over the sale stemmed from his business difficulties, a reason readily distinguishable from casualty or condemnation. Mortgagor was not entirely without choice in resolving his business difficulties. *Perenato v. Pell Sav. & Loan Ass'n,* 419 A2d 620 (1980).

114.45 Right of Subrogation to Mortgagor's or Trustor's Right

California A condominium developer obtained new financing from a bank to pay off three blanket encumbrances on a condominium project. The bank had been promised a first trust deed. A fourth encumbrance was not paid off, but that encumbrancer had agreed to subordinate his interest to the provider of new financing, if the financing met certain conditions. However, the loan from the bank did not do so. The fourth encumbrancer had received and recorded deeds of trust on the property, but the bank's title insurer failed to discover this fact. The fourth encumbrancer foreclosed on the deeds, but the bank sought equitable subrogation to the rights of the three encumbrancers whose claims the bank had satisfied. *Held:* The bank was entitled to equitable subrogation, despite the fact that its refinancing did not meet the fourth encumbrancer's conditions for subordinating his interest. The fact that fourth encumbrancer's deeds were recorded did not matter as long as the bank did not have actual knowledge of the deeds. *Smith v. State Sav. & Loan Ass'n*, 223 Cal. Rptr. 298 (Ct. App. 1985).

114.50 Right of Subrogation to Creditor's Rights

6th Circuit Defendant purchased property subject to an existing mortgage, which permitted mortgagee to pay any taxes on the property unpaid by mortgagor and add the amount to the secured indebtedness. Defendant failed to pay the tax, but mortgagee did not act. Defendant then defaulted on the mortgage. Mortgagee paid the delinquent tax out of the sale proceeds from the property and then sought to recover this amount from the defendant, arguing that it should be equitably subrogated to the claim of the taxing authorities. *Held:* Plaintiff could not be equitably subrogated, because it had not acted to protect its security interest. Mortgagee should have paid the taxes as they came due and added the amounts to the mortgage. *Lincoln Sav. Bank v. Hayes*, 671 F2d 198 (1982).

U.S. District Court, Missouri Alleging that one of its officers had committed fraud, a bank sought recovery under its blanket bond policy. Insurer, alleging only the officer's negligence, in turn sought subrogation against the officer for any payment on the bond that insurer might have to make. The officer moved to dismiss insurer's complaint. *Held:* Insurer's case could proceed. It was not necessary for the third-party claimant, insurer, to have actually made a payment, provided that the third party's claim was contingent upon the success of plaintiff bank's claim. Insurer's allegation of ordinary negligence was also sufficient. *Community Fed. Sav. & Loan Ass'n v. Transamerica Ins. Co.*, 559 F. Supp. 536 (ED 1983).

Arizona Plaintiff guaranteed payments under a retail installment contract for a mobile home at the request of creditor. When buyers defaulted and were evicted, plaintiff not only made good the installment payment, but repaired the home and paid its delinquent parking space rental. Plaintiff then sued buyers for these costs, arguing that there was an implied promise for rehabilitative expenses, or that it was subrogated to the rights of creditor. *Held:* Plaintiff was entitled to reimbursement only for the installment payment. There was insufficient evidence of a contract that might require plaintiff to keep the bank's security intact. More important, in Arizona a guarantor is ordinarily not subrogated to the rights of creditor until the debt has been paid in full. *Mobile Discount Corp. v. Lu Bean*, 656 P2d 639 (Ct. App. 1982).

114.55 Insurance

1st Circuit Plaintiff, owner of a newly constructed apartment complex, purchased an "all risks" coverage insurance policy from defendant. Several of the buildings settled, causing some apartments to become uninhabitable. Defendant avoided payment of the damages claim on the ground that the loss occurred before the policy date, even though it did not inspect the property before issuing the policy. Defendant then canceled the policy on the ground that physical changes had occurred resulting in the property's becoming uninsurable. *Held:* Since defendant had avoided paying the insurance claim on the ground that the settling occurred prior to the policy date, it was in no position to claim later that physical changes occurring after the policy date rendered the property uninsurable. Any physical changes were a fairly predictable consequence of a preexisting condition. Thus, plaintiff was awarded the difference between the premium it had paid defendant prior to cancellation and the higher premium it had to pay for a similar policy from another issuer after defendant canceled. *Roxse Homes, Inc. v. Commerce & Indus. Ins. Co.*, 570 F2d 26 (1978).

7th Circuit Plaintiffs had bought property in what they later learned to be a floodplain; their uninsured houses suffered extensive flood damage. They brought a class action against 27 banks and S&Ls, claiming that these institutions violated Section 4104a of the National Flood Insurance Act by failing to notify plaintiffs of the flood risk when they acquired their loans, and Section 4012a(b) of the Flood Disaster Protection Act by failing to require plaintiffs to purchase adequate flood insurance. *Held:* The statutes cited by plaintiffs did not provide private causes of action. Rather, those statutes direct federal regulators to require banks to include conditions relating to flood insurance in their loans for real estate in flood risk areas. *Mid-America Nat'l Bank v. First Sav. & Loan Ass'n*, 737 F2d 638 (1984), cert. denied, 469 US 1160 (1985).

8th Circuit Plaintiffs took out a FHA insured home mortgage from defendant bank. Neither the FHA nor the bank warned plaintiffs that the house was in flood hazard area or required him to take out flood insurance. The property was later extensively damaged in a flood, and plaintiff sued the bank. The federal Flood Disaster Protection Act of 1973 and the National Flood Insurance Act provide that lenders must give such warnings and require flood insurance. Plaintiffs argued that these statutes created private federal causes of action, and that the National Flood Insurance Act defined a standard of conduct for a state common-law action. *Held:* The federal statutes did not provide a private cause of action. They protected lenders and regulators as much as borrowers, and thus plaintiffs were not members of a specially protected class entitled to sue. However, the case was remanded to determine whether a state common-law action existed. *Hofbauer v. Northwestern Nat'l Bank*, 700 F2d 1197 (1983).

9th Circuit A mortgage insurance company issued policies for a group of residences that creditor's documentation showed to have loan-to-value ratios of about 80 percent and for which the creditor promised to request high down payments. After these mortgages were sold, the insurance company learned that creditor's representations were largely false. When the policies came up for renewal, insurer at first renewed coverage but then attempted to return the premiums and cancel the policies. When creditor refused cancellation, insurer sued. *Held:* Although insurer clearly had a right to cancel, a factual question remained as to whether the right had been timely exercised. Generally, insurers must cancel promptly when they learn that grounds for cancellation exist. *Verex Assurance, Inc. v. John Hanson Sav. & Loan, Inc.*, 816 F2d 1296 (1987).

Indiana A mortgage required that the property be insured against fire loss. Should such a loss occur, mortgagee would have the option of applying the proceeds to the remaining indebtedness, whether or not due. Lessor had an absolute obligation to repair the property, and was entitled to reimbursement from fire insurance proceeds only to the extent mortgagee made the proceeds available. When fire destroyed improvements on the property, mortgagee satisfied the mortgage with a quarter of the insurance money, and mortgagor-lessor sued lessee to make repairs. *Held:* Lessee was required to make repairs at its own expense, and was entitled to apply the remaining insurance proceeds towards the cost. Lessee was equitably subrogated to the rights of mortgagee, but had agreed to take the risk of an accident-induced loss of financing. *Loving v. Ponderosa Sys., Inc.*, 479 NE2d 531 (1985).

Louisiana Six months after a home was destroyed by fire, insurer paid mortgagee. Homeowner filed a timely claim, within 12 months after the fire, but insurer did not pay homeowner. When homeowner's assignee sued on the claim more than 12 months after the fire, insurer argued that the contract of insurance requiring payment within 12 months of the inception of the loss barred the action. *Held:* "Inception of the loss" referred to the time of the fire rather than to the accrual of liability. Insurer did not waive the contractual period by paying mortgagee. *POP Constr. Co. v. State Farm Fire & Cas. Co.*, 328 So. 2d 105 (1976).

Maine A fire insurance policy had a clause voiding coverage if the building were unoccupied for over 60 days, but had the additional condition, "Permission granted for vacancy or unoccupancy without limit of time except as otherwise provided in this policy." The policy also had a clause extending coverage to lender. Owners of the property defaulted on the mortgage, and lender foreclosed. However, lender did not notify the insurance company of the foreclosure, the change of ownership, or the vacancy. The property was vacant for four months, and was destroyed by fire. The insurance company refused to pay. *Held:* Lender was covered. There was no need to inform insurer of the ownership transfer to the lender, who was already insured under the policy. *Hartford Fire Ins. Co. v. Merrimack Mut. Fire Ins. Co.*, 457 A2d 410 (1983).

Mississippi Owners of a house destroyed by fire sought to recover interest that they claimed was unearned, when the holder of mortgage received the insurance proceeds to satisfy the 39 unpaid mortgage installments. While the note and the mortgage did not contain a prepayment clause, they did require that the mortgage be secured by fire insurance payable to the holder of the mortgage. *Held:* Where a lender requires an insurance policy be taken out in its name, it presupposes an intent to pay the entire amount due if the loss occurs, even if there is no prepayment clause. However, lender is not entitled to demand interest beyond the date of such insurance payment. *Oxford Fin. Co. v. Gray*, 317 So. 2d 910 (1975).

New Jersey Mortgagee corporation, which acquired a parcel of improved property by deed in lieu of foreclosure, sought payment for loss caused by fire under a policy issued to the previous owner and still in effect. The policy contained a standard clause stating that any proceeds of the policy for loss would be made payable to mortgagee as his interest appeared of record. The insurance company rejected mortgagee's proof of loss and refused payment on the ground that mortgagee's insurable interest under the policy was terminated when it accepted a deed in full satisfaction of the debt owing to it. *Held:* For plaintiff. Where a mortgagee acquires title to the mortgaged premises by a conveyance from the defaulting mortgagor in lieu of foreclosure, and a fire occurs thereafter, mortgagee-owner is entitled to be compensated for its loss to the extent of available insurance monies. *495 Corp. v. MJ Ins. Underwriting Ass'n*, 413 A2d 630 (1980).

Pennsylvania Plaintiff bank was listed as a mortgagee-beneficiary in the standard mortgage clause of a fire insurance policy. This clause stated that the insurance was to survive foreclosure "provided the mortgagee shall notify the Company of any change in ownership. . . ." Buyers of the property defaulted, and the bank foreclosed. It did not, however, inform the insurance company of this fact. The property was destroyed by fire, and the insurer refused to pay, arguing that the foreclosure was a change in ownership. *Held:* In a case of first impression in Pennsylvania, the court held that the bank was entitled to the insurance, since the foreclosure was an increase of interest rather than a change of ownership. The notification language would apply only when the property was sold to someone other than mortgagee. *Laurel Nat'l Bank v. Mutual Benefit Ins. Co.*, 444 A2d 130 (Super. Ct. 1982).

South Carolina The first mortgage on property specified the amount of insurance that mortgagor was required to obtain; the figure was substantially less than the amount of the mortgage. Mortgagor insured the property for considerably more than was required, but still less than the amount of that mortgage. The second mortgage also required insurance, but did not specify the amount. The property was damaged by fire, and both mortgagees sought declaratory judgments as to how the proceeds should be divided. *Held:* Mortgagees had equitable liens on the insurance proceeds, even if the value of the property exceeded the unpaid balance of the mortgages. First mortgagee would receive the amount of the insurance specified in its mortgage, and second mortgagee would receive the remainder. *Knapp v. Victory Corp.*, 302 SE2d 330 (1983).

Texas A house was sold under a deed of trust, in part for a note payable in installments. The agreement provided that buyers were to maintain an insurance policy on the house payable to seller (who held the note). The house was damaged by fire and the insurance company sent a check to seller, which check buyers asked seller to endorse to them so they could rebuild. Seller refused and buyers sued. *Held:* Seller was not obligated to turn the insurance proceeds over to buyers. The language of the deed of trust raised no doubt that the parties intended lender to have the insurance proceeds. Buyers' argument that good faith and fair dealing required her to do so was too subjective. *English v. Fischer*, 660 SW2d 521 (1983).

Wisconsin Mortgagee failed to renew the insurance policy coverage that he maintained with escrow funds from mortgagor. Plaintiff was injured on the premises and sued mortgagee on several theories: (1) as third-party beneficiary under a mortgage contract, (2) as a fiduciary, and (3) as a direct insurer. *Held:* Although procedural errors caused dismissal of the original complaint, plaintiff was allowed to replead all three theories. *Schell v. Knickelbein*, 252 NW2d 921 (1977).

114.60 After-Acquired Property

U.S. District Court, Louisiana Ewing had secured a loan from the Small Business Administration (SBA) with a mortgage that contained an "after-acquired property" clause for additional security. Ewing claimed that the clause inhibited its ability to obtain further loans and that the clause was invalid under Louisiana statute. The government contended that state law did not apply because of the necessity for uniform decisions, despite evidence that such a clause was not uniformly used across the nation by the SBA. *Held:* State law should determine what security interests the government might obtain, since there was not a significant federal interest in uniformity. The SBA could adapt its security requirements to local law, particularly where the inclusion of the clause for additional security might interfere with mortgagor's ability to acquire additional property. *Ewing v. Small Business Administration*, 359 F. Supp. 16 (ED 1973).

Florida A mortgage and security agreement for a hotel contained an after-acquired property clause granting to mortgagee mortgagor's "right, title and interest" in fixtures and personal property "subject to a conditional sales contract, chattel mortgage or similar lien or claim." The hotel bought computer equipment subject to a purchase-money lien. When mortgagee attempted to foreclose on the hotel and the computer equipment, the computer lienor asserted the superiority of its purchase-money lien. *Held:* Mortgagee's interest was superior. Lienor should have perfected its interest by recording it within 10 days of the equipment's delivery date. *ITT Indus. Credit Co. v. Regan*, 487 So. 2d 1047 (1986).

114.65 Legal Expenses

D.C. Circuit Lender preferred to use the same law firm for all routine home loan transactions and usually charged borrowers for the fee paid to the firm. In 1971, lender decided to waive the fee if borrower used this law firm and paid the firm directly. Borrowers were free to use another firm, but if they did, lender would also employ its own firm and not waive the fee. A group of borrowers brought suit, charging that lender was illegally "tying" the legal services to the mortgage loan. *Held:* Lender had the right under state law to employ its own lawyer and charge borrowers for any fees incurred. Lender's practices were not "illegal restraints of trade," since lender was motivated solely by the legitimate business purpose of safeguarding its security interests. *Foster v. Maryland State Sav. & Loan Ass'n*, 590 F2d 928 (1978), cert. denied, 439 US 1071 (1979).

114.70 Taxes

6th Circuit Defendant purchased property subject to an existing mortgage, which permitted mortgagee to pay any taxes on the property unpaid by mortgagor and add the amount to the secured indebtedness. Defendant failed to pay the tax, but mortgagee did not act. Defendant then defaulted on the mortgage. Mortgagee paid the delinquent tax out of the sale proceeds from the property and then sought to recover this amount from defendant, arguing that it should be equitably subrogated to the claim of the taxing authorities. *Held:* Plaintiff could not be equitably subrogated, because it had not acted to protect its security interest. Mortgagee should have paid the taxes as they came due and added the amounts to the mortgage. *Lincoln Sav. Bank v. Hayes*, 671 F2d 198 (1982).

Kansas A company leased land for the construction of an office building from a city under the authority of an industrial bond ordinance. The company had previously donated the land, and the lease contained an option to buy. When the company went to file notice of the city's interest in the lease, the county registrar interpreted the transaction as a mortgage, and demanded payment of the mortgage registration tax. The company paid under protest and sued for a refund. *Held:* The company was entitled to a refund. The agreement actually was a lease, which the option to buy did not convert into a mortgage. Kan. Stat. Ann. § 79-3102 provides a specific exception from the mortgage registration fee for affidavits of equitable interest filed solely for purposes of notification. *Misco Indus. v. Board of County Comm'rs*, 685 P2d 866 (1984).

114.75 Dragnet Clauses

Alabama A mortgage dragnet clause stated that all future advances from mortgagee-bank to mortgagor-spouses would be added to the amount of the secured indebtedness. The spouses later jointly agreed to guarantee loans from the bank to the husband's business. The spouses were divorced, and the wife informed the bank she would not be responsible for her husband's debts. The bank later made another large loan to the husband. The husband defaulted and the bank foreclosed. The bank sought to enforce the dragnet clause and loan guaranty against the wife. *Held:* The wife was not liable for her husband's postdivorce debts under either the dragnet clause or the loan guaranty. Her notice to the bank was sufficient to prevent her liability for after-occurring debts. *Green v. Southtrust Bank*, 519 So. 2d 1289 (1987).

Alaska Creditor made a large loan to a business, secured by equipment. Creditor later made a smaller loan to the business, secured by real estate. The deed of trust for the second loan included a dragnet clause covering "any and all other indebtedness of the Trustor to the Beneficiary, whether contingent, now due, or hereafter to become due, and whether heretofore or contemporaneously herewith or hereafter contracted, or whether arising by operation of law out of the same or different transactions between the parties hereto or between others." When the business went into default on its loans, the bank sought to foreclose on the secured real estate to recover the amount not just of the second, smaller loan, but also of the first loan. *Held:* The dragnet clause did not cover the preexisting debt. For it to have done so, the loan instrument would have had to specifically mention that debt. Any other rule would make it impossible for junior lienholders to determine the extent of senior encumbrances. *Lundgren v. National Bank*, 742 P2d 277 (1987).

Kansas A $47,000 mortgage promissory note contained a dragnet clause stating that the mortgage would include all subsequent loans up to $400,000 to either or both of mortgagor-spouses. Later, the spouses signed a $300,000 note consolidating all their debts to mortgagee, including the note with the dragnet clause. The larger note had a memorandum space designated "Note Secured By" and listing the dates of previous notes, including the $47,000 promissory note. The spouses defaulted, and the bank sought to collect the $300,000 debt against the mortgaged property. *Held:* The mortgage secured the subsequent debts because this was specifically stated on the face of the new note. The dragnet clause applied to debts contracted before the mortgage. Although the original mortgage was silent as to antecedent debts, subsequent notes specifically indicated they were to be secured by the mortgage. *First Nat'l Bank & Trust Co. v. Lygrisse*, 647 P2d 1268 (1982).

Maine Debtors took out a business loan secured by real estate. The mortgage deed contained a dragnet clause covering future advances from creditor. Debtors subsequently signed a number of notes and debt consolidations, some of which purported to be secured by sources other than the mortgage. When the bank sought to foreclose on the mortgage, debtors attempted to introduce extrinsic evidence to demonstrate the true meaning of the dragnet clause. *Held:* Extrinsic evidence was admissable because a dragnet clause is always ambiguous. At most, it is an offer by the mortgagor to extend the security of the mortgage to new indebtedness. The bank has the burden of showing that the parties intended the subsequent loans to be covered by the mortgage. *Canal Nat'l Bank v. Becker*, 431 A2d 71 (1981).

New York Two brothers purchased property and gave a mortgage to plaintiff bank. The mortgage agreement contained a dragnet clause, providing that the mortgaged property would secure any future loans between the brothers and the bank. After several years, they purchased other property with a loan from plaintiff. Thereafter, they transferred the first property to their mother, who assumed the mortgage and in due course paid it off. In the meantime, the brothers fell into arrears on the second property, and plaintiff brought a foreclosure suit against the mother. *Held:* Over dissent, judgment for plaintiff bank. A dragnet clause, unlike a mortgage for future advances, survives repayment of the original indebtedness. It is a continuing security arrangement for floating debt, whether subsequent debt is separately secured or whether it was contemplated at the time of the original mortgage. *State Bank v. Fioravanti*, 417 NE2d 60 (1980).

Utah A fire insurer of a mortgaged house appealed trial court determination awarding mortgagee judgment for wrongful disbursements of fire insurance proceeds, based on the claim that the insured premises were security for all bank claims by reason of a dragnet clause in the mortgage, and therefore applied to a subsequent, unrelated business transaction of the mortgagor with the bank. The fire insurance company had paid part of the proceeds to the bank to pay off the existing balance on its first mortgage and the remainder to mortgagor for the destruction of the home. *Held:* Reversed. Where evidence showed that the dragnet clause, which applied the bank's security for the first loan to any other indebtedness by mortgagor to the bank, was a boiler plate provision not bargained for by the parties and not in their contemplation when a second loan was made at a different branch of the bank for an unrelated purpose, there was no basis to sustain a determination that the mortgage on the home constituted security for the subsequent security agreement executed by mortgagor in obtaining a business loan. *First Sec. Bank v. Shiew*, 609 P2d 952 (1980).

114.80
Late Fees

Nevada Real estate was sold under a deed of trust and a note to be paid in installments between the parties with a final balloon payment. Buyers missed the last few installments and seller had elected to sell to another, but the parties reached a new agreement. Full payment was made, and title was reconveyed to the original buyers. This arrangement, however, occurred several months after the original agreement had contemplated; and seller sought late charges not only for the missed installments, but for the balloon payment. *Held:* Seller was entitled to late charges only for the missed installment payments. The original agreement had generally distinguished between the late charges and the balloon payment, so it did not seem reasonable to treat them the same in this context. *Sterling v. Goodman*, 719 P2d 1262 (1986).

114.85
Mortgagee's Right to Possession Without Foreclosure

Colorado Unable to physically maintain the premises, borrower, who was defaulting on her mortgages, vacated them and turned the keys over to a junior mortgagee. Junior mortgagee made payments on the senior liens and used the premises for storage. After six years, borrower sued to quiet title. Although the statute of limitations had run for an action based on the default of borrowers' promissory note, junior mortgagee argued that it was entitled as a "mortgagee in possession" to hold the property until the underlying note was paid. *Held:* The court refused to adopt the "mortgagee in possession" doctrine. Colorado has a lien theory of mortgages, so that a mortgagee may take possession only through foreclosure and sale. A mortgagee may take possession of even abandoned property only if it begins a foreclosure action. *Martinez v. Continental Enters.*, 730 P2d 308 (1986) (en banc).

115.00 CONSTRUCTION MORTGAGES

115.05 In General

9th Circuit A California partnership sought financing for a condominium to be built in Los Angeles. It applied for and received a loan commitment from a real estate investment trust (REIT), which was organized under the laws of Massachusetts and had no offices or employees in California. The California firm signed a commitment letter that provided that the loan would be governed by the laws of Massachusetts. All subsequent accounts and disbursements were made in Boston. When the California company brought suit for recovery of usurious interest under California law, the REIT argued that the loan agreement was governed by Massachusetts law, and therefore was not usurious. *Held:* Massachusetts law governed, and the loan was not usurious. The court, applying the rules for a federal court in a diversity case, found that California law respects the contractual choice of law unless (1) the chosen state has no substantial relationship to the parties or the transaction or (2) the application of the law of the chosen state would be contrary to fundamental policy of the state. Here, Massachusetts, the chosen state, had significant contact with the transaction, and the public policy of California was not offended by the adoption of Massachusetts law. *Sarlot-Kantarjian v. First Pa. Mortgage Trust*, 599 F2d 915 (1979).

U.S. District Court, New Jersey A standby loan commitment for the construction of a shopping center gave borrower the option to extend the commitment for an additional six months, provided that the center was constructed according to specifications submitted to lender. The agreement did not have a rental achievement clause, nor was 100 percent completion required. When lender refused to extend for six months because "tenants work" was incomplete, borrower sought specific performance of the financing agreement. *Held:* Because a contract for financing a shopping center is unique, and as it is difficult to calculate damages to a partially rented shopping center, specific performance lies. Furthermore, borrower should prevail because "tenants work" was not to be performed by it and even if it were, these items are minor. Both this agreement and case law provide that once a building contractor has substantially performed, mortgage lender cannot avoid its commitment. *First Nat'l State Bank v. Commonwealth Fed. Sav.*, 455 F. Supp. 464 (1978), aff'd, 610 F.2d 164 (3d Cir. 1979).

U.S. District Court, Pennsylvania Developer obtained a construction loan from a lender, executing a mortgage on the land. Developer submitted false construction certificates to lender and was reimbursed for construction outlays. Before the construction loan was totally depleted, developer entered into a sale and leaseback. The new owner did not assume the mortgage. When the work-completion certificates were found to be fraudulent, the bank accelerated the debt and bought the property at the foreclosure sale. *Held:* Unless a lender specifically assumes the duty of double-checking the veracity of certified construction costs before disbursing mortgage money, lender cannot be liable for aiding and abetting a tenant's fraud. Since the original mortgage agreement did not force the bank to inspect, the new owner could not look to the bank for the money owner had paid to tenant. *Carlsberg Resources Corp. v. Cambria*

Sav. & Loan Ass'n, 413 F. Supp. 880 (WD 1976), aff'd, 554 F2d 1254 (6th Cir. 1977).

Arizona A construction company needed a permanent financing commitment before a bank would give it a construction loan. The company contacted O'Keefe, and assistant vice-president of Mason-McDuffie Company of Southern California, a national mortgage banking institution. After four months of negotiation, the company gave O'Keefe $36,000 as a commitment fee. O'Keefe provided a letter on Mason-McDuffie stationery, and the letter was signed by a Mason-McDuffie officer containing the commitment of Mason-McDuffie Investment Company of Southern California. The letter was a forgery and the *investment* company was nonexistent. The construction company sued Mason-McDuffie for recovery of its losses on the theory that Mason-McDuffie was bound by the acts of its agent, O'Keefe. *Held:* Mason-McDuffie was liable because O'Keefe had apparent authority to transmit a commitment to a construction firm. He was manager of a Mason-McDuffie office, using Mason-McDuffie stationery and business cards and representing Mason-McDuffie in its business dealings. There was ample conduct by which Mason-McDuffie apparently conferred on O'Keefe the authority to extend the commitment in question. *Miller v. Mason-McDuffie Co.*, 739 P2d 806 (1987).

Arkansas Lender had "absolutely and unconditionally" agreed to provide construction loan funds for one year at 9 percent interest, with borrower taking down the loan by periodic disbursements. Lender added a one percent service charge up front. Borrower sued lender, claiming that the service charge was in fact additional interest and that this additional interest pushed the total interest on the loan above the usury ceiling. *Held:* The service charge was additional interest, rather than a true service charge for specific and reasonable expenses of lender. The penalty under state law for this usurious loan was the forfeiture of both principal and interest. *Arkansas Sav. & Loan Ass'n v. Mack Trucks, Inc.*, 566 SW2d 128 (1978).

Florida Borrower desired funds for the acquisition and development of an island in Biscayne Bay. One of the lenders, a Massachusetts business trust, issued a loan commitment for more than $3 million, at 14 percent interest. Lender also received 50 percent of the stock in borrower's corporation, and a commitment fee of one percent. When the project failed, lender joined in a foreclosure action against borrower. Borrower counterclaimed that lender's acquisition of borrower's stock constituted additional interest that made the loan usurious. Lender argued that Massachusetts law (which had no applicable usury statute) rather than Florida law applied, according to the terms of the contract. *Held:* The appeals court refused to apply Massachusetts law, holding that to do so would violate Florida's public policy against usury. The court found that the loan was usurious, and lender was held liable for double the amount of interest as a penalty. *Continental Mortgage Investors v. Sailboat Key, Inc.*, 354 So. 2d 67 (Dist. Ct. App. 1978), disapproved as to penalty imposed, *North Am. Mortgage Investors v. Cafe San Blas Joint Venture*, 378 So. 2d 287 (1979) (forfeiture of interest, not double the amount of interest, was proper penalty).

Nevada Plaintiffs obtained a bank loan for the construction of their house. During construction, plaintiffs noted serious defects in the foundation, so they asked the bank's loan officer to withhold payments until the problems were corrected. The bank refused, apparently without making any investigation. Plaintiffs then sued the bank. *Held:* For plaintiffs. Although a lender normally has no duty to exercise care to identify deficient construction or to withhold payment on request, a lender may not with impunity disregard a borrower's complaint of *substantial* construction deficiencies affecting a project's structural integrity. Although the loan agreement provided that the bank had no obligation to inspect the construction and was not responsible for proper disbursement of the loan, neither provision was sufficient to disavow the bank's implied duty to inspect the work under these circumstances. Lenders, however, should not consider themselves at risk for failure to inspect as a general practice or for failing to investigate complaints of minor defects. *Davis v. Nevada Nat'l Bank*, 737 P2d 503 (1987).

North Carolina Plaintiff, a builder seeking permanent financing as a prerequisite to obtaining a construction loan, executed defendant's application form, unaware that defendant was a mortgage broker and did not actually make permanent loans. Plaintiff then sought a construction loan from a bank, which contacted defendant and was informed that plaintiff's application was being processed and that defendant was committed to financing the permanent loan. When the permanent loan was not forthcoming, plaintiff was forced to negotiate a series of interim loans and make various expenditures in an unsuccessful attempt to obtain permanent financing. He sued defendant for breach of contract to make a permanent loan. *Held:* For plaintiff. He was entitled to recover the cost of additional title insurance, broker's fees, accounting costs, and appraisal fees; additional damages measured by the cash value of the difference between the interest rate available on the date of breach and the contract rate for a 25-year period; and interest he had to pay on the interim loan. *Pipkin v. Thomas & Hill, Inc.*, 236 SE2d 725 (1977).

North Dakota First Federal lent money to Compass Investments to develop an apartment complex on real estate owned by a trust. The trust and Compass entered into a guaranty agreement under which four individuals with interests in Compass agreed to guarantee the completion of the project and agreed that, if it were not completed, they would pay all costs incurred by the trust or the mortgagee in completing the project. When the project was not completed within two years of its inception, First Federal sued guarantors for the amount required to complete the project. *Held:* Action dismissed. First Federal was merely an incidental beneficiary of a contract between the trust and Compass. It was the trust that required the guaranty. First Federal did not require the guaranty, did not give additional consideration for it, and was not a party to the agreement. Mention of its name in the agreement did not give it the right to sue when it was not the party intended to benefit from the agreement. *First Fed. Sav. & Loan Ass'n v. Compass Invs., Inc.*, 739 P2d 806 (1987).

115.10
Operation and Effect

Illinois Defendant developers borrowed $375,000 from plaintiff bank to purchase land. At the time the loan was made, the land was in a land trust with the bank as trustee. A mortgage was given to secure the loan, and a promissory note was executed by the land trustee to evidence the debt. Defendants were guarantors on the note. Later, defendants' attorney forwarded an extension note, which carried a higher interest rate than the original note, from plaintiff to the land trustee. When payment was not made when due, plaintiff sued defendants. The trial court ruled they were not liable because there had been a material alteration of the obligation assumed by the guaranty. *Held:* Reversed. Defendants were experienced businessmen, all of whom had considerable background in land development and in financing such development through banks. They knew they were personally liable on the note and that the trustee was not. They authorized the extension note and, having received its benefits, had waived their defense of "material alteration" of the guaranty instrument. *Bank of Commerce v. Riverside Trails*, 367 NE2d 992 (App. Ct. 1977).

New York Plaintiff and defendant were participating lenders in a large-scale land development venture in Texas. As principal lender, defendant received all loan repayments from the developers and in turn paid over a ratable amount thereof to plaintiff. Under the terms of the loan consortium agreement, accrual of interest was to be deferred in the event of liquidation until after the principal had been recovered. After two years of operation, developers ran into difficulties with the enforcement of outstanding sales contracts, and plaintiff elected to terminate its line of credit. It requested that defendant transmit all principal due on current advances, together with interest. Defendant refused to include the interest, arguing that the cessation of loan activities by plaintiff amounted to a "liquidation" under the agreement. *Held:* Since defendant had elected to waive default and continued to extend credit, there had not been a complete "liquidation [of] investment" as unambiguously contemplated in the agreement. Plaintiff's election to terminate its participation did not effect a liquidation of the entire financing scheme, and therefore the interest accrued by plaintiff should have been paid along with the principal. *Westinghouse Credit Corp. v. James Talcott, Inc.*, 408 NE2d 897 (1980).

Ohio Plaintiffs were buyers of a home that a contractor was building. The bank financing construction and plaintiff's mortgage disbursed funds to the contractor without complying with an Ohio law on mechanic's liens that required construction lenders to obtain from contractors affidavits stating that all labor, materials, and services furnished to the date of disbursement had been paid for. After the contractor misapplied some of the disbursed funds, several mechanic's liens were filed against the property. Plaintiffs sued the bank, seeking compensatory damages for the bank's noncompliance with Ohio law. The bank was granted summary judgment on the theory that its duty to obtain the affidavit did not extend to plaintiffs who were not privy to the construction loan. Plaintiffs appealed. *Held:* Reversed. Its mortgage loan commitment to plaintiffs put the bank on notice that plaintiffs would be harmed by a wrongful disbursement of construction loan funds. A construction lender's statutory duty to obtain affidavits from contractors extends to anyone who could be injured by a breach of such duty. *Takach v. Williams Homes*, 453 NE2d 656 (1983).

Pennsylvania Contractor entered into agreement with developer for a rehabilitation project. Developer had a separate loan arrangement with defendant public agency. After the project was underway, defendant withdrew the financing, citing developer's apparent insolvency. The contractor continued on the project, and brought a declaratory judgment action against defendant. *Held:* The contractor was not a party to the loan, and therefore had no standing to assert any of developer's possible defenses to the loan cancellation. At the same time, contractor was not a third-party beneficiary, nor did it have an equitable lien in the absence of contract privity. Contractor accepted the risk of financial loss by relying on the credit of developer, and could not look to lender for relief. *RM Shoemaker Co. v. Southeastern Pa. Economic Dev. Corp.*, 419 A2d 60 (1980).

Washington Owners of undeveloped land leased it to developers and provided in the lease that the land could be mortgaged for development and construction, and for that purpose, owners could subordinate their fee ownership to the lenders' mortgage. Of $665,000 that developers borrowed, $110,125 was not used for construction, building costs, or other improvements of the land. Owners sued for an accounting of the mortgage proceeds. *Held:* Developers would be liable for money judgment of $110,125 in case of default. Subordination agreements, which are generally part of a mutual enterprise, should be strictly construed according to their express terms. Owners entered into the ground lease and subordination agreement only for the purpose of facilitating construction and development on their property. Nothing in the subordination agreement expressly provided for the loan proceeds to be used for purposes that would neither enhance owners' equity nor provide funds from which they would be paid. *Ban-Co Inv. Co. v. Loveless*, 587 P2d 567 (Ct. App. 1978).

115.15 Priorities

Delaware A mortgage company had given a construction loan, secured by a mortgage, to mortgagor, who was acting as his own contractor. Progress payment advances were to be made to subcontractors at specified stages after mortgagee's agent had approved the work done. The agent gave approval for work that had not actually been done, exhausting the loan before Matthews, a subcontractor, had been paid (although his work was completed before that of other subcontractors who were paid.) When the mortgagee foreclosed, Matthews intervened, claiming priority for his mechanic's lien, for which he had obtained a default judgment. *Held:* Matthews' mechanics's lien had priority over subsequent construction loan advances. The advances made after Matthews had begun work were optional in that they were not required to be paid until mortgagee had approved the work done. Mortgagee had constructive knowledge of the status of the work and wrongfully paid others after Matthews' lien attached. *JJ Kislak Mortgage Corp. v. William Matthews, Builder, Inc.*, 303 A2d 648 (1973).

Iowa A builder-vendor obtained a letter from purchasers' mortgagee advising that it had made a mortgage commitment to purchasers, which letter the builder-vendor used to obtain construction financing. The mortgage commitment was withdrawn, however, because the house violated subdivision restrictions and purchasers could not provide marketable title. Builder-vendor sued for damages. Builder-vendor claimed the letter constituted a letter of credit, which is enforceable by addressee despite a breach of the underlying contract. *Held:* A letter of credit requires a direct promise to pay addressee. Since this letter did not do so, nor was there a commercial setting usual for a letter of credit, the letter was not an absolute commitment, but was subject to the underlying mortgage agreement. When the mortgage was lawfully terminated, the letter became void. *Johnson v. State Bank,* 195 NW2d 126 (1972).

Minnesota A bank loan to a developer was secured by a second mortgage, which contained a clause assigning rents from the property to the bank in the event of default. That mortgage went into default, and the bank foreclosed. During the redemption period, developer did not pay taxes on the property or interest on the first mortgage. The bank sued for the deficiency from the second mortgage, as well as interest on the first mortgage and unpaid taxes. *Held:* The bank was entitled to only the deficiency on the second mortgage. With regard to the other charges claimed by the bank, the assignment of rents was substituted for developer's personal liability. *GGC v. First Nat'l Bank*, 287 NW2d 378 (1979).

New Jersey Assignee of a construction loan mortgagor sought to recover funds assigned to him out of a future advance. The construction loan mortgagee was required to advance funds only if it would receive a first lien of good and marketable title. At the time of the advance from which the assignee sought recovery, mortgagee had notice of the existence of a mechanic's lien and a second mortgage. *Held:* Where first mortgagee has the option to make future advances, it does not receive priority for those advances made after notice of subsequent encumbrances. By statute, to obtain priority, mortgagee was entitled to distribute the advance to the precedent lienholders. (N.J. Stat. Ann. § 2A:44-89). Since this had been done, mortgagor did not qualify for any payment, nor did his assignee, who stood in the shoes of assignor-mortgagor. *Mayo v. City Nat'l Bank & Trust Co.*, 265 A2d 382 (1970).

116.00 ACCELERATION OF BALANCE DUE

116.05 Validity and Operation of Acceleration Clauses

2d Circuit When mortgagors defaulted on a home loan, mortgagee, wishing to enforce the mortgage's acceleration clause, brought an action for foreclosure. Before a final judgment of foreclosure and sale could be entered, mortgagors filed a Chapter 13 petition under the Bankruptcy Code. The U.S. Bankruptcy Court gave mortgagors permission to cure the default via Chapter 13, and mortgagee appealed, citing New York State law allowing lenders to accelerate mortgages in default. *Held:* The Second Circuit held that federal bankruptcy law presided over state mortgage law. The court stated two reasons for holding that the Chapter 13 provisions authorized debtors to prevent acceleration. The first reason stated was that the Chapter 13 provisions were expressly designed to cure defaults on loans and that the power to decelerate is included in the power to cure defaults. The second reason stated was that the power to cure defaults is not limited by the ban against modifying home mortgages, because cures of default are not modifications of claims. *Di Pierro v. Taddeo*, 685 F2d 24 (1982).

5th Circuit A savings and loan association (S&L) elected to accelerate into maturity the full balance of a note secured by a mortgage, and it started foreclosure proceedings 16 months later. One month afterward, debtor filed a Chapter 13 petition in federal bankruptcy court, which stayed the foreclosure proceedings. Debtor proposed a plan calling for the payment of all delinquent and matured amounts in 36 monthly installments. The bank objected, arguing that when a secured note on a homestead has been accelerated and matured before filing the bankruptcy petition, it should not be subject to being reinstated and cured under a Chapter 13 petition plan. *Held:* Policy considerations strongly supported the right of debtor to cure a default by filing a Chapter 13 petition even after acceleration pursuant to the terms of the note, where no sale has occurred. This will avoid "unseemly and wasteful races to the courthouse" in states where a prepetition acceleration is available to lender. *Grubbs v. Houston First Am. Sav. Ass'n*, 730 F2d 236 (1984).

California Guarantor of a note raised as a defense the fact that the acceleration clause was set forth only in the mortgage and not in the note and deed of trust that guarantor signed. *Held:* The several documents constituted a single integrated transaction, and therefore the holder's acceleration was effective against all parties. At the same time, the clause did not fail under the rule against restraint of alienation, but was fully within applicable provisions of the UCC. *Guild Wineries & Distilleries v. Land Dynamics*, 163 Cal. Rptr. 348 (1980).

Florida Purchasers arranged to assume sellers' mortgage and agreed to make the October and November payments through an escrow agent. However, the escrow agent misfiled the closing documents and failed to forward the payments or notify the bank of the assumption. The bank sent notices of default and acceleration to sellers. When purchasers made their December payment, it was refused. *Held:* For the bank, despite prior decisions that apparently conflicted with the holding. Given that neither party was at fault, the equity would not interfere with the enforcement of the bank's contractual rights. The case did not fall within any of the established principles of equity, as set forth in *Campbell v. Werner*, 232 So. 2d 252, under which the trial judge's discretion may be invoked to deny foreclosure on an accelerated basis. *David v. Sun Fed. Sav. & Loan Ass'n*, 461 So. 2d 93 (1984).

Florida A mortgage provided for acceleration of the balance due if any of the property was taken as a result of eminent domain proceedings. A portion of the secured property was in fact taken by such proceedings. The mortgagees then brought suit to enforce the acceleration provision, but failed to allege any impairment of the security. *Held:* The Fourth District Court of Appeals held for mortgagor. Florida courts have consistently denied foreclosure where there has been merely a technical breach of the mortgage that did not impair the security. *Sessler v. Arshak Corp.*, 464 So. 2d 612 (Dist. Ct. App. 1985).

Florida Defendants purchased a bowling alley from plaintiffs. Plaintiffs took back a purchase-money mortgage that provided for acceleration of the outstanding balance in the event of default and a $28,000 discount if the mortgage was paid in full before November 1, 1981. Because of defendants' late payments, plaintiffs filed a foreclosure suit. Two days later, and before November 1, defendants sent plaintiffs a check for the full unpaid balance less the $28,000 discount. Plaintiffs rejected the check, arguing that the acceleration clause preceded the discount clause. *Held:* The mortgage provision that the acceleration clause controlled "anything herein to the contrary notwithstanding," made it clear that the acceleration clause took precedence over the discount clause. Defendants were not entitled to the discount although they paid the loan in full before November 1, 1981. *Quiring v. Plackard*, 412 So. 2d 415 (Dist. Ct. App. 1982).

Georgia Defendants, holders of a promissory note, appealed a judgment that temporarily enjoined them from accelerating the balance of the debt on the land in question. Plaintiffs, before making an interest payment due on the promissory note, demanded release of certain acreage when defendants notified them that they were in default. Plaintiffs based their claim on two provisions in the security deed: "Seller shall release in its entirety the above referred Tract #2 containing 20 acres upon payment in full of the existing first mortgage" and "additional releases based on 110 percent of money paid in with interest and road front proportionate." Defendants contended that they had released Tract #2 but that plaintiffs did not satisfy the second release provision in the note. *Held:* The terms of the note were clear and unambiguous; defendants were not obligated to release the land since plaintiffs had paid only the interest payments and nothing toward the principal. *Honea v. Gilbert*, 223 SE2d 115 (1976).

New Jersey Defendants obtained a mortgage from plaintiff for a house they claimed they would occupy. The mortgage commitment provided that the mortgage would immediately become due if the house was not the primary residence of the owners. When the bank learned that defendants were renting the house to others, it demanded the full balance. When defendants did not pay, plaintiffs sought to foreclose. Defendants claimed that the acceleration clause and the requirement to live in the house were unconscionable. *Held:* Summary judgment for the bank. The clause was a legitimate exercise of the bank's statutory duty to promote home ownership and consistent with the bank's desire to maintain the value of its security because, based on prior experience, owner-occupied properties maintain their value better than rented properties. *Investor Sav. & Loan Ass'n v. Ganz*, 416 A2d 918 (1980).

New Mexico Buyer and seller entered into a note and mortgage that provided for a 60-day default period, but contained no acceleration clause. Buyer ceased making payments, allegedly on the ground that seller had breached an obligation to upgrade an existing road. The trial court ruled in favor of seller, and buyer appealed, arguing that because the note did not contain an acceleration clause, seller could not foreclose on the mortgage for the entire unpaid balance of the note. *Held:* For seller. The absence of a specific clause providing for acceleration is not a bar to a foreclosure action. The trial court's acceleration of, and foreclosure on, the unpaid balance was based on substantial evidence that showed that seller had an obligation to pay and that she was in substantial breach. A suit on the note would have been unavailing since buyer was indigent. *Gonzales v. Tama*, 749 P2d 1116 (1988).

South Carolina Mortgage-backed note contained an acceleration clause stating, "If default be made in the performance of . . . this note . . ., principal sum with all accrued interest thereon shall become at once due and payable at the option of the holder without further notice." On February 14, the bank, which had not received the February 1 payment, placed the note and mortgage with its attorney for foreclosure. On February 22, before the bank had notified mortgagor of its intention to accelerate, the bank received the February 1 payment. Mortgagor argued that the February 22 payment cured the default, since it was made before the bank evidenced to mortgagor its intention to accelerate. *Held:* For the bank. No affirmative act constituting notice to mortgagor was required in view of the "without further notice" provision in the note. When the bank placed the note in the hands of its attorney for foreclosure, mortgagor was in default, and only tender of the full accelerated amount would cure the default. *Allendale Furniture v. Carolina Commercial Bank*, 325 SE2d 530 (1985).

Texas In 1963, plaintiffs borrowed $12,000 from defendant lender to purchase a house. The loan was secured by a deed of trust on the house and land that provided that, in the event of default, defendant had the option to declare the balance immediately due. In 1978, plaintiffs fell into arrears. Defendant notified plaintiffs of the arrearages and that failure to cure by a specific deadline "*may* result in acceleration" of the balance and sale of the property. When plaintiffs failed to pay arrearages, defendants commenced foreclosure proceedings. Plaintiffs, claiming not to have received notice of defendant's intent to exercise its option under the acceleration clause if the default was not cured, sued to set aside the sale. *Held:* While defendant gave plaintiffs notice that the acceleration clause had been enforced when it announced the foreclosure sale, its letter was not prior notice of an unequivocal intent to enforce it. Defendant's letter said only that failure to cure might result in acceleration and foreclosure. *Ogden v. Gibraltar Sav. Ass'n.*, 640 SW2d 232 (1982).

116.10 Due-On-Sale Clauses

U.S. Supreme Court An S&L made loans to three sets of purchasers. All loans were secured by deeds of trust on either residential or commercial property, and were subject to due-on-sale clauses. All deeds of trust also contained provisions that the transactions "shall be governed by the law of the jurisdiction in which the property is located." The three sets of purchasers conveyed the property to the three sets of plaintiffs against whom the S&L sought to enforce the due-on-sale clauses. The S&L contended that state law was preempted by the Federal Home Loan Bank Board (FHLBB) regulations authorizing the enforcement of due-on-sale clauses. *Held:* The California appeals court held that FHLBB regulations authorizing the enforcement of due-on-sale clauses did not preempt state law prohibiting their automatic enforcement. The U.S. Supreme Court reversed, holding (1) that the federal regulations had the intended effect of preempting contrary state laws and (2) that the FHLBB had the authority to issue the regulations. The Court held the regulations to be a valid exercise of the FHLBB's power to protect the financial soundness of the thrift industry. *Fidelity Fed. Sav. & Loan Ass'n v. de la Cuesta*, 458 US 141 (1982).

4th Circuit Plaintiffs purchased a home for $64,000 with a loan of $55,000 from defendant. The term was 30 years, and the interest rate was 10 percent. Two years later, when plaintiffs planned to sell the home, the market rate shot up to 15 percent. As a result, the value of the loan was discounted by 29 percent. Defendant, therefore, notified plaintiffs that it would exercise the due-on-sale clause contained in the deed of trust. Plaintiffs sued to enjoin defendant from doing so, contending that the due-on-sale clause was invalid under Virginia law as a restraint on alienation. *Held:* Due-on-sale clauses, viewed in isolation, cannot be said to create restraints on alienation. Homeowners subject to these clauses are free to sell their homes and realize as much gain as can a homeowner holding the same property free and clear. In fact, during periods of rising interest rates these owners enjoy an economic advantage over free-and-clear owners. Enforcement of the due-on-sale clause in this instance would amount to an unfair protection of this economic advantage at the cost of defendant's loan security. *Williams v. First Fed. Sav. & Loan Ass'n*, 651 F2d 910 (1981).

9th Circuit Metz obtained a discharge in bankruptcy under Chapter 7 of the Bankruptcy Code. His mortgage loan was reduced from a personal debt to a lien against his house. On the day he received his discharge, Metz filed a Chapter 13 reorganization plan in which he proposed to reinstate his mortgage indebtedness but cure the default by repaying his arrearages at market interest over three years in addition to his regular installments. Lender objected on the ground that it had accelerated the mortgage under state law and the entire balance was due and payable. *Held:* For debtor. State law is not permitted to interfere with the result intended by Congress in the Bankruptcy Code. Also, the successive filings were not improper. Although debtor's personal liability had been discharged, his property remained encumbered. That encumbrance was a claim that could be addressed separately via reorganization under Chapter 13. Metz's stratagem did not violate the good faith mandate of Chapter 13. *In re Metz*, 820 F2d 1495 (1987).

9th Circuit A corporate debtor obtained a loan from the Farmer's Home Administration (FmHA). The mortgage contained a due-on-sale clause and a provision authorizing the federal government to commence foreclosure proceedings if debtor failed to discharge any mortgage obligation. Debtor's shareholders sold all their stock without the government's consent, and buyer tried to assume the mortgage at its 8.5 percent interest rate. The FmHA began a foreclosure action in April 1981 after notifying the shareholders that they were in default under the mortgage and providing them with an opportunity to repay the loan promptly. The shareholders argued that the FmHA could not accelerate the debt under Washington law, which holds that due-on-sale clauses are illegal restraints on alienation unless it can be shown the enforcement of the loan is necessary to protect lender's security. *Held:* For the government. Federal, not state, law governs questions involving the rights of the United States under nationwide federal programs. Applying Washington law would limit the remedies available to the federal government. The court rejected the shareholders' contention that transfers of stock do not trigger a due-on-sale clause. Under Washington law, transfer of the stock in a corporation implies transfer of an interest in the underlying assets. *United States v. Med O Farm, Inc.*, 701 F2d 88 (1983).

U.S. District Court, Florida Plaintiff entered into a contract of sale for his property. Paragraph 16 of his mortgage with defendant, a federally chartered S&L, was a due-on-sale clause providing that if a conveyance were to be made "without the written consent of the Association and without assumption in regular form of law," then all money owing would become immediately due. When defendant refused to permit plaintiff's contract vendees to assume the mortgage, plaintiff sued for a declaratory judgment and damages. *Held:* For plaintiff. Although federal regulations permit federal S&Ls to include due-on-sale clauses in their mortgages and preempt state laws to the contrary, Paragraph 16 of the mortgage limited the S&L's right to exercise the due-on-sale provision if the assumption is "in the regular form of law." Here, a clause in grantee's warranty deed indicated grantee's agreement to assume and pay the mortgage obligation. Since that would result in an assumption in the regular form of law, the S&L's option to accelerate was not triggered. *Morse v. City Fed. Sav. & Loan Ass'n*, 567 F. Supp. 669 (SD 1983).

U.S. District Court, New York Defendant, a federally chartered savings and loan association S&L, acquired a mortgage originated by a state chartered S&L. Plaintiff attempted to assume the mortgage from original mortgagor, but defendant wanted to raise the interest rate in exercise of the mortgage's due-on-sale clause. Defendant claimed that, as a federal S&L, it was governed by the federal regulations that preempt state laws that disfavor enforcement of due-on-sale clauses. *Held:* For plaintiff. There was no indication that federal due-on-sale regulations were intended to preempt state law in the case of a mortgage originating in a state S&L and subsequently acquired by a federal S&L. Defendant's contention that the acquisition of the mortgage by a federal S&L changed the law governing it and mortgagor's rights along with it would raise constitutional issues involving impairment of property rights acquired under state law. *Bleeker Assocs. v. Astoria Fed. Sav. & Loan Ass'n*, 544 F. Supp. 794 (SD 1982).

Alabama Due-on-sale clause provided for acceleration of payments due in the event that the mortgaged property was transferred without mortgagee's approval. When mortgagor sought approval of a pending sale and assumption of the mortgage by buyers, the mortgage conditioned its approval upon the payment of a penalty or increased interest. Buyers paid the penalty, then brought suit to recover. Mortgagee appealed judgment for buyers. *Held:* Mortgagee had no justification for refusing to consent to the transfer. The right to accelerate is dependent upon the sale's producing a threat to a legitimate interest of mortgagee. Here, there was no indication that the threatened acceleration was due to an increase of risk or jeopardy to the security. If the due-on-sale clause is to be used to advance the financial interest of lender through requirement of payment of a penalty or an increase in the interest rate, such purpose must be openly stated and bargained for from the inception of the contract. *First So. Fed. Sav. & Loan Ass'n v. Britton*, 345 So. 2d 300 (1977).

California Plaintiffs purchased an apartment building from defendants, husband and wife, who held title to the property in the name of "Dawn Investment Co." Plaintiffs gave defendants a promissory note secured by a deed of trust that contained a due-on-sale clause. When plaintiffs sold the building, defendants notified them they intended to accelerate the balance of the loan. Plaintiffs sued to enjoin defendants from foreclosing on the property. Defendants, claiming to be private, noninstitutional lenders, argued that the rule of *Wellenkamp v. Bank of America*, making due-on-sale clauses illegal in California, did not apply to them. *Held: Wellenkamp* applies to both private and institutional lenders. In both cases, the effect of a due-on-sale clause would be to prohibit the sale or assignment of property. A private lender's security is in no greater need of the protection provided by due-on-sale clauses than is that of the institutional lender. The court also held that *Wellenkamp* applied equally to commercial property and home equity, and that a public policy favoring the protection of home equity was not a basis of the *Wellenkamp* ruling. *Dawn Inv. Co. v. Superior Court*, 639 P2d 794 (1982).

California Guarantor of a note for the purchase of a winery that was secured by separate mortgages on the realty and personalty of the winery and its related cooperage was sued by the mortgage holder after the note was accelerated pursuant to a due-on-sale provision following a second sale of assets by the mortgagor without mortgagee's consent. Guarantor argued that mortgagor could not accelerate payment on the note securing the entire indebtedness because the due-on-sale provision was not present in the real estate mortgage. The trial court ruled for the plaintiff. *Held:* Affirmed. There was no support in the documents comprising the contract for sale that the agreement merely placed a due-on-sale restraint on the separate sale of the cooperage without a sale of the accompanying real estate. The absence of due-on-sale clauses in the real estate mortgage implies only that the realty could be sold separately. However, since the cooperage was also sold, the acceleration clause was effective with regard to the sale of the mortgaged real estate. *Guild Wineries & Distilleries v. Land Dynamics*, 163 Cal. Rptr. 348 (1980).

California Family financed its purchase of real property with a promissory note secured by a deed of trust that included a due-on-sale clause. Subsequently, the family sold this property to plaintiff, who assumed their loan with defendant, the bank that was trustee of the deed. When plaintiff gave notice of the transfer and sent defendant a check in payment of the current installment of the loan, defendant returned the check and notified plaintiff of its right to accelerate the balance of the loan upon transfer of the property. Defendant offered to waive its right to acceleration if plaintiff would agree to pay a higher interest rate, but she refused. Defendant filed a notice of default and election to sell; plaintiff sued to stop the sale. Plaintiff argued that the due-on-sale clause was an unreasonable restraint on alienation. *Held:* Absent a showing of harm to the lender, due-on-sale clauses are an unreasonable restraint on alienation. The court noted that enforcement of these clauses might make it impossible for buyers to get financing when mortgage money is tight. Fluctuating interest rates are a foreseeable business problem that banks should take into account when planning long-term loans. *Wellenkamp v. Bank of Am.*, 148 Cal. Rptr. 379 (1978).

California In 1973, vendors sold two parcels of land carrying secondary financing to plaintiffs. In 1979, buyers sold the land to a third party, and vendors sought to enforce the due-on-sale clause in the promissory note and mortgage. On October 15, 1982, the Garn-St. Germain Depository Institutions Act became law. The act preempted all state judicial restrictions on the enforcement of due-on-sale clauses except for those in loans during the act's "window period"—the time between the date of state restrictive action and October 15, 1982. Buyers argued the due-on-sale clause was unenforceable because it fell into the window period applicable to loans in California. *Held:* For buyers. California's window period began with the 1978 decision in *Wellenkamp v. Bank of America*. There, the California Supreme Court held that due-on-sale clauses are unenforceable as unreasonable restraints on alienation except where a creditor's security is impaired. A 1982 decision declaring *Wellenkamp* applicable to private lenders was simply a refusal to create an exemption from the *Wellenkamp* rule for private lenders; thus, it was not the start of the window period for private lenders. *Lucas v. Jones*, 196 Cal. Rptr. 437 (Ct. App. 1983), cert. denied, 469 US 818 (1984).

California Defendants sold their single-family house to the Lopezes for $49,000, taking a note and deed of trust for $44,000 containing a standard due-on-sale clause. A year later, the Lopezes sold the property to plaintiffs for $62,500. Defendants sought to enforce the due-on-sale clause against the Lopezes. Plaintiffs sought a preliminary injunction to halt foreclosure, arguing that the due-on-sale clause could not be enforced even by individual homeowner lenders under *Wellenkamp* and *Dawn Investment Co. v. Superior Court*, 180 Cal. Rptr. 332 (1982). *Held:* The cited cases bar enforcement of a due-on-sale clause by an individual homeowner who sold his home and took back a promissory note and deed of trust. The quantum of restraint resulting from the automatic enforcement of the due-on-sale clause in this transaction would be just as great as that existing in a transaction with an institutional lender or a larger-scale noninstitutional lender. In either case, borrower would be restrained from selling his property if he could not obtain a new loan. *West v. Buffo*, 188 Cal. Rptr. 535 (Ct. App. 1983).

California On March 29, 1978, plaintiffs purchased commercial real property from defendant, who took back a promissory note secured by a mortgage, each containing a due-on-sale clause. On April 17, 1979, plaintiffs conveyed the property to third parties without defendant's written consent. Relying on the due-on-sale clause, defendant filed a notice of default and began foreclosure proceedings. On October 15, 1982, the Garn-St. Germain Depositary Institutions Act was passed preempting all state judicial restrictions on the enforcement of due-on-sale clauses except for those in loans during the act's "window period"—the time between the date of state restrictive action and October 15, 1982. Plaintiffs argued that the transactions fell into the act's window period. *Held:* For plaintiffs. California's window period began on August 25, 1978, when the state supreme court decided *Wellenkamp*, which held that institutional lenders may not enforce due-on-sale clauses except to prevent impairment of security. The case of *Dawn Investment Co.* that held *Wellenkamp* applicable to private lenders was retroactive to the date of the *Wellenkamp*, so the window for private lenders opened on August 25, 1978. *Miranda v. Macias*, 663 P2d 177 (Ct. App. 1983).

California Defendant, a veteran, and the Department of Veterans Affairs entered into an installment contract for the purchase of a home. The contract provided that if defendant transferred the property without the department's consent, the balance would become immediately due. When defendant conveyed the property without the department's consent, the department demanded full payment and cancelled the contract. In a suit to quiet title, defendant argued that the rule of *Wellenkamp* applied, which invalidated due-on-sale clauses unless the lender can prove impairment of security. *Held:* The department had authority to cancel the contract. The *Wellenkamp* rule is based on Civil Code § 711, which is a general prohibition against restraints on alienation. The department, however, had specific statutory authority under the Veterans' Farm and Home Purchase Act to restrain alienation in ways an ordinary lender could not. *Department of Veterans Affairs v. Duerkson*, 187 Cal. Rptr. 832 (Ct. App. 1982).

California Defendants, husband and wife who had granted more than 20 loans in the previous five years, loaned purchasers $5,000 in exchange for a second deed of trust on purchaser's residence. The deed of trust contained a due-on-sale clause. Purchasers later conveyed the residence to plaintiffs, who were found to be at least as solvent as the original purchasers. Defendants notified plaintiffs that the due-on-sale clause would be implemented and began foreclosure proceedings. Plaintiffs sued to enjoin foreclosure, citing the *Wellenkamp* rule that due-on-sale clauses are unreasonable restraints on alienation. Defendants contended that as private noninstitutional lenders, they were not subject to the *Wellenkamp* rule. *Held:* For plaintiffs. The reasonableness of a due-on-sale clause is not to be determined by the nature of the lender, but by the nature of the clause and the restraint on alienation it imposes. Due-on-sale clauses drafted by private lenders as well as institutional lenders shall not be automatically enforced, but must be justified by showing impairment of lenders' security. Impairment was not shown in this case. *Wilhite v. Callihan*, 175 Cal. Rptr. 507 (Ct. App. 1981), aff'd with directions, 185 Cal. Rptr. 215 (1982).

Colorado In an action for a declaratory judgment as to the rights of the parties under a deed of trust, the trial court ruled that a due-on-sale clause in an installment land contract constitutes an unreasonable restraint on alienation. An appeal was taken. *Held:* Reversed. The trial court decision attached too much weight to the interests of the parties and not enough to the interests of society. A refusal to enforce a due-on-sale clause would result in a loss of money to a state S&L, which would have to be recaptured either by a decrease in the interest rate paid on deposits or by a higher rate on new loans. This would also result in a competitive imbalance between federally chartered and state-chartered S&Ls in that state S&Ls would be forced to charge higher rates than their federal counterparts. Thus, a prohibition of the enforcement of due-on-sale clauses would be inequitable unless the lender engaged in unconscionable conduct. *Income Realty & Mortgage, Inc. v. Columbia Sav. & Loan Ass'n*, 661 P2d 256 (1983).

Colorado Sellers owned a home financed by defendant, a federally chartered S&L, with a $46,000 mortgage at a rate of 8.75 percent per annum. The mortgage contained a standard due-on-sale clause. When plaintiffs purchased the home from sellers, defendant submitted an assumption and modification agreement to be signed by plaintiffs at the closing. Plaintiffs signed the agreement, which raised the interest rate to 11 percent. Afterwards, plaintiffs asked that the interest rate be lowered to 9.75 percent, because Colorado law prohibited rate increases greater than one percent above the existing rate. When defendant claimed that it was not bound by that law because the FHLBB regulations authorized its exercise of the due-on-sale clause, plaintiffs brought suit. *Held:* Defendant, as a federal savings and loan association, was not bound by Colorado restrictions on interest rate increases. The court first cited *Fidelity Fed. Sav. & Loan Ass'n v. de la Cuesta*, 458 US 141 (1982), which ruled that the FHLBB regulations preempt state law. It then ruled that the facts and issues of that case could not be distinguished from the facts and issues of this case. *Haugen v. Western Fed. Sav. & Loan Ass'n*, 649 P2d 323 (1982).

Colorado Purchaser of real property delivered a mortgage to lender that included a standard due-on-sale clause with the language of "sale or transfer of the real property." The property was subsequently conveyed via an installment land sales contract. When lender sought to enforce the due-on-sale clause, purchasers argued that it did not apply to installment sales, but only to outright sales. *Held:* Although an installment sale is different in form from an outright sale, and may take more time to complete, it is a "sale or transfer of the real property" for purposes of the due-on-sale clause. The difference is one of procedure and not of substance. *Krause v. Columbia Sav. & Loan Ass'n*, 631 P2d 1158 (Ct. App. 1981), aff'd, 661 P2d 265 (1983) (en banc).

Connecticut A limited partnership executed a mortgage containing a standard due-on-sale clause, which allowed mortgagee to accelerate the underlying indebtedness on the "sale or conveyance" of the property. In the three years following execution, a new general partner was brought in, and the original general and limited partners all withdrew, transferring their interests to the new general partner. The mortgage holder argued that the change in control of the partnership was a sale or conveyance and moved to accelerate the balance due. *Held:* A limited partnership is a legal entity entitled by statute to acquire and hold property in the partnership name and capable, under certain circumstances, of surviving the withdrawal of a general partner. Thus, the change of membership occasioned by the withdrawal did not constitute a conveyance that would trigger the due-on-sale clause. *Fidelity Trust Co. v. BVD Assocs.*, 492 A2d 180 (1985).

Florida Borrower executed a promissory note and first mortgage in favor of plaintiff S&L. The documents contained a provision that made the principal of the loan immediately due and payable at the S&L's option if the property were sold. Five years later, borrower conveyed the property without the S&L's consent, and the S&L brought a foreclosure action in the Florida courts. Borrower and purchaser defended on the ground that the security had not been impaired and so the S&L had no equitable right to accelerate the debt. The S&L argued that the due-on-sale clause was authorized by the rules and regulations of the FHLBB. *Held:* Despite the FHLBB's rules and regulation authorizing due-on-sale clauses, the S&L could not obtain foreclosure in a Florida court without showing that a violation of the clause had impaired the security of its mortgage. *First Fed. Sav. & Loan Ass'n v. Lockwood*, 385 So. 2d 156 (1980).

Illinois Mortgagors entered into an agreement for deed with a third party. Mortgagee, a federal S&L, moved to foreclose, claiming a violation of the mortgage's due-on-sale clause. At issue was the meaning of the words "change in the ownership of the premises" in the clause. *Held:* The agreement for deed did not constitute a change in ownership. According to the court, the language was ambiguous, so the court resorted to the rule of construction that instruments are to be construed most strongly against their drafters (in this case, mortgagee). Had the parties intended that an agreement for deed be considered a change of ownership, they could have added appropriate language to the due-on-sale clause. The court was also swayed by mortgagor's allegation that the agreement for deed did not increase the risk to mortgagee's security. *Fidelity Fed. Sav. & Loan Ass'n v. Grieme*, 446 NE2d 292 (1983).

Minnesota Plaintiff, an investment partnership, entered into a mortgage agreement with defendant, a federally chartered S&L, to finance its purchase of an apartment complex. The mortgage contained a standard due-on-sale clause. When the S&L invoked the clause to prevent a transfer to a third party without refinancing, plaintiff sought a declaratory judgment that the due-on-sale clause was invalid as an illegal restraint on alienation. *Held:* For defendant. Minnesota law provides that the enforcement of due-on-sale clauses in the transfer of residential property is per se unreasonable unless it protects against impairment of the lender's security interest. The law does not provide for the transfer of investment residential property. Here, the contract was negotiated by two experienced business parties who were equals in bargaining power, and there were no allegations of fraud or overreaching. Thus, the court upheld the due-on-sale clause. *Holiday Acres No. 3 v. Midwest Fed. Sav. & Loan Ass'n*, 308 NW2d 471 (1981).

Minnesota A mortgage involved the sale of commercial property by a contract for deed. Mortgagor agreed that except for leases not exceeding a term of two years, any conveyances or other transfer of all or any part of the interest of mortgagor, in whole or in part, of the mortgaged premises without obtaining, in each instance, the written approval of mortgagee shall give to mortgagee the right, at its option, of declaring the unpaid principal balance of the principal note and interest thereon together with all sums advanced hereunder, if any, immediately due and payable without notice. *Held:* The court held such provision enforceable per se. *Siegel v. Empire Sav. Bank*, 304 NW2d 335 (1981).

Missouri Defendant's property was used to secure two promissory notes. The subordinate note contained a due-on-sale clause. The real estate was sold at a trustee's foreclosure sale under the first promissory note. Holder of the subordinate note sued defendant for principal, interest, and attorney fees, arguing that the trustee's sale of the real estate under the first deed of trust was a sale or transfer that accelerated the due date of the note under the due-on-sale clause. *Held:* Due-on-sale clause was not activated by an involuntary sale by a trustee pursuant to a deed of trust foreclosure. A right to accelerate is given only when there is no reasonable doubt as to the meaning of the terms employed. The due-on-sale clause in question stated that maturity was accelerated when the property "is sold or transferred by the borrower." In this case, the note was not accelerated, since the borrower was not the trustee under the first deed of trust and the borrower vigorously opposed the sale. Additionally, the subordinate note lacked any reference to the note secured by the first deed of trust, and no conditions were expressed that obligated borrower to maintain current payments on the prior note and to perform all acts necessary to avoid foreclosure of the first deed of trust. *Executive Hills Home Builders v. Whitley*, 770 SW2d 507 (Ct. App. 1989).

Nevada Deed of trust provided that trustee's written consent had to be obtained prior to the sale of the encumbered realty or else payment of the balance of the principal and interest would be accelerated. Trustee conveyed the property without trustee's consent, and trustee foreclosed. Trustor brought an action to enjoin the foreclosure sale. *Held:* A due-on-sale clause does not constitute an unreasonable restraint upon alienation and is entitled to enforcement when there has clearly been a sale of the property by the trustor. The burden is on trustor to prove that enforcement of the clause is unreasonable. *First Commercial Title, Inc. v. Holmes*, 550 P2d 1271 (1976).

New Hampshire Plaintiffs purchased some real estate and delivered to defendant a mortgage of $32,800 at 10.75 percent interest, which mortgage contained a due-on-sale clause. When defendant learned that plaintiffs subsequently conveyed the property, defendant notified plaintiffs that it intended either to accelerate the $31,000 balance due on the mortgage or permit the new purchasers to assume the mortgage at the then prevailing interest rate of 14.75 percent. When plaintiff refused to act on defendant's notice, defendant brought an action for foreclosure. Plaintiff argued that the due-on-sale clause was unenforceable as an unreasonable restraint on the alienation of property and as an adhesion contract. *Held:* The due-on-sale clause was not an unreasonable restraint on alienation because it did not preclude plaintiff from conveying the property. It was not unenforceable as an adhesion contract because it was almost identical to the due-on-sale provisions permitted by the FHLBB regulations, and there was no evidence of overreaching or that a mutual meeting of the minds was lacking. *Mills v. Nashua Fed. Sav. & Loan Ass'n*, 433 A2d 1312 (1981).

New Jersey Corporate mortgagor transferred title to its principal stockholder. The property was later reconveyed to corporate mortgagor. Action was brought to enforce acceleration of debt on the ground that transfer of title violated the due-on-transfer clause in the mortgage note. *Held:* Acceleration of the due date of the mortgage note was not justified. The transfer of title did not jeopardize mortgagee's security interest or frustrate the purpose of the clause. The presumed intention of the parties governs, and the parties did not seem to intend acceleration of maturity of the note. *Fidelity Land Dev. Corp. v. Reider & Sons*, 377 A2d 691 (1977).

South Carolina Dozier Associates purchased real property by giving sellers a mortgage that contained a due-on-sale clause. Four months later, Dozier Associates transferred the property to the Doziers, who owned Dozier Corporation, without obtaining sellers' consent. Sellers accepted payments from the Doziers for 17 months before calling in the loan for violation of the due-on-sale clause. *Held:* Sellers were equitably estopped from accelerating the mortgage after accepting payments from transferees for 17 months. The election of the holder to declare the acceleration of the due date of the entire debt represented by a mortgage note containing a due-on-sale clause must be exercised within a reasonable time after notice of default. *Rakestraw v. Dozier Assocs., Inc.*, 329 SE2d 437 (1985).

Tennessee Plaintiffs sold a building to a partnership of four individuals for a cash down payment plus a promissory note containing a standard due-on-sale clause. A disagreement arose among the partners resulting in a withdrawal of two partners. Plaintiffs took the position that the mortgage could not be assumed and that the due-on-sale clause would be exercised upon sale of the property. After blocking a planned sale of the property to the two remaining partners, plaintiffs brought an action to activate the due-on-sale clause. *Held:* For defendants. The withdrawal of two partners, while the business of the partnership was continued in lieu of liquidation, did not amount to a sale or transfer by borrower, even though the partnership had changed by operation of law. A deed of conveyance is not necessary under Tennessee law, but something more than an aborted sale to partnership members is required. *Hodge v. DMNS Co.*, 652 SW2d 762 (Ct. App. 1982).

Virginia The beneficiary under a land trust agreement sought to transfer and assign his interest under the agreement. The trust property consisted of a condominium unit that was encumbered by a deed of trust, which contained a standard due-on-sale clause. Beneficiary moved for a declaration that the transfer or assignment of his interest under the land trust agreement would not trigger the due-on-sale clause. *Held:* On the contrary, transfer or assignment of the beneficiary's interest would trigger the due-on-sale clause. Although the deed of trust was signed by trustees under the land trust agreement, and not by beneficiary himself, beneficiary had control over the property. Beneficiary's attempt to distinguish his interest under the trust agreement from an interest in the property itself was unacceptable sophistry, given the extent of his control of the property. *Barnes v. VNB Mortgage Corp.*, 334 SE2d 531 (1985).

Wisconsin Defendant executed a note and mortgage containing a due-on-sale clause. The clause provided that the note would become due at the option of plaintiff if mortgagor conveyed the premises or if title vested in another party without plaintiff's consent. Defendant sold the property to a different party, buyer agreeing to pay such additional interest as mortgagor would be obligated to pay pursuant to the note. This intervening purchaser assigned all its rights in the property to another property owner. Mortgagee, who was not informed of either transfer until more than a year after the transaction, sued to foreclose based on the due-on-sale provision. Defendant appealed a judgment of foreclosure. *Held:* It was not inequitable to permit mortgagee to declare the entire sum due and pursue its right to foreclose. The due-on-sale provision was not against public policy as a restraint on alienation, nor was the interest rate proposed by plaintiff unfair. Defendant made advantageous transfers without paying the current interest rates, at the expense of plaintiff, and judgment for plaintiff was affirmed. *Mutual Fed. Sav. & Loan Assocs. v. Wisconsin Wire Works*, 239 NW2d 20 (1976).

117.00 TRANSFER OF PROPERTY BY MORTGAGOR/TRUSTOR

117.05
Transfer by Mortgagor/Trustor

Alabama Plaintiff purchaser of rental property executed a purchase-money mortgage with defendant seller. Plaintiff later sold to a third party, who assumed the mortgage and made payments to defendant. Defendant notified plaintiff that he would invoke a due-on-sale clause unless plaintiff's purchaser agreed to pay higher interest rates. *Held:* Over dissent, judgment for plaintiff reversed. Rising interest rates constitute a valid business purpose justifying acceleration of payments. Although mortgage foreclosure is an equitable matter and courts will not permit an inequitable result, the instrument in question was drafted by plaintiff's counsel and its enforcement, therefore, could not be considered unconscionable under the circumstances. *Tierce v. APS Co.*, 382 So. 2d 485 (1979).

Delaware Borrowers executed a bond and mortgage of real property. They later sold the property to grantee, who assumed liability for the mortgage. Lender was not a party to this transaction and did not execute a new contract or instrument releasing borrowers from liability. When grantee's mortgage payments ceased, lender instituted suit against borrowers on their bond. Borrowers contended that lender, by accepting timely mortgage payments from grantee and dealing with grantee rather than borrowers until default, was required to foreclose the mortgage before proceeding against borrowers. *Held:* Absent a release or contract of novation, lender's acceptance of grantee's mortgage payments and related correspondence was insufficient to alter its right to proceed, on default, against the bond. A creditor's knowledge of a debt assumption and acceptance of debt payments from the assumptor is not sufficient to effect a novation or release. The creditor's expressed assent to give up the original debt is required. *Berg v. Liberty Fed. Sav. & Loan Ass'n*, 428 A2d 347 (1981).

Florida Borrower executed a loan agreement with lender, which provided that borrower would not encumber or transfer the real property described in the agreement without lender's consent. Borrower later transferred the property without lender's consent to a third party, who executed a mortgage on the property in favor of the bank. When the third party defaulted on mortgage, the bank sued to foreclose on the property. Lender claimed a superior interest because of the original agreement. *Held:* Lender did not have a superior interest. The agreement not to encumber or transfer the property did not create an equitable lien against the property, but merely constituted evidence of intent to create such a lien. *Manatee Fed. Sav. & Loan Ass'n v. Pace*, 378 So. 2d 95 (1979).

Indiana Defendant executed a mortgage in favor of bank as security for a real estate loan and then conveyed the real estate to a purchaser subject to the mortgage. Without notifying defendant, bank and purchaser agreed to increase the interest rate on the outstanding debt. According to bank, the mortgage provided that, if the property were sold, bank could deal with the new owner and increase the interest rate without defendant's consent. After purchaser defaulted, bank instituted a foreclosure action against both purchaser and defendant. *Held:* Defendant was released from liability under the mortgage because of bank's dealings with purchaser. Defendant became a surety upon the sale of the property. However, if a surety does not agree to a contract change, the surety is released from liability under the contract. Furthermore, the mortgage only gave bank authority to deal with purchaser, without releasing defendant from his obligations, for purposes of forbearance of foreclosure or extensions of time for payment. *First Fed. Sav. & Loan Ass'n v. Arena*, 406 NE2d 1279 (1980).

Maryland Plaintiffs sold real estate to defendants in 1977 and took back a purchase-money deed of trust with an interest rate of 8.5 percent. If defendants sold the property and a subsequent purchaser assumed the deed of trust, plaintiffs or their assignees had the right to charge the prevailing rate of interest at the time of the assumption. Defendants sold the property in 1980 under a purchase-money wraparound deed of trust. Plaintiffs claimed that this transaction was an assumption and tried to raise the interest rate to 14 percent. *Held:* For defendants. Defendants did not intend to assume primary responsibility for the 1977 debt because, first, the 1980 deed of trust expressly provided that it was "subject to" the 1977 deed of trust. Second, the balance of the 1977 debt was included in the 1980 debt through the wraparound feature. Finally, defendants, not assignees, were primarily liable for the 1977 debt. Assignees could, but were not obligated to, make payments directly if defendants failed to do so. *Daugharty v. Monritt Assocs.*, 444 A2d 1030 (1982).

New York As a result of a series of financial transactions, plaintiff received an assignment of a mortgage as collateral security for a promise of indemnification. The underlying note was not assigned. Plaintiff brought an action to foreclose on the mortgage. Defendants moved to dismiss the complaint. *Held:* Plaintiff's actions for foreclosure and deficiency judgment must fail because foreclosure of a mortgage may not be brought by one without title to it. Absent a transfer of debt, the assignment of the mortgage was a nullity. *Kluge v. Fugazy*, 536 NYS2d 92 (App. Div. 1988).

Oregon Bank sought to foreclose a mortgage that had matured 11 years earlier and was subject to an unrecorded extension agreement. The property had since been sold and resold to parties who took subject to, but did not assume, the mortgage. Oregon statute (Or. Rev. Stat. § 88.110) bars foreclosure on mortgaged property after the expiration of 10 years from the recorded maturity date of the mortgage or from the recorded date for extended payments, if later. *Held:* The bank was entitled to foreclose under an exception to the statute that applied when (1) payment on the mortgage was voluntarily made within 10 years of commencement of the foreclosure action; (2) original mortgagor still owned the property, and (3) no lien or right of a third person attached to the property after expiration of the 10-year period. Although the contract vendees had equitable title to the property, this did not carry over in cases such as this involving third-party creditors. *Security State Bank v. Luebke*, 737 P2d 586 (1987) (en banc).

South Dakota Kleinjan mortgaged 580 acres to the bank. The form used was a "One Hundred Eighty Day Redemption" mortgage. Subsequently, the Kleinjans' son bought seven acres of the mortgaged property from his parents. The bank sued to foreclose on all 580 acres. The son argued that he took free of the mortgage since the mortgage was void at inception, because it violated state statute by containing more than 40 acres. The trial court granted summary judgment to the bank, and the son appealed. *Held:* Affirmed. The redemption mortgage was not void because the mortgaged property contained more than 40 acres. The deed given to the son was inferior to the mortgage and subject to foreclosure upon mortgagor's default on the original mortgage. *First Nat'l Bank of Volga v. Kleinjan*, 418 NW2d 327 (1988).

117.10 Assumption of Mortgage or Deed of Trust by Grantee

9th Circuit Defendant agreed to purchase a house and executed an escrow agreement providing for a $16,000 cash down payment to be placed in escrow and the assumption of all mortgage installments subsequent to August 1969. The mortgage contained an acceleration of principal clause if it was conveyed without mortgagee's consent. Subsequently, defendant's husband was arrested for criminal possession of marijuana and the Internal Revenue Service placed an excise tax lien on the escrow money. Mortgagee then informed the parties that it would not consent to the conveyance of the property to defendant, and it exercised the acceleration clause. The property was eventually sold to another purchaser at a greatly reduced price. Plaintiffs brought an action to retain the escrow money as liquidated damages for breach of contract and for the brokerage fee, contending that defendant had agreed to assume the mortgage and was financially responsible when the mortgagee exercised the acceleration clause. *Held:* Defendant agreed only to assume installments on the mortgage and did not assume the entire mortgage principal. Seller was responsible for obtaining mortgagee's waiver of clauses that did not appear in the purchase agreement. *Stewart Title & Trust Co. v. Ordean*, 528 F2d 894 (1976).

11th Circuit Two federally charted savings and loan associations granted loans to home buyers at rates one quarter below the legal maximum. In each case, the home was sold to a subsequent purchaser, who entered into a loan assumption and modification agreement with lender. The interest rate on each loan was raised above the maximum in force at the time of the original loan but within the maximum current at the time of assumption. Each agreement stated that the assumption was not a novation. Subsequent purchasers sued, claiming that because there was no novation, the interest ceiling at the time of the original loans was controlling, and the loans to them were usurious. *Held:* For the lenders. Under Georgia law, the fact that an agreement is not a novation does not prevent its being a new contract. Looking at the substance of the assumption agreements, the court found they were new contracts. Moreover, although Federal Home Bank Board regulations providing that assumptions were new loans took effect after the making of the original loans, the regulations were merely intended to preempt conflicting state law. *Lindenberg v. First Fed. Sav. & Loan*, 691 F2d 974 (1982).

Kentucky A property encumbered by a mortgage was sold at a public auction approved by mortgagee as "absolute" in nature. Mortgagee took no action during the auction to indicate its expectation that purchaser would be bound by an existing mortgage. The contract of sale guaranteed delivery of unencumbered, marketable title. Some time after the auction, after purchasers had made substantial improvements to the property, mortgagee moved to foreclose. *Held:* Mortgagee was equitably estopped from enforcing the mortgage. Its failure to object to the advertised terms of the auction and its delay in seeking to enforce the mortgage induced purchasers to purchase and improve the property. *First Fed. Sav. & Loan Ass'n v. Cundiff*, 704 SW2d 664 (Ct. App. 1986).

New York Plaintiff and defendant bank entered into a mortgage and lease whereby bank leased property owned by plaintiff and financed plaintiffs's construction of a branch bank for defendant. Subsequently, a buyer offered to purchase the property from plaintiff subject to the bank's consent to an assumption of plaintiff's mortgage. The bank refused to permit assumption by purchaser unless he agreed to an increase in the mortgage rate. Plaintiff sued for declaratory relief. *Held:* In a case of first impression, the bank was found to have unreasonably withheld consent to the proposed sale. The mortgage contained a clause prohibiting the bank from unreasonably opposing assumption by a qualified purchaser. Buyer's credit was unobjectionable; the only reason the bank insisted on additional interest was to upgrade its return to current rates. Plaintiff's right to sell her property under an assumption was a bargained-for benefit under the mortgage contract which the bank could not defeat unless its security was jeopardized. *Silver v. Rochester Sav. Bank*, 424 NYS2d 945 (1980).

117.15 Conveyance Subject to Mortgage or Deed of Trust

Georgia Borrower executed a note and security deed to secure the debt to lender for the purchase of real property. When borrower conveyed the property to a buyer, the warranty deed stated that the conveyance was made subject to the loan agreement. When buyer transferred the property to another buyer, that deed contained a clause stating that the second buyer assumed the debt from the loan agreement. When second buyer defaulted, lender brought suit for the debt. The remote buyer argued that he could not be personally liable to lender for the debt because his predecessor in title took only subject to the debt and was not personally liable for that debt. *Held:* The remote buyer was personally liable to lender for the debt. A person should do that which he promises to do, and generally the courts will enforce a promise if it is supported by consideration. If there is valid consideration for a promise, it does not matter from whom it moved. The beneficiary of a contract made between other parties for his benefit may maintain an action against promisor on the contract. *Somers v. Avant*, 261 SE2d 334 (1979).

Massachusetts Purchaser bought a home subject to a prior mortgage. At the time of purchase, he was not aware of a home improvement loan outstanding from the same mortgagee. After paying the loan under protest to obtain discharge of the mortgage, he sued mortgagee for reimbursement of the loan amount, contending that he had no actual knowledge of the loan, and the mortgage priority existed only as long as the property was owned by the original borrower. *Held:* Mortgagee was entitled to mortgage security from subsequent purchaser. Under Massachusetts Gen. L. ch. 183, § 28A, the aggregate amount of the outstanding balances of a home mortgage and subsequent home improvement loan at any one time cannot exceed the amount originally secured by the mortgage. So the principal amount of the mortgage as recorded informs the subsequent purchaser of the limit of indebtedness, and puts him on inquiry to investigate the existence of an intervening loan. The law protects subsequent purchaser against liability for amounts advanced by mortgagee in excess of the original loan. *Zaltman v. Melrose Sav. Bank*, 389 NE2d 1039 (App. Ct. 1979).

Wisconsin Mortgage provided for acceleration if the property was conveyed without lender's consent. Mortgagor sold the property without lender's consent and without notice to it, and two and a half years later, lender elected to accelerate and foreclose. *Held:* Under Wisconsin's lien theory of mortgages, buyer had acquired equitable title subject to both mortgagor-seller's legal title and the lien of the lender's mortgage. The acceleration clause itself did not violate public policy, but the validity of its use in a given case depends on whether such would be equitable. If so, it would be enforceable as a contractual condition of a note and mortgage. *Mutual Fed. Sav. & Loan Ass'n v. Wisconsin Wire Works*, 205 NW2d 762 (1973).

117.20 Wraparound Mortgages

Texas A townhouse was sold, subject to a deed of trust. This deed of trust secured a note that contained a due-on-sale clause previously executed by sellers. The contract for sale provided that buyer would observe all of the obligations under the deed of trust, "excepting the covenant for the payment of the note secured thereby." It was agreed that buyer would make monthly payments to seller, who would make the monthly payments on the note secured by the deed of trust. When the noteholder learned of the sale, it demanded immediate payment of the entire outstanding indebtedness, but neither buyer nor seller was willing to pay the accelerated amount. The noteholder foreclosed under the deed of trust, and buyer sued seller for damages. *Held:* Seller had a contractual duty to pay the accelerated indebtedness. Buyer was entitled to the return of her $20,000 down payment plus attorney fees as compensation for seller's breach of contract. *Lyons v. Montgomery*, 701 SW2d 641 (1985).

118.00 PRIORITIES

118.05 General Rule

4th Circuit Mortgagee, who was owed $360,000, held a second mortgage on debtor's property. When debtor went into bankruptcy, trustee collected rents but failed to make payments on the mortgage. Mortgagee sued for the accrued rent. The question before the court was whether the bankrupt estate or mortgagee was entitled to rents realized from mortgaged property between the time of mortgagor's bankruptcy and foreclosure of the mortgage. *Held:* Recognizing that there is a split among the circuits, the Fourth Circuit adopted the view that mortgagee was not entitled to the rents. The court pointed out that under state law mortgagee must first take possession in order to fix his rights to the rents. Thus, mortgagee is entitled to recover the rental income during the bankruptcy administration only if he has petitioned the bankruptcy court for a sequestration order, obtained the appointment of a receiver to collect the rents, or secured the court's consent to foreclosure. *Golden Enters. Inc. v. United States*, 566 F2d 1207 (1977), aff'd, 440 US 48 (1979).

Alabama Plaintiff landowner borrowed $6,000 from a relative and executed a mortgage on two lots as security for the debt. The agreement included a dragnet clause covering any other debt secured by the mortgage. It also included a defeasance clause, which provided that the conveyance would become null and void if the note were paid in full. Plaintiff subsequently borrowed an additional $32,000 from the relative, who died before either loan was repaid. Her executor attempted to foreclose on the mortgage and claimed the dragnet clause made the property security for the entire debt. Plaintiff asserted that the defeasance clause made the mortgage void once the $6,000 was paid off. *Held:* The dragnet and defeasance clauses, when read together, did not show an explicit intent to cover additional loans. The purpose of the defeasance clause was to identify the conditions under which the mortgage was to cease being security for the debt. The court concluded that the mortgage applied only to the $6,000 loan. *Underwood v. Jarvis*, 358 So. 2d 731 (1978).

Florida Borrower executed a loan agreement with lender that provided that borrower would not encumber or transfer the real property described in the agreement without lender's consent. Borrower later transferred the property without lender's consent to a third party, who executed a mortgage on the property in favor of the bank. When third party defaulted on the mortgage, the bank sued to foreclose on the property. Lender claimed a superior interest because of the original agreement. *Held:* Lender did not have a superior interest. The agreement not to transfer the property merely constituted evidence of intent to create an equitable lien. It did not create such a lien. *Manatee Fed. Sav. & Loan Ass'n v. Pace*, 378 So. 2d 95 (1979).

Georgia Two days before a divorce hearing was scheduled, another judge granted default judgment in favor of bank against husband and imposed a lien of $125,000 against husband's real property. This lien was purportedly effective 11 months before the default judgment. The judge in the divorce action consolidated the cases, set aside the $125,000 judgment, granted the wife a special lien of $15,000 on marital property, and awarded bank a new judgment for $125,000. Bank appealed. *Held:* Divorce judge was justified in setting aside the $125,000 judgment, because bank had not asked for the extraordinary relief of an antedated lien. Because the first judgment was set aside, wife's lien was superior to the bank's. *First Nat'l Bank v. Blackburn*, 329 SE2d 897 (1985).

Kansas A foreclosed property was subject to two mortgages. The first mortgage had a dragnet clause, securing two advances made after the second mortgage was executed. The second mortgagee claimed that its mortgage had priority over the advances. *Held:* The advances were secured under the first mortgage and had priority over the second mortgage to the extent that they, together with the sum owing from the original advance, did not exceed the amount originally advanced. For a debt to be secured under a dragnet clause, either the note must state that the debt is secured by the prior mortgage or the debt must be of the same kind or character. Although the advances here did not meet the second requirement, they did meet the first. *First Nat'l Bank v. Fink*, 736 P2d 909 (1987).

Louisiana Tenant signed a lease, which he never recorded, to a suite in a medical plaza. He later signed and recorded a second lease on a neighboring suite. The leases expressly provided that they were subordinate to any mortgage lien placed on the plaza. The owner of the plaza placed a mortgage on the property. After the mortgage was foreclosed, purchaser bought the plaza at a judicial sale and brought an eviction action against tenant. *Held:* Tenant could be evicted. While tenant may not have realized the legal consequences of consenting to the subordination provision, it constituted an unambiguous stipulation in which he surrendered his superior position to all mortgages. Therefore, one could not reasonably infer from its language that an additional contract was necessary before subordination became effective. *TD Bickham Corp. v. Hebert*, 432 So. 2d 228 (1982).

Minnesota Father and son were majority owners of bank. As part of a divorce settlement, son's wife was given the family farm and $257,705 in lieu of her share of bank stock, but the judgment did not give rise to a judgment lien, nor did the court make provisions to secure the judgment on wife's behalf. During the divorce action, son granted a mortgage on the farm to bank, which was recorded. He also borrowed $100,000 from father, secured by the stock. Subsequently, the court filed an order for judgment requiring son to pay

$100,000 to wife and $232,705 over the next 10 years. The judgment was secured on all of son's stock and real estate. Wife brought an action to determine the priority of the various liens against son's property. *Held:* Father's and bank's valid security interests in the property took priority over wife's judicial lien granted later in time. There is no exception to this general rule based either on equitable principles or the fact that father and bank had actual notice of the divorce proceedings. The undocketed and unperfected judgment did not give rise to an interest in the property of which father and son had notice. Bad faith could not be imputed to appellants merely because a business and family relationship existed between the parties. However, because the money judgment awarded to wife was intended to reflect the value of the shares of stock originally awarded to her, wife had judicial lien of first priority as to those shares. *Oldewurtel v. Redding*, 421 NW2d 722 (1988).

Montana Judgment of foreclosure of a mortgage specifically excepted a prior indebtedness for which the same defendant had executed a trust indenture naming a third party as beneficiary. The said trust indenture described the same 7.1 acres of real property as the mortgage and was recorded prior to the mortgage. The trial court found that the trust indenture constituted a first lien on the property and was not affected by the foreclosure proceedings. *Held:* The purported trust indenture was not a statutory trust indenture as contemplated by Montana law, since the Small Tract Financing Act governing trust indenture at that time authorized transfers in trust of real estate of not more than three acres. In addition, although the defective trust indenture would be enforced between the parties as an equitable mortgage, the lien of such defective indenture was subordinate to the claims of subsequent encumbrances and of judgment creditors who extended credit subsequent to the date of the instrument without actual knowledge of the existence of the indenture. *Amsterdam Lumber, Inc. v. Dyksterhouse*, 586 P2d 705 (1978).

South Carolina Landowner issued a mortgage, which was recorded, to a senior mortgagee as security for an existing indebtedness and for all future advances. Subsequently, landowner issued a mortgage to junior mortgagee. This second lien was also recorded. Junior mortgagee contended that senior mortgagee made additional advances to landowner with actual and constructive knowledge of the junior lien; hence, the junior lien should be held superior. *Held:* Under state law (S.C. Code § 45-55), a holder of a mortgage with a provision for future advances retains his priority as to all future advances made as against a junior or subsequent lienholder even though such advances are made after prior lienholders receive actual notice. *McMillen Feed Mills, Inc. v. Mayer*, 220 SE2d 221 (1975).

Virginia After divorce, husband failed to satisfy judgment for spousal support. Subsequently, husband settled a preexisting debt by giving creditor a deed of trust, conveying his one-half interest in real property owned in common with wife. Creditor recorded the deed without examining the land records, from which creditor could have learned of the docketed judgments in wife's favor. Wife's attorney mistakenly released all judgments. Two months later, husband conveyed his interest in the property to creditor in satisfaction of the deed of trust. Subsequently, wife's judgment was reinstated and she sought adjudication of the interests in the property. *Held:* For the wife. A lien that has been released through a mistake will be restored except if the restoration prejudices the rights of a bona fide purchaser for value without notice. Creditor had constructive notice of wife's judgment when deed of trust was recorded. Because creditor claimed not to have known of the judgment, creditor could not have known that it had been released, and relied on the release when deciding to accept husband's conveyance. Thus creditor was neither a bona fide purchaser without notice nor a party who detrimentally relied on the mistaken release. *Fox v. Templeton*, 329 SE2d 6 (1985).

118.10 Statutory Modification

Texas First National held a prior deed of trust on certain apartments. Whirlpool had supplied and installed appliances, for which it had perfected statutory materialman's liens. Subsequent to the perfection of Whirlpool's lien, First National foreclosed and bought the property, later reselling it to another party. Whirlpool claimed priority and sought permission to remove and sell the appliances to satisfy its lien. *Held:* The materialman's lien statute was intended to encompass realty and such personal property as has been incorporated in or consumed in construction or repair or delivered for such purposes. Accordingly, garbage disposal units and dishwashers were subject to the materialman's lien but refrigerators and ranges were not. *First Nat'l Bank v. Whirlpool Corp.*, 517 SW2d 262 (1974).

West Virginia Lot owner took out two initial trust deeds to begin construction and then made an oral agreement with a plumber. Subsequently, owner executed several other trust deeds on the property, interspersed with oral contracts with materialmen. When two materialmen sought to enforce their mechanic's liens, the issue of priorities between the beneficiaries of the trust deeds and the materialmen arose. *Held:* The order of priority was the two initial trust deeds, the mechanic's and materialmen's liens, and finally the deeds made after construction began. Under Virginia law, general contractors' and subcontractors' liens ordinarily have priority over trust deeds executed after the commencement of work, and materialmen generally have priority over the liens of the contractors; so materialmen should have priority over deeds of trust made after work begins where there are no general contractors and subcontractors. The properly perfected liens of all materialmen and mechanics should date from the time the first mechanic began work or furnished materials and should be of equal priority. *Carolina Lumber Co. v. Cunningham*, 192 SE2d 722 (1972).

118.15 Subordination Agreements

1st Circuit A corporation that owned a restaurant wrote a promissory note for $120,000 and issued a mortgage on the restaurant to secure the note, both of which were eventually assigned to CLIC for $1.00. The corporation, however, did not then borrow the money. Later, Paramount agreed to lend FFSI $30,000 for the restaurant, which it did by writing checks to CLIC. The corporation later became insolvent, and the Small Business Administration (SBA) erroneously paid the full amount of the promissory note ($120,000) to CLIC. An action was brought to determine who was entitled to the $30,000 overpayment on the promissory note. *Held:* Paramount could recover. Since Paramount intended to advance the money to the corporation against the previously executed promissory note and mortgage, Paramount was an assignee of the mortgage. The note and mortgage issued by the restaurant constituted a promise to repay any money CLIC or its assignees advanced to the corporation. *CLIC & Co. v. Goldfarb*, 838 F2d 32 (1988).

Alaska A land sale contract was executed whereby buyer agreed to pay cash and assume sellers' debts equal to approximately one-third the purchase price, with sellers taking back a mortgage on the remainder. The contract provided that sellers agreed to subordinate their lien to a loan to be obtained by buyer for the purpose of developing the land. No further details were stated. After disputes arose, sellers refused to perform, and buyer sued for specific performance. *Held:* For sellers. Although the contract was sufficiently certain to bind the parties legally, the contract did not adequately secure buyer's performance to allow the equitable remedy of specific performance. The subordination clause did not limit the amount of the loan to which sellers subordinated, limit the interest rate or the pay period, or describe the method of repayment. The absence of such provisions failed to provide sellers with adequate security to assure the court that a decree of specific performance would not place an unfair risk of developer's failure upon sellers. *Stenehjem v. Kin Jin Cho*, 631 P2d 482 (1981).

Georgia Plaintiffs sold plot of land to developer, thinking that developer's construction of a shopping center on the land would increase the value of their remaining property. Most of the purchase price was secured by a promissory note and a mortgage on the plot. The mortgage instrument provided that plaintiffs' lien was subordinate to the lien of developer's construction loan covering the property. Each plaintiff signed a subordination agreement, providing consideration of $1 to plaintiffs. When developer defaulted on the construction loan and lender instituted foreclosure proceedings, plaintiffs sought to have the subordination agreements set aside for lack of consideration. *Held:* The subordination agreements did not require independent consideration because they were intended to fulfill plaintiffs' obligation in the mortgage agreement to waive their lien's seniority. The prospect of the enhanced value of plantiffs' remaining property was sufficient consideration to subordinate their senior lien. *Cameron v. Churchill Mortgage Corp.*, 290 SE2d 474 (1982).

Maryland By agreement with borrowers, sellers subordinated their purchase-money deeds of trust to the lien and secured a SBA loan for construction or repair purposes. The subordination agreement did not contain a clause conditioning subordination upon the borrowers' using the SBA loan proceeds for construction or repair; the borrowers used the loan for another purpose. They executed the deeds of trust upon the properties in favor of the SBA to secure repayment of the SBA loan, and they defaulted on that loan. Following a petition to foreclose, sellers intervened as defendants and counterclaimed for a declaration that their purchase-money deeds of trust were entitled to first lien status. *Held:* Sellers' purchase-money deeds of trust did not have priority. In the cases sellers cited, the court noted that subordination was conditional by implication only because of a condition expressed in the agreement's subordination clause of the agreement. Since the instant agreement contained no such subordination clause, sellers' purchase-money deeds of trust were not entitled to first lien status. *Rickhill v. United States*, 418 A2d 197 (1980).

Pennsylvania Landowners sold a tract of land to developer and took back a purchase-money mortgage, which provided for subordination to the lien of any mortgage subsequently given to developer for the purpose of developing the property. Landowners executed a power of attorney authorizing title insurance company to act for them in subordinating their mortgage. Developer obtained a loan commitment from banks and requested that title insurer exercise its power of attorney to subordinate landowners' mortgage to the new financing lien. Landowners sought to enjoin title insurer from subordinating, because developer was in default on their mortgage and they feared developer would use the proceeds of the new loan to pay its general debts rather than for development purposes. *Held:* Title insurer was enjoined from subordinating landowners' mortgage. The banks were not innocent parties with a right to priority of their lien based on their reliance on the power of attorney. The restriction on subordination imposed by landowners' mortgage was a matter of record of which the banks had constructive notice. The case was remanded to determine whether the new loan had a development purpose. *Fierst v. Commonwealth Title Ins. Co.*, 451 A2d 674 (1982).

118.20 Over Mechanic's Liens

1st Circuit Housing project developer defaulted on a mortgage insured by the Department of Housing and Urban Development (HUD), and lender assigned the mortgage to HUD. Title insurance company warranted as to the mortgage's priority over subsequently recorded liens. Subcontractor claimed its mechanic's lien had priority over the mortgage since it was executed first. Under federal common law, the first to record has priority. The bank and title insurance company sued for a declaration that the government's mortgage lien was entitled to priority over subcontractor's mechanic's lien. *Held:* The mechanic's lien had priority. Applying the balancing test set forth in *United States v. Kimbell Foods, Inc.*, 440 US 715 (1979) with respect to choice of law in the absence of federal statute, the court held that a national rule was unnecessary to protect the interests of the federal government and to prevent commercial disruption and adopted Maine law as the federal rule of decision. *Chicago Title Ins. Co. v. Sherred Village Ass'n*, 708 F2d 804 (1983).

Delaware A mortgage company had given a construction loan, secured by a mortgage, to mortgagor, who was acting as his own contractor. Progress payment advances were to be made to subcontractors at specific stages after mortgagee's agent had approved the work done. The agent gave approval for work that had not actually been done, exhausting the loan before a subcontractor had been paid (Although this subcontractor's work was completed before that of other subcontractors who were paid). When mortgagee foreclosed, subcontractor intervened, claiming priority for his mechanic's lien, for which he had obtained a default judgment. *Held:* Subcontractor's mechanic's lien had priority over subsequent construction loan advances. The advances made after subcontractor had begun work were optional in that they were not required to be paid until mortgagee had approved the work done. Mortgagee had constructive knowledge of the status of the work and wrongfully paid others after subcontractor's lien attached. *JI Kislak Mortgage Corp. v. William Matthews, Builder, Inc.*, 303 A2d 648 (1973).

Minnesota Bank issued a $25,000 loan for the construction of a barn, secured by a mortgage on borrower's land. A few years later, borrower obtained a $180,000 loan from the bank for further construction. Several mechanic's liens on the property had been filed after the first mortgage but before the second mortgage. Bank claimed that because the first mortgage was paid off with proceeds of the second mortgage, equitable subrogation should be applied to give the bank priority over the mechanic's liens. *Held:* Equitable subrogation should not be applied, because the bank had not acted under an excusable mistake of fact and granting the bank priority would harm the innocent mechanic's lien holders. Bank's failure to consider potential priority conflicts and to obtain subordination agreements from contractors or materialmen was deemed not excusable. *Carl H. Peterson Co. v. Zero Estates*, 261 NW2d 346 (1977).

New York Owner executed a mortgage to developer to secure payment for improvements developer constructed on owner's lots. After the mortgage was recorded, a contractor installed flooring in houses on the lots and was unpaid. After owner defaulted on the mortgage and foreclosure proceedings were instituted, the flooring contractor filed a mechanic's lien. Contractor argued that the mortgage was a subterfuge to avoid the lien law, and that developer-mortgagee's claim should be subordinate to lienor's. *Held:* The prior recorded mortgage had priority over the subsequently filed mechanic's lien. Although a mortgage knowingly made to avoid the lien law is void against a lien in existence at the time the mortgage was created, here the lien did not exist when the mortgage was executed. Although developer's improvements were covered by the lien law, the mortgage was valid and could not be treated as a lien. *WL Dev. Corp. v. Trifort Realty, Inc.*, 377 NE2d 969 (1978).

North Carolina A deed of trust was executed to secure a note for construction of a motel. Trustees sued to foreclose on the deeds. The general contractor for construction of the motel, one of defendants in the action, asserted that his lien was superior to the deed of trust. *Held:* The deed of trust was superior to the contractor's lien. The general contractor had waived the materialman's lien as consideration for execution of the note and, therefore, did not take priority over the deed of trust. *Miller v. Lemon Tree Inn Inc.*, 249 SE2d 836 (1978).

Ohio Mortgagors signed an open-end mortgage under which mortgagee agreed to make periodic advances up to $2 million for the construction of an apartment complex, provided that mortgagors were not in default. The mortgage was recorded, and mortgagee made 13 advances and then started foreclosure proceedings when mortgagors defaulted. During the interim between the last two advances, subcontractors performed work for mortgagors but failed to file mechanic's liens. The trial court found mortgagee had actual notice of these liens, and ruled that lienors were entitled to priority. *Held:* Reversed. Obligatory advances under open-end mortgages have priority over subsequent liens, regardless of whether lender has notice of them. In this case, mortgagee was contractually obligated to make advances and had no discretion over whether to do so. Thus, it was entitled to priority over the mechanic's liens. *Colonial Mortgage Serv. Co. v. Southard*, 384 NE2d 250 (1978).

Utah On June 14, 1978, mortgagee conveyed real property to mortgagor by warranty deed, and mortgagor executed and delivered a purchase-money mortgage to mortgagee. The mortgage was not recorded until June 27. In the intervening period, mortgagor hired a contractor to perform work on the building. No mechanics' liens were filed as a result of the work. After the mortgage was recorded, mortgagor hired a second contractor to do additional work. The second contractor filed a mechanic's lien. In an action to determine priority, second contractor claimed its lien should relate back to the work performed by the original contractor prior to recording of the mortgage. *Held:* For mortgagee. Tacking of a lien onto an earlier time when work was performed on the property by a different contractor can occur only if both projects were performed under a common plan. There was no evidence the projects were part of the same improvement plan, but rather, were ordinary maintenance work. *Calder Bros. Co. v. Anderson*, 652 P2d 922 (1982).

118.25
Purchase-Money Mortgages

Nebraska A judgment lien for child support attached to McNally's present and after-acquired property. Subsequently, he purchased land to be financed by plaintiff. McNally signed a note to plaintiff and executed a mortgage. The note stated that the funds were advanced to purchase the land, and the deed and mortgage were recorded. McNally later conveyed the property to the Robinsons, who executed a new blanket mortgage to plaintiff and a release of the McNally mortgage; the release and new mortgage were recorded. When the Robinsons defaulted on the blanket mortgage, plaintiff brought foreclosure proceedings, naming McNally and the Robinsons as defendants. McNally's ex-wife intervened, claiming her child support lien had priority over plaintiff's blanket mortgage. She alleged that the release extinguished both the McNally mortgage and its previous purchase-money status. *Held:* For plaintiff. Under Nebraska law, a purchase-money mortgage has priority over judgment liens. The McNally mortgage was a purchase-money mortgage because the note stated that the funds were advanced for the purpose of purchasing the tract. The release and new blanket mortgage continued the McNally mortgage because the mortgages were part of the same transaction and the parties were ignorant of the intervening lien. *Commerce Sav. Lincoln, Inc. v. Robinson*, 331 NW2d 495 (1983).

Utah Plaintiffs sold real estate and took back a purchase-money deed of trust from buyers. At the time of conveyance, plaintiffs knew of outstanding judgments against buyers, including one by the state for unpaid child support. When buyers defaulted on the loan, plaintiffs brought foreclosure proceedings. At issue was whether the exception giving tax liens priority over purchase-money mortgages could be extended to a judgment for unpaid child support. *Held:* For plaintiffs. The crucial factor was the reliance of the lienholder on the underlying security. While a purchase-money mortgagee would be concerned with the real property as collateral, a judgment lienor would not necessarily look to the property, especially where the property was purchased after the judgment was entered. The court refused to extend the exception for tax liens to judgments for child support payments. *Nelson v. Stoker*, 669 P2d 390 (1983).

119.00
FORECLOSURE

119.05
Nonjudicial Foreclosure

11th Circuit Plaintiff appellants in class action were Alabama residents who had borrowed from the Farmers Home Administration (FmHA) under the Housing Act of 1949 (42 USC § 1472). Alabama allows nonjudicial foreclosure. Plaintiffs had either had their homes foreclosed, or had sought to prevent foreclosure. The class action challenged nonjudicial foreclosure on due process and equal protection grounds. A motion for a preliminary injunction to prevent foreclosure was denied. *Held:* Reversed. All requirements for a preliminary injunction were present, including likelihood of success on the merits. Plaintiffs, holders of FmHA loans, had a property interest protected by the due process clause of the Fifth Amendment, which includes a meaningful opportunity to contest an adverse action. However, aspects of administrative procedure might very well not satisfy due process requirements, such as possible bias on the part of the hearing officer. As to the claim of violation of equal protection rights, the FmHA had entered into a consent decree in Georgia that provided that all FmHA loans there were to be foreclosed through judicial process. This raised the likelihood that plaintiffs would prevail on the equal protection issue. *Johnson v. United States Dep't of Agriculture*, 734 F2d 774 (1984).

U.S. District Court, California After purchasing a home with a Veteran's Administration (VA) loan, buyer became unable to make monthly payments. Mortgagee rejected his offer to pay half his unemployment insurance benefits on the loan. The VA representative told buyer the agency was powerless to help. Buyer subsequently found a job and wanted to resume full monthly payments, but the mortgage company claimed that the VA would not allow forbearance on a loan more than four months in default. When buyer's home was sold in a nonjudicial foreclosure sale, buyer sought relief in federal court. *Held:* Foreclosure should be set aside. The VA is empowered to refund to a private lender the unpaid balance of a loan and receive an assignment of the debt. The VA can then grant forbearance to borrower. Since the VA's rules imposed mandatory legal duties on private lenders and on the agency to avoid foreclosure of VA-guaranteed home loans, the VA and lender were remiss in failing to arrange an assignment of the debt. *Rank v. Cleland*, 460 F. Supp. 920 (CD 1978).

Alaska Counsellors bought commercial property from Conrad, and gave him a note secured by a second deed of trust. Counsellors stopped making payments on the note, and Conrad sued for a judgment on the note. The lower court granted Counsellors summary judgment. Conrad appealed, filing a complaint for judicial foreclosure and a deficiency judgment after the lower court removed language in its judgment, which precluded judicial foreclosure. Counsellors made a motion to dismiss, arguing that the lower court decision precluded the subsequent claim, which was denied; and the supreme court agreed to review the denial of motion to dismiss. *Held:* Conrad did not agree to limit his remedy to nonjudicial foreclosure. A secured creditor generally has the option to sue on the note or foreclose the security, unless there is an agreement that limits the remedy. The note in issue stated that Counsellors' party "promises to pay" the sum owed and did not indicate that Counsellors would be relieved of payment in the event of default. Likewise, the trust deed did not expressly preclude a suit on the note. Therefore, Conrad had the right to sue on the note as well as foreclose the security. *Conrad v. Counsellors Inv. Co.*, 751 P2d 10 (1988).

California Owner sold his property to a new owner, who wished to assume the underlying mortgage. The mortgage contained a due-on-sale provision, however, and mortgagee demanded that the entire sum due and owing be paid. When new owner balked, mortgagee followed the applicable state law and began a nonjudicial foreclosure. New owner brought suit, claiming that the state law violated due process under both the U.S. and California Constitutions. At a minimum, he argued, there should be a prior court hearing. *Held:* If mortgagee were proceeding under color of state law to interfere with the traditional right to a prior hearing, then the statute being challenged would have to be struck down. However, the court refused to find "state action," and held instead that morgagee's foreclosure was based primarily on the express terms of the mortgage. The law permitted nonjudicial foreclosure, but only when clearly agreed to by mortgagor. Thus, the court characterized mortgagee's action as based primarily on the underlying contract, rather than on the statute. Purely private conduct and agreements, no matter how arbitrary or discriminatory, are not forbidden under either the U.S. or California Constitution. *Garfinkle v. Superior Court*, 578 P2d 925 (1978).

Washington A trustee in a deed of trust foreclosure action knew that grantors had an action pending against his client, grantee of the deed, and that grantors believed their action halted foreclosure proceedings. Nonetheless, trustee initiated foreclosure and sold grantors' home for $11,784, the amount grantee was due, although the home was worth between $200,000 and $300,000. Grantors successfully sued to have the sale set aside. *Held:* Affirmed. Washington's nonjudicial foreclosure procedure prohibits foreclosure if an action is pending on a debt secured by the deed of trust. Since the trustee knew of grantors' action when he initiated foreclosure, the sale was void. Moreover, trustee's actions alone, along with the grossly inadequate purchase price, were enough to void the sale. A stringent fiduciary duty is imposed upon trustee in a nonjudicial foreclosure; he must act impartially for both grantee and grantor and avoid sacrifice of grantor's property. *Cox v. Helenius*, 693 P2d 683 (1985) (en banc).

119.10 Strict Foreclosure

6th Circuit Federal National Mortgage Association foreclosed plaintiff's mortgage pursuant to the Michigan statute regulating foreclosure by advertisement. The property was sold at a sheriff's sale, and mortgagor failed to redeem the property within the statutory redemption period. Mortgagor sued to set aside the mortgage foreclosure on the ground that the Michigan foreclosure by advertisement statute violated the due process clause of the Fourteenth Amendment. *Held:* The statute authorizing foreclosure by advertisement, the actions of sheriff and registrar of deed, and the conduct of mortgagee did not constitute state action. There was therefore no violation of the due process clause. *Northrigs v. Federal Nat'l Mortgage Ass'n*, 527 F2d 23 (1975).

Illinois Where the mortgage company applied for a common-law strict foreclosure against defendant's property and for appointment of a receiver pendente lite to collect rents and profits from it, the lower court issued a default judgment but held that strict foreclosure had been made unavailable by Ill. Rev. Stat. 1957 ch. 77, §§ 18(c), 18(d). *Held:* Reversed. The statute's provisions neither expressly nor impliedly voided the strict foreclosure remedy, which obviated the necessity for judicial sale. *Great Lakes Mortgage Corp. v. Callymore*, 302 NE2d 248 (App. Ct. 1973).

119.15 Necessary Parties

California A borrower executed a promissory note that was secured by a purchase-money trust deed. When borrower failed to make payments, one cobeneficiary of the trust deed proposed that the widow of the other cobeneficiary join him in executing a notice of default. When she refused, he proceeded to institute a foreclosure and later bought the property at the foreclosure sale through an agent. When the agent brought an action to quiet title, a third party intervened, attacking the foreclosure as invalid since the cobeneficiary's widow had not consented to it. *Held:* The cobeneficiary who bought the property was entitled to quiet title. The foreclosure action was valid, even without the consent of the cobeneficiary's widow, since the cobeneficiaries of the trust deed were tenants in common in beneficial interest under the note and deed. As such, one beneficiary was entitled to protect the common beneficial interest on his own. *Perkins v. Chad Dev. Corp.*, 157 Cal. Rptr. 201 (Ct. App. 1979).

New York Plaintiff and his wife jointly held mortgages on land owned by defendants. Plaintiff's wife died and, on November 17, 1981, executors of her will were appointed. Defendants failed to make a mortgage payment due on October 1, 1981, within the grace period provided for in the mortgages. Plaintiff, in his name only, commenced foreclosure proceedings and served defendants with a summons and complaint on December 2, 1981. Defendants' offer on December 31, 1981, to pay the overdue installment was rejected by plaintiff. On January 24, 1982, defendants deposited the payment with the court clerk. Two days later, plaintiff filed an amended complaint, which joined his wife's executors as additional plaintiffs. Defendants moved for dismissal of the complaint on the ground that the offer to pay the amount in arrears had occurred before a valid election to accelerate the mortgage debt. *Held:* Commencement of the foreclosure action by plaintiff alone on December 2, 1981, did not constitute a valid election to accelerate. If a mortgage is owned by two persons jointly, one of them alone cannot elect to accelerate it. A valid election to accelerate the mortgage did not occur until January 26, 1982, by which time defendants had cured their default. *Lapidus v. Kollel Avreichim Torah Veyirah*, 451 NYS2d 958 (Sup. Ct. 1982).

119.20
Notice

U.S. Supreme Court Plaintiff made a loan and took a mortgage on the property. Without plaintiff's knowledge, the property was sold by the state of Indiana for unpaid taxes. Indiana required notice of a tax sale to be given by posting and by publication. The owner was given notice by certified mail, but there was no requirement of notice to mortgagees. Plaintiff, who was owed money on the mortgage, did not learn of the sale until the statutory redemption period had passed. Plaintiff argued it had not received constitutionally adequate notice. *Held:* Notice to plaintiff was inadequate under the due process clause of the Fourteenth Amendment. Notice via publication and posting was not reasonably calculated to apprise plaintiff of the sale and afford it an opportunity to present objections as required by *Mullane v. Central Hanover Bank & Trust Co.*, 339 US 306 (1950). Personal service or notice by mail was required. *Mennonite Bd. of Missions v. Adams*, 462 US 791 (1983).

9th Circuit The Federal Housing Administration (FHA) guaranteed plaintiff's loan for renovating a hospital she owned. When plaintiff defaulted, the FHA paid lender the balance, and lender conveyed its interest in the property to the FHA. The property was sold at foreclosure for well below market value. Plaintiff sought a temporary restraining order against the sale on the ground that the FHA's failure to notify her in writing violated due process. *Held:* For the FHA. Plaintiff's lack of formal notice of the sale did not matter, because it was clear she had actual notice.

She had asked the FHA several times to delay the sale and her suit was brought immediately after the sale, attesting to her knowledge. A due process claim could not be based on the meaningless formality of written, rather than oral, notice. *Lehner v. United States*, 685 F2d 1187 (1982), cert. denied, 460 US 1039 (1983).

Alaska After assignment, a property remained subject to two deeds of trust: one executed by purchasers, as assignees, in favor of assignors and one executed by assignors in favor of a third party. Purchasers made regular payments for seven years, but assignors fell into default on their deed of trust. When the property was foreclosed under the first deed of trust, trustee sent notice to all record interest holders, as required by statute. However, purchasers had moved in the seven years since recording their deed of trust and had not notified trustee. When the notice to purchasers was returned as undeliverable, trustee made no further attempt to locate them and went ahead with the foreclosure sale. Purchasers learned of the foreclosure sale six months later and sued to set it aside. *Held:* For purchasers. The court interpreted Alaska Stat. § 34.20.070(c), which requires trustee to mail a notice of default to "the last known address" of, inter alia, grantor's successors in interest, as requiring trustee to exercise due diligence to determine the address most likely to give the affected party notice and to treat that as the last known address. Purchasers still lived in the Anchorage area, and could have readily been located by a diligent trustee. *Rosenberg v. Smidt*, 727 P2d 778 (1986).

Delaware Holders of equitable title to real property acquired at a tax sale were not given notice of either a mortgage foreclosure proceeding or a sheriff's sale. *Held:* Holders of equitable title had a significant property interest and therefore a due process right to prior notice of a foreclosure proceeding involving that property. *Gelof v. First Nat'l Bank*, 373 A2d 206 (1977).

Massachusetts Plaintiff was deeded land in Plymouth in 1923. The deed was duly recorded and listed her address in West Newton. In 1966, the town made a purported tax taking of the land for failure to pay a 1965 tax bill of $16.29, which had been mailed to her in Plymouth. When she discovered the taking in 1972, she sought declaratory relief since she had never lived in Plymouth and the tax collector had failed to comply with state law (Mass. Gen. Laws, ch. 60, § 16), requiring him to send a demand for payment of taxes "to the address best known" to him. The tax collector countered that plaintiff failed to give notice of her address to the town clerk pursuant to state law (Mass. Gen. L. ch. 60, § 39). *Held:* Plaintiff's failure to advise the town of her new address would have justified the use of her address appearing in the 1923 deed, but it could not diminish the "best known address" safeguard of Section 16. *Bartevian v. Cullen*, 343 NE2d 851 (1976).

New Jersey Landowner questioned the constitutionality of an in rem foreclosure act providing for notice by publication and posting where the name and address of the owner appear on the tax rolls. *Held:* The provision was unconstitutional as a denial of due process under both federal and state constitutions. Where the name and address are known, the owner must receive notice by mail before his right to redeem his property may be foreclosed. *Township of Montville v. Block 69.*, Lot 10, 376 A2d 921 (1977).

New York After mortgagor had been in default on mortgage payments for several years, mortgagee brought a foreclosure action. After mortgagee's motion for summary judgment was granted, mortgagee mailed copies of the foreclosure judgment and notice of sale to mortgagor's attorney. In addition, as required by New York's Real Property Actions and Proceedings Law, copies of the notice of sale were posted in the towns where the property was located and where the sale was to occur. Notice was also published in a local newspaper for four successive weeks. Despite mortgagee's publication efforts, mortgagor claimed she had not learned of the sale until after it had occurred, and that her attorney never received notice of the judgment or the sale. Mortgagor argued that the sale should have been set aside because she was not personally notified of it. *Held:* Publication of notice, and not personal service, was all that the Real Property Actions and Proceedings Law required. The service of notice by mail was authorized by N.Y. Civ. Prac. L8R 2103, and was effective whether or not actually received by addressee. *White v. Magee*, 446 NYS2d 453 (1981).

Texas Mortgagors financed their home through holder under a deed of trust that contained an acceleration clause that obligated lender to send prior notice to borrower specifying the breach and stating that failure to cure would result in acceleration of the loan. The deed also required notice to borrower of the right to reinstate and to bring a lawsuit. When mortgagors defaulted, notice of foreclosure was sent to mortgagors, but it did not mention their rights to reinstate or bring a lawsuit. Mortgagors sued for wrongful foreclosure. *Held:* For holder. The supreme court cited *University Savings Ass'n v. Springwoods Shopping Center*, 644 SW2d 705 (1982), where a foreclosure sale was upheld despite noncompliance with a recording provision. In *University Savings*, the court found that where no prejudice resulted from failure to comply with a provision in the deed of trust, borrower's action for wrongful foreclosure was barred. Therefore, the court found that actual notice of a right to reinstate and bring a lawsuit was sufficient. *Jaspar Fed. Sav. & Loan Ass'n v. Reddell*, 730 SW2d 672 (1987).

Washington The city foreclosed on two properties for failure to pay assessments. Under former Wash. Rev. Code § 35.50.090, notice of the city's foreclosure suit was given by publication. Notices of delinquency—but not of foreclosure or sale—had been mailed, but were sent to a wrong address. Landowners did not receive notice of right of redemption, right to claim a homestead, or right to demand an upset price. Landowners sued for quiet title, alleging inadequate notice and violation of due process under 42 USC § 1983. *Held:* For landowners. *Mullane v. Central Hanover Bank & Trust Co.*, 339 US 306 (1950) held that due process requires notice reasonably calculated to inform parties of proceedings that directly and adversely affect their legally protected interests. Failure to mail notice of the actual foreclosure proceedings to landowners was a violation of due process. Because of the violation of their civil rights, landowners were entitled to damages and attorney fees, as well as to quiet title. *Brown v. Wells*, 690 P2d 1144 (1984) (en banc).

119.25 Defenses

3d Circuit After a lender obtained a foreclosure judgment against debtors, their house was sold at a sheriff's sale. Subsequently, debtors filed a Chapter 13 bankruptcy petition. Purchasers sought to lift the bankruptcy stay so they could complete their payments and secure a conveyance of the property. *Held:* A home mortgage default may not be cured following a foreclosure sale. Section 1322(b)(5) of the Bankruptcy Code gives a debtor the right to cure a default on a home mortgage. However, when a debtor files a Chapter 13 petition, proposing to use Section 1322(b)(5) after a foreclosure judgment has been filed, there is no longer a contractual relationship between the parties that can be cured. Under state law, the foreclosure judgment had the effect of merging the mortgage into the judgment and extinguishing the contract. Congress did not intend that state law be set aside in this area. In this case, debtors had ample time to file their bankruptcy petition before the foreclosure judgment. *In re Roach*, 824 F2d 1370 (1987).

7th Circuit The Department of Housing and Urban Development (HUD) was assigned the mortgage on a housing project. Although mortgagor continued in default, HUD worked with it for a number of years in an attempt to work out the loan and also provided various subsidies to keep the project running. HUD informed mortgagor that it intended to foreclose, but gave it time to look for a buyer. HUD rejected a proposed sale, because buyers were not putting up enough cash to remedy the project's physical deterioration and to bring the payments on the mortgage up to date. *Held:* HUD was entitled to foreclose. Its choice of foreclosure as the remedy for default was consistent with national housing policy, as embodied in 42 USC § 1441 because, once a mortgagor defaults, concern with promoting the security of federal investment in the loan outweighs the goal of promoting private sector investment in housing. Additionally, when HUD commenced default proceedings, it had full discretionary power and was no longer required to even consider national housing policy. *United States v. OCCI Co.*, 758 F2d 1160 (1985).

8th Circuit In 1978, Congress authorized the secretary of agriculture to defer FmHA payments for farmers who show their inability to repay is due to circumstances beyond their control. Debtor brought suit to enjoin the secretary from foreclosing on his defaulted FmHA loans. He argued that because no procedural or substantive standards had been established to implement the secretary's authority to defer loan payments, he was denied notice of his opportunity to explain why he was unable to pay. *Held:* The elements of adequate notice and the opportunity to be heard embodied in the amendment enacted by Congress could be ensured only by the establishment of uniform procedures and substantive standards. The secretary's failure to establish such procedures and standards warranted an injunction against the foreclosure. *Allison v. Block*, 723 F2d 631 (1983).

8th Circuit Debtors' land was encumbered by a mortgage insured by HUD, which upon default had taken an assignment of the mortgage from the private lenders and paid them off. Debtors argued that HUD's foreclosure suit could not proceed in the face of their Chapter 12 bankruptcy petition. *Held:* Section 517 of the Bankruptcy Code does not apply to the creditors of any debtor under a mortgage insured pursuant to the National Housing Act. Although the mortgage had determined, in that the debt had been satisfied and no further premiums were being paid, it was still a mortgage insured pursuant to the National Housing Act within the meaning of Section 517, so the foreclosure suit could proceed. HUD would be left in an untenable position every time it exercised its option to offer to pay the mortgage insurance if, at that point, the mortgage would be rendered unenforceable by debtors' Chapter 12 filing. *In re Mansion House S. Redev. Co.*, 661 F2d 724 (1981), cert. denied, 457 US 1117 (1982).

Georgia Plaintiff sold real property to defendant and took a note and security deed for part of the purchase price. The note was dated March 15, 1975, but the installments were not to begin until May 1, 1978. A dispute arose as to whether interest was due from the date of execution or was to begin on May 1, 1978, when the first payment was due. Defendant filed an action to reform the note contending that it was the intention of the parties that interest was not to begin until the date when the first payment was due. The trial court denied reformation; plaintiff declared the note in default and instituted foreclosure proceedings; defendant petitioned to enjoin the foreclosure. Defendant paid the first two installments due on May 1, 1978 and June 1, 1978. Plaintiff accepted these payments but refused payments tendered thereafter because the interest from the date of execution of the note until the date of the first installment was not paid. After the judgment denying reformation of the note, defendant tendered the interest admitted to be due from March 15, 1975, to May 1, 1978, in the form of a cashier's check that was retained by plaintiff. *Held:* The note was not in default, because defendant had tendered all amounts due. *Smith v. Cox*, 273 SE2d 610 (1981).

Maine Defendant mortgagors defaulted on a promissory note and a mortgage held by plaintiff mortgagees, and failed to pay real estate taxes on the property for three years. As a result, municipal tax liens were filed against the property. Mortgagee sued to foreclose. Subsequently, mortgagor paid the overdue taxes and obtained a municipal tax deed and sought to use the deed as a defense to the foreclosure action. *Held:* For mortgagee. A mortgagor cannot buy a tax title and assert it successfully against a mortgagee. *Danforth v. Gautreau*, 556 A2d 217 (1989).

Michigan Defendant executed a mortgage to plaintiff covering four separate parcels of land. The mortgage contained a provision that, if the mortgage were foreclosed, mortgagee had the option to sell the four parcels en masse instead of individually. In due course the mortgage was foreclosed, and the parcels were all sold together. Defendant challenged the judicial sale, claiming that it had violated statutory provisions of state law that required that mortgaged parcels be sold individually when this could be accomplished without injury to the parties. *Held:* Judgment for mortgagee. The provision for sale en masse was unambiguous, known to both parties, and not violative of Michigan public policy or state law. It should be given effect in the absence of a showing of bad faith by mortgagee. *Metropolitan Life Ins. Co. v. Foote*, 290 NW2d 158 (1980).

Nebraska Farmers mortgaged their farmland to a bank. The mortgage contract contained a term relinquishing the farmer's homestead rights in the mortgaged land. After the farmers fell behind in their mortgage payments, the bank foreclosed and the property was sold to satisfy the unpaid liens. Farmers filed for bankruptcy and claimed a homestead exemption. *Held:* The foreclosure sale was affirmed. The state statute that allows making the homestead subject to execution or forced sale if executed and acknowledged by debtors does not violate federal bankruptcy law or state constitutional law. It merely recognizes that debtors may wish to increase their borrowing power by waiving their homestead rights when mortgaging land. The bank's foreclosure did not create a "judicial lien" that could be avoided in bankruptcy. The foreclosure procedure does not create a lien but seeks to enforce one that already exists. A mortgage lien is not avoidable merely because it was established by judgment in a foreclosure action. *Federal Land Bank v. Blankemeyer*, 422 NW2d 81 (1988).

Nebraska Buyers purchased farmland from seller and gave him a purchase-money note and mortgage, payable in equal installments. Buyers made all payments until they discovered that seller had previously conveyed a small portion of the farmland to a third party. They computed their loss and deducted that amount from their next installment payment. Seller refused tender and commenced foreclosure proceedings. After the trial court decreed foreclosure and awarded them an abatement, buyers appealed, claiming that foreclosure should not have been decreed because seller breached the contract, and that the abatement awarded was insufficient. *Held:* Under state law, foreclosure is an available remedy for a mortgagor's breach notwithstanding the fact that mortgagor was entitled to an abatement of part of the unpaid mortgage debt. The amount of abatement awarded by the trial court was proper; buyers incorrectly calculated their loss on the basis of the average cost per acre when evidence showed that the missing land had the least value of all the land. *Kuhlman v. Grimminger*, 327 NW2d 104 (1982).

New Hampshire Plaintiff and her husband gave a promissory note secured by a mortgage to corporation, which later was dissolved. After her husband died, plaintiff stopped making mortgage payments. Eight years later, plaintiff sought to discharge the mortgage, contending that corporation and its former sole shareholder were barred from foreclosing the mortgage and enforcing the note because the three-year corporate windup period had expired. *Held:* The former shareholder could commence a foreclosure action or otherwise enforce the note within the 20-year statute of limitation period for actions to enforce a mortgage. Although corporation's right to take action on the note and mortgage ceased at the expiration of the windup period, its right descended automatically to the former shareholder, suing in his individual capacity. *Jenot v. White Mountain Acceptance Corp.*, 474 A2d 1382 (1984).

New York Borrower obtained a loan of $300,000 from lender, which was secured by a mortgage on real property. Within a year, when borrower fell behind on loan payments, a new payment schedule was established by a new loan agreement. The new agreement provided that it could not be modified or terminated orally. When borrower was unable to honor the new payment schedule, lender commenced foreclosure proceedings. In its defense, borrower presented an affidavit stating that lender waived default on the payments when a vice-president of lender orally represented that lender would defer acting on any defaults so long as borrower was able to close a then-pending sale of the mortgaged property to an interested buyer. *Held:* While the parties were prevented from modifying their agreement, nothing prohibited one of them from excusing the other from performing all or part of the agreement. The case was remanded by the New York Court of Appeals to the trial court on the issue of whether or not the events described in the affidavit actually transpired. *Nassau Trust Co. v. Montrose Concrete Prods. Corp.*, 436 NE2d 1265 (1983).

New York In 1960, the Roths loaned $11,000 to Herbert and Lillian Michelson. The Roths secured the debt by taking a second mortgage in the Michelsons' home. Only two payments on the debt were made, in 1961 and in 1973. In 1975 Herbert Michelson declared bankruptcy, and trustee put the house up for sale. The Russos purchased it, subject to existing liens, for $500. When the Roths brought an action to foreclose on their mortgage, the Russos argued the action was barred by the six-year statute of limitations. The Roths argued that Michelson's 1973 payment revived the mortgage. *Held:* Lillian's interest could not be foreclosed because there was no proof she knew of Herbert's payment and could not be charged with reviving the mortgage. Herbert's interest could not be foreclosed even though the 1973 mortgage revived the mortgage, because New York General Obligations Law provides that a payment by a mortgagor does not revive the right to foreclose against a bona fide purchaser. The $500 paid by the Russos, although nominal, was sufficient to make them bona fide purchasers under the statute. *Roth v. Michelson*, 434 NE2d 228 (1982).

Ohio In 1982, defendant's father executed a mortgage in favor of plaintiff, a bank. The legal description of the land mortgaged was not included in the mortgage document at the time of execution. Such information was supplied later. Defendant obtained title to the property in 1983, and subsequently defaulted on the mortgage. Plaintiff began foreclosure proceedings, and defendant argued that the mortgage was defective because it was signed with blank portions to be filled in at a later date. The trial court found that the mortgage was valid and enforceable; the court of appeals affirmed. *Held:* Affirmed. The Supreme Court of Ohio held that a mortgage is not fatally defective when parties knowingly and voluntarily leave portions of the document blank, so long as there is an understanding that the missing information will be filled in at a later date. When one or both of the parties fill in the blank portions within a reasonable time, the mortgage is valid and enforceable. The court also stated that the rule that a deed executed in blank is void does not apply to mortgages because a mortgage does not establish an indefensible title, but rather an equity in grantor. *Security Bank v. Hawk*, 517 NE2d 886 (1988).

Ohio A production credit association and a federal land bank organized under the Farm Credit Act of 1971 brought foreclosure actions against farmowners who had defaulted on mortgages. As a defense, farmowners sought to raise lenders' alleged failure to comply with the provisions of Section 2001 et seq. of the Farm Credit Act. Regulations at 12 CFR § 614.4510 provide among the criteria to be included in bank and association loan servicing policies that "the policy shall provide a means of forbearance for cases when the borrower is cooperative, making an honest effort to meet the conditions of the loan contract, and is capable of working out of the debt burden." *Held:* Citing several decisions by other courts, the Ohio court held that this language did not provide a valid defense to a foreclosure action. The regulation was not a substantive rule, but a general statement of agency policy. In any case, the determination of borrower's ability to work out the debt burden is best left to lender. *Farmers Prod. Credit Ass'n v. Johnson*, 493 NE2d 946 (1986) cert. denied, 479 US 1032 878 (1987).

Oregon Bunnell sold real estate under a land sale contract, retaining title to the realty to secure payment. Bunnell borrowed money from Security Bank and pledged to it his interest in the land sale contract and the property. The bank recorded its interest. Later, Bunnell borrowed money from Chiapuzio and again pledged his interest in the land sale contract and the land as security. Bunnell defaulted on the bank loan and the bank brought foreclosure proceedings on its security interest. Chiapuzio contested the foreclosure on the ground that he was a subsequent bona fide purchaser and had priority, basing his argument on UCC Article 9. The bank argued Article 9 did not apply because the underlying transaction involved Bunnell's assignment of an interest in land, pursuant to UCC § 9-104(j), which provided that Article 9 did not apply "to the creation or transfer of an interest in or lien on real estate." *Held:* For the bank. The exception of Section 9-104(j) regarding perfection of security interests in realty was viewed by the court as inapplicable when the transaction shifted from the creation of a claim directly upon realty to the taking of collateral in an obligation secured by a claim upon realty. Priority in a security interest was governed by Section 9-301(1), which provided that an unperfected security interest was subordinate to the rights of a subsequent purchaser without knowledge of the security interest. Chiapuzio was acquiring an interest in an obligation secured by realty. This obligated him to examine the land records for the status of title. He therefore could be charged with constructive notice of the bank's prior interest and could not claim priority over that interest. Although the security interest in the obligation secured by an interest in realty was separable from the latter interest and, thus, subject to the separate filing requirements of Article 9, the relationship between the two interests was such that priority could still be controlled by information in the land records. *Security Bank v. Chiapuzio*, 747 P2d 335 (1987).

Texas Decedent executed a deed of trust for his home in favor of his brother; and with his wife he executed a financing statement for furniture and appliances in favor of the brother. Upon decedent's death, the brother seized the house and its contents and evicted the wife, foreclosing six months later. The brother also took the wife's car and decedent's last VA check. The wife sued for conversion and trespass. The brother argued that as lienholder on the personal property he had the right to repossess the property in default. He contended that his security interest negated the element of intent to convert. *Held:* For the wife. By definition, the brother wrongfully converted her property. He had no right to claim the residence upon decedent's death. He had to follow certain steps in accordance with law and the deed of trust before the property could be foreclosed upon. Trespass requires proof of interference with the right of possession of real property, and the record reflected sufficient evidence to support the contention that the brother wrongfully interfered with the wife's right of possession. *Cargal v. Cargal*, 750 SW2d 382 (Ct. App. 1988).

Washington Landowners conveyed an undivided 15 percent interest in property located in County *A* to purchaser. Thereafter, the owners used the property, along with property located in County *B*, to secure a loan from lender. Owners defaulted on the loan, and trustee commenced foreclosure proceedings. Both parcels of land were sold to lender at a foreclosure sale in County *B*. Lender then sued purchaser to quiet title, and purchaser asserted that the two parcels had been improperly sold as a unit. *Held:* The parcels of land located in separate counties could not be foreclosed in a single proceeding. The state Deed of Trust Act prohibits the sale of property outside the county in which it is located where contiguous parcels straddle a county line. *Queeen City Sav. & Loan Ass'n v. Mannhalt*, 842 P2d 754 (Ct. App. 1987).

119.30
Foreclosure Sale

U.S. Supreme Court The federal government sought to enforce a tax lien against a deceased taxpayer's estate. The widow objected, citing her homestead rights under the Texas Constitution. In Texas, each spouse has a separate and undivided possessory interest in their homestead that may not be compromised by the other spouse. However, the government cited IRC § 7403, which authorizes a federal district court to order the sale of a home in which a delinquent taxpayer had an interest at the time he incurred his indebtedness, even if the taxpayer's spouse also has an interest and does not owe any taxes. *Held:* Because of the supremacy clause, the Texas Homestead Law could not immunize the property from the reach of Section 7403. Thus, the district court was authorized to order the sale and give the widow her share of the proceeds. However, the language of Section 7403 permitted, but did not require, the court to authorize a forced sale, permitting the court to balance the equities. *United States v. Rodgers*, 461 US 677 (1983).

Minnesota Attorneys handling a foreclosure sale failed to serve the written notice required by the Internal Revenue Code (IRC) and by Minnesota statute that would allow discharge of the junior liens following the redemption period. Purchaser, who bought the property without knowledge of the liens, sued seeking rescission of the sale. *Held:* Mortgagee's failure to notify the state and federal governments of the foreclosure sale rendered the sale voidable by purchaser. The purpose of a mortgage foreclosure sale is to terminate all interests junior to the mortgage being foreclosed, so that purchaser acquires a title identical to that of mortgagor at the time the mortgage was executed; this was not accomplished. *Gerdin v. Princeton State Bank*, 384 NW2d 868 (1986).

New York Plaintiff guaranteed a mortgage securing a loan by defendant to Alvil, Inc. The agreement provided that defendant would be the beneficiary of all casualty insurance policies. Subsequently, the property was destroyed by a fire and the proceeds of the insurance went to defendant; a portion of the mortgage was still left unpaid. The property was sold at a foreclosure sale and was purchased by defendant for the exact amount remaining on the debt. Plaintiff sued to have guaranty declared void, defendant counterclaimed, alleging plaintiff was still liable for the balance of the debt because the purchase price of the property at the foreclosure sale exceeded the actual or appraised value of the property. *Held:* Defendant bid the full amount of indebtedness at the mortgage foreclosure sale, thereby extinguishing the debt and further liability of plaintiff. A mortgagee cannot foreclose on property, receive the full amount of the debt, and then allege that the value of the property was less than its bid, having potentially cut off higher bids at the foreclosure sale. *Alaimo v. First Fed. Sav. & Loan Ass'n*, 383 NYS2d 751 (App. Div. 1976), aff'd, 398 NYS2d 1011 (1977).

North Carolina Plaintiffs, who had defaulted on two notes that were secured by separate deeds of trust on separate parcels of land in the same county, requested that the parcels be sold separately. Instead, the two parcels were sold together. Plaintiffs sued, asking that the foreclosure sale be set aside. *Held:* For plaintiffs. Citing equitable grounds, the state supreme court refused to give effect to state statutes that limited injunctive relief in foreclosure proceedings. Sales of separately indentured land must be conducted separately to maximize proceeds, enable the debtor to satisfy each separate debt before sale is completed, allow upset bids on each property, and apply the proceeds in a proper manner. Purchasers could not claim to be "bona fide purchasers for value without any notice of irregularity" so as to cut off mortgagors' right of redemption, since the advertisement of sale disclosed that two tracts secured by separate deeds of trust were being sold together, which was an irregularity. *Swindell v. Overton*, 314 SE2d 512 (1984).

119.35
—Sufficiency of Price

Iowa Debtors owed $53,000, and the bank obtained a money judgment in this amount. After the judgment was entered, the bank recovered $33,000 in insurance money, because of fire damage to the property the debtors had mortgaged. When the foreclosure sale was held, the bank mistakenly bid the amount of its judgment plus costs, instead of the

$20,000 to $22,000 the fire-gutted property was allegedly worth. After the sale the debtors moved for an accounting of the insurance proceeds. *Held:* Debtors were entitled to have the money judgment reduced by the amount of the insurance proceeds, but the sale was set aside on equitable grounds. Enforcing the sale would have had the unconscionable result of giving a substantial windfall to debtors and imposing an oppressive burden on the bank. *Farmers Sav. Bank, Joice v. Gerhart*, 372 NW2d 238 (1985).

Nevada Joint venturers defaulted on a loan secured by units in a condominium complex. Lender instituted nonjudicial foreclosure on 53 unsold units and obtained a deficiency judgment for the balance of the loan. Joint venturers appealed the trial court's decision to calculate the deficiency judgment based on an appraised value of $42,500 per unit, since it was less than the $60,000 at which lender valued each unit at the time the loan was made. *Held:* Affirmed. Nevada law provides that a deficiency judgment shall be rendered at the amount that the debt exceeds the fair market value of the property at the time of sale. The appraisal took into consideration the area's depressed housing market and the fact that only 31 units sold in two years for an average price of $64,000, despite financial incentives. It would not be sound to base fair market value on the property's value at the time of the loan. *Lee v. Verex Assurance, Inc.*, 746 P2d 140 (1987).

Pennsylvania A lender foreclosed on its junior mortgage and purchased the property for $2,475 at a sheriff's sale. It later sold the property for $35,000. Debtor sued to set aside the sheriff's sale on the ground that it had not received adequate notice of the sale and that the purchase price was grossly inadequate. Lender had sent notice of the sale to plaintiff's place of business, but not to plaintiff's chief officer, even though it had had dealings with the chief officer and should have known that the debtor company was merely a "straw owner" and that the chief officer was the real owner of the property. *Held:* The sheriff's sale was upheld. Since debtor company's name, not that of its chief officer, was included on all documents filed with the Department of State, notice to the company was all that was necessary. The price was not grossly inadequate in light of the fact that the property was sold subject to a large mortgage and was located in an undesirable neighborhood. *Vend-A-Matic, Inc. v. Frankford Trust Co.*, 442 A2d 1158 (1982).

Tennessee A bank foreclosed on mortgaged property and purchased the property for $8,600, the amount the property had been mortgaged for some 10 years earlier. Ten days later, bank resold the property for $30,000. Relying on two very old Tennessee cases, owner brought an action to set aside the foreclosure on the equitable ground that the price was so inadequate as to shock the conscience of the court. *Held:* The old rule was impractical and should be abandoned. If a foreclosure sale is legally held, conducted, and consummated, there must be some evidence of irregularity, misconduct, fraud, or unfairness on the part of trustee or mortgagee that caused or contributed to an inadequate price for a court of equity to set aside the sale. The lone infirmity of shockingly inadequate price did not justify voiding the foreclosure sale. *Holt v. Citizens Cent. Bank*, 688 SW2d 414 (1984).

Washington A construction lender foreclosed on a condominium and purchased the property at the foreclosure sale. Debtor objected and persuaded the trial court to grant an upset judgment based on a per unit valuation. Instead of setting aside the foreclosure sale, however, the trial court confirmed the sale at the upset price, over lender's objections, and entered a deficiency judgment based on the higher, or upset, valuation of the property. *Held:* Although the upset price was not unreasonable, the trial court had no right to confirm the sale at the upset price over the objections of lender-purchaser. If a successful bidder rejects an upset price, Wash. Rev. Code § 61.12.060-.070 contemplates a resale of the mortgaged property at or above the upset price. Unfortunately for the success of its appeal, however, lender had drawn on the funds held by the court in satisfaction of the deficiency judgment that it sought to challenge, thus acceding to the trial court's confirmation of the sale. *American Fed. Sav. & Loan Ass'n v. McCaffrey*, 728 P2d 155 (1986) (en banc).

119.40 —Purchaser's Rights and Obligations

U.S. District Court, New York Plaintiffs, former owners of homes financed by VA mortgages that were foreclosed, sued to enjoin the VA from evicting them. Plaintiffs wished to remain in the homes until they were sold and offered to pay rent. They argued that, as former homeowners, they had a property interest in continued occupancy. *Held:* The veterans' benefit statute, 38 USC § § 1801 et seq., does not provide plaintiffs with a protectable interest in continued occupancy under these circumstances. The VA's responsibility is to guarantee loans for veterans, not to provide housing for rental tenants. *Wells v. United States Adm'r of Veterans Affairs*, 537 F. Supp. 473 (ED 1982).

District of Columbia Developer intervened in a civil action and moved to quash a writ of attachment issued against property that defendant had transferred to it by quitclaim deed. Even though the property had been posted, developer contended that attachment was not perfected since defendant transferred his interest prior to service upon him of the writ of attachment and the endorsement and notice as required by the D.C. Code. *Held:* The delivery of the writ before attachment created only an inchoate lien on defendant's property. Taking by quitclaim deed did not put purchaser on notice that title was defective and did not preclude developer from proving that it was a bona fide purchaser who took the property without notice of the writ of attachment. *Jack Dev., Inc. v. Howard Eales, Inc.*, 388 A2d 466 (1978).

Georgia Purchasers of property brought an action to enjoin bank from foreclosing under a security deed that grantor had previously given the bank. The security deed contained an "open-end" clause securing "any other present or future indebtedness or liability" of grantor to bank. The warranty deed from grantor to purchasers recited that it was given subject to the security deed from grantor to bank, which loan deed purchasers assumed and agreed to pay. *Held:* The open-end clause was valid. Purchasers knew or should have known that their assumption of grantor's deed made the property security for subsequent debts of grantor to bank because of the recitals in their warranty deed. *Commercial Bank v. Readd*, 242 SE2d 25 (1978).

Illinois Plaintiffs purchased an interest in real property at a sheriff's sale following execution of a judgment. In a later proceeding, it was determined that the sheriff had failed to set off debtor's homestead exemption, and the sale was declared void. Plaintiffs thereupon sued the judgment creditor for recovery of the purchase price. *Held:* The doctrine of caveat emptor applied, and the judgment creditor could not be held liable to plaintiff. The failure of title was due to defects in the conduct of the sheriff's sale, and not from any negligence, fraud, or misrepresentation on the part of the judgment creditor.

Dixon v. City Nat'l Bank, 410 NE2d 843 (1980).

Oregon Mortgagors executed a mortgage to mortgagee on parcels of land totaling 62 acres. Before mortgagee commenced foreclosure proceedings, mortgagor had conveyed all but one small parcel to third parties. The circuit court's foreclosure decree prorated mortgagee's judgment among all the parcels according to their acreage. Mortgagor contended the judgment should have been paid first from the sale proceeds of the parcel retained by mortgagor, and the balance charged against each of the other parcels in inverse order of their alienation until the judgment was satisfied. *Held:* The right to invoke the equitable doctrine of inverse order of alienation belongs to the earliest grantee who may use it only to protect himself, not to grantor-debtors. This doctrine could not be used by mortgagors because they failed to show substantial prejudice from the foreclosure decree. *First State Bank v. Meadow Lake Stables*, 640 P2d 662 (1982).

Texas After a foreclosure sale, trustee promised to remain at the courthouse for about 45 minutes so that the high bidder could obtain a cashier's check. Forty minutes later, while the original high bidder was still retrieving his funds, the trustee started another sale and sold the property to another bidder. The original high bidder sued to have the sale set aside, claiming that he was the rightful buyer by virtue of being the highest bidder at the sale. *Held:* For the original high bidder. Trustee had a duty to allow the high bidder a reasonable time to procure funds to cover his bid. Evidence showed that trustee failed to wait a reasonable time, and that the high bidder presented his cashier's check within a reasonable time. The high bidder testified that he returned to the courthouse within 45 minutes, and trustee testified that he proceeded with the second sale 40 minutes after the first sale was completed. Since the trustee told the bidder he would remain at the courthouse for 45 minutes in order to accept the check, the trustee himself had set a "reasonable time." *First Tex. Serv. Corp. v. McDonald*, 762 SW2d 935 (Ct. App. 1988).

Washington A foreclosure sale was properly conducted, except that junior lienholders were not notified of the impending sale. Purchaser, who was one of the junior lienholders, learned of the sale from the notice posted on the property and successfully bid for the property. After the sale, trustee learned that other junior lienholders had not received notice of the sale and sued to void the sale. The junior lienholder that purchased the property claimed to be a bona fide purchaser entitled to rely on the recital in the deed of trust that the sale was conducted properly. *Held:* Junior lienholders enjoy the same right as disinterested purchasers to rely on the recitals in the deed of trust and qualify as bona fide purchasers. However, since purchaser here had constructive knowledge that another junior lienholder had not received notice of the sale, the case should go to trial to determine whether purchaser reasonably relied on trustee's assurances that all statutory procedures were followed. *Glidden v. Municipal Auth.*, 758 P2d 487 (1988) (en banc).

119.45
—Rights to Proceeds of Sale

6th Circuit At a public sale, mortgagee bid on the real property for a sum in excess of the balance due on the mortgage. Mortgagor thereafter filed a voluntary bankruptcy petition. When surplus proceeds of the sale were claimed by other creditors of mortgagor, mortgagee sued to retain the surplus proceeds as costs of the sale and attorney fees. *Held:* An amount bid in excess of principal and interest belongs to mortgagor's estate in bankruptcy, except to the extent that mortgagee can show the nature and extent of reasonable expenses and fees incurred. The Bankruptcy Court is empowered to determine the amount to be allowed out of the foreclosure sale to cover expenses and attorney fees. *In re Bain*, 527 F2d 681 (1975).

Alaska Defendant entered into a land contract for the purchase of plaintiff's property. At nearly all times during an eight-year period, defendant remained in default in spite of cash advances for improvements and changes in the repayment schedule made by plaintiff. Faced with his own bankruptcy, plaintiff was compelled to foreclose and sought the full remedy available under state law. Defendant applied for the aid of equity to protect him from losing the benefits of a nearly six-fold increase in the value of the property. *Held:* Judgment of foreclosure and forfeiture of payments affirmed. Foreclosure was appropriate in view of plaintiff's continuous efforts to assist defendant in the financing of the project. The increased value of the property should not, therefore, inure in equity to buyer. *Curry v. Tucker*, 616 P2d 8 (1980).

New Hampshire Bank agreed to lend company $211,000, and the state's Industrial Development Authority agreed to guarantee the loan up to 28.4 percent of the unpaid balance of the mortgage. The authority's guaranty further provided that, if the company should default and the "net proceeds" of the foreclosure sale plus the amount of the guaranty exceeded the balance due on the mortgage, then the excess was to be deducted from the guaranty. When the company defaulted and the bank foreclosed, the bank claimed almost $20,000 in conservation and foreclosure costs which it deducted from "net proceeds." The authority, which would have lost an additional $10,000 because of the bank's computation of "net proceeds," objected. *Held:* The bank was entitled to deduct only "costs of sale," in this case about $2,000 in advertising and auctioneering fees. "Net proceeds," which were not specified in the guaranty agreement, comprise the gross proceeds of the sale minus the costs of sale. *Manchester Bank v. Industrial Dev. Auth.*, 396 A2d 558 (1979).

Pennsylvania Before all the monies scheduled to be advanced under a construction loan were advanced, the project became troubled. The construction lender foreclosed, purchased the property, and then sold it at a substantial profit. Unpaid subcontractors brought suit against lender, claiming that they had relied on assurances from lender and were entitled to payment under a theory of constructive trust. *Held:* Lender was unjustly enriched to the extent that loan proceeds had been advanced to developer for work actually performed by the subcontractors but not paid to them, at least to the extent that lender recovered the value of such advances in the foreclosure sale. To maintain a claim of unjust enrichment, a plaintiff does not need to prove wrongdoing or misrepresentation, nor the existence of a contractual relation with defendant. *Gee v. Eberle*, 420 A2d 1050 (Super. Ct. 1980).

119.50 Deficiency Judgments

Florida Bank held a second mortgage on motel and, when mortgagor was in default, sued for an accounting for foreclosure and sale to pay for sums outstanding. A judgment of approximately $1.4 million was awarded, and the property was put up for sale. The bank was the sole bidder and bought the property for the exact amount of the judgment. Bank then sued mortgagor for a deficiency judgment, claiming that various fees and expenses after the entry of final judgment of foreclosure should be paid by mortgagor. Bank also argued that since the true market value of the property was less than it paid at the foreclosure sale, the true market value should be the measure for determining the amount of the deficiency. *Held:* The amount paid at the foreclosure sale should determine the amount of deficiency. The amount for which property is sold, whether to mortgagee or to a stranger, is the proper amount to be applied to the debt. The amount of deficiency judgment may not exceed the difference between the amount for which the property is sold and the amount of indebtedness, regardless of the true market value of the property. *Provident Nat'l Bank v. Thunderbird Assocs.*, 364 So. 2d 790 (Dist. Ct. App. 1978).

Idaho After foreclosing on debtors' home, lender waited until after expiration of the three-month statutory period for seeking a deficiency judgment from debtors to demand that guarantor pay the deficiency. When guarantor refused to pay, lender filed a deficiency action against guarantor. Guarantor argued that he was entitled to the same protections afforded to debtors by Idaho law and that lender could not bring the action against him because the three-month period had expired. *Held:* For lender. Guarantor could not claim the protection affored to debtors by the statute because his obligation was independent of theirs. Further, guarantor had expressly waived any right to require lender to proceed against debtors or to pursue any other available remedy. *Valley Bank v. Larson*, 663 P2d 653 (1983).

Indiana Purchasers bought real and personal property, borrowing $70,000 of the purchase price. When they ceased payments a year later, the contract vendor foreclosed, bid $45,000 at the foreclosure sale, and sought a deficiency judgment for $16,000. The appellate court vacated the deficiency judgment, concluding that the contract vendor must prove the real estate purchased at the foreclosure sale was worth less than the presale deficiency. *Held:* Reversed. Requiring a contract vendor or mortgagee who purchases property on which he is foreclosing at sheriff's sale to provide independent proof of market value to obtain a deficiency judgment misplaces the burden of proof. Purchaser's remedy if the price is wholly inadequate is to move to have the sale set aside. *Arnold v. Melvin R. Hall, Inc.*, 496 NE2d 63 (1986).

Mississippi A bank, the only bidder, purchased property mortgaged to it at a foreclosure sale for $85,000. Mortgagor sued, claiming the value of the property at the time of foreclosure was $393,000, based on "market values" in the deed of trust for releasing individual lots to third parties. The bank countersued for a deficiency judgment for difference between the amount owed it and the sale price. *Held:* Mortgagor failed to show the sale price was unconscionable, since the values for release of single lots upon sale by developer were insufficient evidence of the lots' fair market value. The bank was not entitled to a deficiency judgment absent proof that the fair market value was less than the amount owed by mortgagor. *Lake Hillsdale Estates, Inc. v. Galloway*, 473 So. 2d 461 (1985).

North Carolina The land securing a purchase-money deed of trust was released by sellers after the sale, allowing purchasers to resell the land to a third party. When purchasers defaulted on the note, sellers commenced foreclosure proceedings and also sought an in personam judgment against purchasers. Purchasers asserted in defense North Carolina's antideficiency statute, N.C. Gen. Stat. § 45-21.38, which prevents the holder of a purchase-money deed of trust from obtaining a deficiency judgment on account of an obligation secured by the purchase-money deed of trust. Sellers contended that, having released their security interest in the land sold to a third party, the note was no longer secured by a purchase-money deed of trust. *Held:* For purchasers. Expressly rejecting its ruling in a 1940 case, the court ruled that the holder of a note given by a buyer to a seller for the purchase of land and secured by a deed of trust embracing the land sold must look exclusively to the property conveyed in seeking to recover any balance owed; even if the holder has released his security, he may not sue on the note. It would be contrary to the legislature's intent to allow seller to deprive buyer of the protection of the statute by releasing the security and then suing on the note. *Barnaby v. Boardman*, 330 SE2d 600 (1985).

North Dakota Partners of a property development partnership individually guaranteed a mortgage loan to the partnership. On default, mortgagee instituted foreclosure proceedings and also sued the individual partners in their capacity as guarantors. The resulting judgments left the partners personally liable as guarantors to the extent that the price realized at foreclosure fell short of the balance due on the partnership debt. The partners sued to set aside the judgment against them on the ground that it was prohibited by North Dakota's antideficiency statute. They argued that because partners are always personally liable to partnership creditors, the guaranties added nothing to their primary obligation under the partnership debt. *Held:* For mortgagee. Recovery by mortgagee on the partners' guaranties was not precluded by the antideficiency statute any more than recovery on a guaranty by a guarantor unrelated to the primary obligor would be precluded. *Mandan Sec. Bank v. Heinsohn*, 320 NW2d 494 (1982).

South Carolina On first mortgagee's motion, a foreclosure action was commenced and a receiver appointed for mortgaged property, as provided in the mortgage. First mortgagee purchased the property at the foreclosure sale for a nominal fee and agreed not to demand a deficiency judgment. First mortgagee then sued seeking monies accumulated from rents collected while the foreclosure action was pending, to which second mortgagee also asserted a claim under the terms of its mortgage. *Held:* First mortgagee was entitled to the proceeds of the receivership. These proceeds were part of the collateral secured under the terms of the mortgage agreement. As such, they were unaffected by first mortgagee's waiver of its rights to a deficiency judgment. *Sellara v. First Colonial Corp.*, 280 SE2d 805 (1981).

Texas Payee and holder of a promissory note sued maker for a deficiency remaining on the note after a sale of land securing payment. The note provided the maker would be personally liable for its payment during the first two years of its term, after which payee or holder would look solely to the security for the note to satisfy the indebtedness, even if sale of the security did not fully satisfy the debt. Default occurred after one year. The makers claimed that this provision prohibited an action for a deficiency judgment following a foreclosure sale. *Held:* Summary judgment for the note holder affirmed. The parties intended that the maker would be personally liable if default occurred within the first two years of the note. Since there was default within the two-year period, the maker was personally liable for the deficiency. *R&F Enters. v. LaGuarta, Gavrel & Kirk, Inc.*, 596 SW2d 517 (1980).

119.55
Rights of Junior Mortgagees or Trustees

Alaska At a nonjudicial foreclosure sale, a junior lienholder purchased the property for slightly more than the amount owed to the senior lienholder, resold the property at a substantial profit, and sued debtor on its promissory note, which was in default. The trial court responded by attaching funds in debtor's bank account, and debtor appealed. *Held:* Affirmed. Although Alaska law bars a deficiency judgment by a junior lienholder, the junior lienholder loses its security interest upon the senior lienholder's foreclosure and sale, and may therefore sue debtor personally to recover on the underlying note. The fact that the junior lienholder purchased the property, securing its note at foreclosure sale, does not affect this right. The court contrasted Alaska law with the law in other states. *Adams v. Fedalaska Fed. Credit Union*, 757 P2d 1040 (1988).

California Grantor sold a lot on which an office building was to be built for an amount down and the balance on a note secured by a purchase-money deed of trust. Grantee's general partners agreed to waive their protection from deficiency judgments, and grantor agreed to subordinate her prior lien to that of the construction lender. Grantee then transferred the property to MKS, which negotiated a construction loan, and grantor executed a specific subordination recognizing the priority of construction lender's lien. This loan was later foreclosed, and a deficiency was recovered from MKS. Grantor, having had her subordinated purchase-money deed of trust rendered valueless by the foreclosure, filed an action to enforce the written personal promises to guarantee payment of the note. *Held:* When a vendor subordinates a purchase-money lien to a lien securing the purchaser's construction loan during the process of sale and, afterwards, upon default by purchaser, loses the security interest upon foreclosure of the senior lien, the statutory proscription against deficiency judgments does not bar recovery by the junior vendor-lienor of the unpaid balance of the purchase price. *Spangler v. Memel*, 498 P2d 1055 (1972).

Massachusetts Mortgagee foreclosed on a building. The junior mortgagee alleged that it had lost its lien on mortgagor's equity owing to first mortgagee's delay in commencing foreclosure proceedings. The junior mortgagee contended that first mortgagee violated a duty owed to a creditor to exercise due diligence in foreclosing a mortgage. *Held:* The junior mortgagee was not entitled to damages for the delay. There was no finding of bad faith or want of judgment or discretion on the first mortgagee's part. Mortgagee was not compelled to commence foreclosure proceedings promptly after default, since effort and attention were required. *Seppala & Aho Constr. Co. v. Peterson*, 367 NE2d 613 (1977).

119.60 Purchaser's Duty to Pay Attorney Fees Upon Default

Louisiana Borrowers signed a note secured by a purchase-money mortgage. The note obligated borrowers to pay all attorney fees incurred in its collection "hereby fixed at 20 percent of the amount to be collected." When borrowers defaulted, sellers instituted foreclosure proceedings, but agreed to accept the full amount of the unpaid principal and interest plus 20 percent for attorney fees. Borrowers paid, under protest, then sued for reimbursement of the attorney fees, to the extent that they were excessive in relation to the legal work actually performed. *Held:* The reasonableness of the predetermined attorney fees had to be examined against the guidelines for legal fees in DR2-106 of the Code of Professional Responsibility. Although prior case law allowed attorney fees fixed in advance of default on a contract on the theory that they are liquidated damages, the court rejected the idea that attorney fees paid on the default of a debtor are paid as damages. *Leenerts Farm, Inc. v. Rogers*, 421 So. 2d 216 (1982).

119.65
Contractor's Right to Holdbacks

5th Circuit Cost-plus construction contracts between a developer and its contractors mirrored the way monies were advanced to developer under a HUD-insured construction loan. The contractors were paid in installments based on acceptably completed work plus the value of additional materials delivered to the building site, less a 10 percent holdback. On default, mortgagee deeded the properties to HUD. When HUD sold the projects and refused to pay the holdback funds, contractors and their sureties sued, claiming that HUD had been unjustly enriched by the value of uncompensated construction services. They also claimed to be third-party beneficiaries of a contract under which they had performed. *Held:* For HUD. The contractors had no reasonable expectation that HUD would pay the holdbacks if developer defaulted. Developers in both cases were private, profit-making entities, not creations of HUD, and the contractors had an alternative remedy in contract against the solvent owners. The third-party beneficiary theory was also rejected by the court, since to say that HUD's acceptance of the contractor's continued performance was sufficient to make it liable for the holdbacks would mean that the HUD holdbacks were security for the construction work alone, not for repayment of the loan. *Van-Tex, Inc. v. Pierce*, 703 F2d 891 (1983); *United States v. I-12 Garden Apartments*, 703 F2d 900 (1983).

5th Circuit Cost-plus construction contracts and the HUD construction loan agreement for Section 236 low-income housing were on HUD-prescribed forms. They provided that contractors would receive advances based on acceptably completed work, plus the value of additional materials delivered to the building site, less a 10 percent holdback. On default, mortgagee foreclosed and deeded the property to HUD. The subcontractors filed liens against the property, and the surety sued HUD, as subrogee of the subcontractors, to recover the held-back funds from HUD. HUD claimed that it had never assumed the obligations of the building loan agreement, because the foreclosure extinguished the obligations. *Held:* For the surety. The foreclosure could not extinguish third-party beneficiary claims against HUD where the building loan agreement expressly bound HUD to all of its terms. *Commercial Standard Ins. Co. v. Bryce St. Apartments, Ltd.*, 703 F2d 904 (1983).

119.70
Injunction of Foreclosure

5th Circuit Plaintiff real estate developer financed a shopping center through defendant, a savings and loan. Plaintiff gave defendant a promissory note secured by a mortgage on the property. When plaintiff missed several payments, the parties began negotiations to modify the loan agreement, but defendant nonetheless posted the property for foreclosure sale. Plaintiff sought a preliminary injunction against the sale, contending defendant violated state law since an agreement had been reached between them before the posting. *Held:* Plaintiff was entitled to a preliminary injunction. He would suffer irreparable harm should foreclosure proceed before a decision on the merits of the case was reached. Plaintiff's interest in the property was unique and thus no post-foreclosure remedy could substitute for injunctive relief. *Bean v. Independent Am. Sav. Ass'n*, 838 F2d 739 (1988).

Texas A lender appealed a temporary injunction enjoining foreclosure. *Held:* The injunction was an appropriate use of the trial court's discretion. First, plaintiff, a developer, would suffer irreparable injury if the land were sold, since he would lose his equity in the land and suffer damage to his reputation in the industry and be unable to borrow funds. Further, real estate is unique, so that damages would not be monetarily compensable. Second, the equities were in developer's favor, since lender could not show that it had a potential purchaser or that the value of the property was declining. Lastly, the developer had established probable success on the merits since interest rates on the loans in question were usurious. *Guardian Sav. & Loan Ass'n v. Williams*, 731 SW2d 107 (1987).

120.00 RIGHT OF REDEMPTION

120.05 Nature of Right

9th Circuit The state of California filed a tax deed against already encumbered property on which taxes were delinquent. Owner of the property sold half of his interest (in effect, half his right to redeem). The Internal Revenue Service (IRS) then placed a lien against the property for nonpayment of federal employment taxes. When the original encumbrance on the property was foreclosed on, the IRS attempted to redeem the property under 26 USC § 7425. The objection was raised, however, that the portion of the right to redeem that had been sold did not rise to the level of an interest in property to which a federal tax lien could attach under 26 USC § 6321. *Held:* Under California law, the right to redeem is a valuable, transferable pecuniary asset to which a lien could attach. This was supported in this case by the fact that valuable consideration had been given for it, and indeed by the fact it was the subject of a suit. *Little v. United States,* 704 F2d 1100 (1983).

11th Circuit Over a year after the Federal Deposit Insurance Corporation (FDIC) foreclosed on a mortgage acquired from a failed bank, a co-owner offered to pay the arrears and redeem the property (the co-owners had moved and not informed the bank, so they did not receive actual notice of the default). The FDIC, on the other hand, sued to collect on the mortgage note. The co-owner alleged a lack of due process under the Fifth Amendment. *Held:* The right to redeem was indeed a property interest protected by the Fifth Amendment, even though it was not transferable under state law. However, due process had not been violated. The FDIC's actions in the foreclosure accorded with state law. *FDIC v. Morrison,* 747 F2d 610 (1984), cert. denied, 474 US 1019 (1985).

Alabama A delinquent mortgagor challenged the statement provided to her under Alabama Code § 6-5-234, purporting to set out the debt and lawful charges it would be necessary for her to pay to redeem her house. She claimed that some of the items were permanent improvements that went beyond what was necessary to keep the house from deteriorating during the redemption period. *Held:* The questioned items were "necessary permanent improvements." They were valuable and useful additions to the property suited to its reasonable necessities, character, and use. *Moore v. Horton,* 491 So. 2d 921 (1986).

Alabama A husband held one quarter of the tenant in common interest in mortgaged property, and his wife the rest.

They defaulted on the mortgage, and the property was bought by mortgagee at a foreclosure sale; but husband and wife later redeemed it. After their deaths, the husband's heirs claimed a presumptive half interest in the property against the wife's heirs, arguing that the foreclosure sale had ended the original tenancy. *Held:* The husband's heirs received only a one-fourth interest. Alabama law specifies that a redemption restores legal title as if there had been no sale, provided (as in this case) redemption occurs within the statutory redemption period. *Foster v. Hudson,* 437 So. 2d 528 (1983).

Illinois Within a two-year period, mortgagor had twice defaulted on a mortgage and twice been reinstated after paying the arrears plus costs. However, there was a statutory right to reinstatement only once in a five-year period; and when mortgagor defaulted again, mortgagee refused to allow reinstatement. Mortgagor claimed the right to reinstatement nevertheless. *Held:* There was no right to another reinstatement. The five-year rule was not a denial of due process, because it was rationally related to a legitimate governmental interest. Neither did it deprive some suspect group of equal protection of the laws. Additionally, the fact that mortgagee had waived its right to foreclose the second time mortgagor went into default did not constitute a waiver of that right for all subsequent occasions. *First Fed. Sav. & Loan Ass'n v. Walker,* 437 NE2d 644 (1982).

Minnesota Creditor held three consecutive mortgages against property; a bank held a junior lien. The most senior mortgage went into default, and creditor bought the property at the foreclosure sale for the amount of that mortgage. The bank then attempted to redeem the property for the same price, arguing that creditor should have redeemed her junior mortgages when she bought the property. *Held:* The bank was not required to pay off the second and third mortgages in order to redeem the property. Each lien stands by itself and is cut out unless redemption is made under it. *Petition of Brainerd Nat'l Bank,* 383 NW2d 284 (1986).

Minnesota A bank loan to a developer was secured by a second mortgage, which contained a clause assigning rents from the property to the bank in the event of default. That mortgage went into default, and the bank foreclosed. During the redemption period, developer did not pay taxes on the property or interest on the first mortgage. The bank sued for the deficiency from the second mortgage, as well as interest on the first mortgage and unpaid taxes. *Held:* The bank was entitled to only the deficiency on the second mortgage. With regard to the other charges claimed by the bank, the assignment of rents was substituted for developer's personal liability. *GGC v. First Nat'l Bank,* 287 NW2d 378 (1979).

Tennessee A mother pledged her house to secure the indebtedness of her son. They both executed a deed of trust that gave the mother the right to pay the balance and release the indebtedness. The son defaulted, and the mortgage was foreclosed. The mother then tendered payment, but mortgagee refused. She then brought an action to enjoin the foreclosure. *Held:* Mortgagor was entitled to pay the indebtedness. Announcement of foreclosure proceedings does not terminate the right of mortgagor to tender payment and obtain a release. *Horne v. Payne,* 586 SW2d 101 (1980).

Washington A property was purchased at a foreclosure sale but was redeemed 11 months later. The redemptioner challenged the inclusion of delinquent and current irrigation assessments in the redemption price. Although purchaser had paid these assessments and had served the redemptioner with notice that it had made the payments, it failed to comply with Wash. Rev. Code § 6.24.150, which requires a purchaser to file a statement of taxes and assessments paid with the county auditor. This statute provides that if purchaser fails to record the payment of assessments properly, the property may be redeemed without paying the assessments. *Held:* The purpose of the notice requirement was met by directly serving the redemptioner with a statement of purchaser's assessment payments. The court held that redemption statutes are remedial in nature and should therefore be liberally construed to accomplish legislative purpose. Here, the redemptioner received timely notice of the amount required for redemption, and conceded that it did not suffer prejudice from purchaser's deviation from the statute. *GESA Fed. Credit Union v. Mutual Life Ins. Co.,* 713 P2d 728 (1986) (en banc).

120.10 Who May Exercise Right

9th Circuit The Internal Revenue Service (IRS) had a tax lien against property the mortgage on which became delinquent and which passed through several owners. Ten days after the last such sale, the IRS announced its intention to redeem the property for the price obtained at the foreclosure sale. The latest purchaser, who had secured his purchase with a mortgage on the property, sued to enjoin the redemption. *Held:* The IRS had a statutory right to redeem the property, which was taken free of the latest buyer's security interest. The time for determining the existence of encumbrances to which redemption would be subject is the time of foreclosure. *Olympic Fed. Sav. & Loan Ass'n v. Regan,* 648 F2d 1218 (1981).

Iowa Mortgagors, whose appeal of a judgment of foreclosure had been only partially successful, challenged the constitutionality of an 1873 Iowa statute that provided that mortgagors waive their statutory equity of redemption by appealing a judgment of foreclosure (Iowa Code § 628.4). They argued that the right to redeem has long been a recognized property right and that the statute deprived them of recognized property rights, due process, and equal protection. *Held:* The statute was upheld. The right to appeal and the right to redeem are statutory and not constitutional. Although the soundness of the statutory scheme was "debatable," mortgagors' criticisms of it did not rise to constitutional dimensions. Some justification could be found for the statute as a means to cut down the delay that would otherwise be obtained by debtors who pursue frivolous appeals merely to buy time, unfairly extending the redemption period. *Farmers Trust & Sav. Bank v. Manning,* 359 NW2d 461 (1984).

Missouri A contract for sale of a farm required buyer to assume sellers' existing mortgage, but mortgagee was not a party to the contract. Buyer defaulted on the mortgage, and sellers moved to redeem. Mortgagee objected, on the ground that the contract of sale had also transferred the right to redeem. *Held:* Sellers could still redeem. The redemption statute should be read liberally to protect those who would suffer loss, i.e., mortgagors. *State ex rel. LeFevre v. Stubbs,* 642 SW2d 103 (1982) (en banc).

New Jersey Owner of two tax sale certificates covering a single tract of undeveloped land sought to foreclose the right of redemption of two groups, each of whom owned an undivided one-half interest in the property. One group redeemed its one-half interest, but the other group failed to do so. A lower court held that the redeeming group had become tenants in common with the owner of the certificate. The nonredeeming group appealed.

Held: The redeeming group must redeem all the real estate, not merely its undivided interest. If it does, it has a claim against the other group for reimbursement to the extent of its share. *Lonsk v. Pennefather,* 402 A2d 259 (1979).

Oregon A foreclosure proceeding was held that did not include as defendants all creditors claiming an interest acquired after the commencement of the proceedings. After the foreclosure sale, one who had acquired the interests of these nonparty creditors attempted to redeem the property. *Held:* The nonparty creditors had a right of redemption. While the lis pendens on the property did foreclose the security interests of the junior creditors, it did not preclude them from acquiring a lien on which redemption could be based. *Land Assocs. v. Becker,* 656 P2d 927 (1982).

120.15
Effect of Bankruptcy

California The co-owner of land subject to a private foreclosure declared bankruptcy. Cal. Civ. Code § 2924 provides for a three-month redemption period. The co-owner argued that the automatic yearlong stay of proceedings under the Bankruptcy Code (11 USC § 362(a)) tolled the running of the three-month period until the stay was over. *Held:* The Bankruptcy Code did not toll the running of the redemption period. The relevant bankruptcy provision is 11 USC § 108(b), which allows trustee in bankruptcy to cure a default if the period to do so has not expired at the time the bankruptcy petition is filed. Trustee may then cure within the normal period or within 60 days of the filing of the bankruptcy petition, whichever is later. *Napue v. Gor-Mey W. Inc.,* 220 Cal. Rptr. 799 (Ct. App. 1985).

Iowa Farmer obtained a loan from the bank, which loan was secured by a mortgage on his real estate. After farmer defaulted on the note, he filed three successive petitions in bankruptcy, the first two under Chapter 11 and the last under Chapter 12. All three petitions were dismissed, and the bank filed a foreclosure action. While appeal of dismissal of the third petition was pending, the state court held that farmer was entitled to redeem the homestead portion of the real estate under state statute, but could not redeem any remaining portions of the land. Both parties appealed. *Held:* The automatic stay provisions of Chapter 11 extinguish the right of redemption found in the state foreclosure provisions. Iowa provides a right of redemption, which arises at the time of the foreclosure sale if the debtor has not delayed the sale by securing a stay of execution of the foreclosure judgment. Under the statute, the automatic stay in bankruptcy is treated as a stay granted by the state court. The statute does not violate due process or equal protection principles, since it is necessary to prevent the unfair extension of the redemptive period by delaying tactics. Both the equity of redemption and the statutory right of redemption are property of the bankruptcy estate. A debtor who files for bankruptcy before the foreclosure sale retains an equity of redemption. Because this property interest is not forfeited, modified, or terminated by the filing, the state statute is not in conflict with the federal bankruptcy act. *Hawkeye Bank & Trust v. Milburn,* 437 NW2d 919 (1989).

120.20
Waiver of Right

9th Circuit The law of Arizona requires that notice of intent to redeem be given within six months of a foreclosure sale. On the other hand, federal law gives the government the unconditional right to redeem for one year after foreclosure. The Small Business Administration (SBA) tendered the redemption amount 11 months after an

Arizona foreclosure, without having complied with the state notice requirement. *Held:* The SBA's tender of redemption was ineffective. Federal law did not preempt Arizona notice provisions. There was no conflict, since the federal statute did not contain notice provisions. Also, preemption is disfavored. *Dupnik v. United States,* 848 F2d 1476 (1988).

9th Circuit A farmer executed two mortgages on his property to secure loans from the Farmers Home Administration (FmHA). For each mortgage, farmer signed a standard FmHA form with a clause purporting to waive farmer's right to debtor protections under state laws, including the right to redeem following a foreclosure sale. After farmer defaulted, the FmHA foreclosed on the mortgages and scheduled a foreclosure sale. Farmer sued to enjoin the foreclosure and to exercise his right under Washington law to redeem his property within one year of a foreclosure sale. *Held:* For farmer. The court held that the loan transactions were governed by federal law and noted that no federal statute or regulation provided a redemption right. However, it applied a rule that state law will be adopted as the federal common law if it can be given effect without conflicting with federal policy. The court concluded that there was no conflict between the state redemption remedy and the federal policy of helping farmers through financial difficulty. It rejected the government's argument that added operating costs incurred by a recognition of the state law redemption remedy would defeat the federal policy of maintaining a credit fund available to farmers at reasonable rates. *United States v. Ellis,* 714 F2d 953 (1983).

U.S. District Court, Kansas Some FmHA loans contained clauses stating that they were not subject to state redemption laws. When borrowers attempted to redeem foreclosed property, the FmHA claimed that this clause had waived borrowers' redemption rights, and that in any event the loans were governed by federal law. *Held:* Contractual waivers of state redemption rights in mortgages to federal agencies are valid notwithstanding state law. However, borrowers in this case were equitably granted a 180-day postforeclosure redemption period. *United States v. Curry,* 561 F. Supp. 429 (1983).

Michigan A land sale contract went into default, but the parties reached an oral settlement just before the foreclosure hearing. Part of the settlement included a waiver of buyer's redemption right should she default again. She did default again, but tried to redeem after foreclosure anyway. She argued that the waiver was invalid because it clogged the equity of redemption. *Held:* The waiver was valid. The clogging doctrine does not apply to good faith contracts entered into separate from the original loan and for fresh consideration. *Russo v. Wolbers,* 323 NW2d 385 (1982).

121.00 TERMINATION

121.05 Effect of Purchase Subject to Mortgage

Arizona Del Rio had stopped its business activity and made arrangements to sell its land at auction, subject to an existing mortgage. Haumont was the high bidder at the auction, but Del Rio considered his bid too low and refused to accept it. Haumont sought specific performance and additionally asked that Del Rio be required to pay off the mortgage out of the sale proceeds. *Held:* Sale "subject to the mortgage" meant that buyer at the auction, while not personally obligated to pay off the mortgage, would have to pay it off if he wished to retain ownership. *Del Rio Land, Inc. v. Haumont,* 514 P2d 1003 (1973).

California Walker had purchased property from DEI. DEI had used this property as "additional security" in conjunction with a chattel mortgage, and a deficiency judgment against DEI was pending. After Walker had purchased, the bank tried to foreclose its deed of trust on the property. Walker filed to quiet title and enjoin the trustee sale, claiming that Cal. Div. Pro. Code § 726 barred the bank from additional recovery after it had once foreclosed on part of the debt security. *Held:* Foreclosure against the personal property, when both personal and real property secured a single debt, waived the right to foreclose under a trustee deed power of sale. Moreover, had the bank foreclosed first under the trust deed, it would have been precluded from obtaining a deficiency judgment. Attempting to foreclose after the deficiency judgment would go against the intent of Section 726 that all security should be exhausted first. *Walker v. Community Bank,* 518 P2d 329 (1974).

Washington Borrower executed a promissory note to lender for $1.42 million, secured by a deed of trust to several parcels of land. Borrower later conveyed one of the parcels to another purchaser, who had notice of lender's security interest, but did not assume it. When borrower went into bankruptcy, lender sued to foreclose on the parcels, but did not join the later purchasers as defendants. More than three years after the original suit was filed, lender sued the later purchasers. *Held:* Lender could not enforce the lien against the later purchasers because lender with notice of the later purchaser's claim had released the borrower from personal liability on the note. Lender's release diminished the subrogation rights of the later purchaser and thereby discharged the lien against the property sold to them. *MGIC Fin. Corp. v. HA Briggs Co.,* 600 P2d 573 (1979).

121.10
Release

Florida A foreclosure action went to trial, but the action was stayed pending the interlocutory appeal of a discovery order. During the stay, the trial court granted mortgagor's motion to substitute cash to be held by the court for the mortgage. Mortgagee appealed. *Held:* The trial court ought not to have made the substitution during the stay. A mortgagee should not be required to accept a substituted security interest, since a mortgage lien is a property right that cannot be extinguished. Security cannot be substituted except by agreement, judicial sale, or eminent domain. *Mailman Dev. Corp. v. Segall,* 403 So. 2d 1137 (Dist. Ct. App. 1982).

Utah Defendants and their development corporation entered into a financing arrangement with plaintiff bank, providing for release of separate lien mortgages in stages, as individual lots were sold. After all the lots were sold, the release payments failed to satisfy the outstanding indebtedness, and the bank sued for the balance. *Held:* The state "one-action" rule, which limits creditor's remedy through judicial sale or resort to the underlying obligation, is not violated where the credit agreement calls for disposition of the security through release of liens. Since the bank had no discretion as to whether liens were to be released, debtors could be sued in a separate action for the deficiency.

Utah Mortgage & Loan Co. v. Black, 618 P2d 43 (1980).

121.15
Acquisition of Title by Third Parties

Oregon A fraternity chapter was assigned a land sale contract to a house. The chapter borrowed the money for the assignment from its parent fraternity, in return for a mortgage on the chapter's interest in the property. The vendor to the land sale contract knew of the equitable mortgage, but was not a party to the agreement. The chapter abandoned the property when it could no longer make payments under the land sale contract. The parent fraternity, however, claimed that its interest was not extinguished. *Held:* The equitable mortgage was enforceable only while the underlying land sale contract was kept in force by the performance of its terms. The vendor had no duty to protect the parent fraternity's security interest. *Estate of Brewster v. Iota Delta Chapter,* 692 P2d 597 (1984) (en banc).

121.20
Rescission

Florida Contractor built a house for purchasers. At closing, contractor accepted a $7,000 second mortgage to secure payment of certain "extras." At the same time, contractor executed an affidavit in which he falsely certified that there were no outstanding claims against the property by subcontractors or materialmen. On learning of outstanding liens, purchasers sued contractor for rescission of the second mortgage and damages for breach of contract. *Held:* Purchasers were not entitled to rescission. Rescission is only granted if the parties can be restored to status quo ante. Since purchasers received the "extras" they bargained for, restoration was impossible. However, the evidence supported a finding that purchasers would not have given the second mortgage had they known of prior liens. The court therefore allowed the damages incurred by purchasers to be set off against the indebtedness. *Keith, Mack, Lewis & Allison v. Boraks,* 483 So. 2d 560 (Dist. Ct. App. 1986).

PART V
GOVERNMENTAL REGULATION OF TRANSACTIONS

122.00 APPLICABILITY OF SECURITIES LAW TO REAL ESTATE OFFERINGS

122.05 Federal Securities Laws in General

U.S. Supreme Court A shareholder in a real estate investment trust (REIT) brought suit for damages for fraudulent activities and breaches of fiduciary duty in violation of Section 206 of the Investment Advisors Act. The suit attacked the relationship between the REIT and its investment adviser, arguing that the adviser misappropriated profitable investment opportunities for the benefit of other entities affiliated with it, thus preventing the REIT from making the best available investments. Defendants countered that the shareholder could not bring suit under the Investment Advisors Act, since it does not give private individuals a right to bring such a lawsuit. The Ninth Circuit ruled that the shareholder could sue under the act; defendants appealed. *Held:* Section 206 of the Investment Advisor Act does not give a private shareholder the right to sue. Congress did not intend to give private individuals the right to bring this kind of lawsuit for damages. However, under Section 215 of the act, shareholders may still sue for cancellation of investment advisory contracts or for a return of fees. *Transamerica Mortgage Advisors, Inc. v. Lewis*, 444 US 11 (1979).

8th Circuit Buyer of an apartment complex entered into a management agreement with seller that appointed seller as exclusive management agent for the complex. The agreement was effective for three years and could be canceled only if buyer sold his interest in the complex or defaulted under the purchase agreement. When the complex's mortgage was foreclosed, buyer sued the broker, alleging that it had fraudulently induced him to invest in the complex in violation of federal securities laws. *Held:* The transaction did not constitute an investment contract under federal securities laws. The fact that buyer did not have a unilateral right to cancel the management contract was insufficient to convert a sales transaction into an investment contract. There was no absolute reliance on the profit-making efforts of another. Buyer was free to enter into the management contract and, at the end of three years, to negotiate a new management contract with someone else. Buyer retained ultimate control over the complex. *Schultz v. Dain Corp.*, 568 F2d 612 (1978).

10th Circuit Plaintiffs purchased lots in a planned residential community. Some intended to build, while others bought only as an investment. Defendant, developer of the community, represented that the development would become self-sufficient, with shopping, transportation, and recreational facilities. A uniform real estate contract was the only agreement executed between plaintiffs and defendant. Plaintiffs, asserting that the development was "dying on the vine," brought an action under federal and state security laws. The complaint alleged that the sale of the lots constituted the sale of a security, in the form of an investment contract. *Held:* Summary judgment for defendant. For a security to exist, there had to be a common venture or enterprise between plaintiffs and defendant. This requirement was not satisfied, since defendant was under no contractual obligation other than to deliver title. The expectation of a profit or resale did not transform the sale of real property into the sale of an investment contract. *Woodward v. Terracor*, 574 F2d 1023 (1978).

U.S. District Court, District of Columbia A publicly held corporation bought land from a trust for a note and a mortgage. The Security and Exchange Commission (SEC) claimed that the land was worthless and that the transaction was a scheme to defraud the corporation's shareholders. The SEC asserted jurisdiction under the theory that the note was a security, since it was issued by a publicly traded corporation for an investment, and was not given to a party in the business of making loans. *Held:* The note was a security within the meaning of the Securities Act of 1933 and the Securities Exchange Act of 1934. The federal courts of appeals use various tests to determine what constitutes a security, but this note would have satisfied any of them. *SEC v. Diversified Indus., Inc.*, 465 F. Supp. 104 (1979).

U.S. District Court, New York Plaintiff purchased a half-acre plot in a development pursuant to an executory installment sales contract. Plaintiff sued under the Securities Exchange Act of 1934, alleging the property to be worthless and fraudulently advertised, causing her to purchase at an artificially inflated price. She alleged that the representations in the development's advertising that the property was a wise investment that would "rise substantially in value over the coming years" rendered her purchase agreement an investment contract falling within the meaning of the act. *Held:* The agreement was not an investment contract. Although defendants planned improvements that would substantially enhance the value of plaintiff's property, they did not undertake to manage the development so as to generate profits for her. Absent a clear showing of management of the property as an investment, the simple real estate installment sale contract could not be construed to be an investment contract. *Davis v. Rio Rancho Estates, Inc.*, 401 F. Supp. 1045 (SD 1975).

U.S. District Court, North Dakota Plaintiff purchased an apartment complex from a partnership, with defendant acting as broker. The agreement provided that the partnership would manage the property for a sum equal to 5 percent of the gross rental for a term of 36 months. Plaintiff brought action for violation of federal securities regulations, alleging that the profits of the investment were solely dependent on the efforts of the partnership in its management capacity and therefore the transaction constituted the purchase of a security. *Held:* The purchase of real estate in fee simple absolute coupled with a management agreement does not constitute a security and is not subject to federal regulation. *Fargo Partners v. Dain Corp.*, 405 F. Supp. 739 (1975), aff'd, 540 F2d 912 (8th Cir. 1976).

Vermont Plaintiff leased to defendants a combination gas station-retail grocery store. In the lease addendum, plaintiff promised to install a "walk-in" cooler and a "modern island marketer" facility on the leasehold premises, to be financed by an additional monthly rental payment and a $.01 royalty on each gallon of gasoline sold. In plaintiffs' suit for breach of the lease agreement, defendants counterclaimed, arguing that the agreement was, instead, an unregistered investment security. *Held:* The agreement could not be said to involve a security, as defendants' belief that increased profits would result from the acquisition of the facilities could not have included the reasonable expectation that such profits would result substantially from the entrepreneurial or managerial efforts of plaintiff. *Northern Terminals, Inc. v. Leno*, 392 A2d 419 (1978).

122.10
—Cooperatives and Condominiums

U.S. Supreme Court Tenants of a low-income cooperative housing project brought suit alleging violation of federal securities laws. *Held:* Shares of a cooperative housing corporation's stock that entitled tenants to lease apartments in a state-aided nonprofit cooperative housing corporation were not securities within the purview of the federal securities laws. The shares were not "shares of stock," because they did not confer the right to dividends from profits and could not be sold at a profit or pledged. They were not "investment contracts," because they did not derive from an investment in a profit-making venture. The fact that the apartment cooperative offered space at below market rentals did not constitute a basis for a finding of profits in favor of shareholders. Even if a portion of the monthly rental applied to interest on the mortgage was considered profits in view of its tax deductibility, this could not be characterized as "profit" for purposes of the federal securities statutes, because it did not result from the managerial efforts of others. *United Hous. Found., Inc. v. Forman*, 421 US 837 (1975).

U.S. District Court, Colorado Plaintiff made what it believed would be a passive investment in a condominium project. When delays occurred because defendant developer had difficulty obtaining financing, plaintiff sued to rescind the agreement under the federal securities laws, arguing that the agreement was a security or investment contract covered by those statutes. Developer contested this characterization. *Held:* The agreement could be called a security or investment contract for purposes of the securities laws. There was an investment of money, there was a common enterprise involving other investors, and profits were expected solely from the efforts of a promoter or third party. *Woolridge Homes, Inc. v. Bronze Tree, Inc.*, 558 F. Supp. 1085 (1983).

New York Condominium developers bought an apartment building that they leased to people who knew a conversion was imminent. The prime lessees then sublet to people who paid rent and security deposits directly to developers. Developers put together a conversion plan using subscriptions from the prime lessees and started to evict the subtenants. The state alleged that developers had deceitfully manipulated a conversion, using illusory, nonresident tenants in violation of the Martin Act (N.Y. Gen. Bus. Law § 352-c(1)(a)), which prohibits fraudulent securities sales. *Held:* The Martin Act was not violated (though the Rent Stabilization Act may have been). Renting apartments to persons whom the landlord may have believed would not occupy them does not support a prosecution under the Martin Act, even if the landlord selects such "illusory" tenants in order to facilitate a cooperative conversion. There was no evidence of collusion, coercement, or discriminatory inducement in the conversion offering or implementation. *Badem Bldgs. v. Abrams*, 510 NE2d 319 (1987).

New York A cooperative established transfer fees for sales of its shares on a sliding scale, depending on how long the shares had been owned and whether seller had been an original purchaser. A shareholder who sold his apartment sued to recover the fee, alleging that it violated

N.Y. Bus. Corp. Law § 501(c). *Held:* The fee was illegal. Section 501(c) required that each share be equal to every other share of the same class, and the cooperative had only one class of shares. *Fe Bland v. Two Trees Management Co.*, 489 NE2d 223 (1985).

New York A sponsor for a cooperative plan increased the purchase price for unsold apartments but granted each tenant the nonexclusive right to accept the lower price within 30 days. The sponsor orally withdrew the offer from one tenant before the expiration of the 30-day period, but tenant accepted the offer in writing the same day. Tenant sued for specific performance. *Held:* The sponsor successfully revoked the offer. Sales of interests in cooperative apartments are sales of securities governed by the Uniform Commercial Code. Under UCC § 2-205, an offer in a signed writing that gives assurance it will be held open is irrevocable in the absence of consideration during the time stated. Since the offer gave no such assurance, the sponsor effectively reserved the right to revoke the offer. Accordingly, defendant's oral revocation was effective, and plaintiff's power to accept was thereafter extinguished. *Friedman v. Sommer*, 471 NE2d 139 (1984).

122.15
State Securities Laws

Florida Twenty-five people put up the money to buy a tract of land as an investment. Title was in the name of two trustees, but buyers were beneficiaries and each was liable for property taxes and other expenses in proportion to his investment. Nine of these people later sued to rescind, arguing that the purchase violated a state securities act that defined "security" to include a "beneficial interest in title to property." *Held:* The interests of buyers were not securities. Their investment was not designed to produce profits from the efforts of others. *Wiener v. Brown*, 356 So. 2d 1302 (Dist. Ct. App. 1978).

Texas Investors participating in a joint venture involving undeveloped land sued sellers under state securities statute. By the terms of the statute, the underlying interest being sold must fall within the legislative definition of "security." *Held:* The land, as such, was not a security. The mere holding of property in anticipation of appreciation in value is not a statutory security, unless the element of reliance on management, operation, and development efforts by others can be shown. Therefore, where the simple rise in market value of undeveloped land is the sole investment motive, no security can be said to have been sold. *Wilson v. Lee*, 601 SW2d 483 (Civ. App. 1980).

123.00
REAL ESTATE SETTLEMENT PROCEDURES ACT

123.05
Scope and Extent

U.S. District Court, Massachusetts The state passed a law requiring interest payments on certain real estate tax payments. Various federal savings and loan associations challenged the statute, arguing that it violated the supremacy clause, since this area had been preempted by federal law. The state argued that the Real Estate Settlement Procedures Act (RESPA), Section 18 permits the statute. *Held:* The statute violates the supremacy clause and is not permitted under the RESPA. Section 18 of the RESPA provides for the application of state law only when the secretary of the Department of Housing and Urban Development (HUD) determines that the statute gives greater protection to a consumer than does federal law. The secretary of HUD had made no such determination in this case. *Greenwald v. First Fed. Sav. & Loan Assoc.*, 446 F. Supp. 620 (1978).

123.10
Operation and Effect

U.S. District Court, Illinois A bank required customers receiving federally related mortgages to deposit in tax escrow accounts sums in excess of those prescribed by RESPA. One borrower sued for overcharges for herself and other borrowers, arguing that RESPA created a private right of action. *Held:* RESPA did not provide a private right of action. The subject of plaintiff's claim was traditionally a matter of state law, and the legislative history did not indicate any congressional intent to create a private federal right of action. Indeed, a private remedy would be inconsistent with RESPA's statutory scheme. *Allison v. Liberty Sav.*, 535 F. Supp. 828 (ND), aff'd, 695 F2d 1086 (7th Cir. 1982).

U.S. District Court, Michigan Homebuyers brought suit against mortgage lenders, alleging that they had not required closing homeowners to pay one twelfth of the estimated total taxes into escrow reserves, as provided by Section 10 of RESPA. *Held:* There was no violation of RESPA. RESPA permits the closing homeowners to deposit into escrow reserves only a pro rata portion of estimated taxes, corresponding to the number of months from the last date of payment to the date of settlement. This procedure was followed in this case and therefore no violation occurred. *Vega v. First Fed. Sav. & Loan Ass'n*, 433 F. Supp. 624 (ED 1977), aff'd, 622 F2d 918 (6th Cir. 1980).

Hawaii The title insurance agreement covering a real estate construction loan provided for a rebate to developer when all the units were sold; there may have been an implicit understanding that unit buyers would be directed to that title insurer. After this agreement was reached, RESPA went into effect, forbidding kickbacks and unearned fees on settlement procedures. When all the units were sold, insurer refused to make the rebate, citing RESPA. Developer argued that RESPA did not cover the construction loan. *Held:* RESPA did apply, and it prohibited the rebate. While the construction loan by itself would not have been subject to RESPA, that loan and the loans for the units were part of the same package. The unit loans were covered by RESPA because they were made by federally insured banks. *Aiea Lani Corp. v. Hawaii Escrow & Title, Inc.*, 647 P2d 257 (1982).

124.00
STATE LAND SALES FULL DISCLOSURE LAWS

124.05
Out of State Land Sales

3d Circuit The New Jersey Land Sales Full Disclosure Act (LSFDA) regulates the offer and sale within New Jersey or to New Jersey residents of subdivided land located outside the state if the offer and sale are via a common promotional plan. As part of a promotional plan, developers advertised in New Jersey an offer to sell subdivided lots of Pennsylvania real estate. New Jersey officials informed them that the advertisements violated the LSFDA. Developers were given the option of complying with the LSFDA's registration and disclosure requirements or stating in the advertisements that the offering was not open to New Jersey residents. Developers sued, arguing that the LSFDA was unconstitutional. *Held:* Even though the LSFDA applied evenhandedly without regard to seller's citizenship, it violated the commerce clause because it clearly discriminated against interstate commerce. Compliance under the LSFDA for sellers of out of state land was more expensive than compliance under a similar statute that governed the sales of New Jersey property. *Old Coach Dev. Corp., Inc. v. Tanzman*, 881 F2d 1227 (1989).

TABLE OF CASES

[*References are to sections.*]

A

[*References are to sections.*]

[*References are to sections.*]

[*References are to sections.*]

B

[*References are to sections.*]

[*References are to sections.*]

[*References are to sections.*]

[*References are to sections.*]

[*References are to sections.*]

C

[*References are to sections.*]

[*References are to sections.*]

[*References are to sections.*]

[*References are to sections.*]

[*References are to sections.*]

[*References are to sections.*]

[*References are to sections.*]

[*References are to sections.*]

[*References are to sections.*]

D

[*References are to sections.*]

[*References are to sections.*]

[*References are to sections.*]

E

[*References are to sections.*]

[*References are to sections.*]

F

[*References are to sections.*]

[*References are to sections.*]

[*References are to sections.*]

G

[*References are to sections.*]

[*References are to sections.*]

[*References are to sections.*]

H

[*References are to sections.*]

[*References are to sections.*]

[*References are to sections.*]

[*References are to sections.*]

I

[*References are to sections.*]

J

[*References are to sections.*]

[*References are to sections.*]

K

[*References are to sections.*]

[*References are to sections.*]

L

[*References are to sections.*]

[*References are to sections.*]

[*References are to sections.*]

M

[*References are to sections.*]

[*References are to sections.*]

[*References are to sections.*]

[*References are to sections.*]

[*References are to sections.*]

[*References are to sections.*]

N

[*References are to sections.*]

[*References are to sections.*]

O

[*References are to sections.*]

[*References are to sections.*]

P

[*References are to sections.*]

[*References are to sections.*]

[*References are to sections.*]

Q

R

[*References are to sections.*]

[*References are to sections.*]

[*References are to sections.*]

S

[*References are to sections.*]

[*References are to sections.*]

[*References are to sections.*]

[*References are to sections.*]

[*References are to sections.*]

[*References are to sections.*]

[*References are to sections.*]

[*References are to sections.*]

T

[*References are to sections.*]

[*References are to sections.*]

[*References are to sections.*]

U

[*References are to sections.*]

V

[*References are to sections.*]

W

[*References are to sections.*]

[*References are to sections.*]

[*References are to sections.*]

[*References are to sections.*]

X

Y

Z

[*References are to sections.*]

INDEX

[*References are to sections.*]

A

[*References are to sections.*]

[*References are to sections.*]

[*References are to sections.*]

[*References are to sections.*]

[*References are to sections.*]

[*References are to sections.*]

[*References are to sections.*]

[*References are to sections.*]

[*References are to sections.*]

D

[*References are to sections.*]

[*References are to sections.*]

[*References are to sections.*]

[*References are to sections.*]

E

[*References are to sections.*]

[*References are to sections.*]

F

[*References are to sections.*]

[*References are to sections.*]

[*References are to sections.*]

[*References are to sections.*]

[*References are to sections.*]

[*References are to sections.*]

J

L

[*References are to sections.*]

[*References are to sections.*]

[*References are to sections.*]

[*References are to sections.*]

[*References are to sections.*]

M

[*References are to sections.*]

[*References are to sections.*]

[*References are to sections.*]

N

[*References are to sections.*]

O

[*References are to sections.*]

[*References are to sections.*]

[*References are to sections.*]

[*References are to sections.*]

[*References are to sections.*]

[*References are to sections.*]

[*References are to sections.*]

[*References are to sections.*]

[*References are to sections.*]

[*References are to sections.*]

[*References are to sections.*]

[*References are to sections.*]

T

[*References are to sections.*]

[*References are to sections.*]

[*References are to sections.*]

[*References are to sections.*]

[*References are to sections.*]

W

[*References are to sections.*]

Z